ENLIGHTENMENT CONTESTED

Enlightenment Contested

Philosophy, Modernity, and the Emancipation of Man 1670–1752

JONATHAN I. ISRAEL

OXFORD
UNIVERSITY PRESS

Great Clarendon Street, Oxford OX2 6DP

Oxford University Press is a department of the University of Oxford.
It furthers the University's objective of excellence in research, scholarship,
and education by publishing worldwide in

Oxford New York

Auckland Cape Town Dar es Salaam Hong Kong Karachi
Kuala Lumpur Madrid Melbourne Mexico City Nairobi
New Delhi Shanghai Taipei Toronto

With offices in

Argentina Austria Brazil Chile Czech Republic France Greece
Guatemala Hungary Italy Japan Poland Portugal Singapore
South Korea Switzerland Thailand Turkey Ukraine Vietnam

Published in the United States
by Oxford University Press Inc., New York

First published 2006

British Library Cataloguing in Publication Data
Data available

Library of Congress Cataloging in Publication Data
Data available

Typeset by Newgen Imaging Systems (P) Ltd., Chennai, India
Printed in Great Britain
on acid-free paper by
Clays Ltd., St Ives plc

ISBN 978–0–19–927922–7

3

Preface

Was the Enlightenment in essence a social or an intellectual phenomenon? The answer, arguably, is that it was both and that physical reality and the life of the mind must be seen to be genuinely interacting in a kind of dialectic, a two-way street, if we are to achieve a proper and balanced approach to this fundamental topic. Does it really matter how we interpret the Enlightenment? Surely, it does. For while it has been fashionable in recent years, above all (but not only) in the Postmodernist camp, to disdain the Enlightenment as biased, facile, self-deluded, over-optimistic, Eurocentric, imperialistic, and ultimately destructive, there are sound, even rather urgent, reasons for rejecting such notions as profoundly misconceived and insisting, on the contrary, that the Enlightenment has been and remains by far the most positive factor shaping contemporary reality and those strands of 'modernity' anyone wishing to live in accord with reason would want to support and contribute to.

It is consequently of some concern that we almost entirely lack comprehensive, general accounts of the Enlightenment which try to present the overall picture on a European and transatlantic scale; and also that there still remains great uncertainty, doubt, and lack of clarity about what exactly the Enlightenment was and what intellectually and socially it actually involved. For much of the time, in the current debate, both the friends and foes of the Enlightenment are arguing about a historical phenomenon which in recent decades continues to be very inadequately understood and described. In fact, since Peter Gay's ambitious two-part general survey *The Enlightenment: An Interpretation*, published in 1966, there have been hardly any serious attempts, as Gay puts it, to 'offer a comprehensive interpretation of the Enlightenment'. Especially disturbing is that it remains almost impossible to find a reasonably detailed general account of the crucially formative pre-1750 period and that there is nowadays among general historians of the eighteenth century, as distinct from philosophers and specialists in political thought, rarely much discussion of the Enlightenment's intellectual content as opposed to the—according to most current historiography—supposedly more important social and material factors.

The purpose of this present account is to attempt to provide a usable outline survey and work of reference, enabling the general reader, as well as the student and professional scholar, to get more of a grip on what the ideas of the Enlightenment actually were, and one which at the same time denies that the social, cultural, and material factors are of greater concern to historians than the intellectual impulses but does so without simply reversing this and claiming ideas were, therefore, more crucial than the social process. Rather, my aim is to strive for a genuine balance, showing how ideas and socio-political context interact while yet approaching this interplay of the physical and intellectual from the intellectual side, that is running against the nowadays usual and generally received preference. The reason for this contrary emphasis is that the intellectual dimension, it seems to me, is by far the less well-understood side of the equation and hence at present much more in need of reassessment than the social and cultural aspects.

One of the most controversial questions about the Enlightenment in recent years has been that concerning its precise relationship to the making of revolutions, a question closely tied, in turn, to that concerning its relationship to 'modernity' more generally. Odd though this may appear today, it was often claimed, from the late seventeenth to the mid nineteenth century, in books, pamphlets, sermons, and newspapers, that 'philosophy' had caused, and was still causing, a 'universal revolution' in the affairs of men. After 1789, it was usual to link this notion to the French Revolution in particular and view that vast upheaval as the 'realization of philosophy'.[1] But there was nothing new about bracketing 'philosophy' with modern 'revolution' in the early nineteenth century, or indeed earlier, and it is vital to bear in mind that in the decades before and after 1789 there were all kinds of other 'revolutions' beside that in France—not all violent and not all political, but all very closely associated with the unprecedented, and to many deeply perplexing, impact of philosophers and philosophy.

For some time after 1789, the French Revolution and its offshoot upheavals across the European continent and in the Americas, including by the 1820s the major revolutions in Greece and Spanish America, were usually thought of as essentially parts of a much larger and more 'universal' revolution generated by 'philosophy' or, to be more exact, what in the previous century had come to be known as *l'esprit philosophique* or sometimes *philosophisme*. For *l'esprit philosophique*, as a French revolutionary statesman interested in this question, Jean-Étienne-Marie Portalis, pointed out in 1798, was actually something very different from philosophy in general. For most philosophers, including those embracing a strict empiricism and confining themselves to what could be deduced from 'l'observation et l'expérience', as well as those adhering to the German idealist systems, had long sought to curtail philosophy's scope and reconcile reason with religious belief. *L'esprit philosophique*, by contrast, while also a 'résultat des sciences comparées', was defined precisely by its refusal to limit philosophy's scope to specified parts of reality, its sweeping aspiration to embrace and redefine the whole of our reality: revolutionary 'esprit philosophique', in other words, claimed, as Portalis puts it, to be 'applicable à tout'.[2] Above all, as against other sorts of philosophy, *philosophisme* was 'une sorte d'esprit universel'.

Post-1789 attribution of the 'revolution' to *l'esprit philosophique* was frequent but in essence no different from the many examples of pre-1789 complaints about dangerous new forms of thought infiltrating religion, social theory, and politics in such a way as to threaten the basic structures of authority, tradition, faith, and privilege

[1] McMahon, *Enemies of the Enlightenment*, 56.
[2] Portalis, *De l'usage et de l'abus*, i. 114–15.

on which *ancien régime* society rested. Modern historians and students, of course, are apt to dismiss this sort of thing as a figment of the collective imagination of the time, an illusion powerfully fed by ideological obsessions and bias which only very vaguely corresponds to the historical reality. In recent decades, it has been deeply and more and more unfashionable among historians, in both Europe and America, to explain the French Revolution, the greatest event on the threshold of 'modernity', as a consequence of ideas. Marxist dogma with its stress on economic reality and cultural superstructure helped generate this near universal conviction. But another major justification for this in some ways distinctly peculiar article of the modern historian's creed is the growing democratization of history itself: students especially, but professors too, readily take to the argument that most people, then as now, do things for exclusively 'practical' reasons and have no interest in matters intellectual. Any attempt to stress the impact of the *philosophes* is nowadays routinely objected to on the ground that the vast majority knew next to nothing about them or their books and cared even less.

This, of course, is perfectly true. But there is an important sense in which this fashionable objection misses the point. For those who inveighed most obsessively against new ideas before and after 1789 also insisted that most people then, as now, neither knew nor cared anything about 'philosophy'. Yet practically all late eighteenth- and early nineteenth-century commentators were convinced, and with some reason, that while most failed to see how philosophy impinged on their lives, and altered the circumstances of their time, they had all the same been ruinously led astray by 'philosophy'; it was philosophers who were chiefly responsible for propagating the concepts of toleration, equality, democracy, republicanism, individual freedom, and liberty of expression and the press, the batch of ideas identified as the principal cause of the near overthrow of authority, tradition, monarchy, faith, and privilege. Hence, philosophers specifically had caused the revolution.

Throne, altar, aristocracy, and imperial sway, according to spokesmen of the Counter-Enlightenment, had been brought to the verge of extinction by ideas which most people know absolutely nothing about. Most of those who had supported what conservative and middle-of-the road observers considered corrosive and pernicious democratic concepts had allegedly done so unwittingly, or without fully grasping the real nature of the ideas on which the ringing slogans and political rhetoric of the age rested. Yet if very few grasped or engaged intellectually with the core ideas in question this did not alter the fact that fundamentally new ideas had shaped, nurtured, and propagated the newly insurgent popular rhetoric used in speeches and newspapers to arouse the people against tradition and authority. Indeed, it seemed obvious that it was 'philosophy' which had generated the revolutionary slogans, maxims, and ideologies of the pamphleteers, journalists, demagogues, elected deputies, and malcontent army officers who, in the American, French, Dutch, and Italian revolutions of the 1770s, 1780s, and 1790s, as well as the other revolutions which followed proclaimed and justified a fundamental break with the past.

The kind of 'philosophy' they had in mind, like its social and political impact, was plainly something fundamentally new. What was not at all new was the turmoil, violence, and fanaticism accompanying the revolutionary process. For if the common people were perfectly capable of causing all sorts of agitation, instability, and disruption without any help from philosophers, the conceptual overthrow of altar, throne, and nobility was considered, surely rightly, something previously wholly unimagined and inconceivable which, consequently, had little inherently to do with economic need, social pressures, or the allegedly innate unruliness of the plebs. Rather, such upheaval could only stem from a revolutionary transformation in the people's way of thinking.

Not only was the foundational role of 'philosophy' heavily stressed by contemporaries in the early nineteenth century, but there was also a clear grasp of the later obscured, yet perhaps rather obvious, fact that it makes little sense to seek the causes of the 'revolution' in the decades immediately preceding 1789; for a great revolution in thought and culture takes time. One must look back to the century before 1750 to locate the intellectual origins and early development of what transpired in the revolutionary era. It was not popular grievances, economic causes, obsolete institutions, lack of liberty, or any material factor, according to Antonio Valsecchi, in a book posthumously published in Venice in 1816, but specifically *spirito filosofico* which in Italy, as in France and the rest of Europe, had virtually destroyed 'society, commerce, discipline, faith, and throne', a revolution of the mind culminating in Voltaire and Rousseau certainly but whose real origins lay further back, in the seventeenth century. The true originators of the French Revolution, he says, were not Rousseau or Voltaire but 'Tommaso Hobbes d'Ingilterra, e Benedetto Spinosa di Olanda', truly world-shaking and subversive philosophers whose deadly work of corrosion had been continued, again in Holland, by the no less subversive 'Pietro Bayle'.[3]

Yet this interpretation of the revolutionary upheavals of the late eighteenth century in essence scarcely differed from that of another Italian professor, Tommaso Vincenzo Moniglia (1686–1787), at Pisa, who over seventy years earlier, in 1744, warned the Italian reading public that recent intellectual trends in France, inspired by the English 'Deists' Anthony Collins and John Toland, using ideas introduced by Spinoza, were producing a new and dangerous kind of philosophy, one which overturns all existing principles, institutions, codes of custom, and royal decrees. Their ideas, he argued, entail a 'total revolution in ideas, language, and the affairs of the world', leading to a drastically changed society in which *Spinosismo*, or as another Italian writer of the period, Daniele Concina, put it, 'questa mostruosa divinita Spinosiana' [this monstrous Spinozist divinity], would reign supreme, meaning that in place of faith, hierarchy, and kingship everything would henceforth be based on physical reality alone and 'on the interests and passions of individuals'.[4]

[3] Valsecchi, *Ritratti o vite*, 101–2.

[4] Moniglia, *Dissertazione contro i fatalisti*, ii. 21–2; Israel, *Radical Enlightenment*, 523–4.

Moniglia's and Concina's admonitions about *Spinosismo* and 'universal revolution' in the mid eighteenth century, in turn, differed little in substance from other warnings issued still earlier. At the beginning of the century, the Anglo-Irish High Church divine William Carroll, in the second part of his pamphlet *Spinoza Reviv'd* (London, 1711), maintained that philosophy based on what he calls 'Spinoza-principles', meaning militant Deism based on one-substance philosophy, 'fundamentally subverts all natural and reveal'd religion, [and] overthrows our constitution both in church and state'.[5] The earliest avowals along these lines indeed reach back to the late seventeenth century. In 1693, for example, a prominent German court official of wide experience, the Freiherr Veit Ludwig von Seckendorff (1626–92), thought it quite wrong to suppose, as many theologians did, that 'atheistic' philosophy of the kind propagated by Spinoza undermines only religion and theology; for by making life in this world, and individual expectations, the basis of politics Spinozism equally threatened to liquidate all royalty, and their courts and courtiers, as well.[6] In 1681, similarly, the French Calvinist Pierre Yvon (1646–1707) avowed that Spinoza not only destroys theology philosophically, reducing morality to a mere calculus of individual advantage, but that his political theory authorizes everyone to instigate political rebellion.[7]

Across Europe, the radical-minded, as well as many religious thinkers, were quick to grasp that a fundamental revolution of the mind must eventually translate also into political revolution. The threat to the political, religious, and social status quo posed by 'Spinoza-principles' was colourfully alluded to by the anonymous author of the tract *Rencontre de Bayle et de Spinosa dans l'autre monde*, published in 1711 in Holland—though with 'Cologne' declared on the title page—a work designed to tighten the reading public's association of Bayle with Spinoza by implying these two great thinkers shared not just parallels in their lives, both being refugees from Catholic, monarchical intolerance in quest of individual freedom of thought, but also common philosophical aims.[8] In the imaginary dialogue between the two, set in the next world, 'Bayle' assures 'Spinosa' that while some approved the latter's self-portrayal (in his sketch-book, found after his death) in the fisherman's garb of the notorious seventeenth-century insurgent Masaniello—a symbol in Spinoza's day of popular revolt against monarchical oppression[9]—his enemies feared this might imply that 'what Masaniello had brought about in fifteen days [i.e. a democratic revolution], in Naples, you would likewise accomplish in a short time, in the whole of Christendom'.[10]

Later Counter-Enlightenment accusations associating philosophy and the *philosophes* with revolution, then, once stripped of ideological bias, possess

[5] Carroll, *Spinoza Reviv'd Part the Second*, 7.
[6] Seckendorff, *Christen-Staat*, i. 12, ii. 139–41.
[7] Yvon, *L'Impiété convaincue*, 212, 362, 400, 411–12.
[8] *Rencontre de Bayle et de Spinosa*, 21–2, 31.
[9] Meinsma, *Spinoza et son cercle*, 473; Stone, *Vico's Cultural History*, 3, 31, 115.
[10] *Rencontre de Bayle et de Spinosa*, 12; *See also* Stewart, *Courtier*, 95–7.

a considerable degree of cogency and deserve more attention from scholars than they have hitherto received. For the trends towards secularization, toleration, equality, democracy, individual freedom, and liberty of expression in western Europe and America between 1650 and 1750 were arguably powerfully impelled by 'philosophy' and its successful propagation in the political and social sphere; and just as the Counter-Enlightenment affirmed, in the end such ideas were bound to precipitate a European and American revolutionary process, of a type never before witnessed. If, moreover, in recent decades most historians of both Enlightenment and the French Revolution have repudiated interpretations emphasizing the role of ideas, claiming the revolutionary movements were primarily social and cultural phenomena best understood by focusing on social relations and material factors, there remain formidable unresolved difficulties with this conception. For the results produced by recent social historical research hardly seem to justify the continuing emphasis on a primarily 'social' approach. No one has been able to specify what the allegedly profound social changes which lay behind the Enlightenment and Revolution actually were or even how shifts in social structure, given their reality, could broadly and spontaneously translate into a popularly driven 'universal revolution' designed to transform the core principles upon which society and politics rest.

In any case, a reverse shift of emphasis back to the study of ideas in their historical setting may produce useful results for the history of Enlightenment, modern revolutions, and the history of western 'modernity' itself. Recent claims about social structure, material factors, and the people's unawareness of new ideas notwithstanding, it remains fundamentally implausible that the 'modern' core concepts of equality, democracy, and individual freedom sprang directly out of a process of social change or cultural adjustment, or became central to 'modern' society and politics, or could enter the public sphere at all, without being forged, defined, and revised through a process of intellectual debate. And even if some readers remain convinced that socially and culturally driven changes, not ideas, must be the primary factors in the historical process, the intellectual side of the history of modern revolution still remains one of immense drama, complexity, and interest which needs to be surveyed in a more comprehensive fashion than it has been.

In my earlier book, *Radical Enlightenment*, a start was made to describing how philosophical debates in the late seventeenth and early eighteenth centuries generated the radical edge of the western Enlightenment. Here, my aim is to offer a much wider and more general reassessment of the Enlightenment as it developed down to the early part of the battle over the *Encyclopédie* (1751–2), giving particular emphasis to the Enlightenment's essential duality, that is the internal struggle between the opposing tendencies which from beginning to end always fundamentally divided it into irreconcilably opposed intellectual blocs. In doing so, I shall try to demonstrate how, historically and philosophically, the main line in the development of modern 'enlightened' values transferred from the earlier centre in the Dutch Republic to other parts of Europe by the mid eighteenth century and especially France, which, from the 1720s onwards, increasingly presided intellectually and culturally over the emergence and development of radical, democratic, and egalitarian ideas.

Besides seeking to show how ideas of equality, toleration, democracy, and individual freedom came to challenge monarchy, aristocracy, authority, and tradition, this study also deals with the intellectual beginnings of anti-colonialism and the radical critique of European imperial sway over non-European peoples. Additional themes are the Enlightenment's always dual and divided quest to engage with the non-European 'other', and specifically classical Chinese culture and the world of Islam, together with other ramifications of the late seventeenth- and early eighteenth-century revolution in scholarship and ideals of learning.

In the research for, and writing of, this book I have been greatly assisted by the Institute for Advanced Study at Princeton to which I owe an immense debt of gratitude. I would like, in the first place, to thank Susan Schneller, Marian Zelazny, Julia Bernheim Kirstie Venanzi, and Marcia Tucker, all of whom have been wonderfully supportive and in whose debt I shall long remain. For contributing to the further development and modifying of my understanding of the Enlightenment since the publication of my first volume on this subject, through conversation, discussion, and correspondence, I would further like to thank Antony McKenna, Wim Klever, Wiep van Bunge, Sarah Hutton, Wijnand Mijnhardt, Martin Mulsow, Michiel Wielema, Siep Stuurman, Giovanni Ricuperati, Vincenzo Ferrone, Sylvia Berti, Gianluca Mori, Eduardo Tortarolo, Winfried Schröder, Catherine Secretan, Kinch Hoekstra, Vittorio Hösle, Dan Garber, Margaret Jacob, William J. Connell, Piet Hut, Steve Adler, Susan Morrissey, Adam Sutcliffe, Alastair Hamilton, John Hope Mason, Jonathan Scott, Steve Pincus, Veit Elm, Hilary Gatti, Manfred Walther, Paschalis Kitromilides, Irwin Primer, Bill Doyle, and, most of all, and with all my heart, my partner Annette.

Contents

List of Plates

List of Figures

Abbrevations of Library and Archive Locations

ABM	Aix-en-Provence, Bibliothèque Méjanes
ARH OSA	The Hague: Algemeen Rijksarchief, Oud Synodaal Archief
AUB	Amsterdam: Universiteitsbibliotheek
BL	London: British Library
CRL	Copenhagen: Royal Library
GA Amsterdam	Amsterdam City Archives
GA Leiden	Leiden: City Archives
GA Rotterdam	Rotterdam: City Archives
GA The Hague	The Hague: City Archives
GA Utrecht	Utrecht City Archives
GUB	Göttingen: Universitätsbibliothek
HARA	The Hague: Algemeen Rijksarchief
HHL	Harvard University: Houghton Library
HKB	The Hague: Koninklijke Bibliotheek (Royal Library)
HUB	Halle: Universitätsbibliothek
IAS	Institute for Advanced Study, Princeton
KBJ	Cracow, University Library
LDrW	London: Dr Williams' Library
LUB	Leiden: Universiteitsbibliotheek
NBN	Naples, Biblioteca Nazionale
NYCU	New York, Columbia University Library
NYPL	New York Public Library
PBA	Paris: Bibliothèque de l'Arsenal
PBM	Paris: Bibliothèque Mazarine
PBN	Paris: Bibliothèque Nationale
PrF	Princeton, Firestone Library
UCLA	Los Angeles: UCLA Research Library
UCLA-Cl	Los Angeles: Clark Library
UUL	Uppsala University Library
VBM	Venice: Bibliotheca Marciana
WHA	Wolfenbüttel: Herzog August Bibliothek
WLC	Washington, Library of Congress

WUL	Wroctaw (Breslau), University Library
YBL	Yale Beinecke Library
YML	Yale Mudd Library
YSL	Yale Sterling Memorial Library

Other Abbreviations

AGPh	*Archiv für Geschichte der Philosophie*
ANTW	*Algemeen Nederlands Tijdschrift voor Wijsbegeerte*
BAASp	*Bulletin de l'Association des Amis de Spinoza*
BCSV	*Bolletino del Centro di Studi Vichiani*
BHR	*Bibliothèque de l'humanisme et de la Renaissance*
BJEC	*British Journal for Eighteenth-Century Studies*
BJHP	*British Journal for the History of Philosophy*
BJHS	*British Journal for the History of Science*
BMGN	*Bijdragen en Mededeelingen betreffende de Geschiedenis der Nederlanden*
CHRPh	Ch. B. Schmitt and Quentin Skinner (eds.), *The Cambridge History of Renaissance Philosophy* (Cambridge, 1988)
CHSPh	Daniel Garber and M. Ayers (eds.), *Cambridge History of Seventeenth-Century Philosophy* (Cambridge, 1998)
Corpus	*Corpus: revue de philosophie* (Paris X-Nanterre)
DEBPh	J. W. Yolton, J. V. Price, and J. Stephens (eds.), *The Dictionary of Eighteenth-Century British Philosophers* (2 vols., Bristol, 1999)
DHS	*Dix-huitième siècle*
GCFI	*Giornale critico della filosofia italiana*
GRSTD	*Groupe de Recherches Spinozistes: travaux et documents*
GWN	*Geschiedenis van de Wijsbegeerte in Nederland*
HPSGF	Rolf Reichardt and E. Schmitt (eds.), *Handbuch politisch-sozialer Grundbegriffe in Frankreich, 1680–1820* (Munich, 18 parts, 1985–96)
HPTh	*History of Political Thought*
JHI	*Journal of the History of Ideas*
JHPh	*Journal for the History of Philosophy*
LIAS	*LIAS: Sources and Documents Relating to the Early Modern History of Ideas*
MvSH	*Mededelingen vanwege het Spinozahuis*
MSJCW	*Mededelingen van de Stichting Jacob Campo Weyerman*
NAKG	*Nederlands Archief voor Kerkgeschiedenis*
NRL	*Nouvelles de la République des Lettres* (Naples)
OSEMPh	Daniel Garber and Steven Nadler (eds.), *Oxford Studies in Early Modern Philosophy* (from 2003)
RCSF	*Rivista critica di storia della filosofia*
RDF	*Rivista di filosofia*

RDl'E	*Recherches sur Diderot et sur l'Encyclopédie*
RSF	*Rivista di storia della filosofia*
RSI	*Rivista storica italiana*
RSPhTh	*Revue des sciences philosophiques et théologiques* (Paris)
SVEC	*Studies on Voltaire and the Eighteenth Century*
TJEAS	*Taiwan Journal of East Asian Studies*
TTP	Spinoza, *Tractatus theologico-politicus*
TvSV	*Tijdschrift voor de Studie van de Verlichting*

Part I

Introductory

1

Early Enlightenment, Revolution, and the Modern Age

1. *ANCIEN RÉGIME* AND REVOLUTION

Even a cursory study of the French Revolution will soon convince an attentive student that the ideology and rhetoric of revolution in late eighteenth-century Europe, and not least the slogans—'liberty', 'equality', and 'fraternity'—were very intimately connected with the new ideas of the Enlightenment. Pre-revolutionary early modern societies, by contrast, were unquestionably too steeped in tradition, theological doctrine, and the mystique of kingship, as well as too respectful of legitimacy rooted in the past, and idealized conceptions of the community, to embrace 'revolution' in the modern sense of a 'radical change and a departure', as one scholar expressed it, 'from traditional or accepted modes of thought, belief, action, social behaviour or political or social organization'.[1] Still less conceivable in early modern times was a 'universal revolution' of the kind urged by the radical *philosophes* of the Enlightenment, that is revolution moral, cultural, and political, based on schemes for fundamental reorganization potentially applicable to any society.

The basic difference between pre-modern revolts and upheavals and modern revolution, therefore, is that, with the former, justification of social and political change invariably invoked theological *fundamenta*, customary law, and veneration of tradition while modern revolutions quintessentially legitimize themselves in terms of, and depend on, non-traditional, and newly introduced, fundamental concepts. What historians of 'modernity' are really striving to pinpoint when they set out to investigate the phenomenon of 'modernity', then, and within 'modernity' the problem of 'revolution', is the difference between social, cultural, and political renewal expressed theologically, traditionally, and dynastically, on the one hand, and, on the other, far-reaching action and reform justified in secular, non-theological, and non-customary ideological terms.

[1] Cohen, 'Eighteenth-Century Origins', 258; Zagorin, 'Prolegomena', 169–70; with respect to the English Revolution, see Sharpe, 'An Image Doting Rabble', 54–6.

In the sixteenth and seventeenth centuries, as earlier, long-accepted and deep-rooted criteria legal, dynastic, and theological fixed the measure of just and unjust, legitimate and illegitimate, and of what reforms could rightfully be implemented.[2] With a few exceptions, historians have generally accepted that this means that there were, and could be, no real revolutions during the fifteenth, sixteenth, and seventeenth centuries and this seems broadly correct, though many scholars assumed from this that there was, therefore, no real 'revolutionary' outlook before the French Revolution itself which, as we shall see, is certainly incorrect.[3] At the same time, historians mostly continue to think of revolution as something deriving principally from deep-seated social and economic change rather than fundamental shifts in ideas. However, no one has been able to specify precisely what these social and economic shifts were, while talk of deep-seated 'cultural' shifts is usually even vaguer, so that it is surely legitimate, by now, to express some scepticism about whether the prevailing assumption that modern revolutions were essentially social and economic, or at least cultural in origin, rather than intellectual, in reality possesses much cogency. In any case, a plea for a shift of emphasis to a hegemonic role for ideas not in isolation but firmly placed in social context, such as underpins this present work, need not mean a return to older methods of working, although there have always been those who recognized that revolution, conceived as a prime engine of modernity, is chiefly a question of ideas. In this respect (if in no other) Edmund Burke, in his *Thoughts on French Affairs* (1791), was right to assert that what was fundamentally new about the French Revolution, marking it off from all previous known political upheavals, was not popular participation, class antagonism, economic change, cultural shifts, or social pressures but rather the fact that it was 'a revolution of doctrine and theoretic dogma'.[4] Yes, indeed, but the intellectual challenge facing the historian (and philosopher) today is to explain the ideas of the Enlightenment in their precise historical context, a task strangely neglected in recent decades.

All societies, of course, rely heavily on myths, revelations, and basic concepts explaining the principles and justifications on which they are organized, concepts which, in the nature of things, are in varying degrees shared and disputed. Tension rises in proportion as the range of disagreement widens in relation to the spectrum of consensus. But a potentially revolutionary change can arise only with major and thoroughgoing questioning of the validity of justifications and legitimizations that previously commanded wide respect and veneration. Hence, our present attempt to reassess and reinterpret the European Enlightenment starts from the thesis that the institutions, social hierarchy, status, and property arrangements on which a given society is based can only remain stable whilst the explanations that society offers in

[2] Cohen, 'Eighteenth-Century Origins', 263–4; Schouls, 'Descartes as Revolutionary', 9–10; Bonney, *European Dynastic States*, 221–2, 361–3, 416; Wootton, 'Leveller Democracy', 419–20.

[3] Wootton, 'Leveller Democracy', 420; Elliott, 'Revolution and Continuity', 105, 108, 111–13.

[4] Quoted in Zagorin, 'Prolegomena', 153.

justification command sufficiently wide currency and acceptance, and begin to disintegrate when such general acceptance lapses. Both social realities and ideas, then, have to be kept equally firmly in mind. However, basically the same social inequalities, hierarchy, economic hardship, and political forms which fed social discontent and frustration in the eighteenth century already existed, at least in broad outline and essentials, in the sixteenth and seventeenth centuries. Socially and institutionally, *ancien régime* society did not change very dramatically between 1650 and 1789. What did change spectacularly and fundamentally was precisely the intellectual context; and so this is what chiefly needs explaining.

That modern 'revolution' crucially entails a massive intellectual break with the past, importing a whole new interpretative paradigm, is indeed implicit in the way the modern idea of 'revolution' itself first arose. The first example of the onset of a principled, general discarding of authority and traditional premisses, in Europe, was the advent of the mechanistic world-view asserted by Cartesianism which triumphed widely in the later seventeenth century. This great shift in basic concepts, like the slightly later notion of a 'Scientific Revolution' occurring between Galileo and Newton, changed western civilization profoundly and, among innumerable other changes, transformed the meaning of the word 'revolution' itself.

Descartes embarked on a general 'reformation', or 'revolution' as it was called in the early eighteenth century, of knowledge, and the way we look on every aspect of life, or as Turgot expressed the point in 1748, Descartes systematically theorized 'une révolution totale';[5] for, in Descartes, 'revolution' means not just linear, fundamental, and irreversible change, and not just auto-emancipation from the intellectual and cultural shackles of the past, but also, as Turgot's remark indicates, something that changes everything.[6] Especially important in shaping the idea that modern thought begins with Descartes were the claims of Enlightenment writers like Bernard Le Bovier de Fontenelle (1657–1757) who, from 1699 to 1741, served as secretary of the Paris Academy of Sciences and has justly been dubbed first of the *philosophes*, d'Alembert in his *Preliminary Discourse* to the *Encyclopédie* (1751), and Condorcet, that Cartesianism engineered a comprehensive sweeping away of previous scientific and philosophical authority together with all criteria of legitimacy based on past authority, knowledge, and practice.[7] Scorning all existing categories and premisses, and all traditional learning, Descartes and Cartesianism transformed men's way of viewing the world, even if the real change was less stupendous than it subsequently seemed,[8] and for this reason were regarded as a true founding 'revolution'.[9] This 'revolution' then, in turn, helped forge the Enlightenment's deep

[5] Turgot, *Recherches sur les causes*, 134.

[6] Spallanzani, *Immagini*, 46, 60 n.; Gaukroger, *Descartes' System*, 1, 4; Schouls, 'Descartes as Revolutionary', 15–18, 20; Schouls, *Descartes*, 15, 18–19, 73–4, 162–3.

[7] Schouls, *Descartes*, 14–16, 72–3; Schouls, 'Descartes as Revolutionary', 22–3; Williams, *Condorcet*, 93, 95.

[8] Garber, *Descartes' Metaphysical Physics*, 58–62, 308.

[9] Williams, *Condorcet*, 7–8, 14–15, 30; Cohen, 'Eighteenth-Century Origins', 280–1; Porter, 'Scientific Revolution', 290; Harrison, *Bible, Protestantism*, 100–1, 268–9.

conviction that between Galileo and Newton there occurred also a more general 'Scientific Revolution' which, like the 'Cartesian revolution', introduced a supposedly entirely new conceptual and interpretative paradigm creating many additional tensions in thought, culture, education, and theology. Following on from these two great 'revolutions', early eighteenth-century *philosophes* took to using the term 'revolution' to refer to any great, fundamental, and—especially but not necessarily—positive change in the basic thinking and institutions of humanity.[10]

The modern concept of 'revolution' is thus specifically a product of the Early Enlightenment, a fact of the utmost importance for any proper understanding of modernity, though few modern historians, owing perhaps to the profound implications for social, political, and economic history, have been willing to acknowledge this. Moreover, the recent trend among historians of science to question whether there really was a 'Scientific Revolution' of discoveries, new procedures, and instruments which fundamentally changed the substance of scientific debate in the seventeenth century leaves untouched the vast influence of the early eighteenth-century perception of 'Scientific Revolution'. Indeed, it would seem to strengthen the argument that it is precisely in the 'displacement of the conceptual network through which scientists view the world' by an essentially new paradigm,[11] a change in categories and ideas, a philosophical transformation in other words, that one finds the really significant difference between what is pre-modern and what is 'modern'. The more historians of science stress the persistence of older methods, approaches, and categories in the era between Copernicus and Newton, detracting from a 'Scientific Revolution' of procedure and fact, the more it emerges that what actually occurred during the Early Enlightenment was a 'revolution' in ideas and interpretative framework, a reconfiguring of the conceptual context within which scientific data were presented, a powerful intellectual construct in other words in large part invented by Fontenelle, Dorthous de Mairan, Voltaire, Turgot, d'Alembert, and Condorcet—that is, more or less the same authors responsible for the notion that 'Cartesianism' constituted a 'revolution'.[12]

Before 1750, then, Cartesians, Hobbists, Spinozists, Leibnizians, and after them the *philosophes*, did not doubt there had been a 'Scientific Revolution' and that this revolution was conceptual or philosophical rather than 'scientific' in the twentieth-century sense. In fact they did not know or use the words 'science' or 'scientific' in our sense but spoke rather of a 'revolution' in 'natural philosophy'. After the Cartesian and 'scientific' revolutions, moreover, nothing could have been more natural than that Europeans and Americans should quickly familiarize themselves with the reality and challenging implications of conceptual 'revolution' in general, and begin to extend this idea to politics. For the late seventeenth- and early eighteenth-century

[10] R. Kosellek, 'Revolution', in Brunner et al. (eds.), *Geschichtliche Grundbegriffe*, v. 719–20; Reichardt and Lüsebrink, '*Révolution*', 53, 60; Baker, 'Revolution', 50–2; Engels, 'Wissenschaftliche Revolution', 240, 243, 246.

[11] Kuhn, *Structure*, 102–4, 111.

[12] Ibid. 290–1, 300–1, 304, 306–7; Cohen, 'Eighteenth-Century Origins', 266–71.

intellectual ferment not only transformed both the word and idea 'revolution' but accustomed literate society to the notion that powerful new ideas can prepare the ground for, and generate, linear, fundamental change.

This new meaning of the word 'revolution', moreover, entered all the main western idioms, German no less than Latin, French, English, and Italian, precisely in the crucially formative half-century between 1670 and 1720.[13] The idea of 'revolution' as something that embraces, and stems from, change in the basic concepts on which society is based, rapidly became central to European political and institutional, as well as intellectual and cultural life, since the intellectual supremacy of traditional categories, religious authority, precedent, and long-established patterns of learning, besides such traditional governmental and administrative forms as 'divine right monarchy', the 'ancient constitution', and customary law, were as much called into question by the conceptual revolution of the late seventeenth century, implicitly at least, as were traditional astronomy, physics, alchemy, magic, and medicine.

Hence, by the 1670s and 1680s the intellectual and cultural barriers to the idea of a political revolution in the modern sense, while still pervasive and powerfully operative in most minds, had eroded in some quarters to the point that both the feasibility and fear of 'revolution' as a planned, deliberate attempt to replace the existing foundations of society had become a real possibility and was widely recognized as an immediate threat. At risk were not just the traditional forms of monarchy, aristocracy, and ecclesiastical power but also all prevailing moral, devotional, and intellectual systems. In this way, from the 1680s onwards, the term 'revolution' rather suddenly came to be understood and deployed in the new and modern sense—a sure sign that we are moving into a 'revolutionary' era. Modern revolution, accordingly, began as an idea and an essentially philosophical and scientific concept but almost at once came to be rendered into the vocabulary of general politics and theological dispute.

It is perfectly true, as is evident from the vast pamphlet literature published during the years 1688–1700, that most English, Scots, and Irish either, like most continental European commentators, considered the so-called 'Glorious Revolution' of 1688 in Britain, Ireland, and the English colonies in America wholly unjustifiable and illegitimate or else rather half-heartedly acknowledged its outcome as legitimate on a *de facto* basis while seeking to justify it in traditional cyclical terms, as a restoration of the 'true' or legitimate institutional order. Nevertheless, there was also a conspicuous and vocal fringe of radical Whigs and republicans both in Britain and the Netherlands who, with very different premisses and aims in mind, proclaimed the 'late Revolution' a great turning point, a linear transformation, introducing a fundamentally new type of polity justifiable exclusively on the basis of 'philosophical' principles, without drawing any legitimacy from tradition, precedent, royal lineages, or theology; and in the eighteenth century this approach,

[13] Koselleck, 'Revolution', in Bruner et al. (eds.), *Geschichtliche Grundbegriffe*, v. 1714–15; Baker, 'Revolution', 41; Reichardt and Lüsebrink, '*Révolution*', 41.

though by no means dominant in the national mythology of 'the Revolution', nevertheless became increasingly widespread in America and in western Europe.[14]

What was 'revolutionary' about the 'Glorious Revolution' of 1688–91 was that, unlike the first English Revolution, it not only permanently dethroned the House of Stuart but created a fundamentally new type of parliamentary monarchy, one which transformed the role of both monarchy and Parliament in Britain as well as the sway of religious uniformity and the Anglican Church, establishing a general 'Toleration' of churches; it also subordinated Scotland and Ireland to England within a changed legal and institutional context as well as transforming the system, and rhetoric, of British control in North America.[15] It was with some reason, therefore, that its bolder apologists justified all this in terms of the new principles of popular sovereignty, and sought to justify toleration, natural rights, and resistance to tyranny, dubbing the whole business 'a great revolution', as the Scottish republican Sir James Montgomery called it. Admittedly, the term 'Glorious Revolution' itself was coined only later. But the term 'revolution' in the new sense propagated by radical publicists, journalists, and statesmen quickly came to be widely used in connection with 1688.

Nor was the change confined (as has been claimed) to the English-speaking world.[16] Quite the contrary, henceforth the term 'revolution' was widely applied to almost any abrupt but fundamental political change with lasting implications. Hence, the French historian the Abbé Vertot, in 1695, in his *Histoire des révolutions de Suède*, calls both Sweden's separation from Denmark, and break with the papacy, 'revolutions' because they introduced basic and irreversible changes. When the Austrians captured the viceroyalty of Naples from Spain in 1707, causing an unprecedented political situation in that realm, Giannone, looking back on that basic linear change from the perspective of the late 1730s, described it as a *rivoluzione*.[17] In Boulainvilliers's history of Muhammad of 1730, the Islamic conquest of the Near East after the Prophet's death is labelled 'a revolution' in both the original French and the English translation of the following year, being called, in the latter, a revolution 'unforeseen, as it was unimaginable' and one of 'greater extent than any that is recorded in history' precisely because it introduced a wholly new era without any cyclical element, one based on totally new principles which (apparently) had nothing to do with the past.[18] Equally, Mably, in 1751, judged the Arab conquests of the Near East, Iran, and North Africa of the seventh century one of the most astounding 'revolutions' of history because of their linear, transforming character.[19] Significantly, this writer defined political revolution, in his *Observations sur les Romains* (Geneva, 1751), as something sudden and tumultuous which transforms the political character of a state, in some cases at least for the better with the people recovering their 'liberty'.[20]

[14] Reichardt and Lüsebrunk, '*Revolution*', 48–9; Goulemot, 'Le Mot révolution', 429–31, 436–8, 443; Zagorin, 'Prolegomena', 170; Baker, 'Revolution', 43; Israel, *Anglo-Dutch Moment*, 10–38.

[15] Israel, *Anglo-Dutch Moment*, 6–7.

[16] Baker, 'Revolution', 43; Kosellek, 'Revolution', in Bruner et al. (eds.), *Geschichtliche Grundbegriffe*, v. 716, 722; Rachum, '*Revolution*', 131–51, 159.

[17] Giannone, *Opere*, 60.

[18] Boulainvilliers, *Life of Mahomet*, 4; in the *Vie de Mahomed*, 4, he refers to 'cette révolution . . . la plus étendue dont on aît connoissance, et dont la mémoire des hommes aît conservé le souvenir'.

[19] Mably, *Observations sur les Romains*, ii. 271.

[20] Ibid. i. 200, 203, 278.

Likewise, in 1750, Turgot styled the rise of Christianity, in his view the greatest and most decisive linear change in history, 'une révolution générale dans les esprits',[21] a designation no one before the Early Enlightenment would have dreamt of applying to the beginnings of their religion but typical of the Early Enlightenment. Perhaps we find here a lesson for the historian and one we should endeavour to take to heart in what follows. Scholars often say: do not rely on the secondary literature, go back to primary sources. But do we do this enough? Do we sufficiently realize the risks in relying on received wisdom, on what the existing modern scholarly literature states? For it was almost universally agreed, for decades, heavily stressed among others by Hannah Arendt, that the modern concept of 'revolution' as linear fundamental change hardly existed before the French Revolution. This claim has been made in hundreds of publications and is still repeated by some historians today. But any reasonably broad reconnaissance of the primary literature of the early eighteenth century will soon convince the researcher that this view is totally incorrect.

'Revolution', then, in the modern sense, inconceivable in the West until the late seventeenth century, during the early pre-1750 Enlightenment became central to Europeans' understanding of the world, particularly after 1688. Furthermore, as with almost every major aspect of the Enlightenment, the critical change in ideas happened well before 1750. Quite rapidly, the notion of fundamental 'revolution' began to seep in everywhere. 'Fashionable books' and political changes, as well as insidious ambition, predicted Leibniz rather astoundingly in his *New Essays* (1704), were now 'inclining everything towards the universal revolution with which Europe is threatened, and are completing the destruction of what still remains in the world of the generous sentiments of the ancient Greeks and Romans who placed love of country and the public good, and the welfare of future generations, before fortune and before life'.[22] The precise danger, he says, lay in the fact that the 'good morality and true religion which natural reason itself teaches us' were no longer upheld owing to the impact of dangerous new views and attitudes.

In this remarkable passage, Leibniz grants that Spinoza, whom he saw as symbolizing intellectually the main causes of the coming 'universal revolution', had, like Epicurus before him, led an exemplary life;[23] but he doubted whether others similarly undermining belief in the 'providence of a perfectly good, wise and just God', following, like Bayle, in Spinoza's footsteps, would achieve anything good. On the contrary, he deeply feared the 'disease' he detected, warning that should it continue to spread 'it will engender a revolution' that would wreak untold damage, though he also believed that 'Providence will cure men by means of that' and that even if the 'universal revolution' he foresaw, with all its consequences, did indeed occur, 'in the final account things will always turn out for the best'.[24]

Trust in and acceptance of social hierarchy and kings, bishops, and aristocracy was bound to erode and be at risk once revolutionary philosophical, scientific, and political thought systems began to invade the general consciousness, questioning

21 Turgot, *Discours sur les avantages*, 210.

22 Leibniz, *New Essays*, 463; Lilla, *G. B. Vico*, 61; Hösle, *Morals and Politics*, 588.

23 Leibniz, *New Essays*, 462.

24 Ibid. 463.

the ascendancy of established authority and tradition, and eroding deference for supposed ancient constitutions and law codes as well as the ancient consensus that all legal and institutional legitimacy derives from precedent, religious sanction, and traditional notions about the true character of the community. From this followed directly the advent of republican and democratic political ideologies expressly rejecting the principles on which political, social-hierarchical, and ecclesiastical legitimacy had previously rested.

However, the fact that the concept of 'revolution', political, social, and moral, became familiar does not mean, needless to say, that it was welcomed. Far from it. Most men had no more desire to discard traditional reverence for established authority and idealized notions of community than their belief in magic, demonology, and Satan. Doubtless, this is true of both elites and the common people; but it is especially true of the latter. Even those relatively few in society sufficiently swayed by the Cartesian intellectual revolution to adopt mechanistic explanation and mathematical logic as the new general criterion of truth rarely sought to apply it to everything. Just as Descartes with his two-substance dualism created a reserved area for spirits, angels, demons, and miracles, and Boyle and Locke with their emphatic empiricism similarly ring-fenced miracles, spirits, and the core Christian 'mysteries', so the intellectual elites of Europe mostly sought one or another intellectual expedient for having it both ways—that is reconciling the new mechanistic criteria of rationality not just with religion and theological doctrines but also with social norms and notions of education, society, and politics based on custom, usage, and existing law as well as social-hierarchical principles.

Few then sought to apply the new criteria to everything. This is why, from its first inception, the Enlightenment in the western Atlantic world was always a mutually antagonistic duality and why the ceaseless internecine strife within it—between moderate mainstream and Radical Enlightenment—is much the most fundamental and important thing about it. Peter Gay's two-volume survey of the Enlightenment, *The Rise of Modern Paganism* (1966) and *The Science of Freedom* (1969), may be in some respects a towering achievement of the historiography of the 1960s. But arguably it rests on a pivotal mistake revealed in the very opening sentence: 'there were many *philosophes* in the eighteenth century, but there was only one Enlightenment.'[25] This needs to be completely reversed: conceptually, there were always two—and could never have been 'only one Enlightenment'—because of the basic and ubiquitous disagreement about whether reason alone reigns supreme in human life or whether philosophy's scope must be limited and reason reconciled with faith and tradition. Peter Gay was mistaken in supposing 'one' enlightenment but much closer to the mark in asking rhetorically, 'what, after all, does Hume, who was a conservative, have in common with Condorcet, who was a democrat?'[26] For he clearly thought they had relatively little in common. Here, in

[25] Gay, *Enlightenment*, i. 3.

[26] Ibid. i, preface p. x; Himmelfarb, 'Two Enlightenments', 297–8.

any case, lies the central inconsistency which calls in question a great deal of the older Enlightenment historiography.

From the outset then, in the late seventeenth century, there were always two enlightenments. Neither the historian nor the philosopher is likely to get very far with discussing 'modernity' unless he or she starts by differentiating Radical Enlightenment from conservative—or as it is called in this study—moderate mainstream Enlightenment. For the difference between reason alone and reason combined with faith and tradition was a ubiquitous and absolute difference. Philosophically, 'modernity' conceived as an abstract package of basic values—toleration, personal freedom, democracy, equality racial and sexual, freedom of expression, sexual emancipation, and the universal right to knowledge and 'enlightenment'—derives, as we have seen, from just one of these two, namely the Radical Enlightenment; historically, however, 'modernity' is the richly nuanced brew which arose as a result of the ongoing conflict not just between these two enlightenments but also (or still more) between both enlightenments, on the one hand, and, on the other, the successive counter-enlightenments, beginning with Bossuet and culminating in Postmodernism, rejecting all these principles and seeking to overthrow both streams of Enlightenment. Rousseau, initially in the late 1740s and early 1750s an ally of Diderot and a radical *philosophe*, subsequently, in the 1760s, rebelled against both branches of Enlightenment, becoming the moral 'prophet' as it were of one form of Counter-Enlightenment.[27]

Of the two enlightenments, the moderate mainstream was without doubt overwhelmingly dominant in terms of support, official approval, and prestige practically everywhere except for several decades in France from the 1740s onwards. Nevertheless, in a deeper sense, and in the long run, it proved to be much the less important of the two enlightenments. For it was always fatally hampered by its Achilles heel, namely that all its philosophical recipes for blending theological and traditional categories with the new critical-mathematical rationality proved flawed in practice, not to say highly problematic and shot through with contradiction. Cartesian dualism, Lockean empiricism, Leibnizian monads, Malebranche's occasionalism, Bishop Huet's fideism, the London Boyle Lectures, Newtonian physico-theology, Thomasian eclecticism, German and Swedish Wolffianism, all the methodologies of compromise presented insuperable disjunctions and difficulties, rendering the whole philosophico-scientific-scholarly arena after 1650 exceedingly fraught and unstable.

The radical wing who scorned all such dualistic systems, and attempts at adjustment, may have been a tiny fringe in terms of numbers, status, and approval ratings, among both elites and in popular culture, but they proved impossible to dislodge or overwhelm intellectually. Those who reduced the worldly and spiritual to a single continuum and erected a single set of rules governing the whole of reality, beginning

[27] Garrard, *Rousseau's Counter-Enlightenment*, 25–7.

in a sense with Hobbes but especially with Spinoza, were everywhere denounced, banned, and reviled. Yet the universal opposition of churches, governments, universities, and leading publicists, as well as the great bulk of the common people, could not alter the fact that it was precisely these philosophical radicals extending the Galilean-Cartesian conception of rationality, and criterion of what is 'true', across the board, pushing it as far as it would go, and allowing no exemptions whatsoever, who often seemed to evince the greatest intellectual consistency and coherence.

Reason, then, contended the radical *philosophes* of the Early Enlightenment—Bayle, Fontenelle, Boulainvilliers, Meslier, Fréret, Boureau-Deslandes, Tyssot de Patot, Du Marsais, Rousset de Missy, La Beaumelle, Lévesque de Burigny, Mably, Morelly, Diderot, d'Alembert, Helvetius, the marquis d'Argens, and the pre-1754 Rousseau, teaches that human society should be based on personal liberty, equality, and freedom of thought and expression. The radical philosophical underground, however, with its branches in England, Germany, Italy, and the Netherlands as well as France, long remained not just minuscule but fiercely denigrated and persecuted by virtually the whole of European and American society. But precisely because the old learning and scholarship had lost its prestige and all the centre blocs proved intellectually highly unstable, the radical fringe, from the 1660s onwards, was remarkably successful not just in continually unsettling the middle ground, subverting the Republic of Letters, redefining the key issues, and setting the general intellectual agenda but also in infiltrating popular culture and opinion. By the mid 1740s, the radical faction, despite the opposing efforts of Voltaire, had largely captured the main bloc of the French intellectual avant-garde which it continued to dominate down to the time of Napoleon. Vast energy was invested by governments, churches, universities, erudite journals, lawyers, and scientific academies, not to mention the Inquisition and guardians of press censorship, in seeking to prevent, or at least curb, the growing seepage of radical ideas into the public sphere—and eventually the popular consciousness. Leading controversialists of the time, such as Samuel Clarke in England, Jean Le Clerc in Holland, Christian Thomasius in Germany, and the Abbés Houtteville and Pluche, in France, spared no effort to stifle the radical challenge intellectually. Yet the moderate mainstream, countering the radical challenge with Lockeanism, Newtonianism, and—in Germany, Scandinavia, and Russia—with Leibnizio-Wolffianism, simply proved unable clearly and cogently to win the intellectual battle.

Public controversy, moreover, generates its own dialectic. As Condorcet later noted, during the French Revolution, 'cette philosophie nouvelle', by seeking to undermine tradition and re-educate the people, was everywhere ceaselessly assailed by those social groups which exist, as he puts it, only because of 'privilege', error, prejudice, credulity, and persecution'.[28] Yet, for all that, it proved not just impossible to suppress the prohibited concepts or prevent their becoming entrenched at the heart of Europe's intellectual and cultural life, but also to prevent their penetrating

[28] Condorcet, *Esquisse*, 208.

the public sphere more generally. Indeed, it is arguable that from the 'Philosophy the Interpreter of Scripture controversy' which erupted in the Dutch Republic in 1666 down to the 1848 revolutions across Europe, radical thought, defined as 'philosophy' which eliminates all theological criteria, supernatural agency, tradition, magic, and racial and hierarchical conceptions of society, placing the whole of reality under the same set of rules, the question of whether to accept or oppose what the young Karl Marx later called a 'consistent naturalism' unifying whatever is true in both idealism and materialism in a single system,[29] remained uninterruptedly the supreme and basic issue in western intellectual debate.

However, due to the leanings of much recent historiography, as well as the anti-historical orientation of twentieth-century Anglo-American philosophy, the modern reader investigating the rise of 'modernity' as a system of democratic values and individual liberties in the Enlightenment encounters a bewildering and curious paradox. For the crucible in which those values originated and developed—the Radical Enlightenment—has not only, until recently, been very little studied by scholars but at the same time confronts us with a major philosophical challenge in that its prime feature is a conception of 'philosophy' (and indeed of 'revolution') from which during the course of the nineteenth and twentieth centuries western liberal thought and historiography, especially in the English-speaking world, managed to become profoundly estranged. Part of the difficulty, in contemporary Britain and America, is that philosophy's proper zone of activity has come to be so narrowly defined by the intellectual heirs of Locke and Hume that philosophy is generally conceived to be a marginal, technical discipline which neither does, nor should, affect anything very much, let alone define the whole of the reality in which we live, an approach which firmly places 'philosophy' at the very opposite end of the spectrum from the Radical Enlightenment's (and indeed Marx's and Nietzsche's) conception of 'philosophy' as discussion of the human and cosmic condition in its entirety, the quest for a coherent picture, the basic architecture, so to speak, of everything we know and are.

Hence, where the radical thinker Condorcet, looking back on the Enlightenment's achievements from the standpoint of 1793, deemed it certain not just that 'philosophy' caused the French Revolution but that only philosophy can cause a true 'revolution'—which is also the position underlying this present study—this challenging and important proposition remains for most contemporary readers a remote and deeply puzzling idea. Where for Condorcet, a revolutionary shift is a shift in understanding, something which, though ultimately driven by the long-term processes of social change, economic development, and institutional adaptation, is in itself a product of 'philosophy' since only philosophy can transform our mental picture of the world and its basic categories, most modern readers, conditioned by our Lockean and Humean legacy to resist attempts to envisage 'philosophy' as what defines the human condition, our knowledge and self-awareness in their overall contours, see things very differently.

[29] Marx, *Economic and Philosophic Manuscripts*, 156.

However, tentatively to agree with the radical *philosophes* in their understanding of 'revolution' and of history is not necessarily to deny the validity of other conceptions of philosophy in their context, or indeed of the role of social forces, or popular culture, in the making of the Atlantic democratic revolutions of the eighteenth century. To the radical *philosophes*, not only all types of science but also the methodologies of the new human disciplines of economics, social theory, ethics, aesthetics, legal studies, and politics by definition coherently interrelate, every aspect of human knowledge being presided over by what Condorcet terms 'la philosophie générale', a characteristic of all systems which are basically *Spinosiste*.[30] This striving for universality and an overarching coherence, rooted in a conception of philosophy as the sum of knowledge, a force presiding over everything, may be rather alien to the mainstream tradition of Anglo-American thought and may indeed be deeply suspect philosophically, but its power as a shaping force in the Enlightenment, hence as a historical factor, is beyond question.

Asserting the primary role of 'philosophy' in the Enlightenment sense can in any case readily be combined with acknowledging the importance of socio-economic factors and 'cultural-anthropological' dimensions of history- so long as we keep basic concepts at the centre of our picture. 'Philosophy' defined as discussion of the shared and disputed core ideas which both organize and drive changes in human societies does not of course conjure up from nowhere the gross inequalities, deprivation, misery, social revolt, land hunger, commercial rivalries, and resistance to fiscal pressure fuelling the resentment and social unrest which is an indispensable precondition of revolutionary change; but 'philosophy' as defined by the *philosophes* can plausibly be claimed to drive basic change in human societies by channelling social grievances, resentments, and frustrations in one direction rather than another.

Revolutionary ideas in any case can only become a powerful force in history when they are conceived, articulated, discussed, and then developed, propagated, and widely disseminated, highly complex processes linked to, but yet also in some sense clearly distinct from, the social and economic context or the anthropological profile of a society in which new ideas are expressed and debated. This means that a primary aspect of any restructuring of historical studies designed to reconfigure the basic relationship between intellectual history and the rest of history so as to place the former at the centre while simultaneously ensuring a close interaction of ideas with social, cultural, and political history must first reconsider what history of ideas itself actually is. If showing the links between core concepts and broad and long-term shifts in the social and economic environment, as well as popular culture, is the chief task of a restructured historical studies concerned with achieving an integrated, 'joined-up' conception of the past, and if every real modern 'revolution' is indeed caused by a prior and widely disseminated conceptual revolution, then a restructured history of ideas will inevitably eventually replace the current modish

30 Condorcet, *Esquisse*, 200.

preoccupation with so-called 'cultural' and social developments as the study most relevant and decisive for any serious understanding of 'modernity'.

2. HISTORIANS AND THE WRITING OF 'INTELLECTUAL HISTORY'

Consequently, the most urgent priority in any current attempt to devise a methodology of intellectual history capable of serving as a frame for an 'integrated general history' is to redefine the field 'history of philosophy' in a way that enables us satisfactorily to accommodate the Enlightenment meaning of the term 'philosophy'. That is, for the purposes of this present exercise our best course may be to experiment with readopting 'philosophy' in its widest and most opposite sense to that projected by the Anglo-American 'analytical' tradition; for without a dramatic widening of the scope of 'history of philosophy', breaking in this respect with the Lockean and Humean legacy, no historian, or philosopher, can be said to engage broadly with Enlightenment ideas about revolutions and society or deal comprehensively with a 'modernity' of principle conceived as a set of values, attitudes, and ideas generated by the Radical Enlightenment.

All the rival tendencies in the restructuring of historical studies in the last few decades—however much they disagree in other respects—concur that the 'old intellectual history' prevalent down to the 1960s had for urgent and unavoidable reasons become decidedly unsatisfactory. For the 'old intellectual history' separated ideas from social context, taking it for granted, on the basis of current consensus, that we know who the relevant thinkers of a given epoch are, who are more and who less important. In this way, it yielded a highly selective and abstracted 'canon of classics', a 'great-book, great-man' vision of intellectual history, as Robert Darnton called it, which not only removed thinkers and texts from their historical context but tacitly superimposed its own prior intellectual preferences—that is, ideas and intellectual traditions pre-selected as 'key', or as the concepts which most powerfully shaped the historical process, by the historian himself often unconsciously influenced by contemporary debates and preoccupations. The result was an established 'canon', a kind of intellectual mythology, lionizing certain figures while ignoring others, creating a picture potentially remote from contemporaries' real intellectual concerns which, apart from enshrining the dubious notion of 'intellectual influence', revealed little about society or how ideas impact on politics, culture, and the 'common man'.[31] Not only was it unhistorical, this canon was also, and with considerable justification, later widely attacked for building in very real (and, from our present perspective, unacceptable) biases: it was in several respects insufficiently democratic and egalitarian, indeed can fairly be said to have been to a degree

[31] Darnton, *Forbidden Best-Sellers*, 170; Stuurman, 'The Canon', 152–3, 157; Skinner, *Liberty*, 102–6.

patriarchal, Eurocentric, subtly pro-imperialistic, and heavily skewed towards certain particular transatlantic preferences and cultural traditions.

The chief concern of the 'old' intellectual history, or *Ideengeschichte*, then, was to demonstrate how ideas 'influence' the development and propagation of other ideas. Envisaging these as generating or affecting other concepts in a more or less unbroken chain, this older methodology not only left us with a decidedly simplistic and unsatisfactory, not to say unexplained, process of intellectual 'influence' but, even worse, also tended to ghettoize intellectual history by rigidly separating it from virtually every aspect of mainstream social, economic, and institutional history. A widespread revolt followed in which attention shifted decisively away, as Darnton, one of the most influential of Enlightenment historians of recent decades, put it, from the content of ideas to such questions as 'how do ideas relate to the wider historical process?' 'And how do they penetrate and influence society?'[32]

Hence, on both sides of the Atlantic during the last third of the twentieth century, traditional history of ideas came to be widely and justifiably discredited as too narrow, too arbitrary, and insufficiently embedded in context and the wider historical process.[33] However, it was toppled not by one but by several—at least three—different, conceptually widely divergent, methodologies developed largely in isolation from each other. Besides the new kind of cultural-social *histoire de mentalités* (and its Poststructural revisions) developed by the Annales School, in France, there arose in the Anglo-American academic milieu a new approach originally developed at Cambridge in the 1960s, where its chief practitioners were John Pocock who later moved to the United States, Quentin Skinner, Richard Tuck, and John Dunn, a group of scholars who asked how concepts relate to the rhetoric, forms of expression, and 'political languages' in which political debates are conducted, thereby devising a fruitful new method sometimes called 'revolutionary' which they applied in particular to history of political thought. While there were and are differences between these practitioners—Skinner, for instance, to an extent resisting Pocock's strategy of treating different political languages and traditions as essentially autonomous entities and placing greater emphasis on authorial autonomy, a difference sometimes labelled as that between 'contextualists' proper and 'conventionalists', the latter meaning that authors have to express their viewpoints conventionally—they share a broadly common approach to studying the textual and linguistic context of ideas.[34] Their contribution was to identify, clarify, and greatly thicken and enrich 'the context' of discourse surrounding the emergence and deployment of ideas.

A third force, the German school of 'conceptual history' or *Begriffsgeschichte* whose founding figures were Reinhart Koselleck and Rolf Reichardt, envisaged basic concepts such as 'revolution', 'republic', '*critique*', 'civil society', 'civilization',

[32] Skinner, *Liberty*, 106; Darnton, *Forbidden Best-Sellers*, 169; Darnton, *Business*, 1; Richter, 'Towards a Lexicon', 95–6.

[33] Stuurman, 'The Canon', 152; Richter, 'Towards a Lexicon', 96, 101, 103–6, 117–18.

[34] Richter, 'Towards a Lexicon', 105–6, 108; Palonen, *Quentin Skinner*, 65–7, 79; Bevir, 'Role of Contexts', 165.

'liberty', 'liberalism', 'enlightenment', 'toleration', and even 'history' as being crafted, propagated, and adapted amid the cut and thrust of political, social, and economic history and made these key ideas, and their historically determined shifts of meaning, themselves the prime focus of study.[35] While anglophone 'contextualists' have deemed it methodologically questionable, even counter-productive, to isolate particular concepts from their immediate context of linguistic usage, debate, and phraseology in this manner, and historians of philosophy, with equal justification, dislike their tendency to divorce 'basic concepts' active in society from the conceptual battles of philosophers, yet this school of thought has undeniably also helped deepen our understanding of key conceptual components of both intellectual and social history, though Koselleck can certainly be faulted, among other things, for a far too timid application of his own method to the meaning and usages of the term 'revolution' in the late seventeenth and early eighteenth centuries, failing effectively to revise the long prevailing (but wrong) assumptions about this, something which as we shall see has been a major obstruction both to Enlightenment studies and to study of the French Revolution.[36]

Meanwhile, advocates of *Begriffsgeschichte* charged the 'contextualists' with separating the flow of intellectual discourse more than the historian should from the complex dynamics of social and political history.[37] They were far more assertive than the Cambridge School in seeking to pull social and intellectual history together, in particular by dredging a very wide range of sources to focus on shifts in collective expressions and conceptualizations of key ideas.[38] In criticizing Cambridge *Diskursgeschichte* for defining 'historical context' too narrowly and showing insufficient concern for social structures and pressures,[39] German 'conceptual history' here joined forces with the French 'diffusionists', as Darnton calls the cultural-anthropological tendency preoccupied with popular culture, book and print history, and *histoire de mentalités*. Skinner's claim that the meaning of a text arises from the writer's intentions being expressed in terms fashioned by the conventions and usages of his historical context seemed to both of these factions to rely on a notion of 'context' which is too narrowly textual and rhetorical, taking insufficient account of the complex roles of book production, text diffusion, and marketing, as well as of political, legal, and ecclesiastical restrictions and other forms of interference.

Such critics argue that it is not by studying discourse and intellectual debate more or less in isolation, or authors' intentions mediated through textual and terminological conventions, but rather in the wider historical contexts in which ideas are applied, the social and political context, that the real and precise significance of intellectual encounters can be coaxed from texts and the evolution of thought best traced. Authors' 'intentions', they point out, often relate to texts in less clear-cut and

[35] Kosellek, 'Hinweise', 36–8, 42, 44.

[36] Reichardt, 'Einleitung', 62–4; Richter, 'Towards a Lexicon', 107–12; Krüger, '*Geroglifici* und *scrittura*', 353.

[37] Kosellek, 'Hinweise', 45–6; Bödeker, 'Reflexionen', 78–9, 83.

[38] Böleker, 'Reflexionen', 83–4.

[39] Darnton, *Forbidden Best-Sellers*, 170, 175, 178–9; Palonen, *Quentin Skinner*, 39, 65.

unproblematic ways than the 'contextualists' imply, all sorts of circumstantial, societal, and cultural factors intervening which may be beyond authors' immediate awareness, making 'context' discourse itself theoretically more problematic and less useful on its own than Skinner and Pocock claim.[40]

Besides rejecting, like the others, the old straitjacket of a hallowed canon of key ideas expounded in great books, 'diffusionists' have been primarily interested—here unlike the others—in linking attitudes, trends in religiosity, and modes of thought to cultural developments in society generally, seeking to do so in often startlingly new ways by studying not articulated ideas or intellectual 'contexts', but cultures of literacy, publication, and communication in the widest sense, including newspapers and other ephemera, journals, *clandestina*, wills, inventories, jokes, songs, the practices of publishers and distributors. By investigating how texts of all kinds are read and used, and by whom, they scored impressive successes in uncovering the dynamics of readership, attitude formation, cultural reception, and diffusion. Again, the result was to enrich historical knowledge in crucial ways, not least by providing a much more detailed picture of the size and character of the contemporary reading public than was previously available—readers of fashionable literary works in Paris around 1660, for example, being estimated at around 3,000[41]—together with much clearer notions of what was read and by whom.

French 'diffusionists' and Anglo-American practitioners of the 'new social history' have been primarily concerned to locate outlook and attitudes in their social and cultural context and, hence, in reaction to the 'old intellectual history', drastically de-emphasize the role of alleged intellectual leaders. Where willing to concede a place for intellectual history at all, these scholars are chiefly concerned with questions of impact, popularization, social function, as well as quantification of reading and publishing. With their often archivally based methods using evidence of all kinds, they revealed much that is new about the evolution of attitudes and modes of thought in society, hence about *mentalités*— though the concept of *mentalités* itself latterly came to be discarded by most 'diffusionists' as predicated on a degree of structural coherence in the make-up of popular culture which Poststructuralists suspect may not actually exist. A few critics, however, including myself, have expressed unease at their disinclination to study intellectual debates and articulated ideas as such. Darnton, who urges more interaction, if not actually a fusion, between the 'Cambridge' and French 'diffusionist' schools, deemed the almost total segregation of Cambridge contextualism with its intense preoccupation 'with analyzing texts reflecting different languages of discourse' from the 'new' social history of culture with its prime focus on popular cultural entities and the common people as unhelpful and ultimately counter-productive. But while the Cambridge School would doubtless profit from being immersed in more social and cultural history and the 'new social history' in ideas, given the two schools' very different

[40] Palonen, *Quentin Skinner*, 42–6; LaCapra, *Rethinking Intellectual History*, 36–7; Bevir, 'Role of Contexts', 168.

[41] Muchembled, *History of the Devil*, 163.

methodological premisses—and focus, one on society's cultural traits, the other on the intellectual culture of small highly articulate elites—there would seem to be little likelihood of a future merger.

An impressive result of 'diffusionist' research in our present context is our now far more detailed awareness of the reality of the set of cultural shifts driving or—depending on your point of view—reflecting the emergence of new ideas in the seventeenth and eighteenth centuries. A broad transition in north-western European society towards 'enlightened' attitudes regarding magic, demonology, and the Devil, for example, has been conclusively demonstrated and in a detailed manner showing that the crucial changes took place long before 1750—and not in the second half of the eighteenth century as readers of the discarded 'old intellectual history' would be led to suppose. In France, the decades 1720–50 were particularly decisive for this crucial shift, though in Holland and England the same development occurred earlier.[42] The diffusionists are entirely justified, therefore, in asserting that the 'old' intellectual history's notion that the broad onset of more secular ideas began around the middle of the eighteenth century—arising in the wake of Montesquieu's *L'Esprit des lois* (1748) and the first volumes of the *Encyclopédie* in the early 1750s—is not just mistaken but utterly unhistorical and misleading. Equally, though, as we shall see, the diffusionists were themselves mistaken in assuming that the errors of the 'old intellectual history' demonstrate that the articulation of new ideas by the *philosophes* was therefore marginal to the main process and posterior to what they alleged were prior 'cultural' shifts.

While the changes in ideas among the more highly educated strata of society which the French 'diffusionists' demonstrated are broadly in line with the wider cultural trend reflected in literature, their techniques also revealed a growing divergence from the late seventeenth century onwards between elite and popular culture. They confirmed—as only a few, such as Paul Hazard, had previously surmised—that the start of the demystification and the real parting of ways of Enlightenment elite and popular culture began in fact in the later seventeenth century, with belief in Satan, magic, and demonology receding rapidly among sections of the elites but remaining strongly entrenched among the poorer strata and especially the rural illiterate and barely literate sections of the population.[43] Such research also showed that while adherence to a traditional, magical world-view remained strongest among the illiterate and little educated, *anti-philosophie* and Counter-Enlightenment nevertheless also remained entrenched among some more highly educated sections of society. Invaluably, 'diffusionism' was able to prove that only small minorities of elite society confidently and consistently adhered to what contemporaries called a 'philosophical' view of the cosmos, most even of the more highly educated retaining enough of their old anxieties and fear of the supernatural to remain in two minds about the *philosophes* and their rationalizing message.[44]

[42] Ibid. 171; Goulemot, 'Démons, merveilles et philosophie', 1231–7.

[43] Goulemot, 'Démons, merveilles et philosophie', 1226, 1238–40; Muchembled, *History of the Devil*, 163.

[44] Muchembled, *History of the Devil*, 171, 175–81.

But if the 'diffusionist' approach yielded some impressive results, showing that shifts in attitudes over time stand in clear and quantifiable but complex interaction with changes in society, this methodology also reveals a glaring weakness: for it provides no way of knowing whether new views and attitudes derive from, or alternatively drive, structural shifts in society. Rather it tends to carry over from Marxist tradition a rooted bias assuming that ideas must be subordinate to supposedly deeper social realities, professing to replace the discredited economic determinism of Marxist theory with a novel type of social structural or, latterly, cultural determinism while actually leaving it wholly unclear, as between ideas and cultural shifts, which is the cart and which is the horse. In the case of waning belief in magic and demonology, for instance, or the proven decline in ordinations for the priesthood and numbers of new recruits entering French monasteries in the eighteenth century (from the 1730s onwards),[45] clearly documented shifts in practice, beliefs, and attitudes were vaguely attributed to alleged but unseen and undocumented social and cultural pressures and 'sensibility'.

For some time, this vagueness prompted relatively little protest. But as the process of restructuring historical studies continues, a struggle seemingly for the very 'soul' of historical studies, a sharp divergence between two mutually incompatible materialist conceptions of the historical process, has become evident. An expression of the 'diffusionist' approach which especially highlights this growing collision and rivalry between the 'new social history' and its rival, the 'new intellectual history', for hegemony over the new broad, 'integrationist', history the methodological debate is generally striving for, is the method of Roger Chartier, who famously asserted that de Tocqueville rightly claimed eighteenth-century France underwent an 'abandonment of Christian practices unequaled in Europe', and that the Revolution stemmed from a transformed state of mind, but wrongly ascribed this transformation to the *philosophes* and ideas expressed in books. Abandoning the old dogma that the essence of social development lies in changes in control of property and the means of production, Chartier argues there is still a basic, determining set of 'real' social structures, or trends, distinct from ideas which determine the latter, revealing the workings of this 'real' social determinant being the task of what he calls 'cultural sociology'.

The 'new' social history's way of ordering historical studies, focusing on changes in attitude and practice in society while marginalizing intellectual history, its insistence that the impulses and origin behind any great revolutionary restructuring of attitudes such as transformed the West in the eighteenth century cannot be primarily intellectual but must be 'social' and socio-cultural, rests in the end on the claim that in society changes in belief and sensibility are independent of, and prior to, ideas and that these 'deeper' shifts stem from movements in social practice and custom to which the formulation of intellectual doctrines and concepts is posterior and subordinate: 'the most profound changes in ways of being', contends Chartier,

[45] Delumeau and Cottret, *Le Catholicisme*, 407–8; Chartier, *Cultural Origins*, 100–1.

'were not the direct result of clear and distinct thoughts'; for, on the contrary, 'even the most powerful and most original conceptual innovations are inscribed in the collective decisions that regulate and command intellectual constructions before they achieve expression in clear thoughts'.[46] As a theory this may sound plausible and has certainly won widespread support; but while philosophical ideas may indeed often follow inarticulate and deep-seated trends in culture that are not intellectually generated, it remains very difficult to substantiate such claims in a clear and convincing manner and some of its assertions look distinctly vulnerable.

Characteristic of Chartier's 'cultural sociology', as of the new social history more generally, is the attribution of major shifts in beliefs and attitudes to changes in social-cultural practice, fashion, and sociability, unconscious shifts in piety, the decreasingly ritual character of governance and kingship after 1700, and mutations in patterns of marriage, gender relations, sexuality, and birth control. Especially unconvincing is Chartier's insistence on viewing the emergence of ideas from sensibility, through sociability, as a strictly one-way street, compensating for the inevitable paucity and inconclusiveness of evidence about sensibility with what is frequently no more than sheer conjecture. Theoretically, as Marx himself admitted before arriving at his more dogmatic formulations of dialectical materialism, it is by no means obvious why a thoroughgoing materialist and naturalist account of the world should be unable to accommodate a balanced interaction, or two-way traffic, between physical reality and human consciousness. From a practical point of view, moreover, historians are bound to react to the obvious impossibility of demonstrating anything very persuasively about shifts which by are definition silent, inarticulate, and unconscious.

Its built-in, ineradicable vagueness is certainly the Achilles heel of the 'new social history'. When discussing eighteenth-century French secularization, for example, Chartier claims the Revolution marks the culmination of a 'transfer of sacrality which, even before it rose to the surface, had silently shifted to new family-orientated, civic and patriotic values the affect and emotion formerly invested in Christian representations'.[47] Perhaps. But how can anyone cogently demonstrate such a complex and mysterious process from the limited 'social' evidence at hand especially when not only Condorcet and de Tocqueville but virtually all eighteenth- and nineteenth-century commentators insist on the exact opposite, namely that 'philosophy' was incontestably the prime cause of the changes in social attitudes? The enemies of the Enlightenment, furthermore, were just as emphatic about this as the *philosophes*: the 'extraordinary progress which incredulity makes from day to day', exclaimed one Christian apologist in 1751, has no other explanation than the effect of 'la philosophie', that is the kind of philosophy which opposes belief in miracles, revelation, and ecclesiastical authority.[48]

It is easy to mock Chartier's 'inchoate sensibility', 'silent' shifts, and inarticulate risings to the surface. But these are arguably symptomatic of the chronic weakness

[46] Chartier, *Cultural Origins*, 2, 109. [47] Ibid. 109.
[48] [François], *Preuves*, i. preface pp. i–ii.

and defects of the 'new' social history as a method of explaining crucial changes in attitudes in the history of societies. Some claim that such resolute de-emphasizing of ideas and of intellectual history whatever its inherent logic and justification at least far better accords than history of ideas with the democratic tenor of modern society with its insistence that what counts is the common man. Ordinary folk, it is contended, have no interest whatever in ideas and scorn people who do, and to be relevant historical studies must focus on the mass of humanity and render the main processes of history accessible to those who neither know nor want to know about doctrines, concepts, constitutional principles, or intellectual debates. Surely to study the ordinary mass of humanity must always be a more legitimate procedure than to study tiny intellectual elites?

This sounds plausible but is wholly fallacious, being based on a deep-seated confusion between the significance and power of ideas and ability to understand them. For ideas were never confined to elites. Rather, as the radical writer Jean Meslier already pointed out, in the early eighteenth century, the misery, exploitation, and economic hardship suffered by the most downtrodden, and especially the peasantry, illiterate artisans, and labouring poor, despite the fact that they mostly have no inkling of this, are organized and systematized on the basis of doctrines in which they trust implicitly and which theorize, buttress, and legitimize the political, religious, and economic instruments of their own exploitation—doctrines which flourish all the more, and gain a firmer hold, the greater the credulity and ignorance 'des plus faibles et des moins éclairés'.[49] The present modish preference among teachers and students for the 'cultural' and the 'social' over the intellectual in the core mechanics of history may owe much to the, for some, appealing implication that history of ideas is irrelevant to an effective understanding of history, and hence there is no need to bother one's head with complex ideas supposedly the concern only of small and remote elites. But this kind of anti-intellectualism, however many eager converts it wins, does so at great cost: for it has often rendered the 'diffusionists' either willing or, in Darnton's case, as Jeremy Popkin pointed out unwilling allies of the Postmodernist campaign to discredit traditional methods of historical criticism and marginalize, and cast a negative light on, the Enlightenment itself.[50]

The 'new' social history's subordination of the intellectual to allegedly deeper and more powerful social structures is part of a venerable tradition of historical and social thought reaching back via the Annales School in France and Marx all the way to Montesquieu who was the first in modern times to assert that there is such a thing as an underlying set of structures—geographical, climatic, economic, or racial—which generate in particular societies a fixed or slow-moving social and moral disposition generating social forms and structures held to be more fundamental, and more apt to determine the overall shape of historical development, than the supposedly surface froth of mere articulated doctrines, ideas, and elite culture. Such theories marginalize the significance of new intellectual initiatives but

49 Meslier, *Testament*, i. 7.

50 Ibid. 4; Popkin, 'Robert Darnton's Alternative', 105–6, 128.

are also conspicuously unwieldy—as Braudel notoriously was, for example—in accounting for major political events. An astute contemporary objection to Montesquieu's 'structuralism', around 1750, advanced by the Danish *philosophe* Ludvig Holberg (1684–1754), was that it conspicuously fails to account for developments, like the cultural revolution in early eighteenth-century Russia, where there were no relevant prior impulses among the peasantry, townspeople, or the rest of society pointing to a sudden 'revolution' of ideas but where a vast cultural and social transition, transforming every aspect of Russian society, nevertheless occurred, a revolution largely imported in the form of books and intellectuals from outside.[51] Holberg had a point to which Montesquieu could indeed provide no answer. Doubtless real 'revolutions' mostly are caused at least in part by broad social-structural factors. But apparently they do not have to be, if there is powerful external interference, something more obvious in the eighteenth century, perhaps, than it is now.

To integrate intellectual history effectively with social, cultural, and political history, then, it seems likely that what is really needed is nothing like a 'cultural sociology' but rather a new, reformed intellectual history presiding over a two-way traffic, or dialectic of ideas and social reality, and focusing less on finished theories, as one participant in this collective process has aptly expressed it, than the 'reconstruction of polemical, frequently unresolved arguments', a new intellectual history in which the major theorists of the past still figure prominently, though the ranking between them may be greatly altered, but in which the chief emphasis is less on thinkers and theories than on 'thinking' and debates.[52] For once basic concepts about society, taught as doctrines, beliefs, and legal principles, partly shared and partly disputed, are acknowledged to be the key factor in determining, defining, and reassessing social organization, and hence in social change itself, and the true hub of an integrated social and cultural history, the task of reforming intellectual history itself at once becomes even more urgent. Especially requisite is a dramatic broadening of the concept of 'argument' to include not just political, legal, and ecclesiastical interventions in polemical debates but also, and perhaps especially, popular protests and interventions. Needless to say, such a new intellectual history, fusing the advantages and shedding the disadvantages of the Cambridge School, 'diffusionists', and *Begriffsgeschichte*, though an eclectic construction will, at the same time, be a cultural phenomenon of considerable importance not only to historians but also philosophers, social theorists, political analysts, and the lay reader.

The result may usefully be termed the 'controversialist' approach to intellectual history, a methodology envisaging the interaction between society and ideas as a series of encounters in which concepts partly shared and partly disputed are deemed not the sole motor of social and political change, since material shifts remain major factors, but the prime channelling and guiding force. Such a

[51] Holberg, *Remarques*, pp. d2^{v}, e5–e5^{v}; Wolff, *Inventing Eastern Europe*, 204–5.

[52] Stuurman, 'The Canon', 161.

restructuring of historical studies around the 'new intellectual history', in direct rivalry to the 'new social history', would envisage society's system of political, economic, and cultural relations as being continually reassessed, shaped, and reshaped by controversies over basic concepts about authority, tradition, religion, science, and power. The seventeenth century, and to a decreasing extent the eighteenth and nineteenth centuries, were an age in which individuals (despite calls by Kant, among others, to think critically) were not supposed to engage in independent, critical thinking. Basic ideas were proclaimed, taught, and laid down for society by the churches, legal bodies, craft guilds and corporations, schools, universities, the medical profession, artistic bodies, and, of course, princely courts. This, in turn, imparts an overriding significance to public controversies and encounters about books, pamphlets, spoken addresses, and ideas; for it is here that society, government, and the churches, as well as other bodies, most extensively and precisely defined their relationship to intellectual positions and traditions and where linkages between ideas and the 'public sphere' are most distinctly revealed.

Researching publicly approved or condemned views also brings to the fore sermons, synodal proceedings, academic disputations, and other texts which reflect less a given author's thoughts than what groups and congregations were expected to think in response to new ideas. The question who read particular books, highlighted by the diffusionists, will here lose some of its relevance. For focusing on controversies soon demonstrates that society teems with people who have strong views (just as they do today) about ideas articulated in books which they have not read and about which they know very little even though they may well have heard of them. As the French Jesuit journal the *Mémoires de Trévoux* noted during the public controversy over Montesquieu's *L'Esprit des lois*, in April 1749, in France the book was very 'well known' even to people who had not read it and were incapable of properly understanding it.[53]

In other ways too, setting up a two-way interaction between basic concepts and society requires going beyond the question who read particular authors and books and why. Numerous surviving Early Enlightenment texts are anonymous, multi-authored, or given to flights of fancy and elaborate jokes which rely on readers sharing in particular perceptions, and these too need to be studied less as the product of a particular author's mind, or who read a particular author (which is in many ways a false question), than as fragments of a partly shared and partly disputed conceptual framework extending throughout society. The researcher must also learn to read as if participating in a public discussion and on different levels simultaneously. The general ban applying everywhere during the age of the Enlightenment on direct expression of atheistic, anti-Christian, anti-monarchical, and libertine ideas generated complex forms of irony, ambiguity, and sarcasm which—as Quentin Skinner pointed out long ago in the cases of Hobbes and Bayle[54]—one is more likely

[53] *Mémoires de Trévoux* (Apr. 1749), 718.

[54] Skinner, 'Meaning and Understanding', 33–4, 40.

to interpret accurately if one carefully considers how contemporaries read them than by treating them simply as authored texts in isolation.

Contemporary controversies, then, major and minor, are the pivot, the means to grasp not just intellectual history in its proper perspective but, more importantly, the real relationship between the social sphere and ideas. For it is the contemporary controversies which connect philosophers, books, and ideas directly to politics, approved attitudes, and the public sphere, indicating precisely which ideas are penetrating and which not, how they mutate or are simplified when publicized or recycled by lesser intellectual figures, when and how they penetrate, and what the perceived consequences of their propagation might be. Gestures, slogans, images, protests, jokes, court cases, and other marginalia can then readily all be incorporated within this wider fabric of intellectual controversy. The Early Enlightenment period featured numerous highly fraught public controversies, such as the pamphlet war between British and Irish Jacobites and Williamites during the Glorious Revolution, the Rotterdam disputes preceding Bayle's dismissal from his professorship in 1693, the Bekker furore of 1691–3, the heated English Deist controversy in the years 1713–17, Christian Wolff's public condemnation and expulsion from Prussia in 1721, the 'Wertheim Bible' controversy during the later 1730s, the controversy over Voltaire's *Lettres philosophiques* (1734), the demonology controversy in north-east Italy in the 1740s, the so-called 'Querelle de *L'Esprit des lois*' (1748–51), and the quarrels involving church and state over whether to allow publication of the *Encyclopédie* during the 1750s.

A notable advantage of such a 'controversialist' method is the guidance it affords with the perennial problem of determining what is more and what less representative, what is more and what less important, who and what were talked about more and who and what less, in other words what the canon of principal thinkers and ideas *really* was. David Hume, for instance, in retrospect one of the greatest philosophers of the eighteenth century, was practically never mentioned in the major European intellectual controversies in the period down to 1752 covered by this present volume. Retrospective distortion, insularity, a one-sided picture, a 'national' view, anachronistic frameworks superimposed by later epochs, and often ideologically driven prejudgements, are all constant and very serious hazards. If historians can never achieve total objectivity, the quest for objectivity nevertheless remains an inescapable and constant concern and duty.

Examining controversies in detail provides a means of testing possible answers to the most pertinent questions objective to the historical process itself, enabling us to see what was most discussed and what less, who were the most feared thinkers, and why, and who were the most widely admired, and why. As a methodology it employs the general historical process itself to locate the key ideas of the time and sift out those superimposed as 'key' by later schools of thought, and historians. It is more objective than both the 'old intellectual history' and Cambridge *Diskursgeschichte* in starting from the overall European situation, clearly pinpointing the major controversies in a way which puts them in a self-imposed hierarchy: for they define themselves in terms of longevity, quantities of publications, extent of translation into other languages, legal prosecutions, academic disputes, ecclesiastical proceedings, and, generally, the amount of public attention given. Here intellectual history is fully merged with book history, social history, as well as religious and political history; and therein lies its strength.

Controversies took place and provide masses of evidence. Such public events occurred everywhere in the western Atlantic world throughout the Enlightenment era. Minor instances might begin with the appearance of a text advancing an unpopular or innovative point of view precipitating a debate in the journals and involving only a handful of participants but nevertheless exerting a noticeable public impact. Another type of minor controversy was public disputations on university theses in Latin, especially where the issues were then reported in vernacular journals, as often happened in eighteenth-century Germany. At the opposite extreme, as with the Wertheim furore of 1735–8, a controversy might draw in many governments and other authorities across a large slice of Europe and involve literally thousands of participants, including philosophers, historians, philologists, theologians, printers, booksellers, lawyers, courtiers, city councils, and scientists. A middle-sized controversy could begin in a university but, through touching on particularly sensitive issues, draw in ecclesiastical and secular authorities, provoking a substantial public uproar as occurred in Paris in 1752, when the Sorbonne formally censured the thesis of the Abbé Jean-Martin de Prades, an episode which obliged the latter to seek refuge in Berlin and threatened to capsize the whole enterprise of the *Encyclopédie*.

This present study, an attempt to reassess the western Enlightenment applying this controversialist technique in opposition to the claims of the 'new social history', focuses on the broad mass of Early Enlightenment controversies French, German, British, Italian, and Dutch which, taken together, provide a window enabling us to see in a reasonably objective light how structures of belief and sensibility in society interact dialectically with the evolution of philosophical ideas. All of these in one way or another demonstrate how numerous lesser figures came to be bound up with the systems of major philosophers, how diffusion and propagation alters and often simplifies ideas, how 'reception' is fundamentally mediated and shaped by the reactions of churches and governments, and how in the process public exposure and governmental, ecclesiastical, and academic rulings highlighted certain ideas while marginalizing others. The resulting picture turns out to be surprisingly unfamiliar.

3. *L'ESPRIT PHILOSOPHIQUE*

The 'old' intellectual history's creation of historical epochs based on changes in ideas and high culture, nomenclature such as Renaissance, Reformation, Baroque, Enlightenment, and Counter-Enlightenment, should, according to the 'new social history', now be discarded in favour of more 'socially' based designations. What does the man in the street care about Renaissance and Enlightenment? Conversely, restructuring historical studies around the 'new intellectual history' tends exactly in the reverse direction, concentrating more general social significance than before on the designations 'Renaissance', 'Enlightenment', 'Counter-Enlightenment', etc. bringing these out of the confined ghetto of history of thought and high culture, and making these the basic segments of western history. As regards the eighteenth century, the picture was dominated by three great intellectual-cultural impulses: Radical Enlightenment, moderate Enlightenment combining reason and faith, and Bossuet's anti-philosophical Counter-Enlightenment.

By 1700, the Radical Enlightenment was a widespread, formidably entrenched philosophical underground active in Holland, France, Britain, Italy, and Germany alike. It is important therefore not to identify its main thrust, or quintessential ideas, with any particular national or cultural tradition even though it happened to begin in the Dutch Republic and England and even though, after 1720, French language and culture eclipsed all the rest as the medium for diffusing radical ideas in Europe and the Atlantic world more generally. If the centre of gravity was first located in the Netherlands and later shifted to France, this had little to do, *pace* Montesquieu, with inherent 'national' characteristics or cultural sociology. It was simply a function of those countries' recent past and current social and political development, as was, conversely, Britain's remarkable failure, after the 1720s, to play a comparable role to France in the elaboration and propagation of radical ideas.

After the Revolt against Spain, the newly fashioned Dutch Republic underwent a period of rapid further urbanization, commercialization, overseas colonization, growing internal social fluidity, restructuring of artistic life, and dispersal of political power; at the same time the new governing class, the urban regents, created, or rather were forced to permit, a wholly novel climate of religious toleration and relative freedom of thought and expression. If Holland in the later seventeenth century was the place where radical ideas were most fully formulated philosophically, and where they could be most comprehensively developed, explored, and propagated, this was doubtless because it was the first predominantly urbanized society and economy and the first, along with Switzerland, not to be ruled by princes, nobles, and ecclesiastics. At bottom, then, the origins of the Radical Enlightenment lay in a whole complex of connected developments, social, political, religious, cultural, and economic, a new set of structures interacting with ideas.

The comparatively open and tolerant character as well as the academic institutions, bookshops, and publishing facilities of the United Provinces naturally encouraged the arrival and settlement not just of numerous visiting foreign scholars but of many permanent intellectual refugees—Jews, Socinians, and Catholics as well as Protestant dissenters and freethinkers. It was indeed the pressure of intolerance, censorship, and repression elsewhere which brought many of the outstanding intellectual figures of the time to the United Provinces and enabled others, such as Malebranche and Richard Simon who did not settle there in person, to publish works at the time unpublishable in France. Without this influx from abroad the Dutch Early Enlightenment could certainly never have played the pivotal role for all Europe which it actually did. One could, of course, also compose boldly innovative radical works elsewhere. But if so, one was bound to be more circumspect and less direct than was feasible in Holland or, after the Glorious Revolution, England. Neither Boulainvilliers nor Meslier were able to publish their more daring works. The marquis d'Argens, one of the foremost radical publicists of the Early Enlightenment, noted of the *Histoire des oracles* (Paris, 1686), one of Fontenelle's chief contributions to radical thought, that had it been written in Holland or England, and therefore been less guarded, it would have been 'encore plus parfaite'.[55]

Economic change, social mobility, and religious plurality, then, together with the exceptional impact there, after 1650, of Cartesianism and the general advance of the arts and sciences, created what one historian has aptly called the 'New World of the Dutch Republic'.[56] A crucial contributory factor fixing Holland as the original hub of the Radical Enlightenment was the rise, particularly after the Revocation of the Edict of Nantes (1685), of a large and vibrant Huguenot diaspora which was significantly larger than and, particularly in the intellectual sphere, generally eclipsed, the other branches of the Huguenot diaspora located in England, Ireland, Germany, Switzerland, and America. Actually, the French-speaking refugee community which flourished in the Dutch Republic, primarily in Amsterdam, Rotterdam, and The Hague, was not wholly Huguenot in composition. For among them were Jansenist, other Catholic, and ex-Catholic exiles, including several dissident ex-monks fleeing the—for some—repressive atmosphere prevalent in the French monasteries under Louis XIV (reigned 1643–1715).[57]

This exceptionally dynamic, prosperous, and highly educated French-speaking diaspora, not surprisingly, developed a marked aversion to the absolutism of the French court, and, after 1685, firmly aligned politically with the United Provinces, England, and Brandenburg against France. Owing to its own recent experience, it was a milieu which was also viscerally opposed to religious persecution and intolerance. Theirs was a community eager to salvage what it could from France, add to the trade and industry of their new homelands, and preserve such links as they could with the Protestant remnants in France as well as the rest of the Huguenot diaspora. So much so, indeed, that it has been aptly remarked that Bourbon France for several decades after 1685 felt itself to be besieged ideologically and culturally by a whole ring of Huguenot communities scattered from Geneva to Dublin with their headquarters in Holland. For the Huguenots in exile, far more than the British or the native Dutch, were an intellectual and theological, as well as political, foe of the French monarchy—and a francophone one at that.[58]

[55] D'Argens, *Mémoires secrets*, v. 185. [56] Swart, *Miracle*, 3.

[57] Hazard, *Crise de la conscience*, 83–90; Vernière, *Spinoza*, 24–5, 81, 326, 408; Berkvens-Stevelinck, *Prosper Marchand*, 1–6; Mulsow, *Die drei Ringe*, 11; Israel, *Radical Enlightenment*, 575–90.

[58] Hazard, *Crise de la conscience*, 90.

If Huguenot intellectuals based in the Netherlands opposed Louis XIV's militarism and expansionism, they also fought his divine right absolutism and religious policy, generating an external opposition which was simultaneously political, cultural, theological, and philosophical and whose armaments were not guns but ideas, newspapers, tracts, journals, books, and the book trade.

Admittedly, the specifically 'modern' features of the United Provinces were only rarely esteemed abroad. On the whole, Dutch social fluidity, religious pluralism, toleration, and relative freedom of the individual tended rather to fuel the antipathy to Dutch society frequently voiced by foreign visitors at the time. The Lutheran theologian Heinrich Benthem who toured Holland in 1694, while granting that not everything Dutch was bad, nevertheless compiled a remarkably long list of points that appalled him. He expressed revulsion at the relative freedom of women as well as servants and children,[59] and horror at the weak position of the church authorities, ascribing the licentiousness rife in Dutch cities to the public church's inability to compel city governments to close the 'music halls' for which Amsterdam's harbour area was notorious, as well as brothels and other dens of vice, and clamp down on prostitution.[60] He was shocked by the freedom enjoyed by Jews and Socinians as he was by the lack of deference of Dutch workmen for their social superiors and, more generally, the absence of any clearly defined social hierarchy. Lack of clear social stratification in urban life seemed to him to be the root cause of the unprecedented latitude permitted, or at least not prevented, regarding personal lifestyle and dress. Worst of all, though, in his opinion, the festering sore on which all the rest fed, was 'die grosse Religions-Freyheit' [great religious freedom] the regents allowed.

If Benthem disapproved, most foreigners' comments about the Republic in this period were broadly negative, though by 1688 praise of Dutch toleration began to be heard rather more frequently than before.[61] It is hardly surprising, therefore, that when an independent-minded republican and defender of individual freedom like the artist, inventor, and writer Romeyn de Hooghe (*c.*1645–1708) in 1706 declared the Dutch state to be 'verre de loflykste, vryste en veligste, van alle die welke op de wereld bekend zyn' [by far the most praiseworthy, freest and safest of all those known in the world],[62] very few outsiders were prepared to agree and any that did themselves risked becoming objects of scorn and censure. Foreigners who suggested the Republic should be eulogized as a universal model were decidedly isolated voices, usually freethinkers and Deists like the sieur de Saint-Evremond who, exiled from France, resided in The Hague between 1665 and 1670, the 'Epicurean' English diplomat William Temple (1628–99) who praised the Republic in his *Observations* (1672), the freethinking Anthony Collins,[63] and the heterodox Italian Protestant Gregorio Leti (1631–1701), a fervent champion of toleration who spent

[59] Benthem, *Holländischer Kirch- und Schulen-Staat*, i. 7–9.

[60] Ibid. i. 8–9; Bientjes, *Holland und die Holländer*, 22.

[61] Schreiner, 'Toleranz', 537.

[62] De Hooghe, *Spiegel van Staat*, ii. 57.

[63] Collins, *Discourse of Free-Thinking*, 28, 30; Collins, *Discourse of the Grounds*, pp. xxx–xxxii.

his last years in Amsterdam and dubbed the United Provinces of the 1690s the true 'mater gentium'.[64]

No doubt a firmly established comprehensive toleration, as Temple maintained, really does soften age-old confessional antagonism. But not many contemporaries wished to adopt this remedy. Among those who did was Noël Aubert de Versé (1645–1714) who, in his *Traité de la liberté de conscience* (1687), affirms that Amsterdam, the commercial and financial hub of Europe at the time, 'doit sa splendeur et son opulence que toutes les nations admirent à cette chère liberté', claiming no group, sect, or nation was dissident enough to be excluded, provided they conducted themselves as 'sincères, fidèles et bons citoyens'.[65] But then Aubert de Versé himself was an outcast, being a Socinian. Indeed, ironically, soon after penning these words, local intolerance obliged him to flee to Hamburg. In his *Reasons for Naturalizing the Jews in Great Britain and Ireland* (1714), John Toland (1670–1722) similarly eulogized Holland, as a land providing social stability based on 'unlimited Liberty of Conscience'.[66] But then Toland too was universally scorned for his heterodox—that is pantheist, anti-Christian, and freethinking—views, as was Anthony Collins who, complimenting Temple for his views on toleration and the Dutch, asked, 'are not the United Provinces remarkable for liberty and peace? There all men, how different soever in notions live in such peace and friendship with one another, as is unknown to men in other countries.'[67]

Commentators often granted that the 'Dutch model' was the 'freest' in Europe, but with this usually intended no compliment.[68] Nor was it only foreigners who disparaged the comparative tolerance and egalitarianism characteristic of Dutch society and culture. For there was much about the 'New World' of the Republic deeply repugnant to a large part of Dutch society itself. If the institutionalization of what Adriaen Paets (1631–86), the regent who brought Bayle to Rotterdam, called the individual's 'inborn freedom' to decide one's own convictions, for oneself, according to one's own judgement,[69] scandalized outsiders, it also appalled much of the Dutch public, many of whom thought censorship and ecclesiastical authority in their country needed not further dilution but drastic strengthening. Many, especially but not only of limited education, deeply resented the creeping erosion of age-old beliefs and religious authority through freedom of opinion and conversation. Conversation was no less of a problem than books and reading. As Johann Lorenz Schmidt, the central figure in the Wertheim controversy, remarked in 1741, men become 'atheists' just as much through talk as through books.[70]

[64] Leti, *Monarchie universelle*, ii. 525, 527, 559–60; Leti, *Raguagli politici*, 2. ii. 408–10.

[65] Aubert de Versé, *Traité de la liberté*, 55.

[66] Toland, *Reasons for Naturalizing the Jews*, 46.

[67] Collins, *Discourse of the Grounds*, p. xxx.

[68] Temple, *Observations*, 134; Leti, *Raguagli politici*, 2. ii. 408–10; Bientjes, *Holland und die Holländer*, 22; Mulsow, 'Eine "Rettung" ', 86–7.

[69] Frijhoff and Spies, *1650. Bevochten eendracht*, 358, 371; Labrousse, *Pierre Bayle*, i. 172–3.

[70] Schmidt, 'Vorbericht', 76.

Although the loss vastly outweighed the gain according to the traditional-minded, there was a broad consensus by the 1660s that Dutch intellectual culture and higher education had been transformed by the 'New Philosophy'. It was obvious, moreover, that the resulting collision between 'philosophy' and theology could not easily be resolved and that this 'crisis of conscience' was generating powerful new tensions in Dutch society. While the pro-Cartesian Cocceian faction of the Reformed Church blamed the intellectual crisis on the perversion of Cartesianism by 'bastard Cartesians' and 'Spinozists', Reformed theologians of the hard-line Calvinist 'Voetian' mould, as well as many dissenting and Catholic clergy, tended to attribute the whole of what they saw as a social catastrophe to Cartesianism itself. It was due to Descartes, as the Reformed preacher Jacobus Koelman expressed it in 1692, that Holland was now rife with a 'dreadful mass' of 'atheists, libertines, New Sadducees, Hobbists, mockers and the like'; for all of them were intellectually nurtured on Cartesianism, including 'den Cartesiaan Spinosa, ook Coerbach' [the Cartesian Spinoza, and also Koerbagh].[71]

Consequently, pleas for a wider intellectual freedom and religious toleration were routinely rejected not only by the hard-line orthodox opposed to all modern philosophy but also by middle-of-the-road opinion favouring a Lockean-style limited toleration. Most people, not without justification, interpreted arguments urging full freedom of expression as being effectively a plea for the right to propagate freethinking, Spinozism, and philosophical atheism—or what the Zeeland preacher Cornelis Tuinman (1659–1728) termed 'soul-poison'.[72] It was considered a typical ploy of Socinians, freethinkers, and Deists to eulogize Amsterdam, invoking that city as do Spinoza,[73] Temple, Aubert de Versé, Toland, and Mandeville as proof that civic vigour, affluence, and stability are causally linked to toleration, freedom of thought, and individual freedom.[74] Opponents loudly deplored this strategy, reminding interlocutors that Amsterdam was anyhow less tolerant in reality than such mischief-makers claimed, Koerbagh and Aert Wolsgryn, publisher of the second part of *Philopater*, having been justly locked up by the Amsterdam magistrates and left to rot in the Rasphuis for propagating Spinozism.[75]

Dutch freedom of the individual and liberty of conscience, however abhorrent to many foreigners, were actually, as Koerbagh's, Wolsgryn's, and Aubert de Versé's experiences illustrate, far from being 'unlimited', as Toland put it, in practice. Even Jean Le Clerc (1657–1737), a leading intellectual figure at Amsterdam and someone of far more liberal opinions than most contemporaries, held, like his friend Locke, that 'atheists' should not be tolerated and that expression of radical Deist and atheistic views should be rigorously curbed.[76] Socinian refugees from Poland, like Daniel

[71] Koelman, *Het Vergift*, preface p. ix; van der Wall, 'The *Tractatus*', 212.

[72] Tuinman, *Liegende en bedriegende Vrygeest*, 55, 93; Tuinman, *Het helsche gruwelheim*, 271–3.

[73] Tuinman, *Het helsche gruwelheim*, 274; Spinoza, *TTP* 298.

[74] Tuinman, *Het helsche gruwelheim*, 274.

[75] Ibid. 275.

[76] *Bibliothèque choisie*, 10 (1706), 392–3.

Zwicker (1612–1678) and Socinus' grandson Andrzey Wiszowaty (d. 1678), could dwell mostly undisturbed in Amsterdam, and even clandestinely propagate the odd Socinian tract; but they were subjected to constant pressure from the consistories and magistrates, receiving official warnings against expressing their views and being periodically subjected to investigation and interrogations at the town hall.[77]

Allegedly excessive individual freedom and religious fragmentation were seen by many, Dutch and foreigners, as the chief reason why such philosophical heterodoxy as radical Cartesianism, Spinozism, and Koerbagh's libertarianism surfaced in Holland rather than elsewhere. The German Eclectic with Aristotelian-scholastic leanings Christoph August Heumann (1681–1764) at Göttingen, a key figure in the rise of the new discipline of 'history of philosophy', and one of the first European scholars to stress the influence of time, place, and environment on the evolution of ideas,[78] believed each of the European peoples possessed ingrained intellectual characteristics acquired from their milieu. As much as he admired the English for their moderation, and knowing how to reconcile religion with reason in philosophy and science, he scorned the Dutch 'ingenium', or conditioned intellectual nature, which struck him as far inferior, indeed wholly unsound, as he thought obvious from its having produced the likes of Spinoza and Koerbagh.

Heumann's notion that one national 'ingenium' is intellectually 'better' or 'worse' than another, owing to environment, though developed further, was far from a rare opinion at the time. But cultural differences, including differing levels of enlightenment, were more often interpreted as due to temporary circumstances rather than any inherited or innate racial or national characteristics. For the radical-minded, creating a better society was therefore essentially a question of re-education and spreading 'enlightenment'. Different peoples stood at different stages of development in terms of openness to 'enlightened' ideas; but there was little if any difference, it was thought, between the different branches of mankind in intellectual and moral capability as such. 'La raison est la même dans tous les hommes', asserted one radical writer in 1723, 'mais tous ne la consultent pas également.'[79] Spain and Portugal, like Muscovy, were widely considered especially benighted lands—but not due to any innately inferior disposition. Should one day the Spaniards and Portuguese open their eyes, mused d'Argens, and revert back from 'leur aveuglement', they will perhaps have great difficulty in understanding 'comment ils ont pu rester si longtemps sans faire usage de leur raison'.[80]

Heumann, d'Argens, and others had good reason to style Holland the land *par excellence* of dissident and heterodox philosophy. The seditious business of reworking Descartes's duality of substances, extension, and mind into a one-substance materialism—the realm of the physical—subjecting the entire cosmos to the rules of mechanical cause and effect, rules which authentic Cartesians applied to bodies but not to the

[77] Fix, *Prophecy and Reason*, 129–32, 142, 149; Bietenholz, *Daniel Zwicker*, 34–8.

[78] Braun, *Histoire*, 113–15; Kelley, *Descent of Ideas*, 5, 161–3; Albrecht, *Eklektik*, 493–6.

[79] [Bruzen de La Martinière], *Entretiens*, i. 1.

[80] D'Argens, 'Lettre dédicatoire', p. ix.

realm of the spiritual, began in the 1650s and 1660s, at Amsterdam and Leiden. This crucial scientific-philosophical step which was to have vast implications for all Europe and the wider world was taken within a small circle of professional and amateur *érudits* active outside formal academic life. Its chief members were Spinoza, his Latin master Franciscus van den Enden (1602–74), Adriaen Koerbagh (1632–69), the physician Lodewijk Meyer (1629–81), Johan Bouwmeester (1630–80), Petrus van Balen (1643–90), Hadrianus Beverland (1650–1716), the German philosopher Ehrenfried Walther von Tschirnhaus (1651–1708), and the lawyer Abraham Johannes Cuffeler (1637–94). Not part of Spinoza's circle but a crucial influence in the one case on the Spinozists' democratic republican political thought and, in the other, on their science, were the brothers de La Court, at Leiden, and the great scientist and rival of Newton Christian Huygens (1629–95) at The Hague.

While details about the intellectual inception, individual contributions, and relationships between the key members of this 'atheistic' milieu remain sparse for the mid and late 1650s when 'Spinozism' and Dutch democratic republicanism first crystallized, there seems little doubt that Descartes, or rather the stripping down of Descartes, provided the starting point for a fundamental intellectual 'revolution' leading to the construction of a new kind of radical world-view. Cartesianism was a prime ingredient; but it seems fairly clear that the influence of Machiavelli and Hobbes was also of not inconsiderable importance. In outline at least, this group's new conception of philosophy, politics, science, and text criticism, and of the role their ideas would play in revolutionizing the world, already existed by 1660, after which date their system rapidly matured and began to be talked about more widely in society.[81]

After 1670, and the anonymous publication of Spinoza's *Tractatus theologico-politicus*, radical philosophy with its explicit democratic republican agenda spread to much of the rest of western Europe, primarily through Latin and French renderings of Spinoza's own texts but also through the published writings of others of his circle and those of subsequent disciples and acolytes. At the same time, Spinozism as a system began to pervade the Dutch universities and other spheres of local culture. This specifically Dutch process, moreover, seemingly penetrated further than historians have in the past tended to suppose. By the 1690s, it was noticed on passenger barges and in wagons that Spinoza and the 'Spinozisten' were being discussed even by ordinary unlearned folk,[82] in particular regarding the possibility that the Bible might not, after all, be 'true', that there might be no divine judgement or afterlife, and that the Devil, demons, angels, and magic might not actually exist.[83]

In the early eighteenth century, the great Remonstrant *érudit* Le Clerc attributed Spinoza's now considerable (if mainly negative) profile and wide impact in the

[81] Mignini, 'Données et problèmes', 9–13, 20–1; Mertens, 'Franciscus van den Enden', 718, 738; Gelderblom, 'Publisher', 162–6; Wielema, 'Adriaan Koerbagh', 61–3.

[82] Brink, *Ongenoegsame satisfactie*, 4; Molinaeus, *De* Betoverde Werelt *van D. Balthazar Bekker*, 24–5.

[83] Brink, *Ongenoegsame satisfactie*, 4.

Netherlands, something he deemed totally undeserved, to the excessive preoccupation of Dutch academe with the many thorny philosophical problems bequeathed by Cartesianism.[84] Among scholars steeped in Cartesian issues, the Spinozist critique of Descartes had indeed descended like a bombshell. While Le Clerc, no less than Spinoza, considered Descartes's system replete with contradictions, he deeply deplored the way Spinoza had been able to rework its more coherent features into a monist system drawing much of its force precisely from the insoluble difficulties in which the Dutch Cartesians had entrapped themselves. Meanwhile, despite their increasingly precarious position, leading liberal Cocceio-Cartesian theologians such as Christopher Wittichius (1625–87), for many years professor at Leiden, tenaciously stuck to their guns, battling the Voetians to the right and Spinozists to the left, as well as Le Clerc and others challenging them for the middle ground. Among other criticism, Wittichius and his followers had to fend off charges that they were ultimately to blame for the radical threat, by letting Spinoza in on the back of their confident and sweeping but irresponsible and ultimately unviable claims for philosophy.

For a time, as frequent contemporary testimony attests, radical ideas penetrated Dutch society quite widely, spreading during the half-century 1670–1720 before receding again, presumably owing in part at least to the sheer weight of popular and elite disapproval. Many contemporaries, like the Remonstrant minister Johannes Molinaeus, writing in 1692, remark on the unsettling upsurge of philosophical unbelief and libertinism in late seventeenth-century Holland, leading, as he put it, to the 'ruin of the pure teaching of Christ' and loss of countless souls caused by the 'unholy misuse of philosophy' and the latter's seductive power.[85] He did not agree, though, with the frequent tendency at the time to blame the radical breakthrough on Wittichius and the Cartesians. In his opinion, the rot derived not from Descartes but exclusively from Hobbes and Spinoza. The two most harmful books in circulation, in his view, despite their having long been banned (in 1674) by decree of the States, were Meyer's *Philosophia S. Scripturae interpres* (1666) and Spinoza's *Tractatus*: for both works, he says, use philosophical arguments systematically to undermine the status of Scripture.

Spinoza himself, though continually under pressure in the last years of his life, was never arrested or imprisoned. During his lifetime, he was prevented, however, from publishing his masterpiece, the *Ethics*, and given to understand that the authorities would crack down hard should his prohibited Latin *Tractatus theologico-politicus* appear in the vernacular. After his death and the posthumous clandestine publication in 1677–8 of his *Ethics* and other hitherto unpublished works by his friends in Amsterdam, his works, and all summaries (and reworking) of them, were comprehensively banned by decrees of the States General and States of Holland of April 1678. During his last years, Spinoza—whose motto was 'caution'—adroitly steered clear of serious trouble, helped by his premature death at the age of barely 45. Several

[84] *Bibliothèque choisie*, 26 (1713), 311; in 1710, he wrote, 'il n'y a rien que je méprise plus que le système de Spinoza', see *Bibliothèque choisie*, 21 (1710), 40.

[85] Molinaeus, *De Betoverde Werelt van D. Balthazar Bekker*, 24.

allies and acolytes, however, were conspicuously less fortunate. At least five writers and publishers of 'Spinozistic' books—Adriaen Koerbagh, Hadrianus Beverland, Aert Wolsgryn, Ericus Walten (1663–97), and Hendrik Wyermars—were severely dealt with by the secular authorities during Spinoza's lifetime, or during the next decades, receiving draconian prison sentences (the last in 1710), and dying in wretched circumstances, in prison, disgrace, or in exile. Others received warnings, fines, or shorter bouts of imprisonment, while Spinoza's closest friend of his last years, Abraham Johan Cuffeler, could only publish his substantial Latin treatise the *Specimen artis ratiocinandi* (1684) furtively and anonymously.

The shock and dismay caused by the spread of Spinoza's reputation and ideas in the Netherlands, Germany, France, Italy, and to a lesser extent Britain, confronted the main body of European theologians and philosophers with a serious dilemma. Leaving Spinoza's arguments unanswered entailed obvious risk: for as Johann Lorenz Schmidt later stressed, in the preface to his German rendering of Tindal, Lutheran theologians, despite complaining incessantly about the spread of philosophical unbelief and 'atheism' in German society, failed to address the main cause of this phenomenon which, according to him, was their own failure to refute the arguments against revealed religion of the freethinkers and Spinozists.[86] On the other hand, by replying to Spinoza, theologians and academics unavoidably ran the opposite risk of drawing fresh attention to his philosophy. This predicament produced a highly peculiar form of intellectual boycott widely observed over several decades, especially in French-language debates. For polemical purposes, individual Spinozistic arguments were relentlessly attacked but only when detached from Spinoza's system and with his name deleted. Many prominent figures adopted the technique of alluding darkly to certain pernicious writers, and targeting key arguments, but without actually naming the author in question, seeking in this way to counter his burgeoning intellectual legacy without adding to his renown.

This tactic enabled opponents to avoid continually citing the writings of a philosopher universally condemned as the most subversive of the age, the only author more pernicious and damaging to authority, convention, and tradition than Hobbes and Machiavelli, and an influence from whom, it was supposed, readers needed urgently to be shielded. In this way, it was hoped to prevent Spinoza coming to the attention of people who would not otherwise read him. Thus, Le Clerc expressly states, in a letter to the English bishop Richard Kidder, in November 1694, that numerous arguments expounded in his writings are directed against Spinoza specifically rather than others but that he nevertheless took care in those same passages not to mention Spinoza by name.[87] Similarly, Bishop Bossuet, Malebranche, Arnauld, Régis, Fénelon, indeed practically everyone in a position of intellectual authority in France towards the close of the seventeenth century and opening of the eighteenth, warned of the need to avoid drawing attention more than was

[86] Schmidt, 'Vorbericht', 79, 100–3.

[87] Le Clerc, *Epistolario*, ii. 222–3: Le Clerc to Richard Kidder, Amsterdam, 5 Nov. 1694.

absolutely necessary to Spinoza while yet simultaneously seeking to combat his philosophy.

Later, though, this strategy was abandoned. Particularly, after Houtteville's well-known work defending Christian belief against Spinoza of 1722, French apologists for religion, miracles, and ecclesiastical authority no longer tried to hide the fact that the *Spinosistes* were their most formidable and most numerous enemy, the chief category of *esprits forts* and naturalists attacking Christian tradition. Indeed, they now loudly insisted down to the 1750s that the main enemies of authority in France were the followers of Spinoza, though they still sought to minimize his status as a philosopher by claiming much of his power came from his 'obscurity', that his system was a 'galimathias inintelligible' of arid metaphysics, that his disciples mouthed slogans like the 'order of nature' without grasping concepts which are in fact impenetrably obscure; at the same time, they denied there was anything original in his thought, attributing its main elements to the ancient Greeks, variously citing the Presocratics, Stoics, Epicureans, and Stratonists as his source of inspiration.[88]

Spinoza's name and writings then were first, in part, generally boycotted and later firmly equated with the principles of ancient materialism. At the same time, there was among those of more radical disposition, like Walten, Toland, and Schmidt, a powerful motive to avoid being linked to a thinker whose reputation was such that one's own standing was bound to be injured by the least hint that one was a *Spinosiste*.[89] Nevertheless, no one else, not even Hobbes, was denounced as often as Spinoza whether in the late seventeenth, early eighteenth, or mid eighteenth century, or in so many countries; or indeed was so widely known to the public as a universal philosophical bogeyman. In this respect, as Schmidt notes in his preface to his translation of the *Ethics*, in 1744, Spinoza remained the most feared philosopher in eighteenth-century Europe, eclipsing in contemporary perception every other alleged 'atheist' in history.[90]

The result was spreading awareness, discussion, refutation, condemnation, and—especially among the followers of Leibniz and Wolff—also admiration of Spinoza often without his name being so much as mentioned. If most philosophers—apart from Descartes and (in Britain) Hobbes—were known only to tiny elites of the educated, as had always been true of philosophers, this was not the case with Spinoza. Contrary to what twentieth-century writers have often asserted, from the late seventeenth century onwards, his name was widely known in Europe outside scholarly and intellectual circles. There is thus nothing surprising in the statement of a Catholic eulogist of Antoine Arnauld in the mid 1770s about 'ce fameux athée', that 'tout le monde connaît Spinosa'.[91]

During the period covered by this present volume, to 1752, numerous refutations of Spinoza's philosophy appeared in Dutch, Latin, French, German, Italian,

88 [François], *Preuves*, i. 84, 234–6, 267, 276.

89 Rihs, *Philosophes utopistes*, 230.

90 Schmidt, 'Vorrede', 4; Israel, *Radical Enlightenment*, 599–609.

91 *Préface historique et critique, Œuvres de Arnauld*, x, pp. xv–xvi.

English, and even Spanish, Danish, Swedish, and Portuguese.[92] While materialist naturalism and libertinism had in recent decades become rife throughout Europe, had many causes, and, forged by diverse intellectual traditions, took various forms, nevertheless by the 1730s and 1740s it was taken for granted that all coherent philosophical 'atheism'—meaning rejection of supernatural agency, providence, and the miraculous as constituents of the universe tied to a democratic politics, comprehensive toleration, and ideas of equality and individual liberty which is not Epicurean-Gassendist in stipulating a material soul constituted of some subtle substance—is either overtly Spinozist or else, on examination, as with Boulainvilliers, Meslier, Diderot, and d'Alembert, boils down in its essentials to 'Spinozism'.

The sweeping character and comprehensiveness of the general transformation of society, morality, politics, and education that radical ideas envisaged stemmed no doubt from over-optimism as to the power of philosophical reason to defeat established authority and engineer far-reaching social, cultural, and political change. But this belief in the power of *l'esprit philosophique*, and joy in its spread, though over-optimistic, was, as history was to prove, not wholly misplaced. What perhaps is especially striking is that a similar and parallel appraisal of the potential of philosophy was shared in the late seventeenth, eighteenth, and early nineteenth centuries—albeit for them it fed only extreme apprehension and dread—by both the moderate mainstream and the Counter-Enlightenment. In fact all three of the modern West's chief ideological blocs largely converged, whichever of various transitory terms were used to describe it, in seeing the kind of evolutionary materialism projected by 'Spinozism' as apt to overturn and radically transform everything, from erudition to politics, and not only in theory but potentially also in practice. The end result of Spinozistic thinking, irrespective of whether one welcomed or opposed it, was on all sides seen to be a philosophical 'universal revolution', that is a universal re-evaluation of all values in the name of reason, tolerance, and equality.

Where the Counter-Enlightenment reacted by rejecting 'philosophy' altogether in favour of faith, piety, and submission to authority, the moderate mainstream retorted that the *Spinosistes* had got both their philosophy and their history wrong. Their *esprit philosophique* was denounced as a monstrous aberration which violates the principles of true philosophy and causes only catastrophe by making excessive claims for reason. In Germany, Scandinavia, Switzerland, and Russia before Kant, the respectable Enlightenment congregated into two main camps—the Thomasian Eclectics, on the one hand, and the Leibnizio-Wolffians, on the other. Further west, English ideas heavily predominated. The best antidote to aberrant 'esprit philosophique', claimed the Thermidorean Jean-Étienne-Marie Portalis, in 1798, is Lockean empiricism which strictly limits reason's scope and takes 'l'observation et l'expérience' as its guiding principle.[93] This type of enlightenment was throughout emphatically Anglophile in outlook, seeing the main line in modern thought as

[92] Ibid., p. xvi; Goeree, *Kerkelyke en weereldlyke historien*, 667; Israel, *Radical Enlightenment*, 56–8, 63, 489–91, 501, 599–600, 657.

[93] Portalis, *De l'usage et de l'abus*, i. 114.

running through Bacon, Boyle, Locke, Newton, Clarke, Condillac, Montesquieu, Voltaire, and Hume.[94] Radical Enlightenment, by contrast, based according to the moderate mainstream on 'faux systèmes', generally scorned Locke and Newton, looked with growing suspicion on the *anglomanie* of the moderate mainstream, and saw the main line as running from the Presocratics through Epicurus, the Stoics, Strato the naturalist, and Machiavelli and then on to Spinoza, Bayle, Fontenelle, Diderot, d'Alembert, Helvétius, d'Holbach, and Condorcet.

During the eighteenth century, moderate mainstream Enlightenment with its insistence on reconciling reason and religion and support for (modernized) monarchy, aristocracy, and ecclesiastical authority was culturally and politically preponderant in much of the western Atlantic world. But in the end it failed, or at least was thwarted, being unable to overcome its own internal divisions which, according to many, in the Counter-Enlightenment camp as well as on the radical left, flowed ineluctably from its own internal intellectual inconsistencies and contradictions. The veritable Counter-Enlightenment mentality was not reacting to something it did not grasp or failed to engage with. On the contrary, men like the Yale theologian Jonathan Edwards (1703–58), the leading intellectual figure in New England and the Middle Colonies in the mid eighteenth century, were profoundly shaped by reading Locke and Newton, had a thorough understanding of what 'philosophy' entailed,[95] and attacked their outlook in part for its internal contradictions, thereby adding to the difficulties the Arminians faced. If the 'Arminian' Enlightenment of Locke, Clarke, and Le Clerc ultimately faltered, it lost ground owing as much to Counter-Enlightenment attacks showing the pitfalls of mixing faith with reason, and Scripture with philosophy, as to Spinozists and radical Deists attacking the divine authorship of Scripture, providence, and Creation by a divinity.

Rather paradoxically, then, radical thought was powerfully aided in the work of secularizing western thought, culture, politics, and society, by its greatest enemy—the Counter-Enlightenment, the very grouping which most vehemently denounced it. For if the favourite technique of the radicals was 'à mettre en opposition la raison et la foi', as a Swiss adversary styled Bayle's subversive technique in 1733,[96] precisely this antithesis, setting reason against faith, which the moderate mainstream strove so hard to surmount philosophically, underpinned the strategy, advancing from the other side, also of the Counter-Enlightenment. The latter vigorously encouraged popular faith-based hostility to 'philosophy', proclaiming the power and sanctity of tradition; but by attacking reason and extolling the simple faith of the masses, such *anti-philosophie* harshly polarized matters in a way which often played straight into the hands of their radical foes.

Counter-Enlightenment has been little studied by historians and where it has is usually wrongly supposed to be a consequence of the French Revolution. In fact, in

[94] Portalis, *De l'usage et de l'abus*, ii. 93; Jacob, *Radical Enlightenment*, 91–107.
[95] Zakai, *Jonathan Edwards's Philosophy*, 87–90; Kucklick, *History*, 8, 14–15.
[96] Crousaz, *Examen*, 201, 323, 336.

ideological essentials, there is little difference between pre- and post-1789 (or, for that matter, pre- or post-1830) Counter-Enlightenment Catholic or Protestant; for the central thread throughout, from Bossuet's time onwards, is that Christendom is being destroyed by an insidious philosophical conspiracy, and that at the heart of the conspiracy is a new conception of philosophy—*l'esprit philosophique*, a universal threat, undermining the pillars of authority and tradition, that is Christian, royal, and aristocratic society.[97] Hence, the beginnings of Counter-Enlightenment, logically enough, were to be found in the late seventeenth century with the advent of a conscious, self-proclaimed 'Enlightenment'. It was an inevitable and natural reaction to a more or less correctly perceived universal challenge.

An interesting early example of its characteristic psychology at work was the 'conversion' of the dissident Huguenot theologian Isaac Papin (1657–1709). Originally an ardent champion of reason and toleration who studied Spinoza closely, debated with Le Clerc, and explored every path towards a philosophical accommodation of reason and faith,[98] in the end, after years of peregrination in England, Holland, Germany, and Poland, he abandoned such research as self-defeating and hopeless, turning his back on reason and toleration alike. The Enlightenment projected by some he deemed an impossible delusion since, as he put it, there is scarcely one in every hundred thousand people 'qui puisse suivre la voye du raisonnement et de l'examen' [who can follow the way of reasoning and investigation]. Life is too short and the difficulty too great, urged Papin, for the vast majority to be able to choose their religion, or establish their views, on the basis of independent critical thinking and sound reasoning.[99] Hence, tradition and ecclesiastical authority, Papin convinced himself, are the sole reliable pillars of a Christian society based on piety and hierarchy. Since the most imposing ecclesiastical authority—and most opposed to intellectual freedom and toleration—was Catholicism, he resolved to convert to that faith. Received amid great fanfares into the Roman Church at Paris by Bishop Bossuet in 1690, Papin from then on tried to persuade his former Huguenot colleagues that their hopes of finding an intellectually coherent middle path between spiritual submission and Spinoza, however alluring, were just a deadly chimera.[100] Toleration, independent critical thinking, and freedom of thought ultimately mean permitting all opinions and 'by this means', as it was put in an English version of his refutation of toleration, 'you make a chaos, and not a regular society'.[101]

Spinoza and Bayle, held Papin, rightly set faith and reason in irreconcilable opposition to each other. Indeed, all cogent thinkers must finally opt for one or the other—except that the only responsible and Christian choice is to repudiate Spinoza and opt for devout obedience. Later, in the 1780s, this was likewise the message

97 McMahon, *Enemies of the Enlightenment*, 32–7, 189–90.
98 Pitassi, 'L'Écho des discussions', 260–1, 264–5; Zuber, 'Spinozisme', 222–3.
99 [Lévesque de Burigny], *De l'examen*, 39.
100 Zuber, 'Spinozisme', 225, 227; Zuber, 'Isaac Papin', 4–5, 8–12.
101 Papin, *Toleration of the Protestants*, 93; Zuber, 'Spinozisme', 225.

Friedrich Heinrich Jacobi (1743–1819) proclaimed to the German philosophical world: the Thomasians, Leibniz, Wolff, Mendelssohn, and Kant may think they have found a viable middle way, blending faith and reason; but they are deluding themselves. In the end, none of their systems work philosophically; no such reconciliation, he held, can withstand Spinoza's withering logic. All Enlightenment thought is, without exception, either built, like that of Descartes, Locke, Leibniz, Newton, and Voltaire, on a dualism so rife with inconsistency that it must eventually collapse of itself, or else ineluctably reduces into materialism and Spinozism.

Papin and Jacobi, writing a century apart, rightly claimed Spinoza's greatest weapon was his monism and philosophical cohesion. Despite being everywhere banned and condemned by governments and churches, radical thought nevertheless met with considerable success in infiltrating and undermining mainstream intellectual positions.[102] An extremist fringe according to most contemporaries—and indeed most of the historiography since—it was, as I shall try to demonstrate from the intellectual trajectories of Bayle, Voltaire, Diderot, d'Alembert, Helvétius, Lessing, d'Holbach, Kant, and Goethe in this present volume, and its sequel covering the second half of the eighteenth century, the freethinkers, *esprits forts*, and *matérialistes*, particularly adherents of something called 'Spinozism' (which was not quite the same thing as Spinoza's philosophy), who set the pace and framed the agenda of scholarly and intellectual discussion not only during the Early Enlightenment but throughout the Enlightenment era.

Despite the elements of myth-making, make-believe, and stratagem in its attempts to reconstruct the true story of Man's past and *l'esprit humain*, the Radical Enlightenment, then, possessed one concrete advantage in its struggle with both Counter-Enlightenment and the moderate mainstream. It was the advantage monist systems always afford of—real or apparent—intellectual consistency, cohesion, and coherence. Yet this was assuredly its only real resource. At various times and in different places, the mainstream Enlightenment had many governments and churches on their side. The same was true from the 1650s onwards of the always extremely formidable Counter-Enlightenment. But no government, church, or other organization, not even the French Revolution under Robespierre, ever endorsed the authentic programme of the Radical Enlightenment. If, after 1789, the French Revolution embraced radical concepts in part, at the same time it fundamentally perverted its philosophy of liberty, equality, and emancipation of the individual.

The impact in other words was appreciable but the repression and recrimination still greater and more universal. Much of the time, aspiring to change the world through propagating radical ideas must indeed have seemed a thankless, dispiriting, even hopeless task. The pessimism often expressed by Spinoza and Bayle about the common man's capabilities—as well as by lesser figures like Meslier, Tyssot de Patot, Edelmann, Lau, and Schmidt whose approach differed from that of *philosophes* like

102 Israel, *Radical Enlightenment*, i. 565–713; Stuurman, 'Pathways', 228; but see Robertson, *The Case*, 31.

Montesquieu and Voltaire above all in aspiring to change the outlook of the ordinary man—is doubtless largely explained by this. Both Koerbagh's premature death in the Amsterdam Rasphuis, in 1669, and Walten's apparent suicide in prison at The Hague, in 1697, like the gloom of Tyssot's last years, are attributable to despair leading to psychological breakdown. Meslier offers an elaborate theory to explain why even those he calls 'the most enlightened' (*les plus éclairés*), who see clearly the terrible abuse and disorder caused by ecclesiastical sway, princely authority, and aristocratic privilege, mostly find themselves compelled to remain silent. As he saw it, so great was what he calls the 'torrent des erreurs communes' that no one can oppose absolute monarchy, ecclesiastical pretensions, popular belief, or what he calls 'la tirannie des grands de la terre', without sacrificing his own comfort and peace and experiencing massive intimidation and repression.[103] Error, superstition, dread, devout submission, hypocrisy, self-imposed silence, and theological mystification, a towering and colossal edifice of imposture and false doctrine, as Meslier saw it, formed an all-embracing system reaching everywhere, powerfully bolstering the supremacy of tyranny, abuse, exploitation, and vice throughout our world, a labyrinth of error so great that it appeared an all but impossible task to undermine or break it down.

Yet, fitfully, there was also a measure of optimism regarding future prospects for clandestine propagation of radical thought, eventually leading to a restructuring of culture, and remodelling of society, encompassing the common people in a way that Voltaire and the moderate mainstream Enlightenment firmly repudiated. Even the grimly austere Meslier believed, just before his death in 1729, that if he could somehow ensure the survival after his death of his huge manuscript relentlessly detailing the endless 'erreurs, illusions et impostures' of the society in which he lived there was just a faint hope he might thereby ultimately contribute towards shaking the great citadel of theological thinking and monarchical, aristocratic, and ecclesiastical sway.[104] However tentatively and furtively, the Radical Enlightenment designed the overthrow of 'superstition', kingship, 'priestcraft', and institutionalized social hierarchy, and their replacement by democracy, equality, and individual liberty, and believed this *was* conceivable theoretically and one day perhaps also in practice.

If Meslier lived and wrote in almost total isolation and some radical thinkers died in prison or psychologically broken and in lonely desperation, others found no small recompense in the inspiration and support they gave each other and derived from their sense of battling the forces of darkness and prejudice, of being persecuted and yet right. There was indeed satisfaction to be drawn from claiming the moral and intellectual high ground, and pleasurable conviviality to be found in sharing an underground philosophical counter-culture which in late seventeenth-century Dutch towns, according to several accounts, including the clandestine Amsterdam philosophical novel *Philopater* (1697), did not, despite the shared

[103] Meslier, *Testament*, i. 10–14. [104] Ibid. i. 21, 26.

stigma, preclude relaxed gatherings in smoke-filled taverns or coffee- and wine-houses in which books, philosophers, and theologians were discussed in an irreverent but serious spirit.[105] By the 1730s and 1740s the scene had shifted to the Parisian cafés, but the philosophical impulse was the same. Deep down, it was the fervent expectation of all the radical thinkers of the age, including the three principal architects of the Radical Enlightenment—Spinoza, Bayle, and Diderot, that however formidable the difficulties, the world could be revolutionized by philosophy and that, in the end, they would revolutionize it.

And in a way they were right. For it was out of this decried and persecuted underground movement that emerged the values—democracy, freedom of thought and expression, individual freedom, comprehensive toleration, rule of law, equality, and sexual emancipation—which since the late nineteenth century have increasingly constituted the declared quintessential values of western 'modernity', since 1945 even in Germany and since the 1990s, albeit very hesitantly, even in Russia. The 'universal revolution' in ideas, education, culture, social theory, and political reality postulated by radical thinkers was, admittedly, nowhere ever fully carried through, and remains today incomplete not least in the United States. Yet during the twentieth century, western democratic libertarianism and emancipation of the individual slowly strengthened, gaining ground especially through their role in helping overcome Fascism and Stalinism to the point that these values after 1945 became the official ideology of the western world. As such they blunted the edge of nationalism, discredited racist theories, defeated Marxism, and spelt the end of the colonial empires of Britain, France, and the other old colonial powers as well, ultimately, as that in eastern Europe and central Asia, of the Soviet Union.

In the planned sequel to this volume, as indicated in the Preface, I hope to continue further the story of the impact of radical thought in the western Atlantic world, centring around the phenomenon of radical and revolutionary philosophy, after 1752 down to and through the American, French, and Batavian revolutions.

105 *Vervolg van't leven van Philopater*, 140, 174, 194, 207; Maréchal, 'Inleiding', 18–19; Israel, *Radical Enlightenment*, 318.

2

Philosophy and the Making of Modernity

1. SPINOZA AND SPINOZISM IN THE RADICAL ENLIGHTENMENT

Some initial signposting may be helpful to the reader. The *philosophes* labelled in this work 'radical' were those who, prior to 1752—marking the end date of this present volume—openly opposed not just tyranny, intolerance, credulity, superstition, and ecclesiastical sway, like all men of the Enlightenment, but also the moderate mainstream Enlightenment of Locke, Newton, and Voltaire, rebelling so to speak from the 'left'. That is they broadly denied all miracles and revelations and rejected physico-theology, Lockean empiricism, and providential Deism along with monarchy, (in most cases) aristocracy, and all social, racial, and sexual hierarchy as well. These out-and-out intellectual rebels of the Radical Enlightenment writing in French were Bayle (except in his politics), Fontenelle, Boulainvilliers, Tyssot de Patot, Lahontan, Fréret, Meslier, Du Marsais, Lévesque de Burigny, Boureau-Deslandes, de Maillet, Mirabaud, d'Argens, Boindin, Rousset de Missy, Jean-Frédéric Bernard (not be confused with Jacques Bernard), Bruzen de La Martinière, Vauvenargues, Buffon, Diderot, d'Alembert, Helvétius, La Beaumelle, Boulanger, Morelly, Mably, d'Holbach, Rousseau prior to the mid 1750s, and La Mettrie in his materialism though not his politics or moral theory.

The main task of this present volume is to analyse the thought of this sizeable group in relation to a Dutch coterie of writers and thinkers who were their immediate predecessors intellectually and ideologically, namely Spinoza, van den Enden, Koerbagh, Meyer, the brothers de La Court, Cuffeler, Beverland, van Balen, Walten, van Leenhof, and Mandeville, as well as smaller circles of English, German, and Italian writers and thinkers broadly classifiable together with the above as radical republicans, 'atheists', materialists, 'Spinozists', or non-providential Deists. The English group figured Blount, Toland, Collins, Bolingbroke, Tindal, and in some respects also Shaftesbury; the Germans, Tschirnhaus, Stosch, Wagner, Wachter, Edelmann, Lau, Hatzfeldt, Johann Lorenz Schmidt, and, in a more underhand, refined, and academic context, Hieronymus Niklaus Gundling and Johann Jakob Schmauss. The Italians included Giannone, Doria, Conti, Radicati, and, arguably, though this remains fiercely contested, many seeing him as a firmly Catholic thinker, that great and representative figure of his age Giambattista Vico.

Since Spinoza's philosophy and what the Early Enlightenment called 'Spinozism' need to be kept clearly distinct, and both are crucial to what follows, it seems as well to begin by outlining what precisely is meant by these two terms in our present context. Many have argued that there is in fact a very considerable gap between the philosophy of Spinoza, on the one hand, and what before 1750 was termed 'Spinozism', on the other, and that late seventeenth- and early eighteenth-century writers mostly had a remarkably inaccurate and superficial grasp of Spinoza's thought. It is sometimes asserted that talk of 'Spinozism' in the Early Enlightenment in fact means little, if anything, more than that a given thinker or writer is an 'atheist' and 'materialist'. But this widely held view is certainly unsustainable; for several major thinkers of the period, including Cudworth, Bayle (who stresses that Spinoza's one-substance doctrine is not a necessary accoutrement of atheism),[1] Boulainvilliers, Buddeus, and Reimmann, clearly believed both atheism and materialism could be reached via various different philosophical paths and, most certainly, without being a 'Spinozist'. Bayle, by far the most important 'image architect' of both 'Spinoza' and 'Spinozism' between 1680 and 1750, also thought there have been many atheists who had no clear, consistent, and systematic philosophical stance at all.[2]

Bayle was a key thinker rather obsessed with Spinoza from the moment, early in 1679, that he obtained a copy of the recent French translation of the *Tractatus theologico-politicus* clandestinely published in Amsterdam, and of all books found it to be 'bien le plus rempli de doctrines impies que j'aie jamais lu'.[3] Although the once extremely common view among historians and philosophers that Spinoza had virtually no impact on contemporaries, and the following generations, has now been shown to be so wide of the mark, and so thoroughly discredited, as not to merit further discussion, a variant of the older theme remains widespread and influential: namely that the real philosophy of Spinoza was so little understood by contemporaries that what passed for 'Spinozism' down to the mid eighteenth century, no matter how much talked about and widespread in society, utterly deformed his thought to the point that it was little more than an irrelevant caricature. If substantiated, it would then still be possible to argue that Spinoza advanced views, as one scholar recently expressed it, 'which had no real effects in their time because they were overshadowed by the influence of Descartes and his successors'.[4] It would follow also, if correct, that it makes no difference how frequently Spinoza is cited, invoked, or denounced during this period, or how many times his system was engaged with and 'refuted' by his innumerable adversaries, it can still be cogently contended, as one recent scholar claimed, that he was *not* in any meaningful sense a 'herald of the Enlightenment'.[5]

Many or most philosophers today still seemingly subscribe to a view of Spinoza according to which a careful balance must be struck, as one commentator recently

[1] Mori, *Bayle philosophe*, 218. [2] Ibid. 217–18.

[3] Bayle to Minutoli, Sedan, 26 May 1679, in Bayle, *Correspondance*, iii. 180.

[4] Mason, *God of Spinoza*, 248–9, 256; see also Thomson, 'La Mettrie' (1982), 241.

[5] Mason, *God of Spinoza*, 200, 248, 253–5.

put it, 'between the divine and the natural' so that even though Spinoza expressly rules out a knowing God who rewards and punishes in the hereafter or ordained the laws of human morality, there is still, at the heart of his thought, a crucial element of theism.[6] This is a question of rigorous examination of texts and formulations which cannot be gone into exhaustively here; but my own considered view is that it is extremely difficult, after analysing Spinoza's texts with the utmost care, to agree with those who still today find traces of theism in Spinoza. Even if it is true that they are a majority (which is open to question), there are also many others convinced they are mistaken. 'A close look at what [Spinoza] means by nature in the expression "God or Nature" ', as one of the latter recently expressed it, 'should be sufficient to dispel the view that he was a theist of any kind.'[7] God for Spinoza is always and consistently just 'the fixed and immutable order of Nature', something self-creating and evolutionary which never departs from the laws of nature as ascertained by empirical science. 'God's being', held Spinoza, 'coincides with the power by which he exists and "creates" whatever can be conceived.'[8] Hence, in his thought, something clearly evident as early as his *Cogitata metaphysica* (1663), there is, as likewise in Bayle later, absolutely no sense in which God can be said to be a benevolent (or malevolent) rather than a purely neutral force, the totality of all that is.[9]

In any case, all Early Enlightenment thinkers, major and minor, that is many dozens of writers, took it for granted that Spinoza was the pre-eminent 'atheist' of the era and that there is no element of theism in his work. Although Spinoza often used the word 'God', remarks Voltaire, in fact he was a much more openly and consistently 'atheistic' writer than almost anyone else in his time, there being very few truly consistent atheistic writers since many *esprits forts* in practice waver, are sceptical, or vary their views. Spinoza, by contrast, is always the classic rigorous 'atheist', argues Voltaire, because he allows only one substance, totally excludes all divine providence and supernatural agency, and, like Strato (Voltaire is here following Bayle), rejects all teleology and 'argument from design'. Furthermore, he does so allowing no room for doubt, as a complete anti-sceptic.[10] Only La Mettrie, suggests Voltaire in one place, can be compared with Spinoza in this respect. Indeed, Voltaire accounted Spinoza a much more consistent 'atheist' than Epicurus or the vast majority of other ancient Greek thinkers, Strato and Diagoras alone excepted.[11]

Admittedly, Spinoza indignantly rejects the designation 'atheist' but this is because he was not an 'atheist' under the terms of his own (and other Early Enlightenment materialists') redefining of the term 'atheism' to mean refusal to acknowledge the

[6] Mason, *God of Spinoza*, 15, 22–3, 248, 250–1, 254–5, 258; Hubbeling, *Spinoza*, 67–74; Sprigge, 'Is Spinozism a Religion?', 15.

[7] Smith, *Spinoza's Book of Life*, 43; see also Hampshire, *Spinoza*, pp. xxi, xxiv; van Bunge, 'Spinoza's atheïsme', 104–7; Nadler, *Spinoza's Heresy*, 32; Montag, *Bodies, Masses, Power*, 5; Huenemann, 'Middle Spinoza', 216–19; Nadler, 'Spinoza's Theory', 5–7; Lagrée, 'Y a-t-il une théodicée', 198, 204–5.

[8] Lagrée, 'Y a-t-il une théodicée', 198; Verbeek, 'Baruch de Spinoza', 118.

[9] Huenemann, 'Middle Spinoza', 216–17.

[10] Voltaire, *Homélies prononcées à Londres*, 353, 356; Voltaire, *Lettres à son altesse*, 391–2; Voltaire, *Philosophe ignorant*, 36–8.

[11] Voltaire, *Philosophe ignorant*, 37.

natural order and the obligations of the rational man. In terms of what was normally meant by 'atheism' during the Enlightenment, namely denial of all supernatural agency in the cosmos, including rejection of a providential God who created and guides the cosmos, and watches over the actions of men, Spinoza unquestionably *was* an 'atheist'. Hume too, hence, was certainly correct to refer to 'true atheism' as a set of sentiments 'for which Spinoza is so universally infamous'.[12] Nor is there any contradiction, since he identified God with the totality of nature, between Spinoza's asserting that 'God is an extended thing' [Deus est res extensa] and his brusque dismissal of the notion that God is 'corporeal'. As he expresses his view in Proposition XV of the *Ethics*, 'except God, no substance can be or, consequently, be conceived', from which it follows that 'God is unique', that there is only one substance in nature, and that this is absolutely infinite. Since both the modes of extended being and thought cannot be conceived without substance, it follows that both 'modes can be in the divine nature alone, and can be conceived through it alone'.

Consequently, everything is in God and 'nothing can be or be conceived without God'.[13] With this metaphysics Spinoza eliminated all notions of a normative world created by God with the intention that it should function in one way rather than another. God does not and cannot knowingly govern the world or regulate human affairs. Spinoza's one-substance doctrine also eliminates the traditional view that men consist of a separate substance, or combination of substances, thereby possessing a specially close and significant relation to God and his alleged purposes on earth. This in turn removed the ontological gulf between Man and other creatures and products of nature so that men are left superior to other animals and living things only insofar as they wield greater power or contrive to think more complex ideas.[14] Spinoza's philosophy, like that of Hobbes', is inherently empiricist in its premisses at least (and in some respects, perhaps, more consistently so than Locke's), and hence not at all 'rationalist' in the sense Anglo-American philosophers have in mind when they point to the wide gap between 'empiricism' and 'rationalism'—since, as with Hobbes, Spinoza's one-substance doctrine means that all knowledge of reality must necessarily originate in experience, activity, and sensation, given that there is nothing else. Moreover, in contrast to Locke there is no such thing, in Spinoza, as 'faculties' or powers of the mind substantially distinct from the body.

In my *Radical Enlightenment* (2001) may be found a working summary of Spinoza's thought which readers who, at this point, require a more detailed account of his system might wish to refer to.[15] Otherwise, it seems necessary to add here only that his thought is best understood as a comprehensive and consistent system of naturalism, materialism, and empiricism, eliminating all theism, teleology, miracles, and supernatural agency. As such it necessarily implies, without spelling out, some doctrine of nature evolving as a self-creating process and, hence, of evolution of species[16]—notions staunchly opposed by Voltaire, who ridiculed the many

[12] Hume, *Treatise*, 240. [13] *Collected Works of Spinoza*, i. 420.

[14] Walther, 'Philosophy and Politics in Spinoza', 52; Hampshire, *Spinoza*, p. xiv.

[15] Israel, *Radical Enlightenment*, 230–41. [16] Hampshire, *Spinoza*, pp. xxv, xlix–l.

conjectures of his age about fossils possibly demonstrating the extinction or mutation of species by proposing that the seashells and marine fossils found on inland mountains must be the remnants of travellers' picnics or part of the debris left by pilgrims crossing the Pyrenees on their way to Compostella.[17]

It follows that the frequently alleged gap between Spinoza's philosophy and the 'Spinozism' rife in the Early Enlightenment, though it exists, was not nearly so vast as many modern commentators suggest. Admittedly, what was called 'Spinozism' *was* often far sketchier and cruder than Spinoza himself. But one must also bear in mind that Early Enlightenment adversaries of Spinoza, including the Jesuit compilers of the *Dictionnaire de Trévoux*, a compendium characterizing the 'Spinozism of Spinoza's books' as a pot-pourri of rabbinics, Cartesianism, and Protestantism, not infrequently imply that other variants of 'Spinosisme', found elsewhere, were less garbled than the content of Spinoza's own writings.[18] Indeed, rather paradoxically, the Scottish Jacobite Catholic convert and disciple of Fénelon Andrew Michael Ramsay (1686–1743), a philosopher truly obsessed with Spinoza who devoted most of his philosophical efforts in the 1720s and 1730s, whilst living in Paris, to combating his legacy, reckoned the new *Spinosisme* fomented chiefly by French *esprits forts* and materialists, around 1720, but also, he says, being developed by 'les disciples de Spinoza en Italie' and those in Germany, Holland, and Britain, a more pressing philosophical challenge than Spinoza's own exposition of his thought which anyhow he professed to disdain as a 'tissu de plusieurs erreurs': 'all is supposed and nothing demonstrated in his system.'[19] Though undoubtedly differing from Spinoza's own philosophy, especially in presentation and ways of arguing, the important point, stressed Ramsay, was that the new French and other European 'Spinosisme' was a widespread growing and socially (and politically) menacing force.

Ramsay's idea, though it will seem strange, no doubt, to many today, actually had considerable justification. For it is indeed both completely unhistorical and also philosophically questionable to refuse to assign major relevance to eighteenth-century 'Spinozism' merely on the ground that it is not identical to, or so rigorously expressed as, Spinoza's system. For the long-sustained post-1677 Spinozist resurgence could readily be construed as a far greater and more actual menace than Spinoza's own books. On this topic, Ramsay's opinion was not far removed from that of Voltaire who was scarcely less conscious of the penetration of early and mid eighteenth-century French society by what he calls *les spinosistes modernes*, he too considering this a more pressing problem than Spinoza's own thought, since in his opinion Spinozism in general overthrows 'tous les principes de la morale' and, although perhaps not quite so fatal to modern society as religious fanaticism and *odium theologicum*, was yet the most potent philosophical danger at hand and his

[17] Ehrard, *L'Idée*, 199; Alatri, *Voltaire, Diderot*, 422; Dupré, *Enlightenment*, 37.

[18] Puisais, 'Deschamps', 97.

[19] [Ramsay], *Anecdotes*, 443; Ramsay, *Principes philosophiques*, 62, 67–8; Baldi, *Verisimile, non vero*, 324.

own chief intellectual antagonist.[20] Spinoza's system and the Spinozism of the *Spinosistes modernes* may have been two different things, with the latter being more loosely expressed than the former, but both, held Voltaire, were anchored in the same premisses, most effectively expounded by Spinoza himself, and both should be combated with the same arguments, the five most effective refutations in French, he judged, being those of Fénelon, Bayle, Lamy, Condillac, and Pluquet.[21]

Another consideration to bear in mind is that the impression of loose usage has been greatly accentuated by a long and relentless historiographical tradition of dismissing earlier identifications of 'Spinozists' in eighteenth-century writing as inexact and misplaced, a judgement often repeated and passed on to students, but not very well substantiated. This tendency has itself recently increasingly been called into question owing to important scholarly revisions, resulting in key figures now being restored to their 'Spinozist' setting. A major example of such reversion is the important figure of Anthony Collins (1676–1729). He has persistently been represented in the modern historiography as essentially a 'Deist', or a wavering voice suspended somewhere between Christianity and Deism. It was long taken for granted that Collins was shaped intellectually by his friend Locke, and other indigenous influences, and contemporary claims that he was an 'atheist' and his views on ontology, Bible criticism, prophecy, freedom of thought, and determinism essentially 'Spinozist', such as we find in Bishop Berkeley, and the German scholar Urban Gottlob Thorschmid, were routinely dismissed as quite erroneous, even fanciful.[22] However, now that Collins', writings have been more carefully studied, scholars have come to see that actually he was not even remotely a 'Deist' or Lockean, and that it is, rather, the long-standing assumption that he was a Deist, semi-Christian, and Lockean which constitutes the real loose usage, since the veritable Collins unquestionably argued, just as Berkeley claims, 'against the being of a God', subscribing to forms of determinism, rejection of the supernatural, and text criticism very close to Spinoza's.[23]

Indubitably, the 'Spinozism' prevalent in Early Enlightenment culture often derived not from a direct reading of Spinoza's *Ethics* or other works, but from reports in influential intermediaries such as Bayle or Boulainvilliers, from the clandestine manuscripts, or else other underground sources including subversive conversation, and published refutations, sources which frequently distorted or oversimplified Spinoza's positions and arguments,[24] though Voltaire's reference of 1772 to Spinoza's *Ethics* as his 'famous book so little read' should not be taken as wholly accurate for the situation down to the 1740s.[25] Equally, this constant private reconstitution of

[20] Voltaire, *Philosophe ignorant*, 38–40; Voltaire, *Lettres à son altesse*, 391–2.

[21] Voltaire, *Lettres à son altesse*, 390; Voltaire, 'Notes de M. de Morza', 252–3.

[22] Berkeley, *Alciphron*, 9–12, 17, 204; Thorschmid, *Critische Lebensgeschichte*, 76–7; Berman, 'Determinism', 252–4.

[23] Berman, 'Determinism', 252; Berman, *History of Atheism*, 70, 78–81, 94–5; Taranto, *Du déisme à l'athéisme*, 15 n., 16–17, 344–54, 381–400, 435; Berman, 'Disclaimers', 271.

[24] Verbeek, 'Baruch de Spinoza', 119.

[25] Voltaire, 'Notes de M. de Morza', 252.

Spinozism from secondary sources undeniably involved absorbing all sorts of extraneous philosophical elements, and even whole passages of text incorporated wholesale from other philosophers. Hence, that key 'Spinozistic' text the *Traité de trois imposteurs* pasted in large chunks of Hobbes, albeit without this causing serious disjunction by injecting arguments which seriously diverge from Spinoza's particular conception of the origins of organized religion.[26] In most cases, such clandestine propagation encouraged adoption of a tone and style very different from, and mostly more militant than, that of Spinoza himself. However, as we shall see, none of this necessarily means that Early Enlightenment 'Spinozism' lacked coherence, or was intellectually remote from Spinoza's system or departed fundamentally from his ideas. On the contrary, it entirely confirms the correctness of Berkeley's referring to 'Spinosa', in 1732, as 'the great leader of our modern infidels'.[27]

Furthermore, numerous radical writers, including Toland, Collins, Mandeville, Boulainvilliers, Vauvenargues, Lau, and, most importantly, Diderot, where a clear direct or indirect influence can be documented, evince in large parts of their thought an impressive and crucially important proximity to many, if not all, of Spinoza's key points. The same is true of the Huguenot novelist and mathematics teacher of Deventer, Simon Tyssot de Patot (1655–1738), whose 'Spinozism' dates from the 1690s, and, to an extent, of Julien Offray de La Mettrie (1709–51), who matured in the 1740s, stood close to the radical tradition expressed in the clandestine manuscripts, and was certainly a 'Spinozist', as he openly declared, in his ontology and materialism—albeit he simultaneously rejected Spinozist positions in his moral, social, and political thought. In other cases, where there was scant or no direct 'influence' at work, or at least little that can be documented, as with Du Marsais or Meslier, the actual systems of these materialists bear so many parallels and resemblances to Spinoza's system that it is perfectly accurate and meaningful to include them as *Spinosistes modernes* as was usual in their time.[28]

Prophecy is just fantasy and organized religion nothing more than a political and social device, held the 'Spinozists', following Spinoza, adopted for the well-being of men in this world. Integral also to all variants of *Spinosisme* was the doctrine that geometrical 'reason' is the only criterion of truth, so that there can be no limit to the application of reason operating on the basis of experience, and hence of knowledge, short of the furthest bounds of human awareness and perception, but that there is no other source of knowledge available to men. This of course was denied by the Cartesians, Boyle, Locke, and Newton and is what Kant later called their 'lawless use of reason'.[29] All this may be highly reductive. But it is erroneous to see it as seriously divergent from, or a distortion of, Spinoza's basic doctrines, as so many have argued, or just loosely equivalent to 'atheism'. Tyssot de Patot and La Mettrie both

[26] Popkin, *Third Force*, 135–6, 144–8; Berti, 'Introduzione', pp. xx, lvi–lxvi; Charles-Daubert, '*Traité des trois imposteurs*', 274–301; Thomson, 'Déterminisme et passions', 80.

[27] Berkeley, *Alciphron*, 155–6; Olscamp, *Moral Philosophy*, 215–16, 221.

[28] Ricuperati, 'Il problema', 372; Tortarolo, *L'Illuminismo*, 26–30.

[29] Montag, *Bodies, Masses, Power*, 53–4.

summarize 'Spinozism' as the doctrine that nothing comes from nothing, that there is only one substance which while subject to perpetual change is eternal and indivisible governed by a fixed and immutable order of nature, that the whole of reality is hence governed by a single set of rules comprised of interlocking and unchanging scientific laws, so that God is both the 'cause nécessaire' of his works and simultaneously the totality of them. Thought and thinking, hence, cannot be separated from the actions of matter; indeed, mind and body, it follows, are one and the same, men being simply part of nature like all other creatures; finally, there is no ordained, absolute moral law, so that morality is in reality a man-made device needed for the better maintenance of society.[30]

Early Enlightenment 'Spinozism' was thus both a very widespread phenomenon, especially in France, the Netherlands, and Germany, and one broadly faithful to Spinoza's system even if normally also a considerably simplified, thinned-down vulgarization. In addition, it was often perceived as possessing ancient roots but as having been largely submerged from sight until comparatively recently, albeit latterly to have again become a powerful force. As Mandeville expresses this notion in *The Fable of the Bees*, at the same time following Cudworth and Bayle in seeing philosophic atheism as something that comes in very different varieties, 'this doctrine, which is *Spinosism* in epitome, after having been neglected many years, begins to prevail again, and the atoms [of Epicureanism] lose ground: for of Atheism, as well as Superstition, there are different kinds, that have their periods and returns.'[31]

It was this accurately perceived strengthening of 'Spinozism' after 1700 that led to its being taught to theology and other university students at continental Protestant universities: it was felt that future pastors needed to be armed against it. Jean-Alphonse Turretini, an eminent professor of theology at Geneva, summarized Spinoza's doctrine for his students, around 1728, in six main points: for Spinoza there are no miracles, prophecies, or revelations, whatever happens happens necessarily, there is no sin, no soul separate from the body, and no difference between mind and matter; finally, there are no duties for Man ordained by God and no Natural Law other than the desires and appetites of every individual.[32] The perception of Spinozism as a growing force continued much longer in France and Italy than in Holland or Britain, moreover, indeed in mid eighteenth-century France, many Catholic apologists, as for instance the Abbé François-André Pluquet (1716–90), Laurent François, author of the *Preuves de la religion de Jésus-Christ contre les Spinosistes et déistes* (3 vols., Paris, 1751), and Dom Leger-Marie Deschamps (1716–74), who wrote several refutations of Spinoza, wrote of the 'matérialistes et de leur chef Spinoza', portraying 'le Spinosisme' as the philosophical and moral core of the new French materialism of the radical *encyclopédistes* and correctly so, as we shall see.[33]

[30] Verbeek, 'Baruch de Spinoza', 119; Vartanian, *La Mettrie's* L'Homme machine, 46–7, 62–3, 101, 110; Rosenberg, *Tyssot de Patot*, 56, 65–77; Comte-Sponville, 'La Mettrie', 133–4, 138; Israel, *Radical Enlightenment*, 706–8.

[31] Mandeville, *Fable of the Bees*, ii. 312.

[32] Turrettini, 'Réfutation', 192.

[33] Pluquet, *Examen*, ii, preface p. 1, 95; Deschamps, *Œuvres philosophiques*, ii. 522, 613–22; Puisais, 'Deschamps', 97–8, 104–5.

Early Enlightenment 'Spinozism' was also heavily influenced by the account of Spinoza's thought in Bayle's article 'Spinoza', the longest of all the entries in his *Dictionnaire historique et critique* of 1697. This focused on certain aspects of Spinoza's thought, in particular ridiculing his one-substance doctrine, while praising his moral character and ignoring, or oversimplifying, other key features of his system; even so, there seems no good reason to claim Bayle's depiction of Spinoza as the 'virtuous atheist' *par excellence* and deliberately subversive advancement of this topos in European culture, here and elsewhere, seriously distorted Spinoza's message. On the contrary, Bayle's argument that Spinoza's philosophy is the culmination, and most orderly presentation, of all the materialistic and 'atheistic' arguments put forward by philosophers since the Greek Presocratics, and that his chief role was not so much to introduce novel concepts, as to weld everything said by earlier monists and naturalists of ancient, medieval, and early modern times into a more coherent and orderly whole, probably did much to further the impact of Spinoza's actual system.[34] Nor was Spinoza viewed by Bayle as the summation only of western philosophical atheism; for, like Arnauld and Malebranche, Bayle held that Spinozism also had close affinities with the 'atheistic' philosophical tendency prevalent, they believed, since ancient times in Chinese, Japanese, and Siamese thought.

One might object that these latter notions play no part in Spinoza's own philosophy and are, therefore, strictly speaking not 'Spinozist' ideas at all. Yet, it is clear that his system does in fact incorporate ingredients from various ancient sources, especially Epicureanism and Stoicism, as well as from Machiavelli, Hobbes, Descartes, and the brothers de La Court, while none of the other materialists of the Early Enlightenment, not even Hobbes, can be said to have matched Spinoza in orderliness and overall coherence. Bayle's insights, consequently, can be regarded as highlighting features which genuinely characterize Spinoza's philosophy even if Bayle deliberately gave his observations about Spinoza, here and more obviously in his late writings, an elaborate historical context, global orientation, and subversive force Spinoza himself did not.

2. LOCKE, HUME, AND THE MAKING OF MODERNITY

Several distinguished scholars have reacted to my thesis that Spinoza and Spinozism, amplified and further elaborated by Bayle, Diderot, and a host of lesser figures, together formed a powerful collective legacy, forming a continuous tradition extending from the 1650s to the age of Heine, Marx, and Hölderlin, and that it was from this essentially philosophical tradition, the Radical Enlightenment, that the essential values of 'modernity' derive rather than from the more familiar and far more frequently discussed moderate mainstream Enlightenment, by protesting

[34] Bayle, *Écrits*, 21, 29–33; Costa, 'Bayle', 118–19; Mori, *Bayle philosophe*, 218.

that this would seem seriously to understate the roles in the making of 'modernity' of such key Enlightenment thinkers as Locke, Hume, and Voltaire. Consequently, it seems a useful preliminary procedure here also to define further, for the reader, the exact relationship of the Radical Enlightenment to the making of 'modernity' and briefly clarify the relation of Locke, Voltaire, and Hume to the phenomenon of Spinoza and the Radical Enlightenment.

First of all, it should be noted that the phrase 'making of modernity' in what follows designates two chronologically and factually inseparable and partly overlapping, but yet conceptually distinct phenomena, one philosophical, the other historical, which the reader needs to keep notionally apart. Where appropriate, I have tried to ensure that it is clear in which sense the appellation is being used. Philosophically, the 'making of modernity' here means the emergence of an interlocking complex of abstract concepts of which individual liberty, democracy, freedom of expression, comprehensive toleration, equality racial and sexual, freedom of lifestyle, full secularization of all legal institutions and most publicly maintained educational establishments, together with a wholly secular morality based on equity, are the most important and which, it is argued, are predominantly (but not exclusively) derived from the Radical Enlightenment. I say 'not exclusively' because there is undeniably some overlap between the desiderata of the two enlightenments, on the metaphysical front, regarding the need to curtail the authority of miracles, prophecies, and scriptures together with ecclesiastical authority, and on the practical front, as regards toleration, individual liberty, and liberty of the press.

From the standpoint of 'modernity' defined philosophically, as above, the divergences between moderate mainstream and the Radical Enlightenment remain, however, more conspicuous and numerous than the elements of overlap. For, overwhelmingly, the moderate mainstream rejected equality and comprehensive toleration (especially in Locke and Le Clerc), retained the principles of monarchy and empire, and sought to block the route to democracy, as with Hume who, as some late eighteenth-century opponents of the French Revolution pointed out, categorically denies that political sovereignty derives from the people.[35] The mainstream also broadly abjured notions of a purely secular morality, sticking (especially in Locke[36] and Hume) to a very conservative, traditional conception of virtue, and declining to extend 'enlightenment' and emancipation to all men, while at the same time rejecting the Radical Enlightenment's complete elimination of theological criteria and unrestricted application of reason to everything we know or what later came to be called *l'esprit philosophique*.

In the fight for a 'universal toleration' Voltaire, admittedly, stood out. He has been called the 'head of the "party of humanity" ' and a figure at the 'forefront of the Enlightenment movement for religious toleration'.[37] Yet he introduced no new arguments for toleration and took up this cause in earnest only a good many decades after

[35] Bongie, *David Hume*, 107; Porter, *Enlightenment*, 200; Haakonssen, 'Structure', 183, 194–6.

[36] Locke, *Some Thoughts*, 106–7, 129–32, 167–8.

[37] Zagorin, *How the Idea*, 293–4, 298.

Spinoza, Bayle, and, slightly later (and to a lesser extent), Locke had launched the main Enlightenment attack on the bastions of intolerance. Furthermore, his toleration was qualified by two curious but significant counter-tendencies. One was his obsession with the Jews towards whom he felt a deep and abiding hostility which he was never to relinquish.[38] The other was his marked reluctance to endorse toleration of atheism. Throughout his career he considered himself to be the 'enlightened' opponent of the atheists, materialists, and Spinozists, and, at moments, even held it was better for men to live subject to the strangest superstitions, or adore exotic idols, than succumb to atheism.[39] Voltaire's unwillingness to tolerate atheism, moreover, was, as we shall see, linked to his unbending commitment to a strongly providential Deism based on the 'argument from design' which, in turn, further fortified his dislike of theories of biological evolution and endorsement of notions of a divinely intended and moulded hierarchy of species, races, and social orders.

Hume, like Voltaire, vigorously championed toleration and liberty of the press and here, as in his attitude to ecclesiastical authority and scepticism concerning miracles, clearly overlaps with radical thought, even though he saw the rise of British liberty of the press as an almost unique phenomenon (albeit not forgetting to point out that Holland had preceded England in this respect) shaped by Britain's 'mixed form of government, something neither wholly monarchical nor wholly republican'.[40] The altogether exceptional freedom of the press flourishing in early and mid eighteenth-century England, he deemed a crucial safeguard of political liberty: 'the spirit of the people must frequently be rouzed', he wrote in 1741, 'in order to curb the ambition of the court; and the dread of rouzing this spirit must be employed to prevent that ambition.' Nothing else, he believed, was 'so effectual to this purpose as the liberty of the press, by which all the learning, wit and genius of the nation may be employed on the side of freedom, and everyone be animated to its defense'; consequently this freedom was not at all to be taken for granted and needed to be vigilantly and staunchly defended.[41]

Hume, again like Voltaire, is eager to curb theology's sway, albeit, unlike Spinoza, never pronouncing it wholly unreasonable to believe in miracles. Like the radicals and unlike Voltaire, he also casts doubt on the 'argument from design', though, again, in contrast to Spinoza and Diderot, from his sceptical standpoint he could not categorically rule out such a concept.[42] Furthermore, he advances distinctly further than Voltaire towards eradicating supernatural agency, and the transcendental, from the sphere of morality, deeming ethics something which, as far as anyone can know, as he typically says in his sceptical vein, is exclusively the product of human concerns.[43] Where Voltaire always asserts morality to be divinely ordained,

[38] Zagorin, *How the Idea*, 293; Manuel, *Broken Staff*, 193–200; Sutcliffe, *Judaism and Enlightenment*, 7–8, 19, 231–8.

[39] Zagorin, *How the Idea*, 298; Dupré, *Enlightenment*, 14, 254.

[40] Hume, *Essays*, 10; Porter, *Enlightenment*, 192.

[41] Hume, *Essays*, 12; Gay, *Enlightenment*, ii. 72, 74.

[42] Fogelin, 'Hume's Scepticism', 93; Gaskin, *Hume's Philosophy of Religion*, 6, 48, 164–5, 221.

[43] Norton, 'Hume, Human Nature', 156, 158; Taylor, *Sources of the Self*, 344–6.

Hume does nothing of the sort, even though, as a sceptic, he scrupulously combines his basically secular morality with what has aptly been termed an 'attenuated deism'.[44] Hence, it was with perceptibly more justification than Spinoza or Diderot, but less than Voltaire, that Hume could deny, in both public and private, being in the customary sense an 'atheist'.[45]

Nevertheless, Hume devotes his powerful philosophical mind and sophisticated social criticism to essentially conservative political, social, and moral goals and was relentless in his attack on the pretensions of philosophy itself. The ground freed by pruning theology's sway, he proposed to occupy not with 'reason', whose dominion, he, like Locke, strives to curb, and even ridicule, but with custom, habit, and practical good sense. Not only does Hume insist our knowledge always derives from experience, he combined this with sceptical arguments, to extend Locke's attempts to narrow the scope of philosophy, seeking to curb the pretensions of natural philosophy too. Echoing Newton's empiricist strictures, as well as reacting somewhat to the euphoria surrounding his achievements, and the sweeping claims of other philosophers, he asserts in his *Enquiry Concerning Human Understanding* (1748) that 'it must certainly be allowed that nature has kept us at a great distance from all her secrets and has afforded us only the knowledge of a few superficial qualities of objects, while she conceals from us those powers and principles on which the influence of these objects entirely depends'.[46]

Hume sought to restrict the range of philosophy's applicability in the search for truth and, still more, its practical applicability.[47] The latter ensured a head-on clash with the efforts to construct a secular morality and reason-based social theory and politics in Spinoza, Bayle, and Diderot, as we see from his strictures concerning the place of reason in the making and upholding of moral values. Already, in his first major work, the *Treatise of Human Nature* (1739), Hume takes up an argument which subsequently remained a central strand of his philosophy: 'since morals have an influence on the actions and affections, it follows, that they can not be deriv'd from reason; and that because reason alone, as we have already prov'd, can never have any such influence. Morals excite passions, and produce or prevent actions. Reason of itself is utterly impotent in this particular. The rules of morality, therefore are not conclusions of our reason.'[48] He proceeds similarly in his *Enquiry Concerning the Principles of Morals* (1751), the work Hume himself dubbed 'of all my writings, historical, philosophical, or literary, incomparably the best' albeit one which, like his previous works, also 'came unnoticed and unobserved into the world'. Here, Hume firmly eschews all theological criteria, granting that the 'end of

[44] Gaskin, *Hume's Philosophy of Religion*, 7.

[45] Ibid. 219–22; Stewart, 'Hume's Historical View', 195; Box, *Suasive Art*, 213.

[46] Hume, *Enquiry Concerning Human Understanding*, 46; Rothschild, *Economic Sentiments*, 150, 228.

[47] Porter, *Enlightenment*, 178–9; Fogelin, 'Hume's Scepticism', 108, 113.

[48] Fogelin, 'Hume's Scepticism', 100–5; Hume, *Treatise*, 457; Stewart, *Opinion and Reform*, 314; Norton, 'Hume, Human Nature', 163–4; Schneewind, *Invention of Autonomy*, 358; MacIntyre, *After Virtue*, 49, 54.

moral speculations is to teach us our duty, and, by proper representations of the deformity of vice and beauty of virtue, beget correspondent habits, and engage us to avoid the one, and embrace the other'; but he also refuses to accept that any such result could stem 'from inferences and conclusions of the understanding', on the ground that reason has no hold over individuals and cannot 'set in motion the active powers of men'.[49] Custom must do the work.

It remained Hume's firm conviction that whatever morality is current in a given society is valid and is the one to be followed, morality like politics being best based on tradition, custom, and the current status quo. And as with morality, so with Hume's view of equality. The fundamental unity and equality of Man urged by the Radical Enlightenment being based on the idea of a shared reason, and the equivalence of individual volitions or motivation as proved by 'reason', is definitely not for Hume, whose downplaying of 'reason', and insistence on experience and practice, undoubtedly reinforced his anti-black bias and inclination 'to suspect that the Negroes and in general all of the other species of men (for there are four or five different kinds) to be naturally inferior to the whites'.[50] He was likewise strongly prejudiced against the Irish and Jews.[51] Hume may not have thought in terms of a divinely ordained order, like Voltaire, but he did conclude from experience and inductive evidence that nature had formed the races and peoples of the world in an inherently unequal hierarchy.

On the economic front, he offers more liberal sentiments, granting that it 'must be confessed that wherever we depart from this equality we rob the poor of more satisfaction than we add to the rich, and that the slight gratification of a frivolous vanity in one individual frequently costs more than bread to many families, and even provinces'.[52] He concedes also that the ideal of equality had, at least in some degree, been adopted in such ancient republics as those of Sparta 'where it was attended, it is said, by the most beneficial consequences' and in some other Greek cities. However, in general, he contends that such schemes are wholly impracticable 'and were they not so would be extremely pernicious to human society'.[53] For if you leave the individual free, starting from a position of general equality, the natural inequality of men in intelligence, skill, and diligence 'will immediately break that equality' while any attempt to check the effect of these differences in ability will inexorably 'reduce society to the most extreme indigence, and instead of preventing want and beggary in a few, render it unavoidable to the whole community'. On top of this, he warned, with admirable prescience, that the increased authority inevitably required to supervise the maintenance of equality 'must soon degenerate into tyranny and be exerted with great partialities'.[54]

[49] MacIntyre, *After Virtue*, 171–2; Hume, *Inquiry Concerning the Principles*, 5; Rothschild, *Economic Sentiments*, 231.

[50] Hume, *Essays*, 208, 214; Bracken, *Freedom of Speech*, 135; Popkin, *Third Force*, 65–6, 70–5.

[51] Popkin, *Third Force*, 65; Hume, *Essays*, 205.

[52] Hume, *Inquiry Concerning the Principles*, 24–5.

[53] Ibid. 245.

[54] Ibid.; Haakonssen, 'Structure', 198.

Fundamental inequality is justified in Hume on the grounds of the public interest in upholding the moral principles enshrined in tradition and custom which indeed themselves are generally founded on the experience, rather than the principle, of utility. No matter how defective a form of government, it still acquires legitimacy, no matter how violent, illegitimate, and upstart in origin, argues Hume, merely from the fact of 'long possession' of power and through the 'right of succession', a basic principle in Hume's politics and morality as well as theory of property.[55] If chastity and marital fidelity are very widely prized in human societies because the 'long and helpless infancy of man requires the combination of parents for the subsistence of their young' and this in turn predicates the sanctity of the marriage bed, the same experience of the facts of nature, in Hume's opinion, ensures that marital infidelity 'is much more pernicious in women than in men. Hence the laws of chastity are much stricter over the one sex than over the other,' and Hume feels this is as it should be.[56] However, moved by ingrained bias against blacks and belief that one may obtain anything from them by offering strong drink, he noted, in 1748, that one 'may easily prevail with them to sell, not only their children, but their wives and mistresses, for a cask of brandy'.[57]

Though critical of Montesquieu whose books, and especially *L'Esprit des lois* (1748), enjoyed all the success and fame which, until the 1760s, eluded him, elements of Hume's defence of social hierarchy and inequality and the varying utility of different moral systems for different types of society and state, as well as his classification of despotisms, monarchies, and republics, are strikingly reminiscent of those of that 'illustrious writer'.[58] Comparing Britain with France and other continental monarchies with more rigid social hierarchies, Hume remarks that in the latter it is 'family, that is, hereditary riches, marked with titles and symbols from the sovereign' which is the 'chief source of distinction'. By contrast, in Britain which he considers a 'crowned republic' rather than a true monarchy, wealth as such often mattered more. Hume thought both systems of privilege had their advantages and disadvantages and these corresponded in significant ways to the differences in monarchical political structures. 'Where birth is respected, unactive, spiritless minds remain in haughty indolence and dream of nothing but pedigrees and genealogies; the generous and ambitious seek honor and authority and reputation and favour. Where riches are the chief idol, corruption, venality, rapine prevail; arts, manufactures, commerce, agriculture flourish.' Consequently, Hume thought the 'former prejudice, being favourable to military virtue', better suited to monarchies and the latter, being more favourable to 'industry, agrees better with a republican government'.[59]

[55] Haakonssen, 'Structure', 202–3; Hume, *Treatise*, 509–11.

[56] Hume, *Inquiry Concerning the Principles*, 36–7; Gay, *Enlightenment*, ii. 200–1; Schneewind, *Invention of Autonomy*, 36.

[57] Hume, *Essays*, 214.

[58] Popkin, *Third Force*, 65; Wootton, 'David Hume, "the Historian" ', 293–5; Stewart, *Opinion and Reform*, 290–1, 301.

[59] Stewart, *Opinion and Reform*, 292; Hume, *Inquiry Concerning the Principles*, 73.

Hume's very choice of words shows he had no particular fondness for monarchy or social hierarchy *per se*. His preferring mixed government to absolute monarchy was doubtless reinforced by his perception that poverty and inequality extend furthest under absolute monarchy, and that excessive inequality harms society as a whole,[60] though he also believed the social fabric, with all its inequalities, was a delicate thing which could not be sensibly or safely challenged or changed by anything, least of all 'reason'. Above all, he was emphatic in his belief that philosophy and 'reason' have no business in trying to transform the world. His conservative scepticism represents a more systematic attack on the capacity of reason than perhaps any other eighteenth-century assault on *l'esprit philosophique*. Hence, despite the fact that in the long run perhaps no one, next to Spinoza himself, did more to erode belief in miracles, the 'argument from design', and the supernatural, Hume nevertheless must be regarded as a firm anti-democrat and, on the whole, more of an opponent than an ally of the Radical Enlightenment.

Accordingly, where the term 'modernity' is employed philosophically in what follows, it is primarily the Radical Enlightenment which is meant since both the other main intellectual blocs on the threshold of 'modernity'—the moderate mainstream Enlightenment and the Counter-Enlightenment—were in some degree, if not wholly, opposed to its fundamental principles, despite overlap in the areas of toleration, civil liberty, and liberty of the press. However, the designation 'making of modernity' is also employed in this book in another, unavoidable, and more historical sense to designate the altogether untidier, less coherent outcome which actually constitutes the value-system and political orientation of the West today, an outcome shaped by a long process of continual clashes and collision between the rival impulses of Radical, conservative, and Counter-Enlightenment. Looked at ideologically, the picture is one of a continuous triangular conflict in progress from the end of the seventeenth century down to today. Looked at from a practical point of view, the gap between philosophical 'modernity' and historical 'modernity' at the centre of this present study, particularly where western countries say their politics is based on democratic practice, claim to uphold the principle of equality, and profess, as in practically all western countries today, to outlaw ethnic discrimination, and discrimination against women or homosexuals, is primarily a difference between theory and practice.

From a historical, as distinct from the philosophical, point of view, then, there can be no question as to the overwhelming importance of Locke and Hume, rather more doubtless than Voltaire, in the 'making of modernity' and it is in no way my intention to imply that their significance in the making of historical 'modernity' is less than it has generally been taken to be. It is also undeniable that anyone scanning the historiography of the Enlightenment will find that both Locke and Hume are accorded in the existing historiography, and still more in student textbooks, incomparably more weight than Spinoza and Spinozism in formulating the ideas of the

60 Payne, *The* Philosophes, 55–6; Gay, *The Enlightenment*, ii. 356–7; Porter, *Enlightenment*, 251.

western Enlightenment. However, none of this alters the fact that despite being heterodox on religious issues and vigorous advocates of toleration, Locke and Hume, like Voltaire and the great American Deist Benjamin Franklin, were politically, socially, morally, and, in some respects, religiously—and in their views on philosophy's proper scope—essentially conservative thinkers who opposed many or most of the radical and democratic ideas of their age and, as such, were, in the main, opponents of the Radical Enlightenment.

Locke and Hume are two of the very few Enlightenment philosophers who still attract numerous admirers today. Their ideas, persons, and cultural legacies continue to enjoy widespread allegiance. Taking into view the whole of modern times, no one could sensibly deny that they were both great and immensely influential figures. In the next volume where more attention will be given to the 'making of modernity' in its post-1750 historical aspects, further attention will be paid to Locke's legacy, as well as to Hume and the Scottish Enlightenment. But this present volume covers the Early Enlightenment, down to the great international controversy over Montesquieu's *L'Esprit des lois* (1748–52), and the first part of the 'war' over the *Encyclopédie* (1751–2), and in this, arguably the most decisively formative period of the Enlightenment, the evidence of the major continental controversies unequivocally shows that as yet the Scottish Enlightenment had had no impact. Francis Hutcheson (1694–1746) was a major figure in moral philosophy; but he avoided continental influences and debates, his concerns being mainly with Locke, Shaftesbury, and Mandeville, and was, in turn, ignored outside Britain until the 1750s when he was taken up by Lessing and others.[61] Colin MacLaurin (1698–1746) was a prominent expositor of Newtonian physico-theology but again, not one of the better-known commentators on the Continent. Indeed, even Hume, let alone the others—both Adam Smith (1723–90) and Adam Ferguson (1723–1816) were aged only 29 in 1752—was then almost wholly unknown outside Britain until the 1750s, and even there his 'love of literary fame', as he lamented himself, went generally unrequited.

Historically, Locke, eventually Hume, and both the English and Scottish 'enlightenments' *were*, of course, immensely influential. Nevertheless, even from a strictly historical point of view, there is a further point to be made about distortion and lack of balance in the way the figures of Locke and Hume, besides those of Newton, Clarke, Hutcheson, and Adam Smith and other major English, Scottish, and Irish figures of the Enlightenment have come to be presented in the recent literature. For it has become increasingly usual in recent years, among anglophone historians and philosophers when assessing the significance of the eighteenth century, to play down the significance of the French Enlightenment, in an almost chauvinistic fashion, and to lay more and more emphasis on the allegedly overwhelming formative impact of British ideas and inspiration in the making of the western Atlantic Enlightenment as a whole, usually accompanied by a marked de-emphasizing also of the contributions of Germany, Italy, and the Netherlands. Roy Porter, for

[61] Malherbe, 'Impact on Europe', 300.

instance, whether or not there is any justice in his claim that Ernst Cassirer and others, in their older surveys of the Enlightenment, unjustly neglected Britain, certainly leant over the other way when suggesting that Voltaire's passionate intellectual and cultural-Anglophilia typified the 'ardent' enthusiasm of the *philosophes* towards Britain, and British thinkers, and in citing as representative the opinion expressed in a French journal in 1758, that France 'owes' to England the 'great revolution which has taken place in everything which can contribute to render peoples more happy and states more flourishing'.[62]

This tendency of some historians to adopt an insular view of things and far too readily presume that the 'early Enlightenment in England is attested by a body of literature, by controversies and by certain figures in a way that is not true of France, or anywhere else',[63] closing their eyes to the achievements of Bayle, Le Clerc, Fontenelle, Boulainvilliers, and other francophone giants of the Early Enlightenment, is matched by a still more emphatic stance among some recent philosophers of Anglo-American derivation. Driven perhaps by undiminished confidence that the path Anglo-American philosophy took, from Locke onwards, was the right one, and that in leaving the continental system-builders, together with their supposedly 'facile' eighteenth-century French successors—or at least those who failed to venerate Locke and Newton—behind, philosophy, together with science and religion, assumed their truly 'modern' and western guise, emphasis on the supposedly overwhelming centrality of Locke and Hume has been still heavier. In some cases, such views are propagated with a quite remarkable ardour for the Scottish dimension, as with Alasdair MacIntyre who suggests, apparently in all seriousness, that 'in fact, France is from the standpoint of [Enlightenment] culture itself the most backward of the enlightened nations. The French themselves avowedly looked to English models, but England in turn was overshadowed by the achievements of the Scottish Enlightenment.'[64] If we look at the Enlightenment in terms of national contributions, he adds, then, for intellectual range and variety as well as overall importance, neither those of the English, French, nor Germans can 'outmatch David Hume, Adam Smith, Adam Ferguson, John Millar, Lord Kames and Lord Monboddo'.

One might dismiss this as a ridiculous joke were it not part of a wider, deeply serious, and now pervasive tendency. Charles Taylor may be a fairer, more balanced interpreter of the western Enlightenment than MacIntyre; but he too thinks English Deism was massively imported into early eighteenth-century France (a highly doubtful assertion, as we shall see) and that there was a fusion of English influence with French genius, with Voltaire as 'the major architect of this fusion'; and that the result of this merging of streams 'was what we know as the Enlightenment, a bilingual product of the two societies (or more accurately England, Scotland, France, and America)'.[65] Such a view sounds plausible to many but is in fact wildly inaccurate especially in that Voltaire, through his lifelong efforts, knew better than anyone the

[62] Porter, *Enlightenment*, 6–7.
[63] Harrison, *'Religion' and the Religions*, 3.
[64] MacIntyre, *After Virtue*, 37.
[65] Taylor, *Sources of the Self*, 334–5.

real extent of his failure, by the 1750s almost total, to steer the French High Enlightenment onto the track of the 'English ideas' which he so deeply and sincerely venerated.

No doubt total impartiality as between different cultural and intellectual traditions is an impossibly elusive ideal. Nevertheless, the historian's duty is to strive for the most objective and balanced outcome possible and, if in this respect the 'controversialist method' advocated and utilized in this work has any merit, then the summons to the historian to seek balance, fairness, and all the objectivity he is capable of strongly suggests there is serious retrospective cultural distortion at work here which urgently needs to be countered to set the historical and philosophical record straight and avert the tendency of one particular modern intellectual tradition which claims to be the right one to pre-empt and appropriate the Enlightenment for itself. Where Locke, Hume, and Voltaire were, throughout, truly fundamental was in shaping the moderate and conservative Enlightenment. For it was with this kind of enlightenment that England came to be especially associated. Hume's conservative scepticism, and eagerness to restrict reason's scope, were undoubtedly directly connected to his Anglomania; and no one, perhaps not even Voltaire, was a more enthusiastic Enlightenment Anglicizer than Hume, especially with respect to Scotland.[66]

However, when it comes to the Radical Enlightenment, the Enlightenment that matters most for us today, both historically and philosophically, the real picture is quite otherwise. Here Locke, Hume, and Voltaire the Anglicizer were not admired but rather broadly opposed. Hence, one of the main aims of this present work is to function as a Europeanizing and, it is hoped, useful corrective to an aggrandizing and distorting tendency which seriously exaggerates the importance of one particular intellectual and cultural tradition in a way which unhelpfully serves to obscure the real philosophical and cultural background, predominantly continental European—and after 1720, especially but by no means only French—of the accepted values and democratic principles of the egalitarian western world today. A democratic civilization, avowedly based on equality, needs to know its origins correctly.

Moreover, it is not only historically and philosophically inaccurate but also, from a moral and cultural point of view, seriously unbalanced and unjust, as well as deeply misleading, to belittle, as some scholars do, the in reality increasingly preponderant role of the French radical, or materialist, Enlightenment from the 1720s onwards, and, indeed, scarcely any more satisfactory to ignore the indispensable Dutch, German, and Italian dimensions which, as we shall see, did a great deal to amplify and reinforce the wider impact of the incomparable and resounding French achievement.

[66] MacIntyre, *Whose Justice?*, 281–98; Porter, *Enlightenment*, 251.

Part II

The Crisis of Religious Authority

3

Faith and Reason: Bayle versus the *Rationaux*

1. EUROPE'S RELIGIOUS CRISIS

To grasp the full scope of the religious crisis of the late seventeenth century one must bear in mind the extent of the shock and anguish inflicted by the horrific destruction and seemingly incomprehensible confessional stalemate of the Thirty Years War. During three decades from 1618, much of Germany and Bohemia were devastated and large areas brutalized. The cost in men and money to the German lands, Spain, France, Sweden, Denmark, Flanders, Portugal, and parts of Italy was unprecedented. And yet, this terrible struggle, ostensibly between Catholicism and Protestantism in the name of God and religious truth, had no clear-cut outcome. However reluctantly, by the time of the Peace of Westphalia in 1648, Europeans had to accept that the Almighty, for whatever reason, refused to signal which church teaches the true faith, for the time being at least, and ordained, instead, general confessional deadlock reaching from the Americas and Ireland to Poland, Hungary-Transylvania, and the fringes of the Orthodox world, with many lands in between remaining deeply split. Theologically, this was altogether inexplicable and yet a reality that had to be grappled with.

The profound spiritual crisis which ensued after 1650 was partly caused then by an exacerbated but wholly unresolved schism between Catholicism and Protestantism (sometimes nuanced by a growing awareness of the history and doctrines of the eastern churches), but it was due also to the growing fragmentation of the Protestant churches themselves. For besides the three major Protestant churches, the Lutheran, Calvinist, and Anglican, which enjoyed the support of numerous princely, civic, and colonial governments across the western Atlantic world (while in the case of the first two regarding each other with almost as much animosity as all three evinced for Catholicism), numerous dissident Protestant sects—Mennonites, Spiritualists, Socinians, Remonstrants, Quakers, and Collegiants—had arisen since the Reformation which despite widespread persecution and suppression had gained toeholds in parts of Germany, Poland, Hungary-Transylvania, the Netherlands, Britain, and North America.

But this was not all. For even the pattern of broad regional domination by one particular church had begun to disintegrate when first the Dutch, from the 1560s, and then, in the 1640s, the English rebelled not only against kings and courts, claiming peoples owe no allegiance to monarchs who become tyrants, but also against the established, traditionally powerful, ecclesiastical hierarchies of the day, substituting *de facto* toleration, local confessional supervision such as consistories, presbyteries, and church councils, and religious plurality (if not yet any supporting ideas) for the earlier structure of ecclesiastical authority and institutions. These new religious structures fundamentally changed the relationship between state and church, and church and people, while at the same time affording more breathing space to dissenting, fringe Protestant sects. The change also allowed the Jews to re-emerge as a significant presence in western Europe.

Admittedly, few were yet disposed to think there were any valid grounds for toleration, or any positive spiritual meaning behind this splintering of religious uniformity and widespread *de facto* connivance, any more than theoretical justifications had yet been found for abjuring monarchs, curtailing the political role of nobility, or chasing out bishops. During the English Civil War and Commonwealth of the 1640s and 1650s, such champions of religious toleration as Milton still primarily thought, and formulated their views, in theological terms. But by the 1650s a minute fringe of radical dissenters and republicans were beginning to conceive that there might be a purely secular, philosophical rationale for dismantling ecclesiastical authority, freedom of thought, and independence of the individual conscience.

Against this fraught background, it is hardly surprising that the New Philosophy and new science, ushered in by Galileo and Descartes, adduced many fresh complications for theologians, further convoluting confessional polemics, and especially the content of theological debate. Equally, the new intellectual context further aggravated the long-standing tensions between ecclesiastical authority and theological dissent, along with pleas for toleration, within churches. Above all the chronic intellectual agitation fuelled by the New Philosophy and science coalesced with the unresolved pattern of theological schism and fragmentation to create an urgent and overriding need and yearning for a new general intellectual synthesis capable of winning broad acceptance in which traditional modes of thought, and the existing relationship of theology to culture and society, were preserved in essentials. It was precisely because the new religious crisis ran so deep at the individual as well as group level, that the Early Enlightenment era witnessed so many high-profile and highly publicized conversions, as well as fresh splintering of old churches, schemes for new churches, and grandiose projects, like those of Leibniz and Le Clerc, for general church reunification.

By demolishing the previously dominant Aristotelian framework of philosophy and science, the Cartesian 'revolution' of the 1650s shattered an intellectual unity which, outside theology, had survived the great schism of Europe into Catholic and Protestant halves in the sixteenth century for more than a century. By doing so the irruption of the New Philosophy not only stimulated but necessitated energetic new efforts to reconfigure everything—theology, philosophy, and science—into a new and more viable unity. But instead of bringing the clarity and cohesion for which Cartesianism strove, the result was a bitter struggle between Aristotelian traditionalists and Cartesian reformers, most intense at first in Holland, Germany, and Switzerland but soon spreading also to Scandinavia, France, and Italy, and what was even more dismaying for many, a spiraling intensification of philosophical strife. With the philosophies of Hobbes and Spinoza, it became clear that what was being overturned, at least potentially, was all forms of authority and tradition, even Scripture and Man's essentially theological view of the universe itself.

It was perfectly logical, then, that the first stirrings of the Radical Enlightenment, and the *esprit philosophique* it proclaimed, arose amid a generally perceived need in the 1650s to revise and adjust the relationship between theology, philosophy, and science. It was inherent in the situation, furthermore, that theologians should figure centrally in the great intellectual debates of the Early Enlightenment and that theological issues should remain basic to the concerns of all the principal participants—philosophers, scientists, and statesmen no less than theologians—and to the concerns of all three main camps, moderate mainstream, Radical Enlightenment, and Counter-Enlightenment, that emerged in Europe and America from the ensuing controversies.

Theological debate, then, lay at the heart of the Early Enlightenment. Theology dominated the correspondence between Newton and Locke, and was the exclusive topic of conversation when they first met; for while they shared what has been called 'a rationalistic approach to religion', vast work, it seemed clear to both, lay ahead defining precisely what this meant for Man, religion, and society in the new context.[1] Equally, the greatest number as well as the fiercest reactions to Spinoza emanated from theologians, Protestant and Catholic, while, again, it was the theological implications of Bayle's writings which chiefly upset his contemporaries. It was neither science, then, nor new geographical discoveries, nor even philosophy, as such, but rather the formidable difficulty of reconciling old and new in theological terms, and finally, by the 1740s, the apparent collapse of all efforts to forge a new general synthesis of theology, philosophy, politics, and science, which destabilized religious belief and values, causing the wholly unprecedented crisis of faith driving the secularization of the modern West.[2]

If all the great Early Enlightenment intellectual controversies, whether the Bekker furore of 1691–4 in Holland,[3] the French disputes surrounding Richard Simon's Bible criticism, the Newtonian debates, the Deist controversy in early eighteenth-century England, or the German quarrels surrounding the 'Wertheim Bible', in one way or another hinged on the now thoroughly destabilized and problematic relationship between reason and faith, arguably the single most exhaustive treatment of the issues at stake in these furiously contested encounters was the bitter polemic waged from the 1690s down to his death in 1706 between Bayle and his liberal Huguenot theological opponents, known as the *rationaux*.[4] The latter, the cream of the European Huguenot intellectual elite, the foremost of

[1] Westfall, *Life of Isaac Newton*, 199–200. [2] Beiser, *Sovereignty of Reason*, 13–18.

[3] On this, see Fix, *Fallen Angels*, and Israel, *Radical Enlightenment*, 375–405.

[4] Gundling, *Vollständige Historie*, iii. 4007–9; Brogi, *Teologia senza verità*, 15–21.

whom were Le Clerc, Élie Saurin, Jacques Saurin (1677–1731), Isaac Jaquelot (1647–1708), Jacques Bernard (1658–1718), David Durand (*c.*1680–1763), Élie Benoît, Jean La Placette, Jean-Pierre de Crousaz, and Jean Barbeyrac (1674–1744), were so-called because their prime aim was to rebuild precisely that viable and stable synthesis of faith and reason, authority and freedom, science and religion, to which Boyle, Locke, and Newton in England, Malebranche in France, and Leibniz and Wolff in Germany were all so fervently committed. In this confrontation and its ramifications can be seen converging all the factors in the making, and then crumbling, of the fragile reintegration of religion, science, and philosophy which formed the essential backbone of the European mainstream Enlightenment.

Bayle's tortuous and often anguished intellect can be seen as a microcosm, symptomatic of both Enlightenment contested and the ultimate intellectual—if not social and political—victory of the Radical Enlightenment in a particularly vivid sense: the drama of his own life and painful tragedy of his family tellingly reflected both the impact of religious schism and stalemate and the deeply distressing consequences of unresolved deadlock infusing a mind and conscience of rare sensitivity and genius. One of the most decisive developments of his youth was his being sent by a father, who was a Protestant preacher and whom he deeply respected and loved, too late on in his education (due to the family's shortage of money), to the Huguenot college of Puylaurens where he was dismayed by the mediocrity of the instruction and students—as a consequence of which he gravitated to the Jesuit college at Toulouse and, in March 1669, converted to Catholicism.

Bayle felt not only the clash of Protestantism and Catholicism to the very depths of his being, but also the irresolvable dilemma of their incompatible claims and the human misery which so often resulted and which soon assumed a peculiarly acute form in his own case. For to convert to Catholicism meant pitting conscience against, and breaking with, the family he loved and to which he was so closely tied. After a year or so, moreover, though still filled, as his letters of that period show, with a sense of the power of divine providence and foreboding at the ruin and desolation caused by religious schism, he began to doubt the truth of Catholic claims and regret his decision to convert, in particular feeling that the specific reasoning which had swayed him to leave Protestantism had been insufficient and inconclusive.[5]

Since relapse from Catholicism was then a crime in France punishable by being sent to the galleys, he secretly abjured the dominant faith, after seventeen months, on 21 August 1670, fleeing from 'cette ville superstitieuse' (i.e. Toulouse) to Geneva, in order to escape the social consequences of his extraordinary reversion. He reached the Calvinist city republic spiritually elated, assuring his brother, in a letter from Geneva of November 1670, that he had felt the same joy on departing the Catholic Church that those who live in polar regions feel on seeing the sun for the

[5] Bost, *Pierre Bayle*, 12–13; Labrousse, *Pierre Bayle*, i. 83, 92, 107.

first time in six months, yet was also, evidently, deeply fearful and anxious.[6] In Geneva, while expressing strong anti-Arminian and anti-irenicist sentiments, he became seriously interested in philosophy and embraced Cartesianism, an intellectual system then banned from the colleges of France by Louis XIV.

He returned to France, still extremely poor, four years later and in 1675 took up his first professorship, at Sedan, where he publicly taught Aristotelian philosophy while privately remaining a Cartesian and, in part, a *Malebranchiste*. Meanwhile, during the later 1670s, the focus of his spiritual and intellectual striving shifted increasingly from theology to philosophy. Late in 1681, after some months in Paris, and again deeply distressed, following the suppression of the Huguenot college at Sedan by Louis XIV, Bayle left France for ever, settling permanently in Holland and taking up his second professorship, at Rotterdam. There, his attitude to organized religion gradually began to become more elusive and problematic, a long transition only completed in the last years of his life with the publication of his final astounding books, in 1705–6.

After publication of his *Dictionnaire historique et critique* (1697), the supreme publishing success of the Early Enlightenment, Bayle became increasingly suspect to many of his former colleagues and allies. The chief issues pitting the *rationaux* against Bayle, after 1697, were those of whether 'reason' supports the Christian 'faith' or, on the contrary, faith must stand alone, the problem of Christian disunity and schism, whether or not the consensus of the world's peoples proves the existence of a providential God—that is the question of *consensus gentium*, whether the God of the Bible is manifestly a God of goodness and justice, whether the most rational morality is indeed that proclaimed by the Gospels, whether a meaningful human morality can be independent of theology, whether the central 'mysteries' of religion can be accommodated within a scientific and rational view of the world, the philosophical status of 'miracles' and revelation, Socinianism, the issue of the eternal damnation of sinners, and, finally, the cogency of the 'argument from design', the linchpin of the Newtonian physico-theology which for decades everywhere underpinned efforts to reconcile science and religion.

Even after Bayle's physical demise, alone in his book-laden lodgings from which he increasingly rarely emerged in his last years, on 28 December 1706, the unrelenting and acrimonious contest between him and virtually the entire Huguenot moderate mainstream as to whether reason upholds Christianity, and counters freethinking and Spinozism, and whether society, law, morality, and politics inherently require revealed religion, or can rest purely on philosophical reason, not only lingered in the minds of Bayle's followers and adversaries but persisted as unresolved tensions within the Enlightenment for decades.

The importance of this encounter rooted in Bayle's personal experiences of the late 1660s and 1670s, and which unfolded over a quarter of a century from the early 1680s down to his death, in the wider context of western history lies both in its unparalleled

[6] Labrousse, *Pierre Bayle*, i. 94–5; Bayle, *Correspondance*, i. 29–35, 94–5.

intellectual intensity, duration, and scope, and its occurring on the very threshold of theology's loss of hegemony in the eighteenth century. Where Bayle held, on ostensibly Calvinist, anti-Arminian, and 'fideist' grounds, that there is no rational basis for faith, that faith and reason cannot support or buttress each other, and that the essence of orthodoxy is to admit this and rely on faith alone, his theological adversaries replied that nothing could be more ruinous for religion and the primacy of theology in the world than to proclaim such a principle. Each of Bayle's main theological opponents among the *rationaux* had his own particular set of priorities and emphases. But they all shared a common conviction which Bayle rejected, that the new findings of philosophy, scholarship, and science could and must be accommodated within an evolving international Protestant tradition which in their case was heavily influenced by seventeenth-century Dutch and English as well as Huguenot Arminianism.[7]

For the *rationaux* and their Lockean allies the rationality of faith was the crux on which the whole of this immense controversy hinged. No one, they held, should confuse 'faith' with credulity. In their view, having a correct understanding of faith, as something based on reason rather than authority, was, in the words of Élie Saurin, 'le fondement de toutes les véritez'.[8] If the Huguenot *rationaux* acquired from the Cartesians a notion of 'reason' as something autonomous and self-sustaining, and from Locke a method of limiting philosophy's scope and protecting their core 'miracles' of Creation, revelation, and Christ's mission and Resurrection, they inherited from the Dutch Arminians the notion that true Christianity consists in only a small number of fundamental points and that even these do not need to be rigidly defined by ecclesiastical authority, and from this a theologically anchored theory of toleration.[9] From Dutch Arminianism too they drew their fervent commitment to toleration, and ultimate Christian reunification, and the need for a thoroughgoing reform of religious ideas and practice, using the tools of human reason and systematic scholarship to purge what is superfluous and counterproductive from Man's view of the world and religious culture.

At the heart of the *rationaux*'s great project was the notion of 'rational' belief, the doctrine that 'reason' proves the truth of Christianity, and can be shown to be fully consonant with that particular religion, showing it to be evidently the best and most rational basis for human morality and the political order. Basic to their approach was the concept, upheld by Locke, Malebranche, and Leibniz but rejected by Spinoza and Bayle, and afterwards, following them, by Toland and Collins,[10] that there is a valid distinction between theological doctrines 'above reason' but which can be accommodated within a rational system of religion and, on the other hand, doctrines inherently 'contrary to reason'.[11] Such doctrines as the resurrection of the

[7] Heyd, '*Be Sober and Reasonable*', 180–2; Pocock, *Barbarism*, i. 52–7; Spellman, *Latitudinarians*, 31, 55, 98; Tyacke, 'Religious Controversy', 601–3.

[8] Saurin, *Examen*, 76; *Bibliothèque ancienne et moderne*, 2 (1714), 201.

[9] Pocock, *Barbarism*, i. 50–71; Brogi, *Teologia senza verità*, 16–22; Beiser, *Sovereignty of Reason*, 92–9.

[10] Beiser, *Sovereignty of Reason*, 253–4; Taranto, *Du déisme à l'athéisme*, 478–86.

[11] Locke, *Essay*, 687; *Bibliothèque choisie*, 9 (1706), 156–9; Pearson, *Fables*, 54; Spellman, *Latitudinarians*, 151–4; Brogi, *Teologia senza verità*, 35–6.

dead and the Last Judgement, held Le Clerc, are not opposed to reason and do not contradict any of reason's clear principles: thus they are in no way contrary to reason albeit they are 'au delà, ou au dessus de la raison'.[12] While, as they saw it, 'true' Christianity by definition contains nothing contrary to reason, the 'corrupted' religion prevailing in both Catholic and Protestant Europe had been thoroughly muddled and muddied by 'superstition', bogus doctrines, and false 'miracles', as well as superfluous notions of ecclesiastical authority; and while the chief offender in all respects was the Catholic Church, and especially the papacy, all the other major and minor churches, including the Calvinists, Lutherans, Anglicans, and Greek Orthodox, were in varying degrees likewise at fault. Consequently, urged these theological reformers, much was being scandalously distorted and obscured in modern Christendom by useless, meaningless, and irrational theological obfuscation.

It was precisely their insistence on reason, the centrality and indispensability in their thought of scientific and philosophical premisses, which made Bayle's philosophy so immensely troublesome to the *rationaux*.[13] For whether he was a genuine Christian 'fideist', which, after around 1702, they increasingly doubted, or someone using the pretext of fideism for purely subversive purposes, which was increasingly their view (besides that of more conservative Huguenot critics like Jurieu), Bayle's philosophy was wholly corrosive of their intellectual system and reform programme. It was not that they resisted new ideas, disliked novelties, or lacked courage to dissent from prevailing structures. On the contrary, they were open-minded, assiduous in the search for truth, innovative and resolute, indeed had few inhibitions about defying ecclesiastical authority when believing its theological premisses to be at fault, and were also ardent champions of toleration even if they did conceive of toleration differently from Bayle.

Though both preachers of the French Reformed Church in the Netherlands, Jaquelot too had marked Arminian-Socinian sympathies while Bernard, if cautious in doctrinal matters, was likewise close to the Remonstrants, someone who well knew what it was to suffer persecution, having in his youth had to leave France due to Catholic and, later, Switzerland due to Calvinist intolerance. In Holland, he long remained personally close to the Remonstrant Le Clerc, under whom he had studied in Geneva.[14] Indeed, it was precisely the yoke of confessional dogmatism that these intellectually gifted men were eager to cast off. They admired Bayle's acumen as a critical scholar and historian and his vast erudition, sharing his antipathy to traditional humanist scholarship and Aristotelian scholasticism as well as 'superstition' and bigotry.[15] Yet, all this notwithstanding, they saw no alternative but to enter in public combat, and seek to rebut and discredit what they considered the extremely dangerous implications of his books.[16] For them, God and the core

[12] *Bibliothèque choisie*, 9 (1706), 159; Bayle, *Entretiens*, 4–5.

[13] Bots (ed.), *Henri Basnage de Beauval*, ii. 140–2; Lomonaco, 'Jean Barbeyrac et le "Pyrrhonisme" ', 254–5, 260, 262–4.

[14] Brogi, *Teologia senza verità*, 17 n.; van Bunge et al. (eds.), *Dictionary*, i. 83.

[15] [Bernard], *Supplément*, i. 282.

[16] [Bernard], *Nouvelles de la République des Lettres* (Jan.–June 1705), 123–4.

elements of religion must be placed on a rational basis, and fully attuned to philosophy and science, and here Bayle (much more effectively than Papin) stood squarely in their way, indeed directly denied the validity of their whole enterprise, asserting 'que le principe des Rationaux selon lequel il ne faut rien croire sans évidence, conduit au Socinianisme, au Pyrrhonisme, et au Déisme' [that the principle of the *Rationaux* according to which nothing should be believed without evidence leads to Socinianism, Pyrrhonism, and Deism].[17]

Each separate strand of this vastly convoluted contest led back to the same basic issue—whether, as Bayle (and, on the right wing, Papin and Jurieu) maintained, faith stands alone unaided by reason, and is purely arbitrary in that one believes simply because one wants to believe or feels compelled to believe, or whether, on the contrary, faith is buttressed by reason and, insofar as rational religion involves doctrines 'above reason', is justified by rationally incontestable signs, traditions, miracles, and other 'evidence'.[18] For Le Clerc and his allies, genuine religious belief must rest on rational conviction. Such 'evidence' could be natural, as with the 'argument from design', historical, like the unbroken chain of tradition attesting, it seemed to them, to Christ's miracles, or geographical and anthropological as with the beliefs of non-European peoples and the issue of *consensus gentium*. Among the *rationaux*, the theologico-philosophical principle of *consensus gentium* possessed a particular centrality in the theological polemics of the day owing to Le Clerc and others of the group adopting Locke's rigorous empiricism, with its demolition of the Cartesian (and Jesuit) doctrine of the innateness of the concept of a providential God.[19]

Bernard, especially, became preoccupied with this complex question. After emigrating first from France, and then Switzerland, he had found employment as a French Reformed minister at Gouda, then taught philosophy, and finally, in the early 1690s, succeeded his mentor Le Clerc as editor of the Amsterdam *Bibliothèque universelle*. By1699, when he took over the editorship of the *Nouvelles de la République des Lettres* which he retained until 1710, and turned into a vehicle for criticizing its original editor Bayle, he figured among the foremost *érudits* of the United Provinces, in 1712 being appointed professor of philosophy at Leiden, in succession to the formidable Burchardus de Volder. Urging the essential compatibility of Christianity and 'reason', against the Spinozists, Bernard migrated philosophically from orthodox Cartesianism to the conviction, following Le Clerc, that Locke offers the best solution to the problem of how to stabilize the relationship between philosophy and theology. Convinced that for reconciling religion and science on a truly 'enlightened' basis 'la méthode des philosophes anglois étoit la plus sûre',[20] at Leiden he proved, as the curators had hoped, as staunch an ally of 'English' ideas as he was an unremitting opponent of Spinoza and Bayle.

17 Bayle, *Entretiens*, 15.

18 Saurin, *Examen*, 93–8; Brogi, *Teologia senza verità*, 77, 167, 195, 254.

19 Brogi, *Teologia senza verità*, 86–7; Bayle, *Continuation*, i. 18 (all references are to the 1705 edn. unless otherwise indicated).

20 *L'Europe savante* (July 1718), 154; Hazard, *European Mind*, 288.

Bernard's 'fort longue dispute avec Mr Bayle' revolved about two main controversies: first, whether 'le consentement de toutes les nations à croire une Divinité' is, despite Bayle's tenacious resistance, a valid proof of God's existence, and secondly Bayle's highly unsettling contention that atheism is not a worse evil than idolatry.[21] While the first was philosophically the more complex, the second, with its far-reaching moral implications, was religiously and socially the more emotive. For Bayle's claim that atheism was not worse than pagan idolatry, as Bernard noted, excited many against him, and deeply disconcerted others, for most considered atheism was 'la plus pernicieuse disposition d'esprit et de cœur' possible in men.[22]

2. *CONSENSUS GENTIUM* AND THE *PHILOSOPHES*

The dispute about *consensus gentium* permeated the entire conflict. If the idea of a God who creates, rewards, and punishes could no longer be considered innate in Man in the pre-Lockean sense, universal, or near universal, reasoning, or what Le Clerc calls 'raisonnement que tout le monde fait', could serve as a reliable surrogate for what was being discarded. Even if not innate, the outcome of collective human reasoning and experience, held Bernard and the others, must be deemed incontestable and authoritatively binding on every rational person.[23] Hence, while there is no innate concept of God, human reasoning had produced a *consensus gentium* which, according to Bernard, Le Clerc, Élie Benoît, and the other *rationaux*, constitutes a valid philosophical proof of the essential reasonableness of faith not just in God but also in his goodness, omnipotence, and providence, something binding on all men capable of cogent reasoning. Later, Voltaire, while excluding all primitive peoples from the equation, reckoning the beliefs of *sauvages* wholly irrelevant to the case, otherwise concurred fully with this argument, *consensus gentium* being in fact a linchpin of his own philosophical system: 'tous les peuples policés, Indiens, Chinois, Égyptiens, Persans, Chaldéens, Phoeniciens', he maintained, 'reconnurent un Dieu suprême.'[24] Bayle, however, stubbornly denied that 'l'approbation universelle' is in any way a proof that something is true, redoubling his assault on this principle in his last years, in the context of his mounting quarrel with Bernard, Le Clerc, and Jaquelot.[25]

[21] Bayle, *Continuation*, ii. 364; Chaufepié, *Nouveau Dictionnaire*, i. 253–5; Mori, *Bayle philosophe*, 186, 209, 307; Brogi, *Teologia senza verità*, 24, 97–100, 117–19.

[22] [Bernard], *Nouvelles de la République des Lettres* (Jan.–June 1705), 124; Chaufepié, *Nouveau Dictionnaire*, i. 256; Mason, 'Voltaire devant Bayle', 448–9; Pascual López, *Bernard Mandeville*, 89–90.

[23] [Bernard], *Nouvelles de la République des Lettres* (Jan.–June 1705), 126–8; Bayle, *Réponse*, ii. preface pp. 3^{v}–4 and 284–98.

[24] Voltaire, *Homélies prononcées à Londres*, 352; Voltaire, *Dictionnaire philosophique*, i. 389–91; *Corpus de notes marginales*, v. 123–5.

[25] Bayle, *Réponse*, ii. 284; Bayle, *Continuation*, i. 26; Des Maizeaux, *Vie de Monsieur Bayle*, pp. lxxxix, cxiv; *Mémoires de Trévoux* (Feb. 1714), art. xix, p. 239; Zoli, *Europa libertina*, 206–11; Pascual López, *Bernard Mandeville*, 94–5.

For Bayle, unlike Descartes, Locke, Malebranche, Newton, and Leibniz, but like Spinoza, philosophical reason *more geometrico* is the only criterion of what is true.[26] In him, as in Spinoza, natural reason produces 'adequate ideas', that is, ideas which correspond to reality, solely by means of mathematical rationality under which text criticism was subsumed, Bayle too grounding his concept of rational argument on mathematical proportion and exactitude. Holding it undeniable that the whole must be bigger than its parts and that if from equal entities 'on ôte choses égales, les résidus en seront égaux',[27] Bayle sought to exploit to the full reason's scope as an instrument for assessing evidence and determining truth.[28] If, in his Bible criticism, Spinoza had already supplemented 'geometrical' reasoning with the critical sifting and contextualizing of documents and the historical method of establishing 'facts', Bayle strove further to widen reason's sphere of action, grounding text criticism in detailed historical research which was to be a key tool in constructing his politics.

While both mathematical and historical 'truths', held Bayle, are ultimately based on geometrical proportionality, he also speaks at times as if his (and Mabillon's and Le Clerc's) 'vérités historiques', the new dimension of critical historical rationality, constitute something different in kind from mathematical truth based on quantification. For historical certainties, culled by critical sifting of texts, he suggests, may ultimately prove a more reliable safeguard against Pyrrhonism than mathematical knowledge. In his 'Project' for the *Dictionnaire*, of 1692, Bayle points out that it is, after all, ultimately more certain that Cicero really existed outside men's minds than that a perfect circle, or any geometrical concept, truly exists outside our imagination.[29] Hence even if mathematics is the anchor, critical history may provide our surest knowledge.

In any case, mathematical rationality combined with knowledge derived from historical texts, critically evaluated, defines the totality of what is knowable. Faith, meanwhile, is indistinguishable from 'superstition', society's greatest enemy, so that *l'esprit philosophique*, the systematic application of human reason, is actually the only way to distinguish between what is true or false in any aspect of human life and in moral issues.[30] Whatever lies beyond 'certain evidence', such as the Christian mysteries, is by definition incomprehensible and can never be matter for rational discussion, or explanation, nor incorporated into a rational view of the world. Nevertheless, theologians habitually debate their doctrines as if they were susceptible to reason so that Catholic controversialists deny that transubstantiation is contrary to sound reasoning while, equally, the Reformed, no less than they, contradict the Socinian view that the Trinity and the Incarnation 'soient des dogmes contradictoires'.[31] Hence, contends Bayle, theologians in practice negate their own supreme

[26] Marilli, 'Cartesianismo e tolleranza', 577.
[27] Bayle, *Commentaire philosophique*, 87–8; McKenna, 'Pierre Bayle et la superstition', 58.
[28] Bost, *Pierre Bayle*, 32–5.
[29] Bayle, *Political Writings*, 12; Israel, *Radical Enlightenment*, 453–5.
[30] McKenna, 'Rationalisme moral', 262–4.
[31] Bayle, *Commentaire philosophique*, 87.

maxim that theology is a queen 'dont la philosophie n'est que la servante'; for the theologians themselves betray by their conduct that, deep down, without admitting it, they too recognize philosophy as queen 'et la théologie comme la servante'.[32]

Consequently, held Bayle, orthodox theologians (whatever they say), Socinians, and true philosophers *au fond* all concede that philosophy, not theology, is the true 'queen'—only, no one except Spinoza was willing or able to say so publicly. Theological articles can and, in the case of the Christian 'vérités révélées', readers are assured, *should* be believed. But this does not alter the fact that religious doctrine cannot buttress any rational position or principled system of morality and politics. For the sincere Christian, this creates an inescapable moral and political dilemma: for no one can rationally demonstrate that any divine 'vérités révélées' are authentic and not the figment of someone else's imagination. Since there is no way to prove revelations and miracles authentic or inauthentic, nothing prevents one man's 'vérités révélées' being rejected by the next as the most ridiculous 'superstition'.[33] Characteristically, Bayle leaves this irresolvable dilemma wholly intact, indeed shows no interest in resolving what he takes every care to highlight. For his concern, unlike Locke's and Le Clerc's, is not to rescue or reconstitute theology but, on the contrary, compromise it as much as possible so as to justify his detaching morality, social theory, and politics completely from theological tutelage.

Against Bayle, Bernard denies there was any evidence that 'atheistic' peoples existed, insisting that what might be found in still unexplored parts of the world in the future could have no bearing on the current debate. To this Le Clerc added that the existence of 'atheistic' peoples definitely remained unproven and that even if western travel accounts did claim some east Asian societies were 'atheistic', westerners' knowledge of Chinese, Japanese, and other relevant languages remained too rudimentary for *savants* to be certain as to the meaning of reputedly 'atheistic' metaphysical terms.[34] Against this, Bayle claimed incontestable evidence that some peoples of Africa and the Americas, among them the Canadian Indians described by Lahontan,[35] lacked all knowledge of a divinity who is a supernatural and providential agent. But in any case, he insisted, the fact that most people believe something, or even if everyone believes something—the case of *consensus omnium*—is not in the slightest degree proof that such a belief is true;[36] on the contrary, the opposite is more probable. For the common people, he held, mostly believe what is wholly erroneous. Hence, by Le Clerc's and Bernard's criterion, classical Greek and Roman pagans could justly claim the ancient oracles of Delphi and Didyma gave out only the purest truth since in their time practically everyone believed in them.

Meanwhile, the *rationaux*, objected Bayle, ignored the incontrovertible fact that there have always been thinkers who acknowledge only an eternal and necessary

[32] Ibid. 88; Gros, 'Sens et limites', 69. [33] McKenna, 'Pierre Bayle et la superstition', 63–5.

[34] Ibid. 211–12; Bayle, *Réponse*, ii. 299; *Bibliothèque ancienne et moderne*, 28 (1727), 387–8; Belgrado, 'Voltaire, Bayle', 394; Brogi, *Teologia senza verità*, 97–8.

[35] Paganini, 'Avant la *Promenade*', 20; Israel, *Radical Enlightenment*, 580–2.

[36] [Bernard], *Nouvelles de la République des Lettres* (Jan.–June 1705), 128; Bost, *Pierre Bayle*, 104–6.

'cause immanente de tous les effets de la nature', denying such a cause can influence or direct the actions of men or can in any way be an intelligent or free agent, conscious of its actions. Ever since philosophy began, there had been leaders of schools of thought who denied the world was created by what Le Clerc called 'un agent sage et libre'. Among them were many of the foremost Greek philosophers and we know too, from Jesuit accounts, he added, that such philosophies are to be found still in China and Japan. This was sufficiently evident, contended Bayle, without his needing to refer in this connection to Spinoza and his followers, a recent fact 'et si certain qu'il seroit fort inutile d'en donner des preuves'.[37]

To this, the *rationaux* replied that philosophical traditions reaching back to pre-Christian antiquity help little in comprehending the nature of the cosmos, or ascertaining the essentials of moral philosophy, something indispensable for society.[38] Here they were on identical ground with Locke and Clarke; for reason unaided by revelation, they averred, is insufficient to provide many necessary truths about Creation or explain human duties and responsibilities. Core dogmas of religion which have a vital bearing on morality, such as Original Sin and Christ's mission among men, are taught, observed Bernard, only by religion and remain inaccessible to reason, though they are not contrary to it.[39] The moral perfection of Christianity, the *rationaux*, like Locke, maintained, is self-evident and such that Stoicism and Epicureanism are, in comparison, but feeble things of limited capacity for demonstrating essential moral truths.[40] As for the utterances of ancient pagan philosophers about Creation, retorted Bernard, these were just confused imaginings full of darkness and uncertainty which only the Bible dispels.

After 1700, the furore over *consensus gentium* became inextricably entwined, following Arnauld's and Bayle's declarations on the 'atheism' of classical Chinese thought, with the simultaneous Early Enlightenment dispute surrounding Confucius and Confucianism. If Bernard showed little inclination to dispute with Arnauld and Malebranche, as well as Bayle and Toland, over whether classical Chinese thought is inherently 'atheistic',[41] Élie Benoît attacked Toland, whom he regarded as a 'copiste de M. Bayle en la défense des athées', in a treatise published at Delft, in 1712, stating that the Chinese Confucianists, atheists or not, nevertheless insisted on the institution of religion among the common people, seeing that society cannot function without it, a line of criticism later taken up, like so much else initiated by the *rationaux*, by Voltaire.[42]

During the long years of their increasingly bitter struggle, Le Clerc always took particular exception to the article in Bayle's *Dictionnaire* on 'Manichaeism' and the, in his eyes, unmistakable implication it carries that God, if he exists, is manifestly

37 Bayle, *Réponse*, ii. 471; Paganini, 'Avant la *Promenade*', 45–6.

38 *Bibliothèque choisie*, 26 (1713), 344–5.

39 Bernard, *De l'excellence de la religion*, 118–19, 136.

40 Ibid. 141–2, 152–5; Marshall, *John Locke*, 302.

41 Pinot, *La Chine*, 323 n.

42 *Mémoires de Trévoux*, (Feb. 1714), art. xix, p. 256; Belgrado, 'Voltaire, Bayle', 390, 408–9.

not a God of goodness and justice.[43] From long experience, including his early correspondence with Papin, he (like Leibniz) was acutely sensitive to the Spinozist reverberations lurking behind any implication that 'God' is the source of the evil and harm in the world. He was also outraged by what he considered the blatant hypocrisy of Bayle's assurances that he had no intention of undermining religion in attacking, as Le Clerc put it, 'si odieusement la bonté divine', praising the exemplary cogency of the Manichaeans, and defying all the theologians in the world to give a coherent reply to the objections of the Manichaeans 'contre la bonté de Dieu'.[44] In fact, there was nothing, contended Le Clerc, 'de plus ridicule et de plus opposé au Christianisme' than Bayle's 'eulogy' of Manichaeism. To this Bayle retorted that Le Clerc had plunged into a sea of contradiction through coming to see the problematic character of, and effectively rejecting, both Original Sin and eternal torment in Hell, realizing that these cannot be rationally reconciled with any notion of the goodness and justice of God, in defiance of the fact that these are ancient and basic Christian doctrines.[45]

Bayle's arguments against the compatibility of reason and faith, if allowed to stand, would undoubtedly destroy the whole basis of the *rationaux*'s argument for the evident and demonstrable truth of Christianity and irrational, 'superstitious' character of incredulity. For Le Clerc, Bernard, the Saurins, Jaquelot, and also Bayle's friend Jacques Basnage (1653–1723), like Locke and Clarke, held that it is reason, even prior to Revelation, which proves Christianity the true religion. This, for them was an indispensable principle, it being Le Clerc's conviction that infidels are such in general because 'ils ne savent pas raisonner'.[46] Hence, if the Jews could reason properly, laying aside their ignorance and obduracy, they would, through the force of reason, certainly embrace Christianity, their opposition to Paul in Greece arising not from cogent arguments, he maintained, but only arrogance and intellectual inadequacy; equally, other *incrédules* dwelling among Christians are only such due to weak capacity for clear thought.[47]

Equally, Le Clerc's analysis of the interminable catalogue of dispute and schism marring the history of the world's churches—namely, that their wrangling is due to failure to reason cogently—would, should Bayle be vindicated, lose all validity. Were there no 'rational' basis for faith, nor any rationally cogent grounds for regarding Scripture as divine Revelation, why would anyone who wishes to live in accord with reason, and philosophical truth, demands Le Clerc, see the least reason to embrace faith?[48] If consistent reasoning leads no one to Christ, there would be no

[43] [Barbeyrac], *Éloge*, 4–5; Zuber, 'Spinozisme', 225; Pitassi, 'L'Écho des discussions', 266–71; Wilson, *Leibniz's Metaphysics*, 273; Ehrard, *L'Idée*, 639.

[44] Bayle, *Entretiens*, 4, 7, 19; *Bibliothèque ancienne et moderne*, 28 (1727), 390, 393, 398–9; [Barbeyrac], *Éloge*, preface pp. 5, 14–15; Gundling, *Vollständige Historie*, iii. 4010.

[45] Bayle, *Entretiens*, 16, 23; Walker, *Decline of Hell*, 188–93.

[46] *Bibliothèque ancienne et moderne*, 2 (1714), 198; Le Clerc, *De l'incrédulité*, 74, 80, 82.

[47] Le Clerc, *De l'incrédulité*, 80, 82, 117–19; *Bibliothèque choisie*, 9 (1706), 151–3.

[48] Le Clerc, *De l'incrédulité*, preface p. v.

such thing as a set of clear core doctrines—what Le Clerc termed 'le Christianisme en général'—evident to all men of good will and, therefore, no way to persuade Catholics, Lutherans, or for that matter anyone else believing what is 'manifestly false' that they are in error. For, courtesy of Bayle, all can now reply that it can make no conceivable difference what rational arguments you adduce, since all reasoning is equally invalid with respect to issues of faith.

Nor would there then be any way of healing schisms among Christians, since rationalizing Christian doctrine, argues Le Clerc, is the only way of ending such unwholesome bickering and reuniting the churches.[49] He grants that Deists and freethinkers would be right to argue that it is unworthy of any revealed religion, and 'une chose scandaleuse', to cause so many divisions as ensued over the centuries within the bosom of Christendom, were it the case that faith had actually inspired all these 'divisions et le désordre'.[50] But in reality Christianity was merely the innocent victim, he says, of base ambition and vicious personal rivalries, and no one can infer from that any consequence 'désavantageuse à la religion'.[51] This great defect persisted not through any fault of religion as such but purely owing to insufficient and inadequate use of 'reason'.

What divides the world's churches, held Le Clerc, is precisely everything that is irrational and superfluous in contemporary misconceptions of the Christian faith—in other words the unnecessary obfuscation requiring eradication. Therefore, it is precisely what all churches have in common which represents the perfect, pure, rational core dubbed by Le Clerc 'les principes du Christianisme',[52] and it was a fundamental rule of the enlightened theology he, Bernard, Jaquelot, Basnage, Locke, Clarke, and all their allies propounded, that one can only distinguish pure from impure in theology via 'reason'. Hence, should it emerge, as Spinoza and Bayle allege, that 'reason' cannot, after all, separate the bogus chaff of querulous dispute from the wheat of true theology and if reason cannot render superstitious men better followers of Christ, then the splits among the churches are incurable, 'superstition' is ineradicable, and the whole system of enlightened, rational Christianity propounded by the *rationaux* collapses, leaving Spinoza, after all, undisputed victor of the greatest of contests among men.

A further insidious consequence of Bayle's system, held Le Clerc, was that in the fight against the papacy and the Catholic Church, Protestants would be stripped of any means to combat the superstition, credulity, and bigotry of ordinary folk who are readily persuaded by the papacy and Jesuits to believe, and persuade others to believe, in false miracles, fraudulent saints, and absurd doctrines. The fact that innumerable faked 'miracles', and unfounded dogmas—Le Clerc here included 'transubstantiation'—are claimed, especially but not only in Catholic Europe, enables the *esprits forts* to mock the Christian faith, and cast doubt on Christ's 'true' miracles, alleging that Christianity is irrational.[53] Indeed, if reason cannot bolster

[49] Le Clerc, *De l'incrédulité*, 119–25. [50] Ibid. 200.

[51] Ibid.; *Bibliothèque ancienne et moderne*, 2 (1714), 204–10.

[52] Le Clerc, *De l'incrédulité*, 119–25, 200, 207; Israel, *Radical Enlightenment*, 466–7.

[53] Israel, *Radical Enlightenment*, 257–63; Hazard, *European Mind*, 122.

faith then it is impossible to segregate 'true' from bogus 'miracles', or sound doctrine from the superstition to which most ordinary folk are addicted, since there would then be no rational grounds for believing, or not believing, no matter how implausible and contrary to reason such beliefs may be.

Bayle professed not to be attacking religion, merely showing that reason cannot buttress faith; and yet, equally, throughout his career, he no less than the *rationaux* simultaneously contended that 'il n'y a point de ravages', as he put it in August 1704, 'que la superstition ne commette dans le cœur et dans l'esprit'.[54] Who could doubt that Bayle was as averse to 'superstition' as were the *rationaux*? But, this granted, did it not prove, if proof were needed, that Bayle was not a genuine 'fideist'? Indeed, in his philosophy the distinction between what is certain and what doubtful, far from being meaningless, or open to Pyrrhonist objections, is actually fundamental at every step and not just in history, mathematics, philosophy, and science but no less in morality, society, and politics. In fact it was exclusively matters of faith which Bayle subjected to his withering bogus Pyrrhonism. Indeed, so far as Le Clerc could see, his system makes it wholly impossible to distinguish between faith and superstition. The matter was all the more exasperating and paradoxical in that when it came to the gullibility of common folk, Bayle complained more bitterly than Le Clerc or anyone else that 'rien n'a plus de force que la superstition' and that popular credulity 'est une peste très-dangereuse aux societez'.[55]

Another hindrance placed by Bayle in the path of the 'Arminian' Enlightenment was his disdain for, and insinuating critique of, Locke. In resounding contrast to Le Clerc, chief continental supporter of Locke whom he had met for the first time in 1685,[56] Bayle, who also knew Locke personally, seemed more interested in diminishing than enhancing his reputation. Where the *rationaux*—apart from Jaquelot, who adhered to Cartesian dualism,[57] but including Crousaz and Barbeyrac both of whom, like Bernard, were converted to Locke's philosophy by Le Clerc—laboured to build up Locke's continental standing, laying the foundations of the moderate mainstream's subsequent adulation of him, Bayle, who read Pierre Coste's French translation of Locke's *Essay* in the autumn of 1703, when he was starting work on his *Continuation* and seeing a good deal of Shaftesbury (who probably passed on to Bayle something of his own dislike of Locke), was little taken with that work, disagreed with the argument of his *Reasonableness of Christianity*, and generally, like Leibniz, found little to admire in Locke's philosophy.[58]

Where Le Clerc in his 1710 edition of Locke's *Œuvres diverses* appended a hundred-page eulogy to this 'profonde philosophe, qui a pénétré les secrets de l'entendement humain', accompanied by what a Jesuit reviewer called 'des louanges

[54] Cantelli, 'Virtù degli atei', 695–6; Bayle, *Continuation*, i. 'avertissement'.

[55] Bayle, *Continuation*, i. 8–8^{v}.

[56] Evers, 'Jean Le Clerc', 99–100, 102–5; 'Lomonaco, 'Jean Barbeyrac et le "Pyrrhonisme" ', 260; Lomonaco, 'Religious Truth', 422.

[57] Schøsler, 'Jaquelot et Le Clerc', 334–6.

[58] Bayle to Coste, Rotterdam, 17 Dec. 1703, 8 Apr. 1704, 30 Apr. 1705, in Bayle, *Œuvres diverses*, iv. 834, 840–1, 853; Israel, 'John Locke', forthcoming.

infinies à M. Locke',[59] Bayle generally ignores Locke in his writings; even in his correspondence with Locke's translator Coste he tends to skip quickly over any discussion of Locke and where he does cite him, usually does so only to disparage his thought as a welter of confusion resting on weak definitions. Locke, objects Bayle, erases all effective distinction between matter and thought and thoroughly clouds our understanding of matter, reverting to 'l'ancien cahos des scholastiques', by reintroducing a completely senseless distinction between 'substance' and its 'accidents' along with 'autres dogmes absolument inexplicables'.[60]

Locke admits that he does not know what the properties of matter or soul are; yet when one is ignorant about that, urges Bayle, it is impossible to say whether there is in matter an attribute incompatible with thought, 'ni qu'il y ait dans l'âme quelque attribut incompatible avec l'étendue'.[61] How can the *rationaux* regard Locke's system as a reliable barrier against materialism, and a method of effectively uniting philosophy and science with Christianity, when it fails substantially to separate soul and body? Once its confusions are ironed out, contended Bayle, Locke's philosophy collapses more or less of itself into Spinozism, his erosion of the distinction between matter and thought having the result that 'on ne pourra plus conclure que si une substance pense elle est immatérielle'.[62] Le Clerc, followed later by Crousaz, Barbeyrac, Maupertuis, and Voltaire, sought to counter this by claiming that Locke, contrary to Bayle's insinuations, *does* uphold an absolute duality of spirit and body: he *did not* impart to matter the capacity to think, as Spinoza does, but only conjectured that God can perhaps 'superadd' to matter the quality of being able to think.[63] Bayle's disparagement of Locke, in Le Clerc's opinion, was simply yet another instance of his deliberately deploying his mastery of philosophical criticism to advance the cause of the *incrédules*.

The contest between Bayle and the *rationaux* was followed all across Europe. The Dutch and Swiss Arminians, English and Irish Latitudinarians, German Leibnizians, and the vying Huguenot intellectual factions were all acutely aware, through the Dutch French-language journals, that Bayle's stance called in question the entire edifice of 'rational religion', the parallel systems so painstakingly assembled in their different ways in England by Newton, Locke, and Clarke, in France by Descartes, Arnauld, and Malebranche, and in Germany by Thomasius and Leibniz, as also by the Huguenot *rationaux*. For all these thinkers held theirs to be an increasingly 'enlightened' age, in which 'reason' set the agenda *and* ensured that religion, authority, and Christian morality were strengthened and confirmed, by the advances of philosophy and science. In effect, Bayle's philosophy categorically blocked all prospect of a Christian Enlightenment.

[59] *Mémoires de Trévoux* (July 1712), art. xcviii, pp. 113, 117; Evers, 'Jean Le Clerc', 103.

[60] Bayle, *Réponse*, iv. 222.

[61] Ibid. iv. 219–20; Mori, *Bayle philosophe*, 61–2, 71.

[62] Bayle, *Réponse*, iv. 222, 225; Crousaz, *Examen*, 479, 488–9; Schøsler, 'Jaquelot et Le Clerc', 335.

[63] Schøsler, *Jaquelot et Le Clerc*, 337–8; Bayle, *Réponse*, iv. 222; Conti, *Scritti filosofici*, 272; Maupertuis, *Œuvres*, i. 249, ii. 229; Salaün, *L'Ordre*, 172–3.

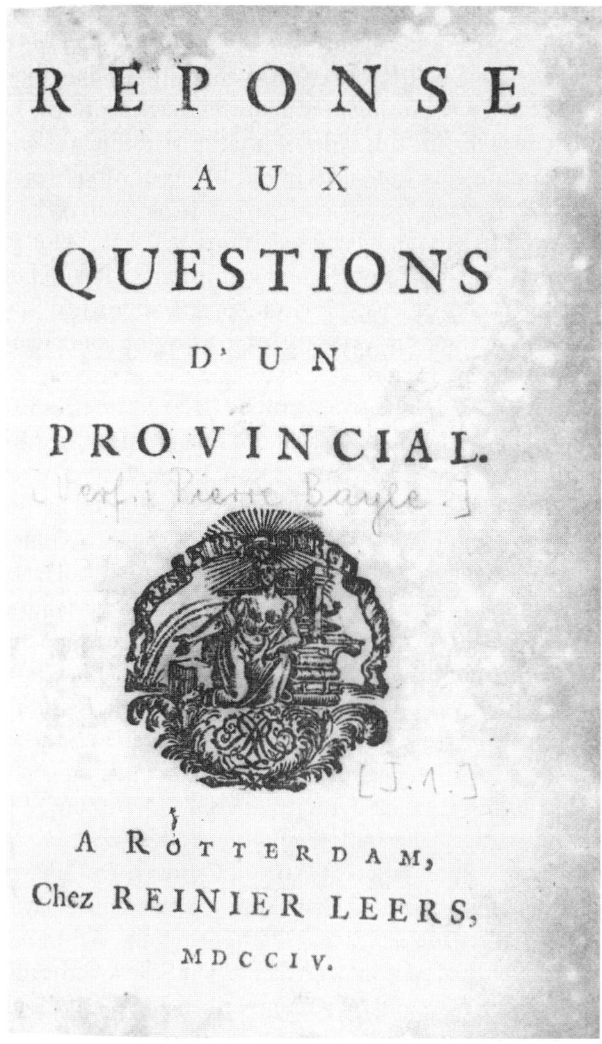

Figure 1. The title page of Bayle's *Résponse aux questions d'un provincial* (Rotterdam, 1704)

Bayle refused to accept that Christianity and 'enlightenment' converge by design of the Creator, or that belief in Christ's miracles, Resurrection, and mission as Saviour rest on irrefutable evidence, historical, moral, and textual, as Le Clerc and Saurin, like Locke and the Dutch Remonstrant leader Philip van Limborch (1633–1712), maintained. He also refused to accept there is any moral imperative for all clear-minded persons schooled in 'l'art de penser en ordre' to embrace Christianity.[64] It almost seemed, objected Jaquelot, that Bayle had made it his life's

[64] Le Clerc, *De l'incrédulité*, 81; Lomonaco, 'Jean Barbeyrac et le "Pyrrhonisme" ', 265–6.

work to plead the cause of the atheists 'et de faire leur apologie', especially since his great ability and immense erudition gave him the means to 'faire lever l'arrêt que le public a prononcé contre eux' [to lift the ban which the public has pronounced against them].[65] The *Dictionnaire*, assuredly, one of the most read books of the era, had a great many admirers but this did not prevent there being very many critics even of that evasive work—as a *mémoire* of his life and works sent from Holland to the Jesuit *Journal de Trévoux* shortly after Bayle's death points out—who strongly suspected him 'd'avoir du penchant pour le Spinozisme'.[66] Jaquelot comments that the article on Spinoza, the longest in Bayle's *Dictionnaire*, would have been more effective in clearing Bayle of suspicion of crypto-Spinozism had it tried to differentiate two distinct substances—one spiritual and one material—which, indeed, it conspicuously fails to do.[67]

Where Le Clerc insisted on the conformity of Christian ethics with the principles of reason and 'natural religion', Bayle not only denies Christianity provides mankind with the best and most rational possible system of morality but propounds, as Jaquelot expressed it, 'une entière et perpetuelle opposition de contradiction entre la foi et la raison' and even, as Barbeyrac pointed out, puts in 'opposition avec la raison, la morale de l'*Évangile*'.[68] Little wonder that Barbeyrac, leading Natural Law theorist and in his mature years a passionate advocate of Locke and especially Locke's insistence on the compatibility of reason, Christianity, and the basic principles of morality, judged that Bayle's real aim was to undermine respect for Scripture and religion, and concluded that 'les derniers ouvrages de Mr. Bayle', as he wrote to Le Clerc in April 1706, referring particularly to the *Continuation des Pensées diverses* and the *Réponse aux questions d'un provincial*, were even more dangerous than 'les livres de Hobbes, et de Spinosa'.[69]

Seeing its ruinous implications for the 'enlightened' synthesis of faith and reason they urged, Le Clerc, Bernard, Jaquelot, Saurin, Crousaz, Durand, and Barbeyrac had little choice, even after his death, but to continue to oppose Bayle's insinuating system. Combating Bayle's ideas was all the more urgent, held Le Clerc, in that, regrettably, the world is full of persons who do actually follow faith without reference to reason in the manner Bayle feigns to recommend, believing without justification, in the fashion of Papin, Bossuet, Jurieu, or Huet, rather than on principle. There are an infinity of persons, complains Le Clerc, who are Christians 'non par lumière et par raison' but merely by birth and through belief; had these same people been born in Islamic lands they would be Muslims, or in India, then adherents of Indian religions. Like Le Clerc and Jaquelot, Élie Saurin saw no merit in faith resting solely 'on authority', or nourished merely by emotion, habit, or fervour, without believers

65 [Jaquelot], *Examen*, 15; *Mémoires de Trévoux* (Apr. 1707), art. xlvii, pp. 702–3.

66 *Mémoires de Trévoux* (Apr. 1707), 'Mémoire sur la vie', 700.

67 Ibid. (Sept. 1707), pp. 1499–500.

68 Ibid. (Sept. 1707) art. cxii, p. 1501; Lomonaco, 'Religious Truth', 422.

69 Le Clerc, *Epistolario*, iii, Barbeyrac to Le Clerc, Berlin, 10 Apr. 1706; *Bibliothèque choisie*, 9 (1706), 403; [Barbeyrac], *Éloge*, 24–6; Lomonaco, 'Jean Barbeyrac et le "Pyrrhonisme" ', 254–5; Lomonaco, 'Jean Barbeyrac als Ausleger', 201; Hochstrasser, 'Claims', 43.

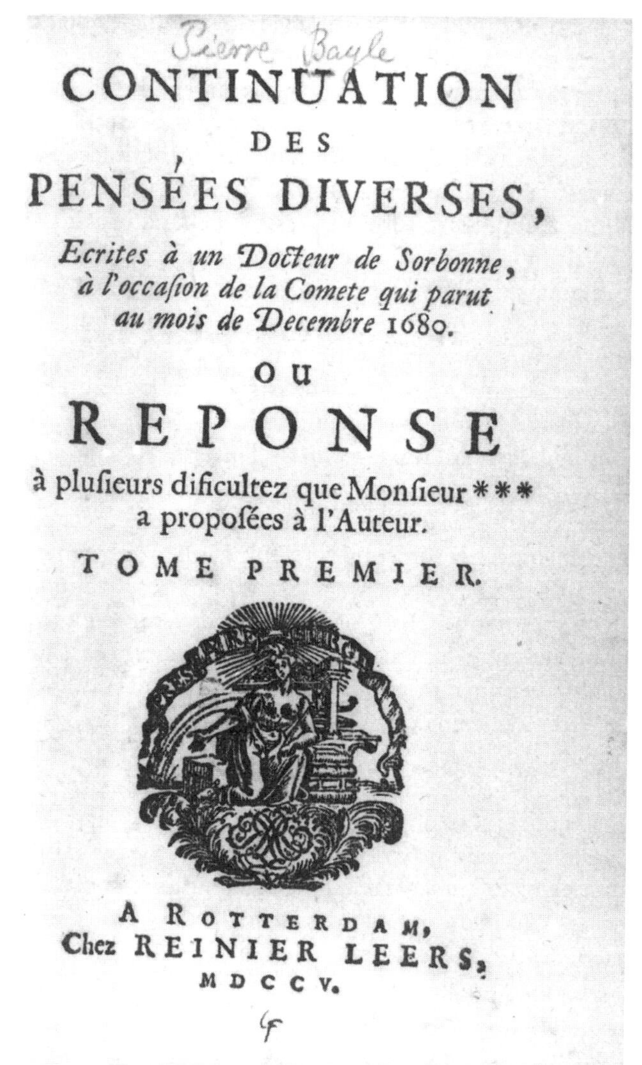

CONTINUATION
DES
PENSÉES DIVERSES,
Ecrites à un Docteur de Sorbonne, à l'occasion de la Comete qui parut au mois de Decembre 1680.
OU
REPONSE
à plusieurs dificultez que Monsieur *** a proposées à l'Auteur.
TOME PREMIER.

A ROTTERDAM,
Chez REINIER LEERS,
MDCCV.

Figure 2. The title page of the first edition of the Bayle's *Continuation des Pensées diverses* (Rotterdam, 1705)

first convincing themselves of the truth of their confession with arguments and 'evidence', while Jurieu's principle that the text of Scripture contains within itself no signs which provide conclusive proof that it is divinely inspired struck him as totally disastrous and apt to lead straight to atheism.[70] Bayle himself notes disdainfully that religion is usually passed down without any interruption, from father to

[70] Landucci, 'Appendice', 77–8.

son, the only reason one religion has more followers than another being that there are fewer children 'dans celle-là que dans celle-ci'.[71]

The unreasoning conformity underpinning the faith of most Christians, held Le Clerc, is a weak and wretched travesty of veritable religion and a social, political, and cultural catastrophe because 'faith' without 'reason' both feeds off and breeds erroneous theology, faked miracles, and ridiculous mystification, producing an ever vaster and more oppressive corpus of false belief and brutal religious power politics driven solely by superstition and the irrational anxieties of men. This kind of religion is indeed a social pest, he maintained, because it is continually apt to foment a universal division and strife among all confessions.

Bayle's post-*Dictionnaire* works were aimed at the whole phalanx of his 'enlightened' antagonists and not least the most learned, Le Clerc. Long rivals, after 1704 the two men became embittered enemies accusing each other not just of error but of pernicious heresy and of fundamentally damaging religion.[72] Le Clerc, held Bayle, was an 'Arminian', 'Socinian', and 'Arrian' who, while posing as a champion of toleration, produced more heat than light and was more fired up with *odium theologicum* than anyone else; someone who, for all the overblown pretensions in theology and philosophy, subverts the integrity of Scripture in all his writings, secretly employing 'the arguments of Spinoza'.[73] Bayle relentlessly assailed the reality of a basic accord between reason and faith underpinning Le Clerc's Bible exegesis, labelling this 'contradiction' typically 'Socinian' and replete with the confusion he discerned in both the *rationaux* and Socinianism.[74] Often repeating the latter smear while also citing Spinoza's undeniably deep influence on Le Clerc's critical method and Bible hermeneutics, Bayle disparaged Le Clerc as a paragon of bad faith, obscurity, and evasion, repeatedly protesting at his (and Jaquelot's) 'chicaneries'.[75] Le Clerc retaliated by charging Bayle with hypocrisy, philosophical incoherence, and deliberately seeking to 'ruiner la religion', labelling his formidable *Continuation des pensées diverses* (1705) 'son apologie des athées'.[76]

Despite the smokescreen of 'fideism' which, indeed, serves no real function in Bayle's philosophy other than categorically to separate philosophy from theology and deflect criticism and outrage by concealing the true implications of his stance, being as Barbeyrac later described it just an 'expedient, dont la mauvaise foi est évidente',[77] Bayle actually bases his thought, as Le Clerc clearly saw, on a radical Cartesian mathematico-historical rationalist foundation, a kind of *Malebranchisme* purged of all theological elements—or, in other words, a type of crypto-Spinozism. Its aim and effect was to bar every route to a rational

71 Le Clerc, *Epistolario*, 130; Saurin, *Examen*, 91; Bayle, *Continuation*, i. 59.

72 *Bibliothèque choisie*, 10 (1706), 379–426; Bayle, *Entretiens*, 14–15; Bots, *Henri Basnage de Beauval*, ii. 141.

73 *Bibliothèque ancienne et moderne*, 28 (1727), 394 Hoogstaten and Schuer, *Groot Algemeen Woordenboek*, ii. B. 108; [Barbeyrac], *Éloge*, preface pp. 15, 22–3; Knetsch, *Pierre Jurieu*, 372; Barnes, *Jean Le Clerc*, 229–30, 232.

74 Bayle, *Entretiens*, 20–3; Labrousse, *Pierre Bayle*, ii. 330–1, 365–7.

75 Bayle, *Entretiens*, 11, 96; Walker, *Decline of Hell*, 188.

76 *Bibliothèque choisie*, 10 (1706), 379.

77 Rétat, *Dictionnaire de Bayle*, 39–40.

theology. Bayle, contended Le Clerc, had entered on a forlorn and lonely path from which there was no escape.

This catastrophe, held Le Clerc, arose from Bayle's outmoded adherence to the mechanistic axioms of Descartes, Fontenelle, and Malebranche and disastrous rejection of the epistemology of the English empiricists.[78] Where Bayle, in Le Clerc's opinion, was secretly abetting Spinoza and leading many to perdition, Boyle, Locke, and Newton with their wise empiricism, deployed to defend a 'rational' Christianity and Christ's miracles, had shown the 'republic of letters' the true path to 'enlightenment'. Like his colleague van Limborch, Le Clerc warmly endorsed Locke's epistemology and toleration, and what mattered even more to them, his method of reconciling philosophy and science with theology as demonstrated in both the *Essay* and the *Reasonableness of Christianity*, a work full of excellent content, remarked Le Clerc in his review of that text, marred only by some omissions and repetitiousness.[79] Le Clerc fiercely denigrated Bayle for failing to take Locke seriously 'sans entendre ses sentiments', as he assured Shaftesbury,[80] and for refusing to see the crucial importance of recent developments in English thought. If one required further proof of Bayle's lack of 'raisonnement solide', he declared years later, in 1717, one need only note his almost total (and in Le Clerc's eyes positively culpable) obduracy regarding English ideas: 'il n'avoit lû aucun livre de la philosophie expérimentale des Anglois, dont plusieurs avoient paru long-tems avant sa mort; ni aucun des livres de raisonnement de la même Nation, excepté quelque-uns de ceux, qui avoient été traduits.'[81]

The gap between Locke and Bayle was unbridgeable. Meanwhile, if Le Clerc and the *rationaux* had ample grounds for hurling the charge of Spinozism back in Bayle's face, and ridiculing his accusation of Pyrrhonism, rebutting the oft repeated charges of Arianism, Pelagianism, Arminianism, and Socinianism proved less easy. For besides the *rationaux* themselves, all their key allies, such as Locke, Clarke, and the Swiss Calvinist titan Jean-Alphonse Turretini (1671–1737) and his friends working for a more tolerant and liberal Reformed Church in Geneva, Basel, and Lausanne,[82] were profoundly influenced by the Arminianism of van Limborch and the Dutch Remonstrants and practically all of them were accused of Socinianism by a wide variety of theological adversaries.

Though still in the first place a Dutch phenomenon, Arminianism in the late seventeenth and early eighteenth centuries became fundamental to the pro-toleration, Latitudinarian tendency in Protestantism throughout north-west Europe. Hence, ironically, Le Clerc's influence came to be intensely felt, among other places, in early eighteenth-century Geneva whence he himself had earlier been forced to flee by

[78] *Bibliothèque ancienne et moderne*, 28 (1727), 389.

[79] *Bibliothèque choisie*, 25 (1712), 398–400; Barnouw, *Philippus van Limborch*, 50; Brogi, *Teologia senza verità*, 18, 35–6.

[80] Barnes, *Jean Le Clerc*, 173.

[81] Sina, 'Le *Dictionnaire historique*', 232; see also Balduzzi, 'Problemi interpretativi', 465–6.

[82] Bayle, *Entretiens*, 15; Trevor-Roper, *Religion*, 211–12; Pocock, *Barbarism*, i. 50–71; van Eijnatten, *Liberty and Concord*, 166.

Calvinist intolerance. Since the Restoration in England, the Arminian intellectual legacy had revived strongly at Oxford and Cambridge and throughout the Anglican Church as well as among the Huguenots in France.[83] There was moreover, a close connection between the Arminian revival in England and the subsequent triumph of rationalizing Latitudinarianism within Anglicanism in the 1690s, after the Glorious Revolution, as well as the subsequent rapid spread of Locke's and Newton's influence in Britain, Ireland, and the American colonies. For Latitudinarianism, as one scholar has aptly put it, was 'clearly Arminian in its theological emphases'.[84] Indeed, even in New England by the middle of the eighteenth century, as a deeply worried Jonathan Edwards noted in 1753, the 'term Calvinistic is, in these days, among most, a term of greater reproach than the term Arminian'.[85]

Foremost among those who opposed the Arminian tendency were the partisans of a traditional Calvinism, Dutch, Swiss, Huguenot, Anglo-Scottish, and American with whom Bayle, quite spuriously in Le Clerc's view, professed to align.[86] This was a force strong also in New England. In opposing 'Arminianism' from a Calvinist standpoint Edwards urged that men should base themselves not on the reason of Le Clerc but on what he calls 'a kind of holy pusillanimity' even with respect to Newton whose science he accepted but towards whose influence in religious matters, and learning generally, he was distinctly on his guard. In his deep suspicion of scientific reason, Edwards stood close to, and warmly admired, the leading Dutch hard-line anti-Cartesian and anti-Arminian Voetian theologian Petrus van Mastricht (1630–1706) whom he considered one of the most important recent European theological writers.[87]

Scarcely less antagonistic to the 'Arminian' tendency were the Anglican high-flyers. When the crypto-Socinian Arthur Bury (1624–1713), rector of Exeter College, caused uproar in Oxford in 1690 with his not especially learned book *The Naked Gospel*, arguing that 'reason' should be our guide, that there persisted 'much corruption in some churches', and that much of what is deemed orthodox had actually been concocted by ecclesiastics centuries after Christ's death, to heighten 'superstition' and illegitimately inflate ecclesiastical authority, he was warmly applauded by Le Clerc but, in Oxford, was excommunicated, fined, deprived of his rectorship, and had his book burnt.[88]

The *rationaux* were much heartened by the post-1688 progress of Arminianism and Latitudinarianism in Britain and, like Voltaire later, clearly saw the connection between this process of liberalization and the emergence of a specifically English scientific-philosophical Enlightenment based on reconciling elements of faith and theology with reason. From Voltaire's perspective, these trends had the added

[83] Van Eijnatten, *Liberty and Concord*, 156, 160; Tyacke, 'Religious Controversy', 601–9, 617–18.

[84] Tyacke, 'Religious Controversy', 618; Lomonaco, 'Jean Barbeyrac et le "Pyrrhonisme" ', 260, 265.

[85] Edwards, *Freedom of the Will*, p. ix.

[86] *Bibliothèque choisie*, 10 (1706), 422; *Mémoires de Trévoux* (Aug. 1707), art. xcix, p. 1364.

[87] Edwards, *Religious Affections*, 264; Marsden, *Jonathan Edwards*, 318, 488.

[88] [Bury], *Naked Gospel*, B2^{v}; Tyacke, 'Religious Controversy', 616–17; Champion, *Pillars of Priestcraft*, 107; Marshall, *John Locke*, 389.

advantage of greatly narrowing the gap between a reformed liberal Christianity and the kind of providential Deism to which he himself adhered. But Bayle, unimpressed by Le Clerc's and Bernard's 'English' strategy, scorned Arminianism and Latitudinarianism no less than the Unitarianism (Socinianism) later particularly favoured by Voltaire. Echoing the many orthodox, whether Calvinist, Catholic, Lutheran, or Anglican, who expressed themselves in similarly contemptuous terms, he deplored this resurgent Anglo-Dutch-Swiss Arminianism as the sewer 'de tous les Athées, Déistes et Sociniens de l'Europe'.[89]

3. VOLTAIRE AND THE ECLIPSE OF BAYLE

The triumphant progress of English philosophy, science, and Latitudinarian theology after 1688, in effect the English Enlightenment of Locke and Newton, was in every way welcomed and applauded by the *rationaux*. Here was an important link between them and Voltaire which was to bind the latter, throughout his career, consciously and closely to the legacy of Le Clerc and Clarke. Henceforth, veneration of Locke, Newton, and Clarke, especially for powerfully coupling reason and theism, became the very touchstone of 'raisonnement solide' for all those who subscribed to the Voltairean Enlightenment no less than that of the *rationaux*, the ultimate test of 'enlightened' principles in effect for large sections of enlightened opinion in France, Switzerland, and Holland, no less than Britain, Ireland, and America. Among the party of Le Clerc and Bernard—just as later, in the 1730s and 1740s among the *parti philosophique* of Voltaire—lack of zeal for 'English ideas' was tantamount to betraying the most basic principles of 'enlightenment', to admitting one was unenlightened, or else a concealed Spinozist.

Le Clerc, Jaquelot, Saurin, and Bernard were all sworn to uphold reason, fight superstition, and promote the cause of philosophy. Yet there was no possibility of peace or compromise with the radical wing despite the fact that both factions were persecuted by the orthodox. For the basic axioms of the two streams remained totally incompatible and antagonistic: one side held there is no such thing as supernatural agency, while the other contended that there are supernatural beings, including angels and demons, only that one should not believe in 'signs', 'wonders', and other doings of spiritual beings without the clearest evidence. Where the Spinozists held there were and are no miracles, nor ever had been, and no evidence to support belief in the Christian revelation, the moderates, proclaiming the truth of revelation and Christ's miracles, and the universality of Christian ethics, sought instead to persuade people to eschew unfounded claims and 'miracles' which, when shown to be fraudulent, merely fortify irreverence, scepticism, and unbelief.[90]

[89] Cited in Walker, *Decline of Hell*, 188; Labrousse, *Pierre Bayle*, ii. 328, 422 n.; see also Tyacke, 'Arminianism', 75, 78.

[90] Bernard, *Superstitions anciennes*, i. 138.

Despite enveloping his meaning in thick layers of irony, ambiguity, and imposture, Bayle was and remained, particularly in the early eighteenth century, deeply suspect; but in this he was far from being alone in that age of intellectual crisis so that contemporary assessments of his work were sometimes themselves scarcely any less convoluted. The Halle professor Gundling, while respectably paying lip-service to Bayle's critics, was yet justifiably suspected of being something of a *Bayliste* himself.[91] The Neapolitan philosopher Paolo Matta Doria (1662–1746), a professed 'Platonist' suspected by some of crypto-Spinozism, readily agreed that Bayle's philosophy amounted to 'atheism' and was, arguably, even more subversive than Spinoza's, but yet held Bayle to be 'tanto buono istorico, quanto falso ed ignorante filosofo' [as good a historian as he was false and ignorant a philosopher].[92] What was certain was that after Bayle's reputation became severely damaged, particularly after 1700, it remained the case for a long period, until Voltaire changed matters, that only hardened intellectual rebels and outcasts from respectable society like Toland, Collins, Mandeville, Radicati, Rousset de Missy, and d'Argens ever ventured to offer unqualified praise and admiration of the 'philosopher of Rotterdam'.

Even so, Bayle never came to be so universally identified as an 'atheist', or so widely vilified, as Spinoza. This was only natural given his frequent evasiveness and paradoxical style. His standing also benefited from the odd circumstance that most professional theologians, Catholic and Protestant, even at the height of his battle with the *rationaux*, when his ideas were widely acknowledged to be subversive, were too shocked by Le Clerc's and his allies' uncompromising rationalism, and assault on 'mysteries' and dogmas, to join with them in assailing Bayle who, after all, purportedly upheld orthodox positions. Jaquelot's appalling theology, complained the Jesuit *Mémoires de Trévoux*, in September 1707, for example, in a long review more than a little inclined to take Bayle's part despite worries about his paradoxes, was so set on changing everything in the name of reason that even semi-Pelagians must shrink back in horror.[93] Similarly, the Lutheran theologian Friedrich Wilhelm Bierling (1676–1728), at Rinteln, a pupil of Christian Thomasius, sharply criticized Le Clerc, Jaquelot, Bernard, La Placette, Leibniz, and Buddeus for not taking Bayle's fideism seriously enough.[94]

Faced by the highly disconcerting challenge of Le Clerc and the *rationaux*, orthodox Catholics, especially in France and Italy, understandably mostly preferred, or found it expedient, to accept Bayle's claim to be a fideist, or at least give him the benefit of the doubt, rather than highlight the extremely subversive and unorthodox implications of his system.[95] This they did despite perceiving what the Jesuits called Bayle's 'trop d'indulgence pour l'athéisme', and knowing full well that *les Spinosistes* frequently hid their necessitarianism behind a veil of Calvinist

[91] Gundling, *Gundlingiana*, iii. 4010–1; Bots, 'Le Plaidoyer', 547–50.

[92] Doria, *Manoscritti napoletani*, iii. 33.

[93] *Mémoires de Trévoux* (Sept. 1707), art. cxii, p. 1526.

[94] Bierling, *Dissertatio theologica*, 6–8.

[95] *Mémoires de Trévoux* (Oct. 1707), art. cxxx, pp. 1739–41, 1747, 1751; Capasso, *Historiae philosophiae synopsis*, 385–6.

predestination. Aspects of Bayle's devastating critique of the *rationaux* were bound to prove useful to their Catholic and High Church opponents, while Bayle's professed fideism appealed to French anti-Cartesians, again especially the Jesuits. Added to this, his well-publicized opposition, in 1688, to Jurieu's summons to Huguenots in, and outside, France to join William III and wage war on Louis XIV further helped his standing in that kingdom, despite the fact that all his works remained officially banned there.[96]

In this way, Bayle's reputation as an irreligious and dangerous author was significantly muted in some quarters even before 1720. Ultimately, the consequence of this papering over of awkward cracks was, once again, a heavy if camouflaged defeat for orthodoxy and tradition, an outcome engineered in the first place by Bayle's extraordinary skill as an intellectual strategist and the deftness with which he everywhere insinuated his crypto-Spinozism. Meanwhile, he continued to exert an unprecedented impact right across Europe down to the middle of the eighteenth century. No one else, not even Locke, was a staple of so many libraries or had so wide a general influence, his writings being everywhere acknowledged to be a prime cause of the tide of scepticism, atheism, and materialism sweeping the west of the continent. The Huguenot Laurent Angliviel de La Beaumelle (1726–73), who spent many years in Denmark, reports that, by the late 1740s, Copenhagen and the Danish court had become a veritable Deistic haven. This, he says, was due to philosophy and there could be no doubt which philosopher had most effectively given expression to the insights, doubts, and questions driving this great cultural change: the Danish 'déistes', who are very numerous 'parmi les gens d'un certain rang', he informed his brother in France in April 1748, were all steeped in Bayle, and forever seeking out his books and reading him, one particular nobleman, the count of Rantzau to whom he was close, speaking incessantly about that philosopher every time he saw him.[97]

The changing situation, as Catholic, Lutheran, and Calvinist orthodoxy all lost ground in north-west Europe during the first half of the eighteenth century, produced a widely perceived and urgent need for new answers to, and techniques for countering, Bayle's influence. The result, from the 1730s onwards, was a powerful tendency to reconstruct Bayle's image and present him as something which he was not. Neither the Deist, nor Protestant, and still less the Catholic moderate mainstream could any longer fight Bayle in the manner of Le Clerc, Bernard, or Jaquelot, stressing the rationality of Christianity; the need now was to develop less overtly theological strategies. Pierre-Louis Moreau de Maupertuis (1698–1759), for example, who, like the *rationaux* and Voltaire, greatly admired Newton, Clarke, and Locke, strongly reaffirmed the values of the moderate mainstream in the late 1740s, notably in his *Essai de philosophie morale*, vigorously joining the battle against Bayle, but was palpably less confident than Le Clerc or Jaquelot that reason could ever finally defeat the *incrédule*s or stop

[96] *Mémoires de Trévoux* (Oct. 1707), art. cxxx, pp. 1737–8. [97] Lauriol, *La Beaumelle*, 139.

the spread of incredulity: were religion 'rigoureusement démontrable, tout le monde seroit Chrétien'.[98]

If Maupertuis still adopted a more explicitly Christian perspective than Voltaire, fully endorsing the *rationaux*'s guiding principle that the true *philosophe* seeks a middle course, 'un juste milieu' between the stance of the *dévots* and that of the *impies*, between blind faith, and the freethinking of the *esprits forts*, he also markedly retreated from the stance of the *rationaux*.[99] Aligning, like them, with Locke, and endorsing Condillac's assault on metaphysical systems, he attacked radical *esprit philosophique* as something philosophically unsound in itself and especially as something inherently incapable of demonstrating any clear 'impossibility' in Christian doctrine. No purely rational system of science and philosophy, held Maupertuis, can ever answer the deepest, most far-reaching questions better than the Church. It is enough to convince us of the impotence of systematic philosophy, he argues, to examine the systems of the leading philosophers of antiquity and of modern times, especially of those independent-minded spirits most noted, he added, alluding to the Spinozists, for being emancipated from every kind of prejudgement, and belief. For Spinoza's followers postulate 'une divinité répandue dans la matière, un Univers Dieu', one single entity in which are comprised all the perfections and all defects, all virtues and all vices, a being 'susceptible de mille modifications opposées'.[100]

Is the God of Spinoza, then, really easier to believe and trust in than the God of the Christians? Maupertuis did not think so. We must simply admit, he concludes, restating his empirico-sceptical creed, that God, Nature, and Man are entities far surpassing our conceptions 'et toutes les forces de notre esprit'.[101] By the 1730s and 1740s, meanwhile, the efforts to check Bayle's influence were helped by the fact that his astounding paradoxes and contorted method of argument were beginning to lose something of their appeal and their force. For as the peculiarly fraught ideological milieu of the 1680s, 1690s, and opening years of the new century which had shaped his philosophical style receded into the past, readers became less attuned and receptive both to his paradoxes and to the constant twists and circumlocutions of which he was the supreme master.

By the late 1740s, the process which eventually led to the eclipse of Bayle's once vast reputation, in the later eighteenth and nineteenth centuries, was already apparent. Much more effectively than Maupertuis, Voltaire powerfully intervened, using various lines of attack to deflate Bayle's standing, styling his *Dictionnaire* a mine of miscellaneous and curious information while pointedly always ignoring his philosophy as such.[102] From 1722, when he first visited Holland, and discussed Bayle, among others, with the latter's former friend, the now elderly Basnage, he frequently harked back to the 'philosopher of Rotterdam', scribbling numerous marginal notes in his own copy of the *Dictionnaire*.[103] But while fascinated by the

[98] Lauriol, *La Beaumelle*, 243–4.
[99] Maupertuis, 'Essai de philosophie morale', 242–4, 246–7. [100] Ibid. 249.
[101] Ibid. 250. [102] Voltaire, *Lettres philosophiques*, 138, 140.
[103] Labrousse, *Pierre Bayle*, ii. 582; Mason, 'Voltaire devant Bayle', 444.

vast success of a writer he deemed a 'dialecticien admirable, plus que profound philosophe', he insisted on projecting him as unversed in experimental philosophy, scornful of Locke, and, most discreditable of all, ignorant about Newton. Slighting his *oeuvre*, he was alienated in particular by Bayle's unwillingness to acknowledge the evidence for divine providence, or any teleology in history.[104] His strategy for combating Bayle, however, was quite different from that of the *rationaux*: for he consistently denied Bayle was insidious or dangerous, preferring rather to recast him as a sceptic (like much of the late twentieth-century historiography). While agreeing that his 'scepticism' sometimes unwittingly functioned as an engine for manufacturing *esprits forts*, producing so many objections to Christian dogmas that many were disturbed by him,[105] he completely rejected Jurieu's view of Bayle as an advocate 'd'idées plus dangereuses que celles de Spinosa'.[106]

Rather, Voltaire continually expressed disdain for Bayle's convoluted style of thought and constant sliding between fideism and other positions, and, while feeling bound to praise his campaign on behalf of toleration, principally valued him as a fund of anecdotes and curious themes, as in *Cosi-Sancta*, one of his first stories, and his remarks about St Bernard in the *Lettres philosophiques*.[107] When in Holland, in 1739, in discussion with the radical-minded marquis d'Argens (who had a much higher opinion of Voltaire the poet, dramatist, and story writer than of Voltaire the philosopher),[108] he tried to persuade him that Bayle had greatly over-inflated his *Dictionnaire* with unnecessary matter and was generally far too prolix, showing a deplorable lack of rigour in argument as well as unfortunate love of irrelevant detail. D'Argens firmly disagreed, insisting Bayle was 'un esprit universel, savant philosophe, habile critique, génie vaste', indeed much more so, he thought privately, than Voltaire.[109] Bayle and Fontenelle, it seemed to him, were the two *philosophes* who had opened up philosophy to society: 'there is an art of discoursing upon the most sublime subject', as a contemporary English translation of d'Argens puts it, 'without soaring out of the reach of common capacities; none have been masters of this art more than Mr Bayle and Mr de Fontenelle; their works are undoubted proofs that the most abstruse subjects may be treated in such a method, as to render them easily understood.'[110]

Since d'Argens thought all this of surpassing importance, Voltaire assured him that he too admired Bayle, that his aim was not to diminish Bayle's reputation (which d'Argens saw perfectly well, in fact, it was), and that he should not bracket him, because he criticized aspects of Bayle among those sworn enemies of the 'philosopher of Rotterdam' who would like to ruin 'à la fois la réputation du philosophe et la bonne philosophie'; but he continued to insist that the copious

[104] Voltaire, *Œuvres complètes*, xxv. 70–2; *Corpus des notes marginales*, i. 231, 235; Voltaire, *Lettres à son altesse*, 349.

[105] Voltaire, *Lettres à son altesse*, 349–50.

[106] Voltaire, 'Notes de M. de Morza', 253.

[107] Voltaire, *Lettres philosophiques*, 89, 241–2; Voltaire, *Romans*, 695; Pearson, *Fables*, 43 n.

[108] D'Argens, *Réflexions historiques*, 357–64, 382.

[109] D'Argens, *Lettres juives*, i. 165; Bush, *Marquis d'Argens*, 66–7; Trousson, 'Voltaire', 230; Minuti, 'Orientalismo', 893–4.

[110] D'Argens, *The Impartial Philosopher*, i. preface p. iv.

writings of 'ce génie facile' would be best boiled down to a single volume;[111] as for Fontenelle, Voltaire, as he later remarked in his story *Micromégas*, thought him an 'homme de beaucoup d'esprit' skilled at providing excellent accounts of the inventions of others but who invented nothing himself.[112] Over the years, there was to be no sign of slackening in Voltaire's campaign to diminish the status of either Fontenelle or Bayle. In 1751, he even dismissed Bayle's first great attack on 'superstition', the *Pensées diverses*, as 'inutile', the designation he applies, in his *Lettres philosophiques*, also to Descartes.[113]

Voltaire was willing to agree that Bayle's life, like Spinoza's, was singularly virtuous;[114] but he did not consider the sedentary life of philosophers who, like Bayle or Spinoza, spend their entire careers contemplating reality from their studies to have much broad significance for society, admiring much more the worldly cut and thrust of an active life like his own. Ridiculing the fact that Des Maizeaux had gone to the trouble of writing a whole book about Bayle's life, he went so far as to suggest that even six pages would have been excessive![115] The question of how to be a *philosophe* and change the world was, of course, a pressing one for Voltaire as for Spinoza and Bayle. In a passage penned in 1766, he again brackets Spinoza and Bayle together as philosophers who searched assiduously all their lives for the truth, albeit by different routes, Spinoza constructing an 'erroneous' system and Bayle attacking, as he puts it, 'tous les systèmes'; also they were writers who in the 1760s still had their readers, even if, as he remarks elsewhere, Spinoza was a philosopher of whom everyone spoke but whom no one read.[116] The paradox he suggested was that both these Dutch-based philosophers had enjoyed huge reputations but yet had had no meaningful impact on society. Why was this? Because men are ruled, says Voltaire, principally by habit and custom 'et non par la métaphysique'. A personality who is eloquent, active, and received in high society can exert a much wider impact among men, he suggests, than a hundred philosophers of the stamp of Spinoza and Bayle 's'ils ne sont que philosophes'.[117]

Bayle, then, for Voltaire, was not in the least a hero or in any way comparable with Locke, Newton, or Clarke in importance. Rather, Voltaire continued Le Clerc's battle with Bayle, only now with new weapons and a new strategy, continually belittling his status as a thinker and portraying his 'scepticism' as pervasive, certainly, but also overrated and thoroughly tedious. One of his favourite quips at Bayle's expense was that when it came to Cartesianism and especially Cartesian 'reason', 'le sceptique Bayle', he put it around 1752, and later repeated several times, 'n'est pas encore assez sceptique'.[118] As virtual head of the *parti philosophique* of

[111] Minuti, 'Orientalismo', 54–5; Voltaire, *Œuvres complètes*, lxxi. 391, 394, xv. 35, 70; Wade, *Intellectual Development*, 408, 467, 649–50; Benelli, *Voltaire metafisico*, 100–1; Cantelli, 'Virtù degli atei', 683 n.; Bartlett, *Idea of Enlightenment*, 14.

[112] Voltaire, *Micromégas*, 133; White, *Anti-Philosophers*, 29.

[113] Mason, 'Voltaire devant Bayle', 445, 451; Mori, *Bayle philosophe*, 133.

[114] Voltaire, *Philosophe ignorant*, 40.

[115] Voltaire, *Œuvres complètes*, xxv. 71.

[116] Voltaire, 'Notes de M. de Morza', 253.

[117] Voltaire, *Philosophe ignorant*, 40; Vernière, *Spinoza*, 497.

[118] Mason, 'Voltaire devant Bayle', 451.

the 1730s and early 1740s Voltaire could not publicly denounce 'le dangereux Bayle', as his Jesuit correspondent Father Tournemine called him in 1735, and as had Le Clerc, but he found a more effective means to criticize Bayle's *oeuvre* and deflate his reputation.[119] Certainly, he loathed Bayle's refusal to acknowledge the rationality of belief in a divine Creator and opposed Bayle's thesis that 'une société d'athées peut subsister' as well as his claiming idolatry is worse than 'atheism', remarking that he would only have been able to agree had Bayle contended instead that *le fanatisme* is worse than atheism.[120] Bayle's view that Chinese society, government, and philosophy were essentially 'atheistic' aroused not just Voltaire's opposition but his indignation.[121] But he saw that Bayle could be most effectively countered by continually disparaging his alleged long-windedness, inconsistency, and tiresome 'scepticism', rather than trying to answer his arguments.

There was just one strand of Bayle Voltaire judged useful and sought to redeploy, a feature he (and Maupertuis) praised several times, a fact which suggests it fitted with an important aspect of their own general strategy, namely Bayle's seeming attack, in his *Dictionnaire*, on Spinoza's doctrine of one substance and metaphysics generally. It is a mistake, held Voltaire, to argue, like Jaquelot and so many others, that Bayle had innocently (or deliberately) misrepresented or distorted Spinoza's argument; he insisted, rather, that Bayle's critique was both sincere and effective.[122] What sort of 'God' would it be, he affirms, echoing Bayle's central objection, that is everything at the same time, gardener and plants, doctor and patient, murderer and murdered, destroyer and destroyed? Remarkably, Voltaire persisted in labouring this point despite himself all along privately doubting, he later admitted in 1771, that Bayle had in fact correctly represented Spinoza's one-substance doctrine.[123]

The most remarkable part of Voltaire's anti-Bayle strategy, however, was his reconfiguring, in a way reminiscent of his later demolition of Meslier, the general drift of his thought. Whereas for Le Clerc, Jaquelot, Bernard, Barbeyrac, and all the *rationaux*, as likewise later for Collins, Radicati, Mandeville, d'Argens, and La Mettrie,[124] Bayle was essentially an anti-religious and crypto-*Spinosiste* writer, Voltaire developed a strikingly contrary position: while granting Bayle had been one of the 'bons esprits' who in the late seventeenth century had begun 'à éclairer le monde',[125] and ruling that many of his opinions, due to his opaque style of argument, were actually impenetrable, fundamentally, he insisted, Bayle's views concerning the key points of natural theology—creation of the universe by a Creator-God, divine providence and immortality of the soul—had been systematically misrepresented. In reality, he propounded, and was an ally of, the same kind

[119] Tournemine to Voltaire, Sept. 1735, Voltaire, *Correspondence*, iii. 206; van Bunge, 'Pierre Bayle', 387; Mason, 'Voltaire devant Bayle', 448–51, 454.

[120] Mason, 'Voltaire devant Bayle', 448–51, 454; Voltaire, *Dictionnaire philosophique*, 388–9; Voltaire, *Homélies prononcées à Londres*, 346; Belgrado, 'Voltaire, Bayle', 400.

[121] Voltaire, *Essai sur les mœurs*, i. 70–1; Pinot, *La Chine*, 314–27.

[122] Voltaire, *Philosophe ignorant*, 36–8, 40; Voltaire, 'Notes de M. de Morza', 252–3; Voltaire, *Lettres à son altesse*, 390–1.

[123] Voltaire, *Lettres à son altesse*, 390–1; Vernière, *Spinoza*, 520, 523.

[124] Wellman, *La Mettrie*, 255–6.

[125] Voltaire, *Dictionnaire philosophique*, i. 560.

of providential Deism as he himself championed. Flatly disagreeing with Barbeyrac, Voltaire ruled it a damaging and intolerable error to interpret Bayle's legacy as one of 'atheism' and propagation of crypto-Spinozism.[126] In pursuing this tactic, Voltaire deftly exploited Bayle's own professed fideism, orthodoxy, and scepticism, all of which enabled him to depict him as a firm advocate of a beneficent God, a divinely ordained morality, and even a limited toleration.

In hastening the waning of Bayle's reputation, Voltaire, over the years, undoubtedly met with a measure of success.[127] After 1750, the epithets 'Baylien' and 'Bayliste' came to be used less than previously and his writings gradually to be less widely read and admired. If he could not wholly remodel the views of his independent-minded royal friend Frederick the Great of Prussia, for instance, he could subtly influence the direction of conversation at Berlin and Potsdam. Introduced to Bayle's *oeuvre* around 1736, whilst still crown prince, by his Huguenot secretary and adviser on books Charles Étienne Jordan (1700–45), Frederick had, early on, been impressed by his writing. Jordan had adopted Bayle as his own 'maître spirituel', imbibing a healthy respect for his powerfully subversive tendency, and passed something of this on to Frederick. Reading Bayle had for Frederick, as for so many others, been a decisive step in his own personal intellectual development and especially his growing disenchantment with the philosophy of Wolff.[128] Consequently, he long continued to regard him as one of the main authors of the Enlightenment: in 1776, writing to Voltaire of his admiration for those who had inspired the profound 'revolution' brought about by the Enlightenment, the king noted that that it was to 'Bayle, votre précurseur', no less than to Voltaire himself, that the glory is due 'de cette révolution qui se fait dans les esprits'.[129] Voltaire could hardly contradict this royal judgement, but he could encourage the idea that Bayle was his precursor in engineering this great 'revolution' of the age, while gradually whittling down the king's admiration for Bayle, work in which he was seconded by d'Alembert who disliked the Huguenot's historical, anti-mathematical bias.[130]

Thus, Le Clerc's conception of Bayle as a philosopher who seeks, as he put it in 1727, to 'renverser la religion chrétienne, en feignant de la défendre' [to overturn the Christian religion while feigning to defend it], general in the first third of the eighteenth century, eventually came to be overshadowed by Voltaire's rigorously pruned and sanitized Bayle.[131] Bayle the crypto-*Spinosiste* came to be replaced by Bayle the fideist and sceptic. By the late eighteenth century, only a few clergy and academics, as well as *philosophes* and *anti-philosophes*, still recalled Le Clerc's, Jaquelot's, Bernard's, and Barbeyrac's older (yet assuredly more accurate) designation of Bayle as the thinker who wrote to justify the *athées*, a deeply subversive thinker who refused to accept that 'atheists' should be deemed rebels against the moral

126 Mason, 'Voltaire devant Bayle', 443, 455–6; Belgrado, 'Voltaire, Bayle', 400.
127 Cabanel, 'Faute à Voltaire', 106–7.
128 Häseler, *Wanderer*, 30, 103–4, 136; Birnstiel, 'Frédéric II', 147, 156.
129 Birnstiel, 'Frédéric II', 144, 154–5.
130 Ibid. 149–50.
131 *Bibliothèque ancienne et moderne*, 18 (1727), 390.

order, who wished to tolerate everyone whatever they believe, who propagated the idea of the 'virtuous atheist', everywhere insinuating crypto-Spinozism, insisting that 'on peut être Déiste ou Athée de bonne foi', indeed may act more morally without any faith than anyone else, since true morality has nothing to do with faith and both morality and toleration, among Man's most precious assets, are the discoveries not of peoples, legislators, prophets, or theologians but rather, being a task for pure reason alone, of the philosophers.[132]

[132] *Journal des savants* (Apr. 1752), 201–4.

4

Demolishing Priesthood, Ancient and Modern

Toleration, purification, and rationalization—that was the agenda of the moderate mainstream. The leading theorists of the liberal Protestant middle ground, such as Le Clerc, Locke, Jaquelot, Basnage, Bernard, van Limborch, Barbeyrac, Formey, Thomasius, and Leibniz, all converged in regarding schisms and splits, theological polemics over secondary issues, superfluous theology, unnecessary claims, and fabricated 'miracles' to be not just pointless obfuscation but a serious and constant threat to true Christianity. Such superfluous 'priestcraft' while particularly disfiguring Catholicism, in their view, marred all the churches in varying degrees while serving no constructive purpose other than to clog the path to Christian reunification and overly inflate ecclesiastical authority.

On one level, their programme was coherent and clear. However, the protagonists of rational Christianity faced a serious dilemma where and whenever they sought to further their agenda. For insofar as they strove to discredit 'superstition', false 'miracles', superfluous theology, and excessive ecclesiastical power, they appeared to attack the very same outer bastions of tradition and ecclesiastical authority as the Deists and Spinozists. The fact that they, unlike their more radical rivals, wished to leave the inner citadel entirely intact was not necessarily obvious to the defenders within. Their problem, then, was not how to segregate themselves intellectually from the radicals but rather how to avoid appearing to endorse and assist the *esprits forts* and freethinkers in their combined assault on what the latter considered unmitigated 'superstition'. The situation, as Le Clerc saw in battling Bayle, Locke discovered in fending off Toland, and Christian Thomasius found in disentangling himself from the Baltic Spinozist Theodor Ludwig Lau (1670–1740),[1] was one which forced the moderate mainstream into the highly uncomfortable predicament of a two-front war. Theirs was a high-risk strategy requiring both new and often seemingly precarious theological arguments.

The dilemma was made all the more acute by the circuitous tactic, initiated by Spinoza, and elaborated by such subversive writers as Blount, Toland, Collins, Bayle, Boulainvilliers, Count Alberto Radicati di Passerano (1698–1737), Johann Lorenz Schmidt, the Dutch Huguenot author and publisher Jean-Frédéric Bernard (1683–1744), and the radical Deist Étienne Gabriel Morelly (*c.*1715–d. *c.*1755?), of

[1] See Israel, *Radical Enlightenment*, 652–4.

differentiating sharply between the impressive ideals of those that found great religions, like Jesus and, in Toland, Radicati, and Boulainvilliers, Muhammad, and in Toland and d'Argens, Moses, and the perversion of their ideals by ambitious and self-seeking 'priests' who through ambition and greed appropriate their spiritual legacy.[2] In this way, the radicals contended that the teaching of the great churches, or any organized religion, in no way corresponds either to pure 'natural religion' or to 'true' Christianity which according to Radicati does not differ from 'natural religion', 'true' Muhammadanism, or 'true Judaism'. This was both a more usual and, in the long run, more typical tenet of the Radical Enlightenment than the more militant and uncompromising view put forward by the late seventeenth-century *Traité des trois imposteurs* with its claims that Moses, Jesus, and Muhammad were all 'impostors' and the religions they founded devised merely to uphold priestly pretensions and ecclesiastical sway.

Thus, Spinoza, in his *Tractatus theologico-politicus*, holds Christ was not a prophet but someone whose mind was adapted 'to the universal beliefs and doctrines held by all mankind, that is to those concepts which are universal and true', in other words was a moral teacher and philosopher whose thought had nothing to do with what ambitious ecclesiastics and theologians have since turned it into; by definition, Jesus' message, according to Spinoza, belonged not to the realm of theology but, insofar as it was true, to philosophy.[3] While he stopped short of explicitly identifying Jesus with his own philosophy,[4] as Toland later equated Moses with 'Spinozism', Spinoza did expressly claim, as Tschirnhaus informed Leibniz, that insofar as Christ was a universal and inspired moral teacher who proclaimed true religion to consist in 'justice and charity' he should not be considered a prophet but 'summum philosophum', the supreme philosopher.[5] Radicati added to this the notion of Jesus as a great social reformer and egalitarian, wisest and most just of legislators, 'le fondateur de la république chrétienne', who desired men to live in 'perfect democracy', his legacy then being totally subverted by the first bishops who used his gospel to secure their own authority and were responsible for destroying the 'democratical government settled by Christ'.[6]

According to Spinozists, the church may once have been inspired by the authentic teaching of Christ and been based on wisdom, a 'religion of love, joy, peace, temperance and honest dealing with all men' but had then degenerated, already with the apostles, into one in which factions incessantly quarrel and battle for supremacy, employing theological dogmas as their weapons.[7] The rise of what

[2] Radicati, *Succinct History*, 21–5; Thomson, 'L'Utilisation de l'Islam', 250; Champion, *Pillars of Priestcraft*, 120–2, 124, 126–7; Harrison, *'Religion' and the Religions*, 84, 166; Assmann, *Moses*, 92–4.

[3] Spinoza, *Opera*, iii. 64; Mason, *God of Spinoza*, 218; Juffermans, *Drie Perspectiven*, 366–9.

[4] Juffermans, *Drie Perspectiven*, 222; Smith, *Spinoza, Liberalism*, 103, 105–6, 108.

[5] Matheron, *Christ et le salut*, 66–7, 69; Mason, *God of Spinoza*, 222; Dupré, *Enlightenment*, 232–5.

[6] [Radicati], *Sermon préché*, 3, 11; Radicati, *Twelve Discourses*, 26, 45–6, 49, 75; Radicati, *Succinct History*, 135; Tortarolo, *Ragione*, 10–11, 14, 17; Venturi, *Alberto Radicati*, 195–6.

[7] Spinoza, *TTP*, preface; Smith, *Spinoza, Liberalism*, 110; Rosenthal, 'Spinoza's Republican Argument', 326–7.

Radicati calls 'ecclesiastic superiority and dominion' went hand in hand with the elaboration of doctrine. 'For as soon as the Church's true function began to be distorted', asserts Spinoza, 'every worthless fellow felt an intense desire to enter into holy orders, so that eagerness to spread abroad God's religion degenerated into base avarice and ambition.' In this way, he complains, 'faith has become identical with credulity and biased dogma' and 'piety and religion' assumed the 'form of ridiculous mysteries, and men who utterly despise reason, who reject and turn away from the intellect as naturally corrupt—are those (and this of all things is the most pernicious) who are believed to possess the divine light!'[8] Consequently, in their debased condition, lacking moral and intellectual status and thoroughly corrupt, the religions of the Christians, Jews, Muslims, and pagans are really all equivalent and all equally damaging to society.

John Toland (1670–1722) proceeds likewise, claiming the 'ambition of the clergy had not only corrupted, but even banish'd a large part of Christianity out of the world, leaving indeed the name, but perfectly destroying the thing'.[9] The bishops and other high churchmen 'miserably perverted the innocency and simplicity' of Christ and the apostles, he maintains, 'creating a proud, unyielding and unforgiving *imperium in imperio*' so that by the time of Julian the Apostate, in the later fourth century, the 'holy religion of Jesus' was hopelessly 'metamorphos'd into faction, superstition, hypocrisy and a mere worldly policy'.[10] Toland deemed it an almost universal error among Protestants critical of the inflated hierarchies of the Greek and Catholic churches to suppose the 'grandeur of the clergy had its rise from Constantine's liberality', contending that in reality ecclesiastics had 'long before divided the world into provinces, and that the dignity of bishops, patriarchs, and such like, was not only so reputable, but likewise so very lucrative, that the canvassing and contests about their elections occasion'd unspeakable animosities and divisions, nay most barbarous battery and bloodshed'.[11]

In perfecting their 'mysteries', held Spinoza, Christian priests employed the 'speculations of Aristotelians and Platonists, and they have made Scripture conform to these so as to avoid appearing to be the followers of heathens'.[12] But why, to use Spinoza's phrase, did mere credulity come to be everywhere 'looked upon as faith'? He argues that it is natural for men driven by emotion rather than reason and 'especially when they are helpless in danger that they all implore God's help with prayers and womanish tears'. In such times men reject reason 'while the delusions of the imagination, dreams, and other childish absurdities are taken to be the oracles of God. Indeed, they think that God, spurning the wise, has written his decrees not in Man's mind but in the entrails of beasts, or that by divine inspiration and

[8] Spinoza, *TTP*, preface; Berti, 'First Edition', 211, 219.
[9] Toland, *Appeal to Honest People*, 7–8, 10–11.
[10] Ibid. 17; Toland, *Christianity not Mysterious*, 159–60; Champion, *Pillars of Priestcraft*, 127, 133–4, 137.
[11] Toland, *Appeal to Honest People*, 4; see also Toland, *Christianity not Mysterious*, 170.
[12] Spinoza, *TTP*, preface; Juffermans, *Drie Perspectiven*, 306–7.

instigation these decrees are foretold by fools, madmen or birds. To such madness are men driven by their fears.'

For it is dread and anxiety, holds Spinoza, here following Hobbes, which engenders and foments superstition. Far from being, as some argue, a confused idea of deities or the Deity, superstition, he avers, stems from emotional frenzy, especially fear, and like all emotional disturbance assumes very varied and unstable forms. But no matter how unstable, the multitude being ruled by superstition more than anything else, superstition remains a constant source of power in the hands of those who know how to channel it to serve their ends by dressing it in pompous and impressive ceremonies. Hence whereas one of the main functions of the worthy and upright state, in Spinoza's philosophy, is 'vulgi iram et furorem cohibere' [to restrain the anger and fury of the common people], ambitious clergy see how to direct that irrational fury against their opponents. This deliberate manipulation of irrational fears and hopes was a theme often taken up later by radical writers, from John Trenchard in his *Natural History of Superstition* (1709) to the brooding French village priest Jean Meslier (1664–1729), writing around 1720, the latter speaking of the 'vain fears' instilled into the people by a relentlessly oppressive priesthood and especially the dread of frightful torments threatened by an implacable God in 'un enfer qui n'est point'.[13] As for the demons which preachers and artists alarm the common people with, and depict under the most hideous aspects, these are pure figments 'qui ne sauroient faire peur qu'aux enfans et qu'aux ignorans', the only real devils and enemies of the people, in his opinion, being the nobles, ecclesiastics, and the rich.[14]

Just as Spinoza portrays true Christianity as something that has lapsed, and Radicati claims the true 'religion of Christ differs not from the religion of nature' but unfortunately 'began to decline from the very time of the Apostles',[15] so Radicati contrasts 'true' Islam, 'whose worship' he deemed 'exceedingly pure', with the corruption by the 'Turkish priests' which followed so that the 'Moslems, notwithstanding the purity of their divine worship, have not failed to imbibe sundry very superstitious, nay even most ridiculous opinions'.[16] Radicati, who knew the Koran in translation and often quotes from Bayle's *Pensées diverses* and *Continuation*,[17] besides Fontenelle on oracles, Machiavelli, Sarpi, Spinoza, Algernon Sidney, Pufendorf, Barbeyrac, Toland, Tindal, Jean-Frédéric Bernard, and Collins, repeatedly compares Islam with Christianity, depicting priests in general, whether pagan, oriental, or Christian, as betrayers who instead of advancing the high ideals of their founders which would have caused them to be 'venerated unfeignedly, as public benefactors',[18] applied themselves instead 'to the forging of

[13] Meslier, *Testament*, i. 32; Champion, *Pillars of Priestcraft*, 160–1.

[14] Meslier, *Testament*, ii. 180–1; Ehrard, *L'Idée*, 521.

[15] Radicati, *Twelve Discourses*, 26, 45, 53; [Radicati], *La Religion Muhammédane*, 1; Wielema, *Filosofen*, 96.

[16] Radicati, *Succinct History*, 42–3.

[17] Radicati, *A Parallel*, 42; Venturi, *Alberti Radicati*, 152–4.

[18] Radicati, *Succinct History*, 23; Ferrone, *Intellectual Roots*, 55, 118, 161, 274–5.

ridiculous fables, abusing therewith the credulity of ignorant people, and extending their own power'.[19] Astounding the popular mind by preaching 'things inconceivable' and 'making childish, nay, scandalous processions', as well as 'bedecking temples with ornaments no less pompous than useless', and instituting sacred precincts in which the laity were not suffered 'to set foot', the better to 'perpetuate the veneration of the people for the sanctuary', the priesthood abandoned the 'very essential of their duty', namely 'instructing the people in matters of true faith and morality'—and Radicati's notion of morality, integrity, and 'true faith' was a wholly secular one—to the philosophers.[20]

This profoundly Spinozistic idea of progressive corruption of an originally pure and pristine religion by priests for their own purposes, leading to more and more layers of accretion, superfluous doctrine, ceremonies, and obfuscation, was exactly paralleled in the case of the Jews in the writings of the marquis d'Argens. During his years in Holland, in the later 1730s, d'Argens, who took a keen and mostly positive interest in the Jews as a people and tradition, while sharing the usual disdain of the Enlightenment for rabbis, Jewish observance, and especially the Talmud, became attuned to what was a real tension within the incipient Early Jewish Enlightenment, at any rate within western Sephardic Jewry, namely the growing clash in this period between orthodoxy and secularism, resulting especially from a growing taste for fashionable pursuits and pastimes outside the Jewish community. The perceived revolt against Jewish religious observance and rabbinic authority, in part taking the form of a resurgence of Neo-Karaism, became a central issue in Sephardic consciousness at this time.[21] D'Argens, needless to say, warmly welcomed all such signs of 'Karaism', leaving no doubt as to his own preferences among the variant strains of Judaism, as we see from his references to Karaites in his texts and his discussion of the ancient Sadducees in the fourth volume of the *Lettres juives*.

Like Bayle—by whom he was strongly influenced,[22]—Bolingbroke, and other early Enlightenment writers,[23] d'Argens portrays the ancient Sadducees as a sect of strict rationalists who reject immortality of the soul, angels, demons, Satan, and all spirits separate from bodies, as well as Heaven and Hell, and resurrection of the dead.[24] He also links these attitudes to Spinozism, the Karaites, and western European Neo-Karaites.[25] The original Karaites, or Scripturalists, were a medieval

19 Radicati, *Succinct History*; [Radicati], *Christianity*, preface pp. ix–x; Jacob, *Radical Enlightenment*, 185.

20 Radicati, *Succinct History*, 23; Radicati, *Twelve Discourses*, 69–70; Ricuperati, *Nella costellazione*, 200 n.

21 Kaplan, 'Intellectual Ferment', 288–314.

22 Bush, *Marquis d'Argens*, 54, 66–7; McKenna, 'Marquis d'Argens', 115, 121, 131–2.

23 On Bayle's and the Deists' usage of the term 'Sadduceeism', see Bayle, *Écrits*, 29; Yardeni, *Anti-Jewish Mentalities*, 203–4; Harrison, *'Religion' and the Religions*, 123; Young, *Religion and Enlightenment*, 172–3.

24 'Les Saducéens . . . ils nièrent la résurrection des corps et l'existence des anges; ils soutinrent que l'âme étoit mortelle, et qu'il n'y avoit d'esprit que Dieu seul', d'Argens, *Lettres juives*, iv. 49–50; see also Nadler, *Spinoza's Heresy*, 56, 175.

25 Hertzberg, *French Enlightenment*, 279; McKenna, 'Marquis d'Argens', 125; McKenna, 'D'Argens et les manuscrits', 109; Sutcliffe, *Judaism and Enlightenment*, 211.

sect for whom d'Argens displays an obvious if a rather artificial sympathy. They had rejected the Jewish Oral Law, the Talmud, as well as rabbinic authority and saw themselves as cultivating a purer Judaism than other Jews. Doubtless his positive appreciation of the Karaites owed much to the recent western Christian rediscovery of this topic, thanks to the labours of Richard Simon, though he may also have heard reports that in 1712, three modern Dutch Sephardic heretics—David Mendes Henriques (alias David Almanza) and the brothers Aaron and Isaac Dias da Fonseca—had been excommunicated in Amsterdam for 'following the sect of Karaites and acting as they do, entirely denying the Oral Law, which is the foundation and underpinning of our Holy Law'.[26]

It was no accident that on that occasion the Amsterdam rabbis employed the same formula of excommunication, their most severe ban, as they had used for the expulsion of Spinoza from the synagogue in 1656. This same threat of the *Karraitas* (i.e. Karaites), moreover, was perceived as a considerable danger to rabbinic authority at the beginning of the eighteenth century also by David Nieto (1654–1728), rabbi of the Bevis Marks Sephardi synagogue in London who noted that 'en este siglo han aumentado los que se desverguençan y hablan mal de su explicacion' [in this century the numbers of those who are shameless and speak against their [i.e. the rabbis'] interpretation have increased].[27] Nieto was a progressive rabbi by the standards of his time, one who expressly approved of Jews studying Cartesianism, and the New Philosophy more generally, while himself favouring the 'Newtonian philosophy'; but, at the same time, he emphatically denounced 'Sadduceeism'—effectively the new trend of 'Deism' which both Christians and Jews then considered broadly equivalent to the ancient Jewish sect—as a 'diabolico veneno, negando premio, y pena espiritual, la immortalidad del alma, y la tradicion de los sabios' [diabolical venom, denying spiritual reward and punishment, immortality of the soul, and the tradition of the rabbis].[28]

Originally, Judaism, suggested d'Argens, was a pure religion unencumbered with irrational dogmas and ceremonies. This pure core had been championed by the Sadducees and, then, the medieval and early modern Karaites, anti-rabbinic and anti-Talmudic reformers who strove to revert to that pure religion; in his day, the age of the Enlightenment, a new 'Reform Judaism' which would thoroughly prune traditional Judaism, using reason, was again conceivable via a Karaite resurgence. In his *Lettres juives*, his fictitious 'Rabbi Isaac' in Constantinople—who, before long, defects from rabbinic Judaism and joins the Karaites—assures his Sephardic friend, visiting Paris, by letter, that all the sects which today divide the Christians ['les Nazaréens'] had earlier been seen among the Jews: 'les Sadducéens étoient en Judée', he writes, what the Deists are today in Paris.[29] In their

26 Kaplan, '"Karaites" in the Early Eighteenth Century', 238–9; Kaplan, 'Intellectual Ferment', 310–14; see also Popkin, 'Les Caraïtes', 143–4.

27 Nieto, *Matteh Dan*, fo. 1ᵛ; Kaplan, '"Karaites" in the Early Eighteenth Century', 276.

28 Nieto, *Matteh Dan*, preface and fo. 1ᵛ; Ruderman, *Jewish Enlightenment*, 185.

29 D'Argens, *Lettres juives*, iv. 51; Bush, *Marquis d'Argens*, 115, 118, 128–30.

correspondence, the Talmud increasingly emerges as a corrupt and oppressive instrument of religious obscurantism responsible for debasing and perverting Sadducean Judaism and then Karaism. The Talmud, contends Rabbi Isaac, 's'éloigne en tout de la première simplicité de notre religion'.[30] 'Considères, mon cher Isaac', he urges his friend, in a subsequent volume, 'combien les écrits des rabbins ont été pernicieux aux Juifs.'[31]

D'Argens, knowingly or unknowingly, wholly obscures the fact that the authentic medieval and early modern Karaism was, in reality, far less rationalist than Scripturalist and fundamentalist, denying the whole interpretative tradition of rabbinic Judaism not from any philosophic standpoint but 'in the name of Biblical literalism', more in the style, as indeed Simon understood, of Protestant reformers reacting to pre-Reformation Catholicism than eighteenth-century Deists combating priestly obscurantism.[32] But if d'Argens's 'Karaites' were a total fiction in one sense, they mirrored contemporary Jewish social reality in another, by echoing the views of some of the new rebels against rabbinic authority and tradition, the 'Neo-Karaites' among the Sephardim of north-west Europe, and by echoing also real fears and anxieties about the challenge of Karaite 'reform' felt by Nieto and other rabbis.

The key point is that in the early eighteenth century, the term 'Karaite', while still partly referring to the Near Eastern and East European Karaites of the past, was also clearly beginning to be used in a quite new sense, to designate not biblical literalism but rather precisely the incipient Deistic tendency among the Jews, those calling for emancipation from the burdens and responsibilities of Jewish observance and the Oral Law.[33] Hence it has been argued, regarding the excommunication of David Almanza and the brothers Dias de Fonseca, in Amsterdam, in 1712, that they were less adherents of genuine Karaism, their knowledge of which was meagre in the extreme, than of an idealized abstraction—of 'Karaites' as 'Juifs épurez', as formulated in late seventeenth-century Christian scholarly literature, particularly by Richard Simon in his *Histoire critique du Vieux Testament*. In any case, Simon's, and now much more subversively d'Argens's, 'Karaites' upheld precisely such a purified, rational, and critical Judaism, spurning what seemed to them the 'false' and superstitious traditions of the rest of Jewry.[34]

If d'Argens's *Lettres juives* and *Lettres cabalistiques* were primarily instruments of general subversion aimed at traditional structures of thought and authority, drawing widely on Bayle and Fontenelle, and the French clandestine manuscripts, several of which, including Du Marsais's *Examen*, he has been shown to have used, this does not mean that d'Argens did not also nurture a genuine interest in the

[30] D'Argens, *Lettres juives*, ii. 35.

[31] Ibid. v. 68; Bush, *Marquis d'Argens*, 125, 128; see further on the issue of so-called 'Karaitism' in early eighteenth century west European Sephardic Jewish history, Petuchowski, *Theology of Haham David Nieto*, 7–8; Kaplan, 'Intellectual Ferment', 311–12.

[32] Popkin, 'Les Caraïtes', 140–1; see Walzer et al., *Jewish Political Tradition*, i. 249.

[33] Gaster, *History*, 104, 111; Kaplan, '"Karaites" in the Early Eighteenth Century', 274–6.

[34] Kaplan, 'Intellectual Ferment', 313.

possibility of Jewish renewal and reform on enlightened lines as well as real compassion for a people he believed had been continually wronged, persecuted, and slaughtered by their Christian neighbours over many centuries. Indeed, in his own personal career, both in Holland and subsequently, in the 1740s, in Berlin, d'Argens seems to have tried to counter the irrationality of anti-Jewish prejudice and encourage the onset of just such a Jewish Enlightenment and reform movement not only through his writing but by fostering contacts with Jews on an entirely new, secular 'philosophical' basis.

Among the latter, in the early 1740s, was Aaron Solomon Gumpertz (1723–69), scion of a prominent family of Brandenburg court Jews who served as d'Argens's secretary and, later, in 1751, gained a university doctorate in medicine at Frankfurt an der Oder. Gumpertz was indeed among the founding figures of the Jewish Enlightenment, a sophisticated man, if largely self-taught, seriously interested in contemporary thought, who had acquired French and Latin besides some mathematics and natural philosophy and continually wrestled throughout his adult life with the difficulties of reconciling enlightenment with Jewish tradition and loyalty to his own people.[35] He also acted for a time as Maupertuis's secretary, at the Berlin academy. It is significant that it was he who, in the mid 1740s, first introduced the young Moses Mendelssohn (1729–86) to the fraught world of contemporary philosophy.[36]

The concern with 'true faith and morality' buttressing d'Argens's vision of an inner Jewish tradition altogether superior to rabbinic Judaism which could be revived and which, in turn, would revive Jewish life itself is closely related not just to convictions about the morally, socially, and intellectually vitiating character of organized religion underlying much of Radicati's, as of Spinoza's, Blount's, Toland's, Collins', Tindal's, and Johann Lorenz Schmidt's attacks on 'priestcraft', but also to their notion of a future role for a purified 'natural religion'. For they accepted that the common people can never be philosophers and can only learn morality from religious teachers. Hence, the final outcome of the radical attack on theology and priestcraft, should it succeed, would not, as they conceived, be the overthrow of organized religion but rather its drastic reform, to align it with their secular principles of equality, equity, and 'natural religion', and also subordinate it, as much as possible, to the political sovereign.[37]

The more irrational their teachings, held Radicati, the greater the priesthood's ability 'to keep the vulgar in subjection and obedience'. Priesthoods in all places and times, Christian, Muslim, Jewish, pagan, and oriental in his view, have acted on the principle that 'the more a thing seemed impossible, the more it was a proper object of faith'.[38] A fervent democrat, Radicati defines the 'stupid vulgar' not as ordinary folk as such but rather Spinozistically, to include that part of the people who blindly

[35] Sorkin, *Berlin Haskalah*, 56; Feiner, *Jewish Enlightenment*, 42–3.

[36] Altmann, *Moses Mendelssohn*, 23–5, 41–2; Sorkin, 'The Early *Haskalah*', 19–25.

[37] Champion, *Pillars of Priestcraft*, 234–6; Ricuperati, *Nella costellazione*, 200.

[38] Radicati, *Twelve Discourses*, 160; [Radicati], *Christianity*, preface p. x.

defer to priests together with all the princes, nobles, and 'pretenders to learning who in matters of religion have no more knowledge than the vulgar' and similarly avoid secular modes of thinking.[39] Priests have always required, he adds, that no one but themselves should investigate matters of faith, everyone else being required only to venerate their dogmas 'as indisputable, even tho they shock'd reason, and were contradictory in themselves'. Christianity, held Meslier, has been the strongest and most successful of religions but also, and for that very reason, dogmatically the most divided and the most ridiculous in doctrine: for there has been no other faith, he claims, 'de si absurde dans ses principes et dans ses principaux points que celle-là', nor so contrary 'à la nature même et à la droite raison'.[40]

Freethinkers, in short, followed Spinoza in depicting priesthoods as professional agents of prejudice, uncritical thinking, and ignorance, teaching the people that 'to obtain the favour of God', as Radicati puts it, 'it was absolutely necessary to believe the most unaccountable propositions, and the most evident contradictions'.[41] Toland held that 'priestcraft' is the very reverse of true religion; in his history of the Druids, written in 1718, he defines 'priestcraft' as the 'design'd abuse and reverse of religion, (for superstition is only religion misunderstood)',[42] and priests men 'who in most parts of the world are hir'd to keep the people in error, being commonly back'd by the example and authority of the magistrate'.[43] Meslier, going still further, argues that all known religions are evidently false since none offers any clear, cogent evidence of the truth of its teaching of a kind any clear-thinking person should accept. He also insists on 'la ridiculité de ces prétendus miracles' related in the New Testament, stressing 'la grossièreté et la bassesse' of the style in which the Gospels are composed.[44] To this Collins added that so ambitious are religious sects to expand their power that they not only reverse 'true religion', turning it into superstition, but also condone 'vice and wickedness to as great a degree as they can conveniently'. For by that means 'they are sure to engage all the rogues and vicious (and by consequence the fools, who will ever be led by them) in their party', thereby growing continually stronger.[45]

While Radical Enlightenment from its inception in the 1650s and 1660s was suffused with vehement republican, anti-monarchical tendencies, and a stress on human equality and personal liberty, and aspired to the wholesale reform of social institutions, philosophy, scholarship, and science, it nevertheless remains true that its chief preoccupation during its first century and a half, and the theme with which it was most preoccupied in print, was its relentless war on ecclesiastical authority, theological ways of viewing the world, and religion seen as an instrument of social and political organization and repression. This seems understandable given the vast reach of ecclesiastical authority and, to their minds, suffocating centrality of

[39] [Radicati], *Christianity*, 2; Radicati, *Twelve Discourses*, 203–4; Alberti, *Alberto Radicati*, 78; Ricuperati, *Nella costellazione*, 128, 171, 200 n.

[40] Meslier, *Testament*, i. 31; Ehrard, *L'Idée*, 442.

[41] [Radicati], *Christianity*, preface p. x; Harrison, *'Religion' and the Religions*, 83.

[42] Toland, *Specimen*, 9; Champion, *Pillars of Priestcraft*, 168.

[43] Toland, *Specimen*, 140.

[44] Meslier, *Testament*, i. 97–101, 117, 174.

[45] Collins, *Discourse of Free-Thinking*, 117.

theological claims in pre-modern European society and culture. To embark on root and branch renewal in the fields the Radical Enlightenment sought to reform both seemed, and was, impossible without first curtailing theological ways of explaining the world and dismantling priestly power.

Accordingly, the radicals' efforts to shake the pillars of 'priestcraft' were frequently conceived as part of an age-old process, of reason fighting ecclesiastical authority in alliance with social hierarchy and oppressive government, reaching back far beyond the beginnings of Christianity, indeed over the millennia to the remotest times, an epic contest viewed as central to the inherent logic of human history. This was Condorcet's endless war of 'la philosophie contre les oppresseurs de l'humanité', something he thought destined to last for as long as there are priests and kings on earth.[46] While earlier, in Blount, for example, it is pagan religion and priestcraft which is chiefly unmasked and Christianity is taken to task only indirectly,[47] later there is a more explicit tendency to reduce all organized religions with an established priesthood to a single category. We see this not least in Toland and other English so-called 'Deists'- a misnomer, actually, since neither Toland, Blount, nor 'that great and good man Mr. Collins', as Radicati dubbed him, did profess 'natural religion and a Creator' as distinct from atheism.[48]

Promoting 'good sense in the world', according to Collins, is something best done, as he remarks in a letter to Des Maizeaux of September 1721, by employing 'the philosophical works' of 'some superior genius [like Cicero] to hinder it from being hissed out of the world by the knaves and fools'. Cicero's works he thought particularly 'applicable to all sorts of folly and superstition by those who have eyes to see and ears to hear; and which must have a good effect on many from the establish'd credit and authority of the author', such clearing away being essentially the same task in his day, it appeared to him, as it had been in Roman times.[49] Ancient and modern credulity and ignorance was all of one piece. This tendency to unite all of history around the battle against superstition whether ancient or modern, pre- or post-Christian, is equally evident in Radicati, Meslier, Jean-Frédéric Bernard, and d'Argens.[50] 'Priestcraft' is interpreted as a method of accruing power and authority over the common people by capturing their emotions and minds with 'fables', false hopes, and myths, dividing all mankind into believers and 'infidels', the former to be saved and the latter damned, and then requiring believers to institutionalize priestly authority and persecute and suppress unbelievers and heretics.

Priests like to eulogize the simple faith of the humble. But according to Meslier, the simple 'faith' which is the foundation of all religions, and which priests urge

[46] Condorcet, *Esquisse*, 66.

[47] Berman, 'Disclaimers', 260, 262; Ellenzweig, 'Faith of Unbelief', 43.

[48] Radicati, *Twelve Discourses*, 2 n.; Gawlick, 'Epikur bei den Deisten', 324, 329; Taranto, *Du déisme à l'athéisme*, 16, 18–19, 399–400, 432.

[49] BL, MS 4282, fo. 184. Collins to Des Maizeaux, 26 Sept. 1721; Champion, *Pillars of Priestcraft*, 184.

[50] Wade, *Clandestine Organization*, 68; Harrison, *'Religion' and the Religions*, 163.

their congregations to cherish, is in reality nothing but a 'principe d'erreurs, d'illusions et d'impostures'.[51] Intellectually, such a faith is not just contemptible but also actually something highly prejudicial to every individual and most of all to society collectively. Furthermore, the simple faith of humility was also considered by the radicals to be fundamentally wrong morally: for it lay at the very heart of the secular morality of the Radical Enlightenment to insist that 'salvation' must be available to all and not reserved for some. If God really created men so that some should be happy and others unhappy in the afterlife, contended Radicati, in order to impress all men with his power, 'je soutiens qu'il auroit été injuste et cruel'.[52]

For the radicals, the psychological mechanism inspiring religious persecution, and the enforcement of dogma, in fact had little to do with the theological content of any particular faith. Toland believed the clergy's age-old pride, ambition, and a spirit of 'emulation', and not Christianity *per se*, was the 'real source of all those heresies, which make so bulky and black a catalogue in ecclesiastical history'.[53] In most societies, he supposed, secular authority as a rule showed very little interest in fomenting intolerance, but the 'clergy (which the superstitious are always readier to obey than their magistrates)' found the suppression of heresy a tool essential to their acquisition of power, and ability to dominate, so that 'seditious adherence to priests against the magistrates' was in fact the 'real source of most persecutions'.[54]

Antiquity, it has been cogently argued, knew nothing of positive toleration of the kind later introduced by the western Enlightenment.[55] During the two centuries prior to Constantine the Great, the Roman empire practiced a prolonged and relentless persecution of the Christians, torturing and killing sizeable numbers with traumatic effects on subsequent generations. Acutely aware of this, Bayle and the Radical Enlightenment, unlike Voltaire, Gibbon, and the moderate Deists, did not seek to characterize religious intolerance and persecution as such as something exclusively or characteristically Christian, even though they mostly considered Christianity more intolerant than the rest. Rather, like Spinoza, they contended that priests of all religions, ancient and modern, habitually seek to mobilize popular rage against dissidents, that is the free and independent-minded who oppose their dogmas, suppressing them, in particular, Radicati notes, by labelling anyone resisting their pronouncements an 'atheist'.[56] Those designated 'atheists' by the 'vulgar, and by those whose interest it is to decry them', he objects, usually in fact 'admit a first cause under the names of God, Nature, Eternal Being, Matter, universal Motion or Soul. Such were', he continued, 'Democritus, Epicurus, Diagoras, Lucian, Socrates, Anexagoras, Seneca, Hobbes, Blount, Spinosa, Vanini, Saint Evremond, Bayle, Collins and in general, all that go under the name of speculative Atheists'.[57] Like Spinoza, Toland, and Collins, Radicati himself considered the 'power of

[51] Meslier, *Testament*, i. 66.

[52] [Radicati], *Sermon prêché*, 21; Carpanetto and Ricuperati, *Italy*, 318.

[53] Toland, *Appeal to Honest People*, 5.

[54] Ibid. 6; Champion, *Pillars of Priestcraft*, 146, 149.

[55] Drake, *Constantine*, 20–3.

[56] Radicati, *Twelve Discourses*, 11–12.

[57] Ibid. 11, 189; Berman, 'Disclaimers', 270.

Nature' the 'very same as that of God, whose right is eternal and consequently unalterable'.[58]

Since all human history, held the radical enlighteners, is a ceaseless struggle of 'reason' against a grasping, power-hungry, and malicious priestly class, orchestrating an ignorant, fearful, and readily enraged populace, they increasingly tended to conflate all periods of history into one single continuum rather than accept traditional notions representing history since Christ as divided spiritually from what transpired before. Contradicting Christian claims, they refused to see that anything of any overriding significance occurred with the rise of the Christian Church, the basic story continuing subsequently, just as before, even if the priesthood from time to time modify the style and content of their 'fables' and ceremonies, instituting fresh 'miracles' and more refined myths. 'Take my word for it', avers Alciphron, Bishop Berkeley's literary recreation mimicking the opinions of Collins, Shaftesbury, and other English 'Deists', composed at Providence, Rhode Island, in the years 1729–31, 'priests of all religions are the same: wherever there are priests there will be priestcraft; and wherever there is priestcraft there will be a persecuting spirit, which they never fail to exert to the utmost of their power against all those who have the courage to think for themselves, and will not submit to be hoodwinked and manacled by their reverend leaders.'[59]

Over time, priestly techniques grew in sophistication but their methodology remained largely the same. Only in this light, it was thought, can the reality of human existence and society be properly grasped. Where the priests of pagan Greece deceived the people by combining magnificent ritual, bogus oracles, superstitious reports, and 'par des possédés que le peuple prenoit toujours pour des illuminés', explained the Amsterdam radical Jean-Frédéric Bernard, the Christian clergy later used similar methods albeit with greater expertise and more elaborate doctrines. The Christian clergy, like their predecessors, sought to convert the people 'pour leurs intérêts', and to make themselves indispensable to the political sovereign, and for this end have always filled the people's heads with meaningless talk of 'miracles', wonders, prophecies, and demons. The same has been, and will be, practiced always and by all religions, asserts the radical Bernard, 'et tant qu'il y aura des hommes'.[60]

Theologians exploit all who 'ont la foiblesse de les écouter', cunningly inculcating the people with credulous superstition, prejudice, rage, and hatred, fabricating prodigies and miracles; 'ils en faisoient ensuite des descriptions extraordinaires', not forgetting to include phrases and formulations which make no sense whatever but perfectly serve to instil awe and wonder in the devout.[61] Error thus put down deep roots, and finally, rulers willingly or unwillingly endorsed such pretensions as it was in their interest to do and it became impossible any longer to resist the priests'

[58] Radicati, *Twelve Discourses*, 190; Ferrone, *Intellectual Roots*, 55, 118; Taranto, *Du déisme à l'athéisme*, 143.

[59] Taranto, *Du déisme à l'athéisme*, 250–5; Berkeley, *Alciphron*, 27; Olscamp, *Moral Philosophy*, 215–22.

[60] [Bernard], *Réflexions morales*, 296.

[61] Ibid. 295.

doctrines 'sans devenir criminel d'état'.[62] Where rulers refused to comply willingly they were either compelled to do so under threat of being overthrown, or actually toppled by priests arousing the enraged populace.

In the first centuries AD, reluctant potentates thus had to 'go over to the strongest side', as Radicati puts it, 'and become Christians'. Among them, 'Constantine submitted to be baptized';[63] and with even emperors, henceforth, subject to clerical sway, only the pope, as pontifical sovereign, remained free of clerical supervision which, in turn, encouraged the papacy to aspire to become 'absolute master of mankind', despite the fact that 'all the authority of the Church over Christian princes and nations is founded', according to Radicati, invoking the sixteenth-century Spanish Dominican Las Casas' harrowing account of the 'destruction' of the natives of the New World, 'upon just the same right as the Spaniards had to butcher the Americans' with a view 'to get their wealth into *their* hands'.[64]

Insisting there is no spiritually significant difference between the pre- and post-Christian eras of human history, or between the Christians or non-Christians, meant that the veritable theme of mankind's history, namely the endless struggle between 'partisans of reason', on the one side, and Radicati's 'sticklers for the sacerdotal profession', on the other—everywhere continues now as it always has. While strife and discord among men have many causes, 'the clergy's usurpations' are proclaimed by the radicals the most important 'cause of all those divisions which have been so long reigning among men, and of those distinctions for which the several sects are, to this very day, furiously contesting'.[65]

A subplot to this theme, again introduced by Spinoza, in the *Tractatus theologico-politicus* where he suggests that 'sacrilegious men' had in ancient times 'adulterated Scripture in many places',[66] and taken up by Toland and Collins, was the idea that it belonged from the outset to the technique of priestly fabrication to pass off as authentic and worthy of the utmost reverence what Collins calls 'pious frauds', that is forged or doctored foundational texts the fraudulence of which no layman, other than the odd philosopher, even suspects. Since priests originally concoct articles of religion, 'and mankind are so stupid as to let them have success', as Collins puts it, 'how can we receive books of bulk (such as the Fathers and Councils) that have gone thro' their hands, and lay any stress or dependence on their authority?'[67] Such doubts as to authenticity were then deliberately fomented not just to undermine the authority and status of such key writings and promulgations, like those of the Church Fathers and early councils, but to undermine also the (Lockean) idea of an authentic and unbroken chain of Christian tradition reaching back to the apostles. Rather than trusting in the received canon of Scripture and other authoritative

62 [Bernard], *Réflexions morales* 295.
63 Radicati, *Twelve Discourses*, 80.
64 Ibid. 43–4; Symcox, *Victor Amadeus II*, 215–16.
65 Radicati, *Twelve Discourses*; Tortarolo, *L'Illuminismo*, 122.
66 Spinoza, *Opera*, iii. 97; Klever, *Definitie*, 198.
67 [Collins], *Priestcraft*, 46; Collins, *Discourse of Free-Thinking*, 91–5; Collins, *Discourse of the Grounds*, 45, 138–9; Gay, *Enlightenment*, i. 378; Champion, *Republican Learning*, 201–3.

texts, radical writers thought it more realistic to assume that 'where they have had an opportunity', as Collins puts it, the theologians 'have laid out their natural talents in alterations, interpolations, and rasures' rather than let anything come down to us 'pure and unmixt'.[68]

Scarcely less grave was the charge of systematic political manipulation against the interests of society generally. In his culminating attack on priestcraft, in the *Tractatus theologico-politicus*, Spinoza maintains that nothing is more fatal 'for both religion and the state than to grant ministers of religion the right to issue decrees or to concern themselves with state business'.[69] For once the clergy obtain a role in government all political stability will end and doctrine and schism will be deployed to engineer more and more violent forms of faction-forming, ambition, persecution, and tyranny. Spinoza ends this his most politically engaged book by alluding to the hard-line Calvinist *coup d'état* in the United Provinces which overthrew the Oldenbarnevelt regime in The Hague in 1618. Not only can freedom of thought be granted without endangering political stability, true piety, or the right of the sovereign power, he asserts here, but it *must* be granted if these are to be conserved. For when the opposite course is followed, and dissenters' opinions are suppressed by those who enforce what the people deem doctrinal rectitude, 'upright dealing and honest loyalty are corrupted, flatterers and traitors are favoured, and opponents of freedom exult because their anger has won acceptance and they have converted the sovereign authorities to their creed, of which they count as the interpreters'.[70]

Adoption of this perspective soon created a whole new and rich literature of political anticlericalism. A tract published in London in 1709, probably by Tindal, accusing the Non-Jurors, and all the 'highflying zealots', of the Anglican Church of plotting counter-revolution and the restoration of the Stuarts, likened their activities to those of the Danish clergy preceding Frederik III's *coup d'état* of 1660. On that occasion, the kingdom of Denmark-Norway was drastically remodelled on a new, hereditary, and fully absolute monarchical basis, the country's previous mixed constitution being entirely set aside.[71] In their treacherous scheming to restore absolutism, 'endeavouring to give up all the British libertys', British Jacobites, charged Tindal, 'have but one excuse in common with the Danes which is that what they have done has been at the instigation of priests, too many of whom have been everywhere active in enslaving their country; and 'tis notorious that by their means, most of the nations of Europe, who within a century had the same libertys, the same Gothick constitution that we enjoy, are reduc'd to a most miserable slavery'.[72]

'These profess'd enemys of toleration', as Tindal calls the Lutheran orthodox and Anglican high-flyers, were depicted as an imminent counter-revolutionary danger to the Revolution Settlement of 1688–9 in Britain. The underlying motive of such

[68] [Collins], *Priestcraft*, 45–6; Taranto, *Du déisme à l'athéisme*, 73–5.

[69] Spinoza, *TTP* 275–6.

[70] (My translation) ibid. 229; Spinoza, *Opera*, iii. 247.

[71] Hope, *German and Scandinavian Protestantism*, 78, 102; Laursen, 'Censorship', 102.

[72] [Tindal?], *New Catechism*, 9–10; Toland, *Appeal to Honest People*, 46; Champion, *Pillars of Priestcraft*, 174–5.

'wicked priests' in seeking 'to enslave their country, by preaching up the absolute power of the prince over the subjects', affirms Toland, was that the monarch would thereby ultimately 'become their subject'.[73] Sweden had followed Denmark down the melancholy route to royal absolutism, the crown being freed from accountability to the Estates, acquiring unlimited prerogatives there, in 1680–2, again allegedly by intercession of the clergy. The 'kings of Denmark and Sweden', comments Toland, 'who not very long ago got the liberties of their subjects surrender'd into their hands, did successively employ their priests to procure this absolute power, as they still make use of 'em to maintain it'.[74] Here was a dire threat confronting the whole Protestant world.

In Catholic Europe by contrast, keeping the 'vulgar in subjection and obedience' required the fabrication of more and more ecclesiastically approved 'miracles', moments of general consternation being especially conducive, allegedly, to such spiritual guidance. Radicati recounts that during the failed siege of Turin, in 1706, one of Louis XIV's heaviest setbacks, a community of monks—the Bernardoni—'gave out' that the Madonna had stationed herself 'upon the cupola of their church and with her hand repelled a number of bombs, which were ready to fall on her temple'. These 'good monks' had then cleverly hung up several bombs in the chapel of our lady 'to authorize this most impertinent story', rendering the populace 'so fully persuaded' that 'our lady' had intervened to thwart the French that all doubters and sceptics were obliged to fall in with it and 'every year on 7 September, the court, senate, magistrates and nobility, and the whole body of the clergy go in procession to this good lady to give thanks'.[75]

Priests whether Catholic or Protestant were regularly compared in radical rhetoric with lawyers and doctors, as manipulators of popular credulity and vendors of magical formulae couched in incomprehensible terminology, in the Catholic case, naturally, in Latin. Indeed, priests, Collins suggests sardonically, should surely be blamed somewhat more than either doctors or lawyers: 'for it is manifest that all priests, except the orthodox, are hir'd to lead men into mistakes. Whereas there are no lawyers nor physicians set apart and hir'd to defend mistaken opinions in those professions.' Doctors and lawyers, moreover, have the same interest in success as their clients whereas, by contrast, where the layman is anxious to know the truth, the 'priest desires to have him of his opinion'.[76] Hence, 'Popish, Mahometan, Lutheran, Jewish, Siamese, and Presbyterian priests', unlike doctors who study medicine as such, 'study their several systems' rather than divinity in general.[77]

Even so, society's three leading professions continued to have much in common. Collins offers one of his acerbic jokes in *A Discourse of Free-Thinking* (1713) about

[73] [Tindal?], *New Catechism*, 14–15; Toland, *Appeal to Honest People*, 46; Champion, *Republican Learning*, 141–2.

[74] Toland, *Appeal to Honest People*, 47–8.

[75] [Radicati], *Christianity*, preface pp. xviii–xix; Ferrone, *Intellectual Roots*, 118; Symcox, *Victor Amadeus II*, 149–52.

[76] Collins, *Discourse of Free-Thinking*, 109.

[77] Ibid. 110.

someone who enquires of an inhabitant of New Jersey, a colony then inhabited by a mere handful of whites, some of whom were Quakers, 'whether they had any lawyers among them?'; and, on being told 'no', nor any physicians or priests, the gentleman exclaimed: 'O happy country! That must be a paradise.' Answering this gibe, Newton's acolyte Bentley indignantly suggested that the British crown surely might consider deporting Collins and all the 'Deists' and, after depositing them for a spell in the 'purgatory of the Spanish American mines', send them on to 'their *Paradise of New Jersey*, where neither priest, nor physician, nor lawyer can molest them'.[78]

The radicals' continually alleging parallels between ancient religions, once venerated but now long scorned as idolatrous and redundant, and the Christian churches deeply offended, by insinuating Christianity might one day seem as derisory to nearly everyone as these ancient and many eastern cults now appeared. Much to Bentley's annoyance, Collins habitually referred to the 'Oracular temples or Churches of the Pagans' and, even worse, placed the Talapoins of Siam 'upon a level with the whole clergy of England', to highlight this general parallel.[79] Declaring the ancient Athenians 'the most civilised people the world ever saw', Radicati judged that if Athens was once the site of sacred cults characterized by 'many fooleries and religious extravagancies introduced there by the administrators of things sacred', and 'if these knowing, these polished people, I say, could fall into horrible idolatry, if their understandings could be sullied and contaminated with ideas no less foolish than superstitious, by the artifice of their knavish priests, ought we to wonder if we now see in the world, errors altogether as gross and as impious, which are yet abundantly better authorised than those of the Greeks?'[80]

An amusing literary conceit, published in 1730, bracketing together the secret ambitions and pretensions of all who claim priestly authority in society, by an anonymous radical writer, styling himself 'l'Abbé de Charle-Livry', was a satirical dialogue (sometimes attributed to Jean-Frédéric Bernard)[81] set in Heaven where various gods and prophets debate different stratagems for further extending priestly power on earth. 'Jupiter' bitterly regrets his loss of authority among men but finds fresh courage in the irreconcilable schisms among Christians and helpful advice of 'Mahomet'. Despite the efforts 'des cabales de philosophes contre les deux Jupiters', that is himself and the Christian God who has usurped his throne, the Jupiter of ancient Rome has not abandoned hope yet that one day his sway on earth will revive. Assured by 'Mahomet' that the Christians cannot resolve their divisions and, teaching dogmas every bit as ridiculous as those of their rivals, cannot attack Muslims or pagans 'sur l'usage de la fable et de l'erreur', 'Jupiter', much heartened, proposes a tripartite alliance in which he, 'Mahomet', and, once they see they cannot win on their own, the Christians join forces to share their sway

[78] Ibid. 108; Bentley, *Remarks*, 30, 33, 47.

[79] Bentley, *Remarks*, 25, 45; Collins, *Discourse of Free-Thinking*, 19; Harrison, *'Religion' and the Religions*, 80.

[80] Radicati, *Succinct History*, 25–6.

[81] Cioranescu, *Bibliographie*, i. 328; Jacob, *Radical Enlightenment*, 212.

on earth by collaborating behind the scenes. Delighted by this suggestion, especially since, at Europe's courts, concluding alliances containing secret articles the public knows nothing about is 'présentement fort à la mode', 'Mahomet' predicts their alliance will have a great impact 'et je crois que ce monde ne tarderoit pas d'être à nous'.[82]

In the mid eighteenth century, Morelly was another who fiercely condemned priestcraft. Despite showing no trace of Diderot's influence and retaining some Deistic tendencies—being hesitant, for example, about whether finally to accept or reject the immateriality and immortality of the soul—Morelly was a militant radical even in his early pre-republican phase, a writer influenced not only by Machiavelli, Fontenelle, Bayle, Shaftesbury, and Condillac but also specifically Du Marsais.[83] Being convinced, like Radicati, Meslier, and Mably before him, that institutionalized social inequality prevents all true liberty, he too insisted, in 1751, that persecution and intolerance are not inherent in Christian teaching as such, or that of any particular faith, but are rather integral to the practice, psychology, and interests of priesthoods generally.[84] He held that ecclesiastical authority is a form of 'dominion' the common people fervently believe is disinterested but which, in fact, is quite the reverse: for it refuses to tolerate loss either of followers, or of sway over them, and seeks to maintain its grip precisely by inspiring in the faithful a fierce hatred and fear of, as well as desire to persecute, other creeds.[85]

By curbing priestly power, radical *philosophes* expected many solid benefits to accrue to humankind, in particular an end to persecution, lessening of despotism, freedom of thought, extending of liberty, and diminution of superstitious credulity. But how exactly was 'priestcraft' to be combated? Firmly subordinating the clergy to the secular sovereign, in matters of morality, education, and even doctrine, as well as politics, is much insisted on in Spinoza's *Tractatus theologico-politicus* and was always central to radical plans. In Catholic lands, from Giannone, Doria, and Radicati onwards, radical writers concocted schemes to diminish the size, property, and economic resources of the clergy.[86] Morelly, in 1751, recommended that the secular authority should impose a strict limit on the number of clergy in each diocese 'necessary for divine service and the instruction of the people', and a cap on ordaining new priests, limiting the clergy's size to the number of vacancies on the authorized list.[87] He also recommends that all the monastic orders, masculine and feminine, which 'la sotise des siècles passés' had so prodigiously enriched, should forfeit both their property and their autonomy, and have their numbers drastically pruned back, with no more property remaining in the hands of the parish and monastic clergy than sufficed for their subsistence. The residue, he urged, should be taken charge of by the state and employed for the upkeep of hospitals and other charitable ends.[88]

82 [Bernard], *Dialogues critiques*, 300–1.

83 Coe, 'Le Philosophe, Morelly', i. 40–1, 61, 158 n.

84 [Morelly], *Le Prince*, ii. 43; Wagner, *Morelly*, 146–7, 173, 356; Dagen, *L'Histoire*, 200–1; Ferrone, *Intellectual Roots*, 275.

85 [Morelly], *Le Prince*, ii. 44, 47.

86 Tortarolo, *L'Illuminismo*, 37, 122–3.

87 [Morelly], *Le Prince*, i. 136.

88 Ibid. 138–41.

It seemed necessary not just to expose priestly ambition and manipulation, and what Collins called 'the forgerys of priests', but also to persuade ordinary laymen to consider more sympathetically the reasons of 'heretics' who question, from a philosophical standpoint, religious doctrines, and popular beliefs and the methods by which these are imposed on society and dissenters are silenced. Since it was only 'those ridiculous, dissolute and barbarous methods of adoring the Eternal Creator' which induced 'philosophers to contemn the religion of the vulgar' in the first place, held Radicati, it is entirely 'unjust to charge them with atheism for their so doing; since it is abundantly more probable, that they conceived a detestation and horror to opinions so very gross, and so incompatible with the nature and essence of the true God, thro' their own sublime ideas of Him, than because they deny his existence'.[89]

Radicati, an inveterate foe of all Inquisition, thought it especially vital that dissidents should no longer be labelled 'atheists' but instead be called 'Deists', 'there being no such thing as an atheist in the world, as the ignorant imagine, and the crafty priests would have believed when they brand with this odious name such as detect their impostures, with the design to expose them to the rage and fury of an incensed populace'.[90] Those denounced by clergy and the people as 'atheists' in reality comprised many excellent men, Bayle and Le Clerc among them. All these thinkers, held Radicati, insinuating his materialist conception of Nature as God, very much as in Spinoza's (and Toland's and Collins') sense, 'admit a first cause under the name of God, Nature, Eternal Being, Matter, universal motion or soul'.[91] This was a point also stressed by Theodore Ludwig Lau: since 'veritas et religio una est; quia ratio una; quia Deus una' [truth and religion are one; since reason is one and God is one], there simply are no 'atheists' and no 'atheistic' books.[92]

Each radical writer had his own slightly different version of how humanity had come to be ruinously enslaved to error, superstition, and priestly manipulation. Among the more ingenious accounts of this process, highlighting the clash of 'reason' and 'theology', besides invoking the intellectual 'Hellenism' which became a frequent theme of radical thought, was that propounded by the 'Wertheim' freethinker Johann Lorenz Schmidt (1702–49). Schmidt, whose highly accomplished translation of Spinoza's *Ethics* into German appeared at Leipzig in 1744, sought to explain how everything in mankind's religious and moral life had become so vitiated as to foster literally dozens of warring churches and sects, expounding irreconcilable and mostly 'absurd' doctrines. Contrasting the confused jumble of doctrine and myth preached by contemporary religion, as he saw it, with the rational, mathematically coherent structure of reality postulated by philosophy and natural philosophy, his narrative of the human mind's tortuous progress includes

[89] Radicati, *Succinct History*, 35; Radicati, *Twelve Discourses*, 11–12.

[90] Radicati, *Twelve Discourses*, 12; Berman, 'Disclaimers', 269–70; Jacob, *Living the Enlightenment*, 83.

[91] Radicati, *Twelve Discourses*, 11; Gundling, *Vollständige Historie*, iv. 6068–9; Carpanetto and Ricuperati, *Italy*, 118; Tortarolo, *Ragione*, 9–10.

[92] Lau, *Meditationes*, theses, 122, 124.

a hint of divine inspiration, though not miraculous revelation in the traditional sense, proclaimed first to the Jews, through Moses, and later Christ.

However, the Jews, alleges Schmidt, an unschooled people definitely not to be counted 'among those who established the *Wissenschaften*' that is, science, philosophy, and text scholarship, lamentably disfigured the truth with popular ideas and were, in any case, disdained by all their neighbours.[93] It was rather the Greeks who, towering over all other nations, and making by far the greatest contribution of any people to the advancement of mathematics, science, and philosophy, had first set out clear principles of morality and knowledge of God. The first to cultivate rational thought, their crowning achievement was the invention of philosophy. Certainly, Greek philosophers too had their schisms, but their competing schools, argued Schmidt (echoing Bayle and Collins), stood in much closer harmony in 'agreeing on crucial truths' than either ancient or modern priesthoods and, hence, afforded mankind more valid insights than any of the world's theologians.[94]

Greek philosophy, then, provides the chief thread of history. However, the Greek thinkers, like all philosophers since, were greatly hampered in their work of benefiting mankind, held Schmidt, by the ignorance, credulity, love of mystery, polytheism, indignation, and superstitious dread of the common folk. This caused a bitter struggle between the philosophers and priests in which the latter soon gained the upper hand, obliging the former to conceal their real insights, reserving their true teaching for tiny coteries of intimates. While the philosophers outwardly were obliged to embrace the 'absurd' beliefs and rites of the multitude, the pagan oracle-priests preferred, even though the more intelligent of them were equally scornful of popular superstition, to refine their methods of deceiving the people, to teaching them anything worthwhile. They especially took care to ensure that the people remained totally ignorant and, instead of assisting the philosophers in teaching moral principles, continually obstructed their efforts.[95]

Even so, superstitious dread was also clearly the instrument whereby 'Providence' ensured the gospel conquered the Graeco-Roman world: for part of the pagan priesthood soon came to see that they would have still more scope for exploiting credulity if they defected from the pagan gods and became Christian priests—much like the Druids later, according to Toland.[96] Since the new priesthood's goal was to extend their sway as much as possible, they set out to corrupt the original Christian teaching with dogmas as contrary to the most elementary rules of reason as they could devise, almost obliterating the precious kernel of truth. Practised deceivers, the Church Fathers systematically concocted 'miracles', 'wonders', and doctrines like the Trinity and resurrection of bodies which the philosophers saw were false since philosophers, as Schmidt puts it, are aware that 'nothing happens in the world without a matching cause (which tenet Archimides had already known)'. But they could not tell the multitude that it is ridiculous to

[93] [Schmidt], *Vest gegründete Wahrheit*, 18; Spalding, *Seize the Book*, 68.
[94] [Schmidt], *Vest gegründete Wahrheit*, 18.
[95] Ibid. 19; Spalding, *Seize the Book*, 185–6.
[96] Toland, *Specimen*, 14.

believe a woman can conceive 'miraculously' without sexual intercourse, or that one must be utterly 'confused' to suppose the Father would really send his son as Saviour to 'reprieve the wrongdoing of others', for the multitude, believing every word, no matter how ridiculous, compelled the philosophers to condone what was generally believed.[97] The result, suggested Schmidt, was a grotesque mix of philosophy and theology, inspired partly by the clergy's efforts to sway the philosophers and partly by the philosophers' attempt to counter the new faith's irrationality.

Strands drawn from revelation, Jewish and early Christian superstition, and sound philosophy as well as debased Platonism and Aristotelianism were thus all thrown together and churned into a grotesque spiritual chaos. Schmidt's vision differed somewhat from the parallel older constructs of Cherbury, Blount, Toland, and Tindal in that instead of highlighting an ancient pure theology, or 'natural religion', of four or five basic doctrines, beginning with the existence of a supreme God, accessible to everyone without priestly intercession or theology, first introduced by Moses but later utterly debased, the stress now was on Hellenism and philosophy.[98] Where the older narrative postulating a primitive religion of Deism, 'pantheism' or Tindal's and Radicati's 'natural religion' spoke of corrupt and vitiated versus pure theology, Schmidt's scenario focuses on a submerged pure philosophy which precariously survives down to modern times, buried beneath layers of theology laced with corrupt philosophy, a shift influenced doubtless by Bayle's stress on the centrality of the rise of Greek philosophy in the history of moral thought. In place of a confrontation of a pure ancient 'natural religion' opposed to priestly and popular religion is substituted Spinozist-*Bayliste* philosophical reason and mathematics pitted against theology reinforced by academic philosophy, a contest commencing with the first Greek philosophers.

A secret wisdom, held Schmidt, had survived among a few coteries dedicated to the sacred hope of one day reforming society, politics, and morality on the basis of a truth which, as in Spinoza and Bayle, is in fact philosophical reason itself. In Schmidt's case, though, there is also more than a hint of genuine Christian Deism, however residual, opposed to the materialism and atheism infusing the work of many other radical writers. A shadowy divine providence which Schmidt considers the basis of moral truth and the overarching coherence of the cosmos remains,[99] though without mitigating in any way the intensity of the attack on priestcraft. The Herculean task of replacing superstition with reason, he acknowledges, will require a stupendous programme of sustained, concerted philosophical and scholarly effort,[100] but must be undertaken for the sake of humanity by those few courageous enough to face the devastating impact of disputing what the people believe on their careers and lives.

[97] [Schmidt], *Vest gegründete Wahrheit*, 21.

[98] Willey, *Eighteenth-Century Background*, 14–15, 17; Assmann, *Moses*, 93–5.

[99] Harrison, *'Religion' and the Religions*, 165–7; Champion, *Pillars of Priestcraft*, 140, 165–8; Beiser, *Sovereignty of Reason*, 229, 244–5.

[100] [Schmidt], *Vest gegründete Wahrheit*, 21–4, 27; [Schmidt], 'Vorbericht', 5.

The residual theism, evident in Schmidt, and the high status of Scripture once purged of superstitious interpretation, makes it hard to decide whether his system was a form of Wolffian Deism or an extreme variant of Socinianism. His Wertheim Bible, so universally decried in Germany on its appearance in 1735, was condemned as both 'Socinian' and 'naturalist'.[101] Typical of radical thought was his elimination of the theologians' ancient dichotomy of believers and unbelievers and its replacement with a new division of mankind based, as with Spinoza, Bayle, Radicati, Meslier, Du Marsais, and Wachter, on the distinction between the 'enlightened' and unenlightened, a dichotomy with a purely worldly significance.[102] But if the essential thread in Schmidt's reconstruction of human history is a heroic, strictly rational, 'philosophical Hellenism' which, as he saw it, lives on eternally in an endless fight for the soul of man between reason and theology, he also aspires to build his society based on truth in part at least on the Bible and Christian morality.

101 Spalding, *Seize the Book*, 99, 105.

102 Wachter, *De primordiis*, 74, 80–3; Schröder, 'Einleitung', 12–13; Israel, *Radical Enlightenment*, 650–1.

5

Socinianism and the Social, Psychological, and Cultural Roots of Enlightenment

The intellectual controversies driving the western Enlightenment took place amid a fundamentally new and rapidly expanding commercial, imperial, and metropolitan setting evolving in the late seventeenth and early eighteenth centuries in the large conurbations of Europe. To begin with the forum of debate that counted was largely confined to just a very few centres, basically the Amsterdam–Leiden–The Hague–Rotterdam conurbation in Holland, together with London and Paris. Before long, though, other fast-growing and fast-changing capitals, such as Berlin, Geneva, Hamburg-Altona, Copenhagen, Vienna, and St Petersburg, where traditional hierarchical social and religious structures were likewise rapidly dissolving, also became part of the newly emerging cultural arena. Enlightenment's specific social context, then, was a widening sphere of cultural plurality, class fluidity, and coexistence of communities, churches, and legal structures, where a new context of 'liberté et égalité', as Montesquieu called it,[1] both created a bracing social reality necessitating fresh modes of social and political thinking, and generated fresh cultural assets and possibilities, encouraging the use of a rapidly emerging new conception of rationality to address these novel challenges.

The progressive breakdown of traditional hierarchical forms in these great international centres was partly just a result of increased mobility, recent urban growth, and rapid economic change. But it was also a question of accelerating country–town migration and wholly new forms of social diversity and broadening religious plurality, caused by unprecedentedly large-scale immigration from abroad. The impact of foreign immigration on the formation of Enlightenment contexts and attitudes was everywhere crucial; indeed, in the most extreme instances, Peter the Great's St Petersburg and Moscow, expatriate communities—especially Lutheran Germans, Dutch, Huguenots, and Italians—may even be designated the principal agents of Enlightenment. For the most novel aspect of this social-structural change, and one of the most decisive effects of metropolitan urban expansion on intellectual life and general culture, was the conspicuous role played by relatively small but dislocated and uprooted expatriate communities, diasporas

[1] Montesquieu, *Œuvres complètes*, 331; Lacouture, *Montesquieu*, 189.

originating elsewhere, impelled by their quest for viable places of refuge and economic need but, at the same time, a powerful new cultural force generating novel kinds of intellectual activity.

Foreign expatriate communities hence became an integral component of the Early Enlightenment metropolitan milieu and one which, especially in the case of diasporas recently ejected from their original native lands, like the Huguenots and western Sephardic Jews, was culturally and psychologically more disorientated and destabilized than other groups. Hence, unsurprisingly, once partly integrated, these foreign immigrants became major agents of intellectual and cultural reorganization and reform. The Huguenots, we have seen, were easily the most numerous and prominent of these recently arrived new communities in northern Europe; another significant if much smaller presence was the 'fringe Jews', both Sephardic and Ashkenazic, to be found in centres such as Amsterdam, Hamburg, Berlin, and London, of the sort described in d'Argens's *Lettres juives*, that is individuals who had to a greater or lesser extent broken with traditional norms of Jewish observance, like Spinoza himself, sometimes, as with Spinoza's comrade of the mid 1650s Juan de Prado, or Salomon Gumpertz in Berlin, highly educated university graduates, immersed in philosophy. Another key diaspora, by no means to be ignored, was the Polish and Polish-German (especially from Danzig) Socinians driven out during the course of the seventeenth century by the now triumphant and ever more intolerant Polish Counter-Reformation increasingly bent on the destruction of religious dissent in that kingdom.

As a factor in the Early Enlightenment, the Socinian challenge needs to be viewed as a theological-intellectual tendency which was simultaneously a social phenomenon still linked, after 1650, to the wave of Polish émigrés to the West but increasingly loosely. Since most of the Polish exiles settled in northern Germany and Holland, the religious movement called Socinianism during the Early Enlightenment in the western world more generally—like Arminianism, an import into England from Holland, whither it spread in the early seventeenth century from Poland—was always regarded as essentially a spiritual challenge rather than as a social problem associated with particular groups immigrating from distant lands.[2] However, the fact that the Socinian question proved particularly acute among other uprooted diasporas, like the Huguenots, strongly suggests that there continued to be a significant connection, psychologically and culturally, between the facts of persecution, emigration, and exile, on the one hand, and attraction to radical reforming theology such as Socinianism, on the other.

In any case, it was the theological implications which chiefly worried and preoccupied contemporaries. In England the so-called 'Unitarian' controversy reached its climax in the years 1687–1700; in 1698, a Parliamentary Act for the 'more effectual suppression of blasphemy' reaffirmed a long-standing ban on

[2] Chaufepié, *Nouveau Dictionnaire*, i. 135; Kerkhoven and Blom, 'De La Court en Spinoza', 153–4; Kühler, *Het Socinianisme*, 135–44, 227–41; Cragg, *Church and the Age*, 153, 169; Tyacke, 'Arminianism', 72, 74; Young, *Religion and Enlightenment*, 26–8, 75–6; Beiser, *Sovereignty of Reason*, 95–101.

expressing anti-Trinitarian sentiments, threatening anyone convicted for a second time with three years in prison.[3] The Anglican Church remained extremely jittery on this issue, moreover, until deep into the eighteenth century, as indeed did nearly all the dissenting churches. Jonathan Edwards, the theologian-philosopher of Yale, a leader of the movement of spiritual renewal known as the 'Great Awakening' which swept New England and the Middle Colonies in the early 1740s, firmly identified Socinianism along with Arminianism, Arianism, Quakerism, and Deism as a principal cause of the 'prevailing of licentiousness in principles and opinions', now scarcely any less evident in New England than in England itself and which his fiery New Light revivalism strove to combat.[4]

If in Britain and Ireland, High Church and moderate Anglicans after the Glorious Revolution often suspected the Socinian menace to be seeping up partly through Latitudinarian circles (including, in the opinion of some, Locke's philosophy),[5] among the Reformed in France and Switzerland, after 1650, the challenge seemed to derive chiefly via the parallel 'Arminian' stream, particularly strong at the Huguenot academy at Saumur. Here, among the professors in the 1660s, taught the noted Arminian-Cartesian Claude Pajon (1626–85), an influential minister later at Orléans and friend of Le Clerc, and leader of a strain of 'rational' philosophical Arminianism, highly suspect to orthodox Calvinists, which soon gradually also gained ground at Geneva and Lausanne.[6] But whatever the exact routes and mechanisms of its propagation, the spread of Socinianism was plainly symptomatic of profound religious crisis. For the core ideas of the Socinians, and especially their rejection of the divinity of Christ and other central 'mysteries' of the faith, as incompatible with reason, manifestly sapped the very foundations of traditional Christian belief, theology, and ecclesiastical authority.

Few doubted there was an inherent link, furthermore, between the diffusion of Socinianism and the late seventeenth- and eighteenth-century upsurge of philosophical incredulity and Deism, some also discerning affinities between Socinianism and the reforming theology of Le Clerc and the *rationaux*. The Abbé Pierre Valentin Faydit, an idiosyncratic French Catholic antagonist of Le Clerc ironically praised, for deep insight (in denouncing Le Clerc), by Bayle, envisaged the 'Spinosistes, Sociniens et Cléricistes [i.e. followers of Le Clerc]' as all advancing along a common line, in employing the newly developed methods of Bible exegesis to undermine belief in the 'mysteries' and the miraculous.[7] Even Bayle himself, usually eager to ridicule whatever is commonly thought, here adopts a conventional stance, condemning Socinian rejection of the Trinity and Christology on the grounds these 'ne sont conformes à la raison', and their general rejection of the 'mystères

[3] Champion, *Pillars of Priestcraft*, 107; Marshall, *John Locke*, 389.

[4] Marsden, *Jonathan Edwards*, 199, 433, 448; Zakai, *Jonathan Edwards's Philosophy*, 261, 268, 325.

[5] Yolton, *Locke and the Way of Ideas*, 10–11, 169–74, 181–3; Marshall, *John Locke*, 345–50; Champion, *Pillars of Priestcraft*, 106–10.

[6] Labrousse, *Pierre Bayle*, i. 154; Simonutti, 'Absolute, Universal', 712.

[7] [Faydit], *Remarques sur Virgile*, 90, 238–9; *Bibliothèque choisie*, 10 (1706), 383; *Bibliothèque ancienne et moderne*, 28 (1727), 394–5.

inconcevables de la religion chrétienne' as pernicious error opening the door as wide as possible 'au pyrrhonisme, au déisme, à l'athéisme'.[8]

The rapid penetration of Socinian influences in the last decades of the seventeenth century was particularly evident among the Huguenot diaspora and, for them, an especially acute problem owing to the sudden rapid proliferation of their congregations in such places as Amsterdam, The Hague, Rotterdam, London, and Berlin, large, new, and unstable congregations located in the very places already most subject to religious plurality and splintering—and the most fertile in tolerationist ideas as well as dissident intellectual influences. The specific social context of the congregations making up the Huguenot Refuge, in other words, stimulated a profusion of doctrinal differences, exacerbating theological clashes and rivalries, rendering it peculiarly difficult to preserve much more than a bare semblance of traditional Calvinist discipline in their ranks.

The United Provinces, where the largest and culturally most dominant part of the Huguenot intellectual elite settled, including well over half, some 363, of the 600 Reformed ministers obliged to leave France after the Revocation of the Edict of Nantes,[9] was to some degree exceptional when compared to London and Berlin, in being previously more exposed to Socinian, Catholic, and Jewish as well as 'Arminian', Collegiant, and Mennonite influences, especially in Amsterdam, The Hague, and Rotterdam where most Huguenots congregated. If Holland remained the chief focus of French-speaking émigré debate, publishing, theology, and philosophical endeavour, that province was also the seed-bed of the ideas and clandestine texts of the radical fringe. But spiritual instability and fragmentation were soon characteristic of all the main Huguenot centres. In London, where the number of Huguenot churches burgeoned from six in 1688 to twenty-six served by nearly fifty ministers by 1700, chronic problems similar to those witnessed in Holland arose from much the same taxing combination of rapid expansion, adjusting to a large and fluid metropolitan area, and endemic doctrinal strife.[10] Before long, a near unmanageable theological ferment extended through virtually the entire Huguenot diaspora which, being as much a cultural and economic, as a religious *Refuge*, and one bitterly resentful of the campaign of intolerance from which it had suffered, possessed few effective means of disciplining or eradicating religious dissidents.

Refugees flocked to the *Églises Réformées* often for professional, economic, and linguistic as much as religious reasons and, not infrequently, were no longer 'Calvinists' in any definite sense. This applied even (or especially) to many of their spiritual leaders; for on reaching their places of refuge, numerous actual or trainee preachers and teachers had, out of expediency, or because there was little else they could do, acceded to the Calvinist formulas of submission, in the Dutch case adjusted to the articles of the Synod of Dordt, while inwardly resisting these doctrines,

[8] *Mémoires de Trévoux* (Aug. 1707), 1363–4; Tinsley, *Pierre Bayle's Reformation*, 302, 305–6; McKenna, 'La Norme et la transgression', 130; Lennon, 'Bayle and Socinianism', 180, 184–6.

[9] Van Eijnatten, 'Huguenot Clerisy', 218.

[10] Gwynn, 'Disorder and Innovation', 253–4.

thereby helping foment an upsurge of theological heterodoxy, especially Socinianism, within the bosom of the Huguenot congregations themselves.[11] The resulting tensions were intensified further by the philosophical imbroglio surrounding Spinoza and Bayle, names well known to much or most of the community and, by the early years of the eighteenth century, often bracketed together as constituting the very quintessence of intellectual insidiousness. Particularly troublesome were these philosophers' theories of toleration and individual freedom and their thesis that whether or not a person is religiously pious makes no difference to their true moral status and prospects for salvation. Also unsettling, noted Jean La Placette (1639–1718), Huguenot minister in the years 1686–1711 at Copenhagen, was the strict determinism taught by Spinoza and hinted at by Bayle, their thesis that freedom of will is not required, as La Placette put it, 'pour agir moralement', a doctrine confusingly resembling the Calvinist doctrine of predestination, which, as Jesuit observers gleefully pointed out, greatly hampered strict Calvinists in the work of combating Spinoza's ethical philosophy.[12]

It is hardly surprising, therefore, that conservative theologians like Jurieu, Gabriel d'Artis, at Hamburg, and the anti-Cartesian Élie Benoist (1640–1728), for many years French Reformed minister at Delft, constantly lamented that traditional Huguenot Calvinist doctrine was everywhere under dire threat. While existing procedures for disciplining the heterodox could be effective in small towns like Canterbury whence, in 1697, a group of Socinian dissidents were obliged to flee to Holland, efforts to suppress Socinianism in London, Amsterdam, and other large centres probably never had much effect,[13] and it soon became obvious in all the main Huguenot centres that some of the French Reformed Church's own ministers were themselves under suspicion of serious forms of heterodoxy including crypto-Socinianism. When the Reformed pastor Louis Maimbourg—not to be confused with the more famous Jesuit historian of the same name (who passed away in France in 1686)—died more or less as a declared Socinian in London in 1692, four ministers, among them Jacques Souverain (d. 1698), author of *Le Platonisme desvoilé* (1700), defied the community's ban on visiting and supporting him on his deathbed: these were then publicly (but vainly) censured by the main body of ministers.[14]

Nevertheless, efforts to enforce uniformity of doctrine continued and the General Assembly of the Huguenot churches of London set up, in 1698, as a counterpart to the 'Walloon Synod' which convened annually in the United Provinces, though mostly concerned with practical questions like communal poor relief, also tried, emulating the French Reformed synods in the Dutch Republic and Switzerland, to find ways to exert greater pressure for doctrinal cohesion.[15] The Walloon Synod in

[11] Ibid. 256–7; Mulsow, 'Views', 44.

[12] *Mémoires de Trévoux* (Apr. 1714), art. xlvi, pp. 619–20, 630–2, 634, 636.

[13] Gwynn, 'Disorder and Innovation', 258–9.

[14] Mulsow, *Moderne*, 269; Gwynn, 'Disorder and Innovation', 257.

[15] Gwynn, 'Disorder and Innovation', 259–61, 269, 271; Israel, *Dutch Republic*, 669, 931–2, 1031.

the United Provinces strove to maintain doctrinal discipline after 1686 by means of a permanent commission of surveillance, consisting of four pastors and four professors of theology, charged with monitoring preaching and publications.[16]

Socinianism, around 1700, was still generally regarded both within and without the Huguenot diaspora with a repugnance verging on that felt for 'atheism' and Spinozism. Fulminating against Socinianism united Lutherans, Calvinists, Catholics, and Orthodox as did little else. As we have seen, among the chief complaints about the Dutch Republic in the late seventeenth century was that there, unlike other Christian lands, Socinians could publish anti-Trinitarian writings and more or less openly deny Christ's divinity and other key Christian 'mysteries' at least *de facto*, albeit, as Aubert de Versé (having already been exiled from France for Socinian leanings) found when being ejected from Holland, and as Bayle remarks in his article on Socinus in the *Dictionnaire*,[17] Socinians were not actually as free to express their opinions there as was generally thought. Even so, the Amsterdam and Rotterdam city governments did turn a blind eye to Socinian activity for much of the time, enabling them to infiltrate the Collegiant movement, as well as the Mennonite and Arminian congregations, and propagate their views at any rate with less constraint than elsewhere.

Like the Jews, Socinians were loudly disapproved of everywhere and, in print, continually attacked from every conceivable direction. Not surprisingly, in these circumstances, whether émigrés from Poland or native Dutch converts, Socinians tended to outdo every other Christian fringe group in their zeal for toleration, and it was just one more conspicuous point of affinity between radical philosophical Deism and Socinianism, seemingly, that the latter, outstripping even the Arminians, urged a practically unlimited toleration. Thus, for example, the firmly anti-Trinitarian theologian Daniel Zwicker (1612–78) from Danzig, whence he had been driven by Lutheran persecution, having subsequently had to leave Poland altogether, owing to mounting Catholic bigotry, emigrating to Amsterdam in 1657, expressly approved toleration of all Christian creeds and even atheists.[18]

Conversely, only via the Enlightenment could the Socinians expect any lessening of the pressure against them. Where Malebranche charged the Socinians with insulting the God of true Christians, and debasing Christianity, by seeking their deepest illumination and moral instruction in someone they considered a mere man, thereby fomenting a new superstition and idolatry, as if a mortal could be humanity's—and the universal Church's—supreme guide,[19] the Deist view was much more positive. Indeed, for moderate Deists of Voltaire's stamp, the rise of Socinianism and English Unitarianism seemed definitely something to celebrate—at least in private. For here, seemingly, was a widely dispersed, spreading movement, deeply embedded in

[16] Cerny, *Theology, Politics and Letters*, 62–3.

[17] Bayle, article 'Socin' from the *Dictionnaire* in McKenna, *Pierre Bayle: témoin*, 466; Tinsley, *Pierre Bayle's Reformation*, 317.

[18] Kolakowski, *Chrétiens*, 226–7; Bietenholz, *Daniel Zwicker*, 14, 28, 71–3.

[19] Malebranche, *Dialogues*, 275–6.

western society, extending from Poland and Transylvania to North America, which assailed, if not the principle of revelation, then certainly nearly all the other roots of traditional theology, eliminating most miracles as well as Christ's divinity and Incarnation. This left men with a universal Creator God who regulates the cosmos, ordains morality, and benignly ordains the fate of men and beasts on earth. Hence, Socinianism appeared to be doing most of the work, as a useful proxy, which Voltaire had in mind for 'philosophy', enthroning 'un Être suprême' who exerts absolute dominion and decrees the moral order, removing all cause for dogmatic strife from among the peoples of the world.[20] In his clandestine text the *Sermon des cinquante*, penned around 1740 but circulating only as an anonymous manuscript (until anonymously published in 1763), Voltaire exults that the western world now positively abounds with ardent religious reformers who embrace a 'Socinianisme qui approche beaucoup de l'adoration d'un seul Dieu *dégagé* de superstitions'.[21]

For the modern historian, all this powerfully poses the question of whether, and especially how, Socinianism may have aided and abetted the rise of philosophical Deism and hence of the Enlightenment both moderate and radical, particularly in its Dutch, Huguenot, German, and Anglo-American contexts. Even if, as seems likely, many contemporaries overstated the links and affinities between Socinianism and the diverse strands of Deism, *prima facie* it would still seem that Socinianism in significant ways lent added impetus and many new recruits to all wings of the Enlightenment. If, moreover, the more extreme variants of Socinianism were only marginally distinguishable from Deistic 'natural religion', consisting mainly, apart from a drastically reduced minimum of core mysteries, of a spiritually intense moral teaching based on Christ's example, and if Socinian Collegiants like Pieter Balling (d. 1669), Jarig Jelles (*c.*1620–83), and the Amsterdam publisher Jan Rieuwertsz (*c.*1616–87) were undoubtedly disciples and allies of Spinoza,[22] is there not a clear case for reckoning Socinianism among the chief factors generating radical no less than the Arminian and Voltairean currents of the Enlightenment?

In the case of Balling, Jelles, and Rieuwertsz, declared Socinians clearly figured prominently in organizing the early printing, translation, and diffusion of Spinoza's works. Since Socinians rejected the doctrine of the Trinity and Christ's divinity, as well as Original Sin, and often also eternal damnation, and God's foreknowledge of each individual's salvation or otherwise, the more rigorous rationalists among them developed a version of Christianity so drastically purged of dogma and 'mysteries' as to be barely distinguishable from providential Deism.[23] No doubt, this

[20] Van Eijnatten, *Mutua Christianorum tolerantia*, 209.

[21] HHL, MS Fr. 79 [Voltaire], 'Le Sermon des cinquante', fo. 26; [Voltaire], *Sermon des cinquante*, 20; Lee, 'Le "*Sermon*" ', 143; in the other Harvard MS copy HHL, MS Fr. 17, p. 31, the word 'Socinianisme' has been corrupted to 'Socratisme'.

[22] See van Bunge, 'Spinoza en de waarheid', 656; Manusov-Verhage, 'Jan Rieuwertsz', 248–50; Israel, *Radical Enlightenment*, 164 n., 170–1 n., 342–58.

[23] Fix, *Prophecy and Reason*, 148–50; Mulsow, 'New Socinians', 49–52.

helped pious Collegiants like Balling, who held man's 'inner light', which he equates with reason, to be 'the first principle of religion',[24] feel comfortable fraternizing with Spinoza who, in any case, probably expressed himself more circumspectly in the 1650s than later, in his *Tractatus theologico-politicus* (1670). By then Balling had died and Spinoza was less guarded; but, even there, while denying miracles, supernatural agency, and revelation, he holds that Christ, though a mere man, had somehow been specially inspired with understanding and moral truth and was therefore not a 'prophet', in his somewhat derogatory technical sense of the term, but rather a unique exception, the inspired 'mouthpiece of God', a doctrine close to that of his friend Jelles and doubtless deliberately formulated to appeal to his Collegiant friends.[25] Jelles was one Socinian who (probably rather exceptionally) seemingly had no objection even to the *Tractatus* and, indeed, paid for its translation into Dutch which, however, remained unpublished, at Spinoza's own special request, to prevent a severe crackdown by the authorities.[26]

After Spinoza's death, Jelles, who wrote the preface to his illegal *Opera posthuma* (1677), still considered his friend's philosophy compatible with his Socinian brand of Christianity. Spinoza's idiosyncratic view of Christ as a uniquely inspired but not superhuman individual the substance of whose message 'consists essentially in moral teachings' has long puzzled commentators of both Christian and Jewish background.[27] 'Miracles' being an absolute impossibility, according to Spinoza, to him Christ's 'miracles' were assuredly no truer than any other alleged 'miracles' reported in history.[28] Yet he plainly looked forward to the day 'when', as he puts it in chapter 11 of the *Tractatus*, church schisms and disputes will cease because 'religion shall be separated from philosophic speculations and reduced to those very few and exceedingly simple doctrines [*paucissima et simplicissima dogmata*] which Christ taught his following'; this happier age, he added, would be 'ab omni superstitione liberam', freed from all superstition, a remark showing that for Spinoza 'religio', or at any rate Socinian religion, is far from being the same thing as 'superstitio' despite its modest status as compared to philosophy.[29]

The most plausible way to interpret Spinoza's account of Christ, and the latter's significance for humankind, is indeed to see it as stemming from a deeply felt need to form a tactical alliance for promoting the kind of campaign he believed could potentially reform society and politics, and institute a true *libertas philosophandi*. For it was only with the Socinian Collegiants whose circle in Amsterdam he frequented for some years (1656–61), after his expulsion from the synagogue, that he could hope to form such an alignment. To an extent, moreover, this strategy

24 Balling, *Het Licht*, 5; Kolakowski, *Chrétiens*, 210–12.

25 Spinoza, *TTP* 64, 107; Nadler, *Spinoza*, 107, 141; Spruit, 'Introduzione', pp. xlv–xlvi.

26 Spruit, 'Introduzione', p. xv; Spinoza to Jelles, The Hague, 17 Feb. 1671, Spinoza, *Briefwisseling*, 292–3; van Bunge, *From Stevin to Spinoza*, 134, 136.

27 Mason, *God of Spinoza*, 208, 212–13; Popkin, *Spinoza*, 62–3; Verbeek, *Spinoza's Theological-Political Treatise*, 84–7.

28 Klever, *Spinoza classicus*, 271, 281, 283–4; Matheron, *Christ et le salut*, 87–9.

29 Ibid. 96–7; Preus, *Spinoza*, 178.

proved successful; some Socinians, like Jelles and Balling, and later in Germany Johann Lorenz Schmidt, Socinians that is who aspired to combine their Christian creed with a systematic rationalist philosophy, merging their thought with elements of Cartesianism, Spinozism, and in Schmidt's case Wolffianism, must be classed as integrally part of the Radical Enlightenment. This is particularly the case where, as with these figures, there is besides denial of Christology a thoroughgoing scepticism about miracles and uncompromising insistence on the need for full freedom of thought and a comprehensive toleration.

Yet too much should not be read into Spinoza's friendship and amicable intellectual relations with such men. There were bound to be large question marks over the viability and stability of any such attempt to combine Socinianism with Spinozism. Despite Spinoza's Collegiant links, and the sympathy for Socinianism expressed also by Meyer and others, all the Dutch radical writers including Koerbagh, who called Socinianism the only true 'reformed' religion,[30] and was very close to his brother Johannes Koerbagh, an anti-Trinitarian theological student who combined marked Spinozist sympathies with participating in Socinian prayer gatherings in Amsterdam,[31] expressed far-reaching reservations about Socinianism, a latent hostility, as it were, which was especially marked in Bayle.

Nor should one suppose that, after Spinoza's death, the Dutch Socinian Collegiants as a group were favourably disposed towards Spinozism. Already in the 1670s, and especially in the 1680s, leading anti-Trinitarians among the Collegiants, such as Frans Kuyper (1629–91), editor of parts of the *Bibliotheca fratrum Polonorum* (1656–92), the most notorious and frequently banned set of Dutch-Polish Socinian writings which he began to publish in 1668, reacted strongly against the Spinozist (and Cartesian) penetration of their movement;[32] and even the most uncompromisingly 'rationalist' wing of the Polish Socinians in exile segregated themselves with growing insistence, both practically and theoretically, from the Deists and Spinozists, calling their doctrine 'rational religion' by which they meant something quite different not just from Spinozist naturalism but also the 'natural theology', or 'natural religion' of Blount, Toland, and Tindal as well as of the providential Deists.[33] If Toland's first book, *Christianity not Mysterious*, can rightly be said to be 'more a Socinian than a deist or materialist work', Toland's subsequent intellectual development diverged sharply, in the direction of materialism, pantheism, and a republican quasi-Spinozism.[34]

The modern historian can agree that Socinianism was what Christopher Hill called 'another route to deism'—but only up to a point and with considerable qualification.[35] Actually, it was most obviously the forebear not of Deism either

30 Koerbagh, *Een Ligt Schijnende*, 154–5; van Bunge, *From Stevin to Spinoza*, 102; Wielema, 'Adraan Koerbagh', 68.

31 Israel, *Radical Enlightenment*, 185–91; Wielema, *March*, 87, 90.

32 Fix, *Prophecy and Reason*, 156–60; van Bunge, *From Stevin to Spinoza*, 114, 136.

33 Kühler, *Het Socinianisme*, 243–8; van Slee, *Rijnsburger Collegianten*, 238–66; Fix, *Prophecy and Reason*, 144–56.

34 Beiser, *Sovereignty of Reason*, 248; Taranto, *Du déisme à l'athéisme*, 43–8.

35 Hill, *Some Intellectual Consequences*, 77.

providential, on the Voltairean model, or radical, but of that specifically early eighteenth-century phenomenon 'Christian Deism', the creed of Thomas Woolston (1670–1733), Thomas Morgan (d. 1743), and Thomas Chubb (1679–1747). Chubb, a Wiltshire artisan who taught himself theology, held that anything 'contrary to reason and equity' is a 'horrid imputation upon the great Maker and Governor of the world', that the 'interest of the clergy' is a very different thing 'from the common interest of mankind', and that in most of the churches, the Catholic above all, 'superstitious practices' had replaced true Christianity;[36] but he still stoutly insisted that rational theology, not philosophy, is Man's chief light, that revelation is our chief guide, and it is here that he stood closest to the Socinians.

While it is true that 'a widespread concern with Socinianism' permeated Enlightenment intellectual debate,[37] even leaders of the Christian mainstream Enlightenment, those eager to carry through a fundamental reform of Christianity, stripping away all superstition, like Le Clerc, Jaquelot, Locke, and the Berlin librarian La Croze, men themselves widely supposed to harbour Socinian sympathies, mostly seem to have felt less sense of kinship with Socinian ideas than was generally assumed and, from their point of view, they were right to reject Socinianism's supposedly 'enlightened' credentials. For while Socinianism assisted the rise of both Enlightenment wings, in a limited way, especially as a source of recruits from among those disillusioned with Socinianism, there was little real affinity of ideas not just between them and the radicals but even between them and men like Le Clerc, a gap most clearly evident in their (generally) very different attitude to philosophy. Hence, despite Bayle's frequent imputations to the contrary, in reality, as Barbeyrac points out, Le Clerc was not at all a 'Socinian'.[38]

The authentic Socinian standpoint was summed up in the key term *religio rationalis* used, among others, by the Polish Socinian—and grandson of Faustus Socinus—Andrzej Wiszowaty (or Wiszowatius or Wissowatius) (1608–78), including as the title of his book published in Amsterdam, several years after his death, in 1685, a work greatly esteemed by Zwicker and reviewed that year by Bayle in his *Nouvelles de la République des Lettres*.[39] The primary difference between Socinian 'rational religion' and Deist 'natural theology' was that where the latter invokes reason alone, the former embraces the guiding principle of divine revelation and the reality of a residue of miracles—at any rate, as with Locke and Le Clerc, where these are attested by historical evidence deemed 'certain' but making no use of philosophical arguments.[40] The creed of men like Wiszowaty, Zwicker, and Frans Kuyper focused squarely on the Christian Bible and, in their eyes, the distinction between supernatural and natural, even if requiring drastic reform, at the end of the day nevertheless remained

[36] Chubb, *A Discourse*, 5, 14, 21, 32, 80; Harrison, *'Religion' and the Religions*, 32, 189 n. 52.

[37] Pocock, *Barbarism*, i. 53–4, 62–3.

[38] [Barbeyrac], *Éloge*, 55.

[39] Kühler, *Het Socinianisme*, 229–30, 236; van Bunge, *Johannes Bredenburg*, 94–5, 251; Bietenholz, *Daniel Zwicker*, 272–3.

[40] Bietenholz, *Daniel Zwicker*, 272–3; Jelles, *Belydenisse*, 1–3; Kuyper *Bewys*, 3–4; Fix, *Prophecy and Reason*, 149.

an essential and wholly valid one. For them, like Locke and Le Clerc, it is the thinking Christian's duty to demonstrate that Revelation comes from God, that it does not contradict reason but complements it, and that it is best explicated through 'reason'; but unlike them, their frame of reference in most cases was Scripture alone.[41] Jonathan Edwards, then, was quite right to discern a fundamental difference between real Deists and Socinians since the latter 'own the Scriptures to be the word of God, and hold the Christian religion to be the true religion'.[42]

Wiszowaty, forced to leave Poland by the growing intolerance of the Polish bishops in 1658, after several years of wandering, in Hungary, Silesia, and the Palatinate, reached Amsterdam in 1661, and, stripping away many or most traditional Christian doctrines, proclaimed *religio rationalis* the sole authentic Christian theology. However, the gap between him and the *Cléricistes*, as well as the Spinozists whose Bible hermeneutics he expressly rejected, remained very considerable. In one respect, it is true, they were much closer to Locke and Le Clerc than to the Spinozists: while they, insisting one can only have a meaningful faith in something made clear via one's reason and not in inexplicable dogmas,[43] firmly repudiated the Trinity, Incarnation, and other core Christian tenets because they conflict with the dictates of reason, they, unlike Spinoza, Meyer, Bayle, and Collins, but like Le Clerc and Locke, also insisted on the distinction between *supra rationem* (above reason) and *contra rationem* (contrary to reason).[44] This was basic to Wiszowaty's, Aubert de Versé's, and most Socinians' theology enabling them, in many cases, as with Kuyper, and like Locke, to claim the existence of angels and demons, eternal reward for the saved and punishment for the wicked, as well as, crucial for all of them, Christ's supernatural status as 'God's Son, our Redeemer'.[45]

As Arthur Bury (1624–1713) stressed, in his *The Naked Gospel*, the book publicly burnt at Oxford in 1690, and later discussed with some sympathy by Boulainvilliers, Socinianism proclaims 'faith' in Christ as the universal saviour of Man.[46] For Socinians, whether Polish exiles like Wiszowaty or Zwicker, or Dutch converts like Balling and Jelles, or Englishmen, Jesus while not God is still a supernatural being, a man so uniquely inspired as to be a direct emanation of God and, in clear contrast to Koerbagh's stance which contemporaries, like van Limborch, rightly equated with Spinoza's, does embody the Holy Ghost and *is* endowed with an element of divinity.[47] Likewise, Wiszowaty asserts the binding truth of the Resurrection, claiming, like Locke and Le Clerc, that the testimony of the large number of witnesses to this event cannot be doubted.[48] Rather than eliminating

[41] Fix, *Prophecy and Reason*, 14; Marshall, *John Locke*, 340–5; Spellman, *Latitudinarians*, 101, 151–2.

[42] Zakai, *Jonathan Edwards's Philosophy*, 261.

[43] Wiszowaty, *Religio rationalis*, 16, 18, 33–5.

[44] Ibid. 82–4; Kühler, *Het Socinianisme*, 235–6; Olscamp, *Moral Philosophy*, 191; Bietenholz, *Daniel Zwicker*, 272–3.

[45] Wiszowaty, *Religio rationalis*, 82–3; Wiszowaty, *Spooren der Deugden*, 31, 42, 69–70, 91–2, 94; Kolakowski, *Chrétiens*, 267.

[46] [Bury], *Naked Gospel*, 12–13; Venturino, *Ragioni*, 135–6.

[47] Koerbagh, *Een Ligt Schijnende*, 217; Jelles, *Belydenisse*, 3, 21–3; Fix, *Prophecy and Reason*, 206–7; Kolakowski, *Chrétiens*, 218; Bietenholz, *Daniel Zwicker*, 60.

[48] Wiszowaty, *Spooren der Deugden*, 134.

theology, there was still an irreducible residue of the miraculous to be accommodated, so that Wiszowaty and others of the Socinian vanguard, including Zwicker, concurred with Locke's principle that faith 'be nothing else but an assent founded on the highest reason' and that on this basis Jesus, in their eyes, was procreated by the Holy Ghost, is the Messiah, and is Man's Saviour.[49] Jelles, in his *Belydenisse*, like Wiszowaty later, took the view that the rationalism of Descartes and Spinoza could be selectively combined with Christianity using the device of 'above reason', prompting Leibniz too to charge him with inconsistency and one modern scholar aptly to characterize his position as that of 'la mystique unitarienne pseudo-rationaliste'.[50] For Spinozists, their stance was indeed pseudo-rationalist.

Bayle for one clearly understood this. If he purposely made the issue of Socinianism central to his dispute with the *rationaux*, this was because at the heart of his critique of Le Clerc, Bernard, and Jaquelot was precisely his argument that reason cannot be the basis of faith. Hence, in his eyes, the Socinian question so agitating the churches was closely akin to that arising from the *rationaux*'s claims that reason must be the judge of theological doctrines and the cornerstone of Bible exegesis.[51] It was what the Socinians had in common with Le Clerc and Jaquelot that was the object of his hostility. Were they to be consistent in espousing reason as their guide, contends Bayle—and his point was that both Socinians and Huguenot *rationaux*, including his friend Basnage, were being inconsistent—both Socinians and *rationaux* (who did not openly deny Christ's divinity and the Trinity) would abjure not only Christ's divinity, Incarnation, and pre-existence, and hence the Trinity, but also his supernatural power to expiate men's sins through his suffering on the Cross, and Resurrection, Original Sin, and the eternality of Hell as well, more generally, as Creation from nothing, divine prescience of contingent events, predestination, and the necessity for divine Grace, since all of these, he says, while historically unquestionably core Christian doctrines, are wholly irreconcilable with reason.[52]

Faith, held Bayle, must stand alone. Were the *rationaux* right to allege that faith requires the aid of reason and that, hence, his own fideism constituted an attack on religion, they would, he argued, simultaneously be vindicating the Socinians' claim that Christianity must be placed on an exclusively rational basis. The effect, should this principle prevail, would be the ruin of all orthodoxy and destruction of conventional Christian belief. For then there would be no orthodox theologian who would not also be attacking religion since there is, and can be, no orthodox minister who does not teach that the Trinity and the hypostatic union are mysteries our reason can never grasp but must simply believe in humble submission 'à l'authorité de Dieu qui nous les a révélez.'[53]

[49] Locke, *An Essay*, 668; Van Eijnatten, *Liberty and Concord*, 165.
[50] Jelles, *Belydenisse*, 1–3; Kolakowski, *Chrétiens*, 217–18; Goldenbaum, 'Leibniz as a Lutheran', 181, 185.
[51] Bayle, *Réponse*, iii. 649–50; Bayle, *Entretiens*, 22–3; Tinsley, *Pierre Bayle's Reformation*, 302–5.
[52] Bayle, *Réponse*, iii. 650; Lennon, 'Bayle and Socinianism', 175.
[53] Bayle, *Réponse*, iii. 643; Bayle, *Entretiens*, 20; Walker, *Decline of Hell*, 28–9.

Bayle's rebuttal of Socinianism implies not just that they wrongly suppose reason must underlie faith but that they are utterly inconsistent in applying their own principles. Already early in his career, Bayle expounded his deeply held conviction that the distinction, common to Le Clerc, Bernard, and the Socinian exponents of *religio rationalis*, between what is above reason and what is contrary to reason is fallacious and that in human life there can be no 'au-dessus de la raison' which is not also contrary to reason.[54] This was a firmly fideist position, assuredly, but was also, of course, Spinoza's and Koerbagh's. While ostensibly denouncing Socinianism because it conflicts with the Pyrrhonism and fideism which he says is the only philosophy compatible with orthodox Christianity, plainly Bayle's real purpose is to lead the reader round to something else. Having first rehearsed Socinian objections to the Trinity and Incarnation with what Le Clerc indignantly called 'beaucoup d'art et de force', under pretence of parading orthodoxy and humbling 'reason', Bayle proclaims the impossibility of demolishing the Socinian case by means of reason while at the same time stressing the absurdity of claiming, as the Socinians, the *rationaux*, and Locke all do, that revelation and miracles are 'above' but not contrary to reason.[55]

In attacking Socinianism, Bayle performs with great dexterity a perfect philosophical somersault: starting by decrying the Socinians for relying on reason, he then pronounces their rational objections to orthodox doctrine rationally unanswerable, after which he complains that with their 'above reason' the Socinians (like Le Clerc, Jaquelot, and Locke) are being irrational in failing to eliminate from their doctrine what is inconsistent with reason. For Bayle, then, like Koerbagh and Meyer, even the most 'rationalistic' Socinians were still inconsistent theologians rather than philosophers, men who, as Koerbagh puts it, 'do not yet in everything entirely use reason'.[56] Where for Koerbagh the Holy Ghost is identical to reason itself and the most perfect of God's gifts, the two are not, or at least not wholly, equivalent for Jelles, Balling, Wiszowaty, Zwicker, Rieuwertsz, and most or all other Socinians.[57] Koerbagh, who advocates a one-substance monism, akin to Spinoza's, and was emphatically a secular freethinker, clearly understood that the Socinians turn the principle of 'above reason' into the very pivot of their system.[58] But employing the notion of 'above reason' to explain their belief in revelation, biblical miracles, and the Resurrection, insists Koerbagh, is invalid 'since nothing either against or above nature can happen', any more than 'visions', he says, can be anything other than wholly subjective mental disturbances in the individuals who experience them.[59]

Despite sympathizing with a sect fiercely persecuted for centuries, Bayle brackets the Socinians along with the *rationaux* as a group trapped in irresolvable self-contradiction; likewise, Koerbagh objects that since they deny Jesus' divinity

54 Labrousse, *Pierre Bayle*, ii.190; McKenna, 'La Norme et la transgression', 129, 133–4.

55 McKenna, 'La Norme et la transgression', 129, 133–4; *Bibliothèque choisie*, 10 (1706), 422.

56 Koerbagh, *Een Ligt Schijnende*, 271; Wielema, 'Adriaan Koerbagh', 68–9.

57 Koerbagh, *Een Ligt Schijnende*, 217; Fix, *Prophecy and Reason*, 206–10.

58 Koerbagh, *Een Ligt Schijnende*, 68, 75–6; Kolakowski, *Chrétiens*, 408, 410; Wielema, *March*, 80, 84.

59 Koerbagh, *Bloemhof*, 447, 647; Wielema, 'Adriaan Koerbagh', 68.

Socinian adoration of Christ amounts to idolatry: 'for to worship a man is idolatry'.[60] Socinian 'reason', in short, was not at all the same thing as Radical Enlightenment 'reason', and Socinian Bible criticism with its deep reverence for Scripture as above and wholly separate from everything else, the Word of God and prime source of truth, was very far from the same thing as radical Bible hermeneutics. It was also far from Le Clerc's conception of text criticism. Actually, as amateurs rather than professional scholars, Socinians mostly practised a rather unsophisticated style of exegesis and often, as with Kuyper and the Rotterdam poet Joachim Oudaen (1628–92), openly scorned 'philosophy', urging men to 'prefer the simplicity which is in Christ', as Bury puts it, 'before all the subtleties which are in the schools'.[61] Daniel Zwicker, a leading theorist of toleration and bold Socinian exegete, was interested, if his personal library allows us to judge, neither in recent scientific developments, nor in Hobbes, nor the exegetical theories of Spinoza and Meyer; a Patristic as well as biblical scholar, one of those who laboured to prove that none of the Fathers prior to Justin Martyr (late in the second century) embraced the dogma of the Trinity, he simply refused to engage with the challenge of recent philosophy, science, or philosophical exegetics.[62]

Some Socinian Collegiants, no doubt, *were* seriously interested in philosophy. Had this not been the case, there would indeed have been no basis for Spinoza's pro-Socinian tactics and theory of Christ's being uniquely inspired by God. Several, like Jelles, Rieuwertsz, the embattled Jan Bredenburg (1643–91), and also Balling who, like Jelles, was a close friend of Spinoza and who translated his commentary on Descartes published at Amsterdam in 1663, were deeply immersed in Cartesianism as well as Spinozism, just as Schmidt, later, was in Wolffianism, and conceived the summons to adopt reason as their tool as an summons to reconcile philosophical and religious truth. Balling's tract *Het Licht op den Kandelaar* [The Light on the Candlestick] of 1662, published under the name of the Quaker leader William Ames, has often been regarded as the first 'Spinozist' publication. But what is most significant about it is precisely the delicate, ambivalent, and also precarious ambiguity of its stress on the 'inner light' and unmistakable mysticism of its identification of 'the light' of reason as Man's true guide with Christ, the 'spirit' and 'the Truth', with which it endeavours to reconcile Cartesian reason, and Spinozism, with Collegiant spirituality.[63] Precisely, this precariousness infused all the efforts of the 'philosophical' Socinians to effect a junction of philosophy with Socinian doctrine.

Unable to bridge the gap between themselves and Spinoza as Bredenburg's efforts, and the bitter internecine quarrel which resulted, proved all too clearly,[64] repudiated by Koerbagh and by Bayle, neither did the 'Unitaires' offer any real basis

[60] Koerbagh, *Een Ligt Schijnende*, 271; van Bunge, *From Stevin to Spinoza*, 102; Israel, 'Meyer, Koerbagh', 203.

[61] [Bury], *Naked Gospel*, 102; Cragg, *Church and the Age*, 153; van Bunge, *Johannes Bredenburg*, 90–8.

[62] Kolakowski, *Chrétiens*, 226; Bietenholz, *Daniel Zwicker*, 271–2.

[63] Balling, *Het Licht*, 4; Fix, *Prophecy and Reason*, 200–5; Klever, *Mannen rond Spinoza*, 20–2; van Bunge, *From Stevin to Spinoza*, 107, 134; van Bunge et al. (eds.), *Dictionary*, i. 46.

[64] van Bunge, *Johannes Bredenburg*, 198–254; Israel, *Radical Enlightenment*, ch. xix.

for an alliance with the Arminians. Van Limborch, like the English and Swiss Latitudinarians, while having no wish to sound intolerant, nurtured powerful objections to Socinianism.[65] Eschewing the harsh condemnation of Jurieu and of the major churches, Le Clerc and the *rationaux* nevertheless viewed Socinianism with scarcely more sympathy or sense of affinity than Koerbagh, Meyer, or Bayle. For the Socinians seemed to Le Clerc, as to Bayle, simultaneously to embrace revelation and miracles and yet deny them. Where Le Clerc's 'rationalism', like Locke's, was structural and formal, deeply concerned with the integration and conjunction of theology with philosophy and science, the Socinians' usually less philosophical approach was often little more than a crude 'common sense' contextual 'rationalism' directed at ironing out particular difficulties in Bible interpretation.[66] Bernard was even more hostile, scorning Socinus' Bible hermeneutics as the remedy of an incendiary who systematically burns down old buildings to save the architects the trouble of repairing them.[67]

A prominent scholar who devoted close attention to the Socinian question was Mathurin Veyssière de La Croze (1661–1739), royal Prussian librarian in Berlin, professor of philosophy, collector of clandestine manuscripts, and correspondent of Leibniz and Bayle. The most gifted of the estranged former monks who absconded from the French monasteries under Louis XIV, La Croze, at the age of 35—and already famous for his erudition—had in 1696 fled the Benedictine abbey of Saint-Germain-des-Prés in Paris, escaping, via Basel where he joined the Reformed, to Brandenburg.[68] Even before that, he had long inwardly abjured Catholicism, ecclesiastical authority, and divine right monarchy, as a result, seemingly, of witnessing royal repression of the Huguenots and Jansenists and perusing 'livres de Hollande', as well as the intellectually bigoted attitude, as he saw it, of his own order. He now construed Catholicism's adherence 'to the pretended Holy See', as it is put in the English version of his *Dissertations historiques* (1707), a 'doctrine so much boasted, and so ill prov'd', as 'the most certain proof of the errors of that Church'.[69] Clerical corruption and bad faith were nowhere clearer, in his view, than in the political intrigues of the Catholic courts: the French royal court 'peut tout à Rome', he complained, while the Jesuits 'peuvent tout à la cour de France'.[70]

Discarding the old certainties, La Croze went fervently in search of the new, in the process acquiring pronounced Deist sympathies.[71] An indefatigable researcher, close to Leibniz from the end of the 1690s, he worked on a vast scale, according to his biographer Jordan covering all the books in his library with dense handwritten annotations. His immense erudition and extensive knowledge of ancient and

[65] van Gelder, *Getemperde vrijheid*, 178, 275; Simonutti, 'Religion, Philosophy and Science', 309, 319; Spellman, *Latitudinarians*, 98, 100–2.

[66] *Bibliothèque choisie*, 10 (1706), 379–80; Kühler, *Het Socinianisme*, 239–40.

[67] Bernard, *De l'excellence de la religion*, 160; [Barbeyrac], *Éloge*, 55.

[68] Jordan, *Histoire*, 10–11, 14; Mulsow, *Die drei Ringe*, 10–11, 14–15.

[69] La Croze, *Historical and Critical Reflections*, 153–4.

[70] La Croze, *Dissertations historiques*, 'preface' p. 3^v.

[71] Jordan, *Histoire*, 79, 227; Geissler, 'Littérature clandestine', 485; Mulsow, *Die drei Ringe*, 17.

oriental languages—to which, however, he failed to add Chinese as Leibniz urged him to do—won admiration but also, along with his undogmatic cast of mind and zealous interest in heretics and outcasts of every hue, and vigorous advocacy of a comprehensive toleration, rendered him widely suspect. Some thought him a sympathizer of Bayle,[72] others a surreptitious propagator of Socinianism, interpreting his interest in Islam and a section of his *Dissertations critiques*, where he compares Socinianism with Muhammadanism, claiming that Islam with its stress on the unity of God is 'so like Socinianism, that it is impossible to distinguish them', as implying empathy for both.[73]

Yet, La Croze too, for all his impartiality and extensive contacts with Socinian scholars, categorically rejected the teaching of what he called 'that unhappy and cursed sect'. More importantly, he evaluated contemporary Socinianism in a way which strongly reinforces the impression that its contribution to the emergence of both the Radical and mainstream Enlightenments was mostly indirect and contingent rather than central or profound. Not unsympathetic, he was nevertheless overwhelmingly negative in his conclusions. By denying Christ's divinity and Resurrection, and speaking 'with contempt of the Fathers', the Socinians, he thought, had left themselves with no alternative but to claim the unparalleled and supernatural significance of Christ's life and example while wholly lacking any dogmatic basis for doing so. The outcome was a cart too precarious for its load, inherently prone to the chronic instability he identified as Socinianism's prime feature. Like Bayle, La Croze attributed this fatal debility to the Socinians' applying reason to matters of faith. Their whole system rested, it seemed to him, on a central contradiction: 'l'existence de Dieu', he points out, again not unlike Bayle, cannot be proved by reason: 'cependant tout dépend de la raison dans le Socinianisme'. Who can fail to see in such a fragile construct 'une porte ouverte à l'athéisme, et à l'abnégation de Dieu'? [74]

Like Koerbagh, Meyer, and Bayle, La Croze charged the Socinians above all with intellectual incoherence. The movement's history, he urged, proves Socinianism had always been an agent of disintegration, the subversive sect of the 'Demi-Judaïzans' having split from the Polish Socinians before spreading, as Socinus himself records, throughout Poland and Lithuania to infect Transylvania.[75] Still more disastrous, in recent times, Socinianism had gained ground in Germany and many other parts: numerous young men in their ignorance had been seduced 'par un amour aveugle pour la nouveauté'. Religion and piety would long continue to suffer grievously from their proselytizing; for experience showed their doctrine leads as a matter of course 'au Déisme et au libertinage'. For while Socinianism never lacks for new adherents often even more zealous than their predecessors, such converts, no matter how ardent at first, rarely show enduring commitment to their creed.

[72] Mulsow, *Die drei Ringe*, 66–85; Mulsow, *Moderne*, 71, 75; Mulsow, 'Views', 29–30, 43–5.

[73] La Croze, *Historical and Critical Reflections*, 156; Häseler, *Wanderer*, 67; Thomson, 'L'Utilisation de l'Islam', 251; Mulsow, *Die drei Ringe*, 72.

[74] La Croze, *Dissertations historiques*, 151; Geissler, 'Littérature clandestine', 485.

[75] La Croze, *Dissertations historiques*, 152.

Even a short time sufficed for many new adherents, once 'appris'd of their [teachers'] wavering state between doubt and knowledge', to become disillusioned and 'like people ready to drown, grasp at the first thing that comes their way'.[76]

The result was a spiritual catastrophe driving these disorientated souls in all directions. Some 'embrace Spinozism', he observes, 'some popery; others go over to Judaism or to Mahometanism, [but] very few of them return to orthodox religion'.[77] Since the Reformation, there had indeed been various recorded instances of Italian, Polish, and German Socinians fleeing Christian for Ottoman lands and embracing the, to them, supposedly familiar tenets of Islam.[78] Likewise the most renowned Jewish convert of the age, the former Lutheran Pietist Johan Peter Spaeth (*c*.1644–1701), having briefly flirted with Catholicism, embraced Socinianism, but, after denying Christ's divinity, soon completely jettisoned his Christian heritage, joining the Jews in Amsterdam and having himself circumcised. Spaeth, moreover, was additional proof that Socinianism fomented Spinozism no less than Judaism: for Johann Georg Wachter (1673–1757), having disputed in Amsterdam with 'Moses Germanus', as Spaeth became known after his conversion, setting out his views in his *Der Spinozismus in Jüdenthumb* (1699), showed this singular apostate to be as much a 'Spinozist' as he was cabbalist and Jew.[79]

Disenchanted Socinians, says La Croze, might become Spinozists, but were equally likely to embrace popery, the most celebrated example in the Huguenot world of defection first to Socinianism and then Catholicism being that of Isaac Papin, a nephew as well as former disciple of the Arminian Pajon. Already deemed *pajoniste* on leaving Bordeaux at the time of the Revocation, Papin, after a spell in England as an Anglican minister, had tried to secure a preaching position in the Netherlands but fell foul of Jurieu who, at the Walloon Synod at 's-Hertogenbosch in 1687, charged him with excessive enthusiasm for toleration as well as suspect theology sullied, he claimed, by Socinian and Deistic tendencies.[80] Papin then migrated to Danish Altona where, for a time, he associated with Aubert de Versé in an Arminian-dominated Huguenot church, headed by the *pajoniste* minister La Conseillère. From there, he emitted a counter-blast, accusing the orthodox Jurieu of predestinarian 'fatalisme', and much less plausibly, one might think, of believing, with Hobbes and Spinoza, 'qu'il n'y a qu'une seule substance', namely matter, and that this substance is God.[81]

Papin's Socinian phase, however, if sensational was brief. He grasped, notes Bayle, that reason cannot demonstrate the existence of one almighty God so that this vital information can be delivered to us only through revelation, a realization which led him utterly to abjure Socinianism.[82] This did nothing to mollify Jurieu, however, who had Papin publicly condemned for heresy at the Walloon Synod at

[76] Ibid. [77] La Croze, *Historical and Critical Reflections*, 198.

[78] Ibid. 212; Thomson, 'L'Utilisation de l'Islam', 251.

[79] Israel, *Radical Enlightenment*, 645–50; Mulsow, *Moderne*, 281, 401.

[80] Bayle, *Réponse*. iii. 717–18; Knetsch, *Pierre Jurieu*, 263–4; Zuber, 'Isaac Papin', 3, 11.

[81] Ibid. 11–12; Labrousse, *Pierre Bayle*, i. 154, 225 n.

[82] Bayle, *Continuation*, ii. 513; Lévesque de Burigny, *De l'examen*, 39, 47–8.

Kampen in 1688. Humiliation in the Netherlands and lack of prospects in Germany doubtless contributed to his subsequent return to France, and abjuring of all forms of Protestantism. But in essence his conversion to Catholicism stemmed from his discarding of Socinian 'reason'. If his reception into the Catholic fold, on 15 January 1690 in Paris, was a publicity disaster for the Huguenots, the setback ensued, according to Jurieu, from misplaced passion for toleration and, to La Croze, from the effects of Socinianism.[83]

Intellectual freedom, the 'way of liberty', held Papin, to which he himself had misguidedly trusted, cannot ground a truly Christian world-view. For 'according to the Protestant principles', as the English rendering of his *La Tolérance des Protestans* (1692) puts it, we must tolerate those who make 'profession to take the Scripture for the rule of their faith, and to have very well examined it'; this, as all Protestants admit, plainly follows from the *sola Scriptura* principle. Hence, Protestants must not only 'tolerate the Arminians, the Pelagians, the Arians, Socinians, and all other hereticks, past and present who all pretend to follow exactly the Holy Scripture' but also Deists and Spinozists who study Scripture independently and then 'declare they do not believe that God hath created the World from nothing, that God is infinite, that Man is born in Original Sin' or that 'Jesus Christ is God equal to the Father, that there are three persons in the blessed Trinity, [or] that Christ Jesus died to satisfie the justice of God for our sins'.[84] For *les Spinosistes*, no less than Protestants, the foundational 'règle de la vérité' is reason and individual judgement and yet, after searching, they find nothing in Scripture to support Christian belief.[85]

'For, either the design which a man hath to follow the truth is sufficient to give him a right to this liberty or it is not.'[86] Since Scripture makes no mention of the Trinity, observes Papin, clearly answering Socinianism can 'have no force but in the mouth of the Catholics'.[87] Only the Catholic Church, he held, can counter the rational-minded Protestant's inevitable progressive slippage from Calvinism to Arminianism, from Arminianism to Socinianism, and from Socinianism to Deism.[88] Jurieu was right, he remarks, 'when he said in a private letter he wrote to me' that it is the 'doctrine of the universal toleration which disfigures our Reformation, and which brings so many different religions into Holland—tis the most dangerous of all heresies, because it comprehends them all'. In retrospect, the only word of Jurieu's here which Papin wished to alter was 'disfigures': 'he would have spoken more truly, had he said, that this doctrine of toleration unmasks the Reformation. For it doth not disfigure it, but makes it appear, and known for what it really is.' The 'Arminians' say they intend a 'universal toleration' of Christians. But their 'way of liberty' leads ineluctably to a general toleration not only of all Christian sects but also 'of Jews, Muslims, Deists and atheists too'.[89]

[83] *Bibliothèque françoise*, 3 (1724), 288; Labrousse, *Pierre Bayle*, i. 72; Knetsch, *Pierre Jurieu*, 307, 311.

[84] Papin, *Toleration*, 40, 58–9, 93; Mori, *Bayle philosophe*, 261.

[85] Papin, *Toleration*, 93; *Journal littéraire*, 1 (1713), 360, 363–71; Vernière, *Spinoza*, 232–3.

[86] Papin, *Toleration*, 105.

[87] Ibid. 49; Simonutti, 'Absolute, Universal', 713.

[88] Papin, *Toleration*, 58–9, 63; Zuber, 'Isaac Papin', 8.

[89] Papin, *Toleration*, 101–2.

It is, held Papin, a sign of the corruptness of human nature that there abound so many different opinions about the most important questions. 'There is nothing else', he urged the champions of toleration, 'but religion which can remedy this disorder, and it cannot do it but in drawing men from a road, or to speak better from a desert cut into a thousand different paths, where Nature leaves men, which is that of the *examen* and the independence'. The only way lies in 'causing them to enter into the road of submission and obedience to an authority divine and infallible'.[90] 'La voye d'authorité' is thus far better than a 'universal toleration' in practice, he urged, as is confirmed 'par l'usage de tous les siècles'.[91] Not the least exasperating aspect of Papin's reversing his own earlier stance, for both Jurieu and Le Clerc, was his concluding by embracing Bayle's proposition that true Christianity means submitting human reason wholly 'à l'authorité de la foi'.[92]

Socinians invoked reason but actually, held Bayle, La Croze, and the post-1690 Papin, grounded their teaching on inconsistency, contradiction, and self-delusion. At war with all the main churches, they could not help but sow dissension throughout Christendom. Where La Croze, like Le Clerc and Leibniz, judged the work of Christian reunification the highest task for all who aspired to ground an 'enlightened' Christianity, Socinians seemingly had nothing to contribute but strife and discord. La Croze, having sent his text to Leibniz, received a long letter from his always sympathetic friend in December 1706, agreeing with him that there was much resemblance between Socinianism and Muhammadanism and also that internal Christian rivalry and splits were the greatest of all ecclesiastical disasters, the churches' own schisms and mutual persecution being responsible for the lightning speed of Islam's conquest of the Christians of Syria, Egypt, and North Africa in the seventh century, a reverse so resounding that still in their day it stood as clear proof that much was wrong in Christendom.[93]

Leibniz agreed also that far from advancing Christian reunification, Socinianism could only further undermine Christian unity by inflaming the disagreements between the churches and exacerbating the tension between theology and philosophy. Besides denying Christ's divinity, Holy Trinity, and the Eucharist, what he calls their being 'too quick to reject everything that fails to conform to the order of nature' often led the Socinians to reject the soul's immortality and wholly subvert 'natural theology' by denying 'Dieu la prescience des choses contingentes' as part of a misguided quest to rationalize religion by removing the age-old dilemma of how a prescient God could possibly condemn Man to Original Sin and sinners to eternal damnation.[94] Their solution, the claim that God does *not* foresee what is contingent and did not, after all, predict Adam's disobedience, struck Leibniz as yielding a wholly inadequate idea of God, one unworthy of the 'author of all things' and again self-contradictory 'so that', as the English rendering of his letter expresses it, 'the

90 Ibid. 185; Landucci, 'Appendice', 71; Mori, *Bayle philosophe*, 261.

91 *Journal littéraire*, 1(1713), 371.

92 Bayle, *Entretiens*, 16–20; Simonutti, 'Absolute, Universal', 713.

93 Jordan, *Histoire*, 79.

94 Leibniz, *Theodicy*, 161; Leibniz, *New Essays*, 498; Mulsow, *Moderne*, 172.

Socinians seem to spoil both natural and reveal'd religion, as well in theory as in practice, and destroy a great part of their beautys'.[95] Socinianism was indeed something calamitous and for the Socinians themselves as much as anyone. Yet none of this justified rulers persecuting them: it is only 'la mauvaise volonté' which should be punished, he concurred with Le Clerc and La Croze, 'et nullement l'erreur'.[96]

According to Bayle too, the notion that God lacks omniscience and prescience is absurdly self-contradictory, a recipe only for subverting God's government of the world without in the end freeing him of blame.[97] Here, for once, Bayle and Leibniz closely converged, both deeming it totally misconceived to claim God cannot, or does not, foresee contingent events.[98] Doubtless the sixteenth-century Socinian founders, men such as Laelio Socinus (1525–62) of Siena and Faustus Socinus (1539–1604) who fled Italy in 1574, and settled in Poland, or Michael Servetus, burnt by the Calvinists at Geneva in 1553, had been sincere and pious in their way. Yet while these Italian and Spanish anti-Trinitarians imagined, concludes Leibniz, that they were completing the Reformation of Christendom initiated by the Germans, in reality 'ils ont presque anéanti notre religion, au lieu de la purifier'.[99]

95 La Croze, *Historical and Critical Reflections*, 254; Leibniz, *Theodicy*, 343; Goldenbaum, 'Leibniz as a Lutheran', 181, 184, 187–8.

96 La Croze, *Dissertations historiques*, 176; Rutherford, 'Leibniz and Mysticism', 36–7.

97 Labrousse, *Pierre Bayle*, ii. 388, 413.

98 Leibniz, *Philosophical Essays*, 323.

99 La Croze, *Dissertations historiques*, 176.

6

Locke, Bayle, and Spinoza: A Contest of Three Toleration Doctrines

1. TOLERATION FROM LOCKE TO BARBEYRAC

The question of toleration constituted a severe problem in Early Enlightenment Europe. The religious stalemate of the Thirty Years War left the German empire in a condition of permanent confessional deadlock with three entrenched, formally acknowledged confessional blocs—Lutheran, Catholic, and Calvinist—solemnized by the Peace of Westphalia (1648). It also removed all immediate prospect of ending the *de facto* partition of the Low Countries into opposed Catholic and Protestant entities, or re-establishing protected minority Catholic worship in Scandinavia and the Baltic, or recognized Protestant worship in the Czech lands and Austria. To complicate matters further a century of steady confessionalization had enabled the major confessions to put down such sturdy roots that wherever princes, or city governments, sponsoring one faith were afterwards replaced by successors of another, as in the Palatinate (whence many Calvinists fled after 1685) or Silesia, divergence of prince and people added fresh layers of disparity to the already acute difficulties posed by religious plurality and minorities. Such changes marooned scattered but deeply rooted Protestant communities in areas like Austria, Alsace, Silesia, and Poland where the sovereign was now more militantly Catholic than before and, conversely, ensconced Catholic pockets in areas like States Brabant, eastern Overijssel, and the Lower Rhine duchies of Cleves and Mark where the sovereign was Protestant. There were even Imperial Free Cities, like Augsburg and Ravensburg, where, under the Peace terms, Catholics and Lutherans enjoyed minutely specified equal rights, nurturing a stifling 'parity mania'.[1]

To complete this bewildering, intractable mosaic of confessional confrontation, suspicion, and tension, there was the effect of commerce which fostered trading communities, especially of Calvinists, Jews, and Greek Orthodox, in major entrepôts and court cities like Hamburg, Venice, Livorno, Vienna, Berlin, Lübeck, Danzig, and Trieste, where petitions for some limited form of legal toleration often precipitated fierce local disputes. In addition to all this, there was the friction generated by sharp

[1] Whaley, 'Tolerant Society?', 180, 182.

disparities of policy on toleration within neighbouring jurisdictions, an extreme instance being the case of Danish Altona where all the main confessions (as well as the Jews, Mennonites, and Arminians) enjoyed an exceptionally wide toleration, adjoining Hamburg where these same minorities were firmly excluded from even remotely comparable rights. Finally, there was the impact of the Huguenot exodus from France, in the mid and late 1680s, besides several lesser expulsions like those of the Jews from Vienna, in 1669, and of around 20,000 Lutherans from the archbishopric of Salzburg in 1731–2. All these further adjustments to Europe's confessional map obliged both advocates and opponents of a wider toleration to argue and reassess the question in a continually changing but extremely fraught context which meant that toleration theories in this period both proliferated and gained more of a footing in political debate, while yet facing a predominant if not almost universal tendency to reject the underlying principle and condemn the cultural and social consequences of toleration.

Resistance to any kind of theoretically grounded toleration remained everywhere extremely tenacious and to the extent that it was broken down was reduced only by a dogged combination of practical pressures and philosophical argument. This simultaneously practical and theoretical quest for local solutions was played out in a wide variety of scenarios across the continent, albeit few were as bitter as that in Hamburg, a Lutheran city with numerous minorities none of which enjoyed a secure toleration, where the arrival of some 900 Huguenot refugees during 1685–6 led to heavy renewed pressure on the city Senate to allow a public Calvinist church and community institutions. Always refused in the past, this time such permission was both more urgently needed and more strongly urged, with the powerful backing of the court in Berlin.[2] Yet, once again, pleas for toleration were resoundingly rebuffed by the city's traditionally intolerant populace and clergy: citing legal precedent, and imperial privileges, as well as theological arguments, formal toleration for Calvinism, as likewise anything beyond hidden, private house synagogues for Jews,[3] and inconspicuous house chapels for Catholics, was firmly rejected.

Popular and ecclesiastical opposition to toleration in Hamburg was so strong that the city's Lutheran pastors, in 1697–8, even managed, against the wishes of the Senate, to secure additional discriminatory enactments against the Jews, further curtailing the limited residence rights granted in the early seventeenth century, and imposing a new special tax specific to them, a measure which so alienated the long-established Sephardic community that its leading merchants and financiers mostly relocated at this time to Amsterdam.[4] A further twist to the already highly convoluted Hamburg toleration debate of the 1690s, as in many other places in northern Europe, was the bitter feuding between strict Lutheran orthodoxy and the confessionally more pliant Pietist movement, the latter, though, in this case being adversely affected by their comparatively liberal attitude towards tolerating

[2] Whaley, *Religious Toleration*, 124–5. [3] Ibid. 75–9, 104; Israel, *Empires and Entrepots*, 351.
[4] Ibid. 212; Israel, *Diasporas*, 502; Whaley, *Religious Toleration*, 79–80.

non-Lutherans. In the 1720s, the issue of toleration was again well to the fore in Hamburg when liberal elements in the Senate, anxious about the city's economic difficulties, and drawing on arguments of Christian Thomasius, the leading theorist of toleration in Germany, Christian Wolff, and others, introduced new proposals for a limited toleration, notably through the reform group known as the Hamburg Patriotic Society.[5] By this stage, philosophy was clearly making its mark; but it was not as strong as traditional arguments opposed to toleration. The Patriots were denounced from the pulpit as 'indifferentists' and advocates of Christian Thomasius' ideas, and again the toleration proposals were thwarted. Renewed efforts to secure a French-speaking church for the Huguenots in Hamburg in the 1740s again came to nothing, neutralized by the argument that if toleration was once granted to the French Reformed, the Senate would come under pressure to accord comparable rights to Dutch Calvinists, Catholics, Jews, and Greek Orthodox as well.

Likewise, in the 1740s, the last Protestant deputies were finally excluded from the national Diet of the Polish kingdom, a land marked by a steady growth in religious intolerance from the early seventeenth century onwards.[6] Intolerance, in fact, won many victories during the Early Enlightenment and by no means only on the European side of the Atlantic. Puritan establishments continued to dominate most of New England. The upheaval of 1688–9 witnessed a resurgence of hard-line Calvinism in the still predominantly Dutch city of New York while, in Maryland, the 'Glorious Revolution' not only overthrew Lord Baltimore's proprietorship but largely reversed the coexistence of Catholics and Protestants in place since 1649, Anglicanism as in neighbouring Virginia henceforth being the established church with Catholics, as in the other colonies, excluded from voting and holding office.[7] Among Britain's North American colonies, only Pennsylvania and Rhode Island were in any meaningful sense enclaves of religious freedom. Toleration in other words was a matter of immediate relevance, great significance, and boundless difficulty for virtually the entire population of late seventeenth- and early eighteenth-century Europe and America, with only a tiny fringe of opinion being yet willing to contemplate adoption of toleration on principle.

At the same time, of course, there was no single principle of toleration. The toleration advocated, despite its inherent philosophical difficulties, by the Hamburg Patriots and other moderate mainstream enlightened groups in Germany was that of Thomasius, that is, the type of partial or guarded toleration proposed by Locke, a toleration subsequently modified, but still carefully restricted, by Jean Barbeyrac.[8] Locke's leading conservative Anglican opponent in the English toleration controversy, Jonas Proast, called his theory a plea for 'an universal Toleration

[5] Whaley, *Religious Toleration*, 39–40, 129; Whaley, 'Tolerant Society?', 182–3.

[6] Müller, 'Toleration', 212–15, 217, 221.

[7] Zagorin, *How the Idea*, 224; Johnson, 'Revolution of 1688–9', 232; Schlenther, 'Religious Faith', 128–9.

[8] Fitzpatrick, 'Toleration', 38–9; Israel, 'Spinoza, Locke', 102–3; Lomonaco, 'Jean Barbeyrac als Ausleger', 204–5.

of religions';[9] but this was hardly exact since Locke's theory stems from theological premisses tied to the quest for salvation in the hereafter, and not all religions expressly offer 'salvation of souls'. Locke's (and Barbeyrac's) theory can hence more accurately be characterized as a 'tollerantismo', as an Italian critic put it, between Christian churches;[10] for while Locke accommodates other revealed religions—notably Judaism—Jews and other tolerated non-Christians cannot be said in his schema to acquire full equality of religious status or freedom of expression.[11]

As Locke's Dutch Remonstrant friend van Limborch remarked, the argument of the anonymously published *Epistola de tolerantia* which appeared at Gouda, in both Latin and Dutch, in 1689, so closely resembles in spirit that developed by the Dutch Arminians since the 1620s, especially by Simon Episcopius (1583–1643) (and van Limborch himself), that Dutch readers, recognizing its positions as characteristically Arminian, could scarcely believe it had not been composed by a Dutch Remonstrant.[12] But this only heightened the enthusiasm with which they embraced it, van Limborch, for his part, rejoicing that 'so scholarly a text and one so serviceable to the common cause of Christianity should be deemed incapable of issuing from anywhere other than the workshop of the Remonstrants'.[13]

Whether or not Locke's thesis was quite as quintessentially Arminian as van Limborch suggests, this key work was certainly written—during the autumn of 1685, whilst lodging in Amsterdam with the Remonstrant and staunchly anti-Cartesian physician Dr Egbert Veen—at a time when the furore surrounding Louis XIV's persecution of the Huguenots was at its height and when Locke found himself fully immersed in the anti-Cartesian, anti-Spinozist, and anti-Baylean 'enlightened' Remonstrant theological world of van Limborch and Le Clerc.[14] This was also the time when he supported van Limborch in his protracted theological encounter with the Jewish controversialist Isaac Orobio de Castro and developed close ties with Le Clerc, another fervent champion of toleration—but again only a limited toleration in accordance with theological rather than philosophical criteria.[15] Locke's Latin text was later personally rendered into French by Le Clerc, appearing in that language in the *Œuvres posthumes de M. Locke*, at Rotterdam, in 1710.[16]

For Locke, each individual Christian is not just directly responsible for seeking the salvation of his or her soul but is required, as Episcopius, van Limborch, Veen, and

[9] Proast, *Third Letter Concerning Toleration*, 9.

[10] Concina, *Della religione rivelata*, ii. 362; van Eijnatten, *Mutua Christianorum tolerantia*, 39; Lomonaco, 'Religious Truth', 422–3, 427.

[11] Whaley, *Religious Toleration*, 4; Matar, 'John Locke and the Jews', 57, 62.

[12] Locke, *Correspondence*, iii. 607–12, 646–50, 681–5; Sina, *L'avvento della ragione*, 344–7; Israel, 'Toleration', 16–22, 28; Israel, 'Intellectual Debate', 18–25; Nuovo, 'Dutch Enlightenment', 769.

[13] Locke, *Correspondence*, iii. 648.

[14] Simonutti, 'Religion, Philosophy, and Science', 315; Simonutti, 'Absolute, Universal', 718–19; Pocock, *Barbarism*, i. 66.

[15] Kaplan, *From Christianity*, 275, 277–8; van Rooden and Wesselius, 'Early Enlightenment', 140–3; van Eijnatten, *Mutua Christianorum tolerantia*, 36.

[16] Zarka et al. (eds.), *Fondements philosophiques*, 102.

Le Clerc likewise insisted, to perform openly that form of worship, and live by that moral code, by which, in their view, redemption is to be sought.[17] Since 'every man has an immortal soul, capable of eternal happiness or misery; whose happiness depends on his believing and doing those things in this life which are necessary to the obtaining of God's favour, and are prescribed by God to that end', it plainly follows that dutifulness in this regard 'is the highest obligation that lies upon mankind'.[18] This is why, when discussing slavery, Locke, relying on the quasi-substantial dualism pivotal to his philosophical system, held that black slaves should be free to attend the church of their choice 'but yet no slave shall hereby be exempted from that civil dominion his master hath over him'.[19] A principled toleration is justified according to Locke, van Limborch, and Le Clerc, primarily on the ground that saving one's soul has priority over everything else in a man's life; since no worldly authority can direct or assume responsibility for saving one's soul, and it would be inappropriate and irrational for anyone to entrust his or her personal salvation to another, the Christian state must grant both the primacy of an individual's religious beliefs, duties, and observances over other concerns and their entire and unrestricted liberty in that sphere.[20]

Locke's theory of toleration, then, is overwhelmingly concerned with freedom of worship, theological debate, and religious practice, insofar as these are an extension of freedom of conscience, rather than with freedom of thought, debate, and of the press more broadly, or indeed for that matter freedom of lifestyle; indeed, Lockean toleration expressly denies liberty of thought to those who reject divine revelation—and, still more, freedom of behaviour to those who embrace a moral code divergent from that decreed for men by revelation.[21] Unwilling to accept that a comprehensive toleration in Bayle's sense is possible or desirable, Locke proposes a system of religious toleration capable of accommodating Christian plurality and strengthening freedom of choice in matters of faith—correspondingly weakening both state control over churches and the state church's standing in society—while refusing to accommodate irreligion, unbelief, and libertine lifestyle.[22] As a system it not only *did* not, but inherently *could* not, concede full equality of religious status and expression to agnostics, Buddhists, Confucianists, Hindus, or Muslims.[23]

As has often been noted, it follows from Locke's theological premisses that he is hampered theoretically, and also by preference reluctant, to extend toleration to certain groups, and, at the same time, expressly rules it out for others.[24] Compared

[17] Episcopius, *Vrye Godes-Dienst*, 37–47; Barnouw, *Philippus van Limborch*, 18, 41–4; Simonutti, *Arminianesimo e tolleranza*, 26–7, 39, 46; Israel, 'Toleration', 20–1.

[18] Locke, *Political Writings*, 421; Zagorin, *How the Idea*, 262.

[19] Glausser, 'Three Approaches', 203.

[20] Dunn, *Locke*, 17; Wootton, 'Introduction', 94–110; Marshall, *John Locke*, 119–54, 329–83.

[21] Wootton, 'Introduction', 105, 109–10; Dunn, 'Claim to Freedom', 174–8; Harris, *Mind of John Locke*, 185–6; Waldron, *God, Locke and Equality*, 209–10; Simonutti, 'Absolute, Universal', 721.

[22] Van Eijnatten, *Mutua Christianorum tolerantia*, 38–40.

[23] Matar, 'John Locke and the Jews', 50–1, 56–7; Paradis, 'Fondements', 29.

[24] Redwood, *Reason, Ridicule*, 83; Wootton, 'Introduction', 104–5; Grell and Porter, 'Toleration', 6–7.

with the full freedom of conscience espoused by Bayle and the Spinozists, Locke's toleration is indeed very substantially curtailed—and by at least six restrictions which, for most pro-'toleration' contemporaries, represented the real soundness and strength of Locke's toleration. First, since his was essentially a 'privilege' or 'immunity' from the form of worship otherwise generally prescribed by the sovereign, through the state church—hence, the Reformed Church in the United Provinces, or the Anglican Church in England—Lockean toleration can meaningfully be accorded only to entities maintaining a publicly constituted form of worship for which exemption can be claimed.[25] Claimants for exemption could be Protestant dissenters, Catholics, Jews, Muslims, or members of other defined faiths. But those subscribing to no organized religion, besides any creed failing to assert immortality of the soul, whether agnostics, Deists, Socinians, Confucianists, or *indifferenti*, while not expressly excluded are relegated to a vague limbo without clear status or acknowledged rights.

Secondly, there is Locke's well-known equivocation regarding Catholics. As an established church teaching supernatural salvation and the immortality of the soul there should be no theoretical difficulty here. But unlike Arminians such as Uyttenbogaert and Episcopius,[26] Locke leaves toleration of Catholics under something of a question mark. For the magistrate, argues the *Epistola*, is not obliged to tolerate churches claiming an authority overriding that of the sovereign, in a way potentially prejudicial to the civil peace, as Catholics do in holding the pope can dispense from oaths of allegiance, depose rulers, and release from promises made to those the papacy considers 'heretics'.[27] Much the same difficulty and doubts arise with regard to Muslims.[28] The tendency in Locke was to deny toleration to Catholics and equivocate concerning Muslims.

A third major restriction integral to Lockean toleration is the exclusion of 'atheists', meaning those who deny divine providence and judgement of men. Since atheists, *Saint-Évremondiste* Epicureans, Stoic materialists, and Spinozists do not acknowledge a knowing, active, providential God and embrace no recognized form of worship, nor seek to save their souls, under Locke's schema they were not, strictly speaking, entitled to toleration.[29] Stipulating, as Locke does, that every human being 'has an immortal soul, capable of eternal happiness or misery' whose redemption depends on fulfilling those things in this life which will secure God's 'favour, and are prescribed by God to that end, it follows from thence, first, that the observance of these things is the highest obligation that lies upon mankind, and that our utmost care, application, and diligence ought to be exercised in the search and performance of them, because there is nothing in this world that is of

25 Dunn, 'Claim to Freedom', 177–9; Marshall, *John Locke*, 367–9.

26 Episcopius, *Vrye Godes-Dienst*, 44; Israel, 'Toleration', 21.

27 Park, 'John Locke: Toleration', 14; Wootton, 'Introduction', 95; Fitzpatrick, 'Toleration', 38; O'Cathasaigh, 'Bayle and Locke', 688.

28 O'Cathasaigh, 'Bayle and Locke', 688–9.

29 Dunn, 'Claim to Freedom', 180–2; Harris, *Mind of John Locke*, 189; Park, 'John Locke: Toleration', 14–15, 17; van Eijnatten, *Mutua Christianorum tolerantia*, 38–9.

any consideration in comparison with eternity'.[30] 'Atheists', since they neither believe this nor participate in the 'stupendous and supernatural work of our salvation', *ipso facto* exclude themselves from those eligible for toleration. Locke, like Le Clerc, Christian Thomasius, Buddeus, Barbeyrac, and the entire moderate mainstream,[31] consistently denied 'atheism (which takes away all religion) to have any right to toleration at all'.[32] 'Those are not at all to be tolerated', insists Locke, 'who deny the being of a God', chiefly because 'promises, covenants and oaths, which are the bonds of human society, can have no hold upon an atheist'. For Locke, precisely as for Le Clerc and Barbeyrac, the 'taking away of God, though but even in thought, dissolves all'.[33]

The fourth major limitation, the conversionist claims basic to the case he makes for tolerating Jews (and presumably also Muslims), again stems from the theological premisses on which Locke's toleration rests. Believing Man's redemption is exclusively through Christ, and that it is the duty of Christians to effect the conversion of non-Christians, including Jews, tolerating Jews is partly justified in Locke's schema, as he explains in his *Second Letter*, against Proast, on the ground this will facilitate the work of bringing the Jews to Christianity.[34] The fifth restriction arises from the interdependence of Locke's toleration with his social contract theory; for this creates the possibility that a society where a majority uncompromisingly adheres to a particular theology could, and presumably would, by agreement of its citizens, as in Hamburg, repudiate toleration in favour of uniformity. Locke's contract theory of government, in short, prevents his consistently upholding even his restricted Christian toleration as a 'universal principle'.[35] Sixthly and finally, Lockean toleration emphatically rejects liberty of lifestyle.

In the past, historians have been so keen to emphasize Locke's liberal credentials, and immense relevance to the development of Anglo-American modernity, that there has been a unfortunate tendency to exaggerate the scope of his toleration and view it as something much wider and more 'modern' than it actually is. Also by exaggerating Locke's importance in promoting the rise of modern freedom of thought, and freedom of the individual, within the wider context of Enlightenment thought, historians have yielded a hostage to Postmodernist critics eager to deny the Enlightenment's credentials as the foundation of a just and comprehensive liberty. In reality, while it greatly appealed to his Arminian friends, and thoroughly infuriated his High Church critics, in the eyes of the *esprits forts*, and men such as Bayle, not to mention *indifferenti*, Jews, Confucianists, and Muslims, Locke's was in essence an ungenerous, defective, and potentially menacing theory. For it is a doctrine which entirely fails to address scepticism, agnosticism, indifferentism, and

30 Locke, *Political Writings*, 421.

31 *Bibliothèque choisie*, 10 (1706), 392–3, 426; Gawlick, 'Thomasius und die Denkfreiheit', 272.

32 Locke, *A Third Letter for Toleration*, 236; Lomonaco, 'Jean Barbeyrac als Ausleger', 201, 205–6; Lomonaco, 'Religious Truth', 424; Gros, 'Tolérance et le problème', 434–5.

33 Locke, *Political Writings*, 426; Lennon, 'Bayle, Locke', 190–1.

34 Matar, 'John Locke and the Jews', 57–62.

35 Michael, 'Locke, Religious Toleration', 27, 38.

Socinianism while fiercely targeting and outlawing 'atheism', and privileging Christian conceptions of proper lifestyle and sexual conduct, in such a way as to promote a particular theological conception of man. By empowering the magistrate to legislate against and suppress such vice and licentiousness as the churches deem detrimental to the work of salvation, an authority potentially affecting everyone's lifestyle, Locke cleared a wide space for sexual, dress, and moral intolerance.

Furthermore, this residual intolerance stems from his conviction that one tradition is not just mankind's most cogent and authoritative moral code but forms the necessary basis of any rational practical moral philosophy since, in his view, before revelation, despite the commendable efforts of the Greek philosophers and Confucian sages, men were largely ignorant of their duties. It was a fundamental principle of Locke's social thought, as he emphasizes in the *Reasonableness of Christianity*, that revelation is in practice indispensable to society since 'it is too hard a task for unassisted reason to establish morality in all its parts upon its true foundation with a clear and convincing light'.[36] In his *Second* and *Third Letter on Toleration*, Locke repeatedly endorses the suppression by the sovereign of what Christians consider debauchery, licentiousness, adultery, and sodomy, and while this notably illiberal doctrine strongly appealed to many Anglican, Remonstrant, and Reformed sensibilities, it plainly curtails freedom of the individual, refusing among other points of lifestyle the right to sexual freedom as conceived by radical thinkers.[37]

However, this was precisely what the moderate mainstream required. At the same time, since Locke's doctrine encourages, even advocates, the advancement of theological plurality, and therefore the weakening of state churches and their authority, at a time when religious scepticism and libertinism were spreading, his doctrine was bound to be disparaged as subversive and socially pernicious by conservative, Non-Juror, 'high-flying', and Calvinist critics. The great fallacy in Locke's theory, held Jonas Proast—and he would add that of Locke's allies, van Limborch and Le Clerc—and one for which Locke could find no remedy,[38] is that in practice many, and probably most, men, including dissolute 'practical atheists' who yet make no profession of speculative atheism, do not, as far as anyone can see, focus their efforts on saving their souls. This is often not a question of unbelief but neglect, ambition, and absorption in worldly pursuits. If some devoutly seek salvation, he urged, 'the impressions of education, the reverence and admiration of persons, worldly respects and the like incompetent motives determine far greater numbers'.[39]

The very fact so many religions exist, each supreme in a different place, proves most men merely follow convention; and while Locke might be right that the state

[36] Locke, *Reasonableness of Christianity*, 170, 172–3; Marshall, *John Locke*, 302.

[37] Marshall, *John Locke*, 378–80, 382–3; Dunn, 'Claim to Freedom', 186–7; Spitz, 'Quelques difficultés', 148–50.

[38] Spitz, 'Quelques difficultés', 129–30, 133, 139.

[39] Ibid. 129; Proast, *The Argument*, 78; Harris, *Mind of John Locke*, 293–4.

cannot compel men to believe what they do not, yet by forbidding some views, and endorsing others, contends Proast, governments can and do cause their subjects to lean one way rather than another. Hence, with calculated intolerance, the ruler ensures more and better adherence to Christian teaching.[40] If one accepts Locke's case regarding salvation, then surely men must be prodded in the right direction, albeit short of outright compulsion, preferably by monarchs powerfully supporting their established churches. When ecclesiastical authority is diminished, as in England since 1688, it is scarcely surprising, he adds, that the land should teem with such books as 'now fly so thick about this kingdom, manifestly tending to the multiplying of sects and divisions, and even to the promoting of scepticism in religion among us', or that there should proliferate 'sects and heresies (even the wildest and most absurd)' including 'Epicurism and Atheism'.[41]

'Atheism' was held by Locke, Le Clerc, Thomasius, Barbeyrac, and many others, gravely to injure civil society so that, while a limited freedom of the press is desirable, such freedom should be allowed, held Le Clerc, only 'lors qu'on ne dit rien qui soit contraire aux lois de la société civile', so that Spinozistic and atheistic books both were and should be banned.[42] While dissenting worship ought be tolerated, there should not be any willingness, as Thomasius stressed in his attacks on Tschirnhaus in 1688, and on Lau in 1720, to tolerate the kind of independent critical thinking which encourages Spinozism, libertinism, and 'atheism'.[43] Indeed, Thomasius' Lockean-style conception of toleration justified him, in his view, in keeping silent when Wolff was expelled from Prussia in 1721. For the fact that Spinozism was integrally involved, and Wolff's philosophy was reckoned by some to be quasi-Spinozistic, meant that, on grounds of 'enlightened' principle, Wolff might not be entitled to acceptance, though ostensibly, at least, Wolff too held that *Atheisterei*, presumably including Spinozism, harms society and should not be tolerated.[44]

Yet however limited, moderate mainstream toleration nevertheless constituted a remarkable new impulse in European and American history. In England, Scotland, and some of the American colonies, headed by Massachusetts, toleration and freedom of the press made impressive strides in the aftermath of the Glorious Revolution.[45] In his *Traité sur la tolérance* of 1762, Voltaire makes four claims about the progress of toleration since the end of the Thirty Years War, all true and all significant. He notes that for the first time in centuries there had, since the signing of the Peace of Westphalia in 1648, been a decisive shift from intolerance to tolerance.[46] This, he thought, contrasted dramatically with the duality previously

[40] Zagorin, *How the Idea*, 266. [41] Proast, *Third Letter Concerning Toleration*, 34–5.

[42] *Bibliothèque choisie*, 15 (1708), 76.

[43] Israel, *Radical Enlightenment*, 640–1, 653–4; Gawlick, 'Thomasius und die Denkfreiheit', 269–72.

[44] Gawlick, 'Thomasius und die Denkfreiheit', 272–3; Schreiner, 'Toleranz', in *Geschichtliche Grundbegriffe*, vi. 556.

[45] Tyacke, 'Introduction', 7–16; Israel, 'William III and Toleration', 129–70; Johnson, 'Revolution of 1688–9', 234, 240.

[46] Voltaire, *Traité sur la tolérance*, 48–55.

characteristic of world history, a bifurcation between whole eras of tolerance as prevailed for millennia in China and Japan, and an unremitting intolerance in lands such as in Portugal and the Spanish empire. Secondly, he sees that this transformation had occurred only in one specific part of the world—Germany, Britain, the Netherlands, and France besides English-speaking America. Thirdly, he points out that the intellectual changes that engineered this breakthrough took place during the period previous to his own, that is during the late seventeenth century.

Finally and most importantly, he attributed this great advance in the history of humanity to a remarkable new and powerful tool—namely 'la philosophie, la seule philosophie' had disarmed the hands which superstition had for so long covered with blood, 'et l'esprit humain, au réveil de son ivresse, s'est étonné des excès où l'avait emporté le fanatisme'.[47] This, of course, was a superficial view at most only half true. The real causes driving Enlightenment toleration were certainly partly social and cultural: the devastation of the Thirty Years War and the complete stalemate resulting from the clash of Catholicism and Protestantism were the prime causes. Bayle and Diderot, in particular, understood that it was the pain, misery, and destruction caused by religious conflict which had been mankind's most effective teacher: a crucial moral lesson had been learnt. Some men had instinctively grasped, as Diderot saw it, even if they could not intellectually comprehend it, that religious doctrines are not what is most central in human life. But it was true that all this could only be rationalized by philosophy and that the final outcome, justified toleration, was unthinkable without first reconfiguring the relationship between theology and philosophy.

However, by insisting on a Lockean format for the new freedom of religion, leading juristic and Natural Law writers, like Jean Barbeyrac, helped ensure that reformist court officials and governments endorsed and sponsored a type of toleration which rigorously limited freedom of thought, criticism, and conduct. The moderate Enlightenment saw good reason to be emphatically Lockean in its approach. But its illiberal implications and hostility to the 'tolérance universelle' of the Radical Enlightenment need to be more stressed by historians and philosophers than they have been.[48] The quest for individual emancipation in the modern sense remained firmly blocked. Indeed, by the mid eighteenth century, Locke's and Barbeyrac's conception, with its stress on the core doctrines of religion as the essential underpinning of the moral order and frame of society, was seemingly being used as much to justify restricting, as promoting, toleration.[49] In this way, respectable moderate mainstream 'toleration' came to be institutionalized as a semi-secular establishment doctrine of authorized governmental intolerance.

47 Voltaire, *Traité sur la tolérance*, 49; [Voltaire], *La Voix du sage*, 414.

48 Paganini, *Analisi della fede*, 197; Paradis, 'Fondements', 34; Turchetti, 'Élie Saurin', 187–8, 197.

49 Rétat, *Dictionnaire de Bayle*, 40; van Eijnatten, 'Huguenot Clerisy', 212; Lomonaco, 'Natural Right', 137–8.

2. BAYLE'S FREEDOM OF CONSCIENCE

Not unnaturally, among the post-1685 Huguenot diaspora, scattered throughout north-western Europe from Dublin to Berlin, pro-toleration attitudes abounded and nowhere more so than in the Huguenots' new intellectual heartland—the Dutch Republic. In the writings of Bayle, Le Clerc, Élie Saurin, Aubert de Versé, Basnage, Basnage de Beauval, Jaquelot, Barbeyrac, and Jacques Bernard—not to be confused with the very different and radical-minded Jean-Frédéric Bernard—the Huguenots produced a body of toleration theory such as had no precedent and no parallel in subsequent European history. In Holland, native Dutch toleration theorists like Bayle's Arminian patron Adriaen Paets, the Remonstrant theologian van Limborch, and the Leiden professor Gerard Noodt (1647–1725) helped enhance the image and broaden the scope of a practical tolerance which ever since the Revolt against Spain surpassed any other known in the West but was nevertheless still only relatively liberal. For even if enforcement remained patchy, late seventeenth-century Holland, with regard to public debate, group discussion, and publication, continued to maintain a broadly framed ban on Socinian, Spinozist, and other anti-christological, atheistic, or sexually libertine points of view.[50]

Yet toleration was undeniably gaining ground. Even in France, as the Abbé Houtteville observed with deep alarm in 1722, though there had been no formal decree of toleration, no observer of French society under the new regency government, headed by the libertine Philippe, duc d'Orléans (1715–23), could fail to be struck by the fundamental change in either attitudes, or realities of religious life, since Louis XIV's death in 1715. Without people even thinking about it, let alone discussing the question, he says, toleration had, on a day-to-day, pragmatic, basis, quietly but rapidly, become socially acceptable to most of the educated. Where before 1715, uniformity in matters of belief and strict doctrinal discipline was generally insisted on, now in the new post-Louis XIV France, in practice if not in theory 'on laisse chacun arbitre de ses opinions particulières et libre de se composer à son gré sa propre religion'.[51] Official persecution of Protestants and Jews had largely ceased, inter-confessional strife and polemics, if by no means ended, certainly eased, and, above all, attitudes in French society generally became more 'tolerant'.

Many applauded. But at the same time, leaders of opinion in all the countries affected reacted with consternation to the extent, speed, and ultimate implications of this great cultural shift. Houtteville, though an ecclesiastic of relatively liberal inclinations, had no doubt that this transition to practical toleration was a crucially important but also potentially catastrophic development, something likely to diminish the church's authority drastically, weaken the ecclesiastical estate, and

[50] Israel, *Dutch Republic*, 499–505, 637–45,674–6, 952–6; Israel, 'Intellectual Debate', 21–35; van Eijnatten, *Mutua Christianorum tolerantia*, 6–20; Velema, 'Introduction', 11–13.

[51] Houtteville, *Religion chrétienne prouvée*, i, p. viii.

concede an excessive and dangerous liberty to the individual. Among the perils lurking behind the new *de facto* toleration, in his view, the most dangerous and insidious stemmed from the practical impossibility of distinguishing rigorously between toleration of other churches affirming the central 'mysteries' of Christianity and toleration of irreligion, impiety, and Spinozism.[52]

Criticizing the tolerant policy of the Orléans regency regime on the grounds that a broad religious freedom undermines the standing of churchmen and nurtures a freedom of thought which inevitably breeds libertinism, Deism, and secular philosophical modes of thought, Houtteville highlighted the central dilemma of the western Enlightenment. If intolerance and religious persecution are inherently wrong and socially undesirable because they engender instability, persecution, and strife, as pro-toleration writers urged, most were equally convinced that atheism, Socinianism, libertinism, and irreligion undermine the social order so that these must continue to be repressed by government. Hence the only toleration theorists respected by the moderate mainstream sought to steer educated opinion towards a guarded toleration, like that theorized by Locke, Le Clerc, and such figures as Noodt[53] and Barbeyrac.[54] As we have seen, the result was to anchor mainstream Enlightenment toleration theory within a judicial and theological framework which could be just as readily used to curtail, as advance, freedom of thought and the moral autonomy of the individual.

For this reason, it is fundamentally incorrect to discern, as some scholars have, a 'surprising convergence' between Bayle's and Locke's theories of toleration; for the two theories are actually totally different and incompatible, the first Protestant, theological, and limited, the latter entirely non-theological and universal.[55] For Bayle, the chief priority in toleration theory, as elsewhere in his system, is to detach morality from faith, which leads him to approach the whole question of toleration quite differently from Locke, Le Clerc, or Barbeyrac. Since his aim is to ground our moral system exclusively on 'la lumière naturelle',[56] he proclaims a freedom of conscience and conversation which far transcended what the moderate mainstream Enlightenment considered permissible and even Voltaire thought excessively broad. While Bayle hotly denied Isaac Jaquelot's charge that his philosophy, having divorced faith *from* reason, actually, if not explicitly, subordinates faith *to* reason, the content of Bayle's social, political, and toleration theories, and especially his views on justice and morality, entirely substantiate Jaquelot's accusation.[57]

In Bayle's arguments for toleration there is no privileging of particular forms of belief over other sorts of opinion and the Christian is not assumed to possess

[52] Houtteville, *Religion chrétienne prouvée*, i, p. ix.

[53] However, it has been argued that 'if we look for Noodt's predecessors [on the subject of toleration] we may possibly find more in Bayle or Spinoza than in Locke', see van den Bergh, *Life and Work*, 226.

[54] van Eijnatten, *Mutua Christianorum tolerantia*, 45–50.

[55] Paganini, *Analisi della fede*, 197–8; Lennon, 'Bayle, Locke', 192–4.

[56] Bayle, *Commentaire philosophique*, 86–90, 94–5; Mori, *Bayle philosophe*, 290; Gros, 'Introduction', 23–4.

[57] Bayle, *Entretiens*, 484, 494; Cantelli, *Teologia*, 342, 368; Lussu, *Bayle, Holbach*, 58–9.

a prior moral superiority over others. In the *Supplément* to his main treatise on toleration, published in the year of the Glorious Revolution, 1688, Bayle held that if, as some think, it is correct that the Christian faith justifies the use of coercive force to bring non-Christians within the fold, then the Graeco-Roman pagan authorities before Constantine were surely no less justified in persecuting the Christians, since Christian doctrine was then not just disrupting the public cults upheld by the state, and publicly defying the laws of the time, but by authorizing coercion in matters of faith disrupting also 'la religion naturelle, les lois de l'humanité, de la raison, et de l'équité'.[58]

Realization of the implications of a toleration theory such as Bayle's, based solely on philosophical reason and notions of 'equity', had by the early 1690s spread quite widely. Before his dismissal from his professorship in Rotterdam in 1693, the Dutch Reformed consistory drew up a detailed list of objections to his philosophy based on his anonymously published *Pensées diverses* of 1683, which, by that date, Bayle openly acknowledged as his. Fifteen 'extravagant propositions' were highlighted, and formally condemned by the assembly at its gathering of 28 January 1693, all of which are redolent of Bayle's refusal to assign any innate moral superiority to Christian positions and his basing social justice purely on philosophical reason.

Especially condemned by the Rotterdam Dutch Reformed consistory, in its report to the city government in March 1693, was Bayle's thesis that nothing was ever less of an inconvenience to society than 'atheism' which is why God enacted no miracles to curb it.[59] Judged hardly less outrageous were his maxims that atheism is not a greater evil than idolatry;[60] that everything in nature being uncertain 'it is best to keep to the faith of one's parents and profess the religion we learn from them';[61] and that, as the original French puts it, 'l'athéisme ne conduit pas nécessairement à la corruption des mœurs'.[62] Totally unacceptable was Bayle's no less notorious proposition that, as the Rotterdam assembly expressed his view, 'een societyt van atheisten ook wel gereguleert kan zyn' [a society of atheists could be well regulated]; and that the Sadducees, though denying immortality of the soul, were morally worthier than the Pharisees,[63] ideas which again all imply Christian doctrines need not be the basis of a well-ordered society.

The public disputes surrounding Bayle from the early 1690s down to the years shortly after his death need to be examined by both social and intellectual historians much more than they thus far have been. For the whole drift of the controversy reveals that in the modern historiography, there has been a most unfortunate tendency to misconstrue—perhaps especially by failing to pay enough attention to his post-*Dictionnaire* writings—what Bayle is actually saying and how his immediate contemporaries understood his words. Shortly after his death, Bayle's intellectual legacy was again formally condemned by the Dutch Reformed Church at the

[58] Bayle, *Commentaire philosophique*, 89; Bayle, *Supplément*, 167–8.

[59] Bayle, *Pensées diverses*, i. 281–2.

[60] Ibid. i. 303; Mori, *Bayle philosophe*, 203–9.

[61] Paradis, *Fondements*, 28.

[62] Bayle, *Pensées diverses*, ii. 5.

[63] GA Rotterdam Acta Kerkeraad, vii. 408–9, 413. Res. 28 Jan., 19 Feb., and 11 Mar. 1693.

gathering of the South Holland Synod, meeting at Leerdam in July 1707. Delegates from the Rotterdam *classis* declared that Bayle's books 'behelsen vele schadelycke stellingen tegen God's Woord en de gantsche Christelycke Godsdienst strydende' [contain many damaging propositions tending against God's Word and the whole Christian faith], urging the synod to press for his books to be banned by the States of Holland.[64] This was a collective judgement made by both Dutch and (in the background) Huguenot preachers and laymen residing in Bayle's immediate urban milieu and should carry far more weight in any proper analysis of his intentions than some modern scholars' totally incorrect assumption that Bayle was really a sincere Calvinist.

Assuredly, matters never went to the point that the States banned Bayle's books. But equally both immediately before and after his death, practically all Dutch and Dutch Huguenot commentators, whether judging his thought from liberal Cocceian and Arminian, or more orthodox Calvinist, viewpoints, condemned it as fomenting the spread of 'atheism' and highly subversive. Nor was this a view only of Protestants. Le Clerc rightly pointed out that the French Jesuits, despite their unrelenting hostility to himself and other *rationaux*, such as Jaquelot, nevertheless agreed with their reading of Bayle's *Réponse aux questions d'un provincial* as essentially a justification of 'atheism'.[65] Paolo Mattia Doria, in the 1740s, may have been a little extreme in styling Bayle even more 'atheistic' than Spinoza but his reasoning was hard to fault: in the *Pensées diverses* and other works, Bayle leaves no distinction between 'religione e superstizione'.[66] In short, in dramatic contrast to much modern scholarship, most scholars between Bayle's death in 1706 and the 1750s unhesitatingly linked him with Spinoza against Locke, Le Clerc, and Voltaire.

The misconception bedevilling the historiography rests on the assumption that Bayle was sincere in his Christian 'fideism'. But while this view is often repeated in the modern literature, it can hardly be said that the grounds for it are very convincing. It is true that one or two contemporary Huguenot preachers who knew him were willing for a time to give him the benefit of the doubt, taking his repeated and adamant professions of religious faith at face value. But to ignore the fact that most immediate contemporaries, after carefully examining Bayle's arguments, concluded that his fideism was just an imposture and a camouflage device, is surely to ignore contemporary 'context' to a wholly indefensible degree. For even those who most loyally defended him against a growing army of detractors, Arminian, Calvinist, Lutheran, and Catholic, such as his friends Jacques Basnage (1653–1723), for many years minister of the Huguenot congregation at The Hague, and David Durand (1680–1763), who in 1711 moved to London, eventually changed their minds as the implications of Bayle's post-*Dictionnaire* writings became clearer, joined the majority, and felt they had been duped by him.[67] By 1707, practically

[64] ARH Oud Synodaal Archief 97, Acta South Holland Synod, Leerdam, July 1707, art. 18.

[65] [Le Clerc], *Bibliothèque choisie*, 10 (1706), 383; *Mémoires de Trévoux* (Oct. 1707), art. cxxx, pp. 1737, 1740, 1744, 1751.

[66] Doria, *Manoscritti napoletani*, iii. 33–6; Paradis, 'Fondements', 28.

[67] Labrousse, *Pierre Bayle*, i. 268–71, ii. 445; Mori, *Bayle philosophe*, 237; Pitassi, 'De la courtoisie', 70.

no one in his immediate context took Bayle's professions of fideism seriously; and his contemporaries had every reason not to. Yet, at the same time, no one could deny that Bayle's was the clearest and most comprehensive defence of toleration of the age, its very effectiveness stemming from his adept use of an ostensibly fideist stance rooted in what was in reality a philosophically radical position, a strategy which proved a highly effective means of promoting toleration.

Historical context was fundamental to Bayle's toleration argument. For his strongest card was precisely the unresolved confessional deadlock prevailing in Europe since the Reformation. 'Bayle's reciprocity argument for religious toleration', as one scholar puts it, 'turns on the frightful results of the Wars of Religion'.[68] By showing that religious persecution and efforts to impose religious uniformity by force wreak terrible havoc on life and property, he persuades the reader that the religious intolerance which justified the Wars of Religion is morally wrong and cannot therefore be advocated by God, Christ, or, justifiably, by any Christian ruler or church. The words of the apostle Luke (14: 23) 'contrains-les d'entrer' [compel them to enter], as Bayle expresses them in his *Commentaire philosophique* of 1686, could be piously proclaimed by any of the rival churches, so that were this admonition to be taken literally, he observes (like La Beaumelle later), all Christian sects would be equally justified in fighting and seeking to exterminate the rest, resulting in a vast and manifestly irrational state of violence, misery, suffering, and strife.[69]

Bayle's toleration theory, hence, rests squarely on the pseudo-fideist argument that there is no way rationally to ascertain which is the true faith—or whether there is a true faith. In a typically brutal Baylean paradox, he simultaneously proclaims the unqualified primacy and total irrationality of faith. Believers are convinced they adhere to the true faith, and that faith is our chief guide; but since there is no way of demonstrating rationally that one's faith is the truth to someone who believes otherwise, everybody's faith is for the interim, even if not ultimately, equally valid and simultaneously someone else's 'superstition'.[70] This argument provides the basis of Bayle's famous doctrine of the 'conscience errante'.[71] Since one cannot know or prove, through reason, the truth or falsity of any religion, or the legitimacy or illegitimacy of any belief, there is no rational means of showing someone who believes in false or even wholly ridiculous doctrines that their fondest convictions have no basis. Were one to take his 'fideism' seriously (which would reduce his system to complete and fundamental inconsistency), it would mean, as Doria remarks, that what is most important in human life is totally indistinguishable from 'superstition' which Bayle considers absolutely the worst and most pernicious of things, a position which is manifestly absurd.

Consequently, the only reasonable course, as La Beaumelle later reiterated, expressly invoking Bayle, in 1748, is to grant the same freedom of conscience, and

[68] Kilcullen, *Sincerity and Truth*, 110–11; Lennon, 'Bayle, Locke', 188.

[69] [La Beaumelle], *L'Asiatique tolérant*, 69–70; Bayle, *Commentaire philosophique*, 130–1, 256–7; Mori, *Bayle philosophe*, 274–5, 279.

[70] Paradis, 'Fondements', 25, 27–8.

[71] Bayle, *Commentaire philosophique*, 300–3, 307, 309–10; Gros, 'Introduction', 28–9.

religious practice, to dissenting minorities, including those whom nearly everyone else thinks mistaken in their beliefs, as one accords to believers in what one considers the true faith.[72] Thus, it is not from contemplating religion but rather from examining history and moral philosophy, according to Bayle, that we learn that reason can never justify persecution and that intolerance, to cite the heading of the second chapter of the *Commentaire philosophique*, is always and incontestably 'contraire aux plus distinctes idées de la lumière naturelle'.[73] Indeed, in Bayle, it is never theological doctrine, love, or forbearance which debar and condemn persecution but solely and exclusively the intrinsic injustice, rationally demonstrated, of oppressing the innocent. In contrast to Locke's theological toleration, toleration in Bayle rests exclusively on the principles of equity and morality which, however, can all too easily be obscured or negated by theological doctrines.[74]

A key component of Bayle's toleration is his argument that while it cannot have been Christ's intention that the church should persecute, all established churches have in practice persecuted, indeed been systematically intolerant. Remarkably boldly, given that he was writing in Holland, he added in the *Supplément* that his thesis that 'l'esprit de persécution a plus régné parmi les orthodoxes, généralement parlant, depuis Constantin, que parmi les hérétiques' applies not just to the Greek, Catholic, Lutheran, and Anglican orthodox but also to the Reformed Church. It was, affirms Bayle, a dreadful and outrageous thing that those who wished to reform the church after its utter perversion by the papacy did not understand 'les immunités sacrées et inviolables de la conscience' but rather adhered to 'le dogme de la contrainte'; and that in the year 1535, at Geneva, the birthplace of the Reformed Church, the Calvinists suppressed Catholicism, expelling everyone who refused to convert.[75] Only the Socinians and Arminians, contends Bayle, were free of intolerance; but these were both tiny, fringe churches: thus the doctrine of tolerance is only recognized as true in a few small corners of Christendom 'qui ne font aucune figure, pendant que celui de l'intolérance va partout la tête levée'.[76] While continually attacking the Socinians for being theologically more muddled and inconsistent than anyone else, it was typical of Bayle that he simultaneously holds that morally they were exceptionally just and upright.

Central to Bayle's system of political and moral thought is his implication that established churches possess no more, and in several significant respects actually less, validity than tolerated fringe churches.[77] For Bayle's toleration, unlike Locke's, has nothing to do with exemption from church structures which otherwise retain a

72 [La Beaumelle], *L'Asiatique tolérant*, 67; Mori, *Bayle philosophe*, 276; Marilli, 'Cartesianesimo e tolleranza', 562–3, 566; Kilcullen, *Sincerity and Truth*, 66–8; Cantelli, 'Virtù degli atei', 696.

73 Bayle, *Commentaire philosophique*, 97–8; Des Maizeaux, *Vie de Monsieur Bayle*, p. xxxvi; Zagorin, *How the Idea*, 285–6.

74 Bayle, *Commentaire philosophique*, 89–91; Bayle, *Réponse*, iv. 276, 289–90, 436, 456; Marilli, 'Cartesianesimo e tolleranza', 566.

75 Bayle, *Supplément*, 239, 254–6; Tinsley, *Pierre Bayle's Reformation*, 307.

76 Bayle, *Supplément*, 228; Gros, 'Tolérance et le problème', 424.

77 Paradis, 'Fondements', 32; Gros, 'Bayle: de la tolérance', 296, 304.

general validity, and was in fact less a theory of toleration—given that he recognized no established or public church in his schema—than a universal freedom of conscience entailing mutual Christian, Muslim, and Jewish forbearance, Catholic acceptance of Protestants, and vice versa; it also entailed all major churches being compelled to acknowledge as equals the lesser dissenting churches and placed no barrier on an indefinite proliferation of churches.[78] Nor was it only Socinians, Jews, and Muslims who could, within Bayle's framework, claim rights of conscience but equally Deist freethinkers, *indifférents*, *Saint-Évremondistes*, and 'atheists', despite Bayle's *de rigueur* but (seemingly) deliberately feeble disavowal: denying his theory is a charter for 'atheists', he perfunctorily adds that should the secular authorities consider 'atheism' incompatible with their laws they can always ban it.[79] But this scarcely alters the fact that strictly in terms of principle, in Bayle's toleration there is no basis for atheists being excluded any more than pantheists, agnostics, Spinozists, Confucianists, or anyone else.[80]

In this, of course, Bayle was emulated practically exclusively by radical writers like Toland, Jean-Frédéric Bernard, Collins, Tindal, Lau, Hatzfeld, Radicati, Morelly, Johann Lorenz Schmidt, Edelmann, La Beaumelle, Diderot, and, later Condorcet apt to think the more churches there are in a society, and the more they neutralize each other, the better off and more stable society will be.[81] No one in the moderate mainstream could subscribe to such a view. Hence, we may be fairly sure (unless he is a Socinian) that if an eighteenth-century writer espouses a more or less unlimited toleration *à la Bayle*, like Bernard Mandeville (1670–1733), in his *Free Thoughts on Religion, the Church and National Happiness* (1720), a work which refers frequently to Bayle,[82] he belongs with the Radical Enlightenment. Republican, anticlerical, pro-Dutch, and in some respects Spinozist, within his small circle Mandeville was a leader of opinion. When Benjamin Franklin met him in London in 1725, he headed a 'club' meeting in a Cheapside tavern 'of which he was the soul, being a most facetious, entertaining companion'.[83] Insisting on a comprehensive freedom of thought and personal liberty, excluding no one, he held, like Bayle, that there is 'no characteristic to distinguish a true church from a false one',[84] adding that the 'greatest argument for toleration is, that differences of opinion can do no hurt, if all clergy-men are kept in awe, and no more independent on the state than the laity'[85]—a strikingly Spinozistic sentiment.

78 Gros, 'Bayle: de la tolérance', 295–6, 308–9.

79 Bayle, *Pensées diverses*, ii. 5–8; Bayle, *Commentaire philosophique*, 272–4, 275–6, 312–13; Lennon, 'Bayle, Locke', 187, 193.

80 Bianchi, 'Religione e tolleranza', 68; Wielema, *Filosofen*, 66; Dunn, 'Claim to Freedom', 188, 190; Schneewind, *Invention of Autonomy*, 279–82; Dagron, 'Toland et l'hétérodoxie', 79, 84.

81 Williams, *Condorcet*, 120; on Toland's 'Spinozistic' broad toleration, see Dagron, 'Toland et l'hétérodoxie', 84, 88.

82 James, 'Faith, Sincerity', 45–7; Jack, 'Religion', 38–9.

83 Franklin, *Autobiography*, 97.

84 Mandeville, *Free Thoughts*, 241; Jack, 'Religion', 34, 42; James, 'Schism', 698, 700.

85 Mandeville, *Free Thoughts*, 241, 246; James, 'Schism', 699; Pascual López, *Bernard Mandeville*, 112–17.

Bayle's formulations imply that the Dutch States General's general decree prohibiting Socinian and other anti-Trinitarian opinion was socially and morally unequitable and unjust, philosophically (as well as theologically) unjustifiable, and ultimately untenable.[86] Not surprisingly, he enjoyed the ardent support of the French Socinian exiled to Holland Noël Aubert de Versé, who, in his *Traité de la liberté de conscience* (1687), recycles whole phrases taken from Bayle's *Commentaire*.[87] But categorical approval proved forthcoming only from those who were themselves unacceptable to mainstream opinion. Le Clerc, an ardent champion of toleration of worship in the style of Locke, admittedly did endorse Bayle's theory of the *conscience errante* initially, but later, as he grew more sensitive to the implications of the latter's subversive philosophy, changed his mind, rejecting Bayle's toleration along with the rest of his thought.

As open antagonism between the two titans of the Huguenot intellectual stage erupted early in the new century, Le Clerc angrily rebuffed Bayle's charge that behind a rhetorical show of tolerance he was really a theorist and practitioner of intolerance but in a way that suggests Bayle was by no means entirely wrong. Le Clerc rejected all talk of inconsistency, claiming never to have opposed, but rather always approved, the public condemnation of those who deny divine providence, ridicule religious belief, 'qui font l'apologie des athées, et qui débitent des choses qui détruisent toute religion, comme [Bayle] fait'.[88] Le Clerc then reiterated the position he shared with Locke that toleration of atheism necessarily damages civil society, one of the chief foundations of which is belief in God. If Bayle thinks toleration should extend to permitting men to attack 'la providence d'un Dieu bon et saint', then Le Clerc repudiates his toleration totally along with all who embrace it. For such persons have no conscience nor any right to complain when they are censured and punished by the authorities.[89] Bayle, complained Le Clerc in 1706, continually harps on the contradiction he sees between Scripture and reason, the aim of his deviousness being to make the first redundant. What, he asks rhetorically, will he put in its place? 'Seroit-ce cette société d'athées, qui devient tous les jours plus célèbre par les écrits de M. Bayle?'[90]

By 1706, even the most liberal Huguenot Calvinist ministers saw in Bayle's theory an utterly pernicious feigned 'fideism' betokening the loss of established status for the largest churches, general elimination of ecclesiastical authority in society, and a purely philosophical stance of strict neutrality not just between religions but, worse still, as between religion, philosophical deism, and atheism. Efforts to refute Bayle's arguments, answer his baffling paradoxes, overcome his separation of morality and religion, and curtail the sweeping 'freedom of conscience' he adduces pervaded the subsequent toleration debate in Europe for many decades, this tension powerfully infusing, for example, Montesquieu's *Lettres persanes*.[91]

[86] Bianchi, 'Religione e tolleranza', 68–9; Mori, *Bayle philosophe*, 289.
[87] Mori, *Bayle Philosophe*, 287; Labrousse, *Pierre Bayle*, i. 212 n.
[88] Bayle, *Réponse*, iv, part ii, 5–16; *Bibliothèque choisie*, 10 (1706), 392.
[89] *Bibliothèque choisie*, 10 (1706), 393. [90] Ibid. 9 (1706), 168–9.
[91] Bianchi, 'Religione e tolleranza', 52–3, 60–1.

But most harmful of all from the *rationaux*'s and Locke's perspective was the sleight of hand by which Bayle effectively evicts all the churches from their traditional status as Man's hitherto undisputed chief guide to moral truth. His sweeping liberty of conscience rests on a formula which dramatically overturns the age-old procedure in human judgements about values. Instead of theologians declaring what is right and wrong in accordance with God's revelation, universal moral principles based purely on philosophical reason, and wholly detached from theological premisses, are made judge of every religious doctrine and ecclesiastical ruling as well as of church history.[92] Eighteenth-century toleration theorists were indeed so sensitive to the fundamental distinction, as they saw it, between a legitimate Christian toleration and the illegitimate comprehensive freedom of thought and conscience proposed by Bayle and Spinoza, that it was found necessary to coin a new form of terminology to express the conflict of basic principle involved. One should clearly differentiate, suggested the Abbé Pluche, between what he calls 'la Tolérance et le Tolérantisme', the first being soundly Lockean, the second signifying a universal indifference to confessional status and theological doctrines to be generally decried.[93]

Only radicals embraced *le tolérantisme*, then, as did Morelly, in 1751, with the added admonition that it should be regarded as an essentially political rather than theological construct, something which has to be imposed, against their wishes, on the churches and sustained by the secular authority.[94] For every church or sect in Europe which in his time endorsed toleration, he contended, would speak very differently were they not obliged by present circumstances to embrace that principle. All clergies, he urges, by their nature are inherently disposed to foment hatred and intolerance, condemning all their rivals as 'idolaters', 'heretics', and 'schismatics'. To curb the ingrained *intolérantisme* of the priesthood, he suggested, princes should never participate in theological quarrels and, whatever theologians may advise or admonish, never encroach on the 'liberté de conscience' of their subjects who must share in it equally.

By contrast, Élie Saurin (1639–1703), minister of the Utrecht French Reformed congregation for over thirty years, and eloquent advocate of a moderate toleration, maintained, like Isaac Jaquelot and Bayle's friend Jacques Basnage,[95] that comprehensive toleration, or what they termed Bayle's *liberté d'indifférence*, is not only something completely different from the moderate toleration they advocated but something intrinsically damaging and pernicious.[96] He considered Bayle's system wholly incompatible with a Christian outlook: for Bayle, in his *Commentaire philsophique*, holds that every individual should act according to his private conscience whether inspired by true religion, or in error, and that no prince can justifiably coerce that individual conscience—except where political sedition flows

[92] Ibid. 306–7; Paradis, 'Fondements', 29–31.

[93] Bots, 'Le Plaidoyer', 557–8.

[94] [Morelly], *Le Prince*, ii. 47–9, 51.

[95] Basnage, *Traité*, i. 55–65; Cerny, *Theology, Politics and Letters*, 113, 303; van Bunge et al. (eds.), *Dictionary*, i. 58.

[96] Des Maizeaux, *Vie de Monsieur Bayle*, p. xcv.

directly from heterodox belief. Hence, objects Saurin, the individual is as free, under Bayle's system, to adopt Sadduceeism, Socinianism, Islam, Hinduism, Judaism, Deism, or atheism as Christianity. This he rejects as totally unacceptable, a repugnant irreligious indifferentism. Carefully distancing himself, and his colleagues, from Bayle, he sought to locate the liberal Calvinist conscience midway, at the 'juste milieu', between what he designates the bigoted 'intolérance absolue' of Jurieu which he, like Bayle, Basnage, and Le Clerc, despised, and the—in his eyes no less loathsome—'indifférence des religions, et l'impiété du *Commentaire philosophique*'. For Saurin, like Le Clerc and even Basnage,[97] Baylean 'tolérance outrée', like that of Lessing in Germany, later, was condemned as something wholly devoid of Christian content, philosophically insidious, and ruinous to religion and morality alike.[98]

Saurin felt reassured to see that within the Walloon (i.e. French Reformed) community in the Netherlands both Jurieu's adherents, 'les intolérants', and Bayle's, 'les indifférents', remained numerically insignificant fringes: in contrast to them, 'la multitude et la foule des Réformés', he remarks, 'tient le milieu entre l'intolérance et l'indifférence'.[99] Where Jurieu uncompromisingly lumps liberal Calvinists like Saurin and Jaquelot together with 'indifférents' like Bayle, his own toleration theory, Saurin maintains, like Locke's, essentially liberty of conscience for all Christians subscribing to the Christian *fundamenta*—in other words the 'Arminian' approach increasingly favoured by liberal Calvinists—rests on Christian charity, unlike Jurieu's bigoted intolerance, while yet wholly rejecting Bayle's damaging unrestricted freedom of thought.

Liberal Calvinists and most Huguenots in northern Europe during the Early Enlightenment, then, adhered to the middle-of-the-road position established and carefully fortified by Locke and the Dutch Arminians, distancing themselves from Bayle no less than Spinoza.[100] Bayle's equal rights for the individual conscience whether Christian or non-Christian—since 'le droit de la conscience errante de bonne foi est tout le même que celui de la conscience orthodoxe'[101]—everywhere aroused the profoundest misgivings. Bayle's reluctance to affirm that it is self-evidently true that Christianity is the true faith, and the unmistakable implication of many of his maxims that he did not in fact think this, sharply segregates his conception of tolerance from that of both the Dutch Remonstrants (and Locke) and the *rationaux*—Le Clerc, Basnage, Saurin, Jacques Bernard, Jaquelot, and Barbeyrac—thus further calling in question the genuineness of his fideism and the sincerity of his allegiance to the Reformed faith.

97 Basnage, *Traité*, i. 98–9, ii. 282; Cerny, *Theology, Politics and Letters*, 297–303.

98 Saurin, *Traité de l'amour*, appendix: 'Récit de la vie . . . de Saurin', 34–6; Turchetti, 'Élie Saurin', 176; Balduzzi, 'Problemi interpretativi', 461; Mori, *Bayle philosophe*, 288; Whaley, 'Tolerant Society?', 184.

99 Quoted in Turchetti, 'Élie Saurin', 177; Lomonaco, *Tolleranza*, 79.

100 Steenbakkers, 'Johannes Braun', 206–7; Frijhoff, 'Religious Toleration', 36–8.

101 Turchetti, 'Élie Saurin', 187; Bayle, *Commentaire philosophique*, 300; Gros, 'Introduction', 29.

3. SPINOZA'S LIBERTY OF THOUGHT AND EXPRESSION

The third major theory of toleration to appear during the Early Enlightenment, that of Spinoza, stood in still sharper opposition to the Christian rationalism of Locke and Le Clerc, in some important respects going decisively beyond Bayle's theory, especially regarding the quest for freedom of speech, expression, and publication. Here, in contrast to Locke, and more than in Bayle, churches and forms of worship recede into the background, Spinoza's stress, as we have seen, being primarily on freedom of thought and of the press rather than of belief.[102] It was always one of his main objectives to demonstrate not only that such freedom can 'be granted without endangering piety and the peace of the commonwealth' but also that the 'peace of the commonwealth and piety depend on this freedom'.[103] Indeed, liberty of worship as such is only marginally touched on in the *Tractatus theologico-politicus*, where Spinoza chiefly expounds his theory of individual freedom and toleration, most extensively discussing the place of religion in society and politics, presumably because he saw this question as being essentially secondary to the wider issue of liberty of thought, and perhaps mainly a political problem, rather than something fundamental to the making of a good society. Religious freedom, in any case, he treats as included in, but subsidiary to, toleration as conceived in terms of liberty of thought and expression.[104]

In his later work the *Tractatus politicus* (1677), he does more extensively deal with liberty of conscience and worship but in a way which again shows that his toleration is chiefly intended to ground individual freedom of opinion, as well as of speech and writing. Moreover, here again he shows a marked reluctance to encourage organized ecclesiastical structures to expand in influence, compete for followers, and assert their spiritual authority over individuals, as well as engage in politics. He begins by distinguishing carefully between toleration of worship, strictly speaking, which is one thing, and empowering religious groups to organize and extend their authority just as they wish which he sees as something rather different. While entirely granting that everyone must possess the freedom to express their beliefs no matter what faith they profess, Spinoza simultaneously urges the need for certain restrictions on the activities of churches. While dissenters should have the right to build as many churches as they want and individuals may freely fulfil the duties of their faith as they understand it, Spinoza does not agree that this means that minority religions should have a free hand to acquire large and impressive ecclesiastical buildings or exercise sway over their members, as the Amsterdam Portuguese synagogue had once sought to dictate to him. Magnificent places of worship should, he thinks, be monopolized by the public religion of the state which, in turn, must be a 'very simple, universal faith' teaching that salvation comes

[102] Walther, 'Spinoza's Critique', 100; Israel, *Radical Enlightenment*, 266–7; Prokhovnik, *Spinoza*, 217.

[103] Spinoza, *TTP*, preface.

[104] Spinoza, *The Political Works*, ed. Wernham, 410–11.

through practising 'justice and charity', that is an idealized universal philosophical religion very different from the public churches which actually presided over Europe in his day.[105]

Moreover, while minority faiths should be kept firmly subordinate, 'no more disastrous policy can be devised or attempted in a free commonwealth' than to render the official religion sufficiently strong that it is able and feels justified in seeking to regulate the views and expression of opinion of individuals. For 'to invest with prejudice or in any way coerce the citizen's free judgment', contends Spinoza, 'is altogether incompatible with the freedom of the people'. Officially condoned persecution justified under pretext of the need to enforce religious truth is an intrusion of the law 'into the sphere of speculative thought' and results in beliefs being 'put on trial and condemned as crimes'.[106] Consequently, he urges, the state should punish men only for deeds and never for their utterances or opinions. In Spinoza's view, the publicly established church as he saw it in his own society, and neighbouring countries, was not an upright, praiseworthy, and justified religious institution but a corrupt body in which what he considered the church's true function, to instruct the people in 'justice and charity', was systematically perverted by 'base avarice and ambition', one in which doctrine was used a weapon to defeat rivals and, by exploiting the people's ignorance and credulity, amass power and control. As a result, says Spinoza, 'faith has become identical with credulity and biased dogma', dogma which degrades human reason, 'completely inhibiting men's free judgment and capacity to distinguish true from false', a system of tenets 'apparently devised with the set purpose of utterly extinguishing the light of reason'.[107]

In the public church, furthermore, 'only patricians or senators should be permitted to perform the principal rites' since it is ruinous, he thinks, in any form of republic to permit anyone but holders of the state's chief offices to be 'ministers of houses of worship and guardians and interpreters of the state religion'. Ideally, there should be no deviation, he argues, from the basic principle of a religion grounded on the 'common good' that 'cultum Dei ejusque obedientiam' [the cult of God and obedience to him] consists in 'sola justitia et charitate sive amore erga proximum' [solely in justice and charity or love of one's neighbour].[108] If the republic permits an organized clergy to evolve, distinct from the ruling elite or democratic office-holders teaching the publicly proclaimed religion, the 'multitude' will always consider the clergy and its leaders an alternative, and higher, source of authority, believing as they inevitably do that ecclesiastics are closest to God.[109] Churchmen, as is only to be expected, will then devise intricate dogmas designed to enhance clerical sway and subordinate secular authority to their judgement and approval. Consequently, a vital safeguard for preserving liberty in a

105 Ibid. 411; De Dijn, 'Spinoza and Revealed Religion', 42–3; Mignini, 'Dottrina spinoziana', 73–4; Sprigge, 'Is Spinozism a Religion?', 138–40.

106 Spinoza, *TTP*, preface.

107 Ibid.

108 Spinoza, *Tractatus politicus*, 411; Spinoza, *TTP* 224.

109 Matheron, *Individu et communauté*, 439–41.

republic, he urges, is to prevent the factions that form among a ruling oligarchy, or the office-holders in a democracy, from dividing into competing sects or churches supporting rival priesthoods and doctrines. For the more they seek the approval and support of clergy in their conflicts with other political factions, the more they will defer to theologians, and the more office-holders will become helpless prey to 'superstition', Spinoza's shorthand for subservience to ecclesiastical authority and theology. In such cases, he held, adherents of religious congregations and doctrines condemned by the dominant priesthood are inexorably sacrificed 'not to the public weal but to the hatred and savagery of their opponents'.[110]

Freedom of religion, then, as distinct from freedom to expand ecclesiastical authority, hierarchy, and property, is fully accommodated in Spinoza's scheme but remains entirely secondary to freedom of thought and expression and is tied to restrictions on sacerdotal independence and the authority of churches over their members. Freedom to embrace a particular faith, practise the religious duties it prescribes, and profess the tenets its clergy stipulate, not only must be respected but is politically useful to the state when well managed, however, only when accompanied by effective safeguards against the danger of religious zeal and intolerance. Preventing the growth of separate, powerful, and unified public priesthood in Spinoza's view is essential in a free republic because the outward forms of religion and religious authority fundamentally affect the cohesion, stability, and orderliness of the commonwealth as well as freedom of the individual and liberty of expression and the press.[111] Where ecclesiastical authority exercises hegemony, the loyalty of the masses will inevitably be alienated from a government which upholds individual liberty, aiding those who thirst for power over others 'so that slavery may return once more' and 'superstition' again reign supreme.[112] Having himself witnessed the street disturbances, and murder of the brothers de Witt in The Hague in 1672, Spinoza knew at first hand the politically disruptive consequences of allowing ministers of religion to denounce office-holders or policies they dislike as ungodly and heretical, thereby inflaming the ignorant and credulous against ministers of state.

Spinoza's toleration, accordingly, while granting freedom of worship aims above all to weaken ecclesiastical sway over the 'multitude'. By contrast, once freedom of worship is accorded and plurality of churches acknowledged, Locke's toleration theory envisages, like much subsequent liberal thought in this area, the withdrawal of the state in the main from the sphere of religious affairs, assuming preaching, staging ceremonies, education, and debate can then safely and beneficially be entrusted to churchmen. Where Spinoza fears that rivalry of political factions in states will enable designing ecclesiastics to extend the sway of theological notions over popular consciousness and ultimately deprive citizens 'of the freedom to express their beliefs',[113] in Locke's conception, the state leaves churches free to compete with each other, enhance their grip over their followers, and widen their influence in

[110] Spinoza, *TTP*, preface.

[111] Moreau, 'Spinoza et le *Jus circa sacra*', 336; Halper, 'Spinoza', 173, 179.

[112] Spinoza, *TTP*, preface.

[113] Spinoza, *Tractatus politicus*, 411.

education, life style, and other spheres as much as they can, on the assumption this benefits rather than harms society.

In Spinoza, freedom of thought and expression is grounded on a particular conception of political power and of the role and functions of the state. Since the right of the state, in his thought, is identical to the power of the state, and since no one can control the thoughts of someone else, it follows that it is impossible to control men's thoughts and it lies entirely outside the competence and proper business of the state to attempt to do so. When setting up the state, argues Spinoza, every individual surrenders, for the sake of added security, cooperation, and also freedom, his or her natural right to act unrestrictedly, as he or she pleases—but not his or her right to reason, judge, and express opinions; and since everybody retains the right to think and judge independently, it follows that it remains everyone's right to express whatever views one wishes about religion, politics, law, and everything else pertaining to the 'common interest' and the state, provided such freedom is exercised without undermining the law or prejudice to the state. Expressing views about this or that decree, event, political decision, or office-holder only becomes subversive and hence liable for punishment, holds Spinoza, if it directly obstructs implementation of laws and decrees.

That there would really be, in practice, so clear and evident a distinction between action, on one side, and thought and expression, on the other, as this theory presupposes may well appear unlikely.[114] When exactly, by Spinoza's criterion, is political or religious propaganda seditious and when not? But however he proposed to substantiate it in particular instances, this divide between action as distinct from thought and expression remained basic to Spinoza's (and the Spinozists') conception of individual liberty. Whatever thoughts, utterances, speeches, and publications can safely be allowed in society should be permitted, he urges, since the fundamental 'purpose of the state is, in truth, freedom' [finis ergo republicae re vera libertas est].[115]

A well-ordered state, holds Spinoza, 'grants to every man the same freedom to philosophize as I have shown to be permitted by religious faith' and indeed draws strength from this freedom.[116] Here we find Spinoza's claim that philosophy and theology are totally separate, and do not conflict, combining with his subversive redefinition of the meaning of 'religious' and 'faith' in terms of his own philosophical system. Asserting freedom of religion and religious practice, Spinoza authorizes individuals to ascribe any and whatever meaning to theological *fundamenta* they like while simultaneously stipulating what, in his view, the scope and limits of 'religion' really are. In his discussion, in the *Tractatus theologico-politicus*, of the essentials of a minimal public confession, or *fides universalis* [universal religion], to which all men of good faith can readily

[114] Balibar, *Spinoza and Politics*, 26–30; Smith, *Spinoza, Liberalism*, 157.

[115] Spinoza, *Opera*, iii. 241; Spinoza, *TTP*, preface.

[116] Spinoza, *TTP* 295; Halper, 'Spinoza', 173.

subscribe, Spinoza proposes seven articles which he says every rational person will approve:[117]

> God, a Supreme Being, supremely just and merciful, exists.
> God is one and unique.
> God is omnipresent and directs everything with a uniformity of justice.
> God alone is subject to no one and has sovereign right and power over all things.
> True worship of God consists solely in the practice of 'justice' and 'charity'.
> All those, and only those, who obey God are saved.
> God pardons sinners who repent.

No one has any rational grounds to object to any of these, he says, provided everyone remains wholly free to interpret them for himself whether philosophically or theologically, without any priesthood or authority defining what they mean. For what matters, as with all religious doctrines in his opinion, is not what anyone thinks, or believes, these articles mean but rather their practical value in terms of maintaining social stability, disciplining conduct, and promoting justice and charity. Indeed, for Spinoza whose explanation of this is surely one of the most astounding passages in his *oeuvre*, it matters not a whit whether one understands these doctrines theologically or philosophically: 'whether God is believed to be everywhere actually or potentially, whether he governs things freely or by natural necessity; or lays down laws as a ruler or teaches them as eternal truths' [deinde nihil etiam ad fidem si quis credat quod Deus secundum essentiam vel secundum potentiam ubique sit; quod res dirigit ex libertate, vel necessitate naturae].[118] Neither does it matter whether one believes men should obey God from free will or by the necessity of the divine decree; or finally, whether the reward of the good and punishment of the wicked is considered natural or supernatural [quod homo ex arbitrii libertate, vel ex necessitate divini decreti Deo obediat; quodque praemium bonorum et poena malorum naturalis vel supernaturalis sit].[119]

In this way Spinoza sought politically to reconcile Man's two intellectually irreconcilable modes of comprehending the universe—the philosophical and theological. The essential point is that no one can or should ever be coerced. Everyone ought to adapt these simple tenets of 'faith' to his own understanding and interpret them in whatever way helps him 'embrace them unreservedly', doing this entirely freely.[120] Spinoza, in other words, denies that theological doctrines contain any truths at all other than allegorically and metaphorically, claiming that whatever theological notions individuals embrace can make no positive difference to society or to prospects for personal salvation. The function of such universal teachings is not to explain truth, or enhance the authority of churches, but solely to inculcate in society maxims of good conduct. Since these

[117] Spinoza, *Opera*, iii. 224; Sprigge, 'Is Spinozism a Religion?', 139; Smith, *Spinoza, Liberalism*, 81, 199–200.

[118] Spinoza, *TTP* 225–6; Spinoza, *Opera*, iii. 241.

[119] Spinoza, *Opera*, iii. 241; Roothaan, *Vroomheid*, 121–2; Israel, 'Spinoza, Locke', 107.

[120] Spinoza, *TTP* 225; Preus, *Spinoza*, 204–5 Lagrée, *Spinoza*, 80–1.

are the substance of true 'religion', according to Spinoza, the only genuine measure of who is 'religious' and who not, the sole universal and valid criteria of true piety are those of 'charity' and 'justice'.[121]

It is not then religious toleration, for Spinoza, but freedom of thought and expression which principally safeguard individual liberty under the state, constituting the most precious possession not just of the wise but of those who are genuinely 'religious'. Unfortunately, this essential point is very rarely grasped among men. To regulate men's thoughts, beliefs, and judgements may be impossible but in his time, as subsequently, it was generally not thought appropriate for individuals to form their own views as to what is true, and what is not, freely and independently. Rather governments and churches took it for granted that individuals have no right to decide the most fundamental matters of belief for themselves; and that what is proper to believe should be enforced and what is incompatible therewith suppressed. Among the various censorship laws, anti-heresy statutes, and decrees of religious uniformity applying in Europe in his day, those which Spinoza himself most directly encountered were the Dutch anti-Socinian laws of 1653, the instrument of censorship by which the books of Meyer and Koerbagh, and his own, were suppressed.

For Spinoza, indeed, the Dutch censorship posed a formidable problem as to whether, when, and how to publish his own writings, something which dogged him in his later years on an almost daily basis.[122] A key aim of his toleration theory, consequently, was to ground freedom to publish one's views however much these are decried by theologians and by the majority. No other Early Enlightenment theory of toleration, not those of Locke or Le Clerc, nor even that of Bayle, endeavours to clear a comparably broad path for liberty of the press.[123] For Spinoza, the principle that society may rightly and justifiably demand of the individual submission with respect to actions, but not regarding thoughts, opinions, and conversation, meant that men should also be free to express their views in print. All efforts to curb expression of opinion and freedom to write and publish, he insists, not only subvert the sphere of legitimate freedom but spell constant danger of instability for the state. The bitter strife between Remonstrants and Counter-Remonstrants in the United Provinces, and overthrow of Oldenbarnevelt in 1618, he maintains, sufficiently proves that in times of spiritual turmoil the 'real schismatics are those who denounce the writings of others and subversively incite the unruly multitude against their authors; and not those authors themselves who generally write only for scholars and appeal to reason alone; and that finally the real disturbers of the peace are those who, in a free commonwealth, vainly seek to suppress liberty of judgement which cannot be suppressed.'[124] His rule that the 'less freedom of judgement is conceded to men the further their distance from the most natural

121 Mignini, 'Dottrina Spinoziana', 68–70, 74; De Dijn, 'Spinoza and Revealed Religion', 42–4.

122 Israel, 'Banning', 3–14; Israel, *Radical Enlightenment*, 278–93.

123 Spinoza, *TTP* 295, 298; van Gelder, *Getemperde vrijheid*, 291.

124 Spinoza, *TTP* 298; Roothaan, *Vroomheid*, 69.

state, and consequently the more oppressive the regime',[125] besides securely anchoring everyone's free right of access to information and ideas in a free republic, also afforded a ready method for evaluating any state.

By thoroughly subordinating freedom of conscience and worship to individual freedom of thought and expression in this way, Spinoza, like Bayle, placed his toleration entirely beyond the pale of respectability. Aside from a few radical Socinians, like his friends Balling and Rieuwertsz, few contemporaries considered such a concept either compatible with a Christian outlook or proper for a well-ordered society. Generally, Locke's toleration was vastly preferred and, in this sense, it is doubtless true that 'Locke provided the theoretical defence of the toleration which would rule the outlook of the coming age'.[126] Yet Locke's 'Christian argument' was decidedly not that of the radical wing; by eulogizing freedom of the individual, and of expression, in preference to freedom of conscience and worship, Spinoza in fact cleared a much wider space for liberty and human rights than Locke and though, until recently, insufficiently acknowledged, cuts a historically more direct and, arguably, more important path towards modern western individualism.

This is evident not least from the fact that it was the toleration of Spinoza and Bayle, and clearly not that of Locke and Barbeyrac, which was espoused by the French Radical Enlightenment of the mid eighteenth century, that is to say by Diderot, d'Alembert, and the *encyclopédistes.* Just as Diderot followed Spinoza in many of his metaphysical preoccupations, and his monism, so he was also the mid eighteenth-century French thinker who most seriously addressed Spinoza's dilemma of how a society based on liberty of the individual, and freedom of thought and personal lifestyle, should conduct itself with regard to ecclesiastical power and the expansive authority the vying churches strive to extend over their members, public institutions, and over society generally.

Diderot could not accept Locke's approach: for the state to withdraw and allow the churches laissez-faire to his mind provided no solution at all. Indeed, here, Diderot goes still further than Spinoza or Bayle, contending that the moral and social influence of Christianity is not actually a positive good but something damaging in bequeathing society two wholly different, conflicting, and incompatible standards as to what is good and what bad.[127] It was not simply, holds Diderot, that this or that religion persecutes, or that most religions are intolerant; the difficulty, in his opinion, was that belief in God, spirits, miracles, and transcendental realities as such harms both society and the individual even where such beliefs are propagated by a church which formally renounces compulsion. This is because such doctrines are then claimed to be the holiest and most fundamental that men can conceive but are yet, at the same time, by definition, incomprehensible, not demonstrable, and definable only by theologians specially trained for this purpose.

125 Roothaan, *Vroomheid*, 69.

126 Cragg, *Church and the Age*, 80; Waldron, *God, Locke, and Equality*, 208–13.

127 Diderot, *Additions*, 67; Cherni, *Diderot*, 488–9.

Confessional faith, indeed all religion, he contends, fosters individual unhappiness and strife by persuading people that chimeras no one understands are more important than the quality and content of individuals' daily lives.[128] Such a perspective could only further sharpen what eventually became a basic Spinozist dilemma: liberty of thought and expression include freedom of belief and religious conviction; but how, in good conscience, can a true *philosophe* countenance the churches' sway over the people without seeking to impose curbs, restrictions proposed by philosophy to safeguard the 'common good' and its secular social morality? Here we see the first seeds of that 'philosophical' intolerance of which the young Turgot, after reading Diderot's first book, the *Pensées philosophiques*, complained in 1746: accusing Toland and Collins of aggression and intolerance towards Christianity, he records that he had heard that Shaftesbury too 'poussait sa haine pour le christianisme jusqu'à l'intolérance'.[129]

Diderot later returned to this dilemma, notably in his article 'Intolérance' written for the *Encyclopédie* around 1759, by shifting the focus of discussion from promoting toleration to curbing intolerance, intolerance being depicted by him as not just a moral evil, indeed an appalling injustice, but also something which, in practice, mostly either takes the form of 'ecclesiastical intolerance', something which, in his view, needs to be treated as a special type of political problem, or else lay intolerance fed by theological ideas. Diderot builds his argument on Bayle's principle that 'men who fall into error in good faith should be pitied, never punished' and on Spinoza's principle that the 'mind can only acquiesce in that which it regards as true', implying that what the people believe is of concern to all. But he gives all this a particular twist of his own, claiming that in much of society it is the clergy and churches which are chiefly guilty of 'impiety', 'irreligion', and 'immorality' because intolerance is basic to their teaching and because it is rank impiety 'to stir up the people, arm nations and soak the soil with blood'; in this way, he ties into his toleration theory a favourite strand from his political thought, the primacy of the 'general will', and one, moreover, which contains just a hint of a revolutionary threat.[130]

In his radical separation of moral truth from the sphere of the churches, and determination to check the latter, Diderot hence reveals himself more *Spinosiste* than Spinoza and more *Bayliste* than Bayle. If one accepts that the sovereign is protector equally 'of all his subjects, and his mission is to make them happy' then for a sovereign to practise or condone intolerance, in alliance with a church, is a complete betrayal of political responsibility. Society thinks that the subject owes allegiance to the prince whatever the latter's views, even if he is an unbeliever; but does this not require, asks Diderot, a reciprocal principle? If the sovereign decrees that a subject who is an unbeliever has no right to life, on that account, is there not then an equivalent 'reason to fear' that the subject might hence conclude that a faithless prince is unworthy to rule?[131]

[128] Diderot, *Additions*, 67–72; Duflo, *Diderot philosophe*, 390–1; Pätzold, *Spinoza, Aufklärung*, 25–7.

[129] Turgot, 'Réflexions', 91.

[130] Diderot, *Political Writings*, 29–30.

[131] Ibid. 30; Proust, *Diderot*, 496; Cherni, *Diderot*, 489; Quintili, *Pensée critique*, 189–90.

Meanwhile, in an age in which the Inquisition was being dismantled and church censorship generally receding before secular state censorship, no one could be confident that Locke's freedom of worship, rapidly gaining ground in much of western Europe and America, particularly after 1715, necessarily entailed a corresponding shift towards greater freedom of thought. Rather, developments in Prussia, Denmark, Russia, France, and elsewhere during the eighteenth century showed that freedom of conscience and worship, no matter how liberally defined, even disregarding Locke's reservations regarding Catholics and Jews, cannot simply be equated with growing freedom of thought and expression. For widening religious freedom clearly did not necessarily mean greater freedom to express ideas—and especially not 'philosophical' arguments in Spinoza's or Diderot's sense of the term—where these sought to weaken churches, curtail ecclesiastical power, contradict the essentials of revealed religion, or, indeed, criticize sovereigns who proclaimed themselves champions of the public churches.[132]

Ultimately, the term 'libertas philosophandi' which appears in the subtitle of the *Tractatus theologico-politicus* denotes everyone's right to examine and, if he so chooses, reject, or argue against and ultimately contribute to toppling, traditional theological and ecclesiastical structures as well as other kinds of opinion and authority. The term 'philosophy' is here already charged with that revolutionary intent with which it was later infused by Diderot and the radical *philosophes*. The shift from a quest for freedom of worship, such as Spinoza's Socinian friends Jelles and Balling espoused, to the pursuit of freedom of thought and expression beginning with Spinoza's philosophy was indeed to become a key defining feature of the Radical Enlightenment. By the second quarter of the eighteenth century, radical *philosophes* in western European countries, at any rate outside Italy and the Iberian Peninsula, no longer complained primarily about lack of religious freedom. The focus of their struggle now was the battle for intellectual liberty and liberty of expression and to publish, a fight which was to prove long and arduous indeed.

The point was expressed with typical adroitness and humour by d'Argens, during the period he lived in Holland, in the later 1730s. His Chinese visitor to the West, reporting back home what he sees as the extraordinarily eccentric behaviour and strangeness of the Europeans, in his *Lettres chinoises*, remarks that it was astonishing but he had often had reason to reflect that were the Greek and Roman philosophers so widely extolled there actually to return, far being admired or permitted to expound their doctrines, they would everywhere in Europe be quickly silenced—immediately imprisoned in Paris and Vienna and burnt in Madrid and Rome: Empedocles, Thales, Anaxagoras, and Pherecydes, he avers, all would suffer the same fate.[133]

[132] Sina, *L'avvento della ragione*, 344–7; Wootton, 'Introduction', 109–10.

[133] D'Argens, *Lettres chinoises*, i. 123; Israel, *Radical Enlightenment*, 118.

7

Germany and the Baltic: Enlightenment, Society, and the Universities

1. THE PROBLEM OF 'ATHEISM'

If the entire moderate mainstream concurred that 'atheism' should not be tolerated in a Christian society, an obvious symptom of spiritual crisis in the Early Enlightenment was the growing stream of both moderate 'enlightened' and Counter-Enlightenment books and debates, from the 1670s onwards, deploring the propagation of what contemporaries called 'atheism'. By this was meant not 'atheism' in today's strict sense, of not believing in any notion of God, but a far more sweeping concept, characteristic of the time, meaning rejection of belief in a personal God who created the world, ordained morality, and rewards and punishes in the hereafter, a notion which also left 'no room', as Locke puts it, 'for the admittance of spirits, or the allowing any such things as immaterial beings in *rerum natura*'.[1]

That the 'atheist' has no awareness of right and wrong, and no respect for justice was an almost universally held conviction. As one theologian, Valentin Loescher, put it in 1708, 'atheism is pernicious both to virtue and the republic';[2] as another put it in 1710, 'atheism' is worse than any other human evil as it overthrows everything in matters both human and divine.[3] Since awareness of God, as it was put in a Marburg disputation in 1725, 'radix est et fundamentum omnis politiae notitia Dei' [is the root and foundation of every polity], 'atheism' was deemed the quintessence of all denial of the existing order.[4] 'Atheism' in this comprehensive Early Enlightenment sense had been known in Germany, according to the remarkably ambitious history of books in German lands published in 1713 by Jakob Friedrich Reimmann (1668–1743), Lutheran superintendent from 1717 at Hildesheim, since the twelfth century when it arose in the wake of Averroism, the Emperor Friedrich II (1215–50), he notes, figuring among its earliest representatives. But for several centuries it had been prodigiously rare and was in no way a serious social problem.

[1] Locke, *Some Thoughts*, 246.
[2] Loescher, *Praenotiones*, 20, 22.
[3] Jäger, *Spinocismus*, A2.
[4] Ries, *Dissertatio philosophica de atheis*, 35; Beermann, *Impietas atheistica*, 139, 144.

Since around 1650, however, the picture had changed dramatically. Previously practically unknown, 'atheism' in 'Germanic' lands had suddenly spread alarmingly in recent decades, though at first, says Reimmann, most representatives of this post-Renaissance, post-Aristotelian, 'atheism' were 'Dutchmen' rather than Germans as such. He cites the artist Torrentius, the chroniclers Olfert Dapper (1639–89) and Lieuwe van Aitzema (1600–69), Isaac Vossius (1618–98), Hadrianus Beverland (1650–1716), Franciscus van den Enden (1602–74), Bayle whose *Dictionnaire* had impressed the young Reimmann but whose bogus fideism he, like the Huguenot *rationaux*, later condemned, and, more surprisingly, perhaps, from a modern standpoint, Bekker who denied not the power of God but only that lesser spirits can work on bodies, and the Socinian Kuyper who denied neither God nor spirits.[5] Reimmann, rejecting Locke's critique of innate ideas, considered the idea of God innate in Man, 'atheism' in his view being a perverse affectation found only among a fatally few corrupted persons who were yet perfectly capable of establishing clandestine networks and corrupting many others.[6]

What then had caused the contagion? Everyone agreed the prime cause was 'philosophy' or else, as with La Croze, philosophy supplemented by Socinianism, much of the blame being attributed to foreigners. While England, Holland, Italy, France, and Poland were all identified as sources of the sickness, England and Holland were generally regarded as the prime sources in recent times, albeit with varying emphasis. The Kiel professor Christian Kortholt, in his *De tribus impostoribus* (1680), highlights the role not only of Hobbes but also, before him, of Herbert of Cherbury, while acknowledging that both came to be overshadowed by Spinoza whom he calls 'impostor omnium maximum'. It was not in fact uncommon to give a particular emphasis to Holland, as Reimmann does both in his history of German books and his later *Historia universalis atheismi* (1725).[7] Likewise, in a disputation on the mounting battle between theology and philosophy for primacy in academic study, held at Tübingen in 1737, Daniel Maichel, the presiding professor, identified Holland as the root of the impulse driving philosophy to challenge and supplant theology and from where 'atheism' had in the past been most energetically propagated. The United Provinces might be a very small place, he commented, but just as it was a great power in international affairs, indeed a 'theatre' of the whole world in politics and diplomacy, so it was also in the 'literary'—by which he meant scholarly, philosophical, and theological—sphere.[8] He illustrated Dutch centrality in the modern clash of theology and philosophy by citing the Bekker disputes of 1691–4 and the struggle between Bayle and the *rationaux* philosopher-theologians Le Clerc, Bernard, and Jaquelot.[9]

[5] Beermann, *Impietas atheistica*, 85, 87; Reimmann, *Versuch einer Einleitung*, ii. 97–8; Zedelmaier, 'Aporien', 103–4; Jaumann, 'Jakob Friedrich Reimmann's Bayle-Kritik', 200–2, 205–6.

[6] Sparn, 'Omnis nostra fides', 83–5, 87.

[7] Kortholt, *De tribus impostoribus*, preface p. xi, and pp. 94–138; Pätzold, *Spinoza, Aufklärung*, 19; Malcolm, *Aspects of Hobbes*, 480.

[8] Maichelius, *De philosophia theologiae domina*, 5.

[9] Ibid. 5–6, 24.

But while England and Holland were identified as prime sources of denial of God, flagrantly defying the *consensus gentium*, no one doubted that the intellectual roots of *Naturalismus* and *Libertinismus* in German society were indigenous as well as foreign, even though it was only after 1670 that a discernible indigenous stream of 'atheists' arose, beginning, according to Reimmann and others, with Matthias Knutzen, who in 1674 administered a severe jolt to the University of Jena with atheistic tracts in Latin and German found strewn on the professors' pews in church, followed by Joachim Gerhard Ram, a Wittenberg student who, in 1688, having composed a last *Testament* denying immortality of the soul, rather perversely committed suicide.[10] Knutzen, son of an organist, from near Eiderstedt, in Holstein, having studied for many years at Königsberg, Copenhagen, and other universities, possessed excellent Latin and tolerable prospects yet 'arrived to such a degree of extravagancy', as the English version of Bayle's *Dictionnaire* puts it, 'as publickly to maintain Atheism, and undertook great journeys to gain proselytes'.[11]

Beset by this new form of politico-religious subversion, Lutheran academe reacted with dismay and some anxiety, particularly to reports that 'atheism' had now become an organized movement in the universities. According to Knutzen, there existed an underground society of some seven hundred sworn atheists, predominantly students, both high-born and commoner, headed by himself, scattered across Europe from Rome and Hamburg to Copenhagen, Stockholm, and Königsberg.[12] He named his 'sect' the *Gewissener* [Conscientiaries] because, he said, there exists no other true God, Religion, or Magistracy than Man's Conscience, the medium by which all men are taught the 'three precepts of justice', as Bayle puts it, precisely recording Knutzen's formula as given in his tracts: 'to do no injury to anyone, to live honestly and give every one his due'.[13] Urging a wholly secular morality independent of revelation, he categorically insisted on the non-reality of Heaven and Hell.

Even if it existed almost wholly as a phantom in the mind, this supposed movement was unquestionably revolutionary. For Knutzen's tracts not only categorically denied God but also the legitimacy of princes, prelates, and magistrates, proclaiming the equality of all men and negating the sanctity of marriage.[14] Reason Knutzen declared a better 'Bible' than Scripture,[15] life after death a fantasy, and churchmen practised deceivers. He went so far as to urge that 'priests and rulers should be

10 Reimmann, *Versuch einer Einleitung*, ii. 98; Meyer, *Närrische Welt*, 38; Pratje, *Historische Nachrichten*, 8; Schröder, *Ursprünge*, 422–3.

11 Pfoh, *Matthias Knutzen*, 26–9; Israel, *Radical Enlightenment*, 630–1, 659–61; Bayle, *An Historical and Critical Dictionary*, iii. 1844.

12 Tietzmann, *Atheismi*, p. B3^{v}; Musaeus, *Ableinung*, 1–2, 4–5, 11, 16; Grossmann, *Johan Christian Edelmann*, 120–1; Glebe-Møller, *Vi Fornaegter Gud*, 46.

13 Knutzen, 'Ein Gespräch', 53–4; Bayle, *An Historical and Critical Dictionary*, iii. 1844; Gundling, *Vollständige Historie*, iii. 3904; Edelmann, *Moses*, ii. 32, 38; Mulsow, *Moderne*, 35, 143.

14 Musaeus, *Ableinung*, 9, 11; Pfoh, *Matthias Knutzen*, 30–1; Knutzen, 'Ein Gespräch', 49–50; Wagner, *Johan Christian Edelmanns verblendete Anblicke*, ii. 97, 195; Grossmann, *Johan Christian Edelmann*, 147.

15 Knutzen, 'Ein Gespräch', 53; Musaeus, *Ableinung*, 13, 19; Edelmann, *Moses*, ii. 53.

driven from the world'.[16] A ducal 'inquisition' was instituted but the culprit escaped without trace and nothing more was discovered about his secret society. Even so, neither the princely, church, nor academic authorities proposed to treat the matter lightly. If Knutzen's tracts were effectively suppressed,[17] at least until 1711 when La Croze reproduced one of his pieces in his *Entretiens*, and then in the 1740s when Johann Christian Edelmann (1698–1767) republished more, memory of the scandal lingered not only among connoisseurs of *clandestina*, like La Croze and Frederick the Great's secretary Jordan, but also, due to Bayle's devoting an article to him in his *Dictionnaire*, in the wider European consciousness.

The subversive thesis, afterwards associated especially with Bayle, that 'atheismum non ducare necessario homines ad morum corruptionem' [atheism does not necessarily lead men to the corruption of morals], which came to be deemed especially fatal, was illustrated with particular reference to Knutzen even before the appearance of Bayle's *Dictionnaire*, as we see from a university disputation held at Wittenberg in March 1696.[18] At Wittenberg, students were being taught to rebut Knutzen's thesis that all mankind shares the most essential moral ideas, and that these can underpin a viable society sustained by reason, education, and conscience alone without divine intervention or ecclesiastical authority. The counter-argument was that any such viable moral framework is inconceivable, if not anchored in 'natural religion', that is, belief in a Creator God who ordains morality and administers reward and punishment in the hereafter, and impossible without a clergy and magistrates to remind us of the divine Creator who made, instructs, and judges the consciences of all.[19]

The most worrying aspect of the contagion, for many, was the incontestable fact that the universities themselves were inherently part of the burgeoning problem of 'atheism'. With thirty universities in the Holy Roman Empire, and several more beyond, in the Baltic, maintaining close ties with those of northern Germany, sharing in a common Lutheran theological and reading culture, the academic world constituted a more substantial sector of society in this part of Europe than elsewhere. Besides training the men who dominated the legal and medical professions, and the body of Protestant pastors, academe was the training ground of most officials staffing the princely bureaucracies and the source of the tutors educating the sons of the nobility. Socially and politically as well as culturally, the universities, in other words, were a major cornerstone of Germany's *ancien régime*.

After Knutzen, further deeply disturbing indications of 'atheism' besetting the Lutheran universities rapidly materialized. If Spinoza's friend Tschirnhaus, and the minor Berlin court official Friedrich Wilhelm Stosch (1648–1704), had presumably been contaminated in Holland rather than Germany, and nothing at all was known of the anonymous 'Magdeburg atheist' who, in 1714, deposited a

16 Knutzen, 'Ein Gespräch' 49; Grossmann, *Johann Christian Edelmann*, 115–16, 125.

17 Pfoh, *Matthias Knutzen*, 27 n., 34; Schröder, *Ursprünge*, 420–1; Schröder, 'Contesto storico', 22; Brogi, *Teologia senza verità*, 160 n.

18 Pritius, *De atheismo*, art. xvi; Weber, *Beurtheilung*, 22.

19 Schröder, *Ursprünge*, 164–5; Hüning, 'Grenzen der Toleranz', 231–2.

comprehensively irreligious discourse there,[20] such notorious personalities as Gabriel Wagner (d. *c.*1717), Lau, Wachter, and Edelmann, the latter once an anti-Wolffian Pietist theology student at Jena who after reading the *Tractatus theologico-politicus*, in the summer of 1740, following a deep personal spiritual crisis, became a devotee of Spinoza,[21] were, like Knutzen, incontestably all products of German-Scandinavian academe. If the Johann Konrad Franz von Hatzfeld (*c.*1685–*c.*1751) gaoled at The Hague in 1745–6 for his book *La Découverte de la vérité* (The Hague, 1745) denying Christ's divinity, calling the biblical prophets and apostles 'deceivers', being of humbler social origin than the others, had never been a university student, he too, having gained a good knowledge of languages, acquired much of his philosophical and scientific knowledge, as well as his opportunities to spread radical ideas, at Leipzig in the late 1720s and 1730s, as a private tutor of English, chiefly among university students.[22]

Solidly academic, and even more shocking than Knutzen's tracts, as well as perhaps the intellectually most formidable text of Early Enlightenment German 'atheism', was the anonymous clandestine manuscript known as the *Cymbalum mundi* or *Symbolum sapientiae* which, according to manuscript copies surviving today at Halle, Erlangen, Berlin, and Parma, was composed in 'Eleutheropolis' in the year 1678,[23] but cannot actually have been written before 1692 since it cites works of Le Clerc published that year.[24] Although composed in Latin, it was indubitably conceived by a German scholar for a Lutheran erudite readership, as was evident from its referring—as Reimmann, a great bibliophile, pointed out—to Luther's Bible and certain typically German turns of Latin phrase, as well as its virtual absence outside Germany.[25] Written probably around 1700, or soon after, Wachter once topped the list of those suspected of having written it, Knutzen has been proposed, and Wagner and Stosch (d. 1704) both seem possible. Whoever the author was he was especially familiar with the juridical works of Christian Thomasius and may have had some connection with Halle.[26]

The *Symbolum* is a major work, not only one of the first but, in argument, one of the most sophisticated and detailed, clandestine texts of the European irreligious Enlightenment. Moreover, it circulated (in manuscript) quite widely within the Empire, being studied among others by both Edelmann and Wachter to whom Reimmann tentatively attributed the work's original authorship in 1731, but who was too young to have written it, given its early date, though he knew the text well, felt a special kinship to it, and inserted additional material into several of the

20 Mulsow, *Moderne*, 35. 21 Ibid. 287–8; Grossmann, *Johann Christian Edelmann*, 111–12.

22 ARH Hof van Holland 5454/13, art. 28. Interrogation: von Hatzfeld, 16 Nov. 1745, 29–36; [Hatzfeld], *Découverte de la verité*, pp. lix–lx.

23 HUB Misc. 8/2. 'Cymbalum mundi ceu symbolum sapientiae, (Eleutheropoli, 1678); the surviving copy at Wittenberg purports to be dated 1668 but this must be incorrect since it refers to Spinoza's *Tractatus* of 1670, Canziani, 'Critica', 36–7; Schröder, 'Symbolum sapientiae', 229.

24 Schröder, 'Contesto historico', 17–19; Mori, 'Athéisme', 187.

25 Schröder, 'Symbolum sapientiae', 229; Canziani, 'Cymbalum mundi', 38.

26 Schröder, 'Contesto historico', 25–7; Mori, 'Athéisme', 187.

manuscript copies.[27] Even if still alive, Knutzen too seems an unlikely candidate since it is written in a very different style from his tracts of 1674 and, unlike these, is explicitly Spinozistic.[28] In the 1740s, at the height of its underground existence, this text was translated into German, probably either by Edelmann who possessed a Latin copy at the time, Wachter, or Johann Lorenz Schmidt, though this vernacular manuscript version is itself now lost.[29]

The *Symbolum*'s message is stated bluntly enough and no one able to read its scholarly Latin could have remained in any doubt as to its inflammatory political and social intent: deception and imposture, graced with the names of revelation and Holy Scripture, rule throughout our world; the common people are forced into drudgery and subjection, and individual freedom is quashed, by an oppressive apparatus of 'superstition' dignified with the name of revealed religion which, whether pagan, Jewish, Christian, or Muslim, is served by a cynical, deceiving priesthood who work hand in hand with the secular authorities in their own interest and that of their princely allies. It has been argued that the *Symbolum*'s anonymous author was no authentic 'Spinozist' since his equation of religion with superstition is too blunt and his anti-Scripturalism too militant, being more reminiscent of the *Traité des trois imposteurs* than of Spinoza's calm reasoning. By presenting revealed religion in a purely negative light, 'quia religio errorum mater est et genetrix' [because religion is the mother and progenitor of errors], and ignoring Spinoza's view of religion and Scripture as socially useful in some respects, by exerting a positive moral influence among those incapable of independent critical judgement, the *Symbolum* does indeed both oversimplify and, to a degree, pervert Spinoza's ideas.[30] Yet in questioning and ultimately seeking to overthrow the pillars of existing society, the text essentially just sharpens and renders more explicit much that is already inherent in Spinoza. In substance, if not in tone, it unquestionably is 'Spinozistic'.

If it omits some of Spinoza's arguments, the *Symbolum*, while leaving the *Ethics* unmentioned, makes no secret of its reliance on the *Tractatus theologico-politicus*, indeed, is essentially a reworking of the *Tractatus*' core thesis. Most obviously Spinozist is the work's total denial of divine providence, divine judgement, and supernatural agency, reducing all reality to a single integrated naturalistic system, conceiving organized religion's social function as being to make the people 'obey' and depicting theologians and priests as a corrupt class of deceivers. Its claims that all revealed religion is 'superstition' and encourages credulity and bigotry, that Scripture is a purely human document and a highly defective one at that, that reason is the only revelation that is authentic and biblical prophecy a form of fantasy, are presented not only giving mostly the same reasons but not infrequently almost the same words as appear in the relevant propositions of Spinoza's treatise.[31]

27 Schröder, *Ursprünge*, 408–16; Schröder, 'Symbolum sapientiae', 229; Mulsow, *Moderne*, 241–3.

28 Schröder, 'Contesto storico', 22.

29 Ibid. 32–3.

30 HUB Misc. 8/2, 'Cymbalum mundi', fos. 68^{v}–70, 78^{r}–78^{v}; Schröder, 'Symbolum sapientiae', 234.

31 Schröder, 'Symbolum sapientiae', 232.

Equally Spinozistic is the *Symbolum*'s wholesale denial of miracles and dismissal of spectres and demons as just chimeras of the deluded imagination, along with the claim that the clergy and princes, whatever their pretexts, suppress freedom of thought and expression which is a basic human right out of ambition and self-interest.[32] Spinozist also, if again sharpened, is the complaint that the dogmas of revealed religion are cunningly manipulated by theologians and princes to incite the common people to persecute and destroy the few who proclaim the truth.[33] The *Symbolum*, then, like Knutzen, challenges the prevailing order in strident, uncompromising tones, pre-echoing Meslier (and Nietzsche) in stressing the supposedly wretched style of the New Testament, deriding its spiritual claims, and deploring the divisive proliferation of sects and heresies arising from its obscurity. Both Knutzen's tracts and the *Symbolum* clearly indicated that the new philosophical 'atheism' arousing such consternation in Germany formed part of a wider propaganda campaign aimed not only against belief in God, revealed religion, and ecclesiastical power but, scarcely less, at discrediting princely authority and denouncing social hierarchy; at the same time, this was plainly a campaign to emancipate the individual from a deeply rooted system of traditional attitudes entailing wide-ranging moral and sexual constraints.

Preachers, professors, and other defenders of the status quo, whether traditionalist or moderately enlightened, were thus largely justified in claiming that the philosophy embodied in such texts threatened to shatter the basic principles on which society, culture, and faith in the Holy Roman Empire rested. They rightly maintained that these attacks on Scripture, miracles, supernatural agency, Christian dogmas, princely authority, and the existing social order formed a single interlocking, comprehensive system of ideas buttressed by a new kind of philosophy, representing a threat which could only be combated by a superior philosophy. While the intellectual seeds of modern naturalism could be traced back to Italian and French writers of the Renaissance, remarked a well-known treatise condemning the growth of incredulity concerning Satan, demons, and witchcraft published at Wittenberg in 1694, Nathanael Falck's *De daemonologia*, in Germany it was actually only since Spinoza, Falck points out, that the confounding of God with the 'secondary causes' of nature in a philosophical mode had gained ground in a decisive, concerted manner, with significant numbers of unbelievers and freethinkers systematically equating God with nature. It may be true that since ancient times there have been countless libertines, impious thinkers, and irreligious scoffers, but only since Spinoza with his 'monstrous opinions' about the Devil, demons, and the supernatural had freethinkers and libertines become so perverse as to preclude outright the existence of all disembodied spirits, ghosts, beings, and apparitions whatsoever and, by so doing, foment a general scepticism about these, paving the way for the Bekker controversies causing so much uproar in Holland and considerable dismay in Germany as well.[34]

[32] HUB Misc. 8/2, 'Cymbalum mundi', fos. 32–4, 35^{v}, 38, 68^{v}–69, 70, 104.

[33] Ibid., fo. 34^{v}.

[34] Falck, *De daemonologia*, 2–6, 58–9.

Spinoza hence came to be associated with what was perceived as a general intellectual malaise permeating the whole of German society. Although Falck worked at Wittenberg, and the shift in attitudes of which he complains was primarily an academic phenomenon, in his mind the menace certainly extended to the whole of society. Likewise, Friedrich Gottlob Jenichen (1680–1735), chronicler of the van Leenhof controversy, depicts 'Spinozism' as a full-scale onslaught on all respectable thinking, lamenting, in 1707, that his age was appallingly 'fertile in Spinozistic writings and paradoxical opinions'.[35] During this period, in Germany, as in Holland and France, Spinoza's name even became to some degree a household word, Edelmann remarking, for instance, in 1740, that not only the Lutheran clergy 'but also the common people—pretending to understand more than they do—grimace with disgust, if by chance someone should mention Spinoza's name'.[36] There were also, though, he adds, a few who though often humble men with little learning, clandestinely, and sometimes openly, dissented from the common view.

Even so, categorical rejection of all supernatural forces, as an argued, systematic stance, *Spinosisterey*, as it was known, remained primarily an academic phenomenon. A Lutheran pastor in a small town near Halberstadt, Johann Georg Leuckfeld (1668–1726), in 1699 published a book on the advent of 'atheism' which, after rehearsing the familiar points about the morally vitiating effects of court life and soldiering, neither at all novel phenomena, focused particular attention on the unwitting responsibility of the Protestant universities for spreading the alleged spiritual and intellectual sickness. In their public lectures and publications, he grants, professors adhered closely enough to received doctrines laid down by the princely and church authorities. But besides failing to curb the heavy drinking and disorderliness rife in universities, the professoriate, he complained, was seriously negligent in not imposing stricter control over the private 'philosophical collegia', mostly given by younger scholars who did not hold 'chairs'.[37] These private classes, objects Leuckfeld, were frequent, very popular with the students, and, what was most worrying, intellectually unregulated; it was these, he argues, which were systematically injecting philosophical ideas and attitudes into discussion of biblical, religious, moral, and social questions previously treated exclusively in theological terms.

Even students attending university without any intention of studying philosophy, concentrating just on Bible, theology, and Church history, so as to become pastors, had in recent years, he observes, been forced to bend to the fashion somewhat since in contemporary German society no one gained respect as a scholar or biblical exegete without some familiarity with the New Philosophy. Professional standing and the academic readership required it. Thus, through their teachers, students were encountering all kinds of newly arrived, foreign ideas 'which are at odds with God's Word'.[38] This now universally prevalent tendency was being

[35] Ibid. 22, 25; Schröder, 'Spinozam tota armenta', 164–6.

[36] Edelmann, *Moses*, ii. 118.

[37] Leuckfeld, *Verführische Atheisten Hauffe*, 249–50.

[38] Ibid. 271.

exacerbated, he complained, by the increasingly divided state of both philosophy and theology faculties, a state of stasis which was the root cause of the bitter quarrels and factionalism now prevalent in academic life. Before the advent of 'Cartesianism', the German academic disputation, he claimed, had been wholly uncontroversial, just an exercise in technical skill, in handling settled categories and agreed concepts in each discipline with an underlying consensus about doctrine. Now the academic disputation was an arena for conflicting schools of thought in which professorial reputations are continually pitted against each other, fomented by a spirit of rivalry and antagonism which both incited students and deepened the strife.[39]

So vehement had the philosophical feuding become that it would be easier, he suggests, to convert a Jew to Christianity than to persuade adherents of the rival philosophical schools—Aristotelians, Cartesians, Eclectics, and Sceptics—to switch allegiance from one sect to another.[40] Such furious divisions inevitably disorientated students, leading some to an incipient 'naturalism' and then further sliding, little by little, finally culminating in atheism. At the heart of the catastrophe, hence, were the universities themselves: for by teaching students critically to examine, and search for objections to all propositions put to them, the university classroom itself fostered a culture of questioning, research, scepticism, and independence, not least by conveying the impression the universities themselves had no clear grasp of the truth.

What we know of the major exponents of radical thought in Protestant German lands would seem to confirm the burden of Leuckfeld's thesis. For just as most of Spinoza's non-Collegiant allies in Holland, like Koerbagh, Meyer, Cuffeler, and (for a time) the Dane Nicholas Steno, initially acquired their radical ideas in the lecture rooms, private collegia, and public disputations about Cartesianism at Leiden and Utrecht, so many of the German radical writers, like Knutzen, Stosch, Lau, Wachter, Wagner, Edelmann, and Johann Lorenz Schmidt, similarly reflect the impact of a philosophically fragmented and deeply divided academic milieu, in a way which suggests the latter indeed made a considerable contribution to shaping the Radical Enlightenment. Wachter, son of the city physician of Memmingen, had studied philosophy and theology at Tübingen, from 1689 until 1693, and then, in the years 1696–7, at Leipzig and Halle. By the time he visited Holland, in 1698–9, where his preoccupation with Spinozism and Judaism was intensified by his arduous dispute, in Amsterdam, with Spaeth, his mind was already filled with academically acquired philosophical erudition; after the appearance of his *Elucidarius cabalisticus* (1706), he was universally considered a 'Spinozist'.[41] The East Prussian radical Lau had studied for many years at both Königsberg and Halle where he was taught by Buddeus and Christian Thomasius.[42]

[39] Leuckfeld, *Verführische Atheisten Hauffe*, 309–10.
[40] Ibid. 250.
[41] Wachter, 'Leben', 162–4; Gundling, *Vollständige Historie*, iv. 4938; Schröder, 'Einleitung (1995)', 17–28.
[42] Israel, *Radical Enlightenment*, 652; Mulsow, *Moderne*, 36–7.

Gabriel Wagner (?1660–*c.*?1717), a man of formidable learning and originality, had studied chiefly at Leipzig, where he had been on close terms with Thomasius until expelled from the university in 1691, apparently after a quarrel with his landlady about rent, leading to a clash with the university authorities and his being gaoled for two years. In 1693, now an avowed enemy of the German university system, he followed Thomasius to Halle; but was disowned by the latter, according to Leibniz, owing to his libertine opinions. Wagner repaid Thomasius by haranguing whoever would listen with vehement denunciations of his former mentor and publishing several tracts, in Latin and German, attacking Thomasius' doctrines.[43] The first of these, *Discursus et dubia in Christ: Thomasii introductionem ad philosophiam aulicam*, published in 1691 under the pseudonym 'Realis de Vienna' with the place name 'Regensburg' falsely declared on the title page, sufficiently impressed Leibniz (who was no friend of Thomasius) to prompt him to try to trace the anonymous author.[44]

After conspicuously failing to secure a permanent teaching post in Berlin where he lived in the years 1693–6, or Vienna, in 1696, he secured a position at the Hamburg civic Gymnasium but again without establishing himself permanently. For some years, he corresponded with Leibniz, who remained sympathetic despite his abrasive personality and freethinking ideas and also helped with money and obtaining a succession of short-lived positions, including one as a cataloguer in the great library at Wolfenbüttel. In their lengthy discussions, Wagner regularly opposed Leibniz's key metaphysical views in favour of the necessity of all that is.[45] Eventually, he managed to quarrel even with Leibniz, as well as clash with Reimmann whom he accused of stealing one of his manuscripts. His bitterest complaints, though, were directed not against individuals but against the universities and prevailing system of erudition and tuition, as well as the German nobility and the ruling princes.

A far-reaching reformation of the academic system was requisite, in his opinion, which would place far more emphasis on mathematics, physics, medicine, and history, and curtail the role of older authorities and especially theology. He rejoiced in the progress philosophy and science had made since Descartes, believing more impressive advances had been achieved in Germany than in France or Italy. Citing the example of medicine, in 1691, he claimed nearly all the university-trained physicians in Germany were now *Eclectics*, meaning medics freed from older doctrines, whereas in France many doctors were still 'Aristotelici, Galenici, Ptolomaici' and in Italy and Spain still more so.[46] A passionate advocate of Cartesian science, he fully shared Thomasius' zeal for the new eclecticism, believing it had emancipated the German universities from the shackles of the past and inaugurated a genuine freedom to philosophize. A contemporary who particularly influenced him was

43 Stiehler, 'Gabriel Wagner', 66.
44 Ibid. 74, 77–80; Wollgast, 'Einleitung', 9–11.
45 Wollgast, 'Einleitung', 20–5; Stiehler, 'Gabriel Wagner', 86.
46 Wagner, *Discursus et dubia*, 2, 65.

the quietly subversive Halle professor Gundling, Wagner especially liking the latter's argument that it was the pagan Greeks who invented philosophy and these 'atheistic' Hellenes who first forged a conception of philosophy as the queen of the disciplines presiding over all other knowledge.

A high priority for Wagner was to secure the total separation of philosophy, experimental and speculative, from theology.[47] According to Leibniz, Wagner believed neither in the Bible, nor in Creation, nor in divine providence, figuring among those for whom reason—which, however, he thought Descartes and Clauberg had wrongly applied—is Man's only guide, that which, next to moral uprightness, is the most 'godly' thing about us.[48] Attacking Thomasius' views on the spirit and the soul, in his again clandestinely published *Prüfung des Versuchs Thomasii vom Wesen des Geistes* (1707), 'Realis de Vienna' accused Thomasius of not applying reason consistently, vitiating all sound, empirically-based reasoning, indeed encouraging the spread of unreason and superstition. Here, he emerges as a more or less thoroughgoing materialist, denying the existence of spirits separate from bodies, embracing the universal necessity of all things, rejecting both the incorporeality and immortality of the soul, and, seemingly, not believing in any God separate from the world.[49]

Adamant that reason must be closely combined with the experimental method, Wagner simultaneously praised Descartes for helping emancipate the human mind while criticizing him for going astray, like Thomasius after him, in distancing reason from the five senses and hence experimental science. Thomasius, whom in his text of 1707 he taunts by asking whether he had not read Descartes, Le Boe Sylvius, Hobbes, and Leibniz, he bitterly reproaches for placing the will beyond reason and betraying his own dictum that 'the senses without reason, and the latter without the former, would be quite useless to men'.[50] Although the only direct references to Spinoza in his published work are in a pamphlet of 1710 which is probably, but not certainly, by him, there are obvious points of convergence between Wagner and Spinoza, though Wagner, like Tschirnhaus, generally puts more emphasis on the need for experiments and mathematical methods, and while wholly segregating philosophy (and science) from faith, does not expressly identify nature with God.[51] A hard-hitting seventy-two-page diatribe against Wagner, published at Halle in 1710 by 'Jucundus de Laboribus', thought to be the Pietist controversialist Joachim Lange (1670–1744), the theologian who, later, in the 1720s, led the campaign against Wolff, highlighting his seeming identification of God and the cosmos, roundly accused Wagner of being a disciple of 'B.d.S.'[52] The reply

[47] Mulsow, *Moderne*, 328; Stiehler, 'Gabriel Wagner', 76–7, 83.

[48] Stiehler, 'Gabriel Wagner', 79; [Wagner], *Discursus et dubia*, 75–6; [Wagner?] F.M.v.G., *Antwort*, 57; [Lange], *Freye Gedancken*, 47–8, 54.

[49] [Jucundus de Laboribus], *Freye Gedanken*, 47–8, 54; [Wagner?] F.M.v.G., *Antwort*, 44–6; Wagner, *Prüfung des Versuchs*, preface and pp. 9, 21–2.

[50] Wagner, *Prüfung des Versuchs*, 9–10, 12; Hunter, 'Passions', 117–18.

[51] Stiehler, 'Gabriel Wagner', 86–7; Wollgast, 'Einleitung', 25, 43, 54.

[52] Wollgast, 'Einleitung', 44; [Jucundus de Laboribus], *Freye Gedanken*, 48, 51.

to this attack, published anonymously the same year under the initials 'F.M.v.G.', presumably another pseudonym of Wagner's,[53] dismisses the charge as *Staupbesenschelm* [calumny], notes that its author had, prior to this, been verbally linking him with Spinoza in conversations at Halle,[54] and remarks, significantly, 'indessen ist Spinosen nicht so viel irrig also die Lästersüchse rufen' [meanwhile Spinoza is not as wrong as the slanderers proclaim].[55]

Wagner aspired to reform not just the universities but German society more broadly. Most of his countrymen, he believed, were afflicted by a pervasive inferiority complex with regard to both foreign nations and their own rulers, supinely submitting to the most abject and humiliating circumstances. Scathing about the cultural preferences of the German courts, especially their zeal for French fashion, language, and manners, and disdain for the German language, he deplored the Empire's fragmentation into often absurdly small and ineffective states and its weakness. The social and political primacy of the nobility he thoroughly detested, insisting nobility of the mind far eclipses aristocracy of birth in worth and merit,[56] a view not at all conducive to extricating his career from its relentlessly ruinous course.

Priding himself on his insights as a political thinker, Wagner boasts, in his reply to Lange of 1710 that were his political philosophy ever to appear (which it did not), he would demonstrate how men, if only they wanted to, could lead morally worthier and happier lives and show that 'a rational state is not as Platonic or utopian as people think'; he would also prove that practically all *ethica, politica*, and *juristica* hitherto taught are a waste of time, that while Spinoza and Pufendorf are two eminently worthy philosophers in this field, Grotius is just a schoolmaster, Naudé a deceiver, Machiavelli unbalanced, and 'Hobbes a visible devil despite the fact that, according to Spinoza, he is cleverer than all the others'.[57] In 1717, Wagner is known to have stayed briefly in Göttingen, and debated intensively with Heumann; after that, all trace of him disappears. Presumably, he died in, or soon after, that year.

2. ACADEMIC DISPUTATIONS AND THE MAKING OF GERMAN RADICAL THOUGHT

By the middle of the century, it seemed clear that philosophical 'atheism' was penetrating more widely in society and also fanning out geographically. In 1751, a Lutheran pastor, Johann Meyer, writing in the small Silesian town of Bernstedt, attested that, during the seventeen years he had been preaching there, 'atheism'—that is not 'practical irreligion' but philosophical atheism—had noticeably 'caught

53 Wollgast, 'Einleitung', 43.
54 [Wagner?] F.M.v.G., *Antwort*, 45–6.
55 Ibid. 46.
56 Stiehler, 'Gabriel Wagner', 71.
57 [Wagner?] F.M.v.G., *Antwort*, 61.

on even with the common man'.[58] The cause of the rot, indisputably, in his opinion, was 'philosophy'. Whereas, until the 1730s, there had been only isolated 'atheists' like Stosch, Lau, and Edelmann, now owing to philosophy and 'through their godless writings, many thousands of others have been led to it also'.[59] Germany, held Meyer, was now awash with *Indifferentismus* and *Libertinismus*, and had joined Italy, France, England, the Netherlands, and Poland as a land of 'atheism'.

The blight was allegedly spreading likewise in Scandinavia. In Denmark, the problem was worst, of course, at Copenhagen where, in the late 1740s, according to La Beaumelle, freethinking was rife among the court nobility. Among other evidence, he notes that the clandestine manuscript *Examen de la religion* (by Du Marsais)—written, La Beaumelle suspected, by d'Argens and against which he wrote a reply (now lost)—was freely circulating in select and bibliophile circles. Bayle, as we have seen, was thoroughly in vogue while the count of Gyldenstern, he reports, was openly an admirer of Fontenelle.[60] All the currently controversial French books were available, albeit at high prices, he adds, in Copenhagen whither they were shipped from Holland, La Beaumelle himself having received by this route his copy of Diderot's banned *Pensées philosophiques*.

Erik Pontoppidan (1698–1764), court preacher in Copenhagen from 1735 and, from 1738, a Pietist theology professor at the university, and then bishop of Bergen (1748–55), in Norway, and probably the most authoritative observer of the spiritual state of Denmark-Norway in the mid eighteenth century, though previously relatively unconcerned about the progress of 'atheism' in Denmark, had become deeply worried by mid century. Earlier he had written an account of parish life on the Danish island of Als, off Jutland, a land where Satanism and belief in witchcraft remained pervasive, while residing there as chaplain to a duke between 1723 and 1734. What chiefly appalled him at that time were its grossly superstitious peasants who still imagined that making the sign of the cross had the magical property of warding off evil and who trusted in the mystical healing properties of consecrated communion wine.[61] Although until recently unbelief had been considerably rarer than 'superstition', and 'atheism' remained less rampant in Denmark than in Holland or Germany, by the 1750s, Pontoppidan had to admit that philosophical 'atheism' had disastrously penetrated there too, so much so that he no longer felt justified, as he formerly had, in keeping quiet about it but, on the contrary, now urged the professors at Copenhagen to target 'atheism', something he deemed vital for the defence of religion, and the social and political order more generally.[62]

A full-scale cultural crisis then, caused by the impact of 'philosophy', had by the 1740s undeniably gained a worryingly wide grip within the Lutheran universities which had themselves become a crucial channel of diffusion of radical ideas. This meant that the social role of the universities had now changed in a significant

58 Meyer, *Närrische Welt*, 'Vorrede', p.C^{v}. 59 Ibid. 38, 274.

60 Lauriol, *La Beaumelle*, 139. 61 Hope, *German and Scandinavian Protestantism*, 149.

62 Pontopiddan, *Abhandlung*, 13–14; Pontoppidan, *Kraft der Wahrheit*, 4; on Pontoppidan, see Hope, *German and Scandinavian Protestantism*, 128.

fashion: previously the source merely of technical and professional training for preachers, lawyers, officials, and physicians; now they were the source of innovating, reforming, and also destabilizing ideas. At the same time, society generally, by the 1740s, took a closer interest than they had in the past in the academic proceedings themselves. University disputations and theses were presented, of course, in Latin. But during the early eighteenth century, German-language periodicals like the *Gründliche Auszüge aus denen neuesten theologisch, philosophisch und philologischen Disputationibus*, published at Leipzig between 1733 and 1745, took to reviewing academic publications in the vernacular, especially those dealing with theological, philosophical, and scientific topics, thereby helping to focus general attention on issues intensively debated between professors and students as well as their way of classifying and categorizing the new and vying streams of thought, and indeed all past thought.

Still more important was the *Fortgesetzte Sammlung van alten und neuen theologischen Sachen* which in 1733, remarkably enough, published a review of the *Symbolum*, a clear indication of that text's widely disturbing dissemination in the German Early Enlightenment.[63] By the 1720s and 1730s there were also several other periodicals specializing in reporting academic proceedings in German, as well as the *Bibliothèque germanique* (50 vols., 1720–41) and its successor, the *Nouvelle Bibliothèque germanique*, published by Pierre Humbert in Amsterdam but largely edited by Huguenot *érudits* in Berlin, which reported German academic disputes in French, helping broadcast them among the German courts as well as abroad.[64]

The five German Calvinist Reformed universities—Marburg, Herborn, Duisburg, Frankfurt an der Oder, and Heidelberg (after 1685, Catholic), the ten Catholic universities—Cologne, Erfurt, Mainz, Freiburg, Trier, Ingolstadt, Bamberg, Paderborn, Dillingen, and Würzburg—and, especially, the dozen Lutheran universities responded to the deepening intellectual crisis by tightening academic discipline and trying to narrow freedom of thought, as well as institute new forms of academic training designed more directly to confront the burgeoning challenge of philosophical radicalism. Gundling, teaching at Halle from 1698, after studying at Aldorf, Jena, and Leipzig, to some extent opposed the attempts to restrict liberty of thought;[65] but most of the leading luminaries, including Thomasius, Buddeus, Leibniz, and Wolff besides Pufendorf who participated in the commission which condemned Stosch, willingly assented to the pressure to impose curbs on intellectual freedom.[66] German universities, not least Königsberg where the young Kant signed on as a student in 1740,[67] remained eclectic, lively, and divided between

[63] Schröder, 'Contesto storico', 31.

[64] Van Eeghen, *Amsterdamse boekhandel*, iii. 181; Berkvens-Stevelinck, *Prosper Marchand*, 48, 117; Goldgar, *Impolite Learning*, 74–86.

[65] Gundling, *Vollständige Historie*, iv. 6066–7; Albrecht, *Eklektik*, 576; Mulsow, *Moderne*, 341–8.

[66] Hüning, 'Grenzen der Toleranz', 229–31, 243–4; Seidler, 'Politics', 232.

[67] Cassirer, *Kant's Life*, 26–7; Kuehn, *Kant*, 67–9; Schönfeld, *Philosophy*, 13.

different currents; but full freedom to philosophize continued to be deemed undesirable and was frowned upon.

Among other things, students required training, it was thought, in how to identify, unmask, and discredit pleas for the wrong sort of freedom of thought. According to a Copenhagen thesis of 1719, Spinoza, Toland, and Collins were the three foremost advocates of full or absolute freedom of judgement, and the main reason they champion *libertas philosophandi* is to try by this means to inject the 'perverseness' of Spinoza, meaning a generalized philosophic naturalism based on freedom of the individual, into the minds of those that sample this dangerous freedom.[68] Unrestricted freedom of thought and expression was deemed pernicious first because such freedom encourages circulation of all kinds of opinions, fomenting *libertinismus theologicus*, thereby encouraging, as it was put in a Swedish disputation of 1738, the propagation of Socinian, Mennonite, Remonstrant, and Spiritualist ideas; secondly, because it foments *libertinismus philosophicus*, encouraging moral and sexual licentiousness; and, thirdly and still more damaging, because it foments 'atheism' which is why Spinoza 'ut princeps atheorum' [as head of the atheists] had been so much in favour of propagating freedom of thought in the first place.[69] No less pernicious than full freedom of thought, in the Lutheran context of the time, then, was the idea of personal liberty of lifestyle. But this then raised questions as to what authentic, legitimate personal freedom actually is.

While it was clear that if certain concepts actively undermine religion, morals, and propriety, then it cannot be permissible to say allowing those ideas conforms to any legitimate form of human freedom, there was an urgent perceived need to find ways more clearly to identify, 'segregate', and exclude philosophical libertinism. Especially the philosophical libertinism expounded by the 'Englishmen' Toland and Collins and the 'Dutchman' Spinoza,[70] which, according to the same Swedish disputation, had now replaced *libertinismus theologicus* as the chief menace to Christian society, had to be clearly marked off from permissible moderate, Christian tolerance or what was called 'genuine liberty'. A key desideratum here was to limit penetration of philosophy into discussion of Scripture. In a disputation of April 1749, presided over by the Eclectic philosopher and anti-Pietist theologian Franz Albrecht Aepinus (1673–1750), at Rostock, where he had taught since 1712, excessive zeal for 'reason', and 'philosophy', were blamed for the progressive invasion of *Naturalismus* and *Indifferentismus* into essentially theological debates. The more philosophical reason takes hold, complained Aepinus, the more the prestige of 'divinely revealed theology' declines. This, he thought, had to be stopped and such 'Misbrauch' [abuse] energetically curbed by the university senates. To show what he meant, he cited the *Philosophia S. Scripturae interpres* of Lodewijk Meyer, published in Amsterdam in 1666, a plain case, he says, of the 'abuse' of subordinating Holy

68 Nannestad, *De libertate philosophandi*, 24–5, 50–1; Gundling, *Vollständige Historie*, iv. 6066.

69 Schröder, *Dissertatio gradualis*, 13, 15–16.

70 Ibid. 14.

Writ to criteria imposed by philosophical reason, something, he urges, which must be generally banned.[71]

The academic authorities agreed on the need to counter influences conducive to the spread of 'atheism'. Yet it was not at all easy to see how to draw a generally acceptable line between legitimate and illegitimate freedom of thought. For even the key term 'atheism' had lately become more complex if not inherently problematic, especially since Gundling's disturbing intervention on behalf of Hobbes, in his essay *Hobbesius ab atheismo liberatus*, of 1707, arguing that Hobbes was not, after all, as most scholars maintained, an 'atheist' and that valuable lessons may be learnt from his writings, as Pufendorf and others laying the foundations of Natural Law had shown.[72] One reason for Spinoza's unrivalled prominence as 'arch-atheist' in German scholarly debate of the Early Enlightenment, as the German controversy around Hobbes suggests, was simply his uniquely unquestioned status when it came to drawing a hard and fast line between what was allowed and what was not. For if even Hobbes could plausibly be held not to be an 'atheist', something absolutely incontrovertible was required enabling the professors to formulate a comprehensive target list of forbidden points covering the whole range of the intellectual challenge the universities were striving to confront.

What Thomasius too called the 'perverseness' of Spinoza in this way became an integral part of the Lutheran world's academic curriculum and an indispensable teaching tool. Hence a crucial part of the new training students received consisted of expounding what 'atheism' is, how to target it, and how thoroughly to discredit those blacklisted as 'Spinozists'.[73] This was the procedure, for instance, in 1707, a year after publication of Wachter's *Elucidarius cabalisticus* (1706), a work purporting to absolve Spinoza of 'atheism';[74] Wachter was roundly denounced as a 'Spinozist' damaging society by teaching 'atheism', and identifying God with nature, in a disputation presided over by Jakob Staalkopf (1685–*c.*1730), at Greifswald.[75]

One effect of the wider social and cultural crisis was to make 'history of philosophy' relevant in a new way. In the first volume of *Gründliche Auszüge*, for example, appeared a German-language account of the 'dissertatio historico-metaphysica', discussing the maxim 'ex nihilo nihil fit' [nothing can be made from nothing], delivered at Altdorf University, near Nuremberg, in June 1732 by Jakob Wilhlem Feuerlein (1689–1766). This concept, much utilized by present-day 'atheists' who reject the Judaeo-Christian conception of Creation, non-Latin readers learnt, had already been familiar to the Greek Presocratics, especially Anaxagoras and Xenophanes, over two millennia before.[76] Bayle having introduced Spinoza into discussion of numerous aspects of ancient philosophy, Buddeus in his early work

[71] *Vollstandige Nachrichten*, 2 (1750), 289–300.

[72] Ibid., Gundling, *Vollständige Historie*, iv. 6071; Mulsow, *Moderne*, 341–8; Malcolm, *Aspects of Hobbes*, 533–4.

[73] Nannestad, *De libertate philosophandi*, 51; Wollgast, 'Spinoza', 171.

[74] Wagner, *Discursus et dubia*, 137, 185.

[75] Staalkopf, *De atheismo Benedicti de Spinoza*, 296–308.

[76] *Gründliche Auszüge*, 1 (1733), preface pp. 252–3.

had then further encouraged this tendency and, in the view of many (possibly including himself), with highly questionable results. For if 'most of the ancient philosophers', as it was put in a Helmstedt disputation in 1742,[77] 'shared the godless set of doctrines of Spinoza', students could scarcely avoid concluding that Spinoza was one of the most pivotal figures in the whole history of human thought, and this could only consolidate his status as effectively chief philosophical antagonist and rival to Christian philosophy. While some orthodox Lutheran theologians, like Buddeus and Reimmann, readily upheld Bayle's appraisal of numerous Presocratic and Hellenistic Greek thinkers as 'atheistic' and 'Spinozistic', others pointed to the risk inherent in adopting such an approach. An Altdorf disputation of 1729, devoted to the figure of Xenophanes, for instance, chiefly concentrates on adducing arguments useful for countering Bayle's and Buddeus' classifying that philosopher as a precursor of Spinozism.[78]

No less problematic was the question of Chinese philosophy. Wolff, as we have seen, got into serious trouble, at Halle, with his *Oratio* of 1721, eulogizing classical Chinese thought for its achievements in moral and political philosophy while simultaneously conceding there are grounds for classifying Confucius' system as 'atheistic'.[79] But if the Wolffians had their fingers burnt, the Thomasians too needed to classify Chinese moral, political, and metaphysical philosophy somehow and decide whether or not it was 'Spinozistic'. Conceding Confucianism is close to Spinozism, as Bayle, Malebranche, and Buddeus urged, and as was thought to be implied by the Confucians' conceiving 'salutem populi supremum esse legem' [the good of the people to be the supreme law], carried the obvious further risk not just of enhancing Spinoza's status and reputation even more but, still worse, of conceding that an 'atheistic' society can be well ordered, viable, and durable. Gundling's intervention here was again subtly subversive: Bayle was right, he maintained, to stress the 'atheism' of ancient Chinese society and culture but also right to assert the excellence of Chinese moral teaching.[80] No less awkward for his colleagues, Gundling rejected Le Clerc's designation of Bayle as an apologist for atheists, but agreed it was widely thought Bayle should be classified among the 'Spinozists'.[81]

A key element in the conundrum confronting the Lutheran universities was the rivalry of moderate mainstream factions, competing and blocking each other as well as collectively seeking to combat atheism, *Naturalismus*, and *Libertinismus*. Some unifying thread of counter-naturalist discourse had to be devised in which would feature a formidable Devil's advocate able to embody, link, and articulate all the diverse and complex strands of radical thought ancient, medieval, and Renaissance and which would serve to train future theologians to concert their onslaught on different aspects of naturalism and libertinism. This academically constructed *princeps* of 'atheism' was needed to help define the principal arguments

[77] *Gründliche Auszüge*, 11 (1743), 284.

[78] Feuerlein, *Dissertatio historico-philosophica*, 45–7.

[79] *Fortgesetzte Sammlung* (1737) ii. 577; Hüning, 'Grenzen der Toleranz', 232.

[80] Gundling, *Historiae philosophiae moralis*, 36–7.

[81] Gundling, *Vollständige Historie*, i. 913, ii. 1643–4, iii. 4011, iv. 4938; Mulsow, *Moderne*, 347.

of 'atheism' and identify the critical points of vulnerability. Such a supreme philosophical libertine would have to bridge a wide range of debates connecting theology, philosophy, science, morality, politics, and social theory and be a more convincing chief foe of religion, society, and the existing political order than Machiavelli, Hobbes, or Bayle. Above all, this philosophical arch-subversive had to be clear and systematic, not a thinker prone to be construed in widely divergent ways. While he need not be the direct inspiration of all the coteries at present constituting the underground German Enlightenment, as the grand unifying figure and most cogent threat to tradition, authority, and religion, his status was bound to be further enhanced by Lutheran academe's focusing their disputations and theses in the first place upon him. Spinoza alone was fitted for this role. Thus, the very spokesmen of orthodoxy and academic institutions most concerned to combat his ideas were partly responsible for instituting Spinoza, rather than Machiavelli, Hobbes, or Bayle, as the principal 'other' in German culture.

Unlike such alleged 'atheists' as Bruno, Vanini, Knutzen, Wagner, Wachter, Lau, or Bayle, or the Socinian dissidents, or indeed Hobbes, the 'atheism' of all of whom could be, and was, contested, Spinoza possessed the unique qualification, from the standpoint of professors of theology, philosophy, Natural Law, and hermeneutics, of being clear, universal, comprehensive, and impressively systematic. In these respects, he had no competitor. Bruno—until Bayle portrayed him as a *Spinosiste* in his *Dictionnaire*—was often construed in Protestant lands as a kind of proto-Protestant; Bayle himself, of course, however widely suspect, was for this purpose hopelessly evasive and slippery, while Hobbes, veiling his meaning to an extent, and having been defended by Gundling, was also unusable. By contrast, no one in a presiding position, in or outside the universities, questioned that Spinoza was an arch-atheist and general threat to the social and religious order. Machiavelli could perhaps rival him here but was a much older writer, less comprehensive, and philosophically unsuitable.

For this purpose, Spinoza would very likely have been preferred to Hobbes even without Gundling's intervention, partly owing to his monarchism and defence of ecclesiastical power and censorship, partly to his equivocation on magic, demons, and spirits, and partly, as the Kiel theologian Christian Kortholt put it in 1680, because Spinoza expressed Hobbes's ideas, or what were taken to be his ideas, 'more clearly' and 'eloquently' than Hobbes did.[82] Buddeus' pupil, the theologian and historian of philosophy Johann Christoph Dorn, similarly observed when explaining why he allotted more space to Spinoza than Hobbes when discussing key propositions introduced by the latter, that 'has [the views of Hobbes] majore astutia ac meliori ordine hactenas nemo tradidit, quam Bened. Spinoza' [no one transmitted thus far with greater astuteness or in better order than Bened. Spinoza].[83]

[82] Kortholt, *De tribus impostoribus*, 149, 196.

[83] Dorn, *Bibliotheca theologia critica*, i. 508; Ries, *Dissertatio philosophica*, 9.

Bayle's thesis, seconded by Buddeus and Gundling, that Spinoza had imposed order and coherence on an immense but fragmentary legacy of philosophical doctrine reaching back to the Greek Presocratics, thereby constructing a negative counterpart to the *prisca theologia* tradition, a veritable *anti-prisca theologia*, made Spinoza indisputably at once the supreme 'atheist' and the most obvious and practicable choice for training university students in theological and philosophical refutation of *Naturalismus*. Early eighteenth-century German academic milieu, doubtless often rather dubiously, frequently devised overarching theoretical edifices of 'atheism' and naturalism in which figures like Pomponazzi, Bruno, and Vanini were integrated (or distorted) into a constructed tradition of thinking; but this approach, making Spinoza the *princeps* of a vast and ancient tradition, through becoming a teaching routine, itself became, whatever its intrinsic intellectual merits, a potent factor in academic discourse.

What the eighteenth-century German disputations show is that in this context, Spinoza, however negatively conceived, remained in Bayle's sense the unrivalled organizing device, the hinge connecting discussion about the Bible, miracles, prophecy, providence, Satanism, magic, witchcraft, freedom of thought, toleration, forms of state, sexual liberty, and secular morality to a coherent overarching framework of orthodox justification and polemics. Hence, it not only made sense but was a familiar procedure that the German materialist, radical Deist, and atheistic writers of the time should, as a matter of course, all come to be located within the framework of the Spinoza debate. This applied to Tschirnhaus, Knutzen, Stosch, the author of the *Symbolum*, Spaeth, Bayle, Wagner, Wachter, Lau, Edelmann, and Schmidt without exception and, as a matter of course, inevitably in the case of every exponent of radical ideas.

Those scholars who argue that the stress on 'Spinozist' influence in the German Early Enlightenment has been exaggerated point out that Spinoza is never cited in the proceedings of the commission appointed to investigate the clandestine publication of Stosch's banned and suppressed book, the *Concordia rationis et fidei* (1692), and that Stosch was not in fact condemned, in Berlin in 1694, for Spinozism but rather for propagating 'Socinian' views.[84] This is perfectly true but it is equally true that the wider German intellectual debate about Stosch in the eighteenth century almost invariably classified him not in terms of Socinianism—or of Bayle or Hobbes—but specifically within the context of the expanding debate about Spinoza and Spinozism.[85] This is not to deny that Stosch had close ties with Socinians, especially the Socinian teacher Johann Preuss, or that his subversive text was secretly published—with 'Amsterdam' on the title page—in the Brandenburg town of Guben an der Neisse where other Socinian writings also appeared.[86] But the emphasis on Socinianism in Stosch's original indictment was rapidly discarded

[84] *Acta Stoschiana*, 641, 649–50, 68, 699–700; Israel, *Radical Enlightenment*, 641–4; Seidler, 'Politics', 232; Schröder, *Spinoza*, 35–7, 41–3.

[85] Schröder, *Spinoza*, 35; Pätzold, *Spinoza, Aufklärung*, 20, 159; Israel, *Radical Enlightenment*, 641–5.

[86] Israel, *Radical Enlightenment*, 641; Schröder, *Spinoza*, 32; Walther, '*Machina civilis*', 210.

and, just a few years after his imprisonment, attention shifted from the earlier concern with Socinianism to his having learnt his naturalism in Holland and his being a 'discipulus' of Spinoza.[87] What is important about Stosch, stressed a Copenhagen disputation in 1732, is that his approach is philosophical rather than theological, that he identifies God with the universe, and that he claims nature creates itself.[88] Men, according to Stosch, had, like animals and insects, originally arisen somehow out of mud or some other basic matter.[89] Johann Preuss, voicing a real Socinian opinion, not only disowned Stosch and his system of thought but rightly insisted that he abolishes all faith and replaces it with philosophical reason alone, and that, consequently, Stosch was not a Socinian at all but a Spinozist.[90] Stosch's thesis that 'Deus est unica et sola substantia' [God is the one and only substance],[91] is what chiefly mattered for contemporaries and it was inconceivable that this matter could have been discussed in Germany after 1694 principally in relation to Socinianism rather than Spinoza.

No German freethinker was better known abroad during the Enlightenment than the East Prussian Lau, or more representative in Germany of what has been called the 'atheistische-pantheistische' stream.[92] A student of Thomasius, after studying for nine years at Königsberg and Halle (1685–94) Lau commanded an extensive erudition. He also angrily repudiated the designation *Spinosista* but, then, so did Wagner and Wachter, as did anyone with claims to respectability in German society at the time.[93] Lau read widely, his thought was influenced by many sources, and it is therefore perhaps not surprising that there has been a trend in recent historiography to detach him from the 'Spinozism' with which he was firmly linked by Thomasius and other contemporaries. Indeed, it has recently been argued that his thought shows no real dependence on Spinoza's philosophy at all,[94] that most contemporaries did not explicitly portray him as a 'Spinozist' but rather as a 'Pantheist, Indifferentist and Deist', stressing that he called himself (as some others also called him) a *Universalista*.[95]

In particular, Lau's borrowings from Toland have been highlighted by way of opposing his designation as a 'Spinozist' and claiming that Toland was Lau's real *spiritus rector*.[96] But if Lau read widely and evidently drew on such varied sources as Epicurus, Lucretius, Bruno, Herbert of Cherbury, Hobbes, Beverland, Bekker, Bayle, and Toland besides Spinoza, [97] the thesis that he was therefore a 'Tollandist',

[87] Buddeus, *Analecta*, 113–22; Loescher, *Praenotiones*, 146–7; Reimmann, *Historia Universalis*, 512–14; Lilienthal, *Theologische Bibliothec*, 259–61; Israel, *Radical Enlightenment*, 644.

[88] Bluhme, *Exercitatio philosophica*, 39.

[89] Stosch, *Concordia*, 2–3, 9; Schröder, *Ursprünge*, 298.

[90] *Acta Stoschiana*, 686, 695–6; Schröder, *Spinoza*, 40.

[91] Stosch, *Concordia*, 35–6, 81; Loescher, *Praenotiones*, 147; Hazard, *European Mind*, 176.

[92] Schröder, *Ursprünge*, 490–1; Mulsow, *Moderne*, 36.

[93] Bluhme, *Exercitatio philosophica*, 278, 282.

[94] Schröder, *Spinoza*, 124, 148, 150; Schröder, 'Spinozam tota armenta', 166–7.

[95] Lau, *Meditationes philosophicae*, 5, 7; Pott, 'Einleitung', 31–2; Otto, *Studien*, 104.

[96] Thomasius, *Elender Zustand*, 273; Pott, 'Einleitung', 59.

[97] Pott, 'Einleitung', 30–1; Thomasius, *Elender Zustand*, 273.

not a 'Spinozist', remains both unconvincing and unhistorical. It would have more force were Toland still considered today a Deist *stricto sensu* rather than an atheistic naturalist but that is no longer the case.[98] Part of the problem no doubt is a certain confusion stemming from an excessively purist reaction against the older German historiography's tendency to emphasize Spinoza's pervasiveness among the radical fringe of Enlightenment culture. But while stipulating that no one should be called a 'Spinozist' unless they replicate his whole system accurately may make sense as a philosophical exercise it is scarcely relevant in the context of a broad, deep-seated cultural phenomenon like radical thought in eighteenth-century Germany. Worse, it produces unhistorical conclusions and distortion.

The radical writers in question mostly do not, of course, embrace Spinoza's system in every respect; often indeed, they only partly understood it. Nevertheless, what these writers stood for was a broad cultural phenomenon called 'Spinozism' and Spinozism is fundamental to a correct understanding of the intellectual context in which it emerged and was read and talked about. In his *Origenes Judaicae* (1709), where he first classifies his own thought as 'Pantheism', Toland himself affirms that Moses was a 'Pantheist', according to Strabo, 'or as we in these modern times would style him a Spinozist'.[99] Moreover, Lau's interest in Toland focused chiefly on his idea that 'all the phaenomena of nature must be explain'd by motion, by the action of all things on one another, according to mechanick principles'.[100] But as was noted by William Wotton, at the time, and several scholars since, all Toland is doing in his discussion of motion in matter is restating Spinoza's thesis that motion is inherent in matter while pretending to criticize him for not expounding that very position.[101]

In a Marburg disputation of June 1725, it is held that Spinoza, being 'princeps atheorum', had many adherents, Toland, whose views on the cosmos were virtually identical to his, prominent among them; here, Spinozism is directly equated with 'Pantheism' and philosophical Naturalism excluding all supernatural agency.[102] It was habitual in Early Enlightenment Germany to classify Toland, Collins, and also Tindal as 'Spinozists', so that Lau can meaningfully be reckoned a radical Eclectic, Pantheist, Tollandist, and Spinozist all at the same time. At Halle, he imbibed, especially from Thomasius, an academic eclecticism leading him to read and ponder very widely; but precisely this same methodology required him critically to sift and then order and amalgamate his gleanings into a coherent whole. Whether one was labelled a Cartesian, Thomasian, Wolffian, or Spinozist hinged on the resulting synthesis. No contradiction was involved, therefore, when Thomasius later devoted a whole tract to demonstrating that Lau, though certainly an Eclectic

[98] Gawlick, 'Epikur bei den Deisten', 324.

[99] Mosheim, *Vindiciae*, preface p. C; *Historie der Gelehrsamkeit unserer Zeiten*, 160; Champion, 'Politics of Pantheism', 270–1; Champion, *Republican Learning*, 1745.

[100] Lau, *Meditationes philosophicae*, 20–3, 26; Pott, 'Einleitung', 40–1.

[101] Wotton, *Letter to Eusebia*, 47–8, 53; Moniglia, *Dissertazione . . . materialisti*, i. 48–55; Lurbe, 'Spinozisme', 44.

[102] Ries, *Dissertatio philosophica*, 8–9; Herslev, *De vera notione miraculi*, 9.

which he readily acknowledged, was nevertheless essentially a 'Spinozista', Spinoza being the prime, though not the only, 'father' of his 'atheistic propositions'.[103]

In a disputation held at Giessen, in July 1719, much was made of the recently coined new term 'universalista' to designate Lau's philosophy. Denounced as a dangerous writer for championing full 'libertas sentiendi et scribendi' [freedom of thought and writing] and a general *Libertinismus*—having stated that the 'first and true status of men is *Libertinismus*'[104]—he was charged also with anti-Scripturalism, believing nature to have been created out of itself not *ex nihilo*, erasing all distinction between believers and infidels in religion, placing all religions and no religion on the same footing, and, finally, making morality and law man-made and relative. The same disputation likewise labelled him an *Indifferentista* and *Naturalista* which plainly he was.[105] But he was then classified as part of the ancient and modern tradition of 'Pantheism' which, in all essentials, we are then told, is identical to 'Spinozismus'.[106] Far from being an instance of a loose usage, viewing Lau (like Stosch, Wachter, and Edelmann) as equivalent or close to Spinoza on this long list of fundamental issues is a complex but perfectly cogent position and an immensely significant historical fact.

Thomasius and Gundling, at Halle, and Pontoppidan, at Copenhagen, all correctly identified Spinoza as the prime influence on Lau's intellectual formation.[107] Thus, from his own 'enlightened' standpoint, Thomasius, as the most celebrated and influential champion of mainstream freedom of thought in Germany, as well as a leading theorist of separation of 'spirits' from matter, was taking an entirely principled and consistent stand when refusing to help defend Lau when the latter's books were banned or oppose his prosecution and expulsion from Frankfurt by the city Senate; for like Locke, Le Clerc, and Barbeyrac, he held that no Christian society can permit expression of 'atheism'.[108] By contrast, Gundling took a more nuanced stance and, like his pupil Johann Jakob Schmauss later, another scholar on the extreme liberal fringe of respectable academe,[109] unmistakably evinced a degree of sympathy for Lau whom he presumably knew from his years at Halle. He pointedly reminded contemporaries that Lau had useful things to say about politics and law and that had he not 'published works in which one sees that he is a Spinozist and an atheist, he would have made his fortune'.[110]

Edelmann, for his part, made no less of a stir in the 1740s, drawing down much vehement condemnation on his own head as well as focusing fresh attention on Knutzen and the whole tradition of German radical thought. His books, like those of Lau, were publicly burnt. His name was regularly linked to Spinoza's in the

[103] Thomasius, *Elender Zustand*, 256–64, 273; Pott, 'Einleitung', 32–3; Otto, *Studien*, 104–5.

[104] Lau, *Meditationes philosophicae*, 2.

[105] Ibid. 7; Arnold, *Universalista in theologia naturali*, 28.

[106] Arnold, *Universalista in theologia naturali*, 2–4; Nieuhoff, *Over Spinozisme*, 266; Pätzold, *Spinoza, Aufklärung*, 20–1.

[107] Thomasius, *Elender Zustand*, 256, 259, 264; Pontoppidan, *Kraft der Wahrheit*, 119, 124; Otto, *Studien*, 104–5.

[108] Thomasius, *Elender Zustand*, 256–8.

[109] Mulsow, *Moderne*, 35, 296–300, 304, 307.

[110] Quoted in Otto, *Studien*, 102.

numerous refutations of his work; and, here again, this linkage represents no loose use of terms or inadequate grasp of Edelmann's derivative, Eclectic, and often not particularly coherent teachings.[111] Several scholars have urged that 'Edelmann was never a Spinozist in a strict sense' and that it will help clarify the position to remove all reference to 'Spinozism' and discuss him rather as a 'Deist'.[112] But denying he was a Spinozist clarifies nothing, rather it obscures the picture: contemporaries labelled him a 'Spinozist' for meaningful reasons which make perfect sense in their historical context.

By classifying Edelmann a 'Spinozist', contemporaries did not mean his doctrines were identical to Spinoza's or that he did not incorporate heterogeneous ingredients from elsewhere. On the contrary, Edelmann's meandering eclecticism and inconsistencies were obvious to everyone, the Silesian pastor Johann Meyer repeating, in 1751, what by then was already a well-worn remark that Edelmann belonged to an ancient tradition of thought reaching back to the 'Pantheisten der alten Welt' [to the pantheists of the ancient world], culminating in Spinoza and Toland's *Pantheisticon*, but also embracing Collins, Tindal, Lau, and numerous others.[113] Edelmann's system, judged another critic, consisted of 'Spinozismo, Naturalismo, Pythagorismo, Sadducaismo, Fanaticismo, Skepticismo und Indifferentismo'.[114] Yet another described his project as being to fuse together 'all the greatest errors which the teaching of Spinoza made especially repellent' [abscheulich] with Hobbes's contribution, Knutzen's offerings, those of Boehm, and also Collins and Toland, and turn this into one 'truth'.[115]

The 'Spinozists', for much Lutheran scholarship in the early eighteenth century, were not just theoretically, but actually, a long-lived ancient and modern 'sect' of which Spinoza was the undisputed *princeps* in the *Bayliste* sense that it was he who gave pantheism its best and most cogent and most unifying arguments so that his texts are those that best resume that tradition, and put everything in order, without implying his are the only relevant texts. Early eighteenth-century commentators, far from being 'loose' in bandying accusations of 'Spinozism', clearly express what the *Spinozismus* of the early *Aufklärung* actually entailed. They were, of course, outraged when Edelmann, parodying their own technique (in emulation of Toland), drew a quite different parallel, labelling the first and truest Christians 'gute Spinozisten' [good Spinozists].[116]

Spinoza, then, served an overarching function in early eighteenth-century German academic debate about the relationship of philosophy to theology and morality to religion because 'atheism', 'Indifferentism', naturalism, pantheism, and 'Universalism' all raised challenging issues concerning divine providence, revelation, prophecy, miracles, freedom of thought, Natural Law, and Natural Religion on which the

[111] Mulsow, *Moderne*, 287–8; Tortarolo, *L'Illuminismo*, 51.

[112] Schröder, 'Spinozam tota armenta', 166; see though Mulsow, *Moderne*, 281.

[113] Meyer, *Närrische Welt*, 259–60; Hazard, *European Mind*, 69; Pätzold, *Spinoza, Aufklärung*, 27.

[114] Pratje, *Historische Nachrichten*, 127.

[115] Wagner, *Johan Christian Edelmanns verblendete Angesicht*, i. 'Vorrede'.

[116] Ibid. ii. 412–14.

'atheistic' or naturalist position was most clearly, concisely, and comprehensively stated by Spinoza rather than anyone else. While Spinozism was universally denounced, deemed by both mainstream and Counter-Enlightenment the archetypal 'atheistic' philosophy, adopting Spinoza and Spinozism as key tools in German philosophical-theological debate during the *Aufklärung* was further encouraged by the form in which his philosophy was cast. For judged from a purely methodological or formal point of view, as a logical system, perceptions of his argumentation were far from wholly negative. Many German university professors harboured, despite themselves, more than a hint of respect for Spinoza's orderly rigour, powerful concision, acumen, clarity, and comprehensiveness. Even while assailing it on every front, Leibniz and Wolff could not help quietly indicating their regard for his reasoning and his striving for coherence; Reimmann, too, felt obliged to admit that Spinoza's philosophy was not wholly bad and that in him one finds 'some gold nuggets although sullied by much dark, godless, self-contradictory debris'.[117]

The 'gold nuggets' evidently glittered all the more for being surrounded by so much dark and reprehensible matter. Meanwhile, the unacceptable 'godless debris' in a paradoxical manner also acquired a kind of official status through being so widely deployed as a tool against *Freigeisterey* (freethinking), anti-Scripturalism, and pantheism. If, to the modern historian of philosophy, it seems inexact to equate pantheism with Spinozism, in early eighteenth-century disputes about Natural Religion, it seemed vital to prove pantheism violates the first principle of Natural Theology, namely that God created the world and regulates its movements, as supposedly demonstrated by reason and not least Newtonian science. In these debates pantheism, which was often associated with Greek Stoicism and not infrequently Xenophanes and other Presocratics, as well as Averroes, needed to be represented by a spokesman who could plausibly be portrayed as the head of an ancient as well as still surviving underground sect.[118]

Artificial construction though it was, Spinoza's range and systematic quality fitted him peculiarly well for the task of linking ancient 'pantheism' with Bruno, Vanini, Toland, and other modern exponents. The pivotal figure in the universal history of 'atheism', freethinking, and pantheism, it went without saying that Spinoza had an exceptionally large number of modern followers. According to Zedler's *Universal-Lexicon* these consisted of two concentric circles of disciples. The inner circle were the 'Spinozists' proper among whom were Stosch, Lau, Boulainvilliers, and Toland as well as the Dutch radical thinkers Cuffeler, van Leenhof, Wyermars, and Pontiaan van Hattem. The outer circle consisted of those 'in Spinozismi suspicionem', that is writers suspected of being corrupted by Spinozistic influence. Again dominated by Netherlanders, according to Zedler, among them Geulincx, Bekker, and Deurhoff, this group included Wachter.[119]

[117] Reimmann, *Versuch einer Einleitung*, iv. 651.

[118] Dorn, *Bibliotheca theologia critica*, i. 508–19; Münter, *Theologiae naturalis polemicae specimen*, 28.

[119] Münter, *Theologiae naturalis polemicae specimen*, 29–30; Zedler, *Grosses universal Lexicon*, xxxix. 86; Israel, *Radical Enlightenment*, 13.

3. AN ALTERNATIVE ROUTE? JOHANN LORENZ SCHMIDT AND 'LEFT' WOLFFIAN RADICALISM

But if Spinoza provided the scaffolding holding up the German academic edifices of *Spinozismus* and *Antispinozismus*, atheism versus religion, and full toleration and freedom of expression versus limited toleration and intellectual freedom, bringing order to the discussion overall, this is not to deny that Socinianism as well as Cartesianism, eclecticism, and Wolffianism contributed to the mix which produced the distinctive German corpus of Radical Enlightenment. La Croze, Leibniz, and Bayle had all convicted Socinianism of being based on an inherent set of contradictions. Beyond this, the question was whether there was some other way these diverse elements could be coherently blended to produce a viable radical stance which yet was genuinely not 'Spinozist' in essence in the early eighteenth-century German signification of the term and which could convincingly incorporate an authentically Christian, or at least Socinian Christian component.

The writer who came closest to doing so, in any case, was assuredly not Wachter, Stosch, Lau, or Edelmann but rather the intriguing figure of Johann Lorenz Schmidt (1702–49), who devoted his adult life and all his intellectual energy to his quest for a stance which would underpin the primacy of reason, end the conflict between philosophy and theology, and uphold a full toleration and freedom of expression in a career which, once again, illustrates the remarkable role especially of the universities of Jena, Halle, and Leipzig as an engine for collating, sifting, and reworking the rival philosophical currents of the time in pursuit of a stable synthesis. Schmidt's closest ally and lifelong friend Johann Wilhelm Höflein (1689–1739), an official at the small court of Wertheim, without whose assistance the Wertheim Bible would never have been published and Schmidt would probably not have escaped lengthier imprisonment, had studied for most of a decade at Halle, Giessen, and Leipzig and, like Schmidt himself, was well known to Wolff.[120] During his own four years at Jena, in the early 1720s, Schmidt studied under the anti-Wolffian Buddeus, after which he moved to Halle where he publicly adhered to Wolff's philosophy at a time when Wolff's reputation stood under a dark cloud.

Schmidt later described how studying philosophy, natural science, and mathematics transformed his own ideas, revolutionized his life, and led him to reject all conventional theology. This inner intellectual revolution, he says, began at Jena in his student days but long remained hidden and unseen, a 'conversion' to philosophical ideas which, outwardly, found no expression prior to 1735.[121] Indeed, as a young man seeking a career, Schmidt, buoyed by his Wolffianism, always aspired to find some role which would enable him to help harmoniously reconcile

[120] Spalding, *Seize the Book*, 26–7, 53–4, 126, 162, 175.
[121] Goldenbaum, 'Erste deutsche Übersetzung', 16–22, 24–5.

religion and philosophy.[122] His inner intellectual conversion also convinced him that Bible exegesis, indeed all theology, must be radically reformed so as to conform to natural philosophy and mathematical reason.[123] It was this which led him to his great project of a new German version of the Pentateuch with a long introductory preface and detailed notes, erasing all unjustified traditional assumptions, published in 1735, at Wertheim where, since 1725, he held the post of tutor to the countess's children.

In calling his rendering of the Hebrew Pentateuch a 'free translation', Schmidt did not mean to imply he was being loose in any way in his translation—on the contrary, he claimed to be more faithful to Scripture than any predecessor—but rather that he worked wholly independently, guided only by 'philosophy', without reference to any ecclesiastical authority. At no point, in translation or notes, was any church or theological principle deferred to. His Pentateuch thus departs dramatically in content and style not only from Luther's standard German version but from all other known versions.[124] Philosophically, as he explains, in the several tracts he published in the years 1735–7 to defend his project, his aim was to show that philosophy and natural philosophy are the appropriate and only correct criterion for interpreting Scripture.

A earnest young man of high integrity, there seems no reason to doubt his later claim that he embarked on his revolutionary Pentateuch project above all with a view to swaying every Deist, *esprit fort*, and anti-Scripturalist by systematically stripping away all the dubious interpolation and questionable renderings with which tradition, ecclesiastical authority, and 'superstition' had so deplorably obscured our understanding of the Bible.[125] His duty, as he saw it, was not to leave the laity in utter ignorance about the real truth about Scripture but place all the incidents of biblical narrative into a rational, causal framework, including even the Creation which he turned into a non-miraculous set of natural processes. He recounted all the scriptural episodes in terms of probable human motives and emotions explained through systematic analysis of the 'affects'.[126] Putting human responses into their 'real' relationship with natural causes showed why these and not other effects ensued, and how they fit together into a single, 'allgemeine Verknüpfung der Dinge' [universal connection of things]. For every aspect of reality, held Schmidt, arises from the 'zureichenden Grund' of its own nature.[127] Since nothing should be believed, he argues, which is not plainly evident to our reason, and since truth, as Leibniz and Wolff taught, cannot be 'divine truth' unless

122 Ibid. 23; Winkle, *Heimlichen Spinozisten*, 29; Schmidt-Biggemann, *Theodizee*, 77–8, 91.

123 [Schmidt], *Vest gegründete Wahrheit*, 'Vorrede', fos. 1–2^v; Zedler, *Grosses universal Lexicon*, xxv. 411–12; Goldenbaum, 'Erste deutsche Übersetzung', 109.

124 *Neuer Zeitung von gelehrten Sachen* (1735), 623–4; Goldenbaum, 'Erste deutsche Übersetzung', 110.

125 [Schmidt], *Vertheidigung*, 6.

126 Ibid. 3, 5; Zedler, *Grosses universal Lexicon*, lv. 602; Sheehan, *Enlightenment Bible*, 122; [Schmidt], 'Vorrede' [1735] 19.

127 [Schmidt], '*Vorrede*' [1735], 12–14; [Schmidt] *Vertheidigung*, 3; [Schmidt], *Vest gegründete Wahrheit*, 2, 5.

it fully coheres with the principles of all other truth; Scripture, held Schmidt, despite what the ignorant devout universally believe, cannot really contain reports or accounts of supernatural 'effects', miracles, or wonders.[128]

With Höflein's help, the preparations for publication proceeded smoothly and without concealment, indeed with the full knowledge, and even patronage, of members of the Wertheim court, despite there having been no prior scrutiny of the text by the local church consistory, as was usual with theological publications. To meet the requirement for some form of approval, Höflein and Schmidt showed the translation—but without the accompanying notes and introduction—to Wolff himself, then at Marburg, and the celebrated ecclesiastical historian Johann Lorenz Mosheim (1694–1755), likewise a pillar of the moderate *Aufklärung* at the Hanoverian university of Helmstedt Their responses, a mixture of lukewarm praise and criticism, were then deployed to vouch for the work's respectability.[129] In this inconspicuous manner commenced if not the most prolonged—that was the Wolffian controversy—then certainly the most intense and spectacular of all the German Enlightenment controversies.

Schmidt's efforts to win over the freethinkers by expounding only what they too, using the same strict mathematico-philosophical criteria of truth as himself, would accept as valid or, as one critic put it, amalgamating all the harmful exegetical methods of 'Spinoza and his followers, all the Deists, Naturalists and Socinians' as well as Grotius and Le Clerc,[130] inevitably dragged him into conflict with every strand of theological opinion other than that of the extreme Socinians. Admiring Leibniz, Wolff, and, as far as moral philosophy was concerned, Spinoza, Schmidt invests unlimited confidence in 'reason'. Everything that is real, he contends, is governed by the same mechanistic set of rules; and to this there can be no (or hardly any?) exception. But as contemporaries all too clearly saw, as soon as the Wertheim Bible appeared, such systematic appeal to reason not only entails denial of miracles, destroys ecclesiastical authority, eliminates all Christology, and destroys the links between the Pentateuch and Christ's mission among men, it effectively denies all demonstrable supernatural agency after the act of Creation and largely eliminates organized religion in any traditional sense, including most of the moral, educational, and belief structures on which society rested. Even his non-Spinozistic doctrines of Creation and divine providence did not seem to his readers either clear or firmly established. As one theologian indignantly enquired, how can anyone possibly expect miracles and the doctrine of the Creation of the universe from nothing to be plainly and evidently reconciled with reason?[131]

Divine providence, to his way of thinking, is essentially the course of nature itself. It was here especially that his 'left' Wolffianism verged on, or failed to clearly distance itself from, Spinozism. The consequence was not simply to screen out

[128] [Schmidt], *Vest gegründete Wahrheit*, 2, 5; Sinnhold, *Historische Nachricht*, 39; Zedler, *Grosses universal Lexicon*, lx. 602; Spalding, *Seize the Book*, 69–70; Tortarolo, *L'Illuminismo*, 51.

[129] Spalding, *Seize the Book*, 37–8, 86; Mulsow, *Moderne*, 337–41.

[130] Sinnhold, *Historische Nachricht*, 8.

[131] [Oeder], *Anmerckungen*, 32, 62.

wonders and supernatural 'signs' but also everything traditionally supposed to have linked the Pentateuch with the Gospels, everything that is taken to refer to Christ, the Church, and the truth of Christianity. Unsurprisingly, the Leipzig theology faculty condemned the Wertheim Bible, in January 1736, as reflecting the opinions of Jews and Socinians as well as encouraging the spread of 'Naturalism and atheism' while, the following June, the Prussian crown banned the book for attacking the 'foundation of the universal Christian faith'. A general imperial prohibition followed, in January 1737, at Vienna,[132] together with orders for Schmidt's arrest and trial and confiscation of all remaining stock of the offending text. Meanwhile, the 'Biblia Wertheimensis' continued to be locally banned in many other states, including, in March 1737, Holstein-Gottorf, which included the University of Kiel, as a work in which the 'system of basic Christian truths and mysteries of faith are undermined by principles adopted from foolish reasoning and futile philosophy in a supremely damnable way', by 'special order of the [British] king and elector' of Hanover, in May,[133] the Bavarian elector, in July, and the king of Denmark, in November.

Recrimination was hurled on Schmidt, still at Wertheim, from every side, though he stuck doggedly to his guns: if Newton revolutionized physics and astronomy with mathematics, his inductive method was what was now needed, he held, to carry out an equally systematic and precise reassessment of Scripture and theological doctrine, using scientific criteria to recast theology. The need for this was obvious given the prevailing confusion about how to interpret many biblical passages and the endless disputes and schisms dividing the churches and sects. On the other hand, there was no need for miracles in a world in which God had revealed himself clearly enough in nature: Schmidt's guiding principle in Bible hermeneutics was that 'alles, was wirklich ist hat seinen zureichenden Grund, aus welchem es sich verstehen und erweisen lässet' [everything that is real has its proportionate cause, from which it can be understood and proven] and to this, he was convinced, there can be no exception.[134] Such philosophical terminology was less Cartesian or Spinozist than Wolffian which, in Schmidt's case, left only the barest margin for theology as traditionally conceived.

Although Spinoza's name was mentioned here and there in the controversy, in this case, unlike those of Stosch, Wachter, Lau, and Edelmann, opponents did not label Schmidt's system as such 'Spinozistic', recognizing the prominence of Leibnizian, Wolffian, and Newtonian elements in his world-view.[135] Imprisoned on orders from Vienna, at Wertheim, in the spring of 1737, Schmidt faced the prospect of being subjected to an elaborate trial in the name of the emperor. Over fifty published attacks, Lutheran, Calvinist, and Catholic, on the *Wertheimische Bibel*

[132] Sinnhold, *Historische Nachricht*, 34–5; Spalding, *Seize the Book*, 105; Goldenbaum, 'Der Skandal', 266–7.

[133] Spalding, *Seize the Book*, 136–41.

[134] [Schmidt], *Vertheidigung*, 3; [Schmidt], 'Vorrede' [1735], 14; [Schmidt], 'Vorbericht' (1741), 40; [Oeder], *Anmerckungen*, 26, 30–2, 60; *Fortgesetzte Sammlung*, (1735), ii. 232–3, 235–9, 310–11.

[135] Schmidt-Biggemann, *Theodizee*, 77–8, 88–91; Otto, *Studien*, 353–4.

and its translator appeared between 1735 and 1738.[136] Nevertheless, the condemned scholar also had supporters, notably at Leipzig and Wertheim, a few of whom briefly spoke up in his defence; and, besides these, Wolff, Mosheim, Johann Christoph Gottsched, and other prominent men of the early *Aufklärung*, even while entertaining reservations about his work, were shocked by the weight of the proceedings against him and had considerable sympathy for his plight. However, such eminent figures could hardly speak out on his behalf without damaging themselves. Indeed, Wolff, who was in considerable difficulty himself at the time, felt obliged publicly to disown and renounce all relations with him, announcing that Schmidt's hermeneutics were not based 'on my philosophy'.[137]

However, the projected trial under imperial auspices never took place. Suddenly during 1738, rumours spread across Germany that Schmidt had somehow escaped, or been released, which turned out to be true. After a year's imprisonment in Wertheim, he got away, in the spring of 1738, with the help of the local count, acting in defiance of the court in Vienna. Passing fleetingly through Leipzig in the summer, by September he had reached the juridical safety of Danish Altona, adjoining Hamburg, where, like Lau and later Edelmann, he was to live relatively undisturbed for much of the rest of his life. He resided for some years in the house of a Jewish doctor and reputed Spinozist, David Gerson,[138] under an assumed name ('Johann Ludwig Schroeter').[139] There he studied, talked, and translated, further refining his concept of natural theology, insisting on the unique moral status of the Bible, and repudiating outright materialism, a stance characterized by residual but definite Socinian tendencies.[140]

His main contribution after 1738 was as an accomplished translator of key radical texts into German, including Tindal's *Christianity as Old as the Creation* (London, 1730), the first work of English 'Deism' to appear in German, in 1741, Spinoza's *Ethics* (1744), and Du Marsais's *Examen* published at Leipzig in 1747.[141] Rumour also attributed to him the appearance of Boulainvilliers's 'Muhammed' under the title *Das Leben Mahomeds*, published at Lemgo in 1747. His preface to, and the excellent quality of, his rendering of Spinoza's *Ethics* confirms the deep sincerity of his radical eclecticism, skill as an expositor, sense of close affinity to Spinoza's moral teaching, and respect for his systematic reasoning; at the same time, he calls Spinoza the 'most frightful' of all the dangerous enemies of Truth, insisting on the skill and effectiveness of Wolff's refutation of Spinoza which he published in the same volume and with which he justified translating and publishing Spinoza's masterpiece.[142] Spinoza, he claimed, could only be overcome by

136 Zedler, *Grosses universal Lexicon*, 636; Tortarolo, *Ragione*, 156–7.

137 Sinnhold, *Historische Nachricht*, 53; Kobuch, *Zensur und Aufklärung*, 72–7.

138 Winkle, *Heimlichen Spinozisten*, 32.

139 Spalding, *Seize the Book*, 174–5; Sheehan, *Enlightenment Bible*, 130.

140 Mori, 'Einleitung', p. xxxviii.

141 Ibid., p. xliv; Hazard, *European Mind*, 75; Spalding, *Seize the Book*, 186, 209; Tortarolo, *Ragione*, 10, 22.

142 Schmidt, 'Vorrede' to B.D.S., *Sittenlehre*, 4.

closely engaging with his system, examining it carefully, and following the reasoning of Wolff. Significantly, his preface also stresses the affinity of Spinoza's moral thought with Christ's teaching, a point he reinforced by including Jelles's original preface to the *Opera posthuma* with its Socinian claim that Spinoza's is in essence a 'Christian' philosophy.[143]

Here and still more forcefully in his preface to his final translation, his German rendering of Du Marsais's *Examen de la religion*, he stuck to his distinction (however much its coherence was doubted by others) between a fully rational—in fact, radical Socinian—Christianity repudiating the supernatural and (all or most) miracles, on the one hand, and the unqualified, pure materialism of Du Marsais and Diderot, on the other. Among the most sophisticated of what have aptly been called 'Links-Wolffianer' [Left-Wolffians],[144] he was eager to integrate his ideas into a comprehensive philosophical and scientific framework which for him integrally included an impressive range of radical literature, featuring Spinoza, Bayle, Knutzen, Woolston, Tindal, Collins,[145] Lau, Edelmann, Du Marsais, La Mettrie, and d'Argens, besides Diderot's *Pensées philosophiques*. Schmidt in short showed how far a highly trained, philosophically orientated Bible exegete could go towards embracing and reworking the radical programme, refusing to submit to any ecclesiastical authority, and embracing a full toleration and individual autonomy of thought, while simultaneously avoiding the metaphysical consequence of Spinozism and resisting the systematic materialism of thinkers like Du Marsais.

Schmidt certainly urged his readers to keep to what he calls the 'middle way' between credulity and incredulity, trusting in a benign Creator-God.[146] The problem was that it was difficult or impossible to see how his principles rescued him from the systematic *Naturalismus* of which he was universally accused. Rejecting belief in the Devil and the idea of revelation in its traditional, miraculous sense, Schmidt clearly opposed what to him was the essence of *Spinosisterey*—the total identification of God with Nature. In its place he advocated a radically attenuated dualism in which God is firmly distinguished from the world and natural theology not wholly replaced by philosophy, and in which the soul's separateness from the body and its immortality are upheld allowing for reward and punishment in the hereafter, though, rather bafflingly, he concedes the soul's materiality.[147] His problem was that his stance simply was not evidently coherent or clear.

Having eked out a long and penurious career as an intellectual fugitive in Altona, Schmidt spent the last three years of his life (1747–9), still under his assumed name, in comparative luxury at Wolfenbüttel, as court mathematician and resident

143 Ibid. 1–5, 9; Spalding, *Seize the Book*, 185.

144 Mulsow, *Monadenlehre*, 130.

145 [Schmidt], 'Vorbericht' (1741), 70–1, 95; Spalding, *Seize the Book*, 298 n. 63.

146 Mori, 'Einleitung', pp. xlii–xliii; [Schmidt], 'Vorrede' [1747], 15, 35, 38; Du Marsais, *Die wahre Religion*, 3–4, 118–19, 121–2 (notes by Schmidt).

147 Schmidt, notes to Du Marsais, *Die wahre Religion*, 230–1, 234; [Schmidt], 'Vorrede' to B.D.S. *Sittenlehre*, 4–5; [Schmidt], 'Vorrede' [1747], 12–13, 22, 54; Sinnhold, *Historische Nachricht*, 6; Mori, 'Einleitung', pp. xlii–xliii.

intellectual, in which capacity he foreshadowed Lessing, frequenting one of the greatest libraries in Europe.[148] Duke Karl I of Braunschweig-Wolfenbüttel (ruled 1735–80) was one of the supposedly 'enlightened' princes of the day and strongly supported the arts, music, Wolffian philosophy, and the library. However, he also spent lavishly on court magnificence and his oversized army, ostentatiously aping the absolutism of Louis XIV. The absurdity of his military and political posturing and his yearly spending of 70,000 *thaler* on his tiny opera when most of the Lutheran pastors of his state lived on yearly stipends of under 200 *thaler* was not lost on his subjects and least of all on the pastors.[149] However, neither Lutheran tradition, nor the prevailing Natural Law doctrines, provided any way of justifying basic criticism of Germany's political structure.

4. NATURAL THEOLOGY, NATURAL LAW, AND THE RADICAL CHALLENGE

In Germany, Natural Law theory, an old field with a growing relevance in this part of Europe, developed into a key arena in the escalating struggle between theology and philosophy, powerfully exacerbating the 'crisis of theology'. The intensification of Natural Law studies in the Lutheran universities down to the mid-eighteenth century was indeed a remarkable cultural phenomenon, driven by the proliferation of university chairs for teaching a subject increasingly viewed, after 1650, as indispensable to the study of civil and public law, and for integrating state, society, church, and bureaucracy more effectively. Strongly encouraged by the chaotic impression given by positive law in a land much of which was a veritable tangle of overlapping jurisdictions and small states, chairs in Natural Law were set up in rapid succession: at Jena, Kiel, and Uppsala, in 1665; at Lund, in 1668; at Königsberg in 1673; Marburg and Greifswald in 1674; Helmstedt in 1675; Erfurt in 1676; Frankfurt an der Oder and, in the far Baltic, at Dorpat in 1690; Halle in 1694; Leipzig in 1711; and Göttingen, in 1734.[150]

The classic contribution in the field during the period was Pufendorf's *De jure naturae et gentium* [On the Law of Nature and Nations], published in 1672. Pufendorf (like Spinoza and Locke) was born in 1632, during the Thirty Years War, his family being directly affected by the devastation and forced to flee several times. The violent, confessionally divided, precarious world in which he grew up is said to have helped inspire his quest for a Natural Law independent of theology.[151] While it would be wrong to suggest that Pufendorf, and Christian Thomasius, deliberately sought to promote a secular ethics, administration, and politics independent of theology with their theories of Natural Law,[152] both undoubtedly

148 Spalding, *Seize the Book*, 194–5; Winkle, *Heimlichen Spinozisten*, 33.

149 Hope, *German and Scandinavian Protestantism*, 268–9.

150 Ibid. 85–90.

151 Seidler, 'Politics', 228–9.

152 Hochstrasser, *Natural Law Theories*, 28.

regarded the subject, like philosophical eclecticism, as a device for limiting the impact of confessional strife, as well as small state rivalries, and constitutional wrangling, while simultaneously blocking naturalism, by creating an autonomous edifice of social and political theory, working in a stable, semi-autonomous relationship to theology. The fundamental Natural Law concepts they introduced into German academic discourse, while resting on ultimately theological foundations, nevertheless weakened in some measure the sway of precedent, tradition, and theological doctrines over law and ethics, thereby helping desacralize law and politics, and strengthen the drive for moderate reformism and toleration. Natural Lawyers and their field of enquiry were consequently attacked by some orthodox Lutheran theologians precisely for seeking to establish morality and law independently of theology.[153]

Pufendorf's approach seemed a particularly effective instrument for instituting a clear, unassailable junction of reason with Natural Theology while segregating both from confessional theology. God's will, claims his celebrated treatise, laid down a particular nature for mankind from which no one can diverge, so that the basic facts of history and society themselves exhibit the laws to which God commands us to adhere.[154] The basis of Natural Law, as he conceived it, was the divine commandment to develop our sociability, men requiring security and mutual help to counter their natural vulnerability, insecurity, and proneness to discord. God as Creator, benign overseer, and a supernatural agent, decreed the laws of human behaviour and sociability but it is men, rationally appraising the facts of history and society, who identify and freely choose to conform to, or disobey, divinely ordained principles, social institutions like marriage, and duties, the dictates of which they acknowledge to be distinct from their own interests or desires. At the same time, Natural Law was a theoretical construct, powerfully influenced by Grotius and Hobbes, grounding legal and moral premisses on Man's primal, natural concern with self-preservation and security, making little attempt to establish a correspondence of its principles to any metaphysically transcendent ideas of reason and justice.

This rendered the entire discipline problematic in various ways. Leibniz, in particular, disliked Pufendorf's uncoupling of Natural Law from metaphysics, attacking his system especially for attenuating the ties between Natural Law and Natural Theology. Pufendorf, he objected, was creating a morass of philosophical difficulty and contradiction by seeking to render Natural Law largely autonomous. Since Leibniz deemed immortality of the soul demonstrable by reason alone but less so from revelation (which Pufendorf denied, claiming this doctrine rests on revelation only), it followed, in Leibniz's opinion, that Pufendorf's approach softens the impact in this life of the theology of reward and punishment

[153] Ibid.; Hunter *Rival Enlightenments*, 88–91; Grunert, 'Reception of Grotius', 95.

[154] Grunert, 'Reception of Grotius', 172–80; Schneewind, *Invention of Autonomy*, 125–31; Westerman, *Disintegration*, 191, 193–4.

in the next, by removing its capacity to lend hope to the good, and instil fear in the wicked, regarding prospects in the hereafter. In Pufendorf's system 'that which remains hidden in the soul, and does not appear externally, is not pertinent to Natural Law'; but this, argues Leibniz, unacceptably limits Natural Law, diminishing its linkage with Natural Theology and undermining the concept of duty. Law for Pufendorf, objected Leibniz, is just a legitimate command from a superior obliging the 'subject to conform his actions to what the law itself prescribes': hence, under his system 'no one will do his duty spontaneously, there will be no duty when there is no superior to enforce rules, and no duties for those who have no superior'.[155]

In expounding Natural Law, held Leibniz, one must 'derive human justice, as from a spring, from the divine, to make it complete'.[156] Being in essence a juristic, anti-philosophical philosophy of politics and law divorcing Natural Law from ethics and metaphysics no less than theology, Pufendorf's construct, to Leibniz's mind, obscures the true conception of justice and, relying too much on Hobbes, leaves men defenceless under illegal and unjust government. The complete impossibility of criticizing the princely courts under Pufendorf's system, even on grounds of basic justice, indeed created a major problem and dilemma for the German moderate mainstream. For while it is true that there was relatively little fundamental criticism of the German system of princely government (something hardly surprising given the dependence of figures like Leibniz, Thomasius, and Wolff, and—no less—Stosch, Wachter, Edelmann, and Schmidt, on the favour of princes), there was nevertheless much suffused disgruntlement in society about conditions in the Empire.

Barbeyrac tried to defend Pufendorf against Leibniz by softening the jurist's stress on primal drives, and natural sociability, and placing more emphasis on God's justice as the foundation of Natural Law.[157] But his answers to Leibniz's strictures seemed inadequate to many, as also did his arguments against the naturalists and Spinozists. The latter, by denying a Creator God that ordains, regulates, and governs, threatened to pull the mat from under Pufendorf's system by denying that it is God's decree that holds society and the state together.[158] According to Spinoza, as also the *Symbolum*, Stosch, Wagner, Lau, and Wachter who, in 1704, published at Berlin a forty-four-page Latin treatise on Natural Law incorporating (without mentioning Spinoza) Spinoza's ethical doctrines, and several phrases verbatim from his *Tractatus politicus*, there can be neither good nor bad in the state of nature, and Natural Law boils down to saying that divine justice is equivalent to divine power, that is the power of nature.[159]

It was always central to Pufendorf's and Thomasius', as later Barbeyrac's, conception of Natural Law, that the sovereign must forbid and suppress the expression

[155] Leibniz, *Political Writings*, 70.

[156] Ibid. 69; Korkman, 'Voluntarism', 196–9.

[157] Westerman, *Disintegration*, 253–4; Korkman, 'Voluntarism', 204–5; van Eijnatten, 'Church Fathers', 19, 22–3.

[158] Ries, *Dissertatio philosophica*, 35, 37; Jäger, *Spinocismus*, 28.

[159] Stosch, *Concordia*, 38–63; Lau, *Meditationes philosophicae*, 38–48.

of 'atheistic' and Spinozistic views.[160] For 'atheism' as understood then directly contradicts the premiss that social and political practices conducive to the good of society, and its tranquillity, derive from naturally established legal principles ordained by God for regulating the affairs of men. Once Spinoza's system is allowed as a conceivable option, the whole of Natural Law as understood in the Early Enlightenment Lutheran world collapses, because under his scheme of thought there can be no such thing as a divinely decreed Natural Law or any inherent duties or absolute right or wrong.

Spinozism means the only natural law is the law of an impersonal, morally neutral nature or as Wachter puts it: 'conservatio sui est juris naturalis' [self-conservation is the law of nature].[161] While no one can contravene what is divinely decreed, if the *jus naturae* is reduced by Spinoza, Stosch, and Wachter, as by Hobbes, to little more than appetite, each individual's power to compete, on an equally justified basis, with any other and the unnaturalness of knowingly working against one's own conservation and security, then providence no longer has a role.[162] Politics and administration then no longer possess any divine authorization in either the theological or the Pufendorfian sense, and can only be rationally based on the 'common good' or what will make people in general 'virtuous and happy' as Wagner expressed it.[163]

If Hobbes was absorbed after a fashion, denial of Natural Theology on the philosophical grounding of 'atheism', or Spinozism, dissolved the whole foundation of moral, political, and legal theory of Pufendorf, as also of Thomasius, Leibniz, Barbeyrac, and Wolff. The ideas of justice and honesty which the 'atheists' seek to formulate without reference to the will of the 'supreme legislator who is not only the author of nature but also the protector of human kind and society' must be rejected, as one professor expressed it, as nothing but feeble and 'groundless chimaera'.[164] For Natural Lawyers, Stoicism rated as an altogether higher system of moral thought than Spinozism because in Stoicism, 'good and bad' are absolutes, defined in terms of the relationship of the individual soul to the world-soul. Stoic morality, much admired by Barbeyrac, focuses on the individual, and the relationship of the individual to the universal, rather than the individual to society, establishing a basis for an absolute, timeless moral standard divinely decreed in a way inconceivable to philosophical 'atheism', and Spinoza, whom Barbeyrac attacked as the supreme 'sponge of religion and morality'.[165]

160 Hochstrasser, *Natural Law Theories*, 198–201; *Nouvelle Bibliothèque germanique*, 5 (1748/9), 329, 343.

161 Wachter, *Origines*, 19–20, 22–3; Jäger, *Spinocismus*, 28–9; Gundling, *Volständige Historie*, iv. 5407, 5477–8, 6061.

162 Musaeus, *Tractatus theologico-politicus . . . examinatus*, 84–7; Wachter, *Origines*, 1, 16, 28–30; Wachter, 'Leben', 289; Hösle, *Morals and Politics*, 36–8.

163 [Wagner?] F.M.v.G., *Antwort*, 61.

164 Beermann, *Impietas atheistica*, 144; Lomonaco, 'Natural Right', 138–40; Hunter, *Rival Enlightenments*, 95; Seidler, 'Politics', 229.

165 Barbeyrac, 'Préface', pp. lxvii–lxx.

Pufendorf may have in part engineered a 'profound "de-transcendentalising" of civil governance',[166] and 'desacralising separation of transcendent morality and civil authority', as one scholar puts it, albeit in Leibniz's judgement fatally separating politics from true morality,[167] but Barbeyrac, fighting Bayle no less than Spinoza and Leibniz, sought to reverse this tendency in Pufendorf, bending Natural Law back the other way. Like Crousaz, he deemed it vital to defeat Bayle's (and Spinoza's) cardinal principle, enunciated in both the *Continuation* and *Réponse*, that 'la politique et la religion étoient incompatibles'.[168] For him, as for Locke and the *rationaux*, the junction of religion and politics was, on the contrary, the very linchpin of an 'enlightened' educational, legal, and social reform programme. 'Natural Law', far from being 'desacralized', needed during the Early Enlightenment convincingly to reinforce Pufendorf's doctrine that such law is the Superior Will's manifestation in the world. Barbeyrac held that, for Pufendorf, as for himself, human conscience, obligation, and respect for duties are all directives imposed on us by God: 'voilà le grand et premier fondement de tout Devoir et de toute Obligation'.[169]

Despite their different objectives, the Leibnizio-Wolffian, and Spinozist-*Bayliste*, attacks on Pufendorfian Natural Law theory were closely linked philosophically. Leibniz's criticism of Pufendorf's principles of Natural Law, of 1706, resembled, and may even have been, in part, prompted by, Bayle's assault, in his *Continuation* of 1705, on precisely that aspect of Pufendorf and Barbeyrac which moral philosophers term 'voluntarism'.[170] For both Leibniz and Bayle argue that if God proclaims our moral categories by his will alone, without these corresponding to universal principles which are metaphysically independent of God, then the 'voluntarist' cannot explain why God should be praised for being 'just' or benevolent.[171] Natural Law voluntarism inevitably blurs our concept of justice also in other ways since anyone adhering to the dictates of fairness and equity in accordance with Pufendorf's theory may be said to do so only because he or she fears a superior power, or sees these as God's commands, and not through awareness of their justness. Equally, such a theory can never guarantee that God's will, seen as the foundation of Natural Law, commands us to do what is, of itself, inherently and eternally just. Hence, the Pufendorfian-Barbeyracian approach leaves it unclear why divine ordinances should not be seen as in some respect arbitrary, or even unjust and negligent, as Bayle implies in his article on 'Manichaeism'.[172] Bayle's and Leibniz's objections to 'voluntarism' combined with the Spinozist critique in effect undermined Pufendorfian-Barbeyracian legal and social theory in its entirety.

166 Hunter, *Rival Enlightenments*, 26, 149–50.
167 Ibid. 95–6, 128–30; Schneewind, *Invention of Autonomy*, 250–1.
168 *L'Europe savante*, 4 (1718), 58–60.
169 Ibid. 138–9; Hutchison, *Locke in France*, 60; van Eijnatten, 'Church Fathers', 22–4.
170 Leibniz, *Theodicy*, 241–3; Labrousse, *Pierre Bayle*, 269–70.
171 Schneewind, *Invention of Autonomy*, 252; Hunter, *Rival Enlightenments*, 96, 129.
172 Hunter, *Rival Enlightenments*, 129–30; Westerman, *Disintegration*, 199, 203, 205–6, 223.

If God has reasons other than his power over us for decreeing moral rules, and endorsing princely legislation, then there must be some independent source of moral truth. But if there is such an independent moral truth, it remains unclear why God's Will is what makes an action morally good or bad. 'Justice does not depend upon arbitrary laws of superiors', held Leibniz, 'but on the eternal rules of wisdom and of goodness, in men as well as in God.'[173] But Leibniz's account, though effective against Pufendorf and Barbeyrac, risked playing into the hands of Spinoza and Bayle by eliminating divine governance of his universal and timeless principles of justice. These were perplexing difficulties and both Barbeyrac's and Leibniz's positions were rendered still more fraught by the failure of the first to link 'voluntarism' in any comprehensible way to his Lockean, contractarian account of political sovereignty and of the second convincingly to demonstrate divine providence.[174]

Barbeyrac's reply to Leibniz, published with the latter's criticism, as an appendix to the 1718 reissue of his French translation of Pufendorf, was that God is necessarily 'just' and that this is inherent in his nature; he cannot do otherwise than be just. But Barbeyrac could not explain the source of the moral law God both proclaims to be 'just' and adheres to himself, or under what sort of necessity he obeys it, or indeed how his nature gives rise to justice as one of his inherent attributes. The Pufendorfian conception of Natural Law, though still immensely powerful in the Lutheran universities as a social and political theory, had by the 1730s become a philosophical cripple, retreating before a rival Leibnizian-Wolffian Natural Law tradition based on a more metaphysical conception of justice and an equally devastating Hobbesian-Spinozist retort, drawing in part on Gundling's reworking of Hobbes, on Stosch, Wachter, and Lau, and, finally, culminating in Johann Jakob Schmauss (1690–1757), a great expert on Grotius, Pufendorf, and all Natural Law theory besides, among other things, Spanish and Portuguese history, appointed professor of Natural Law at Göttingen by George II, King of England and elector of Hanover, with the founding of the university, in 1734.[175]

Scorning Barbeyrac, acutely aware of both Hobbes and Spinoza,[176] Schmauss argued against Pufendorf and Thomasius that the only Natural Law that really exists is Hobbes's and Spinoza's drives, instincts, and impulses. In his private 'collegia' at Göttingen and, at the end of his life, in his notorious, posthumously published, critique of Grotius and Pufendorf, both of whom he sought to unseat from their previous pre-eminence in German academe, Schmauss helped undermine one of the most crucial linchpins of the German conservative princely Enlightenment.[177] He took Pufendorf and Thomasius to task especially for conflating

173 Westerman, *Disintegration*, 199; Leibniz, *Theodicy*, 403; Hochstrasser, 'Claims', 44–6.

174 Hochstrasser, 'Claims', 46; Schneewind, *Invention of Autonomy*, 253–4.

175 Lau, *Meditationes, theses*, 2, 32–3; Schmauss, *Neues Systema*, 'Vorrede' p. 3^v, 316–17, 335.

176 Schmauss, *Neues Systema*, 276–96, 308–12.

177 Ibid., 'Vorrede', 3^v, 390–1, 394, 525; Pontoppidan, *Kraft der Wahrheit*, 321; Reill, *German Enlightenment*, 57–8, 62, 96–7; Grunert, 'Reception of Grotius', 97; Hochstrasser, *Natural Law Theories*, 147–8.

and confusing Natural Law with the moral criteria Man derives from applying his reason and hence with positive law. In effect, he stripped Pufendorf and Thomasius down to a philosophical naturalism which could not, any longer, be coupled with Natural Theology, or indeed separated from Spinoza's 'order of nature'. Natural Law was reduced by Schmauss virtually to what it is in Hobbes, Spinoza, the *Symbolum*, Stosch, Wagner, Wachter, and Lau—the universal law of humanity as inscribed in men's hearts and minds, their character and motivation.

8

Newtonianism and Anti-Newtonianism in the Early Enlightenment: Science, Philosophy, and Religion

1. ENGLISH PHYSICO-THEOLOGY

Amid so great a crisis gripping religion and religious authority in western Europe, it was only to be expected, given the recent stunning advances in astronomy, physics, and mathematics, that theologians and philosophers should turn to a new source—science—for help, guidance, confirmation, and support. This placed the predominant Early Enlightenment grouping in European science—Newton and the Newtonians—in a commanding position at the very centre of the intellectual debate; and they were well equipped to preside over the moderate mainstream Enlightenment in the West since, for them, as the Scottish mathematician and Newtonian Colin MacLaurin (1698–1746) expressed it, it was axiomatic that science, or what they termed 'natural philosophy, is subservient to purposes of a higher kind, and is chiefly to be valued as it lays a sure foundation for natural religion and moral philosophy, by leading us, in a satisfactory manner, to the knowledge of the author and governor of the universe'.[1] Science, held the Newtonians, reveals the handiwork of he whom Newton grandly dubbed 'rerum omnium fabricator ac dominus': scientific enquiry 'is to search into His workmanship; every new discovery opens to us a new part of His scheme'.

Newtonianism, then, entailed a full-scale revolution, not only in physics and astronomy but also philosophy, religion, and all erudite endeavour, his acolytes attributing their idol's unparalleled accomplishment to his scrupulously inductive method and aversion to that unfortunate 'love of systems' deemed to have ruined Descartes, Spinoza, Malebranche, and Leibniz. 'In this philosophy', proclaimed Sir Isaac, 'propositions are deduced from phenomena and made general by induction.'[2] Newton allegedly refused to 'set out with any favourite principle or supposition, never proposing to himself the invention of a system', and supposedly

[1] MacLaurin, *Account*, 3; Willey, *Eighteenth-Century Background*, 135–6; Stewart, 'Religion', 39, 56; Broadie, 'Human Mind', 61.

[2] Newton, *Philosophiae naturalis principia*, 484.

scorned all mere conjecture: seeing 'how extravagant such attempts were', Newton liked 'to call his philosophy experimental philosophy, intimating by the name, the essential difference there is betwixt it and those systems that are the product of genius and invention only'.[3]

Newtonian 'philosophy', then, came to dominate great swathes of the moderate mainstream Enlightenment and claim a general hegemony, indeed its adherents felt that earlier philosophies and philosophers should be altogether discarded as rooted in *esprit de système* where the true 'philosophy' of Newton by contrast, depended exclusively (as Le Clerc and, later, Voltaire also affirmed) on empirical procedures, experiment, and data according to the principles of Bacon, Boyle, and Locke supplemented by the genius of Newton. Yet, paradoxically, despite this great emphasis on strict empirical procedure, Newtonian 'philosophy', it did not go unnoticed, in revealing 'the frame of the system of the world', gained in authority by being 'advanced' 'with a greater shew of certainty'—as one dissenter put it—'than any other', its propositions being presented not merely as 'probable, but as absolutely certain and mathematically demonstrated'.[4] Where earlier thinkers supposedly based their systems on sheer fantasies and dreams, Newtonians with their new and sound methodology provide facts, certain knowledge, and what Le Clerc admiringly called 'des preuves mathématiques'.

Newtonianism, then, was not just an account of the planetary system and the laws of mechanics and gravity but regarded in the Enlightenment as essentially a 'philosophy', demonstrating the overall shape of what we know, and one deemed a powerful weapon against the *esprits forts*. It was enthusiastically embraced as a means of restoring order and certainty, destroying incredulity and materialism, and not least transcending the 'variety of opinions and perpetual disputes among philosophers'. Being devised by 'those who have consulted nature and not their own imagination', Newton's approach was thought to supersede all previous systems of thought while at the same time disclosing why, previously, so much confusion reigned: 'that the fault has lain with philosophers themselves, and not in philosophy.'[5]

Not the least of the merits of 'Sir Isaac Newton's philosophy', held his acolytes, was that 'it altogether overthrows the foundation of Spinoza's doctrine', as MacLaurin puts it, with demonstrations of divine intervention and, especially, by 'shewing that not only there may be, but that there actually is a vacuum; and that, instead of an infinite, necessary and indivisible plenitude, matter appears to occupy but a very small portion of space, and to have its parts actually divided and separated from each other'.[6] By the early years of the new century, overthrowing Spinoza in a clear, demonstrable fashion, in public discourse, appeared both timely and requisite for, as the London-based Huguenot Desaguliers remarked, in Britain (as elsewhere),

[3] MacLaurin, *Account*, 8; Hartsoeker, *Recueil*, 37–8.
[4] Gordon, *Remarks*, 123–4; Hartsoeker, *Recueil*, 76–7, 86.
[5] MacLaurin, *Account*, 100; Voltaire, *Lettres philosophiques*, 97.
[6] MacLaurin, *Account*, 81–2; Clarke, *Demonstration*, 36–47.

there was widespread alarm that materialist and Deistic ideas were rapidly spreading and that 'proselytes are gain'd among the weak and ignorant, or such conceited debauchees as are glad to be supply'd with means to defending their immoralities, by attacking religion with a show of wit and argument'.[7] It was those arguments that could now be eradicated from society by means of a programme of public education of sermons, lectures, and popular expositions.

Before long, Newton, the former recluse of Trinity College, Cambridge, came to be internationally lionized and adulated as not just a scientific giant but head of an all-conquering system which had finally discredited and killed off those ancient philosophers and modern *incrédules* who postulate an idea of God 'sans empire, sans providence et qui ne propose aucune fin', as Le Clerc put it in his effusive review of the influential new edition of Newton's *Principia* prepared at Cambridge and published at Amsterdam in 1714. Le Clerc, now as staunch a champion of Newton as of Locke, vigorously defended Newton against the objections of the Dutch scientist Nicolaas Hartsoecker, claiming he was a philosopher who had shown that 'Spinosa et ceux qui suivent son sentiment', which consists, he says, in not acknowledging any God distinct from the cosmos, and calling by the name of 'God' what was really just Fate or nature, stood in flagrant contradiction not only to religion but also to the findings of modern science, indeed reason itself.[8]

Claiming Sir Isaac's science as the best way to demonstrate divine providence, Newtonians built a highly integrated physico-theological system encompassing not only science, religion, and philosophy but also history, chronology, Bible criticism, and moral theory which became vastly influential throughout eighteenth-century Europe and America, enabling them to speak of the 'materialists', as Clarke puts it, as the 'great enemies of the mathematical principles of philosophy'.[9] But scientific research was deemed vital to society most of all because 'false schemes of natural philosophy', in MacLaurin's words, were what led men 'to atheism or suggest opinions concerning the Deity and the universe, of most dangerous consequence to mankind; and have been frequently employed to support such opinions'.[10]

As a comprehensive system of natural philosophy, Newtonianism can be said to date from 1691–2 when Newton first came into contact with Richard Bentley (1662–1742), an intellectually formidable young Cambridge don, so forceful that he had been selected—very likely at Newton's own prompting—to give the first series of London Boyle lectures. In preparing these, subsequently published under the title *The Folly of Atheism* (1692), Bentley worked together with Newton who, in the early 1690s, was just beginning to gain confidence that his 'new system of the World' would prove decisive in upholding religion and defeating the 'atheists' and Epicureans, developing the new science into a comprehensive system of thought.[11]

[7] Desaguliers, 'A Letter to the Translator', preface to [Nieuwentyt], *The Religious Philosopher*.

[8] *Bibliothèque ancienne et moderne*, 1 (1714), 90–1; Vermij, 'Formation', 197–8.

[9] Clarke, *First Reply*, in *Leibniz–Clarke Correspondence*, 12.

[10] MacLaurin, *Account*, 4.

[11] Guerlac and Jacob, 'Bentley, Newton and Providence', 314–18; Westfall, *Life of Isaac Newton*, 205, 216; Harrison, *Bible, Protestantism*, 137, 172.

The relationship of the sun to the planets 'I do not think explicable by mere natural causes', Newton assured Bentley, in a letter from Cambridge of December 1692, 'but am forced to ascribe it to the counsel and contrivance of a voluntary Agent'. His principal argument was that the 'same Power, whether natural or supernatural, which placed the sun in the centre of the six primary planets' also placed Saturn and Jupiter in the midst of their moons 'and the earth in the centre of the moon's orb; and therefore, had this cause been a blind one, without contrivance or design, the sun would have been a body of the same kind with Saturn, Jupiter and the earth, that is without light and heat.' He dismissed outright the Cartesian hypothesis that suns cool and lose their light and are not in fact in essence different kinds of substance from planets. 'Why there is one body in our system qualified to give light and heat to all the rest, I know no reason, but because the Author of the system thought it convenient; and why there is but one body of this kind, I know no reason, but because one was sufficient to warm and enlighten all the rest.' He was similarly convinced, by inference, that the 'motions which the planets now have could not spring from any natural cause alone, but were impressed by an intelligent Agent.'[12]

It was above all Newton's new way of arguing that the cosmos was created and is governed by an intelligent agent 'endowed with liberty and choice' which seemed to overturn, as Samuel Clarke puts it, 'what Spinoza and his followers have asserted concerning the nature of God'.[13] If initially supported mainly by Low Church Latitudinarian Anglicans, liberal Christian dissenters, and providential Deists, in England Newton's system quickly began to draw very wide support, rapidly conquering first Cambridge and then Oxford and, by 1711, gaining ascendancy at all five universities in Scotland.[14] By around 1715, thanks not least to Le Clerc, Newtonian physico-theology had also established its hegemony among the *rationaux* Huguenot theologians and was becoming pervasive more generally among educated opinion in the Netherlands. There then followed a pause until the later 1720s when Newtonianism began to make rapid headway also in France, Italy, Germany, Spain, and the new Russian Imperial Academy of Sciences at St Petersburg.

In this way Newton built a scientific and intellectual empire, or 'espèce de monarchie universelle' as Voltaire dubbed it,[15] its innate superiority, comprehensiveness, scorn for continental systems, and essential 'Britishness' all alike contributing to generate its special mystique which rested not only on his brilliant insights and capacity for creative synthesis but also the fervour of key supporters, his domineering character, and vigorous and deft 'management' of his books, ideas, influence, and growing authority. Cutting philosophy down to size, and combining it with religion, always lay at the centre of the Newtonians' public agenda, MacLaurin, for instance, not only being one of the founders, in 1737, of the Edinburgh Philosophical Society, but delivering courses of public lectures in 'experimental philosophy' for

12 Newton to Bentley, 10 Dec. 1692 in Bentley, *Works*, iii. 204; Henry, 'England', 203–4.

13 Clarke, *Demonstration*, 46.

14 Wood, 'Scientific Revolution', 100.

15 Voltaire, *Lettres philosophiques*, 123.

the cultured classes of Edinburgh. Meanwhile, supported by a growing army of expositors and popularizers, Newton cleverly confined his own writings to a tiny elite, deliberately using only Latin and abstruse terminology beyond the capacity of most readers even in his non-mathematical sections, by this means creating an aura of lofty insight, or what one critic called 'that almost impenetrable cloud of obscurity', which had the effect of putting 'almost everybody beyond a possibility of disputing his philosophy'. As a result, objected one or two solitary dissenters, men 'received this philosophy as they did of old the dictates of the Magi, or the responses of their oracles, without knowing the meaning of what was imposed upon them, or the reason of what was said to them'.[16]

Their superior methodology, claimed the Newtonians, rested on intellectual modesty, there being much in nature that we cannot know, or do not know yet, so that their cautious empiricism, unlike that of the mere system-builders, frankly acknowledges there are large areas of mystery and darkness which 'natural philosophy' cannot explain: hence 'even the avowed imperfection of some parts of it', held MacLaurin, helps convince us of its excellency and 'conformity with nature'. For 'the great mysterious Being, who made and governed the whole system [of the cosmos]', he contended, 'has set a part of the chain of causes in our view; but we find that, as He Himself is too high for our comprehension, so His more immediate instruments in the universe, are also involved in an obscurity that philosophy is not able to dissipate.'[17] Hence, their very method and principles enabled Newtonians to 'beware of the danger of setting out in philosophy in so high and presumptuous a manner' as had Descartes, Spinoza, and Leibniz.

Leibniz, added MacLaurin, was doubtless a genius in his way but, apart from being misled by grand concepts, had been presumptuous in his criticism of Sir Isaac and had mistakenly 'ridiculed the metaphysics of the English, as narrow, and founded on inadequate notions'.[18] Here, as in other passages, one gains a sense of how Newton eventually came to be viewed by his legions of admirers as an integral feature of Britain's recent meteoric rise to international pre-eminence and imperial dominance, marked annoyance being expressed, for example, at the tardiness with which the French and others acknowledged what the young Voltaire, immensely stimulated by his visit to England, unhesitatingly dubbed 'la supériorité de la philosophie anglaise'. As Voltaire also noted, some Royal Society members openly complained of Fontenelle's presumption in assigning the 'dreamer' Descartes comparable status to Newton in his official eulogy, after Newton's death.[19]

As early as 1672, Newton had begun to greet criticism of his views, including Huygens's critique of his theory of colours, with more than common irritation and impatience.[20] In this instance, Newton's irritation is all the more remarkable in that, as d'Alembert expressed it later, Huygens was someone 'à qui Newton doit peut-être autant qu'à Descartes'.[21] After becoming president of the Royal Society in London

[16] Gordon, *Remarks*, 110. [17] MacLaurin, *Account*, 23.
[18] Ibid. 80–1, 86; Wood, 'Science', 102. [19] Voltaire, *Lettres philosophiques*, 96–101.
[20] Feingold, 'Huygens', 31. [21] D'Alembert, 'Éloge historique', 46.

in 1703, he rapidly extended his personal influence over the upper echelons of the scientific establishment in England—in the process exerting a tight grip over the Royal Society and over such crucial research resources as the astronomical observatory at Greenwich run by the Astronomer Royal John Flamsteed, and the extensive data on the motions of the moon and other astronomical records painstakingly collected there. While Flamsteed and a number of other scientists in London and Cambridge were tyrannized over by Newton in an astonishingly overbearing and despotic manner,[22] reducing them to the level of menial dependants, Newton's store of data to collate with his theoretical premisses was steadily widened and enhanced.

To further develop his system and its sway, in both its scientific and non-scientific aspects—theology, universal history, and biblical chronology—Newton devoted immense energy throughout the rest of his life. By 1750, Newtonianism had become as powerful a force in the Greek, Russian, and Spanish enlightenments as it was in western Europe. This 'new system of the World' has been dubbed 'physico-theology' and that, indeed, is precisely what it was. Although, during the nineteenth and early twentieth centuries, it was mostly assumed one can divorce Newton's scientific research, findings, and reasoning readily from his less compelling theological, mystical, and alchemical concerns (though it was realized that these were pervasive and deep), in fact this hardly seems to be the case. Admittedly, his system was anchored, in part, in an emphatic scientific empiricism akin to that of Boyle, Sydenham, Huygens, or Boerhaave, enjoining a combination of careful observation followed by theorizing and generalization only insofar as accords with observed data; and it is true, also, that he always professed to be powerfully on his guard against the intrusion of metaphysical assumptions. But this aversion to *a priori* metaphysics only really applied to premisses of which he disapproved, and he seemed strangely unaware of how comprehensively unproven metaphysical concepts underpinned his own system as well as there also being strong empirical dimensions to rival 'systems'.[23] He rightly complained that Leibniz accused him of reintroducing 'occult qualities' into science while himself postulating a *harmonia praestabilita* which itself 'is miraculous' and to an extent preferring 'hypotheses to arguments of induction drawn from experiments'.[24] Yet he failed to see that his own 'argument from design' rested, as Leibniz countered, on theoretical (in fact, metaphysical) conjectures about gravity, attraction, inertia, 'absolute time and space', and motion which were equally unproven, indeed stretched beyond anything demonstrable mathematically.[25]

The presumption of absolute time and space, for which he was to be severely (and correctly) criticized by Huygens, Leibniz, and Berkeley, formed—together with his third foundational property of reality, 'inertia'—the conceptual frame for

22 Westfall, *Life of Isaac Newton*, 260–1; Clark and Clark, *Newton's Tyranny*, 55, 86–101.
23 Rogers, 'Science and British Philosophy', 45; McGuirre, 'Predicates', 91.
24 Newton to Conti, 26 Feb. 1716, in *Leibniz–Clarke Correspondence*, 187.
25 Mamiani, 'Rivoluzione incompiuta', 42–4.

linear and unbending trajectories of motion central to Newtonian dynamics. 'Motus absolutus' [absolute motion] is defined by Newton as the transfer of any body from one point in absolute space to another, so that, as conceived by Newton, motion and all dynamics are only explicable, and capable of mathematical expression, within a world frame built of '*spatium absolutum* [absolute space], in its own nature, without relation to anything external [which] remains always similar and immoveable' and what he calls 'absolute, true, and mathematical time, [which] of itself and from its own nature flows equably without relation to anything external' so constructed that 'as the order of the parts of time is immutable, so also is the order of the parts of space'.[26] Newton, while granting that the physical cosmos constituted of matter may be finite, ruled that in any case 'space is infinite and cannot be terminated by any limits' as it was put by his first major continental expositor, 's-Gravesande, in the 1720 edition of his *Mathematical Elements of Physics Prov'd by Experiments*, a text translated and 'revised' by Newton's faithful acolyte Keill.[27]

All beings, held Newton, are placed, planted, or move in relation to this 'true or absolute space' with the exception of God who, because 'He is eternal and infinite, omnipotent and omniscient' and by the same necessity that he exists, 'adest ab infinito in infinitum' [is present from infinity to infinity], every part of the infinity of space being immovable and immutable.[28] For as both absolute space and absolute time are needed to register quantitatively the 'presence and duration of any existing individual thing' so the 'quantity of the existence of God' can be inferred to be 'eternal, in relation to duration and infinite in relation to the space in which he is present'.[29] The proof that space is 'eternal in duration and immutable in nature', for Newton, lay in the fact that 'if ever space had not existed, God at that time would have been nowhere', a notion no less 'repugnant to reason', he argued, than the notion that God's ubiquity somehow arose in time, or that he created his own ubiquity.[30] Such doctrines as absolute motion, absolute space, and *tempus absolutum, verum et mathematicum* are basic to Newtonianism but seemed dubious to Newton's critics, being predicated on an unquestioning but philosophically problematic correspondence between mathematics and reality. For Leibniz, by contrast, absolute time and space are only clear and definite ideas mathematically, as he intimated to the Venetian *savant* Antonio Conti, in 1716, that is, Newton's axioms are logically consistent within themselves and therefore 'true but ideal, like numbers' and hence not necessarily a reflection of physical reality.[31]

The regularity, purposeful intricacy, and coherence of the universe, held Newton, are in themselves proof of supernatural agency in its design: 'this most

[26] Newton, *Mathematical Principles*, i. 9, 12; Shapin, *Scientific Revolution*, 62; Barbour, *Absolute or Relative Motion?*, 19, 22, 30.

[27] 's-Gravesande, *Mathematical Elements*, 1, 9.

[28] Newton, *Philosophiae naturalis principia*, 483; Newton, *Mathematical Principles*, ii. 389–91.

[29] Barbour, *Discovery of Dynamics*, i. 619; McGuirre, 'Predicates', 94–7.

[30] McGuirre, 'Predicates', 92–5; Barbour, *Discovery of Dynamics*, 620; Gaukroger, *Descartes' System*, 102.

[31] Newton quoted in Barbour, *Discovery of Dynamics*, i. 623; *Leibniz–Clarke Correspondence*, 185.

beautiful system of the sun, planets, and comets, could only proceed from the counsel and dominion of an intelligent and powerful Being.'[32] 'All that diversity of natural things which we find', he argued, 'suited to different times and places, could arise from nothing but the ideas and will of a Being necessarily existing.'[33] As the All Souls Fellow William Wollaston (1660–1724) echoed Newton's sentiments, 'the astonishing magnificence of it, the various phenomena and kinds of beings, the uniformity observed in the productions of things, the uses and ends for which they serve, etc. do all shew that there is some Almighty designer, an infinite wisdom and power at the top of all these things.'[34] This 'Almighty designer', asserts Newton, 'omnia regit, non ut anima mundi, sed ut universorum Dominus; et propter dominium suum pantokrator (id est, imperator universalis) dici solet' [governs all things, not as the world-soul, but as Lord over all things; and because of his dominion, he is called ruler of all].[35] If we know God through his works and 'admire His perfections', we 'adore Him on account of his dominion'.[36] Newton's emphatic doctrine of godly 'dominion' in turn grew into a full-blown theory that 'contrary to Spinoza's assertion', as Clarke put it, 'motion itself and all its quantities and directions with the laws of gravitation are entirely arbitrary, and might possibly have been altogether different from what they now are'.[37] This rejection of Spinozist necessity was integral to the Newtonian summons to worship God, for his direct governance of the cosmos indeed infused the whole of Newton's system.

Newton's laws of dynamics directly rely not only on the *a priori* premisses of absolute space and time but also on the externality of motion to inherently inert matter. From this derives the connected idea of 'absolute motion'. It was the doctrine of the externality of motion to matter, that 'all corporeal motions proceed originally from something incorporeal' as Wollaston puts it,[38] which made it a key principle for Newtonians that gravitation—and hence the power which keeps the planets and moon perpetually in their orbits—is not physically caused motion, or force, in the usual sense. While granting that gravity was assuredly not a 'causeless cause', Newton always held 'that it must proceed from a cause that penetrates to the very centers of the sun and planets, without suffering the least diminution of its force; that operates, not according to the quantity of the surface of the particles upon which it acts (as mechanical causes use to do) but according to the quantity of solid matter which they contain; and propagates its virtue on all sides to immense distances, decreasing always in the duplicate proportion of the distances', and that, hence, gravitation has no mechanical or material cause, since 'inanimate brute matter' can and does not, or so Newton contended, move other matter without direct

[32] Newton, *Philosophiae naturalis principia*, 482; Conti, *Scritti filosofici*, 219; Force, 'Breakdown', 147; Markley, *Fallen Languages*, 139.

[33] Newton, *Mathematical Principles*, ii. 391.

[34] Wollaston, *Religion of Nature*, 79.

[35] Newton, *Philosophiae naturalis principia*, 482.

[36] Newton, *Mathematical Principles*, ii. 391.

[37] Clarke, *Demonstration*, 49; Harris, *Of Liberty and Necessity*, 47.

[38] Wollaston, *Religion of Nature*, 108.

physical contact.[39] Hence, 'mutual gravitation or spontaneous attraction', as Bentley put it, 'cannot possibly be innate and essential to matter'.[40] While in his *Principia*, Newton refers only to 'that force, whatever it is, by which the planets are perpetually drawn aside from rectilinear motions, which otherwise they wou'd pursue, and made to revolve in curvilinear orbits', clearly Newton himself, no less than Le Clerc, Bentley, Clarke, MacLaurin, and Wollaston, considered gravity not just different in kind from ordinary motion conceived by them as the effect of 'force' on matter and therefore something, by definition, already transferred to, albeit not inherent in, matter, but as nothing less than a direct emanation of God's general providence.[41] Locke fully concurred, accepting Newton's view that gravity has no physical cause and is explicable only as 'the positive will of a superiour Being, so ordering it'.[42]

'Attraction', echoed Wollaston, 'is not of the nature or idea of matter.'[43] Indeed, gravity was something so distinct from matter which is indeed chiefly distinguished from 'mind or spirit', according to Newtonians, by what MacLaurin calls its 'passive nature, or inertia', that they interpreted gravity as 'a new and invincible argument for the being of God: being a direct and positive proof, that an immaterial living mind doth inform and actuate the dead matter, and support the frame of the world'.[44] This unyielding distinction between mechanical effects based on 'absolute motion' and those based on 'attraction' and certain other unexplained forces such as 'the power of magnetism' and electricity, a duality later replicated by Maupertuis and Voltaire but rejected by the materialists, remained central to Newtonian science, philosophy, and theology and was to be the particular Newtonian doctrine most frequently attacked by Spinozists and materialists like Wagner, Collins, d'Argens, Hatzfeld, Buffon, Diderot, and d'Holbach, as well as neo-Cartesians, Leibnizians, and Wolffians.[45] Not only was there no difference in kind between gravity and other causes of motion, held Newton's critics, but absolute space, absolute time, absolute motion, and the externality of motion to matter—in fact virtually the whole conceptual paraphernalia of Newton's physics and astronomy—far from being empirically proven were not 'scientific' at all and, for all the confident talk of induction and a fundamental breakthrough in scientific method, just figments of the Newtonian metaphysical imagination.

A year before his death, in 1694, Huygens who had long asserted the relativity of all space and motion, at least since the early 1650s, again assured Leibniz, opposing Newton, that 'there is no real but only relative motion'.[46] If correct, as it was, of

[39] Newton, *Mathematical Principles*, i. 76, 84–5 and ii. 392; Westfall, *Life of Newton*, 204–5, 238, 294–5; Shapin, *Scientific Revolution*, 63–4.

[40] Bentley, *Folly of Atheism*, vii. 26; Hatzfeld, *Case of the Learned*, 16–17.

[41] Hartsoeker, *Recueil*, 38.

[42] Locke, *Some Thoughts*, 246.

[43] Wollaston, *Religion of Nature*, 79.

[44] Bentley, *Folly of Atheism*, vii. 30; MacLaurin, *Account*, 100–3.

[45] [D'Argens], *Songes philosophiques*, 176–8, 185; Landucci, 'Mente e corpo', 129–30; Kuhn, *Structure*, 104–6.

[46] Kuhn, *Structure*, 72, 98; Guerlac, *Newton on the Continent*, 49–50; Barbour, *Absolute or Relative Motion?*, i. 673.

course, the whole of the theologico-philosophical framework encasing Newton's science of dynamics, though not his mathematical demonstrations or theory of the universal applicability of gravity, was called fundamentally into question. The unavoidable implication of Huygens's and Leibniz's critique, as Leibniz pointed out, was that the Newtonians were mistaken in supposing the proven 'mathematical principles of philosophy are opposite to those of the materialists'; for 'on the contrary', held Leibniz, 'they are the same'; the only real, meaningful difference between the Spinozists and 'Christian mathematicians', in natural philosophy, he held, being that where the former 'admit only bodies', the latter 'admit also immaterial substances'.[47]

The ineluctable consequence of there being no absolute space, time, motion, or inertia is that all space, time, motion, and location is relative. What this in turn meant, Huygens—whose formerly positive relationship with the Royal Society in London never really recovered from the deterioration in his relations with English scientists during the Third Anglo-Dutch War (1672–4)—and Leibniz could only rather vaguely speculate, leaving suspended in the air a problem scientists subsequently forgot about, for Einstein to grapple with more than two hundred years later.[48] In fact, most of the western world simply assumed that the correctness of Newton's demonstrations of the planetary movements and gravity proves also the soundness of his ideas about space, time, inertia, motion, and force as well, so that the intellectual significance of the many eighteenth-century scientific and philosophical critiques of Newton, debated chiefly on the Continent, long continued to be generally missed or ignored.

How far Spinoza's doctrine that motion, far from being absolute, is inherent in matter, and its chief constituent, derived from Huygens can never be exactly known. It is certain, though, from Spinoza's early *Korte Verhandeling* [Short Treatise] which survives only in a contemporary Dutch version of around 1658 to 1660, that the doctrine that motion 'nog door zig zelfs bestaan noch verstaan kan worden, maer alleen door middel van de Uytgebreidheid' [neither exists nor can be understood in itself but only through means of bodies] was then already basic to his system.[49] Hence it was in direct line from Spinoza that Abraham Joannes Cuffeler (d. 1694)—who may, however, also have independently known Huygens in The Hague—and other Spinozists formulated a physics of motion flatly contradicting Newton's premisses, combining relative motion with the thesis that motion is part of the definition of matter. This basic difference between the systems of the Newtonians and Spinozists extended far beyond the sphere of physics and astronomy not least into the life sciences and psychology. Hence, movements of the mind were explained by Spinozists as internal to bodies, and determined by proportionate cause and effect in the same way as motion itself is intrinsic to matter

[47] *Leibniz–Clarke Correspondence*, 15.

[48] Feingold, 'Huygens', 32–4; Barbour, *Absolute or Relative Motion?*, i. 462, 465, 478, 488–9.

[49] Spinoza, *Korte geschriften*, 288; Spinoza, *Collected Works*, i. 91–2.

and exists only relative to it, whereas for Newtonians mind is something totally distinct from the physical universe.[50]

Newton—not unlike Locke and Henry More (1614–87)—in a way paralleled Descartes (with whom in his earlier years he was much preoccupied), even while repudiating most of his ideas, by postulating a basic ontological dualism encompassing the entire cosmos, central to which is the dichotomy of body and mind.[51] Body and spirit, for Newton, no less than Descartes, are fundamentally different and distinct. Furthermore, his theory of motion formed an integral part of precisely this ontological dualism, motion for him being an active force external to matter, just as, on the opposing side, the conception of motion as something entirely relative and constituent of matter such as one finds in Spinoza, Huygens, and among the eighteenth-century materialists implies a fundamental monism. Indeed, in Newton's system, matter is by definition passive, the active principle in the cosmos, including gravitation or 'attraction', deriving essentially from spirit. For Newtonians, like Bentley and Clarke, it was thus a vital line of defence to be held at all costs 'that sense and perception can never be the product of any kind of matter and motion'.[52]

The opposing Newtonian and Spinozist-Huygensian-Leibnizian conceptions of the time and space frame, motion, and matter—though the latter was not yet coherently formulated but appeared only in fragments[53]—hence stood in diametrical opposition to each other. Matter being wholly inert, contended the Newtonians, the cosmos must be governed by forces regulated by mathematical laws decreed and overseen through God's general providence, though the architect of the cosmos in his infinite wisdom and omnipotence also wields a special providence with which, by miraculous means, he effects the occasional adjustments to the whole he deems necessary and without which the universe would inevitably collapse and crash in upon itself.[54] For Newton's success in demonstrating the laws of gravitation also seemed to confirm God's ceaseless intervention in and dominion of our universe. Even if 'we should allow such attraction to be natural and essential to all matter', held Bentley, yet the atoms of matter could never cohere so as to 'form the present system; or if they could form it, it could neither acquire such motions, nor continue permanent in this state, without the power and providence of a divine being'.[55] The same considerations applied to the origin and reproduction of life. For Newtonians, mechanical causes had no place in explaining the origins of life and Spinozists were mistaken in thinking the 'matter of which an egg consists doth entirely constitute the young one', as Clarke tried to substantiate by invoking the evidence of microscopes to prove the matter of an egg actually provides little or nothing of the body of the living creature 'but only serves it for nourishment and growth'.[56]

[50] Klever, *Mannen Rond Spinoza*, 160–3.

[51] *DEBPh* ii. 650.

[52] Bentley, *Folly of Atheism*, ii. 31; Jacob, 'John Toland', 321–4.

[53] Vilain, 'Espace et dynamique', 21–2.

[54] Maupertuis, *Œuvres*, ii. 239–40; Jacob, 'John Toland', 320–1, 323; Force, 'Breakdown', 147–8; Porter, *Enlightenment*, 135–7.

[55] Bentley, *Folly of Atheism*, vii. 21.

[56] Ibid.; Shapin, *Scientific Revolution*, 157–8.

Externality of motion to matter was one of the most essential aspects of Newton's system. For such an ontological dualism of body and spirit, passivity and force, as Clarke and Wollaston stressed, is necessary if one asserts 'free will', the liberty of the human agent, in a universe ruled by general laws; and 'free will' is indispensable if one claims the absoluteness of good and evil which is likewise requisite if, like the Newtonians, one argues that we can, without revelation, ascertain the existence of an omniscient and omnipotent Deity who actively governs the cosmos.[57] For this reason, Newton and Clarke continually reaffirm, against Leibniz, the principles of absolute time and space, their concepts of 'gravitation' and 'force' requiring, they saw, a fixed frame of reference within which the Creator's 'general providence' operates.[58] Indivisible space is thus taken for granted, indeed expressly asserted by Newton and Clarke, to be one of God's attributes, His 'duration' reaching 'from eternity to eternity; His presence from infinity to infinity'.[59]

Man then, held the Newtonians, dwells in a divinely ordered universe relying on perpetual divine supervision to avoid collapsing into chaos, a structurally unified system which can only be rightly comprehended by a 'philosophy'—in fact, a 'system' which is simultaneously mathematical, ethical, historical, and theological.[60] Newton held that 'a continual miracle is needed to prevent the sun and fixed stars from rushing together through gravity', the constant intervention of the *manus emendatrix* of God, a tenet vigorously seconded by Clarke and William Whiston (1667–1752) as well as Wollaston.[61] In a host of other ways too, the lives of men are universally subject to divine governance. The point of studying biblical prophecy, on which Newton expended immense labour throughout his life, poring over Bibles in Greek, Latin, and Hebrew as well as English and French, and closely examining explanations in the Church Fathers, was precisely to comprehend God's peerless dominion over Man and his history.[62] Indeed, chronology and history in Newton's system, even matter itself as we see from his lifelong obsession with alchemy, was no more secularized than was his physics or astronomy. God, to his mind, exerts a ceaseless rule and judgement over men's activities just as he perennially exercises his 'general providence' to maintain the universe.

While Newton and his followers asserted the permanent miracle of gravitation and the general laws of the universe, accounting God a 'universal ruler' who mostly, in Newton's words, 'was confined to working through natural causes',[63] an apparent constraint on divine omnipotence that worried some, Newtonians were often less willing to speak about miracles in the normal sense of interruptions

57 Wollaston, *Religion of Nature*, 186–91; Clarke, *Demonstration*, 63–4, 74–5, Harris, *Liberty and Necessity*, 58–9; Rogers, 'Science and Philosophy', 45–6.

58 Rogers, 'Science and Philosophy', 45–6, 54–6.

59 Newton, *Mathematical Principles*, ii. 389; Jacob, 'John Toland', 320; Kors (ed.), *Encyclopedia*, i. 256.

60 Voltaire, *Lettres philosophiques*, 118–23; Markley, *Fallen Languages*, 141; Porter, *Enlightenment*, 138.

61 Quoted in Force, 'Breakdown', 147; Wollaston, *Religion of Nature*, 79; Ehrard, *L'Idée*, 175.

62 Force, 'Newton's God of Dominion', 80–1; Markley, *Fallen Languages*, 158–9, 177.

63 Zakai, *Jonathan Edwards's Philosophy*, 103–4.

in the ordinary course of nature. Assuredly, they left room for miracles, and Newton, Clarke, and Bentley, like Locke, were particularly insistent on the authenticity of Christ's miracles. Even so, in however qualified a manner, the tendency to distance themselves from specific miracles, including in some degree Christ's, led gradually to a lessening of emphasis in Newtonian discourse on Christ's unique role and Christology generally. Upholders of traditional religious values had good reason to suspect a corrosive element in Newtonianism apt to sap genuine religious fervour. 'It is beyond doubt', remarked Jonathan Edwards, at Yale, 'that too much weight has been laid, by many persons of late, on discoveries of God's greatness, awful majesty, and natural perfection', for anyone can easily have what he termed 'a sense of the natural perfections of God' without this really humbling the hearts of men, or tending to 'wean them from the world, draw them to God, and effectually change them'. While endorsing the Newtonian view that 'gravity depends immediately on the divine influence', Edwards who put much stress on the efficacy (in contrary directions) of both Satan and angels, found it impossible to approve of Newtonianism as such. For as he saw it, 'their discoveries have worked in a way contrary to the operation of truly spiritual discoveries'.[64] Hence, while Newtonianism was widely held to reinforce the claims of both Christianity and 'natural religion', there was an important sense in which it also inhibited traditional religious fervour and what Edwards calls 'spiritual understanding', meaning the 'moral beauty of divine things' and especially the 'beauty of the way of salvation by Christ'.

This desacralizing Deistic tendency innate in Newtoniansim was then further accentuated in Wollaston's *The Religion of Nature Delineated* (1724), a best-seller which sold over 10,000 copies and admitted that the reality of specific miracles, and God's 'particular providence' affecting individual men, is much harder to prove than demonstrating 'general providence'.[65] While avoiding mention of Newton, Wollaston adopted most of his system in a modified and soon highly influential form which substantially prefigures Voltaire, one which is distinctly Deistic rather than Christian in tone and from which not only is particular, as distinct from general, providence largely discarded but so is virtually all reference to revelation, Original Sin, redemption, and, indeed, Christ.[66] In this reworked, more streamlined, but also more Deistic version of Newtonianism, the rules of morality, like the laws of nature, are still divinely decreed but are now ascertainable purely through reason rather than communicated by revelation.

Consequently, Newtonianism which initially appeared to be a great, overarching new synthesis binding science, philosophy, history, and Christian theology into a vastly impressive and wondrous new unity, a tightly governed intellectual empire capable of dominating whole continents, in fact revealed signs of

[64] Edwards, *Religious Affections*, 190–2, 198; Marsden, *Jonathan Edwards*, 70–4.

[65] Marsden, *Jonathan Edwards*, 110–11, 154–5; Markley, *Fallen Languages*, 98; Porter, *Enlightenment*, 112.

[66] *DEBPh* ii. 971.

profound internal fissures. While most accepted the assurances of Newton, Bentley, and Clarke that science and religion had now been brought into perfect accord, the published Boyle Lectures, the famous series set up in 1692 under Boyle's will and for many years the principal organ for propagating physico-theological Newtonianism in Britain, Ireland, and America, not infrequently seem to have induced in intellectually rigorous readers the opposite effect to that intended. Hence, the young Benjamin Franklin (1706–90), perusing extracts of the Lectures in Boston in the early 1720s, found the 'arguments of the Deists which were quoted to be refuted, appeared to me much stronger than the refutations', attributing his own defection from Christianity to Deism to that encounter.[67] Remarkably, Hume later assured Boswell that reading Clarke had precisely the same effect on him.

There was substantial opposition, then, from the outset to the Newtonian synthesis of science and religion from various directions. Leibniz's critique of Newton's dynamics and complaint that 'M. Newton and his followers believe that God has made his machine so badly that unless he affects it by some extraordinary means, the watch will very soon cease to go',[68] was echoed by the radical German writer and amateur scientist Johann Konrad Franz von Hatzfeld, whose first book attacking Newton and the Newtonians, *The Case of the Learned* (1724), so antagonized members of the Royal Society—he claimed it was formally burnt—that their displeasure contributed to his departure from England soon afterwards.[69] Hatzfeld claimed to have conducted experiments with wheels and weights disproving Newton's dynamics and accused 'Sir Isaac Newton, and his like' of 'denying God to have foreseen, or made provision of all what is necessary in the world, as they do by pretending God to have produced it in such an hyperfection, as not to be able to subsist the least space of time, without His immediate and continual assistance'.[70] The Newtonians' denial that gravity 'be essential to matter', in his opinion, was an error which lands ' 'em into all sorts of absurdities and contradictions', encouraging atheistic conclusions.[71] Back on the Continent, Hatzfeld tried to enlist 's-Gravesande's support for his anti-Newtonian ideas and 'inventions' and later, in Germany, equally unsuccessfully approached Wolff,[72] though this did not prevent his later claiming to have Wolff's support, in his second book, published at The Hague in 1745. Here he restates his anti-Newtonian thesis, claiming that Newton's denial that gravity is an essential property of bodies turns God into the author of all evil 'because he makes Him the immediate cause of all the effects produced in the material world from which one must conclude that He is also the immediate cause of all the effects in the spiritual world'.[73]

67 Franklin, *Autobiography*, 113–14; Morgan, *Benjamin Franklin*, 16–17.

68 *Leibniz–Clarke Correspondence*, 185.

69 ARH Hof van Holland 5454/13, art. 28, hearing 16 Nov. 1745; Tortarolo, 'Hatzfeld', 815–16.

70 [Hatzfeld], *Case of the Learned*, 6–7, 23, 25, 29; [Hatzfeld], *Découverte de la vérité*, 213–14.

71 [Hatzfeld], *Case of the Learned*, 16–17.

72 ARH Hof van Holland 5454/13, fos. 18–19, 29.

73 [Hatzfeld], *Découverte de la vérité*, 165.

2. FROM 'S-GRAVESANDE TO D'ALEMBERT (1720–1750)

The pivotal figure in continental Newtonianism through the 1720s and 1730s down to the appearance of Voltaire's *Élémens de la philosophie de Neuton* (1738) was Willem Jacob 's-Gravesande (1688–1742), professor of physics at Leiden from 1717. 's-Gravesande, who during his visit to England in 1715–16 had met Newton and been elected a Fellow of the Royal Society, and who by that date was recognized as pre-eminent in Dutch science, was initially regarded as an orthodox Newtonian and continued to be for a time,[74] following the publication in 1719 of his general handbook on Newtonian physics, a work rendered into English by Keill the following year. The second most eminent experimental natural philosopher of the Netherlands at this time, Petrus van Musschenbroek (1692–1761), who had also met Newton (in 1717), and from 1723 was based at Utrecht, likewise came out publicly as a Newtonian. But before long, the alliance between these men and the Royal Society in London—like that between Huygens and Leibniz and the Royal Society previously—began to deteriorate owing, in particular, to disagreements concerning the so-called *vis viva* controversy (or 'la Querelle des forces vives'), the disagreement between Newton (agreeing here with the French Cartesians) and Leibniz (again relying partly on the insights of Huygens)[75] concerning the concept of 'force' which persisted long after Leibniz's death in 1716.

Ever since publishing his view of *forces vives* in the Leipzig *Acta eruditorum* for 1686, Leibniz had criticized first the Cartesians, and later the Newtonians, for confusing movement with force and ignoring the existence of the autonomous energy in matter. 's-Gravesande had become involved in this imbroglio after visiting Hesse-Cassel in 1721, where he witnessed the so-called 'perpetual motion machine' devised by the Saxon engineer Ernst Elias Bessler (alias Offyreus).[76] Following experiments of his own in 1722 with dropping copper balls of differing weights in a ratio of three, two, and one down inclined grooves into potter's clay, to assess acceleration and impact, he concluded Newton's account of dynamic force in moving objects was indeed mistaken. He now accepted that 'force' was not proportional to the speed of objects as the Newtonians held but, rather, as Leibniz contended, proportional 'to the square of its speed', so that a body accelerating to double its previous velocity actually quadruples its 'force'.[77] This view, which Kant in 1747 declared to be in general 'false',[78] was also adopted by Musschenbroek, an experimentalist highly reputed in Germany, and in 1747 dubbed by the young

[74] Mijnhardt, 'Dutch Enlightenment', 203, Israel, *Dutch Republic*, 1042; Vermij, *Calvinist Copernicans*, 337–9, 341.

[75] D'Alembert, *Traité de dynamique*, 253; d'Alembert, 'Éloge historique', 56–7; Barbour, *Absolute or Relative Motion?*, 475, 504–5.

[76] Allamand, *Histoire*, pp. xxiv, xxiii; Gori, *Fondazione*, 115–16.

[77] De Clerq, *At the Sign*, 83–5; 's-Gravesande, *Essai*, 217, 228–9; d'Alembert, *Traité de dynamique*, preface p. xvii; Garber, 'Leibniz: Physics', 289–93; Barbour, *Absolute or Relative Motion?*, 503.

[78] Kant, *Gedanken*, 29 n., 139, 181.

Kant himself 'the greatest of the Naturalists of this age', as he explains in his *Beginselen der Natuurkunde* (1736), a work which appeared in German in 1747.[79] Where Musschenbroek, though, continued vigorously to support Newtonian physico-theology, the same is not true of 's-Gravesande.

's-Gravesande, then, early on contradicted Newton's doctrine that 'active impulsive force', as Clarke calls it, must be directly proportional to velocity, that is change in speed multiplied only by the bulk of the body.[80] Herewith he was dragged, somewhat against his will, into the long-standing quarrel over Leibniz's thesis that there is a 'live' force in bodies inherent in matter itself, which continued to agitate the scientific world of the time for two more decades. Body, held Leibnizians and Wolffians, here not unlike the materialists, is something which includes a principle of activity causing motion, the *vis viva*, or live force; this live force, for them, powerfully influences the dynamics of mass in motion, contradicting Newton's principles.

Though the master himself was now too old to respond, his entourage—Clarke, Pemberton, Eames, Desaguliers, and others—indignantly repudiated 's-Gravesande, accusing him of betraying the great Newton by conceiving of 'force' in the manner of Leibniz and by claiming (here against Leibniz, as well as Newton) that perpetual motion is theoretically possible, a position which Hatzfeld also held.[81] Clarke in particular denounced what he termed 's-Gravesande's efforts, in Leibniz's footsteps, 'to raise a dust of opposition to Sir Isaac Newton's philosophy' by insisting 'with great eagerness, upon a principle which subverts all science', and wholly undermines the Newtonian conception of matter as 'lifeless, void of motivity, unactive and inert', by conceding the innateness of motion in matter.[82] Presumably, Clarke was not unaware of 's-Gravesande's Deistic tendencies and scepticism about miracles. It is possible that he seriously believed that 's-Gravesande aimed to subvert Newton's legacy.

While 's-Gravesande reacted coolly, adamantly refusing to accept he was not a 'Newtonian', and claiming to be purely inductive in his scientific methods which surely Sir Isaac would approve of, in fact he entertained growing doubts about not only Newton's dynamics but also other aspects of his system and came to share much of Leibniz's scepticism about Newton's so-called 'mathematicism', or acceptance of the absolute correspondence of mathematical models and language to the time-space cosmic frame. Worse still, in the eyes of Newtonians, he became increasingly reluctant to underwrite the physico-theology so powerfully urged by Newton, Clarke, and Bentley, refusing to see why Newton's laws of gravitation, like the other laws of nature 'si constantes et si générales', should be dogmatically held to be 'miracles', or a 'direct emanation of God', as the Newtonians asserted,

79 Kant, *Gedanken*, 118, 172–5.

80 De Pater, 'Inleiding', 19; Beeson, 'Il n'y a pas d'amour', 905; Barbour, *Absolute or Relative Motion?*, 505.

81 Allamand, *Histoire*, pp. xv–xvii; Gori, *Fondazione*, 296; Tortarolo, 'Hatzfeld'.

82 Tortarolo, 'Hatzfeld', 118, 300–1; 's-Gravesande, *Œuvres philosophiques*, i. 252.

and here once again deferred to the Leibnizians (and Fontenelle) in refusing to acknowledge any such 'occult qualities'.[83]

At the university, without attacking Newton, he invariably presented his physics, and demonstrations, being the products of observations and sense, as something resembling the moral certainties applying in human life rather than the absolute certainties defined by mathematics. The notion of exactitude and certainty in science, he argued, should be conceived not as a sort of mirror but merely as an expedient tool and approximation to physical reality. In this way, 's-Gravesande retreated to what might be termed a pure experimental empiricism such as that postulated earlier by Huygens and other post-Cartesians, that is one theoretically detached from Boyle's, Newton's, and Locke's theological premisses, simply maintaining we know nothing about any substance.[84] This was a stance which seemed to make 's-Gravesande's physics neutral as between the materialists and anti-materialists.

Being a highly experimental physicist and mathematician in his own right, someone whose air-pressure pumps and other scientific instruments, manufactured with the help of the Musschenbroek workshop in Leiden, were renowned all over Europe, 's-Gravesande remained through the 1730s far better equipped than Voltaire—who came to sit in on his lectures during his third visit to Holland, in 1737[85]—to preside over the further propagation of Newtonian methods and the new techniques of teaching and conducting experiments in physics, remaining a respected and influential figure in which he was aided by his fluency in French. But in his philosophical writings, 's-Gravesande, much more than Voltaire, tended to depart from the authentic spirit of Newtonianism, in particular by stressing the centrality of proportionate mechanical cause and effect, as expressed mathematically, in all the workings of nature,[86] and formulating propositions in a way which tended to erode Newton's physico-theological ontological duality of reality based on segregating matter and motion, body and soul, and the necessary from the contingent.

Abandoning physico-theology led 's-Gravesande more or less inevitably into conflict with Clarke; for he appeared to be adopting philosophical principles and a conception of nature which thoroughly blurred the line between the 'materialists' and the 'Christian mathematicians'. A particularly controversial aspect of his speculative work was an argument which figured in his *Introductio* to philosophy of 1736, which appeared to undermine, or at least threaten, the doctrine of free will and raise awkward questions about the Cartesian-Newtonian claim that body and mind cannot interact. He argued that philosophically one cannot avoid ascribing 'necessity' to human decisions, motives, and actions but that the ontological

[83] 's-Gravesande, *Œuvres philosophiques*, 92–4; Ferrone, *Intellectual Roots*, 231–2; Mamiani, 'Rivoluzione incompiuta', 43.

[84] 's-Gravesande, *Œuvres philosophiques*, i. 126, 129; [Lelarge de Lignac], *Élémens*, 237–8, 313.

[85] Vercruysse, *Voltaire et la Hollande*, 36–7, 127.

[86] Vanpaemel, 'Culture of Mathematics', 207–11.

distinction between body and mind is still retained if one distinguishes meticulously between 'la nécessité physique, ou fatale' and 'la nécessité morale'. Some readers, though, judged this to be a devious method of dismantling Locke's and Newton's (as well as Descartes's) dualism altogether.[87] Though he insisted that his aim was merely to clarify the concept of physical 'certainty' in science, suspicion that he was surreptitiously abolishing the distinction between body and soul, and between necessary and free,[88] prompted a campaign of smear and insinuation against him instigated reportedly (if somewhat paradoxically) by hard-line Calvinist divines committed to predestination. In any case, he was publicly accused of 'Spinozism' despite his expressly stating that he believed absolutely in the immortality and immateriality of the soul.[89]

While freedom of the will, plainly, cannot be reconciled with 'la nécessité physique', such as applies in the laws of physics mathematically expressed, it can be combined, held 's-Gravesande, with 'la nécessité morale'.[90] He was not endangering the real distinction between free will and 'necessity' by invoking the necessity by which the mind acts, because in any case something 'contingent' God has foreseen must necessarily happen, despite its being contingent, without this in any way detracting from God's free will, or Man's duty and obligation.[91] Such a distinction, moreover, was requisite, he urged, because something has to cause every determination of the human will, without exception, and the motive which always determines our choice, or decision, is the inevitability of our choosing that which seems best to us. However difficult a decision may be, it is impossible not to choose what seems, on balance, 'le meilleur', meaning what is most likely to conserve our being and advantages. Hence, in contrast to Leibniz who distinguishes between free souls and mechanically determined bodies even though, by divine decree, the two converge harmoniously to produce human actions, 's-Gravesande contends, here closer to Bayle and Spinoza, every human volition is mechanically determined albeit supposedly without this implying our will is not free.

's-Gravesande rejects what he considers the common error 'd'envisager toute nécessité comme si elle étoit fatale'. To prove he was not echoing Spinoza's denial that human liberty is contradicted by necessitarianism, he asks the reader to imagine a man locked in a room from where there is no way of escape: he wants to exit but is forced to remain: 'cette contrainte est physique.'[92] But if we then suppose the cell has an open window which, however, overlooks a sheer and unavoidable precipice ensuring certain death were one to climb out, the case, philosophically, is altered. Again the prisoner is compelled to remain. But the form of compulsion is now different: it is no longer a physical obstacle: 'elle est devenu contrainte morale.'[93] Hence the mechanism regulating human decision-making, concludes

[87] 's-Gravesande, *Œuvres philosophiques*, ii. 8–9, 22; Allamand, *Histoire*, pp. xlvii–xlviii.

[88] Vanpaemel, 'Culture of Mathematics', 210–11; d'Argens, *Thérèse philosophe*, 19–23, 170; Gori, *Fondazione*, 149–51; De Pater, 'Inleiding', 33, 48–9, 51–2.

[89] Allamand, *Histoire*, pp. l–lii.

[90] 's-Gravesande, *Œuvres philosophiques*, ii. 21.

[91] 's-Gravesande, 'Rede', 66, 69.

[92] 's-Gravesande, *Œuvres philosophiques*, ii. 22.

[93] Ibid.

's-Gravesande, determines our actions no less than do physical processes, but we are wrong to infer that an intelligent being whose actions are determined therefore resembles a clock whose movements 'sont les conséquences nécessaires de certaines loix de méchanique'.[94]

This distinction between physical and moral 'nécessité', claimed 's-Gravesande, rescues the well-intentioned philosopher from the irresolvable contradictions and pitfalls generated by the self-contradictory views of Descartes, Malebranche, Leibniz, and (by implication) Newton without entrapping him in Spinozism. But it was insufficiently clear how it enables one to avoid the trap. Like many others, 's-Gravesande construed Spinozism as an ancient tendency long preceded, as regards necessity and liberty, by Stoicism, as well, he affirms, as by 'les Mahometans'.[95] A tract appeared at this point, sometimes attributed to the Dutch Huguenot radical bookseller Jean-Frédéric Bernard, disputing his reasoning, and implying the charge that he was a crypto-Spinozist was justified. This anonymous author praises his contributions to experimental science and unwillingness to be distracted by metaphysical speculations, something which had signally contributed, he says, to ridding mankind of the doctrines equally 'étranges et incompréhensibles' of Malebranche and Leibniz, but then questions whether he is really a Newtonian, since his theory of mind, on examination, turns out to be indistinguishable from that of 'Spinoza et Hobbes'.[96] 'Il me semble, Monsieur', he continued, that your distinction between physical necessity and moral necessity is a wholly unreal one which consists 'seulement en paroles, n'y ayant au fond aucune différence réelle'.

What difference does it make, he objects, whether I am constrained by pulleys or bars or considerations, motives, or emotions which 'déterminent nécessairement ma volonté'? Since 's-Gravesande acknowledges that every intelligent creature is 'déterminé par la volonté', he cannot deny, other than rhetorically, that the will is therefore determined by 'une nécessité aussi inévitable' as is the equilibrium of balanced scales upset by adding a weight to one side.[97] Philosophically, 's-Gravesande was on a path very different from that he professed to be taking: if outside causes work on us no less effectively, and in the same way, as one body impacts on another, and if we are moved by desires and inclinations unaware of this causation, are we not 'véritablement et en effet tels que l'homme de Spinoza?'[98] As far as he could see, he concludes, there did not seem to be any real difference between 'la fatalité Spinoziste ou Mahometane et la votre'.[99]

'Spinoza est clair et précis', the author reminds 's-Gravesande, quoting proposition XXIX of part i of the *Ethics*: 'nullum datur contingens, sed omnia ex necessitate naturae divinae determinata sunt, ad certo modo existendum et operandum' [There is nothing contingent, but all things are determined by the necessity of the

[94] Ibid. ii. 23; De Pater, 'Inleiding', 34.
[95] 's-Gravesande, *Œuvres philosophiques*, ii. 22–4.
[96] [Bernard?], *Lettre à Monsieur G. J. 's-Gravesande*, 7–8.
[97] Ibid. 10–11; De Pater, 'Inleiding', 33–4.
[98] [Bernard?], *Lettre à Monsieur G. J. 's Gravesande*, 18.
[99] Ibid. 20; Gori, *Fondazione*, 152–3.

divine nature to exist and to function in a certain way].[100] 's-Gravesande claims to venerate Newton, and admire his natural philosophy. But the whole edifice of Newtonianism collapses if 's-Gravesande's deviations from Newton's system of cause and effect and views on the human will are endorsed, 'et par conséquent nous serons encore dans le Spinozisme'.[101]

Hence, the philosophical packaging 's-Gravesande wrapped around Newtonian physics came to be recognized as being at certain points crucially distinct from Newton's. While scholars (including myself) have mostly taken him at his word in proclaiming the centrality of divine providence in regulation of the universe, and warning students against Spinoza whose ideas he calls 'très dangereuses' and whose notion of geometric reasoning he scornfully dismisses,[102] and therefore in taking his anti-Spinozism and loyalty to Newton's legacy seriously, aspects of his teaching nevertheless seem to have helped undermine the cardinal Newtonian principle that motion is external to matter, that material impulse, as Newton and Clarke insisted, 'is not the cause of gravity'. Also, in abstaining from Clarke's claims that it had 'been demonstrated even mathematically, that gravitation cannot arise from the configuration and texture of the parts of matter, and from the circumambient impelling bodies', and that therefore, 'some Being that is not material . . . must of necessity be allowed to be the cause of it',[103] 's-Gravesande was effectively lending covert support to the anti-Newtonian critique of the Leibnizians, materialists, and Spinozists.

More emphatically anti-Newtonian than 's-Gravesande, and also important as a bridge between the Cartesio-Leibnizian critique of Newton and the French High Enlightenment,[104] was the stance of the Swiss mathematician and engineer Johann (Jean) Bernoulli (1667–1748), from Basel. Bernoulli had taught in the years 1695–1705 at Groningen where, as we have seen, he clashed with the traditionalist Calvinist bloc, particularly in the 1699 dispute over nutrition and digestion, during which he was publicly accused of Spinozism. At that time, he adhered, as he continued to do later, to a strict Cartesian dichotomy of mind and body, claiming in his *Spinozismi depulsionis echo* (Groningen, 1702) that Cartesianism was a much better barrier to Spinozism than claims that body and soul do interact.[105]

Bernoulli aligned with Huygens and Leibniz against Newton in the dispute about *forces vives* albeit erroneously, according to Kant whose first published work, in 1747, was devoted to refereeing the *forces vives* controversy from a basically pro-Newtonian perspective.[106] After Leibniz's death, in 1716, Bernoulli vigorously pursued Leibniz's quarrel with the English Newtonians, indeed, quipped d'Alembert,

[100] [Bernard?], *Lettre à Monsieur G. J. 's Gravesande*, 20; *Collected Works of Spinoza*, i. 433; Spinoza, *Ethics*, ed. Parkinson, 99; Klever, *Ethicom*, 67.

[101] [Bernard?], *Lettre à Monsieur G. J. 's Gravesande*, 23; 's-Gravesande, 'Rede', 70.

[102] 's-Gravesande, *Œuvres philosophiques*, ii. 22, 355; Mijnhardt, 'Dutch Enlightenment', 203.

[103] Clarke, *A Third Defense*, 846.

[104] D'Alembert, 'Éloge historique', 42, 59–60.

[105] Ibid. 33–6; Israel, *Radical Enlightenment*, 437–9.

[106] Kant, *Gedanken*, 57, 112–13, 150–1.

'avec Angleterre' itself, as well as opposing Newton on the question of magnetism.[107] Denouncing Newtonianism as a science 'obscure et insuffisante', in 1730 he published a prize-winning essay on celestial mechanics and elliptical orbits, vainly attempting, like Fontenelle, to rescue Descartes's vortex theory of 'propulsion' as the vital principle of the cosmos rather than 'attraction'. His main importance, though, lay in his sophisticated application of mathematics to dynamics which proved to be one of the main influences on the approach of d'Alembert himself who, in 1748, delivered a fifty-five-page 'éloge' in his memory in which he admitted having originally acquired his own concept of dynamics from him.[108]

's-Gravesande's subtle revisions with Leibnizian adjustments, and Bernoulli's more explicit anti-Newtonianism, then, contradicted Newtonian doctrine at crucial points. Where Locke and the Newtonians grounded their systems on divine providence, 's-Gravesande and Bernoulli effectively removed the appeal to God's dominion of the world; where Locke and the Newtonians drastically limited the scope of philosophy, 's-Gravesande undid this part of their work, claiming the natural philosopher not only expounds physics but also connects science to the moral and human sphere.[109] Despite the continuing strength of Newtonian physico-theology and MacLaurin's tireless but inconclusive efforts to refute Leibniz's, Bernoulli's, and 's-Gravesande's account of 'force' mathematically,[110] restoring exact proportionality of movement to force, ontological externality of force to matter, and mathematics to the essence of reality, cracks were undoubtedly appearing in Newton's overarching system fusing science and theology together.

In its wider, philosophical sense, as a system of physico-theology, Newtonianism was, by the 1740s, doubtless losing something of its earlier hegemony even in Britain. After Martin Folkes became president of the Royal Society in 1741, reportedly, a noticeable change set in in the outlook of members of the society with a growing divorce between science and religion, a wider propagation of scepticism, and more of what the Newtonian William Stukeley, rector of St George's, Bloomsbury, called 'the infidel system'.[111] Though little notice was taken of his publications at first, by the late 1740s Newtonians and followers of Locke also had to fend off Hume's witheringly sceptical essays 'Of a Particular Providence' and 'Of Miracles', sallies distinctly unsettling for Newtonians as well as Lockeans even if not altogether incompatible, ultimately, with Newtonian physico-theology and the 'argument from design'.

In France, meanwhile, dissolution of Newtonian physico-theology proceeded rather faster. In 1746, Diderot still deemed the works of Newton a convincing proof 'de l'existence d'un Être souverainement intelligent'.[112] But through a process of

[107] D'Alembert, *Traité de dynamique*, 253; d'Alembert, 'Éloge historique', 49–50, 56–7; Walters, 'Querelle', 199.

[108] D'Alembert, 'Éloge historique', 11; Spallanzani, *Immagini*, 114–15; Gaukroger, *Descartes' System*, 159, 173–5.

[109] Gori, *Fondazione*, 70.

[110] D'Alembert, *Traité de dynamique*, preface p. xviii.

[111] Force, 'Breakdown', 151.

[112] Diderot, *Pensées philosophiques*, pensée XVIII; Quintili, *Pensée critique*, 95; Duflo, *Diderot philosophe*, 107–10.

intense debate with his fellow *philosophes*, reading, and inner wrestling, he soon abandoned this view. Partly, this was because he saw Newtonianism as cogent regarding divine intervention in nature but less so in matters of human life and morality, and partly because he became philosophically more attracted to monist and hylozoic explanations. But at the same time, as we shall see, the progress of science itself contributed to toppling Newtonianism, by 1747 at the latest, in the mind of the chief editor of the *Encyclopédie*. For it seemed to him, encouraged no doubt by Buffon's materialism, post-1749 anti-mathematicism, and other strands of anti-Newtonianism,[113] that recent discoveries in French biology and fossil science broadly contradicted the principles of the Newtonians.

Diderot, moreover, preoccupied with the life sciences rather than physics, and with humanity more than with the inanimate, evinced an instinctive anti-mathematicism, to be strongly reflected in his *De l'interprétation de la nature* (1753), as well as his lingering disagreements with d'Alembert. By the time the *Encyclopédie*'s first volume appeared, in 1751, Diderot had come to the astounding conclusion—not one of his profounder insights—that the reign of mathematics was now over and biology in the manner of Buffon had become the presiding model in science.[114] If his rebellion against English ideas was reinforced by the (incorrect) impression that the Newtonians were wholly in error on the issue of *forces vives*, and Leibnizian ideas on the retention of force in matter wholly correct, his anti-Newtonianism seems to have been principally driven by reluctance to concede the centrality of mathematics in natural philosophy, general philosophy, and understanding the reality of the human condition. By the late 1740s, Diderot had in any case emerged as the supreme anti-Newtonian of the High Enlightenment.[115]

113 Roger, *Buffon*, 43, 57–8, 196–7; Larrère, 'D'Alembert and Diderot', 78–9, 82.
114 Larrère, 'D'Alembert and Diderot', 75, 92–4; Diderot, *De l'interprétation de la nature*, 180–1.
115 Cherni, *Diderot*, 226–7; Fauvergue, 'Diderot', 122–3.

Part III

Political Emancipation

9

Anti-Hobbesianism and the Making of 'Modernity'

Diderot was a philosopher of both Man and nature; yet perhaps, ultimately, more of Man than of nature. In any case, social, moral, and aesthetic thought were at the heart of his concerns. Though firmly hostile to Hobbes's anti-democratic stance, in his article on 'Hobbes' for the *Encyclopédie*, Diderot was far from wholly unsympathetic to his general aims, motives, and philosophy. He excuses Hobbes's to his mind overly negative depiction of the state of nature as due to the unusually grim situation facing England during the years he wrote his *De cive* (1642) and *Leviathan* (1651). He praises Hobbes's honesty and insight, and his devising a system which, despite its averred loyalty to revealed religion, seemed to him to be a form of atheistic materialism, that is, something of which (from 1747) he entirely approved. Yet despite these positive and mitigating features, Diderot in the end felt Hobbes erred badly owing to an excessively pessimistic view of humanity: taking a particularly menacing set of circumstances 'pour les règles invariables de la nature', he sums up, he became 'l'agresseur de l'humanité et l'apologiste de la tyrannie'.[1]

Especially in the article 'Citoyen' in the *Encyclopédie*, Diderot strongly objects to Hobbes's refusal to acknowledge any difference between a 'citizen' and a 'subject', and his doctrine that the citizen owes unconditional obedience to the state; equally Diderot expresses antipathy to Hobbes's view that the sovereign may justly deny freedom of expression to his subjects.[2] Anti-Hobbesianism, moreover, that is a deep-seated aversion to Hobbes's anti-libertarianism, anti-republicanism, and scorn for democracy, as well as a general suspicion of his moral philosophy and idea that the 'state of nature is a state of war of all against all', had to a degree always been integral to the Radical Enlightenment from its commencement with the advent of Dutch democratic republicanism, in the work of Johan de La Court, Franciscus van den Enden, and Spinoza, down to the French republican political thought of Boulainvilliers and the young Mably.

[1] Diderot, art. 'Hobbisme, Diderot and d'Alembert', in *Encyclopédie*, viii. 233; Schröder, 'Liberté et pouvoir', 147; Duflo, *Diderot philosophe*, 400, 462, 507–8.

[2] Glaziou, *Hobbes en France*, 142, 147–9; Proust, *Diderot*, 343–4, 427–30; Skinner, *Reason and Rhetoric*, 285–6.

Nevertheless, it is undeniable that major components had been, and continued to be, detached by radical thinkers from Hobbes's system, and perhaps especially his notion that 'democracy' is the first kind of instituted commonwealth 'in order of time' and his doctrine that sovereignty, after the making of the state, is what has been called the 'aggregate of private wills', an idea afterwards centrally adopted by Spinoza. This extracted, more equitable, 'democratic Hobbesianism' to no small degree helped define and refine the theoretical apparatus of the early modern democratic republicans, and hence of the Radical Enlightenment as a whole.[3] James Harrington was certainly not alone among early modern republicans in noting that 'Mr Hobbes holdeth democracy to be of all governments the first in modern order of time.'[4] Furthermore, this has been part of the justification of what in recent decades has developed into an important theme in history of political thought studies—the thesis that, for Hobbes, as it has been put, 'democracy was prior both chronologically and logically to other forms of government',[5] and that Hobbes's sovereign has what has been called 'an elective, republican character', so that, in short, 'Hobbes is the true ancestor of constitutional liberal democracy'.[6]

A founding genius of the New Philosophy, Hobbes fully shared with Descartes, as well as the great thinkers of the radical tradition, like Spinoza, Bayle, and Diderot, a new, practical, and totalizing conception of what philosophy is: its purpose, for Hobbes, like these other thinkers, is to demonstrate, advocate, and promote what is necessary for the preserving and enhancement of human life.[7] Hence, it is—or should be—chiefly concerned with grasping and improving the overall architecture and existing arrangement of everything, that is society, politics, and all that is, and, consequently, is always and at all times (whether men recognize this or not) the pre-eminent intellectual discipline. Hence, Hobbes endeavoured to adjust morality, politics, society, and knowledge generally, in ways which would help secure and stabilize human societies.

Radical authors, then, while mostly viewing Hobbes as an apologist for tyranny, calumniator of republican assemblies, champion of censorship, and a thinker who had drawn an excessively pessimistic picture of natural humanity, and especially its proneness to aggression and conflict, consistently did so in a curiously equivocal, even paradoxical, way, hardly ever altogether disowning him and his system, and often betraying an unmistakably strong sympathy for elements of his thought and writing. As Anthony Collins remarked, however much free thinkers disapproved of what he terms Hobbes's 'High-Church Politicks', meaning his compliant views on ecclesiastical authority and book censorship, as well as monarchical sovereignty, and other 'false opinions', there was no denying Hobbes was what he approvingly styles a 'great influence of learning, virtue and free-thinking'.[8]

[3] Goldie, 'Reception of Hobbes', 603; Malcolm, *Aspects of Hobbes* 37–8; Borrelli, 'Hobbes e la teoria', 243, 262; Hoekstra, 'Lion in the House', section IV, forthcoming.

[4] See Hoekstra, 'Lion in the House', section IV, forthcoming.

[5] Tuck, *Philosophy and Government*, 310.

[6] Ibid. 316; Coleman, *Hobbes and America*, 3; Hoekstra, 'Lion in the House', section IV, forthcoming.

[7] Hoekstra, 'Hobbes on Law', 119.

[8] Collins, *Discourse of Free-Thinking*, 152; Israel, *Radical Enlightenment*, 602; Taranto, *Du déisme à l'athéisme*, 91, 105–6.

Rejection of many—yet not all—of Hobbes's basic positions in morality, politics, and church government is, indeed, central to the radical tradition of thought. Radicati, whose democratic republicanism drew on Machiavelli, Sarpi, Sidney, and 'the ingenious Mr. Toland', besides Bayle and Spinoza, went furthest, of those writing before Rousseau, in assailing Hobbes's notion of the 'state of nature'. Envisaging the 'state of nature' as a utopia of primitive communism, not unlike Morelly, who later spoke of 'le doux empire de la nature et de la vérité',[9] Radicati insists, against Hobbes, that 'savages and brutes of the same species, that follow the laws of nature only, are more sociable among themselves than men that are civilized: since they live together with great kindness and cordiality, and observe the laws of equity in everything; each enjoying the fruits of the earth, and their females and suffering the rest to do so, without envy or ambition, being all equal, and having everything in common'.[10]

There were, of course, real and significant affinities between Hobbes's philosophy and Spinozism and elements specific to Hobbes's discussion of equality and democracy which were in their own right not just highly original but potentially inspiring and formative for advocates of radical thought. His image and reputation were then further tied to the Radical Enlightenment by the particular priorities of its enemies, at any rate during the late seventeenth and early eighteenth centuries. Since Hobbes was widely conceived to be a materialist, as he himself affirmed, and also, despite his avowals to the contrary, an atheist, Christian theologians took to coupling the names of Hobbes and Spinoza continually together, as an obvious step in their crusade against 'atheism', something which was bound to encourage radical thinkers like Bayle, Radicati, Diderot, and Mably, while continuing to repudiate Hobbes's views on major points, simultaneously to seek out what, to them, were his redeeming features. In this spirit Diderot remarks of Hobbes that if he was not an 'atheist' one has to admit that his God 'diffère peu de celui de Spinosa'.[11]

In particular, Hobbes was a key stimulus to the kind of 'anti-Scripturalism', materialism, and atheism which writers such as Bayle, Collins, and Diderot saw as integral to the radical attitudes they strove to propagate. Diderot, for all his criticism of Hobbes's views about society, hence warmly praises his metaphysics and epistemology, recognizing important elements here which he shared with Hobbes. For the latter, as for himself, Bayle, and Spinoza but not Descartes, Locke, or Hume, philosophy and science are ultimately the same thing, and simultaneously wholly separate from theology. To their minds, philosophy ascertains the overall architecture of reality while omitting nothing real which importantly affects the human condition by basing itself exclusively on knowledge gained through sense perception. In essence, it is the art of sound reasoning from premises derived from sensible experience about the structure of everything we know.[12] Consequently, for Hobbes

[9] [Morelly], *Basiliade*, i. 165.

[10] Ibid. 2, 18, 72–4; Radicati, *Twelve Discourses*, 32, 39; Venturi, *Alberto Radicati*, 198.

[11] Diderot, art. 'Hobbisme', in *Encyclopédie*, viii. 241.

[12] Curley, 'I durst not write', 575; Schneewind, *Invention of Autonomy*, 83–4; Garrett, *Meaning*, 103–4, 110.

no less than Spinoza, Bayle, or Diderot, philosophizing cannot be just a purely contemplative exercise. For the rational analysis of causes and connections naturally leads us to deploy knowledge so as 'to be able to produce, as far as matter and human force permit, such effects as human life requireth'.[13]

Hobbes's materialism, empiricism, and the fact that crucial practical conclusions follow from his stance clearly appealed to Diderot and the *encyclopédistes*. Applauding Hobbes's rejection of Cartesian dualism, Diderot remarks that the English thinker, flatly contradicting Descartes, was far from agreeing 'que la matière étoit incapable de penser'; where Descartes had famously said 'I think, therefore I am', Hobbes, observes Diderot, says 'je pense, donc la matière peut penser'.[14] But the feature of Hobbes's system that most of all appealed to radical minds, though rooted in his metaphysics, was at the same time an aspect of his political and social theory, namely that morality and law are not based on divinely given criteria but are purely social constructs, such that, as Diderot puts it, 'les loix de la société sont donc la seule mesure commune du bien et du mal'.[15]

A central feature of Hobbes's *De cive* (and the *Leviathan*), criticized from the moment the book appeared, and something diametrically opposed to radical views, was what one critic termed his desire to unite 'sovereign priesthood with princely power', thereby politicizing religion and reinforcing the sovereign in ways which seemed 'atheistic' to many theologians and struck radical writers as merely a formula for tightening the age-old alliance of throne and altar. At no point did Hobbes seem more obviously to be an agent of despotism. His 'consolidation of the right politic and ecclesiastic in Christian sovereigns' offended radical thinkers by placing in rulers' hands what Hobbes called 'all manner of power over their subjects that can be given to man for the government of men's external actions, both in policy and religion', and the responsibility for the making of all law. None was more repelled by this than Bayle for whom stripping the sovereign of divine right claims and theological justifications was paramount, a necessary prior condition for freedom of thought and conscience, the very foundation for formalized toleration which was the cornerstone of his political thought and which is wholly dissolved by Hobbes.[16]

Yet, once again, Bayle's account of Hobbes is no more predominantly a negative one than is Diderot's. As with most late seventeenth- and early eighteenth-century French authors, Hobbes was not in fact a particularly important source of reference or inspiration for Bayle despite the obvious similarities of their politics. Where Bayle's article on Spinoza is the longest in his *Dictionnaire*, and reveals something of his lifelong obsession with Spinoza, that devoted to Hobbes, even if still substantial

13 Hobbes, *Leviathan*, xlvi, para. i.

14 Diderot, art. 'Hobbisme', in *Encyclopédie*, viii. 233; Dedeyan, *Diderot*, 244.

15 Diderot, art. 'Hobbisme', in *Encyclopédie*, viii. 236; Schneewind, *Invention of Autonomy*, 88–9, 91–2.

16 Labrousse, *Pierre Bayle*, ii. 148, 478–9, 481–2; Goldie, 'Reception of Hobbes', 612–14; Tuck, *Philosophy and Government*, 333–4.

compared to those devoted to the other philosophers for whom Bayle provides entries, is nevertheless very brief by comparison. Hobbes did not have a comparable importance for Bayle to that of Spinoza; nevertheless, he treats him in some respects in an almost parallel fashion, especially when praising his character, viewing him, as the English translation of Bayle's *Dictionnaire* puts it, as a 'great observer of equity' while simultaneously stressing, like Diderot as early as his reworking of Shaftesbury in 1745, that he did not believe in God. Parts of Hobbes's system were clearly regarded by Bayle with considerable sympathy.[17]

Bayle's prime criticism of Hobbes—that he simply went too far in his preference for monarchy—is remarkable for someone who shared many of his strictures about democracy and republicanism. 'Hobbes was enrag'd against the principles of the Parlementarians', he observed, citing this as the reason he 'went to the other extreme, and taught that the authority of kings ought to have no limitation, and that in particular the externals of religion, as being the most fruitful cause of civil wars, ought to depend upon their will'.[18] Bayle noted in this connection that Hobbes's deployment of Thucydides seemed especially intended to inspire the English with a disgust for the republican spirit.[19] Thus, where Spinoza dismisses the English Revolution, and its succumbing to the dictatorship of Cromwell, as failure to face the problem of how to remove monarchy in more than in name, Hobbes deplores it in a quite different and clearly anti-democratic sense, concluding that the worst tyranny is that of popular assemblies. 'The democrats won', echoes Bayle, citing the (later) Latin version of the *Leviathan*, and they established a democracy; but they paid the price of their great crimes by losing it in no time at all. A single 'tyrant'—Hobbes does indeed have a notion of 'tyrant' despite famously denouncing those who abuse the notion of 'tyranny' to oppose rightful sovereigns—'seized control of England, Scotland and Ireland, and confounded their democratic principles (both that of the laity and that of the ecclesiastics)'.[20]

Early Enlightenment reactions to Hobbes confirm the aptness of the claim that 'eventually, the link with Spinoza would come to characterize the terms in which Hobbes was criticized and denounced: extreme naturalism (undermining faith in miracles), radical Biblical criticism (undermining faith in Revelation), and so on'.[21] To this one might add conflation of mind with matter, so prominent in Diderot's appraisal of the English thinker. The fact Hobbes was often for the first time dragged into discussion of such issues after 1670, and hence viewed differently from in the 1640s and 1650s, need not necessarily mean, of course, that Hobbes did not anticipate Spinoza in crucial respects any more than Radical Enlightenment

[17] Bayle, *An Historical and Critical Dictionary*, iii. 1680; Diderot, notes to Shaftesbury's *Essai*, 80; Malcolm, *Aspects of Hobbes*, 484; Duflo, *Diderot philosophe*, 400.

[18] Duflo, *Diderot philosophe*, 510–11; Bayle, *An Historical and Critical Dictionary*, iii. 1679; Schröder, 'Liberte et pouvoir', 154.

[19] Bayle, 'Hobbes', in McKenna (ed.) *Pierre Bayle: témoin*, 203; Hoekstra, 'Lion in the House', section II, forthcoming.

[20] Hobbes, *Leviathan*, xlvii (L), para. 29; Hoekstra, 'Tyrannus rex', 427–8, 433–4, 436.

[21] Malcolm, *Aspects of Hobbes*, 477–8, 480.

authors' partly negative view of Hobbes demonstrates that he did not significantly influence them. However, the contemporary evidence clearly shows that Hobbes played little—perhaps surprisingly little—direct part in the formation of the various materialist and atheistic systems prevalent in France during the Early Enlightenment period.

Indeed, between Bayle's death and the 1750s, Hobbes scarcely figured on the French philosophical horizon. Hardly any French thinkers of this period concerned themselves with Hobbes either as a general philosopher or as a potential democratic influence. Du Marsais does not discuss Hobbes in his atheistic and fiercely anti-Scripturalist *Examen de la religion* and neither does La Mettrie in his *Abrégé des systèmes*, a set of brief outlines of the major philosophical systems of the seventeenth century, or, very much, in his other writings.[22] Significantly, neither in his *Essay* of 1746, on the origin of human knowledge, nor in his highly influential *Traité des systêmes* (1749), a work in which he devotes separate closely argued chapters to demolishing what he perceives as the major systems of the recent past, especially those of Malebranche, Leibniz, and Spinoza, does Condillac show any concern with Hobbes, despite the close similarity of Hobbes's and Spinoza's sensationalist theories of 'perception'.

Condillac's chapter, 'Le Spinosisme refuté', the longest and most substantial of the forays in his *Traité des systêmes*, a section of over seventy pages where he goes all out to demolish Spinoza whose ideas he clearly acknowledges to be a major threat in France, seemingly makes no mention of Hobbes at all.[23] Hobbes, as far as we can see, was scarcely read by the French *philosophes* prior to Rousseau's discussion of him in the 1750s, and seems to have had very little to do with the genesis of the materialistic systems of Du Marsais, Boureau-Deslandes, La Mettrie, and Helvétius, or indeed Diderot, whose materialism, hylozoic monism, and atheism were all essentially formed by 1747 but whose initial engagement with Hobbes seems to date from relatively late on in his career, the mid 1750s.[24]

Admittedly, during the earlier, predominantly 'Dutch', phase of the Radical Enlightenment, Hobbes was, and was acknowledged to be, a much more substantial contributor to the formation of radical thought than he was subsequently, in France. Plainly, the brothers de La Court, Koerbagh, van den Enden, and Spinoza *did* read, absorb, and discuss Hobbes. Indeed, the translation and publication of the 1667 Dutch version of Hobbes's *Leviathan*, at Amsterdam, may be regarded as a deliberately subversive planned radical intervention by friends of Koerbagh.[25] But here too it is possible to question whether the influence of Hobbes, and the underlying affinities between Spinozism and Hobbism, were really so close as contemporary theologians were apt to claim. For churchmen hostile to the radical critique of revealed religion it was, after all, natural to highlight and encourage the perceived linkage of

[22] Vartanian, *La Mettrie's* L'Homme machine, 65; Wellman, *La Mettrie*, 339.
[23] Condillac, *Traité des systêmes*, 139–211.
[24] Glaziou, *Hobbes en France*, 198–200.
[25] Secretan, 'Réception de Hobbes', 28, 43; Israel, *Radical Enlightenment*, 186.

two thinkers whose names were both notorious and whom they were eager to blacken as much as possible especially since what these allegedly most had in common was precisely their perceived 'atheism', materialism, and 'anti-Scripturalism'.

Late seventeenth- and early eighteenth-century Lutheran divines such as Christian Kortholt at Kiel, Nathaniel Falck who defended the claims of demonology at Wittenberg in 1694, and Jakob Staalkopff who publicly refuted naturalism at Greifswald in 1707, not only regularly linked the names of Hobbes and Spinoza but roundly maintained that Spinoza followed in 'Hobbes's tracks'.[26] All this would seem to support the argument that the 'positive European reception of Hobbes for radical purposes' has been underestimated and that Hobbes's influence on Dutch radical thought and republicanism, generally, and Spinoza, in particular, requires more attention and emphasis.[27] But Hobbes's contribution, though undoubtedly important, was balanced by other powerful influences, notably those of Machiavelli and Descartes. Johan de La Court, the first of the Dutch writers to seek to propagate democratic republicanism, though like his brother Pieter undoubtedly interested in Hobbes, cannot really be said to have adopted a basically Hobbesian approach to the central issues of natural right, liberty, popular sovereignty or the question of the relations of state and church.

Undeniably, Hobbes did precede Spinoza and the Dutch republicans, as Pufendorf and the Natural Lawyers pointed out, in equating 'natural right' with power, as well as in ascribing ultimate supremacy, and a presiding role over the religious sphere, to the sovereign state, and stressing the need to prevent theological dissension from disrupting the public peace.[28] But Hobbes also diverged markedly from their insistence that religious repression is never justified, that freedom of individual conscience in matters of worship must be respected, and that, by tolerating all forms of worship which submit to the laws, the state reinforces rather than weakens social stability. The comprehensive toleration central to Spinoza, van den Enden, and the brothers de La Court is neither explicitly recommended by, nor integral to, Hobbes who indeed is more inclined to recommend censorship, imposing uniformity and suppression rather than toleration wherever political stability and the security of the state are threatened.[29]

Unrestricted individual freedom under an (equitable) law, including full freedom of speech and expression, is always fundamental in the radical tradition but is found in Hobbes only in a very restricted sphere concerned with the pursuit of private interests. For he sharply segregates the internal world of freedom, confined to the mind of the individual, and the latter's private dealings, from an external world of public obedience and outward conformity to the law in matters of faith.[30] In Spinoza, and with the democratic republicans generally, in contrast to Hobbes,

[26] Kortholt, *De tribus impostoribus*, 149, 153–4, 196; Malcolm, *Aspects of Hobbes*, 482.

[27] Malcolm, *Aspects of Hobbes*, 515–16.

[28] Schmauss, *Neues Systema*, 276–96; Ehrard, *L'Idée*, 478; Kervégan, 'Société civile', 151.

[29] Malcolm, *Aspects of Hobbes*, 515; Kossmann, *Political Thought*, 70, 78.

[30] Borrelli, 'Hobbes e la teoria', 247–9; Montag, *Bodies, Masses*, 52.

Man's natural right always remains intact under the state 'quod ego naturale Jus semper sartum tectum conservo' [because I always conserve the natural right safe and sound], as Spinoza explains, in his well-known letter to Jarig Jelles of June 1674 a doctrine very closely tied to Spinoza's theory of Man, nature and the *conatus* which pervades all his thought but is most fully developed in his *Ethics*.[31] Hobbes might well have accepted Ericus Walten's way of recycling Spinoza's idea: 'not only are all men naturally born free, but also this natural freedom always remains in its entirety until limited through ordinances, enactments, contracts or laws' [so dat niet alleen alle menschen van natuur vrijgeborene zijn, maar ook die natuurlijke vrijheid altijd in 't geheel blijft, tot datse door voorweerden, provisien, contracten of wetten bepaald wordt];[32] but he would have firmly disagreed with the accompanying notion that obligation to submit to political authority extends no further than the state's capacity to exact compliance which, according to Spinoza and subsequent republicans such as Walten, de Hooghe, and van Leenhof, does not include the power to restrict non-subversive criticism of the state's policies and laws and, moreover, shrinks proportionately the further one retreats from democracy.[33]

Where Spinoza claims liberty of the individual, under the law, is greater in a democracy than under a monarchy, Hobbes denies 'that there is more liberty in *Democraty* than *Monarchy*; for the one as truly consisteth with such a liberty, as the other'.[34] The gap between the Hobbesian conception of the state and Spinoza's, as has been pointed out by Alexandre Matheron and others,[35] is in reality a wide and significant one but is sometimes missed, or underestimated, owing to the long-entrenched misconception in some of the political thought literature[36] that Spinoza's political theory is virtually identical to that of Hobbes. In one recent reiteration of this still lingering notion we are told that 'Spinoza recommended a Hobbesian "state" that provides "peace and security" '.[37] In reality, neither Spinoza, nor his disciples among whom Mandeville belongs, recommend anything remotely like the Hobbesian state; and while one can boil down the essential difference between Hobbes's political theory and Spinoza's to the single clearly divergent point that, in Spinoza, Man's natural right always remains intact, in civil society just as it was under the state of nature, whereas in Hobbes this natural right is wholly surrendered when the state comes into being, under the terms of the supposed contract which forges the state, this divergence in turn opens up in various directions with wide implications for toleration, censorship, participation, and political ambition as well as personal liberty.[38]

31 Spinoza, *Briefwisseling*, 309; Curley, 'I durst not write', 513; Klever, 'Power', 96; Bove, 'Introduction', 34–8.

32 Walten, *Regtsinnige policey*, 6; Walten, *Onwederleggelyk Bewys*, 19.

33 Balibar, *Spinoza and Politics*, 34–6, 38–9, 104; Matheron, 'La Fonction théorique de la démocratie', 268–9; Matheron, 'Le Problème de l'évolution', 264.

34 Tuck, *Philosophy and Government*, 317.

35 Matheron, 'Le Problème de l'évolution', 258, 266; Barebone and Rice, 'La Naissance', 53–6; Klever, 'Bernard Mandeville', 4–5; Smith, 'What Kind', 14–15.

36 Hampshire, *Spinoza*, 135, 137; Barebone and Rice, 'La Naissance', 48, 52.

37 Faulkner, 'Political Philosophy', in Kors (ed.), *Encyclopedia*, iii. 320.

38 Hobbes, *Leviathan*, xiv, paras. 8–12; Matheron, *Individu et communauté*, 293–5.

For Hobbes, as we have seen, as for Spinoza, 'equality' and 'liberty' are both major elements of the state of nature.[39] But owing to the prevailing fear and insecurity in that stage of human development, groups rapidly form and disband, strong leaders are chosen, natural hierarchies form and dissolve, rivals for resources are threatened, despoiled, conquered, or enslaved. Equality and inequality are, so to speak, in a constant and shifting dialectic. But the point to note is that, in Hobbes, it is the inequality which holds out the promise of more security and stability and the basic equality of the state of nature which is in the first instance most menacing, dangerous, and unsettling. Hobbes frequently uses his construct of the state of nature to warn readers about the dangers of liberty, and indeed to diminish liberty's prestige while at the same time undermining the possible attractions of equality. All this is in reverse, as it were, of the radical order of priorities with regard to both liberty and equality.

A related, initially marginal but again ultimately fundamental opposition between Hobbesianism and the core values of the Radical Enlightenment arises from Hobbes's key insight that Natural Law and natural morality, insofar as these can be supposed to exist in the state of nature—and it is not at all his claim that 'right and wrong' exist only under the rule of law, in a constituted state—must be based on the principle of 'equity' and 'reciprocity'. 'The equal distribution to each man of that which in reason belongeth to him' is, declares Hobbes, 'called Equity'.[40] Hobbes defines a law of nature (*lex naturalis*) as a 'precept or general rule, found out by reason, by which a man is forbidden to do that which is destructive of his life or taketh away the means of preserving the same, and to omit that by which he thinketh it may be best preserved'. These laws of nature, including the admonition not 'to hurt without reason' because this 'tendeth to the introduction of Warre', he declares 'immutable and eternal'.[41]

Thus far, the Spinozists were merely following Hobbes's lead. But precisely because natural equality, in his view, is dangerous, destabilizing, and to be avoided in favour of order and social hierarchy, this potential route to a purely secular and autonomous morality under the state, the path chosen by Spinoza, Bayle, and Diderot, is peremptorily blocked off by Hobbes. For he reduces the content of natural morality, underpinning the social contract and the rule of positive law, to an absolute minimum with little applicability to political life under the state, coupling a doctrine of the indivisibility of sovereignty closely aligned with that of Bodin to the idea that 'in the act of our submission consisteth both our obligation and our liberty'. In this way, he interposes an absolute divide between ruler and ruled and insuperable polarity between natural right and law.[42] This creates a considerable gulf between Hobbes and the Radical Enlightenment, leading not just to conflicting views about politics and human freedom but also opposing systems of morality and conceptions of the philosopher's role and of the philosophical life.

39 Kortholt, *De tribus impostoribus*, 196, 210.
40 Hobbes, *Leviathan*, xv. para. 24.
41 Ibid., paras. 3, 5, 8, 19; Hoekstra, 'Hobbes on law', 111–13, 116.
42 Kervégan, 'Société civile', 152; Hoekstra, 'Disarming the Prophets', 129–31; Balibar, *Spinoza and Politics*, 104.

Where for Hobbes the individual's true liberty lies solely in his freedom to do what the sovereign, whether monarchical or otherwise, has not precluded, and liberty itself is viewed as just absence of constraint, in radical thought liberty includes sharing in some way, if only by expressing one's opinion, in the making of constitutions, laws, and important decisions of state which happens the more, the less the state is monarchical. Where in Radical Enlightenment it is axiomatic that kings, ministers, and office-holders are not above the law but subject to it, and the more limited the better, valid legal principles and true morality being defined by the 'common good' of society and not by the sovereign through the processes of legislation, law enforcement, and church policy, in Hobbes the sovereign is always *legibus solutus* and accountable to no one while simultaneously being the source of law, church policy, and morality. Undoubtedly, this is still tied to the 'common good' but a 'common good' more closely restricted to political stability and security broadly understood, and less anchored in 'reason', than Spinoza's.[43]

The sudden definitive loss of 'natural right' by a generalized, permanently binding contract under the state, ultimately the least persuasive part of Hobbes's political theory, is crucial to his system and was perhaps bound to be vigorously countered by later naturalistic-minded political thinkers, as also by Pufendorf and the exponents of Natural Law.[44] The de La Courts, Spinoza, Meyer, and Cuffeler diverged dramatically from Hobbes in maintaining that the individual's natural right corresponds unalterably, hence also under the state, to his desires and power, to what Mandeville called that 'natural instinct of sovereignty, which teaches Man to look upon every thing as centering in himself', albeit this conception still in some sense derives from Hobbes.[45] As Matheron and Negri rightly stress, where Hobbes's concern, with his surrender of the individual's natural right, is to reinforce sovereignty as much as possible, whether monarchical or otherwise, by restricting liberty, Spinoza's political thought enhances liberty as much as possible by dispersing and redefining sovereignty, in particular by depressing the status of monarchy even in states supposedly ruled by kings, albeit he does not question the right to rule of any ruler who does.[46] The gulf between the Hobbesian state and the Spinozan becomes yet more starkly apparent when we consider that, for Hobbes, securing civil peace and harmony is the state's overriding function whereas Spinoza, while granting history teaches that democracies are more prone to disunity, factionalism, and civil strife than monarchy or aristocracy, nevertheless argues that the risk should be borne for the sake of advantages the democratic republic affords.

For Spinoza, the kind of 'peace' imposed by the despotic sovereign who disdains the 'common good', and suppresses freedom of expression, is a wretched thing altogether abhorrent to reason. Civil 'peace' wrought by tyranny and curbing individual

43 Balibar, *Spinoza and Politics*., 55; Dedeyan, *Diderot*, 246; Schröder, 'Liberté et pouvoir', 154; Raphael, *Hobbes*, 37; Hoekstra, 'Lion in the House', forthcoming.

44 Hirschman, *Passions and the Interests*, 15–16, 20, 31–2; Hunter, *Rival Enlightenments*, 187.

45 Cuffeler, *Specimen artis ratiocinandi*, ii. 93–7; McShea, *Political Philosophy*, 58–9.

46 McShea, *Political Philosophy*, 86–91, 143–7; Balibar, *Spinoza and Politics*, 55–6.

freedom he condemns as the 'peace of the desert', not true 'peace' but a state of oppression and slavery: 'nam pax, ut jam diximus, non in belli privatione, sed in animorum unione, sive concordia consistit' [for peace, as we have said, consists not in absence of war, but in a union or concord of minds].[47] Here Spinoza is partly endorsing Hobbes's formulation, as well as partly contradicting it and, in a way, also going beyond it. Hence, where Hobbes advocates an absolute sovereign unconstrained by law—and further to strengthen sovereignty, strong censorship and a powerful ecclesiastical arm (albeit subordinate to the sovereign), Spinoza, like Cuffeler, Walten, and van Leenhof after him, disdains such Hobbesian accoutrements.[48] The true purpose of the state being 'freedom', counters Spinoza, it is less important to maximize security than to secure the advantages of orderly cooperation with other men, including political collaboration, and the maximum of independence for the individual compatible with the general interest.[49] Whenever a state no longer upholds a liberty which adequately protects the individual from the irrationality, selfishness, greed, unruliness, and passions of others, including the sovereign, its citizens *ipso facto* have the right, as well as the motivation, to intervene and change it.

For Spinoza, van den Enden, Cuffeler, Walten, de Hooghe, van Leenhof, and Mandeville, then, government has no more 'right' over its subjects than power over them, whereas Hobbes separates right—of the sovereign no less than the individual—fundamentally, from power, through the device of his social contract.[50] Where Hobbes sees no way of ensuring safety and social peace other than by curbing and repressing Man's impulses through the might of the sovereign,[51] Spinoza (and Mandeville) conceive the state as the product of an evolutionary process constituting a single continuum with the state of nature.[52] Where Hobbes checks the chaos and brutality of the 'state of nature' by assigning the sovereign decisive and overriding power over society, and the individual, Spinoza, again following the brothers de La Court, not only preserves individual freedom as far as possible but, where he delimits it, absorbs and merges the individual's 'right' (and power) and autonomy not into the executive but into the sovereign, redefined as 'the majority of the whole community of which he is part', that is into the state conceived as the collective body of society, laws, and institutions.[53]

These different positions, in turn, generate further striking disparities. Where for Hobbes power can and should be concentrated effectively in a sovereign monarch, for Spinoza true monarchy is literally impossible.[54] Power is always widely dispersed

[47] Spinoza, *Opera*, iii. 298; McShea, *Political Philosophy*, 126, 144–5.

[48] Walten, *Onwederleggelyk bewys*, 42; Klever, 'Power', 96–7; Hoekstra, 'Tyrannus rex', 425.

[49] Spinoza, *Opera*, ii. 241; McShea, *Political Philosophy*, 64–5, 144–5.

[50] McShea, *Political Philosophy*, 138–41; Petry, 'Hobbes', 150–2, 154; Den Uyl, 'Passion, State, and Progress', 390–1; Barebone and Rice, 'La Naissance', 53.

[51] Monro, *Ambivalence*, 187–8, 221, 232–3.

[52] Den Uyl, 'Passion, State and Progress', 371–2, 382–3, 386–8; Pascual López, *Bernard Mandeville*, 184–6.

[53] Spinoza, *Opera*, iii. 195; McShea, *Political Philosophy*, 146–52; Klever, 'Power', 96–7; Petry, 'Hobbes', 154–5; Balibar, *Spinoza and Politics*, 34, 53; van Bunge, *From Stevin to Spinoza*, 86, 88.

[54] Spinoza, *Tractatus politicus*, 317; Blom, *Morality and Causality*, 235.

so that even the most despotic monarchy is really nothing but a concealed, unregulated form of aristocracy or unsatisfactory mixture of aristocracy and democracy. The aggressive and selfish instincts of each individual which Hobbes's sovereign seeks to curb, and which Hobbes views in an essentially negative light, in Spinoza, van Leenhof, and Mandeville—following on from the de La Courts—are instead pitted against each other, in society, and rather than being repressed, are transmuted with the help of Spinoza's mechanics of the passions into positive and beneficial equivalents. As Spinoza expresses this idea in his *Ethics*, 'it is when every man is most devoted to seeking his own advantage that men are of most advantage to one another', an insight, one might suspect, rooted in his early experience as a merchant and in business.[55]

The main difference here between Spinoza and Mandeville is that where the first deems these 'bad' impulses transformed into 'good', the latter sees men behaving at the behest of society in ways perceived as 'good', 'virtuous', or 'chaste' which, however, do not correspond to genuine 'virtue' but rather an elaborate system of hypocrisy. Men do the right things, argues Mandeville, not by and large out of virtue, but rather for 'honour', influence, and to avoid disapproval and 'shame'.[56] But the difference in this case too may be more apparent than real since Mandeville speaks of 'virtue' in the conventional sense while Spinoza, as so often, redefines the term to denote something quite different from what is conventionally meant.

In society, according to both Hobbes and the Dutch radicals, individual interests clash and largely neutralize each other, thereby restricting men's desires. But where, for Hobbes, Man in civil society is essentially a subject, Spinoza renders him an active citizen who, whatever his desires and degree of rationality, participates and contributes through sociability to the civilizing, law-enforcing, morality-generating process. Men being useful to each other in infinite ways, society affords possibilities for satisfying individual desires in a complex manner which Man's 'natural right' left to itself, in the state of nature, would not comparably provide. Hence, the state, and society, in Spinozism, as in Mandeville, not only guarantee security and peace but also provide opportunities and scope for participation and expression, politically and economically, of a different kind, or at least to a greater extent, than does the Hobbesian model.[57] Doubtless both concepts accommodate pride, the quest for glory, and desire for promotion; but Spinoza's construction gives more scope to expression of opposition, political ambition, and faction, as well as desire for public status. However selfish in themselves, such impulses acquire a positive potential and function in civil society with the result that they cease to be purely negative, aggressive, or disruptive, but rather tend to further the 'common good' while simultaneously serving individual greed and desire.[58]

55 Spinoza, *Ethics*, iv, prop. 35, corollary 2; Montag, *Bodies, Masses*, 31.
56 Monro, *Ambivalence*, 126–8, 188; Hundert, *Enlightenment's Fable*, 140–1.
57 Balibar, *Spinoza and Politics*, 111–12; Bove, 'Introduction', 90–3.
58 Hammacher, 'Ambition and Social Engagement', 57; Monro, *Ambivalence of Bernard Mandeville*, 232–3.

Admittedly, Spinoza seems close to Hobbes in considering it ruinous for 'religion', as well as the state, to permit clergy to issue decrees, or concern themselves with legislation or political decisions, and deems it essential not just for society but also 'religion' that 'the highest powers [of the state] must possess the right to determine what is right and what is wrong' [quam necesse sit, tam reipublicae, quam religioni, summis potestatibus jus, de eo, quod fas, nefasque sit, discernendi, concedere].[59] But the sovereign here is understood very differently from in Hobbes, being less the ruler than the supreme legislating body and institutions of the state. Respect for, and compliance with, laws conceived for the 'common good', are elevated by Spinozists above all other duty, and far above submission to kings, aristocracy, ecclesiastical authority, tradition, or belief. But here Hobbes is clearer at least, since Spinoza's conception of sovereignty introduces an unmistakable tension, or element of contradiction, between the power of law-making and the 'common good' especially where these two uncomfortably diverge.

Hence, Dutch and later radical writers typically follow Spinoza, as Du Marsais does in *Le Philosophe*, in redefining 'piety' and 'religion' to denote reverence for the law conceived not as the ruler's will but as expression of the common interest, while simultaneously redefining 'atheism' and 'godlessness' to mean defiance of society's laws and well-being. Despite their divergent vocabularies, this applies also to van Leenhof and Mandeville. True sovereignty for these writers, too, resides less in the executive power than in the legislation produced by the governing body in accordance with society's needs, legislation to which everyone, office-holders and ordinary citizens alike, is subject.[60] Nothing could be more 'atheistic', contends van Leenhof, whose primary concern is for personal freedom, than that 'men koningen boven de wetten stelt' [kings should be placed above the laws].[61]

Consequently, for Spinoza, Walten, and van Leenhof, again quite unlike Hobbes, the primacy of the rule of law, as distinct from the executive, should always be clear and unchallenged. Power, on the other hand, being, despite appearances, always highly diffused, even in the most centralizing of absolute monarchies, is best shown to be divided in an open, formalized, and balanced fashion, so that factions and ambitious men are boxed into a stable equilibrium by committees, collective decision-making, constitutional procedures, checks, and balances.[62] Thus, the only way rule of law can be upheld in monarchies, and 'a people can preserve a considerable measure of freedom under a king', holds Spinoza, here diametrically at odds with Hobbes, is if every conceivable precaution is taken to ensure royal authority is checked by the people's power and armed might.[63] Weapons in the citizens' hands are as vital for defending the people's interest in Spinoza as in van den Enden and the brothers de La Court, crucial that is not only against external enemies but also

[59] Spinoza, *Opera*, iii. 226.

[60] van Leenhof, *De Prediker*, 156, 239; [Du Marsais], *Le Philosophe*, 188; Israel, *Radical Enlightenment*, 80.

[61] van Leenhof, *Het Leven*, 44.

[62] Spinoza, *Tractatus politicus*, 305, 317–19, 339, 364–5; van Leenhof, *De Prediker*, 73–4; van Leenhof, *Het Leven*, 239–44.

[63] Spinoza, *Tractatus politicus*, 305.

one's own king (where one is unfortunate enough to have one), as well as oligarchs and usurpers of whatever sort.[64]

While both Hobbes and Spinoza deem Scripture eminently useful for inculcating 'obedience' into the mass of men in a Christian society, Hobbes here introduces an anti-democratic and anti-libertarian twist quite foreign to Spinoza's, Bayle's, and Diderot's political thought. 'Sacred Scriptures', says Hobbes, 'teach that Christian subjects ought to obey their kings and sovereigns (and their ministers) even if they are pagan, not only on account of fear, but also for the sake of conscience, as ordained by God for our good.'[65] While Spinoza, and still more Bayle, blame religious conflict on the ambitions and the tactics of theologians, Hobbes, while acknowledging rival interpretations of Scripture and competing theologies are a perennial source of strife, does not consider these the only, or even primary, cause of wars of religion, which he dreads, of course, no less than they. Rather, fomenting civil strife generally is to be blamed, in his opinion, no less on Aristotle and much of the rest of the Greek political thought tradition: for he believed much harm had been done by labelling the 'rule of kings tyranny' and inculcating into modern man the, to his mind, pernicious notion that 'only in democracy is there liberty'.[66]

Democracy here embraces, as also in Spinoza, not only participation of all in politics but also of everyone in deciding what is right and wrong, just and unjust. But here, once again, a not inconsiderable gap separates Hobbes from radical ideas. For it was the teaching of Greek authors to 'our youth', in the universities, claims Hobbes, which generated that 'poisonous doctrine' whereby all 'decided about good and evil, just and unjust, laws and religion, each according to his own discretion'. Where Spinoza and his followers encourage such debates, Hobbes considers this inherently harmful because 'in every commonwealth the measure of good and evil is the law', not individual judgement.[67]

The basic divergence between the Hobbesian and Spinozist systems, then, extended far beyond politics. In Spinoza, as in Bayle and Diderot, the ultimate measure of good and evil is not precisely the law, despite our obligation to obey it, and could not be, for laws are not infrequently misconceived, ineffective, disastrous, or despotic, but rather the 'common good', Diderot's 'general will'. This fundamental disagreement about the nature of law is clearly rooted in a no less profound disagreement about the nature of morality. Hobbes, in practice, denies there is such a thing as a secular morality underlying law and politics, since, for him, it is only where men conceive of commandments about good and bad as being divine in origin that they can amount to more than the arbitrary dictates of the sovereign.[68] Here Mandeville may well be closer to Hobbes than to Spinoza. In Hobbes, it is precisely because there is no more than a very rudimentary secular morality deriving from Natural Law that the sovereign's sole right to interpret divine law, as well as to

64 Klever, 'Krijgsmacht en defensie', 150–66.

65 Hobbes, *Leviathan*, xlvi. para. 23.

66 Skinner, *Liberty*, 60, 68, 79–82.

67 Hobbes, *Leviathan*, xlvi. para. 23.

68 Curley, 'I durst not write', 502–3; Lagrée, 'Du magistère spirituel', 604–5; Raphael, *Hobbes*, 75.

legislate civil law, is unimpeachable, rendering the sovereign, and the church which he supervises, sole judges of the criteria of just and unjust in society.

While it is true, then, that Hobbes's contribution to the making of the Radical Enlightenment was appreciable, one cannot say the Hobbesian programme implied as wide-ranging a social and 'cultural transformation' as did Spinozism. In so far as Hobbes's system did entail a major transformation, it was certainly not a libertarian, emancipatory programme tending towards the freeing of the individual, and a generalized egalitarianism, in the manner of the Radical Enlightenment. Hobbes's programme has been called a form of 'enlightenment' and a 'project of liberation'. Not only did 'his ideas supply' the thinkers of Enlightenment Europe 'with some of the materials they needed', it is claimed, 'his project of enlightenment was, in the end, the Enlightenment's project too'.[69] But if we define 'enlightenment' as the Radical Enlightenment did—the organizing of human life on the basis of reason only, for the 'common good', resulting in personal liberty, equality, democracy, a comprehensive toleration, and free expression as essential values, then it seems excessive to portray Hobbes as its original inspiration.

As with 'enlightenment', so also with democracy. There were enough democratic hints and insights in Hobbes's political theory, some modern commentators maintain, to ground the claim that Hobbes marks a new departure, not only holding that all commonwealths were originally democratic but that they also derive their legitimacy from these democratic origins. But it is possible to question the correctness of this view which, in any case, worryingly underestimates the consistency, intensity, and sweep of Hobbes's fervent rejection of democracy. If Hobbes was only in a rather limited sense a forefather of the Radical Enlightenment, equally, he is only to a limited extent the 'true ancestor' of modern democratic republicanism.

[69] Malcolm, *Aspects of Hobbes*, 545.

10

The Origins of Modern Democratic Republicanism

1. CLASSICAL REPUBLICANISM VERSUS DEMOCRATIC REPUBLICANISM

Freedom of thought, then, in both Spinoza and Bayle is rooted in a naturalistic philosophy centring around the liberty of the individual whose life is confined to the here and now. However, in Spinoza, unlike Bayle, freedom of thought is also expressly tied through freedom of expression to an anti-monarchical and anti-aristocratic politics. In fact, Spinoza's political thought seeks to maximize individual liberty under the state by demonstrating, and emphasizing, the positive interaction between Man's individual and collective interests and the power of the sovereign, the state's true strength and stability, in his opinion, depending on the willingness of citizens to identify with, participate in, and support it.

The essential link between individual liberty and politics in Spinoza's philosophy is the idea that personal freedom, and satisfaction of individual desires, is greater or less, and the individual more or less secure, depending on the degree to which the state strives to maintain 'the common good', something which Spinoza argues is inherently more likely to be the case the more the state is broad based and democratic in character. Conversely, the more autocratic the state—though he regards pure monarchy as an impossible fantasy—the weaker it is. A concrete contemporary illustration of this, in practical terms, would be the contrast between the Dutch Republic where he lived and the neighbouring monarchy of Louis XIV. While the latter was styled an 'absolute' monarchy, the Dutch Republic was incomparably stronger in the sense that it could maintain a far larger army and navy in proportion to population—the States' army at the time he wrote his *Tractatus politicus*, for example, being around one third of the size of the French army despite the Dutch state having merely one tenth of France's population. The reason was precisely that decision-making in the Republic was broader based, and the common people more prosperous, enabling the United Provinces to raise considerably more in per capita revenue than France, and do so with less internal stress and fiscal resistance.

Accordingly, there is an inherent link between Spinoza's overall system and a type of democratic republicanism which crystallized in Holland in the late 1650s and

1660s under the stimulus of the political ideas of Machiavelli, Hobbes, and the brothers de La Court. Dutch seventeenth-century republicanism with its predominantly urban social base and strong emphasis (from Johan de Witt onwards) on the natural inclination of republics as compared with monarchies towards peace[1] developed, though, in a strikingly different way from English republicanism in this period, even while drawing on some of the same sources as the English variety, particularly Machiavelli. In view of the existing historiography, one might not think this especially important for the wider western and global intellectual context given that few general discussions of seventeenth- and early eighteenth-century political thought in English, French, Italian, or German assign any great significance to Dutch influences in the wider Atlantic picture. Most of the historiography simply assumes that the so-called 'Atlantic' republicanism of the English gentry is overridingly the most important tradition in post-Renaissance Atlantic republicanism generally, much as Locke and Early Enlightenment English liberalism are assumed, not least in America, to be the real grounding of the modern western liberal tradition.[2]

Yet there are serious grounds for questioning these assumptions and arguing, in opposition to them, that focusing on the Anglo-American republican tradition, screening out, or marginalizing, the de La Courts and Spinoza as well as van den Enden, Koerbagh, Willem van der Muelen (1659–1739), Ericus Walten (1663–97), Romeyn de Hooghe (*c.*1645–1708), Frederik van Leenhof (1647–1713), Jean-Frédéric Bernard, Jean Rousset de Missy, and other Dutch and Dutch Huguenot political writers of the Early Enlightenment period, is an error which substantially impedes a proper understanding of the origins of modern democratic republicanism. For where English republicanism was essentially that of a landed gentry, and rarely emphatically democratic in tendency, Dutch republicanism was plainly not the ideology of a rural elite, aspiring to dominate a national parliament, but rather one of city burghers whose interests were predominantly civic, commercial, and non-agrarian. Hence, Dutch seventeenth-century democratic republicanism, arguably, was distinctively 'modern' in a sense in which no other European republicanism of the period, including Britain's, can genuinely be said to have been.

Furthermore, since agrarian interests in Dutch political thought remained wholly subordinate to urban trade and industry, the implicit basis of social hierarchy inherent in much English classical republicanism is replaced in the Dutch context, with important implications for the whole subsequent history of the Enlightenment, with theories of equality. Attempting to classify all those not dependent on others—that is who are not women, children, and servants—as a single category of 'citizen', the interests of each of which are strictly equivalent to those of the next, Dutch republican writers can be said to have initiated an important new trend in western political thought. Indeed, in one of the most militantly democratic texts discussed

[1] Israel, *Dutch Republic*, 731–3, 744, 762–3, 786–92.

[2] See, for instance, Worden, 'English Republicanism', 443; Harrison, *'Religion' and the Religions*, 3, 176 n. 4; Beiser, *Sovereignty of Reason*, 5–7, 16–17, 326–7; Porter, *Enlightenment*, 4–47, 483–4.

in this chapter, the *Vrye Politieke Stellingen* (Free Political Institutions) published in Amsterdam, by the atheistic schoolmaster Franciscus van den Enden (1602–74), in 1665, we find one of the first general affirmations of the universal rationality and fundamental equality (*evengelykheit*) of all men—of whatever race, colour, or creed—of modern times.[3] Envisioning merchants and wage-earners as the backbone of the citizenry, Dutch democratic republicanism at bottom was a republicanism which pivoted on an egalitarian conception of the 'common good' as the guiding principle of society and politics.

By contrast, the pre-1776 Anglo-American 'classical republican' tradition has been aptly called the republicanism of an opposition-minded gentry—agrarian, anti-commercial, asserting the special status of free property-holders and the duty of the citizenry to participate in government; it was grounded, as one leading authority puts it, 'on the Machiavellian theory of the possession of arms as necessary to political personality'.[4] In this long-lingering tradition of 'Harringtonian republicanism' which has also been called 'English Machiavellism', the ties between land, republican freedom, and the bearing of arms have been deemed crucial. 'As in Machiavelli', so in this kind of republicanism, we learn, 'the bearing of arms is the primary medium through which the individual asserts both his social power and his participation in politics as a responsible moral being: but the possession of land in nondependent tenure is now the material basis for the bearing of arms'.[5]

In concrete terms, this was the ideology of one strand of the land-based, parliamentary gentry which dominated eighteenth-century England, as well as Ireland and parts of North America and the Caribbean, a creed which bears few real affinities with the neighbouring Dutch 'burgher' republican thought when considered in its wider cultural and social setting. This applies to the agrarian dimension but also to the strong and increasing British 'republican' preference in the years after 1688 for 'mixed government'—the view that if absolute monarchy is tyrannical, 'absolute democracy', as one republican writer, Viscount Bolingbroke, expressed the point, 'is tyranny and anarchy both'.[6] The preferences of Dutch radical republicanism were remote from English classical republicanism in these respects and perhaps still more importantly in a way which has been somewhat underemphasized in recent discussion of early modern political thought, namely the strongly aristocratic and anti-democratic drift inherent in a republicanism of a landed gentry as well as its growing connection with empire, and with cultivating a martial spirit among the populace for imperial purposes, a feature characteristic of both the Cromwellian and anti-Cromwellian 'Commonwealth' revolutionary legacy, especially pronounced in the thought of Algernon Sidney.[7]

[3] Van den Enden, *Vrye Politieke Stellingen*, 169; Israel, *Radical Enlightenment*, 180; Klever, *Sphinx*, 147–8.

[4] Worden, 'English Republicanism', 452; Pocock, *Machiavellian Moment*, 386.

[5] Pocock, *Machiavellian Moment*, 390; Kossmann, *Politieke theorie*, 225.

[6] Bolingbroke, *Political Writings*, 127, 156, 230–1; Pocock, *Machiavellian Moment*, 478–80, 485–6; Pocock, 'Dutch Republican Tradition', 189; Levillain, 'William III's Millitary', 322, 332, 349.

[7] Scott, *Algernon Sidney*, 236–7, 259–60; Worden, 'Revolution of 1688–9', 264–8.

The political and social world of English squirearchy, then, was a markedly different one from that of the Dutch urban burgher. Furthermore, given its stress on equality and the civic context, Dutch republicanism needed to be and was philosophically more radical, and more coherently radical, than its English counterpart, or to express the point differently, from van den Enden onwards its 'Spinozist' wing was more closely connected to a particular type of general philosophy than its English counterpart, a crucial difference which has little to do with innate national tastes or aptitudes but much to do with circumstances. For being expressly more anti-monarchical, anti-hierarchical, and more concerned with equality than English republicanism, the Dutch tradition was obliged to seek more and better arguments for rejecting the prevailing hierarchical vision of society generally prevalent in baroque Europe with its customary stress on princely authority, aristocratic values, and ecclesiastical authority.

The difference, in other words, stemmed from the Dutch state being a republic forged by a long and bloody revolt against a fully legitimate monarch, originally a *de facto* republic which, in the 1580s, had step by step, overcoming considerable domestic hesitation and reluctance, been obliged to abjure the principles of monarchy and hereditary possession of the state as well as dispense with bishops and a comprehensive state church like that of England; by contrast post-1688 Britain was a essentially parliamentary monarchy, chiefly managed by a landed aristocracy, with a relatively strong established church which revered the monarch as its head, had a long tradition of praising 'mixed government' and was also accustomed to showing due respect for the principle of aristocracy. These divergent institutional frameworks, not surprisingly, fomented distinct and ultimately rival traditions of constitutional and republican political consciousness.

Furthermore, the Glorious Revolution of 1688–91, crucial for Britain and the United Provinces alike, further widened the divergence between the two traditions of republicanism by softening and, in significant measure, deradicalizing the English variety.[8] Thus, where English compromise devised an increasingly stable balance between king and Parliament, encouraging a particular emphasis in eighteenth-century Anglo-American culture on the singularity and superiority of the British model, internal stresses and the struggle against the absolutism and militarism of Louis XIV, in the Dutch case, kept alive a more radical republican tendency which, after 1750, increasingly resurfaced—through a complex transition in which Dutch-based Huguenots seemingly played a role—in French republican and crypto-republican theorists such as Meslier, Boulanger, Morelly, La Beaumelle, Mably, Diderot who, in the 1790s, was rightly identified as a 'véritable républicain'—albeit one obliged to veil his true political sentiments living as he was under a traditional absolute monarchy,[9] and Rousseau. It was this Dutch–French trajectory, arguably, and not, after all, the British tradition which—despite having been largely submerged

[8] Worden, 'Revolution of 1688–9', 241, 268–72; Pocock, 'Significance of 1688', 277–9.
[9] Tarin, *Diderot*, 139–41.

and ignored in histories of western political thought—may be said to represent the main line in the emergence of modern western democratic republicanism.

Where some pre-1789 Anglophile continental political thought, notably Boulainvilliers and Montesquieu, deemed limited monarchy on the British model the highest possible ideal in politics, British 'mixed government' exerted less attraction on Dutch democratic republicans and less still on the French Radical Enlightenment after Boulainvilliers. Morelly's anonymous *Code de la nature* (1754), having as its subtitle 'ou le véritable *Esprit* de ses Loix', a text usually attributed to Diderot during the French Revolution (and publicly condemned during the trial of Babeuf, in 1797, as one of the prime roots of revolutionary social radicalism), full-frontally attacks Montesquieu's conservative, hierarchical conception of society, seeking to substitute an uncompromisingly democratic, if also thoroughly utopian, vision in its place.[10]

An idealist-materialist and, yet, 'Deist' thinker, Morelly had espoused a radical conception of democracy by the early 1750s, building his democratic vision on typically Spinozistic premisses. These included the ideas that every man seeks his own 'conservation', that a new worldly and sensual morality is needed, that monarchy grows in outward splendour and inner corruption and the *bien général* suffers, the more inequality of status and property in society increases,[11] and that as our needs are equal and wills equivalent so a fundamental equality is the general principle on which a truly secular politics must be structured, nature having shown men 'par la parité de sentimens et de besoins, leur égalité de conditions et de droits, et la nécessité d'un travail commun'.[12] If genuine virtue makes men happy but is undermined by the false virtues proclaimed by the churches, false piety no less than veritable immorality and deception make men unhappy. All this owed much to Du Marsais and possibly Mably, as well as Morelly's deep-seated antipathy to Montesquieu's aristocratic and mixed monarchical proclivities.

Rejection of British limited monarchy, in any case, was inherent in the further development of the democratic republican model. If the turning away from the British model only characterized the political thought of Mably, Diderot, Rousseau, and other *philosophes* after 1750, rejection of mixed government on principle was, nevertheless, from the outset characteristic of what we shall term the 'main line' of development of the western republican tradition. The Brothers de La Court deemed 'Harrington's ideal state of a *regnum mixtum* with a monarch deprived of absolute power', but retaining some influence, thoroughly undesirable and intrinsically 'unstable as well as continually at risk of degenerating into despotic monarchy'.[13] Van den Enden was, if anything, even more contemptuous of mixed monarchy; as later, in his *Spiegel van Staat* (1706), was the staunchly republican and libertine artist, inventor, and political writer Romeyn de Hooghe.[14]

[10] Tarin, *Diderot*, 114–15, 117, 139–40; Morelly, *Code de la nature*, preface and pp. 18–21; Talmon, *Origins*, 17–18.

[11] [Morelly], *Basiliade*, i. 188–95.

[12] Ibid. 24–5; Wagner, *Morelly*, 173, 236–7, 356.

[13] Kossmann, *Politieke theorie*, 222–3; Kossmann, *Political Thought*, 69; Prokhovnik, *Spinoza*, 98.

[14] Van den Enden, *Vrye Politieke Stellingen*, 160–4, 176; Klever, *Democratische vernieuwing*, 46–7.

Spinoza, for his part, considered the English revolution of the 1640s an utter failure which while attempting to remove a tyrannical king had merely substituted, in the person of Cromwell, another and worse 'monarch' under another name.[15] Admittedly, in his late treatise, the *Tractatus politicus*, which lay unfinished at the time of his death in 1677, Spinoza allows that monarchy is redeemable up to a point but only where and when it can be so drastically degraded as to approximate to democracy—and hence to share in democracy's strengths and advantages. In indicating how this should be done, he so utterly emasculates government by kings that what survives is no more than a caricature. The perfect monarchy, he suggests (doubtless tongue in cheek), is constitutional monarchy on the model of the old kingdom of Aragon before it was subverted by the despot Philip II, a kingdom so replete with legal procedures and restrictions that the king lacked the authority even to make an arrest by royal prerogative alone.[16]

Nor were the Dutch radical writers who came after Spinoza any less negative or sarcastic about kings, princely power, and the monarchical principle. Ericus Walten, a friend of the etcher and fellow republican writer Romeyn de Hooghe, and participant as a propagandist on the side of William III in the Glorious Revolution, exhibited increasingly radical tendencies in the early 1690s.[17] Like de Hooghe, he dismisses monarchy in his Orangist tracts of the years 1688–91 as inherently (and always) inferior to republics and an abusive affectation and fiction: 'so that not only has all absolute power [*absolute magt*] which any monarch has ever exercised', he declared in 1689, in support of William III's and the States General's invasion of England, 'been usurped, in violation of the fundamental laws of the state, but monarchical government itself is against God's intention, especially when exercised in the form of a sovereign power in one person alone, since God and Nature lodged the sovereign power in a full gathering of men'.[18] For these writers, all governments, whether rulers admit it or not, 'represent the whole people' and can only derive their legitimacy from the people. Walten and de Hooghe appear to have derived their political ideas from studying Spinoza, the de La Courts whom Walten repeatedly cites, Machiavelli, and also Hobbes but cite no English republican writers.[19]

Both Walten and de Hooghe were democratic republican Orangists strongly opposed to the regent oligarchies which dominated Dutch town government, clashing especially with those of Amsterdam and Rotterdam. An interesting feature of de Hooghe's republicanism is the firm distinction which he draws between the oligarchic republicanism of states such as Venice and Poland and the true people's 'allervryse volks regeering' [fully free people's commonwealth], or states with a genuine 'democratic' element such as he, in common with much early eighteenth-century European usage, considered the United Provinces and Switzerland to

15 Spinoza, *TTP* 227–8.
16 Spinoza, *Tractatus politicus*, 305, 364–5; Blom, *Morality and Causality*, 236.
17 Van Bunge, 'Ericus Walten', 41–54; Israel, *Dutch Republic*, 4, 674–5, 856, 928–31.
18 Ericus Walten, *Regtsinnige Policey*, 20–1, 23; Knuttel, 'Ericus Walten', 351–2.
19 Knuttel, 'Ericus Watten', 362.

possess.[20] In one of his diatribes against the Amsterdam magistracy he accuses them not only of seeking 'het meesterschap over de rest van de Republique' [mastery over the rest of the Republic] but of wanting to turn Amsterdam into another Venice, changing the burgomasters' families into *signori* and *cavallieri* to form a corrupt aristocratic republic ruled by a tiny elite who organize everything in their own interest at the expense of the people.[21]

Fredrik van Leenhof (1647–1713)—an ardent and systematic Spinozist as recent research has shown[22]—was another who believed republics are always better than monarchies and that if one must be saddled with a king, monarchy is rational and justifiable only where the monarch is placed under the law, like everyone else, and can only change a given law 'met gemeene of genoegzaame toestemminge' [with general or sufficient consent].[23] Mandeville, a radical Cartesian medical man from the Netherlands resident in London, likewise aligned with the Dutch republican tradition in rejecting parliamentary monarchies as undesirable since 'mix'd government leads to doubts about where sovereignty lies'.[24] Nevertheless, it has been argued, despite the impressive vitality and originality of late seventeenth-century Dutch republican political ideas, that 'Dutch republican theory did not, so it seems, draw inspiration from its own intellectual past' so that the earlier corpus of theory 'never developed . . . into a peculiarly Dutch intellectual tradition which it would be correct to define as the Dutch paradigm'.[25]

This qualification is surely correct regarding the mainstream, moderate Dutch (and Dutch Huguenot) Enlightenment with its increasingly anti-democratic, conservative, and (by 1813) monarchical tendencies. Preference for the 'British model' and the conviction, as Le Clerc expressed it in 1708, that the ideal political system is one midway between 'pouvoir arbitraire' on the one side and democracy, on the other, and that 'toutes les démocraties sont sujettes à de grands désordres' certainly met with widespread approval and came to dominate the Dutch moderate mainstream.[26] But this arguably misses the point with regard to the further propagation of Dutch democratic republican ideas: for it is precisely the radical character of Spinoza's and the de La Courts' principles—as well as those of van den Enden, Koerbagh, Walten, de Hooghe, van der Muelen, van Leenhof, and Mandeville—which separates what is most original and significant in late seventeenth- and early eighteenth-century Dutch political thought from the more respectable Dutch as well as wider western moderate Enlightenment.

It makes little sense, in other words, to search for a distinctive national 'Dutch republican' tradition based on the de La Courts and Spinoza when the real issue is to differentiate the Dutch Radical Enlightenment clearly from the conservative oligarchic republican and Calvinist-Orangist political ideology which dominated

20 [De Hooghe], *Postwagen-Praetjen*, 5; de Hooghe, *Spiegel van Staat*, ii. 22; Israel, 'Monarchy', 12, 15.

21 Israel, 'Monarchy', 12.

22 Israel, *Radical Enlightenment*, 406–35; Israel, 'Spinoza, King Solomon', 303–17.

23 Van Leenhof, *Het Leven*, 45–6; Wielema, *March*, 118.

24 Mandeville, *Free Thoughts*, 297.

25 Kossmann, *Politieke theorie*, 233; Wildenberg, *Johan en Pieter de La Court*, 51.

26 *Bibliothèque choisie*, 15 (1708), 87–8.

Dutch urban culture during most of the eighteenth century. If only sporadically, the 'Spinozist' republican tradition was revived in the early eighteenth century by various writers in Italy, Germany, and England as well as France and Holland, notably by Radicati and, of course, Mandeville, whose thought is better interpreted as radical, Dutch, and Spinozist (and to an extent also Baylean) than as Hobbesian as it has often been regarded.[27] Where the conservative Orangist Élie Luzac (1721–96), as part of his campaign against the Patriots in the 1780s, unerringly identified the brothers de La Court as a principal target of his publications,[28] the more democratic elements of the pre-revolutionary *Patriottenbeweging* of the 1780s made no secret of their admiration for the theories of the de La Courts, at the same time seeing themselves (and being regarded by their opponents) as adherents of a broad European philosophical radicalism.[29]

Viewed in this light, the political thought of the de La Courts and Spinoza was not, after all, a dead-end. It was on the contrary, the intellectual source of the strand of republicanism which developed ultimately into Jacobinism, and attempted, after 1789, to eradicate monarchy, social hierarchy, and ecclesiastical power by means of revolution. In this connection, it is worth noting the frequency with which works by the de La Courts and Spinoza resurface first in German and later, in numerous eighteenth-century libraries, in French, German, and English editions. Already before 1672, three different major political treatises of the de La Courts appeared in German, the first in 1665, so it is far from surprising Leibniz went out of his way to meet Pieter de La Court, in Leiden, whilst visiting Holland in 1676.[30] During the early eighteenth century, following publication under the supposed authorship of 'Johan de Witt' of Pieter de La Court's *True Interest*, in French and English editions, the de La Courts' books clearly remained widely available.[31]

[27] Den Uyl, 'Passion, State and Progress', 369–95; Dekker, 'Private Vices', 481–98; Israel, *Radical Enlightenment*, 623–7.

[28] Velema, 'Introduction', 136–7.

[29] Leeb, *Ideological Origins*, 34–5, 39; Wildenberg, *Johan en Pieter de La Court*, 47; Velema, 'Verlichtingen in Nederland', 51–3.

[30] These were V.D.H. [Pieter de La Court], *Interesse von Holland, oder Fondamenten von Hollands-Wohlfahrt* (n.p.,1665); [Johan de La Court], *Consideratien von Staat, oder Politische Wagschale mit welcher die allgemeine Angelegenheiten, Haupt-Gründe und Mängel aller Republicken wie sie von langer Zeit biss itzo her gewesen und zugleich die beständigste, nützlichste auch beste Art und Form einer freyen politischen Regierung in gleicher Gegenhaltung erwogen allen verständigen politicis zu fernerer Betrachtung und geschichter Vollziehung dargestellet wird* (Leipzig, 1669), translated and dedicated to a group of Dresden officials by Christoph Kormart; and [Pieter de La Court], *Anweisungen der heilsamen politischen Grunden und Maximen der Republicquen Holland und West-Vriesland* (Rotterdam, 1671), editions discussed among others by Johann Joachim Becher and Nikolas Hieronymus Gundling; see Wildenberg, *Johan en Pieter de La Court*, 55–6, 131; Israel, *Dutch Primacy*, 234, 291, 350.

[31] See 'J. de Witt' [Pieter de La Court], *The True Interest and Political Maxims of the Republick of Holland and West-Friesland* (London, 1702); [Pieter de La Court], *Fables, Moral and Political with Large Explications*, trans. from the Dutch (2 vols., London, 1703); J. de Wit [Pieter de La Court], *Mémoires de Jean de Wit, grand pensionnaire de Hollande*, trans M. de *** (The Hague, 1709); J. de Wit [Pieter de La Court], *Mémoires de Jean de Wit, grand pensionnaire de Hollande* ('Ratisbonne', chez Erasme Kinkius, 1709); J. de Witt [Pieter de La Court], *Political Maxims of the State of Holland* (London, 1743); J. de Witt [Pieter de La Court], *The True Interest and Political Maxims of the Republic of Holland*, trans. John Campbell (London, 1746).

Spinoza who, like Sir William Temple (with whom he very likely held discussions at the time), resided in The Hague during the mid and later 1660s, in 1670 published his *Tractatus theologico-politicus* amidst a highly charged political as well as intellectual atmosphere. This lent his text added intensity and urgency and helped, together with its revolutionary Bible criticism, give the work a much wider European notoriety—but also impact, especially in Germany (where Leibniz filled his copy with handwritten notes which survive today) and France—than could have resulted from a work of pure political theory alone.[32] Indeed, the highly competent French translation, clandestinely produced under three different 'false' titles in 1678, had an unparalleled influence for such a subversive work not just in France but also in the German courts where, among court ladies, the mother of George I of England, the future Electress Sophia of Hanover, was one of Spinoza's first and most enthusiastic readers.

The kind of democratic republicanism expounded first by Johan de La Court (1622–60) in his *Consideratien van Staat* (1660), then, was totally at odds with mainstream Dutch opinion and, again in contrast to English republicanism, showed all the psychological traits of an oppositional temperament albeit directed not against the then government but rather against traditional attitudes and conventional thinking. Despite the undoubted impact of their books in the United Provinces, as well as abroad, practically no pamphleteers or propagandists of the 1660s, 1670s, or later—Orangist or anti-Orangist—and practically none of those who aligned with either main bloc of the Dutch Reformed Church (Voetian and Cocceian), praised the political theorizing of the brothers de La Court or even mentioned them in anything other than a hostile, disparaging fashion. Those who did endorse their approach, like van den Enden, Koerbagh, Spinoza, Walten, and Mandeville, were themselves too radical, and beyond the pale, given their general philosophical stance, antipathy to ecclesiastical authority, and promotion of individual freedom, to be favoured, quoted positively, or recommended, by anyone with any pretension to respectability.

Admittedly, Walten and de Hooghe, while concurring with the passionate anti-monarchism of Johan and Pieter de La Court and the former brother's democratic sentiments, also fiercely criticize Pieter especially for being the mouthpiece of Johan de Witt and the regent oligarchy.[33] Walten did not share the de La Courts' sympathy for the States' faction in Dutch politics, apparently preferring the views of the politically sceptical but highly astute Aitzema, as well as of the Orangist republican Petrus Valckenier (1638–1712).[34] These perspectives enabled him to lend vigorous support to the Dutch intervention in Britain, in 1688, and laud the prince of Orange,[35] while simultaneously proclaiming, like de Hooghe, that people choose the form of state in which they live and can never lose their sovereign 'magt en regt'

32 Israel, *Dutch Republic*, 785–90, 889–22.

33 [Walten], *Wederlegginge*, 4, 51.

34 Ibid. 4–24, 56, 73, 75; Israel, *Dutch Republic*, 674, 684, 759, 786.

35 Walten, *Spiegel der Waerheyd*, 81.

[might and right]. Hence, Dutch democratic republicanism was from its very inception, around 1660, a general outcast and renegade inside as well as outside the Netherlands. Partly this was due to its egalitarianism, advocacy of personal freedom, and antagonism to ecclesiastical authority—as well as its pronounced anti-monarchism—and partly to its close links with radical, that is Spinozist, philosophy more generally. For the democratic republicanism expounded by van den Enden, Adriaen Koerbagh (1632–69),[36] Lodewijk Meyer (1629–81)—probable author of the anonymously published *De jure ecclesiasticorum* (1665),[37] a vehement attack on ecclesiastical status and power—as well as Spinoza, Walten, de Hooghe, van Leenhof, and Mandeville, stemmed directly from, and remained intellectually closely tied to, a philosophical underpinning rejecting all *a priori* authority, miracles, and divine revelation.

2. DEMOCRACY IN RADICAL THOUGHT

To view the emergence of modern democratic republicanism in its proper light, therefore, one must appreciate the direct linkage in radical minds between 'philosophy' as they understood the term—that is something like the *esprit philosophique* of the *philosophes*—and the principles of individual freedom, equality, and democracy.[38] These writers believed realization of their political ideals depended on the prior thorough re-education of the public. Particularly insistent on this is van den Enden for whom popular enlightenment is not just a desirable but, in contrast to the de La Courts,[39] also a feasible and imminent reality so that consciousness of the 'common good' as a political and social imperative in his writing carries much of the weight it later acquires in Diderot, Boulanger, Morelly, Mably, Rousseau, and Condorcet.[40] Indeed, in van den Enden harmony between private interest and the 'common good', rather optimistically, is thought to ensue almost automatically from the establishment of the democratic republic.[41]

But whether zealous and militant, as with van den Enden, or measured and cautious, as with Spinoza, the discrediting and delegitimizing of social hierarchy and elimination of monarchy, hereditary status, and ecclesiastical authority which their systems entail, as well as the replacement of hierarchy with their notional equality

[36] Vandenbossche, 'Quelques idées', 223–40; Jongeneelen, 'Philosophie politique', 247–67.

[37] 'Lucius Antistes Constans' in any case belonged to the circle around Spinoza and shared the same basic premisses, see Tuck, *Natural Rights Theories*, 140–1; Blom, *Morality and Causality*, 105, 282.

[38] Giancotti-Boscherini, 'Liberté, démocratie', 82–3.

[39] Kossmann, *Political Thought*, 69; Klever, ' "Conflicting" Considerations', 5.

[40] McShea, *Political Philosophy*, 191–2; Mertens, 'Franciscus van den Enden'; Israel, *Radical Enlightenment*, 78–80.

[41] Mertens, 'Franciscus van den Enden'; Klever, *Mannen rond Spinoza*, 29–31; Israel, *Radical Enlightenment*, 175–80.

of the 'state of nature', derives from their common espousal of a monist philosophical tendency. Their redefining of Man as an exclusively natural phenomenon determined like other natural phenomena seems, especially in this early formative stage of modern democratic republicanism, to have been a *sine qua non* for its conceptualization, as indeed was the general context of philosophical warfare gripping Dutch society and the Reformed Church at the time.

Democratic republicanism in early modern Europe hence arose from a particular philosophical movement formed within a highly fraught intellectual arena gripped by relentless strife between opposed schools of thought.[42] 'I have observ'd as much hatred and animosity between the Aristotelians and Cartesians when I was at Leiden,' remarks Mandeville, referring to his student days in the late 1680s, 'as there is now in London between High Church and Low-Church.'[43] Such a cultural background meant that incipient democratic republicanism could rely on an energized, alert reading public primed to absorb sweeping intellectual novelties. A radicalized offshoot of Cartesianism, the radical thinkers were the disowned progeny of a broad trend within Dutch culture itself born amid fierce conflict with Aristotelian scholasticism. From this double layer of acrimonious confrontation emerged a modern tradition of political thought, forged not only by political theoretical concepts working within a given social context, but, equally, a powerful impulse toward philosophical renewal, driven by Cartesianism and seeking comprehensively to emancipate the mind from conceptual shackles of the past.

Van den Enden twice makes a point of the sweeping novelty, as well as universal significance, of the democratic republicanism he so powerfully advocates. The first time he does so, in the *Vrye Politieke Stellingen*, he claims that in upholding the cause of the just commonwealth based on equality he had, to his own knowledge, been preceded (albeit only recently) by two other writers in Dutch. Unfortunately, he fails to tell us their names,[44] though presumably he is alluding either to both brothers de La Court or, conceivably, just Johan (whose democratic proclivities were stronger than his brother's, together with the radical Collegiant Zeelander Pieter Cornelis Plockhoy (dates unknown), an associate of van den Enden's in the early 1660s. Plockhoy was already in the late 1650s a fervent republican and egalitarian—albeit from an essentially biblical perspective, like the Levellers—a writer in no way inclined to mince words when discussing kings, aristocrats, and priests, as we see from his English-language pamphlet *A Way Propounded to Make the Poor in these and Other Nations Happy* (London, 1659) written whilst revolutionary democratic fervour was still alive in England, and he resided there, hoping his utopian vision could be realized in that country.[45]

The second occasion van den Enden styled democratic republicanism a fundamentally new idea in the history of political thought occurred a decade later,

[42] Israel, *Radical Enlightenment*, 3–29.

[43] Quoted in Monro, *Ambivalence*, 55.

[44] Van den Enden, *Vrye Politieke Stellingen*, 160–1; see also Mertens, 'Franciscus van den Enden', 725; De Dijn, 'Was Van den Enden het meesterbrein?', 76.

[45] Klever, 'Inleiding', 31–2; Israel, *Radical Enlightenment*, 175–80.

in 1674, after his arrest by the Paris police in connection with the conspiracy of the chevalier de Rohan. Under interrogation at the Bastille by the lieutenant-general of police, the marquis d'Argenson in person, van den Enden was asked to explain the political theory he had expounded in his writings and as a private tutor. This time, he claimed to have invented the new concept himself and to be its chief publicist: over the centuries, he responded, three different kinds of republic had figured in the published literature. These he classed as, first, the 'Platonic republic', secondly, that of 'Grotius'—meaning the oligarchic or regent republic, and thirdly, the 'utopian', that is the ideal of Sir Thomas More. Latterly, though, he added, not without a note of pride, there arose, through his own writings, a wholly novel political construct—the 'free republic' based on equality, freedom of expression, and the 'common good'.[46] The expression 'common good'—'*t gemenebest* in Dutch—was the term van den Enden uses to designate a free commonwealth of the sort he advocates.[47] This was the concept to which he had converted his former pupil and principal French ally the Norman noble Gilles du Hamel, sieur de La Tréaumont.

La Tréaumont was not only van den Enden's chief French disciple but also de Rohan's main co-conspirator and right-hand man in Normandy where the planned revolution was to begin. He was shot and mortally wounded, though, resisting arrest by the royal police, at his Rouen apartment, prior to van den Enden's own capture. The plotters, d'Argenson discovered, aspired to establish in Normandy just such a 'free commonwealth' as is expounded in the *Vrye Politieke Stellingen* and as van den Enden and Plockhoy had hoped to establish in America with their colony at Swanendael (1663–4) on the Delaware Estuary, in New Netherland.[48] Whether La Tréaumont and the other noble conspirators really embraced van den Enden's new democratic republican vision with the ardour he suggested we shall never know. But it is certain at any rate that, on being searched by the police, La Tréaumont's lodgings were found to contain French translations not just of the published part of the *Vrye Politieke Stellingen* but also the unpublished second part and other relevant material, including republican placards, afterwards burnt by the authorities and now lost.[49]

Of van den Enden's two incompatible statements about the origin of the modern 'democratic republic', the earlier seems the more plausible. For in afterwards attributing the invention of the modern democratic republic based on equality to himself, he indefensibly passed over Johan de La Court's *Consideratien van Staat* (1660), incontestably the founding document of seventeenth-century Dutch democratic republicanism. In that work, Johan de La Court not only declares the democratic republic a better, and more appropriate, type of state than monarchy or aristocracy but expressly grounds its superiority on the principles of equality and

[46] *Archives de la Bastille*, vii. 447, interrogation dated 21 Nov. 1674; Israel, *Radical Enlightenment*, 183; Blom, 'Politieke Filosofie', 174; Klever, *Democratische Vernieuwing*, 32–6.

[47] Klever, ' "Conflicting" Considerations', 10.

[48] *Archives de la Bastille*, vii. 420–1, 467; Klever, 'Inleiding', 81.

[49] Van den Enden, *Vrye Politieke Stellingen*, 150–6; Bedjaï, 'Franciscus van den Enden', 293–4.

reason, pronouncing it the 'most natural form of government' [natuirlijkste] and the most rational [redelijkste].[50] It is manifestly the best, being the system which most clearly serves the interests of the community as a whole.[51] Spinoza follows him when he says, in the sixteenth chapter of his *Tractatus theologico-politicus*, that he rates democracy above other kinds of polity 'because it seems the most natural form of state, approaching most closely to that freedom which nature grants to every man' [quia maxime naturale videbatur, et maxime ad libertatem, quam natura unicuique concedit, accedere].[52] Democracy's superiority over other types of government, for Spinoza, as for van den Enden and later Meslier, Morelly, and Mably, stems from its guaranteeing the individual more autonomy than the rest, leaving Man closer to the state of nature than other forms of constitution, and ensuring maximum approximation to equality among individuals, the means by which men will be freer and happier.[53]

This stress on what is most 'natural' and 'most rational' runs like a thread through the entire history of Dutch democratic republican doctrine before resurfacing in the work of mid eighteenth-century French republicans. A typical feature of the tradition, from the de La Courts and van den Enden onwards, was their insistence on a much wider toleration, and freedom of expression, than was then anywhere acceptable to moderate mainstream opinion or admirers of Locke. In the social and political context of their time, such demands for full toleration inevitably entailed a drastic reduction, if not complete demolition, of ecclesiastical power and authority, which meant that their *tolérantisme* was, even in the Netherlands, condemned as dangerously impious to the extent that even the very proposition could not be freely advocated. The chief reason why the States of Holland banned Pieter de La Court's *Aanwijsing der Heilsame Politieke Gronden* (1669), a hard-hitting rehash of his earlier *Interest van Holland* (1662), shortly after its publication, was precisely because of its virtual obliteration of ecclesiastical authority and uncompromising advocacy of a 'free practice of all religions and sects'.[54]

Comprehensive toleration, as we have seen, was not permitted in society anywhere at the time. But it was a common feature of the political thought of the de La Courts, van den Enden, Koerbagh, Spinoza, Temple, Bayle, Walten, van Leenhof, Toland, and Mandeville as well as Radicati, Jean-Frédéric Bernard, Edelmann, Johann Lorenz Schmidt, and other early eighteenth-century radicals Dutch, French, German, British, and Italian. A key difference in political implications between the 'Arminian' toleration of Locke, van Limborch, and Le Clerc, on the one hand, and the broader toleration of the democratic republicans, on the other, was

50 Kossmann, *Political Thought*, 63–71; Matheron, *Individu et communauté*, 361–3; Velema, 'Introduction', 136; Cook, 'Body and Passions', 43–4.

51 Blom, 'Burger en Belang', 109.

52 Spinoza, *Opera*, iii. 195; Hardt and Negri, *Empire*, 185.

53 McShea, *Political Philosophy*, 84, 124; Giancotti-Boscherini, 'Liberté, démocratie', 88; Talmon, *Origins*, 57; Balibar, *Spinoza and Politics*, 32–4, 48–9; Smith, 'What Kind', 22–4.

54 Gemeentearchief Leiden Sec. Arch. 191 Notulen Burgemeesteren, res. 21 May 1669; van Rees, *Verhandeling over de* Aanwijsing, 41–2; Israel, *Dutch Republic*, 786.

the principle, fundamental to the radicals, but rejected by the moderate mainstream, that a stable, enduring toleration requires the assimilation of ecclesiastical power and resources into the state; for if the churches are left with their autonomy in society, politics, and education, the clergy will always, for their own purposes, exploit their position and prestige, as well as popular addiction to 'superstitious' and intolerant notions, to mobilize the masses against any political decision or opponent of which they disapprove.[55] The Counter-Remonstrants had done precisely this in 1618, when, stirring popular opposition and dissent with their uncompromising Calvinist theology, they overthrew and replaced the regime of the Holland regents headed by Oldenbarnevelt.

Accordingly, Lodewijk Meyer, in his *De jure ecclesiasticorum*, and Spinozist radicals more generally, insisted on completely eliminating the independent authority, autonomy, privileges, property, and grip on education as well as the censorship functions of the clergy. In this spirit, Pieter de La Court, especially in his *Aanwijsing* of 1669, combines his plea for a comprehensive religious and intellectual toleration with a passionate critique of ecclesiastical privilege and authority which antagonized many Dutch contemporaries and for which he was sternly rebuked by the Leiden Reformed Church consistory.[56] Similarly, Ericus Walten, likewise an ardent advocate of freedom of thought and expression, denounced by at least one opponent as a crypto-Spinozist,[57] was a fierce critic of the Reformed Church preachers, maintaining there are clear links between the principle of democracy, comprehensive toleration, and the elimination of ecclesiastical autonomy and authority. 'The ecclesiastical', in his view, should come 'under the political government', for if the ecclesiastical authority is not truly subordinate to the political, 'neither would the latter derive from the people'.[58] Hence, if the clergy are assigned a special autonomous status and privileges then the common good and interests of the people cannot be the sole or even main criterion of legitimacy in politics.

While several scholars have commented recently on what has been called 'the powerful influence of the De la Courts on Mandeville', especially with respect to his theory of the passions and human motivation, there has also been a noticeable tendency to downplay, ignore, and sometimes even deny, his radical Deism.[59] As a result, his broad intellectual affinity to Spinozism and the Dutch radical republican stream more generally has been obscured by claims that he was not as radical or Deistic as he sounds. It has even been suggested that his 'religious views are really much more conventional and anodyne than Bayle's'.[60] Yet throughout his works not only does Mandeville regularly rebuke the clergy for meddling in secular affairs,

[55] Van den Enden, *Vrye Politieke Stellingen*, 153–7, 178–81.

[56] Kerkhoven and Blom, 'De La Court en Spinoza', 144–6; van der Bijl, 'Pieter de La Court', 73; Israel, *Dutch Republic*, 760–1.

[57] [Iiritiel Leetsosoneus], *Den Swadder*, 12, 21; van Bunge, *From Stevin to Spinoza*, 144.

[58] Knuttel, 'Ericus Walten', 355.

[59] Cook, 'Bernard Mandeville', 116; see also Hundert, *Enlightenment's Fable*, 24–9; Hundert, 'Bernard Mandeville', 583–5.

[60] James, 'Faith, Sincerity', 51–2.

inciting strife among the laity, and their generally excessive pretensions,[61] but he also advocates the drastic curbing or even complete eradication of ecclesiastical power. Unsurprisingly, Bishop Berkeley, Francis Hutcheson, and many other critics in his own time claimed he was an atheist or radical Deist beyond the pale of respectability and there is reason to think they were right.[62]

Actually, there was much that was radical in Mandeville. Following the brothers de La Court, van den Enden, and Spinoza, his own writings show that he too strove to eradicate theological premisses from society and politics as well as moral and intellectual debate. Just as Spinoza, in the *Tractatus theologico-politicus*, holds true 'faith' to consist solely in obedience to the law, and in 'justice and charity', so 'once for all', echoes Mandeville, 'the Gospel teaches us obedience to superiors and charity to all men', implying this is, in essence, all it teaches.[63] As a student, Mandeville may well have been taught by Bayle in his home town Rotterdam, and, as we know for certain from his published Leiden university thesis *Disputatio philosophica de brutorum operationibus* (Leiden, 1689), presented 'sub presidio B. de Volder', he was steeped in Dutch Cartesianism.[64] While this in itself does not prove an inclination towards radical thought or that he necessarily read Spinoza, it is certain that his principal Leiden teacher, Burchardus de Volder (1643–1709), not only introduced his pupils to the latest Dutch philosophical debates but was widely rumoured to have been a crypto-Spinozist himself and, indeed, as a Franeker anti-Cartesian put it, to have misled 'many a student who later became infected with Spinoza's errors'.[65] Hence, though he refers to him only very infrequently, it is most unlikely Mandeville, whose father was a prominent Cartesian medical reformer in Rotterdam and associate of the radical Cartesian (and suspected Spinozist) Dr Cornelis Bontekoe, did not possess first-hand knowledge of Spinoza's works, or did not participate in discussions about Spinozism as a student, especially since he cites the de La Courts, Bayle, van Dale, and Bekker.[66]

In any case, Mandeville upheld the kind of broad toleration of van den Enden, Koerbagh, Temple, Spinoza, and van Leenhof, which permits the expression of all views, accommodating all religious denominations and heresies as well as atheism and Deism, implying the political sovereign should be indifferent to the saving of souls. Such a standpoint signifies, as Bayle especially stressed, that belief in a providential God is not a prerequisite for the orderly functioning of civil society and upholding of the moral order. What Le Clerc called the 'abominable paradoxe de Mr Bayle', that the moral systems on which all societies depend do not need to be based on religion and that 'les athées peuvent vivre aussi bien que les Chrétiens',

[61] Dickinson, 'Politics', 86–7; Hundert, *Enlightenment's Fable*, 6, 47, 102–3.

[62] Monro, *Ambivalence*, 196–7, 263–5; Primer 'Bernard Mandeville', in Kors (ed.), *Encyclopedia*, iii. 17.

[63] Mandeville, *Free Thoughts*, 246.

[64] Wielema, *Filosofen*, 69–70; Israel, *Radical Enlightenment*, 623, 736.

[65] Israel, *Radical Enlightenment*, 482; Klever, 'Burchardus de Volder', 191–241; Klever, 'Bernard Mandeville', 2.

[66] On Mandeville's 'Spinozism', see Den Uyl, 'Passion, State and Progress', 374–81; Israel, *Radical Enlightenment*, 585–6, 623–7; Cook, 'Bernard Mandeville', 111–18.

in fact underlay the entire tradition.[67] Hence, contemporaries were right to link this kind of toleration with the sort of philosophy advocated by Spinoza, the late Bayle, and their disciples. For in Spinozist eyes, philosophical 'truth' is the only true theology and 'theology', as conventionally understood, is something which possesses no separate truth content of its own; and while, ostensibly, Bayle softened this by declaring merely that faith cannot support, or be supported by, reason so that whatever is explicable by human reason can only be explained philosophically, and not theologically, for all intents and purposes, including questions of toleration and individual freedom, the two positions amount to the same thing. Both strategies were designed to ensure that neither state nor ecclesiastical authority should possess authority to coerce or restrict men's enquiries, beliefs, or the individual's moral conscience.

This grounding of theories of comprehensive toleration in Spinozistic philosophy linked to democratic republicanism is well illustrated by the ideas—and attacks on the ideas—of Fredrik van Leenhof (1647–1712), at Zwolle. A Reformed preacher expounding a moral and social theory rooted in an avowedly republican stance, van Leenhof in 1700 published two books ostensibly about the biblical King Solomon, but in fact about modern society and politics and then followed these up with his *Den Hemel op Aarden* [Heaven on Earth] (1703), a highly controversial work widely condemned in the Netherlands during the first decade of the eighteenth century as a vehicle of popular Spinozism.[68] Steeped in Spinoza since at least the early 1680s, van Leenhof despised kings in general, albeit not Solomon, whom he, like his hero, thought of as a towering exception to the habitual self-centredness and mediocrity of royalty. Linking his political theory to a plea for popular enlightenment and a comprehensive toleration of all beliefs, as well as freedom of expression of all views, van Leenhof publicized the essence of Spinoza's politics in a lightly veiled and undemanding vernacular style.

As one of his numerous outraged critics observed, these works of van Leenhof 'advocate a political religion which consists of just a few basic doctrines designed to secure social peace and love within civil society giving everyone complete freedom to think and speak about religion just as he pleases'.[69] His writings also echoed Johan de La Court's claim that the democratic republic is the 'the most rational' form of government and exhibit yet another characteristic of radical republicanism distinguishing it philosophically and politically from other sorts of republicanism—and Lockean liberalism—namely the claim that 'reason' is the sole legitimate criterion for evaluating the different kinds of polity and forms of political power.[70] For not only divine right monarchy and theocracy but also constitutional monarchy, and all types of oligarchy and aristocracy, affirm the principle of heredity, and other sources of alleged legitimacy, drawing prestige and authority from tradition,

[67] *Bibliothèque choisie*, 14 (1708), 305.
[68] Wielema, 'Ketters en Verlichters', 52–9; Israel, *Radical Enlightenment*, 406–35.
[69] Burmannus, *'t Hoogste Goed der Spinozisten*, 11; Israel, 'Spinoza, King Solomon', 310.
[70] Van den Enden, *Vrye Politieke Stellingen*, 162–3; Israel, *Radical Enlightenment*, 259.

precedent, and ecclesiastical sanction. Indeed, we can be certain of a radical disposition whenever an Early Enlightenment writer follows Spinoza in declaring that in human affairs, including discussion about the best types of constitution, 'reason' is the exclusive criterion of what is good or bad: 'sicuti in statu naturali ille homo maxime potens maximeque sui juris est qui ratione ducitur, sic etiam illa civitas maxime erit potens et maxime sui juris quae ratione fundatur et dirigitur' [just as in the state of nature that man has most power and is most autonomous who is guided by reason, thus also that state will be most powerful and most autonomous which is based on and guided by reason].[71]

Van Leenhof, holding that reason, and not hereditary principle or tradition, must be the exclusive basis of political legitimacy, maintains that 'everything is good insofar as it accords therewith and can rightly be considered divine, everything else being slavery under the appearance of government'.[72] 'Knowledge of matters' he considers the only light by which we can proceed in debate about politics and the exclusive aid to adjusting our lives to the 'nature of God's order and guidance', a typical Spinozist usage, later Morelly's *l'ordre de la nature*, denoting the fixed and rational structure of reality and Man's place in it. Conversely, ignorance and lack of knowledge is in politics, as in everything else, in van Leenhof's opinion, 'the root of all evil'.[73] Reason and 'wisdom', he adds, again employing the populist Spinozist phraseology he had coined, as well as being the key to assessing everything in politics is the path 'whereby we share in God's nature, the highest human good and happiness'.

An exclusively rationalistic philosophy is, for van Leenhof, not just the only authentic grounding for the new doctrine of democratic republicanism but also the path to Man's true redemption. 'Reason' alone can justify equality and show that the 'common good', what Romeyn de Hooghe calls the 'algemeen belang',[74] Diderot the 'general will', and Morelly 'le bien commun', is the veritable and only legitimate standard for legislation; and since reason teaches that the 'common interest' is the sole authentic measure, the inevitable corollary is that serving princes, and cultivating their interests, and devoting oneself to the pomp and circumstance of court life, is, holds van Leenhof (following the de La Courts and van den Enden), inherently reprehensible, corrupt, and morally base.[75] The 'honour' men derive from proximity to kings and their courts is, in his eyes, worthless pomp, flattery, and deceit, something diametrically opposed to the 'common good'. For there can be no kingship, aristocracy, hierarchy, subordination, submission, or slavery, he, like the other Dutch radicals, thought, where power rightfully belongs to all and where laws should be passed by common consent. Genuine 'honour', he proclaims, scorning aristocratic and conventional conceptions of 'honour', is in reality nothing other

[71] Spinoza, *Tractatus politicus*, 287.

[72] Van Leenhof, *Het Leven*, 51, 81; see also van Leenhof, *De Prediker*, 131.

[73] Van Leenhof, *De Prediker*, 84.

[74] De Hooghe, *Spiegel van Staat*, i. 10, ii. 57; Israel, 'Monarchy', 15, 27.

[75] Van Leenhof, *De Prediker*, 132–4.

than 'God en reden, en 't gemeen te dienen' [to serve God and reason, and the community].[76]

Another distinctive feature of democratic republicanism, the wider European Radical Enlightenment, and later also of the age of Revolution (1780–1848), which again derives from a particular kind of philosophy, is the doctrine that there is no absolute 'good' or 'evil', that what is good is what is 'good' for men in society. This concept tied democratic republicanism to the central problems of moral philosophy as conceived by Spinoza, Bayle, and Diderot and it was to retain this close interaction throughout the Enlightenment era, being precisely the linkage signalled by Morelly with his expression 'Code de la nature' which he chose, in 1754, for the title of his most subversive tract.[77]

The political theory thus depended on a particular metaphysics and new kind of *moralisme* and the latter, especially, closely depended, in turn, on the political theory. As early as around 1720, the emergence of a new and fully secular moral philosophy based on Spinozistic premisses was already intimately linked to a republican politics in France, as is apparent especially from the writings of Boulainvilliers, Du Marsais, and Meslier, albeit in Boulainvilliers's case an aristocratic rather than democratic republicanism. A republican politics was clearly integral, even essential, to the purely secular moral stance adopted by these writers. According to Du Marsais, the psychology of life without religion in the conventional sense leads the ideal man, *le philosophe*, to embrace probity and uprightness and the reputation of being upright: 'c'est là son unique religion'.[78] 'La société civile', and its requirements and well-being, argues Du Marsais, become for him the only divinity on earth which he recognizes, and this divinity he cultivates and honours by giving an exact and conscientious attention to his social responsibilities and through his resolve to be a useful member of society. The kind of materialist atheism represented by Du Marsais necessarily creates a context in which the well-being of society becomes simultaneously both the highest political good and the unalterable basis of morality and true 'piety'.

By contrast the man of 'faith' in the usual sense, or the 'superstitieux', as Du Marsais prefers to call such a person, even when raised to positions of the highest responsibility in society, still considers himself in some sense a stranger here on earth, a temporary visitor whose chief responsibility is to transcendent beings, values, and aims rather than the worldly well-being of men, a theme later much expanded on by Diderot.[79] Also, Christian disdain for worldly success, prosperity, and social standing—whatever religious justifications such attitudes may acquire—is, in the end, contrary to what is needed to render a society happy and flourishing. In particular, Du Marsais condemns the ideal of 'poverty' as antisocial and counterproductive, since poverty deprives us of the well-being which makes worthwhile

[76] Van Leenhof, *Het Leven*, 50; Israel, 'Spinoza, King Solomon', 312.
[77] Morelly, *Code de la nature*, 142–4.
[78] [Du Marsais], *Le Philosophe*, 188, 192–4.
[79] Ibid. 198.

pleasures possible: 'elle bannit loin de nous toutes les délicatesses sensibles et nous éloigne du commerce des honnêtes gens'.[80]

Reaffirming Spinoza's principle that the more one lives according to reason directed towards one's own self-interest, the more one is fitted for life in society, Du Marsais holds that the dishonest man is as opposite to the true image of the *philosophe*, conceived as the ideal man of reason, as is a simpleton with scant understanding. Managing the passions, the *philosophe* may be somewhat inclined towards sensual satisfaction and pleasure but never towards crime or antisocial activity.[81] His cultivated reason leads him to display his independence in such a way as never to cause strife or disorderly conduct.[82] The *philosophe* is thus an honest man, holds Du Marsais, 'qui agit en tout par raison, et qui joint à un esprit de réflexion et de justesse les mœurs et les qualités sociables' [who acts in everything according to reason joining a spirit of reflection and justice with morality and the sociable qualities].[83]

Since the republic's laws are the only enforced and politically sanctioned set of guidelines as to what is 'good' and 'bad' in human conduct, they are also if not the foundation (which is reason) certainly the prop and chief support of morality.[84] In this way, the republic's legislation becomes the root of moral obligation, allegiance, and duty, indeed the only valid object of public reverence and obedience, while, conversely, morality in the Radical Enlightenment's sense and, therefore, the 'common good' as defined by Spinoza, Bayle, and Diderot, become the yardstick by which to judge political events and laws old and new as well as suggested amendments. Since there are no divine commandments, according to the Spinozists, or reward or punishment in the hereafter, Heaven and Hell being—as van Leenhof dared affirm (with disastrous consequences for himself)[85]—purely worldly states of mind, there is no other way to uphold order, repress crime, and instil discipline than by means of worldly rewards and penalties proclaimed and enforced by the state and its legislature.[86] This was very much also Mandeville's view.

An important consequence of the claim that human rewards and penalties in the here and now count for more than revealed religion, allegedly divine commandments, and the promise of Heaven and threat of Hell, when it comes to civilizing and disciplining men, and repressing aggression and crime, is a new urgency for the secular polity to be stable, well organized, and efficient. In a striking passage of *Den Hemel op Aarden*, van Leenhof affirms, much like Du Marsais later,[87] that rulers have learnt from experience that theological doctrines instilling dread of divine chastisement in practice exert little effect on hardened criminals and reprobates. Such men mock 'divine' admonitions and entirely set them aside when embarking on their careers of pillage, murder, and other 'mad and bestial passion'. They can be

80 [Du Marsais], *Le Philosophe*, 202. 81 Ibid. 192. 82 Ibid. 83 Ibid. 200.

84 McShea, *Political Philosophy*, 57–7.

85 Van Leenhof, *Hemel op Aarden*, 3–7, 15, 19–20, 33; Israel, *Radical Enlightenment*, 410–12.

86 Israel, *Radical Enlightenment*, 409; van Leenhof, *Het Leven*, 81; van Leenhof, *De Prediker*, 131.

87 [Du Marsais], *Le Philosophe*, 191.

effectively restrained, he contends, only by credible legal deterrents and vigorous policing.[88]

The magistrate who understands what is 'good' and 'bad' for society, he says, 'can do more to curb the godless than all the preachers together', the sovereign power having 'long arms and a thousand eyes through its officials and loyal subjects'.[89] Crime flourishes, he says, where government is weak and the law inadequately enforced: for even in a well-regulated republic only a very few people are truly 'free' and virtuous, that is exercise their own reason adequately, most people obeying the law, as Mandeville later also affirmed, not through love of virtue but merely through fear of punishment.[90] Yet whether government is strong or weak, it is the law-abiding and those who revere the law who are the most 'rational' and, whatever priests may say, also the most 'pious', and this has always been so.

What Mandeville adds to democratic republican theory was his insight that in inculcating obedience to the law, it is not just fear of penalties, and hope of reward, which count but also, and perhaps even more, the mechanics of 'pride' and 'shame'. Preoccupation with 'honour' and 'dishonour', he thinks, is a natural impulse in men which can be effectively exploited to discipline them and spread the legislators' notions of 'good' and 'bad' through society.[91] Hence, 'it was not any heathen religion or other idolatrous superstition that first put man upon crossing his appetites and subduing his dearest inclinations,' he assures readers, 'but the skilful management of wary politicians; and the nearer we search into human nature, the more we shall be convinc'd that the moral virtues are the political offspring which flattery begot upon pride'.[92]

Morality, for these writers, is 'relativistic' only in the restricted sense that there is no God-ordained 'good' and 'evil' and that the criterion of 'good' and 'bad' is what rational men judge beneficial, or not, to Man and what society decides—in van den Enden and Spinoza preferably through democratic assemblies[93]—promotes the 'common interest'. But this purely secular, quasi-utilitarian morality is at the same time universal, and eternally the same, since the 'general good' is as reason dictates and reason, hold Spinozists, is one, all-embracing and unchanging. In this way, the ethical 'relativism' of Spinozist republicanism yields a single moral code invariable and universal, based on reciprocity, equality, and personal freedom, something wholly unlike (and opposed to) the moral relativism of the late twentieth-century Postmodernist 'difference'.

Mandeville, like Hobbes and Spinoza, rules out freedom of the will, arguing that Man is a being determined regarding both motives and actions.[94] Furthermore, it is

[88] Van Leenhof, *Hemel op Aarden*, 108; van Leenhof, *De Prediker*, 249; Israel, 'Spinoza, King Solomon', 313–14; Wielema, *March*, 118.

[89] Van Leenhof, *Hemel op Aarden*, 108.

[90] Van Leenhof, *De Prediker*, 239, 242, 249.

[91] Monro, *Ambivalence*, 126–8, 232–3; James, 'Faith, Sincerity', 54–5.

[92] [Mandeville], *Fable of the Bees*, 34; Norton, 'Hume, Human Nature', 154.

[93] Van den Enden, *Vrye Politieke Stellingen*, 180, 206–8; Prokhovnik, *Spinoza*, 228–30.

[94] Olscamp, *Moral Philosophy*, 178; Den Uyl, 'Passion, State and Progress', 374–6; Klever, 'Bernard Mandeville', 5–8.

precisely this principle that he, like Spinoza and van Leenhof, employs to justify his view that rewards and penalties enacted by the state are the best way to correct, discipline, and civilize men's behaviour. Self-interest is what persuades the criminally inclined to curb their natural unruliness and defer to the law in a well-ordered state. 'There is nothing', asserts Mandeville, 'so universally sincere upon earth, as the love which all creatures that are capable of any, bear to themselves: and as there is no love but what implies a care to preserve the thing beloved, so there is nothing more sincere in any creature than his will, wishes and endeavours to preserve himself.'[95] This, he explains, is 'the law of nature, by which no creature is endowed with any appetite or passion but that which either directly or indirectly tends to the preservation either of himself or his species'.[96] Hence, in Mandeville, no less than Hobbes and Spinoza, the fact that Man is bound to conserve his being, and satisfy his desires, means he can be systematically deflected and deterred from antisocial conduct only by credible warnings of punishment and exposure.

Mandeville's notorious thesis, detested by so many eighteenth-century commentators, including Hume, that virtue is not innate or natural in Man and cannot be taught, is his equivalent of Spinoza's 'infamous' doctrine that 'virtue' is really equivalent to power and is always selfish in motivation and Morelly's claim there are no vices in the universe except avarice.[97] Instead of 'virtue' as something inculcated or learnt, Mandeville substitutes the Spinozistic principle that 'whoever will civilize men, and establish them in a body politick, must be thoroughly acquainted with all the passions and appetites, strengths and weaknesses of their frame, and understand how to turn their greatest frailties to the advantage of the publick'.[98]

Accordingly, respect for the law, integrity, and conscientiousness among office-holders and state officials should never be entrusted to what Mandeville calls the 'virtue and the honesty of ministers', even in the Dutch Republic which he rated distinctly higher than the monarchies of his day, being a state that afforded citizens a more effective rule of law, order, and justice than did the latter. The United Provinces cultivated the public interest, according to Mandeville, by means of 'their strict regulations concerning the management of the publick treasure, from which their admirable form of government will not suffer them to depart: and indeed one good man may take another's word, if they so agree, but a whole nation ought never to trust to any honesty, but what is built upon necessity; for unhappy is the people, and their constitution will ever be precarious, whose welfare must depend upon the virtues and consciences of ministers and politicians'.[99]

Hence in Mandeville, as in Spinoza, the level of probity and respect for the laws and 'common good' among government officials, in a particular regime, stems not

[95] [Mandeville], *Fable of the Bees*, 182. [96] Ibid.

[97] Norton, 'Hume, Human Nature', 154–6; Cook, 'Bernard Mandeville', 104–6; Spinoza, *Ethics*, ed. Parkinson, 63, 228–9, 241; Morelly, *Code de la nature*, 29, 45–6.

[98] [Mandeville], *Fable of the Bees*, 194; van Leenhof, *De Prediker*, 428; Hirschmann, *Passions and the Interests*, 18; Den Uyl, 'Passion, State and Progress', 381–2.

[99] [Mandeville], *Fable of the Bees*, 169–70; Blom, 'Republican Mirror', 114.

from the personal inclinations of office-holders which, broadly speaking, remain always the same, and are all equally liable to corruption, but from the effectiveness or otherwise of regulations, checks, and penalties devised to ensure accountability and respect for the law. Similarly, wrongdoing by individuals is checked only by good government and well-made laws just as, conversely, misconduct thrives on badly framed laws and official neglect. 'The first care therefore of all governments', declares Mandeville, is by severe punishments to curb [man's] anger when it does hurt, and so by increasing his fears prevent the mischief it might produce. When various laws to restrain him from using force are strictly executed, self-preservation must teach him to be peaceable; and as it is everybody's business to be as little disturb'd as is possible, his Fears will be continually augmented and enlarg'd as he advances in experience, understanding and foresight'.[100]

Where English apologists for justified resistance in and after 1688 mostly maintain that sovereignty originates in the people but is wholly relegated, by contract, to Parliament, writers like Walten and van der Muelen held that peoples who install kings or emperors not only never concede an 'absolute of arbitraire magt' but also retain the 'souveraine magt' within themselves, including an inalienable right of armed resistance.[101] This was also the opinion, subsequently, of the Piedmontese republican Radicati who, drawing on Italian sources like Machiavelli and Sarpi as well as Algernon Sidney, Spinoza, and other northern republicans, accounts all monarchical and aristocratic government unnatural,[102] reaffirming Spinoza's principle, in opposition to Hobbes, that the 'natural right' always remains intact under the state. Mandeville, admittedly, is less explicit on the subject of resistance than Walten or van der Muelen; but it was surely not for nothing that Bishop Berkeley denounced him as not just one of 'those pretended advocates for private light and free thought' agitating in early eighteenth-century England but also someone excessive in his 'Revolution-principles', one of those 'seditious men, who set themselves up against national laws and constitutions'.[103]

Meanwhile, the principle of equality fundamental to the new doctrine of democratic republicanism was likewise inherent not only in the moral ideas underpinning Spinozist conceptions of law and sovereignty but also in the radical republicans' view of the general goals and purposes of the state and its rational structure. Hence, yet another typical feature of democratic republicanism in stark contrast to English classical republicanism—as well, observed Boulanger, as ancient Greek republicanism—was its sweeping denial that the state is the guardian or repository of any divinely sanctioned tradition or institutions, or divinely revealed mysteries. Explicit assertion of human, rather than divine, origins was deemed essential, on the one hand, to harmonize with the ideas of those preferring philosophy to 'fables' and, on the other, to safeguard the decision-making machinery, legal

[100] [Mandeville] *Fable of the Bees*, 191; Klever, 'Bernard Mandeville', 7.
[101] Klever, 'Bernard Mandeville', 20; Dickinson, 'Politics', 86, 96.
[102] Radicati, *Twelve Discourses*, 176, 189, 199–200, 213, 240.
[103] Quoted in Monro, *Ambivalence*, 196–7.

terminology, and legislation from priestly interference. In particular, it seemed essential that all public declarations should cite the purpose of political institutions and legislation to be the protection of the security, freedom, order, and heightened opportunities available to all, emphasizing, as Morelly puts it, that a republic's citizens are 'singulièrement et collectivement dans une mutuelle dépendence'.[104] Even in societies where political institutions can only be explained in theological terms, it is still vital, contended radical republicans, that priests be debarred from staging religious ceremonies linked to the state's institutions, and prevented from influencing decision-making, or interfering in legislation. For the laws of the state exist to promote the 'general good' on a basis of equality for all, and hence cannot, or at least not without courting disaster, be publicly dedicated or inaugurated in the name of some purportedly 'sacred', priestly, or mysterious purpose.[105]

Individual passions and interests, as the de La Courts, Spinoza, van Leenhof, Mandeville, and all the participants in the Dutch republican tradition acknowledge, will always pervade the governance of the state. There is no way to ensure laws are 'introduced purely for the common prosperity and well-being without any particular interest being involved'; nor can every eventuality, as van Leenhof observes, be foreseen.[106] But if perfection is impossible, and no republic immune to degeneration, republics still offer humanity immeasurably better prospects for the common interest than other forms of state. Ultimately, it is not the type of state as such which counts but efficacy in serving the 'common good', this being the goal at the heart of the state's *raison d'être*. The Spinozist notion of the 'common good' defined in terms of safety, freedom, and the rule of law, the direct precursor of the mid eighteenth-century 'general will', provided a universal criterion of good and bad by which states of whatever kind could be appraised.[107] 'The best type of state is easily identified', averred Spinoza, 'from the purpose of the political order, which is simply peace and security of life.'[108]

Even the model democratic republic which has long respected the 'common good' can quickly degenerate through the doings of malicious men into something wholly different. No constitution or type of state is infallible; and, no matter how long a regime has functioned reasonably well, nothing remains legitimate that ceases to uphold the 'common good'. By 1770, Mably was warning the Poles that if they wished to rescue their country from the Russians and reconstitute Poland and the Polish constitution on a strengthened and viable basis, then they must take care not to emulate the British who complain continually 'des entreprises de la cour et de la corruption du Parlement', and yet feel they can do nothing to change their defective constitution, preferring to remain 'dans des alarmes continuelles, que de convenir des vices de leur gouvernement, et de les corriger'.[109] In the end, the best kind of

[104] Morelly, *Code de la nature*, 98.

[105] Van den Enden, *Vrye Politieke Stellingen*, 194–205; Israel, 'Spinoza, King Solomon', 313; Bartuschat, 'Ontological Basis', 34–5.

[106] Van Leenhof, *Het Leven*, 51.

[107] McShea, *Political Philosophy*, 107–9.

[108] Spinoza, *Tractatus politicus*, 311.

[109] Mably, *Du gouvernement et des lois de Pologne*, 72–3; see also ibid. 67, 70, 106, 179, 278.

state, Spinozist radicals contended, is simply that which fulfils its basic functions most durably and consistently: 'that is the best constitution', urged Mandeville, 'which provides against the worst contingencies, that is armed against knavery, treachery, deceit and all the wicked wiles of human cunning, and preserves itself firm and remains unshaken, though most men should prove knaves. It is with a national constitution, as with men's bodies: that which can bear most fatigues without being disorder'd, and last the longest in health, is the best.'[110]

110 Mandeville, *Free Thoughts*, 46; Dickinson, 'Politics', 95; Blom, 'Republican Mirror', 113.

11

Bayle, Boulainvilliers, Montesquieu: Secular Monarchy versus the Aristocratic Republic

1. BAYLE'S POLITICS

The pre-1750 Enlightenment fundamentally transformed political thought as it did every other aspect of western civilization and, here, Montesquieu has always rightly been identified as a—perhaps even the—key innovative thinker. Certainly no one had a greater impact than he on the discussion of political theory in mid eighteenth-century Europe. But while granting Montesquieu's originality and incomparable impact which remain undeniable, in the context of a general reassessment of the western Enlightenment such as this, it is requisite not to 'isolate' him, or leave the impression that he springs from nowhere, but rather adequately 'situate' him,[1] which means we must view his *oeuvre* as a response partly to his own experiences but even more to his reading and to prior developments in French and French exile thought. This involves looking especially at the relationship between Montesquieu and Bayle's monarchism, on the one hand, and, on the other, the aristocratic republicanism of Boulainvilliers.

Bayle's politics emerged against a background of local conflict, theological and political, in the Netherlands, in which he remained entangled throughout his most creative years as philosopher and writer. From the moment the 34-year-old philosopher left France never to return, settling in Rotterdam in October 1681, he found himself enmeshed in political controversy affecting not only his own political ideas but his philosophy more generally and not least his paradoxical, convoluted method of writing.[2] On Bayle's career as philosopher, editor, and historian impinged in direct and sometimes surprising ways many of the great political events of the age—the Revocation of the Edict of Nantes, Glorious Revolution, Nine Years War, prolonged toleration debates, and the consolidation of the Dutch stadtholderate.

On taking up his professorship in history and philosophy at the newly created civic 'Illustre School' at Rotterdam, Bayle's chief patron was the Remonstrant-minded

[1] Pocock, *Barbarism*, ii. 341–2.

[2] Labrousse, *Pierre Bayle*, i. 166, 215–34; Knetsch, *Pierre Jurieu*, 274–324.

regent Adriaen Paets (1631–86),[3] a leading anti-Orangist and prominent figure in the highly charged Dutch political world of the time. Advocating a broad Remonstrant-style toleration in the tradition of Episcopius, Paets disliked virtually all institutionalized ecclesiastical authority as well as criticizing the steady accumulation of power in the stadtholder's hands, urging a more neutralist Dutch policy, based on good relations with France. Accordingly, he resisted William III's anti-French strategy during the political crisis of 1683–4, in which Amsterdam, backed by a few other towns, obstructed the stadtholder's statecraft.[4]

The patronage of Paets meant that Bayle enjoyed the support of the Dutch anti-Orangists whom Louis XIV's diplomats styled 'républicains'. After the Glorious Revolution (1688–91), however, the growing weakness of this bloc, not least in Rotterdam where Paets and his allies were fiercely decried by the Calvinist orthodox, left him increasingly isolated, leading Bayle to develop an even more contrived technique of subterfuge and circumlocution in his writing than he had used before. For contrary to what is sometimes claimed, Bayle while residing in exile in Holland was not—and was less and less—able to express his views freely. What has aptly been called his 'tendance innée à la dissimulation' may have originated in the oppressive intellectual environment enveloping his early life in France and Geneva but proved just as indispensable, as his general philosophy became more radical, as a veil of discretion and as political cover, after settling in the 'grande arche des fugitifs', as he famously dubbed the United Provinces.[5]

Pivotal in Bayle's life and career, we have seen,[6] was his public humiliation in Rotterdam, and the loss of his professorship, in October 1693. The Rotterdam Dutch Reformed Church consistory, having circulated excerpts from his *Pensées diverses* (1683) among their assembly, summoned Bayle to explain his views, in what amounted to a full-scale inquisition into his teaching and thought. Privately, Bayle scorned this gathering as largely composed of people who understood neither French nor anything else beyond a few commonplaces of theology, hostile since his arrival in Holland chiefly because his patron, Paets, 'leur étoit fort odieux'.[7] Publicly, though, he remained utterly contrite, despite his writings being condemned all the same as full of 'propositions dangereuses et impies'. The church authorities, disapproving, not unlike Montesquieu later,[8] of his holding 'atheism is not a greater evil than idolatry',[9] were outraged by his claim that one does not need to acknowledge God to lead an upright life and his calling Epicurus 'a most glorious promoter of religion'.[10] No less reprehensible, to their minds, was his proposition that 'l'athéisme a eu des martyrs', Vanini being one such and a heroic one, since he refused to tell lies

[3] Labrousse, *Pierre Bayle*, i. 172 n.; Israel, *Dutch Republic*, 638–9, 790, 834, 858.

[4] Israel, *Dutch Republic*, 830–6; Israel, 'Pierre Bayle's Political Thought', 350.

[5] Labrousse, *Pierre Bayle*, i. 208–9 n.; Schlüter, *Französische Toleranzdebatte*, 208–9.

[6] Israel, *Radical Enlightenment*, 337–8.

[7] Bayle, *Lettres*, ii. 510.

[8] Montesquieu, *L'Esprit des lois*, 698–9.

[9] GA Rotterdam, Acta des Kerckenraedts, vii. 423; Israel, 'Pierre Bayle's Political Thought', 351.

[10] Israel, 'Pierre Bayle's Political Thought', 351; Bonacina, *Filosofia ellenistica*, 22; see also Paradis, 'Fondements', 30.

before his judges, preferring a martyr's death to public retraction which, on his principles, could not harm his prospects in the next world.[11] Equally bad, according to the consistory, was his suggestion that a society of atheists can be well ordered, indeed grounded on sound moral and social principles.[12]

The 'disgrâce de M. Bayle', as Leibniz called it, was widely reported but left a confused impression since no public explanation was given and it remained unclear whether he was deprived of his professorship and pension for heterodoxy, political offences, or some gross impropriety.[13] Under suspicion, and dependent on the financial support of his publisher Leers, Bayle had little choice, in any case, but to remain contrite before the consistories if he was to stay in Holland and continue with his philosophizing and writing relatively undisturbed. Dependent on his publisher and the local Huguenot francophone milieu, French being the only tongue he spoke fluently, he needed, if he was to keep a fixed base and enjoy some tranquillity, to remain within the fold of the 'Walloon' community. This led him, until his final works, to shroud his more challenging 'impieties' in an ever denser fog of distracting circumlocution, the impieties buried in his thoroughly ambiguous and evasive *Dictionnaire* only gradually coming to be recognized by some, as one Huguenot preacher in Switzerland put it, in November 1705, as assuredly the most wicked 'et le plus dangereux livre qui eut jamais été fait'.[14]

Eventually, though, as we have seen, one by one, all the more eminent French Reformed savants, Élie and Jacques Saurin, Le Clerc, Jaquelot, Jacques Bernard, Durand, Crousaz, and Barbeyrac, came to see that he had deliberately deceived their community and was in fact propagating an implied philosophical 'atheism' anchored in Spinoza's maxim 'absolute igitur concludimus, quod nec Scriptura rationi, nec ratio Scripturae accomodanda sit' [thus we absolutely conclude that neither can Scripture be accommodated to reason, nor reason to Scripture].[15] Nor was the danger represented by Bayle purely philosophical; for it was clearly recognized as being political too. Jacques Saurin, a leading figure at The Hague, known for his tolerant views, devoted a whole sermon, entitled 'l'accord de la religion avec la politique', to attacking Bayle's principle that religion must be kept out of politics. Later published at The Hague in 1717, this text quite rightly claims that Bayle's theory of toleration and individual liberty rests on an unprecedented and absolute separation of religion from politics, the dogma that 'la politique et la religion étoient incompatibles', something new and wholly subversive of traditional norms.[16] It was a profoundly challenging stance to which Vico refers on the concluding page of his *Scienza nuova*: 'let Bayle consider then whether, in fact, there can be nations in the world without any knowledge of God.' If religion is lost among the peoples, admonished Vico,

[11] Paradis, *Fondements*, 30; Bayle, *Pensées diverses*, ii. 135–6.
[12] Bayle, *Pensées diverses*, i. 288–9.
[13] Gundling, *Vollständige Historie*, iv. 6069; Cerny, 'Jacques Basnage and Pierre Bayle', 505.
[14] Quoted in Pitassi, 'De la courtoisie', 70.
[15] Spinoza, *Opera*, iii. 185; Moreau, 'Louis Meyer', 75, 83–4.
[16] *L'Europe savante* (July 1718), 58.

'they have nothing left to enable them to live in society, no shield of defense, nor means of counsel, nor basis of support, nor even a form by which they may exist in the world at all'.[17]

Deep contradictions in Bayle's personality, asserted Saurin, led him to the false and unchristian position that the viability of society and the state, and administration of justice, can be independent of faith and religion. Like Montesquieu later, Saurin granted that Bayle was a *grand philosophe*, of vast erudition and brilliance, having read everything that one can read and retained 'tout ce qu'on peut retenir'. But this only rendered him all the more culpable, in his view, a pernicious 'sophiste', championing individual liberty not just with regard to freedom of conscience and thought but, as even his friend Basnage acknowledged, subverting conventional ideas about sexuality and the proprieties, carrying his 'Pyrrhonism' too far,[18] a philosopher using his unparalleled genius 'à combattre les bonnes mœurs, à attaquer la chasteté, la modestie, toutes les vertus chrétiennes'. What could be more insidious and blameworthy than professing to be a loyal Christian while propagating in our century 'toutes les erreurs des siècles passez'?[19]

Bayle's political ideas, observed Saurin, must be examined through the prism of his moral theories, at the heart of which lies the separation of faith from moral principles. Human societies, insists Bayle in the *Pensées diverses*, have long been ravaged by 'superstition' and 'idolatry', irrational ideas which continually cloud human minds and judgement, blighting morality, to everyone's great cost and disadvantage. Yet while loathing ignorance and credulity as the greatest of evils, Bayle judged philosophical reason the only available antidote, the sole instrument capable of redeeming Man from savagery and misery. Christian ideals, argues Bayle, if loftier than the morality taught by reason, are not designed, as Scripture tells us, to ensure well-being and prosperity in this world but only in the world to come.[20] Bayle devoted his life to his roundabout, devious idealization of rational philosophy as Man's finest and only effective tool, a quest which, together with his mocking, subversive pseudo-fideism, or more precisely anti-scepticism disguised as fideism, characterized his *oeuvre*, until in the last few years of his life when, feeling the approach of death, he scarcely troubled any longer, especially in the *Continuation* and the *Réponse*, to veil the crypto-Spinozist reality behind the 'fideist' mask.[21]

No philosopher uses sceptical arguments more than Bayle. But he never employs scepticism, like Montaigne or Hume, to counter the force of reason but rather to undercut grounds for belief, undermine systems based on theological premisses, and ridicule thinkers like Le Clerc, Jaquelot, and Locke whose efforts to blend theology

[17] Vico, *The New Science* (all references are to the 3rd edn. (1744) unless otherwise indicated), 426; Nuzzo, 'Vico e Bayle', 142–3.

[18] Basnage, *Traité*, i. 55–65, 98–9; Cerny, *Theology, Politics and Letters*, 303–6, 313.

[19] *L'Europe savante* (July 1718), 61–2.

[20] McKenna, 'Pierre Bayle: Moralisme', 341–3; Brogi, *Teologia senza verità*, 176; McKenna, 'Pierre Bayle et la superstition', 49–65.

[21] McKenna, 'Pierre Bayle et la superstition', 51–2, 60–1, 63–5; McKenna, 'Rationalisme moral', 266–70.

with philosophy he scorned. No matter how widely held a belief may be, contends Bayle, in the *Pensées diverses*, it may never have been based on anything more than flimsy evidence or no evidence at all. What most people believe does possess a compelling force in society, a 'tradition' or 'superstition' once established can easily dominate vast sections of opinion for millennia; but it does not follow that there are, therefore, any reliable grounds for considering that belief to be true. Most men eschew the laborious task of examining their opinions, and dread, he points out, the stigma heaped on those who oppose what everybody else believes.[22] Most people are much more desirous of not being labelled heretics, rebels, or dissenters than knowing the truth. Hence, while *Consensus gentium* may be a frequently used method of arguing for God's existence,[23] nothing could be feebler, he maintains, than to try to substantiate beliefs of this or any kind on grounds of 'le consentement unanime des hommes'.[24] For the fact something is believed by many, most, or even everyone, far from rendering that belief trustworthy, or certain, generally means there is no reasonable basis for it at all.

By insisting on the total unreliability of what is commonly believed and polarizing reason and faith in this manner, Bayle's 'rationalisme militant', as it has aptly been called, designedly eliminates theology as an eligible or possible basis for evaluating issues of justice, morality, and politics.[25] But precisely this highly subversive strategy Montesquieu and the moderate mainstream were to devote considerable attention to combating.[26] Religion, argues Montesquieu, like Vico, far from being irrelevant is a constant, fundamental, and ubiquitous factor, basic to understanding any society and a prime influence on political institutions and the fabric of politics as well as lifestyle and morality. He began to compose his great masterpiece *L'Esprit des lois* as early as 1727 or 1728, convinced that the variety of laws, institutions, and moral systems in the world is not just random, a matter of chance, but that a particular inner rationale or logic guides the divergent development of particular societies in terms of their own specific conditions and tendencies, adopting as one of his central tenets, from his observations on the relationship of religion to society, that 'le gouvernement modéré', his highest ideal in politics, chiefly flourishes in milieux morally and educationally shaped by Christianity while thriving less in societies rooted in Islamic, Indian, idolatrous, or atheistic beliefs.[27] Christianity was 'praised', as Condorcet later sarcastically put it, by Montesquieu, especially for acting as a brake on despotism and unmitigated monarchy, gentleness 'étant si recommendée dans l'Évangile' that faith, he inferred, mitigates 'la colère despotique' requisite for any harsh and rigid system of rule in ways oriental and other religions do not.[28]

[22] Bayle, *Pensées diverses*, i. 37, 127–8.

[23] Cantelli, *Teologia*, 15–33; Cantelli, *Vico e Bayle*, 11–13.

[24] Bayle, *Pensées diverses*, i. 127; Moreau, 'Les Sept raisons', 23–4.

[25] Gros, 'Sens et limites', 73; McKenna, 'L'*Éclaircissement*', 297, 314–20.

[26] Aubery, 'Montesquieu et les Juifs', 88.

[27] Ibid.; Childs, *Political Academy*, 84; Montesquieu, *L'Esprit des lois*, 698–9.

[28] Montesquieu, *L'Esprit des lois*, 698; [Boulenger de Rivery], *Apologie de* L'Esprit des loix, 33–5; Cottret, *Jansénismes*, 52; Ehrard, *L'Esprit des mots*, 41.

However, the question why one religion, rather than another, takes root in a given part of the world, and why other faiths fail to establish themselves in that region, is explained by Montesquieu in exclusively naturalistic terms and especially terms of climate.[29] For him, it was less in their dogmas and beliefs than their social and moral consequences that religions help shape political realities and that Christianity reveals its superiority to paganism, Indian religions, Judaism, and Islam. Consequently, in *L'Esprit des lois* one finds no claim that Christianity is inherently superior morally, let alone by revelation, to other religions, a feature which shocked many of his ecclesiastical readers.[30] Nevertheless, religion is deemed fundamental to society and necessary for its well-being,[31] a perspective which stood Montesquieu's reputation in good stead later in the century, as the antagonism between church and radical *philosophes* intensified.

For despite the initial wave of ecclesiastical criticism, during the 'querelle' of 1748–53, during the 1760s and 1770s it became usual to ignore the naturalism underlying Montesquieu's treatment of religion and cite *L'Esprit des lois* against the radical *philosophes* as a widely admired work which defends Christianity and the benign influence of organized religion and ecclesiastical authority in monarchies.[32] Already in 1750, one commentator confidently expected Montesquieu's claim that Christianity favours the prevalence of 'le gouvernement modéré', the only kind which promotes human liberty and happiness, while other doctrines do not and Islam 's'accommode mieux à la dureté du gouvernement despotique', would prove extremely useful in helping to silence the *esprits forts* and *Spinosistes* who seek to undermine religion and refuse to submit reason to Revelation. Through being shown that they too enjoy the social and political blessings the Christian religion confers on society, the radicals would now be taught by Montesquieu to respect Christianity 'et à se taire'.[33]

Toleration in Montesquieu's political theory, accordingly, loses the absolute quality as an end in itself that it possesses in Bayle and Spinoza and is, in an important sense, rendered socially conditional. Certainly, Montesquieu, who was married to a Huguenot and descended from Huguenots, detests bigotry and religious intolerance, as his scathing remarks about the Spanish Inquisition show, and judged the spread of toleration in the early eighteenth century in western Europe to be entirely good and desirable.[34] Nevertheless, the logic of his theory led him to urge rulers where religious uniformity, or something close to it, already exists in a given society, or a ruler can easily prevent a new creed or heresy from establishing itself, to maintain uniformity as long as is practicable. Only where it is clearly impracticable to debar a new, or newly encroaching, faith without provoking strife and resorting to oppression should it be tolerated.[35] Hence, despite his denouncing intolerance,

[29] Bianchi, 'Histoire et nature', 298–9.
[30] Ibid.; Lynch, 'Montesquieu', 489–90.
[31] Borghero, 'L'Italia in Bayle', 16,18; Bianchi, 'Histoire et nature', 291–3.
[32] Bergier, *Apologie*, ii. 132–3, 162–5; Kingston, 'Montesquieu on Religion', 380–1, 397.
[33] [Boulenger de Rivery], *Apologie de* L' Esprit des loix, 35; [Risteau], *Réponse aux questions*, 18.
[34] Ehrard, *L'Esprit des mots*, 81–6, 92; Childs, *Political Academy*, 155.
[35] Montesquieu, *L'Esprit des lois*, 708; Bianchi, 'Histoire et nature', 300; Kingston 'Montesquieu on Religion', 392–5.

toleration as such, for Montesquieu, remains *faute de mieux* rather than, as in Bayle, an absolute value in itself.

By contrast, it was precisely by divorcing politics from the sacred, eliminating all theological sanction of institutions, and confining the sovereign within a fully secularized public sphere in which 'good' and 'bad' are fixed by philosophical reason, that Bayle strove to secure the forms of liberty, freedom of thought, belief, and expression he thought chiefly needed safeguarding politically. If Bayle the political and social thinker is known mainly for his sweeping religious toleration and emancipation of the individual conscience, he justifies comprehensive toleration by making the individual conscience supreme arbiter of men's moral and religious conduct, on the grounds that whatever is good and legitimate in our consciences derives from natural reason. Conversely, since intolerance violates reason and natural morality, all efforts by a sovereign to coerce the individual conscience are *ipso facto* illegitimate and unjustifiable. It is, therefore, affirms Bayle, something manifestly opposed 'au bon sens' and to natural reason, that is, to the exclusive criterion, in his thought, of what is right or wrong, in short contrary to the only original and primitive rule 'du discernement du vrai et du faux, du bon et du mauvais', to employ violence to impose a religion on those 'qui ne la professent pas'.[36]

If the Gospel maxim 'Contrains-les d'entrer' justifies kings in enforcing ecclesiastically sanctioned religious uniformity on their subjects, then it would be wholly inconsistent, declares Bayle, to deny ecclesiastics and common people the right, and also the obligation, to compel kings always to submit to the requirements of religion and the church. It is absurd, he insists, for theologians to maintain that Jesus Christ decrees coercion for ordinary individuals, and then refuse to allow that this applies also to kings, denying that 'l'Église ait droit de les déposer';[37] and while Catholic apologists try to circumvent such blatant inconsistency by saying God expressly decrees that 'c'est par lui que les rois règnent', in turbulent times, like the French Wars of Religion, this rule is routinely ignored. Nor, once it is established that individuals must be compelled to submit to theological requirements, argues Bayle, can there be the slightest prospect of political stability for anyone: it is a clear and necessary consequence of the position he seeks to refute, he contends, to spare neither crowned heads, 'ni rien qui soit au monde, quand il s'agit d'avancer la prospérité de la religion'.[38] Here, again, we encounter Bayle's familiar stratagem of setting up a total and unremitting polarity between 'religion' and reason, so as to show the irrationality of regulating society and morality on the basis of the former, only now in the guise of a confrontation between religious authority and political sovereignty.

Having juxtaposed sovereignty, church, and people in this singular fashion, Bayle argues that a general toleration of religions, and *indifferenti* and unbelievers, far from destabilizing the state will actually strengthen it. Rather like the Arminians and Socinians he professes to scorn, but totally unlike the orthodox Calvinists he

[36] Pitassi, 'De la courtoisie', 101. [37] Ibid. 117; Schneewind, *Invention of Autonomy*, 282.
[38] Bayle, *Commentaire philosophique*, 118.

claims to align with, Bayle entirely rejects the common assumption that plurality of sects endangers the body politic, maintaining that society actually becomes less divisive thereby and more stable. If plurality of creeds often foments strife this occurs because each church refuses to countenance the others and seeks to impose its doctrine by force: in a word discord and conflict 'vient non pas de la tolérance, mais de la non-tolérance'.[39] Where Bayle especially differs from Locke, Le Clerc, and the Remonstrants, and indeed also Montesquieu, is in his contention that all organized churches persecute when they can and, hence, that toleration must and can only be a political construct enforced by the secularized state. Toleration, consequently, always finds itself pitted against popular opinion which Bayle deems irredeemably theological and hence inherently intolerant.

Bayle's opponents, the *rationaux*, like Montesquieu and his critics later, scarcely took seriously his claim, in his last works, that he was not attacking religion.[40] But had they accepted him as the orthodox 'fideist' he professed to be and not the crypto-Spinozist or 'Stratonist' they took him to be,[41] his thesis that revealed religion has no grounding in reason, science, or philosophy would have still been wholly destructive of their project of Christian enlightenment. It was axiomatic to the *rationaux* that salvation through Christ is not just the right path for the individual but the universal guide to moral perfection, and therefore the sole proper foundation of the social and moral order. Bayle stubbornly denied this, rendering this question, and his astounding claim that idolatry and even superstition are more harmful than 'atheism', pivotal to the contest between himself and his mainstream Enlightenment opponents.

On these questions, Montesquieu, though somewhere in between, leaned decidedly more toward the *rationaux* than Bayle, expressly rejecting the latter's claim that a society of Christians would be less viable and orderly than an atheistic society and criticizing his argument about idolatry as an unpersuasive paradox.[42] In his *Défense de L'Esprit des lois* (1750), directly contradicting Bayle's thesis that a genuinely Christian society surrounded by non-Christian or insincerely Christian neighbours would not be viable, indeed, being politically and militarily weakened by its Christian ethic, would eventually be overwhelmed, Montesquieu contends that the *principes de christianisme* (a term of Le Clerc's) would, on the contrary, prove more viable and ultimately stronger than the mere worldly moralities of non-Christian republics and monarchies.[43] Furthermore, as we see from his *Spicilège*, a collection of early jottings dating from 1715, Montesquieu had all along disagreed with Bayle's view that revealed religion is unnecessary for maintaining a well-ordered society, judging rather that religious belief and popular credence in Heaven and Hell, and

[39] Ibid. 256–7.

[40] Bayle, *Réponse*, iii. 642–3; Bianchi, 'Histoire et nature', 290.

[41] Bayle, *Réponse*, iv. 139; [Jurieu], *Philosophe de Rotterdam*, 106–7.

[42] Montesquieu, *Œuvres complètes*, 955; Aubery, 'Montesquieu et les Juifs', 88; Bartlett, *Idea of Enlightenment*, 27, 37–8; Kingston, 'Montesquieu on Religion', 389.

[43] Kingston, 'Montesquieu on Religion', 389; Montesquieu, *Œuvres complètes*, 810; Bianchi, 'Histoire et nature', 289–90.

generally in supernatural reward and punishment, are essential to upholding both law and order and morality itself.[44] Hence, it is fair to say that to a certain extent, Montesquieu continued, if in a more secular vein, the *rationaux*'s campaign against Bayle's views on society, morality, religion, and politics.

An integral part of his system, Bayle's politics clearly hinges on his concern to protect individual liberty on the basis of freedom of conscience while safeguarding the security and stability of society. Without order and security, society cannot subsist and the life of the individual becomes unspeakably miserable and wretched. 'Un intérêt capital', he asserts, 'porte les hommes à fuir l'anarchie comme la plus grande peste du genre.'[45] Yet, despite Man's experiments with different kinds of political organization—theocracy, aristocracy, democracy, 'monarchie toute pure', and 'monarchie mixte'—men have never managed to eradicate the constant threat of a resurgence of anarchy: sedition, civil war, revolutions, have been frequent, he says, 'dans tous les états', albeit more in some than in others.[46] In essence, this is because men are irredeemably in the grip of malign passions: 'ils sont envieux les uns des autres; l'avarice, l'ambition, la volupté, la vengeance les possèdent'.[47] Conflicting desires grip men and inevitably clash and generate instability.

Quintessentially Baylean is his claim that sovereigns need unlimited authority in the practical sphere of action, to curb crime and suppress those who harass their neighbours and destroy the public peace 'où chacun doit être sous la majesté des lois', while simultaneously proclaiming the sovereign's total lack of legitimate sway in the sphere of private conscience, morality, and belief.[48] Here indeed is the problematic crux on which Bayle's political thought hinges. For if some features of his system evince radical traits—especially his sweeping toleration, subordination of theology to philosophy, and deployment of atheism—his insistence on the need for unrestricted monarchy in the public sphere, with a free hand to suppress all disorder, unruliness, and opposition, at first sight looks far more Hobbesian than radical.[49]

Yet Bayle's monarchism, though real enough, requires some significant qualification. For it differs in notable respects from the political conservatism of Hobbes, Boulainvilliers, Voltaire, Montesquieu, and Hume. Bayle *does* admittedly consider unrestricted monarchy the safest and most reliable form of political organization and shows no interest at all, unlike Boulainvilliers and Montesquieu, in devising, or even acknowledging the need for, institutionalized constitutional constraints on monarchical power. Indeed, where Montesquieu felt a deep aversion to Louis XIV's policy of crippling or eliminating 'intermediary powers', like the *parlements* and the remaining French provincial estates, Bayle was positively averse to schemes for applying limits to royal authority.[50] Yet he was not an opponent, as Jurieu maintained, of

[44] Montesquieu, *Œuvres complètes*, 396; Kingston, 'Montesquieu on Religion', 389–91.

[45] Bayle, *Continuation*, ii. 558.

[46] Ibid.; Israel, 'Pierre Bayle's Political Thought', 376–7.

[47] Bayle, *Continuation*, ii. 558; Hochstrasser, 'Claims', 32; McKenna, 'Pierre Bayle: Moralisme', 330–1.

[48] Bayle, *Commentaire philosophique*, 261.

[49] Yardeni, 'La France de Louis XIV', 184; Labrousse, 'Political Ideas', 237–42.

[50] Labrousse, 'Political Ideas', 239; Ehrard, *L'Esprit des mots*, 95, 103, Lacouture, *Montesquieu*, 40.

the 'Glorious Revolution' as such. If he was not, like Boulainvilliers and Montesquieu, an enthusiast for the post-Glorious Revolution 'British model', he nonetheless demonstrated his loyalty to the States General and William III and did not criticize the Dutch intervention in Britain as distinct from the Huguenot resort to arms against Louis XIV. Indeed, though not unsympathetic to (the tolerant) James II,[51] his remarks about 'suppositious' royal heirs in the article on François I of France in the *Dictionnaire* damaged the Jacobite cause. For Bayle was no conventional champion of 'l'absolutisme monarchique';[52] in particular, he was never a stickler for the hereditary principle, much less 'divine right' or social hierarchy.[53]

Rather Bayle dreads the disruptive consequences of 'constitutions de gouvernement', fearing that division of legislative power 'entre un prince et un corps de juges' only hinders firm government and obstructs law-making, with judges constantly thwarting what the sovereign intends. He repeatedly cites the disastrous consequences of the French *parlements*' interventions during the Wars of Religion when judges and office-holders sought to curtail royal authority, manipulate administration of justice, and block royal edicts.[54] Denying the *parlements* should form a constitutional check on royal power, and supporting absolutist steps to reduce their powers, Bayle argued that France had never, before or since, been so sunk in disorder and anarchy as during the reigns of Charles IX and Henri III when the crown was, for a time, effectively subjected to constitutional restraints.[55]

Bayle's absolutism, unlike the clerically sanctioned variety propagated at the courts of Paris, Madrid, Lisbon, and Vienna, was thus a purely secular, essentially Bodinian, construct devoid of confessional content. Bayle indeed, considered the principle of divine right monarchy itself profoundly repellent. The cult of sacred kingship, mixing religious ritual with official and popular expressions of veneration for the crown and royal house, as in Louis XIV's France, inspired some of the most withering passages of Bayle's pamphlet of 1686 attacking the French Catholic Church for its 'criminal' complicity in the persecution of the Huguenots. The clergy, he protests, should wholly relegate the work of proclaiming monarchy and flattering kings to officials and magistrates and not interfere 'avec les cérémonies de la religion', because precisely that is the perilous path that leads to idolatry.[56]

Monarchy, holds Bayle, should be absolute but only in what he deems the public sphere. His absolutism encompasses no right to invade the private world of conscience, belief, thought, individual property, or personal lifestyle, is purely functional rather than legitimist, and has no relevance to the sphere of established republics like the United Provinces, Genoa, Lucca, or Venice. For what Bayle is really urging is not monarchical absolutism *per se* but the undivided sovereignty and supremacy of the secular state, however constituted, over lesser authorities, factions, and especially

51 Labrousse, 'Political Ideas', 239–40.
52 Ibid., p. xxxvi; Bost, *Pierre Bayle*, 65–7; Paganini, *Analisi della fede*, 203–6.
53 Burger, 'Prohibition du *Dictionnaire*', 95–6; Jenkinson, 'Introduction', p. xxxvi.
54 Bayle, *Réponse*, v. 37–8.
55 Bayle, *Political Writings*, 111; Labrousse, *Pierre Bayle*, ii. 489.
56 Bayle, *Ce que c'est que la France*, 66; Gros, 'Bayle: de la tolérance', 304.

(but not only) all types of brigandage, lawlessness, factionalism, aristocratic influence, and ecclesiastical power.[57] Above all, his concern is to minimize disturbance in the body politic in the interests of individual freedom and social stability.

Bayle strongly affirms his loyalty to Holland, resort of all fugitives, mother 'et l'azyle des fidèles persecutez', the land which had taken them in 'si cordialement, si charitablement, si libéralement'. He does not hesitate to call the United Provinces 'le rempart de la liberté de l'Europe', the republic which most deserves to prosper given the principles by which it is governed, the professionalism of its troops, and 'l'industrie et la bonne foy de ses habitans', hoping that it will continue to project for centuries 'l'éclat, la puissance et la gloire où Dieu l'a élevée en si peu de tems' through the wisdom and justice of its government.[58] Even so, he judges republics and republicanism inadvisable in the main.[59] While a republican constitution like that of the Dutch or Venetians can function well in a particular context, and remain stable, he seriously doubts, like Montesquieu later, whether republican governments can attain more generally the orderliness and freedom from faction requisite for stability. Here, for once, agreeing with Le Clerc, who thought the ancient republics of Athens and Rome offer no useful model to posterity, Bayle deems self-rule by the people in principle no better, and usually worse, than the sway of an absolute monarch.[60]

The ancient Greek democratic republics Bayle, like Hobbes, reckoned a disaster, though this was less the fault of the Greeks, in his view, than democracy as such.[61] In his *Dictionnaire* article on Julius Caesar's assassin Marcus Junius Brutus, 'le plus grand républicain que l'on vit jamais', Bayle agrees with Dio Cassius that experience shows monarchy to be preferable to democratic government, classical history proving that cities and individuals encounter fewer difficulties and adversities 'sous l'authorité d'un seul, que sous le gouvernement populaire'. Although a few societies have prospered under a democratic government, he adds, that was only until they gained a certain 'point de grandeur, et de puissance', after which they invariably sank into internecine conflict and chaos owing to envy, faction, and ambition. Once Rome's power attained a certain point it became impossible that her inhabitants should not abandon the bridle on their greed and passions 'au milieu de la liberté républicaine'.[62]

Where Montesquieu's political ideal was that of limited monarchy, Bayle was less a defender of monarchical absolutism in the usual sense, and still less of 'divine right', than a supporter of unified, undivided, and uncompromisingly secular sovereignty, preferably monarchical, but, where it works, also republican.[63] This might

[57] Israel, 'Pierre Bayle's Political Thought', 375, 378–9; Paganini, *Analisi della fede*, 203–4.

[58] Paganini, *Analisi della fede*, 114; Bartlett, *Idea of Enlightenment*, 24.

[59] Bayle, *Continuation*, i. 47–51; Labrousse, 'Political Ideas', 238–9; Leroy, 'Le Royaume de France', 173–4.

[60] *Bibliothèque choisie*, 15 (1708), 87–8.

[61] Bayle, *Continuation*, i. 50–1; Israel, 'Pierre Bayle's Political Thought', 373, 377.

[62] Bayle, *Dictionnaire*, i. 717 n. 1 (all references to the 1702 edn. unless otherwise indicated); Bayle, *Political Writings*, 34–5.

[63] Bayle, *Réponse*, v. 37–8; Israel, 'Pierre Bayle's Political Thought', 373; Labrousse, *Pierre Bayle*, ii. 555.

still seem to leave him without radical credentials in politics beyond toleration and individual liberty. But there is a further dimension to his radicalism: for unlike Montesquieu, but like Vico contemplating the *conditio humana* from the standpoint of Naples' unruly history, Bayle sees monarchy as more than just the safest path to a secure and orderly existence for subjects, the highest political good. He envisages it also as the aptest way to establish equality before the law and eliminate privilege, baronial factionalism, and society's disruption by nobles. In Bayle, like Vico, absolutism becomes a levelling instrument invaluable for eradicating factional, aristocratic, and especially ecclesiastical interference with legislation, administration, and enforcement of the laws. It is for this reason especially that mixed monarchy could hold no attraction for him.

Monarchy then, is esteemed by Bayle partly as a tool for disarming noble factions which he, like Vico, considers incorrigibly ambitious, antisocial, and violent. To demonstrate how easily constitutional limits imposed on monarchy can be ruinously exploited, at the expense of everyone else (but the dominant clergy), by a powerfully entrenched nobility, or corrupt legal aristocracy, to further their own power and privileges, Bayle (like Vico and de Hooghe) cites the case of Poland, Europe's most dismal fiasco, to his mind, where the nobility, through opposing royal authority, had virtually emasculated the state and its institutions. What could be more appalling or despicable, he asks, than the demise of a formerly flourishing haven of coexistence and toleration through noble arrogance allied with ecclesiastical ambition and popular credulity, manipulating religious intolerance and office-holders' negligence?[64]

Bayle, then, offers nothing whatever of that partiality for nobility, or checks, limiting agencies, and intermediary institutions, so typical of Boulainvilliers and Montesquieu. Quite the contrary, Bayle deems all hierarchical privilege and priority, noble, ecclesiastical, or judicial, a constant menace to both individual liberty and everyone's tranquillity.[65] For Montesquieu, liberty is in essence the freedom to follow one's natural inclinations and, since a constitution is a product of society's naturally ingrained tendencies, liberty has an innate propensity to flow more readily with, than against, the tide of tradition, and prevailing attitudes, customs, and social hierarchy. The essence of the legislator's task, maintains Montesquieu, is to enact legislation in accord with 'the spirit' [l'esprit] of his society, since society can never do better (where this does not violate the principles of good government) than follow its natural predisposition.[66]

In certain respects, then, Bayle's politics *was* more radical than Montesquieu's, despite being infused with a deep dread of popular religiosity, fanaticism, persecution, sedition, and revolt such as fomented the Wars of Religion and Louis XIV's oppression of the Huguenots. Bayle, much as he resists all theological involvement

64 Labrousse, *Pierre Bayle*, ii. 485–7; Bayle, *Political Writings*, 110–12, 261–2; Mori, *Bayle philosophe*, 315.
65 Ehrard, *L'Esprit des mots*, 20–1; Seif, 'Missverstandene Montesquieu', 155–8.
66 Montesquieu, *L'Esprit des lois*, 642.

in government, denies any right of any segment of society to oppose the ruler in the name of popular sovereignty.[67] The least suggestion of popular participation fills him with dread, the people in his eyes being irretrievably sunk in superstition—and hence devoid of rationality. In his politics, the menace of insurrection, demagoguery, and fanaticism always outweighs that of tyranny, being ineradicably rooted in subservience to theological notions: what would have happened to Europe in the sixteenth century, he asks rhetorically, if the fanatic Munzer 'eût pu gagner deux batailles'?[68]

It was this menace, as Bayle sees it, between popular sentiment and the fearful peril of religious zeal which accounts for the unbending anti-democratic tendency of his political thought. Where Spinoza's philosophy teaches democratic republicanism, and the core radical tradition in the eighteenth century was firmly republican and democratic, especially after 1750, explicitly in Mably, Morelly, and Boulanger, and in Diderot at least in underlying tendency, Bayle rejects democratic republicanism as a plausible option because he thinks the common people, for all the efforts of philosophers, can never be emancipated from the sway of credulity or subservience to religious demagogues. While he envisaged philosophy—as the project of the *Dictionnaire* proclaims—as the chief engine of 'enlightenment' and our best hope if men are ever to be freed from the tyranny of superstition, and hence be civilized and humanized, he evinces nevertheless an unmitigated pessimism regarding the 'multitude'.[69] The deep emotion he invests in the quarrels over *consensus gentium* and whether idolatrous paganism is worse than 'atheism' was rooted ultimately in his insuperable abhorrence of popular zeal as 'une peste très-dangereuse aux societez'.[70]

Constitutional doctrines locating sovereignty in the people, and proclaiming the people's right to resist tyrannical kings, like those of the *Monarchomachi*, strike Bayle as serving no purpose other than encouraging malcontent nobles and clergy to scheme, plot rebellion, and take up arms against kings. Such doctrines, he thinks, foment a basically theological view of politics.[71] What he conceives as the people's ingrained proneness to be manipulated by nobles, churchmen, magistrates, or demagogues urging the dictates of religion emerges with brutal clarity in the article on 'Loyola' in the *Dictionnaire* where he stresses the need to counter what he sees as a constant peril. In France, it was especially the Jesuits, in his view, who proclaim the notion that royal authority 'est inférieure à celle du peuple' and that kings may justifiably be deposed by the people where they, or rather their religious instructors, consider this necessary.[72]

Everywhere, contends Bayle, history records monarchs deposed at the instigation 'ou avec l'approbation du clergé'.[73] Since kings control the forces of law and order,

67 Labrousse, *Pierre Bayle*, ii. 479–88; Hochstrasser, 'Claims', 27, 33.
68 Bayle, *Continuation*, i. 8–9; Israel, 'Pierre Bayle's Political Thought', 375.
69 Bayle, *Continuation*, i. 8; Mori, *Bayle philosophe*, 23; Bouchardy, *Pierre Bayle*, 175.
70 Bayle, *Continuation*, i. avertissement, pp. 8-8v., 158; McKenna, 'Pierre Bayle et la superstition', 51, 63.
71 Labrousse, 'Political Ideas', 256–7.
72 Bayle, *Political Writings*, 157–60; Labrousse, *Pierre Bayle*, ii. 515–16.
73 Bayle, *Dictionnaire*, ii. 1852; Paganini, *Analisi della fede*, 206; Bayle, *Political Writings*, 157.

'tyrants', however objectionable to churchmen, can only be overthrown by mobilizing the people's religious devotion, hence by stooping to demagoguery, conspiracy, and rebellion.[74] Ecclesiastics routinely exploit the people's love of wonders, signs, and holy men, asserting that what the people believe is the truth, that the common opinion must be respected, and that the people's voice 'est la voix de Dieu'.[75] But actually, contends Bayle, consulting the people, or encouraging popular participation to coerce kings, is nothing but an insidious way of inviting men to air their prejudices in an inappropriate setting, rather like asking the majority to decide whether a philosophical proposition is true or false.

Even where sedition is firmly checked, the people's voice continually threatens public tranquillity and good government. No matter how adeptly a constitution is framed, discord and anarchy are never far off. If you try to limit royal authority, moreover, this only increases thirst for 'la puissance arbitraire'; for what is forbidden always excites desire: 'en un mot les uns abusent de l'authorité, et les autres de la liberté'.[76] In the ancient democracies, or any democracy, contends Bayle, the majority habitually shows poor judgement, not least, as Cicero notes,[77] in failing to select those best qualified for office.[78] The tranquillity of the ancient democracies was continually disturbed by commotion, tumults, and revolutions, something inevitable where state business is decided by majority vote whether in assemblies of all the heads of families or just assemblies of a certain number of deputies.[79] All societies are vulnerable to men's ineradicable proneness to ambition, greed, vengeance, and anarchy.

Hence, the prime function of any state is to curb man's propensity to anarchy which would be no threat at all if every individual conformed of himself 'regulièrement à l'équité et à la justice'. But were that happy circumstance ever to apply there would be no need for kings or magistrates.[80] In the real world, the constant curse of disorder must be countered, using man's own particular nature: 'l'homme aime naturellement la conservation de sa vie', observed Bayle, echoing Hobbes and Spinoza, and this drives him to escape from a condition in which one is constantly in arms against everyone else: hence, everyone has an interest 'au maintien des securitez', no one wanting anarchy in his country.[81] Disorder constantly erupts and may prevail for a time but eventually the ceaseless clash of individuals and their private interests 'font que les passions des hommes se repriment les unes les autres'—a strikingly Spinozistic-Mandevillian insight.[82] Consequently, concludes Bayle, we see a natural impulse among men to curb 'l'anarchie générale' and, by and large, it is absolute monarchy free of constitutional checks which best serves the majority by

[74] Bayle, *Political Writings*, 158.
[75] Bayle, *Continuation*, i. 26; Israel, 'Pierre Bayle's Political Thought', 376.
[76] Bayle, *Continuation*, ii. 559; Bayle, *Réponse*, iv. 289–90, v. 37–8.
[77] Bayle, *Réponse*, iv. 289–90, v. 37–8; Israel, 'Pierre Bayle's Political Thought', 376–7.
[78] Bayle, *Continuation*, i. 47–8.
[79] Ibid. i. 50–1.
[80] Ibid. ii. 559; Israel, 'Pierre Bayle's Political Thought', 377.
[81] Israel, 'Pierre Bayle's Political Thought', 377; Bayle *Continuation*, ii. 590–1.
[82] Bayle, *Continuation*, ii. 591.

curbing misconduct, crime, and disorder through laws and penalties, providing the best, fastest, surest, and maximum degree of security for all.

2. EARLY ENLIGHTENMENT FRENCH POLITICAL THOUGHT

As architects of Radical Enlightenment, Spinoza and Bayle—especially the late Bayle of the *Continuation* (1705) and the *Réponse*—converge at crucial points fundamental to the wider evolution of radical thought. Both thinkers justify and uphold, as Locke, Leibniz, and Malebranche emphatically do not, the absolute separation of philosophy from theology, claiming reason teaches nothing about faith and faith nothing about reality construed by reason. They also deny, unlike Montesquieu and Hume, the applicability of tradition, custom, religion, or theological doctrines to determining and regulating the basic principles of morality as well as fixing political guidelines conducive to stability and ensuring the 'common good'. Both thinkers totally reject scepticism (Bayle using sceptical arguments for this purpose), claiming pure reason is the sole criterion of what is true, and are particularly anxious to safeguard individual freedom of thought and belief, urging an exceptionally wide-ranging, comprehensive toleration far transcending that acceptable to most contemporaries.

These elements of convergence between Spinoza and Bayle assume added significance, moreover, when Bayle's conception of politics, and critique of republicanism, are compared with those of Boulainvilliers, the young Mably, and Montesquieu, the key French political thinkers of the first half of the eighteenth century. For commencing with Bayle, the French Enlightenment in the realm of politics continued with Boulainvilliers and his circle, followed by the Entresol group, aristocratic networks which, between 1715 and 1731, when this latter club was suppressed by Cardinal Fleury, firmly re-established in France the practice of studying political institutions, airing the manifest problem, after the experience of Louis XIV, of how men can best achieve 'un juste gouvernement' and 'faire prospérer les rois et les peuples'.[83] Only recently, though, have Enlightenment historians begun gathering the threads of this revived political thought tradition together to uncover the main line in western political theory as it transferred from the Netherlands to early eighteenth-century French thought.

Boulainvilliers, undoubtedly, forms a crucial link between Bayle and Montesquieu and ties both thinkers to the dilemmas posed by republicanism. Convinced that previous political thinkers had made little progress owing to their fascination with Natural Law and what, to him, were simplistic theories of the 'natural sociability' of man, Boulainvilliers felt that the answer was for thinking about politics to become

[83] Boulainvilliers, *État de la France*, i, preface pp. xlix, lii, cviii; Ellis, *Boulainvilliers*, 207; Wright, *Classical Republican*, 26, 147.

more genuinely 'philosophical' and more orientated to the empirical study of history on which he placed a particular stress. By this he meant a study focused on the different stages of Man's natural development as a political being, his gradual emergence, that is, from a primitive phase of statelessness to a phase of minuscule sovereignties and, from there, to larger, more complex structures and, finally, to the great monarchies fitted to provide security of life and rule of law over immense areas, a development which first manifested itself, it seemed to him, in China and Egypt.[84] Hence, the centrality of history and geography, part of what seems so novel in Montesquieu, in fact derived from this older source.

As both thinker and writer Montesquieu, 'le premier homme du siècle' according to his Huguenot acolyte La Beaumelle, long suspected by some of being, like Boulainvilliers himself, a private *Spinosiste*,[85] was undeniably steeped in and heavily indebted to Boulainvilliers, as well as Bayle. For him, as for Boulainvilliers, the 'order of nature' is the fixed norm, the shaping principle determining all human institutions, social and moral systems, and laws.[86] Given this tie to Boulainvilliers, it is hardly surprising that in the controversy which erupted after publication of *L'Esprit des lois* in 1748, Spinoza and Bayle (rather than Hobbes or Locke) were invariably the two principal political and general thinkers invoked, cited, and denounced as being the intellectual sources of Montesquieu's 'naturalistic' theoretical innovations.[87]

In secularizing social and political theory around the concept of an *esprit général*, designating the underlying impulse behind the spirit of the laws in human societies, a guiding tendency or principle of rationality, determining the overall architecture of human institutions, an idea related to that of Natural Law so prevalent in that age but blended with the notion of 'general will', Montesquieu was doubtless influenced by several predecessors and not only Spinoza, Bayle, and Boulainvilliers but also Fontenelle, Fréret, and Doria.[88] But his most original stroke, the point at which he strikes off on his own path, or at least went further than Boulainvilliers, was to combine the idea of a collective logic of societies and institutions, the notion that human nature rather than something decreed or laid down by a divine Creator drives the historical process, pioneered by Spinoza, Boulainvilliers, and Fontenelle, with the notion of divergent variants, each with its own distinct *esprit*, a device enabling him subtly to combine an overall unity of approach with respect for tradition, local diversity, and 'difference'. Hence, in place of the supernatural agents of the past, the prime causal determinants in both Boulainvilliers and Montesquieu are geography, climate, religion, trade, and institutionalized hierarchy, and especially forms of nobility and servitude.

Thus equipped, Montesquieu assails despotism, unjust war, religious intolerance, and slavery, condemning these for their basic irrationality and depriving men

[84] Venturino, *Ragioni*, 25–38.

[85] Lauriol, *La Beaumelle*, 186, 197; Israel, *Radical Enlightenment*, 12–13, 83.

[86] Israel, *Radical Enlightenment*, 49–50, 127, 136; Bianchi, 'Histoire et nature', 292, 296, 302.

[87] Bianchi, 'Histoire et nature', 289–90.

[88] Senarclens, *Montesquieu*, 154–5.

of their liberty,[89] while yet coherently distancing himself from the more radical conception of 'general will' basic to Bayle's and Mably's approach no less than to that of the Dutch democratic republicans. This he does by dropping their insistence on equity and 'equality'. Spinoza and Bayle reduce the basic criteria of the 'common good' to a few simple components which they rigorously apply when evaluating past and present states. Although Bayle modifies Spinoza's 'common good', or 'le bien public' as Mably terms it, from an active concept, in which the populace participate, to a politically passive concept, in effect what he calls 'l'intérêt du genre humain', opposed to which are political disorder, anarchy, and the reign of ambition,[90] his framework remains fully universal. Montesquieu, by contrast, identifies different kinds of social and moral systems as being more or less appropriate to stability and well-being in particular circumstances, depending on conditions of climate, environment, culture, and religion. Compared to Bayle's, Mably's, or Diderot's 'bien public', Montesquieu is always much readier to compromise with hierarchy and theology as well as custom and tradition.[91]

Spinosiste-Bayliste 'general will' in Du Marsais, Meslier, Vauvenargues, Morelly, Mably, Boulanger, and Diderot presupposes a universal, as well as wholly secular, moral base and worldly conception of Man's basic interest. These writers insist not just on the reality of such a secular code anchored in pure reason but also the innate superiority of such an ethics for maintaining societies over the moralities instituted by revealed religions. By doing so they assign to philosophy a crucial responsibility in defining the human condition and fixing the contours of morality; for them, philosophy can, and in favourable circumstances will, serve as a universally applicable tool for improvement in human life, affording not just better moral, social, and political criteria but helping change society itself for the better. Boulainvilliers and Montesquieu, by contrast, each adopt a strikingly different and inherently more conservative stance, the latter in particular blocking the universalist implications of Spinozist 'bien public'.

Boulainvilliers's strategy was to combine a fully Spinozist metaphysics anchored in critical-empirical conception of religion and history which he saw as something shorn of miracles and supernatural agency, with an uncompromisingly aristocratic view of society and politics, and up to a point, but in a more original manner, this is what Montesquieu also did.[92] However, Boulainvilliers, bold and heterodox though he was in his reading, metaphysics, and conclusions about religion and morality, confined these aspects of his intellectual activity to a small private coterie and was chiefly known in France, and internationally, not as a philosopher (which he was) but as a political commentator and historian of French institutions, where his leanings were decidedly unSpinozistic at least in outcome: for he was deeply committed to what, in his eyes, were the authentic realities of noble 'glory' and lineage.

[89] Dupré, *Enlightenment*, 172; Goyard-Fabre, *Montesquieu*, 224–5.

[90] Bayle, *Continuation*, ii. 518–19, 558–9.

[91] Riley, 'General and Particular Will', 184–5, 187–8, 194.

[92] Ehrard, *L'Idée*, 44, 97; Ellis, *Boulainvilliers*, pp. ix, 208, 212.

A dogged opponent of royal absolutism and defender of 'liberty', Boulainvilliers at the same time championed aspects of tradition, in particular urging that men of aristocratic 'birth' and 'virtue' should always be preferred to others for holding high offices of state.

Nevertheless, it would be wrong to infer from this that Boulainvilliers's political thought was largely free of his Spinozist concerns; for in fact he develops his apology for the French nobility starting from clear Spinozistic premisses in a manner rather crucial for the subsequent evolution of French political thought. Since, for him, very differently from Hume, neither theology, nor titles, authority, precedent, privilege, nor custom have any justifying force in themselves, and he is determined to proceed on the basis of reason alone, he feels obliged to begin with the principle of equality which according to his Spinozistic (and indirectly Hobbesian) axioms is the original basis of human society and politics. Even if primitive men dwelt in a world far from idyllic, being prey to constant fear and insecurity, and disrupted by ambition, men's passions being always the same,[93] he contends, 'dans le droit commun tous les hommes sont égaux'; hence such legal categories as nobility, slavery, and common citizenship were, in his system, originally based on nothing more than usurpation, force, and violence.[94] Born of equality such institutions inherently lack all validity.

It was to block the democratic implications of his own reasoning that he appeals to historical circumstances and geography, assigning a particularly pivotal historical significance to the Frankish conquest of Gaul. This Boulainvilliers envisages as the feat not of the Frankish kings but rather of the Franks envisaged as a warrior class, a conquering band which evolved, he contends, into the freedom-loving French *ancienne noblesse*, the elite which forged stable mixed monarchy in France. This they did primarily through regularly convening their general assembly whereby they held the crown in check, doing so in their own interest, assuredly, but also, he holds, for the greater good of society.[95]

Freedom and equality, then, are upheld as key foundational values by Boulainvilliers even though these are then subverted by the inevitable facts of large monarchies, and especially by right of conquest and superior force. Undeniably, the ancient Greeks prided themselves more on being born free and 'de vivre libres' than other ancient peoples and went furthest, despite retaining aristocratic elements in their society too, in upholding a 'general equality' [l'égalité générale]. In fact, he acknowledges, the clear-sighted Greeks considered equality 'le fondement de la liberté'.[96] However, it was precisely here, in his view, that they undermined the political viability of their city-states, through wrongly inferring that the majority

[93] MS Boulainvilliers, *Abrégé*, i. 97, 167–8, ii. 616–17; Ehrard, *Idée*, 524.

[94] Boulainvilliers, *Essais sur la noblesse*, 1; Furet and Ozouf, 'Deux légitimations', 238, 240; Ehrard, *L'Idée*, 97, 509–11, 524; Venturino, *Ragioni*, 78.

[95] Boulainvilliers, *État de la France*, i. 54, 62; Ellis, *Boulainvilliers*, 76, 79–80, 163; Childs, *Political Academy*, 181–2; Ehrard, *L'Esprit des mots*, 142–3.

[96] Boulainvilliers, *Essais sur la noblesse*, 2–3; Venturino, *Ragioni*, 274–9.

can rule. For in reality, held Boulainvilliers, agreeing here with (Hobbes and) Bayle, it was their opting for democracy which led to the ruinous fragmentation of their country into minuscule and ultimately unsustainable city-states and the chronic instability of their republics. Against the failed conception of the Greeks, he offers the example of the great Near Eastern monarchies, especially those of the Babylonians and Persians which were both enduring and stable because, he contends, they wisely reserved all positions of power and influence for noblemen.

The indispensability of noble privilege and esteeming noble birth, in short, is proved, according to Boulainvilliers, by the chronic instability, and vulnerability, of all those states where the nobility 'cesse d'y occuper le premier rang'.[97] Where societies fail to check the natural ambition of each individual by subordinating the multitude to a dominant, hereditary feudal elite, preferably, as with the Franks, of a different ethnic background, they remain fatally subject, claims Boulainvilliers, 'à des révolutions continuelles'.[98] The unparalleled stability of the early Roman republic, and hence its greatness, is attributable, he urges, to the Romans achieving a judicious balance between republican virtue and aristocracy, reserving most high offices and commands for nobles; conversely, the Roman empire's decline is explained by the later emperors' disastrous error in introducing a sort 'd'égalité qui minoit la noblesse'.[99]

Boulainvilliers, then, crucially grants that men are all naturally equal in their share 'de la raison et de l'humanité', but equally adamantly denies one can deduce anything favourable to democracy or republicanism from this, holding that only limited monarchy can effectively guarantee security and personal freedom and, even then, only when access to political offices, and the direction of the state and its armed forces, is confined to nobles.[100] Forming large, stable monarchies, in his view, is the supreme achievement of human history and a highly complex process which advances only slowly after many prior stages of laborious experience and, as a *sine qua non*, must rest on firmly delineated forms of social hierarchy.[101]

In terms of political liberty, stability, and the common interest of society, or what he calls 'le bonheur des peuples', the distance between the classical Greek republic and feudal France actually represents, held Boulainvilliers, a solid gain for humanity. Thus, the true republican spirit, he urges, can be fostered only within a libertarian, virtue-cultivating, and politically responsible noble class. Indeed, he consciously transfers what he considers the best features of the Greek republic to the warlike Franks who, he says, were 'tous libres et parfaitement égaux et indépendens', and the later egalitarian, freedom-loving, intensely political culture he imputes to the old French nobility.[102] Hence, Hume rightly accounts Boulainvilliers 'a noted republican'.[103]

[97] Boulainvilliers, *Essais sur la noblesse*, 7.

[98] Ibid. 2; Boulainvilliers, *État de la France*, i, p. xliii.

[99] Boulainvilliers, *État de la France*, i, p. xci; Senarclens, *Montesquieu*, 54–5; Boulainvilliers, *Essais sur la noblesse*, 5–6.

[100] Boulainvilliers, *Essais sur la noblesse*, 7.

[101] MS Boulainvilliers, *Abrégé*, i. 164–6; Venturino, *Ragioni*, 257–74.

[102] Boulainvilliers, *État de la France*, i, pp. li, 54, 86; Wright, *Classical Republican*, 128–9, 201; Wright, 'Idea', 292, 306.

[103] Baldi, *Verisimile, non vero*, 78 n.

Simultaneously the surest support and chief foundation of stable monarchy, held Boulainvilliers, this feudal elite owes royalty 'ni son établissement ni ses droits'.[104]

Boulainvilliers's juggling of republicanism and Spinozist themes with his vigorous championing of the French nobility led him to stress the importance—here foreshadowing both Montesquieu and Voltaire—of identifying different sorts of cultural context, education, and *mœurs* as something not just relevant, but necessary, for maintaining different kinds of state. Cultivating the right attitudes and *mœurs* enabled the French monarchy to flourish during the Middle Ages, which he conceived as a kind of golden age, prompting Voltaire later to ridicule him for portraying French feudalism as 'le chef-d'œuvre de l'esprit humain'.[105] Since the late fifteenth century (i.e. the reign of Louis XI), however, a combination of adverse developments, argues Boulainvilliers, had lowered the standing and prestige of the *noblesse*. In the sixteenth century, Italian influence had further sapped French aristocratic values, by introducing a deplorable courtly servility and flattery, effeminate refinement, and also the study of Greek political literature. Since Frenchmen dwelt in a monarchy completely opposed 'à l'esprit républicain et aux maximes des Grecs et des anciens Romains',[106] there was, he claims (echoing Hobbes), much that was highly damaging in the elite being educated in Latin and Greek texts. His antipathy to what today we call the Renaissance extended also to Machiavelli, a theorist less of republicanism, in his view, than of base tyranny and moral irresponsibility.[107]

Such were the ironies of Boulainvilliers's paradoxical Spinozistic politics which, starting from premisses of reason and equality, end by reaffirming feudalism, aristocracy, and Italophobia. Readers unconvinced by Boulainvilliers's account of French history but eager to continue his defence of aristocracy, social hierarchy, and mixed monarchy, using only secular arguments, and focusing on the worldly good of society, had to wait for Montesquieu. They had to wait, that is, for a novel vision of institutions, laws, and politics which only fully emerged in *L'Esprit des lois* (1748), but already existed in outline by 1734 when Montesquieu published his book on the Roman republic and whose intellectual origins lay much further back, in his early interaction with the Fontenelle and Boulainvilliers coteries and participation in the 1720s in the Entresol 'club', a gathering of politically active and theoretically engaged nobles meeting in Paris, including the comte de Plélo, the anti-Spinozist Jacobite Ramsay, and the republican-minded marquis d'Argenson, meetings attended, at times, also by the exiled Bolingbroke as well as Montesquieu. Several of these men, including d'Argenson who was impressed with the Dutch Republic which he had visited in 1717, powerfully intensified the group's collective critique of conventional notions of monarchy and nobility.[108]

104 Boulainvilliers, *Essais sur la noblesse*, 11; Furet and Ozouf, 'Deux légitimations', 238–9.
105 Voltaire, *Œuvres complètes*, xxv. 82.
106 Furet and Ozouf, 'Deux légitimations', 288, 290; Senarclens, *Montesquieu*, 55.
107 Venturino, *Ragioni*, 264, 287.
108 Ibid. 201–3; Vernière, *Spinoza*, 397–8; Childs, *Political Academy*, 185–90.

Immersion in Bayle, Boulainvilliers, d'Argenson, and the Entresol debates, as well as Montesquieu, also helped form that other key Early Enlightenment French political thinker Gabriel Bonnot de Mably (1709–85), Condillac's elder brother. The chief task of 'philosophy', held Mably, in his first major work, the *Parallèle des Romains et des François par rapport au gouvernement* (2 vols., Paris, 1740), is to illumine history and, by examining history philosophically, to develop a properly based theoretical politics, that is one concerned to advance the sum of human happiness or what Mably called 'le bien général des hommes' and 'la plus grande utilité du genre humain'.[109] Not unlike Condorcet later, Mably remained a lifelong devotee of Fontenelle's and Boulainvilliers's foundational concept that, however hesitant and halting the phases, there is a gradual rational progress of the *esprit humain*.

The early, pre-1750, Mably agreed with Bayle, Boulainvilliers (who fascinated him), and Vauvenargues that the natural equality and liberty characteristic of the 'state of nature' in no way provide a viable basis for the state since they are not an institutionalized equality and liberty but merely an equality of insecurity, fear, and uncertainty.[110] Like Boulainvilliers, he too considered conventional justifications of monarchy and aristocracy on grounds of titles, tradition, and theological sanction all invalid and irrelevant to the philosopher, the only legitimate reason why monarchy can be preferred to democracy or aristocracy, he held, being that it is the most 'natural' form, the closest to paternal rule in the typical household.[111] An austere, reclusive writer scornful of the more light-hearted, literary side of other *philosophes* whom he mostly judged insufficiently 'philosophical' as well as not political enough, talkers too little given to discussing ideas—in later years, he clashed bitterly with Voltaire[112]—Mably initially shared Boulainvilliers's anti-democratic tendency. He too was convinced aristocratic mixed monarchy is the surest and best form of state, and social hierarchy inherently desirable. To begin with he also judged the greatness of the ancient Roman republic to be due to its wise balancing of the rights and powers of aristocracy and people.[113]

The early Mably's critique of the democratic republic—he was soon to evolve into the foremost of the French Enlightenment republicans—resembles those of Hobbes, Bayle, and Boulainvilliers in stressing that democracy is closest to the state of man in the pre-political period, or the so-called 'state of nature', but also, for that reason, inescapably the closest to 'anarchy'.[114] Liberty of the sort prevailing in democratic Athens he rejected as an empty promise providing little security and less stability, something in reality resembling servitude more than true liberty. Born 'free and equal', citizens of democratic republics are ruthlessly subjected to the tyranny of the majority, and hence the ambition, unruliness, and intimidation deemed by him the inevitable features of democracy. He too, at this stage, judged

109 Mably, *Parallèle*, i, preface p. iv; Dagen, *L'Histoire*, 553–6.

110 Mably, *Parallèle*, i. 50; Bove, 'Vauvenargues politique', 409–10, 412.

111 Bove, 'Vauvenargues politique', 416; Mably, *Parallèle*, i. 48.

112 Galliani, 'Mably et Voltaire', 182–3, 193–4.

113 Ibid. i. 45–8; Venturino, *Ragioni*, 193, 315.

114 Mably, *Parallèle*, i. 46, 48.

monarchy best because it most securely establishes the 'tranquillité publique', providing the protection and stability which are the principal services the state performs for humankind.

During the early stages of Man's political development, monarchy, he agrees with his mentor Boulainvilliers, is also chronically unstable because people's customs and attitudes, their *mœurs*, still contradict the vital principles of hierarchy, *noblesse*, and the 'subordination qu'exige la monarchie'.[115] Man's political history, he affirms, is a slow and painful evolution by stages; only little by little does equality, 'le seul fondement des républiques libres', lose its paralysing grip, recede, and, finally, disappear. The growing gulf between rich and poor, noble and ignoble, and the emergence of more elaborate forms of hierarchy, gradually render monarchy more viable and stable, eliminating all basis for democracy (which is equality) and grounding 'mixed government' after which develops the still higher form, as he conceived initially, of absolute monarchy, an evolution, he argued, which confers benefits on all men in the shape of security, rule of law, and moderation.

Even the Mably of 1740, though, diverged from Boulainvilliers in being more worried by the fact that social hierarchy also creates conditions in which the common people are herded, exploited, and made 'stupide et ignorant', their poverty being now no longer voluntary but institutionalized. As a result, they are now systematically confined to base employments, 'emplois vils', subjecting them more and more to the power of the landed rich while simultaneously debasing their thoughts and opinions. The more the people are subordinated to an elite, the more the feasibility or potential viability of democracy which had earlier been a universal reality diminishes. For besides the turmoil and instability liberty necessarily foments in a large state, in the changed circumstances each citizen would, were democracy restored, bring to the public assemblies not his original awareness of equality, encouraging 'generosity' and 'wisdom', but rather his newly acquired crassness, narrowness, and absorption in private concerns.[116]

Hence, in a large and complex state, emerging at a relatively late stage in Man's development, long after the greatness of Rome, such as medieval and early modern France, monarchy was indisputably best.[117] While subjects were subordinated and conditioned to obey, the young Mably accepted Boulainvilliers's argument that social hierarchy and the specific *mœurs* prevailing in France had ensured that at the same time, owing to the nobility's rightful social dominance, liberty was preserved and French kings could not abuse their power.[118] He disagreed, though, with Boulainvilliers's thesis that the French nobility's decline was a disaster threatening the liberty of all. Mixed monarchy, in his view, was actually not the right form for France, absolutism, he believed then, being both more appropriate and safer.

115 Ibid. i. 32, 50, 53; Wright, *Classical Republican*, 28.

116 Mably, *Parallèle*, i. 53–4, 57.

117 Ibid. i. 240–1, 263, 265.

118 Ibid. i. 57, 265–6; Wright, 'Idea', 297; Wright, *Classical Republican*, 32–3.

Mably had entirely changed his views on liberty, equality, and republics, though, by the late 1740s, presumably partly as a result of seeing the mounting constitutional, organizational, and fiscal difficulties the French monarchy experienced at that time. Envisaging even the consolidation of royal power in France in Richelieu's time as a 'revolution', though it was by no means a sudden or violent event, Mably at this point emerged as a writer particularly concerned with the concept of 'revolution' as a basic, fundamental change of principles. This was a striking point of contrast with, and presumably subdued criticism of, Montesquieu who always studiously avoided using the term in the new sense as amplified by Boulainvilliers, Voltaire, Turgot, and Mably, employing the term only in the plural and in an older and much less significant sense to mean just repeated disturbances particularly in unstable, lawless societies.[119] Mably, by contrast, became especially interested in the general revolt against monarchy, in favour of democracy, in fifth-century BC Greece, a development which struck him as not just a 'revolution' in institutions but a particularly fundamental 'revolution' imparting to the Greeks 'un génie tout nouveau', as he puts it in his first overtly republican work, the *Observations sur les Grecs* (1749), a veritable revolution of revolutions.[120]

Central to Mably's political theory in the late 1740s was his idea that revolutions occur where the laws and *mœurs* of a society are out of step with the form of government in place. Revolutions he saw as the mechanism by which the institutions of government, and *mœurs*, are realigned and, hence, something decisive in determining the degree of 'liberty' or 'servitude' in any given state.[121] What had seemed to him, in 1740, France's tranquillity and remoteness from 'revolution', or 'la perfection du gouvernement françois', he had attributed to the prevailing harmony, as he then saw it, between monarchy and France's society, attitudes, and laws. These gave the king absolute power in theory while, in practice, ensuring the social hierarchy and 'les mœurs qui empêchent qu'il [i.e. the king] n'abuse pas de son pouvoir', preserving the people's liberty.[122] He now seemed to have lost confidence that in France any such harmony actually existed and was carefully exploring the attributes of both 'mixed monarchy' and republics.

By the 1740s, the concepts of 'liberty', 'equality', and 'revolution' had all become basic to French political theorizing in a way which differed strikingly from the trajectory of English political thought of the early eighteenth century. Doubtless this was partly due to the use of different sources, English political writers such as Hobbes, Harrington, Locke, Sidney, Toland, and Bolingbroke being only rarely referred to in the elaboration of French political thought of this period. But it was partly due also to the divergent social and political contexts in which the two traditions of political theory evolved. Classical republican motifs figured centrally in both traditions and both shared a deep preoccupation with *liberté* but the French

119 Ehrard, *L'Esprit des mots*, 122–3, 126–7.

120 Mably, *Observations sur les Grecs*, 11–12; Wright, *Classical Republican*, 16, 39–40.

121 Mably, *Parallèle*, i. 272; Mably, *Observations sur les Romains*, i. 203; Wright, *Classical Republican*, 23, 74–8.

122 Mably, *Parallèle*, i. 272–3; Senarclens, *Montesquieu*, 43–4.

were now unquestionably the more concerned with general problems of equality, aristocracy, and democracy, and especially that of how to balance the interest of the individual against 'l'intérêt général'.[123] Where the English stuck to their own authors, Boulainvilliers was plainly chiefly influenced by Spinoza, Bayle, and Fontenelle, though, through reading Le Clerc and meeting Coste, he also had some awareness of Locke.[124] Montesquieu and Mably likewise grew up in an intellectual world steeped in Bayle, Fontenelle, and Boulainvilliers, conceiving of history as the evolution by stages of 'l'esprit humain' and seeing this as crucial to grasping the nature of the human condition. In his political fragments, written between 1737 and 1747, Vauvenargues likewise bases himself on *Spinosiste* premisses and the work of Boulainvilliers, Fontenelle, Bayle, and Fréret.[125]

3. THE IDEAL OF MIXED MONARCHY

From the 1720s to the 1740s, the two traditions, while remaining separate intellectual traditions reflecting contrasting social and political milieux, nevertheless conspicuously converged in their common veneration of mixed monarchy. Moreover, it was the French discussion of mixed monarchy which was eventually to attract the wider international notice. While the significance of the distinctively French line of development in political theory was largely confined to France until 1748, publication of *L'Esprit des lois* in that year precipitated a vast international public controversy which raged from Rome to St Petersburg, rendering the basic categories of society and politics as formulated by these thinkers the common property of all Europe.

Montesquieu's masterpiece had an unprecedented impact. If Voltaire was distinctly lukewarm, complaining of the work's lack of cohesion, and many factual errors, and the church's *anti-philosophes*, especially the Jansenists and (Italian and Austrian) Jesuits, implacably hostile, all the 'esprits très philosophes', as La Beaumelle put it, enthusiastically lauded Montesquieu's approach, methodology, and ideas.[126] If La Beaumelle accounted his hero, along with Socrates and Luther, one of the three supreme reformers of humanity,[127] Mably, in 1751, if less euphoric, still ranked Montesquieu among the handful of greatest geniuses produced by France.[128] Dubbed by La Beaumelle 'la Bible des Politiques',[129] *L'Esprit des lois* seemed admirably conceived both to demolish conventional thinking about politics, society, religion, and morality, and counter the radical challenge in all these spheres.

123 Bove, 'Vauvenargues politique', 412.

124 Israel, *Radical Enlightenment*, 497–8, 565–74, 689–90.

125 Bove, 'Vauvenargues politique', 403–8.

126 [La Beaumelle], *Suite de la défense*, 149; Masseau, *Ennemis des philosophes*, 121–2.

127 La Beaumelle, *Mes pensées*, 228; Livesey, *Making Democracy*, 36–7.

128 Mably, *Observations sur les Romains*, 170.

129 [La Beaumelle], *Suite de la défense*, 68.

Montesquieu's relationship to radical and republican thought remained, however, complex and deeply ambivalent. To its out-and-out critics, *L'Esprit* seemed to be claiming that the world functions according to a blind and necessary logic, human social and moral structures, as well as legal systems and institutions, being the result of climate, geography, and other aspects of nature, rather than the providential God of the Bible. Hence, from the perspective of the French Jansenists and other *anti-philosophes*, Montesquieu's approach to politics and social theory by no means appeared to be so free of materialist, Spinozist, and *Bayliste* implications as he and his supporters professed.[130] In fact, Montesquieu's naturalism was undeniable, as was a general air of religious *indifférentisme*, evident, for instance, in his contentious claim that Catholicism is better suited to monarchy, especially absolute monarchy, and Protestantism to republics—despite the fact, as one critic complained, that the Venetian, Genoese, and Luccan republics had always remained staunchly Catholic.[131] In other ways too, Montesquieu's disavowals of Spinozism seemed questionable: how can the author of *L'Esprit* be 'donc spinosiste', protested Montesquieu in 1750, having separated the material world rigorously from spiritual intelligences? But it was far from clear, actually, that he did assign any role to purely spiritual beings and forces.[132]

Much influenced by his 'master' Boulainvilliers, and knowing Fréret well, there was nothing surprising about Montesquieu's thought, conversation, and books all reflecting a lifelong preoccupation with issues raised by Spinoza, Bayle, Boulainvilliers, Fontenelle, and Fréret.[133] But if his novel methodology prompted accusations of 'naturalism' and Spinozism from Jansenist opponents, equally his counter-argument that 'il n'y a donc point de Spinosisme dans *L'Esprit des Lois*' was not without force.[134] Claiming he had not challenged the primacy of miracles or theology, or the theologians' interpretations of revelation, but merely deemed such material beyond his scope and expertise, he had after all privileged Christianity over the other religions. Moreover, like Hume, but unlike Spinoza, Bayle, and Diderot, he was clearly a moral and social relativist, developing a kind of social determinism, certainly, but not one applied across the board; he could claim (even if rather questionably) that he had left transcendental spiritual and moral values intact. In any case, the main aim of his theorizing was to forge a new type of liberal aristocratic ideology, and one which was to prove hugely influential in mid and late eighteenth-century Europe and America: for he envisaged nobility as a natural and effective barrier against royal absolutism, serving all of society.[135] In short, Montesquieu

130 Lauriol, *La Beaumelle*, 186–200; Cottret, *Jansénismes*, 61.

131 [La Porte], *Observations sur* L'Esprit des lois, 8, 46, 163.

132 Montesquieu, *Œuvres complètes*, 808; Lynch, 'Montesquieu', 490; Cottret, *Jansénismes*, 62–3.

133 Moreau, 'Malebranche et le Spinosisme', 1–3; Vernière, *Spinoza*, 449–51; Bianchi, 'Histoire et nature', 294; Volpilhac-Auger, 'Nicolas Fréret', 10; Israel, *Radical Enlightenment*, 12, 83.

134 Israel, *Radical Enlightenment*, 68, 71, 76, 144; Smith, *Spinoza, Liberalism*, 11, 211; Cottret, *Jansénismes*, 61; Jacob, *Radical Enlightenment*, 156; Tortarolo, *L'Illuminismo*, 40–1; Bianchi, 'Histoire et nature', 304.

135 Baridon, 'Concepts', 359–60, 364; Senarclens, *Montesquieu*, 54; Seif, 'Missverstandene Montesquieu', 155–6, 165; Himmelfarb, *Roads to Modernity*, 162–3.

adroitly combines enthusiasm for 'mixed monarchy' and the 'British model' with an updated version of Boulainvilliers's *thèse nobiliaire*. With this, his political thought became virtually the socio-political equivalent of Newton's physics, a fundamental pillar of the West's moderate mainstream Enlightenment, the principal reply to the radical politics of the egalitarian materialists, *Spinosistes*, and democratic republicans.[136]

Eager to remodel and strengthen the *thèse nobiliaire* developed by Boulainvilliers and members of the Entresol on a new basis, Montesquieu's conception of politics was closely connected to his and their critique of equality and republicanism. Both the democratic and the aristocratic republic seemed to him to be hampered with insuperable difficulties for any large country like France. While conceding that republics where noble birth is not recognized might perhaps derive some element of political stability from the fact that the plebs will then have no reason to be envious of those to whom it entrusts offices, and from whom it can reclaim authority 'à sa fantaisie',[137] in general he preferred to assume that equality renders the democratic republic even more arbitrary and unstable than the aristocratic and that all republics are, in any case, inherently inferior to 'limited monarchy'. For Montesquieu, as earlier for Bayle and Boulainvilliers, Roman history in particular confirms the non-viability of republics, even aristocratic republics, when organized on any scale.[138]

Even in the case of small republics, there was much to criticize: he saw little to admire in the ancient Greek democracies though he had some praise for the Spartan model, this at least being an aristocratic republic with a royal or princely figurehead.[139] Still less was he enthusiastic about the medieval and early modern Italian city republics despite the impressive stability of the Venetian exemplum which he ascribes to offices of state being consistently reserved to the nobility. Even in optimal conditions making it possible for republics to sustain themselves in the long term, which he, like Boulainvilliers and the early Mably, stipulates as being a combination of smallness and isolation from more powerful neighbours and a firm reliance on nobility, there was still much that was problematic in his view; in particular, he highlights the corrupt and tyrannical character of the commercial republics of Venice and Genoa where, he says 'la liberté se trouve moins que dans nos monarchies'.[140]

More concerned to determine the causes and motives of particular developments, and what adjustments might be more or less suited to particular constitutions, than with what is best in general, the most fundamental distinction between types of governments for Montesquieu was not between monarchies, aristocracies, and republics, or those based on hierarchical or egalitarian principles, but between

136 Gay, *Enlightenment*, ii. 467–9; Venturino, *Ragioni*, 276, 294, 302, 307–8; Pocock, *Barbarism*, iii. 342.

137 Montesquieu, *Œuvres complètes*, 450; Carrithers, 'Democratic and Aristocratic', 144.

138 Montesquieu, *Œuvres complètes*, 452.

139 Ibid. 532–4, 536–7, 1036; Carrithers, 'Democratic and Aristocratic', 110–11, 144–5; Ehrard, *L'Idée*, 513.

140 Ehrard, *L'Idée*, 216, 244, 452, 586; Courtois, 'Temps, corruption', 314.

gouvernements modérés and *gouvernements non modérés*.[141] Consequently, all other political categories and moral systems, in his politics, remained secondary and particular, their origins and effects, even their very meaning, varying according to conditions and their local climactic and moral milieu. As a model, his preference was decidedly for British-style mixed monarchy, a choice doubtless partly inspired by his aristocratic tastes and preferences, and perhaps also by his talks with Bolingbroke whom he had known, and admired, in both Paris and London, though he broke with him later.[142] For Montesquieu, Britain was the key exemplum of wise government, offering prudent checks and balances and an organized division of powers, guaranteeing stable procedures of legislation and justice. But the British constitution was so admirable in his eyes chiefly because what he saw as the true function of the nobility as the appropriate intermediary between sovereign and people was fully acknowledged, the supervisory role of the nobility and gentry, that is, the power of the British constitution to regulate itself, being institutionalized in Parliament,[143] guaranteeing a degree of moderation, stability, and liberty matched nowhere else.

Such a perspective directly clashed with that of the democratic republican tradition as well as the political ideas of Bayle, who also stressed the inherent instability of republics, but would never have endorsed Montesquieu's claim that every state does best to adhere to the forms, traditions, and attitudes for which it is suited by climate, geography, and history, seeing equity, the fundamental and universal principle of morality, as the proper basis of law and social policy.[144] While Montesquieu shared Bayle's zeal for individual liberty, agreeing that the philosopher's task is to ascertain what institutional arrangements best safeguard the individual's tranquillity, freedom of conscience, and in general the liberty which comes with 'gouvernement modéré', the whole tenor of Montesquieu's thesis that liberty is best safeguarded by dividing sovereignty, and institutionalizing intermediate bodies between the king and the people which then serve to balance the power of the king, on one side, and the people, on the other, with the aristocracy as the group best fitted to perform this crucial intermediary role, ran counter to the grain of Bayle's (and Vico's) political thought.[145]

Restricting political authority and rendering it as balanced, deliberative, and even as inert, as possible was central to Montesquieu's conception of a healthy politics, though the particular arrangement suitable in any given context was conditioned by the particularity and special circumstances of any given political constitution. Constitutions being the outcome of a highly complex interplay of

141 Montesquieu, *L'Esprit des lois*, 586–91; Goyard-Fabre, *Montesquieu*, 260–4, 283–4.

142 Hufton, *Europe*, 57–8; Ehrard, *L'Idée*, 508–9, 515; Seif, 'Missverstandene Montesquieu', 153–4; Lacouture, *Montesquieu*, 190–1; Livesey, *Making Democracy*, 34–6.

143 Montesquieu, *Œuvres complètes*, 452, 535, 550, 586–90; Ehrard, *L'Idée*, 508–9; Romani, 'All Montesquieu's Sons', 198–9; Livesey, *Making Democracy*, 36.

144 Spector, 'Des *Lettres persanes*', 120–2; Ehrard, *L'Idée*, 724.

145 Ehrard, *L'Idée*, 460, 493; Carrithers, 'Democratic and Aristocratic', 109–10; Tillet, *Constitution anglaise*, 270–85.

many long-term factors, ranging from climate and religion to social hierarchy and judicial practices, any abrupt change in the 'principes' of a constitution, as Montesquieu liked to say, must always be difficult, dangerous, and generally inadvisable. For such changes are apt to disturb and disrupt by subverting the order of nature as applying in that particular instance.[146] Unsurprisingly, the chief quality required by Montesquieu's reformer or legislator was infinite prudence; for every worthwhile plan for reform necessitated, to his mind, an exceptional fund of insight enabling one to assess how change would affect the intricate network of ties, checks, and balances which determine the character of a state.[147]

Montesquieu's conception of 'mixed monarchy' presupposed a particular kind of social hierarchy, dispersal of power, and moral order. He disavowed any intention to blur the distinction between virtue and vice. But his doctrine that every constitution has its own spirit, the fruit of a complex web of conditions and a particular mix of attitudes, highlighted the indirect, specific, ambiguities of moral principles and traditions in a given context. Thus, for example, Spanish good faith, uprightness, and honesty might be admirable qualities in another context but, combined with Spanish lethargy and aversion to merchants, effectively spoiled all prospect of a dynamic, healthy commerce ruinously for Spain. Their particular *mœurs* enabled other nations to appropriate the seaborne trade with the Spanish Indies, via Cadiz, from under the Spaniards' very noses.[148] This was bound to relativize notions of good and bad, just and unjust, virtuous and vicious, further legitimizing an ideology of 'difference'.

Given his dislike of equality and democracy, Montesquieu's admiration for mixed monarchy and predilection for nobility was especially problematic, philosophically, with respect to morality and questions of basic justice. For according to his own ethical schema, while the highest principle of republics is 'virtue', that of monarchies is 'honour', an aristocratic code of values which, from an ethical point of view, and by his own admission, as well as according to the 'naturalistic' ethical systems of Spinoza, Bayle, and Shaftesbury, disadvantages the majority and represents an altogether lower order of values than 'virtue'. The Abbé de La Roche, one of Montesquieu's foremost French critics during the Querelle de *L'Esprit des lois* of 1748–51, was hence by no means wide of the mark when complaining that, for Montesquieu, Catholicism is the appropriate religion for monarchies while monarchy's supreme *principe* is aristocratic 'honour' which, to any true philosopher, is assuredly a false 'virtue' akin to ambition and pride; here La Roche detected an implicit smear of the Catholic Church through linkage to a dubious code tied to an entirely worldly order of values,[149] rightly identifying an inherent conflict in Montesquieu's system between what promotes the higher virtues and what best buttresses a particular kind of hierarchical social and political system.

[146] Courtois, 'Temps, corruption', 312.
[147] Ehrard, *L'Esprit des mots*, 183.
[148] Montesquieu, *L'Esprit des lois*, 643.
[149] Lynch, 'Montesquieu', 489–90.

Montesquieu protested that in his system, unlike Spinoza's, justice and equity are both absolute and prior to the positive laws made by men, conforming with the premisses of Natural Law; but here he sounded distinctly unconvincing since it remained wholly unclear in what this alleged priority and absolute status consisted. Rather morality and justice in his thought, as another of his foes accusing him of *Spinosisme*, the Jansenist Jean-Baptiste Gaultier (1684–1755),[150] observed, signifies no more than mutually beneficial codes or agreements among men not to follow their individual desires in everything.[151] This could only underline the fact that Montesquieu's ethical schema was altogether relativist as well as more pessimistic and sceptical than those of Bayle and Spinoza, his ethical scepticism, as has been aptly remarked, being nearer to that of Montaigne and the Renaissance than that of the other *philosophes.*[152] As many conservative critics noted during the Querelle de *L'Esprit des lois*, to pool—after making the *de rigueur* disclaimer that the Christian religion is the true faith—all religions and moral systems including Christianity together and treat them as essentially inventions of men closely related to the diverse types of human societies, moulded by the forces of climate, geography, and history, was not just a novel procedure which transforms and secularizes the science of politics, as well as Man's view of history and human culture, but also one that inescapably involves large concessions to the freethinkers' anti-theological conception of reality.

The tension between Montesquieu and radical thought, on the one hand, and Counter-Enlightenment, on the other, with Montesquieu himself caught in the middle, became clearer with the publication of Mably's second overtly republican work, his *Observations sur les Romains* (1751). Increasingly tailoring his politics to his moral theory and general philosophical stance, Mably here argues that the *mœurs* appropriate for a monarchy steering midway between a 'gouvernement libre', that is a free republic, and *despotisme* is essentially a mixture of vice and virtue, corruption and uprightness, the truly noble and austere virtue of the 'republican' being intrinsically unsuited to contexts in which monarchs reign and bestow privilege.[153] It was hard not to read into Mably's discourse the placing of a large question mark over Montesquieu's system, indeed the casting of a moral slur over 'mixed monarchy' itself.

Condorcet, criticizing Montesquieu later, objected that a good law, like a correct proposition in geometry, should be valid for all, and available to everyone equally. Montesquieu, of course, repeatedly disavowed any intention to blur distinctions between just and unjust. Yet, each polity is so distinctive to itself in his schema that, perversely, laws may sometimes be right for some but wrong for others and vice versa,[154] a conception Condorcet judged incompatible with any democratic,

150 Gaultier, Lettres persanes *convaincues*, 34–6, 101; Israel, *Radical Enlightenment*, 12, 729.

151 Montesquieu, *Œuvres complètes*, 809; Gaultier, Lettres persanes *convaincues*, 34; Bartlett, *Idea of Enlightenment*, 33.

152 Senarclens, *Montesquieu*, 139–41.

153 Mably, *Observations sur les Romains*, 203–4; Wright, *Classical Republican*, 40–50, 63–4, 199–200.

154 Wright, *Classical Republican*, 103–4; Larrère, '*L'Esprit des lois*', 151.

universalist, and egalitarian ideal of law or politics. Montesquieu, always impressed by the irreducible diversity and variety of human societies, rarely speaks of the inherent justice or injustice of particular moral, social, or legal systems and does not attempt to construct a scale of better and worse applying to all.[155] Constitutions decay and the problem of what leads to the corruption of a particular polity, the erosion of its principles and *mœurs*, is central to his thought; but his very concept of 'corruption' restricts questions of political deterioration and moral decay to particular contexts rather than relating these to any wider moral or political theoretical framework.[156]

Such wide-ranging particularism to an extent subverts even his key concept of 'liberty'.[157] While *L'Esprit des lois* is in a way a rambling meditation on liberty, the effect of Montesquieu's 'meditation' is to modulate and nuance the concept so as to reveal a bewildering variety of shifts in meaning in different political and moral milieux: 'il n'y a point de mot', affirms Montesquieu, 'qui ait reçu plus de différentes significations.'[158] In fact, the concept was stripped by Montesquieu of any exact meaning, and made indeterminate and contingent rather than something basic to the human condition. Liberty, he holds, is not freedom to do what one wants in some generalized sense but 'cette tranquillité d'esprit' resulting from confidence that everyone is safe in his own possessions and security under the law in a particular polity.[159] The essential principle for him is that 'la liberté politique ne se trouve que dans les gouvernements modérés'.[160]

Consequently, neither monarchy, aristocracy, nor democracy, in the abstract, is specially predisposed, in Montesquieu's opinion, either to enhance or prejudice liberty; human freedom can be promoted or blighted under any system. What matters, he urges, is to grasp that moderation is found only where office-holders do not abuse their power; and that men being so constituted that they always exploit their authority insofar as they can, the only thing that prevents abuse is another power, an institutionalized check blocking the first. Liberty is thus best preserved where exercise of power is most carefully regulated and checked by dispersal of authority, which means instituting as much separation as possible, especially between the executive, legislative, and judicial branches. Mixed government is always best and the supreme guiding principle in politics; and, in this respect, Britain alone was a universal model from which the rest could learn, even though the English constitution too was the product of particular circumstances. By the same token, 'oriental' despotism, though rooted in its own particular circumstances and *mœurs*, is always worst, an emphasis which created a sharp polarity between 'eastern' and 'western' and a definite tension in Montesquieu's doctrine between 'liberty', relative term

155 Senarclens, *Montesquieu*, 133–5, 137.
156 Courtois, 'Temps, corruption', 307–9; Spector, 'Des *Lettres persanes*', 125–6.
157 Goyard-Fabre, *Montesquieu*, 157, 346–8; Senarclens, *Montesquieu*, 136.
158 Senarclens, *Montesquieu*, 136; Montesquieu, *L'Esprit des lois*, 585.
159 Montesquieu, *L'Esprit des lois*, 586; Larrère, '*L'Esprit des lois*', 153.
160 Montesquieu, *L'Esprit des lois*, 586; Goyard-Fabre, *Montesquieu*, 264.

though this was for him, and 'enlightenment', a tension most obviously reflected in his discussion of Russia. For his system clearly implied that there was no clear, necessary, or dependent connection between liberty and enlightenment.

What was most problematic, then, about Montesquieu's 'structuralism' from any 'enlightened' viewpoint—radical or moderate—was that it precluded any absolute standard, or fixed order of justice and liberty, by which it becomes possible to condemn despotism, slavery, or serfdom, and, in sharp contrast, to Boulainvilliers, Voltaire, and Mably, precludes also any mechanism of 'revolution'. Admittedly, Montesquieu's instinctive aversion moves him to make an exception in the case of black slavery, and step momentarily outside his structural framework: since all men are born equal 'il faut dire que l'esclavage est contre la nature'; but literally only for a moment.[161] Slightly further on, reverting to his system of climate and *mœurs*, he suggests that in certain lands slavery too 'est fondé sur une raison naturelle'. With respect to despotism and serfdom, moreover, this difficulty with his system is left completely unmitigated. He expressly disapproved of Tsar Peter I's ruthless way of trying to bring 'enlightenment' to Russia, vaguely suggesting gentler methods would have been more effective.[162] But what he could not explain or legitimize, as Holberg emphasized, is how in a country where climate, religion, *mœurs*, and tradition generate despotism, serfdom, and a clergy like the Russian Orthodox, which he considered ignorant beyond any other, enlightenment in the intellectual sense is conceivable or possible at all and, if it were to prove possible, why and how it would bring about any enhancement of liberty and justice.[163]

[161] Ehrard, *L'Idée*, 735–6; Tarin, *Diderot*, 23; Lacouture, *Montesquieu*, 276–8.

[162] Montesquieu, *Œuvres complètes*, 89, 480; Tortarolo, *L'Illuminismo*, 220; Ehrard, *L'Esprit des mots*, 20; Wolff, *Inventing Eastern Europe*, 158, 190.

[163] Wolff, *Inventing Eastern Europe*, 204–5; Holberg, *Remarques*, d2^{v}, e5–e5^{v}; *Corpus de notes marginales*, v. 742.

12

'Enlightened Despotism': Autocracy, Faith, and Enlightenment in Eastern and South-Eastern Europe (1689–1755)

1. PETER THE GREAT'S 'REVOLUTION' (1689–1725)

The fact that philosophical systems such as those of Montesquieu, Hume, and Voltaire made it difficult or impossible to oppose in principle autocracy, serfdom, or the emphasis on territorial expansion in eighteenth-century Russia lends a particular interest, in a general survey of the Enlightenment, to the *philosophes*' responses to developments in that empire. For newly forged western skills and ideas did in fact make exceptional and impressive progress in Muscovy before 1750 but only, seemingly, due to the exceptional zeal and energy with which one particular despot, Tsar Peter I (reigned 1689–1725), imported new ideas and expertise from the West while expressly setting out to attack custom and tradition. If, moreover, the official ideology of the Russian Enlightenment engendered a new cult of tsarist autocracy, a pragmatic philosophy even more authoritarian than that of the newly 'enlightened' Prussian monarchy of Frederick the Great, or that of Maria Theresa in the Habsburg lands, the only other significant 'enlightenment' in eastern Europe before 1750, that flourishing among the newly thriving south-east European Greek diaspora, was itself fervently Russophile and authoritarian in attitude.

Politically as well as religiously, culturally, and intellectually, the two indigenously east European 'enlightenments' were firmly linked. For Peter's successes opened the way to a wider process of renewal and rationalization, embracing the whole Orthodox world, and while it was not, to begin with, a conscious aim of the Early Russian Enlightenment to project itself to the Orthodox peoples under Ottoman rule, or former Ottoman territory now conquered by Austria, Russia, and Venice, the Greeks in particular saw in Peter's Enlightenment a development of crucial relevance to themselves. The court at St Petersburg then responded, in turn, to their aspirations. A wider eastern European transition was thus set in motion which from the early eighteenth century promoted a powerful new culture of Orthodox 'enlightenment', driven partly by the Petrine reforms and Russian military advances but also by the dynamic new Greek-speaking trading diaspora scattered across the Balkans, southern Russia, and the Ukraine.

The influx of western ideas and methods into the eastern Baltic and Muscovy entered by several different routes but, initially, mainly from northern Germany, Sweden, and Holland. The tsar's determination to Europeanize and 'modernize' his imperial administration, governing elite, Russia's ecclesiastical establishment, and armed forces by adopting new techniques from the West received an especially major boost during the Great Northern War (1701–21) from his conquest of the former Swedish Baltic provinces, thereby absorbing an extensive Lutheran, partly German-speaking, commercially sophisticated cultural component into his burgeoning empire which helped transform the very character of the Russian state. The westernizing cultural cosmopolitanism which the tsar sought to promote was most vividly reflected in the early eighteenth century in the form and dramatic expansion of Russia's new capital of St Petersburg (founded in 1703): as one mid eighteenth-century French compendium put it: 'il y a peu de villes aussi-bien policées.'[1] It was not just that the city was new, modern, and well planned or that formal religious toleration instituted by Peter attracted large number of westerners, Lutherans, Calvinists, and Catholics, or that well before 1750 commerce, the arts, and sciences all began to flourish there imposingly, but, still more, that Russia's new window on the West itself became, by the 1740s, a shop window of the Enlightenment for all eastern Europe.[2]

Peter may have been a brutal tyrant in many respects, and was personally scarcely more of an authentic representative of true 'enlightened' thinking than the bigoted Maria Theresa, or obsessively militaristic Frederick the Great of Prussia. Nevertheless he was by far the most important vehicle of Enlightenment among those eighteenth-century rulers historians have traditionally dubbed 'enlightened despots'. This seemed obvious enough to the *philosophes* themselves in the period down to the 1750s. Tsar Peter's cultural 'revolution' was, from the outset, recognized as a world-historical development of surpassing importance by Leibniz, Wolff, Fontenelle, Voltaire, d'Argens, Montesquieu, d'Alembert, La Beaumelle, and others and was observed by them with mounting enthusiasm and excitement. But where the *philosophes* saw it as a 'revolution' of the first magnitude for humanity generally, modern historians, by contrast, have mostly been surprisingly grudging about acknowledging not its importance as such but rather the inherent relationship of Peter's reforms to the Enlightenment. Peter Gay almost completely ignored Russia in his general reassessment of the European Enlightenment, dismissively describing the pre-1750 changes in Russia as a historical process 'much publicized and much overrated' and the output of the new printing presses established by Peter in his two capitals as a mere 'handful of technical manuals'.[3] Others point to the admittedly rather minor role of both British and French influences in Peter's westernization campaign, mistakenly assuming this proves that the process cannot therefore have belonged 'specifically to the Enlightenment'.

[1] *Abrégé portatif du Dictionnaire géographique de La Martinière* (1762), ii. 38. [2] Ibid. ii. 38.
[3] Gay, *Enlightenment*, ii. 61.

However, the *philosophes* here were certainly nearer the mark. For this 'revolution' in culture and ideas, or shaking off of 'le joug de la barbarie' under which Russia had languished for centuries, as d'Alembert styles it, in the first volume of the *Encyclopédie* in 1751,[4] combined with the rapid expansion of Muscovy's territory and military power, dramatically changed the relationship between western and eastern Europe while, within Russia, fundamentally altering the relationship between autocracy and church, ruler and people, book culture and popular culture, ideas and society. As a Moscow-based 'Baltic German' noted in 1768, Tsar Peter carried through a far-reaching reformation of the monasteries in Russia more than four decades before the new Bourbon monarchy began anything comparable in Spain.[5] Tradition, ignorance, prejudice, and inefficiency were not just things the tsar resented and blamed for reducing Russia to marginality, isolation, and weakness,[6] but an edifice he undertook systematically to dismantle with a 'westernism' imposed relentlessly on every aspect of Russian cultural life, particularly in the main cities and among the upper echelons of society.

Peter, then, from the perspective of the 1750s was unquestionably the foremost of the 'enlightened' despots. He started much earlier than his Prussian, Austrian, Italian, and Spanish counterparts, dealt with a technically more backward realm, impacted on a much larger territory, and easily surpassed the others in the fervour of his assault on traditional, popular, and noble attitudes, practices, and established ways of doing things. If his methods were often ruthless and his schemes in some cases unrealistic and unsuccessful, and if excessive claims have in the past been made for them by nationalist historians, all considered, what was achieved was vast in scope and impact. Professed defenders of custom and precedent, of which there were, of course, a great many, had every reason to loathe and dread his rule, his reforms, and, later, his very memory.

However, the tsar neither rejected Muscovy's past nor admired the contemporary West unselectively or blindly. Rather he generated a logical, clearly worked-out order of goals and preferences, his chief priority being always the enhancement of Russian imperial power and its armed forces, improving the efficiency of his autocratic administration, and expanding Russia's grip on strategic strong points and territory. Hence, nearly all his reforms pivoted on importing technical specialists of many kinds, particularly Protestant Germans, Huguenots, Dutch, Danes, Scots, and also—taking advantage of Venice's hopes of obtaining commercial advantages in the Black Sea, should he succeed in extending Russian hegemony there—some highly expert Venetians and other Italians.[7] He sought to attract especially those skilled in techniques needed to transform Russia's fiscal and recruiting machinery, military technology, shipbuilding, mining, arms manufacture, canal-digging,

[4] D'Alembert art. 'Académie' in Diderot and d'Alembert, *Encyclopédie*, i. 56.
[5] Haigold, *Beylagen*, i, 'Vorrede', 2, 62; Cracraft, *Church Reform*, 251–9.
[6] Riasanovsky, *Image*, 7.
[7] [Katephoros], *Pietro il Grande*, 91.

architecture, and road-making, all with a view to enabling his empire to rival effectively the other European great and (in technology, commerce, and shipping) lesser powers. Urban industries and new commercial processing techniques received much emphasis, Peter importing substantial numbers of skilled textile workers; in several places, he established an Italian-style silk industry and with some success, in St Petersburg, Moscow, and at Yaroslavl, a Dutch Brabant-style linen industry.[8]

Since the two technically most advanced countries at the time were Britain and (until around 1740) the Netherlands, many of those whose skills had to do with shipbuilding, communications, or technological innovations were British and more especially Dutch. It was also mainly to Holland that Russian ships' carpenters, naval engineers, and other technical staff were sent for training. Peter himself began learning Dutch in the early 1690s, practising with the Dutch chemist, engineer, and cartographer Andries Winius who, in 1698, he put in charge of the Sibirskii Prikaz, the office for the development and mapping of Siberia. The tsar also encouraged learning Dutch among the new Russian governing elite more generally,[9] curiously taking to corresponding with his semi-literate favourite of obscure birth, 'Prince' Alexander Menshikov (1673–1729), in a kind of pidgin Dutch.[10] Such was the enthusiasm for Dutch styles, initially, that the interior of Menshikov's palace, the first major aristocratic palace constructed in St Petersburg, was largely decorated (including the ceilings) with Dutch tiles.

In 1697, the tsar spent some months in person studying shipbuilding techniques in the Zaan industrial district of Holland, learning the latest ship and crane construction skills, and studying naval artillery, dredging, windmills, and canals. His considering making Dutch the official second language of his empire, mentioned in some of the secondary literature, was more than an idle whim: for Dutch originally served as the main source of technical, commercial, and maritime terms adopted into Russian and was widely used in St Petersburg, particularly in the navy and naval colleges where many officers were either themselves Dutch—like Cornelis Cruys (1657–1727), the Russian navy's first vice-admiral—or Scandinavians who used Dutch to communicate with their Russian sailors; hence, Dutch, or a mixture of Dutch and German, actually served from the 1690s down to the 1730s as effectively the state's second language.[11] Even Russia's senior English naval officer, George Paddon, recruited as one of Peter's rear admirals in 1717, was approached in part because he 'knows Dutch'.

By introducing the Amsterdam system of all-night street lighting to St Petersburg in which he had been preceded by Louis XIV, and many German cities, Peter instituted a highly visible, conspicuous improvement which (as Voltaire typically

[8] Voltaire, *Histoire*, ii. 259–60; Hughes, *Russia*, 152, 195, 200.

[9] Lewitter, 'Peter the Great's Attitude', 69–70; Wladimiroff, 'Andries Winius', 13–16; Cracraft, *Revolution*, 21, 38, 72.

[10] Hughes, *Peter the Great*, 35–6.

[11] Raptschinsky, *Peter de Groote*, 159; Cracraft, *Church Reform*, 9, 31; Cracraft, *Petrine Revolution*, 278–81, 290, 377–485; Driessen, *Tsaar Peter*, 110.

observed) had not yet at that point been adopted in Rome.[12] Another notable import from Holland were the Dutch 'fire-engines', employing metal pumps with wooden levers, and long hoses, capable of hurling up powerful jets of water from rivers and the newly constructed canals. This was technology developed in the 1670s by the artist-inventor Jan van der Heyden (1637–1712), whose workshop was amongst those the tsar visited whilst in Amsterdam in 1697, and from whom he bought several engines, though he failed to persuade van der Heyden himself to come to Russia.[13]

Above all, as Montesquieu noted in 1721, and Voltaire stressed in his *Histoire de l'empire de Russie sous Pierre-le-Grand*, officially commissioned by Peter's daughter, the Tsarina Elizabeth, in 1757, based on French translations of Russian documents specially sent from the Russian court for this purpose, Peter laboured to raise the prestige and enhance the glory of the Russian empire internationally.[14] To further territorial expansion and conquest, he sought the best administrative models, borrowing his general regulations for the fiscal and civil administration largely from his chief western military rival, the neighbouring and smaller but technically more advanced Swedish empire. But however pragmatic, Peter was no mere technocrat who supposed administrative and technological skills, as well as new productive techniques, could simply be conjured up without an educational, intellectual, and scientific base capable of producing in considerable numbers young men suitably educated to be administrators, officers, engineers, educators, doctors, architects, and naval experts.

Peter grasped that to transform Russia into the kind of state he envisaged presupposed creating new educational and scientific institutions, cultivating mathematics, the sciences, geography, critical text scholarship, western medicine, Latin (to provide access to western academic books), and modern languages as well as drastic reform of the country's existing education system. But given there was not, as yet, any 'enlightened' higher culture and learning worth mentioning published in Russian, it was inevitable that there should long be an entrenched bifurcation between the new empire's 'enlightenment' culture expressed in German, Latin, French, and Dutch, on the one hand, and Russian Enlightenment in a more specifically national sense, on the other. The impulse within Russian society itself being largely lacking, it was not, for example, until 1755 that the first even partly Russian university was founded.

Peter, in other words, consciously carried through a 'revolution' of practice based on a 'revolution of the mind' at a time when there was only the slenderest basis for this within Russian culture and society. Yet in this grand undertaking, he met, thanks to a large influx of foreign expertise, with a fair degree of success. Above all, he succeeded in transforming Russia's international standing, his defeat of the Swedes at Poltava, in 1709, rendering Russia the leading power in eastern Europe

[12] Hughes, *Russia*, 220; Voltaire, *Histoire*, ii. 257; Israel, *Dutch Republic*, 681–2.

[13] Israel, *Dutch Republic*, 681–2; Wladimiroff, 'Andries Winius', 18; Hughes, *Russia*, 220; Driessen, *Tsaar Peter*, 42–4.

[14] Montesquieu, *Œuvres complètes*, 89; Voltaire, *Histoire*, i, avant-propos.

and dramatically changing western perceptions of Muscovy and its potential. Leibniz, writing to the Russian envoy in Vienna at the time, noted how the 'great revolution' in the north had utterly astounded the court of Hanover. Voltaire writing half a century later justly dubbed the transformation effected before 1740 by new ideas and skills in Russia 'une révolution générale dans les esprits et dans les affaires'.[15] Through Peter's project of enlightenment, Muscovy and the eastern Baltic was figuratively dragged from what Voltaire, like the tsar, deemed their wretched and brutal past into a world transformed by science, technology, learning, administration, new juridical codes, higher education, printing, and books.

The emphasis on reform based on reason, learning, and science engendered a culture of intellectual and educational renewal which soon powerfully ramified through the higher strata of Russian society.[16] Specialized institutions of a technical character, providing skills the tsar was eager to stimulate, like the Moscow School of Mathematics and Navigation founded in 1700, and military and naval colleges for training officers, were supplemented by more specifically academic, philosophical, and scientific instruments of cultural change. In response to Leibniz's urging the creation of a 'museum' in his capital to serve not just as an object of curiosity but actively help promote awareness of the sciences, Peter purchased several major collections of exotic 'curiosities', naturalia, coins, medals, and pictures, in Amsterdam, including, in 1716, the (still surviving) collection of preserved embryos and human organs of the celebrated anatomist Frederik Ruysch (1638–1731);[17] likewise, a collection of scientific instruments arrived from Musschenbroek's workshop in Leiden. The Museum Imperialis Petropolitanum, Russia's first public cabinet of curiosities with its library of scientific books (many captured in Riga and the recently conquered Baltic provinces), was established, near the imperial palace, in 1714, and already that year widely publicized, though the first published Latin catalogue of the 'Musei Imperialis Petropolitani' did not appear until 1741.[18] In three sections—the library, coin collection, and 'cabinet' of exhibits including models of the planetary system—the imperial 'museum', under the tsar's German librarian Johann Daniel Schumacher (1690–1761), was officially opened to the public in 1719.

Commencing with a number of manuals and maps printed in Russian at Amsterdam, Peter embarked, from around 1700, on a remarkable drive to organize translation of substantial quantities of practical material into Russian. Requiring a simplified Russian alphabet, this initiative led to the devising, in Amsterdam, of a new font for the new Russian print culture, the old Russian format being henceforth reserved for religious literature.[19] Printing houses using 'modern' Dutch technology were established in Moscow and, from 1714, at St Petersburg. Rendering

15 Voltaire, *Histoire*, i. 354; *Corpus de notes marginales*, v. 742; Hughes, *Peter the Great*, 86.

16 Riasanovsky, *Image*, 8–9.

17 Driessen, *Tsaar Peter*, 55–6.

18 *Mémoires de Trévoux*, 13 (June 1714), art. lxxix, p. 1106 and (Aug. 1714), art. cx, p. 1475; Vucinich, *Science in Russian Culture*, 58.

19 Raptschinsky, *Peter de Groote*, 125; Driessen, *Tsaar Peter*, 105–7; Cracraft, *Petrine Revolution*, 68–71, 298.

technical and scientific literature into Russian, it is often claimed, proved difficult, and translations into Russian supposedly remained very sparse down to the 1750s.[20] But in reality, rendering into Russian (and no less important, German) of works on technical, scientific, naval, military, historical, and philosophical subjects, as well as progress with reforming the Russian language by supplying equivalents for new technical, scientific, naval, cultural, artistic, and scholarly terms, proceeded at an impressively brisk pace: the Russian National Library in St Petersburg today preserves copies of several hundred books translated into Russian from western languages published at Moscow and (from 1714) St Petersburg just down to 1725.[21] Among the earliest printed at the new capital were the Petersburg Dutch–Russian dictionary of 1717 and a dual-language version of Erasmus' *Dialogues* (1716) with the Dutch and Russian text set in parallel, on divided pages, to assist Dutch speakers to learn Russian and Russians acquire Dutch.[22]

According to the French Jesuit *Mémoires de Trévoux* in June 1714, the two languages principally used for fixing the thousands of new Russian equivalents were Dutch and French. However, it is doubtful whether, in Peter's reign, French ever in fact rivalled Dutch or German as a vehicle of enlightenment in Russia. After 1725, German remained firmly predominant in philosophy and Natural Law, moreover, and continued largely to shape the new imperial Russian high culture down to the 1750s, as also, in third place (though the standard histories of Russia often fail to mention this), did Latin, albeit the expansion of Latin studies decreed by Peter proceeded much more slowly than he wanted, being broadly resisted by both the nobility and clergy. Peter's reliance on those nobles at the Russian court, often Baltic Germans, who thought along lines similar to his own, and the new emphasis on technical training, acquisition of modern languages, and state service, rapidly formed a new polyglot imperial official elite.

Though relatively few, Russian supporters of the tsar's 'enlightenment project' did exist. Among them was the diplomat Fedor Alekseevich Golovin (1650–1706) who accompanied Peter to Holland in 1697–8 and, though reportedly attached to the 'old ways', to an extent, did not 'reject new customs where he saw they were useful;[23] he built one of the first western-style aristocratic palaces in Moscow, completed in 1702, and, despite himself having had a traditional Muscovite education, sent his son to Holland and Leipzig for finishing, ensuring that he learnt French, English, German, and Dutch. The two best read of Peter's Russian state servants, judging by their libraries, had, like himself and Golovin, acquired their 'enlightened' outlook through travelling abroad and contact with foreigners. One of these was Dmitrii Mikhailovich Golitsyn (1663–1737), an early companion of Peter's, descended from the Lithuanian grand dukes, sent to Venice to study naval techniques in 1697. Appointed governor of Kiev in 1707, he developed into a staunch patron of the

[20] Gay, *Enlightenment*, ii. 61–2.

[21] *Mémoires de Trévoux*, 13 (June 1714), art. lxxix, p. 1106 and (Dec. 1714), art. clxvi, pp. 2171–2.

[22] Cracraft, *Petrine Revolution*, 290.

[23] Hughes, *Russia*, 290.

Latin Academy there and helped establish studies in a wide range of new topics, including Grotius, Pufendorf, and Locke.

Golitsyn's personal library, totalling around 3,000 volumes, around one third in French, included many works on contemporary political subjects in Latin;[24] during the succession crisis of 1730 in Petersburg, he was accused of wanting to turn the Russian empire into an aristocratic republic on the model of Poland or post-1720 Sweden. Also well known was the 1,300-volume library of the diplomat Andrei Artamonovich Matveev (1666–1728), who spent the years 1699–1715 as Russian ambassador to Holland and the Holy Roman Empire. Matveev, a key agent of Peter's reforms, among other capacities as president of the new Naval Academy of St Petersburg (founded in 1715), was similarly an ardent advocate of general intellectual 'enlightenment' in Russia, his books, mostly in Latin and French, including works of both Bayle and Locke.[25]

Among the governing elite, a key lever for extending knowledge of western languages, and heightening awareness of the latest European learning and philosophy, was being sent for naval training to Holland. A noteworthy Ukrainian example was Andrei Federovich Khrushchov (1691–1740), an officer of a noble family educated in one of the new gymnasia in Moscow, sent to Amsterdam in 1712; after being posted for some years to Berlin, he became a senior official of the St Petersburg admiralty. Of his library of six hundred books, around half was devoted to technical subjects connected with his professional expertise, including mathematics and the science of fortifications; but the rest reflected the cosmopolitan tastes of an early eighteenth-century 'enlightened' western European courtier, including works by Gassendi, Descartes, Hobbes, Spinoza, Fénelon, Malebranche, and Locke's *Reasonableness of Christianity*, mostly in French translation.[26]

Such libraries illustrate the fact that while the Petrine reforms were essentially about creating new structures of power, and building a modern state, an integral effect was to bring western philosophy and a taste for French literature into at least a core of official and noble households of St Petersburg and Moscow. Meanwhile, the new Petrine elite was by no means composed merely of scions of old noble families. Besides 'Baltic Germans', numerous other newcomers, including several men of obscure background, rose to high station, among them Baron Peter Pavlovich Shafirov (1669–1739), son of a foreign converted Jew who worked for the court as a translator of documents into Russian. Having impressed the young tsar with his languages, diplomatic skills, and deftness in handling complaints, Shafirov rose rapidly; created a baron in 1710, he was appointed chief Russian negotiator at the 1713 Peace of Adrianople with the Ottoman Porte. His career was cut short, however, when in 1724 he was suddenly disgraced, convicted of misconduct, and had his possessions, including his library, confiscated. The inventory of his books shows that he was an enthusiast for literary works, of which he had many in French,

[24] Hughes, *Russia*, 325; Okenfuss, *Rise and Fall*, 122–3.

[25] Okenfuss, *Rise and Fall*, 123; Hughes, *Sophia*, 145, 266.

[26] Okenfuss, *Rise and Fall*, 125.

including Molière and several plays of Voltaire, as well as others in German, Polish, and Italian; of philosophical works he had Descartes and Pufendorf besides Leibniz's *Théodicée*, again mostly in French.[27]

Central to Peter's Enlightenment was the work of curbing in certain respects the immense influence of the Orthodox Church. The tenth and last patriarch of Muscovy, Adrian (patriarch from 1690 to 1700), had insisted that while the tsar has power on earth, the priesthood possesses authority both on earth *and* in Heaven and that all the Orthodox, including the tsar, are the patriarch's 'spiritual sons'; moreover, he had opposed Peter's 'newly introduced foreign customs', including the pressure for men to shave off their beards. On his death in 1700 the patriarchate was simply suppressed by imperial decree.[28] Senior clergy sharing Adrian's fervent traditionalism were repudiated at court and prevented from securing high rank in the church. In fact, after initially opposing his reforms, the Russian Orthodox Church had little choice but to bow to the tsar's wishes, at least up to a point. Nothing could be done to prevent loss of revenues, increased supervision, or the tsar's promoting the use of Latin, German, Dutch, and French in officer training and higher education, as well as the senior levels of the administration. The church was equally powerless to curb the influx, and influence, of the substantial numbers of Lutheran Germans and Scandinavians, as well as Calvinist Swiss, Dutch, and Huguenots, imported into the administration and officer corps of the army and navy, or the establishment of Catholic as well as Lutheran and Reformed churches in St Petersburg and elsewhere.

In general, the tsar, like his chief adviser in ecclesiastical, cultural, and propaganda matters, the Ukrainian Bishop Feofan Prokopovich (1681–1736), was better disposed toward Protestants than Catholics.[29] By the mid eighteenth century, it was normal in the West to speak of 'la liberté de conscience dont on jouit à Petersburg'.[30] However, the efforts of Voltaire and others to highlight toleration as one of the striking accomplishments of the Petrine 'revolution' involved considerable oversimplification.[31] For Peter's toleration was of a strictly limited kind. Non-Orthodox were not permitted to proselytize, or convert, the Orthodox; non-Orthodox churches were permitted only in a few cities; freethinking attitudes were discouraged at court; and, in other ways too, the state upheld the general hegemony of the Orthodox Church. Traditional Russian heresies remained banned and it was never the tsar's intention to accommodate Islam in the newly conquered areas around the Black Sea and the southern Volga. During his stay in Holland, he also rejected proposals that Jews dwelling in the Ukraine or Ottoman territory brought under Russian control should be permitted to settle in Muscovy proper, justifying this on the ground that a Jewish presence was something his traditionally minded people

[27] Ibid. 124; Hughes, *Russia*, 429–30; Cracraft, *Revolution*, 8–9, 70–3.

[28] Prokopovich, *Peters des Grossen*, 163–4; Haigold, *Beylagen*, i. 14–15, 17, 36.

[29] Lewitter, 'Peter the Great's Attitude', 72.

[30] *Abrégé portatif du Dictionnaire géographique de La Martinière* (1762), ii. 38.

[31] Voltaire, *Histoire*, i. 90–1, 156–7, 196; Wladimiroff, 'Andries Winius', 20; Lewitter, 'Peter the Great's Attitude', 65.

would never tolerate; an effective bar on toleration of Jews in Muscovy, as Diderot noted, during his visit to St Petersburg in 1773, subsequently continued.[32]

Voltaire remarks that while reforming the church is generally believed to be extremely difficult, Peter, after the death of Patriarch Adrian, took matters in hand and with astounding speed decisively reduced ecclesiastical influence in Russian society, suppressing the patriarchate and the patriarchal court. But this, too, requires qualification. For while the tsar did remove administration of church lands and revenues from ecclesiastical hands, bringing these functions directly under the crown, and set up a new permanent synod for regulating church affairs and making higher ecclesiastical appointments, placing this also indirectly under his own control,[33] in reality all this did little more than strengthen the long-standing links between church and state while tilting the balance towards the tsar's authority and diminishing the church's control over higher education. The same is true of the system of 'inquisitors' instituted in 1721, to supervise the activities of the prelates and clergy and ensure conformity to the new procedures, attitudes, and forms of discipline.

The reform of the monasteries was justified by Prokopovich on the ground that the Greek Christian emperors (whose heir Peter proclaimed himself to be) had been too lenient in the matter of allowing monks to move from remote places into the towns. This had resulted in their being insufficiently self-supporting and mostly idle. The Byzantine emperors' failure to ensure that monks devoted themselves to hard work and fulfilled a range of social functions was alleged to have seriously weakened the Christian Greek empire with disastrous consequences for Orthodoxy. He and his colleagues even claimed that the allegedly excessive number of monks had so sapped the Greek army as materially to assist the Muslim capture of Constantinople in 1453. Peter's reforms supposedly put this right, restricting the number and property of the monasteries, enforcing heavier work schedules, better education, and more social welfare functions; the number of monks and nuns in Russia was nearly halved from a total of 25,207 in 1724 to 14,282 by 1738.[34] As d'Argens put it in his *Lettres chinoises*, if Peter could not make the Russian priesthood 'wiser', he did at least make them fewer and poorer.[35]

The impact of Peter's reform of the Russian monasteries was thus considerable, as Diderot later confirmed during his visit to Russia, even though the initially drastic overall reduction in numbers of monks and nuns was subsequently counteracted by a fresh expansion, in the 1740s and 1750s.[36] The monasteries' traditional independence was certainly greatly curtailed and although it was the bishops who were now responsible for them, they had become in part agents of the state. Among the new social functions the monasteries acquired, at Peter's insistence, was the obligation to maintain orphanages and hospitals and house disabled former soldiers unable to

[32] Raptschinsky, *Peter de Groote*, 127–8; Israel, *European Jewry*, 206–7; Tortarolo, *Ragione*, 68.

[33] Voltaire, *Histoire*, i. 75, 217–20, ii. 284; Hughes, *Russia*, 337–43; Wolff, *Enlightenment*, 141.

[34] Cracraft, *Church Reform*, 251–2; Haigold, *Beylagen*, i. 62, 82–3, 85–7, 90–2.

[35] D'Argens, *Lettres chinoises*, iii. 39–40.

[36] Cracraft, *Church Reform*, 258–9; Hughes, *Russia*, 337–48; Tortarolo, *Ragione*, 67–8.

work. If, among the *philosophes*, the Russian Orthodox clergy long retained their reputation for unmatched ignorance, the new seminaries Peter established in Moscow and St Petersburg did somewhat improve the education and training of both priesthood and monks.[37]

The new governing synod of the church, set up in September 1721, comprised court officials besides prelates to ensure its expertise was more than just theological and traditional. In this way, Peter inserted the sway of lay administrators often more knowledgeable about western Europe and Catholic and Protestant affairs than about Greek ecclesiastical matters, though a Greek prelate, Anastasius Nausii, was also nominated to the governing synod that year, to help reinforce the Greek religious factor. Having organized his synod and drawn up its regulations, Peter then wrote to the patriarch of Constantinople, claiming a high degree of conformity of his measures with both Byzantine precedent and continuing Greek tradition and requesting his approval. The patriarch saw little alternative but to comply.[38]

It was never Peter's aim to compromise the simple piety of the common people, however, or remove most schools from ecclesiastical control, or indeed try to secularize Russian culture in the way that Soviet-era historians frequently asserted.[39] For Peter's reforms not only left intact but reinforced traditional structures of thought and belief in most of Russian society, urban as well as rural. The tsar did not challenge the church's overwhelming ascendancy over popular attitudes as such; at the same time, he willingly accepted stringent limits to the 'toleration' he imported from the West. Since priests, particularly as deliverers of sermons, were the main intermediaries between state and people, the church remained strongly placed subtly to influence the image of the sovereign and his court, as well as his aims and attitudes, in the chief cities no less than in smaller towns and countryside. While traditional ceremonial and imagery of the Russo-Byzantine tradition of tsarist power was, at the tsar's instigation, put aside, particularly in the court context, what replaced this older iconography in Russian culture was by no means a secular conception of autocracy but a new form of glorification and sacralization, a systematic clerical exaltation of the imperial image, firmly ignoring the Latin Roman imperial motifs introduced from the late 1690s in courtly displays, and on coins and medals. Leading churchmen, under Peter, represented the tsar as the conqueror of the Tartars, Turks, and Lutheran Swedes, the 'sculptor' of a new Russia, a supernaturally guided, unswervingly Orthodox ruler reviving the greatness of Justinian and other Greek Christian emperors and, above all, the heroic champion of the ideals of the church.[40]

If Montesquieu discovered, in conversation with a Danish officer who had once been one of the tsar's naval commanders, that Peter was both brutal and apt to fly

[37] Haigold, *Beylagen*, i. 60; Holberg, *Memoirs*, 126.
[38] Haigold, *Beylagen*, i. 24–5, 31; Prokopovich, *Peters des Grossen*, 150.
[39] Hughes, *Russia*, 334–5.
[40] Ibid., 96–7; Riasonovsky, *Image*, 10–13.

into terrible rages, he was also told that he 'n'avait aucune religion' and was in the habit of ridiculing Orthodox no less than Catholic and Protestant churchmen.[41] Yet the Russian priesthood fervently supported the tsar in his wars and great undertakings of state, especially against Lutheran Sweden and the Ottoman sultan, as well as the latter's Tartar and other Turkic allies, continually stressing the tsar's allegedly fervent faith, piety, and reverence for the church.[42] If this bent the truth somewhat, it was also what a deeply loyal and orthodox populace wished to hear. The church largely succeeded in linking Peter's image among the people to traditional popular notions of the tsar as the supreme promoter of orthodoxy and Christian virtues, a ruler who relentlessly combats Tartars and Turks, and Islam generally, and also combats hateful infidelities like Socinianism, Anabaptism, Deism, the Russian Old Believers, and Judaism.

The prelates also managed to limit the impact of Peter's cultural revolution among Russia's elites. The tsar thought it essential for reorganizing Russian society and the state that Latin be taught and cultivated as a vehicle of instruction, reading, and scholarly interaction.[43] A particularly important strand in this programme was the scheme for fostering Latin colleges, or gymnasia, in Kiev, Moscow, St Petersburg, and Novgorod, though here he mostly built on pre-existing institutions, like the Slavonic-Greek-Latin Academy in Moscow (founded in 1687) and the Kiev Academy, founded to counter the Jesuit Counter-Reformation in the Ukraine, in the 1630s, institutions which, in fact, remained under ecclesiastical control.[44] The tsar chiefly wanted Latin as a tool for instruction in technical subjects and promoting the study of western mathematics, science, and philosophy. The church, however, fearful of the potential effect of the Roman classics and modern philosophical and scientific works in Latin on Russian society and anxious lest the teaching and learning of Latin encourage the further penetration of Roman Catholicism in the Ukraine, and other border lands between Russia and Poland, quietly but firmly opposed its broader use in Russian higher education. Indeed, virtually no classical pagan Latin or Greek texts were published in Latin or Greek in the Russian empire, much less translated into Russian, before the 1760s.[45] Through the church's guardianship of education and culture, pagan antiquity in general, whether literary, historical, philosophical, or scientific, was effectively deleted from the Petrine 'revolution'.

Peter the Great's cultural engineering entailing, as it did, learning new languages, subjects, and skills, permitting the establishment of Protestant churches, and the setting up of the Petersburg Academy, directly encouraged the introduction of western moderate mainstream philosophy, especially Leibniz, Wolff, Bilfinger, Pufendorf, Locke, and Newton, among the imperial governing elite; equally plainly, though, the tsar and his advisers were far from sharing the ideals of Radical

41 Montesquieu, *Œuvres complètes*, 412.
42 Ibid. 16–17; Riasanovsky, *Image*, 13, 16.
43 Okenfuss, *Rise and Fall*, 97–101, 116–17; Hughes, *Russia*, 298, 300, 344.
44 Hughes, *Russia*, 300; Haigold, *Beylagen*, i. 59.
45 Okenfuss, *Rise and Fall*, 94–101.

Enlightenment *esprit philosophique*. The tsar's personal library, amounting by the end of his life to some 1,663 titles, clearly illustrates this. It was as up to date, eclectic, and pragmatic in orientation as its tumultuous owner; but technical and factual subjects like mathematics, architecture, geography, history, and the science of fortification heavily predominated. His books did include works by Newton and Pufendorf but lacked Galileo, Spinoza, Bayle, and Locke; if they reflected the tsar's personal interest in ancient Greek and Byzantine studies, they also concentrated, as regards Greek authors, on history, the Church Fathers, and works of traditional piety, showing scant interest in pagan Greek philosophy or science. He possessed hardly any works in English or French.[46]

Given this convergence of Peter's reforms with a tightening of links between church and state, it is apt that the most representative figure of the Petrine Enlightenment should have been a liberal-minded Orthodox churchman, Bishop Prokopovich, whom some consider 'after Peter himself the most important figure of early modern Russian history'. A graduate of the Kiev Latin Academy who had also studied at Jesuit colleges in Poland as well as at the Greek college of St Athanasius in Rome,[47] after returning to the Kiev Academy where he taught philosophy, mathematics, and science, he eventually became its rector. Then, in 1716, the tsar summoned him to St Petersburg to serve as court preacher, a role in which he excelled, becoming first bishop of Pskov, and then, in December 1720, being raised to the rank of archbishop.[48] Fervently extolling absolutism, his modernized version of 'divine right' and autocracy exhorted obedience, powerfully stressed the dangers of ecclesiastical insubordination, and constantly cited the failings of the Emperor Justinian's reign which were now to be surmounted.[49]

Reflecting the growing tension between Russian tradition, on the one hand, and learning and science, on the other—a cultural war between the Russian popular mentality and 'enlightenment' which has continued down to the present day—Prokopovich, most of whose own foreign erudition was Italian and German, contemptuously attacked the long-established pretension of many Russian clergy that learning, especially when foreign, should be regarded with suspicion because it foments heresy.[50] Such a view is 'silly', he argued (rather remarkably), because in the dark ages following the fall of the Roman empire, the age of ignorance *par excellence*, everything had been in much worse shape than in times 'enlightened by the light of the sciences' such as in Greece down to the fourth century AD when, in Constantinople, bishops and monks had not been so 'inflated' as later and when learning had flourished splendidly, in a way that it ceased to do in the later Byzantine empire.

46 Ibid. 129; [Katephoros], *Pietro il Grande*, 362.

47 Voltaire, *Histoire*, ii. 285, 293; Hughes, *Russia*, 431; Riasanovsky, *Image*, 12–13.

48 Haigold, *Beylagen*, i. 36.

49 Cracraft, *Petrine Revolution*, 239–40; Prokopovich, *Peters des Grossen*, 163–4.

50 Prokopovich, *Peters des Grossen*, 203–4; Cracraft, *Church Reform*, 54–6; Hosking, *Russia*, 209.

Were it true, he contended, that erudition harms the church, the best Christians would not have devoted themselves to study whereas, in fact, the most venerable of the (Greek) Church Fathers, like Basil the Great, John Chrysostom, and Gregory the Theologian, were expert, he stressed, not just in Scripture and theology but also in non-Christian science and 'philosophy'.[51] In his recommendations for the education of the tsar's heir, the future Peter II, Prokopovich greatly emphasized the importance of teaching the elements of 'natural theology' first, showing that God exists, that his adoration is what is required of men, and that divine reward of the good, and punishment of the bad, occurs primarily in the next world. Such fundamentals, he held, in outright (if unconscious) opposition to Bayle, must be taught from the consensus and experience 'of all the peoples of all parts who have always believed in and still believe' in a divinity.[52]

According to Prokopovich, 'all Europe' had been utterly sunk in darkness and ignorance between the fourth and fifteenth centuries AD, an era in which 'almost all the sciences' had been in a woeful state of decay, from which religion and society had been rescued by the revival of Greek learning and philosophy in Italy and elsewhere.[53] Since then great improvements had been achieved but, despite this, 'rhetoric, philosophy and the sciences', by which he meant erudition generally as well as physics and mathematics, had remained chronically deficient and backward in many places, including Russia, resulting in the Russians being looked down on as 'barbarians' in the West, disdain which Prokopovich himself much resented. To overcome 'superstition' and ignorance and produce a better, more orderly, and more Orthodox society in the empire what was needed, he proclaimed, was a general reform of education, promotion of the study of both Greek and Latin, and close attention to mathematics, physics, and political science. For society, nothing is worse, though, than the kind of 'false knowledge' based on mere scraps of erudition used by the ambitious to secure power and rank: for 'superficial learning is not only useless but also very harmful to the friends of learning, one's country and the Church'.[54]

Prokopovich's own library of around 3,000 titles was reckoned to have no equal among the private libraries of Russia. A pillar of moderate mainstream Enlightenment, he was convinced that promotion of science and the war on 'superstition' mattered just as much as the struggle against libertinism and atheism; like Locke, he also fervently believed that Christian revelation more effectively teaches morality, and teaches a higher morality, than had the pagan Greek philosophers; it is striking, though, that his library contained few works by British authors, his Early Enlightenment orientation being predominantly Leibnizian-Wolffian rather than Newtonian or Lockean.[55] Above all, he was a doughty champion of autocracy in the

[51] Prokopovich, *Peters des Grossen*, 205.
[52] Prokopovich, *Vorschläge*, 4–7; Hughes, *Russia*, 290, 432.
[53] Prokopovich, *Peters des Grossen*, 206, 208, 214–15.
[54] Ibid. 207.
[55] Prokopovich, *Vorschläge*, 11, 41–5; Hughes, *Russia*, 431–2; Okenfuss, *Rise and Fall*, 110–13.

Russian context, believing it to be vitally important as much for the spiritual as worldly well-being of the common people and all the Orthodox peoples.[56]

Prokopovich combined a measured disdain for Russia's traditions and past with an emphatic orthodoxy in theology, admirable competency in Latin and Greek, and a fierce dislike of (especially Polish) Jesuits who had earlier been allowed to establish colleges in Archangel and Moscow as well as St Petersburg but whom the tsar subsequently expelled from Russia,[57] doubtless with his encouragement. He also showed a keen interest in such central European theological trends as Socinianism and Halle Pietism. More directly relevant to his credentials as a leading European advocate of moderate mainstream Enlightenment, he had not only read but possessed a good teaching knowledge of Descartes, Pufendorf, Leibniz, and Wolff.

2. EUROPE AND THE RUSSIAN ENLIGHTENMENT (1725–1755)

After 1725, there were understandable fears among supportive onlookers in the West, as Le Clerc remarks, in his *Bibliothèque ancienne et moderne* in 1727, that with the tsar's death, his project to re-educate and 'polish' the Russian people would lapse. Yet there was no sign of this happening. On the contrary, 'on a vu, avec étonnement', as Le Clerc remarked two years later, that the court in St Petersburg had continued vigorously with the same 'enlightened' policies.[58]

Western technology, science, medicine, literature, and administrative methods were all major stimuli and Peter himself, at heart, had certainly been a passionate pragmatist, not a philosopher; even so, it is arguable that 'philosophy' was nevertheless, as one historian has expressed it, 'the principal western intellectual influence on the Russian elite in the eighteenth century'.[59] For this is what drove and shaped the entire cultural 'revolution'. But what sort of philosophy? Prominent among those who claimed Peter the Great's 'revolution' was inspired principally by 'philosophy' was Voltaire; but he attributed the great breakthrough mainly to 'Newtonian philosophy and science'. English ideas, he insisted, were decisive and had already captivated Peter during his visit to England in 1698, when Newtonianism was still virtually unknown outside Britain.[60] But here he was clearly misrepresenting the picture for his own purposes. In fact, the prime philosophical impulse in the Russian Enlightenment before 1750 emanated from German lands, as many in the West were quick to point out. As early as August 1714, the French Jesuit *Mémoires de*

[56] Riasanovsky, *Image*, 12–13; Cracraft, *Church Reform*, 57–61; Hosking, *Russia*, 199.

[57] Okenfuss, *Rise and Fall*, 113; [Katephoros], *Pietro il Grande*, 319–20.

[58] *Bibliothèque ancienne et moderne*, 27 (1727), 208–10.

[59] Raeff, *Origins*, 150.

[60] Voltaire, *Histoire*, i, avant-propos and pp. 63, 201, ii. 257; Wolff, *Inventing Eastern Europe*, 89, 155, 170, 190.

Trévoux remarked that, in transforming Russia, the tsar 'prend les conseils de l'illustre Monsieur Leibnitz, à qui la Moscovie devra autant que le reste de l'Europe'.[61]

Leibniz, for his part, leapt at the opportunity to advise the tsar, assuring a correspondent that it mattered more to help guide one absolute ruler, like Peter, towards enlightenment and 'the perfection of humanity' than win a hundred military battles,[62] a noble sentiment if not one for which Peter himself had much time. Leibniz personally met and conferred with the tsar on several occasions and at great length, the first time in 1697. He fully succeeded, moreover, in implanting a lasting influence at the Russian court. The Imperial Academy of Sciences, for which Peter had already started recruiting internationally known scholars able to provide high-level teaching as well as promote debate and research (particularly in mathematics and physics) in 1721, was inaugurated in 1724, essentially along the lines proposed by Leibniz and his disciple Wolff. Its first session was attended by sixteen newly appointed academicians, thirteen of whom were German; none was British or Russian.

In most branches of philosophy, throughout the later years of the tsar's reign, and still more in the decades after his death, in 1725, Leibnizio-Wolffianism in fact remained by far the dominant intellectual stream in Russia and while Wolff (twice) declined the emperor's invitations to come to St Petersburg in person, he became the academy's first honorary member and, over the years, continued to send detailed advice, not least about appointments, which was often acted on.[63] In political thought, meanwhile, Prokopovich, the tsar's chief ideologist, proclaimed Pufendorf Russia's most favoured thinker; and in the next generation Pufendorfian and Thomasian Natural Law gained an even stronger grip.[64] Indeed, the preponderance of German intellectual influence in the Russian Enlightenment generally became still more marked after Peter's death than before, though its hegemony never went unchallenged.

While Germans constituted the vast majority of its original membership, the academy's first secretary and president, Wolff's confidant the Moscow-born German physician Laurenz Blumentrost, had himself trained at Leiden and was a pupil of Boerhaave, and remained an advocate of Dutch medical methods. Consequently, he also sought advice in Holland (including from Boerhaave) and tried to balance the Leibnizio-Wolffian ascendancy with a substantial contingent of French, Huguenots, Swiss, and Dutch besides some German anti-Wolffians several of whom were, in fact, ardent Newtonians.[65] Prominent among the latter was the noted Protestant Swiss mathematician Leonhard Euler (1707–83) who arrived in Petersburg in 1727 and remained until 1741, a European celebrity who published his works in French, German, and Latin, employing Russian only for private letters. Though Euler

61 *Mémoires de Trévoux*, (Aug. 1714), art. cx, p. 1475.

62 Neverov, 'De Collecties', 18.

63 Mühlpfordt, 'Petersburger Aufklärung', 493, 497; Vucinich, *Science in Russian Culture*, 67–71, 126; Cracraft, *Petrine Revolution*, 243, 249–50.

64 Prokopovich, *Peters des Grossen*, 214–15; Cracraft, *Church Reform*, 58, 265; Raeff, *Origins*, 155.

65 Prokopovich, *Peters des Grossen*, 67, 71, 76; Richter, *Leibniz*, 126–7; Hughes, *Peter the Great*, 188–9; Cracraft, *Revolution*, 109–13; Driessen, *Tsaar Peter*, 109.

adopted a wave rather than a particle theory of light, his *Mechanica* (1736) was broadly Newtonian. However, very few other non-German celebrities were willing to come. Blumentrost invited 's-Gravesande (who was later also unsuccessfully approached by the Berlin academy), in a letter of February 1724, but he declined, preferring to remain in Holland.[66]

The Petersburg academy began its formal proceedings in December 1725 with a paper by Christian Wolff's leading disciple and chief advocate in Russia Georg Bernhard Bilfinger (1693–1750), on longitude.[67] Feuding, sometimes ill mannered, between the rival Wolffian and Newtonian blocs, and particularly between Euler and Bilfinger, long remained characteristic of the St Petersburg academy. Under its charter, the academy had a permanent secretary and librarian and was scheduled to convene twice weekly in closed session and, for the more direct edification of Petersburg's social elite, three times yearly, in public. Attached was a 'Latin' secular *gimnaziia* founded the same year. In the late 1720s, the Russian Imperial Academy, besides reassuring foreign commentators, like Le Clerc, that Peter's death had not ended the process of enlightenment in Russia, won some renown in the West under Euler's and Bilfinger's lead as a lively focus of philosophical debate and especially as a principal centre of European mathematics, publishing (in Latin) ten volumes of its *Mémoires* between 1726 and 1750 (see plate 15).[68] The Imperial Academy's library, already comprising some 12,000 volumes in western languages on opening in 1725, long remained by far the largest and most important 'philosophical' library in eastern Europe (see plate 18).[69]

Under the Empresses Anna (reigned 1730–40) and Elizabeth (reigned 1741–61), the process entered a crucial new stage. Gradually, a wider circle of the Russian nobility began to embrace 'enlightened' ideas. The court at St Petersburg consolidated its predominantly western appearance, transforming Russia's aristocracy into a very different thing from what it had been before Peter; in polite society, at least, much was also achieved to soften the former 'esclavage du beau sexe' as d'Argens called it.[70] At the same time, there was a marked slackening in the pace of government-inspired reforms and, as a result, more scope for criticizing the court and the policies of the previous reign. Under the Tsarina Elizabeth, in the 1740s, the academy acquired the only half-literate Count Razumovsky as its president and perceptibly faltered, temporarily alarming the *philosophes* in the West who were convinced, as d'Argens puts it, that no retreat from Peter's enlightened goals was possible without Russia sliding back into 'la barbarie'.[71] However, the academy revived after a few years and, by the 1750s, had regained its position as a respected centre of natural philosophy and learning.

[66] Allamand, *Histoire*, p. lix; Driessen, *Tsaar Peter*, 17.

[67] *Bibliothèque ancienne et moderne*, 21 (1727), art. x pp. 207–10; [Katephoros], *Pietro il Grande*, 362–3; Hughes, *Peter the Great*, 188–9.

[68] D'Alembert, 'Académie', in Diderot and d'Alembert, *Encyclopédie*, i. 55–6; Terrall, *Man who Flattened*, 36.

[69] Driessen, *Tsaar Peter*, 63–4; Hughes, *Russia*, 324–5.

[70] D'Argens, *Lettres chinoises*, iii. 96, 99.

[71] Ibid. iii. 207–8; d'Alembert, 'Académie', in Diderot and d'Alembert, *Encyclopédie*, i. 56.

It also began, for the first time, to absorb a significant Russian intellectual presence. The first major native *érudit* was the Marburg-trained physicist Mikhail Lomonosov (1711–65) who long remained a presiding influence not least on the activities of the attached *gimnaziia* (grammar school).[72] At the same time, more learned and literary translations began to appear in the Russian tongue, though it was still difficult to bridge the yawning gap between an imperial 'enlightened' culture transplanted to Petersburg, Moscow, and a few aristocratic country houses which was basically western in character and the authentic cultural traditions and idioms of Russia itself.[73]

Only very slowly did French intellectual and cultural influences challenge the earlier German-Dutch ascendancy, and it was apparently not until the mid 1750s, when Elizabeth's current favourite Ivan Shuvalov (1727–97) emerged as head of a pro-French faction in the imperial palace which also acted as a powerful engine for promoting the reputations of Montesquieu, Voltaire, and other moderate *philosophes*, that one can speak of a shift towards French cultural primacy. Prior to 1740, one of the few Petersburg academicians known to have been systematically reading Enlightenment authors in French was a Portuguese of New Christian extraction, Dr Antonio Nunes Ribeiro Sanches (1699–1783), later known for his *Dissertation* on venereal disease which appeared at Paris in 1750. Fleeing Portugal and the Inquisition, Ribeiro Sanches had studied medicine for three years at Leiden, from where he proceeded to the Russian court in 1731, on the recommendation of Boerhaave. Remarkably, he rose to become a personal physician of both Anna and then Elizabeth. However, in 1747, his Jewish origins suddenly came to light, causing something of a scandal, and he was immediately ejected from Russia by the tsarina.

Among the first French philosophical writers to figure in Russian was Fontenelle, whose *Entretiens sur la pluralité des mondes* (1686) appeared, in 1740, in a translation by the Moldavian prince and poet Antiokh Kantemir (1709–44).[74] Fontenelle was known all over Europe as an admirer of Peter the Great. Indeed, the French *philosophes* moderate and radical alike, and not least d'Argens writing in 1739, remained deeply appreciative of Peter's achievement, something which in their eyes had dramatically transformed Muscovite society and culture for the better. To them, the 'revolution' in Russia seemed all the more awesome and extraordinary in that they firmly believed Russian traditional, popular, and religious culture to be even more benighted, barbaric, and superstitious than popular culture elsewhere. Almost to a man, they considered the Russians undoubtedly 'le peuple le moins poli et le moins spirituel de l'Europe', as d'Argens expressed it, and one which was hence also exceptionally intolerant and arrogant.[75]

D'Argens granted that remarkable progress had been achieved, in twenty to thirty years, especially in half Dutch, half German St Petersburg, and that intellectual enlightenment, toleration, and less blatant tyranny over women, as well as

[72] Okenfuss, *Rise and Fall*, 165. [73] Raeff, *Origins*, 142–3.

[74] Okenfuss, *Rise and Fall*, 97, 179.

[75] D'Argens, *Lettres chinoises*, iii. 33–4, 147–52; Trousson, 'Cosmopolitisme', 24–5.

devotion to the 'sciences', were gaining ground. But he saw the transformation as being exclusively due to western intellectual influence. If much had been accomplished in twenty years it would need only fifteen, he remarked, with all the foreigners removed, for Russia to slide back into the state of total and brutal 'ignorance' prevailing before Peter. The imperial court knew this perfectly well according to reports reaching him, and hence did everything possible to favour the foreign contingent, especially, he notes, the Germans, whereas the ordinary people, for precisely this reason, loathed and increasingly resented the non-Orthodox who dominated their high culture.[76]

In both Petersburg and Moscow, Protestant German officials and ideas broadly maintained their hegemony down to the 1750s. A key figure was Count Heinrich Johann Friedrich Ostermann (1686–1747), son of a Westphalian Lutheran pastor and a graduate of Jena, whom Peter had entrusted with drafting the 1721 imperial Table of Ranks. He also drew up, at around the same time, a programme for the education of the tsar's heir, Peter II, who was 10 when his father died in 1725—the boy subsequently dying himself, of smallpox, at the age of only 14 in 1730. Ostermann's educational recommendations for the young prince placed a remarkable emphasis on physics, mathematics, and acquiring three key western languages of the Russian Enlightenment—German, French, and Latin. He earnestly hoped Peter II would admire the scientific work of the new scholarly institutions his father had created, urging that the future tsar should be encouraged from early on to fund scientific *experimenta* along the lines then fashionable for courts to subsidize at Paris, London, and elsewhere.[77]

In 1730, Ostermann rose to a pre-eminent position first as one of the three principal ministers of the Empress Anna and then, from 1735, as her chief minister. He continued to preside over foreign policy and the general administration until overthrown by a palace coup in 1741. In foreign affairs, as in cultural matters, his attitude was broadly pro-Austrian, pro-British, and anti-French. He possessed a substantial library, including many works in Latin acquired in Germany and Holland,[78] and, in general, continued the regime's sponsorship of a basically German-style intellectual Enlightenment, though he also read widely in ancient and modern literature, including, among modern English novels, *Robinson Crusoe* and *Gulliver's Travels*.

Eventually, though, by the 1740s, the overwhelming domination of German, Latin, French, and Dutch among the empire's intellectual elite, and the conspicuous weakness of native scholars and the Russian language in the Russian Enlightenment, generated its own reaction. The first noteworthy 'Russian' figure, Lomonosov, was also among the first to press for a campaign of Russification. Nevertheless, this son of a fisherman from the Archangel area, an arrogant man who adopted the air of a nobleman and opposed broadening the social base of those entering the new higher

[76] D'Argens, *Lettres chinoises*, iii. 34, 39–40.

[77] Ostermann, *Einrichtung der Studien*, 5, 8, 36; Prokopovich, *Vorschläge*, 41–3, 45; Mühlpfordt, 'Petersburger Aufklärung', 505.

[78] Okenfuss, *Rise and Fall*, 125.

education institutions from which he personally had so singularly benefited, was himself clearly a product of the German Enlightenment. After graduating from the Kiev Slavo-Graeco-Latin Academy in 1734, and the St Petersburg *gimnaziia* in 1736, he had studied for several years in Germany, including, at Marburg, under Wolff in person (1736–9); the expertise and teaching skills in chemistry, physics, mineralogy, and other sciences which he acquired there and at other German universities then governed his own intellectual apparatus and outlook for the rest of his life.[79] A strong supporter of religion and ardent foe of 'atheists and their leader Epicurus', his personal library, heavily loaded with Wolff and Boerhaave, included practically no French or English books.[80]

None of this prevented Lomonosov, however, from reacting passionately against the domination of Russia's intellectual life by Germans if not against German, or at least Wolffian, philosophy. An energetic ally of Shuvalov, in organizing the efforts which eventually led, in 1755, to the establishment in Moscow of the first genuinely Russian university, he continually strove to expand the Russian content of the 'Russian' Enlightenment. Yet even this university was 'Russian' only in a minimal sense. Its students—a mere handful of sons of the nobility and priests' sons who knew some Latin—were Russian, but a majority of the professors were Lutheran German, among them a certain Dilthey, a 'student of Pufendorf', from Leipzig. Some faculties, notably that of jurisprudence, were almost entirely German dominated.[81]

Besides Lomonosov, the first generation of native Russian products of the Enlightenment included a soldier's son, S. P. Krasheninnikov (1711–55), a graduate of the Petersburg *gimnaziia* who acquired good Latin and much expertise on Siberia, becoming a full academician in 1750, and Dmitrii Ivanovich Vinogradov (1720–58), a priest's son sent, in 1736, together with Lomonosov, to study under Wolff at Marburg. Vinogradov also studied chemistry at Freiburg and later, back at Marburg, also mining. Abroad until 1744, he combined his professional expertise as an expert metallurgist with an impressively broad 'enlightened' culture, his personal library including works by Boyle, Fénelon, Boerhaave, and 's-Gravesande besides the ubiquitous Wolff and numerous other German men of learning.

Lutheran German high intellectual culture, then, continued to dominate down to the 1750s. No doubt it was this powerful current shaping the Early Russian Enlightenment that prompted Rousseau's remark in the *Contrat social* (1762) that Tsar Peter 'tried to turn [his subjects] into Germans or Englishmen instead of making them Russians'.[82] Directly contradicting the favourable judgements of Fontenelle, Doria, Voltaire, d'Argens, Montesquieu, La Beaumelle, Holberg, and others, Rousseau denigrated Peter as a despicable tyrant, a reformer who lacked

79 Ibid. 179–80; Vucinich, *Science in Russian Culture*, 58, 105.

80 Okenfuss, *Rise and Fall*, 174, 178–80.

81 Ibid. 166, 168.

82 Quoted in Wolff, *Inventing Eastern Europe*, 199–200; Riasanovsky, *Image*, 47; Garrard, *Rousseau's Counter-Enlightenment*, 59.

'true genius', and a thoroughly unoriginal mind, attempting a task which was bound to fail. Far from extolling his undertaking, like the *philosophes*, as a truly great 'philosophical' project apt to produce lasting amelioration for Russia and all humanity, albeit simultaneously begrudging his being insufficiently philosophical and too harsh, Rousseau disparaged the tsar's efforts as comparable to those of a typical French tutor failing to nurture the true character of the child in his care, someone who regrettably 'sought to civilize his subjects' rather than develop the specific education and care appropriate to them.

It took time for the wide-ranging implications of Russia's top-down Enlightenment fully to penetrate the consciousness of the West. Initially, in the late 1690s, only the Dutch States General styled Peter 'emperor' and 'His Imperial Majesty'; after Poltava, Queen Anne of England followed suit and, eventually, other western courts, albeit often slowly and reluctantly, acknowledged the tsar in new and more elevated terms.[83] A thoroughly grudging attitude to Russia's emergence as the dominant power in eastern Europe long persisted, Frederick the Great, for instance, reacting to being sent Voltaire's history of Peter's reign by informing the author he had no intention of wasting his time reading about 'barbarians'.[84] It was in fact chiefly the philosophers, beginning with Leibniz and Wolff, who were quick to grasp the surpassing significance of Peter's transformation of a society deeply entrenched in theology and tradition deemed by them, alongside Spain, the most priest-ridden and credulous in Europe.

Fontenelle's oration on the life and accomplishments of Peter, delivered before the Académie des sciences in Paris, shortly after the tsar's death, in 1725, and read out by a proxy owing to the author being ill, included some distinctly unflattering remarks about the Russian people designed to lend emphasis to the tsar's achievement. Having been 'perpetual secretary' of the Académie since 1697, Fontenelle was a man of international prominence and what he said on such an occasion, inevitably, was very widely reported. The Russian ambassador in Paris, Prince Curakin, was so angered by his comments that he announced his intention to visit Fontenelle to demand an explanation in person. This prompted the Danish *philosophe* Ludvig Holberg, then also in Paris, to wonder whether the printed version would be significantly amended, a question he put to Fontenelle in conversation. The latter's answer was that his text would be 'printed word for word as it was spoken'.[85]

For Montesquieu, however, the 'revolution' in Russia was problematic in a way that it was not for Fontenelle, d'Argens, Voltaire, or d'Alembert. Already earlier, in his *Lettres persanes* in 1721, he remarks, like Voltaire later, that the Muscovites were more deeply attached to their old ways than other peoples but that the tsar, with awesome determination, 'a voulu tout changer', personally intervening to shave off the beards of recalcitrant court nobles and forcing everyone at court to adopt

[83] Hughes, *Russia*, 97. [84] Wolff, *Inventing Eastern Europe*, 170.
[85] Ibid. 123; Cracraft, *Petrine Revolution*, 20, 302.

western dress, thereby precipitating a still unresolved and vast cultural contest.[86] If the clergy fought back no less hard, as Montesquieu puts it, 'en faveur de leur ignorance', a perspective fully shared by d'Argens and Voltaire, despite the latter being required, in his official history of Peter, to confine remarks about the Orthodox Church to a minimum, it was they, not Peter, who reflected the genuine *esprit* of Russia.[87]

According to Montesquieu, in *L'Esprit des lois*, 'la religion a plus d'influence' in an outright *despotisme* like Muscovy than in other types of state. Hence, it seemed to him that any campaign to curtail the power of religion and the church, such as that which Peter had embarked on was not only praiseworthy in itself but automatically amounted to striving to 'sortir du despotisme' through establishing the rule of law, moderating penalties for crimes, and encouraging education; at the same time, though, popular opinion, climate, and especially religious belief, in his view, must inevitably obstruct such efforts at reform. But here Montesquieu's theoretical model appeared to lapse into an obvious muddle, as was pointed out, in print, by Holberg and in the marginal notes to his own personal copy by Voltaire: for however much Russia remained in the grip of ignorance, 'superstition', age-old *mœurs*, and religion, a vast cultural and social transition had nevertheless been engineered by the tsar, and Russian society, or part of it, had been rapidly changed, through the force of new ideas from outside.[88]

Rather like Doria earlier, Montesquieu was both impressed by but yet also critical of Peter's approach and especially of his violent temper and tyrannical methods. Where Doria thought Peter lacked true 'philosophical' understanding,[89] Montesquieu, horrified that any monarch should manhandle noblemen, believed the Russians, like all other men, would surely respond better to gentle persuasion, example, and education. 'Les moyens violents qu'il employa', he complained, were uncivilized and ultimately counter-productive: the work of introducing 'enlightenment' to Russia would surely succeed as well or better 'par la douceur'.[90] Here, though, La Beaumelle, writing around 1750, flatly disagreed with his mentor. It is unreasonable to expect respect for the individual or toleration, held La Beaumelle, not to mention the highest political ideals which were, in his view, constitutional monarchy on the British model, without first dragging men against their will to a certain level of 'civilization'.

For Montesquieu, as Holberg stressed, developments in Russia were a contradiction not least because the whole tenor of his thought sought to play down the role of great individuals in history in favour of structure and underlying trends,

[86] Montesquieu, *Œuvres complètes*, 89, 480; Wolff, *Inventing Eastern Europe*, 158, 190; Tortarolo, *L'Illuminismo*, 220; Voltaire, *Histoire*, i. 226.

[87] Voltaire, *Histoire*, i. 82, 217; d'Argens, *Lettres chinoises*, ii. 39–40, 69, 147; Wolff, *Enlightenment*, 138–9.

[88] Holberg, *Remarques*, d2^{v}, e5–e5^{v}; *Corpus de notes marginales*, v. 742; Wolff, *Inventing Eastern Europe*, 204–5.

[89] Doria, 'Il commercio mercantile', in *Manoscritti napoletani*, iv. 349–51.

[90] Montesquieu, *Œuvres complètes*, 606, 643–4; Wolff, *Enlightenment*, 139; Wolff, *Inventing Eastern Europe*, 204; Tortarolo, *L'Illuminismo*, 220.

to which we may add that he eschewed the idea of 'revolution'.[91] Voltaire, on the other hand, did not doubt that Peter's reign counts among those 'révolutions frappantes qui ont changé les mœurs et les lois des grands états',[92] a 'revolution of the mind' which from time to time in history completely 'revolutionized', as he puts it, the laws, attitudes, customs, culture, and way of life of societies. His history of Peter the Great by no means ranks among his better works, consisting mostly of just a recital of the tsar's military exploits—despite his own oft-stated disparagement of histories narrating battles and treaties instead of the story of peoples, knowledge, ideas, and *mœurs*.[93] A mediocre and deeply inaccurate work, it exaggerates the victories and oversimplifies Peter's 'Enlightenment' Nevertheless, it conveys some sense of the great scope of the transformation Peter carried through and, given the work's disproportionate influence in shaping western perceptions of Russia in the mid eighteenth century, his labelling the episode a great 'revolution' proved significant, powerfully contributing to the Enlightenment's own newly forged myth of Peter the Great which had begun with Fontenelle's eulogy before the French Académie in 1725.[94]

Peter was an overbearing tyrant, grants La Beaumelle, but one whose tireless efforts on behalf of enlightenment were greatly to be welcomed; for only such a tyranny can sufficiently civilize and westernize what he considered Russia's intellectually, culturally, and politically deplorably benighted people and prepare the ground for a truly 'enlightened' society. The fact the tsar had striven to change the old ways and import ideas, techniques, and experts from the West sufficed to convince La Beaumelle that Peter had ultimately wished to end tyranny, oppression, and corruption. Peter's efforts, and those of Anna and Elizabeth, he urged, deserved the unwavering support of all true *philosophes* and all well-intentioned men: 'la cause de la nation russe est la cause de l'humanité.'[95]

3. LOCKE, NEWTON, AND LEIBNIZ IN THE GREEK CULTURAL DIASPORA

Though rarely stressed since the eighteenth century, there were crucial connections between the Russian and Greek Enlightenments and between the rising Greek trading diaspora in Russia, the Balkans, and central Europe, from the end of the seventeenth century, and the onset of the early Greek Enlightenment. The links were cultural, religious, and educational but also commercial and political. From the 1690s, and especially the Russian capture of Azov (1696) onwards, it was obvious Peter designed to destroy, or curtail, the Ottoman empire if he could, and, moreover,

91 Ehrard, *L'Esprit des mots*, 143.
92 Riasanovsky, *Image*, 19; Iverson, 'La Guerre', 1414.
93 Condorcet, *Vie de Voltaire*, 151.
94 Wolff, *Inventing Eastern Europe*, 203–5, 208–9.
95 La Beaumelle, *Mes pensées*, 51, 62.

as the Greek historian of his reign, Antonios Katephoros, put it, that 'all the Greek subjects of the Turk would, at the first opportunity, rise in his favour'.[96] However, Muscovy's great push southwards was dramatically reversed, for the moment, by the heavy Russian defeat at Turkish hands at the Pruth, in 1711; even so, Russia's southwards expansion and efforts to gain control of the Black Sea in Greek eyes offered the most alluring prospects.

Since the late seventeenth century, the Greek merchant colonies in Venice, Vienna, Trieste, Budapest, Brașov (founded in 1678), Sibiu, Bucharest, and Moschopolis, and around the mouth of the Danube, in Romania, at Jassy, as well as Kiev and Moscow, had been growing in both economic and cultural importance and, desiring to train the sons of their merchants and business agents in foreign languages, mathematics, and Greek literacy, felt the need to expand and upgrade their network of secondary schools scattered throughout this vast region.[97] Among these high schools were the Greek community educational centre known as the Flanginian Institute in Venice, founded in 1664, a school linked to the university at Padua, the school (1656) and library (1661) founded at Hermannstadt (Sibiu), in Transylvania, that founded in 1677 at Ioannina by Emanuel Giounma, that of Bucharest, and the soon widely renowned Greek school, founded in 1714, in Jassy (Moldavia).[98] The growing and increasingly prosperous Greek merchant diaspora, supplemented by other Orthodox merchants of Vlach, Albanian, Serbian, or other Slavic origin who in this period were acculturated into the trans-Balkan Greek-speaking milieu, also patronized liturgical and sometimes secular printing to an extent which had no precedent in previous Greek history. Greek-language publications of the Enlightenment began to gather momentum from the 1740s, appearing especially at Vienna, Venice, and Trieste.[99] The schools and publishing facilities together with the merchant communities created a framework within which scholars, mostly secondary school teachers who were also priests, began to explore the world of western philosophy and science and also rethink the ancient legacy of Greece itself.

A further factor in the making of the Greek Enlightenment was the affinity with Greek learning, much stressed by Prokopovich, inherent in the Petrine 'revolution' in Russia. The new cultural era among the Greek diaspora in effect began with the series of heavy Turkish defeats at the hands of three European powers, Austria, Venice, and the rising empire of Peter the Great, in the later 1680s and 1690s. For the Austrian advance across Hungary and Serbia, the temporary Venetian conquest of the Peloponnese (1684–1716), as well as the arrival of Russian power on the shores of the Black Sea, suddenly rendered the Greek diaspora in the Balkans, Italy, and at Vienna, as well as southern Russia, the Ukraine, and the Crimea, the chief intermediary, not only in commerce but also in administration and diplomacy, between the shrinking

[96] Ibid. 245; Kitromilides, 'John Locke', 222.

[97] Kitromilides, *Enlightenment as Social Criticism*, 20; Gavroglu and Patiniotis, 'Patterns', 576.

[98] Henderson, *Revival*, 29, 39, 76, 89; Cicanci, *Campanile Grecești*, 165; Candea, 'Les Intellectuels', 200–2.

[99] Dimaras, *Grèce*, 104–5.

Ottoman empire and Europe in a way that it had not previously been. Alongside the growing Greek involvement in maritime coast-to-coast trade among the islands and in the eastern Mediterranean, overland trade routes linking Greece with Vienna, via Sarajevo and a north-east Balkans trade route leading to Kiev and Moscow, now acquired a much enhanced significance for the entire Greek diaspora in south-eastern Europe, and at the same time so did languages, literacy, and numeracy.

An interesting figure linking Greek culture, the new learning of the West, Russian reform, and the development of commerce in pre-Petrine Muscovy was the Moldavian Greek Nikolai Spatharios-Milescu (1636–1708), tutor of the young Matveev, who had been educated in Italy as well as Constantinople and also spent periods in Germany, Sweden, and France. After entering Muscovite service in 1671, he proposed a number of educational and translating projects which, however, were mostly condemned and blocked by conservative ecclesiastical opponents as inconsistent with traditional Muscovite and Greek Orthodox values. Under the ascendancy of the leading pre-Petrine reformer, Prince Golitsyn, in the 1680s, Spatharious emerged as a notable figure in the efforts to 'liberalize' Russia's commerce whereby he contributed to the spread of the new Greek diaspora in southern Russia.[100]

Repeated heavy defeats forced the Turks to negotiate with the Christian powers from a position of weakness and also more frequently and in a more 'European' fashion, which meant relying more than in the past on Greeks. The most famous Greek 'intermediary' between the powers was Alexander Mavrocordatos (1636–1709), a highly cultivated Greek Ottoman official from Istanbul and, from 1673, 'Grand Dragoman' of the Porte, who accompanied the Turkish army which unsuccessfully besieged Vienna, in 1683, and returned to Vienna in 1689, in a failed attempt to extricate the Porte from the war on moderate terms; he again served as chief Turkish negotiator at the Karlowitz peace conference of 1699.[101] His higher education at Padua and Rome had added Italian, French, and Latin to his original Greek, Arabic, and Turkish,[102] providing the kind of expertise needed, along with familiarity with Ottoman ways, to render him and his type indispensable to a Turkish empire suddenly now half ejected from the Balkans. It was, in turn, his diplomatic services on behalf of the sultan which afforded other Greeks the opportunity to gain positions as interpreters, agents, and transporters.

The complex interplay between the Ottoman empire's shrinkage, after 1683, the Greek diaspora's economic expansion, and beginnings of the Greek Enlightenment is aptly illustrated by the career of Alexander's son Nikolaos Mavrocordatos (1670–1730) (see plate 13), who succeeded his father as Grand Dragoman at the Ottoman court (1698–1709) and was the first Greek to become governor (*hospodar*) of Moldavia (1709–16), the prime administrative office, under the Porte, in

[100] Hughes, *Sophia*, 110, 116, 181, 265.

[101] Setton, *Venice, Austria and the Turks*, 262, 367, 389; Henderson, *Revival*, 21.

[102] Candea, 'Les Intellectuels', 229.

what is now Romania. In that capacity, he resided at Jassy.[103] Later, he held the corresponding position of governor of the adjoining region of Wallachia. Well versed in 'philosophy', Mavrocordatos gathered a small circle of Greek-speaking Christian scholars of various nationalities at his miniature court at Bucharest, among them his secretary Antionios Epis.[104] Accomplished in Latin, French, and Italian, as well as diplomacy and administration, Nikolaos, like his father, built an impressive library, which included runs of Le Clerc's journals, and works of Locke, Newton, Richard Simon, and Barbeyrac's reworking of Pufendorf,[105] a library the fame of which eventually reached the ears of the scholars of Leipzig and Hamburg. His praises were sung in print in western Europe among others by Jean Le Clerc, through whose journals he probably first learnt about Locke's philosophy, the role of which in the early Greek Enlightenment was to be fundamental.[106] Mavrocordatos corresponded with Le Clerc, from Wallachia, through the years 1720 to 1727, in particular so as to obtain books.[107]

Comparing atheism to madness and denouncing immorality, Mavrocordatos at the same time sternly denounced 'superstition', assigning a high status to 'philosophy'. He wrote several works, including a philosophical novel *Philotheou Parerga* translated into French as *Les Loisirs de Philothée*, penned between 1717 and 1720, a copy of which was dispatched to Le Clerc in 1721. This was a work intended, as the author explained in a letter to the German translator of the Latin version published at Leipzig in 1722, to promote a reform of attitudes and especially cultivate virtue among modern Greeks. Several characteristic features of the Greek Enlightenment were here already plainly evident. Without wholly discarding the Aristotelianism in which he had been steeped in his youth, but disdaining Arabic philosophy and *πλατωνικὴ μυσταγωγία* [Platonic mysticism], Mavrocordatos announced his allegiance to modern thought: *θαυμάζω καὶ δι' ἐπαίνων ἄγειν οὐ παύομαι τοὺς Νεωτέρους* [I admire and never cease to praise the moderns].[108] But what he means by 'modern' thought was chiefly the empiricism of Locke and ideas of 'the most wise Bacon', a particular favourite.[109] A defender of orthodox theology and tradition, and intensely conservative in social and political matters, Mavrocordatos's repudiation of democracy, individual liberty, and republican oligarchy was passionate and total.[110] But he was also acutely conscious of the major changes in thought now under way in the West, as in Russia, and believed these could in no way be ignored.[111]

At one point he remarks that if Aristotle were to come to life again he would gladly acknowledge his own obsolescence in both physics and moral philosophy

[103] Mavrocordatos, *Loisirs*, 18–20; Setton, *Venice, Austria and the Turks*, 367.

[104] Mavrocordatos, *Loisirs*, 27; Henderson, *Revival*, 22; Candea, 'Les Intellectuels', 229, 641–2.

[105] Bouchard, 'Relations épistolaires', 75–7.

[106] Kitromilides, 'John Locke', 221–2.

[107] Bouchard, 'Relations épistolaires', 67, 75.

[108] Ibid. 78–9; Mavrocordatos, *Loisirs*, 120.

[109] Mavrocordatos, *Loisirs*, 86–7, 121, 127, 219; Bouchard, 'Nicolas Mavrocordatos', 241; Kitromilides, 'John Locke', 221.

[110] Mavrocordatos, *Loisirs*, 202–3; Kitromilides, 'Tradition, Enlightenment', i. 31.

[111] Dimaras, *Grèce*, 22–3.

and agree to become a disciple of the new philosophers.[112] Moreover, he genuinely appears to have believed in the principle of independent study and thought, and in a degree of freedom of judgement (for scholars) even about matters of religious doctrine and Bible exegesis in which he was intensely interested.[113] At the same time, Mavrocordatos also took a vigorous pride in the greatness and continuity of Greek culture, stressing the depth of Renaissance Italy's debt to the many Greek scholars who took refuge there after the fall of Constantinople to the Turks.[114] A son of Nikolaos, Konstantinos Mavrocordatos (1711–69) succeeded his father as governor of Wallachia and continued his father's efforts to promote a strongly conservative Greek Enlightenment.

Meanwhile, the first notable figure of the cultural revival in the Greek lands proper was Vikentios Damodos (1700–1752) of Chavriata in Kephallonia, a scholar who, after studying at the Greek colleges in Venice and Padua, returned to Kephallonia, devoting himself to teaching the new philosophy and science, and cultivation of the spoken vernacular Greek of his day.[115] Proclaiming the ascendancy of 'reason', Damodos wrote several works which, however, long languished only in manuscript, including a textbook of physics based on Cartesian principles and a *Synopsis of Moral Philosophy* unpublished until 1940. A more controversial Cartesian was Methodios Anthrakites (*c.*1660–1736), who likewise studied in Italy and resided for a time in Venice before returning to Greece where, influenced in part also by Malebranche, he taught in schools at Ioannina, Siatista, and Kastoria, expounding mathematics and philosophy.

Some among the clergy, however, deemed the likes of Anthrakites too inclined to make excessive claims for philosophy and philosophers, considering him a threat to traditional piety as well as to Aristotelianism, the doctrine traditionally nurtured by the Greek Church. Formally condemned for heterodoxy (i.e. Cartesianism) by the Holy Synod of the patriarchate at Constantinople, in 1723, he was unfrocked and forbidden to teach. Appealing against this harsh judgement, he initially won the support of Chrysanthos, patriarch of Jerusalem, who, however, changed his mind after examining Anthrakites' notebooks.[116] Despite his continually affirming his orthodoxy, and the supremacy of the ecclesiastical arm in all matters intellectual, Anthrakites' condemnation for philosophizing 'differently from the Aristotelians' was confirmed and he was obliged to recant his ideas;[117] moreover, his notebooks were burnt in the courtyard of a church and he was made to sign a declaration acknowledging Cartesianism to have been inspired by Satan. After a period of exclusion, in 1725, he was allowed to resume teaching in exchange for his promise to instruct pupils only in the Peripatetic philosophy.

112 Mavrocoradatos, *Loisirs*, 129–1; Henderson, *Revival*, 25.

113 Bouchard, 'Relations épistolaires', 75, 90–1.

114 Mavrocordatos, *Loisirs*, 116–17; Bouchard, 'Nicolas Mavrocordatos', 241.

115 Kitromilides, 'Tradition, Enlightenment', i. 39–40.

116 Kitromilides, *Enlightenment as Social Criticism*, 21, 26.

117 Henderson, *Revival*, 36–7.

The next major figure of the Greek Early Enlightenment was Eugenios Voulgaris (or Bulgaris) (1716–1806), a native of Venetian Corfu who began his studies on the island of Zante (Zakynthos), under the priest Antonios Katephoros, author of the history of the reign of Peter the Great published at Venice in 1736, in Italian (and in Greek translation, the following year). Voulgaris too was destined to be strongly orientated towards Russia. A scholar who knew Amsterdam, and had accumulated much western as well as Greek erudition,[118] Katephoros had taught in the Greek high school in Venice; later, on Zante, he established his renowned school where modern philosophy and mathematics were taught and an intellectual atmosphere created in which Bacon, Locke, Newton, and Clarke were the prime influences.[119]

As with Katephoros, it was through his Italian higher education that Voulgaris acquired his knowledge of Cartesianism and of English 'experimental philosophy', and very likely it was by the same route that he first learnt about Leibniz and the other German intellectual influences so central to developments in Russia. An Italian survey of the European intellectual scene which particularly contributed to Voulgaris' teaching was Genovesi's *Elementa metaphysicae* (1743) which he used extensively in formulating his teaching in Greece. Locke was undoubtedly the principal inspiration behind the Greek Enlightenment as conceived by Voulgaris, though like the rest of the Greek Enlightenment, Voulgaris had no use at all for Locke's *Second Treatise* or any aspect of his political thought. In their zeal for combining Enlightenment with conservative social policies and religion, these men essentially followed a parallel line to Prokopovich, the one major difference being precisely in the area of epistemology and scientific concepts where the Greek emphasis was from the outset heavily English in orientation.

From 1742, for some years, Voulgaris was head of the Maroutsaian school in Ioannina in Epirus which, owing to its close commercial and cultural ties with Venice, was the closest thing to a Greek cultural and educational capital in the eighteenth century.[120] Always self-consciously an agent of modernization, Voulgaris zealously advocated Newtonian science and philosophy, but also insisted the Greek intellectual revival under way must remain irreproachably conservative theologically and socially, and while mostly very critical of the effect scholastic Aristotelianism had exerted on recent Greek intellectual life, even wanted to retain certain strands of Greek neo-Aristotelianism. In politics, he deeply venerated Byzantino-Russian autocracy. Indeed, he dreamt of an intellectually updated, comprehensive Russo-Bulgaro-Greek Orthodox empire under Russian tsarist domination and leadership and Greek spiritual inspiration—in full harmony with the teachings and concerns of the Orthodox Churches.[121]

The evidence shows that Voulgaris used Locke's epistemology extensively in his teaching.[122] Indeed, during the years between returning to Greece from Italy

[118] Henderson, *Revival*, 39, 43.

[119] Kitromilides, 'Tradition, Enlightenment', i. 37; Kitromilides, 'John Locke', 222.

[120] Kitromilides, 'Tradition, Enlightenment', i. 42; Kitromilides, 'Athos', 259.

[121] Dimaras, *Grèce*, 65–6; Gavroglu and Patiniotis, 'Patterns', 578–80, 586–7.

[122] Kitromilides, *Enlightenment as Social Criticism*, 31–3.

in 1742 and the mid 1750s, he translated a large part of Locke's *Essay Concerning Human Understanding*, as far as chapter ix of book III, into Greek, probably from Coste's French rendering, or else from the Latin version.[123] Locke's epistemology, furthermore, was central to Voulgaris' most important work, his *I logiki*, a 586-page Greek-language *tour de force*, the foremost achievement of the Early Greek Enlightenment the first draft of which was composed during the 1740s,[124] at Ioannina, and which he was eventually able to publish at Leipzig in 1766. Voulgaris follows Locke in rejecting innate ideas and embracing a strict empiricism and also stresses his functions of the mind. This, he concludes, leaves men with three essentially separate sources of knowledge and categories of ideas: those we know from revelation unconnected with human agency; those we know from the actions of the mind, reflection, judgement, remembrance, etc.; and third and last those that originate in sense and the body.[125]

However, Voulgaris could not leave his epistemology and logic there. A key feature of his project, linked no doubt to his and Katephoros' veneration of Peter the Great and the new Russia, was his concern that a revived Greek intellectual culture should adequately reconcile Locke and Newton with the Leibnizian and Wolffian currents dominant in Russia. The published text of his *Logic* strongly reflects this quest to blend Locke with Leibniz; but it is interesting to note that already in Epirus, in the 1740s, Voulgaris taught his students about Leibniz and Wolff, as well as Locke and Newton, and seems to have accepted parts at least of the Leibnizian-Wolffian critique of Newtonianism, encountering difficulty especially with Newton's conception of 'absolute time'. Having carefully studied the Leibniz–Clarke correspondence of 1715–16, and Madame Du Châtelet's interventions on behalf of Leibniz and Wolff, he tried to forge an intermediate position enabling him to continue with his allegiance to Newton's system while at the same time accommodating Leibniz.[126]

Besides his epistemology, it was especially Locke's technique for restricting philosophy's scope and his educational ideas which seemed most relevant to the Early Greek Enlightenment. Later, another notable Greek Newtonian, Iosipos Moisiodax (*c*.1730–1800), originally from Cernavoda in the south-east of present-day Romania, student of Voulgaris at Athos in the years 1753–6 and later in the years 1765–77, rector of the Greek school in Jassy, a thinker much concerned with problems of education, wrote a treatise on this topic and one again heavily reliant on Locke, a text which appeared at Venice in 1779.[127] Locke, then, and Newton whose legacy Voulgaris and Moisiodax studied in large part through the latter's Dutch interpreters Willem Jacob van 's-Gravesande (1688–1727), whose introduction to Newtonian physics Voulgaris translated into Greek, and Petrus Musschenbroek (1692–1761), supplied together with Bacon the philosophical grounding of the Greek Enlightenment. The Newton on which they insisted was of course less

[123] Batalden, 'Notes', 7–8, 16. [124] Ibid. 8; Henderson, *Revival*, 46.

[125] Henderson, *Revival*, 57, 61, 99, 102; Kitromilides, 'John Locke', 224.

[126] Henderson, *Revival*, 66–7; Ware, *Eustratios Argenti*, 6–7, 171–2; Gavroglu and Patiniotis, 'Patterns', 582, 584–8. [127] Henderson, *Revival*, 90–1; Kitromilides, 'Athos', 263.

Newton the scientist in the modern sense than Newton the physico-theologist, prizing especially his stress on divine dominion and providence and his shielding of miracles.[128]

Unlike Mavrocordatos and other predecessors, Voulgaris, prodded by his reading of Locke, also recommended a very limited degree of religious toleration and freedom of thought, but one effectively denying toleration to religious heretics as well as 'atheists'.[129] His was a conception of toleration rather more tightly delimited and hedged around by restrictions than Locke's or even that of Prokopovich. A certain discreet philosophical freedom of thought was, of course, indispensable if philosophy and the sciences were to progress but this, he thought, should be confined to the educated elite. For society more generally there can only be one acceptable, and therefore tolerable, way of thinking: nevertheless, any properly pious person setting out to defend faith, held Voulgaris, ought to practise an 'attitude of gentleness and clemency', and employ only reasonable means to curb and correct error, heresy, and heterodoxy, rejecting all violent and cruel methods. Toleration for Voulgaris is not really a willingness to coexist with attitudes and beliefs with which we disagree but rather an appeal to defend piety and attack ideas we repudiate non-violently.[130] Crucial for him is the distinction between active persecution, on the one hand, and ensuring orthodoxy by persuasion and good example, albeit effectively backed by threats of excommunication and social ostracism.[131]

True enlightenment, as Voulgaris understood the term, must be tightly restricted intellectually and also carefully delimited socially and culturally. Linked to his distinctively Orthodox conception of toleration and opposition to a wider freedom of thought, for example, were his views on the development of the Greek language. Given the aims of the Greek Enlightenment as he conceived it, it seemed to him, like Mavrocordatos but unlike Katephoros, and his own foremost pupil Moisiodax, that there were no good grounds for teaching or writing in the demotic tongue used by the common people for this could only have undesirable consequences, causing a ferment among the populace. He preferred rather to resurrect ancient Attic into a tool of modern intellectual discourse but one firmly separated from the life of the people and confined to a small, highly educated elite.[132]

A distinctly ironic feature of Voulgaris' Enlightenment outlook, in the light of post-1750 developments, is that for many years his ardour for Newton and Locke led him, despite his theological conservatism, to admire and defend Voltaire. For during his most formative decade, the 1740s, it was natural to assume that Voltaire, whose stock in the Rome of Pope Benedict XIV was high, who was made an honorary member of the St Petersburg Academy of Sciences in 1746, and who was not only Newton's most fervent advocate on the Continent but the most ardent champion of English ideas generally, must therefore be an irreproachably conservative

[128] Gavroglu and Patiniotis, 'Patterns', 580. [129] Henderson, *Revival*, 70–1.

[130] Ibid. 70–2; Kitromilides, 'Tradition, Enlightenment', i. 47.

[131] Henderson, *Revival*, 71–3; Kitromilides, 'John Locke', 229–30. [132] Henderson, *Revival*, 95–6.

and Christian thinker opposed to all dangerous 'atheistic' tendencies.[133] This, and the fact that Voltaire was a great eulogist of Peter the Great whose standing at the Russian court remained high in the 1750s, led Voulgaris, even after 1760, to resist the disturbing reports that the French thinker had begun to assume the public profile of an out-and-out foe of religion and the church.

After Ioannina, Voulgaris taught at Kozani (Macedonia) and, from 1753, at the new college established at this juncture by Patriarch Cyril V on Mount Athos.[134] But his ideas were regarded as too novel by most of the clergy and the growing opposition to his teaching eventually forced him, in 1759, after less than six years, and amid much acrimony, to abandon his career as an educational reformer in Greece. His rebuff in Greece led to his subsequent long years of residence in Halle, Leipzig, Berlin, and, from 1771, the last thirty-five years of his life, in Russia. In Germany and Russia, he absorbed more of Leibniz and Wolff and gradually discarded his earlier veneration of Voltaire, though he long continued to insist Voltaire had written many 'good' as well as some inadmissible things.[135] After becoming librarian to Catherine the Great in 1772, he turned hostile to the French apostle of Locke and Newton, condemning him as a propagator of impiety and freethinking; but he continued to see the combination of Locke, Newton tinged with Leibniz, and Russia autocracy as the key to all true Enlightenment.[136] He ended his career in Russia as archbishop of Slavensk and Cherson, a new archdiocesan seat created especially for him.

[133] Ibid. 69, 73–4; Wolff, *Inventing Eastern Europe*, 198–9.

[134] Gavroglu and Patiniotis, 'Patterns', 580, 587; Henderson, *Revival*, 43, 46, 56–7; Ware, *Eustratios Argenti*, 6–7; Kitromilides, 'John Locke', 223.

[135] Henderson, *Revival*, 70; Dimaras, *Grèce*, 64–6, 68; Ware, *Eustratios Argenti*, 172.

[136] Henderson, *Revival*, 73–4.

13

Popular Sovereignty, Resistance and the 'Right to Revolution'

The concept of 'popular sovereignty' was an extraordinarily difficult notion for the early modern mind to adjust to and accept. This was so in Britain no less than in Europe. For here was a clearly potentially revolutionary concept that ran directly counter to centuries of ecclesiastically and royally sanctioned political doctrine. For radical republicans—few though these were compared with divine right legitimists convinced of the sacredness of their actual constitution—it was axiomatic that government is from and of, as well as for, the people, so that the common people inalienably possesses the right to choose whatever kind of government it wishes.[1] According to such reasoning, where a regime ends, loses its grip, or is overthrown, responsibility for making a new government automatically then devolves upon the people. 'If the government be dissolved', as the point was expressed by the veteran republican activist Sir John Wildman in January 1689, during the Glorious Revolution, 'no one can claim the crown; the royal family is as it were extinct; the people may set up what government they please, either the old, or a new; a monarchy absolute or limited; or an aristocracy or democracy.'[2] Where a revolutionary procedure is the only way to end a tyrannical regime, monarchical or otherwise, then such a revolution is *ipso facto* justified and legitimate.

Much more familiar, authoritative, and deeply rooted for Orthodox, Anglicans, Calvinists, Lutherans, and Catholics alike was the maxim that political power and the supremacy of princes, as the Huguenot preacher Jean La Placette proclaimed in 1699, derives not from the people but from God.[3] During the Glorious Revolution of 1688–91, as before and after, most English, Scottish, Irish, and American commentators, whether Whig or Tory, roundly refused to acknowledge any right of popular resistance, or principle of popular sovereignty, deploying a variety of doctrinal devices for rigorously excluding from respectable and admissible 'revolution principles' both 'popular sovereignty' and the right of resistance.[4] During the first

[1] Kenyon, *Revolution Principles*, 14–17, 103–4; Porter, *Enlightement*, 190–1.

[2] [Wildman?], *A Letter to a Friend*, 14–15; Scott, *England's Troubles*, 192–3, 221.

[3] La Placette, *Traité de la conscience*, 53; Mazzotti, 'Newton for Ladies', 122, 133–5, 137.

[4] Goldie, 'Revolution of 1689', 484, 486–7, 489–90.

year of the Revolution in England, 1688–9, it is remarkable that while Tory and Jacobite pamphlets each accounted for slightly over a quarter of the total number of political pamphlets published, and pro-Revolution Whig pamphlets slightly under 50 per cent, not only did all the former eschew 'popular sovereignty' but practically all the latter expounded what is termed '*de facto* theory' of one sort or another, often of a rather contrived kind, precisely to avoid the need to espouse this then still generally shunned but later quintessentially 'modern' principle.[5]

An astonishingly tiny fraction, barely ten authors (including Locke), even went so far as to propound a right of deposition on the ground of violation of 'primary natural rights' let alone develop an argument of full-blown popular sovereignty.[6] Most embraced theories of 'desertion' or 'abdication', though each of these was a blatant fiction; for it was wholly untrue that James II and his heirs had abdicated or voluntarily 'deserted' the throne. On the contrary, William III and his invading army, together with his English supporters, had captured the kingdom and control of the royal forces, forcibly expelling James from the country, or as Toland preferred to put it, the prince of Orange came 'generously to rescue us from popery and slavery, and to secure us for ever hereafter from those worst of plagues'.[7] Besides the fictions of abdication and 'desertion', another available strategy was to admit more openly that there had been an invasion. Thus, a notable Scottish theorist of the Revolution, the lawyer Francis Grant (1658–1726), who had studied in the Netherlands, at Leiden, during the years 1684–6, not unlike several English counterparts, invoked the 'right of conquest in war', as defined in Grotius' rules of *ius naturae* [Law of Nature], to render lawful the transfer of sovereignty from James II to King William, and justify James's and his heirs' permanent forfeiture of the throne, without conceding that the interests of the people entered in any way into the legal equation.[8]

Of those who, on the contrary, did advocate 'popular sovereignty' and right of resistance many had long lived in exile abroad. Wildman returned from Holland together with other veteran English and Scottish opponents of the Stuarts, on the Dutch armada of November 1688, openly in arms against their reigning monarch. But these men belonged to an ageing, fast dwindling, faction of Commonwealth men implicated in the first English Revolution of the 1640s and 1650s who had subsequently lived in the Low Countries, unable to return to Britain, for decades, so that, while uncompromisingly republican in stance, they represented a strand of opinion increasingly unrepresentative within Britain itself. Wildman, an out-and-out republican, judged the people had the right to change the form of government, by revolution, and should proceed to do so in the most open, public, and consultative fashion possible. The 'way of doing it', he contended, 'must be great, awful and

[5] Ibid. 484, 487. [6] Ibid. 509; Kidd, *Subverting Scotland's Past*, 1–15.

[7] [Toland], *Art of Governing*, 41; Worden, 'Revolution of 1688–9', 262–3.

[8] Speck, *Reluctant Revolutionaries*, 140, 165; Jackson, 'Revolution Principles', 107–11; Kidd, *Subverting Scotland's Past*, 40–1, 64.

august, that none may be able to quarrel it', for this reason recommending that the makers of the Revolution should proceed by means of a grand 'National Convention made up of representatives of the community'.[9] To ensure this National Convention was accepted as representative and 'truly national', he, like John Humfrey, Robert Ferguson, and other radicals, urged that 'it must be larger than a House of Commons ordinarily is' and must, since this 'grand council of the nation' would exert 'more power than a parliament, and is it's creator, have a larger body'.[10] However, such a view was exceptionally rare at the time.

Of course, in a republic like the United Provinces where there was no monarch, inhibitions about appealing to the interests of the people were assuredly less. But here too the Reformed Church held that political power is from God, while the reality of everyday civic politics being wholly oligarchic and in the hands of unelected 'regents', any expression of a permanent right of popular resistance or theory of 'popular sovereignty' long remained problematic and difficult to square with both received opinion and prevailing political reality. Even so, the path to 'popular sovereignty' there lay somewhat more open. Hence, like Wildman and Toland, Walten, de Hooghe, van der Muelen, and several other Dutch and Dutch Huguenot political writers who commented on the events of 1688 roundly contended that the people can never lose the right to repudiate any government which neglects to safeguard the laws and freedoms it was delegated to uphold.[11] In the work of the radical-minded Utrecht regent Willem van der Muelen (1659–1739), one encounters a wide-ranging right of resistance to monarchical oppression, or bad faith, in breach of that contract which seemingly (even if rather vaguely formulated) extends to every individual and is inalienable, the natural right of man, as in Spinoza, being carried over from the 'state of nature'.[12]

Walten in fact saw no difficulty in justifying a universal and wide-ranging 'right' of armed resistance to tyranny of whatever sort. Hence, kings, and for that matter all other forms of regime, he proclaims subject to the laws, and not above them, arguing that 'not only may kings and regents be punished if they have deserved it, but that subjects may also always resist them, if they do something illegal and attack them in their religion, freedoms or property'.[13] For whoever has the 'power and right' to entrust an office to someone, also has the 'magt en regt' [might and right] to demand compensation and retribution where abuse of office, corruption, despotic conduct, or maladministration damages the public interest. All this is based on what Walten calls the 'natuurlijke vryheid des menschen' [natural freedom of the individual] and the 'law of nature', a term to which here and there he gives a distinctly Spinozistic twist by speaking of 'God's law, or the Law of Nature'.[14] More remarkable still this 'law of nature' always prevails over other sources of authority. Thus Christians may

[9] [Wildman?], *A Letter to a Friend*, 15.

[10] Ibid.; Ashcraft, *Revolutionary Politics*, 566–7.

[11] Walten, *Onwederleggelyk bewys*, 9, 11–13, 44; de Hooghe, *Spiegel van Staat*, ii. 12–13; Gregg, 'Financial Vicissitudes', 77–8.

[12] Kossmann, *Political Thought*, 97, 103–6.

[13] Walten, *Regtsinnige Policey*, 6; Walten, *Onwederleggelyk bewys*, 11–12.

[14] Walten, *Onwederleggelyk bewys*, 18–19, 21.

rest assured that the Bible is God's Law. But Muslims and heathens are equally convinced that the Christian texts are just 'Fabelen en Woorden der Menschen' [fables and the words of men] and they too have 'van Natuur het selve regt' [from Nature the same right] to proclaim the Koran of Muhammad canonical and command their preachers and teachers to abide by its ordinances, for the law of nature is the only right which reason can recognize as applying universally.[15]

The most strikingly democratic element in Walten's political thought is indeed the concept that the '*meerder getal* [majority] of a society or nation', though not of a city or locality within it, 'always has *magt en regt*, to change [the form of] religion and Laws', and petition the government to legislate new laws upholding the new form of religion they have chosen.[16] Should the government refuse, 'de meerder getal die het meerder getal uitmaken' [those who constitute the majority], and have chosen another form of religion, have the 'magt en regt' to compel the political authorities to comply or else set them aside and choose a new regime.[17] In Walten's and de Hooghe's political thought, the men of the government, and church ministers, however constituted, merely 'represent the whole people'.[18] Where the people remove the authorities, the new representatives 'must be chosen and delegated through general agreement' for the laws exist for the sake of 'the majority of a kingdom, state or republic' and not otherwise.[19]

Throughout the Atlantic world of the time most opinion undoubtedly remained averse to all constructions vesting the power to choose and discard governments in the people, as well as claims that the proper basis of legitimacy in politics is what Walten called the 'natural freedom of Man'.[20] It was understood that what was at issue here was nothing less than the validity of custom, authority, and a theological view of the world. The Reformed preacher Leonard Ryssenius roundly denounced Walten's doctrine of 'natural right' which he attributed to Hobbes as well as Spinoza, and especially Walten's principle that any society or nation has an inherent and inalienable right to change its laws, its government, and even its religion. Walten requires government to conform to the people's wishes in matters of faith as well as government, irrespective, protested the shocked preacher, of whether the new faith is authentic Christianity, debased Christianity, or a wholly 'false' religion. Not only 'divine right' but established tradition and ecclesiastical authority are dissolved by such a doctrine. Walten's political theory, held Ryssenius, thus stripped William III of everything that is royal, making him a mere servant of Parliament: 'gy set Koning William [*sic*]', he added sarcastically, 'een schoone kroon op het hooft' [you set a fine crown on King William's head].[21]

Dutch and Huguenot propagandists aided the Glorious Revolution by tarnishing the international image of Louis XIV and James II, and their courts, branding them

15 Ibid. 46–8. 16 Ibid. 9, 13. 17 Ibid.

18 Ibid. 13; van Gelder, *Getemperde vrijheid*, 17.

19 '... door algemeene toestemminge daar toe moeten verkoren en gedeputeerd worden', for the laws are on behalf of 'het meerder getal van een koningrijk, staat of republijk', Walten, *Onwederleggelyk bewys*, 9.

20 Ibid. 20. 21 Ibid.; Ryssenius, *Dagon*, 21–2; Blom, 'Our Prince is King', 50–1.

ambitious and greedy tyrants, persecutors, and despots, ridiculing the very idea of divine right monarchy as well as the legitimist principles proclaimed by the Anglican Church (particularly scorned by Walten), and by trying to discredit organized religious persecution, indeed any principle of enforced religious uniformity. In this respect they achieved a considerable propaganda success, casting the perceived menace of 'absolute macht' [absolute royal power] and religious intolerance in a thoroughly negative light in numerous pamphlets recycled in a variety of languages.[22] They also helped head off the initial signs of resurgent regent opposition to the prince, at Amsterdam, following James's overthrow, and William's elevation to the throne jointly with Mary, by decrying the stadtholder's Dutch opponents as selfishly motivated oligarchs who did not have the public interest at heart.[23]

A characteristically anti-Hobbesian feature of Walten's and de Hooghe's, as of Wildman's, resistance theory was their notion that where, through neglect or 'blindness', a people is so ill advised as to entrust absolute power to a king, or prince, and swear unbounded obedience to him, directly contradicting the light of reason, and 'the letter of Scripture', in a contract of the sort Hobbes postulates, then the people can in no way be held to any such misguided transaction later on when the light of 'pure reason' and their improved understanding teaches them the erroneousness of what they have done.[24] For all princely and royal power, they argue, is always and by definition illegitimate where proclaimed to be 'absolute'. A crucial difference between Spinoza and Hobbes was precisely that Spinoza held, contrary to Hobbes, that no contract or constitutional arrangement can bind a future generation which does not wish to be bound by it, a view shocking to most contemporary opinion but inherent in the democratic republican stance.[25] Hobbes's idea that, once delegated, the people altogether lose their sovereign right is anathema to Walten, de Hooghe, and van der Muelen.[26]

Such principles doubtless appeared expedient, in the stadtholder's eyes and those of his entourage, at least for a time. For the parliamentary procedure depriving James of his throne and putting William and Mary in his place was not just unprecedented but from any established legal or constitutional point of view totally unconvincing. The only conceivable way to press home a meaningful and cogent justification of the 'late Revolution' was to assert on democratic republican grounds that 'tyranny' dissolves all obligation on the part of the people. French counter-propaganda, meanwhile, loudly denounced William as a deceiver, impostor, and upstart, the 'Nouveau Cromwell' whose machinations were aimed at subverting republican liberty in Holland no less than at toppling monarchical legitimacy in Britain, admonitions readily taken to heart by many.[27] English, Scots, and Dutch

[22] Walten, *Wederlegginge*, 39–40; Rosenberg, *Nicolas Gueudeville*, 44–9, 51–2.

[23] [De Hooghe], *Nieuw Oproer*, 19–20, 22; [de Hooghe], *Postwagen-Praetjen*, 5; Knuttel, 'Ericus Walten', 359–60; Rosenberg, *Nicolas Gueudeville*, 48, 54; Israel, *Dutch Republic*, 854–7.

[24] Walten, *Regtsinnige Policey*, 78, 93; [Walten], *Wederlegginge*, 4; Knuttel, 'Ericus Walten', 351–2.

[25] Spinoza, *TTP* 239–41; Yvon, *L'Impiété convaincue*, 411–12.

[26] Walten, *Wederlegginge*, 27, 42; Israel, *Dutch Republic*, 856.

[27] Israel, *Anglo-Dutch Moment*, 43; Blom, 'Our Prince is King', 45.

radical republicans replied by stressing the prince's supposedly infinite respect for the rights of the English and Scots, his veneration for Parliament, the Anglican Church, and England's laws and liberties, and (even less plausibly, one might think) his lack of dynastic ambition. Just as he had assisted the English by ejecting their despotic king James II, so, once enthroned, William would impeccably conform to the great new principle enshrined by the Revolution: 'non est princeps supra leges', as van der Muelen formulates it, 'sed leges supra principem' [the prince is not above the laws but the laws above the prince], and the ultimate source of authority of the laws is the sovereignty of the people.[28]

Here was a genuinely revolutionary concept and one reinforced by Walten's insistence that if one generation acts so unwisely as to entrust their affairs to an absolute monarch in perpetuity, their descendants where these develop into a people who acknowledge 'for their exclusive guide' the power of 'natural reason and the light of divine revelation'—for Walten (and Spinoza) these were identical—are in no way required to 'obey such an authority, or subject the subsequently clear thinking of their understanding to the blind impulses and defective judgment of their forebears'.[29] Not only must a constitutional monarch, or any prince whose rule is legitimate, proceed in accordance with the laws, held Walten, but also in accord with Plato's rule that 'royal power is subject to reason'.

Proclaiming the intrinsically evil character of divine right monarchy and religious intolerance on the French model consequently became a stock in trade of Dutch, Huguenot, English, and Scottish republicans. Louis XIV became the very epitome of a universal tyrant. Briefly, the dramatic strategic circumstances of 1688–9 encouraged a situation in which radical republican ideas were extensively utilized by both the Dutch and the new British government so that, for the first time, it became possible widely to propagate the principle that monarchical conduct violating the freedoms and liberties of the people may justifiably be resisted by all available means including armed revolt. In the circumstances, this carried the obvious implication that it was also proper for neighbourly governments to assist such rebellions even where popular resistance is insufficient to overthrow absolutism, unconstitutionality, and intolerance on its own. This could only mean that a people then has every justification for calling in a foreign invasion to help.[30]

This radical reading of the Revolution, needless to say, was fiercely opposed and contested everywhere and continued to be down to 1789, not least in Britain itself. It was resisted not just from the right, by the Counter-Enlightenment, but rigorously, consistently, and strongly also from the centre ground. Many Anglican divines, appalled by the dethroning of James, William III's toleration, and press freedom, came to regret, and often reverse, their initial support for 'the Revolution', emerging increasingly as detractors of 'Revolution principles'. Toland, and later Mandeville, fiercely rebuked these ecclesiastical backsliders that they should 'so soon damn what

[28] Blom, 'Our Prince is King', 56–8; Blom, *Morality and Causality*, 52, 259.

[29] [Walten], *Wederlegginge*, 39–40; [Walten], *Spiegel der Waerheyd*, 39.

[30] Knuttel, 'Ericus Walten', 349–52; Kossmann, *Political Thought*, 97, 99, 103.

they themselves and the whole nation had been acting at the Revolution'.[31] Increasingly unpopular among the English, as well as the Scots and Irish, William needed to show extreme caution, until the end of the war with France in 1697, in managing Parliament and the gentry, which meant distancing himself from whatever they strongly disapproved of.[32] This obliged the new monarch and his entourage to backtrack from their condoning of radical ideas quite soon after the initial success of the Revolution. Just as, in practical politics, William quickly felt obliged to ditch his more radical Whig supporters and seek the support of the middle ground, so equally, particularly after the battle of the Boyne and the decisive defeat of James and the Jacobite cause in Ireland, in 1690, the stadtholder-king moved to espouse more traditional Anglican and constitutional ideas and attitudes.[33]

This broad reaction against radical thought and the concept of 'popular sovereignty' was greatly reinforced by the tide of Tory chauvinism and antagonism towards the Dutch which welled up in the country due to the continued presence of the Dutch troops and the influx of Dutchmen, Huguenots, and Jews who, in the wake of the stadtholder's ascent of the English throne, crossed over from Holland to seek their fortunes in London. By the summer of 1689, ill feeling towards the Dutch was so strong in England that it became a significant factor in itself. Andrew Fletcher, a Scots republican who held that 'nothing can so effectually oppose the great and growing power of France, as the united and neighbouring force of England and Holland',[34] and who, on republican and universalist grounds, opposed an incorporating union between Scotland and England, preferring a looser federative arrangement in which Scotland would retain its own Parliament and militia, accusing the English of 'inveterate malice against the Scots',[35] sourly observed of this other antipathy that 'since the time of the late Revolution which was effected by the assistance of the States [General], and saved these nations from utter ruin, you [i.e. the English] can hardly endure the name of Dutchman and have treated them on all occasions with such scurrilous expressions, as are peculiar to the generosity of your people.'[36]

Mounting dissatisfaction with the political settlement, the Toleration, and Dutch influence, voiced in particular by broad sections of the landed gentry and Anglican clergy, resulted in an increasingly emphatic rejection of the principles of justified resistance and popular sovereignty.[37] During the 1690s, practically all government and church leaders now preferred the Tory fictions of 'desertion' and 'abdication' as a way of constructing a façade of apparent legitimacy and tradition, increasingly discarding the notion that William had, as Bolingbroke put it, 'received the crown

31 Toland, *The Jacobitism, Perjury and Popery*, 4; Dickinson, 'Politics', 89; Israel, 'William III and Toleration', 162.

32 Israel, *Anglo-Dutch Moment*, 128, 134, 142–6; Scott, *England's Troubles*, 219, 479–80.

33 Scott, *England's Troubles*, 219, 478–80; Ashcraft, *Revolutionary Politics*, 596–7.

34 [Toland], *Art of Governing*, dedication; Fletcher, *Political Works*, 261.

35 Fletcher, *Political Works*, 411; Pocock, *Virtue, Commerce and History*, 237–9; Kidd, 'Constitutions', 41, 43; Armitage, *Ideological Origins*, 161–2.

36 Fletcher, *Political Works*, 410; see also Toland, *An Appeal to Honest People*, 40; Israel, *Anglo-Dutch Moment*, 142–6.

37 Bennett, *White Kennett*, 26, 56.

by gift of the people'.[38] This gentry-inspired, court-supported boycott of the principle of popular sovereignty outraged Samuel Johnson, a defrocked radical Whig cleric and staunch defender of the right of resistance, imprisoned by James II but released with the Revolution in 1688.[39] Though men of influence prefer the doctrine of 'desertion', he complained in a tract of 1692, it was 'manifestly false' and while not so base and reprehensible as the 'hypotheses' of 'usurpation' and 'conquest', was equally designed to undermine the Revolution and the 'king's throne, as if he had no rightful title to it'.[40] Talk of 'desertion' and 'abdication' was being insisted on, contrary to the reality of justified resistance, held Johnson, who was also an expert on Julian the Apostate and had once been chaplain, Bayle notes, to the Lord Russell executed by Charles II, in 1683, after the Rye House Plot, 'merely to cover the [Anglican] doctrine of Passive Obedience, and to keep that safe and sound, notwithstanding the Prince and the whole nation had been engaged in resisting oppression, and defending their rights'.

'Desertion' was proclaimed to protect Tory sensibilities but at great cost to society, insisted Johnson, since such Anglican notions 'leave nothing of liberty or property in the nation'.[41] Tory and Whig moderates alike were now refusing to acknowledge that 'the people of England did actually abrogate or dethrone King James the Second for misgovernment', added Johnson scornfully, 'and promoted the Prince of Orange in his stead'; being unable to 'make their slavish doctrine of Passive Obedience agree with the Revolution', they therefore went to work to make the Revolution agree with their doctrine, trying by this means to 'reinstate us', as he put it, ' just in the condition we were in five years ago' [i.e. before the Dutch invasion].[42]

The rapid reorientation in court and parliamentary rhetoric together with William's growing alliance with moderate Whigs and the Tories in politics, and the Anglican Latitudinarians in church affairs, led, from the early 1690s, as has been shown, to an increasingly close alignment of the Williamite court, Anglican Church, and Newtonian physico-theology. Here was a cultural configuration which helped lay the foundations for the dramatic progress of the Newtonian-Lockean Enlightenment in Britain, Ireland, and America during the 1690s and early decades of the next century and spectacular spread of British intellectual influence worldwide in the early eighteenth century. During Queen Anne's reign (1702–14), the reaction to republican, freethinking, and radical ideas grew stronger still. 'We all know', as Radicati puts it, 'what a bellowing the clergy made during her whole reign, incessantly roaring out every where, that the Church was in danger.'[43] This served

[38] Bolingbroke, *Political Writings*, 102; Kenyon, *Revolution Principles*, 6, 10, 31; Goldie, 'Revolution of 1689', 488–9; Pocock, *Virtue, Commerce and History*, 65, 77; Speck, 'Britain', 177–9.

[39] Goldie, 'Roots', 199; Goldie, 'Revolution of 1689', 506; Ashcraft, *Revolutionary Politics*, 318–19.

[40] Kenyon, *Revolution Principles*, 31; Johnson, *Argument*, 17.

[41] Johnson *Argument*, 11, 15–16; Straka, 'Sixteen Eighty-Eight', 150, 154; Rachum, '*Revolution*', 136.

[42] Johnson, *Argument*, 18, 47; Goldie, 'Roots', 227–8, 230–2.

[43] Radicati, *Succinct History*, 57; Zurbuchen, 'Republicanism', 56; Champion, *Republican Learning*, 126, 136.

further to impart a traditionalist, Anglican, and anti-democratic stamp to the political face of much of the British Enlightenment.[44]

Mainstream supporters of the Glorious Revolution, and Hanoverian Succession, persisted over subsequent decades in seeking to discredit the radical reading of what had happened. Edmund Burke did so, for instance, when attacking the pro-American dissenter Richard Price (1723–91), a publicist who in the 1770s and 1780s was, in fact, rather more radical than most of his American admirers, scorning 'Dr Price's principles of the Revolution', a package he adumbrated as a 'general right to choose our own governors; to cashier them for misconduct; and to form a government for ourselves'.[45] The principle of popular sovereignty, and right of resistance, opponents were not slow to point out, whatever Price and other republicans might say, were nowhere authorized in the Revolution Settlement of 1689 or other official publications of the Revolution. As far as Burke was concerned the Glorious Revolution had nothing to do with 'popular sovereignty', right of resistance, or the common interest. On the contrary far from being a popular uprising or a Dutch invasion, the Glorious Revolution in his opinion was the occasion when the prince of Orange, 'a prince of the blood royal in England, was called in by the flower of the English aristocracy to defend its ancient constitution'.[46]

But if the moderate mainstream dominated the scene, radical writers, Dutch, English, and Huguenot, among them Nicolas Gueudeville,[47] rapidly marginalized but in 1688–9 working briefly with official support, succeeded in widely propagating the idea that where popular sovereignty is invoked, there is no requirement for ecclesiastical sanction, legal judgements, or constitutional precedents to oppose dynasts no matter how legitimate their titles, nor any need for a religious rationale to justify armed revolt. Removal by revolutionary force of a legitimate monarch who is a despot is always justified when undertaken by the people.[48] In this way was born the eighteenth-century radical 'myth' of the 1688 'Revolution' as a people's revolution, a theme which, after Price, was taken up during the French Revolution by Condorcet, who published a pamphlet on the subject of the Glorious Revolution in Paris in 1792.

Reminding readers that 'la Révolution d'Angleterre' was occasioned not by the people but by a foreign invasion led by William III, he nevertheless held that such a procedure does not detract from the fundamental legitimacy of that or any revolution provided the principle of 'popular sovereignty' is duly invoked as, according to him, it was: for William, he claims (rather dubiously), seeing he could not legitimately assume the throne merely at Parliament's bidding, secured a legitimizing popular mandate by obtaining the endorsement of the civic corporations.[49]

[44] Kenyon, *Revolution Principles*, 10–17, 31; Pocock, *Virtue, Commerce and History*, 65.

[45] Burke, *Reflections*, 20–1; Paine, *Rights of Man*, 40; May, *Enlightenment in America*, 158, 171; Porter, *Enlightenment*, 453.

[46] Burke, *Pre-Revolutionary Writings*, 317.

[47] Rosenberg, *Nicolas Gueudeville*, 24, 29, 48, 58; Tillet, *Constitution anglaise*, 59.

[48] Kossmann, *Political Thought*, 102–4; Blom, *Morality and Causality*, 252, 228–60; Blom, 'Our Prince is King!', 50–5.

[49] Condorcet, *Réflexions sur la Révolution*, 4, 6; Israel, *Anglo-Dutch Moment*, 4–5, 123–5.

Though William did in fact, in December 1688, secure the prior backing of the city of London, and other cities, this, of course, given the invading army at his side, was a fanciful argument. The subsequent reaffirmation of monarchy, hierarchy, tradition, and the absolute sovereignty of Parliament, along with the abandonment of principle by many former republicans after 1689, and still more after the Hanoverian Succession (1714), led Condorcet to dismiss the final outcome of the Glorious Revolution as an affront to the rights of 'natural equality'.[50]

After the consolidation of the new parliamentary monarchy in Britain, asserting a generalized right to revolution with the Glorious Revolution as a model remained, then, a fringe position both in the English-speaking world and on the Continent. Yet a clear, entrenched, and tenacious tradition of radical republican resistance theory had been established and it seems that, on the Continent, support for popular sovereignty and the right to revolution in the early and mid eighteenth century was more tenacious and widely influential than historians have tended to acknowledge. Radical political opinions were upheld in various Huguenot and other exile intellectual coteries among others by Gueudeville, Radicati, Rousset de Missy, Saint-Hyacinthe, and La Beaumelle and, in Germany, by radical publicists like Wagner, Wachter, and Hatzfeld. In 1719 Saint-Hyacinthe published at The Hague a pamphlet denouncing 'divine right' principles along with Spanish support for the Jacobites, emphatically reaffirming the principle of popular sovereignty, expressly justifying removal of the Stuarts from the British thrones by popular resistance and revolution. The people's 'droit de se révolter' against a despot he bases on the purely secular notion that men should act always 'pour le plus grand bien', in his eyes the only valid way of grounding political and constitutional legitimacy.[51] La Beaumelle, writing in the wake of *L'Esprit des lois* (1748), though a disciple of Montesquieu, was decidedly more radical than his hero in several respects, especially in his conviction that political revolution is not just permissible but the chief path to human freedom and happiness.[52]

In the Holy Roman Empire, discreet admiration of British mixed government and the 'revolution' which had produced such propitious results was widespread, but also powerfully muted by the need to stress the sanctity and naturalness of the German system of princely power and hence the entirely exceptional character of English circumstances.[53] In fact, in these decades, the Empire was mostly undergoing a trend in the opposite direction towards absolutism and stronger princely authority. Traditionalist and constitutionalist, such criticism of the system as there was predominantly justified itself on the basis of the long-established procedures of the Empire. Overt approval of British 'mixed monarchy', naturally enough, featured particularly at the new university of Göttingen founded in 1734 by George II, king

[50] Condorcet, *Réflexions sur la Révolution*, 7–8.
[51] Carayol, *Saint-Hyacinthe*, 59–63; Israel, *Radical Enlightenment*, 583.
[52] La Beaumelle, *Mes pensées*, 26–7.
[53] Israel, *Anglo-Dutch Moment*, 9; Bödeker, 'Debating the *Respublica*', 237.

of England, in his German capacity as elector of Hanover. One its professors, Gotlieb Samuel Treuer (1683–1743), had earlier, in 1719, published a 230-page eulogy of *monarchia mixta* which, rather unusually, praised Locke's political theory and even the militant republican Algernon Sidney.[54] Another Hanoverian admirer of the British constitution was Schmauss who, combining liberal constitutionalism and subversive views on Natural Law with an anti-Wolffian eclecticism and reverence for Gundling,[55] had earlier, at Halle, expressed firmly positive sentiments about the Glorious Revolution, albeit without mentioning the legitimacy or otherwise of popular resistance.

Moderate 'enlightened' eulogy of the Glorious Revolution stressed specificity and tradition, contracts, and constitutionality rather than 'natural rights', though doubtless a few commentators were more radical in private than they were able to reveal in print as is implied by a number of remarks of Gundling, Treuer, and Schmauss. In any case, just as adherence to a fully comprehensive *tolérantisme* could be found only among a small fringe of *esprits forts* and Spinozists which, by the 1750s, included Lessing, so unequivocal support for the people's right to defend the 'common good', in opposition to dynastic principles, was encountered in Germany, as elsewhere, practically only within the ranks of the Radical Enlightenment.[56]

Even so, overt republican sentiment and thoroughgoing questioning of princely legitimacy and the court system prevailing in the Empire was not as rare or unthinkable as is often assumed. Indeed, it was hardly to be expected that a large, populous empire dotted with hundreds of princely courts all rivalling each other's ceremonies, armies, and splendour would not generate some deeply felt, more comprehensive political protest. In fact, indignant, across-the-board rejection of the country's existing institutional framework, totally denying the legitimacy of the system of arbitrary power the princes represented, became a solidly entrenched underground tradition in the late seventeenth and early eighteenth centuries beginning with Knutzen and the *Symbolum sapientiae*, and continuing with Wagner, Wachter, Lau, Hatzfeld, and Edelmann.[57]

Where Thomasius, whose political and legal writings were composed in the service of the princes, sought to alter judicial procedures, widen toleration, and improve administration, Wagner's anti-Hobbesian political philosophy,[58] on which he greatly prided himself, aspired to replace the entire system of *Kleinstaaterei*, small states and princely courts, with a single regime, or 'einfache Regierung', a Reich conceived as vigorous administratively, culturally, and academically rather than militarily. He thought such sweeping reform requisite for social, economic, and cultural reasons, and especially to secure personal liberty and freedom of thought, though his countrymen had, in this regard, in his view, already progressed beyond Catholic

[54] Von Friedeburg, 'Natural Jurisprudence', 141, 152–3, 158.

[55] Hochstrasser, *Natural Law Theories*, 144, 147; Bödeker, 'Debating the *Respublica*', 237, 240.

[56] Bödeker, 'Debating the *Republica*', 238–9; Whaley, 'Tolerant Society?', 175, 184; von Friedeburg, 'Natural Jurisprudence', 152–3, 158.

[57] Israel, *Radical Enlightenment*, 630–1, 661–2.

[58] [Wagner?] F.M.v.G., *Antwort*, 61.

France and Italy.[59] The Empire's defects and inadequacies he blamed squarely on the princes and their, to his mind, despicable policies, devised, so far as he could see, merely to further their own petty interests and a vast replication of superfluous court luxury.

Wachter's main contribution to political thought, entitled *Origines juris naturalis*, has clear affinities to Spinoza's last work, his *Tractatus politicus*.[60] It appeared at Berlin in 1704, dedicated to the count of Wartenberg and other Prussian ministers, and congratulated the court in Berlin on its having opposed Louis XIV's absolutism since the Revocation of the Edict of Nantes (1685). In particular, it praised Brandenburg-Prussia's participation in the Glorious Revolution, expressing obvious satisfaction that in 1688 Brandenburg together 'with the English and Dutch' had freed whole 'peoples from tyranny'.[61] Few readers seem to have noticed, though, that under guise of discussing Natural Law, Wachter quietly smuggles in whole chunks, sometimes quoted almost verbatim, from Spinoza's *Ethics*, *Tractatus theologico-politicus*, and *Tractatus politicus* (1677), obliquely propagating radical ideas about politics as well as personal freedom. Wachter's maxims, slightly reformulating Spinoza, among them 'virtus est potentia mentis ex solo ductu rationis vivendi' [virtue is the power of the mind for living solely under the guidance of reason],[62] though subtly worded, urged men to act from virtue in a cosmos where nothing is divinely ordained, and devise a politics aimed at helping the individual preserve his being by means of the guidance of reason, and do so from the foundation of seeking one's own advantage. The text constructs a system of virtue and freedom aspiring to maximize individual well-being under the law and the state.

Knutzen, the *Symbolum*, Wagner, Wachter, Lau, Hatzfeld, and Edelmann endeavoured to integrate philosophy and science within an anti-theological cosmology, morality, and social criticism and combine all this, despite the forbidding circumstances of a society saturated with the ideology of God-given princely authority, and insistence on unquestioning submission and obedience, with a veiled, and sometimes not so veiled, radical politics. Among the most forceful of the German advocates of 'popular sovereignty' and revolution undertaken by the people against the princes was Hatzfeld who, born in Calvinist Nassau-Dillenburg, was orphaned at the age of 10 or so and raised, near Koblenz, as a page by the burgrave of Wechtersbach. There he acquired the skills which enabled him to become *premier valet* to a succession of diplomats.[63] Acquiring fluent French, English, and Dutch, he was present throughout the great European peace congress at Utrecht (1712–13), which negotiated an end to the War of the Spanish Succession (1702–13), as chief valet to the envoy of the grand duke of Tuscany. Friendly, among others, with the

59 Wagner, *Discursus et dubia*, 2; Stiehler, 'Gabriel Wagner', 104–12, 114; Wollgast, 'Einleitung', 64–5, 67–9.

60 Schröder, 'Einleitung' (Wachter), 25.

61 Wachter, *Origines*, dedication; Schröder, *Spinoza*, 64.

62 Wachter, *Origines*, 2; Spinoza, *Collected Works*, i. 558; Klever, *Ethicom*, 504–5.

63 ARH Hof van Holland, MS 5454/13/I, hearing 29 June 1745.

English ambassador's secretary, on leaving Utrecht he joined the staff of the British ambassador to Vienna, Lord Strafford.[64]

Eventually, though, he decided to use his English and French in a different way and prompted by what he called his 'liefde voor de waarheyt' [love of truth], as well as by the stream of Protestant Germans (Handel among them) who gravitated to London in the wake of the Hanoverian Succession, Hatzfeld resigned his career as a liveried servant, moving to Britain to devote himself to the pursuit of philosophy and science. There, he became acquainted with various members of the Royal Society, including the Huguenot Newtonian Desaguliers, whom he tried to persuade that Newton's philosophy 'ne vaut rien'. After returning to the Continent, in 1726, he resided during the late 1720s and 1730s mostly at Leipzig, punctuated by periods in Hamburg and Berlin, earning his living teaching English to noblemen's sons. There, he also devised 'inventions', disputed with numerous professors, including Wolff whom he met several times after the latter's recall to Halle from Marburg, in 1740,[65] and also, he later admitted, propagated his fierce anti-Newtonianism and radical 'views about religion' among the students.[66] His 'inventions' included an infallible method of resealing diplomatic letters so that breakage of the original seal stays undetected and the 'best and most effectual means for cleaning and preserving the teeth'.[67]

His second book, composed in French, *La Découverte de la vérité et le monde détrompé à l'égard de la philosophie et de la religion*, appeared clandestinely in Holland, at The Hague, in 1745, under the pseudonym 'Veridicus Nassaviensis'. Condemning political oppression in the Holy Roman Empire and deploring the fact that 'la liberté de la presse' remained unknown in most of Europe, he there extolled the precious liberty prevailing in England, since 1688, and especially English freedom of the press, though he also praises Frederick the Great for boldly establishing a near comparable press freedom, since 1740, in Prussia.[68] Press freedom, he asserts, is the foremost instrument of human enlightenment, and enlightenment based on philosophy 'le fondement de tous les arts et sciences', the chief means to a general amelioration of society and reordering of politics and institutions.[69]

Much was wrong with European society, in Hatzfeld's view, especially the rule of title and absurd fact that most men prefer to have the grandest and richest persons for their superiors and sovereigns, something all the more irrational in that titles and marks of honour 'ne sont de nulle signification' if they are not based on virtue and merit.[70] His loathing of the German courts and absolutism, and resentment at the lack of liberty of expression, was closely linked both to his anti-Newtonianism

[64] ARH Hof van Holland, MS 5454/13/I, art. 15; ARH Hof van Holland, MS 5454/3 'attestation of 23 July 1713 of Marquis Charles de Rinuccini'.

[65] [Hatzfeld], *Découverte de la vérité*, 50.

[66] ARH Hof van Holland, MS 5454/13/I, art. 29 and art. 34; ARH Hof van Holland, MS 05664, fos. 52^{r-v}; [Hatzfeld], *Découverte de la vérité*, preface, pp. lix–lx and p. 6.

[67] ARH Hof van Holland, MS 5454/13, exhibitum 16 Nov. 1745.

[68] [Hatzfeld], *Découverte de la vérité*, preface pp. x, xxxii.

[69] Ibid., preface, pp. xxvi–xxvii and p.11.

[70] Ibid. preface, p. xxxiv; Tortarolo, 'Hatzfeld', 824.

and anti-Pufendorfian politics. If, as Pufendorf held, God's command is the source of our duties, and there is no universal justice independent of God, not only is morality then just a matter of passive and blind obedience to divine command, it is hard to see on what grounds any government zealous in religion, and insistent on its theological credentials, but otherwise defective and spendthrift, or even thoroughly tyrannical, can be criticized or opposed as 'unjust' or contrary to the 'common interest'.[71]

Hoping one day to publish a treatise on politics that would deal especially with 'gouvernement limité (which never appeared), he prepared the ground for it, in his preface of 1745, by roundly denouncing the princes and their courts, ridiculing them as so enamoured of their petty 'pouvoir arbitraire', and so hardened in their aversion to constitutional limits, that many would rather employ a devil than a man who favours 'un gouvernement limité'.[72] The basic political problem of 'pays esclaves', like Germany, he held, was that the people are saturated in theologico-political doctrines which make them believe 'sovereigns are installed by God Himself so that they are convinced they must let themselves be flayed alive, and stripped of everything, rather than think of resisting their princes'.[73] The 'imposteurs d'état et d'église' easily persuade the 'pauvres ignorans' who make up most of society to believe whatever they wish, so that the crassest exploitation everywhere thrives and is nowhere opposed. Most imagine, laments Hatzfeld, that the ignorance and 'mauvaise disposition' of the princes can be corrected by finding more competent and honest ministers of state, not realizing rulers choose their ministers according to their own interests and disposition.[74]

The root of all political and social evil, as he saw it, was lack of freedom of expression and of the press. Extolling the English for their courage and 'discrétion supérieure' in rebelling against absolutism and ecclesiastical tyranny, Hatzfeld urges other Europeans to follow their 'auguste exemple', and establish limited monarchy or republics by popular initiative and by means of force in more and more lands.[75] In Germany, the only path to real, enduring improvement, he asserts, is to spread more enlightened ideas and, via rebellion, compel the princes to submit to the will of the people.[76] So far, only Britain had, through its admirable revolution, 'found the method to shake the tyrannical yoke of state and church' prevailing in most of the rest of Europe. Unfortunately, the present yoke happens to suit, or at least be tolerable, to countless persons with neither 'l'esprit ni le courage' to follow the English example. In Germany, most people justify their own 'lâcheté et manque d'esprit', by foolishly calling the English 'rebels', accusing them of having neither 'foi ni loi' because they had the courage to take up arms and resist the most ridiculous 'idolatrie et gouvernement despotique'.

[71] Hunter, *Rival Enlightenments*, 144–5; Hochstrasser, *Natural Law Theories*, 79–80; Korkman, 'Voluntarism', 209–11.
[72] [Hatzfeld], *Découverte de la vérité*, pp. lx–lxi.
[73] Ibid., p. xlv.
[74] Ibid., pp. xxxvi, xlv.
[75] [Hatzfeld], *Découverte de la vérité*, preface, pp. x, xviii, xxvi, xlv.
[76] Ibid., preface pp. xxxvi, xlv, lxi–lxii.

What prevents a wider breakthrough to popular sovereignty and 'gouvernement limité', and, consequently, general amelioration in the fortunes of men, he contends, is nothing other than the people's ignorance. The German people, he laments, are just too 'ignorant' to reform their worthless political and ecclesiastical institutions, something which cannot be done without a thoroughgoing change in attitudes. Meanwhile, the slightest hint of revolt against the prevailing laws, forms, and maxims of government 'et systèmes de religion établis pour les tenir en bride' is severely repressed by the authorities.[77] Even in England there was a risk of reverting. Warning against excessive complacency about their 'constitution', Hatzfeld urged the English to strengthen their guard against unscrupulous courtiers, admonishing that if they were not vigilant, agents of royal reaction and clerical tyranny would surely restore the yoke, 'qui a coûté tant de sang à vos ancêtres pour s'en défaire.'[78] He even flattered himself that his hard-won insights might help remedy English overconfidence. Just as it fell to him, or so he believed, to point out the failings of 'votre prétendu divin Newton' so his own 'système politique' would surely assist the English further to reform their political institutions.[79]

The only way to conquer the ignorance, false teaching, and maxims of despotism prevalent in Germany and even Britain is through liberty of the press; but precisely this is generally lacking. Aside from Britain and Prussia, only the Dutch, he says, were an exception, though even there some *libraires* complained about growing constraints.[80] Should the Dutch fail to defend their precious 'liberté de la presse', he admonishes, both their political and personal freedoms would assuredly lapse and be replaced by tyranny.[81] Even scientific academies, he notes in his preface, attacking in particular the Royal Society in London, bodies supposedly set up expressly 'pour favoriser la découverte de la vérité', actually hamper free enquiry and insidiously block and oppose the views of whoever is beyond their particular chosen circle.[82]

In relying on the Dutch press regime for protection, Hatzfeld miscalculated. Pressing his assault on the 'argument from design', Newton, 'la philosophie Newtonienne' and 'le fripon Clarke', he made the mistake of also openly denying Christ's divinity. The 'inventors' of this Son of God, he declares, were 'aussi sots, que perfides', as appears from the manifest contradiction 'qu'il y a dans leur invention',[83] meaning the doctrine of the Trinity. He likewise impugned the Bible's authenticity, insulted the Reformed preachers, was scathing about Moses and the prophets, and labelled the twelve apostles 'grands imposteurs et blasphémateurs'.[84] The outraged preachers of The Hague mobilized the judicial authorities, who promptly arrested Hatzfeld, his printer, and Huguenot corrector, seizing and destroying nearly all the

77 Ibid., preface pp. lxi–lxii.
78 Ibid., preface pp. xlv–xlvi, lxiii.
79 Ibid., preface p. xlvi.
80 Ibid., preface pp. c–ci.
81 Ibid., preface pp. ci–ciii.
82 Ibid. 30, 46.
83 Ibid. 186; ARH Hof Van Holland, MS 5454/13, hearing 16 Nov. 1745.
84 [Hatzfeld], *Découverte de la vérité*, 186, 188, 224, 239–40; ARH Hof van Holland, MS 5454/13, hearing 16 Nov. 1745; Tortarolo, 'Hatzfeld', 825; Wielema, 'Johann Conrad', 89–90.

one thousand copies of the book he had had printed with his earnings from Leipzig.[85]

His corrector, Pierre Antoine de Saint Hilaire, a mathematics teacher at The Hague, was also tried before the high court of Holland, in his case for colluding in a publication depicting the prophets and apostles as 'impostors' without informing the authorities of such blasphemy. Urging banishment from the country for life, Holland's *Advocaat Fiscaal* argued that, under Dutch law, not just the author of an illicit book but also those collaborating in its production are subject to severe punishment; after a few months' imprisonment, though, Saint Hilaire was fined 100 guilders and released.[86] Hatzfeld, having refused to retract his blasphemous views at his hearing on 21 December 1745 was sentenced to 'perpetual imprisonment' in The Hague,[87] though after a few months in the Gevangenispoort prison, his health deteriorated so rapidly that, in January 1746, the court mitigated his sentence to perpetual expulsion.

Well before 1750, then, an entrenched, underground tradition existed in Germany and France, proclaiming 'popular sovereignty' along the same lines as could somewhat more openly be done in Holland and Britain. Justified resistance and right to revolution had taken root at least as an underground current of opinion and may well have been a stronger force in western culture before 1750 than historians have generally been willing to concede. The Dutch Revolt and the Glorious Revolution for some became part of a new kind of political mythology, exerting a cultural and intellectual impact which extended far beyond the confines of Protestant north-west Europe, imparting a decisive new twist to western European thinking about society and politics. 'Among modern rebellions worthy of eternal praise', exclaimed Radicati in 1732, 'are those of the Hollanders, the English, the Switzers, and the Genevans.'[88] The Huguenot political writer La Beaumelle, raised mainly in Denmark, was another who, like Radicati and Hatzfeld, did not doubt Britain's success in acquiring the freest and best political constitution of the age was due to the willingness of the people to offer armed resistance to tyranny and through their own efforts initiate revolution leading to fundamental change in their political institutions.[89]

Louis XIV's persecution of the Huguenots, and absolutism generally, French, British, or Danish, La Beaumelle viewed with utter repugnance. The point of the Glorious Revolution to his mind was to teach the lesson that all kings 'sont sujets; tous les peuples sont souverains'.[90] Kings may sometimes have been chosen by peoples; but no people, he maintains, can ever have wanted 'des rois despotiques', such

85 ARH OSA 189, Acta Synodus Noord-Hollandiae, Edam, 27 July/5 Aug. 1745, p. 28; ARH Hof van Holland, MS 5454/13, hearing 29 June 1745, fo. 2ᵛ.

86 Ibid., MS 05452/9, fo. 2 and MS 05664, fo. 58ᵛ.

87 Ibid., fos. 57ᵛ–58ᵛ; MS 5454/13, hearing 13 Jan. 1746.

88 [Radicati], *Philosophical Dissertation*, 41.

89 ARH Hof van Holland, MS 5454/13, fos. 29, 149–51, 153–4, 156–7, 167; Tillet, *Constitution anglaise*, 301.

90 [La Beaumelle], *L'Asiatique tolérant*, 105.

as the unfortunate Danes acquired in 1660. Reporting a discussion in which he participated in Denmark in 1748, La Beaumelle says he defended 'la liberté des peuples' and right to instigate revolution wherever monarchs oppress them. Meeting with the retort 'and who will judge entre le prince et le sujet?', he held a king is always at fault when most of his subjects consider him to be; but what, then, demanded his interlocutor, is the criterion of legitimacy? This, he responded, can only be reason and 'le droit naturel' of all men.

Most Danes, like most other Europeans, admits La Beaumelle, showed very little sympathy for such reasoning. In his post-1660 Danish *patrie* where absolutism had become solidly entrenched, he remarks, if one allows that 'patrie et roi arbitraire ne *soient* pas termes contradictoires', irrational, arbitrary force effectively decides every question, since *droit naturel* has no place in a land where the power of reason is stifled, as it always must be under untrammelled monarchy where freedom of thought and expression is not permitted.[91] Without a 'revolution of the mind' the common people will always remain not just ignorant and steeped in 'superstition' but also oppressed and wholly unaware of their own interests. This he sees as an astounding paradox of human life. What a strange thing it is, he observes, that when one urges, in a disinterested fashion, what is plainly in the interest of 'je ne scai combien de millions d'âmes', proclaiming the benefits of reason, toleration, individual freedom, and limited, constitutional monarchy, one finds hardly anyone willing to agree. The 'sacred name of liberty', he asks, which men exclaim with such pleasure, is it nothing but a vain utterance? We are born free of chains: 'n'aimons-nous à vivre que dans l'esclavage?'[92] Is not independence of self and mind 'naturelle à l'homme'? 'L'*England*', he exclaims, curiously mixing English and French, is that land the only country 'où les mortels pensent?'[93]

This avid student of international politics expressed frank astonishment that mankind had taken so long to rebel against the institution and principle of monarchy and not earlier made up its collective mind to 'établir des républiques ou de limiter les monarchies'. In Europe, lamentably, the 'esprit de liberté' had for centuries abjectly bowed down before 'l'esprit de domination'.[94] Why, he wondered, is it so difficult for men to grasp that 'la dépendence d'un seul fait nécessairement le malheur de tous'. Yet such an utterly irrational state of affairs as prevailed in mid eighteenth-century Europe could not continue for ever. Downtrodden and wretched, the common people, La Beaumelle does not doubt, would eventually rise up against their royal and noble oppressors and assuredly possess every right to do so.[95] Even so, the prospect of violence and civil war disturbed him. At one point in his discussion, he wryly suggests that the best outcome would be for princes to suppose the people *do* possess the right to revolt against oppressive sovereigns and peoples to continue to believe they do not.[96]

91 [La Beaumelle], *L'Asiatique tolérant*, 106; Vernière, *Spinoza*, 465; Lauriol, *La Beaumelle*, 131.

92 [La Beaumelle], *L'Asiatique tolérant*, 108.

93 Ibid.; Lauriol, *La Beaumelle*, 143, 170, 181.

94 La Beaumelle, *Mes pensées*, 116.

95 Lauriol, *La Beaumelle*, 526.

96 Ibid. 144–5; [La Beaumelle], *L'Asiatique tolérant*, 120; La Beaumelle, *Mes pensées*, 74.

The common people adore monarchy. But the person who exercises sovereign power is not sacred, asserts La Beaumelle, and rules only on trust, subject to the people's approval since he governs on their behalf. England was never more free, he insisted, nor showed more clearly that she is a land of liberty, than when Parliament declared the throne vacant in 1689, forcibly ejecting the Stuarts, and enthroning William and Mary.[97] This he saw as an enduringly significant, admirable, and decisive act. Revolt against oppression is not just a universal right, he argued, but also a universal reality. In some French provinces, he observed, the unjust distribution of the *taille* was having the cumulative effect of leaving the land denuded of men willing to till the soil. The tendency for fiscal pressure to increase, he predicted in 1751, would eventually lead to a degree of pressure on the common people that would provoke revolt and lead to a massive and violent denouement. A people worthy of being free, he predicted, 'a toujours droit de l'être, et trouve toujours les moyens de le devenir'.[98]

[97] La Beaumelle, *Mes pensées*, 181; Lauriol, *La Beaumelle*, 181.
[98] La Beaumelle, *Mes pensées*, 152.

14

Anglomania, *Anglicisme*, and the 'British Model'

1. ENGLISH DEISM AND THE RECOIL FROM RADICALISM

Once ensconced on the three thrones of England, Scotland, and Ireland from 1689, William III's political priorities soon led him and his entourage to distance themselves from the more far-reaching republican principles associated with 1688–9. Despite being the most committed to upholding the revolutionary settlement, 'the Toleration', and exclusion of the Stuarts, radical Whigs, republicans, and freethinkers rapidly became a liability to the new regime. Their ideas clearly enjoyed only minimal support in the country; for with the rapid growth of Jacobitism, in England as well as Scotland and Ireland, from the summer of 1689, and the new monarch's deepening unpopularity among broad sections of English and Scottish opinion, it became abundantly evident that most greatly preferred traditional and religious criteria of legitimacy to radical modes of thought. Nevertheless, the lasting constitutional and libertarian successes of the Glorious Revolution of 1688–91 were, undoubtedly, in themselves a major reason for Britain's cultural pre-eminence, as well as rapid political, economic, and military expansion, during the early Enlightenment. The triumph of mixed monarchy, the moderate mainstream, and the ideas of Locke and Newton rendered England the anti-absolutist and tolerationist model *par excellence*.

Indeed, the Glorious Revolution of 1688–91 proved in many ways a severe, even irreversible setback to absolutist ideologies everywhere, fatally wounding divine right monarchy and the 'Anglican Counter-Enlightenment' in the English-speaking world and damaging all forms of *ancien régime* beyond.[1] While prudently keeping remarks about the dethroning of a legitimate dynasty to a minimum, Voltaire, in his *Lettres philosophiques* (1734), proclaimed the Glorious Revolution the very foundation of the spectacularly successful new Britain which had emerged since the late seventeenth century, the grounding of its constitutionality, toleration, free press, financial and military power, and stable rule of law. The English nation was the only one on earth, he argued, much like Boulainvilliers earlier and Montesquieu subsequently, which

[1] Israel, *Anglo-Dutch Moment*, 1–43.

had been able to check the power of kings, 'en leur résistant', and the only one to forge a viable and durable compromise between monarchy, aristocracy, and democracy, the outcome being so well crafted, balanced, and wise that, since 1688, the monarch in Britain had always been effectively regulated, the nobles 'sont grands sans insolence et sans vassaux', while the common people participate in elections and the parliamentary process to a small degree and in an appropriately restricted fashion without causing 'confusion'.[2]

After 1688, and especially the defeat of the Jacobite uprising of 1715, full-blown Jacobite Counter-Enlightenment had few immediate prospects anywhere. Admittedly, many in early eighteenth-century England, as well as in Scotland and Ireland, or in exile on the Continent, especially Anglican Non-Jurors, and Catholic Jacobites, but also others who reviled the Revolution and all it stood for, still strove to blend High Church Anglican and Catholic principles with a firm devotion to dynastic legitimacy and princely divine right. Jacobite ideology continued to evolve, crystallizing around the Stuart court in exile, first in Paris and later Rome, subtly combining its Anglican and Catholic dimensions with a fond, nostalgic image of social hierarchy and courtly harmony sometimes effectively contrasted with the raucous factional strife and party politics rampant in Williamite and early Hanoverian England.[3] One of the Catholic Scottish Jacobite exiles in Paris, Ramsay, contributed notably to the intellectual life of France in the 1720s and 1730s, specializing in highlighting the new and universal danger, as he saw it, posed by Spinozism. But while political Jacobitism and support for reactionary 'high-flying' Anglicanism remained far more vigorous in England as well as Scotland and Ireland after 1700 than historians once supposed, within Britain itself both the Non-Juror (Jacobite) and barely Williamite 'High Church' streams found themselves trapped and humiliated, and in varying degrees targets of the new regime. The Glorious Revolution precipitated a sustained government-driven, official disparagement and delegitimization of divine right ideology, absolutism, and High Church notions of political legitimacy and ecclesiastical power. At the same time, both politically and through its decisive widening of toleration, the Revolution greatly strengthened the Latitudinarian tendency within the Church of England vis-à-vis traditional Anglicanism, thereby fragmenting the doctrine, as well as diluting the authority, of the national Church.[4]

The prestige of English culture and learning burgeoned along with the growing predominance of Britain as a world power at sea, on land, and in international politics. The situation was indeed exceptionally favourable to a rapid expansion of British and Anglo-Irish cultural and intellectual influence in Europe and America on a scale never witnessed before. This applied in particular to England's moderate mainstream Enlightenment of Bacon, Boyle, Locke, Newton, Clarke, and Bentley which, from the 1690s onwards, achieved spectacular progress on both sides of the Atlantic, rapidly conquering Scotland and Ireland, gaining firm early footholds on

[2] Voltaire, *Lettres philosophiques*, 53, 57, 66–7, 73; Salmon, 'Liberty', 87.

[3] Szechi, 'Image of the Court', 56–9.

[4] Beiser, *Sovereignty of Reason*, 227–9; Champion, *Republican Learning*, 238–47.

the European continent both among the Huguenot diaspora and in the Dutch universities, and, by the 1720s, penetrating as far as Rome, Russia, the Ukraine, and Greece. Yet English political and intellectual culture could still be viewed as a vigorous duality. For there was also a strengthening, at least for a time, of the more marginal radical and republican tendency, the intellectual luminaries of which were Shaftesbury, Toland, Collins, Bolingbroke, Tindal, Robert Molesworth (1656–1725)—an Anglo-Irish nobleman, ally of Toland and warm admirer of Shaftesbury upon whose views he believed he had some influence[5]—and the Anglo-Dutch Mandeville.

This radical bloc was impressive in its own way not only for its intellectual power, originality, dedication to a lay, republican 'virtue', and skill in publicizing its views but also for its erudition and role in the wider European intellectual debates and culture of the time. Shaftesbury, Bolingbroke, Toland, and Collins were the most 'universalist' and 'philosophical' of the English freethinkers and culturally the most cosmopolitan.[6] All these men had extensive continental ties. Collins owned one of the best private libraries in England and, besides parcels of books, in French and Latin, from Holland, regularly received news from Paris, and cases of wine (Montepulciano) from Tuscany. Among his closest allies was Pierre Des Maizeaux (1673–1745), the London-based Huguenot editor and biographer of Bayle, at the time a key cultural intermediary between England and the Continent.

If the Lockean-Newtonian Enlightenment went from strength to strength in the early eighteenth century and remained heavily predominant, Shaftesbury, Toland, Molesworth, Collins, and Mandeville, the 'club'—as Bentley disdainfully called it—of radical 'Deists' who opposed divine providence, physico-theology, and Newtonianism, and criticized the Revolution and its Toleration, from the left, insisting these had not gone far enough, were also a faction to be reckoned with, at least down to the 1720s. They were also a major force in European thought more widely. Toland and Collins especially exerted a substantial influence on such figures as Giannone, Radicati, and Rousset de Missy,[7] while, as we shall see, Shaftesbury's legacy greatly influenced Diderot's formation. Even so, this 'club' was caught in a curious set of political, social, and intellectual dilemmas which progressively weakened its position in relation to the British and continental moderate mainstream and, after 1720, led to its gradually losing ground both at home and internationally.

Certainly, toleration, freedom of the press, and secularization in Britain all expanded rapidly after 1688 and, among other things, this materially furthered the propagation of republican, freethinking, and non-providential Deist ideas.[8] The English so-called 'Deists'—Bentley, like Berkeley, rightly mainained that Collins was really an 'atheist',[9] as indeed was Toland—enjoyed a growing notoriety and won

[5] Molesworth to Toland, near Dublin, 25 June 1720, in Toland, *A Collection*, ii. 461–3.

[6] Venturi, *Pagine*, 40.

[7] Venturi, *Alberto Radicati*, 191–3; Jacob, *Radical Enlightenment*, 117, 185–9, 213–14; Ricuperati, *Nella costellazione*, 127–32.

[8] Venturi, *Pagine*, 33–4; Jacob, *Radical Enlightenment*, 84–7; Davies, 'L'Irlande et les Lumières', 19–20, 34–5.

[9] Berman, 'Disclaimers', 271; Taranto, *Du déisme à l'athéisme*, 425–37.

some notable triumphs in the intellectual controversies of the day, holding their own in moral philosophy, history of religion, critique of 'priestcraft', and Bible criticism, while powerfully linking their philosophical challenge with a still vigorous republicanism. There were significant differences of view between these men, of course, but it is arguable that what they shared and repudiated outweighed their differences, despite Mandeville's public attack on the deceased Shaftesbury after 1723. For in Mandeville's *Free Thoughts* of 1720, Shaftesbury is cited only with approval and, even after Mandeville rejected Shaftesbury's moral and social philosophy, the scope of the disagreement was not such as to erase many remaining similarities and concurrences of view.[10]

Republican in attitude, all these writers shared a disappointed, deeply ambivalent attitude toward the Revolution. They agreed it had 'secured our hitherto precarious liberties', as Shaftesbury put it, and 'removed from us the fear of civil commotions, wars and violence, either on account of religion and worship, the property of the subject, or the contending titles of the crown'.[11] But the compromises entailed and corruption thriving in its wake aroused only their bitter contempt, Toland denouncing that 'bare-fac'd and openly avow'd corruption which, like a universal leprosy, has so notoriously infected and overspread both our Court and Parliament',[12] to the 'disgrace', as he later put it, 'of the Revolution (in itself the best cause in the world)'.[13] He later called for a curbing of the 'corruption of elections by private entertainments, public feasts, and bribes' and fairer, more even, representation in Parliament by reforming the 'rotten boroughs' and assigning constituencies in new towns like 'Manchester, Leeds, and Halifax' where representation was (and long remained) lacking. Convinced 'freedom of elections, and the frequency, integrity and independency of Parliaments', as Bolingbroke expressed it, were the core 'essentials of British liberty', Toland early on urged annual choosing and assembling of parliaments as a way of improving and strengthening the system.[14]

All of these men appreciated the importance of current ideological and political developments in Europe as well as Britain: reviling French and Stuart absolutism, Shaftesbury, Toland, and Mandeville, like Mably or La Beaumelle later, viewed the advancement of humanity's cause, as they understood it, as part of a vast international struggle in which the fate of their 'Revolution', and republican principles, was closely entwined with developments elsewhere and Britain's alliance with the Dutch Republic conceived as something of cultural and ideological, as well as strategic, significance. Shaftesbury especially took an elevated view of the global Nine Years War (1688–97) with Louis XIV and James II, convinced 'our alliance and union with the Dutch' would contribute to the future 'happiness of Europe, by carrying the point of liberty and a balance further than first intended, or thought of; so as to bring not

10 Primer, 'Mandeville and Shaftesbury', 126–7, 130–3, 137, 141.

11 Shaftesbury, *Characteristics*, 97; on the correlation between Deism and radical republicanism in England in the wake of the Glorious Revolution, see Pocock, *Machiavellian Moment*, 476–7.

12 [Toland], *Danger of Mercenary Parliaments*, 3; Israel, *Anglo-Dutch Moment*, 30.

13 Toland, 'A Large Introduction', p. vii.

14 Bolingbroke, *Political Writings*, 101; [Toland], *Art of Governing*, 76, 78, 121.

Europe only but Asia (which is now concern'd) and in a manner the whole world under one community; or at least to such a correspondence and intercourse of good offices and mutual succour, as may render it a more humane world than it was ever known and carry the interest of human kind to a greater height than ever'.[15] The 'interest of human kind' was indeed among their shared ideals.

Shaftesbury quickly became disillusioned, though, with the mundane, mercenary, and blinkered attitude of most of those who had helped unseat the Stuarts, especially by the sight of 'so many of those, who were zealous for the Revolution, so much pervert the design of it', as Toland reports his feelings, 'and so willfully endeavouring to frustrate the chief ends of it, that he could attribute it to nothing but court-influence, which at length turn'd his stomach at times against the court itself'.[16] If for Shaftesbury 'the Revolution' remained a great moment when 'a happy balance of power was settled between our prince and people', the job had been left unfinished. Resentfully, he continued to press for 'frequent parliaments',[17] openly lamenting the betrayal of the Revolution by 'Apostate-Whigs, who became servile and arbitrary', as Toland put it, 'to please court empirics', leading to his eventual 'hearty contempt and detestation of many [former] Revolutioners'.[18]

Shaftesbury's conception of the 1688 Revolution, which he judged the decisive moment the English won their liberty and the power of 'doing good' in the world, was rooted not only in his republican ideology but also his—and Molesworth's, Toland's, and Collins's—lifelong quest, profoundly influenced by the Greeks, to construct 'a system of virtue independent of religion, or the belief of a Deity'.[19] While Shaftesbury's professed theism was doubtless genuine, and fervent 'benevolence' and aristocratic sensitivity too much for the down-to-earth Mandeville, divine providence in his philosophy, differently from in Voltaire, nevertheless plays hardly any part in fashioning the new moral, political, and cultural order he aspired to build on human nature alone. A declared opponent of 'atheism', reluctant to be associated with the less respectable Toland and Collins, he too nevertheless sought to uncouple morality and politics from theology and firmly approved Bayle's principle 'that Atheism has no direct tendency either to take away and destroy the natural and just sense of right and wrong or to the setting up of a false species of it'.[20]

Shaftesbury's 'natural' morality, based on the 'moral sensibility' he discerned in man, was wholly independent of supernatural agency and based on a particular vision of lay sociability. In characteristically anti-Hobbesian mood, whilst in Bayle's Rotterdam, in August 1698, he jotted in his notebook: 'the end and design of nature in man is society, for wherefore are the natural affections towards children, relations, fellowship and commerce but to that end?'[21] Like Bayle, whose importance he

15 PRO 30/ 24/ 27/23, Shaftesbury Papers, 'Two Letters', fos. 7v–8; Shaftesbury, *Characteristics*, 100.

16 Toland, 'A Large Introduction', pp. vii, xv.

17 Ibid., pp. viii, xx; Shaftesbury, *Characteristics*, 97; Klein, *Shaftesbury*, 134–5.

18 Toland, 'A Large Introduction', p. xvi.

19 PRO 3030/24/27/23, Shaftesbury Papers, 'Two Letters', fo. 8; Klein, *Shaftesbury*, 27–8.

20 Klein, *Shaftesbury*, 157; Leland, *A View*, iii. 17, 21; Schneewind, *Invention of Autonomy*, 303–7.

21 PRO 30/ 24/27/10, Shaftesbury Papers, part 1, Notebook (Rotterdam, 1698), 31.

well understood and with whom he remained on cordial terms, he venerated the Greek achievement in all branches of philosophy but, unlike Bayle (and Hobbes), admired also the Greek achievement in politics. Most of all, though, he admired the ancient 'Grecians' grasp of moral issues which he thought altogether superior to ours. By turns hopeful and gloomy about his contemporary world, he accounted the classical Greeks 'more civilized and more polite than we ourselves, notwithstanding we boasted so much of our improv'd wit and more refined manners'.[22]

Shaftesbury showed a keen eye for the weaknesses as well as the strengths of Early Enlightenment British culture when viewed from a 'philosophical' and international perspective. Besides his disappointment at what he considered the failure of the Revolution to complete its task, he harboured many wider worries and reservations. He loved his country but was deeply disturbed by the intensifying insularity, xenophobia, superiority complex, philistinism, and resistance to intellectual influences from outside, traits no less characteristic of the politically articulate classes of county gentry and clergy than of popular attitudes. These negative traits, later frequently remarked in France, Holland, and elsewhere, Shaftesbury deemed serious defects, indeed a fundamental threat to an authentic republican spirit and set of institutions, the true ideals of the Glorious Revolution, as he saw it; indeed these were traits directly contradicting the potential but as yet unrealized true English republican and international cultural superiority to which he aspired.[23]

The narrow insularity, chauvinism, monarchism, and growing philistinism of the gentry, London coffee-houses, and indeed Oxford and Cambridge, the menace of small talk, complacency, and a vacuous sociability, filled him with deep pessimism, lending a special edge to his fierce anti-Toryism and dislike of much of his own Whig party: 'our best policy and breeding is, it seems, to look abroad as little as possible', he observed sarcastically, in his *Characteristics*, 'contract our views within the narrowest compass and despise all knowledge, learning or manners which are not of a home growth'.[24] Yet, in a way, Shaftesbury himself, true republican idealist and freethinking cosmopolitan though he was, was part of the problem. A man of admirable sensitivity, learning, and refinement, his particular attitude to 'enlightenment' reveals, as Diderot grasped later, a delicate reclusiveness and elitist, anti-democratic tendency, linked to an increasingly gloomy view of the prospects for truly advancing liberty and enlightening and civilizing the masses.[25]

In deteriorating health, Shaftesbury early on retired from politics but persevered to the last with his philosophical efforts. Admiring Bayle,[26] he knew Locke intimately but, after 1694, refused all further relations with him, scorning his epistemology and despising his (in his view) vain, unprepossessing character; in

22 PRO 30/24/27/23, Shaftesbury Papers, 'Two Letters', ii, fo. 1v.

23 Black, *Convergence*, 156–7; Bell, *Cult of the Nation*, 44–5; Shaftesbury, *Characteristics*, 403–4.

24 Shaftesbury, *Characteristics*, 404; Klein, *Shaftesbury*, 96–101.

25 Pocock, *Machiavellian Moment*, 514; Porter, *Enlightenment*, 368–9; Duflo, *Diderot philosophe*, 416–22; Quintili, *Pensée critique*, 56–66; Taranto, *Du déisme à l'athéisme*, 110–11.

26 PRO 30/24/27/22, Shaftesbury Papers, Basnage to Shaftesbury, Rotterdam, 17 Jan. 1706, fo. 2.

correspondence with others he freely ridiculed Locke's efforts, especially his constant dithering, from edition to edition of the *Essay*, regarding 'liberty and necessity' and categorical rejection of 'innate ideas', which he firmly opposes in his *Characteristics* (1711).[27] In fact, he considered Locke's empiricism too simplistic and unconvincing to require much time discussing. Antagonistic to Spinoza and Hobbes and especially the latter's authoritarian politics, and more suspicious than they of 'reason', he freely granted that Hobbes, unlike Locke, was at least a 'genius in philosophy'.[28]

Collins, for his part, was as boldly radical as any Early Enlightenment writer, in those fields in which he directly engaged—freedom of opinion, miracles, religious authority, and whether, if the will is determined rather than free, one can speak of human liberty. Discarding Locke's ontological quasi-dualism and 'talk of the essences of things being unknown' as 'a perfect mistake',[29] he long battled Clarke (and Locke) on the freedom of the will. 'There are', as he put it in 1707, 'causes that ever determine the Will, on appearing good or evil consequences', so that men's choices are hence 'always the result of what seems good or bad to them, with respect to their own interest'.[30] Consequently, he concludes, contrary to Locke but like Mandeville, 'man is a necessary agent'. In Holland, his *Philosophical Inquiry Concerning Human Liberty* (1717) was instantly denounced as 'Spinozistic';[31] spurning all talk of 'free will', Collins doggedly opposed the predominantly theological approach of his age, bracketing himself closely with Bayle (whom he especially admired), Spinoza, Mandeville, and also Hobbes.

For Collins, like Mandeville, 's-Gravesande, and indeed Spinoza, the fact everything we undertake is determined by what seems good or bad, better or worse, to us, in no way contradicts our liberty, as Locke, Clarke, and the theologians maintained. For 'there can be no liberty', he held, 'but what supposes the certainty and necessity of all events. True freedom, therefore, is consistent with necessity, and ought not to be oppos'd to it but only to compulsion.'[32] Yet Collins made little effort to explore further how men can be emancipated from needless hindrances, so that his kind of 'compatibilism' of freedom and necessity can equally well be classified as Hobbesist or Spinozist, justifying Clarke in classifying Collins's 'liberty of will' as a conception attributable to 'both Spinoza and Mr Hobbes'.[33] Very likely, it was precisely the strand of Spinoza closest to Hobbes and most readily reconciled with his gentleman's lifestyle, and rather conservative political and social outlook, which was most palatable to him and other early eighteenth-century British 'Deists'.

[27] PRO 30/24/27/23, Shaftesbury Papers, 'Two Letters', fos. 3^{v}–5; Klein, *Shaftesbury*, 27–8; Himmelfarb, *Roads to Modernity*, 27.

[28] PRO 30/24/27/23, Shaftesbury Papers, 'Two Letters', fo. 3^{v}; Porter, *Enlightenment*, 160–1.

[29] Collins, *A Philosophical Inquiry*, 62–72; Landucci, 'Mente e corpo', 128.

[30] Collins, *A Philosophical Inquiry*, 22–3, 59–60, 141; Beiser, *Sovereignty of Reason*, 228.

[31] Collins, *A Philosophical Inquiry*, 74, 86; De Vet, 'Spinoza en Spinozisme', 24–5.

[32] [Collins], *An Essay*, 48, 50; Taranto, *Du déisme à l'athéisme*, 351–4; Harris, *Of Liberty and Necessity*, 54–5.

[33] Clarke, *Demonstration*, 63; Ellenzweig, 'Faith of Unbelief', 44.

Collins, as was often remarked in Holland and Germany, figured among the era's most powerful advocates of freedom of thought and expression and was as scathing a critic of ecclesiastical authority as could be found. To his vigorous polemical style he added a refined and cutting rhetorical wit. Incensed by his claims of 'pious frauds of ancient Fathers and modern clergy', prominent churchmen and academics, Bentley, Berkeley, Benjamin Hoadly, and Jonathan Swift all well to the fore, regularly targeted his pronouncements which, indeed, seemed specially crafted to infuriate them. His detractors ridiculed his confidence in philosophical reason, one insisting 'what there is of knowledge and true religion among men is principally where Christianity is professed', adding, like Locke in his *Reasonableness of Christianity*, that the Christians had far surpassed the ancient philosophers in the great work of establishing in the world 'a pure system of morals, containing the whole of our duty with respect to God, our neighbours, and ourselves'.[34] Collins was admonished that the ancient Greek philosophy schools were more hopelessly fragmented than the Christian churches and sects had ever been.

Greek freedom to philosophize, and the resulting 'variety and altercation among them', answered Collins, 'whetted and improv'd the wits of Greece, insomuch that Athens by their means became the theatre of learning and politeness, and was visited by great numbers of foreigners, who, either as travellers or students sent thither by their parents and guardians, came to be instructed by the philosophers'.[35] Unlike the schisms of ancient and modern churchmen, moreover, pagan Greek philosophical controversy never entailed interventions 'to gain the common people to bawl in behalf of any set of notions' which, he observed, greatly differs from the 'state of things among us Christians': 'our disputes with one another, for want of impartial liberty,' he held, 'make convulsions in government, involve neighbourhoods in feuds and animosities, render men impolite, and make conversation among friends, of different sentiments, often disagreeable'.[36] Had we full freedom of expression and less ecclesiastical authority, 'there would then be nothing to raise or feed the spirit of contention', 'enthusiasm' [i.e. zeal] would exhaust itself, 'knavery would want its spur, and gross nonsense, when unsupported by enthusiasm and knavery, would sink and fall by being inquir'd into and expos'd'.[37]

However, his materialist philosophy stopped there, Collins evincing little desire, despite his scorn for Jacobitism,[38] to connect his bold theses about liberty of thought and religious authority to a wider package of social, moral, and political issues. He admired Holland, as a country 'remarkable for liberty and peace',[39] but (unlike Shaftesbury, Toland, and Mandeville) did not make a point of arguing that its benefits stemmed from a particular institutional framework, or set of attitudes, which could be usefully emulated elsewhere. Nor did he take up the issues

[34] Leland, *A View*, iii. 63, 65; Locke, *Reasonableness of Christianity*, 172–5.

[35] [Collins], *Discourse of the Grounds*, p. xxv. [36] Ibid., p. xxvi.

[37] Ibid., pp. xxvii–xxviii; Beiser, *Sovereignty of Reason*, 257–9.

[38] Taranto, *Du déisme à l'athéisme*, 56, 72, 111.

[39] [Collins], *Discourse of the Grounds*, p. xxx.

of parliamentary and legal reform espoused by Toland, Shaftesbury, and Molesworth, or, like Toland, champion the legal status of the Jews in England, or indeed attack any of the 'philosophically' questionable elements of eighteenth-century Britain whether empire, slavery, taxation, divorce, or Ireland.

Around 1720, British 'Deism' looked a dynamic cultural and intellectual force; but it tended to recede, from the 1720s, both in local vitality and from continental philosophical debates. If, from Blount onwards, British 'Deism' bore Spinoza's, as well as Hobbes's, imprint even in the case of Shaftesbury who expressly repudiated their thought, in the longer run, non-providentialist Deism in Britain notably failed to integrate a comprehensive toleration, freedom of thought, individual liberty, rejection of religious authority, republican virtue, democratic republicanism, and equality into a coherent radical intellectual system by means of the monist philosophical apparatus at hand. British Deism, despite its republicanism, perhaps revealed itself to be *au fond* more Hobbesian and Humean in orientation than Spinozist.[40] If some British, as well as most continental, observers clearly saw that 'the most applauded Doctor of modern atheism, Spinosa' had, as Leland put it, also 'taken the most pains to form it into a system',[41] in Britain, it was precisely that broad radical intellectual system with its attendant democratic and egalitarian consequences which was avoided.

In any case, by the mid eighteenth century the so-called 'Deist controversy' had largely spent itself and ceased to be central to British culture.[42] At the same time, republican radicalism, as we have seen, did not so much disappear as adjust to the changing British political reality in compliant and compromising ways.[43] In his later years, Toland became the tireless apologist of a faction which tried to merge republicanism with monarchism, rendering it not merely compatible, but closely integrated with, a monarchical, aristocratic, and imperial world system.[44] He had all along helped publicize the suitability and dynastic claims of the House of Hanover but little by little this became more central to his endeavours, gradually softening his republican edge.[45] With his spate of tracts of the years 1711–14, claiming that the Hanoverian Succession by permanently excluding Stuart divine right monarchy, entrenching toleration and civil liberty, and curbing the High Church reaction of Queen Anne's reign (1702–14) would best secure what he and his allies judged the main gains of the Glorious Revolution, the ideological fusion of republicanism with a new version of British mixed monarchy was already largely complete.

If, as a critique of revelation and miracles, British 'Deism' retained much of its vigour into the mid eighteenth century and beyond, maturing in particular into the sceptical philosophy of Hume and anticlerical historiography of Gibbon, Hume's

[40] Ellenzweig, 'Faith of Unbelief', 44.
[41] Leland, *A View*, iii. 21.
[42] Brown, 'Introduction', 10; Porter, *Enlightenment*, 97–8.
[43] Pocock, 'Significance of 1688', 278, 291; Champion, *Republican Learning*, 116–17.
[44] Champion, *Republican Learning*, 133–6; Zurbuchen, 'Republicanism', 50.
[45] Pocock, *Machiavellian Moment*, 449, 476–7, 483; Champion, *Pillars of Priestcraft*, 171–3, Champion, *Republican Learning*, 116–18, 120, 123–4, 129–30, 132–5.

politics and social and moral thought were even more conservative than those of Shaftesbury, Toland, Molesworth, and Collins and, by his time, rejection of the radical approach to social and moral issues had become predominant within, and typical of, British Deism generally. At the same time, it seems this broad retreat from the wider-ranging republican legacy of the recent past, and decreasing participation in the continental intellectual debates, resulted not from any specifically intellectual factors but was due rather to social, cultural, and political conditions in Britain, Ireland, and America.

Historically, there were several reasons for what, by the mid eighteenth century, had become a major divergence of paths between the British and western continental 'philosophical' trajectories. Five, in particular, would seem to be of major consequence. First, there was the political dimension already mentioned: Toland and his allies, in aligning with the Hanoverian court, were not only drawn into the intricacies of court politics and the existing parliamentary system but increased post-1714 English republicanism's proneness to become inward-looking and abandon discussion of general theoretical issues.[46] While the Hanoverian Succession did check the High Church reaction of Anne's reign, it also resulted, under the Septennial Act of 1716 (replacing the Triennial Act of 1694), fixing elections at every seven years—with the support, ironically enough, of both Toland and Trenchard—in less, instead of more, frequent parliamentary elections and further reinforcing royal patronage, and the ministry, in relation to Parliament. The Act in effect materially advanced, instead of curbing, the more corrupt, oligarchic, and negative features of the British monarchical-parliamentary system.[47]

Toland always insisted that it was just a detail that Britain was 'ordinarily stil'd a monarchy because the chief magistrate is call'd a king' and that in fact it was a fully-fledged 'commonwealth', opposed to 'arbitrary' monarchs, a 'mix'd government' which was 'shared between the Commons, the Lords, and the Supreme Magistrate (term him King, Duke, Emperor, or what you please)'.[48] For all their apparent differences, he liked to think Britain and the United Provinces were natural allies, and more alike than most people realized, being 'the two most potent and flourishing commonwealths in the universe', both being 'mixed' monarchies in this particular sense.[49] But the gentry and the common people in the main would have none of this and, as Toland himself admitted, 'so besotted are some people by education, custom or private interest, that they are often heard to say they wou'd rather see England an absolute monarchy than the most glorious republic, as in the late reigns they were taught to say they wou'd sooner be papists than presbyterians'.[50]

After 1716, it was hard to deny that the best-known radical ideologues in Britain were complicit in the very political corruption of which they themselves so bitterly complained. That after Anne's death the Whigs were more resolute in supporting

46 Champion, *Republican Learning*, 159; Worden, 'Revolution of 1688–9', 266–73.

47 Pocock, *Machiavellian Moment*, 473–4; 478–9, 483; Hoppit, *Land of Liberty?*, 48–9, 151, 398.

48 [Toland], *Art of Governing*, 150.

49 Speck, 'Britain', 181.

50 Ibid.; Zurbuchen, 'Republicanism', 50.

the ruling dynasty, the Hanoverians, than the Tories, moreover, placed radical Whigs and republicans in the paradoxical position of being more vocal and principled supporters of monarchy, or at least the newly renovated British monarchy, than traditionalists, Non-Jurors, Jacobites, and crypto-Jacobites, all those that is who rated the incoming German royal house of dubious legitimacy compared with the Stuarts. Republicans like Toland and Molesworth, contributing to the growing respect for monarchy in both Britain and America characteristic of the mid eighteenth century,[51] now fully supported monarchy tempered by Parliament and what, by their own admission, was a reprehensible system of oligarchic politics, placing themselves in diametrically the opposite position—and to all appearances a less principled one—to that which they professed in the 1670s and 1680s.[52]

All this helped the pervasive myth which existed earlier but waxed stronger after 1714, that the Revolution, and dethroning of the Stuarts, only restored the glorious particularity and ancient continuity of English 'mixed monarchy'—and, curiously, a parallel but quite separate mythology of Scottish 'mixed monarchy'—supposedly reaching back to remote times. The Revolution thus came to be widely conceived as merely a brief corrective disturbance restoring the true English constitution, in reality no revolution at all,[53] a view with which Montesquieu tended to agree, arguing that climate and physical causes had long before fomented the disposition of mind, Protestantism, and general ambience favouring the rise of British mixed monarchy and separation of powers.[54] Such marginalizing of 'the Revolution' was further advanced by a growing stress on the benefits of mixed monarchy among English republicans themselves, bolstering what might be called the Hobbesian, anti-democratic strain in English freethinking which had earlier pervaded the aristocratic outlook of personalities like Sidney and Rochester.[55]

Hence, democracy itself came to be disparaged by republicans. Walter Moyle, a republican earlier active against the crown in the so-called 'standing army' controversy of the late 1690s, concluded that most 'men can no more judge of their own good than children', some being 'too dull, and some too negligent'.[56] Praising the mixed constitution of ancient Sparta for providing firm safeguards against what he saw as the shortcomings of democracy, Moyle came to prize the aristocracy, or at any rate the English aristocracy, as the natural mediator between kings and peoples, and 'bold assertors of their country's liberty'; for the French nobility, it seemed to him, had under Louis XIV sunk to the level of 'ensigns and ornaments of tyranny'.[57] Thus, the Revolution during the early Hanoverian period came to be 'appropriated' by an alliance of resurgent popular royalism, a traditionalist gentry Whig and Tory, and

[51] Worden, 'Revolution of 1688–9', 266–7; Wood, *Radicalism*, 14–16, 27–8, 98–9.

[52] Hoppit, *Land of Liberty?*, 45–7; Champion, *Republican Learning*, 130–5, 144–6.

[53] Pocock, *Machiavellian Moment*, 450, 473, 482; Wright, *Classical Republican*, 126; Kidd, *Subverting Scotland's Past*, 74–80.

[54] Holberg, *Remarques*, C5–6, D4.

[55] Worden, 'English Republicanism', 452, 463–4.

[56] Moyle, *The Whole Works*, 54–5, 57; Zurbuchen, 'Republicanism', 50.

[57] Moyle, *The Whole Works*, 162–3.

grudging Anglican Church. Men preferred to speak of 'our liberty' or 'English liberty' rather than liberty in general, characterizing the British constitution as a uniquely wise division of political sovereignty and authority between king, peerage, gentry, and people.[58] After the spectacular victories during the mid-century global wars, the glow of self-congratulation and heightened national pride created a mood in which the British constitution came to be seen as inherently so superior to, and removed from, those of the rest of mankind as to be altogether unique and even in a way—a view encouraged by some clergy—supernaturally fashioned and regulated.[59]

The spectacular burgeoning of the British empire during this period increasingly rendered 'empire' and an imperial sensibility, along with feelings of superiority, particularly (but by no means only) over the non-white races, integral to the nation's outlook.[60] This added a further layer of hierarchy psychological and social to a culture already built around the entrenched and privileged position of the aristocracy and gentry. This could only encourage the deepening xenophobia and insularity which so greatly disturbed Shaftesbury. Hence, the Revolution created not only a new political context but also a new cultural framework in which the cult of English exceptionalism tinged with antipathy to the Dutch and French became an integral feature. Liberty might be a universal human preoccupation but, as an English author put it in 1757, 'the spirit of liberty' had produced 'more full and complete effects in our own country, than in any known nation that ever was upon earth'.[61] The avoidance of continental debates and authors (even Bayle and Spinoza), so deplored by Shaftesbury, and noted also by Rousset de Missy, in the preface to his 1714 French translation of Collins's *Discourse of Free-Thinking* (1713), became habitual, even an essential part of a wider cultural and imperial system.

Finally, there was the combined Anglican and Nonconformist religious revival. The radical impulse was certainly in part squeezed out from the 1720s onwards, in Britain (as in the United Provinces), by a strengthening public reaction against irreligion and freethinking and smoother coexistence of the churches and sects. Misled during his English visit in 1729 by the scoffing at vicars he found among his aristocratic friends, Montesquieu wrongly supposed Britain a country virtually devoid of piety.[62] Doubtless Britain did strike foreign visitors as less devout than France or Italy. But the 'Deist' freethinking movement nevertheless aroused intense indignation among the public while, after the 1690s, the Anglican Church expanded its reach, slowly accepting, in part prodded by the crown, the irremovable presence of the dissenting churches and bridging its Latitudinarian and 'High Church' wings sufficiently to prevent an excessively damaging rift.[63]

58 *Lettre du Chevalier . . . à Mylord*, 3.

59 Schilling, *Conservative England*, 18, 20–2, 83–4; Black, *Convergence*, 143–4.

60 Greene, 'Empire and Identity', 219–20, 222.

61 Quoted in Kidd, 'Constitutions', 46; see also Wood, *Radicalism*, 13–14, 146.

62 Montesquieu, *Œuvres complètes*, 334; Earle, *World of Defoe*, 87–9.

63 Porter, *Enlightenment*, 97; Hoppit, *Land of Liberty?*, 236–41.

Newly enforced flexibility brought a new vitality and momentum which extended also to New York, Maryland, Virginia, and the Carolinas besides the West Indies. Especially after 1714, recently founded Anglican-sponsored societies for the propagation of the gospel, reformation of manners, combating of prostitution, and promoting the religious education of children, as well as missionizing and catechizing overseas and among slaves, sprang up all over the English-speaking world. By 1750, catechizing, establishing charity schools, and publishing spiritually edifying literature, besides sending out clergy, missionaries, teachers, books, and money to the colonies, flourished as never before.[64] Popular attitudes, meanwhile, hardened markedly towards freethinkers, Socinians, 'atheists', and all those commonly deemed beyond the pale of acceptable dissent, as also the Catholic and Jewish minorities and nascent homosexual subculture furtively subsisting in early eighteenth-century London (and urban Holland).

In addition, there was the special relationship between scientific culture and the national Church, in England, pulling science in a different direction from that characteristic of Holland and France. Especially the Latitudinarian wing of the Anglican Church positively welcomed the new developments. Thomas Sprat, first historian of the Royal Society and its 'experimental learning', even went so far as to claim that the 'Church of England therefore may justly be styl'd the Mother of this sort of knowledge'.[65] In any case, in England, as Bentley put it in 1713, 'superstition' had been defeated not by philosophers and 'no thanks to Atheists, but to the Royal Society and College of Physicians; to the Boyle's and Newton's, the Sydenham's and Ratcliff's'.[66] The Royal Society in London, emerging, in the 1660s, from a turbulent and fraught theological context, was from the first strongly committed to promoting attitudes at once experimental, anti-dogmatic, and doctrinally minimalist, without anchoring this vigorous empiricism—about which Shaftesbury for one had considerable reservations—in any particular intellectual or theological system. Anglican preference for institutional forms over dogmatic coherence, and English suspicion of grand, far-reaching philosophical constructs in general, in this way helped prepare the ground for Locke and Newton.

2. FRENCH *ANGLICISME*

Montesquieu esteemed Britain's recent political evolution especially for having ensured a stable and balanced division of power with 'moderation' as its watchword; England, though no longer a real monarchy, in his opinion, was nevertheless something powerfully distinct from both democracy and oligarchy, with the role of

[64] Hoppit, *Land of Liberty?*, 66; Schlenther, 'Religious Faith', 141–4.

[65] Porter, *Enlightenment*, 132, 135–7; Hill, *Some Intellectual Consequences*, 62–3; Henry, 'Scientific Revolution', 198–203; Beiser, *Sovereignty of Reason*, 184–6, 201–5.

[66] Bentley, *Remarks*, 33.

nobility, kingship, and church all being pivotal.[67] Nor did Montesquieu think Britain's burgeoning maritime and commercial empire would hamper future preservation of its newly reinforced liberty.[68] The originality of his conception was to see that the political stability and liberty afforded by English mixed monarchy derived not from any contract or accord but from accommodating competing forces in society and balancing tensions between rival blocs.[69] To prove that were there no king in England 'les Anglois seraient moins libres', he pointed to developments in the Netherlands. Since the death of William III in 1702, who, in his opinion, represented as stadtholder the monarchical element in the Dutch constitution, the Dutch, he claimed, had been 'plus dans l'esclavage' than previously. For the regent oligarchs in each voting city governed as 'de petits tyrans', a view with which Dutch democratic republicans did not disagree.[70]

Removing absolute monarchy, securing mixed government, entrenching toleration, weakening ecclesiastical power, and widening freedom of the press (and the theatre), as well as ensuring, after 1697, that in peacetime Britain should maintain only a very small 'standing army', the Glorious Revolution, as La Beaumelle noted in 1748, engineered a vast cultural change.[71] Such a general 'revolution of the human mind' was precisely the kind of revolution Voltaire, Montesquieu, Maupertuis, Réaumur, and all the moderate *philosophes* aspired to introduce more generally. Since the Glorious Revolution in Voltaire's eyes had defeated 'superstition' and enthroned the experimental philosophy of Bacon, Boyle, Newton, and Locke as the supreme expression of true, valuable and useful knowledge, a world of thought vastly superior, to his mind, to the scholasticism, obscurantism, and intolerance of the past, post-1688 Britain could and should be considered the prime instance of those modern 'révolutions de l'esprit humain' which Voltaire prized as the great positive steps in mankind's history, the stages by which men learn to think, and impose rational order on lifestyle, manners, and 'esprit'.

Voltaire's 'revolutions' of the human spirit represented a sporadic, tortuous form of progress by phases from theocracy—rated by him the lowest form of tyranny—to British-style civil liberty, in his view the highest and most civilized form of society.[72] Such a 'revolution' Voltaire hoped to inspire also in France and it was to this that he dedicated his literary efforts and philosophical life's work. He appreciated, he suggests in several plays and stories, that a comprehensive change in culture and attitudes can only be precipitated by some decisive occurrence or action,[73] though he never claims these should amount to an anti-absolutist struggle or involve violence or indeed, in essence, be political at all. Such a 'revolution of the mind' could be achieved in France and elsewhere, he believed, by means of a

[67] Ibid., 200–1; Montesquieu, *Œuvres complètes*, 537; Bartlett, *Idea of Enlightenment*, 29.
[68] Armitage, 'Empire and Liberty', 43.
[69] Goyard-Fabre, *Montesquieu*, 216–18.
[70] Montesquieu, *Œuvres complètes*, 537; Fockema Andreae, 'Montesquieu in Nederland', 179.
[71] [La Beaumelle], *L'Asiatique tolérant*, 114.
[72] Voltaire, *Essai sur les mœurs*, 246, 815–17, 906.
[73] Wade, *Intellectual Development*, 367.

vigorous, well-judged literary and intellectual campaign apt to capture the minds of the society's elites, thereby creating a freer, more tolerant, and culturally flexible society.

If English cultural influence was more pervasive in Germany in the eighteenth century, especially in the smaller Protestant principalities, and in Spain and Italy, than often supposed,[74] it was especially in France and Holland that the Enlightenment seemed, for a time, likely to be comprehensively based on the 'British model' philosophically, culturally, and scientifically. During the 1720s, French, Dutch, and Italian thinkers came to regard Cartesianism and *Malebranchisme* as outdated and began to espouse Locke and Newton. Montesquieu, Réaumur, Voltaire, and, following his visit to London in 1728, Maupertuis, former musketeer, able mathematician, and, since 1723, member of the Académie des Sciences who later, in the years 1745 to 1753, was to be first president of the Prussian Royal Academy of Sciences in Berlin, all figured prominently among those who powerfully propagated Anglophile views in France.

While the English radical 'Deist' writers remained very little known in France, several works of English providential Deism exerted a marked impact in French, notably, in 1726, Wollaston's *Religion of Nature Delineated*, a translation favourably reviewed in the Parisian *Journal des savants* the following year.[75] Certainly, French, like Italian and Spanish, enthusiasm for English ideas was initially both constrained and discreet. But from 1732, Maupertuis initiated a more open phase, challenging the Académie des Sciences by directly attacking the 'Cartesian' principles still (publicly) espoused by Fontenelle and Dorthous de Mairan. Rejecting the Cartesian-Malebranchian doctrine of 'impulsion', viewing impact of bodies as the common denominator of the laws of motion, Maupertuis substituted Newton's principle of 'attraction' and laws of gravity and motion. Like Voltaire subsequently, Maupertuis interpreted 'attraction' as a general but 'non-essential' quality of bodies, something which God imparts, or superadds, to matter.[76] Henceforth, Maupertuis continually promoted a British-style physico-theological Enlightenment based particularly on Bacon, Boyle, Locke, Newton, and Clarke. But his influence as superintendent of Newtonian and Lockean ideas first in France and, after 1745, in Prussia, later came to be hindered by his difficult and quarrelsome temperament. His relations with the other *philosophes*, moderate and radical, deteriorated markedly in the early 1750s when he clashed bitterly with both Voltaire and Diderot.

Maupertuis, though, was just the first of a crowd. Montesquieu's visit to England, where he arrived in the company of Lord Chesterfield in October 1729, and remained until early in 1731, though he knew very little English, proved much the most formative leg of his European tour. In London, he met prominent Newtonians and associates of Locke, including the latter's translator, Pierre Coste (1668–1747), and, despite finding London an ugly city where there are 'de très belles choses', compared to Paris, a handsome city marred by some very ugly things, he too quickly

[74] Umbach, *Federalism and Enlightenment*, 31–57, 65, 67, 100.

[75] Ehrard, *L'Idée*, 418 n.

[76] Ibid. 140–2; Vamboulis, 'La Discussion', 162–3.

became a declared Anglophile, if a less ardent one than Maupertuis or Voltaire.[77] He especially admired the dynamism of London's rapidly growing metropolitan society. The great centre of what he calls 'liberté et égalité', meaning an unprecedented personal freedom, London, seemed to him the space *par excellence* where men can behave and develop freely without being constricted by a rigid social order; the same could be said of Paris but to a lesser degree, while Venice, in his view, offered no more than private liberty to live 'obscurement' and frequent prostitutes.[78]

'Liberté et égalité' indeed figure centrally in Montesquieu's political thought, but by these terms he meant something quite different from the democratic republicans. To him, 'freedom' and 'equality' were the prime criteria of the best type of social and cultural milieu, a context at once metropolitan and cosmopolitan, freeing the leisured individual to live a more independent, varied, and socially mobile life than had been possible in the past. This distinctly aristocratic notion of liberty and equality led him greatly to prefer English 'liberty', an emphatically hierarchical milieu where peers and gentry ran Parliament and set the tone more generally, to the socially less stratified 'liberté de Hollande', a context with which he was also familiar at first hand but disliked, 'la liberté de la canaille', as he thought of it, a dismal and debased liberty forged for the common man.[79]

He did not doubt that English-style mixed monarchy and separation of powers surpassed all other political forms in excellence and best guaranteed the personal liberty he so esteemed. 'L'Angleterre', he declared, around 1730, 'est à présent le plus libre pays qui soit au monde, je n'en excepte aucune république.'[80] Its superiority was especially evident, he thought, here concurring with Hobbes and Bayle, when its constitution was compared to those of the turbulent democratic republics of ancient times in which 'le peuple avait une puissance immédiate'. No agitator or demagogue would get far, in his opinion, attempting to stir popular passions for political ends in Hanoverian England.[81] The sheer weight of aristocracy, county gentry, and clergy, and flexible but yet firmly hierarchical character of English society, and the residual but restructured power of monarchy, all helped bolster the stability of its political and legal institutions, blocking the path to all unwelcome popular pressures and demands. This was no less vital for preserving liberty in his sense than had been curtailing the royal prerogative in 1688.

Privately, Montesquieu had always scorned French royal absolutism of the kind forged by Louis XIV; but he realized too that his own emerging political *anglicisme* could be propagated in the France of the 1730s and 1740s only very slowly and circumspectly. The disadvantages of pushing too far or fast were shown, in 1734, by the furore over Voltaire's *Lettres philosophiques*, a text which, too stridently proclaiming

[77] Montesquieu, *Œuvres complètes*, 331.

[78] Ibid.; Tillet, *Constitution anglaise*, 85–6, 99,118, 147; Courtney, 'Montesquieu and English Liberty', 275.

[79] Courtney, 'Montesquieu and English Liberty', 275; Himmelfarb, *Roads to Modernity*, 15; Montesquieu, *Œuvres complètes*, 331.

[80] Montesquieu, *Œuvres complètes*, 334; Himmelfarb, 'Two Enlightenments', 311–12.

[81] Montesquieu, *Œuvres complètes*, 647–50; Courtney, 'Montesquieu and English Liberty', 286.

English superiority in institutions, culture, commerce, and social structure, provoked unnecessary indignation, obliging its author hastily to flee Paris.[82] After his own return from England in 1731, Montesquieu had spent the next two years quietly at his château near Bordeaux, composing his second major work, the *Considérations* on the Roman republic and empire (Amsterdam, 1734). At around the same time, he also drafted his famous eulogy of England's mixed monarchy later incorporated in a shortened form in his *L'Esprit des lois*; but this he carefully refrained from publishing for the moment, indeed withheld for the next decade and a half. He likewise left unpublished another brief text penned at this time, entitled *Réflexions sur la monarchie universelle en Europe*, where he observes that had the designs of a certain *grand prince* (Louis XIV) not been checked by a 'great defeat' (Blenheim, 1704), and that ruler had eventually succeeded, after a series of terrible wars, in founding a *monarchie universelle*, nothing would have been more calamitous or 'plus fatale à l'Europe'.[83]

Voltaire, France's most brilliant stylist, coming to the intellectual fore in the mid 1730s, rapidly eclipsed Maupertuis, Montesquieu, and Réaumur as France's chief advocate of English philosophy, science, social norms, and culture. Since 1722, mixing with a Deistic coterie, including the brothers Lévesque, which was probably the first in France to study Newton and English experimental science, and knowing Bolingbroke,[84] Voltaire from the outset repudiated both the *anti-philosophisme* of the *dévots* and Jansenists, on the one hand, and the *Spinosisme* of the Boulainvilliers coterie, on the other. After his return from England, urging his compatriots to embrace a wholly new cultural system based on Lockean empiricism, physico-theology, English-style realistic drama, toleration, liberty of commerce, and freedom of expression, he was soon also at odds with the anti-Newtonian neo-Cartesians and *Malebranchistes*. For the rest of his career, he remained an ardent Anglophile, though, compared to Montesquieu, it was chiefly England's philosophy, science, and literature, and its toleration and freedom of expression, which he admired rather than its parliamentary institutions and politics.

For Voltaire, the philosophical dimension was paramount. From this point on, he accounted himself a 'grand admirateur de Locke', in his eyes 'le seul métaphysicien raisonnable', the thinker who not only abolished innate ideas but effectively disqualified all prior philosophy, subjecting everything to the force of the new empirical epistemology.[85] He fully subscribed to the Lockean-Newtonian doctrine that 'natural theology' and science are conjoined by an omniscient and omnipresent divine providence of which gravitation and 'attraction' are the outward attributes. For Voltaire, no less than Locke and Newton, the universe is directly governed by a Creator who is intelligent and benevolent and decrees our obligations and duties, as well as rewarding and punishing men in the hereafter. This led

[82] Courtney, 'Montesquieu and English Liberty', 277; Rahe, 'Book', 55–6.
[83] Rahe, 'Book', 64–5; Montesqueiu, *Œuvres complètes*, 192, 196.
[84] Barber, 'Newton de Voltaire', 118.
[85] Voltaire, *Mémoires*, 39.

him to align with Locke and Newton also in defending 'free will' against the determinists. Also basic to his system were Newton's absolute time, place, and motion, and the externality of motion to matter. Further, he consistently upheld the divinely fixed character of animal and plant species which he saw as guaranteeing the absolute divide between animate and inanimate bodies, and men and animals, as well as motion and matter.[86] He was more tentative, though, regarding immortality of the soul. The question of 'miracles' he avoided altogether.

For Voltaire, Britain remained the very quintessence of 'modernity'.[87] His allegiance, moreover, clearly exemplifies a key feature of the 'British Enlightenment' of the early eighteenth century in both its Anglo-American and French manifestations: namely, its capacity to accommodate both Latitudinarian or Arminian theology, on the one hand, and, on the other, a providential Deism which confines doubt about miracles and revelation to the social and intellectual elite. Voltaire secularized the Lockean-Newtonian construct, as it developed in France, first by discarding Locke's doctrine that the unbroken chain of testimony confirming Christ's miracles, and those of his apostles, provides unassailable grounds for credence in Christ's messiahship and, secondly, by denying Locke's (and Clarke's) claim that Christianity had been decisive in enabling mankind to institute the basic principles of morality, Voltaire here staunchly upholding the credentials as moral reformers of Confucius, Zoroaster, Epictetus, and the Brahmins.[88] Otherwise, he preserved intact the core principles of 'ce sage Lok, ce grand Neuton', as well as Clarke, including major elements of the theological core, arraying his proofs of the existence of a providential God around the 'argument from design'.[89] His Deism showed affinities to Shaftesbury's but was closer to that of Wollaston.

Voltaire entertained grave doubts as to whether the 'enlightenment' he and his entourage sought to introduce among France's nobility and administrative elite should, or could, be extended to the common people. Mostly, he opposed the idea of 'enlightening' ordinary folk, being convinced, not unlike his foes Rousset de Missy and Saint-Hyacinthe, that upholding the social and moral order involves retaining basic elements of traditional religion, especially belief in 'free will' and eternal reward, and punishment, in the hereafter.[90] The essentials of traditional belief and authority, he felt, needed to be retained provided clerical pretensions to control the independent-minded, critically thinking individual are firmly curtailed and the power of superstition, and intolerance, along with the clergy's appetite for property and revenues, curbed.

Although the Glorious Revolution figured less in his thinking than the achievements of Locke and Newton, he acknowledged the Revolution's centrality to the English model he so admired and pivotal role in England's toleration and freedom of expression.[91] Though for him, like Boulainvilliers and Montesquieu,

[86] Ehrard, *L'Idée*, 199; Fichera, *Il Deismo critico*, 100.
[87] Dziembowski, 'Défense du modèle', 93.
[88] *Corpus des notes marginales*, ii. 650–1, 657.
[89] Benelli, *Voltaire metafisico*, 70–2.
[90] Payne, *The* Philosophes; Pearson, *Fables*, 10–11.
[91] Wade, *Studies on Voltaire*, 190.

'la démocratie ne semble convenir qu'à un très petit pays',[92] and he remained broadly a monarchist, he respected some republics where these were appropriately small, holding ancient Athens and modern Geneva in particular esteem. Still, he tended to contrast what he took to be the primitive character of republics with the sophistication and grandeur of modern 'enlightened' monarchy, something he viewed as the product of a long civilizing process which, by its very nature, renders society progressively more hierarchical.

Voltaire's enthusiasm for the Glorious Revolution, always marginal, was later further muted by his anxiety lest the *philosophes* be perceived as working against the court and governing class. If he is to wage war on superstition and intolerance effectively, the *philosophe*, he believed, must align with the ruler and aristocracy. While he always judged superstition 'le plus horrible ennemi du genre humain', he saw no good reason to oppose monarchs, aristocracy, or social hierarchy in principle. Indeed, there is no example on earth, according to Voltaire, of a true philosopher opposing the will of princes.[93] Disorder, disputes, calamities, turmoil, and upheaval, he maintained, are invariably the fruit of superstition, irrationality, and fanaticism, never philosophers' thoughts.

Following the collapse of Cartesianism and *Malebranchisme*, in the 1720s and 1730s, Maupertuis's and Voltaire's promotion of Locke, Newton, and the 'British model' in France won considerable success.[94] But it never achieved the decisive breakthrough for which they, and allies like Réaumur and, later, Turgot, hoped. Rather a noticeable slackening of enthusiasm for English philosophy and culture set in in the mid 1740s, caused partly by a change in mood following the resumption of the bitter global struggle between England and France after a prolonged interval of peace. After 1745, Anglophilia in France was politically less acceptable than before and soon also less fashionable. At the same time, however much they nourished patriotic pride within Britain, as personalities, neither Locke nor Newton was especially suitable to serve as an iconic hero abroad. Lacking the courtly status of Leibniz, rhetorical skills of Bayle, and literary brilliance of Voltaire, they could be idolized internationally solely for their learned accomplishments.

Where supporters of radical ideas could readily lionize Spinoza and Bayle, turning them into secular saints of philosophy unjustly persecuted by a host of credulous fanatics, inspiring examples to all who reject received thinking and wish to live by reason alone, Locke and Newton were not much of a match for them as role models. Image could of course be tailored to what society required but is hard nevertheless to counterfeit totally, and the reports circulating on the Continent about their unprepossessing personalities were bound to inhibit their lionization there. Newton, undeniably, was an inflexible tyrant who ruthlessly manipulated underlings and colleagues, irritably rebuffing all criticism, including that of Huygens and Leibniz, while Locke's written style and general manner seemed to many pedestrian

[92] Quoted in Pomeau, *Politique de Voltaire*, 40, 182, 185.
[93] [Voltaire], 'La Voix du sage', 427.
[94] Spallanzani, *Immagini*, 50–1; Firode, 'Locke et les philosophes', 58, 63, 71–2.

and prolix to the point of taxing all patience, qualities little admired in aristocratic *ancien régime* France. On top of this, Locke was so vain, Montesquieu was assured by Coste, when in London,[95] he could hardly live without being constantly flattered, a defect Shaftesbury confirmed, ascribing it to his having resided for years in rural places surrounded only by 'des inférieurs'—though Montesquieu was also told by Coste that Locke's treatises on government, which he had not then read, were of great relevance to his own work.[96]

Most problematic of all, Newton's passion for abstruse theology, obsession with alchemy, and speculations in biblical chronology and bizarre esoterica, though all key dimensions of his work, scarcely epitomized the image his British, Dutch, and French supporters sought to foster of a supremely wise and modest experimentalist, the very embodiment of scientific reason and sound sense and religion, someone who always put 'plain facts above mystifying metaphysics'.[97] In Britain, this made scant difference; for there nothing could there withstand the tide of public adulation that surrounded him. His funeral, on 28 March 1727 at Westminster Abbey where he was assigned a resting place of notable prominence, an occasion at which Voltaire was present, was a highly symbolic event, the pall being carried by the Lord High Chancellor, the dukes of Montrose and Roxborough and the earls of Pembroke, Sussex, and Macclesfield, all Fellows of the Royal Society.[98] Newton was praised to the skies as the 'greatest of philosophers, and the glory of the British nation'. But precisely such patriotic fanfares were of little help to spreading his cult abroad at a time of global wars and great power rivalry, though he remained, of course, one of the most influential (if least read) cultural figures of the age.

The high tide of English cultural and intellectual influence in France lasted from the later 1720s for some two decades through to the later 1740s. By 1740, the triumph of the 'British model' in France looked assured and on the verge of becoming as complete as in the Netherlands.[99] However, after 1745, a powerful contrary current set in, as we shall see, and it eventually became clear that Voltaire had, after all, failed to capture the Parisian philosophical avant-garde or consolidate his position as head of the *parti philosophique* in France.[100] From the late 1740s, the French High Enlightenment drifted rather towards monistic philosophy, materialism, and anti-Lockean sensationalism and determinism steered not by Voltaire or the other Anglicizers but by Diderot, d'Alembert, Helvétius, Boulanger, Du Marsais, Boureau-Deslandes, Grimm, and Buffon.

At the heart of the differences between the two vying factions was the 'argument from design', something fundamental to Newtonianism which remained, for Voltaire, an almost sacred tenet but which came to be wholly rejected by Diderot

[95] BL, MS 4282, fo. 125. Collins to Des Maizeaux, Hatfield Peverel, 28 Feb. 1716; Klein, *Shaftesbury*, 65–7.

[96] Montesquieu, *Œuvres complètes*, 988; Schøsler, *Bibliothèque raisonnée*, 57–8.

[97] Porter, *Enlightenment*, 136–8; Westfall, *Life of Isaac Newton*, 111–19, 122–3, 300–4, 311; Clark and Clark, *Newton's Tyranny*, 9, 13, 86–7, 90, 110, 116, 141–2.

[98] Clark and Clark, *Newton's Tyranny*, 142; Westfall, *Life of Isaac Newton*, 312; Barber, 'Newton de Voltaire', 121.

[99] Dziembowski, 'Défense du modèle', 90.

[100] Ibid. 96–7.

and the *encyclopédistes*. Adamant that 'a watch proves a watchmaker', Voltaire battled for the whole of the rest of his long literary, scientific, and philosophical career to rally support for his Newtonian physico-theological creed, holding that the order and harmony of the universe plainly demonstrates a knowing Creator and that matter by itself is, as Newton and Clarke so clearly showed, wholly inert so that, the arguments of the materialists notwithstanding, motion and the active principle can only emanate from God while morality is divinely ordained, the human will free, and thought only divinely superadded to matter, just as 'le sage Loke' maintained. The gulf between the two wings, moderate and radical, proved of course unbridgeable for, as we have seen, these two rival conceptions of enlightenment were grounded philosophically in totally opposed ways and entailed quite different moral, political, social, and intellectual consequences. Nevertheless, Diderot and Voltaire both needed to avoid an open schism and (with the help of their enemies) succeeded in ensuring that this struggle for the very soul of the French High Enlightenment, whatever its wider implications, remained largely screened off from the public and internal to the *parti philosophique* itself.

The stability of the moral and social order, held Voltaire, demands acknowledgement of a benign Creator. What transpires in our universe, he insisted, follows not from the unalterable laws of nature of the 'atheists' but from the will of God, so that (following Locke) even the possibility of miracles must be admitted.[101] Hence Voltaire's unbending maxim that 'if God did not exist, it would be necessary to invent him', though this was actually an old topos in French thought, Bayle attributing to Bodin the remark that if God did not exist the interest of the human race would require men to be ignorant of this truth, 'et qu'ils se persuadassent le contraire'.[102] Though perceptibly more sceptical than Voltaire about the existence of a providential God and divine origin of morality, Montesquieu too insisted on the social and political indispensability of organized religion: if it is not certain there is a God, he once remarked, if philosophy leaves us in some doubt about that, at least 'il faut espérer qu'il y en a un'.[103]

3. *ANGLICISME* AND ANTI-*ANGLICISME* IN THE MID EIGHTEENTH CENTURY

Voltaire, Montesquieu, and Maupertuis, the giants among the French *philosophes* in the mid 1740s, were, in their different ways, all ardent protagonists of the 'British Enlightenment'. Around 1745, the movement which d'Alembert dubbed *anglicisme* was indeed at its zenith, d'Alembert himself frequently extolling Newton and Locke

101 Fichera, *Il Deismo critico*, 89–92, 97; Roe, *Voltaire versus Needham*, 69–71, 75.

102 Roe, *Voltaire versus Needham*, 86; Bayle, *Continuation*, ii. 519.

103 Quoted in Kra, *Religion in Montesquieu's* Lettres persanes, 213.

in these years while the young Diderot joined in with his part translation and part reworking of Shaftesbury's *Inquiry Concerning Virtue* (1699), published in 1745. Somewhat distorting Shaftesbury's thought and firmly aligning at this stage with Voltaire, Diderot, in his notes and preface, highlights the allegedly wide gulf separating Shaftsbury's *théisme* from the atheistic stance of Toland and Tindal—which at that time he himself repudiated, as he puts it, with 'horror'. Shaftesbury's philosophy may be something different from Christianity but (especially in Diderot's version), with its emphasis on an active and beneficent divine Creator, it nevertheless converged, he held, with the 'fondement de toute religion', and hence ultimately with Christianity too.[104]

Philosophically, the critical moment of failure for Voltaire's 'English' strategy occurred between 1745 and 1749 and resulted, seemingly, from the increasing confidence and penetration of the *parti philosophique* of a still publicly reticent but philosophically ambitious countervailing faction descended from the clandestine coteries around Fontenelle and Boulainvilliers. This 'determinist', anti-scriptural, and *matérialiste* grouping included Fréret, Boindin, Mirabaud, Lévesque de Burigny, Vauvenargues, Du Marsais, La Mettrie, and soon also Diderot and d'Alembert besides the aristocratic naturalist Georges-Louis Leclerc, comte de Buffon (1707–88), who is known to have rejected the notion that the human soul is a spiritual substance and become a private materialist already prior to 1739, and, from the mid 1740s, tended to become increasingly anti-Newtonian and anti-Lockean in attitude.[105]

If French educated opinion more generally responded enthusiastically to Voltaire's book expounding the scientific discoveries of Newton in 1738, Buffon was distinctly unimpressed. (Voltaire later covered his copy of Buffon's early volumes of natural history, preserved today in St Petersburg, with equally disparaging comments about the latter's work.) A protracted behind-the-scenes contest between pro- and anti-Newtonian factions began to develop in a variety of milieux including such fashionable Parisian cafés as the Café Gradot much frequented by Maupertuis and the celebrated Café Procope. The latter, opened by a Sicilian in 1689, and originally the home of a mostly literary clientele, during the 1730s also become a favourite of 'philosophical' personalities including again Maupertuis and the 'atheist' Nicolas Boindin (1676–1751). Boindin, reputed 'un des plus beaux parleurs de Paris', and a noted literary scholar, like Fréret, a member of the Académie des Inscriptions, and long a star of the Procope, was especially forthright in argument, as were Diderot and Rousseau who, in the years 1746–50, were also often to be seen there.[106]

Even the Café Procope or Gradot could not be used, though, for undisguised expression of irreligious, materialist, or atheistic ideas. Holding forth in the cafés,

[104] Diderot, *Essai sur le mérite*, 22–4.

[105] Ehrard, *L'Idée*, 176, 182–4; Roger, *Buffon*, 32,43, 438; Landucci, 'Introduction', 42–5.

[106] Terrall, *Man who Flattened*, 22–4; Trousson, *Rousseau*, 143, 197, 200–1.

Boindin apparently veiled his remarks with coded terminology designed to confuse police spies and, when propagating his materialist 'athéisme' more openly, reportedly took to convening open-air discussion groups, in particular in the Luxembourg gardens.[107] Probably the best-known 'apostle' of atheism in Paris in the 1740s, he stood poles apart from Voltaire on almost every issue,[108] the three heroes from whose premisses he had built his system being Descartes, Bayle, and Fontenelle.[109] La Beaumelle, who spent much time at the Procope during 1750, recalled witnessing a heated debate between Boindin and an adversary over the execution of homosexuals, a highly vexed issue at the time in Holland and England as well as France. On that occasion, Boindin maintained that sodomy is no more evil than masturbation and that were it 'contrary to nature', it would have been roundly condemned by all ancient and modern peoples who have respected and venerated the voice of nature, including the Greeks, Persians, and Romans, whereas, actually, homosexuality has been severely condemned and punished only by Christians.[110]

By the mid 1740s Paris had become a vibrant but also fiercely contested intellectual arena where it was progressively harder to sustain the hegemony of Bacon, Boyle, Newton, Locke, and Clarke, owing especially to this behind-the-scenes materialist-determinist intellectual opposition. Those who genuinely esteemed Locke and Newton as the prophets of a philosophical and scientific reform movement capable of engineering a viable conjunction of faith with reason, Nature with supernatural agency, and secular values with ecclesiastical authority, also conceived of the Glorious Revolution and British mixed government as the way to wean monarchy and nobility from divine right and an obsolete metaphysics and recast these in a valid, modernized, more effective form, readily defensible against radical, republican and democratic ideas. However, weakened by Voltaire's long absences from the scene, and Maupertuis's departure for Berlin (1745), as well as the War of the Austrian Succession (1740–8) which pitted France against England, as well as Prussia, the Newtonians lost ground after 1745, as a new generation of *matérialistes* came to the fore and increasingly questioned the Anglophiles' intellectual leadership.

In this, they were influenced by personal ties with older atheistic materialists—d'Alembert, for instance, being close to Du Marsais and Diderot a warm admirer of Buffon.[111] In this way began the complex process of their evolution into 'Nouveaux Spinosistes' as Diderot dubbed what became the hegemonic, directing group of *encyclopédistes*. Before long, Diderot, Helvétius, Boulanger, La Mettrie, and d'Alembert had all effectively abjured Locke's epistemology and moral thought and, even more, Newtonian physico-theology and theory of matter, as well as Voltaire's Creationism and conception of divine providence. They also rejected Locke's notions of mind and 'free will', ideas which had strongly influenced their

[107] Lauriol, *La Beaumelle*, 175–6.

[108] La Mettrie, *L'Homme machine*, 117; Hazard, *European Mind*, 108, 131;Vartanian, *La Mettrie's* L'Homme machine, 229.

[109] Larousse, *Grand Dictionnaire*, ii. 877.

[110] Lauriol, *La Beaumelle*, 176.

[111] Larousse, *Grand Dictionnaire*, vi. 1372.

own early careers,[112] albeit publicly they continued to eulogize Locke, Clarke, and Newton, seeing this as essential to placate court, police, universities, and church.

The tactic of continually invoking Locke and Newton while departing radically from their ideas provided an excellent pretext for rejecting tradition and 'innate ideas' and hence the entire metaphysical apparatus of the past, urging new research, experiment, and further investigation as the path to more and better-grounded knowledge. Did not Voltaire himself insist that with Locke and Newton we possess a completely new framework which renders everything that came before invalid and obsolete? Loudly invoking Locke and Newton, they airily dispensed with any further need to justify their sweeping away the entire body of traditional metaphysics, ethics, and science. Untypical in other ways, the physician La Mettrie was characteristic of the group, at least before fleeing to Berlin in 1748, in regularly invoking Locke while simultaneously subverting Locke's basic positions.[113] Philosophically, 'the materialism of *l'Homme machine*', as one specialist on La Mettrie puts it, 'did not derive from Locke';[114] but rhetorically La Mettrie's repeated appeals to Locke still mattered as a way of neutralizing readers' shock and indignation and placing a fig-leaf over his adoption, in his metaphysics, of a blatant materialism rooted in part in Herman Boerhaave's physiology.[115] Far from reflecting English influence, La Mettrie's conception of nature and physical reality actually reflects that particular conjunction of Dutch and French radical impulses which combined in the later 1740s to unseat the Newtonian Enlightenment.

From the mid 1740s, the avant-garde of the *parti philosophique* turned against physico-theology and Lockean epistemology, repudiating Voltaire's providential Deism and monarchism, and towards materialist, atheistic, and *Spinosiste* doctrines, and perhaps already began to cool in their ardour for English culture more generally, but as yet there was absolutely no reaction against the British political model and mixed monarchy. The Glorious Revolution and the British parliamentary system continued to be admired by virtually the whole of the *parti philosophique* into, and through, the 1750s. While several writers, including La Beaumelle and, after his break with Cardinal Tencin, whose secretary he had been, in 1747, Mably, were already being converted to republicanism in the late 1740s, these still continued to view the Glorious Revolution, and the rise of constitutional monarchy, as the most positive modern development in politics. In his *Observations sur les Grecs* (1749), for example, Mably celebrates the benefits of blending monarchy, aristocracy, and democracy, as exemplified first in ancient Sparta,[116] in his case still at this stage combining this model with the idea of an immutable providential order decreed by a beneficent Creator. In this connection, Mably in 1749 warmly praised Barbeyrac, the foremost popularizer of Locke's political, social, and moral thought in French.

[112] Postigliola, *Città della ragione*, 115, 135–9, 146–8.

[113] Vartanian, *La Mettrie's* L'Homme machine, 62–3; Wellman, *La Mettrie*, 120–6, 149–61.

[114] Vartanian, *La Mettrie's* L'Homme machine, 62.

[115] Ibid. 62–3.

[116] Wright, *Classical Republican*, 41–2.

Political as distinct from philosophical *anglicisme* only began to recede after a fresh wave of Anglophobia swept France in the mid 1750s preceding the outbreak of the Seven Years War in 1756,[117] during which featured a new theme: Britain's imperial arrogance and aggression. By the 1770s, the British political model was as much out of favour with the French intellectual avant-garde as was the Lockean-Newtonian construct, Mably among others having, by then, performed a complete ideological volte-face, and come to regard the British crown as Europe's and the world's foremost 'ennemi de la liberté publique'. His shift from Anglophilia to antipathy towards Britain led to his suggesting the court in London had now so corrupted England, and perfected the arts of bribery and flattery, as to be capable of perverting the constitutional principles of 1688 altogether and perhaps eventually even restoring 'le pouvoir absolu' and producing a new, and no less monstrous, Henry VIII.[118] Hélvetius and Diderot similarly came to believe that England's constitutional 'checks and balances', so admired by Montesquieu, actually encouraged new, more refined forms of manipulation and political corruption.[119]

By the 1770s, Mably had come to see Britain's ascendancy as something that not only oppressed America and Ireland but generated a politics which 'agite, trouble et déchire l'Europe'.[120] Writing to John Adams, during the American Revolution, he proclaimed himself an ardent enthusiast for 'votre heureuse révolution' and advocate of equality, warmly applauding the American breakaway from subjection to England, though not yet wholly won over to the cause of democracy.[121] Not only did he openly encourage the Americans in their Revolution against the British crown and empire, Mably also repeatedly reissued his warnings to the Americans, Poles, French, and even the British themselves not to emulate British institutions, stressing the alleged perils from which 'l'Angleterre est menacée'.[122] Diderot became just as hostile, he too now perceiving Britain as the most oppressive of the colonial powers outside Europe and that which treated the blacks worst.[123] Criticizing Helvétius for remaining, as he saw it, too favourably inclined towards England, the older Diderot held that it was not just in its colonies that Britain was oppressive but also in Scotland and Ireland.[124]

The Glorious Revolution eventually came to be sweepingly rejected by the Radical Enlightenment precisely because it had cemented a powerful new British patriotic consensus, combining elements of modernity with tradition so as to entrench rather than subvert monarchy, aristocracy, imperial sway, and the state church. Earlier an inspiration to writers like Toland, Bolingbroke, Wachter, Hatzfeld, Radicati, Rousset de Missy, La Beaumelle, and Mably, in the end the Glorious Revolution came to be perceived by radical thinkers as basically negative,

[117] Dziembowski, 'Défense du modèle', 90–1.

[118] Mably, *Observations sur le gouvernement*, viii. 382–3.

[119] Ibid. viii. 381–3; Dedeyan, *Diderot*, 341–2, 347–51; Wade, *Structure*, i. 160–1; Wootton, 'Helvétius', 314; Salmon, 'Liberty', 99, 105–6.

[120] Mably, *De la législation*, in *Collection complète*, ix. 2, 15, 32.

[121] Mably, *Observations sur le government*, viii. 340–2, 364–6; Dedeyan, *Diderot*, 348–50.

[122] Mably, *Du gouvernement et des lois de Pologne*, 278.

[123] Ibid.; Firode, 'Locke et les philosophes', 69–70.

[124] Dedeyan, *Diderot*, 347–53.

a process culminating in Condorcet's *Réflexions* of 1792 on the Revolution of 1688 where, as we have seen, he claims the Revolution ended by betraying the very principles of popular sovereignty and natural equality which had originally inspired it. The heirs of the Revolution, according to Condorcet, Diderot, Mably, Helvétius, and others, had ended by condoning the ancient abuse whereby the crown vitiates the constitution with impunity, enhancing the power of privilege while denying the people all legitimate means to assert liberty and curb despotic authority.[125]

The mid and later eighteenth-century French reaction against the Anglophilia of the 1730s and early 1740s, then, developed by stages into a full-scale revolt against everything which Voltaire, Maupertuis, Réaumur, Turgot, and their allies stood for. French *anglicisme* while amply flattering British pride, had, as d'Alembert pointed out, been essentially a critical tool devised by *gens de lettres* seeking to target aspects of their own society which they opposed and hoped to reform, an intellectual device but one which eventually became outmoded, in philosophy and science as early as the late 1740s. It was to certain reformers of thought, natural philosophy, natural history, political thought, and literary affairs, remarked d'Alembert in 1753, alluding to Maupertuis, Réaumur, Montesquieu, and Voltaire, 'that the English nation is principally indebted for its prodigious success among us'.[126] While the French, in his opinion, had continued to outshine their neighbours in matters of taste and design, he entirely agreed that England had for decades surpassed France, indeed continued to do so until a few years before, in the 'great number of excellent philosophers' it had produced and had instructed the French in the use of 'that precious liberty of thought from which reason profits, which some people abuse, and of which fools complain'.[127] But well before 1750, he thought, the relevant lessons had been learnt.

Earlier, in the 1730s and early 1740s, French writers extolled the English with such ardour that our 'eulogies seem to have diminished the old national hatred', he added, 'at any rate on our part'.[128] Yet here, remarked d'Alembert, the French appeared to be somewhat in advance of their neighbours across the Channel, the latter returning remarkably few compliments in exchange for the adulation the French had heaped upon them. 'Cette réserve', mused d'Alembert, in 1753, is it not in reality 'un aveu de notre supériorité?' The two countries were engaged, he thought, in a process of mutual exchange of cultural influences in which the French, having been intellectually 'instruits et éclairés' by the English, were now beginning to rival and perhaps overtake them, especially, he thought, in exact sciences like mathematics and theoretical dynamics (his own particular speciality), while, simultaneously, the English, through more frequently visiting France, had acquired greater aptitude for elegant living, design, and the arts.[129] The French should beware, he joked, lest the English outstrip their teachers in matters of taste, as the French were now overtaking the English in natural philosophy and philosophy.

125 Condorcet, *Réflexions sur la Révolution*, 12–13.

126 D'Alembert, *Mélanges de littérature*, ii. 119 (references are to the 1770 edn. unless otherwise indicated).

127 Ibid. ii. 120.

128 Ibid.; see also Bell, *Cult of the Nation*, 44–7.

129 D'Alembert, *Mélanges de littérature*, ii. 121.

Helvétius may have remained somewhat more positive towards Britain than Diderot, Mably, or d'Holbach,[130] but he too criticized Britain's global role in a way integral to his own increasing radicalism in the 1760s and 1770s. In his *De l'homme* (1773), for example, he asks—as if continuing Shaftesbury's reflections on Britain's contribution to 'enlightenment'—whether, with all its power, prosperity and many advantages, England had in fact, over recent decades, contributed in political, social, and moral thought 'toutes les lumières qu'on devoit attendre d'un peuple aussi libre?' His answer was that, unfortunately, it had not. Rather, its overwhelming maritime, colonial, military, and economic successes had gone to the heads of its people so that now they gave little thought to improving the wider frame of things, or initiating basic change at home or abroad. 'Enivrés de leur gloire', he says, 'les Anglois ne soupçonnent point de défaut dans leur gouvernement actuel.'[131]

After Britain's stunning victories in the mid-century colonial wars, imperial pride and self-congratulation were unsurprising as was the tendency for such global success to encourage a more narrowly national and less self-critical and wide-ranging public psychology than that of the French who had to cope with massive and unprecedented global defeat. Helvétius agreed with d'Alembert and Diderot that it was indeed now the French, not the British, who in social and moral theory were developing what he was to call 'les idées les plus grandes et les plus étendues'. French writers on philosophical topics had become 'plus universellement utiles que les écrivains anglois' not owing to any innate characteristics but primarily because the imperial and cultural contexts were so different. The British still wrote excellent works, 'mais presqu' uniquement applicables à la forme particulière de leur gouvernement aux circonstances présentes et enfin à l'affaire du jour'.[132] The French, by contrast, had vastly less to congratulate themselves about. But France was not so utterly overwhelmed by poverty, ignorance, and superstition, observed Helvétius, or military defeat, that men were reduced to despair, intellects stunted, and philosophy stifled. Rather 'le malheur' was at a sufficiently bearable level to stimulate rather than crush the *philosophes*; and this too, he thought, was in a way an advantage, enabling them to take the lead philosophically and in political theory.[133]

The receding of French *anglicisme* from the mid 1740s was a historical development of fundamental significance which has been very little studied. Doubtless this is in part because most intellectual and general historians (and philosophers) have long taken for granted the supposed primacy of originally English ideas in the making of the western Enlightenment. Were the conventional view about this really correct there should not, of course, have been any receding of English inspiration and influence as the High Enlightenment entered its most creative phase, and numerous are the historians who have implied or assumed that nothing of the kind occurred. According to one scholar, Locke was the 'supreme formative influence on the France of the eighteenth century';[134] according to another,

130 D'Alembert, *Mélanges de littérature*, ii. 344; Wootton, 'Helvétius', 313–15, 347.

131 Helvetius, *De l'homme*, ii. 565.

132 Ibid. ii. 586.

133 Ibid.; Wootton, 'Helvétius', 321.

134 Quoted in Schouls, *Descartes*, 177.

Crane Brinton, 'the importance of Locke for the world view of the Enlightenment can hardly be exaggerated'. 'Bacon, Locke and Newton' were, he asserts, the 'originators, the adventurers in ideas which the French did no more than develop and spread'.[135] Needing to replace the discarded systems of the past, states Peter Gay, the 'men of the Enlightenment constructed a new mystique: they satisfied their need for a representative figure, their craving for a hero, through Isaac Newton'.[136] 'The new currents of thought', agrees Norman Hampson, 'all seemed to flow together in Newton's friend, John Locke' and just as 'Newton had seemed to substitute a rational law of nature for unpredictable and often malevolent forces, Locke appeared to have disclosed the scientific laws of the human mind', as well as laid the foundations for 'toleration' and 'acceptance of the potential equality of man' which would 'allow men to reconstruct society on happier and more rational lines'.[137]

This pervasive assumption of the special and unparalleled pre-eminence of Locke and Newton in the making of the western Enlightenment is part of a long and venerable but also complex and partisan tradition which reaches all the way back to the 1730s. As with many commonplaces, its very simplicity conceals a good deal of oversimplification and distortion. In particular, though rarely pointed out, the more radical (and, after 1745, the dominant) wing of the *parti philosophique*, the Radical Enlightenment, the chief grounding of the modern concepts of toleration, equality, individual freedom, freedom of expression, sexual liberation, and anti-colonialism, shared hardly at all, in reality, in this indeed very widespread cult of Locke and Newton, a fact of overriding importance for a proper understanding of the real character of the western Enlightenment. For the presiding intellectual heroes of the radical *philosophes*, as we shall see, were invariably figures of very different stamp.

This is not to deny that veneration of England, British parliamentary monarchy, and British philosophy, learning, and science continued to permeate society and culture almost throughout eighteenth-century Europe and America. Indeed, the eighteenth century was a century everywhere saturated in Anglophilia. But usually, after 1750, this was a conventional rather than critical way of thinking and, with each passing decade, such attitudes became more specifically the preserve of one branch of the moderate mainstream, and a typical accoutrement of aristocracy, a tendency which itself became socially and politically more conservative as republican, universalistic, and democratic impulses gained in strength. Such moderate and conservative Enlightenment thus came to be powerfully confronted by a Radical Enlightenment, once predominantly Dutch and English but now primarily French in character, which combined materialism and monist philosophy with the view that democracy and equality are the true basis of just social theory and an adequately grounded morality, and popular sovereignty both an achievable goal and something apt to benefit both particular societies and mankind as a whole.[138]

[135] Edwards, *Encyclopedia of Philosophy*, ii. 519, 523.
[136] Gay, *Enlightenment*, ii. 128.
[137] Hampson, *Enlightenment*, 38–40, 97–9, 113.
[138] Wright, *Classical Republican*, 75–7; Rachum, '*Revolution*', 187–9.

15

The Triumph of the 'Moderate Enlightenment' in the United Provinces

1. THE DEFEAT OF DUTCH RADICAL THOUGHT: THE SOCIAL CONTEXT

A wide-ranging Dutch- and French-language movement of Radical Enlightenment arose in the United Provinces, beginning in the early 1670s, characterized (by those who remarked on its existence) as the *Spinosisten or Spinosistes*. In Amsterdam and The Hague but also in other Dutch cities, radical circles formed at that time composed of academics, students, physicians, lawyers, and also at least a handful of the literate but less highly educated non-Latin-reading public. While the evidence remains impressionistic, recorded comments about this urban intellectual phenomenon are numerous enough for us to be reasonably clear that this current grew over the course of around half a century or so, until about 1720, and then, effectively checked, largely receded again.[1]

This is an astounding fact and one of central importance for understanding the history and structure of the western Enlightenment. It is remarkable not least because—apart from his exposition of Descartes—all Spinoza's works, as well as summaries and reworkings of his thought, were definitively banned by decrees of the States General and States of Holland of 1674 and 1678. Of course, one should not suppose that awareness of Spinoza's ideas between the 1670s and the 1720s in the Netherlands relied on conversation and a handful of illicitly printed and sold copies. Assuredly, there were other available sources. If Johannes Colerus' biography of Spinoza, which appeared in Dutch in 1705, failed to circulate widely, research into Dutch library inventories down to 1720 shows that Bayle's long article on Spinoza's life and thought from his *Dictionnaire*, which was published in separate book form as 'Pierre Bayle, *Het Leven van B. de Spinoza*' (Utrecht, 1698) by François Halma (1653–1722), was widely known, indeed one of the most frequently owned books in the country during the early eighteenth

[1] Nieuhoff, *Over Spinozisme*, 40; Israel, *Dutch Republic*, 916–25; Mijnhardt, *Over de Moderniteit*, 23; Mijnhardt, 'Construction', 231–4, 245–62; van Eijnatten, *Liberty and Concord*, 240; Vermij, 'Formation', 189–92.

century, far more so indeed than anything else by Bayle.[2] The Dutch version of Wittichius' *Anti-Spinoza* also circulated widely.

Among the first to comment on the spread of Spinozism in Dutch society, in September 1678, a little more than a year after Spinoza's death, was the vicar-general of the Dutch Catholic Church in the years 1661–86, Johannes van Neercassel. Reporting to Rome about the clandestine publication of Spinoza's *Opera posthuma* at Amsterdam a few months before, Neercassel observes that the only real effect of the recently introduced States of Holland ban on Spinoza's books had been to cause his fame—and the price of his works—to soar, albeit not among 'our Catholics' who, he assures the Vatican, remained scrupulous custodians of the faith, thoroughly detesting all profane novelties. Rather Spinoza's reputation was spreading, he says, specifically among those many Protestants in Holland who presumed to judge questions of faith and religion not according to Christ's teaching but by way of 'philosophy and the inane fallacy of the method of the geometricians, following worldly principles and Euclid', on the basis of reason, that is, and material and mathematical evidence.[3]

Two years later the Utrecht regent and Cartesian Lambert van Velthuysen (1622–85) reported that 'many men who are neither wicked nor stupid' had abandoned their faith in a providential God who presides over his Creation in consequence of Spinoza's arguments.[4] Still clearer was the Amsterdam Sephardic philosopher and physician Isaac Orobio de Castro (1620–87), writing in 1684: for he expressly admits to having been mistaken in his earlier prognosis that Spinoza's impiety would not have a wide impact. Previously, he had judged Spinoza's philosophy too deficient for the learned and too abstruse for ordinary folk. Experience, however, had proved him wrong: not only had some erudite men been swayed by Spinoza's teaching but also not a few among the common people had been convinced by his 'pestilential dogmata'.[5]

One of the chief contemporary assessments of the status of Spinozism as a movement in Dutch society is that of Balthasar Bekker, in his outline summary of general church history of 1686. Here Bekker summarizes Spinozism under six core articles, adding that 'one has to admit that Spinoza's opinions have spread and become rooted all too far and too much in all parts and social orders, so that they have infected many of the best minds, including among the residences of the great; and that people of very ordinary status have been enraptured by them and brought to godlessness, as if to something divine. In consequence, the number of those who profess religion and religious doctrine only to conform outwardly, and rather from human than divine considerations, increases; and if that continues, God help us, what a blow through the heavy fall of such a mass of people will be given to the frame of God's House.'[6]

2 Israel, *Dutch Republic*, 924; Leeuwenburgh, 'Meten is weten', 82, 84.

3 Neercassel to Cardinal Francesco Barberini, 13 Sept. 1678, in Orcibal, 'Les Jansénistes face à Spinoza', 467; Israel, *Radical Enlightenment*, 293–4.

4 Velthuysen, *Tractatus de cultu*, dedication.

5 Orobio de Castro, *Certamen philosophicum*, 389.

6 Bekker, *Kort Begryp*, 39; Koelman, *Het Vergift*, preface p. 9.

In 1687, the heterodox popular theologian, basket-maker, and shopkeeper Willem Deurhoff (1650–1717) added his observation, from first-hand experience, that besides sophisticated libertines, some humble, and even very simple, folk had become attracted to Spinoza's doctrines.[7] His testimony is especially relevant in that Deurhoff figured prominently in the theologico-philosophical anti-church culture which proliferated so luxuriantly in the Netherlands in the late seventeenth century in open defiance of the orthodoxies of the Reformed, and other main confessions, and was someone who read a good deal of Descartes, Geulincx, and Spinoza in translation. A local spiritual leader, he was, in a sense, a direct competitor to the dead philosopher in the contest to sway this new constituency of independently minded, self-reliant, and potentially freethinking individuals who desired to judge the truth about God, faith, and religion for themselves, on the basis of 'certain evidence', without being directed by authority or any established church. He knew the mood and thoughts of the many humble but independent-minded in Dutch society.

The staunch Calvinist preacher Jacobus Leydekker, in his *Dr Bekkers Philosophise Duyvel* of 1692, a work which argues that the Bekker controversies then agitating Dutch urban society so severely abundantly proved the dangers of giving too much licence to modern philosophy, likewise concludes that Spinozistic atheism was spreading in the Netherlands, although he says especially among the affluent, the poor having no access to his books.[8] In 1695, introducing the Dutch rendering of Wittichius' *Anti-Spinoza*, the Cocceian minister David Hassel exclaimed, 'who Spinoza was and what heresy he followed, I do not believe can be unknown to anybody. His books are to be found everywhere and are, in this restless age, owing to their novelty sold in nearly all book-shops.'[9] Still more remarkable is Hassel's comment about the social penetration of Spinozism: 'and Spinoza left behind a no smaller and no less prolific crowd of followers than the best Greek Sophist, adherents who, with their wanton nature and character, and driven only by the itching of their restless intellects and thirst for fame, strive single-mindedly at inculcating the ruinous doctrines of their new master into everyone, spreading them far and wide. Moreover, they succeeded, for within a short time this venom has spread almost through most parts of the Christian world and daily it grows and creeps further and further.'[10]

The Utrecht bookseller Halma justified publishing his translation of Bayle's account of Spinoza in Dutch in 1698 by pointing out that the banned second part of the Spinozist novel *Philopater*, brought out at Amsterdam the year before, imparted a further boost to the already widespread Spinozist following so that a powerful antidote was needed.[11] In 1700, the Zeeland preacher Willem Spandaw (1667–1708), briefly reviewing the entire history of the world's 'godlessness' running from the Greek thinkers through the Italian Renaissance to Vanini, concludes by saying: 'however

[7] Deurhoff, *Voorleeringen*, p. 5.

[8] Leydekker, *Dr Bekkers Philosophise Duyvel*, 117–19.

[9] Hassel, 'Voorreden', p. i; De Vet, 'Spinoza en Spinozisme', 13.

[10] Hassel, 'Voorreden' p. i.

[11] Halma, *Aanmerkingen*, 20, 26, 78.

no-one brought godlessness to a higher point, putting it on the throne and erecting its banners everywhere than the cunning Spinoza. France, England—the cadet-school of monstrous opinions, yes the Netherlands and also other lands produce a vast horde who venerate him as something "marvelous". The greatest minds have imbued his views and without fear openly reveal themselves to be atheists.'[12] If impiety is age-old, he added, Spinoza had given new shape to philosophical godlessness and was nowadays venerated in both Holland and neighbouring countries by whole crowds who embrace his ideas and 'fearlessly and openly proclaim themselves unbelievers'.[13] In a book published during the van Leenhof controversy of May 1704, the Enkhuizen preacher Franciscus Burmannus, son of the famous theologian Frans Burman, agreed that Spinoza's ideas were spreading widely in Dutch society and that 'it is all too true that there are already many Spinozists, that is wicked and vile atheists, in our country'. In 'some of the main cities', disastrously in his opinion, 'meetings of these vermin of the state, and all sound morality, are held so that young people who are still unfocused and ignorant are being unwittingly indoctrinated with Spinoza's principles and his atheism. If measures are not taken soon we will greatly regret it.'[14]

The next year another Reformed preacher, Joannes Aalstius, at Beverwijk, declared unrelenting war on the freethinkers. Explaining why he was proceeding in such an outspoken manner, he expressed a strong sense of alarm and urgency: 'we must under [Christ's] banner take the field against the unbelievers and free-thinkers, and use every means to make them abandon their wicked ideas and ways, and submit to the truth. We will not have much difficulty in tracing them to their hiding places, since this tribe, at present, proliferates massively, and as a result has become so bold that they not only reveal themselves in their lifestyle but also speech and text.'[15] He explicitly identifies this army of freethinkers, encountered, if not throughout, then certainly in large parts of the Dutch urban context as 'Spinozisten', claiming Spinoza's adherents openly boast of their superior grasp not just of philosophy but of things generally. Keeping quiet would merely render the 'Spinozists' still bolder and more confident, a worry exacerbated by a widespread and growing perception that despite the many refutations that had appeared, including Bayle's, these had not, either singly or collectively, actually performed the task of demolishing Spinoza.[16]

Some years later, in the 1716 edition of his post-biblical Jewish history, Bayle's friend, Jacques Basnage observed that Spinoza left 'une secte qui a adopté ses principes' but that it was impossible to say how numerous it was because it consists of people dispersed in different places 'qui ne sont ni corps ni société'; but one could not simply ignore those who now venerate the dead Spinoza, especially since often 'c'étoient des artisans'.[17] Also in 1716, Christoph August Heumann, examining

12 Spandaw, *De Bedeckte Spinosist Ontdekt*, 'Opdragt'. 13 Ibid., 'Dedicatie'.

14 Burmannus, *'t Hoogste Goed der Spinozisten*, 20; Wielema, *March*, 81.

15 Aalstius, *Inleiding*, 4–5. 16 De Vet, 'Spinoza en Spinozisme', 15–16.

17 Basnage, *Histoire des Juifs*, ix. 1035; Leemans, *Het Woord*, 297.

Bayle's objections (in note 't' to his long article on Spinoza in his *Dictionnaire*) to the claim that Spinoza's 'sectateurs soient en grand nombre', made in Stouppe's *La Religion des Hollandois* (1673)—the first known account of Spinozism as a movement—rejected Bayle's conclusion that Stouppe was wrong.[18] In saying Spinoza had 'un grand nombre de sectateurs, qui sont entièrement attachés à ses sentiments', Stouppe had perhaps exaggerated; but Bayle gave the wrong impression in denying this, concludes Heumann, citing the famous Dutch professor of theology Herman Alexander Roëll (1653–1718), who had vigorously contradicted Bayle on this point, declaring 'Spinosam tota armenta (in Belgica nostra) sequuntur ducem' [in our Netherlands whole herds follow Spinoza as leader].[19]

In 1719, more than forty years after Spinoza's death, the Zeeland minister Cornelis Tuinman (1659–1728) confirmed that the number of 'Spinosisten groeit leider aan in ons gantsche Vaderland' [Spinozists increases unfortunately in our whole Fatherland].[20] This continuing dissemination was helped, he alleged, by the insidious duplicity of the dissident theologian Pontiaan van Hattem (1645–1706) who, like van Leenhof, had supposedly camouflaged the new popular Spinozism in Christian-sounding phrases as was manifest, he maintained, from the recent compilation of van Hattem's writings entitled *De Val van's Wereldts Af-God* (The Hague, 1718), clandestinely edited and published by the remarkable Jacob Roggeveen (1659–1729), discoverer of Samoa and, in April 1722, of Easter Island. A self-confessed former Spinozist, Roggeveen claims, however, in his preface to have been brought back to religion precisely by van Hattem.[21]

Tuinman complained about the spread of Hattemism and the inefficient manner in which Roggeveen's edition of van Hattem's writings had been suppressed by the States of Zeeland.[22] Publishing a reply to Tuinman, Roggeveen while conceding that Spinoza was an 'atheist' insisted on major differences between Spinoza's and van Hattem's ideas, championing the latter. But he also defended Spinoza, praising his ethical and social theories which buttressed, he held, an irreproachable morality.[23] A pivotal figure in the propagation of Hattemism, Roggeveen's views about that creed, and also Spinozism, are not without a certain social relevance: Roggeveen, when not at sea, reportedly spent most of his time lounging in Middelburg coffee-houses, convenient terrain for spreading seditious views which he did, according to the Reformed consistory, 'like an instrument of the Devil'.[24]

Finally, in 1724, reviewing the recently published history of classical pagan philosophy by Jean Lévesque de Burigny (1692–1785) in his *Bibliothèque ancienne et moderne*, a journal read all over Europe, Le Clerc concurred in Lévesque's statement that Spinoza, however pernicious, had 'attiré bien de gens après lui', a remark

[18] Heumann, *Acta philosophorum*, iv (1716), 650.

[19] Ibid., i. 651; Schröder, 'Spinozam tota armenta', 157.

[20] Tuinman, *Korte Afschetzing*, 13.

[21] Ibid. 7–8; Vermij, *Secularisering*, 72–3; Wielema, *March*, 172–4; van Eijnatten, *Liberty and Concord*, 42–3.

[22] Tuinman, *Korte Afschetzing*, 7.

[23] Roggeveen, 'Voor-rede' to vol. ii and 'voor-rede' to vol. iii, p. 3 of van Hattem, *Den Val van 's-Wereldts Af-God*; Wielema, *March*, 195.

[24] Wielema, *March*, 193–4.

which presumably applied to the Netherlands as well as France, as Lévesque had recently resided there for much of 1720.[25] Undoubtedly, then, the penetration of Spinozism into Dutch culture between the 1670s and the 1720s, especially initially, was faster and deeper than historians have tended to appreciate. There were more, and more complicated, controversies about Spinoza and Spinozism in Holland than in neighbouring countries. By around 1700, though, something comparable, the signs are, was beginning also in France and Germany. Whereas twenty years before, noted the Dresden scholar Valentin Loescher (1673–1749) in his theological journal in 1701, in Germany men heard with amazement about the outpouring of 'Hobbes, Houtuyn, Spinoza, Acosta, Beverland and their writings' in the Netherlands, there being at that time nothing comparable in Germany, now the German situation was so dire, he admonished, that even Holland was beginning to look pious by comparison.[26] And if this was an exaggeration, German Spinozism being largely confined to the academic context, what was called 'Spinozism' in Germany was obviously spreading.

No doubt it was hardly to be expected that the extraordinary intellectual vitality of the Dutch radical thought between the 1660s and the death of Bayle, in 1706, could be sustained indefinitely. After van Leenhof's death, in 1713, there were no more Dutch or Dutch-based radical thinkers of much stature, apart from Mandeville who lived in London and wrote in English. But there remained several other active propagators and two truly major radical publicists, writing in French, the utopian novelist and author of the notorious *Voyages de Jacques Massé* (*c*.1714), Tyssot de Patot, and someone who exerted a still wider impact internationally—the *libraire* and editor Jean-Frédéric Bernard (1683–1744). This Bernard developed into a particularly dexterous amplifier of Spinoza and Bayle and one who worked on an impressive scale. Bayle had taught readers that there are circumspect but effective ways to propagate subversive ideas; but few succeeded in continuing his one-man quest as skilfully and successfully as the (until very recently) long neglected and ignored Bernard.[27] This Bernard, son of a Reformed *pasteur* originally from near Marseilles, entered the Dutch book trade in the first decade of the eighteenth century as the Amsterdam factor of the 'société des libraires de Genève'.[28] Complimented by Frederick the Great's secretary Jordan, who got to know him while touring the Amsterdam bookshops, in 1734, as a *libraire* possessed of both intellect and erudition, he described him as someone who 'aime peut-être trop l'étude pour son négoce', implying, given the sort of study he was involved with, that in his case, love of profit yielded not just to love of scholarship but also to his personal crusade to liberate mankind from slavery to superstition.[29]

[25] De Vet, 'Spinoza en Spinozisme', 3.
[26] Quoted in Krakauer, *Zur Geschichte des Spinozismus*, 21–2.
[27] Wade, *Clandestine Organization*, 209.
[28] Van Eeghen, *Amsterdamse boekhandel*, iii. 18–19, v. 89, 120.
[29] Cited ibid. iii. 19; see also Häseler, *Wanderer*, 86.

His anonymous and overtly anti-Christian *Réflexions morales, satiriques et comiques, sur les mœurs de notre siècle* (1711), published purportedly at 'Cologne' by 'Pierre Marteau' but, in fact, covertly at Amsterdam, was a work which, as has been pointed out, almost certainly served—along with Marana's *L'Espion turc* (1684)—as a model for Montesquieu's *Lettres persanes* (1721).[30] These fictitious letters from an imagined Persian philosopher touring Europe are both earlier and considerably more radical, if also less polished, than Montesquieu's book. The text strongly savours of Bayle, especially the idea of the 'virtuous atheist', and expresses a radical standpoint on a wide range of social, religious, and intellectual issues.[31] The *Réflexions morales* were followed by his notably free translation of the *De peccato originali* 'du fameux Adrien Beverland' which appeared, under the title *Histoire de l'état de l'homme dans le péché originel*, at Amsterdam in 1714 and was reissued in 1731. Here, Bernard deliberately sharpens Beverland's attack on theologians, holding that universal ignorance has created a system in which 'la superstition devint un art' by which the few govern the many leading them as if they were children.[32] In 1730, he published his hard-hitting *Dialogues critiques et philosophiques*.[33]

Meanwhile, Bernard helped edit the *Nouvelles littéraires contenant ce qui se passe de plus considérable dans la République des Lettres* (12 vols., 1715–20), published in Amsterdam by Henri de Sauzet (*c*.1686–1754),[34] who, like Bernard, was a private scholar as well as publisher. He was also a correspondent of the leading Huguenot editor in London, Pierre Des Maizeaux, a close ally of Anthony Collins. Among other works, de Sauzet published Sallengre's *Mémoires de littérature* of 1715, and the Abbé de La Bléterie's *Histoire de l'empereur Jovien* (1735), with its extracts from the works of Julian the Apostate, later one of Gibbon's chief sources on Julian, which appeared in Amsterdam anonymously.[35] Among other projects on which Bernard and de Sauzet collaborated were the *Histoire critique des journaux* (Amsterdam, 1734), supposedly by Denis François Camusat, and the *Bibliothèque françoise, ou Histoire littéraire de la France* (1723–46) which appeared first under Bernard's name until 1730 and then under de Sauzet's.[36]

Although he seems not to have worked with The Hague radical publishers and editors Charles Levier, Thomas Johnson, Saint-Hyacinthe, and Sallengre, Bernard did collaborate closely with the radical-minded engraver Bernard Picart (1673–1733), notably on the most important and best-known of his projects, the monumental *Cérémonies et coutumes religieuses de tous les peuples du monde* (13 vols., Amsterdam, 1723–43).[37] This immense undertaking, lavishly illustrated by Picart, was one of the most ambitious and impressive, as well as subtly subversive, publications of the Early Enlightenment and one on which, between 1721 and 1733, Picart spent much

30 Jacob, *Radical Enlightenment*, 212.
31 Bernard, *Réflexions morales*, 22–3, 189.
32 [Beverland], *État de l'homme*, 5–6, 19, 22, 45; Benítez, *Face cachée*, 20, 68 n.; Conlon, *Siècle*, iii. 114.
33 Conlon, *Siècle*, iii. 33.
34 Van Eeghen, *Amsterdamse boekhandel*, iii. 108; Berkvens-Stevelinck, *Prosper Marchand*, 113, 206.
35 Bowersock, *Julian the Apostate*, 6.
36 Van Eeghen, *Amsterdamse boekhandel*, iii. 107–8.
37 Ibid. ii. 122, 170–1, iv. 41–2; Graesse, *Trésor des livres*, ii. 104; Jacob, *Radical Enlightenment*, 212.

of his time, as did another luminary of the Amsterdam Huguenot publishing world, Bernard's collaborator Antoine Augustin Bruzen de La Martinière (1662–1746), an expert on the French book trade and censorship who also held radical opinions and who, in 1736, asserted in print that black slavery existed 'to the shame of the human race'.[38] This key publication also subsequently appeared in an English version *The Ceremonies and Religious Customs of the Various Nations of the Known World* (7 vols., London, 1733–4) and in 1754 in German.

Much used by the marquis d'Argens to describe the Chinese rites in his *Lettres chinoises* a few years later,[39] Bernard's, Picart's, and Bruzen de La Martinière's *Cérémonies et coutumes religieuses* was designed to combat superstition and advance toleration, religious scepticism, republican ideas, hostility to ecclesiastical authority, and especially knowledge of non-European peoples and religions, by describing in detail and vividly illustrating the vast array of organized cults, doctrines, and religious practices existing in the world.[40] Though a costly, seemingly respectable undertaking, numerous remarks gently insinuate the editors' subversive aims: 'are all these different forms of worship, all these romantic notions', asks Bernard, citing the infinite forms of human idolatry in the first volume, 'less agreeable to the Supreme Being than the infidelity of an Atheist? The matter will admit of dispute,' he concludes, citing 'the celebrated Bayle' as asserting that atheism is less offensive to God than idolatry.[41]

Discussion of the Canadian Indians in the first volume provided the editors with an opportunity to draw attention to Lahontan's ideas, much as, when dealing with Muhammad, in the fifth, they adduce the more subversive side of Boulainvilliers. Among the themes illustrated by Picart with engravings executed for the series in the early 1720s was the alleged divorce ceremony of the Canadian Hurons included as part of a wider reportage of Lahontan's comments on the Indians' easygoing attitude to sex and casual style of marriage.[42] One of the more spectacular examples of Picart's purely imaginative work highlights what Lahontan says about the offerings and ceremonies surrounding the Huron cult of 'l'Esprit Universel' or the 'Grand esprit, otherwise known as Kitchi-Mautou'.[43] But if much was at least semi-fictitious, there was also a great deal of carefully researched material including objective and unprecedentedly accurate representations of contemporary Jewish life in Amsterdam. The Mennonites and Socinians too were given their due: characteristically, Bernard inserts into the fourth volume, published in 1736, an anti-Trinitarian *Dissertation* recounting the practices of the 'Polish Brethren', based on an actual Polish Socinian text, in Latin, composed in the year 1642, entrusted to him, Bernard reports, by 'un savant unitaire'.[44]

[38] Seeber, *Anti-Slavery Opinion*, 26–7. [39] Minuti, 'Orientalismo', 898–9, 901.

[40] Israel, *Dutch Republic*, 684, 1040, 1048; Israel, *Radical Enlightenment*, i. 724; Artigas-Menant, *Secret des clandestins*, 35–6, 41–2.

[41] [Bernard], *Cérémonies et coûtumes religieuses*, i. 8–9; *Ceremonies and Religious Customs*, i. 12.

[42] *Ceremonies and Religious Customs*, i. 58.

[43] Ibid. iii. 80; [Bernard], *Cérémonies et coûtumes religieuses*, i. 53–4.

[44] Skrzypek, 'Libertinisme polonais', 515–16.

A great and incorrigible publicist, ideologue, and collator who combined wide reading of a non-academic kind with an unrivalled knowledge of the book trade, Bernard, together with Bruzen de La Martinière, was also an important link connecting the clandestine worlds of Paris and Amsterdam (as well as Geneva), notably through his publishing collections of clandestine manuscripts obtained from Paris, his *Dissertations mêlées sur divers sujets* (Amsterdam, 1740), among other pieces, including the first printed version of Mirabaud's *Opinions des anciens sur le monde*.[45] In quiet, circumspect ways, Bernard regularly defended both Bayle and Spinoza, ridiculing Houtteville, for instance, in his review of the latter's *La Religion chrétienne prouvée par les faits* (1722).[46] When, in 1728, discussing the French translation (1717) of Clarke's *A Demonstration*, a work greatly esteemed by Le Clerc and later Voltaire, Bernard styles Spinoza 'le plus célèbre défenseur de l'Athéisme de notre tems', summing up his teaching as being that there is no plurality of substances and that the material world, in its entirety and all its parts, 'est un Être existant par lui-même, et qu'il n'y a point d'autre Dieu que l'Univers',[47] a fair summary, seemingly, of Bernard's own view.

In the 1720s and 1730s there were indubitably numerous Spinozists and *Baylistes* among the student body as well as the publishing, bookselling, and teaching professions in the United Provinces. Yet the general trend in Dutch culture and society militated increasingly against their way of thinking and during the second quarter of the century, the Dutch moderate mainstream, with the aid of Orangism, the churches, schools, universities, and welfare institutions, decisively defeated and stifled the radical challenge. This rapid receding of Spinozism is perhaps best explicable as part of a wider process of cultural adjustment and realignment in the Dutch Republic during the first half of the eighteenth century which saw the rapid decline, and soon virtual extinction, also of most of the other fringe movements characteristic of the later Dutch Golden Age, including the withering of the Collegiant movement at Amsterdam and Rotterdam.[48] What occurred, in other words, was a general reversal of the spectacular growth during the last decades of the seventeenth century of a whole spectrum of semi-underground popular urban, lay religious splinter groups, such as the Deurhovians at Amsterdam, the 'Hebrews' in Zeeland, Hattemism in Zeeland and parts of South Holland, and the Collegiants, their appeal lying in their regular discussion groups, in private homes, in which literate, independent-minded, but mostly not very highly educated people, often artisans or shopkeepers, could unburden themselves of their views in an intimate milieu of high moral earnestness.[49]

Viewed as a cultural and social phenomenon, the proliferation of these various groups, including Spinozism, was certainly the direct result of spreading dissatisfaction and frustration at the overly tradition bound, rigid, and unresponsive posture of the Dutch Reformed Church and the other main churches in the late seventeenth

45 *La Lettre clandestine*, 3 (1994), 357.

46 [Bernard], *Bibliothèque françoise*, 11 (1728), 341.

47 Ibid. 12 (1728), 291–2.

48 Van Eijnatten, *Liberty*, 45, 181; Wielema, *March*, 203.

49 Wielema, *March*, 143–4, 147, 195–6; van Eijnatten, *Liberty*, 40, 42, 67.

century. Stuck in a groove as it were, and excessively absorbed in the confessional polemics of the past, as well as the split between Voetians and Cocceians within the public church, the main churches had been unable to meet the needs of an urban culture moving away from confessional polemics and seeking to come to terms with the newly emerging culture of toleration, new kinds of theology, philosophy, and science. All these spiritual currents reflected a strong and comprehensive awareness of the importance of recent intellectual developments and, perhaps, above all, Cartesianism, much of the attraction of which lay in its promising ordinary folk great things from philosophy, asserting in easily read vernacular language books that it was the Cartesians who could unlock the door to true knowledge and a correct understanding of Scripture. If Cartesianism lay at the root of the Bekker controversies of 1691–4 over whether Satan, magic, and witchcraft really existed, Cartesian philosophy was also proclaimed the key, in vernacular medical works like those of Cornelis Bontekoe and Heidenryk Overcamp, not just to a general reformation of medicine and surgery but to improved lifestyle and even to longer life. In their quest to engage with these new influences, most of the splinter groups, and by no means only the Hattemists and Bredenburg faction among the Collegiants, while firmly rejecting Spinoza's 'atheism' and determinism tended to nurture a much more positive view of his moral philosophy and social ideas and hence encouraged exploration of Spinozism.

But the deep dissatisfaction which caused the post-1670 proliferation also explains the post-1720 reversal of the process. For the Dutch Reformed Church and mainstream urban culture as a whole changed fundamentally during the early eighteenth century, spurred by new social pressures, especially rapid economic decline, and urban decay. If the proliferation of heterodox religious sects and philosophical coteries reflects a prior expansion of the Dutch urban context and literacy in the late Golden Age, the post-1720 decline of the Dutch urban separatist movements, including Spinozism, seems to have ensued from a broad cultural shift driven by the severely negative consequences of economic and demographic decline on the Dutch urban landscape.[50] The general reversal of the factors which had previously powered the Dutch urban expansion was chiefly caused by the sustained bout of hugely expensive warfare in which the Republic engaged between 1688 and 1713 in its efforts to block the expansionism and mercantilism of Louis XIV, and severe disruption of Dutch shipping and overseas trade that followed, made worse by Britain's—but also France's, Sweden's, and Prussia's—increasing success in wresting the initiative away from the Dutch in many markets both in Europe and overseas. The resulting loss of dynamism and momentum of Dutch overseas trade and urban industry set in motion a general process of urban decline. Between 1713 and 1740, the contraction of the Dutch cities, with the textile cities of Haarlem and Leiden well to the fore, was

[50] Israel, *Dutch Republic*, 1006–12; Israel, *Dutch Primacy*, 399–402; De Vries and van der Woude, *First Modern Economy*, 681–2.

both the principal factor shaping Dutch society and the chief influence on Dutch intellectual culture.[51]

At the same time, much of the Dutch populace grew more resentful of the rule of their regent oligarchy while the court in London became increasingly dissatisfied with the Dutch Republic as an ally and prop to British power.[52] This domestic political disaffection—as abundantly shown by the pamphlets of the 1747–8 Revolution—was again chiefly the result of the post-1713 decay of trade, shipping, and industry. Here was a wide-ranging, comprehensive process of decline creating for the first (but not the last) time in European history a predominantly urban society with high levels of affluence and literacy which was being relentlessly squeezed by loss of prosperity, trade, shipping, and markets, contracting urban industry, rising unemployment, and loss of specialized skills, if not yet large-scale destitution and pauperism.[53] Again and again, during the 1747–8 disturbances, the citizenry and their leaders cited the withering of employment in the textile workshops of Amsterdam, Haarlem, and Leiden as the foremost social issue fuelling their disgruntlement.

The urban populace had long been inured to rule by a narrow oligarchy which had become almost hereditary in character, and deemed itself unaccountable to the citizenry, but regent high-handedness began to look conspicuously more blatant, corrupt, and unaccountable in the new circumstances. Urban decay generated a growing awareness, and criticism, of regent profiteering from the municipal lands, buildings, and jobs they controlled politically, as well as abuse in administering the tax-farms and underassessing of their own fortunes on the tax rolls. Like the deterioration of the army and navy, and the economic decline itself, the corruption of regent government encouraged the notion, widespread in the Republic in the decades after 1720, that all states, however successful, are subject to decay and erosion of their basic principles which can then only be restored by concerted effort and with great difficulty. Many drew the conclusion that the all too visible decline of their cities could be reversed only by a moral, social, and political 'revolution' and especially a return to first values and principles. One of the Dutch pamphlets published in 1747 repeatedly invokes Voltaire's *Henriade* in this context, emphasizing Voltaire's view that all states are subject to decay, and a falling away from the *principes* on which their greatness rested, and that only an outstanding leader, like Henri IV after the Wars of Religion, in France, can then lead the way to putting things right.[54] General revival was understood to mean in the first place moral restoration based on godly values linked to a broadly religious agenda.[55]

[51] De Jongste, *Onrust*, 11–64; Israel, *Dutch Primacy*, 359–404; Kloeck and Mijnhardt, *1800: Blueprints*, 31–4, 39–41, 162–4; Israel, *Dutch Republic*, 998–1118.

[52] Israel, *Dutch Republic*, 994–6; Palmer, *Age*, i. 39.

[53] Israel, *Dutch Primacy*, 377–404; Israel, *Dutch Republic*, 998–1018; Prak, *Gezeten burgers*, 94–5; Mijnhardt, 'Dutch Enlightenment', 207–10.

[54] *De Eerste en Voornaamste Oorzaken* (Knuttel 1775), 4–5, 12–13, 17, 27; De Jongste, 'Restoration', 57.

[55] Mijnhardt, 'Construction', 232; Mijnhardt, 'Dutch Enlightenment', 212.

This changed Dutch urban and social context in turn explains the fundamentally new element in the Dutch mainstream Enlightenment of the mid eighteenth century, and the Revolution of 1747–8, namely, the intervention of the common people as the chief agent in social debate and politics. The much greater role of the people is certainly the most conspicuous difference between the Dutch 'revolution' of 1747–8 and the Glorious Revolution of 1688, and chief ground of its special relevance to students of the Enlightenment today. For while the Revolution of 1688–9 was undoubtedly a greater turning point in history and great power politics, and encouraged thinking in terms of 'revolutions', no one could claim the common people, popular opinion, or ideas of popular sovereignty had much to do with it other than in the minds of a few radicals. Dramatically different was the Dutch 'revolution' of 1747–8. For the first time in the western world, the common people clearly and indisputably occupied centre stage from first to last, or as some shocked commentators expressed it in 1748, 'commence à régler les affaires des Provinces-Unies', much as the 'insolent Janissaries' dictated the decisions of the Ottoman Porte.[56] The 'common people', it suddenly dawned on contemporaries, far from being merely passive were, at least in an urban context, an extremely powerful and active shaping force.

Absolute economic decline, deindustrialization, and loss of work generated an unprecedented psychological and social crisis which deeply affected a predominantly literate, religiously very plural urban population. The answer to such problems, the urban populace seem to have felt consciously and unconsciously, was no longer the confessional polemics and doctrinal preoccupations of the past but a reformed and revived religious culture of Protestant consensus, convergence, and moral authority, accompanied by a strengthening of social support, guilds, and poor relief. The link between religious and economic revival seemed clear to most contemporaries: prosperity would return with God's favour. Crowds demonstrating in Amsterdam, Haarlem, and Leiden, and in many smaller towns, during the Revolution, though driven by economic frustration (and fear of the French) compounded by resentment at the shortcomings of regent government, expressed their exasperation in significant part also in theological terms, airing long-established prejudices, certainly, but, more frequently, yearning for a broad religious reawakening, more social consensus, and a stronger social discipline.

Hence, during the upheaval of 1747–8, calls for more Reformed preachers of the 'old study', that is authoritarian Voetians, to help restore the country's moral fibre and curb corruption, as well as revive the Republic's lagging military and naval strength, were countered by pamphlets warning against sowing division, hatred, and intolerance; the solution was to balance the impulse for more Voetian guidance against the Cocceian tendency and build on compromise. It was strongly urged that Amsterdam should reintroduce a formalized, automatic balance of alternating

[56] Raynal, *Histoire du stadhoudérat*, 208.

preaching appointments, 'so that one half [of the Reformed preachers] should be from the old, and the other half those of the new or Cocceian study', as was the practice at Utrecht, so as permanently to defuse the theological clash between 'Voetians' and 'Cocceians'.[57]

Restoring the country's moral fibre was almost universally considered the key to arresting the country's decline, the link between moral renewal, religious rectitude, and the welfare of the citizenry seeming clear to most. It was an impulse that also lent an unparalleled urgency and intensity to the quickening Dutch moderate mainstream Enlightenment, enabling it to become culturally heavily dominant after around 1720. Calls for a broad toleration, irenicism, and reconciliation of (especially) the Protestant churches, including to a significant extent even the Mennonites and Collegiants—and in guild and militia contexts even to a degree the Catholics—became closely tied to a new insistence on the Bible being God's Word and the key to comprehending divine providence and the Almighty's governance of the cosmos. This heightened pressure for more unity within the Reformed Church and more harmony between all the churches was assisted by a marked softening of the confessional polemics of the past and the triumphant progress of the 'argument from design' as the centrepiece of a new shared Christian consciousness which simultaneously weakened confessional dogmatism and squeezed out Spinozism.

The remarkable sway of physico-theological books in eighteenth-century Holland, in some cases Leibnizio-Wolffian as well as Newtonian in flavour, has led one recent historian to comment that the 'ultimately successful campaign against the Cartesian radicals was organized not by the orthodox Voetians, but by moderate philosophers and theologians'.[58] This seems to be correct except that the new irenicism of the early eighteenth century, often inspired by the tolerant, and originally Cartesian, Cocceian 'consensus theology', developed in the late seventeenth century by such theologians as Salomon van Til (1643–1713) at Dordrecht, and by Röell first at Franeker and later at Utrecht,[59] also encompassed the Voetians. Hence, it may be more accurate to say that in the Netherlands the Radical Enlightenment was squeezed out less by the moderate mainstream, as such, than by a new kind of non-confessional urban culture built on a concerted alliance of Cocceian-Newtonian theology and philosophy together with a revived but softened Voetianism. Whereas before 1700, the moderate—then predominantly Cartesian—mainstream, locked in fierce dispute with the Voetians, had sought by attacking the Spinozists to 'blunt the attack of the Voetians on themselves',[60] by the 1730s and 1740s, the 'enlightened' Dutch mainstream, now basically physico-theological, and Lockean-Newtonian, was so preponderant, and the Voetians so debilitated, there was no

[57] *Antwoord aen den Opstelder* (Knuttel 18001), 4, 7–8; *Aan de Weledle Grootachtbare Heeren Burgemeesteren*, 3.

[58] Mijnhardt, 'Construction', 231; van Eijnatten, *Mutua Christianorum tolerantia*, 208–9; van der Wall, 'Religious Context', 51.

[59] Israel, *Dutch Republic*, 898–9, 932, 1030; van Sluis, *Herman Alexander Röell*, 74, 153–4; Kloeck and Mijnhardt, *1800: Blueprints*, 23, 172–4.

[60] Mijnhardt, 'Construction', 232.

longer a risk that the former could mobilize the semi-literate in a sustained attack on them. Rather, the warring wings of the Dutch Reformed Church were now able to sink their differences, or sufficiently adjust them, as was done especially during the 1730s and 1740s, to form a combined front to reform society, manners, and culture. This then hastened the receding of Voetianism in the city governments, church councils, and universities, driving a further broadening of irenicism and toleration. By 1740, there were even liberal Reformed theologians, like Herman Venema (1697–1787) at Franeker, prepared to imply, if not declare outright, that Socinians should be tolerated.[61] A new urban popular culture evolved in this way, characterized by irenicism with regard to the minority churches, and strengthened sense of a shared creed, paradoxically combined with a heightened intolerance of fringe phenomena which could not be assimilated into the new moderate 'enlightened' consensus.[62]

Much energy went into demonizing what was doctrinally too far beyond the pale to be accommodated within the new broad tolerationist consensus. In their examinations of theology candidates hoping for preaching careers, the provincial synods and classes of the Reformed Church continued their formalized campaign wholly to eradicate the influence of Bekker and van Leenhof, laying down clear markers for theology students and candidates for the pulpit, for decades, down to the 1750s and beyond. Meanwhile, a strong emphasis on physico-theology had been a pronounced feature of Dutch culture ever since the publication of Jan Swammerdam's *Historia generalis insectorum* in 1669; but after 1715, this type of scientific philosophy, even perhaps to a greater extent than in Britain, enjoyed an extraordinary vogue. A key example of the genre was *Het Regt Gebruik der Wereltbeschouwingen* (Amsterdam, 1715) [The True Use of World-Concepts] 'to persuade the impious and irreligious' by the resolutely anti-Spinozist Purmerend regent Bernard Nieuwentyt (1654–1718), one of the most widely influential Dutch books of the eighteenth century, a text which appeared in eight editions between 1715 and 1759.[63]

The emphatic anti-Spinozism of Nieuwentyt's books was always central to the newly emerging Dutch intellectual culture of consensus cemented by physico-theology and Lockean empiricism.[64] A second major work, the posthumously published *Gronden van Zekerheid* (1720), again built around a critique of Spinoza, further emphasized the differences between the strict empiricism of the approved 'experimental method', confirming physico-theology, and Spinoza's procedures. The kind of 'enlightenment' embodied in these books, with their stress on Lockean empiricism and a mild theology of harmony and tolerance, was a construct which had learnt its techniques and debating style, as Nieuwentyt himself had, from

61 Vermij, *Secularisering*, 93–101; van Eijnatten, *Mutua Christianorum tolerantia*, 82, 84, 86, 208.

62 Van Eijnatten, *Mutua Christianorum tolerantia*, 168–71; Mijnhardt, 'Construction', 234–6.

63 Vermij, *Bernard Nieuwentijt*, 30–1; Vermij, *Secularisering*, 127.

64 Petry, 'Nieuwentijt's Criticism', 7–8; De Vet, 'Spinoza en Spinozisme', 20, 23; De Vet, 'Spinoza's "systema" ', 28–9, 33, 38n, 58.

directly disputing, at university and outside, with the 'godless' *Spinozisten*. Nieuwentyt's argument that Spinoza's 'geometrical method' is essentially a speculative fiction, not based on experiment or empirical investigation at all, perfectly fitted the churches' new way of arguing their claim that Spinoza's method contradicts Newton's mathematical principles and any true notion of natural philosophy.

Spinozism was now condemned not just as unchristian and subversive, as before, but also as something scientifically invalid, offering no viable basis for conclusions about God, demonology, the world, or society and at the same time something socially and morally corrosive, an immediate threat to Dutch society, something directly opposed to an aroused populace thoroughly schooled in a new kind of intolerance expressly aimed at atheism, Spinozism, and materialism.[65] It was a form of Enlightenment which fully triumphed amid the growing economic anxiety, an integral part of a new popular mentality nurtured on a theology stressing, in place of the old confessional dogmatism, the equivalence and perfect harmony of reason and faith and the vital importance of natural theology. Extolling the virtues of the experimental method in science as opposed to the more philosophical approach typical of the Cartesians and Spinozists—an insistent empiricism was combined with a relentless condemnation of 'atheism' as something deeply pernicious and injurious to society which cannot be permitted in a respectable society and an emphatic Anglophilia fired not just by zeal for Newton and Locke but also by English Latitudinarian theology.[66] Typical of this new ideology as expressed, for instance, in Le Clerc's last journal, the *Bibliothèque ancienne et moderne*, was the expounding of scientific and philosophical arguments designed to address general problems of the relationship of science to religion, denouncing the 'evil' of Spinoza and the Spinozists in terms of scientific and mathematical arguments tied to a moderate, generalized Protestant rationalism stressing divine providence, and the divine harmony of the universe.[67]

2. INTELLECTUAL REALIGNMENT WITHIN THE HUGUENOT DIASPORA

Remarkably but perhaps not surprisingly, this intensification and broadening of the Dutch moderate mainstream extended not only to the Huguenot diaspora but also to the 'enlightened' Sephardic Jewish intellectual elite. The Amsterdam Jewish 'academy' headed by the young Sephardic *philosophe* Isaac de Pinto (1717–87) from the late 1730s spent much of its time discussing how to overcome the challenge of Spinozism, heavily inclining to physico-theology as its favoured antidote.[68]

[65] De Vet, 'Spinoza en Spinozisme', 20, 23; Israel, *Dutch Republic*, 1041; Vermij, *Bernard Nieuwentijt*, 22–3, 34–5; Mijnhardt, *Over de moderniteit*, 24–5.

[66] Mijnhardt, *Over de Moderniteit*, 76–80, 99–104; Wielema, *March*, 203–4.

[67] Mijnhardt, 'Dutch Enlightenment', 203; van Bunge, *From Stevin to Spinoza*, 162.

[68] Nijenhuis, *Joodse* philosophe, 11–12.

Many intellectual leaders of the French-speaking community in the Netherlands, meanwhile, powerfully reflected the new tendency to reconcile Arminian and Socinian with Calvinist and providential Deist strands. Huguenot 'Arminian Enlightenment', striving to reform the Reformed Church and advance toleration, while simultaneously seeking to combat radical ideas, found itself compelled, during the opening years of the eighteenth century, to find new ways to overcome and transcend the old debilitating splits and feuding long troubling relations between the Calvinist orthodox and the Arminian, Cocceian, and Socinian tendencies, so characteristic of the 1680s and 1690s.

From the 1680s until the opening years of the new century, the Huguenot diaspora was increasingly divided by bitter and intractable doctrinal disputes such as those between Jurieu and Élie Saurin, French Reformed preacher at Utrecht, with Jurieu passionately decrying Saurin's *socinianisme*, *Pélagianisme*, and allegedly ruinous *tolérantisme*, before the synods.[69] Isaac Jaquelot, who preached at The Hague between 1686 and 1702 and there wrote his *Dissertations sur l'existence de Dieu* (The Hague, 1697) against Spinoza, was another who was targeted by the orthodox wing owing to his zeal for toleration and other doctrines deemed pernicious by strict Calvinists. Charged by Jurieu before the Walloon Synod, in 1691, of asserting the salvation of virtuous pagans—something dear to the hearts of the 'enlightened' but shocking to the orthodox,[70] besides harbouring anti-Trinitarian leanings, his fiercely resented 'Arminianism' eventually forced him, in 1702, to quit Holland for Berlin, where he became a court preacher to the Prussian king.[71] Yet Saurin and Jaquelot were expounding views which, within a few years, became profoundly typical of Dutch Huguenot culture as a whole.

The men of moderation very quickly came to typify the whole; but they succeeded in part by demonstrating a new and more effective way to overcome the challenge of Spinozism. Jaquelot, for instance, unwilling to compromise his toleration principles, also for many years refused to participate in the campaign against Bayle, and always stressed his respect for his person and erudition, until, by 1704, he became so alarmed by Bayle's, to him, now obvious crypto-Spinozism and imposture that he felt obliged to come out publicly against him.[72] At the same time, he perfectly grasped the futility of combating Bayle and the Spinozists with conventional theological arguments. Rather, like Le Clerc, Locke, Bernard, Basnage, Barbeyrac, and later Luzac, he held that philosophy and science must be demonstrated rationally to lead men to God and that it was incumbent on public representatives of the Word of God, like himself, to present clear, cogent, and comprehensive philosophical rebuttals in popular scientific terms and halt their theological feuding.[73] Where Bayle held that faith cannot buttress reason, Jaquelot answered that reason cannot contradict, or fail to converge with, faith.[74]

69 Saurin, *Traité de l'amour*, appendix: 'Récit de la vie et de la mort de Mr. Élie Saurin', 15–17.

70 Vernière, *Spinoza*, 64.

71 Van Eijnatten, 'Huguenot Clerisy', 220–1.

72 [Jaquelot], *Conformité*, 23–5; Vernière, *Spinoza*, 64; Brogi, *Teologia senza verità*, 24.

73 Brogi, *Teologia senza verità*, 18, 28–9; Vernière, *Spinoza*, 64.

74 *L'Europe savante*, 4 (1718), 58–62; Des Maizeaux, *Vie de Monsieur Bayle*, pp. xcvi–xcvii; Bots, *Henri Basnage de Beauval*, ii. 140.

The mechanistic world revealed by natural philosophy, held Jaquelot, like Le Clerc and Jacques Bernard, has its own strict boundaries. Assailing the Spinozists for being so enamoured of their mechanistic vision of reality as to blind themselves to the clear evidence of reason, imagining the laws of motion to suffice to explain 'la formation de l'univers', he insisted they were wrong scientifically. To demonstrate this, he challenged them to answer two fundamental questions on their premisses: 'l'une, quelle est la cause du mouvement, l'autre quel est l'auteur des règles du mouvement?'[75] They cannot reply, he maintains, since only the 'argument from design' provides cogent as well as Christian answers. It was, insists Jaquelot, the *Spinosistes*, and Bayle, not the Christians, who repudiated the guidance of science and right reason.

The question whether Bayle's 'fideism' is genuine or a form of imposture—which again preoccupies scholars today—increasingly came to seem a superfluous one to Jaquelot. For, any close examination shows that Bayle's professed 'Christian fideism' cannot have been intended as a *bona fide* stance, since he so exaggerates the non-rationality of Christian belief that to be a Christian 'de la façon de Mr Bayle', as Jaquelot puts it, one must virtually cease to be human. Bayle's idea of a Christian life requires 'à chaque pas abandonner les lumières de la raison'.[76] Jaquelot rightly attributed to him separation of faith and reason, protested Bayle, but wrongly accused him of saying religion is 'toujours obligée de reculer devant la raison'; this was sheer calumny.[77] Another newcomer to the campaign against Bayle was his former friend David Durand (*c.*1680–1763), a great foe of superstition and bigotry and an exceptionally irenic preacher in Rotterdam and The Hague, as well as later in London.[78] Durand was so liberal that he approved of van Dale and judged Fontenelle's *Historie des oracles* a treasure.[79] Yet, like Jaquelot, he too, once convinced Bayle had abandoned religion and represented a dire intellectual threat, saw it not just as a pressing duty to help unmask Bayle's insidious paradoxes and deception but as a way of unifying Huguenot opinion. Just as Spinoza had feigned being a Cartesian, and Spinozists today employ the same veil 'pour anéantir la liberté et introduire la fatalité stoïque', Bayle, he alleged, had counterfeited his 'fideism' the more effectively to propagate illicit ideas.[80]

Toleration and irenicism, but also social renewal and communal solidarity as well as the strong Anglophilia typical of the mainstream outlook of the post-1700 period, were still more clearly reflected in the thought-world of Jean Barbeyrac. A native of Béziers in the Languedoc whence his family fled France with the Revocation when he was aged 11, Barbeyrac grew up in French-speaking Switzerland, studying both there and at Frankfurt an der Oder. Beginning his career teaching classics and philosophy (numbering Formey among his pupils) at the Collège Français,

75 Bots, *Henri Basnage de Beauval*, ii. 124.

76 [Jaquelot], *Conformité*, 238; Brogi, *Teologia senza verità*, 43–4.

77 Bayle, *Réponse*, iii. 688; Bayle, *Entretiens*, 47–9.

78 Wielema, *Filosofen*, 93.

79 Durand, *Vie et sentiments*, 170.

80 Ibid. 176; Labrousse, *Pierre Bayle*, i. 267 n.; Cerny, *Theology, Politics and Letters*, 112 n.

in Berlin, where La Croze also taught, his hope of rising socially from teaching to becoming a Reformed *pasteur* had been thwarted, due to doubts about his orthodoxy, an experience which only reinforced his lifelong advocacy of Lockean-Arminian toleration and the need to restrict ecclesiastical authority.[81] After a period teaching at Lausanne in the years 1711 and 1717, but ill at ease with the *Formula consensus*, the Calvinist articles to which academics as well as clergy had to subscribe there at the time,[82] he moved on to the Netherlands where he spent over three decades, from 1717, as professor of Natural Law at Groningen.

His celebrated French translation of Pufendorf's masterpiece having appeared in 1706, from Groningen, Barbeyrac answered Leibniz's attack on Pufendorf and consolidated his position as Europe's foremost exponent of Natural Law theory in French. While undoubtedly harbouring pro-Socinian, pro-Mennonite, and pro-Arminian tendencies in private, Barbeyrac vigorously battled Spinozism throughout his public career and was rightly recognized as a firm champion of religious authority and the public church in a general, interdoctrinal sense. He advocated a moderate toleration, like that of Le Clerc, Noodt, and especially his hero Locke,[83] from which Bayle had to be completely excluded because his final books, the *Continuation* and the *Réponse*, were deemed an essentially crypto-Spinozist, destructive influence.[84]

Even before the main shift within Dutch culture became visible, the particular pressures of the Huguenot diaspora, especially the challenge of Spinoza and Bayle, prodded Calvinist orthodox and liberal Huguenots alike, after decades of furious strife and recrimination, into seeing the necessity of consensus and of joining forces. Whether or not Jurieu was right that it was only Bayle's hypocrisy and extravagant displays of contrition before the *consistoire*, complete with abject avowals of humility and tears, that enabled him to wriggle out of 'la condemnation de ses impiétez',[85] it was only after 1706 that there was there a wider, and more general, reaction against him and his philosophical legacy among the Huguenot *consistoires* in the Netherlands. It then took several more years before this became general throughout the Huguenot diaspora. At Geneva, formal condemnation of his books and reputation occurred only in 1713, an event all the more significant in that previously, in 1697, and again in 1702, prior that is to the marked liberalization in attitude and shift towards irenicism noticeable at Geneva after 1700, the Reformed pastors there had not seen fit to condemn Bayle's *Dictionnaire*. It was precisely during their more tolerant phase, then, that the Genevan preachers denounced Bayle's work as apt to 'inspirer l'impiété et l'athéisme', corrupt morals, and promote *libertinage*, going so far as to request the Genevan republic to ban his *Dictionnaire*.[86]

[81] Häseler, *Wanderer*, 26; Huussen, 'Onderwijs', 164; van Eijnatten, 'Huguenot Clerisy', 209.

[82] Israel, *Radical Enlightenment*, 33–4; van Eijnatten, 'Church Fathers', 16.

[83] Van Eijnatten, 'Huguenot Clerisy', 212; van Eijnatten, *Mutua Christianorum tolerantia*, 47.

[84] [Barbeyrac], *Éloge*, 10–11, 22–3.

[85] [Jurieu], *Philosophe de Rotterdam*, 48.

[86] Ibid. 70–6.

At the heart of the Huguenot intellectual crisis pivoting on Spinoza and Bayle was these thinkers' denial that reason and faith can and must be conjoined. If, on the surface, Bayle's manner of stating this position sounded traditional enough, by 1713 it had been by grasped by the *consistoires* in Geneva, Berlin, and Copenhagen, no less than in Holland, that this was not, in reality, a theological stance at all but a devious philosophical strategy, the aim of which was to underpin an ambitious anti-theological system concerned with society, toleration, history, and politics, and in which true morality derives not from religion but what Bruzen called 'la raison universelle', in a manner wholly destructive not just of ecclesiastical authority, theology, and tradition but of the entire edifice of the *rationaux*'s mainstream Enlightenment. As realization of what Bayle was really doing dawned, the polarization between him and the whole body of Huguenot preachers in Holland became practically total. Even Basnage, who had staunchly supported him against Jaquelot and loathed Jurieu, and who remained his mildest critic, came to accept that Bayle's toleration and attitude to sexuality were unacceptable and that he had 'pushed his sagacity too far'.[87] Almost all the rest were much more sweeping. Nothing was more dangerous or more capable of destroying religion, contended Jaquelot, than to claim it is always 'contraire et opposée à la raison' and that to be religious one must abandon reason, and 'abjurer le sens commun, pour se mettre à l'abri de la foi'.[88]

In this new situation, after 1705, the coming together of the hardline Calvinists and 'Arminians', to form what Bruzen de La Martiniere called 'une ligue aussi injuste que violente',[89] to fight the common enemy, or, as Bruzen scathingly put it, sacrifice him as a victim to God while violating the most sacred of his laws 'qui est l'équité', produced some astounding ironies which indeed no one would have relished more than the much decried Bayle himself. For his extraordinary brand of 'fideism' had by 1705 not only ranged the *rationaux* against him but forced Jurieu and his supporters into the undignified and theologically absurd procedure of first calling a truce and then forming a public alliance with the very *rationaux* whose theology, as well as 'leurs axiomes philosophiques', he had continually decried and heartily scorned. But the 'pope' of Huguenot orthodoxy came to realize that he had little choice but to halt the battle between orthodox Calvinists and the 'Arminians' if he was to stabilize authority within the Huguenot community and fight Bayle and Spinoza effectively, and these represented a way of thinking he feared and abhorred even more than what, to him, were the ruinous heresies of Le Clerc, Jaquelot, and Saurin.

The Jesuit editors of the *Mémoires de Trévoux*, delighted by the astonishing spectacle of Jurieu being claimed as a soul-mate by Bayle while yet embracing Le Clerc, Bernard, and Jaquelot instead, could scarcely believe the evidence of what they read: for only a short time before, as they gleefully pointed out, M. Jurieu had had to suffer 'des railleries de l'un et des invectives de l'autre', that is of both Bayle

87 Cerny, *Theology, Politics and Letters*, 112–13, 115, 308, 313.

88 [Jaquelot], *Conformité*, 265; Cantelli, *Teologia*, 342, 368; Mori, *Bayle philosophe*, 204.

89 [Bruzen de La Martinière], *Entretiens*, ii. 553–4.

and Le Clerc.[90] Still more amazing, though, from a seventeenth-century standpoint, is the fact that the right-centre ideological coalition against Bayle, once formed, endured and strengthened even though the latter's stance—rejecting philosophy and insisting that faith must stand alone—approximated far more to Jurieu's views than did those of Le Clerc, Saurin, Jaquelot, Basnage, Barbeyrac, and (Jacques) Bernard. Glorying in this paradox, Bayle in his last years convoluted everything further by continually reminding readers that his separation of faith and reason was an orthodox Reformed position, like that of Jurieu, a pretension rejected by the latter as the very acme of hypocrisy and imposture.[91]

The *rationaux*, having long opposed Jurieu's claim that faith must rest on an inner movement initiated by the Holy Ghost, held that true faith, on the contrary, depends on evidence, signs, traditions, attested miracles, and not blind trust.[92] Bayle, rejecting this, declared himself for the anti-*rationaux* whatever his personal differences with Jurieu, and, presumably most infuriating of all for that paragon of orthodoxy, even had the effrontery, particularly in the *Réponse*, to cite him against the *rationaux*.[93] Jurieu was quite right, held Bayle, to denounce Élie Saurin's Pelagianism and Nestorianism as well as his Arminian-Lockean doctrine that the Christian faith must proceed 'toujours à la clarté de l'évidence'. The idea that the 'true principle of faith' is not to believe on someone else's authority but only via rational arguments, justly condemned by Jurieu, is indeed wholly disastrous for faith, averred Bayle, and something which unavoidably leads 'au Socinianisme, au Pyrronisme, et au Déisme'.[94]

Bayle's taunts could only further antagonize Jurieu who, by 1706, considered this foe even more fatal to the Huguenots (and all society) than Spinoza himself since where the latter, he says, attracts only disciples already susceptible to his blasphemies, the philosopher of Rotterdam with his witticisms, tricks, and paradoxes continually traps the unwary. Where Spinoza seems bent, he says, on antagonizing his readers with his monstrous principles and obscurities, Bayle had found a way 'qui luy a mieux réussi'.[95] Jurieu's new strategy entailed wholly reversing his public attitude to the likes of Jaquelot as well as Le Clerc whom he 'hated mortally', as both Bayle and Des Maizeaux remarked, but whom, as Bayle observes in one of his last letters, to Shaftesbury, he now went so far as to praise publicly.[96] When Bayle assailed Le Clerc's Arminianism, and deplored his 'Socinianism', Jurieu, despite for decades having himself denounced him as an 'Arminian' and 'Socinian', rallied to Le Clerc's support, pronouncing it absurd that an 'atheist' and 'ennemi déclaré de toutes religions' should charge with heresy

90 *Mémoires de Trévoux* (Oct. 1707), art. cxxx, p. 1747.

91 Bayle, *Entretiens*, 9–10, 35; Bayle, *Réponse*, iii. 813, iv. 139; [Jurieu], *Philosophe de Rotterdam*, 106–7; Labrousse, *Pierre Bayle*, ii. 444.

92 Saurin, *Examen*, 93–8.

93 [Bayle], *Entretiens*, 11–12, 18; Knetsch, *Pierre Jurieu*, 372–4.

94 Bayle, *Réponse*, iii. 659; Saurin, *Examen*, preface p. 1 and pp. 76, 91, 98.

95 [Jurieu], *Philosophe de Rotterdam*, 137; Knetsch, *Pierre Jurieu*, 374.

96 Bayle, *Entretiens*, 12; Bayle to Shaftesbury, Rotterdam, 29 Oct. 1706, in Bayle, *Œuvres diverses*, iv. 883–4; Des Maizeaux, *Vie de Monsieur Bayle*, pp. civ–cv.

an author who, even if not always sound in doctrine, at any rate 'croit un Dieu et une providence'.[97]

Bayle accused Le Clerc of denying his 'Socinianism' to avoid expulsion from Holland, noted Jurieu indignantly; but if Bayle publicly avowed his atheism something much worse than exile would befall him![98] Unlike Jurieu, the *rationaux* did not state in print, or so many words, that they considered Bayle an 'atheist', though Le Clerc repeatedly claimed he was a defender of atheists. Nevertheless, those who read their recent works against Bayle, observed Jurieu, could plainly see this was their meaning.[99] No doubt it cost Jurieu much to extol Le Clerc's learning as superior to that of Bayle. But this too was now requisite. Le Clerc knew Hebrew and other oriental languages, declared Jurieu, which Bayle did not; moreover, Le Clerc had good Greek, knew the Church Fathers, and cited them extensively whereas the despicable Bayle lacked enough Greek 'pour citer les auteurs grecs en original'.[100]

Part of the paradox was that by adopting this extraordinary course Jurieu materially assisted a general tendency, discernible in these years throughout the Huguenot diaspora, for the Church's liberal, Arminian wing to gain rapidly in influence and for the spirit of toleration to become much more widely entrenched. This occurred in Geneva, Berlin, and St Petersburg no less than in Holland and London. Yet, however bizarre and risky for a rigid Calvinist to attack an ostensibly hardline Calvinist stance, in alliance with former opponents he had attacked for decades, Jurieu never subsequently retreated from the painful contortions he now entered into. For combating Bayle and Spinoza now overrode everything else and, in the circumstances, the only effective way to fight radical ideas was for Calvinist orthodoxy to join hands with the hated 'Arminians'. Intellectually, this put him at a double disadvantage: for in the prevailing cultural climate in Holland, with readers expecting rational 'certainties' which they could evaluate themselves, only the *rationaux* possessed the philosophical apparatus needed to theorize toleration, irenicism, and reconciliation while simultaneously intensifying the assault on Spinoza and Bayle.[101] Hence, the changing cultural milieu in the Netherlands after 1705 was one bound further to marginalize strict Calvinism and strengthen the moderate Enlightenment. Indeed, through a bizarre twist of strategy, the post-1705 Jurieu became one of the main architects of the moderate mainstream Enlightenment's triumph throughout the Huguenot diaspora.

As the joint orthodox-Arminian campaign against radical thought intensified, the Huguenot intelligentsia became ever more obsessed with the threat of underhand subversion. Thanks to Bayle, Spinozism seemingly threatened Huguenot society almost as much through its elaborate tactics of entrapment and deception as through its basic principles. Durand highlights the example of van Leenhof, 'autrefois ministre de Zwol et aujourd'hui déposé', a crypto-Spinozist who by

[97] [Jurieu], *Philosophe de Rotterdam*, 41; Knetsch, *Pierre Jurieu*, 390, 412.

[98] [Jurieu], *Philosophe de Rotterdam*, 96.

[99] Ibid. 5, 18; Labrousse, *Pierre Bayle*, i. 264–5.

[100] [Jurieu], *Philosophe de Rotterdam*, 40.

[101] Ibid. 4–5.

deception and concealment had for a time successfully propagated Spinozism under false labels among the common people but finally been found out and, by 1711, thoroughly disgraced. In Bayle, he says, imposture had become a finely crafted subversive strategy, though he too had eventually been found out and was now being systematically combated. Other notable instances were not lacking. For most of his life, few knew anything of the secret Spinozism of Simon Tyssot de Patot (1655–1738), mathematics teacher at Deventer and anonymous author of the clandestinely published *Jacques Massé*, one of the most notorious and overtly Spinozistic novels of the Early Enlightenment. He was only eventually exposed owing to a fatal ambition to share something of Bayle's celebrity. His *Lettres choisies* (1726), where he pulls aside the veil enough to afford a glimpse of his real views, precipitated a local scandal in Deventer leading to his being publicly denounced for Spinozism, obscenity, and denying the immortality of the soul, earning him dismissal from his post and the permanent blighting of his reputation.[102]

In this atmosphere it seems unlikely that those who took the risk clandestinely to publish openly Spinozistic works did so merely out of a desire for profit or other ordinary motives. A case in point, among the Huguenots, is that of Charles Levier (d. 1734) and his collaborators responsible for the illegal printing of *La Vie et l'esprit de Mr Benoit de Spinosa* at The Hague in 1719. Levier and his friends knew that printing such blatantly anti-Christian texts was a head-on challenge to their community as well as Dutch society more generally. Marchand remarks disparagingly of Levier with whom he had collaborated over many years that he not only traded in *clandestina* but was someone extremely 'infatué du système de Spinosa', albeit having no profound grasp of his system.[103] It was in 1711, at Rotterdam, from a then very rare manuscript copy belonging to the English Quaker Benjamin Furley, Marchand also reports, that Levier copied out his versions of Lucas's biography of Spinoza, and the *Traité*, the most infamous of the clandestine manuscripts, a piece, probably by Lucas, dating from around 1678.[104] The text was then 'retouché et augmenté' by Levier together, reportedly, with Rousset de Missy,[105] Levier, according to The Hague publisher, Gaspar Fritsch specializing in such clandestine work.[106]

In 1719, Levier secretly printed the slightly expanded *Traité* together with the Lucas biography under a new title—*La Vie et l'esprit de Mr Benoit de Spinosa*. Levier's motives have been questioned by at least one modern scholar who argues *La Vie et l'esprit* was probably just a ploy by an experienced book-dealer seeking to make money by exploiting the market for *clandestina*.[107] This is a conclusion seemingly supported by Marchand's observation that Levier's entitling his illicit edition *La Vie et l'esprit de Spinosa* was fraudulent, his aim being to trick unwary bibliophiles, unaware this new text differed only slightly from the manuscript version, into

[102] Rosenberg, *Tyssot de Patot*, 3, 26–35, 60–1, 92–3; Israel, *Radical Enlightenment*, 594–5.

[103] Marchand, *Dictionnaire historique*, 324–5; Laursen, 'Politics', 281.

[104] Charles-Daubert, '*Traité der trois imposteurs*', 119–20.

[105] Fritsch to Marchand, Leipzig, 7 Nov. 1737, ibid. 65.

[106] Berti, 'First Edition', 203.

[107] Charles-Daubert, '*Traité des trois imposteurs*', 76, 82.

paying exorbitant prices for both. Yet after printing the illicit text, Levier disposed of his stock of copies so cautiously that Marchand, on inheriting Levier's papers after his death in 1734, found most of the print run, of some 300 copies of the forbidden text, still stored unsold in Levier's shop. These he then burnt to avoid becoming an accessory to evasion of the States' ban on Spinozistic literature.

But Levier's remarkable caution in putting copies of the *Traité* into circulation hardly tallies with the charge that he was motivated mainly by greed. Rather than profiteering the affair smacks more of the intensifying climate of cultural repression in the Republic with regard to radical ideas, freethinking, and Spinozism. So overwhelming was the general condemnation of Spinozism by 1719, claims Levier in his preface, that one hardly dares proceed 'contre le torrent, en rendant publique *La Vie et l'Esprit*'. Any author or publisher who seeks to write about Spinoza, 'ou en sa faveur', he adds, must hide his tracks with as much care, and as many precautions, as if he were setting out to commit a murder.[108] Levier also remarks that the publishers had intentionally had only a few copies printed so that the work would remain no less rare than 's'il étoit resté en manuscrit'.[109] His following comment that it was to such capable persons as were qualified to refute its arguments 'qu'on aura soin de distribuer' this small number of copies, rather than a clandestine publisher's subterfuge, is more probably an ironic way of saying that the copies printed were meant less for the market than the shrinking fraternity of adepts.

Nothing better vindicates the *esprits forts*, holds Levier in his publisher's *avertissement*, than the glaring contradiction in their adversaries' rhetoric. Opponents profess to dismiss the *esprits forts*' arguments with contempt, as devoid of cogency, while doing everything possible to suppress the books containing these same arguments 'qu'ils trouvent si méprisables'.[110] But by denying the *incrédules* freedom to express their opinions are they not feeding the suspicion 'qu'on redoute leurs raisonnemens', and that the authorities lay and ecclesiastical find it easier to prohibit their books than demonstrate their fallacies? This point sounds less like imposture than a genuine argument not dissimilar to that of the *Essai sur la liberté de produire ses sentimens* (1749), a forthright Huguenot statement of the right to freedom of speech, expression, and to publish, thought to be by Luzac. Both texts deny one can claim the triumph of even 'des plus importantes vérités' while society forbids the atheists, 'esprits forts', and other people of that sort to lift their pens.[111]

In view of the Amsterdam magistrates' decision in 1710 to imprison Hendrik Wyermars for fifteen years for publishing his Spinozistic book, Levier had reason enough to conduct himself with extreme prudence. No doubt his friend, and collaborator in printing *La Vie et l'esprit*,[112] the Scot Thomas Johnson (d. 1735), was also cautious. Marchand lumps Johnson together with Levier, as both being 'remplis d'irreligion',[113] and it is easy to see what he had in mind. For it was

108 *La Vie et l'esprit*, 6. 109 Ibid. 2. 110 Ibid.

111 *Essai sur la liberté de produire ses sentimens*, 26; Van Vliet, *Élie Luzac*, 307, 313.

112 Charles-Daubert, '*Traité des trois imposteurs*', 48, 76, 120, 153.

113 Berti, 'First Edition', 4; Laursen, 'Politics', 282, 292; van Bunge, *From Stevin to Spinoza*, 151.

Johnson, at The Hague, who published Toland's *Adeisdaemon* in 1709, and the French version of Sir William Temple's *Memoirs* in 1713, as well as, in 1715, the first edition of Marchetti's Italian version of Lucretius, a work banned by the Inquisition and unpublishable in Italy.[114] It was probably also Johnson who produced Tyssot de Patot's clandestine novel *Jaques Massé* around 1714,[115] and who, in 1722, brought out Tyssot's Spinozistic *Discours sur la chronologie* in The Hague *Journal littéraire*.

As publisher (and an editor) of the *Journal littéraire*, one of the most prestigious French-language journals of the era, Johnson was a notable figure in Dutch cultural life.[116] This periodical was a collaborative enterprise with an editorial board, secretary, *président*, and rules governing its meetings which took place, though increasingly irregularly, from 1713 down to 1722. While conviviality and drinking were part of the concept, and while the editors—besides Johnson and Marchand, Albert Henri de Sallengre (1694–1723), Justus van Effen (1684–1735), Saint-Hyacinthe, and the great physicist 's-Gravesande—did not all share the same views, they did see themselves as participating in a common enterprise of 'enlightenment'.[117] The preface to the journal's opening issue, in 1713, asks anyone offended by 'la liberté de nos critiques' not to approach any particular editor since they had resolved 'unanimement' to change nothing, for any one member, approved 'à la pluralité des voix'.[118]

The *Journal littéraire*'s editorial policy clearly reflects the cultural and psychological pressures at work in Dutch society and growing predicament of the Dutch radical stream. The editors felt compelled to pursue a 'safe' strategy of ambiguity and veiled insinuation. For this was the only way they could publish a critical and literary journal at the time and, however marginally, promote freethinking. Marchand reports an editorial disagreement, citing 's-Gravesande as his source, concerning a review, by the latter, of a book about the Resurrection. Nothing in the review even hinted at querying the reality of this 'miracle', objected Saint-Hyacinthe to the spuriously Christian tone affected by 's-Gravesande, a review which not only failed to reflect his own and their views but infringed, he thought, their agreed neutrality in theological matters. Saint-Hyacinthe, a more overt 'Déiste' than 's-Gravesande, held that a *journaliste*, like a historian, should 'laisser ignorer de quel parti il est' and should not appear to take the veracity of the Resurrection for granted.[119] 's-Gravesande, who, as Marchand remarks, was later to be publicly accused by Voetian preachers of 'Spinosisme',[120] and seems to have been more radical in inclination than historians have assumed but held a respected position in Dutch society, rejected this, claiming Saint-Hyacinthe was taking their agreed 'indifférentisme' too far. The editorial board, of course, supported him; and,

[114] *Journal littéraire*, 7 (1715), 458.

[115] Rosenberg, 'Introduction', 28; Rosenberg, *Tyssot de Patot*, 90 n., 72–3, 172, 174.

[116] Rosenberg, *Tyssot de Patot*, 92–3.

[117] Berkvens-Stevelinck, *Prosper Marchand*, 170–1; Vermij, *Seculisering*, 117.

[118] *Journal littéraire*, 1 (1713), 'Preface' p. xvi; Carayol, *Saint-Hyacinthe*, 35.

[119] Marchand, *Dictionnaire historique*, i. 241.

[120] Ibid. i. 239.

indeed, what other choice was there? For neither the *Journal littéraire*, nor any Huguenot journal, could evade the rigorous surveillance of the *consistoires* or publicly refuse to conform to conventional expressions of belief.[121]

3. THE ORANGIST RESTORATION (1747–1751)

Spinozism, then as a stream within Dutch society and culture, was increasingly squeezed out from the 1720s onwards. While a certain radical republican activism might still be possible in Holland in certain circumstances, not much was left of the Dutch Radical Enlightenment as an intellectual package by the 1740s. What Rousset de Missy chiefly had in mind, in later life, when extolling *l'esprit philosophique*, as against the theological outlook, was what he thought of as the legacy of Bayle.[122] By this, he meant neither Pyrrhonism, nor Christian fideism, and certainly not mere encyclopedism. It signified rather Bayle's fierce independence, stress on liberty of thought and toleration, and insistence on separating politics and religion, to which Rousset added his own robust democratic tendency. Pantheist, *Bayliste*, foe of all churchmen, and veteran publicist, Rousset de Missy kept a close eye on intellectual developments in Paris and was quick to denounce any anti-Dutch bias he encountered in French authors. Implacably opposed to what he called 'le détestable sistême de l'intolérance', he was above all a declared foe of all 'adversaires du célèbre et illustre Bayle'.[123] But this was essentially a private not a propagated standpoint.

Rousset continued to express radical sentiments but mainly in his personal correspondence. When towards the end of the 1730s, d'Argens reverted to a more aristocratic style of life and began to play the courtier, Rousset remarked acidly that in his new garb, exchanged for his former simple habit 'de philosophe', no one any longer recognized the author of the *Lettres juives* who condemned 'si hautement les bagatelles'. The glibness of the mainstream Enlightenment's stress on the divine harmony of the cosmos thoroughly irritated him. The highly popular mid eighteenth-century *Dictionnaire historique et critique* (1750) of Chaufepié, supposedly a supplement to Bayle, he scorned utterly: how does the name of 'Bayle', he asked, come to be placed in the title of so dreary a work which reflects neither the 'sistême, ni le stile, ni la manière de Bayle'?[124] Disappointed by the first volume of the *Encyclopédie* (1751), and missing much of the significance of its subversive strategies, he wondered, writing to Marchand, whether such a paltry result was worth all the fuss made about it. To his mind, it just replicated Chaufepié's insipidity.[125]

[121] Van Eijnatten, 'Huguenot Clerisy', 223.

[122] Ibid. 73, 130.

[123] [Rousset de Missy], *Chevalier*, 60; [Rousset de Missy], *Intérêts*, 21; Charles-Daubert, *'Traité des trois imposteurs'*, 78.

[124] Rousset to Marchand, Zwanenburg, 1 Oct. 1751, in Berkvens-Stevelinck and Vercruysse (eds.), *Métier*, 130.

[125] Rousset to Marchand, 10 Jan. 1752, ibid. 136.

But the Parisian *philosophes* were undoubtedly even more perplexed by Rousset's and Dutch democratic republicanism's devotion to Orangism. Why during the Revolution of 1747–8 did Rousset help to revive the power of the stadtholder hand in hand with politically and socially more conservative Enlightenment spokesmen, like Luzac and Isaac de Pinto, the latter now a figure of some influence at the Orangist court and someone who even ventured to tell his French correspondents that the stadtholder was a champion of equality?[126] Despite the criticism of the corruption, nepotism, and inefficiency of the oligarchical regime of the regents, outside the Republic, there was little grasp of how and why any philosophers, let alone the republican tendency, should back the Orangists. In this respect there is perhaps a direct parallel with the fate of English republicanism: just as the political creed of Toland and his allies was compromised internationally by their long-standing alliance first with William III and then the House of Hanover, so Dutch democratic republicanism became internationally isolated and inexplicable through its vigorous alliance, forged in 1688, and lasting until 1748, with the House of Orange.

For here was a local alignment which seemed to contradict the wider play of forces within the Enlightenment overall. All non-Dutch *philosophes* commenting on the Dutch political context either, like Montesquieu or Hume, urged restoration of the stadtholderate because their views were anti-republican and they wished to see a strengthening of the monarchical and courtly element in the Dutch constitution so as to weaken the principle of popular sovereignty; or else, as with radical commentators, like Mably or La Beaumelle, hoped the Dutch would sooner or later rediscover their true democratic and republican credentials and openly reject the stadtholderate, privilege, and Orangism. La Mettrie, for his part, offered a third possibility; for he seemed to take no interest in the upheaval which he witnessed whilst residing at Leiden in 1747–8, his particular strain of atheist materialism being essentially non-political except insofar as he wished to see fanaticism banished from France as from Holland and freedom to philosophize, for those, such as himself, who think differently from the rest, respected.[127] The 'revolution' meant nothing to him, convinced as he was that reason can not make Man happier, securer, or more virtuous.

On visiting the United Provinces in 1729, at a time when his own ideas were crystallizing, Montesquieu took an almost immediate dislike to the country. A land of rampant political corruption, the most urban (and least aristocratic) of the provinces, Holland, was in his opinion 'la plus mal gouvernée'.[128] Encountering at Amsterdam a widespread disgust with the regents, he predicted that the Republic 'ne se relèvera jamais sans un stathouder'.[129] All this contrasted sharply with his subsequent positive experience of England so that despite maintaining in

[126] Nijenhuis, *Joodse* philosophe, 12–13. [127] Wellman, *La Mettrie*, 44–5, 228, 233–4.

[128] Ibid. 577; Childs, *Political Academy*, 192–3; Montesquieu, *Œuvres complètes*, 328.

[129] Montesquieu, *Œuvres complètes*, 330; Hufton, *Europe*, 205; Fockema Andreae, 'Montesquieu in Nederland', 179.

L'Esprit des lois that the 'république fédérative', as found in the Netherlands and Switzerland, is superior to the unitary republic, he never really considered the Republic a model for emulation by others.[130] Highly significantly, he initially included a paragraph in his *L'Esprit des lois*, in 1748, congratulating the Dutch on their good sense in restoring the stadtholderate which he then, for reasons of prudence, deleted from the published version, since his view contradicted the French crown's attempts to prevent the consolidation of Orangist and British influence in the United Provinces; the fragment was subsequently omitted also from the English, Italian, and other translations, and was later lost, so that only its general tenor remains known today.[131]

Numerous, particularly foreign observers hoped and expected to see a marked strengthening of the courtly, hereditary, and aristocratic tendencies in Dutch life, a socio-political transformation which actually occurred in the wake of the 1747–8 disturbances. Montesquieu considered mixed monarchy on the British model a far better guarantee of 'liberty' than any pure republic could offer while Hume, in his essays published in 1741–2, where he discusses whether 'politics may be reduced to a science', was equally convinced that liberty in general, and 'the extreme liberty, which we enjoy in [Britain], of communicating whatever we please to the public, and of openly censuring every measure, entered into by the king or his ministers', far surpassed anything offered by the political systems of 'Holland and Venice'. The British model's superiority, since the 'British constitution' had been transformed by 'the Revolution' and the '*Accession*, by which our ancient royal family was sacrificed to it',[132] held Hume, lay in the fact that 'our mixed form of government, which is neither wholly monarchical, nor wholly republican', is inherently more conducive to liberty than a 'government altogether republican, such as that of Holland'.

For in the Dutch system 'there is no magistrate so eminent as to give jealousy to the state' and therefore no danger in entrusting the 'magistrates with large discretionary powers'. If the disadvantages of absolute monarchy on the French model were obvious, the drawbacks of the Dutch system, according to Hume, were more subtle. For the Dutch system did afford solid advantages, he grants, 'in preserving peace and order'; yet, it also laid 'a considerable restraint on men's actions' making 'every private citizen pay a great respect to the government'.[133] The lesson, urged Hume, was that 'our mixed form of government' is simply the best while the 'two extremes of absolute monarchy, and of a republic, approach near to each other in some material circumstances'.[134] This rather resembles the view in *L'Esprit des lois* where Montesquieu claims democracy, like aristocracy, is not by nature an 'état libre': 'la liberté politique', he holds 'ne se trouve que dans les gouvernements modérés'.[135] Should the Dutch then modify their constitution by bringing back the House of Orange, thereby reintroducing the courtly and monarchical factor,

[130] Montesquieu, *L'Esprit des lois*, 577–8. [131] Ibid.
[132] Hume, *Essays*, 10; Straka, 'Sixteen Eighty-Eight', 143–4, 146.
[133] Hume, *Essays*, 10–11. [134] Ibid. 11. [135] Montesquieu, *L'Esprit des lois*, 586.

Hume, like Montesquieu, tended to think, Dutch liberty would be the better for it.[136]

The Dutch Revolution of 1747–8, triggered by the rout of the Dutch troops facing the French in the southern Netherlands and a French invasion of North Brabant, began in Zeeland with riots that quickly led to the restoration of the stadtholderate in that province. This was followed by major rioting in Rotterdam, and then Dordrecht, Haarlem, and Amsterdam, before long obliging the regents of these cities likewise to yield to the popular pressure. Thoroughly intimidated, the States of Holland restored the stadtholderate with all its judicial functions on 3 May 1747, naming the prince of Orange to that capacity along with command of the army and navy as captain-general of the Union. At this juncture William IV, prince of Orange, effectively took over the government of the country. After this, the States of Utrecht and Overijssel, the last two provinces of the Union without a stadtholder, also bowed to the rioters and reinstated the stadtholderate. By mid-May 1747, William was the first prince of Orange ever simultaneously to have held the stadtholderate of all seven provinces. Nothing could be clearer than that the common people adored the House of Orange and wanted back a princely court, princely command, and more social hierarchy. The news was greeted with jubilation in England, William reputedly being in thrall to his wife Anne of Hanover (1709–59), daughter of George II, and strongly pro-British in attitude.

However, the 'revolution' was not over. As Raynal expressed it in his *Histoire du stadhouderat* (1748), 'on croyait la révolution finie et à peine elle commençoit'.[137] The people's wish for a restored stadtholderate and Orangist court had been granted. The monarchical element in the constitution was restored; but, beyond this, it soon emerged the people also wanted the regent city governments and tax-farmers to be punished, and measures taken to strengthen the fabric of the public church and ease the fiscal burden. It was clear to the prince's advisers, headed by Willem Bentinck van Rhoon (1704–74), that the vast popular euphoria surrounding the return of the court to The Hague, and the strengthening of aristocratic hierarchy in Dutch society, with the accompanying surge of patriotic zeal and religious emotion, had raised expectations in a way which would eventually force the prince to act against the city governments and do at least something by way of a gesture towards reforming the country's civic and fiscal institutions. The agitation led to a series of massive popular demonstrations, continuing for many months, and much further rioting in the main cities, as well as an unprecedented air of political excitement and organized debate marked by assemblies, speeches, and pamphlets.

In Amsterdam, the popular agitation soon divided into two divergent streams. On the one hand, Orangist agents and publicists, encouraging the people's veneration of dynasty and court, concentrated on organizing demonstrations to intimidate the

[136] Hume, *Essays*, 11; Fockema Andreae, 'Montesquieu in Nederland', 179, 181.
[137] Raynal, *Histoire du stadhoudérat*, 209.

regents and provincial States so as to consolidate the stadtholder's authority still more, and restore the now heavily disrupted effectiveness of the state's fiscal and military machinery. But some of the pamphlets issuing from the presses, denouncing the regents as selfish and corrupt oligarchs, concerned only with lining their own pockets and monopolizing municipal offices, while also supporting the prince, sought to steer the artisans and shopkeepers into pressing for a wider reform of the urban administration and tax system, and restoring what they called 'Dutch freedom' [Nederlandsche Vryheit] and 'het algemeene welzyn' (the general good). The latter also increasingly sought redress from the stadtholder as a kind of universal 'healer', someone called on to restore a sick body politic by taking extensive reform measures. This more radical bloc urged that restoration of the stadtholderate be combined with moves towards a democratization of the Dutch city governments and urban militias.[138]

Political theory, especially theories of popular sovereignty, in this fraught context, assumed a new importance. During the Amsterdam disturbances of 1747–8, it was especially the popular democratizing tendency, the movement of the *Doelisten*, led by Hendrik van Gimnig, aimed at breaking the oligarchic hold of the long-established regent dynasties in the city which Rousset de Missy sought out and which, on its side, drew inspiration from his ideas and publicizing skills.[139] Having narrated the revolution's early stages in his *Relation historique de la grande Révolution arrivée dans la république des Provinces-Unies en 1747* (Amsterdam, 1747), where he observes that the stadtholderate was restored without any of the ugly violence marring the Orangist upheaval of 1672, he went on to play a principal role in Amsterdam, helping to stir up the popular unrest, seeing it as a wholly justified reaction against oligarchic corruption and one which he hoped would produce a decisive and lasting change in Dutch politics and history.

Rousset was undoubtedly a political as well as philosophical radical. He detested the memory of Louis XIV, loathing all absolute monarchy: so long as the French and Spaniards made no move to change their absolute monarchies, neither of those peoples, in his opinion, had any right to complain about their huge losses in dead and wounded in recent wars or the immense drain on their national treasuries. Does not everything which a Frenchman or Spaniard possesses belong to his king? Does not each of them glory in being stripped bare for the sake of his prince?[140] In Dutch politics, he aimed for as broad a toleration as he could get together with more press freedom and a general reform of Dutch urban government.[141] A lifelong antagonist of what he termed 'pouvoir absolu et arbitraire', on the one hand, on the other, he was equally a foe of regent oligarchy (and their tax-farmers), being convinced the middle way was best and that in the United Provinces the common interest required that it should be presided over by a stadtholder.[142]

138 *Nadere Aanmerkingen op de Drie Artykelen* (Knuttel 17984), 23–4, 43, 44–5.
139 De Jongste, 'Restoration', 46, 51, 58; Israel, *Dutch Republic*, 1070.
140 [Rousset de Missy], *Intérêts*, 47.
141 Ibid. 73, 103, 130; Berkvens-Stevelinck, 'L'*Épilogueur*', 983–4.
142 De Voogd, *Doelisten Beweging*, 83, 101, 219; De Vet, 'Jean Rousset de Missy', 135.

But here he was to be gravely disappointed. Everyone, in his view, had both an interest in, and a responsibility for, promoting the 'general interest' and this was now to be his guiding concept. An ardent disciple of Bayle, Rousset saw distinct possibilities also in Locke's theory of justified resistance.[143] Espousing the cause of popular sovereignty, Rousset hit on the notion of bringing out a new revised version of David Mazel's translation of Locke's *Second Treatise on Government* which was indeed eventually published at Amsterdam in 1755, under the title *Du gouvernement civil.* Mazel's abridged and renamed translation (which fails to mention Locke as the author) having already been 'subtly changed', as Peter Laslett put it, 'in the direction of Enlightenment and eighteenth-century Revolutionism', and originally published in Amsterdam in 1691, had been reissued at Geneva in 1724 and at Brussels in 1749.[144]

But Rousset required something still more radical. Introducing his version, anonymously, under mysterious initials he used also on other occasions—L.C.R.D.M.A.D.P. [Le Chevalier Rousset de Missy, Académie du Plessis]—he further slanted Locke's text in a republican and democratic direction, seeking to turn it into a stimulus to revolutionary action.[145] In his preface, he distinguishes the Dutch Republic from the other early modern republics, insisting on the particular 'excellence de la constitution républiquaine' of the former with its restored stadholderate, especially because it guarantees its citizens 'plus pleinement des avantages de la liberté personelle et de la paisible possession de leurs propriétés' than the—in his opinion—deplorably defective and oligarchic 'républiques de Venise, de Gênes, de Pologne' where those distinguished from the rest 'par le titre de nobles' hold everybody else in a slavery 'plus ou moins insupportable'.[146] Its elimination of nobility from effective political influence, at any rate in Holland and Zeeland, he considered (not without justification) as the foremost glory of the Dutch Republic.

Of course, institutionalized nobility still existed, at least marginally, in the United Provinces and was now strengthened by the Revolution of 1747–8. But Rousset argued that equality was nevertheless still the true principle of the Republic, the basis of its civic ideals and success in establishing the rule of law and liberty. Indeed, the Dutch nobles, he contends, 'sont citoyens comme le reste des habitans', having no more to say than the magistrates established 'par la constitution', which is a happy remnant of 'la première installation de la société'.[147] Having prepared his version of Locke during the 1747–8 Revolution, seeing the *Second Treatise* as an apt vehicle for promoting popular sovereignty and spreading political consciousness among the citizenry, as well as means to justify the rioting,[148] on 26 June 1748 Rousset, at that point at the height of his success in Amsterdam, wrote reminding

[143] Rosenberg, *Nicolas Gueudeville*, 133; Berkvens-Stevelinck, 'L'*Épilogueur*', 977, 979, 983.

[144] Christophersen, *Bibliographical Introduction*, 21–2; Laslett, 'Introduction', 12, 14; Hutchison, *Locke in France*, 42; Laursen, *New Essays*, 10; Jacob, *Radical Enlightenment*, 256; De Jongste, 'Restoration', 57.

[145] De Jongste, 'Restoration', 110–11; Jacob, 'Radicalism', 226; Wright, *Classical Republican*, 80.

[146] [Rousset de Missy], 'Avertissement', p. xvii; Jacob, 'Radicalism', 230.

[147] [Rousset de Missy], 'Avertissement', p. xviii.

[148] Ibid., pp. xv–xvi; Jacob, *Living the Enlightenment*, 97; Israel, *Dutch Republic*, 1067–78.

the stadtholder's chief minister, Bentinck, nominally his political supervisor, of a meeting at The Hague some time before when they had agreed on the need for a cheap new edition of Locke's second treatise for Dutch popular consumption. Rousset had now arranged with an Amsterdam publisher for an inexpensive edition adapted for a relatively unsophisticated readership,[149] and was only awaiting Bentinck's signal, he says, before proceeding. Bentinck, however, withheld permission, having had second thoughts about the utility of the doctrine of popular sovereignty from the prince's standpoint.

In the end Rousset's efforts came to naught. After months of turmoil, the States of Holland urged the stadtholder, on 31 August 1748, to go to Amsterdam in person to 'restore order' by whatever means he deemed appropriate. Holding talks with the heads of both riotous factions, the prince found himself distinctly out of sympathy with van Gimnig's popular campaign against the regents and civic corruption, and complaints that the burgers were being oppressed in their rights, pockets, and in every other way. While the huge popular demonstrations forming the backcloth to the prince's visit showed that support was shifting from the moderate to the radical *Doelisten*, the prince indicated by his attitude that he had no wish to serve the aims of the radicals and preferred spending his time being wined and dined by the regent oligarchy. Obliged though he was to purge the city government and change the burgomasters, the stadtholder kept the purge to a minimum, changing only seventeen out of the council of thirty-six and ensuring that even some of these, including all four new burgomasters, came from old-established regent families.[150]

This intervention, and the prince's refusal to set up a militia council independent of the city government to represent the citizenry's wishes, gravely disappointed a considerable part of the Amsterdam populace. Further huge demonstrations took place on 9 and 10 September 1748, demanding a 'free' militia council, but the stadtholder refused to yield, returning to The Hague, leaving a confused and thwarted city behind him. New rioting erupted in the autumn at Amsterdam and also Haarlem and Leiden where the stadtholder finally agreed to purge both city governments, albeit only moderately. He rejected most of the rioters' other demands, though, and when, on 10 November, yet another serious commotion erupted in Leiden, and the city government again urgently requested military assistance to disperse the mob, the stadtholder who on previous occasions had steadfastly refused to use force against the crowds, not wishing to alienate popular support for his own authority, this time dispatched 1,000 troops to quell the disorder. These entered Leiden on 16 November and restored quiet, enabling the Leiden magistracy to ban all further meetings and demonstrations. With this ended the 'grande révolution' of 1747–8.

The radical popular movement of Rousset de Missy and van Gimnig thus ended in suppression by the army and bitter disillusionment. Van Gimnig and Rousset,

149 BL, MS Eg. 1745, fo. 486, Rousset to Bentinck, Amsterdam, 26 June 1748; Israel, *Dutch Republic*, 1074.

150 De Jongste, *Onrust*, 180–3; De Vet, 'Jean Rousset de Missy', 139–40.

though scornful of the people's reverence for tradition, existing laws, and precedent, had continually echoed their fervent Orangism while constantly urging the need to 'adapt the laws to the circumstances and character of the people', as van Gimnig put it, rather than the other way around, putting forward a variety of proposals for political, administrative, and economic reform, the ideological inspiration for which in several cases derived from Rousset.[151] But while these radical leaders both roused the people and clearly reflected the Radical Enlightenment's rejection of what has been called the 'ideology of the normative past',[152] they were caught in a political trap of their own making from which, in fact, there was no way out. For they were inextricably tied to the prince, who had no sympathy for their aims. Then, in May 1749, occurred a definitive break: Bentinck wrote to the stadtholder, informing him of reports that, behind the scenes, Rousset had worked against the Prince's interest, in Amsterdam.[153] Soon afterwards, his disgrace was announced and orders issued for his arrest, though he managed to flee before he could be seized, escaping to Brussels, where he remained, under sentence of a heavy fine and banishment from the States' territory, until 1751, when he was allowed to return on condition of good behaviour. He took no further part in politics, living the remainder of his days in his quiet rural retreat, at Maarssen on the Vecht, near Utrecht.

Among radical-minded *philosophes*, outside the Dutch Republic where knowledge of Dutch domestic circumstances was both superficial and overly depicted in terms of Anglo-French factional rivalries, the course of the revolution seemed deeply baffling. Rousset's brand of popular political radicalism in 1747–8 was something new and significant, it was widely grasped, but its fervent Orangism seemed a contradiction in terms; to those with republican sympathies, the suppression of the popular movement using troops in the autumn of 1748 and Rousset's subsequent disgrace and banishment by the prince of Orange appeared to make much more sense. Champions of the principle of popular sovereignty were naturally predisposed to think that true republicans should oppose the stadtholder, though at the time this view was stridently decried in Britain, as typically French and self-interested.[154] Foreign republicans failed to understand that given the outlook of the people and clergy, and the entrenched position of the regent oligarchy, the politicized mass radical tendency could only operate by adopting the rhetoric of popular Orangism.

In any case, defeat of the radical popular movement in the Dutch cities put everything in a clearer perspective. La Beaumelle, for example, who visited the Republic for several weeks in the autumn of 1750, *en route* between Paris and Copenhagen,[155] carrying in his baggage ninety copies of his sequel to Montesquieu's *Défense de* l'Esprit des lois, with its favourable references to Spinoza, took a very different view

151 Ibid. 46; Jacob, 'Radicalism', 234; De Jongste, 'Restoration', 57.

152 De Jongste, 'Restoration', 58; Zagorin, 'Prolegomena', 171.

153 Berkvens-Stevelinck and Vercruysse (eds.), *Métier*, 9, 12; De Jongste, *Onrust*, 295; Jacob, *Radical Enlightenment*, 258, 271, 292; De Vet, 'Jean Rousset de Missy', 136.

154 Raynal, *Histoire du stadhoudérat*, 202–3.

155 Lauriol, *La Beaumelle*, 194, 213, 216.

of the Orangist revolution of 1747–8 from his mentor, flatly refusing to see it as in any way a positive step or legitimate echo of the Glorious Revolution of which he was a fervent admirer. The triumph of Orangism and the people's deep veneration of the House of Orange he construed as a disaster for the cause of liberty everywhere, but in the United Provinces most of all, charging the Dutch with disgracefully betraying their republican principles and their own interest. The citizenry, he lamented, had abjectly lost their old love of liberty and now appeared set only on obsequious deference to the great and what he called the 'despotisme du stadhoudérat'.[156]

La Beaumelle radicalized Montesquieu's thought, as we have seen, in particular by urging more toleration, greater personal liberty and, as befitted a *philosophe* with probably more pseudonyms than any other (at least ten), greater freedom of expression. But the Orangist Revolution of 1747–8 seemed to him to subvert all republican values. When free, before 1747, the Dutch press had been a means more apt than any other to recall a people to a real awareness of political realities, and its own traditions of liberty; but now, under the thumb of William IV, it had become just an instrument, it seemed to him, of court interests and oppression. While he admired the British constitution and the 'admirable' Swedish revolution of 1719–20 which had similarly balanced monarch, council, Riksdag, and people, to produce a mixed government of precisely the sort recommended by Montesquieu and Hume, he denigrated the Orangist Revolution, on the basis of what he himself saw and heard in Holland, precisely for restoring mixed government, more social hierarchy, and the hereditary principle.[157]

An enlightened view of politics to his mind meant proclaiming the sovereignty of the people, which in turn must mean accepting that the state is a society of men established 'uniquement pour procurer les uns aux autres la conservation et l'avancement des intérêts civils'.[158] How could placing power and command of the army in the stadtholder's hands, restoring the court, and promoting the mystique of the House of Orange benefit liberty, toleration, or the interests of the people? Not even the British government would benefit from a revolution which it had vigorously supported, seeing it as an apt instrument for extending British power. For he doubted that the restored stadtholderate would really lead to an expansion in the size or improvement of the quality of the Dutch forces, in preparation for further conflict with France, as the British hoped. Rather the prince of Orange, he predicted, would employ the army the people had put into his hands 'to prepare the complete ruin of the constitution itself'.[159] These Dutch burgers, he complained, who had defied the whole might of Spain in the heroic sieges of Haarlem, Leiden, and Alkmaar, during the Revolt against Philip II, had now shown with their contemptible Orangism during the late 'revolution' that they had wholly lost their old republican integrity, all sense of their own interest, and even the will to defend

[156] Lauriol, *La Beaumelle*, 99–100, 171.

[157] La Beaumelle, *Mes pensées*, 259.

[158] [La Beaumelle], *L'Asiatique tolérant*, 44.

[159] La Beaumelle, *Mes pensées*, 99.

their homes against the Germans and Swiss hired by the States General supposedly to 'protect' them. While the press had lost its freedom, and the merchants, he thought, were thoroughly intimidated, deference to the court had become general and flattery and hypocrisy firmly reintroduced while the preachers, he sneered (though himself a Huguenot), were as always 'au service du plus fort'. 'Eh bien! Puisqu'ils le veulent, ils auront un despote.'[160]

The United Provinces, held La Beaumelle, were now inescapably trapped between 'le despotisme du stadhoudérat' (and British dominance), on the one side, and the menace of French retaliation, if not conquest, on the other.[161] Only courage and forthright action could revive the Republic's former liberty and splendour, but this to him seemed a slim hope. Either the process of revolutionary uprising would soon be resumed by the people, and in a very different direction from before, or the power now accruing to the prince made the demise of the Republic's former freedom, and an inexorable slide into 'l'esclavage', inevitable. Either the Republic would promptly recover its liberty through a people's insurrection, he admonished, or else 'la perdra bientôt pour toujours'.[162]

[160] Ibid. [161] Ibid. 100; Raynal, *Histoire du stadhoudérat*, 204.
[162] Montesquieu, *Œuvres complètes*, 99.

Part IV

Intellectual Emancipation

16

The Overthrow of Humanist Criticism

1. *ARS CRITICA*

Of the three main components identified by Paul Hazard, in 1935, as generating the 'crise de conscience européenne'—the New Philosophy, the 'Scientific Revolution', and the new text criticism—the last, perhaps better called the 'new scholarship', has generally received the least emphasis from later historians. Hardly anyone today would wish to deny that Cartesianism, and the New Philosophy more generally, with its systematically mechanistic conception of the world had a profoundly innovative and permanently transforming effect on European thought. If many nowadays would question whether there really was a 'Scientific Revolution' of actual practice and procedures of the sort scholars used to assume, it can scarcely be doubted that in the Early Enlightenment, intellectual leaders like Fontenelle, Maupertuis, and d'Alembert, and equally the Newtonians, were convinced such a 'revolution' had occurred and that its discoveries, perspectives, and criteria exerted a vast influence on the science and thought of their age.

By contrast, the 'revolution' real and perceived in scholarship has received much less recognition despite being integrally linked to both the other revolutions, in philosophy and science, and, arguably, of comparable importance. Certain specific aspects, of course, have been explored. The new Bible criticism of Spinoza, Le Clerc, and Richard Simon (1638–1712) has long been acknowledged as a pivotal development in the history of learning. Likewise, Le Clerc's efforts to reform the rules of text criticism have not gone unnoticed, any more than the new craft of close critical analysis of historical documents of Dom Jean Mabillon, or Bayle's introduction of a new kind of critical historical encyclopedism. Recently, historians have also begun to investigate the beginnings of the modern study of history of philosophy reaching back to the researches of Jakob Thomasius, Buddeus, Heumann, and Gundling, leading on to the first great 'critical' history of philosophy, that of Johann Jakob Brucker (1696–1770) published in 1744.[1] But these various strands are not usually brought together and considered as a wider phenomenon, the general transformation of European erudition between the 1660s and the 1720s which, from the perspective of many Early Enlightenment thinkers and scholars, in fact occurred.

[1] Kelley, *Descent of Ideas*, 148–50, 164–8; Hochstrasser, *Natural Law Theories*, 11–12, 14, 18–20.

Here again there would seem to be a problem with the historiography of the Enlightenment. For it hardly seems possible to doubt, when examined, that the various strands of this general 'critical' revolution indeed had a collective impact which forms a crucial part of the Enlightenment as a whole. If this is correct it means there continues to be an insufficient awareness among historians of the late seventeenth century's claims to a scholarly breakthrough, repudiation of humanism, and disclosing of the limitations, both real and imputed, of all earlier hermeneutics and text scholarship. It seems best to add 'imputed' here because Renaissance historians may well feel that there was an element of exaggeration or distortion in the mostly overwhelmingly negative view that great critical scholars of the period like Simon, Le Clerc, Vico, and Bentley took of the work of their humanist predecessors. Yet even where they exaggerated, the abruptness of the break and the vastness of the perceived gulf between themselves and the humanists requires the historian to examine the 'revolution' as it appeared to them in order to assess the scope and impact of the new *critique* and its significance for the Enlightenment.

The new perspectives and approaches were arguably far-reaching, indeed radically transformed whole fields of knowledge, including such vital areas as Bible hermeneutics, comparative history of religions, history of philosophy, study of the Church Fathers, ancient Greece and Rome, Jewish history, Islam, and Chinese civilization. But this was by no means all; for, as we shall see, the revolution in text criticism and erudition had a major impact also on the practice of philosophy itself and on the developing struggle between the two enlightenments.

Viewed in this light, the upheaval in Bible criticism in the 1660s and 1670s can fairly be considered paradigmatic for the revolution in scholarship more generally. Spinoza's *Tractatus theologico-politicus* has, not without reason, been called 'the most important seventeenth-century work to advance the study of the Bible and religion generally' and one with an enduring importance for 'modern' societies, being the work which 'disarmed the religious interpreters who would enforce conformity'.[2] Spinoza, followed by Richard Simon and Le Clerc, transformed Bible hermeneutics in the late seventeenth century partly by insisting on the need for scholars to approach the subject wholly independently, free of all prejudgments about its meaning and significance, acknowledging allegiance to no chain of tradition and authority whether Jewish, Catholic, Protestant, or Muslim, and partly by emphasizing the importance of the distinction—never really previously systematized—between the intended or 'true' meaning of a passage of text and 'truth of fact'. Spinoza warned 'lest we should confuse the true sense with the truth of things, the former is to be discovered only from the use of language, or from reasoning which acknowledges no other basis than Scripture itself'; as a result it was inherent in the new historical-critical method of exegesis that it should remain wholly independent of, and hence apt to be at

[2] Goetschel, *Spinoza's Modernity*, 53–4, 56–7; Preus, *Spinoza*, p. x.

odds with, received opinions accepted *a priori* and thus also all established authority and the prevailing common sense of the day.[3]

Spinoza was undoubtedly right in claiming that in his own age, and in the past, the 'true' meaning of biblical as of other texts, and 'truth of fact', had generally been 'confused'. According to his rules of criticism, it is insufficient to know the language in which a text is composed, and be familiar with its characteristic idioms, usages, and grammar. One must, of course, be able to fix the literal meaning of a text as precisely as possible but then also be able to see this *sensus literalis* as a fragment of a wider complex of beliefs and ideas, a self-defining and contained if rarely coherent human system of notions about the world which, in turn, needs to be viewed as a product of nature and natural forces. Here was an idea which depended on a prior theory of culture and religion such as is set out in Spinoza's *Ethics*. For Spinoza, a religion is a belief system concerned with imagined transcendental realities which answer to men's deepest psychological and emotional needs. It is, therefore, a natural phenomenon in the sense that human emotions, as he argues in the appendix to part i of the *Ethics*, are so structured as to lead us to attribute anthropomorphic and teleological explanations to natural phenomena and all occurrences we do not comprehend and then assume from this that there really exists a transcendental order corresponding to our imaginings outside our imaginations, on high.[4]

Broadly, understanding a text, for Spinoza, is not a question of ascertaining what is 'true' in it or searching for what is authoritative, but rather a historical-critical and linguistic exercise anchored in a wider naturalistic philosophical standpoint. What was both quintessentially 'modern' and revolutionary in Spinoza's text criticism (and also what chiefly sets it at odds with the text criticism of all varieties of contemporary Postmodernism) is precisely its insistence that there can be no valid understanding of a text, and therefore no genuine scholarship, which is not in the first place a 'historical' understanding, the 'historical' in Spinoza's terminology, which is also the characteristic 'modern' meaning, being in fact conceptually impossible until, philosophically, all supernatural agency and magical forces are consciously eliminated from the perceived historical process, something far from the minds of the great majority of early modern thinkers and writers. Placing all writings in 'historical' context effectively meant, in Bayle and Le Clerc no less than Spinoza, reassessing them within Cartesian-Spinozist mechanistic conceptions of natural cause and effect systematically excluding every miraculous, magical, and revealed factor, explanation, and criterion.

To reconstruct the meaning of a text, held Spinoza, every relevant historical detail about its author or authors, composition and redaction, reception, and subsequent preservation and copying, besides changes in language usage, terms, and ideas, must be carefully studied.[5] One must allow for the fact that language is

[3] Spinoza, *Opera*, iii. 101; Walther, 'Biblische Hermeneutik (1992)', 642–3; Walther, 'Biblische Hermeneutik (1995)', 650–1; Walther, 'Spinoza's Critique', 110–11; Preus, *Spinoza*, 160–1; Hösle, 'Philosophy', 194.

[4] Spinoza, *Collected Works*, i. 439–46, 123; Preus, *Spinoza*, 169–71, 196–7.

[5] Preus, *Spinoza*, 160–1; Spinoza, *TTP* 141–54; van Rooden, 'Spinoza's Bijbeluitleg', 126–7.

used differently not only in different periods but also by the learned and unlearned, and while it is the former who replicate and preserve texts, it is not they who chiefly fix the meaning of words or how they are used. While it often happens by intention or error that scribes and scholars alter the significance of passages, or give them a new interpretation, no one can change the way words and phrases were, or are, used and understood in a given society, so that by correlating everything relevant to a given usage within its historical context, a method arises for detecting subsequent interpolation, misinterpretation, and falsification.

While the chief strength of Spinoza's Bible criticism was doubtless its rejection of *a priori* assumptions about Scripture's status and its stringent empiricism, it is wrong to infer from this, as has been claimed, that his was, therefore, basically a 'bottom-up, inductive approach—more British-looking than Continental'—or propose that 'Spinoza wants to start not with general presuppositions, whether theological or philosophical dogma, but with particulars and facts—with history—and then work his way up to broader generalizations'.[6] Far from contrasting his approach with that of the Cartesians, or likening it to that of 'Bacon, whose works Spinoza knew in detail', the unyielding differentiation between the natural and supernatural of Spinoza's naturalism derived its force, and power to innovate, precisely from his reworking of Cartesian conceptions of nature and substance. Had Spinoza really emulated Bacon (of whom in fact he was openly disdainful)[7], or subscribed to Bacon's criteria, and the experimental empiricism of the Royal Society, then he, like them, would surely have failed to envisage history as an exclusively natural process devoid of magical action, spirits, supernatural agency, or miracles, and adhered to a literalist, deeply reverential notion of the Bible as Bacon, Boyle, and Newton all actually did.

Far from repudiating 'general presuppositions' Spinoza's text criticism was, on the contrary, uncompromisingly anchored in his metaphysics. Without this, his novel conception of history as something shaped exclusively by natural forces wholly devoid of supernatural agency and magical forces would have been inconceivable.[8] Spinoza's philosophical system and his relentlessly empirical text criticism, therefore, are thus wholly inseparable. But this does not alter the fact that his particular metaphysical premisses, rooted in one-substance doctrine, resulted in an extremely rigorous empiricism, based on conflating extension (body) with mind (soul) in such a fashion that it was he, and not members of the Royal Society, who reduced, doing so in a way that Lockean empiricism could not follow, the entirety of human experience, the world of the spirit and belief no less than the physical, to the exclusive level of the material and empirical. This was Spinoza's principal innovation and strength as a text critic. But it is also an inherent feature of his system and hence widely separates him from the main line of British thought. Yet at the same time it was integrally part of a much wider revolution in text criticism which obliged

[6] Preus, *Spinoza*, 61–2, 64; Strauss, *Spinoza's Critique*, 259; Rosenthal, 'Persuasive Passions', 262–4.

[7] Spinoza, *Letters*, 62; Gabbey, 'Spinoza's Natural Science', 170–2, 176.

[8] Walther, 'Spinoza's Critique', 101, 107, 110–11.

leading scholars of the time like Simon, Le Clerc, Bentley, and Jakob Thomasius to approach the intellectual and religious manifestations of the past using essentially the same novel techniques even where they totally rejected the metaphysical underpinning of a Spinoza, Bayle, or Vico.

The general principles guiding Spinoza's text criticism, he stresses, are the same as those he applies to the study of nature so that, at least in his terms, his Bible criticism was conceived as 'scientific' in a radically new sense. As also with Bayle, it is fundamental in Spinoza that natural processes are shaped by purely mechanistic cause and effect and that mind and human belief are part of the natural process; hence, for him, history, study of religion, and generally what in German are called the *Sozial- und Geisteswissenschaften* are in principle no different methodologically from the other sciences: 'Dico methodum interpretandi Scripturam haud differre a methodo interpretandi naturam, sed cum ea prorsus convenire' [I say that the method of interpreting Scripture scarcely differs from that of interpreting nature, but rather absolutely agrees with it].[9] This was merely one of many different manifestations in the late seventeenth- and early eighteenth-century West in the field of scholarship of the prior 'revolution' in philosophy rooted in Descartes and Hobbes and then carried further by Spinoza, Bayle, and many others, changes that transformed text criticism, and hence the foundations of all scholarly erudition, and, for the first time, made hermeneutics a fundamental aspect of philosophy itself.[10]

Cartesian text scholars, neo-Cartesians, and Spinozists, and also Le Clerc, Vico, and the German Eclectics, rejected the conventions of traditional humanist scholarship in a sweeping and often contemptuous manner. Both enlightenments directly participated in this process of renewing the foundations of text criticism, those committed to securing a rational junction of faith and reason no less than the freethinkers and Spinozists. The former did not merely follow but actively challenged their radical opponents in developing the new criteria of text criticism. Why should the orthodox—Calvinist, Lutheran, or Catholic—fear methods designed to seek out the truth, asked Reform-minded Cartesio-Cocceians, like Wittichius at Leiden? Wittichius held that whatever in the Bible relating to natural phenomena conflicts with what philosophy tells us should not be understood literally but interpreted instead according to the prejudices of the common people of the time.[11] Though not always as bold in this respect, Buddeus, Mosheim, the great Hamburg philologist, Johann Albrecht Fabricius (1668–1736), and many other leading German scholars agreed that there can be no conflict between erudition and truth,[12] acknowledging the urgent need for reform of critical methods and confidently expecting, using these, to repair the walls of authority breached by Spinoza, Bayle, and Le Clerc.

[9] Goldenbaum, 'Philosophische Methodendiskussion', 153–5; Goetschel, *Spinoza's Modernity*, 61–4.
[10] Hösle, 'Philosophy', 181, 192–5.
[11] Wittichius, *Consensus veritatis*, 3, 11, 14, 357–8; Scholder, *Birth*, 124–5.
[12] Mulsow, 'Eine "Rettung" ', 70–1; Reventlow, 'Johann Lorenz Mosheims Auseinandersetzung', 99–100, 105–6; Blair, 'Practices', 69.

According to Fabricius, an expert on Bible exegesis and the *pseudepigrapha* who possessed one of the largest private libraries (32,000 volumes) in Protestant Germany, Bible scholarship must henceforth proceed along radically new lines, reconstructing ancient belief structures, scrutinizing terminology, and meticulously examining the wider context of defunct Near Eastern cults and their literature. For personal conviction that Scripture is divine revelation, or taking it for granted that everyone accepts Christianity is true, and the Pentateuch the authentic Word of God, no longer suffices either adequately to explain Scripture's meaning or to defend what, for most men, were still undoubted verities against libertines, Spinozists, Deists, and sceptics.[13] Hence the methods of Spinoza, Simon, and Le Clerc had to be used against them.

Nor would Fabricius have disagreed with van Dale's argument that were false claims and imposture, like the *Oracula Sibyllina* and *Testimonium Flavium*, to continue to be defended, as they had formerly, citing spurious texts and interpretations, in the end, in the new intellectual climate, no matter how pious the motives, the only result would be to reinforce freethinking rather than devotion.[14] In this sphere, then, the outcome in terms of 'modernity' arose less from radical thought as such than the fierce interaction over issues of text exegesis and scholarship between the two enlightenments. The common denominator was the perceived need radically to reform the whole of humanistic learning. Hence, though this has rarely been recognized by scholars, the Neapolitan giant Giambattista Vico (1668–1744), in openly aspiring to establish a fundamentally 'new science' of erudition, sweepingly rejecting the basic principles and overall legacy of humanist learning, and doing so specifically under the stimulus (and challenge) of Cartesianism, Spinoza, Bayle, and Le Clerc, however innovative, was at the same time, no less than the German Eclectics, profoundly representative of the deepest scholarly tendencies of his time.

The Early Enlightenment 'revolution in text criticism', then, had a powerful and perhaps exaggerated sense of its own 'revolutionary' character. The two greatest failures of humanist scholarship, in Le Clerc's opinion, were unsatisfactory translation of ancient texts and a rooted, structural inadequacy in explaining what they mean. Humanists, he grants, *had* produced a few serviceable translations; but 'most of 'em', as it is put in the English version of his *Parrhasiana* (London, 1700), 'are not faithful enough, and often misrepresent the sense of the original; because few of them are made by very learned men'. The foremost humanists, unfortunately, had disdained translation as 'a tedious labour which was beneath them' whilst those who undertook the task, essential if society is to possess reliable renderings of the main works of literature, philosophy, history, medicine, and science, whether classical, early Christian, oriental, or medieval, had mostly lacked the understanding needed to translate faithfully and accurately. If the great Isaac Casaubon (1559–1614), grants Le Clerc, rendered Polybius, Aenaeas Tacitus (a Greek writer

[13] Hamilton, *Apocryphal Apocalypse*, 246–7, 292, 294–5; Mulsow, *Moderne*, 252.

[14] Rabus, *Griekse, Latijnse*, 9–10; Evers, ' "Orakel" von Antonius van Dale', 235.

on the art of war), and Theophrastus' *Characters* superbly, most humanist translation had utterly failed to provide the renderings an 'enlightened' humanity needs and has every right to expect.

Besides saddling humanity with masses of inaccurate and misleading translation, the Greek and Latin editions provided by humanists, complained Le Clerc, had mostly been devoid of 'notes on all the difficult places', as well as explanations of terms and beliefs unfamiliar to the modern reader. This major handicap applied also to the first compete modern translation of the Koran, André Du Ryer's French rendering published at Paris in 1647, a text widely used during the Early Enlightenment and, in 1716, one of the first texts to appear in Russian translation at St Petersburg; a book in great demand all over Europe, the usefulness of Du Ryer's rendering was, however, severely curtailed by its lack, as it was put by George Sale, whose own translation of the Koran into English appeared in 1734, of 'notes to explain a vast number of passages, some of which are difficult, and others impossible to be understood, without proper explications, were they translated ever so exactly'.[15] Although matters had improved somewhat since the mid seventeenth century, observed Le Clerc, and recently there had been 'published in Holland three Greek authors, *cum notis variorum*, which one may approve of; because they contain the entire notes of several learned men. I mean Diogenes Laertius, Longinus and Callimachus',[16] and a few Greek authors had lately also appeared in England, 'with the ancient scholia, and some critical notes' which however were not 'to be compared to those of Holland, either for order, or the excellency of the notes, tho' they are not at all to be despised',[17] this was all far too meagre.

The edition of Callimachus of Cyrene, chief librarian of the great library of Alexandria for some twenty years until his death in about 240 BC, and one of the pre-eminent grammarians and poets of Hellenistic Egypt, was the work of the celebrated German professor based at Utrecht Johannes Georgius Graevius (1632–1705), originally from Naumburg, and member of the Utrecht philosophical circle the 'College der Scavanten'. Ardent Cartesian (and firm anti-Spinozist), Graevius, like Bayle and Bekker, wrote opposing popular superstition concerning comets, and was reckoned among the foremost classical philologists in Europe, indeed one of the architects of the new criticism. Appearing at Utrecht, in 1697, this edition was equipped with a huge apparatus of explanatory notes, far exceeding in bulk the original Greek text, with facing Latin translation, notes supplemented by multiple indexes to authors, antiquities, Greek words, and general context, assisting the layman with some Latin and general erudition thoroughly to orientate himself.[18]

[15] Hamilton and Richard, *André Du Ryer*, 107, 117.

[16] Benthem, *Holländischer Kirch- und Schulen-Staat*, ii. 454–5; Gundling, *Vollständige Historie*, i. 191–7; Knuttel, *Balthasar Bekker*, 150; Hubbeling, 'Inleiding', 47; the Longinus edition Le Clerc cites was of the Utrecht classicist Jacob Tollius (d. 1696) published by Halma, under the title Dionysius Longinus, *De sublimitate commentarius* (Utrecht, 1694).

[17] Le Clerc, *Parrhasiana*, 174.

[18] *Callimachi hymni, epigrammata, et fragmenta ex recensione Theodori J. G. F. Graevii cum eijusdem animadversibus* (2 vols., Utrecht, 1697).

Scholars prior to the last quarter of the seventeenth century, then, according to Le Clerc, had utterly failed to introduce and expound ancient literature to educated lay society. Instead of rendering the Greek and other classics accessible and part of general culture by translating and elucidating, most humanists had disastrously concentrated on issues of style and grammar, thereby, in the opinion of the new *critique*, helping obscure from view, as far as most readers were concerned, the precious legacy of humanity's past, tightly restricting it to a mere handful of professional scholars. More devastating still was the Early Enlightenment assessment of humanist exegetical skills. The humanists had competently studied ancient languages and philology but, held the new critics, had done so mainly to recover and edit texts so as to promote eloquence and literary style, cultivate poetry, and eulogize moral qualities. Where there *was* a serious scholarly, as opposed to rhetorical, purpose in humanist study, as with Lorenzo Valla's fideism, or Erasmus' Christian humanism, the prime concern was still mainly to exhort pious submission and emulation, not explore meanings.

A typical refrain of Enlightenment disparagement of older scholarship, the complaints about humanist preoccupation with rhetoric were frequent and scathing. Jean-Frédéric Bernard scorned above all the humanists' stuffing their heads with 'une infinité de mots Grecs et Latins', collecting vast stores of useless phrases which they then employed for pedagogic, decorative, or convivial purposes, arranging phrases and expressions from ancient authors 'presque toujours au hazard', encouraging everyone to misconstrue or attribute the most fantastic meanings to the texts they so abused.[19] Rhetoric is fine for antiquarians, pedants, and muddle-heads incapable of grappling with difficult ideas; but of what use it for those interested in clear thinking and real human issues? No one, held this radical Bernard, can be a true *érudit* and *humaniste*, 'sans être bon philosophe; sans avoir de justes idées de la vertu et du vice', without knowing oneself and others.[20] The humanists of early modern times, by constantly skirting round the fundamental questions in human life, to his mind negated the whole purpose of investigating ancient texts. Inability to free themselves from basically theological, traditional, and magical views of the world had left them imprisoned within what he saw as a hopelessly disfigured and superficial perspective not just on antiquity but likewise philosophy, morality, ecclesiastical history, and history of thought and culture generally.

Humanists, then were judged largely oblivious to the need to reconstruct the context of beliefs and ideas ancient texts embody and elucidate the assumptions, superstitions, and fears which shaped them, as well as ill equipped to develop the kind of historically based exegesis indispensable for achieving such goals. Mostly, they endeavoured to avoid, or play down, the basic antagonisms and tensions in ancient literature. Valla did see philosophy and faith as being in conflict; it was more usual, though, to assume there was no underlying antagonism between philosophy and theology but, on the contrary, an abiding harmony or general convergence of

[19] Bernard, *Réflexions morales*, 312. [20] Ibid. 310–11.

prisca theologia and *prisca sapientia* so that, in essence, ancient philosophy prefigures Christianity, seamlessly connecting with the dictates of religious orthodoxy.[21] Inspired by this ideal of *pax philosophica*, most humanists were nevertheless less concerned to demonstrate the happy junction of truths, or remove difficulties with it, than shelter with as little disturbance as possible under the presumption of an ultimate harmonious union of theology and philosophy.

Humanist discussion of Graeco-Roman Stoicism was a case in point. Stoic morality was extolled, and by the end of the sixteenth century enormously influential; but the monistic, determinist, and materialist doctrines on which it rested were ignored and Stoic, like other pre-Christian concepts of God, Providence, soul, and free will, systematically if mostly unwittingly misrepresented in a conventionally Christian sense.[22] Justus Lipsius (1547–1606) may have been a great scholar who did more than anyone to promote the austere Christian neo-Stoicism fashionable in European high culture in the late sixteenth and early seventeenth centuries, but he too expounded Stoicism, like innumerable lesser contemporaries, as essentially a preparation and paving the way for Christianity.[23] Nor by any means, from the perspective of a Jakob Thomasius, Le Clerc, or Bayle, were these the only shortcomings of his approach. For his very concern with screening out everything contradicting Christian theology encouraged him to ignore, as he did, the earlier surviving Greek sources, and focus instead on later Latin accounts, especially Seneca,[24] thereby intruding extraneous ingredients, including an infusion of Platonism and Neoplatonism, partly so as to impart negative connotations to matter and nature and imply, quite falsely, Stoic commitment to a transcendent spirituality even where, in the eyes of later scholars, such interpretation blatantly contradicts authentic Stoic doctrine.

A key instance of humanism's anachronistic Christianization of pre-Christian thought was indeed precisely this tendency to subsume Platonism, and also Stoicism, into Christian Neoplatonism and generally overstate the parallels and similarities between Platonism and early church dogma. This tradition persisted in the later seventeenth century among the Cambridge Platonists, Plato's philosophy being viewed by them as profoundly akin to, and essentially a preparation for, the thought-world of the early Church Fathers. For all his vast erudition and penetrating insights, Cudworth figured in this respect among the principal offenders. Despite the growing sophistication of seventeenth-century erudition, this long-hallowed tradition of scholarship was not challenged, and perhaps could not have been, until the new *critique* based on wholly fresh philosophical criteria arose towards the end of the seventeenth century. But once the rupture occurred, the implications were far-reaching and of immense consequence.[25]

21 Holmes, *Florentine Enlightenment*, 136; Krop, 'Northern Humanism', 154–7; Stinger, *Renaissance in Rome*, 301–2; Häfner, 'Jacob Thomasius', 141, 152–3, 157.

22 Poppi, 'Fate, Fortune, Providence', 647.

23 Ramond, 'Ne pas rire', 120; Tuck, *Philosophy and Government*, 48, 54–6; Long, 'Stoicism', in Inwood (ed.), *The Cambridge Companion to the Stoics*, 379–82.

24 Long, 'Stoicism', in Inwood (ed.), *The Cambridge Companion to the Stoics*, 381; Häfner, 'Jacob Thomasius', 154–5, 157.

25 Vieillard-Baron, 'Platonisme et paganisme', 440.

Even where basic theological and scholastic premisses were only marginally concerned, humanist scholarship had proven remarkably slow to challenge and supplant all manner of fanciful suppositions, fabrications, and received traditions passed down through texts, including notions which, to the Early Enlightenment mind, were full of gullibility, uncritical acceptance of authority, and not infrequently sheer fantasy. This occurred even where some humanists had from early on nurtured suspicions of fraud and non-authenticity, there being a prevailing unwillingness rigorously to follow up such doubts. A prime and rather serious instance was the Italian Platonists' cultivation of the *Corpus Hermeticum* long venerated, from the time of Pletho and Ficino, as the fount of ancient Egyptian wisdom emanating in a secret chain of pristine theological tradition from its great, archetypal figure 'Hermes Trismegistus' down to the present.

Trust in hermeticism, endorsed by various humanists, was at its peak in the late sixteenth and early seventeenth centuries and if, in 1614, the great philologist Casaubon intervened devastatingly to discredit this powerful learned myth, employing the most advanced humanist techniques which he shared with the great Scaliger to show that the Hermetic Books were not a clandestine source of pristine wisdom reaching back to the beginnings of civilization but a late antique forgery concocted long after the rise of Neoplatonism and Christianity, he and Scaliger (who was even more aware of the extent of Hellenistic, Jewish, and early Christian forgery)[26] nevertheless did relatively little to dent seventeenth-century scholarship's commitment to the myth. For Casaubon's sally failed to sway much or most learned opinion, as regularly happened with the critical breakthroughs of the Renaissance;[27] and, in any case, it was later largely countered by Cudworth who held that Casaubon had blundered in considering the *Corpus Hermeticum* a single compilation, arguing that while three or four of the books were indeed 'nothing but Christian cheats and impostures' the rest must be accepted as genuine.[28]

A wider and deeper rejection of Hermetic and ancient Egyptian 'wisdom', as of the authenticity of the Orphic hymns translated into Latin by Ficino, and many other erudite traditions, fables, and myths accepted, if not revered, by most humanists, swayed the Republic of Letters at large only towards the end of the seventeenth century.[29] After 1700, by contrast, scholars became more and more scathing. Vico had no doubt that an ancient Egyptian tradition of wisdom had survived. But he judged first that thrice-great Hermes referred to a collective tradition of Egyptian popular thought spread over several ages lasting more than a thousand years; secondly, that this popular Egyptian wisdom had nothing to do, originally, with the Neoplatonism later injected into it by Greek philosophers; and, thirdly, that neither

[26] Grafton, *Joseph Scaliger*, ii. 706–8.

[27] Grafton, 'Availability', 768; Harrison, '*Religion' and the Religions*, 132–3; Hofmeier, 'Cudworth versus Casaubon', 572, 582–3; Jehasse, *Renaissance*, pp. xiv, 195, 259, 264, 546.

[28] Yates, *Giordano Bruno*, 169–70, 398, 400–7, 422–3; Stinger, *Renaissance in Rome*, 303; Hofmeier, 'Cudworth versus Casaubon', 581–5; Assmann, 'Rehabilitierung', 44–6.

[29] Grafton, 'Availability', 775, 785; Patrides, *Cambridge Platonists*, 7–8; Assmann, *Moses*, 18–19, 84–5.

the original popular Egyptian tradition, nor pre-Christian Neoplatonism, had anything to do with predicting Christian truths.[30] By the early eighteenth century, as Lenglet Dufresnoy observed, hermeticism, like alchemy, still persisted in some quarters but was no longer deemed respectable, having to a large extent been driven underground and become a furtive hangover from the past.[31]

It may be because twentieth-century historians were themselves long reluctant fully to acknowledge the pervasive influence of Renaissance occultism, and the preoccupation with such arcane sources as the *Hermetica*, Orphism, Pseudo-Dionysius (Corpus Dionysiacum), Cabbala, Chaldaic Oracles, and the *Oracula Zoroastris*, as well as the belief that Homer, Plato, Virgil, and other ancient poets and philosophers were divinely inspired with *prisca theologia* and 'contain hidden allusions to Christianity',[32] that there has been a general lack of appreciation of the importance of the new text criticism of the Early Enlightenment. A long-standing bias towards understating the role of mysticism, magic, and occultism in the Renaissance, and overstating the modernity and critical autonomy of the humanist, in other words, seems to have contributed to a failure to recognize how closely humanism was tied to a cultural system steeped in authority and credulity and how profound was the subsequent break wrought by the Early Enlightenment.

To Le Clerc and the exponents of the new *critique*, wherever authorities such as Patristic literature, or early ecclesiastical history, lent their sanction, the humanists seemed doubly or trebly obtuse, having generally failed to perceive, let alone reject, such obvious forgeries and late compilations as the *Orphica*, Sibylline Chronicles, the third-century AD 'Chaldaean Oracles', innumerable dubious reports of miracles and visions of saints and the Virgin Mary, besides Josephus' supposed testimony to Christ's miracles and Resurrection and Aristeas' supposedly historical account of the translation of the Septuagint. Nothing is harder, contends Bayle, than to re-evaluate critically what has long been believed, or what everyone believes, especially when such credence is rooted in tradition and universally attested in books. 'N'est-ce rien', he declared in his 'project' for the *Dictionnaire* published at Rotterdam, in 1692, 'à ne pas croire légèrement ce qui s'imprime? N'est-ce pas le nerf de la prudence que d'être difficile à croire?'[33] This indeed was the nub of the difference between the new *critique* and the culture of humanism.

Although humanists were often genuinely worried by the disjunction between classical culture and Christianity, as, for example, the Huguenot savant and connoisseur of Greek poetry Henri Estienne was by the frivolity, immorality, and fancifulness of much Greek lyric poetry viewed from a Christian perspective, the typical pre-enlightened response was to resort to extraneous expedients to avoid the intellectual implications. Estienne, who compiled the leading Greek *thesaurus* of early modern times, published in five volumes in 1572, and was in his time

[30] Vico, *The New Science*, 40, 132, 282–3.

[31] Lenglet Dufresnoy, *Histoire de la philosophie hermétique*, i. 441.

[32] Yates, *Giordano Bruno*, 78–9, 89–91; Ford, 'Classical Myth', 339–43; Hamilton, *Apocryphal Apocalypse*, 30–1; Schmidt-Biggemann, 'Platonismus', 205–7.

[33] Bayle, *Projet et fragmens*, 37.

unsurpassed in his knowledge of Greek grammar, philology, and poetry, was, like his colleagues, less interested in addressing the basic conflict of values, of which he, like Erasmus and others, was uneasily aware, than as far as possible massaging it away by seeking to legitimize pagan myths and tales, as Estienne was fond of doing, by allegorizing them in Christian terms.[34]

The great Italian and French humanists, like their northern counterparts, were thus not so much blind to the deeper intellectual challenges inherent in a close study of classical texts as compelled by the practical impossibility of compromising or questioning the fundamental beliefs of their age to adopt an evasive and non-committal philosophical stance. Their passionate involvement with rhetoric and allegory so scorned by the Enlightenment seemingly arose in large part precisely from their needing a self-imposed carefully contrived superficiality with which to screen out underlying or suppressed worries about the authenticity of traditions and texts. They elaborated a florid culture of emulation and analogy, allowing a comfortable coexistence of humanistic studies with theology and scholastic thought, in this way avoiding risk of scandal, outrage, controversy, and a brutal clash of values.[35] Despite the evident boldness of Erasmus' editing and publishing the Greek text of the New Testament, and commenting on the defects of the Vulgate, cohabitation designed to paper over major theological and philosophical problems, not systematic investigation and exploration of ideas, remained the predominant strategy.

One newly rediscovered strand of Greek thought which the humanists did investigate with more resolve was ancient scepticism, especially Pyrrhonism. However, scepticism, as has been pointed out, was made much of by the humanists precisely because it appeared useful as a device for defending theology's hegemony against the encroachments of less welcome strands of ancient thought. Thus Estienne published the *Hypotoposes* of Sextus Empiricus, in 1562, primarily as a way of discrediting the ancient philosophy schools and neutralizing their naturalistic and 'atheistic' views.[36] After the Reformation, moreover, study of Scripture, the Church Fathers, and early church history all came to be heavily overshadowed by the ruthless exigencies of a highly polemical age which further inhibited both Protestant and Catholic scholars from dispassionate study of the early sources.[37] If, by the mid seventeenth century, some humanists felt that the 'age of criticism and philology has passed and one of philosophy and mathematics has taken its place',[38] it was only the old criticism of humanism which receded, crumbling along with the reign of theology and scholastic philosophy. For the rise of Cartesianism and the New Philosophy also meant that a new philosophically and scientifically grounded criticism was being nurtured, a *critique* using the techniques of philology

34 Boudou, 'Poétique d'Henri Estienne', 575–9; Jehasse, *Renaissance*, 73–82.
35 Holmes, *Florentine Enlightenment*, 136; Krop, 'Northern Humanism', 154.
36 Popkin, *History of Scepticism*, 20–1, 33–4; Grafton, 'Availability', 790.
37 Hamilton, *Apocryphal Apocalypse*, 226.
38 Grafton, *Defenders*, 3; see also Grafton, *Bring out your Dead*, 101, 317.

but now chiefly concerned with the impartial, systematic study of the arguments and belief structures revealed by ancient texts rather than testimony, dogmatic formulation, rhetorical exercises, usage, and stylistic matters for their own sake.

2. SECULARIZATION OF THE SACRED

Exponents of Early Enlightenment *ars critica* claimed fresh perspectives and knowledge would flow from re-examining the Bible, Septuagint, Samaritan version, Apocrypha, early church history, mythology, Greek and Roman pagan philosophy, classical religion, Christian Neoplatonism, the eastern churches, pre- and post-Christian Judaism, ancient Egypt, ancient Mesopotamian cults, Manichaeism, and Islam using the newly devised techniques.[39] Seeking to systematize the rules of hermeneutics on a new basis, the exponents of the new methodology dramatically contrasted what they considered novel methods with those of humanist exegesis. To the tools of humanist erudition and philology, they added the requirement for historical contextualization—elucidating the opinions and customs of each age, learning to distinguish different theological, philosophical, and historiographical ideologies, and showing how these tend to govern phraseology and vocabulary. Much attention consequently shifted to the intellectual grounding of polemics and motivations behind text editing, fabrication, and alteration as well as researching the historical origins of names, institutions, laws, and beliefs.

In the writings of the past, held Le Clerc, 'there are innumerable allusions to customs and opinions of their times' which unless fully investigated and explained by modern interpreters will leave us forever unable to understand correctly what they wrote.[40] To put matters right, much historical erudition is required, but equally essential, he believed, was to undertake criticism, as he put it in a letter to Locke (whose philosophy of language was a major influence on his historical-philological method), in a manner 'bien plus philosophique' than in the past.[41] More 'philosophical' elucidation involved painstaking scholarly research, enquiring into cultural milieu and examining poetic expressions using broad comparative techniques. For Le Clerc, whose own Bible criticism was directed partly against Richard Simon and Spinoza but whose critical rules at the same time borrowed heavily from Spinoza (as well as Locke),[42] this applied equally to sacred and profane literature.

Given that ancient writers only rarely explain the beliefs and customs of those among whom they live, ancient texts mostly fail to reveal what we need to know to understand them correctly. Since authors usually refer to prevalent beliefs peripherally or obscurely, critical examination and reconstruction of the suppositions and mental processes underlying what they say is indispensable, held Le Clerc, if one is

[39] Hamilton, *Apocryphal Apocalypse*, 227–8.

[40] Le Clerc, *Ars critica*, i. 48; Pitassi, *Entre croire et savoir*, 13–14.

[41] Lomonaco, 'Tra erudizione e critica', 165.

[42] Ibid. 165–6; Mannarino, *Mille favole*, 102.

to coax the true meaning from texts.[43] Editors and translators must strive to do this when preparing their editions; but enquiring readers, he urged, must also learn to do this for themselves by utilizing the growing but still far from adequate stock of reference works, lexicons, and encyclopedias containing the necessary background knowledge without which exact meanings would frequently elude even the highly erudite. To exemplify the ideal type of lexicographical compilation requisite for the new 'enlightened' style of reading, Le Clerc cites Graevius' imposing twelve-volume *Thesavrvs antiqvitatvm Romanorvm* (1694–9) published and sold at Utrecht and Leiden by François Halma and Pieter van der Aa.[44]

High on Le Clerc's long list of objections to humanist scholarly culture was that in seeking to determine correct usage and grammar, humanists remained generally blind to the discrepancies and ambiguities arising from the way identical or similar words and phrases acquire different meanings over time or are assigned fresh meanings by rival religions, sects, and philosophy schools. Just as 'Holy Scripture' means the Hebrew Old Testament to Jews where, for Christians, the term denotes the Old and New Testaments plus the Greek Apocrypha which they joined to the Old Testament,[45] so innumerable examples of key concepts—fate, soul, 'the light', grace, angel, demon, salvation, Trinity, spirits, prophesy, messiah, providence, God[46]—may be cited where Christian, Jewish, Platonic, Stoic, Aristotelian, and Pythagorean usages of the same expressions are charged with very different meanings. Here the humanist approach seemed still rooted in that of such Hellenizing Fathers as Justin Martyr and Clement of Alexandria; for the Fathers, held Le Clerc, Gundling, and others, had hopelessly confused the debate about the Trinity by indiscriminately mixing Platonic, Neoplatonic, Jewish, and Christian ideas.[47]

Virtually ignoring the problem of divergent belief structures, humanists either conferred Christian signification anachronistically or else, no less commonly, muddled everything up through failure adequately to reconstruct and classify the thought systems of the ancient world. In this way, humanist mastery of verbal usage was completely offset by inability to understand historical context. So deficient was their grasp of ancient systems of belief and thought, claims Le Clerc, that all their various editions of the *Lives and Opinions of Eminent Philosophers* of Diogenes Laertius (AD *c*.200–250), a text vital for studying the ancient philosophy schools, first published in Greek in the West in 1533, were practically useless.[48] There was good reason to be grateful, he added, for the recent critical edition published at Amsterdam in 1692, a version which subsequently long remained, according to Johann Georg Walch, in his survey of *historia philosophica* of 1727, the only reliable as well as best annotated edition of Diogenes.[49]

[43] Le Clerc, *Ars critica*, i. 398. [44] Ibid, i. 58; Bietenholz, *Historia and Fabula*, 276–7.

[45] Le Clerc, *Règles de critique*, 329; Le Clerc, *Ars critica*, i. 249.

[46] Le Clerc, *Ars critica*, i. 274, 415–19; Le Clerc, *Règles de critique*, 351; Sina, *Vico e Le Clerc*, 24–5, 30.

[47] Le Clerc, *Lives*, 69–81, 95–6; Gundling, *Vollständige Historie*, i. 933–4, 936; Cantelli, 'Mito e storia in Leclerc', 275–6; Mulsow, 'Gundling *versus* Buddeus', 115.

[48] Le Clerc, *Ars critica*, ii. 449–50; Blackwell, 'Logic of History', 106–8; Piaia, 'Brucker *versus* Rorty', 76–7; Kelley, *Descent of Ideas*, 91. [49] Walch, *Einleitung*, i. 5.

Particularly deplorable, held Le Clerc, were the deficiencies of humanist Bible scholarship. In his view, all the main churches in recent centuries were equally guilty of obscuring the true meaning of many passages of Scripture with their unscholarly, uncritical, and highly inaccurate readings and translations. So far-reaching in its implications was this defect that he judged it the chief reason, along with the fatal influence of Neoplatonism on the Fathers, for the proliferation of schism and strife plaguing ancient, medieval, and modern Christendom. Such was his confidence in the new *ars critica* that he believed it would eventually resolve the age-old divisions among the churches provided what he called 'les principes du Christianisme', the points of doctrine which all the churches shared, were recognized as inherently rational: if the theologians of the various denominations studied Scripture suspending judgement, as one should, and as is so reasonable and just, until one has completed a careful examination, 'il n'y auroit plus de controverses entre nous'.[50] If there was much that was credulous, irrational, and 'manifestement faux' not only in Catholic teaching but in everything divisive, or peculiar to, the teaching of each particular church, all this irrationality was wholly confined, he urged, to what divides the churches.[51] If one asked what then would be reason's instrument for separating 'le christianisme en général' from falsity, credulity, and superstition, the answer, of course, was *ars critica*. Le Clerc deemed it the highest task of the dawning new age of enlightenment that it should, armed with its new critical apparatus, actively drive the reunion of the churches.[52]

Humanism's worst defect, held Le Clerc, Bayle, van Dale, and Bentley alike, given that 'to forge and counterfeit books, and father them upon great names', as Bentley put it, 'has been a practice almost as old as letters' and that the 'greatest part of mankind are so easily imposed on in this way',[53] was its failure effectively to expose even the most obvious and damaging fabrications and deceptions foisted on humanity by ancient textual authority. Hence the real work of discrediting and disposing of the *Oracula Sibyllina*, Chaldaean chronicles, and Orphic hymns, even though generations of *érudits* had interested themselves in these purportedly pre-Christian pagan verse prophesies and mysteries, seemingly only really began, as Diderot noted in 1751, in the 1650s when the Huguenot scholar David Blondel (1590–1655), much respected later by Bayle, the elder Vossius' successor at the Remonstrant academy, published his treatise on the *Oracula* in Amsterdam.[54] If Casaubon and other humanist scholars saw grounds for scepticism about the *Oracula* as supposedly pre-Christian texts genuinely prophesying the future history of the world, the coming of Christ, and downfall of Rome, throughout the fifteenth, sixteenth, and early seventeenth centuries, most humanists, and most of society, had still continued to revere them as precious confirmation of Christian claims

50 Le Clerc, *Règles de critique*, 377.

51 Le Clerc, *De l'incrédulité*, 205–7, 240.

52 Ibid. 205; Le Clerc, *Règles de critique*, 377; Bots and Evers, 'Jean Leclerc et la réunion', 54–67.

53 Bentley, *Works*, ii. 136–7.

54 Gundling, *Vollständige Historie*, i. 775, 778; Gundling, *Gundlingiana*, iv. 318; Prades, *Thèse*, 63; Yvon et al., *Apologie*, seconde partie, 285.

deriving from an unimpeachable, if mysterious, pagan source—the ten venerable Sibyls.[55]

Indeed, in the late seventeenth and early eighteenth centuries there was still formidable resistance to those who questioned their authenticity. Clement of Alexandria, Origen, St Justin Martyr, and other Fathers had insisted, as Bolingbroke puts it, that the 'ancient and venerable Sibyl . . . was extraordinarily inspired "by almighty God" ', and this still counted for more than Blondel's objections for several more decades in the minds of many.[56] 'What clumsy cheats, those Sibylline Oracles now extant', commented Bentley, noting their long sway, 'and Aristeas's story of the Septuagint', and these 'passed without control even among very learned men!'[57] In Holland, only after van Dale's devastating critique in his *De oraculis veterum ethnicorum* (1683) were the *Oracula Sibyllina* finally discredited.[58] By the second quarter of the eighteenth century, in France too the battle was over: which theologian, asked Diderot in 1751, would dare today use the evidence of the Sibylline Chronicles as a weapon 'contre les Déistes de nos jours'?[59]

Most deplorable of all, Clement, trusting in the *Oracula Sibyllina* and other dubious sources, complains Le Clerc, continually 'cites suppositious writings as if they had been acknowledged by every body'.[60] Lamentably, he adds, such misuse of all manner of texts was 'general among the Fathers'; yet the humanists had failed to expose all of this.[61] 'What today would seem want of honesty', noted Le Clerc, 'was the custom of many ancients, to make use of all sorts of arguments and books to bring over men to their opinions.'[62] This was obvious to him and his contemporaries but, regrettably, had not been to the humanists. Overcoming paganism, in the eyes of the Fathers, justified forgery and deceiving the people. But Le Clerc doubted whether the truly wise could ever approve such devout manipulation. Indeed, the deficiencies of Patristic methods, he held, probably in the end hampered rather than helped the Christian cause: for 'several people believe that the want of sincerity of some Christians, and the credulity of some others, did very much contribute to the keeping up of paganism'.[63]

These and other strictures about the Fathers' treatment of history, originally published in Le Clerc's *Bibliothèque universelle*, ramified especially in Britain where his text appeared in translation, under the title *Lives of the Primitive Fathers* (1701), and Germany where, a few years later, Gundling reworked his account of the Fathers' misuse of Platonism and, in 1721, a German rendering of his text appeared on the initiative of Christian Thomasius.[64] Still better known, Le Clerc's *Ars critica*

[55] Yates, *Giordano Bruno*, 16 n., 42, 364, 427; Ford, 'Classical Myth', 339–40; Stinger, *Renaissance in Rome*, 308–12.

[56] [Faydit], *Remarques sur Virgile*, 93; Goeree, *Mosaize Historie*, ii. 667; Rabus, *Griekse, Latijnse*, 96; Bolingbroke, *Philosophical Works*, iii. 38.

[57] Bentley, *Works*, ii. 138.

[58] Grafton, *Defenders*, 167, 172–3.

[59] Yvon et al., *Apologie*, seconde partie, p. 285.

[60] Ibid. 49; Clement of Alexandria, *Protreptikos*, 113, 141, 161, 167; Lenglet Dufresnoy, *Méthode*, ii. 445.

[61] Le Clerc, *Lives*, 39–40.

[62] Ibid. 50.

[63] Ibid. 204.

[64] Häfner, 'Johann Lorenz Mosheim', 232; Mulsow, *Moderne*, 289–91.

(1697), where he goes furthest toward formulating the rules of the new criticism, remained a classic of the new learning, throughout Europe, until deep into the eighteenth century.[65] The aim of criticism, he held, is to uncover the true meaning of texts; and if humanists might agree with that in broad terms, they would certainly have eschewed his requirement that sound exegesis must chiefly rest on a 'philosophical' approach to reality including Scripture rather than mere philology, and must employ 'philosophical' reason to elucidate historical circumstance, evaluate arguments, and assess the invoking of signs, wonders, fables, and miracles. A historico-philological method and a 'philosophical' approach are seen in Le Clerc as key pieces of apparatus that must be 'perpetually conjoined' if any worthwhile result is to ensue.[66]

A striking feature of Le Clerc's *Ars critica* is its merging of Scripture for purposes of critical appraisal with the rest of ancient literature, as in Spinoza, Boulainvilliers, and Collins, thereby turning Bible criticism into a quasi-secular activity indistinguishable from other kinds of text study.[67] Ever since first reading the *Tractatus theologico-politicus* in 1681, Le Clerc had simultaneously absorbed and combated Spinoza's criticism.[68] Applying the same critical rules to study of Scripture as applied to other texts underlay his strategy of reconciling modern philosophy and theology by removing the obstacles, as he saw it, to a fully 'rational' Christianity. Reducing the miraculous core of Christianity to an irreducible minimum, and segregating this from the rest so drastically as to make even his ally Locke uneasy,[69] he freed himself to subject most of Scripture—and all the Apocrypha, *pseudepigrapha*, and Patristic literature—to the full sweep of his historico-critical rigour, as well as to sacrifice numerous previously accepted miracles.[70] He boldly discarded Moses' authorship of the Pentateuch, like the radical Cartesians, and adopted Spinoza's view of the parting of the Red Sea as due to exceptionally strong winds.[71] For Le Clerc, the Bible is God's Word but not all of it is free from corruption, and not all is authoritative.

The consequences of the new *critique* ramified in all directions, one of the most important being the new discipline of 'history of philosophy'. Here Bayle was among the founding fathers. For Bayle, as for Spinoza, Le Clerc, van Dale, and Gundling, the only cogent way to interpret an ancient source, and usefully assess claims encountered in the religious, philosophical, and scientific literature of the past, is to apply the criterion of natural causality, using the historico-critical method to

[65] Jaumann, *Critica*, 176; Pocock, *Barbarism*, i. 218; one may well query whether 'it summed up two centuries of work on textual and historical criticism', see Grafton, *The Footnote*, 215.

[66] Le Clerc, *Ars critica*, foreword; Jaumann, *Critica*, 178–9; Poulouin, *Temps des origines*, 360–3.

[67] Poulouin, *Temps des origines*, 361–2; Funkenstein, *Theology*, 220–1; Lagrée, 'Le Thème des deux livres', 24–9, 36–7; Pitassi, *Entre croire et savoir*, 51–2, 57–8.

[68] Meinsma, *Spinoza et son cercle*, 523–4; Simonutti, *Arminianesimo e tolleranza*, 78; Pitassi, *Entre croire et savoir*, 25, 48.

[69] Champion, 'Père Richard Simon', 39.

[70] Pitassi, *Entre croire et savoir*, 13–15, 24–5, 81–2; Brogi, *Cerchio*, 37–8.

[71] [Le Clerc], *Sentimens*, 126–7; [Faydit], *Remarques sur Virgile*, 239; Wijngaards, *De 'Bibliothèque choisie'*, 5; Pitassi, *Entre croire et savoir*, 24–5, 82.

uncover not just false ideas but also the whole structure of assumption, imposture, prejudice, fear, and tradition on which the distorted belief structures of the past rest.[72] But from collating basic texts, he saw that one can go on to reconstruct the wider story of the history of human thought and render this an indispensable branch of philosophy. Partly prompted by his insights and provocative theses, Jakob Thomasius, Buddeus, and others began the detailed work of critically evaluating ancient thought later taken up by Fabricius, Gundling, Heumann, and Brucker for whom history of philosophy, to be valid, must be, in Bayle's, Le Clerc's, Boulainvilliers' sense, both 'critical' and 'philosophical', that is evaluated in terms of historical context, natural causality, and precise classification of terminology and traditions.[73]

In Bayle, text criticism is thus integral to both historical study and philosophy. Unlike Descartes, Malebranche, Locke, and Le Clerc, but like Spinoza, for Bayle, natural reason is the only allowable criterion of what is true or untrue.[74] Furthermore, while philosophical reason—mathematical and historical—is ultimately all one and based on geometrical proportionality, as in Spinoza, for him nevertheless, as we have seen, 'vérités historiques', the sifting out of historical facts using the new critical-historical method, even if ultimately anchored in the mathematical criteria of proportion and quantification, provide men with a certainty of fact and rationality found nowhere else, not even in mathematics or physics. No one can contradict our knowing that Caesar defeated Pompey without abandoning all scholarship and reason, whereas we must all contend with 'l'incertitude réelle et absolue' of mathematics, the possibility that mathematical proofs are only 'de beaux et brillans fantômes' offering no 'utilitez morales' as demonstrable historical *vérités* do.

This means, in Bayle's opinion, that historical criticism and research is not just indispensable but central to the process of meaningful philosophizing itself.[75] Hence, in Bayle, there is a close connection between the new 'critique' and his push to transform the relationship between theology and scholarship generally as well as dramatically widen the scope of the 'philosophical' beyond what is susceptible to mere quantitative treatment: mathematical rationality must be supplemented, if one seeks a truly 'philosophical' approach to reality, by knowledge drawn from historical texts critically evaluated.[76] In fact, only historical criticism, in his eyes, provides the true philosopher with what is knowable insofar as men can know things truly, reliably, and solidly. Whether discussing political thought, morality, toleration, atheism, or anything else that affects men, the philosopher can only do worthwhile work on the basis of historical knowledge.

Despite their mutual antagonism, then, Le Clerc and Bayle pulled very much in the same direction in the sphere of criticism, though this did not prevent Le Clerc

[72] Popkin, 'Spinoza and Bible Scholarship', 11–13.

[73] Proust, *Diderot*, 248–9.

[74] Marilli, 'Cartesianismo e tolleranza', 577.

[75] Bayle, *Projet et fragmens*, 35–7; Chaufepié, *Nouveau Dictionnaire*, i. 254; Cassirer, *Philosophy*, 204–7; Grafton, *The Footnote*, 195–6, 209–12.

[76] Fontius, 'Critique', 12; Jaumann, *Critica*, 135, 137, 179.

denigrating Bayle's reviews as too diffuse and unsystematic.[77] Both considered the quest for historical factuality, and the historico-critical method of sifting documents and retrieving facts, the basis of hermeneutics, and hermeneutics as basic to philosophy. They saw their critical methodology as the means to steer between the narrow mathematical dogmatism of Cartesianism, on the one hand, and the theological dogmatism of the churches, on the other, a method which therefore must be both itself 'philosophical' and, simultaneously, a vital instrument of philosophy.[78] In effect the *esprit philosophique*, the systematic application of human reason, with the new *critique* as one of its two primary tools, came to seem to Spinoza, Bayle, and Le Clerc alike, hence all three leading figures of the Dutch Early Enlightenment, the tool by which mankind can authentically know what is true and what is false, what is real and what is fantasy in Man's memory, myths, and texts.

3. MAN AND MYTH

Secularization and eradication of magic were central to the *vera eruditio* in a way that was not the case with humanist scholarship. During the age of humanism which extensively overlapped with the era of the Reformation and Counter-Reformation, theology presided over all intellectual endeavour, and even the pagan poetry of the Greeks had in some sense to be critically evaluated in terms of a Christian world rooted in Scripture. But with the rise of the new criticism this procedure was largely, and on the radical wing altogether, blocked. Where Estienne construes ancient Greek poetic fables as allusions to truth, meaning the Christian truths embodied in Scripture,[79] Spinoza and Le Clerc, albeit not without outraging most contemporary opinion, analyse Scripture as if it were just any manifestation of the human and natural world. The new critical methodology, then, was part of a wider cultural revolution and was not at all, as is sometimes claimed (but more often just assumed), a gradual, more or less straightforward outgrowth of humanist techniques.

The difference between old and new was to be found not in philological tools, technical apparatus, or use of languages but in intellectual outlook. As Fréret expressed it in 1724, 'la vraye critique n'est autre chose, que cet esprit philosophique appliqué à la discussion des faits', a form of enquiry which in examining texts and historical facts follows the same procedure that 'les philosophes employent dans la recherche des vérités naturelles'.[80] The idea that true historical criticism is primarily a philosophical activity, and hermeneutics central to philosophy, though profoundly

77 Lomonaco, 'Tra erudizione e critica', 161.

78 Lomonaco, 'Readers of Locke', 105; Pitassi, *Entre croire et savoir*, 90, 93.

79 Boudou, 'Poétique d'Henri Estienne', 590.

80 Quoted in Grell, 'Nicolas Fréret', 58; Pocock, *Barbarism*, i. 159–60; Poulouin, *Temps des origines*, 21.

un-Cartesian, and often strange to us today, was central to the Early Enlightenment and, hence, the intellectual construction of 'modernity'. By labelling itself 'philosophical' *and* 'historical', the new criticism both highlighted essential features of the cultural revolution of the Early Enlightenment while no less emphatically rejecting the rhetorical-literary-philological criticism of the humanists.

The new *critique* obviously had sensational results for Bible criticism but had dramatic consequences also in many other scholarly fields. For it crucially transformed distinctions between true and false, sacred and secular, supernatural and natural, magical and non-magical, rendering the whole of humanity's past a single continuum of interrelated development. It was a form of rationality which required all claims to authoritative tradition, supernatural inspiration, miracles, divine and demonic intervention, as well as knowledge of visions, prophecies, and revelations found in ancient and less ancient sources, to be explained in terms of historical context understood as the evolution of a humanity subject only to natural rather than supernatural causality. This, in turn, required elaborate 'philosophical' explanations as to why writers of the past continually invoke supernatural agency, hidden forces, signs, wonders, visions, magic, and providential happenings to account for how things happened as they did but which the new criticism felt obliged to discuss (even where, as with Le Clerc, Buddeus, or Fabricius, they were believers) as if all occurrences and alleged miracles were, or might have been, nothing but natural phenomena.[81] In the field of myth, the new exegesis tried, often rather crudely, to uncover the now expected underlying natural—or 'historical'—realities behind the poetic notion encased in the story.[82]

The new *vera eruditio* thus presumed as a matter of course that ancient, medieval, and early modern writers shared outlooks based on predominantly incorrect, misconceived, and credulous notions, and wished to know why and how humans have practically always, and so widely, erred in their most cherished convictions and assumptions. By the same token, the scholarly standards of humanist criticism, having operated within a very different set of rules and criteria, came to be viewed as fundamentally unreliable and suspect. Renaissance interpretation and editions of classical texts seemed to exponents of the new *critique* to be inherently prone to misinterpretation, corruption, unjustified insertions, and systematic distortions of meaning, passed on from generation to generation and now burdening humanity with an immense edifice of error and confusion requiring a root and branch pruning by the new methodology.[83]

The task of uncovering past belief structures, superstitions, and irrational assumptions, and demonstrating the mechanisms by which such structures capture human minds and pervade their texts, was tied to the wider agenda of explaining, rationalizing, and improving the world which the Early Enlightenment set itself. The artist and art historian Arnold Houbraken, an admirer of van Dale's efforts to

[81] Labrousse, *Pierre Bayle*, ii. 14; Preus, *Spinoza*, 209–10.

[82] Cantelli, 'Mito e storia in Leclerc', 279; Cantelli, 'Nicola Fréret', 264–5; Lilla, *G. B. Vico*, 139–40, 143, 175; Porter, *Enlightenment*, 234–5.

[83] Le Clerc, *Ars critica*, ii. 245, 404–5.

de-demonize the ancient Greek oracles,[84] in his *Philalethes Brieven* of 1711 granted that over the centuries there had been a gradual strengthening of human rationality and improvement in scientific, historical, and other knowledge; but he also thought that, more recently, there had been a sudden and decisive shift. It was only in 'our days', he says, that there occurred 'een geheele te niet doening van de heidensche bygeloovigheyt, die de weerelt dus lang heeft betoovert gehouden' [an entire demolition of the pagan superstition which until now has held the world bewitched] with 'all truth' finally being uncovered in the open.[85] Houbraken is here endorsing the historical-critical technique of Spinoza, van Dale, Bekker, and van Leenhof, the tool which engineered the widespread and well-documented collapse among parts of Dutch urban society at the end of the seventeenth century of belief in angels, demons, witchcraft, and the satanic as active forces in human life.

Some aspects of the revolution in scholarship generated relatively little friction between the two wings of the Enlightenment. A field where the humanists seemed to champions of the new exegesis to have wasted much time and effort, leaving intact a legacy of credulity but which could now rapidly be swept clean, was hagiography.[86] Re-evaluating the sayings and opinions of the Fathers seemed suddenly urgent business in both 'enlightened' camps, albeit on the moderate side perhaps less because generations of ancient, medieval, and early modern hagiographers had urged unquestioning reverence for them as paragons of 'wondrous and extraordinary holiness' as the English version of Le Clerc's treatise on this topic expresses it, than because Patristic literature revealed much of the early character of the church, was thought to be the source of much credulity Christians would be better off without, and had been continually 'invoked in the controversies which divide Christians'.[87] Countless supposed 'miracles', visions, and apparitions were now examined critically. 'On n'attaque point la puissance de Dieu', as Lenglet Dufresnoy restated Le Clerc's aims half a century later, by questioning wondrous happenings and marvels 'dont la vérité n'est pas certaine'.[88] Working in a Catholic context, Lenglet Dufresnoy urged the necessity of applying strict critical rules such as he then adumbrated 'pour discerner les véritables révélations, et les véritables apparitions' and to help readers think more critically about the great mass of falsely pretended 'miracles' and visions.[89] What remains when the entire incrustation of spurious wonders and 'miracles' is stripped away by the new scholarship, the theory went, is then incontrovertibly trustworthy.

An intellectually more complex set of problems, bound to aggravate tensions between mainstream Enlightenment and radical thought, concerned how to interpret classical allegorizing and the meaning of the innumerable myths found in classical and other ancient texts. Plainly, both allegory and myth permeated Greek

[84] Goeree, *Mozaise historie*, i, 'Voor-reden', p. k2 and vol. ii, 'Voor-reden', fos. 1^v–2; [Houbraken], *Philalethes Brieven*, 164–5, 227–36.

[85] [Houbraken], *Philalethes Brieven*, 126–7.

[86] Le Clerc, *Lives*, 3; Häfner, 'Johann Lorenz Mosheim', 232.

[87] Le Clerc, *Lives*, 1–3.

[88] Ibid. 1; Lenglet Dufresnoy, *Traité historique et dogmatique*, i. 159.

[89] Lenglet Dufresnoy, *Traité historique et dogmatique*, i. 158–67.

and much other ancient literature. Le Clerc derides Clement of Alexandria for resorting to allegory to explain episodes in Jewish history where, like the Jewish writer Philo (by whom he was greatly influenced), he discovered complex doctrines hidden in stories where nothing of the sort was ever intended. But it was the pagan Greeks, held Le Clerc, who had introduced allegory as a method of elucidation to lend dignity to fanciful poetic stories about gods and spirits which otherwise would be gross, trivial, and immoral.[90] Philo and the Fathers had then eagerly adopted the technique of allegory, partly to infiltrate and share in the prestige of great pagan poets like Homer and Hesiod, and, partly to connect Bible exegesis with the world of classical literature.[91] The result was thick layers of obfuscation encrusting the entire Old Testament, superadded by Jews and Christians alike.

The humanists had mostly explained classical myths as allegories embodying timeless truths often deemed approximate to Christian doctrines and viewpoints. The new text scholarship, by contrast, especially Le Clerc, Simon, Boulainvilliers, Fontenelle, Vico, and Fréret, held that myths were not timeless allegories but poetic, unreflecting, expressions of themes infusing primitive historical experience, or mistaken conceptions more or less invented in order to bring the common people to accept doctrines they could not understand through reason. However, Le Clerc leaned heavily towards Euhemerism, the argument taken from the third-century BC Greek Sicilian philosopher Euhemerus, that mythological deities are primitive and distorted representations of ancient heroes, denying they have any profound moral significance, while Fréret and Vico judged myths to be allegorical records not of personalities, or events, but rather deeply felt metaphysical notions, social changes, institutions, and collective discoveries, such as the advent of new arts and techniques.[92]Boulainvilliers combined elements from both theories.[93]

Patristic literature had favoured Euhemerist explanations of pagan myth as a way of persuading pagans of the spiritual emptiness and insignificance of their deities.[94] The Euhemerist tendencies in Le Clerc, and perhaps in the moderate mainstream Enlightenment more generally, can perhaps be interpreted as a way of reforming that tradition, thereby marginalizing the problem of myth. The anti-Euhemerist tendency in radical thought, by contrast, stressing the distorted and changing character of men's perceptions of timeless metaphysical, social, and physical realities, reflected a strongly subversive tendency in writers such as Fontenelle, Boulainvilliers, Vico, and Fréret to construe human development as an evolving, if halting, single human continuum. Myth, for them, was an early form of documenting social structure and change, a striking example being Vico's path-breaking evaluation of Homer's epics as an accumulation of primitive poetic wisdom expressed in myth, justifying and extolling the hierarchical social system and institutions of archaic Greece.

[90] Ibid. 53; Lamberton, *Homer*, 11, 15–16; Brogi, *Teologia senza verità*, 150.

[91] Le Clerc, *Lives*, 51–2; Lamberton, *Homer*, 78–9; Cantelli, 'Mito e storia in Leclerc', 277–8.

[92] Morrison, 'Vico and Spinoza', 55; Pompa, *Vico*, 35–6; Brogi, *Teologia senza verità*, 114; Dupré, *Enlightenment*, 195–9; Cantelli, 'Nicola Fréret', 271–2, 282, 406.

[93] Brogi, *Cerchio*, 100–2.

[94] Cantelli, 'Nicola Fréret', 277.

Ancient myths needed to be radically reassessed. But with the rise of the erudite journals after 1680, in both Latin and vernacular languages (primarily French, German, and Dutch), the new exegetical methods also came to be applied to the business of reviewing recent literature and the political 'myths' of the contemporary age. This development further intensified what were already crucial impulses of the new criticism: the appeal to scholarly impartiality when judging the deepest issues, an increased focus on the current international intellectual scene, and the notion that every text should be interpreted and placed within the context of an ongoing debate linking past and present. The journals also served to familiarize the public with the principles of competent criticism while intensifying the cautionary and moralizing tendency of the new exegesis.[95]

Having revolutionized Bible studies, galvanized theological debate, and transformed classical and Near Eastern studies with new types of 'comparatism', the new 'philosophical' hermeneutics also contributed to the reforming agenda of the Early Enlightenment including its most radical wing in other ways. In particular, the new *critique* made a noteworthy contribution to unmasking fraud and discrediting imposture operating by means of fabricating the myths of 'absolute monarchy'. The deprecation of myth and fable which often accompanied exposure of how these had been used over millennia as vehicles to propagate entrenched forms of error, tended to encourage a questioning attitude toward divine right theory and other political doctrines buttressed in popular culture by biblical, classical, and mythical parallels and accounts of supernatural intervention. Suspicion of rhetoric, and the impulse to disencumber the gullible masses of myth-based pretensions and fantastic claims, generated an extended 'enlightening' critique reaching into virtually every sphere of activity.

Mankind needed to be awoken to the perils of officially authorized deception, systematic imposture, and manipulation of popular gullibility as perpetrated in modern literature, official documents, and politics no less than in ancient texts. Here, Nicolas Gueudeville stands out as a notable figure. A former monk using erudition as a vehicle of both general and self-emancipation, he employed the new literary hermeneutics in his celebrated critique of Fénelon's *Télémaque*, the first part of which appeared in 1700, to mount a sustained attack not just on imposture and deception packaged in elevated writing for public consumption, but on what he considered the fraudulent pretence underlying the rhetoric of absolutism pervading the whole of European culture at the time.[96] He harshly criticized Louis XIV's war-mongering, insisting he had not ruled in the interests of his subjects.[97] He sought to unmask what he considered the deceptive psychological and intellectual basis on which so oppressive and morally reprehensible a system as divine right monarchy is constructed, in a critical *tour de force* which, of course, was immediately banned in France but for all that, notes Bayle, 'a été fort applaudie'.[98]

[95] Woitkewitsch, 'Thomasius' "*Monatsgespräche*" ', 662–3.

[96] Rosenberg, *Nicolas Gueudeville*, 44–5; Jaumann, *Critica*, 212, 252.

[97] Gueudeville, *Critique du premier tome*, 102–4.

[98] Rosenberg, *Nicolas Gueudeville*, 38.

Enlightenment *ars critica*, plainly, was inseparable from the late seventeenth-century wave of scepticism about not only the Fathers and Scripture, but also 'Mosaic philosophy', Platonic affinities with Christianity, early church history, demonology, hermeticism, ancient accounts of the origins of Rome and other peoples, *prisca theologia*, and also divine right monarchy.[99] As such, the new exegesis not unnaturally provoked fervent opposition from two quarters: on the one hand traditionalists among philologically trained humanists, students of rhetoric, poetry, and classical literature who resented the demolition of the culture of humanism, and, on the other, proponents of Counter-Enlightenment attitudes who felt impelled to try to expose the new critique as a fraudulent device tricking men into acceptance of the removal of supernatural spiritual forces from everyday reality. After publishing the first edition of his *Ars critica* in 1697, Le Clerc became entangled in a dispute which lingered for a decade with Jacob Voorbroeck, better known as Perizonius, a leading classicist who bitterly resented the aspersions cast on humanism and what he saw as unjustified meddling by someone who lacked proper training in philology. He fiercely contested Le Clerc's statements about the Church Fathers, claiming such far-reaching criticism could only encourage more scepticism and libertinism.[100] Gundling saw in this quarrel plain evidence of the small-mindedness of many Dutch academic philologists of the time, men who had progressed, it seemed, only with regard to their technical apparatus but failed to widen their intellectual horizons; he pronounced them unworthy to have in their midst such a great and eminent critic as Le Clerc.[101]

Even staunch defenders of tradition and ecclesiastical authority whose views bordered on those of the Counter-Enlightenment, such as the Abbé Pierre Valentin Faydit (1640–1709), claimed (rather dubiously) to be using the same critical methods which their adversary Le Clerc employed 'pour recevoir ses erreurs', to defend Catholic truth, the operation of supernatural and magical forces in history, and the integrity of the Fathers.[102] A former Oratorian and great admirer of Augustine, dismissed from the Congregation in 1671 for incorrect views on the soul, Faydit fully conceded, in 1705, that Le Clerc's *La vraie critique* had now effectively conquered the French scholarly world: 'il y a peu de gens de lettres en France', he grants, 'qui n'ayent lû l'*Ars Critica*, les *Parrhasiana*, et les *Bibliothèques choisies* de Mr Le Clerc'. In France as elsewhere scholars now predominantly embraced the new critical criteria.

The great danger in this, in Faydit's view, was that few grasped the true motives of those, like Le Clerc, responsible for devising the new critical methods.[103] The peril, in his opinion, was much greater than was yet generally realized, and it was only by turning against the new exegetes their own techniques of explicating Scripture and Patristic literature, as well as ancient poetry, that Catholics would be able eventually

[99] Grell, 'Nicolas Fréret', 52; Blair, 'Practices', 69; Poulouin, *Temps des origines*, 158–74.
[100] Lomonaco, 'Readers of Locke', 106–7.
[101] Gundling, *Vollständige Historie*, i. 981.
[102] [Faydit], *Remarques*, preface p. v.
[103] Ibid., preface p. iv; Wijngaards, *De* 'Bibliothèque choisie', 50–1.

to defeat 'Messieurs les Spinosistes, Arminiens, Pelagiens [et] Sociniens' along with the Quietists and 'Clericistes, ou Disciples de Mr le Clerc' who, according to Faydit, was in essence an 'Arminien-Spinosiste'. Equally adjustments to critical techniques and reading were needed to enable the Catholic faithful to check the dangerous opinions 'de quelques Catholiques de grande réputation tels que sont Monsieur Simon et le P. Malebranche'.[104]

An open enemy of Malebranche, Simon, Fénelon, and Bossuet, the widely read if eccentric Faydit believed solid erudition applied to classical pagan poetry could help repel the poison of Le Clerc's 'pernicieuses erreurs', and all 'détestable Socinianisme, et Arminianisme'.[105] Spinoza and Le Clerc admit, he argues, that the authors of the sacred books of Scripture and the greatest pagan poets all employ language which attributes everything to God and that they continually represent him acting directly 'par luy-même sur le cœur et sur la volonté des hommes', inspiring men with the thoughts and desires which they have and determining them infallibly to do 'ce qu'il veut qu'ils fassent'.[106] Pagan poets and sacred writers alike, say Spinoza and Le Clerc, do this to excite wonder and a sense of the sublime, presuming there is less 'grandeur et d'élévation d'esprit' in describing things straightforwardly, in human terms, and in attributing everything that happens in human life to secondary and proximate causes, than explaining events in terms of 'causes supérieures', that is bringing God or the gods into our affairs.[107] Hence, they insinuate that stories of divine and other supernatural intervention are just poetic fancies whereas Virgil and Homer, rightly interpreted, actually prove divine providence is constantly operative, swaying men first this way and then that.

Spinoza and Le Clerc assert that when Scripture says God does something one should not believe this refers to anything other than what normally occurs according to the usual operations of nature.[108] When Scripture states men's sins are the cause 'de la stérilité de la terre', or that through faith the blind were cured, or that God became angry or repented of having done something, one should not suppose, hold Spinoza and Le Clerc, that this signifies anything beyond the ordinary course of nature. They say biblical expressions implying a direct intervention 'et une volonté particulière pratique de Dieu' should never be interpreted in their literal sense, but rather that all such phrases invariably mean that whatever happened occurred naturally and is attributed to God because he is 'l'auteur des loix générales de la Nature' as a consequence of which the thing happened, and that 'ce n'est pas entendre le style de l'Écriture, que d'en juger autrement'.[109]

But if this way of interpreting sacred history is authorized, protests Faydit, then all ancient texts and classical poetry are by the same token completely stripped of the supernatural, the inevitable consequence of which is to eradicate the direct working of divine providence and all supernatural agency from the totality of

104 [Faydit], *Remarques*, 105–6; Kors, *Atheism in France*, i. 294–5.

105 [Faydit], *Remarques*, 106; Vernière, *Spinoza*, 179, 181 n.

106 [Faydit], *Remarques*, 102–3.

107 Ibid. 103.

108 Ibid. 105; Vernière, *Spinoza*, 180–1.

109 [Faydit], *Remarques*, 106–7.

ancient literature, early church history, and the Patristic books. Le Clerc, he says, chides St Augustine for taking literally the New Testament words about Lydia, the woman vending purple cloth whom Paul encountered at Philippi, in Macedonia, 'and the Lord opened her heart to heed the utterances of Paul'; Le Clerc says it was just the natural eloquence of Paul's words that swayed her, 'sans que Dieu s'en mêlat en façon quelconque'.[110] But if this sort of exegesis is legitimate, retorted Faydit, the final result must be the total destruction of all faith, all theology, and all ecclesiastical authority.

Spinoza and Le Clerc claim that all the visions and dreams in which God, angels, or demons appear, recounted in Scripture, must be deemed 'expressions poétiques' for describing natural phenomena. Yet it is certain that the entire early history of the church and all the older Church Fathers attest that the greater part of the ancient pagans 'venoit à la connoissance de Dieu' by means of visions and dreams in which the Lord summoned them to the faith.[111] In Origen, Tertullian, Eusebius, and other Patristic authors, we find countless narratives of conversions due to wonders, miracles, signs, visions, and supernaturally inspired dreams. Spinoza and Le Clerc contend, and Malebranche implies, that none of this really happened and that such things cannot occur given the 'loix générales que Dieu a établies en créant le monde'.[112] But does not Greek and Latin pagan poetry, one of our most precious treasures, conclusively prove them wrong? Homer and Virgil, the greatest of poets who, with no motive at all to support Christianity, nevertheless continually invoke wonders, visions, and the supernatural whereby they, no less than Scripture, substantiate the essentially theological view of the world taught by the apostles, Fathers, and the church, agree that it is God who sends dreams 'et qui parle à l'homme dans le sommeil'.[113]

Both wings of the Early Enlightenment were as contemptuous of the anti-philosophical strategies and arguments of Faydit, Baltus, Huet, and others of their ilk as they were of those Fathers who 'despised Socrates, Plato and all the heathen philosophers', as Le Clerc put it,[114] and the wider tendency, even among those Fathers more favourably inclined towards some currents of Greek thought, to try to minimize the significance of Greek pagan thought overall. The Greek philosophers, according to Faydit, may agree with Spinoza that θαύματα μωροῖς [wonders are for fools],[115] but where he totally refused to allow the Greek philosophers to stand as the prime spokesmen of antiquity, arguing that they were all sufficiently contradicted by Homer and Virgil, both the moderate mainstream and the radicals joined together to raise the prestige of Greek philosophy and depress the spiritual significance for men of the poetic thought of Homer and Virgil. If all the Fathers had to some extent colluded in depressing the status of the ancient philosophy schools, both parts of the Enlightenment made it their business to restore their prestige.

110 [Faydit], *Remarques*, 107; Acts 16: 14.

111 [Faydit], *Remarques*, 136; Kors, *Atheism in France*, i. 295 n.

112 [Faydit], *Remarques*, 137–8.

113 Ibid. 141.

114 Le Clerc, *Lives*, 197, 204.

115 Ibid. 247.

How ridiculous, insisted Le Clerc, was the notion of Justin Martyr, Clement, and Eusebius that the ancient Greek world borrowed its key ideas from other peoples. According to them, the Greeks learnt their astronomy from the Babylonians, geometry from the Egyptians, and many things from the Persians while procuring most of the rest of their knowledge from the Jews, as Clement, observes Le Clerc disdainfully, 'endeavors to prove in a thousand places; and 'tis well known that this was the common opinion of the Fathers, who undertook to censure the philosophy of the Greeks. The Jews said also the same thing.'[116]

Nothing could be more absurd, held Le Clerc, than Clement's failure to realize that 'many things were clearly spoken of in Greece before the Jews spoke of 'em after the same manner; and that the latter began to express themselves as the Greeks only since they conversed with them'.[117] But if both streams agreed thus far, deep disagreement was bound to set in as soon as the discussion about ancient philosophy and its relationship to Christianity was entered into any further. As it turned out there was a great deal to argue about.

[116] Ibid., 21–3; Clement of Alexandria, *Protreptikos*, 148–51, 159–61, 167; Bolingbroke, *Philosophical Works*, ii. 157–8; Lenglet Dufresnoy, *Méthode*, i. 202; Lamberton, *Homer*, 78–9.

[117] Le Clerc, *Lives*, 23.

17

The Recovery of Greek Thought

1. 'RATIONALIZING THE GODS': DISPUTING XENOPHANES

Realization that it was the ancient Greeks, not the Mesopotamians or Egyptians, who invented philosophy lent Greek thought and culture a wholly new status in the history of Man. Humanists had granted the Greeks and Romans a unique status as regards rhetoric, eloquence, and literary achievement but not as regards Man's spiritual and intellectual development. Whether one viewed the matter from a neo-Eclectic perspective like Heumann, or accepted Bayle's sweeping claims about the achievements of the Greek philosophers, these new perspectives now assumed a critical importance in intellectual life. For Bayle's conception, in particular, imparted a potentially crucial significance to a Greek 'revolution' perceived by some as being Man's first great 'enlightenment'—the Presocratics' discovery of philosophical argument and criticism.

Among the most vigorously debated of the Presocratics before 1750 was Xenophanes of Colophon (*c*.570–*c*.478 BC), the Ionian poet-philosopher born, it is thought, around 560 BC but who seemingly lived down to the 470s. Most of Xenophanes' literary and intellectual output was produced probably towards the end of the sixth century, or soon after, but survived only in a few fragments and brief reports by later authors. For the Early Enlightenment the question what precisely he had thought developed, for the first time since the Hellenistic age, thanks especially to the historico-philosophical enquiries of Bayle, into a full-scale controversy.[1] Whether one classes Xenophanes, as a few modern scholars have, among the more influential, as well as earliest, representatives of the Presocratic 'Enlightenment', or believes his role has been exaggerated, the Enlightenment turned him into one of the most important precursors of the *esprit philosophique* of the eighteenth century as well as most active in transferring the centre of gravity in human knowledge, following the Persian conquest of Anatolia, to the Greek fringes of Italy and Sicily.

From both the moderate and radical perspectives, Xenophanes became a key exemplum. His native Colophon, about the founding of which he reportedly composed a poem, stood near Ephesus not far from the then thriving maritime city

[1] Cantelli, *Teologia*, 232–3, 239.

which became the world's first centre of philosophical endeavour—the Miletus of Thales and Anaximander. The roughly forty-five surviving fragments of his philosophical poetry constitute, as it has recently been put, 'the first sizable body of Presocratic writing'.[2] Noteworthy in itself, this assumed a particular significance for Bayle for whom the populace of ancient Greece dwelt in 'la plus crasse barbarie' until 'les premiers philosophes les eussent humanisez'.[3] According to him, humanity's first great philosophical revolution served to bring civilization to utter 'sauvages', which is what in his eyes, like Fontenelle's, the archaic Greeks were prior to the rise of philosophy. Philosophy, he believed, taught them above all the vital difference between religion and morality, and how to tailor institutions, laws, and politics to the needs of men.[4] Here was a revolution crucial intellectually, morally, religiously, and politically.

Exiled in his youth by a local tyrant, around 555 BC, Xenophanes reportedly lived in nearby Miletus until, around 540, he joined a wave of migration from Asia Minor's Persian-dominated western littoral to southern Italy.[5] According to Diogenes Laertius, in the third century AD, Xenophanes was remembered in late antiquity mainly for his critique of popular ideas, as reflected in Homer and Hesiod, about the gods, omens, and divination.[6] He says Xenophanes was 'the first to maintain that everything that comes into being is mortal and that the soul is the breath of life' (πρῶτός τε ἀπεφήνατο ὅτι πᾶν τὸ γινόμενον φθαρτόν ἐστι καὶ ἡ ψυχὴ πνεῦμα),[7] a claim supported by a surviving fragment of Xenophanes' own verse affirming 'for all things are from the earth and to the earth all things end' (ἐκ γάιης γὰρ πάντα καὶ εἰς γῆν πάντα τελεῖται).[8]

From the 1690s, Xenophanes again seemed important for his critique of the gods, alleged monism, and, as Antonio Conti put it in the 1740s, for being the first to employ doubt as an instrument of philosophy and the acerbic, sarcastic style of satirical poems known as *silloi*.[9] He was already celebrated for these accomplishments by the third-century BC sceptic Timon of Phlius, a satirical poet and intimate of Pyrrho of Elis (*c*.365–275 BC), the official founder of scepticism as a philosophical school. Timon, who was pivotal in fixing Pyrrho's reputation as the chief exponent of total scepticism, stressed Xenophanes' alleged invention of scepticism as a philosophical technique, as well as his notoriety as a critic of Homer's treatment of the gods, claiming these were crucial to Pyrrho's own intellectual development.[10] Where pre-Enlightenment historians of philosophy, notably the late humanist Gerardus Vossius, merely recorded Xenophanes (echoing Diogenes Laertius) as a thinker who taught that the 'substance of God was spherical, in no way resembling

[2] Lesher, *Greek Philosophers*, 12; Barnes, *Presocratic Philosophers*, 82–99.

[3] Bayle, *Continuation*, i, avertissement, pp. 8^{v}–9; Bayle, *Réponse*, ii. 329.

[4] Bayle *Réponse*, ii. 329, iv. 348, 366–7.

[5] Steinmetz, 'Xenophanesstudien', 28–9, 33.

[6] Diogenes Laertius, *Lives of Eminent Philosophers*, ii. 426–7.

[7] Ibid.

[8] Lesher, *Greek Philosophers*, 15; Lesher, *Xenophanes*, 32–3, 124–8; Osborne, *Rethinking*, 353.

[9] Conti, *Illustrazione*, 22, 24; Zeppi, 'Intorno al pensiero di Senofane', 386.

[10] Diogenes Laertius, *Lives of Eminent Philosophers*, ii. 424; Steinmetz, 'Xenophanesstudien', 24, 35–7, 58.

Man, all seeing and hearing but not breathing, the totality of eternal mind and thought',[11] but went no further, Bayle and those who followed restored Xenophanes, along the lines sketched by Timon, as a pre-eminent philosophical innovator, religious reformer, and also sceptic.[12]

In his *Dictionnaire*, Bayle devotes an entry to Xenophanes noting that this Greek thinker-poet taught that 'all things are one which is the immutable and true God who was never born, and is eternal and of spherical shape'.[13] For Xenophanes, he asserts, Nature has no beginning or end, and will remain always the same.[14] Citing chiefly Cicero and Plutarch, Bayle made sure that what chiefly impressed Early Enlightenment readers about Xenophanes was the rigorous monism apparent in his thought.[15] Thus Bayle's thesis that the Colophonian held that there is only one Being in the universe and that God is everything, from which it follows that 'toutes choses étoit Dieu',[16] largely replaced Cudworth's contrary view (following Clement of Alexandria) that Xenophanes had been an early monotheist. The Dordrecht preacher Johannes Aalstius, in his introduction to ethics of 1705, states that Xenophanes taught that 'everything is one, that everything is unchangeable, and was never created; yes, that it is God'.[17] 'Xenophane', affirms Lévesque de Burigny, in 1724, teaches there was only 'une substance dans l'univers qui étoit Dieu',[18] adding that Xenophanes was among the first, together with 'Parmenide, Melisse, Zenon, Empédocle, Anagore, Ocellus Lucanus, Démocrite, Diogène l'Apolloniate, Aristote', and others, who fixed the principle that 'rien ne se fait de rien'.[19] Xenophanes, held Jean-Frédéric Bernard, conflating the universe with God, maintained that it had never begun and would never end.[20]

Professing horror, Bayle had added that Xenophanes' philosophy was even more pernicious than Spinoza's, 'un Spinozisme plus dangereux que celui que je réfute dans l'article de *Spinoza*'. 'More dangerous' because Spinoza's hypothesis provides its own antidote in the continual mutability and corruptibility of the divine nature through the modalities, an argument at odds with common sense, he says, which persuades no one.[21] Xenophanes, by contrast, presents the absolute immutability of eternal and infinite being which he calls God as a purely theological dogma which, consequently, he remarks (sarcastically), will prove infinitely more seductive.[22]

[11] Diogenes Laertius, *Lives of Eminent Philosophers*, ii. 426–7; de Grau, *Historia philosophica*, 318; Diderot, *Œuvres complètes*, xiv. 194–5.

[12] Vossius, *De philosophorum sectis*, 294; Conti, *Illustrazione*, 22–4; Bayle, *Écrits*, 129–31.

[13] Diels (ed.), *Poetarum philosophorum fragmenta*, 32; Vossius, *De philosophorum sectis*, 294; d'Argens, *Impartial Philosopher*, i. 178; [Bernard], *Le Monde, son origine*, i. 36; Conti, *Illustrazione*, 22; Cleve, *Giants*, 10.

[14] Bayle, *Dictionnaire*, iii. 3034; Bayle, *Écrits*, 130; Barnes, *Presocratic Philosophers*, 83.

[15] Barnes, *Presocratic Philosophers*, 83; Brucker, *Historia critica philosophiae* (1742), i. 1149; Cantelli, *Teologia*, 230; Mori, *Bayle philosophe*, 165; Israel, *Radical Enlightenment*, 136.

[16] Bayle, *Continuation*, i. 334; Reimmann, *Historia universalis*, 203; Mori, *Bayle philosophe*, 165.

[17] Aalstius, *Inleiding*, 35; Conti, *Illustrazione*, 3, 5.

[18] [Lévesque de Burigny], *Histoire de la philosophie payenne* (1724), i. 69.

[19] Ibid. i. 246; *Gründliche Auszüge*, i (1733), 253.

[20] [Bernard], *Le Monde, son origine*, i. 35–6.

[21] Ibid.

[22] Bayle, *Dictionnaire*, iii. 3043.

In other ways, too, Xenophanes' thought was apt to prove more contagious than 'le Spinosisme'. For Xenophanes, finding his reasoning blocked by contradictions, takes refuge in scepticism, in being 'incapable de rien comprendre', something Spinoza utterly disdained but a great many admire.[23] The Venetian radical Antonio Conti restated Bayle's interpretation in detail in 1743.[24]

Bayle, of course, displays his obsession with Spinozism throughout his *Dictionnaire* and other writings, demonstrating this philosophy's supposed affinities to a whole lineage of Greek thinkers. But he—and, following him, Buddeus and Diderot—is rarely so emphatic in linking Spinoza with any Greek thinker as with Xenophanes: with regard to God, as he summed the matter up, his teaching 'n'est guère différente du spinozisme'.[25] Many agreed, among them moderate thinkers, including some of Bayle's most vocal opponents. His interpretation was echoed by Buddeus, in a disputation held at Jena, as early as 1701;[26] the Swiss Jean-Pierre Crousaz, one of Bayle's fiercest critics, while dismissing Xenophanes' thought as contemptible, still reiterates Bayle's opinion that it was the original sketch 'du Spinozisme'.[27] Admittedly, there were also dissenting voices who questioned the alleged parallels between Xenophanes and Spinoza. A few opponents followed Cudworth in contending that, for Xenophanes, God, though inextricably pervading the cosmos like the deity of the Stoics, is nevertheless pure mind and hence not identical with nature as in Spinoza.[28]

But, for decades, Bayle's claim that Xenophanes' doctrine 'unum esse omnia' signifies that there is in the universe only one substance, everything else that we see or know 'nihil aliud esse quam unius, sive substantiae, modificationes' [being nothing other that the modifications of the one, or of substance], dominated the scene.[29] Even in his later work, Buddeus claims nothing favourable can be said about Xenophanes or the Eleatics: for Xenophanes, he held, was a systematic monist, one of those Presocratics who, like Parmenides, Melissus, and Zeno of Elea, the principal teachers of the Eleatic school, 'maintained that there is only one substance' and that 'all things are one'.[30] Comparing Xenophanes to Spinoza, one of the main predecessors to the *Encyclopédie*, the seven-volume Dutch general lexicon, the *Groot Algemeen Historisch, Geographisch, Genealogisch en Oordeelkundig Woordenboek* (Amsterdam, 1733) of David van Hoogstraten and Jan Lodewijk Schuer likewise states that Xenophanes' view of the divine nature 'largely agrees with that of Spinoza'.[31]

[23] Ibid. [24] Conti, *Illustrazione*, 25–6.

[25] Bayle, *Dictionnaire*, iii. 3034; Bayle, *Écrits*, 129; Hoogstraten and Schuer, *Groot Algemeen Woordenboek*, vii, X, p. 6; Bouchardy, *Pierre Bayle*, 250–1, 282. [26] Buddeus, *Elementa*, 61–5.

[27] Crousaz, *Examen*, 427.

[28] Reimmann, *Historia universalis*, 203; Fabricius, *Delectus argumentorum*, 300; Mosheim, 'Notes', i. 456; Häfner, 'Johann Lorenz Mosheim', 243–5.

[29] Buddeus, *De Spinozismo ante Spinozam*, 321; Buddeus, *Theses theologicae*, 40.

[30] Buddeus, *Traité de l'athéisme*, 112; Buddeus, *Theses theologicae*, 40; Buddeus, *Elementa*, 29–32; Häfner, 'Johann Lorenz Mosheim', 241.

[31] Hoogstraten and Schuer, *Groot Algemeen Woordenboek*, vii, X, pp. 6–8.

As Xenophanes abused the word *nature*, asserts Saint-Hyacinthe, in his *Recherches philosophiques* (Rotterdam, 1743), Spinoza abused the term *substance*, trying, nearly two thousand years after Xenophanes, to 'rétablir le système de ce prétendu philosophe'.[32] If, like Strato, Spinoza was a philosopher who recognized as God only 'une Nature naturée et naturente', some correctly observe, he says, that Xenophanes already held this position earlier, likewise arguing that nature is the entire universe yet 'n'est pourtant qu'une substance unique', simple and indivisible, except that Xenophanes deemed it spherical while Spinoza gives it no limits.[33] Parmenides, disciple of Xenophanes, and Melissus, Parmenides' disciple, adds Saint-Hyacinthe, also taught 'la même doctrine que Xénophanes'.[34] Slightly varying the theme, Pluquet, in his *Examen du fatalisme* of 1757, claims Spinoza wavered 'entre le sentiment de Straton et celui de Xénophanes'.[35]

There is nothing arbitrary, accidental, or new, then, in Diderot's remark, in the article on Xenophanes in the *Encyclopédie*, that 'ce système n'est point éloigné du spinozisme'; on the contrary, he is merely summing up a long tradition of both radical and anti-radical thought reaching back over half a century.[36] Despite the corrective efforts of Brucker, the Enlightenment down to the 1750s generally classified Xenophanes as what an Italian scholar called 'un panteista-monista' of Eleatic stamp.[37] Today, if the approach is different and no one brackets Spinoza and Xenophanes, the latter is still recognized as a religious critic, reformer, and sceptic much as the Early Enlightenment saw him. 'He is important', affirms one modern scholar, 'because the surviving fragments of his works contain the first certain statements of a theology which in sixth-century Greece was new and revolutionary'.[38] With his new sceptical reasoning about the divine, Xenophanes inferred from the fact that different peoples conceive the gods differently—and after their own likeness—that they imagine (if not fashion) their gods after their own image, unthinkingly imputing anthropomorphic qualities to them.[39]

In a fragment cited by Clement of Alexandria, Xenophanes objects: 'but mortals think the gods are born, and have their own clothes, voice and body'.[40] Xenophanes is in fact the very first thinker known to have argued that because men conceive the gods in their own likeness they also credit them with their own desires and aspirations and, consequently, their own limitations and failings. In seeking to strip away such anthropomorphic encrustation and raise the level of men's thinking about the divine, Xenophanes joined his efforts to those of Heraclitus, Parmenides, and, a little later, Empedocles.[41] For men to think of the gods in their own likeness, he held (winning posthumous applause here from Clement and other Church

[32] Vernière, *Spinoza*, 337. [33] [Saint-Hyacinthe], *Recherches philosophiques*, 57.
[34] Ibid.; Bonacina, *Filosofia ellenistica*, 30, 52. [35] [Pluquet], *Examen*, ii. 33.
[36] Diderot, *Œuvres complètes*, xiv. 195. [37] Zeppi, 'Intorno al pensiero di Senofane', 388.
[38] Hussey, *The Presocratics*, 13.
[39] Ibid.; Barnes, *Presocratic Philosophers*, 92–3; Bietenholz, *Historia and Fabula*, 38; Harrison, *'Religion' and the Religions*, 180, 241 n. 269. [40] Lesher, *Greek Philosophers*, 13.
[41] Empedocles, *Extant Fragments*, 22, 60, 254.

Fathers), is neither logical nor fitting.[42] He censures Homer's gods on moral grounds in particular and was reportedly also critical of Thales, Anaximander, and Pythagoras for doing too little to combat traditional notions of divinity.[43] As Sextus Empiricus reports Xenophanes' words: 'Homer and Hesiod ascribe all the things to the gods which are considered disreputable among men: stealing, fornicating and cheating others.'[44] Bayle, in his article, praises Xenophanes' verses criticizing Homer and Hesiod for thoroughly exposing 'les sottises qu'ils ont chantées des dieux'.[45]

It is illogical and unfitting, judged Xenophanes, to suppose that immortal gods are born and die.[46] Sometimes misleadingly styled the earliest western apostle of a radical monotheism,[47] it was he who is first recorded as having written—albeit without clearly discarding polytheism—that there is an 'Heis Megistos', an overriding God constituted of both body and mind who far surpasses all the rest in power. The much debated fragment containing this assertion is open to divergent readings and has provoked considerable disagreement.[48] But however rendered, it is undeniably striking testimony to the force of Xenophanes' intellect. As Clement reports his words (albeit misrepresenting him as claiming that God is one and also 'ἀσωματος' [without body]) which he plainly does not say), Xenophanes taught:

εἷς θεὸς ἔν τε θεοῖσι καὶ ἀνθρώποισι μέγιστος,
οὔτε δέμας θνήτοισιν ὁμοίιος οὔτε νόημα.

[There is among gods and men one God, the greatest, neither in body nor mind like mortals.][49]

Lesser gods, if they existed at all, play no particular role in Xenophanes' cosmos, so that this and other tentatively reconstructed fragments do certainly suggest that Xenophanes advocated, if not the doctrine that there is only one God, then certainly the still revolutionary idea that there exists one particular god of incomparable 'power, consciousness and cosmic influence' towering infinitely above the rest.[50] Both Enlightenment and modern scholars concur, then, in claiming that Xenophanes' authentic position revolved around the concept of a great god in some sense

42 Algra, 'Beginnings of Cosmology', 59–60; Broadie, 'Rational Theology', 209–10; Lamberton, *Homer*, 15–16, 49, 260; see also Clement of Alexandria, *Protreptikos*, 48–9; de Grau, *Historia philosophica*, i. 301.

43 Boureau-Deslandes, *Histoire critique*, ii. 302; Diderot, *Œuvres complètes*, xiv. 194; Steinmetz, 'Xenophanesstudien', 1–15; Mogyoródi, 'Xenophanes', 267.

44 Hoogstraten and Schuer, *Groot Algemeen Woordenboek*, vii, X, p. 7; Häfner, 'Johann Lorenz Mosheim', 244; Kirk et al., *Presocratic Philosophers*, 168; Cleve, *Giants*, 8; Hershbell, 'Oral-Poetic Religion', 128–39; Lesher, *Xenophanes*, 22–3.

45 Bayle, *Dictionnaire*, iii. 3035.

46 *Algemeen Historisch, Geographisch*, viii. 474; Broadie, 'Rational Theology', 210.

47 Broadie, 'Rational Theology', 210; Barnes, *Presocratic Philosophers*, 89–92; Cleve, *Giants*, 6–9.

48 Lesher, *Xenophanes*, 96–7; West, 'Towards Monotheism', 32–3.

49 Buddeus, *Elementa*, 65; Cleve, *Giants*, 8; Kirk et al. *Presocratic Philosophers*, 169; Hershbell, 'Oral-Poetic Religion', 125, 129–31; Lesher, *Greek Philosophers*, 13–14; Lesher, *Xenophanes*, 30–1.

50 Lesher, *Xenophanes*, 99, 102; Zeppi, 'Intorno al pensiero di Senofane', 388–9.

embodying physically and spiritually the whole physical universe. Xenophanes' God, though coextensive with the universe, seems, moreover, not to have been identical with it but rather some sort of pervasive cosmic force. God remains in one place always, held Xenophanes, but does not rest, being in a relationship of rest to nothing.[51] Hence, perpetually in motion internally, seeing and hearing without breathing, as Diogenes Laertius expresses it, he remains unmoving externally. As the sixth-century AD pagan Neoplatonist philosopher Simplikios reports this remarkable concept: ἓν τὸ ὂν κὰι πᾶν (καὶ οὔτε πεπερασμένον οὔτε ἄπειρον οὔτε κινούμενον οὔτε ἠρεμοῦν) [the Being is one and all (and neither finite nor infinite nor moving nor resting) held Xenophanes of Colophon, teacher of Parmenides, says Theophrastos].[52]

Because all living organisms are conceived in Xenophanes as growing out of and returning to this body of God, it appears that everything there is, for Xenophanes, is comprised in the body and mind of God, a true 'ἓν καὶ πᾶν' [one and all] in Lessing's famous formulation. Xenophanes, says Simplikios, lays down as his μίαν δὲ τὴν ἀρχὴν ἤτοι ἓν τὸ ὄν καὶ πᾶν . . . τὸ γὰρ ἓν τοῦτο καὶ πᾶν τὸν θεὸν ἔλεγεν ὁ Ξενοφάνης [only principle the Being to be one and everything and this 'one and all' Xenophanes therefore called God].[53]

Both Xenophanes and Spinoza, then, apparently saw rest and movement as inseparable from the totality of reality and nature as creating itself: 'Xenophanes the leader, and then Spinosa', affirms Archbishop Melchior de Polignac, the noted Cartesian polymath, connoisseur of antiquities, and Early Enlightenment pioneer of archaeology, in his epic poem the *Anti-Lucretius sive de Deo et Natura*—much of which he wrote at the abbey of Anchin, near Lille, around 1720—seek the principle of movement not, like Epicurus, in the particles of matter separated each from the next, but in the sum of particles, in the mass and body of matter.[54]

Xenophanes in this way overthrew the gods of mythology and, much as he demythologized divine power, sought to demythologize natural phenomena. Clouds he explains as vapour lifted from the sea by the sun;[55] in one of his longest surviving fragments, the sea is depicted as the source of all water and of wind: πηγὴ δ'εστὶ θάλασσ' ὕδατος πηγὴ δ'ἀνέμοιο [the sea is the source of water, the source of wind];[56] by 'begetting' clouds and wind, the sea spreads water and fills rivers.[57] His quest to rationalize nature also led him to wonder about the significance of marine fossils found on high ground about which he is seemingly the first recorded as having ever speculated.[58]

[51] Broadie, 'Rational Theology', 211. [52] Cleve, *Giants*, 15. [53] Ibid. 25.

[54] Polignac, *L'Anti-Lucrèce*, 352–3; Boureau-Deslandes, *Histoire critique*, ii. 306–7.

[55] Diogenes Laertius, *Lives of Eminent Philosophers*, ii. 426–7; Feuerlein, *Dissertatio historico-philosophica*, 30.

[56] Kirk et al., *Presocratic Philosophers*, 176; Steinmetz, 'Xenophanesstudien', 62; Lesher, *Xenophanes*, 134–7; Lesher, *Greek Philosophers*, 15.

[57] Hershbell, 'Oral-Poetic Religion', 126; Lesher, *Greek Philosophers*, 15.

[58] Kirk et al., *Presocratic Philosophers*, 177.

If some of his surviving fragments seem cryptic or baffling, impressively clear is his couplet on the rainbow: 'and she whom they call Iris, this too is by nature a cloud, Purple, red, and grassy-green to behold.'[59] Since the rainbow counted among the foremost portents of popular religion in his time, this suggests Xenophanes deployed naturalistic explanations in whole, or in part, to attack the hitherto unchallenged culture of omen-reading and interpreting portents prevalent in his time.[60] Such fragments imply he more or less ruled out the secret communication of gods with men, and provision of cryptic warnings, revelations, and prognostications through oracles, auguries, and mysterious intimations. If rain, the movements of clouds, and rainbows are purely natural phenomena, mechanistically caused, there is neither reason nor requirement to attribute such occurrences to supernatural interference or action.[61]

Xenophanes was clearly struck by the vast gap between what most men believe and the insights at which he and his colleagues had arrived, and the slowness of Man's progress in knowledge. In one of his most celebrated couplets, he depicts the halting improvement of our knowledge as the result of men slowly discovering, if not actually searching for, knowledge: 'indeed not from the beginning have the gods revealed all things to mortals, but with time, searching, they discover better.'[62] His primal god seems to be knowable in some degree, being coextensive with the physical world, but only up to a point since, like the God of the Stoics, he cannot be identified with the whole of reality but is, rather, in some sense a separate consciousness who, apparently, can be prayed to as a personal God. Since body and mind in his thought are inextricably integrated, all bodies and minds grow out of, and return into, God.[63]

That Xenophanes held God to be a sphere is confirmed by several authorities, including Alexander of Aphrodisias, Simplikios, Clement, and other Christian writers.[64] Xenophanes' divine sphere, described as unmoving and surrounded by an infinite nothing, is the body of *Heis Megistos* and is finite; but surrounded by nothing, this spherical and hence finite being is in a certain sense also infinite. While the combination of such cogency with scepticism has sometimes seemed baffling to modern commentators, appearing to contradict his bold theology,[65] it seemed entirely logical to Bayle who, obliged by the cultural context in which he lived to profess to condemn the monist proclivities of the Eleatic school out of hand, nevertheless saw few grounds for rejecting their stance philosophically. The tenets of Zeno of Elea, holds Bayle in his article on Zeno in the *Dictionnaire*, closely resembled those of Xenophanes and his pupil Parmenides regarding not just the unity and immutability but also the final incomprehensibility of all things: the

59 Ibid. 173; Lesher, *Xenophanes*, 36–7, 139–44.

60 Steinmetz, 'Xenophanesstudien', 67; Lesher, *Xenophanes*, 141, 153–4; Lesher, *Greek Philosophers*, 16.

61 Barnes, *Presocratic Philosphers*, 96.

62 Kirk et al., *Presocratic Philosophers*, 179; Cleve, *Giants*, 28; Curd, *Legacy*, 45; Lesher, *Greek Philosophers*, 17.

63 Lesher, *Greek Philosophers*, 27.

64 Barnes, *Presocratic Philosophers*, 98–9; Cleve, *Giants*, 10–14.

65 Cleve, *Giants*, 28–9; Hussey, *The Presocratics*, 32–3.

whole Eleatic school 'croyait avec lui l'unité de toutes choses et leur immobilité', adding that he thought that it was perhaps from there that the doctrine the sceptics have praised so much, namely that our senses deceive us 'et qu'il ne faut pas se fier à leur témoignage', first originated.[66]

A close link thus developed between Xenophanes' notion of the unity of all things, and the deceptiveness of appearances, systematic doubt originating in the realization that much of reality is for ever hidden from us by an impenetrable veil of 'seeming'.[67] Although Buddeus, Loescher, and other Lutheran theologians endorsed Bayle's general interpretation of Xenophanes and the Eleatics, some of the German neo-Eclectics strongly demurred. Reimmann, in his *Historia atheismi*, argues the contrary, as did Mosheim and the great Calvinist scholar Fabricius.[68] Reimmann reproached Buddeus for being too deferential to Bayle whom he considered a pure 'Indifferentist', here as elsewhere, and, hence, insufficiently respectful towards the Church Fathers, indeed willing to imply they had utterly misconstrued texts, mistakenly exculpating the Eleatics of monism and the crime of 'atheism'.[69] Vindicating the Church Fathers could here be neatly combined with attacking monism and the proto-Spinozist leanings of the Presocratics.

Jakob Wilhelm Feuerlein, presiding over a disputation at Altdorf, near Nuremberg, in December 1729, on the nature of Xenophanes' cosmology, pronounced him a praiseworthy monotheist who heralded the future triumph of Christianity. Feuerlein considered Xenophanes a more substantial thinker than pagan antiquity had been willing to allow, someone unjustly neglected by the ancients, prior to the Church Fathers, owing precisely to the outmoded polytheistic and pantheistic prejudices of pagan writers, tinged in Aristotle's case with professional jealousy.[70] Bayle Feuerlein accused of grossly distorting our picture of Xenophanes by insidiously and deliberately linking him to monism and 'Spinozistic atheism'.[71] In fact, concludes the Altdorf disputation, Xenophanes, though not immune from 'Deistic errors', expounded 'many sane doctrines about God' and in particular established that 'God is the author of this universe' and purely incorporeal.[72]

2. STRATO, SPINOZA, AND THE *PHILOSOPHES*

Bayle rounds off his discussion of Xenophanes by remarking that it was hard to understand 'par quel tour d'esprit' so many ancient philosophers could believe that there is only one substance in the universe.[73] In an accompanying footnote,

[66] Bayle, *Écrits*, 130, 131.

[67] Hussey, *The Presocratics*, 35–6; Mori, 'Interpréter la philosophie de Bayle', 319.

[68] Münter, *Theologiae naturalis polemicae specimen*, 13–14.

[69] *Auserlesene theologische Bibliothec* (Leipzig, 1724/5), section xii, p. 1018.

[70] Feuerlein, *Dissertatio historico-philosophica*, 44–5.

[71] Ibid. 45, 47.

[72] Ibid. 40–1, 46.

[73] Bayle, *Écrits*, 134–5.

he suggests the Greek thinkers reached this totally unaccountable, 'strange', and impious notion by presuming nothing can be produced from nothing, that everything that exists exists necessarily: 'qu'il est donc éternel et infini, et que l'infini doit être unique', leaving the reader scant opportunity to disagree.[74]

Still more often tied to Spinoza during the Early Enlightenment than Xenophanes was the third-century BC philosopher Strato of Lampsacus. Indeed, the question of Strato, successor of Theophrastus and third head of the Athenian Lyceum which he headed for nearly two decades from 287 BC until his death around *c.*269 BC, highlighted by both Bayle and Leibniz, played a not inconsiderable role in the evolution of eighteenth-century materialism.[75]All the writings of Strato were lost during late antiquity; and while there survive a few reports by other classical authors, these—as has often been pointed out—are too few and disparate to provide a coherent picture or even a definite outline of his philosophy. Among the few things that can be said about him with certainty is that he was more critical of Aristotle's views concerning weight, time, and space than his mentor Theophrastus.[76] Commonly called the φυσικός—the 'Naturalist' (sometimes misleadingly translated 'the physicist')—because he devoted himself with particular zeal to the study of nature—Strato was still a noted authority in Athens and Alexandria, the Greek world's chief intellectual centers, down to the time of the Neoplatonist Simplikios in the sixth century AD.[77] Later, his thought was almost wholly forgotten.

His name meant little or nothing to the Middle Ages or the Renaissance humanists. Thomas Stanley in the mid seventeenth century provides a brief entry on Strato in his *History*, but beyond saying 'he prescribed all divine power to Nature' tells us nothing about his ideas.[78] Then, in the late seventeenth century, interest in the 'Naturalist' strongly revived and for one particular reason: contemporaries were greatly struck by the affinities between his supposed system and that of Spinoza. Almost overnight the parallel drawn between Stratonism and Spinozism rendered Strato one of the most intensely debated of all ancient Greek thinkers.

Though Gerardus Vossius, in his great work on pagan religion *De theologia gentili* and his posthumously published *De philosophorum sectis liber* (1657), already states, relying on Cicero and early Christian accounts,[79] that Strato identified God with nature but conceived of nature as acting blindly, without intelligence or design, spontaneously generating all living things,[80] the real debate began with Cudworth's *True Intellectual System of the Universe* (1678), a masterpiece aimed against all forms of predestination and necessitarianism.[81] Master of Christ's College, Cambridge, since 1654, and reckoned 'un des plus habiles hommes du XVIIe siècle' by Bayle, Ralph Cudworth (1617–88) was the first to investigate 'a certain form of

[74] Ibid.; Cantelli, *Teologia*, 239. [75] Geissler, *Boureau-Deslandes*, 87–9.
[76] Simplicius, *Corollaries*, 108–9; Brunschwig and Lloyd, *Greek Thought*, 830.
[77] Gottschalk, *Strato of Lampsacus*, 127. [78] Stanley, *History of Philosophy*, ii. 398.
[79] Rademaker, *Life and Work of Gerardus Johannes Vossius*, 329–30.
[80] Vossius, *De theologia gentili*, ii. 163.
[81] Barnouw, *Philippus van Limborch*, 14, 19; Patrides, *Cambridge Platonists*, 22, 30.

atheism, never before taken notice of, by any modern writers, which we call the Hylozoick: which notwithstanding, though it were long since started by Strato, in way of opposition to the Democritick and Epicurean hypothesis; yet because it afterwards slept in perfect silence and oblivion, should have been here by us passed by silently; had we not had certain knowledge of its being of late awakened and revived, by some, who were so sagacious, as plainly to perceive, that the atomick form could never doe their business, nor prove defensible: and therefore would attempt to carry this cause of atheism, in quite a different way, by the life and perception of matter'.[82]

He was convinced that this newly revived modern 'Stratonism' 'in all probability, would ere long publickly appear upon the stage, though not bare-faced, but under a disguise',[83] an allusion to the welling up of Spinozism in Holland (and potentially England). This danger was something to which Cudworth and his ally Henry More were alerted in the early 1670s by van Limborch, and which grew following the perceptible impact of Spinoza's *Tractatus theologico-politicus* in Cambridge in the mid 1670s, the years immediately prior to the appearance of Cudworth's *magnum opus*.[84] Cudworth makes only one direct reference to Spinoza in the *True Intellectual System*, deploring 'that late *Theological Politician* who, writing against miracles', claims a 'miracle is nothing but a name, which the ignorant vulgar gives, to *Opus Naturae insolitum*, any unwonted work of Nature, or to what themselves can assign no cause of', and that 'were any such thing done, contrary to nature or above it, it would rather weaken than confirm, our belief of the divine existence'.[85] There, he professes to find this 'discourse every way so weak, groundless, and inconsiderable, that we could not think it here to deserve a confutation', were it not proving rather vigorous, though his later references to Spinoza show that actually the modern Stratonist's 'discourse' worried him a good deal.

In fact, no more than van Limborch or Le Clerc did Cudworth underestimate the gravity of the challenge. He confirmed privately that his allusion was to a 'sagacious' reviver of Stratonism, 'Spinoza', a philosopher who 'discarding Hobbianism, was transformed into a kind of Hylozoick Atheist, [and who] attributing a kind of life to all matter, explodes liberty of will, as an impossibility, and contends for universall necessity'.[86] Despite its brilliant insights, the *True Intellectual System* for many years failed to appear in any continental language due to its great size and complexity, until finally it was published in a Latin version, rendered by Mosheim, at Jena in 1733, albeit with adjustments to text and notes, diluting what the German scholar considered Cudworth's inadequate arguments against atheistic materialism, and

[82] Cudworth, *True Intellectual System*, i, preface p. ix; Simonutti, 'Premières réactions', 135; Tomasoni, 'Il "sistema" ', 650; Mori, *Bayle philosophe*, 222.

[83] Cudworth, *True Intellectual System*, i, preface p. ix.

[84] Mosheim, 'Notes', ii. 863; Simonutti, 'Premières réactions', 130; Hutton, 'Introduction', p. xix.

[85] Cudworth, *True Intellectual System*, ii. 707; De Vet, 'Learned Periodicals', 29–30; Tomasoni, 'Il "sistema" ', 651 n., 658–9; Assmann, 'Rehabilitierung', 50.

[86] See Cudworth on 'Liberty of Will' in BL, MS Add. 4982, fo. 55; Hutton, 'Introduction', p. xix.

urging on readers the eclecticism and fideism Mosheim judged a better answer to Spinoza and Bayle.[87]

Even so, by the early 1690s, the substance of Cudworth's argument through personal contacts, correspondence, and knowing some English had been summarized, in French, by Le Clerc, and, in 1703, published in the second volume of his *Bibliothèque choisie*.[88] This French abstract, closely studied by Bayle, Jacques Bernard, and others, played a considerable role in the subsequent debate.[89] It was on the basis of this abstract that Bayle, who, like most continental scholars at the time, knew no English, praised Cudworth as a scholar who combined 'une lecture prodigieuse et une pénétration d'esprit extraordinaire'.[90] Appearing as it did between Bayle's initial references to Strato as an ancient counterpart to Spinoza in his *Dictionnaire* and his major discussion of Strato in the *Continuation* (1705), it was this abstract of 1703 which prompted Bayle during the last years of his life to adopt Strato and 'Stratonism' as key components of his own philosophy.[91]

Cudworth ingeniously differentiates the corpus of ancient Greek philosophical 'atheism' into four main categories or types—a procedure later emulated in numerous early eighteenth-century discussions of ancient philosophy.[92] His typology comprised 'first the Hylopathian or Anaximandrian, that derives all things from dead and stupid matter in the way of qualities and forms, generable and corruptible'; secondly, 'the atomical or Democritical' where the creative force in nature is 'fortuitous mechanism' of atomic movement; thirdly, 'the Stoical or Cosmoplastick' supposing 'one plastick and methodical but senseless nature, to preside over the whole corporeal universe'; and finally, and least understood and discussed by previous modern writers, the 'Hylozoick or Stratonical'.[93] This finely wrought quadrangular schema was faithfully reproduced, but, this time, making Cudworth's allusion to Spinoza explicit, in Le Clerc's summary and, from then on, this remarkable categorization heavily influenced the entire Enlightenment debate about ancient Greek philosophical 'atheism' right down to the 1770s and after, readers of the unsigned article on (and condemning) 'Hylozoisme' in the eighth volume of the *Encyclopédie* of Diderot and d'Alembert, for example, being directed straight to Le Clerc's abstract as the first item of further reading.[94] Of the four main varieties of

[87] Under the title *Systema intellectuale huius universi seu de veris naturae rerum originibus commentarii*, Hutton, 'Introduction', p. xxxiii; Tomasoni, 'Il "sistema" ', 630, 658–60; Schmidt-Biggemann, 'Platonismus', 203–4; Häfner, 'Johann Lorenz Mosheim', 235, 243.

[88] Simonutti, 'Bayle and Le Clerc', 152; Mori, *Bayle philosophe*, 219.

[89] Bayle, *Continuation* (1721), iv. 103; Simonutti, 'Bayle and Le Clerc', 153–4.

[90] Bayle, *Réponse*, iii. 1235.

[91] Bayle, *Continuation*, ii. 430, 502–4, 525–36; Brucker, *De Stratonis Lampsaceni atheismo*, 313; Labrousse, *Pierre Bayle*, ii. 244 n.; Cantelli, *Teologia*, 240, 254; Simonutti, 'Bayle and Le Clerc', 152; Mori, *Bayle philosophe*, 134, 219 n.

[92] Cudworth, *True Intellectual System*, i. 133–4; Bayle, *Continuation*, i. 88–9; *Bibliothèque choisie*, 2 (1703), 181–22, 57, 61; Gundling, *Vollständige Historie*, iv. 4985–6; Patrides, *Cambridge Platonists*, 323 n.; Taranto, *Du déisme à l'athéisme*, 356.

[93] Cudworth on 'Liberty of Will', BL, MS Add. 4982, fo. 60; Cudworth, *True Intellectual System*, i. 134; Schlosser, *De Stratone Lampsaceno*, 23–4; Algra, 'Beginnings of Cosmology', 64 n. 22.

[94] Diderot and d'Alembert, *Encyclopédie*, viii. 392; Proust, *Diderot*, 125.

Greek materialist atheism, Cudworth rated the last and least known, the hylozoic, the 'most considerable' philosophically, as well as most pernicious morally and theologically.[95]

Whereas the second most dangerous category, 'the Atomick Atheism' of Democritus and Epicurus, 'supposes the Notion or idea of Body to be nothing but extended resisting bulk, and consequently to include no manner of life and cogitation in it; Hylozoism on the contrary makes all body, as such, and therefore every smallest atom of it, to have life essentially belonging to it (natural perception and appetite) though without any animal sense or reflexive knowledge, as if life, and matter or extended bulk, were but two incomplete and inadequate conceptions, of one and the same substance, called body'.[96] These second and fourth varieties of Greek atheism, the former well known but the latter almost entirely unheard of, represented 'two schemes of atheism, very different from one another; that which fetches the original of all things from the mere fortuitous and unguided motion of matter, without any vital or directive principle; and that which derives it from a certain mixture of chance and the life of matter both together, it supposing a plastick life, not in the whole universe, as one thing, but in all the several parts of matter by themselves; the first of which is the atomick and Democritick atheism, the second the Hylozoick and Stratonick'.[97]

This 'Stratonick and Hylozoick atheism which attributes to all matter as such the only substance and first principle of all things', buried in oblivion since Justinian's time,[98] struck Cudworth as 'an hypothesis so prodigiously paradoxical, and so outrageously wild, as that very few men ever could have atheistick faith enough, to swallow it down and digest it'.[99] That was why, he thought, it had remained so obscure and 'found so few fautors and abettors, that it hath look'd like a forlorn and deserted thing'. Indeed 'we should not have taken any notice of it at this time, as a particular form of atheism, nor have conjured it up out of its grave, had we not understood, that Strato's ghost had begun to walk of late, and that among some well-wishers to atheism, despairing in a manner of the atomick form, this hylozoick hypothesis, began already to be look'd upon, as the rising sun of atheism—et tanquam spes altera Trojae, it seeming to smile upon them, and flatter them at a distance, with some fairer hopes of supporting that ruinous and desperate cause'.[100]

This was an astounding insight on Cudworth's part. For not only did hylozoism, just as he conceived, reappear in Spinoza's one-substance monism but it then took the lead in Early Enlightenment philosophical atheism and materialism, emerging, finally, in the refined drawing-room *hylozoïsme* of Diderot, with its most detailed

95 Cudworth, *True Intellectual System*, i. 145.

96 Ibid. 105; Patrides, *Cambridge Platonists*, 323; Baldi, *Verisimili, non vero*, 187–8.

97 Cudworth, *True Intellectual System*, i. 109; Brucker, *De Stratonis Lampsaceni atheismo*, 313.

98 Cudworth on 'Liberty of Will', BL, MS Add. 4982, fo. 60; see also Gundling's definition of Strato's 'novum systema atheismi', Gundling, *Vollständige Historie*, i. 4986 n.

99 Cudworth, *True Intellectual System*, i. 145.

100 Ibid.

and consummate reworking in that author's *Le Rêve d'Alembert*, of 1769.[101] 'Now the first and chief assertour of this hylozoick atheism', explains Cudworth, 'was, as we conceive, Strato Lampsacenus, commonly called also *physicus*, that had been once an auditor of Theophrastus and a famous Peripatetick, but afterwards degenerated from a genuine Peripatetick, into a new-formed kind of atheist.'[102] Strato's God, held Cudworth, was 'no other than such a life of Nature in matter, as was both devoid of sense and consciousness, and also multiplied together with the several parts of it'.[103] Strato denied the world was made by a Deity, 'yet he differed notwithstanding from Democritus, giving a different explanation of the origin of things, providing an active principle, and cause of motion as well as explaining the consistent uniformities of nature', asserting 'an inward plastick life in the several parts of matter, whereby they could artificially frame themselves to the best advantage, according to their several capabilities, without any conscious or reflexive knowledge'.[104]

Hence, Cudworth's fourth category, dubbed *atheismus Stratonicus* by Mosheim, was something completely different from the other atheistic varieties. All the varieties of Greek atheism, in his opinion, were not only false but wholly incompatible with each other, this entire 'quadripartite atheism' of ancient Greece being a veritable 'Kingdom of Darknesse divided, or labouring with an intestine seditious war in its own bowels, and thereby destroying itself'.[105] Meanwhile, during the 1680s and 1690s, the conception shared and propagated by Bayle that Spinoza had derived his doctrine of the unity of all substance, and the self-creativity of Nature, from the ancients, welding everything into a more coherent system than any predecessor, took hold.[106] Wittichius already asserted in 1682 that Spinoza had drawn his chief 'errors' from 'Cleanthes, Zeno's disciple, Chrysippus, Seneca, Strato of Lampsacus, and others'.[107] Shortly afterwards, *'t Mom-Aensicht der Atheisterey Afgerukt* (Amsterdam, 1683) by Adriaen Pietersz. Verwer (1654–1720) depicts Spinoza as the systematizer of an ancient tradition of thought reaching back to the Presocratics, and then passed down eventually to Vanini and Hobbes.[108] The Dordrecht physician Petrus Jens asserts, in his refutation of Spinoza of 1697, that Spinoza represents the summation of the whole history of philosophical atheism since ancient times.[109]

This Dutch background doubtless helped shape the thesis introduced by Bayle in his *Dictionnaire* but further elaborated during his last years that Spinozism marks

101 Mihaila, 'L'*Hylozoïsme* de Diderot', 186–8.

102 Cudworth, *True Intellectual System*, i. 107; *Bibliothèque choisie*, 2 (1703), 27; Reimmann, *Historia universalis*, 187; 'on attribue à Straton de Lampsaque', echoes the *Encyclopédie*, 'l'origine de ce sentiment', *Encyclopédie*, viii. 391.

103 Cudworth, *True Intellectual System*, i. 145; Schlosser, *De Stratone Lampsaceno*, 25.

104 Cudworth, *True Intellectual System*, i. 108; Diderot and d'Alembert, *Encyclopédie*, viii. 391.

105 Cudworth, *True Intellectual System*, i. 142.

106 Van Hassel, 'Voorreden', pp. iii–iv; Goeree, *Kerklyke en Weereldlyke Historien*, 627–3.

107 Jenichen, *Historia Spinozismi Leenhofiani*, 30.

108 [Verwer], *'t Mom-Aensicht*, 6–9.

109 Jens, *Examen philosophicum*, praefatio, p. v.

the culmination of a long process reaching back to Xenophanes, the Eleatics, and numerous other ancient and medieval thinkers and sects,[110] but especially parallels Stratonism, the most formidable of the ancient variants, vesting as it does all creative power in matter, envisaging 'une nature nécessaire et continue qui avoit la faculté' to produce everything that is produced in the universe without the intervention of any external factor.[111] Having previously cited Strato only in passing, in the *Dictionnaire* where Stoicism and Epicureanism function as the main ancient equivalents of Spinozism, in the *Continuation* Bayle judges Stratonism the most cogent Greek system and that which the Aristotelians and other Hellenistic schools found hardest to refute.[112] It was thus once again especially Bayle, albeit building on Cudworth and Wittichius, who elaborated the parallel between Strato and Spinoza in the Early Enlightenment consciousness;[113] and it was in the years 1703–4 that Stratonism came to the forefront of Bayle's thought and hence became relevant to his fight with Le Clerc, Bernard, and Jaquelot. There is a much greater gap, argued Bayle, between nothingness and extended being than between extended being and movement, or other modifications of extension, and if existence is something ordained by a Creator, Strato (or Spinoza) can then cogently enough reply that it goes against the nature of things that matter should exist 'en mouvement par elle-même, et que son mouvement ne fut déterminé'.[114]

Where the 'rationaux' advanced the 'argument from design' against his own (ostensible) fideism, assuring 'les non-rationaux' that the cosmos has a rational, coherent order and structure revealing the work of divine providence, Bayle maintains that they were in fact undermining their own position without realizing it. For their stance conceded far more to Strato-Spinoza than they grasped. This plainly emerged, he held, from an analysis of Cudworth's doctrine, approved by Le Clerc, of 'plastic forms', a concept the Master of Christ's College had devised purposely as a way of overcoming all varieties of atheistic thought, including hylozoism. For unless the Almighty directly communicates his design to those entities below who carry out the divine intention, held Bayle, the 'plastic forms' which implement his wishes are really in exactly the same position, being themselves unknowing, blind, and unintelligent, as if no one at all knows about the divine scheme.[115] A Stratonian, held Bayle, can easily refute Cudworth by saying God can, you grant, impart to created things the faculty of producing 'd'excellens ouvrages, séparés de toute connoissance'.[116] Why then can you not admit there is no necessary connection between ability to produce wonderful works of nature 'et l'idée de leur essence'. How can one claim these two things cannot be separate in nature and that nature

110 Cantelli, *Teologia*, 239, 254, 249–50; Mori, *Bayle philosophe*, 165.

111 Bayle, *Réponse*, iii. 1237–8, 1242; Bayle, *Continuation*, ii. 524–36.

112 Bayle, *Continuation*, ii. 502, 508; Bayle, *Réponse*, iii. 1237, 1242–3; Cantelli, *Teologia*, 254–6; Paganini, 'Tra Epicuro e Stratone', 91–2; Mori, *Bayle philosophe*, 219.

113 Mosheim, 'Notes', i. 102; Spink, *French Free-Thought*, 264; Paganini, *Analisi della fede*, 348–53, 379–80; Piaia, 'Brucker versus Rorty', 79.

114 Bayle, *Réponse*, iii. 1240–2.

115 Ibid. iii. 1283–4; Tomasoni, 'Il "sistema" ', 655.

116 Bayle, 'Mémoire Communiqué', 183–4; Labrousse, *Pierre Bayle*, ii. 216.

cannot do by herself what 'plastic natures', you maintain, can do 'par un don de Dieu'? Later, Le Clerc warned Lady Masham, Locke's friend and Cudworth's daughter, that in thus attacking her father's system, Bayle implicitly smeared him with the taint of atheism while himself inspiring atheism.[117]

Le Clerc and Leibniz insisted that Bayle was mistaken in his reasoning, and Cudworth not so easily toppled;[118] Toland, on the other hand, followed Bayle in pronouncing Cudworth's 'plastic life' a useless circumvention. Cudworth, asserts Toland, understood his Platonic 'plastic life' as something 'not material, but an inferior sort of spirit without sensation or thought, yet endued with a vital operation and energy'. Toland too dismissed this as 'seeming to differ with the Hylozoicks only about words, tho' pretending a mighty disagreement, to keep clear, I suppose, of the absurd or invidious consequences charg'd on their opinions', much as the Jansenists affect 'a mighty disagreement with the Calvinists about Predestination despite having a virtually identical opinion on this subject as their opponents'.[119]

If Epicurean atomism renders the world a product of chance, Strato's, held Bayle, makes everything follow an eternally fixed order of necessity, inherent in matter itself; moreover, Strato did not teach that the cosmos is something recent or, like the atomists, that it is 'produit par le hasard', but rather, says Bayle, 'comme font les Spinozistes', that Nature had fashioned it 'nécessairement et de toute éternité'.[120] Strato allows no First Mover distinct from Nature, holding that everything that happens occurs necessarily and that there is no innate 'good' or 'bad' in the cosmos.[121] Like Vossius, Bayle stressed Strato's denial that the cosmos is a living being with intention, intelligence, or sensibility,[122] claiming he saw Nature as containing within itself the origin of all conception, growth, and decline, vested in spontaneous movement innate in matter itself. Bayle's Strato acknowledges no other divine power than that of nature, 'et il soutint que la nature étoit toute corporelle'.[123]

While nothing in the surviving sources proves Strato really did thus conceive of Nature's overall rational coherence, something of the sort can perhaps be legitimately inferred from the fact that no ancient commentator suggests he advocated, like Epicurus, any doctrine of chaos or random contingency.[124] From both the fragmentary historical Strato and Bayle's highly coherent 'Strato' emerges a rationally unified architecture of Nature created by no intelligent power, and devoid of all bodiless spirits and spiritual forces.[125] Motion appears to be the effective motor of all creation, growth, and decay and hence the sole source of Nature's creativity.

[117] Barnes, *Jean le Clerc*, 232–5; Labrousse, *Pierre Bayle*, i. 264.

[118] Leibniz, *Theodicy*, 245.

[119] Toland, *Letters to Serena*, 211–12.

[120] Bayle, *Continuation*, ii. 524–6; Diderot, *Œuvres complètes*, xiv. 581–3; Badaloni, 'Vico', 341–2.

[121] Crousaz, *Examen*, 411–15.

[122] Gatzemeier, *Naturphilosophie*, 106, 108, 111; Furley, 'Cosmology', 416; Bouchardy, *Pierre Bayle*, 282.

[123] Bayle, *Continuation* (1721), iv. 139; Buddeus, *De Spinozismo ante Spinozam*, 319; Bolingbroke, *Philosophical Works*, ii. 38–9; Paganini, 'Tra Epicuro e Stratone', 91; Gatzemeier, *Naturphilosophie*, 109, 119; Simonutti, 'Bayle and Le Clerc', 157.

[124] Gatzemeier, *Naturphilosophie*, 109.

[125] Bayle, *Continuation* (1721), ii. 502; Paganini, 'Tra Epicuro e Stratone', 91–2.

The innateness of motion in matter was of course vigorously denied by the entire moderate mainstream, preceded here by Cudworth.[126] 'Thus the atheists universally', he observes, 'either assigned no cause at all for motion, as the Anaximandrians and Democriticks; or else no true one, as the Hylozoists; when to avoid incorporeal substance, they would venture to attribute, perfect understanding, appetite or will, and self-moving power, to all senseless matter whatsoever. But since it appears plainly, that matter or body cannot move itself; either the motion of all bodies, must have no manner of cause, or else must there of necessity, be some other substance besides body, such as is self-active and hylarchical, or hath a natural power, of ruling over matter.'[127]

For movement, the origin of creation, in Bayle's Strato arises solely from universal, immutable, and purely natural causes like weight, pressure, and especially heat and cold, as is consonant with the Greek sources.[128] There, heat is identified as the chief cause of movement in Strato in particular by the Palestinian Jewish Christian convert and heretic-hunter Epiphanius (AD *c*.320–402), an enthusiast for monasticism who became metropolitan of Cyprus in 367: 'Στράτων ἐκ Λαμψάκου τὴν θερμὴν οὐσίαν ἔλεγεν αἰτίαν πάντων ὑπάρχειν [Strato of Lampsacus said that hot substance is the cause of all things]. Since weight naturally presses down, lighter objects, according to Strato, are forced up by those that are heavier: Στράτων μὲν προσεῖναι τοῖς σώμασι φυσικὸν βάρος, τὰ δὲ κουφότερα τοῖς βαρυτέροις ἐπιπολάζειν, οἷον ἐκπυρνιζόμενα [Strato ascribed natural weight to bodies, the lighter to the heavier being uppermost, as if they were being burnt out].[129] Unlike Aristotle, therefore, who defined lightness as an active principle contrary to weight which strives naturally upwards, Strato saw lightness as just a lesser degree of weight.[130] Inferring that variations in weight result from differences in density owing to matter being interspersed in various ways with void and that no void exists naturally, he derived his theory of suction: if a void is created, surrounding matter will rush in to fill it unless prevented by some obstructing mechanism which, when removed, releases a violent shift of energy.[131]

One sentence of Epiphanius' account of Strato, furthermore, appeared expressly to link heat and movement with the inception of mind in living creatures: ἄπειρα εἶναι τὰ μέρη τοῦ κόσμου καὶ πᾶν ζῷον ἔλεγε νοῦ δεκτικὸν εἶναι [he said that the parts of the universe are infinite and that every living creature is capable of receiving mind].[132] Leibniz, like Buddeus and later Boureau-Deslandes,[133] agreed

[126] Bayle, *Continuation*, ii. 430, 553–4, 760; Schlosser, *De Stratone Lampsaceno*, 30; Gundling, *Vollständige Historie*, iv. 4986 n.; d'Argens, *Impartial Philosopher*, i. 178–9, 184; Maréchal, *Dictionnaire des athées*, 284; Rodier, *Physique de Straton*, 113; Cantelli, *Teologia*, 230, 240, 263; Paganini, 'Tra Epicuro e Stratone', 91–5; Gatzemeier, *Naturphilosophie*, 143.

[127] Cudworth, *True Intellectual System*, ii. 668; Patrides, *Cambridge Platonists*, 325.

[128] Reimmann, *Historia Universalis*, 187; Long, *Hellenistic Philosophy*, 119, 152; Long and Sedley, *Hellenistic Philosophers*, i. 287 n.

[129] Wehrli, *Schule des Aristoteles*, v. 19 (fr. 51); Wolff, 'Hipparchus', 474, 508.

[130] Hankinson, 'Science', 141, 144; Gatzemeier, *Naturphilosophie*, 118–19.

[131] Gottschalk, *Strato of Lampsacus*, 106, 127–9.

[132] Wehrli, *Schule des Aristoteles*, v. 18 (fr. 48).

[133] Geissler, *Boureau-Deslandes*, 87.

with Bayle that the Spinozists are the 'modern Stratonists', and that Strato and Spinoza alike hold 'that all has come about from the first cause or from primitive Nature by a blind and geometric necessity, with complete absence of capacity for choice, goodness and understanding in this first source of things'.[134] But, disputing Bayle's insistence on the intellectual coherence of Stratonism, in the *Continuation*, Leibniz denied Strato's system was as internally consistent as Bayle maintains, saying, on the contrary, that it is 'not to be feared', and that there are valid philosophical grounds for opposing the neo-Stratonian vision of the universe.

In particular, objects Leibniz, Bayle fails to consider the superior cogency of a conception of the 'predetermined harmony of the universe', such as in his own metaphysics, as compared with a simple determinism where God's governance is reduced 'to the dominion of necessity, and a blind necessity (as with Strato) whereby everything emanates from the divine nature, while no choice is left to God and Man's choice does not exempt him from necessity'.[135] Bayle argues 'that one might with Strato' reasonably infer that the world could have acquired its regularity and coherent structure 'through blind necessity'.[136] But since the range of abstract possibilities for ordering the universe includes both the regular and the irregular, replies Leibniz, 'there must be a reason for the preference for order and regularity, and this reason can only be found in understanding'.

Moreover, the geometric truths on which the universe rests, counters Leibniz, 'can have no existence without an understanding to take cognizance of them; for they would not exist if there were no divine understanding wherein they are realized'; hence, 'Strato does not gain his end which is to exclude cognition from the origin of things.'[137] Clarke complained that in Leibniz's system God has no choice but to adopt the best and therefore acts according to necessary laws. Crucial for Leibniz, however, and his rebutting the Newtonian thesis, was the distinction between moral necessity by which God freely chooses the most perfect, albeit he cannot do otherwise, 'and the brute necessity of Strato and adherents of Spinoza, who deny to God understanding and will'.[138] The examples Leibniz offers to illustrate his distinction hardly seem conclusive though: God, he says, could have opted for laws of motion other than those he did choose, his choice having been guided by his desire to choose the best. The reason that there are only three dimensions, however, he thought to be quite different, being determined 'by a geometrical and blind necessity'.[139]

Bayle's claim that Stratonism is the most coherent of systems based purely on reason with its, to most minds, sinister implication that Spinozism, the modern reincarnation of Stratonism, reunites Greek with modern philosophy reinstating that cogency, met with a variety of responses. One was to accept the equation of Stratonism and Spinozism and then, like Leibniz and Voltaire, reject both, on

[134] Leibniz, *Theodicy*, 67, 245, 336, 349; Mosheim, 'Notes', i. 102–3.

[135] Leibniz, *Theodicy*, 349; Schlosser, *De Stratone Lampsaceno*, 28, 30; Paganini, 'Tra Epicuro e Stratone', 96–7; Schröder, *Ursprünge*, 51; Israel, *Radical Enlightenment*, 514.

[136] Leibniz, *Theodicy*, 246. [137] Ibid. [138] Ibid. 336. [139] Ibid.

metaphysical grounds, contending that 'design' proves cognition and excludes Stratonic 'blind necessity'. Alternatively, one could endorse Bayle's thesis with all its implications as a way of heightening suspicion of philosophy in general, which was the reaction of Buddeus initially and of diverse sceptics and fideists. Buddeus and Gundling in fact largely agreed with Bayle about Strato, the first in his *De Spinozismo ante Spinozam* (Halle, 1701) stating that while Strato differs from Spinoza in some not inconsiderable points, he was nevertheless the first genuine precursor of Spinoza.[140] Bayle was right, says Buddeus, to say Strato approaches much closer to Spinozism than Epicurus, and anticipated Spinoza in many things, especially concerning motion and sensibility being inherent in the material world where Stratonism and Spinozism contrast sharply with Epicurus' atomistic universe in which matter is inert and lifeless and the origin of life problematic.[141]

Toland thought likewise, as did the rest of the Radical Enlightenment. Collins expressly sanctions Bayle's interpretation of Strato in his early tract *An Answer to Mr Clark's Third Defence of his Letter to Mr Dodwell* (London, 1708), where he defends both Spinoza and Bayle against Clarke.[142] 'As far as I can judge of the opinions of Strato, Xenophanes and some other ancient atheists from a few sentences of theirs that yet remain, and of that sect call'd the *Literati* in China,' he maintains, 'they seem all to me to agree with Spinoza (who in his *Opera Posthuma* has endeavour'd to reduce atheism into a system) that there is no other substance in the universe but matter, which Spinoza calls God, and Strato Nature.'[143] In Strato's system according to Cudworth and Bayle, life and mind inhere in matter while motion explains actions of the mind as all other happenings in nature. Hence, Strato was widely deemed—at least until Brucker intervened to defend him against the charges of 'atheism' and affinity to Spinoza[144]—the most consistent atheist, materialist, and naturalist among the ancients. This was despite there being no real evidence that his 'hylozoism' did actually entail his denying the existence of the lesser gods and despite the fact that he himself would presumably have been horrified by any suggestion that he was, as the Hellenistic Greeks understood the term, an 'atheist'.[145]

That movement in Strato's system generates not only animate from inanimate matter but equally mind is confirmed by the well-informed sixth-century AD pagan Alexandrine scholar Simplikios, one of the defiant last seven philosophers who sought refuge at the court of the Persian king Chosroës during the final suppression of non-Christian philosophy under the Emperor Justinian. Strato's conception of

[140] Buddeus, *De Spinozismo ante Spinozam*, 317, 319; Brucker, *De Stratonis Lampsaceni atheismo*, 313; Gatzemeier, *Naturphilosophie*, 109.

[141] Buddeus, *De Spinozismo ante Spinozam*, 319–20; Schlosser, *De Stratone Lampsaceno*, 27.

[142] Israel, *Radical Enlightenment*, 617; Taranto, *Du déisme à l'athéisme*, 385.

[143] Taranto, *Du déisme à l'athéisme*, 332; [Collins], *An Answer*, 89; Hazard, *Crise de la conscience*, 33; Vernière, *Spinoza*, 351.

[144] Brucker, *De Stratonis Lampsaceni atheismo*, 317–18; Brucker, *Kurtze Fragen*, 883–4; Brucker, *Historia critica philosophiae* (1742), i. 846, 849.

[145] Rodier, *Physique de Straton*, 112; Schröder, *Ursprünge*, 51.

mind, reports Simplikios, was directly linked to his naturalistic cosmology and physics and entailed the complete dissolution of Aristotle's hierarchical structure of sense, soul, and mind.[146] According to Strato, continues Simplikios, ἀεὶ γὰρ ὁ νοῶν κινεῖται ὥσπερ καὶ ὁ ὁρῶν καὶ ἀκούων καὶ ὀσφραινόμενος. ἐνεργία γὰρ ἡνόησις τῆς διανόιας καθάπερ καὶ ἡὅρασις τῆς ὄψεως [he who thinks is always in motion like him who is seeing, hearing, and smelling; for thought is an energy of mind just as seeing is of vision]. From this Strato concluded, says Simplikios, that the mind's motions are basically the same, when recalling something seen or heard, presented to it by the senses, and when 'thinking is moved of itself', prompting his remark that one cannot think of things, creatures, or places one has not seen or heard about.[147]

Strato, then, abolishes Aristotle's distinction between physical movement and mental activity, reducing all actions of the mind to forms of sense and perception, which means he also eliminates, as both More and Cudworth scornfully remark, all conceivable basis for the immortality of the soul.[148] Vossius had already noted that, for Strato, mind is a function of sense.[149] Bayle and his contemporaries relied in part on Sextus Empiricus' clear (but perhaps oversimplified) remark that among Greek thinkers there were two rival views regarding the origin of mind, those who distinguished thinking from the sensations, as most did, and those who derived thought from sense perception, as a stretching out, like the tones of a flute. 'This dissenting view', says Sextus, 'began with Strato the Naturalist and also Aenesidemus.'[150] 'But this Hylozoick Atheism', objected Cudworth, 'thus bringing all conscious and reflexive life or animality, out of a supposed senseless, stupid and inconscious life of Nature, in matter, and that meerly from a different accidental modification thereof, or contexture of parts, does again plainly bring something out of nothing, which is an absolute impossibility.'[151]

Bayle's reconstruction of Strato's philosophy might be interpreted as something never intended as a serious historical exercise but rather a device adopted for exclusively philosophical purposes.[152] However, he was a teacher of history as well as philosophy and a main architect of the new historico-critical method. It would have meant taking a considerable risk, in that erudite age, had he really devised a purely fictive 'Stratonism' for such highly questionable purposes. Since he drew for most of what he knew about Strato from Le Clerc's account of Cudworth's historically source-grounded arguments, it seems unlikely, despite the weakness of his Greek, that he would rely on his own imagination for the components of a 'Strato' and 'Stratonism' which were henceforth to play a vital

146 Repici, *Natura*, 34.

147 Wehrli, *Schule des Aristoteles*, v. 25 (fr. 74), 71; Gatzemeier, *Naturphilosophie*, 132; Repici, *Natura*, 33–4.

148 Wehrli, *Schule des Aristoteles*, v. 71, 75; Gatzemeier, *Naturphilosophie*, 132–3.

149 Vossius, *De theologia gentili*, i. 468.

150 Wehrli, *Schule des Aristoteles*, v. 33 (fr. 109); Repici, *Natura*, 12–13.

151 Cudworth, *True Intellectual System*, ii. 839; Patrides, *Cambridge Platonists*, 323–4.

152 Labrousse, *Pierre Bayle*, ii. 245 n.; Paganini, 'Tra Epicuro e Stratone', 92–5; Mori, *Bayle philosophe*, 218–19, 221; Mori, 'Interpréter la philosophie de Bayle', 320–2; Bouchardy, *Pierre Bayle*, 101 n., 282, 290.

role not just in his own thought but in the wider European debate about history of philosophy.

That Bayle's final position approximates to a modern Spinozism shorn of the doctrine of one substance, with 'Stratonism' the only coherent response to the great metaphysical questions,[153] need not be incompatible with his having engaged in a genuine historical-critical quest to uncover the true Strato. Rather, the role of the historical Strato both as successor to Theophrastus and as a resolute critic of Aristotelianism seems to have been important to Bayle.[154] The real Strato, attacking the Peripatetics, as it were, from within, argued his way out of an Aristotelian context just like the modern critical philosophy to which Bayle (who had once taught Aristotelianism professionally, at Sedan) devoted his life while simultaneously combating Epicureanism and the Stoic concept of God.[155] For Strato represented—in both antiquity and the Enlightenment—a necessitarianism inherent in the power and coherence of nature entailing a rational structure to all reality—'une nature nécessaire et continue qui avoit la faculté de produire ce qui se produit dans l'univers'.[156]

Stratonism for Bayle and the French materialists was both an ancient reality *and* a modern polemical device. 'Straton', asserted Boureau-Deslandes in 1737, did not stop at materialism: he went from there to a doctrine even more absurd: 'ce fut de vouloir prouver qu'un être intelligent n'a jamais pu créer le monde.' Boureau-Deslandes (in fact himself a materialist and a radical), like Bayle, held that Strato was a direct precursor of Spinoza and the principal Greek exponent of the idea that a blind and unintelligent nature created and creates everything in the universe, animate and inanimate. Leibniz did not disagree with the historical aspect of this analysis, dubbing the *Spinozisten* of his own day the 'Stratoniciens modernes'. Lévesque de Burigny agreed that for Strato, that thinker whom 'M. Cudworth appelle le chef de l'athéisme hylozoique', and who believed Nature 'étoit la seule divinité', God takes no part in what goes on in the world.[157] Jean Meslier, the most systematic and emphatic French materialist writer before Diderot, did not hesitate to rank Strato, with Leucippus, Democritus, and Epicurus, among the first rank of those Greek philosophers who tried not only to integrate everything which is real but, as he saw it, heroically strove to strip away the veil of prejudice and save philosophy from the theologians, someone whose precious teaching—his message (like Meslier's own) being too devoid of marvels for 'des imaginations amoureuses des chimères'—being subsequently brutally stifled amid the 'conjectures fabuleuses des Platon, Socrate, des Zenon'.[158]

If one trusts in reason alone, requiring of philosophy only coherence and consistency, held Bayle, then philosophy can lead the scrupulously cogent thinker to no other

[153] Mori, *Bayle philosophe*, 219; Bouchardy, *Pierre Bayle*, 313.
[154] Bayle, *Continuation*, iv. 130; Paganini, 'Tra Epicuro e Stratone', 91.
[155] Bayle, *Continuation*, ii. 649, 710–11, 726–7. [156] Ibid. ii. 502–4.
[157] Lévesque de Burigny, *Théologie payenne*, i. 50, 115.
[158] Quoted in Rihs, *Philosophes utopistes*, 117.

conclusion than that Stratonism, or ancient Spinozism, is true.[159] Were two young Athenians aged 25 to embark in all seriousness on an unremitting exercise to discover the true nature of Creation, reality, and God, avoiding every pitfall in reasoning, and all distraction, admitting nothing that is not subject to pure reason alone, they might take wrong turns, so arduous a task might take five years, but, if in the end they make good all mistakes, they would conclude at the age of 30 by embracing Stratonism.[160] Only Christian revelation can rescue these two earnest young Athenians from so dreadful a denouement; how unfortunate, then, adds Bayle sardonically, that the gospel benefits only those born after Christ, living where children imbibe Christianity, and not, for whatever inscrutable reason, the rest of mankind.

Stratonism, held Bayle, cannot be defeated by philosophical reason. Impregnable philosophically, it is a form of atheism, he concludes, that boils down to this general perspective: that nature is the cause of all things, that she exists naturally and of herself, and that she acts according to the full extent of her powers obeying immutable laws of which she knows nothing. Nothing, it follows, is possible that nature has not performed; nature produces everything that is possible; everything happens by unavoidable necessity ('par une nécessité fatale'); nothing is more natural than anything else that actually occurs 'ni moins convenable à la perfection de l'univers'—a formula vital, it is worth noting, for a correct understanding of sexuality. Finally, whatever state the world is in, it is always 'tel qu'il doit être et qu'il peut être'.[161] This lacks the doctrine of one substance, it has been pointed out, but otherwise contains the essentials of what in the early eighteenth century was meant by both Spinozism and Stratonism.

3. SPINOZISM: A REWORKING OF GREEK STOICISM?

No other classical writer was cited as often or insistently as Strato in the role of chief ancient precursor of Spinoza, though all sorts of other ancient writers besides Xenophanes, Strato, and Epicurus were adduced in this capacity. The Neapolitan philosopher Paulo Mattia Doria (1662–1746) claimed it was the Roman naturalist Pliny the Elder (AD 23–79), author of a massive and wide-ranging *Natural History* and another author who supposedly conflates body and spirit, who stood closest to Spinoza, referring repeatedly to the 'sistema di Plinio, il quale poi e stato rinovellato da Spinosa' [the system of Pliny which was later renewed by Spinoza].[162] However, the most usual parallel, and liveliest controversy, next to those pertaining to the Eleatics and Stratonians, involved Stoicism.

[159] Leibniz, *Theodicy*, 67, 245, 349; Cantelli, *Teologia*, 239–40, 249–50, 254; Yuen-Ting Lai, 'Linking of Spinoza', 169.

[160] Crouzas, *Examen*, 415; Cantelli, *Teologia*, 254–6; Mori, *Bayle philosophe*, 52; Mori, 'Interpréter la philosophie de Bayle', 324.

[161] Quoted in Mori, *Bayle philosophe*, 220–1.

[162] Doria, *Manoscritti napoletani*, iv. 71–2, 253–4, 367, 371, 377–8.

Bayle refers, in the *Supplément* to his *Commentaire philosophique* in 1688, to the Stoic God being enchained by an inevitable destiny which is scarcely 'meilleur que le Spinozisme',[163] while others insisted no less on the two systems' alleged proximity. Hassel, Bernard, and van Til all charge Spinoza with subversively reintroducing Stoic teaching without declaring his sources or real purpose. In 1690, David Hassel, Cartesio-Cocceian theologian and author of the anonymous preface to Wittichius' *Anti-Spinoza* (1690), asserted that no egg more resembles another than does Spinoza's system that of the Stoics which this supreme impostor had the temerity to rehash and serve up as his own.[164] It was this system of the Stoics, held Bernard in 1692, which Spinoza had renewed, there being nothing so similar 'à sa doctrine, que celle des Stoïciens'.[165] Van Til, like Wittichius a Cartesio-Cocceian, and also writing prior to Bayle's *Dictionnaire*, pointed to the similarity between Stoic doctrine and Spinoza's identification of God with the totality of the universe, citing the Stoic Seneca the Younger's maxim 'Totum hoc, quo continemur et unum est, et Deus' [this everything, which includes us, is one and is God].[166] At the heart of Spinoza's metaphysics, he identified 'een Stoisch nootlot' [Stoic fate], like Hassel, expressing concern lest such doctrines, buried for centuries, should now re-emerge in a new and highly subversive fashion. Who would have imagined, he asked, that those long forgotten ideas should thus revive in our time, 'an age of so much light and clarity'? Buddeus at Jena likewise held that for all the Stoics' fine-sounding phrases about piety and virtue, at bottom their system when examined does not differ much from Spinozism.[167]

Earlier, characterizing Stoicism as wholly alien to the Christian tradition would have sounded far less persuasive. It was only since Jakob Thomasius' pioneering researches on Stoicism, published at Leipzig in 1676, that earlier humanist attempts to reconcile Stoic (as well as Platonic and Aristotelian) doctrine with Christian teachings came to look confused and irrelevant and that it emerged there was now an urgent need for a rigorous re-evaluation of Stoic fatalism.[168] Bayle already suggested parallels between Spinoza and Stoicism whilst editing his *Nouvelles de la République des Lettres* (1684–7) and again in his *Dictionnaire*,[169] and, while later he abandoned this parallel, preferring that with Strato, others continued to see in Stoicism the ancient school most proximate to Spinozism. Gundling compared with Spinoza the first Stoic philosopher, Zeno of Citium (*c.*333–*c.*262 BC), from Cyprus, who arrived in Athens around 311 BC, a decade after Aristotle's death,

[163] Bayle, *Supplément*, 203; Bonacina, *Filosofia ellenistica*, 27–32.

[164] Hassel, 'Voorreden', pp. iii–iv; Hase and Lampe, *Bibliotheca* (1719/20), 3rd classis, p. 479; De Vet, 'La "Bibliothèque universelle" ', 92–3, 107.

[165] De Vet, 'La "Bibliothèque universelle" ' 110 n. 67; *Bibliothèque universelle*, 23 (1692), 325; De Vet, 'Spinoza en Spinozisme', 3.

[166] Van Til, *Voor-Hof der Heydenen*, 257; van Til, *Vervolg op het Voorhof*, p. 92, 131–4; Sluiter, *Idea theologiae Stoicae*, 58–60; see also [Rabus], *Boekzaal van Europe* (Jan.–June 1697), 158.

[167] [Rabus] *Boekzaal van Europe* (Jan.–June 1697), 27–8; Bonacina, *Filosofia ellenistica*, 46.

[168] Bonacina, *Filosofia ellenistica*, 50; Thomasius, *Exercitatio*, 166–76; Thomasius, *Dissertationes*, 14–15, 22, 35; Häfner, 'Jacob Thomasius', 152.

[169] Bayle, *Écrits*, 70–1; Labrousse, *Pierre Bayle*, ii. 199, 355; De Vet, 'Spinoza en Spinozisme', 10–11.

establishing his own school in a row of Stoa (porches) to the side of the Athenian agora.[170] According to Lévesque de Burigny, for whom Stoic teaching 'ne différoit pas beaucoup de celle-là [i.e. of Spinoza]', Zeno's chief followers, Chrysippus, head of the Stoa from 232 BC until his death around 205, chief codifier of Stoicism, and Posidonius (*c*.135–50 BC), from Apamea on the Orontes, in Syria, who, after studying in Athens, established a thriving branch of the school in Rhodes, both taught that the cosmos 'composoit la substance de Dieu'.[171]

Fréret avers that Stoic thought subjects everything to a fatalism and 'hylozoïsme' or 'matérialisme, peu différent du dogme de Spinosa'.[172] Both in his *La Philosophie du bon sens*[173] and *Mémoires secrets* d'Argens asserts that there is no other difference between the Stoic system and 'celui de Spinoza que la diversité de termes'.[174] But there were also those who sharply disagreed. Roëll roundly denied the Stoics reduce God to Nature like the Spinozists,[175] as did Doria (until towards the end of his life), who praised the Stoics for acknowledging, not unlike the Pythagoreans and Platonists, a God immanent in the world, infinite and yet intelligent.[176] Doria, like Vico later, changed his mind about this and equated Stoicism with Pliny's system or that 'renewed in our days by Benedict de Spinoza'.[177] Vico likewise abandoned his earlier favourable view of Stoicism[178] in his *New Science*, lambasting 'the Stoics, who (in this respect the Spinozists of their day) make God an infinite mind, subject to fate, in an infinite body'.[179]

In modern times, the case for regarding Spinoza as a 'new Stoic' has been reiterated by Dilthey, the Dutch scholar K. H. E. De Jong in 1939, and others since, including Oskar Kristeller.[180] Recently, sweeping affinities have again been claimed, especially as regards equating of God with Nature, and the immanence of God in every part of nature, as well as the Stoic distinction between an active and passive aspect of nature often likened to Spinoza's '*natura naturans* and *natura naturata*'.[181] If the Stoics tailored their teaching to the popular polytheism of their day, interpreting stories of the lesser gods as a primitive way of classifying natural forces, Spinoza does something not dissimilar in explaining the origins of polytheism.[182] Further seeming similarities lie in the rigorous determinism both apply to everything in nature, that is to everything there is, including humans,[183] with the resulting

170 Gundling, *Gundlingiana*, v. 189, 239, 242; Reimmann, *Historia universalis*, 160–1.

171 [Lévesque de Burigny], *Histoire de la philosophie payenne*, i. 70.

172 Fréret, *Œuvres complètes*, xvi. 228.

173 D'Argens, *Impartial Philosopher*, i. 201; see also i. 199–200, ii. 119.

174 D'Argens, *Mémoires secrets*, ii. 252.

175 Heumann, *Acta philosophorum*, xi (1720), 814.

176 Doria, *Difesa della metafisica*, i. 30, 149–50, 160, ii. 116, 274; Doria, *Filosofia*, i. 35, 37, part 2, pp. 306–7 and ii. 48, 54, 103.

177 Doria, *Manoscritti napoletani*, ii. 204, 236, v. 182–3.

178 Vico, *De antiquissima Italorum sapientia*, 68–79; Doria, *Difesa della metafisica*, i. 150, ii. 116.

179 Vico, *The New Science*, 98; Croce, *Filosofia di Giambattista Vico*, 78, 85; Mazzotta, *New Map*, 7.

180 Long, 'Stoicism', in Inwood (ed.), *The Cambridge Companion to the Stoics*, 369; De Jong, *Spinoza en de Stoa*, 1–2, 33–4.

181 De Jong, *Spinoza en de Stoa*, 4–5; James, 'Spinoza the Stoic', 291–4; Nadler, 'Spinoza's Theory', 17, 19.

182 Bayle, *Continuation*, i. 125, ii. 649; Kristeller, *Greek Philosophers*, 70.

183 De Jong, *Spinoza en de Stoa*, 7; Spanneut, *Permanence du stoïcisme*, 293–4; Sandbach, *The Stoics*, 103–4; Forschner, *Die stoische Ethik*, 105–8.

tension between Man's liberty and the determinacy of human conduct.[184] Affinities between Spinozism and Stoicism were again stressed in an essay published in 1993 by Susan James, where the author holds that 'much of the substance and structure of [Spinoza's] *Ethics*—its central doctrines and the connections between them—constitute, as I shall show, a reworking of Stoicism'.[185]

Spinoza, like the Stoics, draws moral conclusions from a concept of nature envisaged as the totality of what is,[186] so that their ethical systems do converge in part.[187] To be virtuous, for both, is the same as being happy; and virtue, however differently defined, is the sole source of *eudemonia* [happiness].[188] Happiness, likewise, is, for both, Man's highest good. When Spinoza affirms in the *Ethics* that 'happiness is not the reward of virtue but virtue itself' he appears to be echoing the Stoics.[189] Virtue is attainable, moreover, only when one knows what is 'right' and 'wrong' which is possible only for the wise man; hence happiness, for Stoics and Spinoza alike, depends not on anything one obtains in the outside world but rather on cultivating a rational attitude towards those things.[190] The happiness achieved via the rational pursuit of 'virtue' is in both cases what promotes attainment of a smooth and tranquil life. The tightly linked chain of reasoning characteristic of Stoicism since Chrysippus, 'second founder of Stoicism',[191] and the rigour with which ethics is derived from natural philosophy, seem to foreshadow Spinoza's closely knit *more geometrico* argumentation, similarly integrating cosmology, natural philosophy, and the human condition. 'One is reminded' when contemplating the impressive coherence of the Stoic system, as one scholar put it in 1971, 'as so often in Stoicism, of Spinoza'.[192]

While these modern scholars do not, of course, share the motives which inspired earlier comparisons of Spinozism with Stoicism, the effect, were their reading correct, might well be similar. For by labelling Spinoza a 'Stoic', Early Enlightenment critics questioned both his originality and integrity, reminding readers that Christianity had long since disposed of the arguments of the Stoics, back in late antiquity. Whatever was valid in Stoicism had, they were confident, been absorbed into Christian Stoicism and whatever was invalid been discarded. Spinoza, viewed in this light, however impious his system, was just a shadow threat, rehashing old matter, and not, after all, a major new challenge.

At first glance, the parallels and affinities do indeed look striking. The universe, held the Stoics, is pervaded by reason (λόγος), the active principle which infuses

[184] Stough, 'Stoic Determinism', 203, 207, 224–5; Nadler, *Spinoza's Heresy*, 132, 135–6.

[185] James, 'Spinoza the Stoic', 291; see also James, 'Reason, the Passions', 1374–5; Long, 'Stoicism', in Millet and Inwood (eds.), *Hellenistic and Early Modern Philosophy*, 10.

[186] Long, *Hellenistic Philosophy*, 185.

[187] Kristeller, *Greek Philosophers*, 23, 85; Spanneut, *Permanence du stoïcisme*, 294–5; Sévérac, 'Convenir', 105; Hubbeling, *Spinoza*, 88; Miller, 'Stoics, Grotius', 129, 134.

[188] Sandbach, *The Stoics*, 28–9; Long and Sedley, *Hellenistic Philosophers*, i. 376–7, 382–3, 394–400; Long, 'Stoicism', in Inwood (ed.), *The Cambridge Companion to the Stoics*, 374–5.

[189] Spinoza, *Ethics*, part v, prop. 42; Klever, *Ethicom*, 719.

[190] Sandbach, *Stoic Ethics*, 29; Long and Sedley, *Hellenistic Philosophers*, i. 394–7; Nadler, *Spinoza*, 239.

[191] Sedley, 'The School', 17.

[192] Long, *Stoic Studies*, 139.

nature, and is God. 'Piety' or true 'religion' for them, as for Spinoza, depends on acquiring the right notions about God and revering God-nature, as it is.[193] As in Spinoza, there is neither any act of Creation nor an independent, free Creator. The Stoic God, noted Burmannus in 1688, is strictly subject to fate and wholly immanent in the world and in no sense separate from it.[194] God not being detachable from the totality of reality, divine providence in Stoic parlance is just a way of designating the course of nature itself.[195] Gundling, Brucker, and Diderot all recognized the Stoic God as the dynamic force immanent in matter and therefore nature and hence a concept closely proximate to that of Spinoza.[196]

In Stoicism, there can be no disembodied spirits or supernatural forces any more than in Spinoza—indeed a striking parallel.[197] Both Stoics and Spinoza saw men as determined in their thoughts, desires, and conduct, motivated by *conatus*, or their inevitable and natural striving to conserve themselves. This nurtures a pattern of appetite and aversion which shapes Man's will and all his thoughts and desires.[198] Another affinity is the systematic monism of the Stoic vision, in marked contrast to Aristotelianism and Platonism. Reality constitutes a single coherent whole in Stoicism, no less than Spinozism, and one governed by the same set of rationally ordered rules from which nothing is exempt, or as Diderot expresses it in his article on Stoicism in the *Encyclopédie*, 'ce tout est un'.[199] In both, this identification of God with a rationally structured Nature unencumbered by any purely spiritual dimension is characterized by conceptually distinct, but actually combined, active and inert aspects of nature—Spinoza's *Natura naturans* and *Natura naturata* echoing the Stoic 'principe actif', or God, as Barbeyrac expresses it, as distinct from inert Stoic matter, 'le principe passif'.[200] All this and partiality for a rhetoric of 'providence' seemingly make good the claims of a close parallelism.[201]

Both philosophies scorn 'superstition' and credulity, though the Stoics defined 'superstition' differently from Spinoza or Bayle, and Doria was mistaken in supposing Stoics rejected divination, astrology, and the ancient oracles.[202] At the heart of both systems lies the apparent paradox of strict determinism applying to everything, including human actions, balanced by a powerful ethical impulse rooted in

193 Brucker, *Historia critica philosophiae* (1742), i. 964; Algra, 'Stoic Theology', 157–9, 177–8.

194 Burmannus, *Exercitationum academicarum pars prior*, i. 29, 31–2.

195 Ibid.; Doria, *Filosofia*, i. part 2, pp. 306–7, ii. 48; De Jong, *Spinoza en de Stoa*, 6–7; Furley, 'Cosmology', 449.

196 Diderot, *Œuvres complètes*, xiv. 835; Gundling, *Gundlingiana*, v. 189; Brucker, *Historia critica philosophiae* (1742), i. 926–7, 938; Algra, 'Stoic Theology', 167–8.

197 Rutherford, *Meditations of Marcus Aurelius*, 188–92.

198 James, *Passion and Action*, 151, 270–2; Bove, *Stratégie du conatus*, 14–15; Long, 'Stoicism', in Inwood (ed.), *The Cambridge Companion to the Stoics*, 374–6.

199 Von Arnim, *Stoicorum veterum fragmenta*, i. 27; Diderot, *Œuvres complètes*, xiv. 836–7; Schober, 'Diderot als Philosoph', 39–40.

200 Barbeyrac, 'Preface', p. lxvii.

201 Ruyter, *Funus philosophico theologicum*, 113–14; Todd, 'Monism and Immanence', 139–41; Forschner, *Die stoische Ethik*, 26–7; Long, 'Stoicism', in Inwood (ed.) *The Cambridge Companion to the Stoics*, 370–4.

202 Bayle, *Continuation*, ii. 726–7; Doria, *Filosofia*, i, part 2, p. 308; Algra, 'Stoic Theology', 173; Frede, 'Stoic Determinism', 184.

human liberty.[203] Bayle remarks of Stoicism in his *Dictionnaire* that no thinkers stressed more 'la fatale nécessité des choses', nor spoke more splendidly, at the same time, of man's liberty, than the Stoics.[204] Exactly this same apparent paradox also permeates Spinozism.

In his late work, though Bayle ceased identifying Stoicism as the prime ancient parallel to Spinozism, citing Stratonism instead, he also highlighted what he now saw as serious inconsistencies in Stoicism, comparing these to contradictions he found in Jaquelot's arguments and others of the *rationaux*. Bayle now held not that the doctrine of the necessity of all things conflicts with human liberty, for in Strato, as in Hobbes, Spinoza, and Collins (and his own late thought), it does not, but rather that it is the Stoic (and Christian) idea of divine providence which cannot be reconciled with our freedom.[205] In the *Continuation* (1705), Bayle states that the Stoics, unlike Strato, acknowledge matter to be 'un principe passif distingué de Dieu', so that they actually believe not only that God 'étoit l'âme ou l'entendement de la matière' but that he does, after all, in some sense govern the cosmos.[206]

All the affinities between Spinoza and the Stoics in the end, Bayle came to see, are more apparent than real. For the Stoic cosmos is ruled, as well as permeated, by the living force of a divine intelligence which not only plans but actively directs all that happens down to the smallest detail.[207] 'The cosmos is a living being, rational, ensouled, thinking', proclaimed Chrysippus, a doctrine afterwards endorsed by Posidonius in the early first century.[208] For all their limitations in other respects, Vossius and Stanley clearly grasped this vital feature, seeing that for the Stoics the world is animal, intelligent, and sensitive.[209] This was also Boyle's view, while Cudworth, in his *True Intellectual System*, if perhaps too emphatic, was nevertheless close to the mark in holding that Zeno and Chrysippus conceived their God as 'an Intellectual Nature' and the 'supreme architect and master-builder of the world'.[210]

The Stoic universe, says Cudworth, was 'neither a meer heap and *congeries* of dead and stupid matter, fortuitously compacted together; nor yet a huge plant or vegetable, that is, endued with a spermatick principle only; but an animal enformed and enlivened by an intellectual soul'. Although the Stoics, being 'corporealists', sometimes called the whole world itself God 'yet was the God of the Stoicks properly, not the very matter itself, but that great soul, mind and understanding, or in Seneca's language, that *ratio incorporalis*, that rules the matter of the whole

[203] Long, 'Freedom and Determinism', 173–4; Garrett, 'Spinoza's Ethical Theory', 305; Nadler, *Spinoza's Heresy*, 135; Frede, 'Stoic Determinism', 192–205.

[204] Bayle, *Dictionnaire*, i. 925; Bonacina, *Filosofia ellenistica*, 29.

[205] Bayle, *Réponse*, iii. 802, 806.

[206] [Bayle], *Continuation* (1721), iv. 220–1, 228; Gundling, *Vollständige Historie*, i. 887–8; Paganini, 'Tra Epicuro e Stratone', 103 n.; Diderot, *Œuvres complètes*, xiv. 835–6.

[207] Bayle, *Continuation*, ii. 537, 710–11; Diderot, *Œuvres complètes*, xiv. 835; Forschner, *Die stoische Ethik*, 106; Long, *Stoic Studies*, 203–4; Long and Sedley, *Hellenistic Philosophers*, i. 319, 323–32.

[208] Von Arnim, *Stoicorum veterum fragmenta*, ii. 191–4; Furley, 'Cosmology', 449–50.

[209] Vossius, *De philosophorum sectis*, 310; Vossius, *De theologio gentili*, ii. 162; Stanley, *History of Philosophy*, ii. 478–9 ; Brucker, *Historia critica philosophiae* (1742), i. 940–2.

[210] Boyle, *A Free Enquiry*, 48, 51, 158; Cudworth, *True Intellectual System*, i. 153.

world. Which Stoical God was also called, as well "good as mind", that which is a most moral, benign and beneficent being.'[211] Meticulously distinguishing the strands of ancient thought, Cudworth subtly differentiates between authentic Stoics 'such as suppose a Deity, that acting wisely, but necessarily, did contrive the general frame of things in the world' such as was taught by Zeno and Chrysippus, 'whom the Jewish Essenes seemed to follow', and a few later Stoics who should be classed as 'atheists'.[212]

Hence, for Cudworth, as later Mosheim, most, and especially the earlier, Stoics were not 'atheists'.[213] They seemed to confound God with Nature, grants Cudworth, calling God the τὸν σπερματικὸν λόγον τοῦ κόσμου [the spermatic reason of the world],[214] but held nevertheless that 'Zeno and others of the chief Stoical doctors, did also many times assert, that there was a rational and intellectual nature (and therefore not a plastic principle only) in the matter of the universe; as likewise that the whole World was an animal, and not a mere plant: therefore we incline rather to excuse the generality of the first and most ancient Stoicks from the imputation of atheism'.[215] The Stoic universe-God, moreover, is inherently teleological in character and, to a greater degree than Spinoza's, accommodates the notion of Creation in time by an intelligent Creator.[216] 'The Stoics', affirms Cudworth, envisage a general connection 'of causes necessitating all events which chaine of causes they suppose was framed by one principle which, having sett thinges in such a posture at first' determined all that followed.[217] Everything thus has its appointed place and function. If the fruit of trees provides food for men and animals and contains seeds which eventually produce more fruit, proving the universe to be a planned hierarchy of life forms and levels of activity, culminating in Man and (perhaps) the gods, this idea more resembles the 'argument from design' than the blind causation driving Spinoza's, Bayle's, and Diderot's universe. Epictetus (*c.*AD 55–135) of Hieropolis in Asia Minor, foremost of the late Stoics, a former slave who learnt his Stoicism in Rome, asks who fitted the sword to the scabbard, and scabbard to the sword, meaning that if male and female have reciprocal sex organs and yearn for intercourse, surely this is by design? How can anyone, he says, answer 'no one' to the question who created the universe? It is from artefacts that we see that 'the work is always that of some artisan and has not been randomly created'.[218]

All this shows that Zeno's God, observes Brucker, is immanent in the world in a very different sense from Spinoza's.[219] If, for Stoics, the idea of divine creation of

[211] Cudworth, *True Intellectual System*, i. 423; Algra, 'Stoic Theology', 170–3.

[212] Cudworth, *True Intellectual System*, i. 4.

[213] Mosheim, 'Notes', i. 505–9.

[214] Diogenes Laertius, *Lives of Eminent Philosophers*, ii. 240–1; Kristeller, *Greek Philosophers*, 29.

[215] Cudworth, *True Intellectual System*, i. 133.

[216] Ibid. 448–9; Todd, 'Monism and Immanence', 144.

[217] BL, MS Add. 4981, Cudworth Papers, fo. 17.

[218] Arrian, *Epictetus' Discourses*, i. 40; Long, *Epictetus*, 143–8, 155.

[219] Brucker, *Otium vindelicum*, 143–5, 149; Brucker, *Historia critica philosophiae* (1742), i. 937–8; Wolfson, *Philosophy of Spinoza*, i. 323; Bove, *Stratégie du conatus*, 150–1.

the universe is just a metaphor, the idea of God as ἀρχή of all things, the guiding principle pervading the cosmos, is not. As Vossius asserts, to them 'God is totally infused in the world, the mind of the world itself; the world is God's body.'[220] Just as reason, in Man, occupies the highest place, so the highest place in the world (το ἡγεμονικόν) is occupied by the divine mind, or spirit.[221] Here, Stoicism is more precisely 'pantheistic' than Spinozism. 'The Stoics looked at God partly as the divine mind, separate from his work, that is the world,' noted Vossius, 'and partly as that spirit, mixed in with the world which animates and governs it.'[222] When, on the other hand, Spinoza says all things are in God, he means not that there is a divine spirit permeating the whole but that the parts cohere into the whole and the whole governs the parts. The Stoic world-soul is replaced by a blind, unknowing, mechanistic process.

Integral to the Stoic notion of immanence is the idea that the active, becoming principle in matter is—if not actually, then notionally and metaphysically—exterior to it. Hence, Buddeus observed that Aristotle, like the Stoics and the others who 'attach God to matter, made Him dependent on matter'.[223] Whereas, for Spinoza and the Spinozists, including Diderot, there is—and can be—no such exteriority of the active principle, or notion of penetration, or impregnation, by any spiritual force. Rather the living force of things, and sensibility from which thought arises, is strictly interior to matter and unknowing. Hence, in Spinoza and Diderot, 'motion', and the capacity to evolve, remain inherent in, and part of, the concept of matter itself.[224] For both, there is between 'sensibilité inerte' and 'sensibilité active' no essential difference. Recognizably living matter evolves imperceptibly from what is inert.

Identification of God with Nature in Spinozism is more total than in Stoicism and the monism more consistent.[225] A clear divergence between Stoic divine providence and Spinoza's determinism (and Bayle's Stratonism), and one which, according to Bayle in the *Continuation*, entails an insoluble contradiction, is that where evil remains strictly neutral, in Strato and Spinoza, an unavoidable necessity for which no one is morally responsible, the difference between good and bad, virtue and vice, being like that between pleasure and pain,[226] it is quite otherwise in Stoicism. For the Stoics, argues Bayle, must claim the evils afflicting men are essential to the health of the universe, 'et à la félicité de Dieu'.[227] Upholding divine providence, like Zeno, Chrysippus, and Epictetus, it is unavoidable, however difficult, to claim God intends only the good and frowns on evil and, therefore, that

220 Bove, *Stratégie du conatus*, 310; see also Doria, *Manoscritti napoletani*, ii. 24–7.

221 Vossius, *De philosophorum sectis*, 310; Vossius, *De theologia gentili*, ii. 162–4; Ruyter, *Funus theologico philosophicum*, 114; Doria, *Filosofia*, i. 35, 37; *Algemeen Historisch, Geographisch*, viii. 489.

222 Vossius, *De philosophorum sectis*, 309–10.

223 Buddeus, *Traité de l'athéisme*, 72–4.

224 Schober, 'Diderot als Philosoph', 40.

225 Algra, 'Stoic Theology', 167–8; Long, 'Stoicism', in Inwood (ed.), *The Cambridge Companion to the Stoics*, 371.

226 Bayle, *Continuation*, ii. 757–8.

227 Bayle, *Réponse*, iii. 971.

what seems evil to us cannot be evil to him. Chrysippus' efforts on this question Bayle dismisses as absurdly contradictory and those of the philosopher-emperor Marcus Aurelius (ruled AD 161–80) even more so.[228]

Another point of divergence is that, for the Stoics, divination, astrology, and even prayer, as well as the cult practices accompanying these, are appropriate in a way inconceivable to the Radical Enlightenment.[229] If Epictetus pushed this 'religious' impulse further than his predecessors, he was by no means venturing beyond the bounds of the tradition reaching back to Zeno and Chrysippus.[230] For divination was sanctioned by the entire Greek Stoic tradition except for Posidonius' teacher Panaetius of Rhodes (*c.*185–109 BC), scholarch of the Stoic school of Athens from 129 BC who reportedly expressed strong objections to this reasoning.[231] Exteriority of spirit to matter, and the resulting teleological dimension of Stoicism, always had, then, far-reaching moral, social, and political implications. What has aptly been termed the 'transcendent naturalism' of the Stoics is anchored in their conception of human life as part of a rational whole which meant that for them, no less than for Aristotle, there is a τέλος, or goal of life which frames their moral philosophy, except that in Aristotle the 'end' of Man is a more localized phenomenon less tied to the world order than in Stoicism.[232] Zeno, records Diogenes Laertius, was the 'first to say the goal is to live in agreement with nature, which is to live according to virtue' [τέλος εἶπε τὸ ὁμολογουμένως τῇ φύσει ζῆν, ὅπερ ἐστὶ κατ' ἀρετὴν ζῆν].[233] For nature drives us to virtue.

Since our natures inhere in the Nature of the universe, 'to live consistently with Nature', ὁμολογουμένως τῇ φύσει ζῆν, means living according to one's own nature *and* that of the universe, doing nothing forbidden by the divine principle of the whole 'which is right reason penetrating all things'. And to live thus, 'according to the harmony of the divinity in each of us with the will of the administrator of the universe', is the life of virtue ensuring a smooth and happy flow of life.[234] Hence, in Stoicism divine providence both wills and expects a particular ethical response from Man and this is why, in Stoicism, virtue is unitary and indivisible—something one either has or lacks.[235] This claim that Man's soul is part of God struck Bayle as a thoroughly 'mauvais dogme'.[236]

228 Ibid. iii. 972; Bayle, *Continuation*, i. 285–7, ii. 710–11; Long, 'Stoicism', in Inwood (ed.), *The Cambridge Companion to the Stoics*, 370–1.

229 Algra, 'Stoic Theology', 160; Frede, 'Stoic Determinism', 184; Long, 'Stoicism', in Mille and Inwood (eds.), *Hellenistic and Early Modern Philosophy*, 14.

230 Long, *Epictetus*, 143–5.

231 Bayle, *Continuation*, ii. 726–7; Sedley, 'The School', 24.

232 Frede, 'Stoic Determinism', 184, 201; Inwood, 'Stoic Ethics', 684.

233 Von Arnim, *Stoicorum veterum fragmenta*, i, fr. 179; Diogenes Laertius, *Lives of Eminent Philosophers*, ii. 194–5.

234 Diogenes Laertius, *Lives of Eminent Philosopher*, ii. 196–7; Brucker, *Historia critica philosophiae* (1742), i. 954: 'finis vero hominis est naturae convenienter vivere'; Inwood, 'Stoic Ethics', 685; Long, *Stoic Studies*, 202–3.

235 MacIntyre, *After Virtue*, 168–9.

236 Bayle, *Continuation*, ii. 749.

Spinoza, on the other hand, as Nietzsche was later delighted to discover,[237] spurns all teleology, Stoic, Aristotelian, or any other, in depicting nature.[238] This results in an unbridgeable difference between the two ethical structures, the actively providential structure of the Stoic cosmos consciously framing the principles of human nature and virtue in ways inconceivable in Spinoza.[239] Admittedly, Spinoza grants that all creatures are motivated by their *conatus*, or internalized drive for self-preservation and advantage. But he does not maintain, like the Stoics, that this is ordained by an all-seeing, rational providence which ensures that creatures should so function and evolve, thereby imparting an absolute quality to the concepts of 'good and 'bad'.[240] Moreover, where Stoic *conatus*, stressing preservation and realization of the self, was formulated partly against Epicureanism with its claim that pleasure is the universal basis of human motivation, Spinoza merges the previously opposed Stoic and Epicurean principles, subsuming pleasure within his conception of Man's instinctive pursuit of happiness, and avoidance of unhappiness, the driving mechanism of Man's *conatus*.[241]

Another point of divergence is that Spinoza uses the notional equivalence of each person's individual will, like Bayle later, to buttress equality, and human universality, which then, in turn, become principal pillars of their common moral theory, and idea of common good, as well as of their divergent political doctrines. Spinoza and Bayle, in other words, held that 'tous les hommes veulent être heureux' and that while this entails perennial conflict of wills and interests it is also what makes societies fearful of anarchy and willing to curb individual desires in the interest of the collective whole, inducing men to constitute moral and political systems.[242] The consequence drawn by both philosophers is that a realistic morality must be purely natural, eschewing all teleology as well as the supernatural, entrenched in the principles of individual freedom and the fundamental equality of all men.

Humans, according to the Stoics, as the highest and noblest part of Nature, alone possess the privilege of (potentially) understanding the rationality of Nature and adhering to it, thereby contributing through cultivation of virtue both to its fulfilment and to the perfecting of their own natures. Virtue is thus explained in terms of the rationale of the cosmos as a whole.[243] Because 'virtue' and a correct mental attitude meant, for them, revering this presiding higher and wider rationality, the moral qualities they esteemed most, unsurprisingly, were the lofty and remote

[237] A discovery which greatly excited him in 1881; see Curley, *Behind the Geometric Method*, 128; Moreau, 'Spinoza's Reception', 425; Garrett, 'Spinoza's Ethical Theory', 308, 314.

[238] *Collected Works of Spinoza*, i. 439–43; James, 'Spinoza the Stoic', 306; Long, 'Stoicism', in Inwood (ed.), *The Cambridge Companion to the Stoics*, 377–8.

[239] *Collected Works of Spinoza*, i. 439–43; Long, *Stoic Studies*, 141–3; Mori, *Bayle philosophe*, 195.

[240] Brucker, *Historia critica philosophiae* (1742), i. 954–7; Long, 'Stoicism', in Inwood (ed.), *The Cambridge Companion to the Stoics*, 378.

[241] Diogenes Laertius, *Lives of Eminent Philosophers*, ii. 192–5; Bayle, *Continuation*, i. 20, ii. 590–2; Curley, *Behind the Geometrical Method*, 114–15; Bove, *Stratégie du conatus*, 34–5.

[242] Bove, *Stratégie du conatus*, 16–17, 316; Bayle, *Continuation*, ii. 590–2; Israël, *Spinoza: le temps*, 269–70.

[243] Inwood, 'Stoic Ethics', 682–3.

ones—constancy, imperturbability, and perseverance, attributes recognized as classic Stoic virtues ever since. Stoicism hence comes closer than Aristotle to espousing Socrates' maxim that virtue arises from wisdom.[244] Since Stoic virtue is the practice of what perfects human nature by leading us towards a universal code—conduct consonant with the nature of the cosmos—morality, it follows, can be instilled and improved through education.

There is an urgent need, held the Stoics, to inculcate morality through education since men are readily corrupted by wrong ideas and attitudes. Their moral training aims to anchor a complex of logically entwined doctrines and moral precepts in the mind, ideas which both elucidate, and further enhance, the rationality of the cosmos. Since the effects of education can at any moment be spoilt by an eruption of emotion, the most vital technique to be learned is how to free oneself from the irrational 'passions'.[245] Typically, the passions are seen by the Stoics not just as a surfeit of emotion producing wrong decisions but as something wholly at odds with, and remote from, rational thought—the mental equivalent of bodily illness. Not only the obviously harmful passions of greed, fear, melancholy, and envy but all emotion, they contended, is best eradicated. To be gripped by 'passion' was, for Chrysippus, to suffer a disease of the soul. The physician of the soul is the hardened Stoic philosopher who helps others cultivate a correct mental attitude, fortifying souls against emotion, and, when providing therapy, uses persuasive techniques to undermine the misconceptions that feed emotional frenzy.[246]

It was not easy to reconcile Man's moral autonomy, free will, and capacity to enhance his virtue with an otherwise systematic, thoroughgoing determinism which explains everything. Critics ancient and modern denied it could be done at all.[247] If everything, including human actions, is predetermined in a strict sequence of cause and effect, how can a man be said to exercise autonomy in choosing one course of action rather than another, and be praised or blamed for doing so? Man's moral autonomy in Stoicism arises, though, precisely from man's power to train himself and our rational will being independent of emotions. What happens may be unalterable but our attitude towards what happens, our feeling of freedom, or lack of freedom, in adjusting to the reality of things, is, they held, determined by our will influenced by the rewards and punishments society imposes.[248]

Spinoza, then, did not exaggerate the differences between his philosophy and Stoicism in the preface to the fifth part of the *Ethics* where he criticizes the Stoics for holding that the emotions 'depend entirely on our will, and that we can have absolute rule over them', remarking that 'experience protests against this, and forced them, in spite of their principles, to confess that much practice and a [different]

[244] Inwood, 'Stoic Naturalism', 346; Sandbach, *The Stoics*, 41; Sedley, 'The School', 11, 21.

[245] Von Arnim, *Stoicorum veterum fragmenta*, iii. 108–10.

[246] Doria, *Filosofia*, i. 36; Donini, 'Stoic Ethics', 712–14; Graver, *Cicero*, 160–3.

[247] Bayle, *Continuation*, ii. 744; Long, 'Freedom and Determinism', 178–83.

[248] Long and Sedley, *Hellenistic Philosophers*, i. 385–94; Frede, 'Stoic Determinism', 186, 192, 195–6, 201.

application are needed to restrain and moderate them'.[249] There is indeed a wide gap between Stoicism and radical thought as regards the passions, and how reason curbs emotion which was made a point of also by Du Marsais, in his *Le Philosophe* of around 1720, where he wanted the ideal man still to be a man; the Stoic ideal, he says, is impossible, just a phantom. Where the Stoics seek to eliminate the passions, which is impossible and senseless, Du Marsais wants to put the passions to use and employ them constructively.[250] Where true *philosophes* glorify Man, Stoics are ashamed of humanity.

Reason alone cannot curb emotion, and the only way to master a passion in Spinoza and Du Marsais is by summoning up another, stronger impulse.[251] Mostly, men are led more by appetite than reason, and this is why politics and the state are needed to reinforce reason and supply the restraints society needs, but reason can ally with, deflect, and modify passions already present, demonstrating one's true self-interest; and insofar as damaging impulses are checked, Man becomes more rational. The goal of the rational man, in Spinoza, is not, as with the Stoics, to live without emotion but rather to build on unavoidable impulses: 'in so far as the mind understands all things as necessary, to that extent it acquires greater power over the emotions, or suffers less from them.'[252] A striking difference between Spinoza (and Descartes) and Stoicism is that where, for the latter, all the passions are collectively negative and detrimental, in Spinoza—as later in Bayle, Mandeville, Diderot, and Mably—not only are the passions always fundamental in everyone's life but all emotion without exception is in itself morally neutral, possessing a positive as well as negative aspect.[253] This follows from Spinoza's doctrine that 'desire is appetite accompanied by consciousness of itself, so that appetite is the very essence of man in so far as his essence is determined to such actions as contribute to his preservation'.[254]

Just as the immanence of the Stoic God in nature differs from Spinoza's single substance, so the relation of body and soul (*pneuma*) in Stoicism, despite Stoic monism, and acceptance of the mortality of the soul, diverges widely from Spinoza's. Stoic ideas of the soul's corporeality and mortality, and their marked divergence from Plato here, previously heavily understated by generations of Christian Stoic commentary, were shown to be crucial to Greek Stoicism by Jakob Thomasius.[255] But where, for the Stoics, our minds are an aspect of the cosmic intellect, an emanation or fragment of God,[256] and its reason seeks to harmonize

249 *Collected Works of Spinoza*, i. 595; Spinoza, *Ethics*, ed. Parkinson, 287; Ramond, 'Ne pas rire', 121; Nadler, *Spinoza's Heresy*, 207.

250 [Du Marsais], *Le Philosophe*, 200.

251 Spinoza, *Ethics*, part iv, prop. vii; McShea, *Political Philosophy*, 47; Hirschman, *Passions and the Interests*, 21–3; Den Uyl, 'Passion, State and Progress', 375–6.

252 Spinoza, *Ethics*, part iv, prop. vi; Klever, *Spinoza classicus*, 23.

253 Hampshire, *Spinoza*, 167–8; Curley, *Behind the Geometrical Method*, 94.

254 Spinoza, *Ethics*, part iii, prop. ix scholium and iii, 'definitions of the Emotions'.

255 Thomasius, *Dissertationes*, 177, 227–8; [Brucker], *Historia philosophica*, 97–100.

256 Sluiter, *Idea theologicae Stoicae*, 88; d'Argens, *Mémoires secrets*, ii. 291; Diderot, *Œuvres complètes*, xiv. 838, 842; De Jong, *Spinoza en de Stoa*, 8; Long, 'Freedom and Determinism', 192–4; Long and Sedley, *Hellenistic Philosophers*, i. 318–19.

with that wider rationality so that in learning to live according to nature one proportionately moves towards God, for Spinoza mind is simply identical to body under another aspect, that is the body's sensibility.

Neither does the mind control the body, held Spinoza, who also criticizes the Stoic doctrine of the soul in his early treatise *De intellectus emendatione* of around 1660–1,[257] nor the body the mind; rather all one's thoughts are absolutely coincident with fluctuations in the body.[258] Men are governed, like everything else, by their *conatus*, the term Spinoza uses to designate 'that striving by which each thing seeks to persevere in its own being' or the 'actual essence of the thing'.[259] Where Stoic virtue, while contributing to happiness, has a transcendent moral quality, beauty, and fineness apart from any utility or instrumental value, there are no naturally uplifting moral qualities in Spinoza, and Spinoza's happiness (*laetitia*) is merely awareness of one's success in conserving one's own being, and of passing to a higher state of completeness, or perfection, while sadness, conversely, is a falling away from one's perfection. Whereas in Stoicism, virtue is diminished in some sense by being assessed by its practical results for oneself, or others, rather than as a pattern of behaviour, orientated to what is intrinsically rational and fine in itself, reinforced by practice, the whole flowing from a disposition directed towards nature's (divine) rationality, Spinoza's 'virtue' lacks this transcendent quality.[260]

Since desire, or *conatus*, is the fundamental drive, in Spinoza, it is the motive force behind rationality also. Rationality is inherent in man; but he conceives of it as also a passion at odds with other passions. Unlike the Stoics, Spinoza (like Bayle) sees both rationality and virtue as anchored in self-interest and the individual's basic drives.[261] Accordingly, Spinoza, in one of his most characteristic moves, introduces a radically naturalistic definition of virtue: the 'more each person searches for what is useful to him, that is to preserve his being, and is able to do this, the more he is endowed with virtue'.[262] This is a tenet, like Mandeville's similar concept later, utterly remote from the spirit of Greek moral philosophy generally, and not just Stoic and Christian ethics. In Spinoza, there is no innate 'good' or 'bad', or any 'Natural Law' distinct from the mechanics of the *conatus*, and while rationality shows the wise what is just, or conducive to the common good, there can be no generally agreed rules for a collectively adopted code of 'good' and 'bad' except within a particular society, under the laws of a particular state. A vital role is assigned, therefore, to the shaping functions of society, a role which had, and required, no counterpart in Stoicism while, conversely, Stoicism postulates a conception of 'natural law' without parallel in Spinozism.[263] For the Stoics, since passions are disturbances of the soul best eliminated, what is

257 De Dijn, *Spinoza: The Way to Wisdom*, 112–13.
258 Spinoza, *Ethics*, part iii, prop. ii; Ramond, 'Ne pas rire', 121.
259 Spinoza, *Ethics*, part iii, prop. vii.
260 Forschner, *Die stoische Ethik*, 160–5; Inwood, *Ethics*, 118–20; Irwin, 'Stoic Naturalism', 347–8.
261 McShea, *Political Philosophy*, 50; Mori, *Bayle philosophe*, 195.
262 Spinoza, *Ethics*, part iv, prop. xx; Hampshire, *Spinoza*, 165–6; Nadler, *Spinoza*, 240.
263 Schmauss, *Neues Systema*, 28–30; Watson, 'Natural Law', 222–8; Irwin, 'Stoic Naturalism', 347–8.

required to promote virtue and happiness is less politics and law than individual education, especially in logic, physics, and ethics.[264]

Despite the vague association of Stoicism with opposition to imperial tyranny at Rome, Stoic thinkers mostly saw no need to enter politics, to alter legislation, or change the state, or social conditions, to improve men's conduct. Rather Stoics conceived of men as dwelling in a universal community in which all are spiritually our fellow-citizens.[265] With its reverence for the rationality of the whole, Stoicism, moreover, was inclined to a fatalistic outlook, whereas Spinoza's conceived of an unknowing nature whose often threatening and damaging effects men can best counter by mobilizing an organized, collective response. For Stoics, as Hume observes, even the greatest disasters, when properly understood, are 'in reality, goods to the universe'.[266] Marcus Aurelius' admonition τὸ γὰρ δυσχεραίνειν τινὶ τῶν γινομένων ἀπόστασίς ἐστι τῆς φύσεως, ἧς ἐν μέρει αἱ ἑκάστου τῶν λοιπῶν φύσεις περιέχονται [For to complain against anything that happens is a rebellion against Nature, in each part of which are bound up the natures of all the rest][267] is thus thoroughly Stoic but breathes nothing of Spinoza's spirit.

264 Sandbach, *The Stoics*, 147.
265 Watson, 'Natural Law', 220.
266 Algra, 'Stoic Theology', 171–2.
267 Marcus Aurelius, *Meditations*, 38–9.

18

The Rise of 'History of Philosophy'

1. PRE-ENLIGHTENMENT 'HISTORY OF PHILOSOPHY'

In recent years, several historians have drawn attention to a major but hitherto (aside from R. G. Collingwood) remarkably little-mentioned new development in the history of European thought—the rise of 'history of philosophy', or *historia philosophica*, as a separate discipline.[1] It was, as we shall see, a crucially important new intellectual tool. Mostly, the scholars who pioneered this novel study were contemptuous of, and reacting against, the pervasive syncretism and notions of a general harmony of currents, or convergence of *prisca sapientia* and *prisca theologia*, which dominated Renaissance conceptions of the previous history of human thought. Armed with the apparatus of the new *critique*, scholars such as Jakob Thomasius, Le Clerc, Buddeus, Heumann, and Gundling, a critic, avowedly tied neither by *praeiudicium antiquitatis* nor by *autoritatis*,[2] were convinced the humanists had entirely failed to uncover the key features of the story or even correctly grasp its most basic rudiments, but rather that Italian authors like Ficino, Pico, and Agostino Steuco, with their muddled Platonism and Neoplatonism, had so confused everything as to leave men immersed rather in error than in light.[3]

No doubt Enlightenment historians of philosophy were overly scornful of the humanists, insufficiently appreciating such bold critical spirits of their time as Scaliger and Casaubon; even so, their complaints about the humanists, including Lipsius, were far from groundless. For Renaissance culture, deeply inhibited, from Petrarch onwards, by the ceaseless tension between Christian revelation and ancient pagan thought, was never at ease with pagan Greek themes. Forging intellectually precarious compromises, the Renaissance Italian and northern could never really free itself from seeing ancient philosophy as it thought it ought to be, selecting and adjusting ancient sources to fit Christian and conventional criteria, rather than seeing them for what they were.[4] While the hierarchical relationship between theology and philosophy instituted by medieval scholastics had earlier afforded

[1] Collingwood, *Idea of History*, 61–3; Albrecht, *Eklektik*, 493–6, 507–8, 539–58; Schneider, 'Eclecticism', 83–102; Hochstrasser, *Natural Law Theories*, 11; Kelley, *Descent of Ideas*, 141–68; Kelley, *Fortunes*, 75.

[2] Heumann, *Acta philosophorum*, 6 (1716), 1033.

[3] Gundling, *Vollständige Historie*, i. 933–41; Blackwell, 'Logic of History', 106–9; Häfner, 'Jacob Thomasius', 141, 149, 154–5.

[4] Jehasse, *Renaissance*, pp. xiv, xvii, 114, 668–70.

some autonomy, permitting investigation of a range of questions within stipulated limits, on purely philosophical grounds, Renaissance philosophy, especially the *philosophia perennis* [perennial philosophy] tradition reaffirmed by Ficino, Pico, and Agostino Steuco, with its stress on the idea of Adamite wisdom and on Moses as the supreme teacher, tended to erase rather than reinforce precisely this hesitant demarcation between philosophy and the sacred.[5]

By 1700, humanist attitudes were being increasingly ravaged by the new *critique*. The fashionable but highly contrived literary contest of the *anciens et modernes*, for example, partly a vestige of humanist concerns, eventually lost much of its prestige as a theme and ability to interest the public because of its heavy emphasis on style and presentation rather than content. By the 1730s, the whole business had come to seem ridiculously irrelevant and superficial. Participants championing antiquity, remarked Fréret scornfully, heaped praise on the ancients; but the high accomplishments they celebrated were exclusively to do with the purely decorative skills of rhetoric, poetry, and eloquence, that is to his mind were unimportant. Of concepts and understanding they said nothing.[6] Equally, the series of 'pre-critical' surveys of the history of thought written in Europe between the 1650s and 1680s vividly illustrate both the humanists' pious traditionalism, and placid syncretism, in intellectual matters and the total bankruptcy of humanist intellectual attitudes and tastes in the face of late seventeenth-century *critique*.

The authors of these often bizarre late Renaissance overviews freely admitted having turned to history of philosophy specifically in response to the intellectual crisis brought on by the New Philosophy. Vossius' posthumously published *De philosophia et philosophorum sectis* (1658) originated, he explains, in worries about Cartesianism, as did his urging adoption of an eclecticism combining strands from diverse modern and ancient schools of thought.[7] The Leiden Cartesians Adriaen Heereboord (1614–61) and Johannes de Raey (1622–1707), and the Franeker anti-Cartesian Abraham de Grau (1632–83), similarly wrote in response to Descartes's impact, particularly on university teaching.[8] The first history of philosophy in English, by Thomas Stanley (1625–78), stemmed from his perplexed response to Gassendi.[9] It was surely not 'unseasonable at this time', he explains, 'to examine the tenets of old philosophers, when so great variety of opinions daily spring up; some of which are but raked out of the ruines of antiquity, which ought to be restored to their first owners; others being of late invention will receive addition, when advanced to such height we look down to the bottom from which philosophy took her first rise, and see how great progress she hath made, whose first beginnings are almost inscrutable'.[10]

[5] Schmidt-Biggemann, *Philosophia perennis*, xviii. 32–6, 169–73, 413–14, 428–34.

[6] Fréret, *Œuvres complètes*, xvi. 201–2.

[7] Brucker, *Historia critica philosophiae* (1742), i. 35; Rademaker, *Life and Works of Gerardus Joannes Vossîus*, 329–30; Schneider, 'Eclecticism', 85; Kelley, *Descent of Ideas*, 147.

[8] Schneider, 'Eclecticism', 85–6; Kelley, *Descent of Ideas*, 151.

[9] Heumann, *Acta philosophorum*, 6 (1716), 1049, 1054; Brucker, *Historia critica philosophiae* (1767), i. 35–8.

[10] Stanley, *History of Philosophy*, i, preface.

The pioneer of the new 'history of philosophy' was undoubtedly Leibniz's teacher Jakob Thomasius (1622–84) at Leipzig and, aside from Bayle and Le Clerc in Holland, most key practitioners of this new speciality worked in German Lutheran universities.[11] Only decades later did this form of study catch on strongly elsewhere. The particular geography of this decisive shift in perspective, in turn, prompts several questions: first, what exactly caused the change from a 'pre-critical' to a critical conception of 'history of philosophy', as conceived by Thomasius, Bayle, Le Clerc, Buddeus, Gundling, and Heumann? Secondly, why did those who developed the new discipline consider it both critical-historical and 'philosophical' in a way Renaissance history of philosophy had not been, and also a study indispensable to the practice of philosophy itself?

Bizarre perhaps from the perspective of the twentieth-century Anglo-American analytical and pragmatic schools (which reduce most history of philosophy to the history of error), later French Enlightenment practitioners of this new craft also claimed, like Croce in the twentieth century, that only through this kind of study broadly conceived, dubbed by Fontenelle, Boulainvilliers, Fréret, Diderot, and Condorcet 'l'histoire de l'esprit humain', can philosophy meaningfully be practised. Mankind, since primitive times, it seemed to them, had experienced successive phases of developing intellectual awareness interrelated in highly complex ways—social and intellectual. Exponents of the new *historia philosophica* concluded that only this kind of study can foster genuine philosophical understanding of a sort serviceable to mankind. Hence, the radical *philosophes* in France, no less than the conservative Eclectics in Germany and Italy (especially Genovesi), concurred that relevant, practical, and up-to-date philosophy is impossible unless anchored in study of what Boureau-Deslandes designated 'histoire critique de la philosophie'.

The humanists, judged the new historians of thought, had erred disastrously chiefly owing to their inability to detach philosophy from theology, magic, alchemy, and demonology.[12] If Gerardus Vossius' immensely erudite writings were a partial exception, preoccupation with theological 'mysteries' and with the supernatural heavily permeated the other 'pre-critical' histories, leading to their rapidly falling into contempt. The *Historiae philosophicae libri septem* (Leiden, 1655) by Georgius Hornius (1620–70), a scholar from the Palatinate who held a chair at Leiden (1653–70), a pre-Cartesian work and the first of the mid seventeenth-century attempts to survey the history of thought, was disposed of particularly ruthlessly. Armed with Le Clerc's rules of criticism,[13] Heumann, who taught at the Göttingen gymnasium from 1714, and, from 1734, as professor of history at the newly founded university there, the scholar who established the first European erudite journal devoted specifically to history of philosophy, the *Acta philosophorum* (1715–23), deemed Hornius' worthy intentions his only redeeming feature; for,

[11] Albrecht, *Eklektik*, 494–6, 540–51; Mulsow, 'Gundling *versus* Buddeus', 104, 119; Kelley, *Descent of Ideas*, 147–53, 160–8.

[12] Gundling, *Vollständige Historie*, i. 909–20; Le Clerc, *Ars critica*, ii. 449–50.

[13] *Bibliothèque choisie*, 25 (1712), 2nd part, p. 396.

preceding Vossius into print, he was, at any rate, the first since ancient times who 'proposed to bring *historiam philosophicam* into a proper system'.[14] His account, beginning with Adam who, according to him, was endowed by God with the original pure *sapientia naturalis* [natural wisdom], struck Heumann as perfectly preposterous, and completely ruined by fixation with demonology, magic, and theology besides 'many useless digressions', and his abysmal grasp of doctrines. Worst of all, as Brucker and Diderot later also thought, was Hornius' complete lack of historical-critical sense. Typically of mid seventeenth-century scholarship, Hornius, complained Heumann, 'examines almost nothing but simply throws together everything he has learnt or read', uncritical acceptance of everything found in his favourite theological authors joining hands with his deep conviction that the impious, 'atheistic' tendencies of Greek thought were inspired by Satan himself.[15]

Demonic also, to Hornius' mind, was the spirit of faction everywhere prevailing among the Greek philosophy schools, the cause of ever more contests and bickering, and forming of yet more 'sects'. Eager to reinforce the Bible's authority and minimize the role of the Greeks[16]—apart, that is, from Aristotle whom he called *princeps philosophorum* on the grounds that he had synthesized all the elements of philosophy 'into one body and system'[17]—Hornius detected the origin of all philosophy and sound reasoning, as Diderot noted sarcastically, in Adam before the Fall. Adam's legacy was subsequently passed down, albeit only fragmentarily, by Noah and his sons, via the Hebrews, Egyptians, Babylonians, Assyrians, Persians, and Indians, the role of Moses in instructing men in philosophy, as much else, being especially crucial.[18]

Another little respected pre-Cartesian history was the *De scriptoribus historiae philosophicae* (1659), by the Holsteiner Johann Jonsius (1624–59), an author rated by Heumann someone who had no idea at all what 'history of philosophy' is.[19] The Dutchman Abraham de Grau, while again defending Aristotelian scholasticism against the Cartesians, and leaning heavily on Church Fathers like Clement of Alexandria and Eusebius, scored slightly higher owing to his having consulted more Greek sources and said more about the Greek philosophy schools' rival doctrines.[20] But he too, stressing Thales', Pythagoras', and other Greek philosophers' allegedly heavy dependence on the Hebrews and Egyptians, and the presiding role of Moses, was scorned as a typical product of pre-enlightened humanistic erudition.[21]

[14] Heumann, *Acta philosophorum*, 6 (1716), 1046–7; Malusa, 'First General Histories', 256; Kelley, *Descent of Ideas*, 85.

[15] Hornius, *Historiae philosophicae libri*, 47–9; Heumann, *Acta philosophorum*, 6 (1716), 1046–9; Gierl, *Pietismus*, 492; Kelley, *Fortunes*, 75; Malusa, 'First General Histories', 251–3.

[16] Hornius, *Historiae philosophicae libri*, 135.

[17] Ibid. 194.

[18] Ibid. 59–61, 104, 139, 127–30; Diderot, *Œuvres complètes*, xiv. 4–7.

[19] Heumann, *Acta philosophorum*, 3 (1715), 161.

[20] Ibid.; Malusa, 'First General Histories', 276; Kelley, *Descent of Ideas*, 151.

[21] De Grau, *Historia philosophica*, i. 32–3, 40, 120; Brucker, *Historia critica philosophiae* (1742), i. 36.

Marginally better still was Stanley's *A History of Philosophy* (3 vols., 1655–60). Stanley, a royalist poet, translator, and scholar, dispensed with most of the demonology characteristic of the others and explained more of the conceptual differences between the ancient schools. He also tried to move beyond the chaotic account of the Greek systems in Diogenes Laertius, a work 'sans méthode comme sans critique', according to Fréret,[22] deemed by men of the new *critique* the ancient counterpart of humanist muddle, confusion, and lack of proper grasp of the ancient systems,[23] by setting out the doctrines of key thinkers 'into better order'. Stanley's account, reissued in further English editions in 1687 and 1701, in Dutch translation (1702), and in a Latin version published at Leipzig in 1711, continued to be widely consulted well into the eighteenth century, Diderot acquiring his copy in 1748.

Nevertheless, Stanley too relied excessively on Diogenes and, while scoring some points for following Casaubon in denying Plato was inspired by Hermes Trismegistus and for firmly acknowledging the 'forgery of those books which seem by some impostor, to have been compiled out of the works of Plato, and the Divine Scripture',[24] this was more than counterbalanced by his reaffirming that 'Plato received some light from Moses', and agreeing with Philo and several Church Fathers that Plato was basically just 'Moses speaking Greek'.[25] This conclusion he thought, citing Aristobulus, Josephus, Justin Martyr, Clement, Eusebius, St Augustine, and Numenius in support, was grounded 'with much greater authorities' than the stories about Hermes Trismegistus. In other ways too, he seemed largely devoid of critical discernment.[26] Heumann dubbed him the 'English Laertius', meaning he lacked 'judgment both historical and philosophical', and 'yields nothing to Laertius' in credulity.[27]

The Cartesian De Raey, for his part, held that an original *prisca philosophia* descending from Noah had been bequeathed to the Greeks via the Egyptians, Chaldaeans, Persians, and others. This pristine tradition of knowledge, he too thought, had later been hopelessly corrupted, especially due to the jealousies and splits of the Greek philosophy schools.[28] As an orthodox Cartesian, who also retained the scholastic idea that philosophy is a narrow speciality, De Raey had no difficulty in reaffirming theology's supremacy over philosophy and made a point of denying the practical applicability of philosophical reason. Given that in his Leiden lecture room he faced such earnest young students, all passionately debating the Cartesian 'revolution', as Pieter de La Court, Koerbagh, Lodewijk Meyer, Cuffeler, and very likely, around 1656–7, Spinoza himself, it is of particular significance that

[22] Fréret, *Œuvres complètes*, ii. 38.

[23] Le Clerc, *Ars critica*, ii. 449–50.

[24] Stanley, *History of Philosophy*, i, preface; Heumann, *Acta philosophorum*, 3 (1715), 537–8; Kelley, *Descent of Ideas*, 97–8.

[25] Stanley, *History of Philosophy*, i, preface.

[26] Ibid. i. 160; Heumann, *Acta philosophorum*, 3 (1715), 529; Brucker, *Historia critica philosophiae* (1742), i. 36, v. 30; Proust, *Diderot*, 240.

[27] Heumann, *Acta philosophorum*, 3 (1715), 538–9; Gundling, *Vollständige Historie*, i. 919.

[28] See de Mowbray, 'What is Philosophy?'; Schmidt-Biggemann, 'Bruckers philosophie-geschichtliches Konzept', 117.

he adamantly rejected the idea that philosophy can be used to re-evaluate and change the world outside the lecture room, being a purely academic activity wholly segregated from theology and such vocational disciplines as medicine, law, and politics.[29]

2. GERMAN ECLECTICISM AND THE RISE OF A NEW DISCIPLINE

Thanks to Jakob Thomasius 'who in his time scarcely had an equal in history of philosophy', notes Brucker,[30] followed by the contributions of Bayle and Buddeus, the new field of study blossomed as an authentically critical-historical endeavour, developing on a wholly new basis.[31] As a result, theological premisses, *prisca theologia* and supernatural agency, demonology, magic, and slavish deference to authorities finally came to be firmly separated (and in the case of the radicals wholly eradicated) from what was now viewed as the immensely arduous evolution of human reason. Within a short space of years, beginning in the 1660s and 1670s, it became *de rigueur* to debate the history of knowledge and thought in secular, non-supernatural terms.

The main thrust was in Germany. But given the broad European character of the intellectual crisis, the impulse to historicize the welter of new philosophical problems is best viewed as an international rather than purely German phenomenon. Frequent German references to Bayle's and Le Clerc's evaluations of ancient, medieval, and Renaissance philosophers show that their roles, both stimulating and provocative, were pivotal to the rise of 'history of philosophy' in Germany as elsewhere. Walch's *Philosophisches Lexicon* cites Bayle as a principal, and sometimes the sole, modern authority on numerous philosophers, including Thales, Anaxagoras, Xenophanes, Democritus, Zeno of Elea, Diogenes the Cynic, Chrysippus, Epicurus, Zoroaster, and Averroes, as well as Machiavelli, Pomponazzi, Cardano, Grotius, Hobbes, and Spinoza.[32] If Giambattista Capasso's *Historiae philosophiae synopsis* (Naples, 1728) was heavily indebted to Buddeus, and mediocre, Genovesi's grand philosophical historical surveys were major contributions.[33] Dissatisfied with Aristotelianism, Cartesianism, Leibnizianism, and Locke's empiricism alike and convinced, like his German counterparts, that the fragments of truth are widely scattered, Genovesi put his main effort over many years into studying history of philosophy, believing that accurate delineation of past schools of thought would help identify those admissible into a viable Christian philosophy while avoiding

[29] Verbeek, *Descartes and the Dutch*, 72–3; van Bunge, *From Stevin to Spinoza*, 62–3, 93.

[30] Brucker, *Historia critica philosophiae* (1742), i. 35; Tomasoni, 'Critica al Cartesianesimo', 148.

[31] Gundling, *Vollständige Historie*, i. 909–10; Brucker, *Historia critica philosophiae* (1742), i. 35–8; Braun, *Histoire*, 91–100, 104–5; Schmidt-Biggemann, *Theodizee*, 38–41; Bonacina, *Filosofia ellenistica*, 43–4.

[32] Walch, *Philosophisches Lexicon*, iii 'Anhang', 16, 31, 47, 56, 60, 69, 85, 96, 109, 134, 157, 161, 168.

[33] Donini, 'History', 20; Albrecht, *Eklektik*, 541–3.

both the Scylla of the Renaissance humanists' uncritical syncretism, on the one hand, and the Charybdis of impious naturalism, on the other.[34]

Jakob Thomasius and Le Clerc were basically agreed on the great significance of eclecticism as a philosophical method even if Thomasius did not share the latter's enthusiasm for the ancient school of Potamo of Alexandria, and the support for this school voiced by Clement of Alexandria (*c.* AD 150–*c.*215) and Lactantius (*c.* AD 240–320).[35] Clement could not have chosen a better method 'for a Christian philosopher', judged Le Clerc, 'because there is not one philosopher of whom all the dogmata are agreeable to the Gospel; although a system, that will come up very near to that of the Christian doctrine, may be made by collecting out of all the philosophers what they said agreeably to the light of nature, or some ancient traditions current almost through the whole world'.[36] Le Clerc warmly approved Clement's, and Lactantius', proposition that it is God who bestows philosophy on men and their insisting this cannot mean the doctrines of any one school, 'neither that of the Stoicks, nor that of the Platonicks, nor that of the Aristotelians' but rather the eclectic gathering of those 'truths scattered among the sects' which conform to Christianity and reason 'and which may lead to justice and piety'.[37] But the eclecticism which played a formative role in the moderate mainstream Enlightenment in Germany, the eclecticism of Jakob and Christian Thomasius, Buddeus, Mosheim, Heumann, and Brucker, did not see itself as the descendant of the eclecticism of Potamo, Clement, and Lactantius.

Unlike its ancient counterpart, Thomasian eclecticism urged not just open-minded review of all possibilities, and eschewing of dogmatism, but a rigorous critical exercise, employing reason and a 'free and pure capability of judgment', to evaluate all the doctrines of the past.[38] This necessitated a great deal of new research. By 'philosophy', the German Eclectics had in mind not the evolution of the various compartments of existing philosophy such as ethics, logic, epistemology, natural science, or astronomy, but rather the history and interaction of all-embracing, comprehensive systems of thought negotiating the whole of reality. Moses while a great prophet was not, to their way of thinking, a philosopher, and philosophy, as they defined it, far from descending from Noah via the Hebrews, Egyptians, and Babylonians, stemmed from the special genius of the Greeks—just as several ancient authors had claimed.[39]

This applied, they held, even to ethics, which, like the rest of philosophy, had now to be functionally uncoupled from theology. Though conservative minded in his theological views, Heumann, warmly eulogizing Socrates, did not hesitate to assert that ancient Greece was 'die Mutter der Moral-Philosophie'.[40] His student Brucker,

34 Albrecht, *Eklektik*, 561; Israel, *Radical Enlightenment*, 56–8.

35 Israel, *Radical Enlightenment*, i. 11–12; Donini, 'History', 16, 20, 31; Albrecht, *Eklektik*, 79–85.

36 Le Clerc, *Lives*, 12.

37 Ibid.; Albrecht, *Eklektik*, 80–1; Kelley, *Descent of Ideas*, 51.

38 Gierl, *Pietismus*, 494–6; Schneider, 'Eclecticism', 86.

39 Heumann, *Acta philosophorum*, 2 (1715), 286–97 and 6 (1716), 24–32, 1038–9; Kelley, *Descent of Ideas*, 162.

40 Heumann, *Acta philosophorum*, 2 (1715), 286.

equally keen to reconcile history of philosophy with Christian tradition through pure reason, held that the only true eclectic is he who lays aside all prejudgements based on authority and antiquity, embracing only *clara et evidentes principia*, that is whatever is clearly demonstrated wherever he finds it.[41] This applied as much to defining the limits of the field as to exploring its content. These men, then, fully agreed with Bayle and Le Clerc that the true philosopher is someone whose mind is open to all the philosophies of the past, who explores and accurately delineates them, and absorbs their significance, and finally selects as true only what conforms to the most exacting rational criteria.

Henceforth, pursuit of truth depended as much on vast erudition as acuteness of mind. Jakob and Christian Thomasius, Bayle, Le Clerc, Heumann, Buddeus, Gundling, Fréret, Boureau-Deslandes, Genovesi, and Brucker, then, rightly insisted on a wide gulf between their *historia philosophica* and that of humanist scholarship. Thomasius' enterprise was partly prompted by the growing fragmentation of the German academic world, disarray bound to be receptive to so accommodating a structure as the new eclecticism.[42] In the Eclectic methodology he taught his students at Leipzig, Thomasius saw the most promising path to restoring an enduring framework, upholding theology's ultimate primacy intact. He sharply differentiated, however, unlike ancient Eclectics, between syncretism, something vain and empty in his view, and such eclecticism as accurately identifies and sifts earlier ideas, selecting only what can be cogently reassembled without uselessly trying to bring basically incompatible doctrines into harmony. The quest to reconcile what cannot be reconciled, obvious in the efforts of those who 'absurdly' seek to combine Aristotelianism with Platonism, or Aristotelianism with Cartesianism, he dismissed as typifying an obsolete scholarship devoid of true *critique* and grasp of *historia philosophica*.[43]

At the same time, he and his successors saw themselves as participants in a relentless war of philosophies. For the new discipline was not just regarded as a field of study, and intellectual tool, but also a polemical weapon in the ideological wars of their age. Like Heumann later, Thomasius sought to reform philosophy by coherently reintegrating all 'true' fragments from past and present systems, thereby constructing not just a better philosophy but also an engine of war capable of repelling the philosophical challenges attacking the edifice of contemporary religion, authority, and education. Among modern systems, he chiefly rejected Cartesianism and Spinozism, and, among those of the past, the 'uncritical' syncretism of the Italian Renaissance, especially scorning Ficinean Platonism. Ficino's idea that the veritable traditions of pagan and Christian philosophy converge in a single line of *pia philosophia*, indissolubly uniting faith and reason, and the sacred and secular, held Thomasius, indiscriminately 'mixes truth with what is false'.[44] Equally, he despised

[41] Brucker, *Historica critica philosophiae* (1742), iv, part 2, p. 4; Albrecht, *Eklektik*, 548–9; Hochstrasser, *Natural Law Theories*, 171–2; Kelley, *Descent of Ideas*, 156.

[42] Kelley, *Descent of Ideas*, 141–2.

[43] Ibid. 148–9; Albrecht, *Eklektik*, 298–300, 394, 438–9.

[44] Albrecht, *Eklektik*, 297–300; Malusa, 'Renaissance Antecedents', 15–19; Tomasoni, 'Critica al Cartesianesimo', 151; Kelley, *Descent of Ideas*, 148–53; Mulsow, *Moderne*, 259, 291–9.

the kind of modern syncretism which, like Heereboord's, combined scholasticism with strands of the New Philosophy, in his view a senseless concoction of irreconcilable elements.

Thomasius' efforts to retrieve authentic Platonism, Aristotelianism, Stoicism, Epicureanism, and other traditions from the layers of distortion left by the uncritical scholarship of the humanists, and his reasons for doing so, impressed Leibniz, and, through him, to an extent influenced the whole Leibnizian-Wolffian tradition.[45] 'Tu non philosophorum, sed philosophiae historiam dabis' [you render the history not of philosophers, but of philosophy], Leibniz remarked of his old tutor, wholeheartedly agreeing that truth is scattered widely, must be meticulously searched for, scrupulously selected, and authentically blended, to deliver a genuine synthesis of ancient and modern, and East and West.[46] Throughout his career, Leibniz adhered to the idea that true philosophizing must accommodate a critical appraisal of what everyone else, past or present, has thought and thinks and hence be based on dialogue, erudition, and historical awareness besides acuteness of mind.

While all Enlightenment blocs battled to advance toleration, combat superstition, and secure greater freedom of thought from theological and political authority, critical historians of philosophy had special grounds for eyeing the exclusive claims to truth of most modern and ancient systems with suspicion and laid particular stress on the need to be undogmatic and to leave no niche unexplored in the work of scholarly scrutiny. The result was a rapid expansion of research into a great range of ancient, medieval, and oriental texts in an impressive mix of languages.[47]

One of Bayle's chief aims as a historian was to demonstrate the unity of the philosophical undertaking across the centuries, cultures, and religions, seeing this as a method of demonstrating its ultimate independence from theological underpinning and perennial role in the task of enlightening and civilizing men. Though many of his discussions were intended to advance specific critiques of Aristotelianism, Cartesianism, *Malebranchisme*, or Spinozism, a constant theme of these discussions was his concern to show the impossibility of reason aiding faith, or faith reason. Another typical Baylean topos, especially in the *Dictionnaire* and the *Continuation* (1705), as we have seen, was his incorrigible identifying of proto- and quasi-Spinozist tendencies supposedly permeating the thought of the Greek Presocratics, Stoics, Epicureans, and Strato, besides Averroism and other strands of medieval, Islamic, and Renaissance philosophy.[48]

Another outstanding advocate of history of philosophy as a means of resolving current philosophical challenges was Franz Buddeus (1667–1729), from 1705 academic doyen of Jena, champion of a moderate 'enlightened' Lutheranism whose eclectic vision of history was strongly influenced (like Brucker's) by Jakob Thomasius.[49] Buddeus too detested credulity and 'superstition' but, like Heumann,

45 Israel, *Radical Enlightenment*, 555–62.
46 Collingwood, *Idea of History*, 62–3; Albrecht, *Eklektik*, 95; Braun, *Histoire*, 91.
47 Schneider, 'Eclecticism', 90.
48 Canziani, 'Philosophes', 143–64; Braun, *Histoire*, 104–5, 107; Mori, *Bayle philosophe*, 133–88.
49 Tomasoni, 'Critica al Cartesianesimo', 148, 168.

was even more concerned that modern philosophy should be kept free of what he regarded as the contagion of freethinking, Deism, and Spinozism. As with all the moderate mainstream, he saw himself as locked in a two-front contest, on one flank fighting the hard-line traditionalists who censured the Eclectics' reformism and tolerationist leanings, and, on the other, the *esprits forts*. Popular religion, even in Lutheran lands, being still marred in his view by much gross superstition that needed clearing away, Buddeus considered a vigorous programme of rationalization and educational reform to be the indispensable way forward. In his *Theses theologicae de atheismo* (1717), he declared it impossible truly to counter Spinozism and other 'atheism' unless Christianity was first purged of disfiguring 'superstition' lingering from the past; because, until this was done, Spinozists, when disputing Christianity with Christians, could readily link Christianity to naive credulity, thoroughly confusing the ignorant with fruitless debates.[50]

Even were a clear differentiation between credulity and rational religion established, combating philosophical 'atheism' would remain a difficult and risky undertaking in which success would remain elusive without a sound grounding in *historia philosophica*. Much of the difficulty, as Buddeus saw it, was the validity of Bayle's demonstrations that 'atheistic' ideas reach back in an almost unbroken chain to the origins of philosophy itself: the founding thinkers of Miletus—Thales, Anaximander, and Anaximenes—being, just as Bayle claimed, all materialists and 'atheists'.[51] Yet while conceding many of Bayle's points, often disagreeing with Heumann, Buddeus also worried lest some of the new research ultimately serve merely to inflate the number of Greek, Roman, Chinese, medieval, and Renaissance philosophers whose systems, as it is put in the French version of his *Theses*, 's'accordent avec celui de Spinoza, ou du moins en approchent fort' [agree with that of Spinoza or at least closely resemble it].[52]

Following Bayle's death, and the growing awareness of the implications of his battle with the *rationaux*, attitudes towards Bayle in German Eclectic circles palpably hardened, not least due to the warnings of Buddeus himself. The older Buddeus came to feel that in his own early work he had perhaps too readily accepted Bayle's arguments regarding the Presocratics, Hellenistic thinkers, and Neoplatonism.[53] In particular, he refused to accept Bayle's linking of Plotinus to his purported wider ancient Greek impulse towards one-substance doctrines and proto-Spinozism.[54] While, on the one hand, still defending much of Bayle's research into 'history of philosophy' against numerous critics, he also conceded that in places Bayle seemed to be providing the Spinozists with additional arguments and even, sometimes, not to be combating them 'sérieusement et du fond de son cœur'.[55] But whatever the difficulties, he did not doubt that in the end meticulous investigation

[50] Buddeus, *Traité de l'athéisme*, preface pp. xiv–xv.

[51] Ibid. 10.

[52] Ibid. 72–4, 77.

[53] Ibid., p. vi.

[54] Bayle, *Écrits*, 128–9; Buddeus, *De Spinozismo ante Spinozam*, 330–2; Häfner, 'Johann Lorenz Mosheim', 241, 243–4; Canziani, 'Philosophes', 163.

[55] Buddeus, *Traité de l'athéisme*, 72–4, 77; Schröder, *Ursprünge*, 69.

1. Benedict de Spinoza (1632–1677). Anonymous portrait. (By courtesy of the Herzog August Bibliothek, Wolfenbüttel)

2. The 'Glorious Revolution'. An Imagined Recreation of the Dutch Army entering London, in December 1688. Print by Romeyn de Hooghe. (By courtesy of the Print Room of the University of Leiden)

3. Pierre Bayle, the 'philosopher of Rotterdam'. Painted portrait (By courtesy of the Herzog August Bibliothek, Wolfenbüttel)

4 (*above*). The Visit of Czar Peter the Great to the 'Museum Wildianum', the Collection of Jacob de Wilde, in Amsterdam, on 13 December 1697 (By courtesy of the Rijksmuseum, Amsterdam)

5 (*right*). Frontispiece of a surviving manuscript copy of the *Abregé d'histoire universelle*, composed in 1700 by M.L.C.D.C.D.B. [ie. Boulainvilliers] copied in 1707 (By courtesy of the Historical Studies Library, Institute for Advanced Study, Princeton)

ABREGÉ

D'HISTOIRE

VNIUERSELLE

PREMIER VOLUME

Composé par M.L.C.D.C.D.B. et copié sur l'original de l'Autheur au mois de Fevrier 1707: et recorrigé en 1715.

Si fortuna deest, probitas virtus que rependit

Ex Libris Ludovici Le Bouthillier De Pont Chavigny.

6. John Locke. Portrait after G. Kneller. (By courtesy of the Governing Body of Christ Church College, Oxford)

7. Gottfried Wilhelm Leibniz (1646–1716). Engraved portrait. (By courtesy of the Herzog August Bibliothek, Wolfenbüttel)

8. B. de Fontenelle (1657–1757). Engraved portrait after H. Rigaud (courtesy of the Herzog August Bibliothek, Wolfenbüttel)

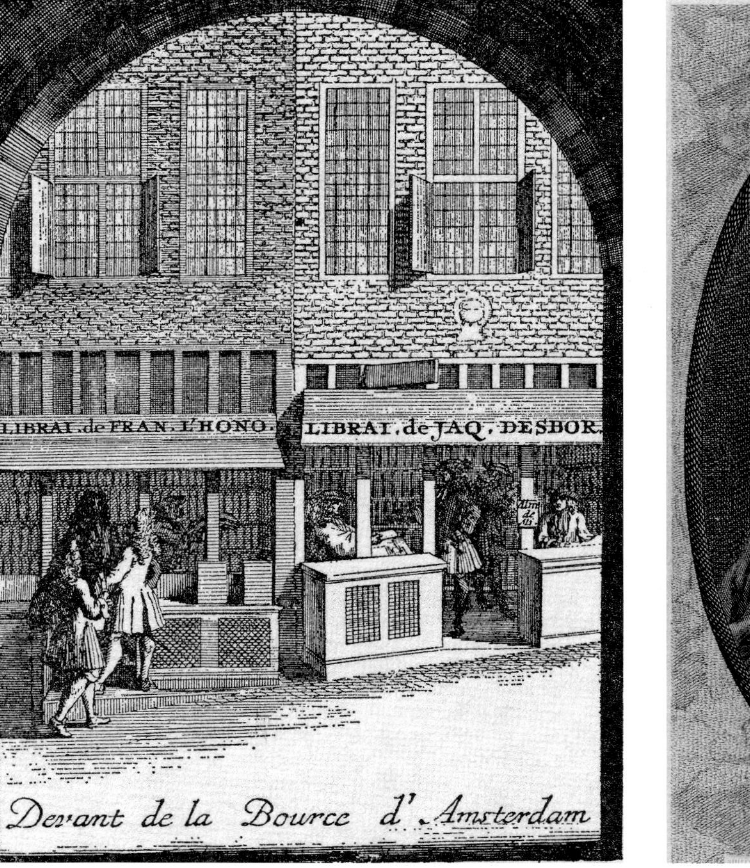

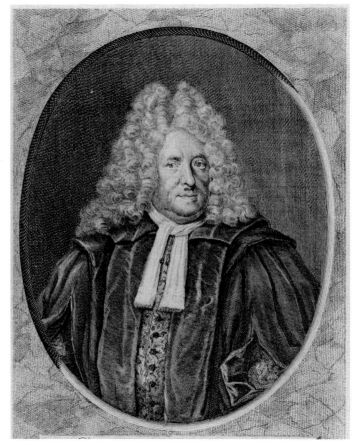

9. The Book-shops of François L'Honoré and Jacques Desbordes, opposite the Bourse in Amsterdam, around 1715

10. Christian Thomasius (1655–1728). Engraved portrait. (By courtesy of the Herzog August Bibliothek, Wolfenbüttel)

1738. C. Fritsch sculps: Hamb. Ihro Königl. Hoheit zu Hollstein Hof Kupferstecher.
Nicolaus Hieronymus Gundlingius,
ICtus Potent. Regi Boruss. a consil. intim. et Ecclesiast. Profes
Jur. Ord. in Reg. Fridericiana. Obiit Pro Rector Magnificus
d. IX Dec. MDCCXXIX. natus d. XXV. Febr. MDCLXXI.

11. Niklaus Hieronymus Gundling (1671–1729). Engraved portrait by C. Fritsch (courtesy of the Herzog August Bibliothek, Wolfenbüttel)

12. Newton in 1712. Painted portrait (By courtesy of the Herzog August Bibliothek, Wolfenbüttel)

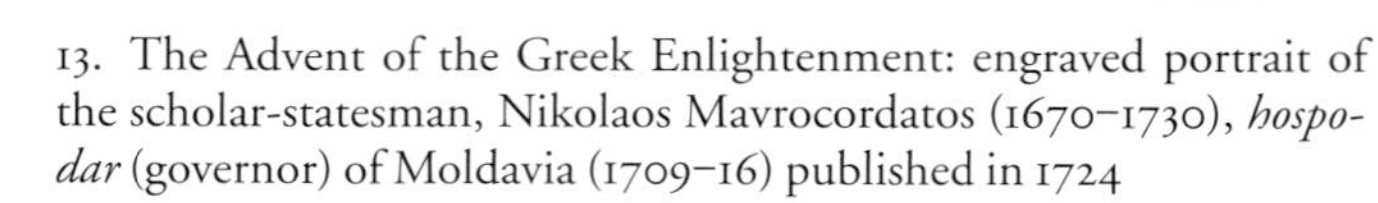

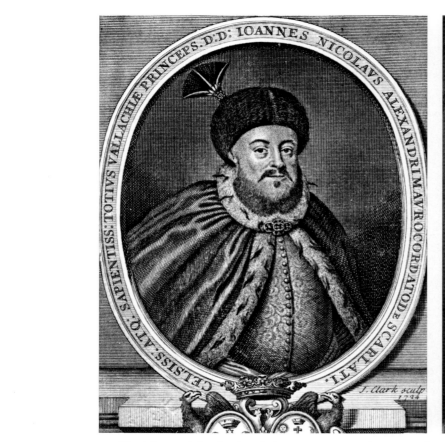

13. The Advent of the Greek Enlightenment: engraved portrait of the scholar-statesman, Nikolaos Mavrocordatos (1670–1730), *hospodar* (governor) of Moldavia (1709–16) published in 1724

14. Montesquieu in 1728 (courtesy of the Chateaux de Versailles et de Trianon)

15 (*right*). Title-page of the first volume of Proceedings of the Russian Imperial Academy of Sciences of Saint Petersburg (Petropolis) published at Saint Petersburg in 1728. (Courtesy of the New York Public Library)

16 (*far right*). Title-page of Alberto Radicati's radical text *A Succinct History of Priesthood* (London 1737). (By courtesy of the Beinecke Rare Book Library, Yale University)

COMMENTARII
ACADEMIAE
SCIENTIARVM
IMPERIALIS
PETROPOLITANAE

TOMVS I.
AD ANNVM cIɔ Iɔcc XXVI.

PETROPOLI
TYPIS ACADEMIAE
cIɔ Iɔcc XXVIII.

A
Succinct History
OF
PRIESTHOOD,
ANCIENT and MODERN.
Humbly inscrib'd
To the Ever-illustrious, and most Celebrated
SECT of
FREE THINKERS.

By ALBERTO RADICATI,
Count DE PASSERAN and DE COCCONAS, a *Piemontæse*
Exile now in HOLLAND, a Christian *Free-Thinker*.

Hâc urget Lupus, *hâc* Canis.
HOR. *Sat.* 2. *lib.* 2.

LONDON:
Printed by H. GORHAM in *Fleet-street*, and Sold by
the Booksellers and Pamphlet Shops, 1737.
[Price 1 s.]

17. Voltaire in 1744. Marbled bust sculptured by Jean-Baptiste Lemoyne (1704–78) (By courtesy of the Musée d'art et d'histoire, Geneva)

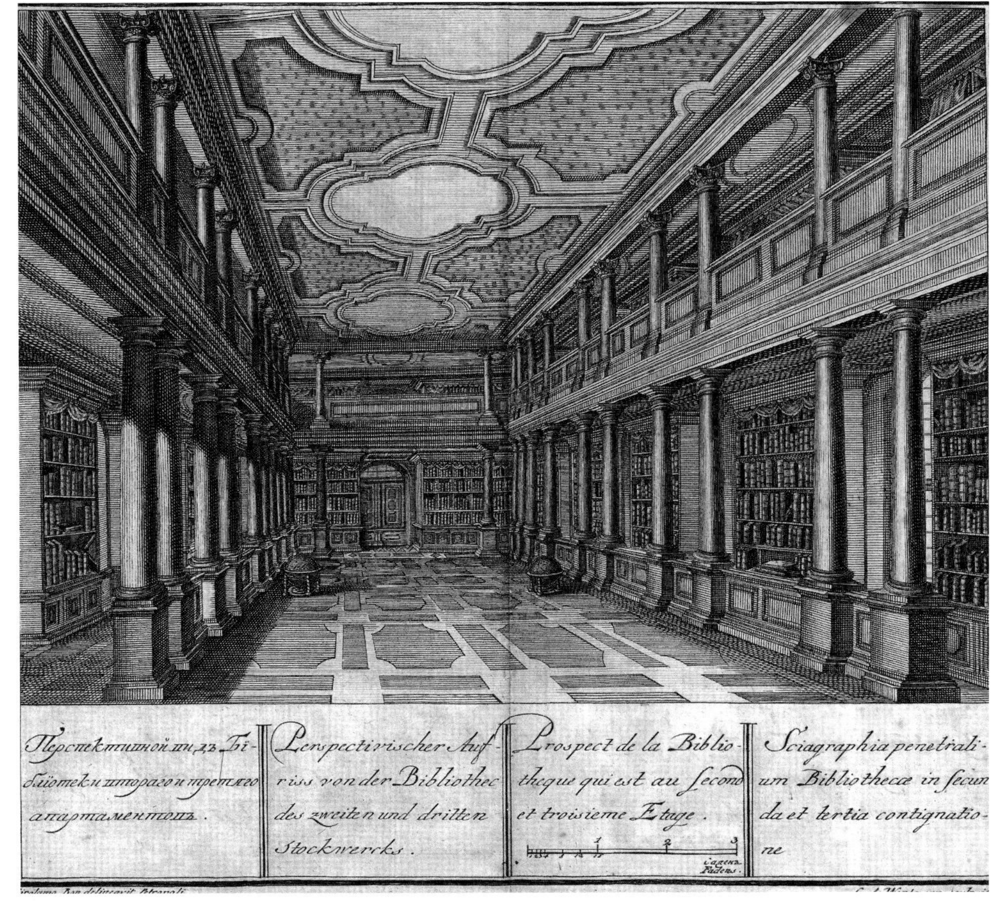

18. The Library of the Russian Imperial Academy of Sciences in Saint Petersburg, around 1740 (By courtesy of New York Public Library)

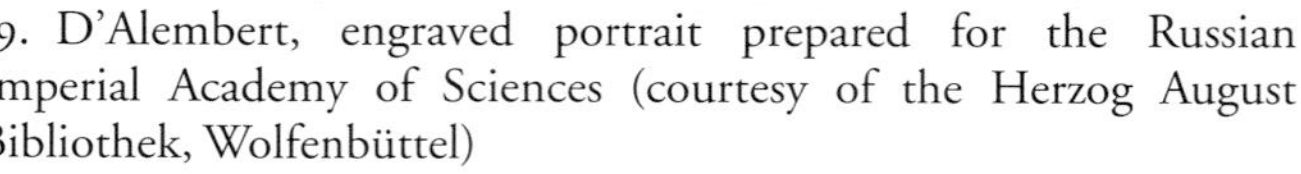

19. D'Alembert, engraved portrait prepared for the Russian Imperial Academy of Sciences (courtesy of the Herzog August Bibliothek, Wolfenbüttel)

20. Rousseau in 1753. Portrait by Maurice-Quentin de la Tour (1704–88) (By courtesy of the Musée d'art et d'histoire, Geneva)

21. Engraved Frontispiece, designed by B. L. Prévost in 1765, for the 1772 edition of the *Encyclopédie* of Diderot and d'Alembert, allegorizing learning, science, the arts and the crafts

22. Denis Diderot (1713–1784). Portrait by Louis Michel van Loo (1707–71) (By courtesy of the Louvre)

of past thought would set the record straight, establish a sound philosophy, solve the riddle of Bayle's ambivalence, and secure final victory over Spinozism.

Much harsher in their criticism of Bayle were Heumann, Brucker, and Johann Jakob Zimmermann (1695–1756), a today little-remembered Zurich Reformed professor of theology, who played a prominent role in the early eighteenth-century German-language debates about history of philosophy. Brucker, in his *Kurtze Fragen* of 1731, rejected even Bayle's most carefully crafted projection of ancient quasi-Spinozism, emphatically absolving Strato from the Huguenot's imputation of proto-Spinozism and 'atheism'.[56] Brucker's impressive *Critical History of Philosophy*, published in four bulky volumes between 1742 and 1744, marks the culmination of the Early Enlightenment project to place history of philosophy on a sounder basis. While Brucker's aims were solidly eclectic and conservative, rather ironically his work became a major reference resource in the hands of the radical *encyclopédistes*. Diderot and d'Alembert, in particular, relied heavily on Brucker's analyses in compiling their many articles on history of philosophy.[57] In this way, *historia philosophica* and the new methods of interpreting the philosophy of the past, and non-European world, as well as affinities between particular modern and ancient philosophy schools, became internationally central to the task of philosophy itself and crucial no less to the contest between the opposed wings of the Enlightenment.

3. 'RADICAL RENAISSANCE'

Within this wider context one of Bayle's major contributions to Early Enlightenment discourse was his introducing, first in his *Dictionnaire*, a powerful new construct which may usefully be termed 'Radical Renaissance'. The term 'Italian Renaissance' itself had, of course, not yet been coined and neither Bayle nor his contemporaries took much interest in many of the features of the Renaissance which later came to make it appear so significant an epoch. Least of all did the Early Enlightenment muster any enthusiasm for Italian humanism or its Platonism or Aristotelianism. But the Italian Renaissance naturalist, libertine tradition culminating in Pomponazzi, Bruno, Vanini, and that key anonymous clandestine text the *Theophrastus redivivus* (1659), was a different matter and its study, by Bayle and the German Eclectics especially, lent a wholly new significance to late Renaissance philosophical naturalism which, though Aristotelian, looked also subversive and atheistic in orientation.[58] At the same time, the potential impact of this remarkable initiative of Bayle's was then, in turn, largely neutralized by a marked anti-Italian bias running through much of particularly the French Early Enlightenment, from

[56] Brucker, *Kurtze Fragen*, 882–3.

[57] Ibid. 164–8; Donini, 'History', 18–19; Kelley, *Descent of Ideas*, 40, 154; Fauvergue, 'Diderot', 111–12.

[58] Ricuperati, 'Il problema', 386–8; Bianchi, 'Pierre Bayle', 256, 263–4.

Boulainvilliers to Diderot and d'Alembert and the *Encyclopédie*'s consequent tendency to de-emphasize the roles of the Italian thinkers and scientists, even Galileo.[59]

Bayle includes numerous figures from the Italian Renaissance, including Savonarola and Machiavelli, in his *Dictionnaire*. Among articles of specifically philosophical significance, it is striking that he takes little interest in the Platonism and syncretism of Ficino and Pico.[60] What he and the Radical Enlightenment found meaningful and important in Italian thought, rather, was the strain of naturalism, producing clandestine anti-Christian and 'atheistic' tendencies, as well as a complete separation of philosophy from theology, and founding of a secular morality detached from God-ordained ordinances, immortality of the soul, and theology.[61] Broadly, the Early Enlightenment's portrayal of Italian Renaissance thought can be said to have evolved in three stages, beginning with Bayle's 'Radical Renaissance' construction, continuing with the German Eclectic response to that construct, and ending with the French Radical Enlightenment's rather muted espousal of Bayle's construct with adjustments taken from the Germans, especially Brucker, and insinuated for radical purposes, in particular by Diderot, into the *Encyclopédie*.

Bayle, in constructing his 'Radical Renaissance', focused on a group of sixteenth-century figures and their early seventeenth-century followers who seemed to have actively sought to undermine the traditional relationship between Aristotelian scholasticism and theology. He considers, in particular, Pietro Pomponazzi (1462–1525), Girolamo Cardano (1501–76) whom he deems one of the wisest of philosophers, Andrea Cesalpino (1524–1603), Jacopo Zarabella (1533–89), Giordano Bruno (1548–1600), Cesare Cremonini (1550–1631), and Giulio Cesare Vanini (1584–1619), all figures whom, in one way or another, he explicitly links with Spinoza.

Contemporaries were often baffled by his remarks. Why does Bayle think Cardano's reflections on piety and religion have a special solidity?[62] What was Bayle's aim in eulogizing the universally reviled Vanini as a 'martyr de l'athéisme', in a manner afterwards emulated by Mandeville?[63] In his *Pensées diverses* (1682), Bayle had claimed that atheism produces its own martyrs, citing Vanini as an instance of an upright 'atheist' who had gone to the stake rather than compromise his principles. What was his purpose in so blatantly offending conventional opinion? Not the least bizarre feature of the *Dictionnaire* was the argument that many Renaissance as well as ancient and medieval 'atheists' deserve praise and admiration for their exemplary lives. Bayle sometimes even seems deliberately bent on emphasizing the positive, rather than the negative, features of even the most decried dissidents and heretics.[64]

David Durand figured among those who queried both Bayle's motives and the accuracy of his research and Bayle himself granted, at the end of his life, in 1706,

[59] Proust, *Diderot*, 248; Venturino, *Ragioni*, 264–5.

[60] Canziani, 'Philosophes', 143–4.

[61] Ibid. 157; Mori, *Bayle philosophe*, 201n.

[62] Göbel, 'Lessing und Cardano', 171–4.

[63] Mandeville, *Fable of the Bees*, i. 214–15.

[64] Holberg, *Memoirs*, 187–8; Jaumann, 'Jakob Friedrich Zimmermanns Bayle-Kritik', 203.

that his account of Vanini, in the *Pensées diverses* attributing to him an austere morality, was not well informed.[65] How could Bayle, asked Durand, extol Vanini, a writer who declared—'Ô Blasphème execrable!'—that the Virgin Mary had conceived Christ through carnal union with an ordinary man who was not her husband?[66] Bayle was right, though, Durand agreed, that the basic concept underlying the thought of the 'incrédules de notre temps' is the identification of God with nature and that a proto-Spinozism is found rudimentarily expressed in many earlier thinkers. But this made it all the more reprehensible that he should exalt Vanini, deliberately misleading readers by failing to mention that Vanini's philosophy was Spinozistic or warn that this Italian 'atheist' held that the world's princes 'ont inventé les religions'.[67] Durand's book contributed to compromising Bayle's reputation after his death, and tightening the public's association of Bayle with Spinoza. Voltaire later added his censure, remarking that Vanini was neither virtuous nor an atheist.[68]

Giordano Bruno 'was a man of great parts', as it is put in the English version of Bayle's *Dictionnaire*, but 'made an ill use of his knowledge; for he wrote against Aristotle's philosophy, at a time when such a thing could not be done without occasioning great disorders and exposing one's self to many persecutions, but also against the most important truths of religion'.[69] For Bruno, declares Bayle, 'the whole universe is but one being'. Cremonini, who died of the plague in Padua in 1631, likewise seems to be deliberately selected by Bayle for his Averroism, rumoured 'atheism', preoccupation with Aristotle, and unacceptable views. 'Cremoninus', relates the English version of Bayle's *Dictionnaire*, 'was accounted a Libertine, who did not believe in the immortality of the soul and whose opinions about these matters were not in the least consonant with Christianity.'[70] Contemporaries had indeed denounced Cremonini before the Inquisition, for rejecting immortality of the soul, the Incarnation, and other key dogmas.[71] Leibniz too mentions Cremonini in this context, in his *Theodicy* (1710), concurring (however much he may have disapproved of Bayle's intentions) with Bayle's 'Radical Renaissance' construct.

'Cremoninus, a philosopher famous in his time', though rapidly forgotten after his death, adds Leibniz, was one of the 'mainstays' of the clandestine 'Averroist' sect, entrenched in the Italian universities since the later Middle Ages, who 'disputed this conformity of faith with reason which I maintain', denying immortality of the soul as well as setting theology and philosophy 'at variance'.[72] Traces of this subversive Italian 'Averroism' which Bayle, adds Leibniz, had linked also with Cardano had surfaced in the writings of Gabriel Naudé (1600–53), a French libertine who alleged Pomponazzi to have been an 'atheist' (and who both influenced and greatly

[65] *L'Europe savante*, 4 (1718), 100; Foucault, 'Pierre Bayle', 231, 235; Mori, *Bayle philosophe*, 201 n., 204.

[66] Durand, *Vie et sentiments*, 176; *L'Europe savante*, 4 (1718), 100; Rétat, *Dictionnaire de Bayle*, 38–9.

[67] Durand, *Vie et sentiments*, 130.

[68] Harris, 'Answering', 242 n.

[69] Canziani, 'Philosophes', 159–63; Bayle, *An Historical and Critical Dictionary*, i. 728–9.

[70] Bayle, *An Historical and Critical Dictionary*, ii. 1031.

[71] Charles-Daubert, 'Fortune de Cremonini', 174, 184, 190.

[72] Leibniz, *Theodicy*, 77, 80–1.

fascinated Bayle), all this proving to Leibniz that 'Averroism still lived on when this learned physician was in Italy'.[73] The *Encyclopédie* of Diderot and d'Alembert, here as in so much else, adopted Bayle's approach, declaring the basis of Cremonini's system to be the same as that of Cesalpino.[74]

Bayle's deliberately bracketing these figures with Spinozism was readily enough accepted by many in the world of Lutheran scholarship. Designating Spinoza chief of the modern *athei speculativi*, or philosophical atheists, Hector Gottfried Masius (1653–1709), from 1686 a court preacher at Copenhagen, claimed this 'atheist' had two major predecessors who were both Italians living in the early sixteenth century—Pietro Pomponazzi (1462–1525) of Mantua and Niccolò Machiavelli (1469–1527).[75] It was by no means unusual at the time to cite Italy as the original home of 'atheism'—or, indeed, Pomponazzi and Machiavelli as two principal representatives of that new contagion,[76] a view echoed in Buddeus' *Theses theologicae* and by Reimmann, in his *Historia universalis atheismi* (1725). As Lutherans, Masius, Buddeus, and Reimmann clearly felt at home with the idea that the contagion of modern 'atheism' had originated in Italy in no small part owing to the effect of Catholic 'superstition' and corruption of religion promoted by the papacy, Catholic hierarchy, and what Reimmann termed Jesuit 'Machiavellismus'.[77]

Since the late fifteenth century, study of Aristotelianism at Padua had shifted to an investigation of original Greek texts, terminology, and commentators, and Pomponazzi was a major exponent of this return 'to the original Greek', a devotee, in particular, like others whom Bayle identifies as denying the immortality of the soul, of the third-century AD Anatolian Peripatetic Alexander of Aphrodisias.[78] In the case of Pomponazzi, Bayle had merely renewed an old controversy, defending him against charges of 'atheism' but yet supporting him, on fideist grounds, in his naturalistic arguments, claiming that Creation and the immortality of the soul cannot be proved and detaching philosophy from theology.[79] A naturalist in the Renaissance more than the anti-magical Early Enlightenment sense, Pomponazzi believed in a causal nexus between the super and sublunary spheres and the validity of astrology. Nevertheless, he also lent the new, non-scholastic Aristotelianism a marked tendency to screen divine providence, prophecy, demonic and angelic intervention, and miracles out of the discussion, replacing these with superlunary astral influences. The stars, according to Pomponazzi, rule not only nature but also history and even the rise and fall of religions.[80]

[73] Leibniz, *Theodicy*, 81; Göbel, 'Lessing und Cardano', 173; Canziani, 'Philosophes', 144; Schröder, *Ursprünge*, 60 n.

[74] Yvon, 'Aristotélisme', in Diderot and d'Alembert, *Encyclopédie*, i. 670.

[75] Masius, *Dissertationes*, 9–11.

[76] Reimmann, *Versuch einer Einleitung*, ii. 97; Reimmann, *Historia universalis*, 354–77; Davidson, 'Unbelief', 55–6.

[77] Reimmann, *Historia universalis*, 352–4; Colombero, 'Andrea Cesalpino', 348; Ricci, 'Bruno "Spinozista"', 53–4.

[78] Leibniz, *Theodicy*, 80; Brucker, *Historia critica philosophiae* (1743), iv. part 1, 167; Canziani, 'Philosophes', 151.

[79] Labrousse, *Pierre Bayle*, ii. 307; Bianchi, 'Pierre Bayle', 255–7, 266; Lohr, 'Metaphysics', 617.

[80] Ingegno, 'New Philosophy', 242–4; Walker, *Spiritual and Demonic Magic*, 110–11; Trinkhaus, '*In our Image*', ii. 550; Gregory, 'Pensiero medievale', 162; Copenhaver, 'Astrology', 272–3.

Pomponazzi's Aristotelianism came under suspicion for raising doubts about miracles as well as the existence of immaterial beings like demons, angels, and immortal souls.[81] His 1516 treatise on the soul's immortality where he affirms 'no natural reasons can be brought forth proving that the soul is immortal', contravening the Lateran Council decree of 1513 which ruled that immortality of the soul can be proved,[82] ranged a number of senior churchmen, as well as his former colleague Agostino Nifo, against him, though there were also defenders who argued that his statements that the soul's immortality and other points of theology could not be demonstrated philosophically subscribed to the sound doctrine of 'double truth', or separate realms of truth. Designated a 'fideist', holding that faith enjoins us to believe the Church's teachings without reference to reason or philosophy,[83] a view palatable to conservative colleagues who insisted the only 'true philosophy' is the Christian faith, he stood his ground. As regards the competing philosophy schools, Aristotle should be preferred to the other schools, many felt, since he starts from sense perception, confining himself in the main to investigating nature. Even so, efforts to crush Pomponazzi and uphold the Lateran decree continued down to the mid 1520s.

After his death the battle dragged on inconclusively over the centuries. Regarded by Campanella and others as the philosophical counterpart of Machiavelli's moral and political naturalism, Pomponazzi's demystifying arguments doubtless did help prepare the way for the Enlightenment materialism of the future.[84] The controversy about him and his writings in any case gained fresh vitality during the Early Enlightenment, thanks to Bayle, in the first place. Regarding angels and demons, according to the English version of Bayle's *Dictionnaire*, Pomponazzi held 'they were only particles of God united to a very subtil matter: nay, he pretended that the souls of men and of beasts, were part of the substance of God'.[85] Although many now found it expedient to decry Pomponazzi as a freethinker and libertine, as in the early sixteenth century, some no less vigorously defended him. Most disturbing of all, in the eyes of some, was that despite it all there was no consensus: Pomponazzi simply remained what he had been for two centuries—an enigma, as Reimmann put it, 'a multi accusatus et defendus', both accused and defended by many.[86]

He was defended with particular vigour by Zimmermann, an exponent of the new *critique* who considered Spinoza's philosophy *falsissima, ineptissima*, and a universal threat to Christianity and society. 'Atheism' and naturalism posed frightful dangers. But Zimmermann's researches into history of philosophy convinced him there was also a need to alert readers to the opposite menace, namely of being dragged into Bayle's, to Zimmermann's mind, scarcely less insidious

[81] Brucker, *Historia critica philosophiae* (1743), iv. part 1, 180–2; Namer, *La Vie et l'œuvre*, 265–7; Davidson, 'Unbelief', 66.

[82] Pomponazzi, *De immortalitate*, 377; Brucker, *Historia critica philosophiae* (1743), iv. part 1, 162–3.

[83] Pomponazzi, *De immortalitate*, 379; Kessler, 'Intellective Soul', 503–6; Bianchi, 'Pierre Bayle', 254–5; Bouchardy, *Pierre Bayle*, 162, 214–15.

[84] Gregory, 'Apologeti', 3, 9; Brann, *Debate*, 449.

[85] Bayle, *An Historical and Critical Dictionary*, ii. 927.

[86] Reimmann, *Historia universalis*, 361–2.

'Atheistenmacherei' [fabricating of atheists].[87] He had a valid point to make which was that unless one adheres to the most scrupulous scholarly standards 'nothing is easier' than to concoct 'dangerous' sounding systems from the 'obscurer and more difficult phrases of ancient authors'.[88] Having himself been suspected of heterodoxy, due to his taste for Arminian authors like van Limborch and Le Clerc, he had come to believe no one should be denounced for atheism 'quo pestilentior error non datur' [than which there is no more pestilential error] without the most unambiguous and definite proof.[89]

Bayle and Buddeus rightly held that identifying crypto- and quasi-Spinozism counts among *historia philosophica*'s main tasks; but Zimmermann demanded greater caution than Buddeus showed in his *De Spinozismo ante Spinozam* (1701), a work he blamed for what he considered its superficial analysis.[90] Zimmermann saw a particular need to redeem Pomponazzi, whom Heumann, in his *Acta philosophorum*, had firmly labelled an 'atheist' and 'Spinozist' while Bayle and Buddeus had not definitely classed him as either but only insinuated as much.[91] Heumann, like Morhof before him, argued that, for Pomponazzi, nature alone moves all worldly occurrence, so that not only is the soul's immortality denied but miracles are eradicated and exclusively natural causes given to explain biblical wonders, including Christ's cures: 'da haben wir also', held Heumann, 'den *Spinozismum* ante *Spinozam*' [there we have then Spinozism before Spinoza].[92] Zimmermann countered by pointing out that nowhere does Pomponazzi expressly deny the possibility of miracles as such, or advance philosophical grounds for doing so.[93]

Furthermore, there was reason to question the relevance of this. Where Pomponazzi, held Heumann, 'introduces a horrible doubt about the existence of angels and demons', Zimmermann, trimming the definition of 'atheism' to cover strictly only denial of God's existence, deemed this objection irrelevant too. The notion of *Spinozismus ante Spinozam*, he argued, must be regarded with deep suspicion, being, in part, an insinuating device of Bayle's, abetted, albeit unwittingly, by Buddeus and Heumann, for raising the status and enhancing the centrality of Spinozism; consequently, he refused to allow that Pomponazzi should be classed as an 'atheist' and proto-Spinozist.[94] Zimmermann's objections, however, were then countered by Brucker who emphatically confirmed Pomponazzi's naturalism, impiety, and opposition to Christianity.[95]

Heumann's and Brucker's notion of Pomponazzi as a giant of sixteenth-century thought at war with theology and a proto-Spinoza became, through Boureau-Deslandes and especially Diderot, the view of the *Encyclopédie*. There, in the first volume, published in 1751, Pomponazzi appears as an 'atheist' and enemy of

[87] Von Wille, 'Apologie', 215, 220–1, 236.
[88] Quoted ibid. 216–17.
[89] Ibid. 215; Mulsow, *Moderne*, 300.
[90] Von Wille, 'Apologie', 218–19, 221, 229.
[91] Bayle, *Écrits*, 115–18, 170; Heumann, *Acta philosophorum*, 9 (1718), 337–8; Labrousse, *Pierre Bayle*, ii. 11.
[92] Heumann, *Acta philosophorum*, 9 (1718), 361.
[93] Ibid. 350–4; von Wille, 'Apologie', 226–7; Pine, 'Pietro Pomponazzi's Attack', 146–9.
[94] Heumann, *Acta philosophorum*, 9 (1718), 355–6; von Wille, 'Apologie', 221–2, 235.
[95] Brucker, *Historia critica philosophiae* (1743), iv. part 1, 171–80.

religion, notably in the long article on Aristotelianism by the Abbé Claude Yvon. Yvon claims Pomponazzi denied miracles, divine providence, and human liberty as well as magic and the immortality of the soul while simultaneously deriding the fideist doctrine of double truth, adding that he cannot comprehend how Pomponazzi's defenders could seriously maintain that he held his libertine view only intellectually, 'en philosophe', while, as a Christian, unquestioningly believing all the 'dogmas of our religion'.[96]

Yvon, recycling Bayle under Diderot's guidance, claims Cesalpino too 'seems' to have preceded 'Spinosa dans plusieurs de ses principes impies'.[97] Bayle remarks that Cesalpino was a 'very learned man' but 'very bad Christian with respect to his opinions. His principles differ'd but little from those of Spinoza.'[98] (Bayle and Leibniz also both say he preceded Harvey in discovering the circulation of the blood.) Not only did Cesalpino deny divine providence, held Diderot's team, but he identifies 'God' with the whole of reality and even 'n'admettoit qu'une substance'.[99] One cannot, the reader is told, read 'sans horreur' what he says about God and men's souls; for he even surpasses Averroes in his 'impieties'. Almost all scholars, concludes the *Encyclopédie*, accuse Cesalpino 'de Spinosisme'. There remains, however, remarks Yvon, one important difference between Cesalpino and Spinoza. The former's one substance is confined to the single world-soul which infuses also every human and all spirituality but does not conflate spirit and matter like Spinoza's: 'mais qu'importe?' Cesalpino's views 'ne détruit pas moins la nature de Dieu, que celle de Spinosa'.[100]

Zimmermann's research, like Brucker's, provided a major corrective to much that was written earlier and much that came to be recycled in the *Encyclopédie*. Yet, there was also a contrary risk inherent in his efforts to dismantle Bayle's 'Radical Renaissance', among much else by rehabilitating Pomponazzi. For if he was right to hold Pomponazzi was not an 'atheist' *stricto sensu*, recent scholarship also shows that Bayle was closer to the mark than he in portraying Pompanazzi as a Naturalist, denier of miracles and immortality of the soul, and, by insinuation, someone attacking the premisses of revealed religion and church authority.[101] Hence, while further research into *historia philosophica* could be useful to the fight against 'atheism' by thinning an overflowing canon of philosophical 'atheists' and proto-Spinozists, such a procedure could also help vindicate real 'atheists' and Naturalists, thus inadvertently helping corrupt whole areas of culture and thought. Hence there were two suspect paths in the new *historia philosophica*.

Among those suspected of surreptitiously pursuing Bayle's campaign to align whole segments of Greek and Renaissance Italian thought with Spinozism was

96 Yvon, 'Aristotélisme', in Diderot and d'Alembert, *Encyclopédie*, i. 665–7.

97 Ibid. i. 669; Bayle, *Écrits*, 120–1.

98 Bayle, *An Historical and Critical Dictionary*, ii. 925–6; Leibniz, *Theodicy*, 81.

99 Lohr, 'Metaphysics', 623–4; Yvon, 'Aristotélisme', in Diderot and d'Alembert, *Encyclopédie*, i. 669–70.

100 Yvon, 'Aristotélisme', in Diderot and d'Alembert, *Encyclopédie*, i. 669–70; Leibniz, *Theodicy*, 81; Labrousse, *Pierre Bayle*, ii. 199.

101 Pine, 'Pietro Pomponazzi's Attack', 145–8.

Gundling.[102] Teaching throughout his career at Halle, in the shadow of Christian Thomasius, Gundling is mostly remembered today in connection with Eclectics like Christian Thomasius and Buddeus.[103] Yet, on key issues, as has been recently pointed out, he aligned with Bayle rather than these authors, making it more accurate perhaps to class him, at least to an extent, rather as a discreet academic advocate of radical thought, like De Volder,'s-Gravesande, and Schmauss, than a man of the middle bloc, though Buddeus, despite their disagreements, remained throughout on friendly terms with him.[104] Gundling's fondness for Bayle,[105] approach to Greek and Renaissance thought, and defence of Hobbes against the charge of 'atheism', as well as stress on freedom of thought, placed him in a different category from other Eclectics and on a collision course with Zimmermann.

Critics were especially indignant at his endorsing Bayle's identification of the great Neoplatonist Plotinus (AD 205–70) as a proto-Spinozist and, worse, claiming Platonism itself is, at bottom, monist and Spinozistic.[106] In the controversy about Platonism stoked up by the publication of Jacques Souverain's *Le Platonisme desvoilé* (Amsterdam, 1700), and persistent efforts of Le Clerc to discredit much of the theology of the Church Fathers, the incorrigible Gundling leapt in, carrying Souverain's and Le Clerc's subversive propositions even further than they did. In 1706, he published his argument that Plato was an 'atheist' whose system, despite its different terminology, in fact closely resembles that of Spinoza.[107] Developing this thesis further in his article 'Plato atheos', published in the Halle journal *Neue Bibliothec* in 1713, Gundling attempted fundamentally to transform the image of Plato in western thought, by amalgamating the arguments of Souverain, Le Clerc, Bayle, and Wachter into a broad thesis convicting of blindness, perverse error, and confusion the entire Plato scholarship of twenty centuries. This piece subsequently reappeared, in 1728, in the fifth volume of his collected *Gundlingiana*.

His thesis hinges on the claim that Plato's God is the immanent cause pervading the cosmos and the world's *causa efficiens necessaria* [necessary efficient cause] just as fire is of warmth, acting in the world blindly and necessarily: 'est enim Deus Platonis mundus, et mundus Deus' [thus the God of Plato is the world, and the world God].[108] Hence, he concluded, Plato's God does not in fact create or form matter but merely pervades it like the Stoic God which, as Buddeus had already confirmed, closely resembles Spinoza's.[109] As Gundling summed the matter up,

[102] Heumann, *Acta philosophorum*, 6 (1716), 1033.

[103] Gierl, *Pietismus*, 523; Kelley, *Descent of Ideas*, 150.

[104] Gundling, *Vollständige Historie*, i. 887, 913, 919; Gierl, *Pietismus*, 523; Mulsow, 'Gundling *versus* Buddeus', 110–14, 117–18.

[105] Gundling, *Vollständige Historie*, i. 913, ii. 1643–4; Jaumann, *Critica*, 218; Albrecht, *Eklektik*, 576–7; Mulsow, *Moderne*, 297.

[106] Gundling, *Gundlingiana*, ii. 312–15, v. 189–91, 222–44; Gundling, *Vollständige Historie*, i. 919–36, iv. 4907–8; Mulsow, *Moderne*, 235, 288–91, 300–13.

[107] Mulsow, *Moderne*, 290; Gundling, *Vollständige Historie*, iv. 4936–7.

[108] Gundling, 'De atheismo Platonis', in *Gundlingiana*, v. 222, 234, 237.

[109] Ibid. v. 190, 300; Brucker, *Historia critica philosophiae* (1742), i. 680, 682.

Plato 'unum omnia et omnia unum statuit; Spinoza unam substantiam' [declared one to be all things and all things one; Spinoza (declared) one substance];[110] incorporating strands of Souverain, Le Clerc, and Wachter, he unhesitatingly identified Plato himself, and with him the entire Platonic and Neoplatonic legacies, as being in the context of the philosophical history of the world broadly in line with Spinozism.

This convergence between the post-*Dictionnaire* Bayle and Gundling, in condemning all ancient, medieval, and Renaissance Neoplatonism,[111] and Plato himself, dismayed but also puzzled the Republic of Letters. For in his *Observationum selectarum ad rem litterarium* (1704), where he praises 'the very acute Le Clerc' for his critical method, Gundling had also expressly approved Le Clerc's contention that while all atheists are necessarily materialists, not all materialists are necessarily atheists. Gundling acknowledged then, like Cudworth and Le Clerc, but unlike Buddeus, that if, as with Stoicism, a materialist postulates a divine force which pervades the matter of which the cosmos is formed, and possesses intelligence, that materialist is then not an 'atheist'.[112] Yet, despite having himself previously pointed out the parallels between the Stoic and Platonic conceptions of divine Providence, and the immanence of God in matter, Gundling now stubbornly refused to concede that the Platonic God therefore possesses the will and intelligence which would exonerate all forms of Platonism from the charge of 'atheism'.

The matter was all the more baffling in that where the Stoic God himself permeates the cosmos, in Plato's *Timaeus* it is rather the world-soul emanating from God that pervades the world.[113] Gundling's refusal to accept that Plato differentiates between the cosmos and God, and his unrelenting attack on Plato and Platonism over nearly a quarter of a century, seemed all the more perverse in that it issued from the pen of someone who simultaneously insisted, contrary to received opinion, that Hobbes was *not* an atheist.[114] It was scarcely any more credible, in his case than Bayle's, that he was unconscious of the devastating and frightening implications of his argument. Nor can he have been unaware that by tenaciously sticking to his opinion, despite mounting scholarly opposition, he was in effect reinforcing Bayle's thesis that it is not after all Christianity but rather Spinozism which represents the main line in both ancient and Italian early modern philosophy. Gundling appeared also to be endorsing the Socinians', Le Clerc's, and the *esprits forts*' claim that the orthodox Christian churches do not speak for authentic Christianity: for if Gundling diverged widely from Souverain, as well as received opinion, he entirely agreed with him, and with Le Clerc, that the second-century Church Fathers and their successors with their zeal for Platonic conceptions and 'fables' had brought 'much misfortune on Christendom'.[115] Scarcely less disruptive, Ficino and Pico

[110] Gundling, 'De atheismo Platonis', in *Gundlingiana*, v. 239; Gundling, *Vollständige Historie*, iv. 4936.

[111] Bayle, *Continuation*, ii. 509; Mulsow, 'Gundling *versus* Buddeus', 118.

[112] Gundling, *Observationum selectarum ad rem*, i. 64, 67–8; Mulsow, *Moderne*, 301–2.

[113] Mulsow, *Moderne*, 300.

[114] Ibid. 291; Mulsow, 'Gundling *versus* Buddeus', 115–16.

[115] Gundling, *Vollständige Historie*, i. 931–4.

della Mirandola, in Gundling's opinion, had then superadded to this whole new layers of error and confusion.[116]

Gundling regretted his inability to sway Buddeus with regard to Plato, Plotinus, and Renaissance Neoplatonism.[117] What was at stake here was the whole of what remained of the *prisca theologia* tradition and the thesis, vital to the Leibnizians and Wolff as well as Buddeus, for whom, as Le Clerc notes, 'Natural theology' was of great significance,[118] that the unifying element in the history of humanity, and all its civilizations and languages, is Natural Theology. Rather, Buddeus doggedly adhered to his judicious middle position, assigning much of ancient Greek philosophy to the Spinozistic category, but, like Leibniz, viewing Pythagoras and authentic Platonism as well as Plotinus and Ficino as embodying the pristine wisdom of a divine Creator and the essence of Natural Theology, thereby approximating to Christianity.

The only way to sort out such a tangle of fundamental disagreement was for the scholarly community to sharpen their critical tools still further and resolve their differences by means of cogent textual arguments and demonstrations. This was a spur to quoting larger and larger chunks of Greek. Among those who challenged Gundling's interpretation was the great Hamburg philologist Johan Albrecht Fabricius (1668–1736), a scholar who supported Jacques Bernard's efforts to defend the *consensus gentium* argument against Bayle.[119] Fabricius held that Buddeus and Reimmann had greatly exaggerated the number of speculative 'atheists' in the Middle Ages, and in early modern Italy, as well as the Spinozistic tendency in Greek antiquity. Not only Plato and Plotinus, affirmed Fabricius against Bayle and Gundling, but also Xenophanes, and Parmenides had been grotesquely misrepresented and in reality 'stood far from Spinozism'.[120] Meanwhile, Brucker, in one of his early writings, the *Historia philosophica doctrinae de ideis*, published at Augsburg in 1723, strongly supporting Jakob Thomasius' and Buddeus' judgement that Plato was *not* an 'atheist' but conceived rather of an intelligent, free, and providential God like the Christians, held that Platonism also teaches, much like the Stoics, that man's soul is immortal and that souls emanate directly from God.[121] However, while rejecting the Bayle–Gundling thesis, Brucker largely accepted Souverain's and Le Clerc's case that the Church Fathers' efforts to Christianize Plato and Platonize Christianity had introduced severe distortions into Christian doctrine as well as Gundling's harsh judgement of the allegedly confused syncretism of the Renaissance Platonists, especially Ficino.[122] Like Jakob Thomasius and Heumann, Brucker especially stressed the need to define ancient philosophical positions more precisely and clearly distinguish Platonism from Neoplatonism, and both of these from Patristic theology.[123]

116 Gundling, *Vollständige Historie*, i. 936–41.
117 Ibid. i. 934; Kors, *Atheism in France*, 242; Otto, *Studien*, 67.
118 *Bibliothèque choisie*, 7 (1705), 378; Mulsow, *Moderne*, 301.
119 Fabricius, *Delectus argumentorum*, 299–300.
120 Ibid. 300, 306; Häfner, 'Das Erkenntnisproblem', 122–3.
121 Brucker, *Historia philosophica*, 46, 51, 94–8.
122 Hutton, 'Classicism and Baroque', 225–6.
123 Schmidt-Biggemann, 'Platonismus', 203.

None assailed Gundling's reading of ancient and Renaissance *philosophia platonica* with more vigour and persistence than Zimmermann, for whom 'Plato certainly did not confuse God with matter', was not a fatalist, did not assert one substance, and did differentiate God from the cosmos.[124] Where Spinoza holds that all things follow necessarily from God's nature, including the cosmos itself, Plato teaches that God is moved to create matter only out of the goodness of his being.[125] Where Spinoza denies freedom of the will, Plato asserts it. Zimmermann all but accuses Gundling of deliberately distorting Spinoza's ideas on divine Providence and God for the malicious purpose of linking him with Plato directly against the literary evidence.[126] He bitterly reproached Gundling for aiding Bayle and the Socinian Souverain, against orthodox opinion, again linking Gundling's claims about Plato's materialism and atheism with the wider tendency initiated by Bayle to discern monist, quasi-Spinozist impulses in vast tranches of ancient, medieval, and oriental thought. Such sweeping suppositions, resting on dubious scholarship, were bound, he thought, to wreak havoc on all study, faith, and authority.[127]

But if Ficino and Pico were successfully rescued, the arena of Italian Renaisances thought, from the moderate mainstream viewpoint, still looked distinctly bleak. As an intellectual rebel, Bruno, like Pomponazzi and Cardano, grew prodigiously in notoriety after 1700, his posthumous reputation being heavily influenced, once again, by Bayle's intervention. Earlier, Bruno's image in Protestant lands had benefited from the papacy's banning his books and burning him alive in Rome in February 1600. His published writings being all but unobtainable, accurate knowledge of his doctrines scarcely existed, which only encouraged the tendency to view him as a quasi-Protestant executed for denouncing Catholic 'corruption' of religion, as did the Inquisition's secrecy as to the reasons for his trial, which in fact had little to do with magic or hermeticism, as Francis Yates maintained, but mainly concerned his doctrines of the plurality of worlds and eternity and infinity of the cosmos as well as his Copernican heliocentrism, denial of Creation, Christ's divinity, and the immortality of the soul (individual souls for Bruno being 'operations' of the 'universal soul'), and his heretical identification of the Holy Spirit with an eternal world-soul something like the Stoic *anima mundi*.[128]

Bayle's bombshell that Bruno was not a quasi-Protestant heretic victimized by papal tyranny, or a magician, but a philosophical monist, atheistic naturalist, and denier of miracles, demonology, and the immortality of the soul whose 'hypothèse est au fond toute semblable au spinozisme', and that both Bruno and Spinoza 'ne reconnoissent qu'une seule substance', was therefore far closer to the mark than

124 Gundling, *Vollständige Historie*, i. 934; Brucker, *Historia critica philosophiae* (1742), i. 680, 689–90; Otto, *Studien*, 67–8; Zimmermann, *Vindiciae dissertationis*, 413–14.

125 Zimmermann, *Vindiciae dissertationis*, 423; Plato, *Timaeus*, 42–5.

126 Zimmermann, *Vindiciae dissertationis*, 476–81.

127 Ibid. 381–2, 423.

128 Yates, *Giordano Bruno*, 349–55; Ricci, 'Bruno "Spinozista" ', 46; Firpo, *Il processo*, 80–6, 89, 103–4; Finocchiaro, 'Philosophy', 60–1, 78–9.

most historians would have been willing to accept until recently.[129] For Bruno *did* believe that substance is eternal and can neither be created nor destroyed but merely changes its manifestations;[130] and was rightly recognized by Bayle and Toland as a precursor of Spinoza's conception of motion innate in matter.[131] Their reinterpretation of Bruno set off a long and remarkable philosophical-historical controversy which again persisted down to Brucker's day.[132]

Like Bayle, Toland, who spent much time studying the question of Bruno, reworked Bruno's system into what has aptly been called 'a hylozoic natural philosophy devoid of mystical symbolism'.[133] During his visits to Holland and Germany in 1701–2 and 1707–8, he carried around with him, and showed to interlocutors, his own copy of Bruno's then very rare *Spaccio della bestia trionfante* (of which even Bayle had no direct acquaintance),[134] drawing Leibniz, La Croze, and others into intensively debating a figure he helped reconfigure into a pantheist who rejected 'toute religion révélée en général'.[135] His argument was accepted by some, including the Prussian royal librarian La Croze, who reacted to the attempts to rehabilitate Bruno with alarm, believing the consequences could be serious should scholars fail to register the true nature of Bruno's heresies; but there was also much opposition. For many, Bruno continued to be depicted as a heroic proto-Protestant combating Catholic 'superstition' who was tyrannically suppressed by Rome and now was being infamously betrayed by Bayle and Toland. Others, including Leibniz, preferred to defend Bruno in other ways, as a Neoplatonist and hermeticist convinced that the active principle in matter is an all-pervading divine force unifying material reality in a way first grasped by the ancient Egyptians.[136]

The problem of how to categorize Bruno engaged the scholarly world for decades. La Croze, notes Brucker, gathered all the relevant documentation he could find, showing great erudition in correcting mistakes of detail in Bayle's article (which itself introduced much new material), but finally corroborating his, and Toland's, view.[137] Bruno, he declares, in his *Entretiens* of 1711, if certainly 'un génie extraordinaire', was an 'atheist' and systematic naturalist. Bayle had been inexact neither in describing his philosophy nor in claiming Bruno's thought 'ne s'éloignoit pas beaucoup du Spinozisme'.[138] The Leipzig *Acta eruditorum* further

[129] Finocchiaro, 'Philosophy', 61; Mendoza, 'Metempsychosis', 273–4, 278–9, 297; Schettino, 'Necessity', 299–300, 312–13,

[130] Schettino, 'Necessity', 299–300, 312–13, 325; Firpo, *Il processo*, 82, 103.

[131] Jacob, *Radical Enlightenment*, 29–32, Brogi, *Cerchio*, 247–8; Ricuperati, *Nella costellazione*, 127, 171 n.

[132] Ricci, 'Bruno "Spinozista" ', 46–8; Labrousse, *Pierre Bayle*, ii. 199; Giuntini, 'Toland e Bruno', 209–10; Bayle, *Écrits*, 118–19.

[133] Mendoza, 'Metempsychosis', 276–9; Jacob, 'John Toland', 313, 316.

[134] Jacob, 'John Toland', 313–15; Giuntini, 'Toland e Bruno', 204–7, 212; Ricci, 'Bruno "Spinozista" ', 48.

[135] Ricci, 'Bruno "Spinozista" ', 43–6; Champion, *Pillars of Priestcraft*, 150–4; Brown, 'Monadology', 385.

[136] Yates, *Giordano Bruno*, 350; Assmann, *Moses*, 111, 207; Giuntini, 'Toland e Bruno', 201, 212, 220.

[137] Giuntini, 'Toland e Bruno', 204; Brucker, *Historia critica philosophiae* (1742), iv, part 2, 15; Häseler, *Wanderer*, 63.

[138] Brucker, *Historia critica philosophiae* (1742), iv, part 2, 15; Heumann, *Acta philosophorum*, 8 (1717), 385, 397–8; Ricci, 'Bruno "Spinozista" ', 49; Mulsow, *Die drei Ringe*, 68.

publicized La Croze's judgement, categorically condemning Bruno's *pestilentissima principia*.

Heumann, however, persisted in opposing this view. Having gathered several of Bruno's texts, he published his enquiry in four instalments of his *Acta philosophorum*, in the years 1715–18. He granted that Bruno is frequently obscure and held some bizarre tenets, like infinity of the universe, animate life in stones and other inanimate objects, the reality of other inhabited worlds created by God, and his strange idea (preceding La Peyrère) that only the Jews descend from Adam; but he considered him far from being a proto-Spinoza, or deserving inclusion in the rapidly burgeoning *catalogus atheorum*. Rather, Bruno was credulous, a believer in magic which all right-thinking persons should readily forgive, he urged, in that he clearly believed in spirits, demons, and sorcery proving, noted Heumann with approval, that he was not in fact impious. While Bruno's texts do contain phrases construable as equating God and nature in their more poetic passages, Heumann did not think this fault amounted to more than wayward poetic licence.

Suggesting La Croze had been insufficiently 'critical' in assessing key passages, Heumann firmly contradicted his thesis that Bruno held 'Spinozische Principia' or considered 'Deum et Naturam pro synonymis'.[139] On the contrary, he interpreted Bruno as devout if also an 'enthusiast' moved on occasion by poetic transports, someone who left Italy disgusted by the 'false' teaching of the Catholic Church, a Christian martyr who defied papal oppression and bore witness to the truth.[140] This was immediately contested by La Croze and also by Buddeus, in his *Theses theologicae*. Many thinkers of the past, including the Stoics, the latter reminded readers, had conceived 'Deum et mundum esse unum idemque' [God and the world to be one and the same], producing systems in essence Spinozistic, and among these was Bruno.[141] Heumann refused to let it lie, though, and the controversy dragged on inconclusively through the 1720s and 1730s.[142]

Among the later participants in this debate was the Huguenot preacher, bibliophile, biographer, and eventually secretary to Frederick the Great Charles Étienne Jordan (1700–45). A pupil of La Croze (about whom Jordan later wrote and, in 1741, published a biography),[143] Jordan, though born in Berlin, was almost entirely a product of francophone, rather than German, Protestant culture. After an erratic student career in which his fiery temperament caused him to be 'sent down' from Geneva in 1720, for causing a scandal in the city's main church of St Pierre, he had been appointed preacher to the French Reformed congregation at Potzlow, in Brandenburg, where, however, he scarcely bothered to hide his boredom with his flock and took to spending most of his time with his books. A noted bibliophile

139 Mulsow, *Die drei Ringe*, 67; Heumann, *Acta philosophorum*, 8 (1717), 381; Ricci, 'Bruno "Spinozista" ', 51–2.

140 Ricci, 'Bruno "Spinozista" ', 54–5; Heumann, *Acta philosophorum*, 8 (1717), 398–9.

141 Ricci, 'Bruno "Spinozista" ', 53.

142 Ibid. 56–7; Gundling, *Vollständige Historie*, iv. 6064–70; Schröder, *Ursprünge*, 62 n.

143 Goldgar, *Impolite Learning*, 219–20; Mulsow, *Moderne*, 71–2.

and connoisseur of the clandestine philosophical manuscripts, his prospects improved immeasurably with his appointment to the entourage of the crown prince Frederick in 1736.

Jordan's intellectual world was alive with unresolved philosophical antinomies between the religious and irreligious, public and clandestine, naturalist and anti-naturalist.[144] Intervening in the dispute about Giordano Bruno with his *Disquisitio historico-literaria de Giordano Bruno* (1731), after locating some rare texts by the Neapolitan which had eluded even La Croze, Jordan, rather typically, refrained from endorsing either Bayle's thesis that Bruno was a virtual *Spinosiste* and 'atheist', or Heumann's contrary view. He concentrated rather on presenting extracts and reinforcing Bruno's destabilizing significance as a 'philosopher'.[145] It may be true, as has been claimed, that fundamentally Jordan sympathized more with Socinian positions than with the Spinozism of a Stosch or Lau;[146] but it was also characteristic of him to soften and obscure the borderline between materialist and fringe Christian positions, in the process creating a culture of studied ambivalence and ambiguity hovering indeterminately around that border.

The Bruno, Pomponazzi, and Cardano debates thus all ended inconclusively. Yet the enhanced position philosophy had enjoyed since the rise of Cartesianism gave debates of this sort a broad new significance and status in the cultural life of the age. In the introduction to his *Acta philosophorum*, in 1715, Heumann explains why he thought it important students should study this new discipline and why the public should engage with the debates about *historia philosophica* gripping the German universities and which he was helping to publicize in German.[147] There had previously been scant need for the ordinary layman to learn how to distinguish 'good' ideas from 'bad', or 'useful' concepts from 'harmful', he suggested, but this was now no longer so. It had become necessary for a basic knowledge of sound concepts to spread more widely in society to counter the tide of impiety and libertine doctrine sweeping Germany.

More research into ancient, medieval, and Renaissance philosophy, averred Heumann, was a pressing desideratum, Cartesianism being one area requiring further investigation, not least to put readers on their guard against the perils lurking in the writings of numerous little-discussed but pernicious fringe thinkers. The entire inventory of current ideas must be brought out of the closet, dusted down, and exposed to view. With this rationale, Heumann dutifully alerted readers to the 'atheism' of a wide range of often little-known dissidents including Koerbagh, Dirk Sandvoort, and Hendrik Wyermars.[148] Wyermars is a particularly curious instance. For all memory of this already largely forgotten young Spinozist imprisoned in Amsterdam in 1710, most copies of whose impious *Den Ingebeelde Chaos* had been destroyed by the Amsterdam magistrates, would, before long, ironically, have lapsed

144 Häseler, *Wanderer*, 40, 46, 65. 145 Ibid. 63–5. 146 Ibid. 46.

147 Heumann, *Acta philosophorum*, 1 (1715), preface; Piaia, 'Brucker versus Rorty', 74.

148 Heumann, *Acta philosophorum*, 7 (1716), 121, 128 n; Schmidt-Biggemann, 'Bruckers philosophiegeschichteiches Konzept', 119–21; Longo, 'Geistige Anregungen', 162–3.

wholly without trace, had not the zealous Heumann in effect rescued him from oblivion.[149] The public, he thought, had to be warned. This new 'Pseudo-philosophus Wyermars', he records, giving the details of his life,[150] 'out of fear of the authorities, now and then pretends to be refuting Spinoza when, in fact, he only puts forward the latter's doctrines even more plainly [than Spinoza does] or at least differently'.[151] He was 'one of the mangy herd of Spinozists of whom there are rather a lot in Holland, striving to overthrow the *articulos fundamentales* of human wisdom'.[152]

Historia philosophica, held Heumann, summing up the German conservative enlightened eclectic agenda which in substance was that of Buddeus and Brucker too, equips students and the wider public to discern the true character and pedigree of ideas, and their implications, and hence determine whether they are 'good' or 'evil', 'Christian' or 'unChristian', desirable or undesirable, 'corrupt Catholic' or 'upright Protestant'. History of philosophy, he, like they, urged, is a way of defending faith, authority, and tradition critically and reasonably without relying on mere authority, indeed freeing the mind from the shackles of 'authorities' while simultaneously opening the door to genuine philosophizing. For these thinkers believed only the modern Eclectics, sifting the full range of what is available with expertise, discernment, and a Christian conscience, deserved to be called true 'philosophers'. Here was a crucial new ideal in the history of mankind which Heumann deemed part of a wider transformation of modern thought and culture, one which he attributed above all to the younger Thomasius who, in his eyes, had set out to and succeeded in reforming everything in the world of erudition and thought in the right direction—ideas, criticism, history of philosophy, and the education of the general public—and doing so by means of the incomparable new Eclectic method. Christian Thomasius, he proclaimed, was truly the 'Luther' of philosophy.

149 See Israel, *Radical Enlightenment*, 322–7.

150 Heumann, *Acta philosophorum*, 7 (1716), 121–3.

151 Ibid. 119–20.

152 Heumann, 'Nachricht von einem neuen Spinozisten, Henrico Wirmarsio', ibid. 7 (1716), 115–19, 121–44.

19

From 'History of Philosophy' to History of *l'Esprit humain*

1. FONTENELLE, BOULAINVILLIERS, AND 'L'*HISTOIRE DE L'ESPRIT HUMAIN*'

The Thomasian Eclectics explored the vast span of human thought searching for the nuggets from which to construct a coherent, stable, and viable new system of thought. This turned out to be a partly shared and partly contested goal also of the Radical Enlightenment. There was a crucial difference in ultimate aims, of course, in that the Eclectics sought to conjoin philosophy to revelation, ecclesiastical authority, and princely sway, leaving room for miracles and 'mysteries', whereas the 'Spinosistes' wished to order the successive stages of Man's intellectual development in a linear, unified, and self-sufficient fashion wholly dispensing with doctrines of divinely authored Creation, revelation, and redemption and altogether excluding the supernatural. But in terms of methodology, research, and historico-critical criteria the two streams were identical.

The philosophers who developed the revolutionary new idea of 'l'histoire de l'esprit humain' as a unitary process encompassing the whole of the human condition were Bayle, Fontenelle, Boulainvilliers, Fréret, Lévesque de Burigny, Mirabaud, Boureau-Deslandes, d'Argens, and Boulanger, culminating in the young Diderot who during the 1740s and 1750s not only became an experienced encyclopedist but also a key exponent of a monistic hylozoism which he himself recognized as having affinities with ancient Greek materialism as well as to Spinozism. Diderot did not hesitate to call himself an 'eclectic' and, from 1750, uninhibitedly plundered, as well as subtly reworked, Brucker's researches.[1] For him, the key to understanding all thought and feeling was to link it to matter. 'Selon moi', Diderot assured an ally in October 1765, 'la sensibilité, c'est une propriété universelle de la matière.'[2]

Since the late 1740s, this had been his consistent view and, as he well knew, in the climate of the times, amounted to an admission of Spinozism, pitting him against most contemporaries, and the entire legacy of Christian thought. But it also

[1] Dagen, *L'Histoire*, 455–6; Albrecht, *Eklektik*, 562–6; Bonacina, *Filosofia ellenistica*, 69–70.

[2] Mihaila, 'L'*Hylozoïsme* de Diderot', 189.

powerfully linked him, or so he believed, to an ancient tradition stretching back via Lucretius and the Hellenistic age to the Presocratics as well as to strands of ancient Indian and Chinese philosophy.[3] Since fragments of this evolving truth were scattered everywhere and only by means of a careful *critique* could the diverse strands composing it be collated, the new eclecticism became an indispensable tool of an intellectual strategy which aspired to universality but working from a particular philosophical standpoint, albeit eschewing dogmatism and admitting its own shifting, provisional character. This flexibility and desire to remain as inclusive as possible was a distinctive characteristic of Diderot's thought.

Diderot's historical-philosophical eclecticism, then, was certainly nothing new in French culture but rather built on the already extant naturalist philosophical-historical tradition reaching back to Bayle and Fontenelle. While only a few radical thinkers and writers were professional scholars, those who were, like Bayle, Fréret, Lévesque de Burigny, and, in Germany, Gundling and Schmauss,[4] figured prominently among those putting *historia philosophica* to work for philosophical purposes. In one of several essays in history of thought, preparatory to a larger work about Socrates which in the end he never wrote, Fréret, sifting all the surviving ancient reports, found that traditional accounts of the historical Socrates seriously distort our picture, projecting too Platonic an image. This view was later shared by Diderot for whom Socrates was an iconic figure and whose Apology he translated, from Plato's original Greek, while in prison at Vincennes in 1749.[5] For these men, long-sanctioned and received views about great thinkers who were public icons were an obvious target and means of precipitating public controversies employing what—since Bayle's *Dictionnaire*—had become highly fraught, even explosive material.

After Bayle, it was easy to claim that many ancient, medieval, and Renaissance philosophers stood closer to the non-providential Deists, materialists, and Spinozists of the Early Enlightenment than to the great bulk of humanists, theologians, and university professors presiding over early modern European intellectual culture. Such drastic revisionism threatened to turn upside down ideas about not only classical culture but also Chinese, Indian, and Arab philosophy, which were all also relentlessly dragged into the battle along with the string of western medieval and Renaissance thinkers whom Bayle had identified as crypto-atheists and quasi-Spinozists. At the same time, history of philosophy afforded radical *philosophes* ample opportunity to highlight the forgeries and distortions which, according to them, had been contrived by the Church Fathers, and later theologians, to mislead, manacle, and exploit the rest of humanity.

The most decisive move, though, in the Radical Enlightenment's deployment of *historia philosophica* was to merge it fully into the new concept of *histoire de l'esprit humain*, a term coined and introduced by Fontenelle in the wake of his *Histoire des fables*, a short treatise written, it is thought, between 1691 and 1699, though not

[3] Ibid. 191–3. [4] Mulsow, 'Gundling *versus* Buddeus', 118; Mulsow, *Moderne*, 296–7.

[5] Diderot, *Œuvres complètes*, xiv. 810–26; Casini, 'Diderot et les philosophes', 36–7; Buck, 'Diderot', 135, 139.

published until 1714 and even then not widely propagated until republished in 1724.[6] Despite its brevity it was a text brimming over with novel ideas with unusually wide-ranging implications. A naturalist to the core, Fontenelle, for whom the only true 'marvel' is the progress of science,[7] here attempted to provide a psychological account, in terms of primitive Man's wonder, musings, fears, and ignorance, of how mythological thinking originally emerged and how primitive mythology sets down deep roots in the human psyche, forging beliefs of exceptional power, durability, and capacity to shape the subsequent history of religion which, however, are fundamentally erroneous and misconceived.[8]

In this way, Fontenelle turned the history of myth and fable which, he suggests, subsequently evolve, among most peoples, into 'religion', into what he dubs 'l'histoire des erreurs de l'esprit humain', even though, in his *Histoire des fables*, he makes no reference beyond subtle insinuation to Spinoza's thesis about the origins of organized religion and does not expressly incorporate religion and theology, as distinct from fables and ancient mythologies, in his schema.[9] His essay, in short, was an attempt at a scientific explanation as to how 'error' became so powerfully entrenched in the human mind, coming to dominate all societies, unmistakably implying also, as Fontenelle did again in another text published under a pseudonym in 1695, on the diversity of religions, that all the world's religions were concocted by humans.[10]

He describes a process of auto-mystification reaching back to the earliest experiences of men but does not go on to argue that studying its vestiges should be part of the task of critical historical research in the same way that the queries about nature are part of scientific research. A notable feature of Fontenelle's approach was his idea that all men, wherever they are in the world, closely resemble each other; and that it is precisely what they have in common, rather than their differences, that most requires elucidation: in their primitive stages all peoples have developed in the same way, passing through the same levels, as it were, of exploration, awareness and knowledge.[11] Hence, the Greeks, he says, for all their genius, when still a primitive people did not think 'plus raisonnablement que les barbares d'Amérique', a perception which led him to conjecture that in other circumstances, had the Spanish *conquista* not occurred, the American Indians might eventually have learnt to think 'aussi finement que les Grecs'.[12]

But why do all peoples remain for millennia steeped in 'fables', or false religions, which bear scant relation to truth?[13]As civilization slowly advanced, a profound change occurred in human awareness albeit only little by little. As ignorance receded, men witnessed fewer and fewer 'wonders' and 'prodigies', accounts and

[6] Funke, *Studien zur Reiseutopie*, i. 322; Mothu, 'Un morceau', 37.
[7] Hazard, *European Mind*, 70, 158–9; Ehrard, *L'Idée*, 263–4.
[8] Fontenelle, *De l'origine des fables*, 34.
[9] Ibid. 39; Mothu, 'Un morceau', 37.
[10] Fontenelle, 'De la diversité', 87, 93–4; Hourcade, 'Jet de plume ou projet', 19–20.
[11] Fontenelle, *De l'origine des fables*, 40; Baridon, 'Concepts', 361; Poulouin, *Temps des origines*, 353–4.
[12] Poulouin, *Temps des origines*, 353; Hourcade, 'Jet de plume ou projet', 20–1; Poulouin, 'Fontenelle', 39.
[13] Fontenelle, 'De la diversité', 96; Niderst, 'Fontenelle', 162.

explanations became less fabulous, fewer and fewer false systems were fabricated.[14] Humanity had thus experienced a long infancy, youth, and maturity but apparently no decline or old age. Fontenelle took the view that men broadly undergo a single, linear progress in their awareness,[15] punctuated by difficulties and setbacks; but without, in Fontenelle's relatively optimistic vision, any degeneration or catastrophes so severe as to prevent subsequent generations building on the discoveries and knowledge of their predecessors.

Men, however, experience great difficulty in discarding false systems of doctrine embraced at earlier stages, as he had stressed also in his *Histoire des oracles* (1687), and progress is achieved only very hesitantly.[16] In this way, Fontenelle introduced a conception of human history and history-writing which itself becomes part of an ongoing cultural struggle encompassing the whole of humanity, one which assigns no space for the feats of kings, princes, and aristocrats, or wars and diplomatic treaties. For if these were the topics which had always preoccupied conventional history-writing, they had no place in the new history of 'l'esprit humain'. Further demystification, in the modern age, will inevitably be a complex and arduous therapeutic process requiring erudition, skill, and a balanced 'philosophical' conception of reality, commodities in very short supply; moreover, before the process can go further, a wholly new conception of history and history-writing has to replace prevailing notions about what history is which, in Fontenelle's opinion, merely fortify the errors, myths, and superstition rampant in the world.

The real mechanics of history, the process of natural cause and effect which explains the rise and fall of myths, religions, systems of thought, and styles of conduct, taste, and morals, thus remain mostly hidden from men and can be penetrated only by a process of 'philosophical' understanding.[17] With this new conception of history, polemical and ultimately optimistic but hardly erudite, Fontenelle bequeathed to the radical *philosophes* a potent instrument for linking together their various campaigns against hierarchy, tradition, superstition, and ecclesiastical sway, and in favour of reason and science, into a coherent whole.[18] The concept forged by Fontenelle was then reworked and lent added depth by Boulainvilliers, who shared many of the same insights but was more of a real historian. The full consequences of Fontenelle's and Boulainvilliers's identification of history of philosophy and science with the universal history of Man, explaining revealed religion, following Spinoza, as the outcome of men's primitive anxieties, took time to seep through but slowly matured through the first half of the eighteenth century.

The contribution of Boulainvilliers and, after him, Fréret and Lenglet Dufresnoy involved working through, in broad historical context, the implications of his own conversion to Spinozism in the years around 1700. Inconceivable without Spinoza's

14 Fontenelle, *De l'origine des fables*, 37; Poulouin, 'Fontenelle', 40–1.
15 Hourcade, 'Jet de plume ou projet', 25; Ehrard, *L'Idée*, 757.
16 Ehrard, *L'Idée*, 759–60; Poulouin, 'Fontenelle', 41.
17 Hourcade, 'Jet de plume ou projet', 26, 28; Poulouin, *Temps des origines*, 199.
18 Hazard, *European Mind*, 158–9; Mazauric, 'Fontenelle', 96.

conflation of the sacred and natural by means of a monistic, one-substance doctrine, Boulainvilliers merged sacred history seamlessly into secular history, proclaiming the outcome 'histoire universelle'. In his *Abrégé de l'histoire universelle*, a text completed around 1705, and one that, though never published, had a considerable diffusion in France as a clandestine manuscript,[19] all opinions that any men have ever had about God, the gods, demons, and angels, as well as the myths, visions, and revelations that broadcast them, are transformed by Boulainvilliers into what he called, borrowing a phrase from a grammarian, *omnium philosophiae disciplinarum parentes*—'les pères de toute philosophie'.[20]

The cursory nature of Fontenelle's treatment, and his air of 'Cartesian' disdain for history as a field of endeavour, could easily discourage deeper study. Fontenelle cared little for historical-critical erudition as such. Yet his idea that myth, fable, and—at least by implication—religious doctrines reflect in complex ways, and directly arise from, collective early experiences and important events in fact stimulated new forms of erudition, as the subsequent endeavours of Fréret, Lévesque de Burigny, Boureau-Deslandes, Boulanger, and Diderot demonstrate.[21] For whilst such a 'philosophical' study remained lacking, it was impossible to uncover the exact process by which superstition and error came to dominate the outlook, education, and attitudes of all human societies and, consequently, impossible also to dismantle the fortified edifices of error which block human progress. Worried onlookers were assured, for example, by Lenglet Dufresnoy—a writer who plagiarized extensively from Boulainvilliers, in his *Méthode pour étudier l'histoire* (4 vols., Paris, 1729)—that 'on n'attaque point la puissance de Dieu', in rejecting the events and marvels 'dont la vérité n'est pas certaine' and that sound history, unlike most historical writing, must be 'philosophical' history and cannot dispense with the most stringent critical criteria.[22]

Fontenelle's and Boulainvilliers's approach imparted a new unity and universality to human history but one which would, at the same time, serve to integrate and justify specialized study of many hitherto ignored, or forgotten, areas of ancient, eastern, and other remote history. When first introducing the phrase 'histoire de l'esprit humain' to describe the overall process, in 1707, Fontenelle commented that the history 'des progrès de l'esprit humain' was one of the most rewarding forms of history 'et sans doute la plus philosophique'.[23] Religious history and classical mythology were in this way brought into conjunction and inseparably linked to history of philosophy, in a dialectical interdependence. Fontenelle and Boulainvilliers had abolished *a priori* the miraculous, inexplicable, and supernatural from the real processes of historical cause and effect, replacing them with a mixture of psychology, worldly circumstances, and geographical context with which Boulainvilliers in

[19] Sheridan, *Nicolas Lenglet Dufresnoy*, 99; Israel, *Radical Enlightenment*, 690; Brogi, *Cerchio*, 28.

[20] Brogi, *Cerchio*, 107.

[21] Poulouin, *Temps des origines*, 358, 365; Poulouin, 'Fontenelle', 42–4, 46; Cristani, 'Tradizione biblica', 118.

[22] Lenglet Dufresnoy, *Méthode*, ii. 159; Sheridan, *Nicolas Lenglet Dufresnoy*, 99–100.

[23] Dagen, *L'Histoire*, 18; Mazauric, 'Fontenelle', 92.

particular pointed forward to Montesquieu.[24] They applied to universal history Spinoza's doctrine of the impossibility of any supernatural causes, magical power, or knowledge, prophecy being explained by Boulainvilliers, as by Spinoza, as 'imagining' inspired by glimmerings of intuited truth, albeit Muhammad is depicted by him far more positively than Moses.[25] All of human history, therefore, forms a single continuum governed by a single set of rules. There was never any idyllic 'golden age' at the dawn of humanity.[26]

In short, for Fontenelle and Boulainvilliers there is not, and cannot be, any form of mythology or religious development not integrally part of history of philosophy conceived as *histoire de l'esprit humain*, that is a process determined exclusively by natural causes in which all supernatural agency is purely imagined. Religion nevertheless remains, in Boulainvilliers's schema, vital to society but now exclusively in the Spinozistic sense of affording the social basis for discipline, morality, law, and obedience. 'Les utilités de la religion', says Boulainvilliers at one point, 'surpassent celles de toutes les autres découvertes humaines.'[27] According to Boulainvilliers's *Abrégé* and brief *Histoire de la religion et de la philosophie ancienne*, philosophy can never dispense with religion; yet, only 'philosophy' in its new critical-historical format can discern 'le faux ou le vrai, aussi bien dans le sens dogmatique que dans le moral'.[28] It is not the dogmas or doctrines, or even the moral principles, of religions that matter, or that men need, at any rate where religions are considered from a strictly philosophical standpoint, but only their effects on men's conduct and especially their power to curb murder, rapine, and pillage.[29] This prompted Boulainvilliers to make the startlingly dissident and Spinozistic remark that among religions 'la plus vraie est la plus propre à rectifier les mœurs'.[30]

Fontenelle's and Boulainvilliers's elimination of the miraculous from history and conflation of sacred and secular history produced a new linear vision of the human past in which the overall trend is cumulative and basically positive. In this they were followed by Fréret who carried over their firmly anti-theological approach, and concern to show the reality underlying myths and fables, into his own conception of history.[31] Both this linearity, and tendency to view the whole of human history as a unitary process, as well as the departure from traditional idealizations of original man, and of golden ages, culminated in the discussions and theories of the 1740s and early 1750s, initiated among others by the young engineer Nicolas-Antoine Boulanger (1722–59) and by the young Christian *philosophe* Turgot. Turgot partly accepted Fontenelle's idea of 'histoire de l'esprit humain' and Boulainvilliers's 'histoire universelle', and frequently employs both these terms in his philosophical

[24] Mazauric, *Fontenelle*, 46; Ehrard, *L'Idée*, 695; Venturino, *Ragioni*, 83, 87–8; Poulouin, *Temps des origines*, 517–18.

[25] Wade, *Clandestine Organization*, 109; Brogi, *Cerchio*, 39, 43, 46–7, 113, 119.

[26] Brogi, *Cerchio*, 499–500; Ehrard, *L'Idée*, 524 n.

[27] Boulainvilliers, *Œuvres philosophiques*, i. 313.

[28] Ibid.

[29] Ibid. 308, 312; Venturino, *Ragioni*, 148–50.

[30] Boulainvilliers, *Œuvres philosophiques*, i. 313.

[31] Furet and Ozouf, 'Deux légitimations', 238; Grell, 'Nicolas Fréret', 59–60; Poulouin, *Temps des origines*, 497–8, 517.

writings (nearly all written in the years 1746–51). But while he agreed with Fontenelle and Boulainvilliers that human progress has been a halting, wavering, and precarious thing, and is a single process, he importantly both qualified and opposed their picture in two ways: first, by claiming the evidence of history shows the hand of divine providence at every step, supernatural intervention being much more real in Turgot's account than in Vico, and, secondly, by insisting on the need to examine 'les progrès de l'esprit humain dans toutes ses révolutions' and especially what he considered the greatest of all moral, social, and legal 'revolutions'—the rise of Christianity.[32]

Boulanger, very different from Turgot, being a thoroughgoing materialist, wrote a text, the *Anecdotes de nature*, penned probably between 1749 and 1753, which remained unpublished but circulated in manuscript particularly among his 'naturalist' friends and sought to explain the earliest traditions and myths of men. He focused particularly on the biblical account of the Flood, emphasizing the collective trauma and the submerged but terrified memory of vast natural catastrophes wreaking havoc with human life, activities, and villages, long pervading Man's consciousness.[33] A veritable obsession, the Flood, to his mind, was not just a terribly real, actual event but a 'terreur universelle' which had everywhere wrought immense damage and left a long legacy of fear, forming the basis for the rise of organized religions.

Noted for his knowledge of fossils and geology, contributor of several articles to the *Encyclopédie*, and someone described in a Paris police report as closely linked to 'Messieurs Diderot, d'Alembert et Helvétius', Boulanger showed no desire to soften the anti-theological tilt introduced into the discussion of primitive 'fables' by Fontenelle, Boulainvilliers, and Fréret; quite the contrary. Described by one contemporary as 'un des plus grands ennemis du christianisme',[34] Boulanger sought systematically to explain the prolonged grip of myth and theocracy in Man's history in terms of general apprehension and feelings of terror. This schema enabled him to draw a clear line—rather importantly in the development of French Enlightenment republicanism—between, on the one hand, ancient republics which he granted were chronically volatile and unstable but owed their instability, he contended, to being theocratic in character, and the modern republic, based on reason, equity, and toleration, which is not based on fear and religious cults, and therefore not unstable, on the other.[35]

By the early 1750s, Boulanger had developed a kind of premonition of the coming struggle between *ancien régime* society (allied to kingship and religion), on the one hand, and philosophy, or what he called 'l'esprit général', for the leadership of humanity and cultural hegemony. What was particularly revolutionary in his

[32] Turgot, *Plan de deux discours*, 276–7, 298; Dagen, *L'Histoire*, 415, 434, 438.

[33] Cristani, 'Tradizione biblica', 95–6, 98–9; Belgrado, 'Sulla "filosofia della storia"', 63; Roger, *Buffon*, 419; Poulouin, *Temps des origines*, 393.

[34] Bianchi, 'Impostura', 263 n; Hampton, *Nicolas-Antoine Boulanger*, 44.

[35] Hampton, *Nicolas-Antoine Boulanger*, 139–40; Venturi, *L'antichità svelata*, 44–7.

thought was his fervent commitment to the idea of the basic unity of all mankind and the idea that the same syndrome of fear and psychological injury lay at the root of all 'les erreurs capitales' which block the emancipation of men and bolster the various types of political despotism which disfigure the face of humanity. For these, he thought, like the world's religions with which they are intimately associated, are closely tied to this all-pervasive tissue of delusion.[36] Scorning Rousseau's idealization of primitive man, and still more his defection from the *parti philosophique*, Boulanger ardently looked forward to what he called 'le triomphe de la philosophie'.[37]

Diderot's contribution was to make use of the work of the German Eclectic historians of philosophy, especially Brucker, to effect a more comprehensive and genuine fusion than his predecessors had attempted between history of philosophy and *histoire de l'esprit humain*. Such a procedure was unthinkable for the Thomasians for whom history of philosophy remained only part of the moral, intellectual, and spiritual history of Man, the rest being the domain of theology and salvation. In Diderot's hands, the new 'critical' history of philosophy became quintessentially an instrument of the Radical Enlightenment, being merged with Fontenelle's and Boulainvilliers's history of the human mind, that is the general progress of reason and Man's slow emancipation from myth, theocracy, superstition, despotism, and ignorance. At the same time, for the radical *philosophes* no less than the German Eclectics, *historia philosophica* became a primary tool for carrying out the tasks of philosophy itself and also a key polemical weapon to be wielded against rival systems of thought which, for the radicals, meant the mainstream currents of the day.

Besides Brucker, Bayle, Fontenelle, and Boulainvilliers, Diderot used the work of André-François Boureau-Deslandes (1690–1757), a radical materialist and Spinozist, who had been a particular friend of Fontenelle from before 1713 and had absorbed his particular conception of *histoire de l'esprit humain*.[38] Author of the first full-scale history of philosophy in French, significantly entitled *Histoire critique de la philosophie* (3 vols., Amsterdam, 1737), this was a work which preceded Brucker's *magnum opus* by several years, and though far less learned, and often superficial, nevertheless represents an important step in the advance of 'philosophical' thinking about history and history of thought. Published in France without a royal licence, clandestinely, it was subsequently reissued in 1742 and 1756; a German translation appeared at Leipzig in 1770. Applauded by d'Argens who at once recognized in Boureau-Deslandes an ally, it was a work fiercely decried by churchmen.[39]

Drawing on Bayle, Boulainvilliers, Fontenelle, and Lévesque, Boureau-Deslandes clearly grasped what the task of a fundamentally new 'critical history of philosophy',

[36] [Boulanger], *Recherches*, 54, 74–5, 108; Dagen, *L'Histoire*, 449–51; Belgrado, 'Sulla "filosofia della storia" ', 61.

[37] [Boulanger], *Recherches*, p. vi; Hampton, *Nicolas-Antoine Boulanger*, 114.

[38] Geissler, *Boureau-Deslandes*, 11–12; Piaia, 'Bruckers Wirkungsgeschichte', 227–8; Geissler, 'Boureau-Deslandes, historien', 137.

[39] Geissler, 'Boureau-Deslandes, historien', 148; Gueroult, *Histoire*, 301; Deneys-Tunney, 'Roman de la matière', 94.

such as he envisaged, would involve.[40] His three guiding rules were the need always to respect historical context so as to avoid incongruously mixing ancient, medieval, and modern philosophical systems; rigorously to eschew details and literary discussion which does not help clarify the basic character of philosophical systems; and, thirdly, the requirement to assess philosophies not in the light of what is currently known but rather what was known when they were articulated.[41] His approach embodies that total separation of reason and faith, and history from theology, in fact a systematic secularization of human history, which was the hallmark of radical 'history of philosophy'.[42]

Like Fontenelle, Boureau-Deslandes believed the philosophies of the past have a particular relationship to the existing state of knowledge, and wider cultural context, and that, as science and knowledge progress, philosophy reflects this general evolution so that, when studied correctly, history of philosophy uncovers the development, and real nature of Man and his mind, experience, and knowledge.[43] From this point on, it remained a guiding conception of the French Enlightenment, later central also to Condorcet's 'progrès de l'esprit humain', that the history of the human spirit must be simultaneously an intellectual and practical evolution, a refining of the physical context of human life and of Man's mind.[44] Condorcet sought to show how the development of agriculture, industry, commerce, and the arts leads of itself to the maturing of human reason which, in turn, enables philosophy to evolve in stages, first challenging, then wearing down, and finally overwhelming authority, tradition, and credulity to revolutionize by means of philosophical 'reason' the whole of human society on the basis of liberty, toleration, equality, and a fully secular conception of the cosmos and humanity.[45]

2. DIDEROT AND THE HISTORY OF HUMAN THOUGHT

Bayle, Fontenelle, Boulainvilliers, Fréret, and Boureau-Deslandes thus initiated a process which culminated in Diderot's articles on history of philosophy in the *Encyclopédie*, articles which, with the help of Brucker's volumes (which he is known to have borrowed from the Bibliothèque du Roi, in Paris, in November 1750), as well as Fréret, Boulanger, Boureau-Deslandes, and other recent contributors, were mostly sketched out in the early 1750s.[46]

Profoundly influenced by both Bayle and Fontenelle, Diderot saw these articles as part of his publicizing and didactic activity so that it would be wrong to expect

[40] Deneys-Tunney, 'Roman de la matière', 137; Albrecht, *Eklektik*, 552; Kelley, *Descent of Ideas*, 80, 102, 143.

[41] Gueroult, *Histoire*, 303; Geissler, *Boureau-Deslandes*, 44–8.

[42] Geissler, 'Boureau-Deslandes, historien', 138–40, 144.

[43] Ibid. 136–7; Gueroult, *Histoire*, 304–6.

[44] Geissler, 'Boureau-Deslandes, historien', 145–6.

[45] Condorcet, *Esquisse*, 1–2, 208–9, 212; Williams, *Condorcet*, 92–3.

[46] Vernière, *Spinoza*, 587; Bonacina, *Filosofia ellenistica*, 108–10; Proust, *Diderot*, 247.

from them the same level of scholarly rigour as one finds in Buddeus or Brucker.[47] His main concern in these pieces is subtly to render the Spinozistic premisses underpinning his radical 'naturalism' and concept of 'history of the human mind' unobtrusively yet transparently obvious. Thus, he explains the term *Naturaliste* as meaning someone who (like himself) believes the whole of reality consists solely of 'une substance matérielle, revêtue de diverses qualités' and hence that 'tout s'exécute nécessairement dans la Nature comme nous voyons'; the term 'naturaliste', he adds, is 'synonyme à athée, Spinoziste, matérialiste, etc.'[48] While often merely employing these articles as a propaganda tool to smuggle in interpretations and arguments supporting his own naturalist neo-Spinozist philosophy,[49] they are at the same time also more than mere propaganda, being intended to provide a reliable scholarly grounding and contribute to a deeply serious philosophical undertaking, as well as reflect a deeply felt fascination with Greek antiquity.

Diderot judged eclecticism the best method to practise philosophy and most natural way of coaxing human reason, and hopefully men collectively eventually, towards the neo-Spinozism he advocates. But he does not simply borrow the erudite findings of Thomasius, Bayle, Gundling, Heumann, and Brucker, all of whom he praises. For where Heumann and Brucker urge the eclectic historian of philosophy to purge all prior respect for academic authorities, antiquity, tradition, and convention from his mind when assessing ideas and evidence, they would never have gone so far as Diderot who exhorts his eclectic researcher to eschew 'le préjugé, la tradition, l'ancienneté, le consentement universel, l'autorité, en un mot, tout ce qui subjugue la foule des esprits', summoning every aspiring scholar to think only independently and admit nothing 'que sur le témoignage de son expérience et de sa raison'.[50] Hence, Diderot's radical eclecticism is an uncompromising absolute, totally excluding *all* authority, including—indeed especially—theological and ecclesiastical authority. Consequently, despite his extensive borrowing from Brucker, his historical eclecticism ultimately turns out to differ markedly from the German variety.

Diderot distinguishes between *l'éclectisme expérimental*, the sphere of pedestrian minds, but necessary for the progress of *l'esprit humain* which, however, is in itself inadequate, and *l'éclectisme systématique*, the sphere of *hommes de génie*, inspiration which, however exalted, is again insufficient on its own. A third necessary function is the ability to combine the two, a classifying capacity which, he thinks, only very few philosophers, such as Democritus, Aristotle, and Bacon, have possessed.[51] Like Buddeus and Brucker (but unlike Boureau-Deslandes), Diderot utterly disdains the ancient eclecticism of Potamo and his Alexandrian school who, he thinks, were uncritical, incoherent, and ridiculously addicted to mystification and

[47] Proust, *Diderot*, 265.
[48] Diderot, *Œuvres complètes*, xiv. 547.
[49] Proust, *Diderot*, 265, 289–90; Quintili, *Pensée critique*, 189–90.
[50] Diderot, *Œuvres complètes*, xiv. 94, art. 'Éclectisme'; Casini, 'Diderot et les philosophes', 34; Albrecht, *Eklektik*, 562.
[51] Albrecht, *Eklektik*, 565; Diderot, *Œuvres complètes*, xiv. 142.

shallow syncretism.[52] Authentic 'critical' eclecticism such as he advocated was a very different thing, insists Diderot, from all types of superficial syncretism.[53]

In seeing his radical eclecticism as applying to our interpretation of the whole of reality, he believed he shared the real outlook 'des bons esprits depuis la naissance du monde'.[54] Unlike his German counterparts but like d'Argens, he conceives modern eclecticism as having its true ancient counterpart not in Potamo but in a tradition of philosophizing caught up in ceaseless strife with the proponents of the kind of syncretism he dismisses as 'platonico-péripatético-stoïcien', that is the ancient precursors of the modern moderate Christian Enlightenment, the men who mix philosophy with theology like Christian Thomasius, Buddeus, Heumann, and Brucker. Where for the Thomasians, ancient eclecticism attained its zenith in the broad movement for reconciling Christianity with Greek philosophy, Diderot reverses this, stressing what he calls the almost general aversion 'des philosophes éclectiques pour le christianisme' and their, to his mind, heroic efforts to withstand the popular tide.[55]

The most capable eclectics of antiquity, philosophers often developing the thought of Plato in a particular direction, Diderot adumbrates as Plotinus, likewise identified by Bayle and Gundling as a proto-Spinozist whom Diderot promotes to major status,[56] and his student Porphyry (AD 232–305), 'cet ennemi si fameux du nom chrétien', despite the latter's defence of the oracles and traditional pagan religious cults;[57] further, he lists Julian the Apostate (emperor 360–3), Maximus of Ephesus, Proclus (*c.*410–85), and (in a passage revealing distinct traces of Toland's wording) that extravagantly praised heroine Hypatia (AD *c.*370–415), a fourth-century female pagan philosopher and disciple of Plotinus, extolled by the radical stream ever since Toland recounted her assassination by an enraged mob of followers of St Cyril of Alexandria.[58] It was impossible not to notice that the list of pre-eminent ancient eclectics offered by the director of the *Encyclopédie* included not a single Jewish or Christian writer.

Diderot also eulogizes numerous earlier Greek thinkers, notably Xenophanes, Democritus, Heraclitus, Anaximander, Anaxagoras, Parmenides, Leucippus, and Epicurus, and generally the Stoics who, for him, are true materialists and *fatalistes*. These were all men who 'avant Spinosa', as Lévesque put it, taught 'l'erreur qu'il a renouvelé'.[59] D'Argens held that it was especially Democritus, Epicurus, and Empedocles who had pioneered the monist and naturalist systems culminating in

[52] Donini, 'History', 21; Kelley, *Descent of Ideas*, 143; Albrecht, *Eklektik*, 565.

[53] Albrecht, *Eklektik*, 563–4; Diderot, *Œuvres complètes*, xiv. 96, 141; Bonacina, *Filosofia ellenistica*, 61–2, 70.

[54] Bonacina, *Filosofia ellenistica*, 108; Diderot, *Œuvres complètes*, xiv. 97; Dagen, *L'Histoire*, 456.

[55] Diderot, *Œuvres complètes*, xiv. 117.

[56] Ibid. xiv. 147–8.

[57] Ibid.; Frede, 'Monotheism', 66–7.

[58] Diderot, *Œuvres complètes*, xiv. 135–8; Dagen, *L'Histoire*, 455–6; Albrecht, *Eklektik*, 45; Kelley, *Descent of Ideas*, 40.

[59] Lévesque de Burigny, *Théologie payenne*, i. 81; Dagen, *L'Histoire*, 454; Duflo, *Diderot philosophe*, 196, 412.

modern Spinozism, on the one hand, and the occult categories of the Aristotelians which had been revived and given new terminology 'par les Newtoniens', on the other.[60] In much the same spirit, the baron d'Holbach, later expressly setting himself against the Cartesians, Lockeans, Newtonians, and Voltaireans, claimed both ancient and modern antecedents, above all Strato, Democritus, Diagoras, Hobbes, Spinoza, and Bayle.[61] When Diderot notes parallels between ancient philosophers he thinks important and key moderns, the affinities he highlights are mostly, as with Bayle, parallels with Spinoza, though in the case of Parmenides his parallel is with Leibniz.[62] Locke, though not entirely ignored, receives only a relatively short and unenthusiastic entry in the *Encyclopédie* and, generally, in Diderot, as previously in Bayle—in sharp contrast to Voltaire—is never accorded an important place in the history of *l'esprit humain*.[63]

While the 'philosophical' history of all the peoples cited by Diderot in the *Encyclopédie*—the Chaldaeans, Chinese, Egyptians, Ethiopians, Greeks, Indians, Japanese, Jews, Malabars, Persians, Phoenicians, Romans, 'Saracens', and Scythians—is represented as a curious mix of religion, superstition, mystification, and philosophy, history of philosophy and of *l'esprit humain* are placed by Diderot in absolute conjunction to form a single continuum. The result is a panoramic vision of a long process of error, mystique, and confusion gradually receding before the onset of rational thought. Philosophy becomes the chief tool with which the emancipation of men from fables, doctrines, and apprehensions which are damaging, oppressive, useless, or degrading, that is notions engendered by mythology, superstition, magic, and theology, is achieved.[64] However inhibited, the impulse towards reason is always there, from the most primitive beginnings onwards, so that, for Diderot, as for Fontenelle, Boulainvilliers, and Boulanger, there is never a time when the history of philosophy is not the same thing as the history of human consciousness itself.

The history of all peoples, for Diderot, is always history of philosophy integrated with history of 'l'esprit humain'. Hence an age steeped in mythology prior to the rise of formal philosophy, like that of the archaic Greeks before Thales, Diderot calls that of 'la philosophie fabuleuse des Grecs'.[65] His entry on the Ethiopians is subtitled 'philosophie des', that on the Indians 'philosophie de', that on the Persians 'philosophie des' and even that on the 'Scythes, Thraces, et Gètes' is 'philosophie de'.[66] He even goes so far as to subtitle his article 'Antédiluvienne', a piece drawn from Brucker but inspired by Fontenelle and Boulanger, 'ou état de la philosophie avant le Déluge'.[67] Hence, Diderot while dismissing the search for the origins of formal philosophy before the Flood, or in the time of Noah, in the manner of Hornius,

60 [D'Argens], *Songes philosophiques*, 185.
61 Dagen, *L'Histoire*, 503.
62 Ibid. 454; Diderot, *Œuvres complètes*, xiv. 194–5, 547, 556, 560.
63 Diderot, *Œuvres complètes*, xiv. 500–7, art. 'Locke'; Dedeyan, *Diderot*, 277–88.
64 Dagen, *L'Histoire*, 452–3.
65 Diderot, *Œuvres complètes*, xiv. 240.
66 Ibid. xiv. 231, 318, 589, 806, 940.
67 Ibid. xiv. 2, art. 'Antédiluvienne'; Proust, *Diderot*, 548; Jehl, 'Brucker', 250–1.

as ridiculous, nevertheless fuses history of philosophy with history of 'l'esprit humain' even in the context of primitive and inarticulate Man.

According to Diderot 'l'esprit humain' has its infancy and maturity, which means vast tracts of Man's experience on earth have been devoted to acquiring kinds of knowledge which will always remain wholly prior to the study of philosophy as such.[68] In primitive and archaic periods magic and theology predominate. But as primitive Man develops, literature, knowledge of languages, the arts, and antiquities advance, preparing the ground for a more conscious, rational evaluation and classification of everything, that is for the rise of philosophy. Eventually, philosophy emerges and, as Diderot sees it, begins to challenge theology's hegemony. 'Car c'est une observation générale', he remarked, in a sentence of his article on the Saracens which the censors excised from the *Encyclopédie*, that religion 's'avilit à mesure que la philosophie s'accroît' [shrinks (in importance) as philosophy grows].[69]

Where mythology and theology create a wide divergence of human contexts, cultural, political, and moral, the progress of philosophy, or what, for Diderot, is the same thing, the progress of *l'esprit humain*, inevitably has the opposite effect—since truth is one and universal—and increasingly brings out the underlying unity of Man. Accordingly, as they become more rational societies also become more alike, if not aesthetically, or the outer packaging of culture, then certainly as regards fundamentals. Referring to the high moral principles of the Zoroastrians, Diderot claims there is nothing here which is not 'conforme au sentiment de tous les peuples' or which inheres more to Zoroaster's teaching than to that of any other philosopher.[70] Since love of truth is the impulse of all philosophies, and advancement of virtue the goal of all legislative systems, 'qu'importe', he asks, 'par quelles principes on y soit conduit?'[71] This underlying unity and convergence which increasingly characterizes 'l'histoire de l'esprit humain' connects with Diderot's idea that morality is vital to men but also natural, something learnt by stages from nature, something originating in human reason itself and anchored in the general will: 'l'utilité générale et le consentement commun' should be the two great rules governing our actions.[72]

While *l'histoire de l'esprit humain*, in Diderot's sense, is certainly a form of progress, intellectual but also political, moral, and social, it is driven neither by any supernatural agency nor by some Hegelian inner spirit which transcends society itself, nor like Turgot's by religious ideals.[73] While everything that happens is a necessary consequence, there is nothing necessary about the progression towards a more rational state of mind and affairs as such. Indeed, it is by no means only ignorance, the immaturity of societies, and barbarian invasions which for long

[68] Diderot, *Œuvres complètes*, xiv. 143.

[69] Ibid. xiv. 948–9; Gordon and Torrey, *Censoring*, 55, 79; Proust, *Diderot*, 276, 278, 554.

[70] Proust, *Diderot*, 278; Diderot, *Œuvres completes*, xiv. 948.

[71] Diderot, *Œuvres complètes*, xiv. 604.

[72] Ibid. xiv. 225, art. 'Epicuréisme'; Spallanzani, *Immagini*, 47; Duflo, *Diderot philosophe*, 412–16.

[73] Dagen, *L'Histoire*, 452–3, 461; Poulouin, *Temps des origines*, 545.

periods thwart and reverse the advance of *l'esprit philosophique* but also catastrophes and especially periodic relapses into fanaticism caused by 'les disputes de religion', 'l'intolérance de la superstition', and the sort of mystical 'philosophie pythagoréo-platonico-cabalistique', as he sarcastically calls it, which corrupts and undermines all sound reasoning. Throughout the history of *l'esprit humain*, says Diderot, there have been huge setbacks, sometimes terrible and sometimes merely obfuscating, as in the late seventeenth century when such 'théosophes' and 'syncrétistes' as Francis Mercurius van Helmont and Pierre Poiret perverted theology, blighted philosophy, and generally clouded the human mind.[74]

Having approached maturity, humanity will hopefully continue to progress, and not fall back into 'son déclin, sa vieillesse et sa caducité'. But Diderot is by no means certain that it will progress.[75] Experience shows how readily everything can deteriorate. The greatest interruption in the progress of mankind, he thought, was the suppression of philosophy, by theology, at the end of antiquity. The result, as by 1751 Mably also thought, was that Man's most precious assets, free independence of mind and critical thought, were obliterated by 'erreurs' and remained forgotten until the sixteenth century.[76] Then, 'nature' which had for a millennium, as if exhausted, remained quiescent strove anew, and finally produced some men who revived liberty of thought: 'l'on vit renaître la philosophie éclectique'.[77] This great revival, holds Diderot, began with the heroic Giordano Bruno of whose views about God, he says, echoing Bayle, Toland, and La Croze—and contradicting Brucker who had declared Bruno's system 'non Spinozisticum'—'il restera peu de chose à Spinoza'.[78] The revival then continued with such eminent personalities as Cardano, Bacon, Descartes, Hobbes, Leibniz, Christian Thomasius, Gundling, Buddeus, Le Clerc, and Malebranche.

In a way profoundly characteristic of radical thought, Diderot views his lifelong contest with theologians, academics, and royal courts, much like Blount and Toland in England or Stosch, Lau, and Wachter in Germany, before him, as simply a fragment of an unending, age-old contest between reason and credulity, and the interest of corrupt elites versus the general interest, reaching back in an unbroken chain over the millennia to the dawn not just of philosophy but of human history itself. This radical perspective envisaging a single history of 'l'esprit humain' integrating modern with ancient, medieval, Renaissance, and oriental history, furthermore, opened a remarkable and important fresh path of attack on the mainstream Enlightenment.

Where Cartesianism, Malebranchism, Newtonianism, and Locke's empiricism did not, as a rule, cultivate *historia philosophica*, and were prone to consign the philosophy and science of the 'ancients' to the rubbish bin, Radical Enlightenment refused to reject the thought of the past in this wholesale manner. Descartes and

74 Diderot, *Œuvres complètes*, xiv. 890.

75 Ibid. xiv. 143.

76 Ibid. xiv. 140, 143; Mably, *Observations sur les Romains*, ii. 231–2, 266–70.

77 Diderot, *Œuvres complètes*, xiv. 139–40; Proust, *Diderot*, 255–7, 276.

78 Diderot, *Œuvres complètes*, xiv. 140; Vernière, *Spinoza*, 559, 588.

Newton each deemed his own system the unique gateway to truth, requiring a wholly fresh start, while Locke's followers and the Thomasians, if more modest in this respect, nevertheless also believed most past philosophers had gone astray through ignorance of the rules and limitations of 'reason'. The radical tendency, by contrast, at least from Bayle, Boulainvilliers, and Fréret onwards, culminating in Diderot, Helvétius, d'Holbach, and Condorcet, took a dramatically different view. Fréret, in one of his essays, actually sets out to enquire what could be the reason for the disdain 'pour les anciens, considerés comme philosophes', affected by most of those who today apply themselves to the 'sciences exactes'.[79] In his opinion, 'modern' disparagement of the ancients flowed from intellectual myopia combined with the arrogant and mistaken notion that our superior mathematics had unlocked whole vistas of reality totally hidden from earlier generations.

If Cartesians, Lockeans, and Newtonians urged philosophers and scientists to forget the past, supposing themselves vastly superior in understanding to the 'ancients', to men of Boulainvilliers's, Fréret's, and Diderot's, as indeed of Thomasius' or Brucker's, cast of mind, such scorn is not just unjustified but tantamount to abandoning the task of philosophy itself. Hence, where Cartesians and Newtonians conceived of 'enlightenment' essentially as a process of learning new things which were unknown before, radical thought understood 'enlightenment' as a process of retrieving more and more men from the clutches of fear, ignorance, superstition, and prejudice by teaching them to grasp truths which, even if now formulated in a more accurate, comprehensive, and refined manner than previously, in essence a few have always intuited, and been able to articulate from the moment clear conceptions first emerged from the fog of primitive myth, fable, and what Vico called 'poetic wisdom'. However dubious his claim, Fréret even contended that the basis of Newton's system, once stripped of its mathematical apparatus and technical terminology, boils down to that of the Greek philosopher Empedocles (*c.*492–432 BC). Time, effort, and experience have widened our knowledge and improved our techniques, but it is far from clear, he insists, that they have given us 'de nouvelles vues générales'. Mostly new methods have only prompted us to renew ancient opinions subsequently forgotten, ignored, or 'décriées depuis longtemps'.[80]

Radical Enlightenment, then, unlike the Cartesio-*Malebranchiste*, Lockean-Newtonian-Voltairean, and Leibnizio-Wolffian streams, became philosophically eclectic during the age of Diderot, embracing a universalism which excluded no aspect of Man's past. While the style and method of systems varies and different terminologies are useful in different contexts, all historical contexts typify a particular stage in the evolution of *l'esprit humain*, and the core of truth, which as time goes on becomes slowly clearer to more and more men, is cosmic, unchanging, and ultimately shared by all. 'Truth' in this context, is unrelentingly monist and materialist, that is hylozoic, 'Stratonist' in the sense propounded by the late Bayle and by Diderot in his articles on *l'histoire de l'esprit humain*. With its penchant for

[79] Fréret, *Œuvres complètes*, xvi. 202. [80] Ibid. 212.

putting ancient philosophy to work to disclose this 'Spinozistic' hidden core in surreptitious ways, radical thought here reveals itself to be as much, or more, the heir to the tradition of *libertinage érudit* as the pupil of the German Eclectics.

Radical-minded historians of thought, while agreeing that truth is something widely scattered, merely glimpsed over the ages in a succession of outward forms each of which exercises a powerful hold, temporarily, and in specific historical contexts, also insisted, here unlike the German Eclectics, that just as true ideas relate to real things so the many setbacks and meanderings of *l'esprit humain* are due to concrete causes, namely inadequate thinking, specific obstacles natural, social, and political heavily obstructing a fixed route which has always been the same. The progress of human knowledge 'est une route tracée', held Diderot, from which it is almost impossible for the human spirit 'de s'écarter'.[81] Every age has its own special characteristics and kind of philosophers. But where, for mainstream Eclectics, philosophical progress must needs centre around the reconciling of philosophy with theology, and must always include an inherent ontological dualism, and has therefore changed since Christ's coming, for radical writers there is a single primary core of reasoning no part of which can be expressed in theological terms and which, for those who venerate only reason, is eternally the same and our only authentic guide. Where, for the German Eclectics, philosophers have a major, if auxiliary, role to play in helping shape education, law, politics, and human society, they wanted no part of the radicals' claim that there is only one virtue, as Diderot puts it, namely justice, and only one goal of human life, to be happy, and that the exclusive teachers of men are the philosophers, they who are the true 'souverains sur la surface de la terre' as Diderot says, reviving a Greek topos, the only men who remain in the state of nature 'où tout étoit à tous'.[82]

Thus, the new discipline of 'history of philosophy' simultaneously inspired one of the main blocs of the moderate mainstream—Thomasian eclecticism—and, from Bayle to Diderot, also fundamentally shaped and guided radical thought. For both wings, the task of the philosopher and historian of philosophy tends to converge. For both, philosophers were now thrust into a wholly new arena where scholars dust down, and disclose to view, previously veiled or submerged fragments of truth scattered across human history. From the perspective of both the Thomasians and the Radical Enlightenment, true philosophers must now incorporate *historia philosophica* in creative ways into their own thought or else become largely irrelevant. Both charged those who sweepingly dismiss past philosophy and science with arrogant obscurantism, contending that philosophers ignorant of 'history of philosophy' cannot philosophize meaningfully since any realistic philosophy must be grounded in the evolving dynamic of what Brucker calls *historia intellectus humani* and the radicals 'l'histoire de l'esprit humain'.

The dynamic of the Enlightenment itself, however, worked more against the Thomasians than against the radical wing. For the former never extended their

[81] Diderot, *Œuvres complètes*, xiv. 140.

[82] Buck, 'Diderot', 140; Donini, 'History', 19.

influence internationally and lost ground in Germany itself from the 1740s. This made little difference on the surface, since other segments of the moderate mainstream, Lockean-Newtonian or Wolffian, with the support of governments, churches, and most opinion, dominated most of European culture. But it left the Radical Enlightenment with uncontested possession of the concept of *l'esprit philosophique*, an important asset. Hence, philosophy and the lessons of philosophy had, for conservatives, during the later eighteenth century, to be redefined as something totally different from *l'esprit philosophique* which hence came to mean exclusively the consistent application of materialist and naturalistic principles to the entire human reality.

Conservative abandonment of history of philosophy doubtless stemmed from a growing realization that Spinoza, Bayle, and Diderot had won this part of the battle and shown that philosophy on its own, as Jacobi and others pointed out in the 1780s, without help from outside forces, cannot overcome or marginalize Spinozism whether strictly defined or broadly conceived in the manner of Bayle, Boulainvilliers, and Diderot. To many, research into history of philosophy, far from blocking, seemed positively to encourage the insight that reality comprises a single coherent structure, governed by a coherent set of rules in which contingency is impossible, all cause and effect being mechanistic and also hylozoic so that nature evolves creating itself without any external authority, providence, or supernatural power. The inevitable consequence was that philosophy's province becomes everything—science, religion, politics, morality, and social theory. It was a vision of what Einstein in the twentieth century was to call the 'orderly harmony of what exists', the totality of reality functioning without divine or supernatural intervention.[83]

[83] Clark, *Einstein*, 502.

20

Italy, the Two Enlightenments, and Vico's 'New Science'

1. ITALY EMBRACES THE MAINSTREAM ENLIGHTENMENT

With the election, in Rome in 1740, after a long conclave, of Prospero Lambertini as Pope Benedict XIV (pope 1740–58), moderate mainstream Enlightenment can be said to have secured a preponderant position in Italy. Previous popes had supported scholarship and the arts; but few could compete with Benedict as a reformer, man of the world (being a seasoned diplomat), or man of learning in his own right (being an acknowledged expert in ecclesiastical history). By 1740, it had become obvious also north of the Alps that Italy was changing fundamentally. Confidently expecting further significant changes in the general cultural atmosphere in Italy, both Voltaire, who wrote to him several times, and the well-connected Montesquieu succeeded during the 1740s in establishing links with the papacy and acquiring enclaves of support within the Vatican.[1]

Besides strengthening the papal libraries and adding to the architectural splendours of his capital, the new pontiff made a point of reviving studies at the Sapienza University in Rome, and encouraging a sense of intellectual renewal. This was part of a wider movement of renovation already evident at the universities of Naples, Pisa, Padua, Turin, and elsewhere, adopting more up-to-date perspectives in established disciplines while adding chairs in natural philosophy, botany, Natural Law, and *Historia juris*, crucial new fields previously neglected.[2] With the appointment at the Collegio Romano, in 1740 of the young Ragusan Jesuit Ruggiero Boscovich (1711–87), an expert in Newtonian astronomy and physics and especially planetary orbits, a vigorous, internationally respected Newtonianism became powerfully entrenched in Italy, at the heart of the papal state itself. This official adoption of Newtonianism by the liberalizing wing of the church was accompanied—Newtonian works, even in Italian, were never placed on the Index despite their heliocentrism[3]—by an intricately worded and carefully planned partial rehabilitation

[1] Macé, 'Lumières françaises', 21; Godman, *Geheime Inquisition*, 262–3.

[2] Zambelli, *Formazione filosofica*, 309–10; Ferrone, *Intellectual Roots*, 263, 297 n. 10; Israel, *Radical Enlightenment*, 524–7.

[3] Godman, *Geheime Inquisition*, 219, 223–4, 252.

of Galileo. Henceforth, the Inquisition—which Benedict tried to rein in also in other respects, albeit often with unclear and contested results—was directed to cease all proceedings against authors alive and dead expounding the earth's motion around the sun. Leading intellectual figures, like the anti-Jesuit Ludovico Antonio Muratori (1672–1750), a pre-eminent lay advocate of Catholic Enlightenment of these years and a figure who had been in some difficulty with the Inquisition, now found themselves under the pope's particular favour and protection.[4]

The reforming papacy of Benedict XIV adjusted to new circumstances not least in its relations with the viceroyalty of Naples, seat of the pre-1700 'Cartesian' phase of the Italian Enlightenment, where prior to 1740 there had been an arduous jurisdictional struggle between the papacy and the (since 1734) restored Spanish Bourbon administration over clerical privileges, taxation, and powers of censorship. Under the concordat of 1741, Benedict accepted an appreciable curtailment of ecclesiastical control, immunity, and privileges in numerous areas including the running of Naples University where Vico taught and supervision of press censorship. As part of the new arrangements, in 1746 the Neapolitan seat of the Roman Inquisition became the first branch of the Inquisition anywhere to be formally abolished. Censorship of books, though, in Naples, as in Rome and Tuscany, nevertheless remained tight, the ban on Giannone's *Historia civile del regno di Napoli* and other key Early Enlightenment works continuing, as before.

Although it is true that Newtonianism as such had been intensively cultivated among the intellectual elite in Rome from the second decade of the eighteenth century, for some time discussion of Newton's ideas on gravity and force had proceeded only in a rather veiled, inhibited manner.[5] Moreover, there seems to have been relatively little awareness of Locke in Italy until after the publication of the new edition of Pierre Coste's translation of the *Essai* in 1729, an event which precipitated a remarkable surge of interest as well as prompting the irascible Doria's tirade against Locke of 1732.[6] According to the Pisan professor Tommaso Vincenzo Moniglia (d.1787), who defined a *materialista* as a *Spinosista*, by the early 1740s the *Locchisti* were to be found everywhere in Italy, many academics and clergy being convinced that Locke's stress on the transcendence and immateriality of God and 'proof' that matter, once at rest, cannot move of itself was the best philosophical defence available against the *materialisti* and *Spinosisti*.[7]

The surge of interest in Locke combined with the efforts of Boscovich and other Roman scholars, and their 'enlightened' colleagues in Naples and Florence, lent a powerful new momentum to Enlightenment based on 'English' ideas in the Italy of the 1730s and 1740s, an intellectual impulse, like its vigorous counterpart, the Leibnizio-Wolffian stream, particularly marked in the universities and among

[4] Bertelli, *Erudizione*, 172, 414–15, 417–19; Tortarolo, *L'Illuminismo*, 37.

[5] Ferrone, *Intellectual Roots*, 18–39, 122–82.

[6] Doria, *Difesa della metafisica*, i. 328, ii. 228–32, 262.

[7] Moniglia, *Dissertazione contro i fatalisti*, i. 41–2, 53, 143, 167; Moniglia, *Dissertazione contro i materialisti*, i. 47, 239, ii. 231–2, 235.

churchmen, attesting to one of the chief social changes in Italy since the late seventeenth century—the dramatic shift in much of the country to higher levels of education among the clergy. In the case of the viceroyalty of Naples, the efforts of three archbishops between 1667 and 1702, including the austere anti-Cartesian Cardinal-Archbishop Cantelmo (archbishop 1691–1702), had brought the proportion of university graduates among male clerics up from around 3 per cent in the early seventeenth century to no less than 20% by 1702.[8]

The ground for an Italian moderate Enlightenment had by 1740 been well prepared, especially in Naples, Florence, Venice, and at Rome itself. Florence, capital of Tuscany, had, since the death of the morbidly pious Grand Duke Cosimo III (ruled 1670–1723), switched from out-and-out reaction to a moderate reformism under the last of the Medici, Gian Gastone (ruled 1723–37), and become an increasingly important publishing centre, being the place, along with Venice, where the Italian version of Voltaire's exposition of the philosophy of Newton, the famous *Metafisica di Neuton*, appeared in 1741–2. Gian Gastone, who had spent some time in Germany where he acquired a taste for the philosophy of Leibniz and Wolff, was a prince of the moderate Enlightenment and introduced various reforming measures, among other things easing the stifling Counter-Reformation restrictions on the Jews as well as censorship. In addition, he had made a point of snubbing Benedict's conservative predecessor, in 1734, by erecting a handsome monument to commemorate Galileo in one of Florence's main churches, Santa Croce.

But only after 1740 did moderate Enlightenment become as it were official in Italy. If Locke's epistemology ring-fenced miracles, immortality of the soul, and divine providence—the Holy Office's earlier, and soon forgotten, ban on his *Essay* (1734) and *Reasonableness of Christianity* (1737) condemned his theology (and verbosity) not his philosophy[9]—Newton's thought was especially esteemed for asserting the dominion and wisdom of God and 'proving' matter wholly inert.[10] English physico-theology in general was much in favour, an influential vehicle in Italian translation published at both Florence and Naples being the works of William Derham (1657–1735), a vicar and friend of Newton much interested in microscopic studies.[11] Lockean epistemology, Newtonian astronomy and physics, and physico-theology: here was a robust new ideological framework well suited to an Italy emerging culturally from the rigid, ghettoized world of the Counter-Reformation but where both princes and church were determined not to proceed too far or fast and in particular to ensure that increased flexibility and freedom was balanced by entrenchments formidable enough to protect the basic structures of authority, belief, and power.

In tune with the new mood of papal realism and the needs of a specifically Catholic Enlightenment, combining tradition and dogma with the new moderate currents of thought, the papacy also made some telling adjustments to its diplomatic

[8] Sella, *Italy*, 117; Israel, *Radical Enlightenment*, 50.

[9] Costa, 'Santa sede', 66, 69–70, 103.

[10] Genovesi, *Lettere filosofiche*, i. 32.

[11] Moniglia, *Dissertazione contro i materialisti*, ii. 223; Derham, *Dimostrazione*, 381; Ferrone, *Intellectual Roots*, 78–9.

relations with the European courts. Especially notable was Benedict's distancing the papacy politically from the House of Stuart. During the period of improved relations between Britain and France, after the death of Louis XIV, the Stuart court had transferred, in 1718, from Paris to the Papal States, first to Urbino and then, in 1719, to the Palazzo Muti in Rome. Benedict, while financially more supportive of the Stuarts than previous popes, nevertheless took advantage of the Stuart pact with France (now at war with Britain) in 1745 to rid himself, as a neutral, of his Stuart alliance and establish friendly relations with the Hanoverian court in London, thereby building yet further bridges to England and English culture.[12] Among much else, this made it easier, especially after the definitive Jacobite defeat at Culloden, in 1746, for well-connected English visitors to come to the Papal States and savour the splendours of the papal city. Although the Stuart court remained at the Palazzo Muti, the Grand Tour now flourished as never before, lending fresh impetus to the intellectual Anglophilia pivotal to the new papacy's cultural policy.

The change meant that the papal court was generally perceived as having abandoned its former unstinting support for the principle of divine right monarchy for a more pragmatic stance. But the election of Benedict above all helped clarify the overall character of the Italian moderate Enlightenment, and the nature of the divide between the acceptable Enlightenment of the reforming Italian courts and radical thought. It marked the transition from an older world in which, as a Venetian observer put it, Protestants, Jews, and Muslims were the chief enemies of the church, to a new ideological climate in which individuals and books teaching materialism and *incredulità* were the papacy's main target.[13] No one could now suppose that the Catholic Church as an institution was opposed to the Enlightenment of Locke, Newton, Leibniz, Wolff, and Voltaire. The conflict between moderate and Radical Enlightenment in general, as well as in Italy, now became more concrete and formalized, with one side publicly and copiously receiving the sanction, so to speak, of papal blessing.

Primed with substantially altered instructions about what to allow and what to suppress, the Inquisition was henceforth obliged sharply to differentiate the intellectual world of Bacon, Boyle, Locke, Newton, and Voltaire, the good 'enlightenment of English ideas'—and also those of the Thomasian Eclectics and Leibnizians—from the intellectual world of impiety, sedition, irreligion, and Deism which the cultural and educational machinery of the papacy now became increasingly focused on trying to combat. This meant that a green light was given for the publication of moderate 'enlightened' works provided their opposition to materialism, radical Deism, and Spinozism was made quite clear. Among the many works published in Italy in the 1740s which could not have appeared earlier was the *Arte magica dileguata* (Verona, 1749) by the aristocratic savant, antiquary, and historian of enlightened views Scipione Maffei (1675–1755), a bold attack on popular superstition, belief in sorcery, and witch trials (still an issue in the extreme north-east of

[12] Gregg, 'Financial Vicissitudes', 77–8.

[13] Concina, *Della religione rivelata*, preface p. ix.

Italy) which, however, carefully avoided denying outright the Devil's power to intervene in the affairs of men.[14] It was a work which effectively defined the Italian moderate mainstream's position on the subject of magic, soon backed up by a *Dissertazione* on this topic by the now aged Costatino Grimaldi (1667–1750), one of the leading legal reformers and opponents of the Inquisition at Naples, posthumously published at Rome in 1751. These publications made clear that the now approved and respectable Italian Enlightenment deplored the excessive popular superstition and credulity of the past but with equal emphasis condemned the 'naturalist', Bekkerite, and 'atheistic' stance that there are no demons and there exists no magic at all. All outright rejection of demonology, Satanism, and the Devil's intervention in men's doings remained strictly forbidden and banned.[15]

As in the sphere of magic, sorcery, and witchcraft, so in the world of high philosophy, the Italian moderate mainstream was now able, from 1740, both to consolidate its intellectual dominance and define its characteristic positions with a new assurance and precision. A key figure here was the great Neapolitan philosopher and reformer Antonio Genovesi (1712–69). By the 1740s, Genovesi had carried out a thorough study of all the main philosophical currents in Europe since Descartes—French, British, German, and Dutch. His major survey works, the *Elementa metaphysicae* (1743) and *Elementorum artis logicocriticae libri V* (1745), explained in detail all the main intellectual streams at work in Italy, including the materialist ideas of the *increduli, fatalisti, spiriti forti (esprits forts)*, and *Spinosisti*, which were strictly forbidden, the whole first part of *Elementa* being devoted, as he puts it, to overthrowing the systems of the ancient and modern atheists, and in particular Spinozism as the most powerful threat.[16] But if defining the new enemy was a relatively straightforward matter, Genovesi encountered great difficulty in providing clear guidance as to how to resolve the disagreements between the rival systems of the permitted, moderate *moderni*.

Genovesi had warm words of praise for Locke, Newton, Leibniz, Wolff, the Thomasians, *Malebranchistes*, and for Voltaire the advocate of Newton, but, at the same time, detected fatal flaws in all their systems, albeit the Cartesian stream (earlier particularly strong in Naples) seemed to him the most flawed since it was the source from which came 'Bekkerianismus et Spinozismus'.[17] What emerged all too clearly from his books was that while in Italy several moderate mainstream currents of thought were now largely (albeit by no means wholly) dominant, at the same time, these were irreconcilably divided and at odds with each other. Newtonianism, though now heavily entrenched in Rome, Naples, Florence, and Venice alike, worried Genovesi as it seemed to him a system which verges too much on pure mechanism, endangering miracles.[18] Unlike Moniglia, he was not

[14] Ferrone, *Intellectual Roots*, 61, 94, 320; Maffei, *Arte magica*, 12–14, 39.

[15] Moniglia, *Dissertazione contro i fatalisti*, i. 166–7; Israel, *Radical Enlightenment*, 744.

[16] Genovesi, *Lettere filosofiche*, i. 31–2.

[17] Genovesi, *Elementorum artis*, 530; Genovesi, *Elementa metaphysicae*, ii. 9.

[18] Genovesi, *Elementa metaphysicae*, ii. 9; Genovesi, *Lettere filosofiche*, i. 37–9; Venturi, *Illuminati*, v. 13–14.

particularly reassured by the strength of support for Locke either owing to what he regarded as the weakness and vagueness of the latter's doctrines of the mind, free will, and immortality of the soul.[19] He could not see how Newton or Locke, despite what so many were claiming, could really be a reliable barrier against Spinozism and materialism.

Part of the danger inherent in such disarray, held Genovesi, was that the *Locchisti* and other blocs were hampering each other from attacking the *fatalisti* forcefully enough.[20] Moniglia, who pleaded for a closer alliance of the *Neutoniani* and *Locchisti* with the supporters of Leibniz and Wolff all joining hands to fight off the dire challenge of Spinozism, also believed the disarray was highly undesirable.[21] But what precisely was the challenge? Moniglia, in 1744, described Spinozism as a universal revolution of the whole of society, authority, law, customs, and politics, 'un roversciamento totale nelle idee, nel linguaggio e nelle cose del mondo' [a total reversal in ideas, language, and the affairs of the world], placing everything on the basis of individual interests and passions.[22] According to the impressively well-read Venetian ecclesiastic Daniele Concina in 1754, the 'splendour and truth of revealed religion' in Italy was now locked in a universal, total struggle with thousands of 'ateisti, Deisti, Materialisti, Naturalisti, Indifferentisti e Latitudinarii' who supposedly all 'believe that men are so many material machines that move according to the laws of mechanism', the leader (*maestro*) of this host of *spiriti forti* being Spinoza.[23]

Meanwhile, inevitably, there was deep resentment and indignation in conservative circles, at such a rapid and general intellectual, cultural, and social liberalization. The result, something almost unprecedented, was the emerging of an incipient (and, for now, largely veiled) Catholic ideological opposition, within the Vatican, at Naples and abroad, an opposition criticizing the papacy from the right. For Benedict wholly failed to reform the Inquisition to the extent he would have liked. But if the criticism inside the Vatican was the more effective for the moment, opposition abroad, including France, was often the more strident. When Voltaire's play *Mahomet* was dedicated to Benedict, in 1742, and the pope reportedly replied, addressing Voltaire as 'mon cher fils', praising his efforts against materialism and atheism, this was too much for the French Jansenists who felt bound to protest. Bitterly reproaching a pope who refused all contact with them while amicably communicating with Voltaire, their clandestine journal, the *Nouvelles ecclésiastiques*, acidly exclaimed: 'Voltaire lui-même a t-il pu n'en être pas étonné?'[24]

Meanwhile the campaign against radical ideas continued unabated, though in Italy the Radical Enlightenment presented a difficult target, owing precisely to the mask, or mental 'discipline', the Inquisition, and church more generally, had been

[19] Genovesi, *Elementorum artis*, 274–5, 514–30; Genovesi, *Elementa metaphysicae*, i. 25–6, 41–56, 98–105, ii. 11–38.

[20] Genovesi, *Lettere filosofiche*, i. 30–2.

[21] Moniglia, *Dissertazione contro i materialisti*, ii. 309–11, 314–16.

[22] Moniglia, *Dissertazione contro i fatalisti*, ii. 22.

[23] Concina, *Della religione rivelata*, i. 3, 7, ii. 371–2.

[24] *Nouvelles ecclésiastiques* (1746), 61 (17 Apr.); Pappas, *Berthier's* Journal, 91; Godman, *Geheime Inquisition*, 262–3.

able to impose on everyone.[25] Part of the problem was camouflaged sedition intruding from outside, Concina describing Bayle as a 'masked unbeliever' whose 'pestiferous books' were daily increasing the number of unbelievers.[26] There were of course one or two Italian radical writers who openly defied the church and princes. But these had all had to flee abroad out of the Inquisitors' reach and their books were all but unobtainable in Italy so that they posed no immediate threat. Radicati had burnt his bridges with the church, as well as the court, at Turin; and he was now dead. The publications of Pietro Giannone (1676–1748), who had lived in exile, mostly at Vienna, since his flight from Naples in 1723, were unobtainable and his major radical work, apart from the *Historia*, an investigation of Scripture questioning its divine origin and miracles called the *Triregno*, a text penned between 1731 and 1734 and much influenced by Spinoza, Le Clerc, and Toland, remained in manuscript. A brief stay in 1734–5 at Venice, where he conferred with Conti, ended with his summary deportation from that state; when he again tried to enter Italy incognito, from Geneva, in 1736, he was lured into a trap and imprisoned by Victor Amadeus II of Savoy who, since his concordat with the papacy in 1727, had become one of the most rigid foes of intellectual freedom among Europe's absolutist princes.[27] The prisoner remained incarcerated at Turin out of deference for the papacy for the rest of his life, even Benedict XIV refusing to relent in the case of such an offender. After twelve years of confinement, Giannone died in his cell in March 1748.[28]

Radicati and Giannone denied miracles and rejected ecclesiastical authority, denouncing 'priestcraft' and the economic privileges of the church, in a direct, abrasive manner. But there were also other, more subtle and diffuse ways of questioning the church's theological view of the world which were harder to identify and eradicate. Antonio Conti (1667–1749), who had shown Montesquieu around Venice during his stay there in 1728, having spent many years abroad before returning to Venice in 1726, had an excellent knowledge of recent philosophical and scientific developments in France, Germany, and England; he lived relatively undisturbed in Venice thanks to his noble birth and connections, and his discretion, albeit at the price of curbing both his pen and his tongue, an ominous brush with the Inquisition in 1735 leaving him under constant surveillance.[29] Others, inevitably, were still more prudent and less easily curbed. How was the church to eradicate those who remained in Italy, employing Nicodemist methods to remain beyond the Inquisition's reach while nevertheless attempting to propagate seditious ideas inconspicuously?

[25] Ricuperati, 'Il problema', 371; Tortarolo, *L'Illuminismo*, 192.

[26] Concina, *Della religione rivelata*, i. 23–4; Conti, *Scritti filosofici*, 102, 241.

[27] Symcox, *Victor Amadeus II*, 221–2; Giannone, *Opere*, 991; Badaloni, *Antonio Conti*, 190–2; Ricuperati, *Nella costellazione*, 171.

[28] On Giannone's imprisonment, see Giannone, *Opere*, 267–88, 326–8; Israel, *Radical Enlightenment*, 674–7.

[29] Costa, 'Bayle', 118–19; Badaloni, 'Vico', 354–5; Nuzzo, 'Vico e Bayle', 170–1; Caporali, 'Ragione e natura', 161, 173, 188–9; Israel, *Radical Enlightenment*, 664–83.

Besides Giannone, there were, we have seen, grounds to include several other members of the Early Neapolitan Enlightenment among the ranks of the radicals, and, in particular, two of its leading lights, Vico and his staunchly republican friend Paolo Mattia Doria (1662–1746). But here ecclesiastical surveillance became entangled in a whole knot of intellectual and practical difficulties. For Vico, though undoubtedly a 'great man', as Doria remarked towards the end of both their lives,[30] was also an author who continually, and seemingly deliberately, failed to express his meaning clearly, an obscurity in no way admired by Giannone. One might explain his lack of lucidity at crucial points simply in terms of an innately convoluted style tending, in the words of Isaiah Berlin, 'to be baroque, undisciplined and obscure'.[31] He venerated classical poetry and rhetoric and was fond of using poetic expression in his own work. But it seems more likely, given he dwelt in a land where the Inquisition presided over intellectual matters, and was a respected professor, having the examples of Giannone whom he knew personally, as of Radicati and Conti, before him, that he felt certain concepts were best expressed obliquely rather than directly.

Many modern commentators have remarked on Vico's convoluted expression and lively poetic streak—often noting that few front-rank thinkers of the past lend themselves more readily to widely divergent interpretation.[32] Unsurprisingly, a great many students of his *oeuvre*, partly misled by Isaiah Berlin's claim that Italy's greatest philosopher was a precursor of 'Counter-Enlightenment', have taken his (occasionally) pious-sounding turns of phrase to mean that Vico's project constitutes an 'original and bold counter-discourse to modernity', driven by suspicion 'of philosophy's own temptation of power and concomitant delusion about its pretended superiority over other forms of knowledge', maintaining that his *Scienza nuova* 'encompasses a critique of philosophy's delusion of power: it unveils philosophy's claim to be the privileged and sovereign discourse of the modern age as well as its project to submit Christianity to its critical scrutiny'.[33] In fact, exactly the opposite is true: with his 'new science' Vico aspired to engineer a 'revolution' in the world of learning, sweeping away the conventional world of historical and literary erudition, revealing his essential 'modernity' not just by rejecting the metaphysical baggage of Descartes, Locke, and Newton but through his remarkable faith in the great power of 'philosophy'.

Despite what numerous Catholic scholars have claimed, if one examines the intellectual context and controversies in which Vico and Doria developed their philosophies, neither can convincingly be said to have been 'anti-modernist', traditionalist, or deferential in their attitudes toward contemporary ecclesiastical authority or society in general. Vico and Doria harboured few of the moderate mainstream (i.e. conservative) preferences and social attitudes typical of Muratori

[30] Doria, *Manoscritti napoletani*, iv. 182. [31] Berlin, *Three Critics*, 21.

[32] Ibid. 22–3; Ricuperati, *Nella costellazione*, 30.

[33] Mazzotta, *New Map*, 222; Miner, *Vico*, 70; see also Morrison, 'How to Interpret', 256–7, 260; Marcolungo, 'L'uomo e Dio', 83; Robertson, *The Case*, 380–1.

and Genovesi, quite the contrary. The label 'anti-moderns' seems especially inappropriate when we consider Vico and Doria's attitude to science. Vico was greatly impressed with modern astronomy and believed his own 'new science' to be a twin component of that of Galileo while Doria profoundly venerated Galileo who, he says, had 'marvelously clarified the system of Copernicus' and thought his own (rather confused) geometric and mechanistic theories to be a continuation of Galileo's project.[34] Similarly, he endorsed much of Descartes's and Newton's mathematics (which, in any case, he believed had been largely borrowed from Galileo—albeit without sufficient acknowledgement),[35] like Vico rejecting mainly Descartes's doctrine of substance and Newton's physico-theology.[36] The cult of Newton undeniably irritated both men but this is not a proof they were engaged in a revolt against modernity.

As for Doria's and Vico's post-1729 antipathy to Locke, a thinker who genuinely aspired to curb modern philosophy's arrogance, and limit its role,[37] this indeed went deep, but at a time when Locke and Newton were becoming conventional thinking among many of the Italian clergy, their hostility was merely symptomatic of their being both thoroughly out of sympathy with the prevailing intellectual context of their time. Meanwhile, the 'Galilean' or mathematical model of thought about the universe undoubtedly figured centrally in the construction of their thought. Doria's veneration for Galileo, moreover, illustrates a further remarkable aspect of his and Vico's thought—their Italian cultural patriotism. Doria employs a seeming rhetoric of 'anti-modernism' but what often lay behind it was his deep resentment at the way Italy had become intellectually, culturally, economically, and politically marginalized by other European nations, and at the low esteem in which Italian culture was now generally held in the north. Cartesianism, Locke's empiricism, and Newtonianism were regarded by them with a jaundiced eye partly because they saw these as invading forces from beyond the Alps reducing Italian savants, it seemed to them, to a merely slavish and unedifying emulation. Doria was fired by the 'passione che io ho per la Gloria della nostra Italia' [passion that I have for the glory of our Italy] and, like Vico, inspired by a belief that there was such a thing as 'l'antica Italica sapienza' [the ancient Italian wisdom], a philosophy Euclidean and also Platonic representing the most important line of western thought, and one humanity needed urgently to revive.[38]

Aside from Italy, the other European lands of which Doria clearly approved were Sweden and Holland, hardly archetypes of anti-modernity. Indeed, it is typical of Doria's 'modernity' that he regards the Dutch Republic (unusually in his time) as

[34] Vico, *On the Study Methods*, 10–11; Doria, *Manoscritti napoletani*, ii. 24–5, 125–6, 421–2; iii. 276; Sina, *Vico e Le Clerc*, 61; Ferrone, *Intellectual Roots*, 46–7, 214–18.

[35] Doria, *Ragionamenti e poesie*, iv; Doria, *Manoscritti napoletani*, ii. 186, 418, 422, 426, iv. 19, v. 20.

[36] Doria, *Filosofia*, i. 56–7; Doria, *Manoscritti napoletani*, ii. 312–14, 426; Belgioioso, 'Introduzione', 43; Ferrone, 'Seneca', 6, 43.

[37] Zambelli, *Formazione filosofica*, 313–17; Pompa, *Vico*, 80, 98 n.; Verene, *Vico's Science*, 203–6; Miner, *Vico*, 4–5, 85.

[38] Doria, *Manoscritti napoletani*, v. 21–2; Carpanetto and Ricuperati, *Italy*, 106.

well as Sweden more favourably than England, or other monarchies, albeit, by the early 1740s, he has become aware that the United Provinces too had seriously declined. During its Golden Age, he thinks, the Dutch Republic had been a kind of modern Athenian republic with laudable democratic tendencies, a republic which in 1672–3, and again in the Nine Years War, had confirmed 'quella virtù, colla quale ha acquistato la libertà' [that virtue with which it had gained its liberty] by successfully resisting the arrogance, expansionism, and Catholic militancy of Louis XIV, a monarch for whom he cherished only contempt. Unfortunately, the Dutch, or rather those that managed their affairs, had subsequently succumbed to a spirit of luxury and aristocratic pride, and begun to aspire 'a mutare la Repubblica Democratica, in Repubblica Aristocratica, soggiogando la libertà del popolo' [to change the democratic republic into an aristocratic republic, subjugating the liberty of the people].[39] Around 1700, Holland and Sweden had also still been economic models for an Italy suffering deeply from severe economic problems of loss of dynamism and stagnation. By 1700, all the Italian trading republics had been reduced to marginality by British, Dutch, and French mercantile competition while the formerly great urban industries of Venice, Florence, Milan, and Genoa had all either stagnated or as with the woollen cloth of Venice and Florence all but collapsed.

Viewed in this context, there was nothing unmodern about Doria's dislike of the colonial empires of the British, French, and Dutch, whose armed trading systems, promoted by powerful navies, he saw as one of the main reasons for Italy's decline and for the profound distortion of what he thought of as more natural international trading patterns. At the same time, Doria, like Giannone, loathed monarchy and thoroughly applauded Sweden's political volte-face of 1718–20 when it had regained 'la sua antica libertà' [its ancient liberty] by putting an end to absolute monarchy. He was also critical of the current state of the principality of Naples, where a disaffected and insubordinate rural baronage, often fiercely hostile to the viceregal regime in Naples, had become a severe social problem and one which Doria labels 'un chaos di confusione'.[40] In particular, Doria, again like Giannone, though of (Genoese) noble lineage himself, was vehemently critical of the Neapolitan nobility whose selfishness and rapaciousness he too vigorously denounced.[41] To this he added an extremely low opinion of the old and stagnating aristocratic republics of Venice and Genoa, the latter of which, he thinks, has been totally corrupted by the Jesuits in alliance with the nobles, thereby becoming a place where severe inequality of wealth, placing too much in the hands of a few aristocratic houses and leaving everyone else excessively poor, had reduced the republic to a dismal tyranny.[42]

39 Doria, *Manoscritti napoletani*, v. 68; Carpanetto and Ricuperati, *Italy*, 99; Mastellone, 'Italian Enlightenment', 113–14; Pii, 'Republicanism', 256.

40 Pii, 'Republicanism', 257; Doria, *Manoscritti napoletani*, i. 61–2.

41 Doria, *Manoscritti napoletani*, i. 54, 71–2, 104–6, 286–8; Ferrone, 'Seneca', 40, 65.

42 Doria, *Manoscritti napoletani*, iv. 329, 344, v. 29–31, 35–6; Pii, 'Republicanism', 257.

Doria was equally contemptuous of the, to his mind, abysmal aristocratic republic of Poland which he considered a land of bigoted, grasping, and despicable nobles who had reduced the peasantry to slavery.[43] 'Enlightened' too were Vico's and Doria's views on education. Vico wanted to restructure higher studies in far-reaching ways. Doria in fact nurtured rather 'modern' views of women's place in society, sexual freedom, and the kind of education appropriate for girls.[44] Among the contemporary institutions towards which he was most antagonistic was actually the Society of Jesus, the Jesuits having in his opinion had a negative effect on education, not least among the Neapolitan clergy, and constructed for themselves, through their colleges, 'un repubblica più ricca, e più potente di qualunque fra le repubbliche secolari, che sia nel mondo' [a republic richer and more powerful than any of the secular republics that there are in the world]. But if contemptuous of the Jesuits, he was equally so of the Jansenists.[45]

Doria and Vico were allies in a way neither thinker ever was with Giannone or Conti and were close particularly during the earlier stages of their development, Vico styling Doria in his autobiography, 'as fine a philosopher as he was a gentleman' and 'the first with whom Vico could begin to discuss metaphysics'.[46] While we have abundant evidence that the two joined forces early on to attack Cartesianism, *Malebranchisme*, Deism, naturalism, and Locke, as well as the physico-theology of Newton—and some have taken all this as clear proof of their 'anti-modernism'—in reality, they denounced most of the world's systems of thought, deftly wrapping this up as an attack on all forms of non-providential Deism, Vico claiming to devote all his energy to fighting, 'la filosofia Epicurea Spinosista, e Deista de' moderni autori' [the Epicureo-Spinozist and Deist philosophy of the modern authors].[47] But there are reasons for investigating exactly how they envisaged their campaign against the schools of thought they chose to combat.

For Doria and Vico reject 'our modern authors of new philosophical sects', arguably, not because they are 'modern' but because they fail to answer the challenges of the modern sciences, or Spinoza and Bayle, producing a spiritual chaos redeemable, they argue, only by recovering an ancient Italo-Greek metaphysics deriving from Plato.[48] Locke is haughtily dismissed by Doria as a purveyor of confusion which can only be resolved into Spinozism, and by Vico (who, like Bayle, mostly ignores him), as just an insignificant 'Epicurean'.[49] The *Locchisti* (Locke's followers), however influential in the Italy of the 1730s and 1740s, all find themselves suspended between two poles and hence ultimately, held Doria, are either 'Epicurei, o del sistema di Plinio' [Epicureans or followers of Pliny], the latter being

43 Doria, *Manoscritti napoletani*, iv. 346–7, v. 84.

44 Doria, *Lettere e ragionamenti*, ii. 332–8; Israel, *Radical Enlightenment*, 92–3.

45 Doria, *Manoscritti napoletani*, i. 298, iii. 218–29, v. 435–6; Carpanetto and Ricuperati, *Italy*, 100.

46 Vico, *Autobiography*, 138; Carpanetto and Ricuperati, *Italy*, 100–1.

47 Doria, *Manoscritti napoletani*, iii. 5.

48 Ibid.; Belgioioso, 'Introduzione', 27, 29.

49 Doria, *Difesa della metafisica*, i. 9–10, Doria, *Filosofia*, i, part 2, p. 300; Vico, *Autobiography*, 126; Belgioioso, 'Introduzione', 29–30, 33, 36–7, 41–2.

the same, he explains, as 'Spinozists'.[50] The 'only and true way to convince, and confound, Epicureans and Spinozists, and all materialist and sensualist philosophers', he insists, 'is to confront them with the Platonic system'.[51] Doria, like Concina and Moniglia, claims 'Spinoza is the author of the sect of the Deists',[52] and principal source of modern Man's intellectual corruption, while Plato he sees as the guide who leads us out of this fatal labyrinth. 'Even the strangest and faultiest minds', he maintains, 'can never derive scepticism, atheism, or Deism from Plato'.[53]

Once Spinoza is soundly rebutted with Platonic arguments, then *ipso facto*, argues Doria, Locke and all the other *sensisti* [empiricists] who maintain *Nil in intellectu, quod prius non fuerit in sensibus* lapse with him. For Spinoza and Locke, he thinks, must be bracketed together as 'sensualists who deny (the existence of) innate ideas in the human mind' thereby abolishing absolute justice and other virtues which Doria—like Shaftesbury, whom he knew personally and with whom he and Vico shared their Platonism—passionately advocated.[54] While it is true that Doria himself exclaimed in old age: 'I combat all the modern authors, and against all the moderns I hurl myself',[55] one should not conclude from this that therefore he favoured pre-Lockeian ideas, medieval ideas, or indeed ancient ideas. For Vico and Doria had no great sympathy for the Middle Ages, being dismissive of the main medieval intellectual trends of the past, and were highly antagonistic towards medieval and Renaissance Aristotelianism, a school of thought dubbed by Doria one which left men more ignorant than if they been under the Ottomans, a remark intended to be highly uncomplimentary.[56] Both scorned traditional erudition, Doria, in particular, also abhorring monasticism and many aspects of the Catholic Counter-Reformation.[57]

While Doria does call himself an 'antiquo', and both he and Vico cultivated the ideal of a supposed 'ancient Italian wisdom', this does not mean that either was broadly favourable to the Greek philosophy schools. Although professing to be hostile to Bayle both follow him in characterizing most of ancient Greek thought, other than that of the Pythagoreans, Plato, Aristotle, and the Stoics, as atheistic and proto-Spinozistic.[58] Epicurus, Democritus, Parmenides, Diogenes of Apollonia, Anaximander, Archelaus, Leucippus, and Anaximenes are included among the many who, according to Doria, acknowledged only a corporeal 'God' 'devoid of intelligence and providence' and therefore philosophers who must be classified together with what Doria characteristically calls 'filosofi Spinosisti metafisici

[50] Doria, *Discorsi critici filosofici*, 113, 134–5; Doria, *Difesa della metafisica*, i. 61, 149, 233, ii. 272–3, 287; Doria *Filosofia*, i, part 2, 301; Doria, *Manoscritti napoletani*, iii. 7–10.

[51] Doria, *Filosofia*, i, part 2, p. 301; see also. p. 300; Doria, *Ragionamenti e poesie*, 234, 238, 252; Doria, *Difesa della metafisica*, ii. 146, 271–2, 284, 287; Doria, *Manoscritti napoletani*, iv. 67–70.

[52] Doria, *Manoscritti napoletani*, i. 31, v. 154.

[53] Doria, *Discorsi critici filosofici*, 130.

[54] Doria, *Manoscritti napoletani*, iii. 15.

[55] Doria, *Manoscritti napoletani*, ii. 421.

[56] Vico, *De antiquissima*, 60; Doria, *Manoscritti napoletani*, i. 327, 367, iii. 276.

[57] Doria, *Manoscritti napoletani*, i. 231–473; Ferrone, 'Seneca', 40–1; Ferrone, *Intellectual Roots*, 240.

[58] Doria, *Difesa della metafisica*, i. 30, 61, 149–50, 160, 232, ii. 271–4; Doria, *Ragionamenti e poesie*, 236–7; Doria, *Filosofia*, i, part 2, pp. 298–9, 301.

materiali e corporei' [Spinozistic metaphysical philosophers, materialists, and corporalists].[59]

The fact that both thinkers frequently extol Plato is, admittedly, a particularly significant feature; but Vico's and Doria's Platonism, like that of Gianvicenzo Gravina (1664–1718), earlier, at Rome, who, in this respect, as in others, may be seen as a predecessor of Vico,[60] is by no means of a traditional kind and there are sound reasons not to equate it with hostility to 'modernity' as such but rather as a philosophical buffer device, hardly justifying the claim that Doria's 'system, supposedly based on Plato, led him to clash not just with Descartes, but with all modern culture'.[61] For their appeal to Plato was not meant to express any sort of attachment to the pious Platonism of Ficino and the Italian Renaissance, and entails no invoking of the supernatural, but was rather a highly artificial construct designed to attack most existing structures of thought in Italy and especially the northern metaphysicians.

Tactically, Vico and Doria were in a tight corner from the moment, in the early years of the new century, that they rebelled against the Cartesianism formerly dominant in Naples, as in the early Venetian and Roman 'enlightenments'. Having originally been fervent Cartesians themselves, their volte-face was bound to drag them into painful and difficult personal clashes and quarrels. Thus Doria became estranged from many who had once been close allies within the Neapolitan Enlightenment, including the Cartesian Leonardo di Capoa (1617–95) who, he says, he had formerly admired but eventually repudiated as a 'filosofo scettico, ed Epicureo'.[62] As time went on, his proud and prickly temperament led him into antagonism also with other Italian *érudits* whom he viewed less as rivals than plagiarists intent on stealing his ideas for themselves, personal grudges poisoning his relationship, among others, with Maffei and Conti.

If Doria was a mathematician and admirer of Galileo, Vico, reading mostly in Latin and gleaning much of his awareness of what transpired in intellectual life beyond the Alps from the Leipzig *Acta eruditorum*, was the master of the new text criticism in the tradition of Spinoza, Bayle, Mabillon, and Le Clerc. Like the latter he aspired to achieve a 'philosophical philology' based on the insight that to retrieve the true signification of ancient terms one must reconstruct the evolution of meaning through successive historical contexts.[63] These stimuli and that of the classicist Gravina encouraged Vico to explore the problem of primitive man and archaic thought, envisaged as a stage in human development, an uncovering of origins directly related to that subversive dimension in Vico's thought which has been aptly dubbed his 'unmasking frame of mind'.[64] Its chief feature is his refusal to take past

59 Doria, *Difesa della metafisica*, i. 149, 232; Doria, *Manoscritti napoletani*, iii. 251, iv. 32.
60 Gardair, *Le 'Giornale'*, 145–51; Gravina, *Orationes*, 25–30.
61 Ricuperati, 'A proposito di Paolo Mattia Doria', 274–5; Ferrone, 'Seneca', 63.
62 Doria, *Manoscritti napoletani*, iv. 109.
63 Sina, *Vico e Le Clerc*, 22, 24, 30, 47, 52; Nuzzo, 'Vico e Bayle', 177–8.
64 Sina, *Vico e Le Clerc*, 25.

accounts of history, societies, and especially origins at face value, a determination, despite the difficulties, to unravel and coax out the true meanings of ancient myths, arcane laws, and poetic thought. In particular, prevailing accounts of history, including official chronicles, struck Vico as being thoroughly distorted by strategies of concealment, designed to glorify and enhance particular faces of authority, hierarchy, and power.

It followed directly from Vico's insight that the ancient 'theological poets were the sense and the philosophers the intellect of human wisdom' that the age-old idea, so prized by Renaissance humanists, of *prisca theologia*, a notion still widely credited around 1700, the concept as he puts it 'that the wisdom of the ancients made its wise men, by a single inspiration, equally great as philosophers, law-makers... and poets' is a total myth.[65] Vico ridicules the age-old conviction that a veritable *prisca theologia* reaches back to the remotest times, having been passed down in recondite fashion through a succession of ancient schools and traditions. This school of thought, culminating, he says, in Pierre-Daniel Huet's *Demonstratione evangelica* (1679)—a refutation of the New Philosophy highly prized by conservative Catholic writers in Italy, aimed in particular at Descartes and Spinoza—seemed to him not just wrong but utterly absurd.[66] Indeed, the 'unmasking' Vico cheerfully 'disposes of all the opinions of the scholars concerning the matchless wisdom of the ancients', discarding as ridiculous 'fraud the oracles of Zoroaster the Chaldean, Anarcharsis the Scythian..., the *Poimander* of Thrice-Great Hermes, the Orphics (or verses of Orpheus), and Golden Verses of Pythagoras, as all the more discerning critics agree'.

Equally ridiculous, he thinks, are the 'mystic meanings with which the Egyptian hieroglyphs are endowed by scholars, and the philosophical allegories they have read into the Greek fables'.[67] At the same time, while scornful of most philosophies and most existing accounts of the past, Vico, like Doria, has no time for scepticism as such, displaying great confidence in the powers of critical reason, and especially *vera eruditio*, the new methods of text criticism, methods dramatically supplanting those of humanism, not least as a means of surmounting scepticism. 'Modern philosophical *critique*', avows Vico, in his *De nostri temporis studiorum ratione* of 1709, 'supplies us with a fundamental verity of which we can be certain even when assailed by doubt. This *critique*', he confidently proclaims, 'could rout the scepticism even of the New Academy.'[68] Nowhere, in fact, does Vico display his triumphant 'modernity' more fully than in his uncompromising rejection of scepticism on the grounds of the superior rationale of the new *critique* which in his thought, as in Spinoza's, Bayle's, and Fontenelle's, is directly tied to the idea of the essential parallelism of ideas and things—a concept basic to Vico and Doria but also, as has repeatedly been pointed out (even by those who insist on his anti-modern and anti-secular leanings), one which Vico frequently restates and consciously connects with Spinoza.[69]

[65] Vico, *The New Science*, 297.

[66] Vico, *The First New Science* (1725), 24–5, 64, 255, 280.

[67] Ibid. 22, 24; Vico, *The New Science*, 37, 40, 134, 137.

[68] Vico, *On the Study Methods*, 9; see also Vico, *Disputation*, 182–3.

[69] Israel, *Radical Enlightenment*, 669; Miner, *Vico*, 39, 90; Stone, *Vico's Cultural History*, 306.

Vico's formulation of this principle of correspondence as the key to understanding reality, with its striking affinity with proposition VII of part ii of Spinoza's *Ethics*, is that the 'order of human ideas must proceed according to the order of things' [l'ordine dell'idee deve procedere secondo l'ordine delle cose].[70] Vico's account of the emergence of modern reason, indeed his whole conception of human attitudes and culture moving in stages that become progressively more rational, here, closely parallels Fontenelle's conception of the evolution of *l'esprit humain* from primitive imaginings, and is anchored in Spinoza's idea that ideas are an articulation of feeling and sense perception and, no matter how confused and inaccurate, invariably correspond to actual real things.

Vico and Doria carefully studied Spinoza—Doria himself tells us that he read Spinoza's *Ethics* as well as the *Tractatus theologico-politicus* and clandestine *Réfutation des erreurs de Benoît de Spinosa* (1731),[71] as well as Bayle and Le Clerc, Vico admiring the latter despite also deeply resenting the prejudice he had been expressing 'for nearly fifty years, namely that Italy produced no works that could stand comparison for wit or learning with those published in the rest of Europe'.[72] He was in innumerable ways influenced by these men, and it is more than coincidence that crucial features of Spinoza's approach to Scripture, and especially the idea that it reflects a historically conditioned stage in a society's development, its wonders, allegories, and fables constituting a pre-rational form of poetic thought, are strikingly paralleled in Vico's treatment of the Homeric epics in the *Scienza nuova*.[73] This was in contrast to Hobbes who (unlike both Spinoza and Bayle) was largely ignored by Vico and rarely mentioned by Doria, though both linked him closely to Machiavelli, classing him among the modern 'Epicureans'.[74] In Moniglia and Concina, similarly, Hobbes though allocated several pages is always subordinate to Spinoza as the leader of modern atheism, materialism, and radical Deism.[75]

Where Spinoza alleges that Scripture teaches only piety and obedience and is not concerned to teach what is true, Vico, the iconoclast, finds in Homer a 'complete absence of philosophy', notwithstanding the claims to the contrary of generations of Platonist and Neoplatonist allegorists.[76] Interpreting Homer as not one but rather a group of poets, or collection of poetry, reflecting the rude wisdom of the archaic Greeks in a heroic age, Vico chides Plato especially for planting in the minds of generations of scholars the spurious notion that Homer was a fount of ancient esoteric wisdom, finding absurd 'that all the other philosophers have followed in his train'.[77] Given that the *vera eruditio* of the new *critique* totally rejected *prisca theologia*, Vico here is presumably referring to the humanists and likes of Cudworth, More, and Huet.

[70] Stone, *Vico's Cultural History*, 302; Spinoza, *Opera*, ii. 89; Vico, *The New Science*, 78.

[71] Doria, *Manoscritti napoletani*, iv. 42; on this text, see Israel, *Radical Enlightenment*, 570, 684.

[72] Vico, *Autobiography*, 159; Pompa, *Vico*, 35–6.

[73] Morrison, 'Vico and Spinoza', 55; Stone, *Vico's Cultural History*, 303–4.

[74] Doria, *Manoscritti napoletani*, iii. 16, 35, v. 29–33, 355; Lilla, *G. B. Vico*, 62; Malcolm, *Aspects of Hobbes*, 511.

[75] Concina, *Della religione rivelata*, ii. 307–8, 381, 396, 398–401.

[76] Vico, *The New Science*, 308.

[77] Ibid. 301; Verene, *Vico's Science*, 34–5; Mazzotta, *New Map*, 142–3, 145.

But this still leaves open the question of whether Spinoza mattered to Vico only as a teacher of the new historico-critical method, and participant in the debate about mythical thought, or whether Vico also imbibed, in some deeper sense, a crypto-Spinozism reminiscent of that of Bayle.[78] Those who interpret Vico as a Catholic 'anti-modern' are obliged to argue that, for him, Scripture, as sacred history, constitutes an altogether higher and purer order of truth than other documents of the past, despite the obvious difficulties with this. For Vico only rarely refers to either the Old or New Testament and, still more striking, in the final redaction of the *Scienza nuova* (1744), as earlier, invokes Christ and Christianity with astonishing infrequency, a feature also of Doria's voluminous writing.[79] Even more significant, where Vico does refer to the Bible, it is far from clear that he distinguishes between sacred and secular history, or even means seriously his somewhat bizarre assurances as to Scripture's absolute veracity and reliability.

It is almost impossible, for instance, not to suspect masked sarcasm lurking when, whilst discussing the dramatically discrepant claims of ancient peoples regarding their own antiquity, and the age of the world, Vico assures readers we need not worry too much since sacred history thankfully rescues us from all possible confusion by revealing that the world is really much younger than is asserted, obviously falsely, by the Chaldaean, Scythian, Egyptian, and Chinese chronicles. 'This is a great proof', he affirms, offering no proof whatsoever, 'of the truth of sacred history';[80] the *non sequitur* is so blatant this must surely be a reverse affirmation in the style of Bayle. Elsewhere where Vico again presents supposedly incontrovertible evidence proving 'the religion of the Hebrews more ancient than those by which the *gentes* were founded, and hence the truth of the Christian religion', he again offers no supporting arguments and must surely have known that in the fraught scholarly field of ancient chronology of his time no attentive, questioning reader could possibly see this as anything other than a deliberately negligent demonstration of the truth of Christian and papal claims.[81]

2. VICO'S 'DIVINE PROVIDENCE'

Vico's insight that in the earlier stages of development men did not and could not reason in abstract terms but instead devised their religions, laws, and institutions through 'poetic thinking' was the conceptual key to his 'new science'. It was a critical tool, he says, which it took him twenty years to develop.[82] Man, in the archaic and heroic stages of human development, he explains, needs and uses the same basic ideas as he later refines into abstract concepts but expresses them more rudimentarily,

[78] Costa, 'Bayle', 118–19.
[79] Mazzotta, *New Map*, 251.
[80] Vico, *The New Science*, 35, 61.
[81] Ibid. 8.
[82] Verene, *Vico's Science*, 66–7; Jacobitti, *Revolutionary Humanism*, 16; Hösle, *Philosophiegeschichte*, 173–4; Preus, 'Spinoza, Vico and the Imagination', 86–7.

in the form of poetic wisdom, fable, myth, and revelations, again a quintessentially Spinozist (and Fontenellian) conception.[83] Man's 'needs and utilities', moreover, are defined by Vico, in the earliest version of the *Scienza nuova*, as something evolving in a logical order from the primary ends or rather first motive of individual man, that is his 'wanting to conserve his nature'—once again, again a strikingly naturalistic and Spinozistic conception. Ability to reason evolves only haltingly and with great difficulty from primitive sensibility and *universali fantastici*. Later he calls this primary motivation, and the sequence of stages which drives the process, the 'two sources of the natural law of the *gentes*'.[84]

Vico's notion that primary human motivation and human needs were the motor of social evolution was doubtless shaped in part by the work of Gravina and the Natural Law tradition of Pufendorf and Christian Thomasius with which he was familiar from the pages of the Leipzig *Acta eruditorum*. But he also complains that writers on law and society such as Grotius, Selden, and Pufendorf had, like the ancient Stoics and Epicureans, altogether failed to take account of 'providence' and this had prevented their extending their reach far enough.[85] Since he regarded his 'new science' as the key to knowledge of humanity—and philosophy as the exclusive means of finding and deploying that key—philosophy for him plainly possessed a status more exalted than it enjoys in the thought-world of Pufendorf or Thomasius, something comparable rather to what we find in Spinoza, Fontenelle, Bayle, or Diderot. In his *De nostri temporis* Vico does not hesitate to pronounce philosophy 'the mother, midwife, and nursling of all sciences and arts', a sentiment close to *l'esprit philosophique* of the Radical Enlightenment.[86] Here was a confidence in the universality and unique power of 'philosophy' which Vico shared with Doria, Spinoza, Bayle, Fontenelle, and Boulainvilliers, which diverged markedly from the views of Locke and Hume.

Nor can this be seen as just a feature of Vico's early development. 'To be useful to the human race,' he says, in the 1744 edition of the *Scienza nuova*, 'philosophy must raise and direct weak and fallen man, not rend his nature or abandon him in his corruption.' At first sight, such wording looks pious. On closer inspection, given Vico's failure to invoke theology, indeed both he and Doria practically never invoke either theological arguments or ecclesiastical authority, one is amazed Vico should think philosophy possesses the power to 'raise and direct' which can only mean reshape 'fallen' humanity.[87] It masks a sentiment closely resembling Doria's maxim 'che la filosofia è la sola ed unica madre della virtuosa umana politica, e della virtuosa libertà' [that philosophy is the one and only mother of the human politics of virtue, and of virtuous liberty].[88]

[83] Preus, 'Spinoza, Vico and the Imagination', 76–9; Sina, *Vico e Le Clerc*, 71; Caporali, 'Ragione e natura', 189.

[84] Vico, *The First New Science*, 31–2; Vico, *Scienza nuova terza* (1744), 63, 103–4; Caporali, 'Ragione e natura, 189–90.

[85] Vico, *The First New Science*, 14–16, 40; Verene, *Vico's Science*, 60–2.

[86] Vico, *On the Study Methods*, 74.

[87] Vico, *The New Science*, 61.

[88] Doria, *Manoscritti napoletani*, iii. 275.

It would seem, then, that Vico's frequent attacks on 'philosophers' have less to do with restricting the scope of philosophy in the manner of Boyle, Locke, and Hume, or subordinating philosophy to theology in the manner of Huet and Baltus, or rejecting 'modernity', than with a fervent conviction that, through lacking the proper method, philosophers had hitherto failed to grasp what must be grasped to practise philosophy successfully. What that proper method is, is explained in the *New Science* where 'Vico seemingly endows history with much the same intelligibility and precision as the *De antiquissima* ascribes to geometry';[89] seeing the centrality of history for any meaningful philosophy, Vico thinks it is the overarching intelligibility and meaningfulness of the human experience which is absent from the endeavours of previous thinkers.[90] Criticizing 'the philosophers', Vico claims they 'failed by half' through contemplating only pure reason, and its uncertain abstractions, instead of contemplating the 'facts', the certain knowledge philologists, historians, and critics derive from languages, texts, and history.[91] Consequently, 'philosophers' had failed in the philosopher's most essential task: to consider the knowledge accessible to us. This is a perfectly valid criticism of what most professional and academic philosophers then did, and indeed still do—namely by ignoring the natural history of Man and the world, and the evolution of society, they wholly marginalize philosophy. But it was certainly not intended as a criticism of 'modern' philosophy and its potential as such.

Since Vico neither uses theological arguments nor refers much to Scripture, the clash between Vico's Catholic commentators and those who locate Vico among the anti-religious philosophical current of the Early Enlightenment in the end almost entirely hinges on the seeming contradiction between Vico's 'claim that human history is the work of man' and his 'simultaneous and frequent insistence that it is the work of Providence'.[92] Despite being often repeated, though, the idea that Vico was essentially a conservative, Catholic, and 'anti-modern' thinker because he constantly invokes divine providence is hardly better grounded than the other aspects of this argument. For the same authors who rebuke 'secular interpreters' of Vico for 'imposing their prejudices on Vico', at the same time admit that it is extremely difficult to see how Vico actually reconciles his supposedly emphatic 'Catholic piety' and anti-modernism with what looks at times like an 'eminently secular if not heretical philosophy'.[93] As a way out, one scholar has suggested that even if references to Thomism in the *Scienza nuova* are very rare, and, where they occur, anodyne,[94] it may be that Vico's anti-modernism and allegedly profoundly Catholic perspective can still be rescued if we envisage his philosophy as ordered on Thomist lines, that is one stipulating a God who is transcendent but also immanent as an efficient cause in all that occurs.[95]

89 Sina, *Vico e Le Clerc*, 60–1; Miner, *Vico*, 82.
90 Lilla, *G. B. Vico*, 144.
91 Vico, *The New Science*, 63.
92 Pompa, *Vico*, 51.
93 Fisch, 'Introduction', 44; Pompa, *Vico*, 51–4.
94 Pompa, *Vico*, 9–10, 14; Mazzotta, *New Map*, 251–2.
95 Pompa, *Vico*, 54, 58; Croce, *Filosofia di Giambattista Vico*, 111; Vasoli, 'Vico, Tommaso d'Aquino', 5–6.

Yet there is no evidence that it was ever Vico's intention that his 'providence' should be understood as divine in a Christian sense. On the contrary, it makes much better sense to accept that Vico's *Provvidenza*, like Spinoza's and Boulainvilliers's providence,[96] neither involves, nor was ever meant to imply other than rhetorically, anything miraculous, supernatural, or transcendent, or any form of supernatural agency. That Vico and Doria often refer to 'providence', then, far from proving 'Vico wants to ascend from human beings to the contemplation of God' and that Vico 'does not postulate a secular world, but assumes a primordial connection between the human and the divine',[97] actually proves nothing of the sort, any more than does Vico's saying 'divine providence' enables the philosopher to steer confidently, as he puts it, between Stoic determinism and Epicurean indeterminism. Both actually refer not to divine guidance but to the general effect of the innate drives in humans, and collective drives in society, working 'through the dictates of human necessities or utilities',[98] that is human wants and needs. A careful reading of the *Scienza nuova* will soon convince the objective reader that there is not a single instance of Vico's using the term 'divine providence' in a way which unambiguously entails any transcendent, supernatural action; and while Vico calls this universal collective striving 'divine', on examination, it emerges that this civilizing process, something he considers innate in all societies, is in his system much less of a theological concept even than in Voltaire: for, in Voltaire's thought, 'providence' always plainly involves intervening supernatural force which in Vico it *never* unequivocally does.

The action of providence in history, says Vico (incomprehensibly if one thinks he is expressing a Catholic view), is what most previous thinkers have entirely failed to grasp. 'Divine providence', he asserts, is something explicable only through the study of civil institutions and laws: for it is the collective logic, or impulse, a hidden but by no means mysterious tendency inherent in social, legal, and institutional development.[99] His *Scienza nuova*, declares Vico, 'must therefore be a demonstration, so to speak, of what Providence has wrought in history, for it must be a history of the institutions by which, without human discernment or counsel, and often against the designs of men, Providence has ordered this great city of the human race'. Although some suppose Vico *is* here invoking divine intervention, and calling 'for humility', against the 'pride of the moderns', maintaining Vico should be considered 'the Augustinian Christian he claimed to be', a profoundly Catholic thinker who 'rejects both fate and chance in favour of providence',[100] it surely strains the plain sense less to construe him here as meaning that even though individuals act primarily in their own interest, the collective result is to generate laws and institutions which promote the needs and security of all through a collective logic which no one planned but which is at the same time

96 Venturino, *Ragioni*, 55–6; Nadler, 'Spinoza's Theory', 6–7.

97 Venturino, *Regioni*, 83–4.

98 Vico, *The First New Science*, 13–14, 39–40; Manuel, *Prophets*, 23, 49.

99 Vico, *The First New Science*, 14–16, 40; Verene, *Vico's Science*, 60–2.

100 Miner, *Vico*, 136, 141.

devoid of non human intervention.[101] Actually, few dispute that this is what the passage seems to mean, the major objection from those who insist on Vico's 'anti-modernism' being that 'it would be strange if Vico, sensitive and hostile, as he professed to be, to the metaphysical determinism he saw in Spinoza and the Stoics, should be advocating what is, in the end, a determinism of a very similar kind.'[102] Such interpreters are simply missing the point. It may be impossible to question the allegedly Catholic and traditional character of Vico's 'providence' without implying that 'despite his own claims, Vico's idea is fundamentally Spinozistic'; but, given Vico's great work departs dramatically in every way from the biblical account of Creation and the origins of Man, this hardly seems much of an objection.[103]

Vico and Doria being far from holding a theological or genuinely Catholic position, the Catholic Counter-Enlightenment, being already a highly developed cultural tendency in Italy in their time, never for a moment made the mistake of including them among the thick ranks of their heroes. On the contrary, for a genuinely theological mind it was not hard to smell a rat. Giovanni Francesco Finetti (d. 1780) observed in the mid eighteenth century that not only does Vico try to degrade primitive man to the status of an animal but his examples of the operation of 'divine providence' are totally unconvincing as instances of divine intervention, and in reality amount to nothing more than saying this or that result was due to 'providence' as could equally well be claimed by any 'Naturalista o Fatalista'.[104] In fact, by collecting the natural development of all peoples comparably into three evolving stages, irrespective of specific time, place, and status, thereby identifying his 'divine providence' with a universal order in history, Vico, objects Finetti, far from bolstering Christian piety, thoroughly undermines trust in the centrality of miracles, revelation, and the action of the supernatural in Man's past, and so decisively that it is impossible not to suspect that precisely this was Vico's aim.[105]

Equally, protests Finetti, Vico's universal order of Man's evolution by stages of cultural and intellectual development was bound to encourage others similarly to seek to explain Man's history without referring to miracles, supernatural agency, or divine intervention.[106] Exactly this implication of Vico's *Providenzza*, indeed, is what attracted Antonio Conti to his work.[107] Hence, Vico's Providence is the unconscious, collective, impulse which coherently impels, essentially as in Spinoza, Fontenelle, and Mandeville, the whole in a given direction without anyone or anything directing or intending such a result. 'For Vico', as has been remarked, 'the creative principle was mind, and mind, or God, was immanent in the world.'[108] Furthermore, in Vico, the direction, at least in certain stages of development, is

[101] Badaloni, 'Vico', 352–3; Caporali, 'Ragione e natura', 184–5; Luft, 'Genetic Interpretation', 153, 168.

[102] Pompa, *Vico*, 54.

[103] Ibid., 55; Zambelli, *Formazione filosofica*, 261, 278.

[104] Finetti, *Apologia*, p. viii; Croce, *Filosofia di G. B. Vico*, 286, Mazzotta, *New Map*, 235–6; Hösle, *Philosophiegeschichte*, 171.

[105] Finetti, *Apologia*, pp. ix, 8–9.

[106] Ibid., xii; Croce, *Filosofia di G. B. Vico*, 286.

[107] Badaloni, *Antonio Conti*, 14, 215; Badaloni, 'Vico nell'ambito', 258–9, 261–4.

[108] Luft, 'Genetic Interpretation', 165.

towards both greater rationality and greater equality, justice, and security. Part of the meaning of Vico's 'divine providence' then is that it is mankind itself which, in scattered groups, prompted by needs and wants, creates laws and institutions, including marriage and family structures—as well as religions rendering possible, at least in cycles, and where conditions are favourable, development to a higher level of order, security, and equality as well as culture.[109]

It is striking, moreover, that the more developed references to 'providence' in the *Scienza nuova*, as has been noted, mostly occur in connection with Vico's repudiation of 'Stoic and Epicurean theories of causation'.[110] The Stoics are taken to task, along with the Epicureans, for denying 'providence', 'the former chaining themselves to fate, the latter abandoning themselves to chance'.[111] The result, contends Vico, is that neither Epicureans nor Stoics, who, he says, were 'in this respect the Spinozists of their day' making 'God an infinite mind, subject to fate, in an infinite body', could provide a proper basis for the study of civil society, institutions, and law.[112] Whatever else it is, Vico's 'providence' clearly underpins his claiming his system demonstrates how to steer meaningfully between the Epicureans' theologically objectionable materialist 'indeterminism' and no less reprehensible and materialist Stoic determinism.[113]

Whereas the mature Vico and late Doria are especially emphatic in rejecting Stoicism which they rhetorically equate with Spinozism, earlier they had been more favourable to Stoicism than Epicureanism. In his *De antiquissima italorum sapientia* of 1710, a work owing much to early metaphysical discussions with Doria, and dedicated to him,[114] Vico repeatedly refers positively to the Stoics while Doria prior to the 1740s is nearly always favourably disposed toward them. Vico's new mode of equating the Stoics with Spinozism in fact curiously coexisted for some time, until Doria aligned with Vico on this point later, in conspicuous contrast to Doria's continuing habit of equating Spinozism not with the Stoics but the Epicureans.[115]

'Since divine Providence has omnipotence as minister', declares Vico, 'it must unfold its institutions by means as easy as the natural customs of men. Since it has infinite wisdom as councillor, whatever it disposes must, in its entirety, be due order. Since it has for its end its own immeasurable goodness, whatever it institutes must be directed to a good always superior to that which men have proposed to themselves.'[116] He ends this noteworthy passage by repeating that the result proves 'to the Epicureans that their chance cannot wander foolishly about and everywhere find a way out, and to the Stoics that their eternal chain of causes, to which they will have it the world is chained, itself hangs upon the omnipotent, wise and beneficent

109 Preus, 'Spinoza, Vico and the Imagination', 90.

110 Ibid. 51–2; Vasoli, 'Vico, Tommaso d'Aquino', 27–30; Robertson, *The Case*, 237–8.

111 Vico, *The New Science*, 5, 61, 103; Lilla, *G. B. Vico*, 62–3; Miner, *Vico*, 79.

112 Vico, *The New Science*, 98, no. 335; Croce, *Filosofia di G. B. Vico*, 78, 111; Mazzotta, *New Map*, 7, 19.

113 Vico, *The New Science*, 103, 235, 425; Pompa, *Vico*, 17, 22–3, 52, 54, 58–60, 158.

114 Vico, *Autobiography*, 150–2; Palmer, 'Introduction', 29.

115 Doria, *Discorsi critia filosofici*, 52; Zambelli, *Formazione filosofica*, 307–8.

116 Vico, *The New Science*, 102, no. 343.

will of the best and greatest God'.[117] But none of this demonstrates a genuine belief in supernatural intervention—any more than it means the lesser gods of pagan antiquity were as real as the Greeks and Romans trusted them to be. It does though genuinely seek to steer between a purely mechanistic determinism and the idea that all results from random chance.

Vico's 'providence' is essentially the outcome of nature in interaction with human aspirations, customs, and concerns. Time after time Vico invokes providence as the manifesting of reason in human institutions, laws, and religions, guiding men equally whether they are Christians, pagans, or whatever, through the pull of their belief in the divine.[118] Vico's 'divine providence' is, above all, a guiding force which, however men perceive and venerate it, actually manifests nothing at all that is 'divine' in a Christian or any monotheistic sense. If more than just an '*ironic* metaphor', it is nevertheless merely a rhetorical device employed to smuggle in a wholly secular conception of the historical process, rendering the latter something self-producing, rational, and immanent which, even if not intended as a radical Spinozist-Baylean thesis (which, in fact, I take it to be), inevitably means, as Finettti saw, ending the distinction between secular and profane history, the complete secularization of human experience and thought, and an inevitable slide, in consequence, into Spinozistic conceptions of politics and society.[119]

One illustration of this was the striking way Vico's conception of history was paralleled by Nicolas-Antoine Boulanger, the republican friend of Diderot, Helvétius, and Morelly, active among the *parti philosophique* by the late 1740s, whose posthumously published *L'Antiquité dévoilée par ses usages* (3 vols., Amsterdam, 1766) became one of the most discussed historico-philosophical works of the French High Enlightenment. Boulanger's naturalistic conception of the human spirit developing through stages, and expressing itself first in terms of myth and fable, owed much to earlier French erudite debates in which scholars like Lévesque de Pouilly and Fréret injected a new dynamism into the study of origins of peoples, mythology, etymology, and oriental languages with a view to resolving thorny questions bequeathed by Fontenelle, Huet, Boulainvilliers, and others regarding the relationship between the various branches of mankind and the ontological character of human history.[120] Boulanger's reconstruction of Man's past, following Spinoza, attributes the origins of priestcraft, and organized religions, chiefly to the fears and anxieties of primitive men. His account exhibits obvious republican and anti-Christian proclivities and was eagerly studied in the radical coteries of Helvétius and d'Holbach;[121] But, at the same time, it also struck Italian *érudits* as being so close to Vico's conception (without Vico being mentioned), as to engender accusations of outright plagiarism.[122]

[117] Vico, *The New Science*, 103, no. 345.

[118] See for example, ibid. 347, no. 948; Jacobitti, *Revolutionary Humanism*, 21–2.

[119] Badaloni, 'Vico nell'ambito', 255; Morrison, 'Vico and Spinoza', 52; Israel, *Radical Enlightenment*, 6.

[120] Venturi, *L'antichità svelata*, 15–21.

[121] Ferrone, *I profeti*, 263–4; Tortarolo, *L'Illuminismo*, 44.

[122] Venturi, *L'antichità svelata*, 125–30; Hampton, *Nicolas-Antoine Boulanger*, 123–9.

While this charge cannot be wholly discounted, there is no sign Boulanger had actually read Vico, Gravina, or knew enough Italian to read anything in that language. Probably, it was just a case of two thinkers proceeding along parallel lines, starting from similar premisses in Spinoza, Bayle, Le Clerc, and Fontenelle. But for Finetti, one of those who stressed the parallel, whether or not Boulanger plagiarized from Vico was not really the issue. What mattered, rather, was that Boulanger, a known foe of the church, materialist, and atheist, should reach a similar concept of humanity's development, openly declaring how immensely damaging to the Christian viewpoint such a vision of history is. Where Scripture declares truths wholly contrary to the claims of the libertines, contends Finetti, Vico's system, by contrast 'favours them, at least indirectly'.[123]

While Vico is among the foremost, and most innovative, philosophers of religion of the Early Enlightenment, one surely cannot ignore the reality that he says practically nothing whatever about Christianity.[124] Instead, he uses a mere label, that of 'divine providence', rather like Bayle employs his 'fideism' to cover the stark nakedness of what he is doing: for under the veil, he reduces Man's religiosity to the status of a purely natural phenomenon but in a brilliantly novel manner by applying the new conception of reason as something that emerges by stages from sensibility by way of 'imagination', and employing the new *critique*, across a very broad canvas and multiplicity of historical contexts. In this way he is able to bring poetry, institutions, social classes, and philosophy all into direct interaction with each other. Spinoza's account of biblical prophecy as essentially poetic imagination was, as has been noted, taken up by 'Vico with the notion that among the Gentiles as well [as the Jews], real prophets existed, but that they were called "augurs and soothsayers" '.[125] Vico, then, elaborates this idea far beyond anything suggested by Spinoza, though there is, also, an important difference in how Spinoza and Vico respectively apply their common doctrine of 'imaginative universals'. If the first explores the function of the imagination in generating prophecy, and also historicizes the phenomenon by explaining, as Vico also does, that those among whom prophets appeared 'were a *primitive* people whose thought processes were on that account essentially different from our own', Spinoza sees prophets and common people as alike incapable of 'adequate ideas' because they are insufficiently schooled in the ways of 'reason', that is are ignorant and philosophically unsophisticated.[126] In Vico, by contrast, though the stress on historical context is the same, all explicit reference to 'adequate ideas' is removed from the scene but inadequate ideas now evolve collectively towards more 'adequate' conceptions through a complex and unconscious, socially driven evolution.[127]

[123] Finetti, *Apologia*, p. xii. [124] Preus, 'Spinoza, Vico and the Imagination', 71–2.
[125] Ibid. 82; Luft, 'Genetic Interpretation', 166–7.
[126] Preus, 'Spinoza, Vico and the Imagination', 85.
[127] Ibid.; Costa, 'Bayle', 118; Pompa, *Vico*, 22–3, 52–7.

While Spinoza lacks an explicit philosophy of history in the manner of Bayle, Fontenelle, Boulainvilliers, Gravina, and Vico, he too claims the meaning of texts is governed by what is thought and believed in 'each age'.[128] Spinoza conceives of nature as constantly in motion; for him, living beings emerge from the inert, and men's sensibility is in principle comparable to that of animals. Accordingly, in his philosophy it is possible to coalesce human history and nature in a way foreclosed to believers in revealed religion. When discussing the true method of interpreting Scripture, he argues (in a key passage inadequately rendered in the available English translations) that sound philosophical knowledge of nature depends on studying the 'history of nature' which includes within it the history of man: 'nam sicuti methodus interpretandi naturam in hoc potissimum consistit, in concinnanda scilicet historia naturae, ex qua, utpote ex certis datis, rerum naturalium definitiones concludimus; sic etiam ad Scripturam interpretandam necesse est ejus sinceram historiam adornare, et ex ea tanquam ex certis datis et principiis mentem authorum Scripturae legitimis consequentiis concludere' [For just as the method of interpreting nature consists chiefly in arranging the history of nature, from which we deduce the conclusions about natural things which follow evidently from certain data, so likewise it is necessary for the interpretation of Scripture to prepare its faithful history and, from that, in the same way interpret from assured data the thinking of biblical authors with legitimate inferences].[129]

Spinoza thus establishes much the same relationship between reason, nature, and historical facts underpinning Vico's revolutionary conception of history: while the foundations of philosophy consist of universal ideas drawn from nature, the real meaning of religion, 'historiae, et lingua, et ex sola Scriptura, et revelatione petenda' [must be sought in history and languages, and must be sought only from Scripture and revelation].[130] For Spinoza, as for Vico, 'the practice of religion was to be understood through history' albeit with 'history' being understood as human development directly (and exclusively) linked to the processes of nature.[131] Nothing is more requisite for evaluating any text, including any biblical or other passage held to be sacred, argues Spinoza, than knowing the time and circumstances of its composition. Denying as he does the reality of supernatural revelation, it follows that all revelations are purely human, historical phenomena which can only be correctly understood as such.[132] Hence psychological, cultural, and spiritual factors, while not in themselves material causes, are nevertheless an inherent part of nature and hence linked to material factors.[133] Furthermore, Spinoza's analogy here, as expressed in his telling phrase *historia naturae*, is just as central to his as to Vico's system of thought. No doubt Vico did further 'historicize' Spinoza's idea, and Bayle, Le Clerc's, and Fontenelle's reworking of it, developing the theme that

[128] Preus, 'Spinoza, Vico and the Imagination', 86.

[129] Morrison, 'Spinoza and History', 178, 193–5; Spinoza, *Opera*, iii. 98.

[130] Morrison, 'Spinoza and History', 181; Spinoza, *Opera*, iii. 179.

[131] Morrison, 'Spinoza and History', 192–3; Mason, *God of Spinoza*, 181–2.

[132] Morrison, 'Spinoza and History', 173.

[133] Mason, *God of Spinoza*, 179.

primitive thought is more imaginative and poetic than that of men with more 'civilized' and developed intellects; but in essence the conception was the same.

3. A RESTORED ITALO-GREEK WISDOM?

If Vico and Doria present secular philosophies with a Spinozistic core, to be intellectually effective this had, in the Italy of their time, to be encased in a wide-ranging and emphatic rhetoric of anti-Spinozism and anti-materialism. Their rhetorical counterweight they call Platonism. True 'Platonism' Doria regarded as a positive antidote to the ills of modern philosophy and also a guide to a healthy politics 'which condemns tyranny and promotes the virtuous liberty of the people, something equally useful to peoples and to just princes'; by contrast, Spinozism, which he always explicitly presents as the opposite of his Italo-Greek Platonist tradition, eliminates not just the intelligence and providence of God but also all moral absolutes and innate ideas, along with angels, demons, and 'and all other spiritual forms created by God'. As such it is the essence of the 'modernity' Doria pledges to combat, 'quel Spinosismo, o sia Deismo, il qual' è seguito da una gran parte de' nostri moderni filosofi' [that Spinozism, or Deism which is followed by a large part of our modern philosophers], and which he and Vico loudly professed to condemn.[134]

To grasp this we must remember that their bold intellectual course was not without tangible risks. Doria was repeatedly accused of Spinozism during his career. Besides Francesco Maria Spinelli, Principe della Scalea, acolyte of the Cartesian Gregorio Caloprese who in his *Riflessioni* of 1733 accused Doria, on the basis of an early manuscript text of his which had been left with Caloprese, of being a 'Spinozist',[135] there had, since 1724, as Doria himself reports, also been others in Naples, and elsewhere, who claimed 'che la mia filosofia sia simile a quella di Spinosa' [that my philosophy is similar to that of Spinoza].[136] Still others, complains Doria, supposed because Plato acknowledges an infinite God, and the divine presence in all eternal forms (and therefore in everything), 'che Spinosa . . . sia stato uniforme a Platone' [that Spinoza agrees with Plato], doubtless an allusion to Gundling no less than Conti with whom he felt obliged to enter into a public dispute about Platonism.[137]

What Vico and Doria needed was an unobjectionable method of bridging the gap between pagan antiquity and Christian tradition, and between body and spirit,

[134] Doria, *Manoscritti napoletani*, iv. 22; Nuzzo, 'Vico e Bayle', 150, 164, 169.

[135] Spinelli, *Riflessioni*, 2, 115–17; Doria, *Manoscritti napoletani*, v. 172; Ricuperati, 'A proposito di Paolo Maria Doria', 263, 275; Belgioioso, 'Introduzione', 37; Stone, *Vico's Cultural History*, 310.

[136] Doria, *Discorsi critici filosofici*, 24–5, 111; Doria, *Difesa della metafisica*, i. 30; Belgioioso 'Introduzione', 22, 27n.; Israel, *Radical Enlightenment*, 672.

[137] Doria, *Filosofia*, i. 26; Zambelli, *Formazione filosofica*, 306.

leaving philosophy independent of theology and effectively supreme but without appearing to merge spirit with body. This is why both men, arguably, came to impart an overriding significance to Platonism which alone seemed capable of bridging the opposite worlds of pagan and Christian thought, pagan and Christian religion, pagan and Christian virtue, body and spirit, mathematics and free will. Other Greek philosophical movements which seemed to Doria to approach Platonism in this respect and likewise foster virtue and 'religion' were those of Pythagoras and, as we have seen, for most of his career also, the Stoics. The outward quarrel between Doria and Spinoza (and Locke) is whether everything boils down to body, and mind is, therefore, only sense and sensibility, or whether innate ideas, and the higher world of 'spirit'—without which all ideas of justice, love, charity constancy, and prudence have no absolute reality and status—are only relative notions.[138]

In fighting this battle, Descartes and Malebranche, holds Doria, are entirely useless: only Platonism, or rather his Platonism, can do the work of retrieving moral absolutes from Spinoza and (when his confusions are straightened out) his subordinate, Locke. Bayle, he adds, merely agrees with and at the same time corrects and elaborates Spinoza (indeed a perfectly accurate assessment).[139] In fact, in Doria's eyes, Plato or Spinoza are the only real alternatives anyone searching for a solution in the Enlightenment context of his day really has, the rest—Descartes, Malebranche, Leibniz, Locke, and Newton—being lost in contradictions which, once resolved, automatically collapse, he says, into Spinozism. Thus, Vico and Doria did not think their 'Platonism' inimical to scientific research or experimental work but, on the contrary, a way of presupposing the essential unity and order of the universe, favouring the advance of science and mathematics, while eluding the compromises with theology entailed by Locke's empiricism and Newton's physico-theology and supposedly avoiding unacceptable 'atheistic' monism associated with much ancient philosophy, such as Epicureanism and Stoicism, as well as Spinozism.[140]

Of all the moderns, Malebranche, Doria suggests, came closest to rescuing innate ideas, spirit, and the Divine Intelligence but fell at the last hurdle, leaving it finally unclear 'se egli sia stato Spinosista, ovver Platonico' [if he is a Spinozist or Platonist], a remarkable formulation.[141] Malebranche, he observes, was 'more similar to Plato than any other philosopher of our times' but finally founders so that it becomes impossible in the end to know whether one is dealing with 'substantial forms' which are at once both body and spirit, and therefore Platonic, or, alternatively, 'l'estensione materiale di Spinosa' [the material extension of Spinoza].[142] The paradox, of course, in Doria's dramatic confrontation of the great modern alternatives, in

138 Doria, *Manoscritti napoletani*, iv. 19–21.
139 Ibid. iv. 25; Ferrone, *Intellectual Roots*, 240, 244.
140 Pompa, *Vico*, 80; Belgioioso, 'Introduzione', 38–9.
141 Doria, *Manoscritti napoletani*, iv. 22.
142 Doria, *Ragionamenti e poesie*, 238; Zambelli, *Formazione filosofica*, 306–7.

philosophy, is that in the end the distinction between Platonic conflation of body and spirit and Spinozist pure sensibility and materialism became a very fine distinction indeed.

This same paradox, of the effective proximity of Platonism and Spinozism, reappears in Doria's sixty-page treatise on classical Confucian philosophy, an important text composed in the early 1740s. Here again, what is chiefly at issue, says Doria, is whether Confucius approaches closer to Spinoza or Plato; for Doria, this being always the primary question.[143] The debate about Confucius, as we shall see, formed part of a major European controversy over Natural Theology, the relationship of philosophy to theology and the universality of human norms. In that Sinophile age, numerous philosophers hoped to demonstrate the validity of their own systems of metaphysics by showing affinities with traditions of 'Natural Theology' in non-Christian parts of the globe. Doria believed the Confucian ideal of a ruler guided by a class of officials steeped in classical philosophy provided an inspiring model reminiscent of Plato's Republic and hence strove to refute those, like Arnauld, Bayle, and Malebranche, who considered Confucianism 'Spinozistic'. Predictably, Doria concluded by declaring Confucianism something very positive and closer to Plato (and his own philosophy) than Spinoza but yet, at the same time, he readily admitted that in many respects it was not easy to tell whether it was the one or the other.[144]

Vico's and Doria's Platonism is paradoxical also in another way. The wider European discussion of Platonism during the early Enlightenment had not only discredited humanist Platonism, and the Church Fathers' use of Plato, but also revealed serious distortions in traditional ways of interpreting Plato. The point of invoking Plato, for Vico and Doria, was to protect them from any accusation that their 'nature' was not composed of both 'spiritual' and physical forces. But it remains unclear how far, if at all, they genuinely saw their Platonist anti-Spinozism as a way of upholding any form of supernatural intervention, disembodied spirits, and Christian doctrines and values.[145] In the wake of Souverain, Le Clerc, and Gundling, as well as Mosheim and Brucker,[146] pagan philosophers, including Plato and his pre-Christian followers, had begun to speak for themselves and function more autonomously from Christian tradition, producing a new and in some respects highly fraught and bitterly contentious Plato.

Gundling, as we have seen, had followed Bayle in identifying the authentic Plato (as well as Plotinus)—that is the Plato they thought the humanists had lamentably distorted—as something close to Spinozism: 'est enim Deus Platonis', held Gundling, 'mundus, et mundus Deus' [for the God of Plato is the world and the

143 Doria, *Manoscritti napoletani*, iv. 31–90; see, in particular, iv. 32, 71.

144 Ibid. iv. 40, 71, 89–90; Stone, *Vico's Cultural History*, 290.

145 Doria, *Manoscritti napoletani*, iv. 37, 39, 41, v. 360, 445–6; Ferrone, 'Seneca e Cristo', 60, 62–3.

146 Ferrone, 'Seneca e Cristo', 60, 62–3; Gundling, *Vollständige Historie*, i. 931–4; Gundling, *Gundlingiana*, v. 190–200, 234, 237–8; Schmidt-Biggemann, 'Platonismus', 197–9, 203; Hutton, 'Classicism and Baroque', 225–6.

world God].[147] Spirit here is just the activating force in matter leaving just one substance, much as in Spinoza. Moreover, in rejecting the edifice of Christian and Renaissance interpretation, Bayle and Gundling pepper their discussions of Platonism with references to Spinoza and Spinozism, tying the Early Enlightenment controversy about Plato inexorably to that surrounding Spinoza. At the same time, conservative scholars around Europe still battled to maintain the view that Plato's thought, as Heumann put it in 1726, 'seems to come closest to Holy Scripture'.[148] In a Catholic context especially, the prestige of the Church Fathers being what it was, it was in practice impossible to uncouple Platonism from authentic Christian tradition. No doubt this was part of Platonism's particular usefulness and attraction to Doria and Vico. But the instability and sharply contested character of Plato's image in Early Enlightenment Europe nevertheless provided such subtly seditious philosophers as Vico and Doria with a respectable signature readily put to subversive uses.

The espousal of Pythagoras, Plato, and Platonism which figures so centrally in the work of Doria and Vico seems to entail a double revisionist thesis, asserting, on the one hand, that true Italo-Greek Pythagoro-Platonism should not be confused with the corrupted Platonism of Ficino and the humanists, and, on the other, that those recent scholars seeking to tie Platonism to Spinozism were distorting the veritable face of Plato.[149] But if it was impossible to uncouple Platonism from Christianity, in the fraught intellectual context of the Early Enlightenment, it was equally impossible, thanks to Bayle, Gundling, and Conti, to uncouple Platonism from Spinozism. It is not, therefore, surprising, that Doria should complain of a group of 'ridicoli Democriti' at Naples who 'confodendo poi Platone coll'empio Bendetto Spinosa, hanno detto che la mia filosofia sia simile a quella di Spinosa' [confusing then Plato with the impious Benedict Spinoza, have said my philosophy is similar to that of Spinoza].[150]

Furthermore, the rhetoric of 'Platonism' locked Vico and Doria into a controversy, reaching back to Gravina, which was confined to Italy and had no currency beyond the Alps. The crucial difference between Platonism and Spinozism, supposedly, was that the latter is a purely materialist philosophy whereas Platonism is idealist; but precisely this thesis was now being widely contested and was apt to raise fresh questions about them. For while Vico speaks of prior metaphysical forms lying behind all actual physical processes and events, given that the actual world of appearances is the only sphere accessible to us, precisely this, he realized, could arouse suspicion that for him too material substance is not ultimately separable from the substance of God.[151] For Vico, Doria, and Conti, Platonism was the best

[147] Gundling, *Gundlingiana*, v. 237, 243–4; Mulsow, *Moderne*, 289–91, 296.

[148] Heumann, *Acta philosophorum*, 17 (1726), 794, 800–1.

[149] Doria, *Difesa della metafisicia*, i. 31, 149–50, 160, 232–3.

[150] Ibid. i. 30–1, ii. 116, 146; Doria, *Filosofia*, i. 26; Doria, *Discorsi critici filosofici*, 111–14.

[151] Pompa, *Vico*, 82–3; Agrimi, 'Paragrafi', 101, 124, 126–7, 130; Lilla, *G. B. Vico*, 26–7; Miner, *Vico*, 76.

expedient available for countering Descartes, Locke, Leibniz, and Malebranche, while also circumventing Spinozism, but one which was nowhere else, outside Italy, debated as a meaningful option.[152]

Especially awkward was Doria's clash with Conti over Platonism, particularly from 1739 when the latter published the first volume of his *Prose e poesie*, a work which seemed to Doria simultaneously to distort, and plagiarize without acknowledging, his own Platonic philosophy.[153] Doria accused Conti of disastrously narrowing the gulf between 'Platonism' and Spinozism, obliterating the crucial distinction between substantial forms and purely corporeal substance, with insidious consequences. He summons him urgently to reconsider lest he be 'incolpato di Spinosista' [accused of being a Spinozist].[154] His problem was that, for Conti, like Spinoza and Locke, ideas are purely hypotheses of the mind, and can only arise out of sensibility and experience, having no independent existence.[155] Ideas for Vico and Doria, by contrast, were professed to be absolute abstractions which really exist outside the mind and are innate and eternal. When, in 1743, Conti published his study of the *Parmenides*, the dialogue Doria considered the key to grasping Plato's metaphysics,[156] the Venetian seemed to have gone out of his way to antagonize him further, claiming, like Gundling, that Plato had not yet been properly interpreted, that for this a thorough knowledge of Greek is essential, and that Plato's God is wholly immanent in the world, a world-soul, pervading matter much as the Stoics too conceived him, so that it is pointless for Christians to search in Plato for the God 'which we adore'.[157]

The clear implication was that Doria had either sadly misunderstood or was purposely misrepresenting Plato and that his, and Vico's, philosophies therefore inexorably unravel into something indistinguishable from Spinozism. Doria had little choice but publicly to rebut these arguments. Those who claim Vico and Doria were 'anti-moderns' might perhaps cite this rupture between Doria and Conti as evidence of the former's genuine hostility to radical thought of which Conti was certainly representative. But if Conti was a radical fusing elements of Bayle and Malebranche into a discreet *Stratonismo*, he too had become deeply immersed, since his researches in Paris where he resided in the years 1718–26, in Platonism and, at the same time, was among the first and most ardent admirers of Vico.[158] From a surviving letter he wrote to Vico of January 1728, it plainly emerges he was both a genuine enthusiast and a vigorous promoter of Vico's reputation both at Venice and in France.[159] Conti, like Vico, thought one of the philosopher's main tasks is to comprehend humanity's beginnings and the slow emergence of human

[152] Vico, *On the Most Ancient Wisdom*, 49, 67, 123–4, 163; Conti, *Illustrazione*, 9, 30–1, 37, 123–4; Conti, *Prose e poesie*, ii. 215, 223–4; Badaloni, *Antonio Conti*, 13.

[153] Doria, *Manoscritti napoletani*, iv. 174, 184, 191, 203, 266–7; for Maffei, see v. 12–13.

[154] Doria, *Manoscritti napoletani*, iv. 189, 193–4.

[155] Belgioioso, 'Introduzione', 39.

[156] Doria, *Manoscritti napoletani*, iv. 192, 202, 368, v. 205, 356.

[157] Conti, *Illustrazione*, 9, 30–1, 37; *Journal des savants* (Aug. 1749), 511, 516–18.

[158] Vico, *Autobiography*, 185; Badaloni, 'Vico', 341; Levene, 'Giambattista Vico', 71.

[159] Vico, *Autobiography*, 184; Badaloni, *Antonio Conti*, 112–13, 149–50.

reason, so that the modern philosopher must make 'the true system of the human mind his principal study' by learning the methods of true criticism, how to research the history of philosophy, and how 'to transport oneself into the remotest and earliest ages of the world', indeed a thoroughly Vichian sentiment, if also one influenced by Fontenelle and Boulainvilliers.[160]

In any case, with its vision of geometrically ordered ideal forms pervading the material world of nature, animating the universe as it were from within, and ensouling nature postulating a single infinite substance in which motion, and all life, are imminent,[161] the Platonism of Vico, Doria, and Conti, it seemed to some, represented something ultimately not very far removed from Spinozism.[162] The supreme difference between Plato's and Spinoza's single substance, according to Doria, is that Spinoza's one substance is 'material' while Plato's is ultimately 'spiritual' entailing, like Stoicism, a knowing God where Spinoza's 'God' lacks intelligence; likewise Doria's and Vico's vision supposedly entails a intelligent and conscious 'providence' while Spinoza's is wholly unconscious and lacks intelligence.[163] But, as we have seen, a close search of Vico shows that this 'intelligent' providence is extremely elusive, to put it mildly. Yet, for both Doria and Vico, it is only philosophy that yields rationally meaningful knowledge; theology, being based on revelation and miracles, cannot make the church's divine mysteries comprehensible to reason. Where Plato, contends Doria, teaches truths men need to know and is 'intelligibile', holy revelation 'non è mai intelligibile dalla mente umana' [is never intelligible to the human mind].[164]

[160] Conti, *Illustrazione*, 123–4.

[161] Doria, *Filosofia*, i. 26, 52–3, 184–6.

[162] Badaloni, 'Vico', 355; Marcolungo. 'L'uomo e Dio', 99; Agrimi, 'Paragrafi', 126–30; Belgioioso, 'Introduzione', 39.

[163] Doria, *Difesa della metafisica*, i. 30, 149–50.

[164] Ibid. iii. 11–12.

Part V

The Party of Humanity

21

The Problem of Equality

1. ENLIGHTENMENT AND BASIC EQUALITY

Among the most divisive and potentially perplexing of all basic concepts introduced by the Radical Enlightenment into the make-up of modernity, and one of most revolutionary in its implications, was, and is, the idea of equality. Assertion of universal and fundamental equality was undoubtedly central not just to the Radical Enlightenment but to the entire structure of democratic values espoused by the modern West. Yet, neither the philosophical nor the historical grounding of this idea, that is its intellectual origins and roots, is at all obvious and this whole issue has been, to a quite remarkable extent, shrouded in neglect in the historical academic literature.[1] Surprisingly ignored as a cultural phenomenon, claiming the basic equality of men and women also continues to be widely opposed and rejected in much of the world today.

As Tom Paine points out in his *Rights of Man* (1790), the notion of basic equality is impossible without first demonstrating, and winning assent to, the idea of the 'unity of man' and forging the corresponding concept of a 'general interest' in which all share equally. For without this, there is no way of coherently arguing that men, as he put it, 'are all of one degree, and consequently that all men are born equal, and with equal natural right'.[2] Homeric and other archaic societies may have nurtured a conception of equality, and shared status, within particular groups, usually nobles in opposition to and above commoners, an ideal still powerfully lingering in the thought of Boulainvilliers,[3] but to develop a conception of general equality is quite another matter. Indeed, at first glance nothing could be less obvious than such a fundamental 'unity of man', something first proposed—and with great brilliance—by Hobbes;[4] or, indeed, less obvious than its presumed consequence: that men share (often without acknowledging the fact) in a universal equality applying at all times and places irrespective of historical context and social structure and essential to any genuinely secular system of politics, law, morality, and society.

In a Europe long dominated by kings, princes, and nobles, saturated in the culture of courts and courtiers, to speak of fundamental equality and the unity of man—after the state of nature—must have seemed to almost everyone, aside from

1 Waldron, *God, Locke, and Equality*, 1–4.
2 Paine, *Rights of Man*, 66.
3 Venturino, *Ragioni*, 307, 310–11.
4 Hösle, *Morals and Politics*, 36.

the radicals, to be going against the grain of reality, to be lost in chimeras. The churches with their doctrine of immortal souls perhaps came closest to establishing a notion of equality; but they too had, nevertheless, always proclaimed a fundamental duality or spiritual hierarchy, based on New Testament authority, between those who believe and those who do not, as well as, ultimately, between those who are 'saved' and those condemned to eternal damnation. In the gospel, Salvation is proclaimed to be through faith, creating an immovable, indeed eternal, yardstick segregating the saved from the damned, those who possess the kingdom of Heaven from those who will not; and even if living men have no way of ascertaining for sure which is which in this life, in practice, the saved hardly seemed likely to encompass self-confessed unbelievers, atheists, agnostics, idolaters, infidels, Confucianists, heretics, reprobates, adulterers, and schismatics.

Locke's (and the Arminians') stress on equality of human consciences may, then, perhaps have helped ground the mainstream Enlightenment's conception of toleration and made some wider contribution to the new ideal of equality, but it is not clear that it did and, if so, it can have been only a subsidiary contribution. For Locke's vision of humanity was too deeply anchored in theological concerns to be secularized in the direction required by more radical, democratic, and republican thinkers. In addition, the fact that Locke's political ideas arose in the entourage of the first earl of Shaftesbury, in circumstances connecting him not just to the world of colonial enterprise, and the expansion of black slavery in the Americas, as numerous historians have pointed out, but also to the centrality of hereditary aristocracy in the functioning of English mixed monarchy, was an inevitable barrier.[5] His great patron, Shaftesbury, had backed Parliament against Charles I, and then supported Cromwell; but he was also one of the movers of the royalist Restoration of 1660. However resolute against royal absolutism, at bottom, he, like Locke, stood for mixed government, limited monarchy, and institutionalized aristocracy.

For Locke, what basic equality between men and women, and between social superiors and inferiors, besides fundamental inequality between men and animals, ultimately amounts to is Man's capability of mind insofar as this renders men universally fit to organize this life and to learn the 'way that leads to a better', that is 'knowledge of their Maker, and the sight of their own duties', a stance tying his philosophy inextricably to theological premisses.[6] By contrast, it was not, as we shall see, religious conviction, or indeed compassion for the poor, which pushed the more radical *philosophes*, almost in spite of themselves, into formulating and discussing theories of equality but the powerful logic of their radicalized versions of the new philosophy itself.

The principle of equality was fraught with innumerable difficulties. Some radical *philosophes*, like various of the clandestine manuscripts, such as the *Traité des trois imposteurs*, expressed a certain generalized sympathy for the multitude, for the

[5] Dunn, *Political Thought*, 27–9, 56–7; McNally, 'Locke, Levellers', 88–90, 92–3, 108–10.

[6] Locke, *Essay, 45;* Waldron, *God, Locke, and Equality*, 78–82; Dunn, 'What History can Show', 448–50.

common people, as victims of impostors, scheming priests, and princes, who, for millennia, had been deviously but systematically exploited economically, politically, and intellectually. But, almost in the same breath, such sympathy usually merged with expressions of scorn for the people's ignorance and subservience—and dread of popular superstition and credulity. For these qualities, whether inextricable or just hard to eradicate, were the basic fodder of the bigotry, fanaticism, and intolerance which, in their view, like Spinoza's and Bayle's, had so disfigured human history.

For the providential Deists and entire moderate mainstream, anyhow, the case for equality was never in any real sense a priority. Dramatic changes might be needed, especially in the context of hardened tyranny and intolerance or long-entrenched civil strife, so that occasionally a thoroughgoing reformation or selective revolution must be contemplated. But if needed, the model of revolution should be either that of the Glorious Revolution in Britain—that is, an initiative led by noblemen to remodel monarchy and church—or else, better still, a restoration of order, toleration, and stable constitutional norms, orchestrated by an intelligent, enlightened well-meaning monarch like Henri IV, celebrated by Voltaire in his first major serious work, *La Henriade* (1723–6).[7] The tension between the moderate mainstream and Radical Enlightenment was certainly a schism between Deism and atheism, belief in supernatural agency and materialism, and over whether the *philosophes*' fight was solely against intolerance, superstition, and censorship, or also against existing structures of authority. But, at a deeper level, it was perhaps especially a struggle about whom and how far 'to enlighten' and ultimately, as we shall see, a contest between hierarchy and equality.

If the underlying strategy of Diderot's and d'Alembert's *Encyclopédie*, cleverly half-veiled beneath the outward rhetoric, was an egalitarian quest for the general projection of knowledge, or what has aptly been termed a 'democratization' of the rights of reason and understanding throughout society as a whole, most contemporaries including the whole moderate mainstream categorically disowned any such objective: as Voltaire reminded d'Alembert, in a letter of 2 September 1768, as far as he was concerned 'on n'a jamais prétendu éclairer les cordonniers et les servantes; c'est le partage des apôtres'.[8] Political sophistication, the arts, civilization itself being inseparable from hierarchy in Voltaire's schema, he tended to be bitingly sarcastic about the concept of equality. In a 'state of nature', such as primitive man had once shared with the quadrupeds, birds, and reptiles, he was willing to grant, Man had doubtless lived in a state of perfect equality. There 'domination' would indeed have been unthinkable, an absurdity. But, as far as he could see, in any more developed society, the concept was not in any way constructive or in the least appealing: 'l'égalité', as he summed the matter up, 'est donc à la fois la chose la plus naturelle, et en même temps la plus chimérique'.[9]

[7] Pomeau, *Politique de Voltaire*, 190.

[8] Martin-Haag, *Aspect de la pensée*, 147–58; Le Ru, *D'Alembert philosophe*, 191.

[9] Le Ru, *D'Alembert philosophe*, 209–13; Voltaire, *Dictionnaire philosophique*, 172–3; Payne, *The Philosophes*, 151–3, 162; Pomeau, *Politique de Voltaire*, 213.

German Natural Law theory and Barbeyrac, while, like Hobbes, certainly proclaiming a fully secularized 'natural equality' in the pre-political status of Man and one applying universally, were scarcely less disdainful of equality under society and the state than Voltaire. Anxious to underpin the patriarchal family, aristocracy, and kingship, these theorists immediately cancelled their starting point of 'natural equality', asserting the 'natural' inequality ordained by God in his highly unequal distribution of authority, family sway, status, and property.[10] By the 1740s, Humean scepticism, as we have seen, likewise evinced a marked proclivity to affirm the fundamental lack of equality between races, different peoples, and the sexes, Hume seeking to justify this new kind of hierarchy dividing humanity by formulating differences supposedly on the basis of empirical investigation and hard-headed induction.[11]

Moderate mainstream Enlightenment generally, then, tended to uphold the principles of monarchy, aristocracy, empire, and racial hierarchy. Anne Robert Jacques Turgot (1727–81), baron de l'Aune, one of the socially most select *philosophes*, a thinker-statesman who sketched out his general conception in the late 1740s, delivered two Latin lectures expounding his ideas at the Sorbonne in July and December 1750, firmly agreeing with Voltaire that history's course shows men were never intended by the divine Creator to be equal.[12] An ardent devotee of Locke, Newton, and Condillac as well as Montesquieu, and a true pillar of moderate Enlightenment in every way, as well as himself from an old Norman noble family with a training in theology, Turgot fully shared the views on the indispensability of religion, for society, expressed in *L'Esprit des loix*, indeed was even more inclined than Montesquieu to stress the 'advantages' Christianity has bestowed on humanity. In the—for France—intellectually decisive years 1746–8, rendered dramatic by the first major interventions of Diderot, Buffon, and La Mettrie, as well as Montesquieu's L'*Esprit*, he sternly took both Diderot and Buffon to task for betraying the 'simplicity and wise reserve' of Locke and Newton and plunging us back 'dans la nuit des hypothèses' besides being grossly irresponsible in dismissing Christianity as 'superstition'.[13]

Though he wished, at least for a time, to participate in the *Encyclopédie* and, at d'Alembert's request, did later pen five articles, including the article 'Existence' (1757), for the sake of his career at court, but also on intellectual grounds, he preferred to keep his distance from Diderot, d'Alembert, and the *encyclopédistes* with whom, indeed, he eventually broke. He was undoubtedly a vigorous anti-traditionalist for all that, indeed someone ardently supportive of development, growth, and change. A great champion of toleration and the progress of reason from 1748, he was a classic instance of an exponent of *anglicisme* and moderation caught in the French crossfire: after 1757 spoken of harshly by Diderot, on the one side, as a defector, after becoming one of Louis XVI's chief ministers, as comptroller-general,

[10] Hochstrasser, *Natural Law Theories*, 6; Stuurman, *François Poulain de La Barre*, 295.

[11] Popkin, *Third Force*, 65, 70–2.

[12] Haechler, *L'Encyclopédie*, 283–4; Manuel, *Prophets*, 25; Dagen, *L'Histoire*, 407; Dakin, *Turgot*, 10.

[13] Turgot, *Œuvres*, i. 90–7, 110–11; Dagen, *L'Histoire*, 409–10, 417, 420.

in 1774, he was equally denounced by the *dévots*, on the other, for his earlier ties with the *encyclopédistes*.[14]

Turgot, like the radicals, embraced the idea of the progress of *l'esprit humain* but qualified it by reinstating divine providence, like Voltaire, and, like Montesquieu, the centrality of religion. He further adjusted the concept by stressing besides Montesquieu's influence of climate and milieu the enhancing capacity of technological inventions like printing and the new textile machinery. For Turgot, new technology together with Newton's *Principia* were the two greatest human breakthroughs of recent times. He forged a conception of general human progress in all fields, or progress as such, which he calls *histoire universelle*, a progress in which aristocracy as well as Christianity are both key positive shaping forces.[15] Just as growing inequality is an essential engine of progress, in his opinion, nobility he conceives as an incontestably valid principle. A minor but telling symptom of the developing ideological schism was his reaction to Diderot's preference for omitting ecclesiastical, official, and noble titles from the lists of what, in the end, totalled 184 contributors to the *Encyclopédie*: after finally agreeing to participate, Turgot, like Montesquieu (but unlike most of the other thirty-four noble participants), insisted on formal acknowledgement of his aristocratic status and is hence referred to there as 'le Chevalier de Turgot'.[16]

Exploration, experiment, trial and error, discarding of dogma, ceaseless innovation, and accumulation of knowledge are conceived by Turgot as the essence of human history. But these impulses, he explained in 1750, are inseparable from the creation of hierarchies of types, classes, and peoples. As with Voltaire, the primitive savage is at the bottom of Turgot's pyramid while some or most more developed societies are always more inert and slower to progress than others.[17] As progress is achieved, more and more inequality becomes essential, especially in societies at the forefront of progress, like England and France. Peasants, he thought, contribute little other than at a very basic level.[18] Similarly, progress in the common crafts seemed to him comparatively easy because artisans and mechanics were very numerous. More difficult is moral, scientific, intellectual, political, and artistic progress, and here specialized kinds of education, breeding, refinement, and good taste are indispensable.

Among other typical patterns of divergence and opposition between mainstream and Radical Enlightenment, Turgot's perspective fully reflects the *angliciste* mainstream's preference for shifting the emphasis away from 'philosophy' and fundamental new ideas as the engine of progress to the 'genius' of specially gifted individuals, newly discovered techniques, and forms of practice and sociability, as well as religion. A favourite theme of Turgot, already in 1748 when he penned some

14 Dakin, *Turgot*, 16, 128, 135; Haechler, *L'Encyclopédie*, 283–4.

15 Manuel, *Prophets*, 13–14, 20–2, 40; Dagen, *L'Histoire*, 411–15; Kelley, *Descent of Ideas*, 119, 121.

16 Haechler, *L'Encyclopédie*, 175, 180.

17 Turgot, *Plan de deux discours*, 295–6, 303–5; Dagen, *L'Histoire*, 421; Manuel, *Prophets*, 34.

18 Manuel, *Prophets*, 36–40; Turgot, *Recherches sur les causes*, 132, 139–40.

notes on the subject, was the idea that it is less 'erreur' in Diderot's sense which hampers advancement of the truth and better government than the indolence, unexamined routines, inertia, and resistance to change rooted in so many societies.[19] While superstition, 'intolerance', and what he considers the natural cruelty and barbarity of primitive men are doubtless also barriers to human progress, rather than the credulity, ignorance, and priestcraft continually decried by the *encyclopédistes*, on the whole inertia seemed to him mankind's greatest defect.

There was much to obstruct formulation of a universal concept such as equality. Nevertheless, this idea had intermittently begun to be employed in politics over the century from the time of the English Levellers, in the 1640s, down to the Dutch 'revolution' of 1747–8, if only among the urban conglomerates at the western fringes of the Continent where social hierarchy was beginning to erode. If the Levellers were too preoccupied with the idea of 'free-born Englishmen', and too rooted in theology, to produce a truly universal conception of the unity of Man, the same may be true of the renewed democratic tendency, during the Orangist 'revolution' of 1747–8, seeking secular arguments for grounding the political accountability of the oligarchic regent governments of Amsterdam and other cities to the citizenry. Even so, exalting the 'general interest' and citing this as the ground for insisting on the accountability of the city governments, Daniel Raap and other Amsterdam *Doelisten* found themselves contending that here the 'lowest burger must be considered equal to the most eminent, retaining his freedom to express his opinion before the community', everyone having an equal stake in the upkeep of society and the state.[20]

Equality then served an actual, perceived, and strongly felt social and political need in north-west European urban social contexts but could only be shaped by 'philosophy'. The quest for equality was hence driven by need for an abstract conceptual device with which to justify schemes of mass politics and an incipient secular morality, especially notions of popular sovereignty and accountability to the people. True virtue as conceived by the moral philosophy of the Radical Enlightenment is something which by definition has no basis in custom, tradition, revelation, or theological doctrines, and is only found, as one scholar observes of the argument of Morelly's *Basiliade* (1753), in the philosophical principle of the natural equality of all men.[21]

Meanwhile, as has been aptly remarked, it was the democratic radical wing of the Enlightenment which invented the exclusively modern idea that an end to poverty is possible.[22] All the truly revolutionary ideas of the Enlightenment developed well before 1750 and the elimination of poverty was plainly no exception. Radical writers began to focus on the seeming injustice of the vast contrasts of wealth typical of early modern Europe. Morelly, like Radicati, Meslier, the young Rousseau, and others, held that institutionalized inequality of property and status destroys liberty,

[19] Turgot, *Recherches sur les causes*, 133; Dagen, *L'Histoire*, 416.

[20] Raap, *Korte Schets of Dag-Verhaal* (Knuttel 17961B), 90–1.

[21] [Morelly], *Essai sur le cœur humain*, 196–200; Wagner, *Morelly*, 190.

[22] Stedman Jones, *End to Poverty?*, 9–10.

upsets natural harmony, and renders society divisive, resentful, and oppressive.[23] But this social preoccupation remained relatively muted at first. Inequality *per se* was nothing new and the compassion for the poor found in these writers was only beginning to stimulate new thinking about social structure during the Early Enlightenment. For the moment concern with equality as a conceptual device in the abstract, as something required for moral and political theory, greatly preponderated over the question of how to redistribute wealth.

Hence, it was not the age-old economic pressures of deprivation which transformed equality into a fundamental preoccupation of western society but rather metropolitan erosion of social hierarchy combined with *l'esprit philosophique* resulting in the concept of 'equality' which led on to the idea that poverty can and should be eliminated. Doubtless a further factor behind the rise of 'equality' was the advent of Bayle's and Le Clerc's independent critical thinking, conceived as the key to truth and something potentially available to everyone, and applicable to everything, including political institutions. For autonomous individual judgement became inseparably linked to the criteria of impartial reasonable debate and exchange of views in an atmosphere of structured dialogue and listening; and this new ideal of dispassionate debate with counterparts with whom one disagrees, in a manner both parties consider impartial, balanced, and reasonable, is conceivable only on a basis of fundamental equivalence of the disputants accepted *a priori*. Reasonable debate, held Bayle, means deeming the contending parties equal in principle, otherwise examining, judging, and resolving differences ceases to be exclusively on the basis of reason and *critique*.[24] Consequently, a society proclaiming reason the sole criterion, and in which there is fundamental disagreement, is simultaneously obliged to adopt equality as axiomatic in a fundamentally new sense. Here again, reason forges the idea of equality; this then intensifies trends in society from which it first arose.

By the late seventeenth century, then, great controversies about thinking had evolved to a point where one could no longer avoid asking what this fundamental principle of equality, irrespective of particular societies and epochs, stemming from humanity's essential attributes actually means. With theology's hegemony seriously brought into question if not yet generally toppled, the question became intellectually urgent, creating a fertile terrain which was bound to be dominated, by the very nature of the material, by philosophers and political thinkers rather than preachers, lawyers, or administrators.[25] The question, reaching back to Grotius and Hobbes, was not in essence about legal status, political rights, religious duties, or economic opportunities but something still more profound and comprehensive: if no God-ordained order exists, or at least cannot be demonstrated philosophically, what meaningful alternative is there to grounding morality, politics, and social theory on

[23] [Morelly], *Basiliade*, i. 18, 33–4, 37–8; Ehrard, *L'Idée*, 538–9, 772–3; Lestringant, 'L'Utopie amoureuse', 83.

[24] Fontius, 'Critique', 12–13; Jaumann, *Critica*, 137.

[25] Clarke, 'Introduction', 9–10; Smith, *Spinozism, Liberalism*, 22–6; Waldron, *God, Locke, and Equality*, 9; Cherni, *Diderot*, 423.

a systematic, generalized radical egalitarianism extending across all frontiers, class barriers, and horizons?

Many late seventeenth-century thinkers, by no means only Spinoza and the Spinozists, contributed to the rise of the concept of basic equality. Descartes's two-substance doctrine, for instance, implies bodily characteristics, including sexual differences, play no part in shaping the powers and characteristics of the human mind, so that Cartesianism could be used to deny that men as distinct from women, men of one race or colour rather than another, or the healthy more than the sick, possess greater innate aptitude for the use of reason.[26] Cartesianism lent theoretical support to Poulain de La Barre's categorical assertion of the general equality of women, in his *Discours physique et moral de l'égalité de deux sexes*, of 1673, strengthening the idea that freeing the human mind from prejudice is an intellectual or educative emancipation unconnected at bottom with the individual's social status, race, wealth, bodily capacity, or religion.

Descartes, however, nowhere integrates his conception of the human mind into a theoretical structure requiring and justifying the fundamental moral and political equality of men in society. Here Hobbes came closer with his path-breaking concept of a general equality in the 'state of nature', an invaluably flexible analytical tool, afterwards taken up by Spinoza and to a degree also by Locke. 'When all is reckoned together', Hobbes affirms in the *Leviathan*, the differences between men in their faculties of body and mind are 'not so considerable as that one man can thereupon claim to himself any benefit to which another may not pretend as well as he'.[27] Roughly speaking, men are equal in terms of their power and even more equal in their minds than their bodies. If one is stronger, another may be more cunning, and 'such is the nature of men', observes Hobbes, 'that howsoever they may acknowledge many others to be more witty, or more eloquent, or more learned, yet they will hardly believe there be many so wise as themselves'. This is because we know the details of our own thoughts, he suggests, but mostly oversimplify the reasoning of others: 'but this proveth rather that men are in that point equal, than unequal.'[28] 'From this equality of ability', contends Hobbes, 'ariseth equality of hope in the attaining of our ends.'

Precisely this 'equality of hope' in fulfilling our aspirations was to dominate the democratic republicans' gradual construction of a general political theory of equality. For as Hobbes again observed, 'if a man be trusted to judge between man and man, it is a precept of the law of nature that he deal equally between them'.[29] Even in Hobbes, this budding principle of fundamental equality is in a few respects carried over to life under the commonwealth, notably regarding administration of justice, 'so as the great may have no greater hope of impunity when they do violence, dishonour or any injury to the meaner sort, than when one of these does the like to one

[26] Clarke, 'Introduction', 25; Schouls, *Descartes*, 31–4; Stuurman, *François Poulain de La Barre*, 7–10, 13–15, 87–92.

[27] Hobbes, *Leviathan*, 74–5, 96–7; Raphael, *Hobbes*, 31.

[28] Raphael, *Hobbes*, 49; Hobbes, *Leviathan*, 75; Waldron, *God, Locke, and Equality*, 78.

[29] Hobbes, *Leviathan*, 97.

of them'.[30] Significantly, Hobbes, for whom all subjects are and should be alike in status under the absolute monarch, even tries to argue for an 'equality of imposition' in matters of taxation, asserting the illegitimacy of all forms of exemption or privilege on the basis of noble, ecclesiastical, or other special social status, regardless of the fact that in the great majority of continental Europe at the time no such fiscal equivalence of subjects actually existed.[31]

Locke, of course, in his *Second Treatise on Government*, likewise asserts that 'all men by nature are equal'.[32] But for both Hobbes in large part, and also Locke, this 'equality of men by nature' effectively ceases with the advent of the state and has no reformist social implications and few other than strictly constitutional consequences in society constituted under a ruler;[33] and where it does, it persists in Locke primarily as an equality of conscience and the duty of salvation. Hobbes was undoubtedly the first general theorist of equality in the state of nature; but, by insisting, as he does, on the huge qualitative change that occurs with the transition, through the social contract, to life under the state, it is equally correct to say that he constructs a naturalist theory of structured, justified inequality: 'the inequality of subjects', he affirms in the *Leviathan*, 'proceedeth from the acts of sovereign power', something which, for him, overrides most of the natural rights preceding the state of society and politics. Locke too immediately claws back from his statement 'that all men by nature are equal', listing 'birth' rather obscurely as one important qualification, meaning certainly subjection of children to parents, and women to men, but implying at least also subordination of those of lower social status to royalty and nobility.[34]

In Locke, moreover, unlike Spinoza, there is no sustained effort to deploy basic equality to argue that democracy is the most 'natural' and fitting kind of state or press for freedom of lifestyle, expression, and publication.[35] Where Locke *does* attach wider political and social consequences to his notion of equality, this occurs mainly with respect to religious as distinct from other kinds of toleration. His vision of equality thus remains anchored in theological assumptions of a sort unsuited to help underpin a purely secular conception of basic equality. Locke's equality, moreover, is only provisionally universal, not applying in practice to those found not to believe in God or belong to churches. To ground legal and moral axioms independently of revelation and theological criteria, the radical *philosophes* needed very different arguments from those of Hobbes and Locke. From the perspective of both Enlightenment and modernity, Locke's equality certainly belongs, as one commentator expressed it, to 'what is dead' in his political thought.[36]

Spinoza, van den Enden, Koerbagh, Lahontan, Tyssot, Poulain de La Barre, Radicati, and Meslier, by contrast, are intensely preoccupied with the idea of basic

30 Ibid. 226. 31 Ibid. 227–8; Raphael, *Hobbes*, 37, 58; Hösle, *Morals and Politics*, 36.

32 Locke, *Second Treatise*, 269–70, 304; Marshall, *John Locke*, 209–10, 262, 298; Ashcraft, 'Locke's Political Philosophy', 230, 239, 242; Waldron, *God, Locke, and Equality*, 11.

33 Dunn, *Political Thought*, 100, 225–6, 250; Malcolm, *Aspects of Hobbes*, 49.

34 Locke, *Two Treatises*, 304; Marshall, *John Locke*, 298–9.

35 Wootton, 'Introduction', 87–8, 113, 115–16, 119; Waldron, *God, Locke, and Equality*, 116–17, 137.

36 Waldron, *God, Locke, and Equality*, 13, 226–7; Bronner, *Reclaiming*, 50–1.

equality as applied to society, politics, and freedom of expression. This entails complete rejection of the Hobbesian (and in part also Lockean) idea of the loss, or transfer, of Man's natural equality, and natural right, in the transition from the 'state of nature' to life in political society, as well as Locke's remnant of 'equality' carried over into society being essentially an equality of religious freedom, and freedom of conscience, within the bounds of revealed faith. Where Hobbes's contract emphatically sanctions structures of monarchical power without participation of those governed, and formal subordination of classes by the sovereign, indeed institutions of aristocracy and slavery, as well as censorship and ecclesiastical power, as also do Locke's, radical (i.e. Spinozist) thought privileges the democratic republic, holding this to be the form of state closest to nature and the natural equality of men.

In Spinoza, 'right' and power are equated in a distinctive and surprising fashion. Since, for him, only nature possesses a sovereign right over all things and 'the universal power of Nature as a whole is only the power of all individual things taken together, it follows that each individual thing has the sovereign right to do all it can do; that is, the right of the individual is co-extensive with its determinate power'.[37] In principle, then, there is no difference between the natural 'right' of men and animals, nor limit on either, beyond what men and all other creatures can actually do. If men rule the animal realm, this is solely because of their greater power, precisely as, through history, men have relegated women to inferior status, and often drudgery, merely through possessing greater physical strength. Such a thoroughgoing naturalism, equating men with all living creatures, enabled Spinoza to devise a theory of basic equality without floundering in a morass of difficulties over species and type distinction, or how to fix boundaries between men and other creatures, problems which bedevilled Locke's egalitarianism, necessitating resort to theological criteria to underpin his equality.

Basic equality in the Radical Enlightenment, then, is grounded on a principle of moral equivalence, given definitive metaphysical expression in part iii of the *Ethics*, 'unaquaeque res, quantum in se est, in suo esse persevare conatur' [Each thing, insofar as it is in itself, endeavours to persist in its own being].[38] In claiming men and animals possess individually a sovereign and equal right to exist and pursue their own advantage, each as naturally determined, Spinoza draws no distinction, as he says, between Man guided by reason and the madman, fool, or emotionally unbalanced, or indeed between such as proclaim divine inspiration and those who do not.[39] Under his rule of nature, men who acquire their moral sense through reason enjoy neither any more, nor less, right to conduct their lives as they choose than those who, unrestrained by reason, live 'under the sole control of appetite'. One's beliefs, degree of rationality, and sanity or insanity are all equally irrelevant to the

[37] Spinoza, *TTP* 237; Walther, 'Philosophy and Politics in Spinoza', 51–2; Smith, *Spinozism, Liberalism*, 136.

[38] Spinoza, *Opera*, ii. 146; Walther, 'Transformation des Naturrechts', 75, 83; Bronner, *Reclaiming*, 55.

[39] Spinoza, *TTP* 237.

fundamental equality of men and animals, as is what Locke calls 'knowledge of their maker' or its lack, under the state no less than in the state of nature.

Spinoza agrees with Hobbes that men opt to make a society chiefly because they 'desire to live in safety, free from fear as far as possible' but does not agree with him (or Locke) that the decision to form a state entails surrendering the individual's 'natural right'. For according to Spinoza, a deterministic conception of human motivation whereby every individual will in all circumstances choose what at that moment seems, from their standpoint, the greater good, or lesser evil, to him or her necessarily means no one willingly surrenders more of their natural right, or *potentia agendi* (power to act), than they must to secure advantages, or avoid disadvantages, greater than what is yielded.[40] Hence, no contract or agreement of any kind in human life has any force or validity, without some means of demonstrating that the cost of violating it exceeds the burdens of conforming to it. 'Natural right', then, held Spinoza, cannot be dissolved by reason of forming a society under the state or by any contract.

In his letter to Jarig Jelles of June 1674, where he explains the difference, as he saw it, between Hobbes and himself in political theory, emphasizing that, unlike Hobbes, he always preserves the natural right in its entirety, Spinoza added: 'and I hold that the sovereign power in a state possesses right over a subject only in proportion to the excess of its power over that subject. This is always the case in the state of nature.'[41] Here it emerges that for Spinoza, very differently from Hobbes and Locke, transition from the 'state of nature' to life under the state was less as a decisive, transforming shift, or event, or irreversible institutional change, than something essentially gradual and inherent in Man's nature, and hence in the course of nature itself.

All the radical writers, explicitly or not, followed Spinoza down this path, this being one of the defining traits of the radical tendency. Meslier asserts general equality with his usual force, claiming men are equal 'by nature', having all equally the right to live and walk upon the earth, and equally to enjoy 'leur liberté naturelle', share in the fruits of the earth, and work 'pour avoir les choses nécessaires et utiles à la vie'. The transition from the state of nature to society must, perhaps, entail a certain dependence or subordination of some to others: but it is also essential, he contends, that any such subordination 'des uns et des autres soit juste et bien proportionnée', by which, like Morelly later, he meant that only those who contribute most to the well-being and prosperity of all deserve positions of leadership, as well as respect, admiration, and status.[42] What this implies, both Meslier and Morelly argue, is that some should not be too much elevated and others not pressed down too far, nor should some be unduly flattered, and others trodden under, nor should society award the wealth of the earth inordinately to some 'et ne rien laisser aux autres', nor, finally, allocate all property and pleasure to one group and heap on

[40] Ibid. 239–40; Walther, 'Philosophy and Politics in Spinoza', 52.

[41] Spinoza, *Letters*, 258; Malcolm, *Aspects of Hobbes*, 49.

[42] [Morelly], *Basiliade*, i. 38–9; Meslier, *Testament*, ii. 170.

the rest all the drudgery, cares, and penury, 'tous les chagrins et tous les déplaisirs'. For such unbalanced inequality and subordination is manifestly 'injuste et odieuse et contre le droit de la nature même'.[43]

Diderot, in his political articles for the *Encyclopédie* in the early 1750s, needed to adopt a milder, more cautious tone; for he was not writing, like Radicati, Meslier, and Morelly, for others clandestinely or posthumously, and hence uninhibitedly. Nevertheless, for him too, Man's nature and passions change little owing to the shift from 'state of nature' to life in civil society,[44] the transition being one of gradual evolution whereas Rousseau, while attacking, and in a sense inverting Hobbes, nevertheless like him regards the change as pivotal and decisive. The great difference between Rousseau and Hobbes, of course, is that this was less a shift from darkness to light, for the former, than almost the reverse—from something morally positive to something apt to erode and degenerate. Both Diderot and Rousseau, accordingly, reject Hobbes's 'state of nature' but only Diderot continues along the 'evolutionary' line introduced by Spinoza.

Being something they conceived as having evolved naturally out of Man's nature and needs,[45] the collective decision of groups of men to congregate in political society cannot have been, held Spinoza, like Vico, Mandeville, and Diderot subsequently, a rational, calculated choice, made at a particular time. Hence it should not be regarded as a formal or binding 'social contract' or 'compact' as we find it in Hobbes and Locke. What is equal in the life of men, according to this conception, is neither men's individual desires or strength, and still less their degree of rationality or sanity, but primarily the equivalence of their wills, aspirations, and motivation, individual free wills which hence remain equal also after the formation of the state.

In essence, much the same concept had been expressed earlier by the brothers de La Court and van den Enden in his *Kort Verhael* (1662) and *Vrye Politieke Stellingen* (1665) where basic human equality, male and female, is argued not in terms of rationality, wealth, status, or supposed innate rights, but as 'natuirlijcke evengelijke-vryheit' [natural equal freedom] which the best type of commonwealth should then formalize and preserve as best it can in civil society, not just to secure the safety and freedom for which it was set up but also to minimize the discontent and opposition which would otherwise progressively impede its own functioning.[46] Similarly, in his *De jure ecclesiasticorum* (1665), Meyer holds, contrary to Hobbes, '*aequalitatem omnium hominum naturalem*' [natural equality of all men], something effective not only in the state of nature but which also 'remains integral and intact' when a state is formed so that no special social status, whether aristocratic, ecclesiastical, or any other, has or can have an intrinsic validity, or external origin, being just a political

43 Meslier, *Testament*, ii. 171; Ehrard, *L'Idée*, 520–1.

44 Proust, *Diderot*, 361; Hope Mason and Wokler, 'Introduction', pp. xiii–xiv.

45 Balibar, 'Jus, pactum, lex', 122; Den Uyl, 'Sociality and Social Contract', 21; Pascual López, *Bernard Mandeville*, 142–4.

46 Van den Enden, *Kort Verhael*, 30; van den Enden, *Vrye Politieke Stellingen*, 168–9; Bedjaï, 'Franciscus van den Enden', 299–300; Klever, 'Inleiding', 54–6; Klever, *Sphinx*, 148–9.

device and nothing more.[47] This means no 'inequality', as he calls it, possesses a legitimacy or authority that overrides the people in determining the shape of the polity.

An indispensable feature of a state organized for basic equality in this sense, argues van den Enden, is that no one can be permanently tied to any servile or menial occupation by law or assigned rank; rather all persons in lowly occupations have the prospect where they possess the necessary capacity and intelligence to emancipate themselves through work and negotiation from every form of dependence and servility.[48] In principle, this applies to women as well as men, and while Spinoza, notoriously, denies there is any known example of women participating in politics on an equal footing with men, or ruling over them, and on this ground, along with van den Enden (and Harrington), relegates women, like servants (and for the same reason, of dependency), to a permanently dependent status, denying them the right to participate in his democratic republic, his argument leaves open the possibility that should women somehow, some day, assert their independence from fathers and husbands, and act as equals to men, they would then be entitled to vote and participate in politics.[49]

Typical of van den Enden, Meyer, and Spinoza is the idea of the interdependence of the state's highest interest with the liberty and security of the individual—and conversely of the individual's prospects of freedom and security with supporting and defending the state.[50] The more a government departs from promoting the 'general interest', namely that of the majority, the more grievance and opposition will impede its functioning. In practice, no state can entirely escape the logic of democracy as the best and most natural form of human compact: for the pressure of the majority interest, acknowledged or not, is always at work in the political process.[51] If society is founded on the acting power of equal and initially free individuals, it follows, held Spinoza, that the power of a society and of its government is nothing but the impulse of all the citizens' power amalgamated together which will always be at its greatest when the citizenry is most united in its desires. Consequently, to fit the institutions and laws of the state to the human condition in the most effective way possible, legislators should consciously adjust the realities of human passions, inclinations, and motivation to the greatest good of the whole, all being deemed equal.

The quest for the 'general good', or what the Amsterdam *Doelisten* in 1748 called *het algemeene welzyn*, as essential in Diderot as Spinoza, inevitably leads to embracing the concept of basic equality, defined as the equivalence of human wills; for unless the principle of equivalence and reciprocity is adopted by law-makers, they

[47] [Meyer], *De jure ecclesiasticorum*, 38, 42–3, 52, 55; Bordoli, *Ragione e scrittura*, 93–4.

[48] Van den Enden, *Vrye Politieke Stellingen*, 158–9, 178.

[49] Matheron, 'Femmes et serviteurs', 376–80; Klever, 'Een zwarte bladzijde?', 40–2.

[50] Van den Enden, *Kort Verhael*, 3, 31, 69; van den Enden, *Vrye Politieke Stellingen*, 149, 169; Bedjaï, 'Franciscus van den Enden', 299; Smith, *Spinozism, Liberalism*, 130–7.

[51] Klever, 'Een zwarte bladzijde?', 39; Walther, 'Philosophy and Politics in Spinoza', 53.

will be precluded from devising a moral code, or constructing a sufficiently equitable rule of law, to meet with broad acceptance and minimize opposition. It is assuredly no accident that the modern idea of basic equality first emerged in the later Dutch Golden Age. For as Gregorio Leti, and later Mandeville, noted, a meaningful discourse of equality before the law requires a particular kind of administrative and judicial strength, anchored in the civic context.[52] By equalizing the protection and freedom afforded by the law which the monarchies and aristocracies of the day scarcely aspired to do, the United Provinces set a crucial example. As the Dutch Huguenot radical Jean-Frédéric Bernard had his Persian philosopher remark in 1711, 'cette égalité de protection', which he considers the most impressive feature of the Dutch Republic, 'est fondée sur le droit qu'a le citoien, comme membre de l'état'.[53]

Spinoza's doctrine then provides a means of instituting, and universalizing, a secular morality without relying on, or referring to, any teleology, supernatural agency, prior authority, ancient constitution, or precedent. Exactly this non-teleological doctrine of basic equality was adopted by Bayle to underpin his generalized freedom of conscience because, as he saw it, only such an innate, natural, fully secular morality proclaims a universalism from which no one, anywhere, whatever kind of property relations they participate in, and whatever their opinions, can be excluded. Bayle's toleration rests on the principle that there is a true universalism of basic equality, grounded on the notions of fundamental equity and justice, applicable to every individual and that this is the only effective ground for a comprehensive toleration. All our laws of morality, as he expresses this idea in his *Commentaire philosophique*, really depend on 'cette idée naturelle de l'équité', something innate in us, part of our natural heritage which illumines 'tout homme venant au monde'.[54]

Bayle judged faith and reason to be wholly non-compatible and mostly in opposition. Equally important, though, Bayle, on precisely this ground, sets faith wholly apart from and, to no small degree, also in opposition to morality. Faith cannot be explained, buttressed, or justified by reason, held Bayle, but far from meaning, as so many commentators have claimed, that this shows he was a true fideist and conscientious believer, this meant, in his opinion, that the basic rules of ethics which are essential to society and human life are explicable only by reason and never by faith. On the fundamental rationality of human morality, in fact, Bayle refuses to compromise and is never sceptical, though some modern scholars have indeed fallen into the trap of assuming—as was alleged (without evidence) by his enemy Barbeyrac—that he is a sceptic on moral issues. The unchallengeable primacy of natural reason in revealing to us what Bayle calls the 'les premiers principes généraux des mœurs' is alike natural, necessary, and universally valid; for it is the only way Man can ever

[52] Leti, *Raguagli politici*, II. ii. 408–10; Israel, *Dutch Republic*, 4.

[53] Bernard, *Réflexions morales*, 263.

[54] Bayle, *Commentaire philosophique*, 90; Gros, 'Bayle: de la tolérance', 306; Mori, 'Scepticisme', 277.

construct the moral system he perennially requires. Thus, in ancient Greece great progress was made in promoting morality but not at all owing to the pagan cults, which Bayle deemed inherently irrational and corrupt, but solely, he thought, to the efforts of the philosophers who, relying on reason alone, established the principles of ethics, of which equity and reciprocity are the chief.[55] This, of course, is the very reverse of scepticism.

No matter how erring and muddled the Socinians may be, argues Bayle, in his *Commentaire philosophique*, in applying reason to speculative matters, there can never be any limit, even when discussing the Bible, when applying reason to moral issues.[56] For him, autonomous reason is the only criterion when establishing and evaluating morality. God himself, he says, must conform to our basic notions of justice, equity, and goodness, for the logic of the moral law is a necessary and unalterable one not something subject to the divine will and something by definition independent of any divine ruling: hence, without exception 'il faut soumettre toutes les lois morales à cette idée naturelle d'équité, qui, aussi bien que la lumière métaphysique, illumine tout homme venant au monde'.[57] So important is the principle of basic equality in Bayle's conception of a secular morality divorced from all teleology, divine ordinance, or prior transcendental order that it prompts him to affirm, as he does repeatedly in his last works, that primitive societies based on equality—such as he took Lahontan's Spinozistic Canadian Indians and the ancient Scythians to be—must *ipso facto* be inherently of a higher ethical level than more hierarchical societies.[58]

Hence, while the man of faith, says Bayle, rightly insists the fundamentals of Christianity cannot be explained by reason, and this should never be attempted, the central mysteries of the Christian religion having no connection with reason, matters are exactly the opposite when it comes to discussing any question of morality. Here, holds Bayle, because only reason can adjudicate ethical issues, faith has no relevance at all, and everything must be settled exclusively on the basis of reason with no appeal to faith being allowed. In the *Réponse aux questions d'un provincial*, Bayle defines the human conscience as that 'jugement de l'esprit 'which leads us to do certain things 'parce qu'elles sont conformes à la raison', and debars us from others 'parce qu'elles sont contraires à la raison'.[59] The function of 'fideism' in his system being tactical only, and exclusively limited to rendering questions of faith uncertain, Bayle is in no way being inconsistent when affirming, in his *Commentaire*, that a strict rationalism, reason that is defined as the 'principes généraux de nos connoissances', is for us always the absolute and only guide when weighing and judging those moral issues posed in, and by, the Bible, since reason is 'la règle matrice et originale' of all Bible exegesis and, moreover, 'en matière de mœurs principalement'.[60]

55 Bayle, *Continuation*, i, *avertissement* pp. 8^v–9, and pp. 20, 238–9, 241.

56 Bayle, *Commentaire philosophique*, i. 89–90; McKenna, 'Norme et la transgression', 122.

57 McKenna, 'Norme et la transgression', 123; Bayle, *Commentaire philosophique*, i. 89–90.

58 Bayle, *Continuation*, ii. 427–30, 574, 591.

59 McKenna, 'Norme et la transgression', 121.

60 Ibid. 121; Bayle, *Commentaire philosophique*, i. 85.

Once basic equality, as introduced by the Spinozists, and espoused by Bayle and the radical stream generally, is conceded, men wield an objective, or at least common, criterion or touchstone for evaluating the human condition and political constitutions in whatever setting. Proclaiming the concept of basic equality, Spinoza, Bayle, and Diderot, the three greatest architects of Radical Enlightenment, fix the purpose of the state as the maximization of peace, security, and freedom for the majority, a criterion which in turn provides a universal benchmark by which to judge the actions of regimes of whatever hue or character. Indeed, with the introduction of this criterion every regime, in theory, automatically falls into one of two categories—either promoting or failing to promote the 'common good' or what Diderot calls the *volonté générale*. It was precisely this Spinozistic dualism of good and bad political systems evaluated in terms of the 'common good' which Paine later invoked when contrasting 'governments which arise out of society, in contradistinction to those which arose out of superstition and conquest'.[61]

Where, for Descartes, human minds are equal because they are intrinsically separate from bodies and equally capable of reason and, for Locke, because each soul is equally valid and potentially redeemable through spiritual striving, in van den Enden, Spinoza, Mandeville, and Diderot, with their one-substance monism, there is an altogether neater conjunction of instinct, appetite, will, and mind. Whether men act rationally or irrationally, whether they are primitive or sophisticated, ignorant or knowledgeable, ultimately makes no difference. Man's motivation is always the same and men's wills always equivalent. Whether a given mind has clear and distinct ideas, or is confused, it 'endeavours', as Spinoza expresses the point in proposition ix of part iii of the *Ethics*, 'to persist in its own being over an indefinite period of time and is conscious of this *conatus*' [Mens tam quatenus claras, et distinctas, quam quatenus confusas habet ideas, conatur in suo esse perseverare indefinita quadam duratione, et hujus sui conatus est conscia].[62]

Democracy is deemed by the first modern democratic republican theorists, Johan de La Court, van den Enden, and Spinoza, to be the best form of state because it is the closest to nature 'approaching most closely to that freedom which nature grants to every man',[63] so that in a democracy nobody surrenders his natural right to anyone else to the extent he can no longer influence opinion and decisions. What he surrenders, he yields, moreover, not to any group or individual, but to the majority of the commonwealth of which he is part, so that as citizens living under and protected by the state 'all men remain equal, as they were before in the state of nature'.[64] What is remarkable in Spinoza's, and later Diderot's, theory of equality is its strategic role in buttressing the entire structure of right and wrong, the passing of laws, and the conduct of the state. When a system of laws is created by a democracy, that is by the majority of the community, and receives the allegiance of all,

61 Paine, *Rights of Man*, 70.

62 Spinoza, *Opera*, iii. 147.

63 Van den Enden, *Kort Verhael*, 3, 31, 69; Spinoza, *TTP* 243.

64 Spinoza, *TTP* 243; Walther, 'Philosophy and Politics in Spinoza', 54–5.

held Spinoza, it enjoys moral authority, that is, convinces everyone that it is in their private interest to conform to those laws to the extent that its system of justice is based on the principles of equity and inequity. One concurs, says Spinoza, because 'those appointed to judge lawsuits are required to hold all men as equal with respect to persons, and to uphold equally everyone's right, neither envying the rich, nor despising the poor'.[65] Equality, therefore is the fundamental principle of democracy which, despite the constant risk of succumbing to sectarian strife, and provided the citizens remain vigilant, affords the best prospect of living well in a well-ordered state based on liberty, security, and stability, being the system which makes most explicit the underlying logic articulating every more or less stable state.[66]

Equality is adopted as a fundamental principle in van den Enden's elaborate schemes for democratic republics in New Netherland, in America, as well as Holland and later Normandy. Spinoza adopts egalitarianism because it provides the best, indeed only, way of justifying and establishing, without recourse to theological criteria, the principle of equality under the law, reciprocity as the basis of morality, equivalence of right in the framing of legislation, and freedom of expression as the basis of politics.[67] Since equality is the essential principle of democracy, and because democracy was judged the strongest, most efficient, and most sovereign form of state, equality became, for the Spinozists, a principle of paramount significance; and for the same reasons, the later Radical Enlightenment of Diderot, d'Alembert, Boulanger, and Helvétius similarly espoused egalitarianism together with the rest of the Spinozist legacy.

Equality thus became an inalienable 'natural right', carried over from the state of nature. Tom Paine echoed this radical tradition when asserting that Man's 'natural rights are the foundation of all his civil rights'.[68] Fundamental equality is therefore always applicable and the perennial criterion of *l'esprit de critique* whether particular societies or individuals in a society acknowledge this or not. At the same time, equity must be incorporated into the decisions and laws of the state if it is to pursue its own and its citizens' best interests. Equality before the law is an aspect of this equality of principle which may or may not exist in any particular state and which can become institutionalized only where the principle of equality, including equality in the free expression of opinion, and right to publish, is expressly upheld and fought for by society.

The *gemeene beste*, *gemeene interest*, or 'common good' in the Spinozist tradition, rejecting all presuppositions of a prior transcendental order, resting on a conception of basic equality which negates the innate rights and duties postulated by the Natural Law theorists but insists on a concept of 'general will', resurfaces in Radicati, Mably, Morelly, Diderot, and then Rousseau.[69] However, Rousseau,

[65] Spinoza, *TTP* 244.
[66] Ibid. 243, 252–4; van den Enden, *Kort Verhael*, 30–1; Israël, *Spinoza: le temps*, 301–3.
[67] Bedjaï, 'Franciscus van den Enden', 297–303; Mertens, 'Franciscus van den Enden', 723–4.
[68] Paine, *Rights of Man*, 68.
[69] Vernière, *Spinoza*, 483; Mertens, 'Franciscus van den Enden', 723.

already in his *Discours sur l'inégalité* of 1754, somewhat diverges from Diderot and the Spinozist legacy in his conception of the 'general will', and in his estimate of natural man and the impact of the state on him and society, and while joining Mably, Morelly, and Diderot in rebuking Hobbes for his excessively negative picture of natural man, also, by implication, criticizes them (and expressly criticizes Mandeville) for conceiving of morality as an essentially social and political construct rather than issuing directly from the natural sensibility of Man.[70] While, like the radicals, scorning the Natural Law tradition of Grotius, Pufendorf, Locke, and Barbeyrac, and while agreeing with Diderot that in the 'state of nature' there is no consciousness of moral right and wrong, it was nevertheless there, he argues, that morality, arising from Man's natural compassion and pity, had its primary and real origin.[71]

On the subject of equality, though, Rousseau largely aligns with Diderot and the radical tradition. Given that he was especially close to Diderot during the years 1746–50, it seems likely his ideas on equality developed at least partly through group discussion among Diderot's café and dining circles. Consciously or unconsciously, Rousseau, in any case, advanced much the same ground for the essential superiority of the democratic republic as Johan de La Court and Spinoza, and indeed echoes their argument: the democratic republic is the best form of state being the closest to the state of nature in that there Man's natural liberty remains most intact and inequality, and the distortions which inequality generates, the least. He too uses the idea of the General Will as a primary criterion. The laws of the democratic republic, held Rousseau, must be based on 'la volonté générale', something conceived as quite distinct from, albeit linked to, the will of the majority: in a democracy, the majority's will is simply what is actually decided; the General Will, on the other hand, has a fixed, unalterable quality and can diverge sharply from what the majority decides in any given case, being roughly equivalent to the timeless general interest, an abstract good which must always exist however well or badly men recognize it.

Rousseau proclaimed 'la volonté générale' infallible in that it must, by definition, tend to the public advantage defined as the common good.[72] Here indeed, as Johan de La Court, van den Enden, and Spinoza already saw in the early 1660s, is an idea relying for its efficacy on the principle of basic equality as an equivalence of wills, enhancing the effectiveness and positive influence of the state the more there is a pooling of those wills.[73] A sceptic might object that there need be no connection at all, in practice, between what the majority decides and the true interest of all. The force of Spinoza's idea that majority votes will relate to the General Will, later adapted by Rousseau, relies, however, on the principle of the equality of wills and the calculation that private interests, no matter how crass, selfish, and narrowly

[70] Rousseau, *Discourse on the Origin*, 75.

[71] Proust, *Diderot*, 361.

[72] Rousseau, *Social Contract*, 203.

[73] Van den Enden, *Kort Verhael*, 3, 31; Mertens, 'Franciscus van den Enden', 723; Walther, 'Philosophy and Politics in Spinoza', 55.

concerned, will continually clash and cancel each other out, thereby tending to produce consensus only for what is most likely to serve the public interest.[74]

It is for this reason Spinoza thinks that in the democratic republic 'there is less danger of a government behaving unreasonably' than in any other form of state; for in his view, it is unlikely (though by no means impossible) for the majority 'to agree on the same piece of folly'.[75] To promote the influence of the general interest over the conduct of the majority, as both Spinoza and Rousseau equally stress, a full and equal freedom of speech and expression must be accorded to everyone. Here, yet again, both the conception of a General Will as the sum of all individual interests, and the idea of curbing of private interests with other private interests, wholly depends on the equivalence, liberty, and reciprocity of individual wills, that is the idea of basic equality.

2. ARISTOCRACY, RADICAL THOUGHT, AND EDUCATIONAL REFORM

In 1709, the Anglo-Irish High Church Anglican William Carroll, in a virulent attack on Locke and others he considered Spinoza's English disciples, indignantly denounced the consequences of Spinoza's thought for ecclesiastical power and clerical privilege. The tract *De jure ecclesiasticorum* (1665), which he had just read and wrongly attributed to Spinoza (rather than Meyer) but correctly judged Spinozistic in character, proclaims the principle, diametrically against Hobbes, that 'the natural equality of mankind is not in private persons chang'd by the institution of a commonwealth'; this necessarily implies, should such reasoning be correct, nothing less than that 'all the inequality betwixt Man and man in civil society' is by no means divinely ordained, or intrinsic, but purely man-made and derived from questionable legislation and dubious motives.[76] Carroll's main worry was with the consequences of such a doctrine for the Anglican establishment. For the obvious inference, he saw at once, is that 'no sort of privileges or divine institution can be found in the Holy Scriptures of the Old and New Testaments which can rightly or truly be ascribed to the clergy' and that all the power and privileges of the clergy so imposing over so many centuries are reckoned to be 'deriv'd, no less, nor otherwise than that of other citizens: and that there is no difference betwixt the latter and the former'. In effect, Spinozism means the end of the ecclesiastical estate.

Radical writers despised the clergy and their privileges; but they were equally hostile to the principle of aristocracy. Exactly the same unremitting demolition of

[74] Spinoza, *TTP* 242–3; Rousseau, *Social Contract*, 203–4; Vernière, *Spinoza*, 483; Cobban, *Aspects*, 24, 148.

[75] Spinoza, *TTP* 242.

[76] Carroll, *Spinoza Reviv'd*, 9; [Meyer], *De jure ecclesiasticorum*, 38; *Bibliothèque choisie*, 21 (1710), 42; Bordoli, *Ragione e scrittura*, 94.

status as Meyer performs on the ecclesiastical estate was wrought by Spinoza, van den Enden, Koerbagh, and Mandeville, besides Knutzen, the *Symbolum*, Radicati, Vico, Wachter, von Hatzfeld, Edelmann, Meslier, Morelly, Mably, and other French writers, on the nobility. Meslier, like Morelly later, claims the forefathers of those who in his day 'font tant de bruit et tant de cas de leur noblesse' were actually nothing but cruel and bloody oppressors, brutal robbers, tyrants, and murderers. It was thus a blatant abuse and 'injustice manifeste' to seek to establish on such a ridiculously flimsy basis and pretext 'une si étrange et si odieuse disproportion entre les différens états et conditions des hommes' as existed in his day in France.[77] Aristocracy and the consequent gap between noblemen and those over whom they tyrannize is inherently unjust, holds Meslier, being 'nullement fondée sur le mérite des uns, ni sur le démérite des autres' and thoroughly odious because, in those society designates nobles, institutionalized inequality chiefly inspires arrogance, ambition, and conceit which in turn only engenders envy, hatred, feuding, and vengeance.[78]

Listing the main factors underpinning arbitrary government, authoritarianism, and petty absolutism in Germany, in 1745, Hatzfeld included, beside the machinery of absolutism itself, and the system of princes and courts, and the imposture of priestcraft, a third great pillar of political slavery—namely, the common people's ingrained admiration of social hierarchy and veneration of high rank. Commoners might be ruthlessly and brutally treated by courtiers; but ordinary folk nevertheless still go in perfect awe of those of 'high birth' while in their ignorance utterly scorning philosophers. It is, held Hatzfeld, a dreadful abuse that most men always prefer the richest, grandest, and most exalted persons to be their rulers rather than the most meritorious, conscientious, and knowledgeable, something all the more senseless in that 'titles and marks of honour are of no significance unless they rest on virtue and ability'.[79] Titles, he says, amount to absolutely nothing in themselves; yet the common people are utterly fascinated by and humbly respect them.

The project to delegitimize aristocracy follows directly from the idea of basic equality adopted at the outset by radical thought in the 1660s. Who is 'noble and who ignoble' asserts Koerbagh in his *Bloemhof* of 1668, is a matter requiring careful consideration. For most men, it would appear, have dismally unsound and incorrect notions on this point. In his opinion, the 'ignoble' is merely he who is unlearned and lacks understanding even if incontestably descended 'from the greatest king': by contrast, 'edel is hy die wijs en geleerd is alwaar dat hy vande de armste bedelaar voortgekomen was' [noble is he who is wise and learned even if he is descended from the poorest beggar].[80] Aristocratic birth, he suggests, in reality counts for nothing, the assumption that noble birth is something very fine and legitimate being just a popular superstition.

[77] Meslier, *Testament*, ii. 173, 178; [Morelly], *Basiliade*, i. 18, ii. 133; Ehrard, *L'Idée*, 523, 538.
[78] Meslier, *Testament*, ii. 169.
[79] [Hatzfeld], *Découverte de la vérité*, p. xxxiv.
[80] Koerbagh, *Bloemhof*, 346.

Yet those who inherited the Spinozist thesis, the radical *philosophes* of mid eighteenth-century France, were not incendiaries preaching revolt against kings, priests, and aristocrats and did not consider it their business to stir up social discontent and unrest. Nor, indeed, would they have been permitted to do so if they had. Even so, Diderot and d'Alembert, unlike Boulainvilliers, were no apologists for the existing social order and, unlike Voltaire, refused to be flatterers of kings and courts.[81] To a greater extent, perhaps, than historians have tended to allow, if usually in a quiet and subtle way, they, along with writers such as Meslier, Mably, Morelly, Vico, Boulanger, and Rousseau, engaged in a remarkably wide-ranging social and cultural critique aimed at exposing the shortcomings, diminishing the prestige, and ultimately lessening the influence of the aristocracy. Moreover, they were not just criticizing particular nobles or nobilities for being ignorant or neglecting their proper duties, or reproaching some for failing to live up to the elevated ideals of others. Rather they advance the principle of basic equality as part of a wider philosophical *critique* of contemporary society, culture, and education not with the aim of directly inspiring a movement of social revolt but rather the objective of exposing what they saw as the basic injustice and irrationality of aristocracy and undermining its legitimacy and respect for it.

A powerful objection raised by d'Alembert in 1753 was the flawed character and results of aristocratic education. It was a rooted prejudice of the society in which he lived, he states, that aristocrats supposedly enjoy an education greatly superior to that provided to others and were consequently considered, when judging literature and the arts, to be 'des connoisseurs plus éclairés'. But, in practice, such assumptions prove altogether false. The education of young nobles, being restricted to mere externals, doubtless equipped them 'à imposer au peuple', as he puts it, 'mais non pas à juger les hommes'.[82] Regrettably, it was the custom in France continually to remind young *seigneurs* of the illustriousness of their names, and glory of their birth, thereby fostering an entrenched, institutionalized arrogance harmful to society instead of inspiring in them 'de motifs plus réels et plus nobles' and, in particular, reminding them 'sans cesse que les autres hommes sont leurs égaux par l'intention de la nature'.[83]

Many nobles, he complains, scarcely suspect that there exist numerous commoners who far surpass them in judgement, expertise, experience, and talent. The falsity and speciousness of aristocratic culture seemed to d'Alembert nowhere more evident than in discussions about literature. Lamentably, most writers and poets in France had been thoroughly schooled in the arts of flattery and servility. This d'Alembert conceives as a vicious form of social corruption stemming from a brutally imposed but completely false conception of noble worth. No matter how

81 Shklar, 'Jean d'Alembert', 647; Hope Mason, 'Materialism and History', 154–5.

82 D'Alembert, *Mélanges de littérature*, ii. 100.

83 Ibid. ii. 100–1; Gordon, 'Great Enlightenment Massacre', 142–3.

mediocre, the *homme de lettres* who bows and dances in attendance the most around aristocrats is in their eyes, he remarks scathingly, the best in his profession.[84] In this way, a literary culture evolves which nourishes the very prejudice and imposture on which the false status and power of aristocracy rest: for it is then flattery and deference which gain men positions and advancement in society. In adding that experience shows that even philosophers are not exempt from such servility, d'Alembert perhaps had Voltaire in mind: for even *philosophes*, he remarks, cultivate prejudices not least by flattering nobles where these are useful to themselves and sometimes with as much energy as they show in combating 'ceux qui leur nuisent'.[85]

But if the pomposity generated by nobility was the most pernicious of all, it was not the only source of organized affectation and speciousness. D'Alembert and Diderot ridiculed all the contrived expression, grandiloquence, and pedantry flourishing under the rigidly hierarchical cultural system of their time along with its overblown legal, medical, artistic, literary, and other professional jargon. No great admirer of Newton, at one point Diderot aligns with those who had for decades criticized the deliberate obscurity of the latter's *Principia*, holding that calculated aloofness and obscurity serve only further to inflate what is specious and interpose a thick veil between the people and knowledge of reality. Obscure authors like Newton and Stahl, he complains, write only for a few initiates when it would have cost them only a month of toil to render their books clear and comprehensible to all, a month sparing three arduous years of study 'à mille bons esprits'.[86] There then, are not three thousand years of work wasted through sheer arrogance which could have been profitably put to work in other ways?

Re-educating the public, in this regard, hence became a primary radical objective. Diderot, in his *De l'interprétation de la nature* of 1753, the same year in which volume iii of the *Encyclopédie* came off the presses, revived the old war cry of van den Enden, Koerbagh, and Meyer: 'hâtons-nous de rendre la philosophie populaire'; and precisely this distinctly subversive social and political strategy lay behind his whole conception of the *Encyclopédie*.[87] Diderot summons scientists, medical men, academicians, and philosophers to abandon completely the scholasticism and obscure metaphysical terminology of the past and make themselves accessible to the ordinary reader. Clarity of writing, he insisted, not only facilitates comprehension and speeds up the process of understanding their work but helps diffuse their findings more widely.

In this way, radical philosophy became inseparable from a general reformation of knowledge and enlightening the people.[88] Yet, such zeal for promoting equality of knowledge and understanding, denying the superior judgement of the aristocracy,

[84] D'Alembert, *Mélanges de littérature*, ii. 102; Goodman, *Republic of Letters*, 37–8; Mortier, 'Diversités culturelles', 28.

[85] D'Alembert, *Mélanges de littérature*, ii. 97.

[86] Diderot, *Œuvres philosophiques*, 216; Martin-Haag, *Aspect de la pensée*, 148, 153, 158, 160.

[87] Diderot, *Œuvres philosophiques*, 216; Vandenbossche, 'Adriaan en Jan Koerbagh', 182–3; Le Ru, *D'Alembert philosophe*, 187–8, 193, 195; Martin-Haag, *Aspect de la pensée*, 48, 176.

[88] Martin-Haag, *Aspect de la pensée*, 48, 176; Goodman, *Republic of Letters*, 25–7.

clergy, lawyers, academies, and other more or less self-appointed elites, had little to do with praising the common man or seeking to idealize popular culture and attitudes; it was a stance wholly remote from present-day society's adulation of the common, the ordinary, and the popular, in terms of both taste and opinion.[89] Veneration of aristocratic grandeur had earlier moved Meslier to deplore the multitude's crassness and credulity, their ignorance being the chief reason they scarcely suspect the 'natural rights' of the human condition, 'ni le tort et l'injustice qu'on leur fait'.[90] In his opinion, it is the 'errors' prevalent among ordinary folk which chiefly compel even 'les personnes sages et éclairés' to remain silent and inactive despite their seeing clearly the injustice and abuse of the existing social and political order.[91] Similarly, Diderot and La Mettrie regarded the common man as in no small part author of his own woes and oppression through a superstition and ignorance embraced devoutly, lovingly, even fanatically.

The people then are given a wholly new status; but not the ideas or culture of the people. Indeed, Diderot openly scorns *la sagesse populaire*, the people's common sense, as the most useless thing in the world.[92] For besides lack of understanding, credulity, superstition, vulgarity, and fondness for priests, ordinary folk revere the supposedly noble and high-born and prize as great practical good sense commonplaces which are, in reality, totally fatuous or false. Offering two examples of such fatuousness, he quotes the familiar maxim 'there is nothing new under the sun' and the popular injunction 'il ne faut point disputer des goûts'.[93] Both expressions, he says, are, for anyone who thinks, completely absurd. The latter, he remarks, is often taken to mean that there is neither good nor bad in matters of taste, an opinion which could not be more mistaken.

Writers and poets fabricate a specious culture of flattering aristocracy which damages society as a whole. All men, avers d'Alembert, whatever the claims of pride, flattery, and popular foolishness, 'sont égaux par le droit de nature'.[94] What he terms 'le principe de cette égalité' resides in the need which all men inevitably perceive to associate with, and depend on, each other and 'dans la nécessité où ils sont de vivre en société'. But if this principle holds good, as it does, how then is this 'égalité naturelle' systematically set aside, at least in appearance and on the surface, 'par une inégalité de convention' introducing an elaborate hierarchy of ranks into every known developed society with each rank being assigned a widely different level of status and 'devoirs extérieurs'?[95] D'Alembert stresses the word 'exterior' because, he like Diderot, following Spinoza and Bayle, insists the interior, universal, and real obligations of men 'sont d'ailleurs parfaitement égaux pour tous'.[96]

[89] Martin-Haag, *Aspect de la pensée*, 181–2.

[90] Meslier, *Testament*, ii. 220–1.

[91] Ibid. i. 11–13, ii. 220.

[92] Diderot, *De l'interprétation de la nature*, 238; Le Ru, *D'Alembert philosophe*, 192.

[93] Diderot, *De l'interprétation de la nature*, 238–9; Martin-Haag, *Aspect de la pensée*, 65–6, 68.

[94] D'Alembert, *Mélanges de littérature*, ii. 125.

[95] Ibid.; Goodman, *Republic of Letters*, 36–7.

[96] D'Alembert, *Mélanges de littérature*, ii. 125–6.

Those who deny basic equality are gravely in error but adduce a show of plausibility in the great variety and variation in human ability and talent: 'c'est en effet dans [les talens] que consiste la vraie différence des hommes.'[97] Yet the system of inequality dominating society is not based on the difference in men's abilities. The reason, he argues, why the existing system of inequality, indeed any long-institutionalized hierarchy, despite lacking all basis in nature and human reality, nevertheless remains powerful and endures is chiefly, he thought, one of psychological and social expediency. A fixed, decreed hierarchy of orders, bogus, bizarre, and utterly unjust though it is, yet provides, he notes, an expedient which difference in abilities does not, for justifying the jarringly disproportionate inequalities of status and possessions prevailing in the world. For to him it seemed inconceivable men should ever have acquiesced without at least some plausible explanation, however specious, in 'un préjugé onéreux au plus grand nombre', resulting in institutionalized and lifelong drudgery, destitution, and injustice for most.[98] Only better education and a philosophical strategy of encyclopaedism can combat such vast, all-embracing error.

Descartes had already highlighted the idea that Man's self-enlightenment, through philosophy, is the way to free the human mind, both individual and collective, from the shackles of the past; and, although he barely explores this point, it is implicit in his argument that such an intellectual process must also be a great equalizer. Here was the genesis of a conceptual strategy destined to generate a universal philosophical egalitarianism in modern society, and one devoted to the cause of intellectual 'enlightenment'. For, as time would show, the advent of the New Philosophy had been not just an intellectual 'révolution totale' as Turgot unhesitatingly calls it, but also something bound to engender a project to emancipate men from error and prejudice. But how was emancipation of the intellect to be translated into a general education of the illiterate, ignorant, and the poor, and more generally of women, removing their instruction from the hands of religious bodies, theologians, and scholastics, providing moral and social guidance according to the precepts and maxims of *la philosophie*? If the true aim of philosophy, as Morelly expressed the point in 1745, is to summarize what men know while seeking also to extend and 'à dissiper l'obscurité' which envelops our knowledge, education's true goal must then be to subject 'notre cœur à l'examen de l'esprit' and subject it to the principles 'que lui dicte la raison'.[99]

General re-education, then, of a consciously revolutionary kind, was a key aim of Diderot, d'Alembert, and the Radical Enlightenment. Because everyone is equal, all must be allowed the same access to knowledge and understanding and all the more so because nothing is more apt to overthrow the democratic republic than 'superstition' and ignorance, though van den Enden had paid considerably more attention to the problem of the relationship between basic equality and education than had Spinoza himself.[100] The need to democratize knowledge is the main reason for

[97] D'Alembert, *Mélanges de littérature*, ii. 126. [98] Ibid. ii. 127.

[99] Morelly, *Essai sur le cœur humain*, 155.

[100] Van den Enden, *Kort Verhael*, 3^{v}; Bedjaï, 'Franciscus van den Enden', 298.

van den Enden's and Meyer's vehement hostility to the closed professional character of law and medicine, and especially their use of technical jargon all but impenetrable to the uninitiated. Convinced that a new kind of education, weaning the common people away from prejudices encouraging credulity and inequality, would strengthen liberty, toleration, and democracy, in particular by exposing and discrediting the deceit of priestcraft, kingship, and aristocracy, van den Enden proclaims equality an inestimable truth and precious social reality ever vulnerable to being obscured and subverted by imposture and deception. Revealing the methods and idioms by which the people are misled must therefore be the paramount concern of all true educationalists.[101]

If all radical thought held that education in its traditional format systematically perverts and obscures men's view of our cosmos and the human condition, and hence also leads men to contravene the basic principles of morality, this view was expounded with particular emphasis and force by Bayle. Bayle, always fascinated by the question of how a notion contradicting the most elementary rules of natural reason can be believed by almost everyone in a particular group, offers a cultural explanation, maintaining that credulity, superstition, and defiance of the rules of reason stem principally from traditional structures of education.[102] Conventional education, he argues, easily erases awareness of the fundamental laws of reason which means also, the two being so closely linked, that it readily obliterates all foundations of equity and justice, substituting the most monstrous injustice in the name of peoples, religions, rulers, or groups provided this is supported with mysterious terminology and theological explanations.

This combined with his doctrine of *conscience errante*, and the moral integrity of the sincerely ignorant, led him to assert that society must accept the moral innocence of those taught to think even the most ridiculously irrational things no matter how destructive, and who are then encouraged to discriminate, foment hatred, and persecute. For their education leads them innocently to imbibe mistaken doctrines while depriving them of any means to cope with the consequences of such error. How then, can society combat intolerance, bigotry, and credulity in the common interest? In the *Commentaire philosophique*, Bayle deliberately leaves this question in the air but, presumably, means the reader to infer, without his spelling it out, that education itself must therefore be fundamentally reformed and, especially, removed from the hands of theologians.

Radical Enlightenment equality urged the democratization of knowledge and making the same ideas, techniques, and critical methods available to the poor and unprivileged as the rich and privileged had access to. Yet a Postmodernist claiming this rhetoric of equality was really just an arrogant quasi-colonial, western 'Enlightenment discourse', designed to master the cultures and traditions of others, might still raise the objection that this was a bogus equality extended to white

[101] Van den Enden, *Kort Verhael*, 3^{v}; van den Enden, *Vrye Politieke Stellingen*, 153–5, 175–6; Klever, *Sphinx*, 149–50.

[102] Bayle, *Commentaire philosophique*, 345; Mori, *Bayle philosophe*, 285–6.

Europeans and Americans but not to the rest of mankind. Was not the greater part of the world falling under European domination by the later eighteenth century? Yet it is precisely here, with its stress on the fundamental unity of mankind, that the Radical Enlightenment opposed the new varieties of hierarchy—racism and imperialism—with which more conservative elements of the Enlightenment, and their nineteenth-century heirs, were to exert their greatest and most pervasive impact on the history of the next two centuries.

Pre-1750 radical thought, then, as one scholar aptly has expressed the point, 'produced the first truly universalist concepts of equality'.[103] Undoubtedly. But this crucial fact makes it imperative to differentiate radical from conservative Enlightenment in a far clearer and more comprehensive fashion than historians are accustomed to do. Van den Enden's, Poulain's, and Meslier's assertion of equality of the races was reinforced in the 1740s, in French materialist circles, by means of one particular reading of Buffon. For Buffon compiled, in the long treatise on the varieties of the human species *Histoire naturelle de l'homme*, published shortly after Diderot's *Lettre* in 1749, an imposing array of empirical evidence showing that 'le genre humain n'est pas composé d'espèces essentiellement différentes entre elles', and that, on the contrary, there was originally only one race of men and women that could and still can readily breed between its different branches.[104] Only later, held Buffon, after dispersing across the face of the earth, and through undergoing the different influences of climate and environment, did groups of men undergo 'différents changements' affecting skin colour, hair, and other features of physiognomy which, however, remain superficial rather than essential traits.

The important point for those intent on interpreting Buffon's findings in an egalitarian fashion (there were also other readings) was that such hereditary traits as skin colour are of the sort that would eventually fade away were the environmental factors responsible no longer to apply. Admittedly, Buffon also develops a theory of degeneration to explain the deterioration of certain subgroups of animals, including men, where conditions are allegedly unfavourable. He does in fact seem to have thought that black Africans have less intelligence than Europeans and, while appalled by the institution of slavery, provides no systematic 'philosophical' condemnation of it either.[105] But, for the universalists, this still left intact his essential thesis that the human race is a single entity, derived from a single type, and that in principle everyone has the same fundamental characteristics and drives.

The principle of basic equality after the 'state of nature', then, was from the outset, and throughout, fundamental to the Radical Enlightenment and was forcefully and eloquently expressed by a impressively large number of writers, beginning in the 1660s with Spinoza, Meyer, Koerbagh, and van den Enden. After 1700, this legacy is further nurtured in the writings of Bayle, Mandeville, Vico, Doria, Radicati, Du Marsais, Meslier, Boureau-Deslandes, and Hatzfeld, and then, in the

103 Stuurman, 'How to Write a History of Equality', (forthcoming).

104 Ibid.; Roger, *Buffon*, 157, 177–80.

105 Roger, *Buffon*, 181; Cherni, *Buffon*, 90–1.

1740s and 1750s, in Diderot, d'Alembert, Mably, Morelly, Boulanger, Helvétius, and others. Few historians, it is true, have duly inferred from this that the principle of equality proclaimed so forcefully by the French Revolution was actually an outcome, and grew directly out of, the pre-1750 European Enlightenment. Indeed, it remains quite usual, despite a growing mass of evidence demonstrating the historical incorrectness of such claims, to maintain 'that this new faith in human equality did not arise directly from the Enlightenment'.[106]

Obviously, the prevailing general image and reputation of the western Enlightenment today often lags seriously behind the reality that historical research, over recent decades, has actually uncovered a gap between the state of our knowledge and how this crucially important episode in the history of humanity is thought about and discussed, which remains at present, in the western world, just as much as elsewhere, a rather serious social and political as well as intellectual and cultural obstacle.

[106] Hampson, *Enlightenment*, 255; Hardt and Negri, *Empire*, 77–81.

22

Sex, Marriage, and the Equality of Women

1. CARTESIANISM AND FEMALE EQUALITY

Simon Tyssot de Patot's second Spinozistic novel, *La Vie, les avantures et le voyage de Groenland du Révérend Père Cordelier Pierre de Mésange* (Amsterdam, 1720), includes a long description of a polar underworld utopia called Rufsal where the public religion is Spinozism.[1] In this underground society, there was no talk of divinely decreed laws or institutions and the sovereign power over Man is nature itself. Here only the highest moral standards prevail and celibacy is regarded as wholly ridiculous or outrageous. Moreover, as the novel's hero is astounded to learn, everyone, men and women alike, is regarded as equal, polygamy having been abolished long before and equity being the most essential principle of the moral system.[2]

Tyssot de Patot evolved gradually into a convinced Spinozist from the late 1670s through the 1680s.[3] It was, however, not Spinozism but Cartesianism which produced the first systematic theory arguing for the equality of women. It was, moreover, precisely one of the philosophically most problematic features of Descartes's system, his rigid dualism, which, for the first time, made it possible to circumvent traditional ideas affirming the natural subordination, dependency, and weaker character of the female sex. Cartesian dualism did this by postulating a wide gulf between body and mind and by denying all possibility of interaction between these distinct substances. Exploiting this dualism, François Poulain de La Barre (1647–1723) published three major Cartesian feminist treatises, in Paris, in the years 1673–5, commencing with his *De l'égalité des deux sexes* (1673), path-breaking texts asserting the fundamental equality of women. Descartes's emancipating impact, his dissolving traditional structures of thought, and his radical scepticism concerning received ideas, together with his claim that there is no natural hierarchy of human intellects and that human reason is autonomous and, in principle, equal, in this way fused with his substance dualism to provide a basis for wholly new arguments about the character of the female mind.

1 Delon, 'Tyssot de Patot', 712, 597.

2 Tyssot de Patot, *La Vie, les avantures*, i. 207–35; Rosenberg, *Tyssot de Patot*, 143–8, 155.

3 Rosenberg, *Tyssot de Patot*, 10–13, 59–77.

Hence, although Descartes himself never formulates such a conclusion, it emerges ineluctably from his substance metaphysics that the human mind has no gender.[4] Poulain, going further, continually asserts that differences in the physical make-up of men and women have no relevance to the question of woman's intellectual capabilities. Reason and mind, for both Descartes and Poulain, are what give men their superior status to animals and define their ultimate spiritual status; reason is also what ensures a person's capacity for moral action and understanding religious doctrines. Hence, it fundamentally affected any and every debate about religion and morality, as well as philosophy and science, that 'l'esprit', in Poulain's words 'n'a point de sexe'.[5]

One of the obscurer problems of Cartesianism concerns how the body, and bodily differences, relate to the mechanics of the passions. It seemed clear, though, that the origin of the passions lies, for Descartes, in the mind (soul) so that the passions, as such, therefore, have no gender characteristics either. The relationship between reason and the passions is thus basically the same in men and women, so that women are as capable of understanding the effects of the passions as men, and just as able to manage them through use of reason and by making moral judgements. The conclusion Poulain drew from this was that the education of boys and girls ought, therefore, to be broadly the same.[6] Indeed, while concentrating his attention on reforming girls' education, he refused to specify a curriculum that would, by its nature, be specific or exclusive to women. The revolutionary implications of such reasoning are clear and nowhere more so than in Poulain's argument that girls should be taught grammar, philosophy (starting with Descartes), mathematics, physics, and independent critical thinking, exactly like boys.

Here, we hit upon another key distinction between moderate and Radical Enlightenment. Based on equality, 'natural equity', and a reform of female education so as to fit women for life in society, the latter, following Poulain's recipe (usually without knowing anything of him), tends to argue, as in Doria's *Ragionamenti* of 1726, for example, that women are equal to men 'in almost all the most important virtues', and should be trained morally and intellectually in the same way.[7] By contrast, the moderate mainstream while not always following Fénelon, the major French Catholic educational authority of the time, in claiming women's intellectual powers are intrinsically weaker than men's, does tend to assume the moral qualities desirable in women are different and that female education should, hence, be kept quite separate from men's.

Society's unjust subordination of women to men is due, explains Poulain, to the power of tradition and prejudice allied with the self-interested tyranny men have through the ages exerted over women, all buttressed by the weight of state and legal

[4] Leemans, *Het Woord*, 261; Stuurman, *François Poulain de La Barre*, 94–5.

[5] Stuurman, *François Poulain de Barre*, 4; Clarke, 'Introduction', 25–7.

[6] Clarke 'Introduction', 28–9; Stuurman, *François Poulain de La Barre*, 138–41, 147.

[7] Doria, *Ragionamenti . . . ne' quali si dimostra*, 216–17, 228–9, 372–90; Stone, *Vico's Cultural History*, 171; Israel, *Radical Enlightenment*, 93–4.

institutions. So potent is custom and tradition, he adds, that women themselves mostly accept their inferior status meekly, without questioning or demur, even though their alleged inferiority lacks all basis in reality.[8] The only effective weapon against such a fortress of prejudice, he states, is that of new forms of education. Reforming girls' education, he thought, would eventually help emancipate women from their traditionally narrow domesticity, ignorance, and propensity to waste time on frivolities, as well as love of gossip, by widening the range of their activities. Proper training of women's minds and intellects was what was required. The qualities needed for a good ruler or administrator, adds Poulain, have nothing to do with bodily characteristics: for they are exclusively capabilities of mind, the result of adequate training and knowledge. If women can administer complex entities like convents, then they must be equally competent to govern other large organizations or even whole provinces.[9] For the same reason, he suggests, women are no less suited than men to become priests and to preach.

Meanwhile, Descartes's insight that self-enlightenment begins with the freeing of the mind from prejudice and misconception served to revolutionize notions as to what truly effective and meaningful teaching is. In Poulain's opinion, authentic education principally means training in how to think critically and independently, being taught *esprit de critique* which, as we have seen, was itself a major impulse behind the radical stream's preoccupation with equality.[10] It seemed to him, moreover, that the education currently provided for men, even among the higher social strata, was itself too deficient to provide a genuine intellectual superiority for any group, indeed that men's usual assumption of intellectual superiority over women with less schooling was even now wholly unreal and especially bogus with regard to discernment and distinguishing between 'what is true and evident from what is false and obscure'.[11] Most men, receiving the kind of education then available, he contended, were in fact dismally 'obscure and confused in their discourses', wholly lacking in cogency, and liable to do far more harm emotional and social to those around them than even the most wretchedly educated women since it is precisely their defective ideas and 'obscurity', he maintains, that enables men to 'dominate and attract the trust of simple and credulous people'.[12]

However, if the physical sway of men over women is *not* sanctioned by nature, and still less by reason or capacity for knowledge and judgement, the same rigid separation of substances which makes the female intellect equal to that of the male condemns women, in their physical condition, to an unalterable position of inferiority and subordination within marriage, in the non-domestic crafts, and under the law, as well as in the wielding of arms, sports, and in sexual and economic life. Poulain does urge the need to reform marriage law so as to render it less one-sided

[8] Poulain de La Barre, *Equality*, 51–5.

[9] Ibid. 73; Stuurman, *François Poulain de La Barre*, 149–50; Clarke, 'Introduction', 19.

[10] Stuurman, *François Poulain de La Barre*, 141, 145, 147–8.

[11] Poulain de La Barre, *Equality*, 64–5.

[12] Ibid. 65.

and firmly rejects the generally prevailing view of writers like Pufendorf and Locke that although marriage is a form of mutual contract, authority within marriage 'naturally falls to the man's share, as the abler and stronger'.[13] Nevertheless, his practical proposals to mitigate male tyranny over women were limited to the suggestion that there should be better and fairer adjudication of disputes within marriage. He did not propose any fundamental reform of the institution of marriage as such, or (at this stage) challenge its indissolubility. Neither did he question the doctrine of Original Sin and the sinfulness of sexual relations outside of marriage. Nor, finally, did he claim women are as entitled to erotic satisfaction as men or criticize the principle of enforcing female chastity while accepting a quite different code regarding male fidelity. Actually, the whole question of sexual practices within and outside of marriage is in his works largely omitted from the discussion.

Indeed, Poulain de La Barre especially esteems unmarried women for being more inclined to chastity and an austere lifestyle than unmarried men, maintaining that women, to a greater extent than men, tend naturally to 'avoid worldly companionships and distractions' and deserve deep respect for this. Even in the case of the most praiseworthy monasteries, he argues, there is still a gender difference; for in good convents women's 'retreat from the world is greater, their penitence more fervent'.[14] At the same time, holds Poulain, women 'are more suited to marriage than we are', more capable of managing a home at a younger age, and more inclined than men to restrain their spouses' passions and guard them against 'debauchery' by their modesty and chastity.[15] Thus, despite his egalitarianism and 'modernity' in certain respects, clearly for Poulain 'virtue', unlike education, is still something heavily gendered, different for men and women and, in the latter case, orientated towards sexual denial, abstemiousness, and avoidance of worldly pleasure.

Moreover, Poulain's Cartesian philosophical stance left him vulnerable to the equally Cartesian counter-argument, offered, for instance, by the Bremen Calvinist preacher Theodore Undereyck (1635–93), that while naturally more moderate in their passions, and more inclined to submissiveness and piety, qualities he esteems no less than Poulain, women excel in these moral qualities mainly owing to what he deemed the fortunate circumstance that they have far less opportunity than men to read, study, and travel. It was precisely through having a much more 'restricted understanding' of the world and its affairs that women are as a rule spiritually wiser, more sensible, and also less at risk than men—by which he meant less prone to libertine lifestyle and ideas.[16] Women of easy virtue and whores exist, he argues, but have usually been seduced, debauched, and adversely influenced by irreligious men.

Undereyck, like Poulain a professed Cartesian, puts no less stress than he on the idea that a woman's body and sexuality cannot in any way affect her mind or render her inferior intellectually.[17] However, he employs Descartes's substance dualism

[13] Ibid. 22; Locke, *Two Treatises*, 321; Stuurman, *François Poulain de La Barre*, 168.

[14] Poulain de La Barre, *Equality*, 73.

[15] Ibid. 72–4.

[16] Undereyck, *Närrische Atheist*, 279–82.

[17] Ibid. 286–302.

very differently from Poulain, his chief goal in championing the feminine intellect using Cartesian mind–body doctrines, in his long discussion of women and the education of girls, being to ensure that female piety and chastity is not harmed by being derided as foolish by libertine men on the false ground that women are intellectually inferior. If the mind has no sex, this did not prevent Undereyck arguing that women process the passions otherwise than men and, by benign decree of God, are not only less given to sexual desire but also generally relate to the outside world more abstemiously. On Cartesian grounds, then, he proceeds in the opposite direction to Poulain, extolling female dependency and subordination, and seeking to confine them still more to the home and further strengthen the control exercised over women by their fathers and husbands.

Hence, there is less reason than some scholars claim to argue that Cartesianism as such provided a sufficiently supportive philosophical grounding for female equality or fully grounded the startlingly innovative feminist conclusions Poulain arrived at. Rather only monist systems could supply criteria capable of consistently underpinning a comprehensive doctrine of female equality. Spinozism in particular could combine criticism of tradition, conventional morality and existing structures of authority with the independent critical thinking urged by Cartesianism, in such a manner as to ground a more balanced female equality which included the sphere of worldly experience, activity, reading, and pleasure, besides marriage, family relations more generally, and admittance of women to more occupations, as well as attitudes to sex and chastity. Monist philosophy also provided a better rationale for segregating moral philosophy from theology—a key precondition for ending such questionable institutions as the cult of female chastity, indissolubility of marriages, and the stigmatizing of illegitimate births, as well as established practices for fortifying female chastity within marriage and without.

2. MARRIAGE, CHASTITY, AND PROSTITUTION

Initially, though, in Spinoza, all this remained largely implicit. Bayle's innovative discussion of female sexuality, much criticized by his friend Basnage for implanting obscene images in the mind and encouraging fantasies about lascivious women,[18] was indeed an integral part of his radical critique of Christian morality and fundamental to his system. Female sexual modesty and the cult of chastity, including scrupulous covering of the female bosom, in his view, have nothing to do with authentic morality, the real reason women eschew sexual encounters and promiscuity more than men, and avoid displaying their bodily charms more than they do, being that, historically, men have generally (but not always) insisted a woman's

[18] Cerny, *Theology, Politics and Letters*, 112–13.

reputation should depend on 'la chasteté'.[19] Were women permitted to satisfy their natural lusts without disfiguring their reputations, they would most certainly do so and with as much or more zest than men. However, Bayle's detaching morality from theology and tradition is not linked to any wider plea for female equality. Rather his discussion of women and sexuality, though of considerable interest, is also characterized by an unmistakable strain of misogyny, as we see from his comments about women being generally less inclined to philosophy and learning than men, bias evident (even if in a veiled fashion) where he observes that atheism is something that 'n'a presque point d'exemples parmi les femmes', a remark here not intended as a compliment.[20]

Yet, Bayle's moral philosophy, his contention that social attitudes and laws are just a means of regulating the passions and ensuring social stability with little inherent relevance to the content or character of true virtue,[21] proved advantageous to the further progress of radical thought in this area. Among his foremost philosophical heirs, for example, was Bernard Mandeville, whose works are not only studded with numerous references to Bayle's publications but fully share his determination to separate morality from Christian doctrines, and true morality from social norms of 'proper' behaviour, while at the same time engaging in a more extended debate about the position of women in society, marriage, and sexuality and, this time, firmly introducing the principle of equality.[22]

In Mandeville, women, no less than men, are encouraged to strive for self-knowledge and an ability to understand the true motives of their own conduct, as well as that of others, as a means to managing the passions better and striving for self-improvement.[23] Mandeville, unlike Poulain, thought men and women entirely equal (or equally lacking) in virtue and notoriously argued that much of what society considered to be 'virtue' is merely the outcome of natural circumstances and hypocrisy tailored to the pressure of popular prejudices. It is, he thinks, absurd to assess the moral quality of a woman by her reputation for chastity. 'The fear of children and the scandal of being counted a whore', he notes, 'often prove sufficient guards to the most wicked and lascivious women.'[24]

Mandeville expressed feminist views in several works and especially in his first prose work in English, *The Virgin Unmask'd* (1709). The opening part of this remarkable text consists of a dialogue between 'Antonia' and her aunt over the propriety, or otherwise, of following recent feminine fashion and exposing part of the bosom to view. Questions of prudery and female modesty, however, are entirely

[19] Bayle, *Pensées diverses*, ii. 81; [Buzen de La Martinière], *Entretiens*, ii. 593; McKenna, 'Pierre Bayle: moralisme', 332; Pitassi, 'Entre *libido* et savoir', 313–14.

[20] Pitassi, 'Entre *libido* et savoir', 309, 311, 316, 318; Leemans, *Het Woord*, 261.

[21] McKenna, 'Pierre Bayle: moralisme', 333–4.

[22] Primer, 'Mandeville and Shaftesbury', 129–30; James, 'Faith, Sincerity', 52–6; Pascual López, *Bernard Mandeville*, 48, 50–1, 73–4, 86, 88–90.

[23] Vichert, 'Bernard Mandeville's *The Virgin Unmask'd*', 5.

[24] Mandeville, *Free Thoughts*, 9; Berry, 'Lusty Women', 417–18.

secondary to the question of woman's status more generally. Mandeville does not doubt what Toland before him called 'the parity of the intellectual organs in both sexes', and that woman's wit is equal to man's, and was equally persuaded that only education can improve woman's lot;[25] but for the moment, he saw the relationship between the sexes as utterly unequal both in the physical and intellectual spheres and especially in the field of debate and discussion. This was not due to any difference in mental calibre, or incisiveness of intellect, but simply circumstances. Women, as Toland had pointed out, lacking the 'advantages of education, travel, company, and the management of affairs' that men enjoy, were quite unable to keep up with men in most kinds of discussion, especially conversation about politics, law, and the arts and sciences. Here then was a species of feminism which, unlike Poulain's, was not limited to the mental sphere but tended toward a genuine equality of independence, moral status, and aspiration to well-being in the world.

Mandeville, moreover, was a stern critic of marriage as then constituted: 'is not every woman that is married', he exclaims, 'a slave to her husband?'[26] The *Virgin Unmask'd* continually harps on the utter defencelessness under the law of women trapped by marriages to cruel, selfish, and domineering husbands. The submission and obligatory chastity imposed on females within marriage did not, from woman's point of view, impress him as admirable or beneficial qualities. His deep preoccupation with socially conditioned false virtues, or 'virtues' which are really selfish devices of hypocrisy and social advancement, in turn fed his insistence on a deeper analysis of motives and interests in moral conduct and his setting up an apparent opposition of 'private vices, public benefits', designed not, as many outraged contemporaries supposed, to encourage vice or immoralism but, on the contrary, by stripping away prejudices and discrediting false 'virtues' which are not really virtues at all, to promote awareness of what should count as genuine virtues, thereby advancing his highly innovative utilitarian morality geared toward social benefits.[27]

Much of this typically Spinozistic and *Bayliste* moral and social logic, with its emphasis on society as an autonomous, dynamic construct built on the passions, and therefore the vices more than the virtues, of men, infuses his notorious and, at the time, highly controversial discussion of prostitution expounded most fully in his *Modest Defense of Publick Stews* (1724), a tract which fiercely derides Anglican 'societies for the reformation of manners', which were a notable feature of the era in England. Here, Mandeville recommends the establishment of a government-regulated and supervised system of brothels to eradicate unsupervised and uncontrolled prostitution which he sees as a social pest apt to make various kinds of disease, infanticide of illegitimate children, and other problems worse than they need be. Prostitution, in his opinion, cannot be eliminated from society and, in any case, performs a useful social function by protecting respectable married, and

25 Mandeville, *Free Thoughts*, 4–5; Wotton, *Letter to Eusebia*, 74; Champion, *Republican Learning*, 52–3.

26 [Mandeville], *Virgin Unmask'd*, 127–8.

27 James, 'Faith, Sincerity', 54–7; Leemans, *Het Woord*, 267–72.

unmarried, women from the passions of frustrated males, reducing the incidence of harassment and rape.

Mandeville seems to have envisaged the world as having a coherent design but perhaps not a benevolent providence to guide it.[28] Morality of both the bogus, conventional kind, and true morality, can be known only from analysing men, both as individuals and in society. The inevitability of whoring was something no one could change but its form and effects, human sexual desire in effect, could be regulated, and doing so, he thought, would have a positive, rather than negative, effect on the moral order, even though men looking for extramarital satisfaction would be able to find it more easily. The benefit would come through protecting more respectable women and unmarried girls, curbing pimping, and reducing infanticide of the illegitimate. Earlier, in much the same vein, Mandeville argued in his *Fable of the Bees* that there is a 'necessity of sacrificing one part of womanhood to preserve the other, and prevent a filthiness of a more heinous nature'. From this he thought he could prove his 'seeming paradox' that in society 'chastity may be supported by incontinence, and the best of virtues want the assistance of the worst of vices'.[29]

The enforced subservience to husbands imposed on women by prevailing marriage patterns and laws, holds Mandeville, generates vast unhappiness and is far from being something any rational person, considering the matter soberly, would wish to have imposed on themselves.[30] This was to become a typical theme of the Spinozist and materialist Radical Enlightenment. In particular, denial of the right to, or near unavailability of, divorce was considered a formidable obstacle to personal emancipation and freedom, masculine and especially feminine. It caused, affirms Meslier, 'une infinité de mauvais et malheureux mariages', ensuring a land teeming with mediocre and unhappy households full of discontented, reluctant, and unsupportive wives and husbands, a state of affairs prevailing, in Meslier's opinion, essentially due to the decrees of the church.[31] The children of such countless flawed marriages, he argues, through the grudging attitude of both unhappy mothers and fathers, were often miserable too, or at least neglected and left in ignorance.

Similarly, Boureau-Deslandes, who thought sexual pleasure should be honoured and eulogized,[32] decries theologically and legally imposed indissolubility of marriage in his *Pygmalion*, as does d'Argens in his *Songes philosophiques* (Berlin, 1746). D'Argens here describes an egalitarian republic of apes where a very simple and natural 'virtue' holds sway, proclaiming that apes should love their fellow apes, and no one should do to another what he would not wish done to himself, and where the dogma of indissoluble marriage unto death is universally viewed with horror. In d'Argens's republic of the apes, anyone who is virtuous is a 'priest of truth' and consequently of the Supreme Being who is himself equivalent to reality and the truth;

[28] Monro, *Ambivalence*, 263–5; Taranto, *Du déisme à l'athéisme*, 112, 433.

[29] Mandeville, *Fable of the Bees*, 70; James, 'Faith, Sincerity', 61; Laqueur, *Solitary Sex*, 287–8.

[30] Vichert, 'Bernard Mandeville's *The Virgin Unmask'd*', 4–6, 9.

[31] Meslier, *Testament*, ii. 219–21.

[32] [Boureau-Deslandes], *L'Apothéose du beau-sexe*, 128.

divorce, moreover, is always readily attainable, since the apes, being 'wise legislators', make laws exclusively to make all the apes happy 'et non pas pour leur forger de nouveaux supplices'.[33] Morelly similarly condemns indissolubility of marriage, along with the fetish of 'virginity' at the point of marriage, for females, and paternally arranged marriages, in his lengthy two-volume *Basiliade* (1753), an erotic reverie published in Amsterdam in February 1753 (whilst he was, apparently, staying in Hamburg) and, also, a few months later, clandestinely, at Paris.[34]

In England, somewhat in contrast, it remains puzzling, given the generally uninhibited zest Toland, Collins, and other freethinkers show in attacking the Anglican Church, clergy, and theology, how rarely, aside at least from the Dutchman Mandeville, these writers expressly attack the rigidity of the English divorce laws and dogma of the indissolubility of marriage. England's law of divorce compared highly unfavourably with those then prevailing in other Protestant lands,[35] and was so rigid that adultery on the part of the wife (not the husband) remained the only accepted grounds for dissolving a marriage, though even that required extraordinarily strict standards of proof which usually acted a deterrent to any thought of applying for such legally formalized separation. Toland, though otherwise an exemplary pillar of radical attitudes in his generally positive treatment of feminine capabilities and intellect, nevertheless seems to have avoided this issue. So did Collins who despite his intellectual boldness, and antipathy to the Church Fathers' view that 'second marriages' should be considered 'a kind of adultery',[36] generally refrains from voicing social criticism or discussing discrimination against particular groups. The providential Deist Wollaston, while granting the authority of husbands over wives 'has been carried much too high', at the same time expressly endorsed indissolubility of marriage, even without claiming any ecclesiastical sanction.[37]

Furthermore, an immediate consequence of the downplaying of reason and drive to restrict the scope of philosophy increasingly prevalent in early and mid eighteenth-century British culture was a tendency for this reticence to reinforce precisely those conventional notions of 'virtue', and the stress on female chastity, denounced by Beverland, Bayle, Radicati, Meslier, and Mandeville. This is especially evident with Hume for whom custom, not reason, was the proper and essential basis of the moral order. Spurning the efforts of 'certain philosophers' to demonstrate morality's content by reason, Hume wholly rejects the idea that 'this science may be brought to an equal certainty with geometry or algebra'.[38] 'Since vice and virtue are not discoverable merely by reason', he contends, 'or the comparison of ideas', our notions of what is right and wrong must result from our perceptions and in essence be matters of sentiment: 'morality, therefore', he concludes, 'is more

[33] Boureau-Deslandes, *Pygmalion*, 69–70; [d'Argens], *Songes philosophiques*, 11; Coulet, 'Présentation', 23.

[34] [Morelly], *Basiliade*, i. 27–9, ii. 126–8; Wagner, *Morelly*, 53–4.

[35] Earle, *World of Defoe*, 268–71; Hoppit, *Land of Liberty?*, 62–3; Porter, *Enlightenment*, 274.

[36] Collins, *Discourse of Free-Thinking*, 14; Bentley, *Remarks*, 23.

[37] Wollaston, *Religion of Nature*, 156–9.

[38] Porter, *Enlightenment*, 463; Stewart, *Opinion and Reform*, 141–50.

properly felt than judg'd of'.[39] Particular *mores* apply in different societies, and are adhered to, through sensibility and sentiment, not reason. As with the modesty and strict 'virtue' society imposes on women but not men, we would indeed not count such 'virtues' as being moral at all, Hume concurs with Bayle and Mandeville, if one appraised morality according to the yardstick of reason. However, contends Hume, that is not the point. Particularly strong emotions attach to the matter of female modesty because that is what favours stability of the family and the self-interest of husbands and fathers who hence impose and enforce chastity on their wives and daughters.[40]

Hume, even while denying the validity of its ultimate moral claims, was perfectly prepared to accept subordination of women, and the one-sided attitudes to sexuality such a custom-based moral system entails. The radical idea, advocated by Beverland, Tyssot de Patot, Radicati, Meslier, Boureau-Deslandes, d'Argens, Morelly, and Diderot, that everyone, man or woman, should enjoy the same sexual freedom, is, in Hume's opinion, unrealistic and to be rejected out of hand. Societies have structures of traditional values which must be respected. Yet while reason cannot sustain a universal morality, it still remains a necessary tool for regulating the predominant moral ideas within particular social contexts, giving rise to an entrenched tension in Hume's thought between moral sensibility, on the one hand, and the partly spurned dictates of reason, on the other.[41] Here, Hume becomes more than a touch inconsistent. At least sporadically, he admits a utilitarian notion of 'interested obligation' as a principle of morality: usefulness to society and the happiness of men become criteria which we sometimes have to apply, as with polygamy, a topic which had earlier also caused Montesquieu embarrassment (since his theory seemed to some to verge on justifying it in the case of warm climates);[42] Hume judges polygamy detrimental to humanity's natural needs and goals, no matter how rooted in some cultures. Overall, then, when judging the morality of a practice, Hume winds up with no consistent criterion for judging between virtues and vices.[43]

Since morality, for Hume, rests on custom, occasionally stiffened with a utilitarian judgement as to what most favours a stable, flourishing society, we are left with an ungrounded hint of universal principles, embedded in a moral culture chiefly based on tradition. Hence it is never entirely clear to what extent morality should be organized around existing mores and circumstances. Hume defends the cult of female chastity but not the doctrine entrenched in Catholic and Anglican societies of indissolubility of marriage. It would be much better, holds Hume, here not unlike Meslier or d'Argens, to adopt 'liberty of divorces' which would then serve not just as a 'cure to

[39] Porter, *Enlightenment*, 470; Darwall, 'Hume', 67–8; Norton, 'Hume, Human Nature', 162–3.

[40] Hume, *Treatise*, 570–3; Gay, *Enlightenment*, ii. 200–1; MacIntyre, *After Virtue*, 232; Berry, 'Lusty Women', 422–3, 431–2; Stewart, *Opinion and Reform*, 196–206, 314.

[41] Stewart, *Opinion and Reform*, 141–2; Darwall, 'Hume', 60.

[42] Montesquieu, *L'Esprit des lois*, 625–6; Ehrard, *L'Idée*, 734.

[43] Gaskin, *Hume's Philosophy of Religion*, 196; MacIntyre, *After Virtue*, 230–2; Dupré, *Enlightenment*, 132–3.

hatred and domestic quarrels' but also as an 'admirable preservative against them'. Beyond this, though, he adheres to his view that different societies justifiably uphold different concepts of what marriage is, calling it a 'mere superstition to imagine, that marriage can be entirely uniform, and will admit only of one mode or form'.[44] While socially and culturally discrete, it is nevertheless philosophically incoherent for any thinker to reject, along with Spinoza, Beverland, Bayle, Radicati, Mandeville, Meslier, d'Argens, and Diderot, 'celibacy, fasting, penance, mortification, self-denial, humility, silence, solitude, and the whole train of monkish virtues' as being no genuine virtues while at the same time failing to provide a clear principled moral framework, as those writers do, to support such utilitarian adjustments and innovations as our pragmatic empiricist recommends.[45]

3. THE EROTIC EMANCIPATION OF WOMAN, AND MAN

On questions of marriage and sexual mores, as in other areas, Hume stands fairly close to the characteristic positions of Montesquieu whose tendency is likewise to preserve social and political hierarchies as something particular to given societies and also innate in Natural Law, as he defines it. Adopting such principles, the philosopher must unavoidably accept that quite different codes of marriage and sexual conduct have both long applied and will, quite properly, in existing societies, in the future. Montesquieu considers chastity, abstinence, and shame not only something generally enforced more on women than men but also something chiefly appropriate to the female sex, 'all nations' being 'equally agreed in fixing contempt and ignominy on the incontinence of women'.[46]

Montesquieu likewise holds that different societies naturally and justly develop different systems of marriage, and do so, as he sees it, especially because religion and local law exert a strong influence on the regulation of marriage in each particular society. The intervention of priests and religion in fixing forms of marriage, he argues, stems from society's need to explain why certain things are 'impures ou illicites' and enforce acceptance of this.[47] Marriage sacraments and ceremonies, he notes, are society's device for enabling theology to regulate what is allowed, or not, and how relations between the sexes should be organized. Marriage, concubinage, banning casual relationships, and fixing family degrees within which marriage is allowed, even if enforced by civil courts, is always legitimized by religious law.[48]

Here we see moderate Enlightenment philosophies not just defending custom, tradition, religion, and positive law as the basis of the moral order but standing

[44] Hume, *Essays*, 181–2, 187–90; Box, *Suasive Art*, 130–2.

[45] Gaskin, *Hume's Philosophy of Religion*, 196–7; Schneewind, *Invention of Autonomy*, 374–5; Taylor, *Sources of the Self*, 343–7.

[46] Courtney, 'Montesquieu and Natural Law', 59–60.

[47] Kingston, 'Montesquieu on Religion', 401 n. 18; Montesquieu, *Œuvres complètes*, 714.

[48] Montesquieu, *Œuvres complètes*, 714.

squarely against all possibility of female equality or the liberation of the human libido. Montesquieu stresses the central role of social factors in impelling religious law not just to fortify the institution of marriage, and indirectly parental control over the choice of marriage partner, but in causing parents to fill children with revulsion 'pour tout ce qui pouvait les porter à l'union des deux sexes'.[49] Unless adolescents, and in particular adolescent girls, are taught to regard extramarital sexual intercourse with horror as something surpassingly abominable, the whole system of sanctity of marriage, paternal control, cult of virginity, and parents' confidence that those chosen to marry their daughters will not get to know them or have any familiarity with them, prior to the wedding ceremonies, breaks down.

Hence, only Radical Enlightenment could expose and reject the entire system of social pressures and theological pretexts men devised to legitimize what Boureau-Deslandes called 'la prééminence et l'autorité sur la femme' which men unjustly arrogated to themselves almost everywhere since the remotest times; only the radical stream assailed this whole vast socio-religious, psychological framework, conceptually repudiating what Diderot later called the 'cruelty' with which the laws of most societies treat both married and unmarried women.[50] Radicati denounced the cult of female virginity as an unnatural 'evil' which is trebly cruel: cruel to young women, cruel in causing illegitimate babies to be 'killed or abandoned because of the stigma of unchastity', and cruel in driving young men often against their initial inclination to homosexuality.[51] Egalitarian pleas by Beverland, Radicati, Tyssot de Patot, Mandeville, Meslier, Boureau-Deslandes, d'Argens, Diderot, and later Morelly, served to propagate, in simplified form, central ethical ideas drawn chiefly from Spinoza and Bayle and promote the idea that a totally different order of society, morality, and sexuality is possible, or at any rate conceivable, under which a fairer, more natural, and more equitable justice and morality would prevail. Such a society based on equality, justice, and charity, from which divine reward and punishment, as well as monarchy, aristocracy, and ecclesiastical authority, are eradicated, was thought to emancipate the individual and enrich his or her life intellectually, socially, and also sensually and sexually.

A vital consequence of enshrining 'natural equity and justice' in this way was the resulting freeing of the human libido. The first writer systematically to attack the doctrines of Original Sin, and sinfulness of sexual pleasure outside marriage, was Adriaen Beverland (1650–1716) who, as we have seen, was arrested and then expelled from Holland, in 1679, for insinuating lascivious thoughts into the minds of the young, in his Spinozistic *De peccato originali* (1678). This work subsequently became widely known in Europe after reappearing, at Amsterdam in 1714, in a French-language version prepared by Jean-Frédéric Bernard which was again reissued in 1731 and 1741.[52] An expert classicist, Beverland had spent years researching

[49] Ibid. 715.

[50] [Boureau-Deslandes], *L'Apothéose du beau-sexe*, 73; Quintili, *Pensée critique*, 458.

[51] [Radicati], *Philosophical Dissertation*, 71–3.

[52] Israel, *Radical Enlightenment*, 87–8; Leemans, *Het woord*, 151–2.

the subject of erotic life in the classical world in the Dutch and English university libraries and composed a long manuscript on ancient eroticism, entitled *De prostibulis veterum*, subsequently confiscated and suppressed by the Leiden University authorities.

In his *De peccato originali*, Beverland argues, citing Hobbes and Spinoza, that the story of the Fall had been misunderstood for millennia and is nothing more than a poetic allegory describing Adam and Eve's discovery of sexual intercourse.[53] Developing a form of philosophical pantheism embedded in a general theory of eroticism, Beverland strove to liberate readers from negative feelings regarding the private parts and the sex act.[54] Central to his argument was the idea that desire for sexual pleasure is a basic drive in all men and women and that whatever form it takes, and however much it may be suppressed, it remains a universal human trait. From this he deduces that the traditional cult of female 'purity' and chastity, and the prevalent idea that women are naturally less given to sexual desire than men, are completely artificial constructions which have no basis in reality but only in tradition, religion, and prejudice. He concludes that women feel the same desires as men, and the same longing for physical satisfaction, but in most cases are obliged by society to mask their true feelings 'comme contraire à la pudeur et à la modestie des femmes'.[55]

Since men and women are created with the sexual urges which, after puberty, they must experience, nothing could be more irrational, held Meslier, like Diderot later, than to threaten them with eternal punishment for what are decried by theologians as their sexual transgressions.[56] In Spinoza himself, Boulainvilliers, Du Marsais, and Meslier, the emphasis remained on removing the stigma and association of sexuality and sexual activity outside of marriage with sin, perversity, and crime; in Beverland, Radicati, Boureau-Deslandes, and Morelly, on the other hand, as also in Diderot's diverting illicit fantasy novel *Les Bijoux indiscrets* (1747), anonymously published in January 1748, and, still more, in d'Argens's *Thérèse philosophe* (1748), the emphasis is transferred to the erotic as such. Sexual intercourse, masturbation, and especially male and female orgasm, become a completely licit, natural, and shared pleasure to be encouraged and savoured in full, and as much by women as men. This new erotic discourse was accompanied by a fierce ridiculing of chastity and prudery and, more generally, of the influence of the Christian religion on attitudes toward sexuality.[57]

Boureau-Deslandes contends that the structure of ancient pagan religions, the psychological roots of which, as with all religions, were 'dread and ignorance', had already long ago locked woman into an inescapably inferior position. It was evident that the fair sex had every right 'de se plaindre et de crier à l'injustice'.[58] If the

53 [Beverland], *De peccato originali*, 4–6, 17, 105, 110; Elias, 'Spinozistisch erotisme', 287.
54 [Beverland], *État de l'homme*, 127–8.
55 Ibid. 107, 308–10; Elias, 'Spinozistisch erotisme', 109–10; Leemans, *Het woord*, 251–2.
56 Meslier, *Testament*, ii. 160–1.
57 Coe, *Morelly*, 70; Lestringant, 'L'Utopie amoureuse', 86, 98–9.
58 [Boureau-Deslandes], *L'Apothéose du beau-sexe*, 123.

irrationality and extreme injustice of men are ever to be put right, making it possible for men and women to live in a more just world, women would be honoured for their capabilities *and* their beauty, a change which would render both sexes happier and depart from all the social systems recorded in history. The ancient Greeks and Romans worshipped Priapus but had no female equivalent; yet there is nothing, he argues, which so effectually calms the brutality of soldiers and roughness of sailors as the female vagina. What could be more natural, he asks, than for society to hold in veneration 'l'organe de la production des êtres raisonnables'?[59]

D'Argens, a writer for whom the mind is material and simply part of the body, came to regard sexual exploration and philosophical investigation as closely related activities.[60] Reason can enlighten us and help us understand the reality of things but it does not determine men's conduct. Like Bayle and Mandeville (following Spinoza), he thinks self-love, pleasure hoped for, and the pain one hopes to avoid, 'sont le mobile de toutes nos déterminations'.[61] For him too, good and bad cannot be defined in terms of divine decrees, the will of God, or any prior transcendental order, but only in relation to men and to society. The 'bien de tous', and the desire, among those who think, to contribute to this common good, is the only veritable basis for a universal moral criterion; and this makes women and men equal as autonomous moral agents no less than equal in their understanding and intellect, the drives that determine their conduct, and their love of sensual pleasure.

Merging mind and body, reconstituting society's moral system, and removing the stigma from the sexual act, and sexual desire, led to eulogies of sexual pleasure, for men and women alike (and, by implication, also for homosexuals and lesbians), composed in the later 1740s by d'Argens, Diderot, and La Mettrie. This transition then, in turn, produced the thesis, featuring at the heart of *Thérèse philosophe*, as well as Diderot's writing, and Morelly's *Basiliade*, that sexual pleasure must intrinsically have a positive rather than negative or purely neutral value. Re-evaluating the erotic in this way also meant bringing sex education and sexual enjoyment directly into view as positive values, something which, additionally, necessarily entailed distinguishing between different kinds of sexual pleasure, and ordering these into morally acceptable and unacceptable categories.

New ideas, then, new philosophies, and new thinking certainly contributed, even if historians will disagree as to the extent of their contribution, to the remarkable phenomenon that, during the early eighteenth century specifically, masturbation both male and female, which previously, over many centuries, had remained a secret vice, and a secret problem, practically never discussed, suddenly came into general view as a major social and moral issue, indeed came to be widely referred to and discussed in print.[62] The 'new social history' and the new 'intellectual history'

59 Ibid. 54–5, 69–70.

60 [D'Argens], *Thérèse philosophe*, 140; see also Venturi, *Utopia and Reform*, 74.

61 Ibid. 146–7; Israel, *Radical Enlightenment*, 95–6.

62 Darnton, *Forbidden Best-Sellers*, 103, 113, 222; Porter, *Flesh*, 233–4, 242, 270–1; Laqueur, *Solitary Sex*, 18–20.

must and will undoubtedly clash here, as to whether intellectual or social factors engineered this striking shift, although they can readily agree on a starting point, that this phenomenon has to do with 'how the morally autonomous modern subject was created and sustained' as one scholar put it.[63]

That said, many or most will undoubtedly prefer to highlight alleged social-cultural shifts, such as the suggested effect of the (well-documented) growing hostility in most of society to homosexuality, leading to a conjectured need to secure 'new boundaries for heterosexuality', and a campaign against masturbation on the part of an expanding and more influential medical profession.[64] This sort of thing appeals widely but is highly conjectural. Others will find more plausible a quite different explanation: namely, that nothing at all changed in society as such linked to the rise of the masturbation debate that was essentially social or cultural in origin. Rather, the huge emotional and cultural disturbance generated in the middle decades of the eighteenth century by the public debate about self-relief was entirely driven by the advent of the—for most people at the time totally unacceptable—new moral philosophical thesis that sexual pleasure, including masturbation, is neither intrinsically sinful nor morally deviant, but rather an inevitable and positive accoutrement of human life. Here was a profoundly unsettling change of intellectual perspective of a sort guaranteed to provoke fierce controversy and widespread disapproval. Not only was it totally opposed to received thinking and values, it was a thesis which could never have been formulated by or propagated in the early and mid eighteenth century without a deep-seated prior philosophical revolution reaching back to the great philosophers of the late seventeenth century and in particular Spinoza and Bayle.

The erotic revolution, entailing a whole new culture of desire, voluptuousness, and pleasure, postulated by Beverland, Bernard, Boureau-Deslandes, d'Argens, La Mettrie, Diderot, and Morelly, is perceived by them as physiologically requisite if women are to enjoy equal satisfaction, since the elusiveness of female orgasm requires a culture of erotic finesse and coaxing and gentleness unlikely to emerge from a traditional atmosphere of repression and which needed now to be nurtured as something morally positive. Its ethical value lay in the first place through removing frustration and advancing the satisfaction and self-enrichment of individuals, and their partners, where mutuality, reciprocity, and harmony are furthered without harm to individuals or the wider fabric of society. Besides softening men's aggression and furthering tranquillity, additional benefits included the lifting from the lives of adolescents left by church and family without the least understanding of what Diderot called 'l'origine des désirs obscurs' that troubled them, of a frequently extremely disturbing anxiety and uncertainty, heightened by ignorance, including feelings of guilt and shame about masturbation.[65] Further, the new code could help with forms of emotional disturbance, caused by sexual repression, especially types of hysteria among women which, in Diderot's opinion, often took the form of dangerous religious exultation.[66]

[63] Laqueur, *Solitary Sex*, 21.
[64] Ibid. 267–9, 269–72.
[65] Martin-Haag, *Aspect de la pensée*, 24–5.
[66] Quintili, *Pensée critique*, 457.

If there is no Original Sin, only innocence, and if sexual relations of whatever kind are simply part of nature and integral to it, then sexual life has to be ordered and classified in an entirely new fashion and this research then becomes, in itself, a not unimportant new kind of investigation. For the radical *philosophes* by definition reject, as Mandeville does explicitly, the purely spiritual conception of love postulated by the Platonic ideal, as much they renounced love of God conceived as a purely spiritualized value. To them love must be sensual and spiritual at the same time and therefore sensual love had now to be elevated to a new level morally, Platonic love discredited, the sexual act and the sexual organs of men and women had to be given a new place in aesthetic and intellectual life, and female voluptuousness had to be assigned a value it had not possessed since the rise of Christianity.[67]

In this new context, as Morelly imagines it, women no longer blush or feel ashamed to initiate and display their enjoyment of sexual intercourse.[68] He harshly denounces the old adage 'omne animal post coitum triste' [every creature is sad after coitus], saying men, swayed by their prejudices, had confused the gentle languor of post-coital relaxation of effort with the furtive tiredness and depression of engaging in something shameful and hidden.[69] Placing the quest for sensual enjoyment within the framework of a general secular morality, as do Radicati, Boureau-Deslandes, d'Argens, Diderot, and Morelly, based on the furtherance of the 'bien de tous', necessarily gives rise to the model of the *libertin vertueux*, the man or woman who through visual and tactile exploration of reality unifies all reality through their being, in a manner which is simultaneously sensual, rational, and free, satisfying to themselves and yet at the same time accords equivalent liberty, and right of consent, to others.[70]

This type of sensual, materialist *moralisme* not only rejected many of the ethical priorities of Christianity, accusing the churches of creating a moral prison for men, and still more for women, and encouraging *imposture* and *de ruses perfides*, but also, especially in Meslier, Morelly, Boureau-Deslandes, d'Argens, and Diderot, blamed theology for directly fomenting moral disorder, rapine, and violence, by diverting nature from its proper course and inflicting on men and women repression, frustration, grievance, and resentment.[71] Their new hierarchy of sexual values not only rejects all forms of abstinence and austerity, insisting, contrary to what the 'vulgar' suppose, that there is nothing shameful about the human genitals,[72] and stigmatizes sexual repression, but also seeks to vilify the purely egoistical and selfish voluptuousness of the cynical individualist, such as La Mettrie's distinct brand of hedonism was perceived to represent. For far from collaborating with the work of constructing a viable ethical frame for the new values, based on equity, La Mettrie seemed to seek a path by which the philosopher could justify, or at any rate morally

[67] Israel, *Radical Enlightenment*, 96; Coe, *Morelly*, 71.

[68] [Morelly], *Basiliade*, ii. 134.

[69] Ibid. i. 21, 25, ii. 134.

[70] Quintili, *Pensée critique*, 139.

[71] [Morelly], *Basiliade*, i. 29–30; Coe, *Morelly*, 69; Martin-Haag, *Aspect de la pensée*, 52–5.

[72] [Beverland], *État de l'homme*, 127–8; [Boureau-Deslandes], *L'Apothéose du beau-sexe*, 29, 54–5.

neutralize, sexual harassment, rape, degradation, and plain cruelty as well as the most ruthless forms of seduction.

In terms of the general development of the Radical Enlightenment, therefore, the kind of sexual utopia or paradise on earth, a thoroughly anti-Hobbesian 'state of nature' postulated by Morelly in his *Basiliade*, a place where there is no social hierarchy or nobility and everyone has an equal civil status and where 'les termes infâmes d'inceste, d'adultère et de prostitution' are all unknown,[73] and where the unmarried girl who becomes pregnant feels not the least shame nor even dreams of murdering her unborn infant,[74] however remote from reality and bizarre, has a certain wider philosophical, literary, and social significance. Morelly's outlook was thoroughly 'revolutionary' in that he believed all the past legislators and 'réformateurs' of humanity instead of making men happier had merely added to their wretchedness by piling up yet more errors, prejudices, and vices and laws based on wrong principles.[75] Seeing only an infinity of sorrow and suffering caused by superstition, credulity, and lack of philosophical 'enlightenment', he vowed to devote all his strength to assailing those 'cherished phantoms', the ideas and doctrines on which existing society was built, to his mind all products of 'l'imposture et la tirannie'.[76]

Morelly's *utopie amoureuse*, warmed by a sunny, benign climate, rests on a sensual-utopian code according to which the Supreme Being never becomes angry or expresses dissatisfaction with men and where just as worldly fruits lie all about for all its inhabitants to share, so the bodies of the most beautiful, men and women equally, seem to belong to all. Morelly's is a utopia where a totally new ethics requires a particular moral belief structure. Above all, it requires the willingness of all to share equally and obey a set of clear but simple rules based on nature, equality of the sexes, and 'l'amour du bel ordre', principles 'brèves, précises, uniformes et constantes'.[77] At the heart of these rules are the principles of sharing and equity, based on a pastoral economy but extending also to sexual life. Decrying feminine *pudeur* (modesty) as an irrelevant hypocrisy, it is a culture which encourages nudity as a moral good in itself and indeed foments a general *panoptisme*, characterized by ubiquitous *voyeurisme* and exhibitionism, allowing everyone to drink in the beauties of everyone else both individually and when copulating, a utopia in which the loveliest delight in giving pleasure to others.[78]

Here, the marriage laws apply to everyone, no one is permitted to remain celibate between reaching sexual maturity and the age of 40 except where 'nature or their health' rules otherwise; although there is no requirement of fidelity, first marriage is to be indissoluble for ten years after which divorce is available at the request of

73 [Morelly], *Basiliade*, i. 33, 37–8; Lestringant, 'L'utopie amoureuse', 93.

74 [Morelly], *Basiliade*, i. 31–2.

75 Ibid., preface pp. xl–xli and pp. 45–6; Ruyer, *L'Utopie*, 200–3.

76 [Morelly], *Basiliade*, i. 2.

77 Ibid. i. 27–34; Ruyer, *L'Utopie*, 200; Coe, *Morelly*, 71–5, 140; Wagner, *Morelly*, 180–1; Lestringant, 'L'utopie amoureuse', 84–5.

78 Lestringant,' L'Utopie amoureuse', 86, 100–1; [Morelly], *Basiliade*, i. 18, 28, 31.

either party.[79] Divorce, in Morelly's utopia, is thus eventually available but rarely used since marriages are based both on mutual attraction and tested compatibility and so tend to last much better than traditional marriages, particularly since there are no jealous obsessions with sexual 'infidelity' to undermine them. All this is placed in stark contrast to societies more familiar to Morelly's readers where love-making had been reduced to 'quelque chose d'infâme' and structures of belief, thought, and authority rendered a true eroticism impossible, relationships between husbands and wives, clients and prostitutes, and unmarried young single men and women all being so strained, corrupted, and unnatural, and attitudes toward love-making, of men and women alike, being generally 'peu raisonables'.[80]

79 [Morelly], *Basiliade*, i. 27–9; Ruyer, *L'Utopie*, 202; Lestringant, ''L'Utopie amoureuse', 84, 100.
80 [Morelly], *Basiliade*, ii. 125–6.

23

Race, Radical Thought, and the Advent of Anti-colonialism

1. ENLIGHTENMENT AGAINST EMPIRE

In the opening years of the eighteenth century, the Huguenot radical writer Nicolas Gueudeville denounced the 'cruautés horribles' practised by the Europeans against indigenous inhabitants in the Americas as a crime even worse than their treatment of the inhabitants of Africa and Asia. For they had stripped the Amerindians—natives whose sole crime was to use legitimate means to defend what he terms 'leurs droits naturels', of the most precious of their possessions—'je veux dire la liberté'.[1]

His ringing affirmation of the universal equivalence of human rights was characteristic of a new style of thought which turned on asserting the fundamental equality of all men and rejecting, as Gueudeville does unreservedly, all theological justification for subjugating the heathen. Even the most different should be respected as equals, including the Hottentots of southern Africa whom Gueudeville robustly defends, despite their seemingly very primitive way of life and reported love of indolence, declaring them 'philosophes sans le savoir'.[2]

Colonial empires entailed conquest, political subjection, and vast economic exploitation, as well as ruthless systems of racial hierarchy. By the late seventeenth century, a number of contemporary observers had become acutely sensitive to this. 'The greatest [European] empires of Asia', held Poulain de La Barre in the 1670s, commenting on the doings of the Portuguese, Spaniards, and Dutch in the East, were, from the beginning, 'the creation of usurpers and thieves'.[3] Yet no matter how brutal the exploitation, and harmful its consequences, in the eyes of such contemporaries, it was by no means easy, for even colonial expansion's most exploited victims and most critical onlookers, to construct a comprehensive anti-colonial theory, tying together the political, military, economic, cultural, social, and moral strands of the question. Prior to the 1660s, there simply existed no theoretical basis for such a construct. The empires of Spain, Portugal, France, the Dutch, Danes, Sweden, Britain, and Russia, reaching back to the fifteenth and sixteenth centuries, were rapidly bringing most of the globe within their grasp. Highly complex systems

[1] Rosenberg, *Nicolas Gueudeville*, 89. [2] Ibid. [3] Poulain de La Barre, *Equality*, 54.

of imperial subjugation and subjection had developed across much of the world in the construction of which the colonizing powers utilized various blends of ideology and institutions, exploiting to the full the mystiques of monarchy, aristocracy, and religious justification as well as newer notions of racial hierarchy and mercantilist doctrines of national prosperity.

These ideological-institutional constructs were extremely formidable structures of authority. Consequently, it was only in the century from roughly 1660 to 1750, specifically in the wake of the Radical as opposed to the mainstream Enlightenment, as the empires themselves strengthened and spread further, that a coherent critique of empire acquired the depth, breadth, and momentum requisite to build a fully-fledged anti-colonial thesis. For in the cultural context of early modern empires, there was only one conceivable way in which a comprehensive anti-colonialism could evolve—and that was by means of a systematically monist philosophy embracing moral, social, and political concepts powerful enough comprehensively to challenge the tightly interlinked strands of justification of empire. For anti-colonialism to evolve into a comprehensively revolutionary political and moral thesis, it had to be anchored in forms of philosophy built on blanket denial of a prior transcendental order and affirming the fundamental equality and unity of Man. Only by negating all the religious, dynastic, and racial hierarchical components used to justify and organize empire, insisting as, for instance, Lau does, that all men 'are the people of God', that all equally have reason and that all their views and religions are of equal status,[4] could such a rival system of thought emerge.

It is true that up to a point the moderate Enlightenment also possessed philosophical resources capable of sensitizing the moral conscience and producing a wide-ranging critique of unprincipled subjection and exploitation as well as intolerance, overblown ecclesiastical authority, unrestrained mercantilism, and war-mongering. But while it showed some capacity to highlight and deplore the excesses of the European conquerors in the Indies, and as in Montesquieu and Hume cast doubt on the legitimacy of black slavery, moderate enlightened thought was prevented by its own philosophical premisses from fully overcoming or disqualifying the theological, monarchical, mercantilist, and race-hierarchical justifications of empire on which the various European imperial ideologies rested. Turgot, for instance, had no desire to justify slavery and bitterly deplored the scale of the misery, destruction, and oppression visited on the Indians and 'slaves' of the New World by the Spaniards, Portuguese, English, Dutch, Danes, Swedes, and French alike. In his *Discours sur les avantages que l'établissement du christianisme a procurés au genre humain* (1750), originally presented in Latin at the Sorbonne, in July 1750, he deplored the 'scènes d'horreur et de cruautés' which had blighted whole peoples, causing untold horrors and suffering; yet the theological dimension of his thought proved an insuperable barrier to pushing his critique any further. For to his mind, as to most of his audience, these unspeakable ravages were ultimately amply compensated for, and justified, by

4 Lau, *Meditationes philosophicae*, 9–10.

the blessings brought by the Christian religion. What for him began as a profound moral dilemma was resolved once the theological dimension was brought into the picture: however terrible their sufferings, the Amerindians, black slaves, and all the peoples of the universe, he urges, should submit with open arms to the preachers of a faith of love which 'enlightens' the spirit, 'qui adoucit les mœurs, qui fait régner toutes les vertus et le bonheur avec elle'.[5]

An equally formidable barrier was the mainstream's tendency to erect a hierarchy of races and human types, setting the more civilized and supposedly more 'rational' vastly above allegedly inferior and less 'rational' peoples. The systems of the empiricists, in particular, proved useful for legitimizing the facts of imperial subjection and constructing hierarchies of human types. Attacking the materialists, Locke dismissed as 'senselessly arrogant' all reasoning which supposes 'Man alone knowing and wise, but yet the product of mere ignorance and chance' and all the rest of the universe likewise the outcome of chance.[6] How can the materialists and Spinozists presume to know the true order of things? Rather, he argued, our world was created by an almighty God with Man having a special status marked by the 'great and inestimable advantage of immortality and life everlasting which he has above other material beings'.[7] Hence while Locke acknowledged a restricted kind of equality and universality binding all men together, he conceived it to be purely spiritual in character, and hence invisible to us, there being no outward sign of it in terms of shape, feature, or colour. 'What sort of outside', asks Locke, 'is the certain sign that there is, or is not such an inhabitant within?'[8]

Locke, accordingly, felt justified in combining his notion of Man as a creature bearing a 'rational soul' not just with rejection of 'innate ideas' but with casting doubt on the notion of the essential unity of mankind whenever considering essentially worldly situations: 'wherein then, would I gladly know, consists the precise and unmovable boundaries of that species? 'Tis plain', contends Locke, 'if we examine, there is no such thing made by nature, and established by her amongst men.'[9] Locke did not necessarily mean by this that blacks, or any particular group of non-whites, were not fully human but did urge that we differentiate empirically between groups rather than seek to bracket the human species generally, urging that we 'quit the common notion of species and essences', defining humans 'as they exist and not by groundless fancies that have been taken up about them'.[10]

This kind of step-by-step empiricism ran full-frontally against that of the Spinozists, highlighting difference rather than what was universal. It also vividly illustrates how very dubious it is to claim, as many scholars have, that Locke figures among the 'equality-radicals' of the Enlightenment and was a philosopher who upheld 'basic equality'.[11] Locke's 'equality' was real enough but was exclusively theological in character. In his treatment of the Amerindians, for instance, one finds a

[5] Turgot, *Discours sur les avantages*, 205. [6] Locke, *An Essay*, 621. [7] Ibid. 571.
[8] Ibid. 572. [9] Ibid. 454, 571–3; Harris, *Mind of John Locke*, 217–18; Muthu, *Enlightenment*, 271.
[10] Muthu, *Enlightenment*, 271; Locke, *An Essay*, 454. [11] Waldron, *God, Locke and Equality*, 5.

studied emphasis on their supposed ignorance, illiteracy, and incapacity for 'general propositions', as well as their economic inefficiency, his insistence on the latter carrying at least a hint of justification for appropriating their lands and resources without their consent.[12] The philosophies of Locke, Voltaire, Montesquieu, and Hume, in fact, could all be fairly readily utilized as devices of imperial legitimization owing to their stressing the divergent varieties of men. 'I am apt to suspect the negroes', remarked Hume, in 1748, 'to be naturally inferior to the whites. There scarcely ever was a civilized nation of that complexion, nor even any individual eminent either in action or speculation. No ingenious manufactures amongst them, no arts no sciences.'[13] Hume spoke of 'an original distinction between these breeds of men', adding that 'there are Negroe slaves dispersed all over Europe, of which none ever discovered any symptoms of ingenuity, tho' low people, without education, will start up amongst us, and distinguish themselves in every profession'; on this ground, he compared the blacks unfavourably even with the ancient Germans and Tartars.[14]

If Hume was no enthusiast for empire, and expressly warned of the dangers of imperial overstretch, his main worry was certainly about the effects of the empire on British liberty and the constitution rather than its impact on others.[15] Moreover, Hume's pragmatic monarchism, justification of empire, and conservative politics and social thought in general, tended to assist the process of imperial dominion and ranking of human races in ways typical of much eighteenth-century transatlantic thinking. The guiding principle of Hume's political thought, namely that 'when there is no form of government establish'd by long possession, the *present* possession is sufficient to supply its place, and may be regarded as the second source of all public authority', religion being the first, could do no other than bolster existing structures of imperial rule outside as well as absolute monarchical rule within Europe. Outside Europe, indeed, it effectively legitimized even the most oppressive institutions of empire.[16] While it is doubtless true that Hume privately considered black slavery reprehensible and 'barbarous', at any rate in his later works, his maxim that 'right to authority is nothing but the constant possession of authority, maintain'd by the laws of society' for most intents and purposes publicly sanctioned slavery, racial subjection, and the despoliation of the Amerindians no less than the institutionalized religious intolerance, including the ghettoizing of Jews, then still prevalent in most of continental Europe. His politics was a denial of basic equality no less than of popular sovereignty.[17]

Voltaire, for his part, rather like Boulainvilliers, was inclined to the view that only the more refined and civilized parts of mankind can be formed into large, stable, and enduring monarchies capable of attaining high levels of political development.

[12] Tully, 'Rediscovering America', 168–73, 178, 185, 195; Squadrito, 'Locke and the Dispossession', 102–4; Uzgalis, 'An Inconsistency', 85–9; Stedman Jones, *End to Poverty?*, 12.

[13] Hume, *Essays*, 208; Chukwudi Eze, *Race*, 3, 6, 33, 35–6; Muthu, *Enlightenment*, 183; Young, *Colonial Desire*, 94, 123.

[14] Popkin, 'Philosophical Bias', 245–6.

[15] Stewart, *Opinion and Reform*, 220, 307–8; Armitage, *Ideological Origins*, 189–93.

[16] Hume, *Treatise*, 557.

[17] Ibid.; Popkin, *Third Force*, 69–72; Stewart, *Opinion and Reform*, 185–7, 301.

Africa and the Americas, not parts of the world (in contrast to China) for which he cherished great esteem, being populated by Amerindians, Hottentots, 'les Cafres', and other dark peoples he deemed savage and primitive were, in his opinion, bound to produce, where left to themselves, only very crude political entities which, he remarks disdainfully, 'sont des démocraties', while the Barbary corsair states of Tripoli, Tunis, and Algiers, if less primitive, were still in his eyes lawless as well as minuscule and unstable 'republics' of soldiers and pirates.[18] He too insisted on 'difference' between the races, meaning that the differences were intrinsic and fundamental and not just to do with climate or other conditioning factors.

The only way to form a moral and political rationale strong enough to counter what was effectively a general convergence of theological justification, mercantilist considerations of national interest, and theories of race superiority and inferiority, was to adopt the principle of equality and the unity of mankind on the basis of 'la raison universelle' as Bruzen de La Martinière calls it.[19] Declaring universal equality the 'holiest' law of morality, as the latter puts it, something overriding every other claim or justification, the radical stream offered an avowedly 'universalist' moral-political standpoint intellectually robust enough to underpin a general system of anti-colonialism which was to culminate during the Enlightenment in the final version of the Abbé Raynal's *Histoire philosophique et politique des établissements et du commerce des Européens dans les deux Indes* of 1780, a ringing denunciation of Europe's ruthless conquest, despoliation, and subjection of Africa, Asia, and the Americas in which the hardest-hitting sections were written by Diderot. The origins and roots of this type of anti-colonialism, however, are clearly recognizable much earlier in the writing of van den Enden, Poulain de La Barre, Lahontan, Gueudeville, Bayle, Fontenelle, Radicati, Tyssot de Patot, Doria, Jean-Frédéric Bernard, and Bruzen de La Martinière, as well as Diderot. For the only way intellectually to undermine such systems of subjection was to uphold the essential equivalence of all individual hopes, wills, and status, and therefore of all peoples and religions, excluding no one, not even unbelievers, heretics, neophytes, and atheists and not even the most primitive nomads. Hence, anti-colonialism as a strand of modernity both actually derived from, and could only derive from, forms of radical thought based on materialist monism.

One way to foment anti-imperial thinking was through the medium of the utopian novel. A particularly remarkable exposition of the Spinozist idea that true morality and 'religion' is a universalism applying everywhere, and assigning an equal value to all, found expression in the novels of the dissident Huguenot Simon Tyssot de Patot, at Deventer, a writer who, besides Descartes, Spinoza, and some Hobbes, was also acquainted with the works of Fontenelle, Bayle, Bekker, van Leenhof, and Lahontan.[20] At one point in his most successful fictional work, published around 1714, the *Adventures of Jacques Massé*, Tyssot's hero is imprisoned in

[18] Voltaire, *Essai sur les mœurs*, i. 6–8; Pomeau, *Politique de Voltaire*, 186, 210–13.
[19] [Bruzen de La Martinière], *Entretiens*, i. 1, ii. 553, 598–9.
[20] Rosenberg, *Tyssot de Patot*, 52–4.

the Inquisition dungeons at Goa. There he meets an extraordinary Chinese prisoner who speaks Portuguese and had once been a Catholic, having as a youth been educated by Jesuit missionaries. This Chinese teaches that all men are equal and, having learnt from bitter experience what harm religious bigotry does, abjures all denominational creeds, including the name of 'Christian', preferring to label himself a 'universaliste', or devotee of the religion 'des honnêtes gens'. Where the Holy Office which had deprived him of his liberty rules a dark and gloomy world of fanaticism, irrationality, credulity, and torture, Tyssot's noble-minded inmate proves the philosopher can be free even in prison and that the intolerant theological dogmas in which most men believe while wreaking great havoc in the world do not in reality possess even any meaning, let alone value.

Tyssot's Chinese, as a professed *universaliste*, makes no distinctions of a qualitative kind between one society, people, or religion and another: for there are no peoples without both beauties and blemishes, nor any religions, 'et je suis persuadé', he says, that there is no path by which 'l'on ne se puisse damner ou sauver'.[21] This concept pervades his moral philosophy and, just in case any reader had missed the point, the profession of this inspiring *universaliste*, we are told, was that of grinding lenses for microscopes, by which labour Spinoza had earned his bread.[22] Tyssot's principal idea is that morality depends not on revelations or confessions but on equality, equity, and reciprocity. In conducting his life, his Chinese behaves towards others, he explains, as he would want them to behave towards himself.[23] The colour and look of Men's faces may differ but, in reality, he assures Massé, men diverge no more in behaviour or thoughts than in basic physique.

'Universalism', avers Tyssot, is the first precept of all 'true religion'. The notion that 'true religion' differs radically from any actually existing organized creed was, we have seen, a characteristic Spinozist theme and one Spinoza himself uses in an anti-colonial context, in the *Tractatus theologico-politicus*, in his brief *excursus* on Europe's relations with Japan. Denying sacraments like Holy Communion and others common to Christians were instituted by Christ or the apostles, implying they were just the inventions of later theologians avid to extend their authority, he maintains that it is unnecessary to participate in any church's established rites to attain salvation.[24] No one wishing to live 'a blessed life', holds Spinoza, but failing to participate in 'religious' rituals and ceremonies, or who lives in solitude, or under a government hostile to Christianity, like that of Japan, can be harmed thereby nor is anyone bound by the directives of any church no matter which. So as not to contravene Japanese law, 'the Dutch who live there', he says, 'are required by the East India Company to refrain from practicing any external rites',[25] but this cannot affect their spiritual status for no one's well-being can be affected by performing or not performing Holy Communion or any other religious ceremony.

21 Ibid. 116–17; Tyssot de Patot, *Voyages et avantures*, 171.

22 Tyssot de Patot, *Voyayes et avantures*, 177; Rosenberg, *Tyssot de Patot*, 116–17.

23 Tyssot de Patot, *Voyages et avantures*, 171.

24 Spinoza, *TTP* 66–7.

25 Ibid. 119, 249.

But it was arguably Bayle, more than any other writer of the Early Enlightenment, who most effectively deployed the principle of moral universalism which so impressed Tyssot as a way of discrediting theological justifications for empire, military conquest, and religious expansion in the Indies. Bayle was probably the first major philosopher, apart from Locke, to use the burgeoning travel literature of the age to assess and evaluate the relationship between Europe and the non-European world. However, in contemplating relations between Europeans and non-Europeans, he came to dramatically different conclusions from Locke. For the latter even though he refrained from justifying dominion over lands once belonging to Amerindians on the ground of their being 'utterly strangers to Christianity', stipulating that their idolatry and ignorance 'gives us noe right to expel or treat them ill', nevertheless, as we have seen, judged that the biblical injunction to 'replenish the whole earth', and claims based on the argument from effective vacancy, *did* stretch to legitimizing dispossession of the natives.[26] Bayle, by contrast, thought that only universal moral criteria could be brought to bear in such a case, questioning the moral, cultural, and political legitimacy of European colonization especially where this was based on theological claims.[27]

Bayle, proceeding from the same monist philosophical premisses and categorical universalism as Spinoza and van den Enden before him, and Meslier and Diderot later, seems, in several parts of his *oeuvre*, to have a special axe to grind, regarding the missionizing ambitions of the Jesuits in the Far East. He vehemently deplores what he considers the arrogant and unjust proceedings of the missionaries as well as colonial companies, merchants, seamen, and soldiers, clearly implying that China, Japan, Siam, India, and other parts of Asia would not just be morally, culturally, and politically better off without not just these European intruders with their warehouses, goods, ships, and guns, but should certainly also rid themselves of the missionaries who were importing an intolerant and aggressively proselytizing new faith, theology, moral system, and education.

Despite being bound to do so in partly veiled terms, Bayle emphatically endorsed the refusal of the Japanese to allow the Spanish and Portuguese friars to resume their quest for converts there, after their expulsion by the shogunate, in the 1620s and 1630s, in what Bayle significantly chooses to interpret as a struggle to defend the integrity and independence of Japan from European colonial ambitions and pretensions. Bayle, in his most insinuatingly sardonic fashion, pronounces it extremely 'unfortunate' that the Japanese, 'not having sufficient illumination to renounce their false religion', failed to make the correct decision as 'between persecuting and being persecuted' and, opting for the former, expelled the Christian missionaries. Despite having made such a disastrously wrong choice, though, he adds, they can perhaps draw some slight comfort from knowing they could 'have preserved their traditional government, customs and worship only by ridding themselves of the Christians'.

[26] Squadrito, 'Locke and the Dispossession', 101–24; Armitage, *Ideological Origins*, 90–1, 97–8.

[27] Charnley, *Pierre Bayle*, 140.

This might not amount to much compared to redemption through Christ, he agrees, but at least the Japanese grasped that the Christians, as soon as they were militarily strong enough to do so, and able to arm their Japanese proselytes, would assuredly have devastated all their traditions, laid waste their land, and destroyed their state and their entire independence.

No sooner did they gain the upper hand, he says, than the Christians would certainly have overpowered and persecuted everyone who refused to submit to them. Indeed, had the 'true faith' after all been successful in Japan, holds Bayle, it is certain the Christians would have practised what he calls the 'cruel maxims' of the Spaniards, and before long 'by means of slaughtering and hanging, as in America, have brought all Japan under their yoke'.[28] Bayle's antipathy to missionaries and efforts at conversion is equally manifest in his discussion of China.[29] Astoundingly, he suggests the only reliable solution for the thorny problem facing the Chinese, in his day, was immediately to expel all the Christian missionaries. In his *Commentaire philosophique*, he imagines a Chinese imperial council discussing the Jesuits and advising the emperor to eject them all from his dominions 'comme des pestes publiques'.

Bayle's imagined Chinese advisers press the emperor never to allow them to return: for to do so would be to introduce into his realms 'la semence perpétuelle du carnage et de la désolation des villes et du plat pays'.[30] If permitted to stay, the missionaries would doubtless behave impeccably to begin with, peacefully preaching, teaching, and flattering their hosts—apart, that is, from promising Paradise, and threatening Hell, in the afterlife. But no sooner did they command enough proselytes to seek dominance politically and militarily, averrs Bayle, than they would undoubtedly suppress, coerce, persecute, and kill everyone standing in their way or who preferred indigenous Chinese religions. To secure the upper hand, they would also spread sedition on all sides and organize armed insurgency against the emperor and his advisers. Should the emperor attempt to resist, they would threaten to summon whole 'crusades' from the West. Slaughtering large numbers and trampling all opposition under foot, they would replace the emperor, once overwhelmed, with another of their choosing and one more willing to submit to the eternal truths proclaimed by the church.[31]

Were the Chinese emperor indeed to banish the missionaries, held Bayle, this would be 'avec raison et justice'.[32] They would have been ejected not because the Chinese were intolerant but exactly the reverse, because the Jesuits were. These remarks were, in a way, extremely prescient. For the papacy, ruling on the problem of the Chinese Rites controversy, after a long debate in 1700–1, overruled the Jesuits, declared Confucianism 'atheistic', and forbade Chinese Catholics to participate in

[28] Bayle, *Political Writings*, 132; Muthu, *Enlightenment*, 324 n. 38.
[29] Charnley, *Pierre Bayle*, 115–19.
[30] Ibid. 116–19, 162; Bayle, *Commentaire philosophique*, 122–3.
[31] Bayle, *Commentaire philosophique*, 124, 130.
[32] Ibid. 125; Pinot, *La Chine*, 316–18; Minuti, 'Orientalismo', 904, 908–10.

Confucian rites.[33] On hearing of this, the Chinese emperor, K'ang-Hsi, retaliated by expelling the missionaries. The papacy's shift to a more confrontational, intolerant stance toward Confucianism in turn reinforced the prevailing impression in Europe that the Chinese neo-Confucianists were indeed, as Arnauld, Malebranche, and other critics of the Jesuits urged, 'atheists' and 'Spinozists'.[34] The expulsion of the Jesuits from China, with Christianity's intolerance being cited as the reason, was later approved by Voltaire and d'Argens, in terms precisely echoing those of Bayle.[35]

Denouncing the Crusades, and the Spanish conquest of the Americas 'par des cruautés qui font horreur', Bayle predicted that the missionaries' zeal would wreak comparable havoc in the future in whichever parts of the world faith 'n'a pas encore ensanglanté'. In singling out for special censure European colonial initiatives using requirements of faith as their justification for imposing western dominance and intolerance,[36] his chief concern, clearly, was to discredit use of theological arguments as justifications for any kind of conquest, despoilment, enslavement, or empire. But by discrediting what was still the principal Catholic and Protestant defence of colonial expansion, slavery, and subjecting non-European peoples, Bayle fundamentally called into question one of colonialism's main ideological pillars, helping focus attention on colonialism's unjustified arrogance, cruelty, sanctimoniousness, intolerance, and destructiveness.

The idea that the true 'universalist' morality has no theological grounding and the connected principle of universal equality may truly be said to be the twin guiding principles of Early Enlightenment anti-colonial theory. Egalitarian, libertarian, and philosophically monist moral concepts forged by Spinoza, Bayle, and Fontenelle, and then amplified by secondary figures like van den Enden, Poulain de La Barre, Tyssot de Patot, Lahontan, Gueudeville, Radicati, Jean-Frédéric Bernard, Doria, and Meslier, laid the basis of a fully-fledged radical Early Enlightenment anti-imperialism. At the same time, their stance encouraged greater appreciation and more extensive study of primitive societies, indeed a thoroughgoing re-evaluation of primitive man as a moral and political being. Here it was van den Enden, and specifically in his *Kort Verhael* (1662), which includes a remarkable eulogy of the Amerindians of New Netherland, who first initiated, well in advance of Lahontan, Gueudeville, Bayle, Radicati, and Morelly, the myth of the morally admirable and upright noble savage or as Gueudeville characterized the type, in 1706, 'un de ces hommes qui suivent le pur instinct de la nature'.[37]

General equality denies the legitimacy of slavery in whatever shape or form. But it also asserted the dignity and equal worth of non-European peoples, the Amerindians, Africans, and Asians, including primitive peoples in whatever remote, isolated parts of the world. Here was a context which figured increasingly in

[33] Kors, *Atheism in France*, 174–5

[34] Wing-Tsit Chan, 'Study of Chu Hsi', 560; Mungello, 'Malebranche and Chinese Philosophy', 553.

[35] Voltaire, *Traité sur la tolérance*, 51; Minuti, 'Orientalismo', 904–5.

[36] Bayle, *Commentaire philosophique*, 13; Mungello, 'Malebranche and Chinese Philosophy', 130–1.

[37] Rosenberg, *Nicolas Gueudeville*, 127–8.

European travel literature, raising a host of new questions about the true nature of man, the 'state of nature', and *consensus gentium*. Yet it was virtually only radical writers who took the significant step of asserting the equal, and in some respects superior, moral worth of primitive men. If Hobbes, asserted Radicati, had investigated the 'state of nature' with greater care, he would have changed his opinion regarding its alleged brutishness and blatant inferiority to society under the state. 'Witness the ancient inhabitants of the Canary-Islands', he remarks, 'who, before they were discovered by the Christians had always lived in the blessed state of Nature. For they fed upon herbs and fruits, lay upon leaves in the forests, went naked, and their women, and all other things were in common amongst them.'[38]

In his account of New Netherland, van den Enden deplored all forms of human subjection, pointedly eulogizing the Amerindians.[39] His Amerindians are self-sufficient, peaceful, dignified, modest, and truthful men exuding a powerful awareness of equality and liberty. Besides this, they avoid, or so he claimed in 1662, lying and swearing and are 'uit 'er natuur zeer vry, en edelmoedigh van aert' [from nature very free and naturally noble], exactly the sort of material, he insists, from which ancient Athenian and Roman democracy was built 'welke ons ordeels ook mede ver de beste voorde gemeene, en volx vryheit te achten is' [which in our opinion is to be considered by far the best [form of state] for the common and popular freedom].[40] The Indians, held van den Enden, detested living in subjection to anyone.

In this way, a new kind of quintessentially 'modern' myth was born. Among such noble *sauvages*, held van den Enden, like Lahontan, Gueudeville, Radicati, and Bernard later, there was far less difference of status, deference, and diffidence, as well as flattery, than 'among us', moving them to say they cannot understand how, in Europe, one person counts for so much more than another.[41] They (supposedly) dwelt in perfect harmony largely free of disputes and it was their admirable custom to take important decisions only in accordance with the view of the majority.[42] Hence, in van den Enden's opinion (despite his never having been to America), the New Netherland Indians could be said to represent a superior society to that of the Europeans. But there was nothing innate, or ethnically determined, about this superiority which was essentially moral and social in character. For if Europe is marred by inequality, authority, credulity, and luxury but might improve so, equally, the Amerindians might readily be corrupted and deteriorate. Human imperfection has nothing to do with Original Sin, according to van den Enden, but is no less ubiquitous on that account, arising, as he saw it, from lust to dominate through violence, deception, and pillage as well as thirst for riches and glory, lusts which, alas, are universal.[43]

[38] Radicati, *Twelve Discourses*, 39.

[39] Van den Enden, *Kort Verhael*, 26, 29–30; Klever, 'Inleiding', 37–8; Klever, *Mannen rond Spinoza*, 38.

[40] Van den Enden, *Kort Verhael*, 19–22, 30–1, 69; Klever, 'Inleiding', 34.

[41] Klever, 'Inleiding', 34; van den Enden, *Kort Verhael*, 19, 30.

[42] Klever, *Sphinx*, 147.

[43] Mertens, 'Natural Man, Colonialism', (forthcoming).

A *Spinosiste* writer who signally contributed to developing the radical conception of the unity and equality of mankind was Louis-Armand de Lom d'Arce, baron de Lahontan (1666–1715), a former army officer who spent some eleven years in French Canada, from 1683 to 1694, and who, after certain acts of insubordination, had to flee not just Canada but the French empire, absconding to England and Holland where he poured out his rancour against the French colonial system at The Hague, becoming one of the best-known writers on North American Indians of the Early Enlightenment.[44] His account of the Hurons, Iroquois, and other Canadian Indians, first published in 1703, and appearing in English in 1705 and German in 1709, in several respects bears a striking resemblance to van den Enden's portrait of the Indians of New Netherland, especially as regards their alleged ardour for liberty and equality and scorn for Europe's stratified society based on money, rank, and a hierarchy of orders.

No doubt, much of Lahontan's account of Canada in the 1680s, with its scathing exposé of the 'despotisme spirituel' of the Catholic clergy and Jesuits, of the corruption of colonial administration, and ill consequences of excluding Huguenots with their skills and hard-working habits, could be viewed as an indictment of one particular colonial system rather than European colonialism *per se*. He accuses the Catholic clergy of so thoroughly manipulating the secular administration as to be the real rulers of the country, amassing power and wealth, and imposing a truly appalling intolerance and narrowness of spirit.[45] Particularly 'insupportable', in his opinion, was the clergy's campaign against books of which they disapproved, in an effort to confine all reading matter in Canada to works of Catholic devotion. The Indians, he maintains, especially blamed and deplored the clergy, lamenting the 'empire despotique' exercised, by them, over both themselves and the country generally.[46] These were abuses which, in theory, could be corrected by the crown, and Lahontan himself does not directly challenge French royal possession of Canada as such.[47] But, in places, particularly the interpolations inserted in the 1705 edition, reported by Jean-Frédéric Bernard and others to be by Gueudeville,[48] the indictment extends further, to encompass colonial rule itself and subjection of native peoples by Europeans generally. As with van den Enden, Tyssot de Patot, Radicati, and Bernard, the case hinges on the concept of fundamental equality, human reason being accounted an 'attribut essentiel de nôtre esprit', something universal among nations and peoples everywhere.[49] In the dialogue between the baron and the Huron 'Adario', heavily doctored, probably by Gueudeville, 'Adario' maintains that he and his people recognize no superior and no master, living as they do 'sans

[44] Mertens, 'Natural Man Colonialism', (forthcoming) Betts, *Early Deism*, 129; Ehrard, *L'Idée*, 748.

[45] Lahontan, rev. Gueudeville, *Voyages du baron*, i. 68–9, ii. 74–5.

[46] Lahontan, *Nouveaux Voyages*, ii. 72–4; *Histoire des ouvrages des savants* (1702), 350.

[47] Muthu, *Enlightenment*, 31; Lahontan, rev. Gueudeville, *Voyages du baron*, ii. 74–5, 83–4.

[48] Rosenberg, *Nicolas Gueudeville*, 125.

[49] Lahontan, rev. Gueudeville, *Voyages du baron*, ii. 242; Rosenberg, *Nicolas Gueudeville*, 89, 127–8; Muthu, *Enlightenment*, 29–30, 68.

subordination et dans une égalité parfaite'. Hence, they are 'incomparablement plus nobles en cela' than the French nation which is nothing but a vast mass of slaves 'sous la volonté absolue d'un seul homme'.

Lahontan idealized Indian society as one based on equality and fully in accord with nature and, like van den Enden before him, claimed the Indians despised Europeans for assigning much more to some than others and for deferring more to those who possess most than to anyone else. Men being created equal by nature, the Hurons and Iroquois, he reported, desired no distinction of ranks or subordination in their society.[50] Indeed, exclaims the exiled baron, they thoroughly deride and ridicule 'la grande subordination qu'ils remarquent parmi nous'.[51] The French king claimed sovereignty over Canada and hence over the Indians and the French living there. Adario, who emerges here as a veritable anti-Hobbes, expounding a rigorous positive naturalism, dismisses such claims as being as ridiculous as they are unjust. By what right did Louis XIV acquire his pretended sovereignty over us? Have we sold ourselves to him? 'Avons-nous stipulé que nous lui obéïrons et qu'il nous protégeroit?'[52] Not at all. Rather it was the French who, without justification, came with their guns and 'usurped' lands belonging to the Indians since time immemorial, who, consequently, have every right to reverse matters and impose their rule on the Europeans.

All the Iroquois, claimed Lahontan, regarded themselves as 'aussi grands maîtres les uns que les autres', saying that since all men are cut from the same block, there should not be any 'distinction ni de subordination entre eux'.[53] Another conspicuous feature in Lahontan-Gueudeville is the alleged absence of superstition among the Amerindians. Ridiculing Jesuit reports that the Iroquois shared in the demonology prevalent in Europe, these writers contend 'le Diable ne s'est jamais manifesté à ses Amériquains', a claim also made earlier by van den Enden about the *naturellen*, as he calls the Indians of New Netherland.[54] The implication once again was that the Christians are actually more superstitious than the Indian heathen.

Lahontan's Amerindians also regulate sexual life and marriage more rationally than the whites. Young women are left entirely free to choose, or agree to, their own husbands without any tyranny of the family. Divorce, as Jean-Frédéric Bernard reminded readers, recycling Lahontan's material in his great compendium on the world's religions of 1723, is readily available but rarely required since their marriages, being better founded, last longer and develop more satisfactorily than those of Europeans.[55] Whereas European men boast of their sexual exploits but impose on women an exacting code of chastity and modesty, and a ruthless surveillance of reputations, a double standard entailing a heavy stigma where women are suspected of

50 Lahontan, *Nouveaux Voyages*, ii. 38; Ehrard, *L'Idée*, 524; Muthu, *Enlightenment*, 24–5.

51 Lahontan, *Nouveaux Voyages*, ii. 97; Hazard, *European Mind*, 28–9; Tortarolo, *L'Illuminismo*, 215–16; Israel, *Radical Enlightenment*, 581.

52 Lahontan, rev. Gueudeville, *Voyages du baron*, ii. 244; Tortarolo, *L'Illuminismo*, 216.

53 Lahontan, *Nouveaux Voyages*, ii. 98.

54 Ibid. ii. 126–7; Betts, *Early Deism*, 129; Klever, *Sphinx*, 148.

55 Bernard, *Cérémonies et coutumes*, i. 58; Muthu, *Enlightenment*, 26–7.

extramarital intercourse, the Canadian Indians, allegedly, made no fetish of virginity or chastity, leaving young women and men free to experiment sexually both before and after marriage.

Lahontan's Iroquois and Hurons, furthermore, are convinced Christianity is 'un ouvrage humain' since this religion has divided into so many rival sects.[56] Despite its marked utopian dimension, Lahontan's, Gueudeville's, and Bernard's construct was plainly designed to undermine Hobbes's emphatic separation of the 'state of nature' from life in society under a form of political organization, in effect to merge the two, to create a society close to the state of nature but harmonious and free of internal disputes, allowing maximum liberty to all.[57] Herein lies its essentially radical and Spinozistic character. Lahontan, stiffened by Gueudeville, and then recycled by Benard and Bruzen de La Martinière, urged that Amerindian egalitarianism and rejection of imperial subjection were integrally linked to their rationality and being free of 'superstition'.

Indeed, native Americans are depicted by them as adherents of a highly rational Spinozistic practical philosophy 'de bon sens', identifying God with nature and with all things, a creed supposedly maintaining that humanity must never strip itself of the benefits of reason, this being 'la plus noble faculté dont Dieu l'ait enrichi'.[58] A critical response to Lehontan's book in the *Histoire des ouvrages des savans* notes that Lahontan's Amerindians deride the Europeans' religion, supposedly amazed at French credulity in believing in the reported 'miracles du Vieux et du Nouveau Testament', deeming this 'une simplicité dont les sauvages du Canada auroient honte'; this point was later recycled in 1751, by one of Diderot's assistants, the Abbé Pestré, in his contribution to the article 'Canadiens', a piece heavily infuenced by Lahontan's perspective, in the third volume of the *Encyclopédie*.[59]

The basic injustice of French royal and ecclesiastical 'tyranny' over the egalitarian, freedom-loving Iroquois and Hurons of the Great Lakes is grounded by Lahontan and Gueudeville on arguments for the basic equality and unity of mankind and republican rejection of monarchy itself. Both the colonial system and the specific 'tyranny' of the Catholic clergy ultimately rest, they contend, on the principle of royal absolutism. Hence in Canada, as in France, it is not the well-being of the nation 'qui est la loi suprême, c'est la volonté du monarque', a wholly false principle from which the majority in society derive no benefit.[60] Uninhibitedly criticizing France, Gueudeville's 'Adario' is scornful that so large a nation should live under the will of a single man; indeed, he can conceive of nothing 'de plus bizarre, ni de plus contraire à la droite raison'.[61]

[56] Lahontan, *Nouveaux Voyages*, ii. 119–20; van Eijnatten, *Liberty and Concord*, 246.

[57] Van Eijnatten, *Liberty and Concord*, 25–6; Ehrard, *L'Idée*, 491–2.

[58] Lahontan, *Nouveaux Voyages*, ii. 117; Ehrard, *L'Idée*, 452, 745.

[59] *Histoire des ouvrages des savants* (Aug. 1702), 349; Diderot and d'Alembert, *Encyclopédie*, ii. 581–2; Spallanzani, *Immagini*, 66, 96.

[60] Lahontan, *Nouveaux Voyages*, ii. 260; Ehrard, *L'Idée*, 491–2.

[61] Lahontan, *Nouveaux Voyages*, ii. 261; Muthu, *Enlightenment*, 24–5.

Writers like van den Enden, Poulain de La Barre, Fontenelle, Bayle, Lahontan, Gueudeville, Tyssot de Patot, Radicati, Meslier, Morelly, Diderot, and later Condorcet, while granting that different human societies stand at strikingly different levels of civilization and technology, also held, unlike Locke, Voltaire, Montesquieu, or Hume, that this in no way implies a moral or legal hierarchy of races. Drastic differences in levels of culture, they maintained, provide no grounds for whites claiming any innate superiority over more primitive men or other non-Europeans. In fact, assessed on the basis of equality and universalism, Europeans could perhaps claim an element of authentic moral superiority over (some) others only in one respect. Poulain at least thought 'reason' was less besieged and persecuted by superstition in Europe than elsewhere in that women in recent times were less subordinated and oppressed there than among 'almost all the nations of Asia, Africa and America', and sound philosophy was now strengthening their position further.[62]

Radical rejection of racial hierarchy derived partly from an ardent conviction that Man's progression from the primitive to the civilized—as Fontenelle was the first clearly to state—is basically a matter of time and place not of race or inherent characteristics. The concept of *l'histoire de l'esprit humain*, forged by Fontenelle, Boulainvilliers, and Boureau-Deslandes, envisages the natural course of development of human reason as being everywhere essentially the same. For Montesquieu, Voltaire, and Hume, by contrast, differences between peoples and races were conceived, whether rooted in environment or climactic conditions, religious traditions, or else innate racial differences, as inherently much more fundamental.[63]

2. SLAVERY AND THE EARLY ENLIGHTENMENT

That the roots of radical anti-imperialism lie in the late seventeenth century is, in itself unsurprising. For this was an era which witnessed a tremendous escalation in the scale of European, and especially British, colonial settlement as well as overseas rivalry and war. By the mid eighteenth century, the whole Indian subcontinent, Australasia, and much of Oceania was on the verge of joining much of the Americas, Africa, and South-East Asia under the political and military domination of Europeans. Simultaneously, this period was one of dramatically expanding involvement, especially by the British, in the enslavement, transportation, and exploitation of black slaves.[64] From 57,000 slaves transported from Africa to the New World in the 1670s, the comparable figure, for the decade, had risen to nearly a quarter of a million, or some 242,000 individuals, by the 1720s.[65] The proportion

[62] Stuurman, *François Poulain de La Barre*, 193.

[63] Hourcade, 'Jet de plume ou projet', 20–3; Stuurman, *François Poulain de La Barre*, 203.

[64] Hoppit, *A Land of Liberty?*, 268; Richardson, 'British Empire', 441.

[65] Richardson, *British Empire*, 442.

of the Atlantic slave trade controlled by Britain, relative to the rest of Europe, moreover, rose steadily to considerably over half of the total by the 1760s. By then, Britain had gained an unparalleled domination of the world's major sea-lanes as well as of North America, the Caribbean, West Africa, India, and Australasia. If was indeed an empire on which the sun never set and geographically the most extensive that had ever existed.

While it is perhaps not entirely fair to depict Locke as an ideologist of empire and claim that he was 'the last major philosopher to seek a justification for absolute and perpetual slavery', it was extremely difficult writing at the heart of the most successful of the colonial powers and the one for whom colonial expansion did most during this period both to boost national prosperity and help shape the developing sense of national identity not at least to some degree to condone the burgeoning empire and its institutions. Locke did endorse slavery at any rate by implication, not least in his financial dealings, and was a significant shareholder in the Royal Africa Company in which he invested the then very large sum of £600 in 1672, besides being among the eleven chief investors in the Bahamas Adventurers Company established in the same year.[66] But his investment in slavery was not just financial: a philosopher who clearly favoured steeply stratified social hierarchy and wide property inequality, there was undeniably an element of hesitation, even perhaps contradiction, in his comments on slavery.[67]

As secretary to the Lords Proprietors of Carolina in the years 1669–75, Locke played a prominent part in drawing up the first *Fundamental Constitutions of Carolina* (1669), a key objective of which was to 'avoid erecting a numerous Democracy'. The colonizers of Carolina planned to root social hierarchy strongly in this new milieu, designing an elaborate system of hereditary white 'landgraves'—a term probably coined by Locke who, in fact, became one of them, as well as of Indian 'cassiques', for this anti-egalitarian purpose.[68] In this planned social pyramid, moreover, black slaves were to be an integral if lowly component without this impinging in any way on Locke's concept of Man's spiritual equality before God. For in his thought, the work of saving our immortal souls, though overridingly important, has no bearing on civil status. The constitutions adopted by the Lords Proprietors stipulated that 'every freeman of Carolina shall have absolute power and authority over his Negro slaves, of what opinion or religion soever'.[69]

Locke also worked on the revision of the Carolina constitutions of 1682, reaffirming both titled hierarchy and slavery just when completing his *Two Treatises on Government*, thereby further helping consolidate what Burke later called the 'high

[66] Farr, 'So vile', 267; Glausser, 'Three Approaches', 200–1.

[67] Laslett, 'Introduction', 105–6; Dunn, *Political Thought*, 174–7; Marshall, *John Locke*, 117–18; Davis, *Problem of Slavery*, 45; Waldron, *God, Locke and Equality*, 149.

[68] McNally, 'Locke, Levellers', 92–3; Farr, 'So vile', 263–5; Glausser, 'Three Approaches', 203; Armitage, 'That Excellent Forme', 14.

[69] Armitage, 'That Excellent Forme', 14; Farr, 'So vile', 263, 265–6, 272; Tully, 'Rediscovering America', 171–2; Uzgalis, 'An Inconsistency', 82; Montag, *Bodies, Masses, Power*, 110.

aristocratick spirit of Virginia and the southern colonies'.[70] He often cites the British plantations in the West Indies and North America, colonies dependent on various forms of forced labour, in ways fully implying acceptance of the principles on which these colonies were founded.[71] Restored to royal favour after the Glorious Revolution, Locke also served during the years 1696–1700 as a commissioner on the Board of Trade which involved, among other tasks, drafting instructions for the governor of Virginia in 1698, directing him assuredly to restrain 'inhumane severities' towards black slaves but also requiring him to support the Royal Africa Company, an enterprise principally dealing in slaves while, at the same time, promoting 'conversion of negroes and Indians to the Christian Religion'.[72] Condoning of black slavery may not have been a basic feature of Locke's philosophy, but it was an integral part of his life and outlook.[73]

But possibly, no great intellectual figure of the age more typically combines liberal tendencies with the dilemmas and contradictions of conservative enlightenment than Montesquieu whose huge, rich, and in some respects ambiguous *L'Esprit des lois*, stressing differences between law, morality, and customs in different milieux, shaped by differing conditions, lent itself with peculiar facility to contradictory readings in different parts of the globe. While Montesquieu's work does contain one of the earliest sustained attacks on slavery from an 'enlightened' philosophical standpoint, as something contrary to the law of nature, his critique of slavery also acquired a not wholly undeserved reputation for being weak, self-contradictory, and even rather flippant.[74] Nor was it difficult to find among pro-slavery circles of the French West Indian planter elite, or anywhere in the New World, publicists keen to rework his ideas, liberally citing from his text, appealing to special conditions and the influence of climate and environment, to buttress pleas for racial hierarchy and justification of slavery, just as, in Russia and Poland, the suitability of serfdom, in the appropriate context, was later defended by invoking Montesquieu. This was *not* justification of slavery in terms of basic principle, but it *was* justification in Montesquieu's terms of special local needs, social structures, and environmental circumstances warranting forms of subjection and forced labour otherwise lacking any rationale in terms of reason, justice, or basic morality.[75]

No doubt, it *was* twisting Montesquieu's texts to present him as a defender of colonial empire, racial hierarchy, and slavery. But it was not twisting him so far as to prevent a purportedly 'enlightened' view based on *L'Esprit des lois* becoming integral to French Caribbean colonial ideology in the later eighteenth century. Such a pseudo-Montesquieuan perspective inspired, for instance, the writings of M. L. E. Moreau de Saint Méry (1750–1819), a lawyer who compiled several studies of

70 Armitage, 'That Excellent Forme', 15.

71 Locke, *Two Treatises*, 237, 283–5; Tully, 'Rediscovering America', 168, 171.

72 Farr, 'So vile', 269.

73 Ibid. 281; Glausser, 'Three Approaches', 203–4.

74 Popkin, 'Philosophical Bias', 30–3; Ehrard, *L'Idée*, 735–6; Tarin, *Diderot*, 23; Peabody, '*There are no Slaves*', 66–7, 101–2; Ghachem, 'Montesquieu in the Caribbean', 12–14.

75 Ghachem, 'Montesquieu in the Caribbean', 24–5; Parker, *Agony of Asar*, 55.

different parts of the West Indies and served as deputy for Martinique in the French Constituent Assembly, in 1790, presiding for a while over the Paris commune. Moreau, invoking Montesquieu, 'violently denounced the Abbé Grégoire, the *Amis des noirs*, and the French mulattoes agitating for equality of rights in the Caribbean colonies'.[76] It was thus a poetic double irony that he was mistakenly reported, in Martinique, at one stage as having urged emancipation of the slaves, in a speech delivered in Paris in May 1789, a misunderstanding which quickly blighted his reputation among the French planters.

It is clear then that the systems of Locke, Montesquieu, Hume, and, even that of Voltaire, provided no real hindrance or opposition to the continuing prevalence of theological justifications for slavery, argumentation which remained widely familiar in the early and mid eighteenth century. This is not to deny that there were also important theological arguments against slavery; but these tended to be cultivated mainly among dissenting, fringe churches. The royal codes systematizing the administrative systems of the Indies promulgated by all the European powers, in any case, made a point of interlacing their political and mercantilist aims with theological doctrines legitimizing their methods of rule and those institutions, such as black slavery, which were specific to the colonial context. Thus, for example, Louis XIV's *Code noire* of 1685, fixing the terms of French Caribbean slavery, combines the ideologies of monarchy, aristocracy, and the 'civilizing' mission with religious aims much as was done also in the legal and administrative terminology employed throughout the viceroyalties and governorships of Spanish and Portuguese America. Faith was being widely used to justify not just empire but also slavery, racial dominion, and the new types of social hierarchy, all supposedly instruments of salvation for the heathen newly converted to the 'true' faith; for such institutions kept the recently converted under effective theological tutelage well segregated from soul-destroying 'heresies' which in the French Caribbean were taken to include Calvinism and Judaism as well as African heathenism.[77]

The foremost black Christian theologian of the Early Enlightenment period, Jacobus Johannes Capitein (1717–47), a Dutch-speaking ex-slave and man of considerable learning and skill with Latin who had studied for five years at Leiden (1737–42), was one of the many who vigorously defended the principle of innate black inferiority and the institution of slavery against the flurries of anti-slavery sentiment then welling up in the Netherlands. Sent out by the Dutch West Africa Company to preach at the Dutch base at Elmina and serve as a Reformed missionary in West Africa, he systematically opposed the principle of racial equality and basic human freedom, doing so on purely theological grounds. Original Sin played a large part in his argument, as it once had in Augustine's; and so did the biblical curse of Ham and other tenets. But the real historical importance of Capitein's *Staatkundig-godgeleerd onderzoekschrift over de slaverny* (1742) [Political-theological treatise about slavery]

[76] Ghachem, 'Montesquieu in the Caribbean', 22–4; Davis, *Problem of Slavery*, 187–8.
[77] Stuurman, 'François Bernier', 10–11, 14; Stuurman, 'How to Write a History of Equality', 23–38.

lies in his thesis that black slavery does not and cannot contradict 'Christian freedom', which must be understood as wholly spiritual rather than physical.

'It is clear beyond doubt', held Capitein, 'that most Dutchmen wish to persuade themselves and others in debate that Christian freedom can in no way walk in step with slavery in the proper sense.'[78] Indeed, the idea was gaining ground, he says, that 'worship of God must necessarily be cultivated not only with a pure mind', which he argued was sufficient, 'but indeed also with a free body'.[79] To this he retorted that it was 'incumbent on all true Christians to promote diligently those means which help this conversion of the heathen, God willing, to develop', that is that the 'Gospel must be spread in our time wherever the dominion and power of Christians' clears the way.[80] From this, one sees the error, he held, of those in Holland 'who, led astray by some unknown spirit, have determined that evangelic freedom cannot coexist with servitude of the body'.[81] If on Dutch soil, slavery was illegal, this was due to the particular laws of the Republic, not any point of Christian teaching. If in England, as distinct from its colonies, 'harsh slavery had been abolished', nevertheless there were still legally indentured white servants and apprentices, like those bonded to work 'just like slaves, for a period, on a contract basis' continually being sent to the West Indies.[82]

Those persons in Holland who make it their business to denounce slavery, Capitein denounces as 'fanatics' and persons who confuse 'spiritual freedom' with bodily freedom. He grants that 'according to Natural Law' the common condition of 'early mankind permitted equal freedom to all humans' but insists that since the Fall and Curse of Ham such philosophical considerations entirely cease to apply. At the same time, this theological emphasis in much of the defence of slavery was bound to lead to accusations of blatant hypocrisy. 'Christians' who should love all other men as themselves, remarked Jean-Frédéric Bernard caustically, in the 1731 edition of his reworking of Beverland, go every year to buy and sell other men whom they carry to market like animals, considering 'the lives of these slaves less valuable than those of dogs'.[83]

To strengthen his case that Christian 'spiritual freedom' can have no bearing on the question of physical freedom or slavery, Capitein adduces Calvin, Bodin, Henry More, and Christian Thomasius.[84] Nor was there any shortage of other Protestant preachers in the early and mid eighteenth century offering similar justifications. The pre-eminent mid eighteenth-century Danish Lutheran theologian Erik Pontoppidan similarly argues, defending the Royal Danish West India Company which shipped black slaves from Africa to the Danish West Indies (St Thomas, St Jan, and St Croix), from where slaves were re-exported elsewhere, that heathendom is something far worse than even the worst (i.e. Catholic) form of Christianity. Hence slavery stands justified: for through this means most slaves will 'get to know

[78] Capitein, *Political-Theological Dissertation*, 103. [79] Ibid.
[80] Ibid. 82; Smith, *Religion and Trade*, 127. [81] Capitein, *Political-Theological Dissertation*, 93.
[82] Ibid. 129. [83] Beverland, *État de l'homme*, 226.
[84] Capitein, *Political-Theological Dissertation*, 112, 115.

God and His Kingdom better, thereby becoming liberated in Christ, though servants of men'.[85] Anglicanism, whether in London, the West Indies, or the Carolinas, adopted much the same stance as did the Calvinists of New England.[86] Jonathan Edwards, at Yale, while granting the 'spiritual' equality of Africans and Indians, in 1741, nevertheless felt obliged (even if reluctantly), to sanction slavery, observing that slavery is not condemned anywhere in the New Testament where everything truly evil is 'expressly mentioned and strictly forbidden'.[87]

Very different was the standpoint of the Radical Enlightenment. Denouncing slavery as wholly contrary to reason, justice, and the basic equality of man,[88] van den Enden is adamant that all peoples are equally capable of reason, learning, and basing their societies on true foundations, with the exception possibly only of the Hottentots, should travellers' reports that they lack human reason prove correct.[89] It is sometimes claimed that the special ardour of van den Enden's condemnation of slavery on grounds of human equality has no real parallel in the Early Enlightenment and should for this reason be considered unrepresentative, an isolated instance rather than something integral to any wider radical impulse towards a comprehensive equality and anti-colonialism.[90] But this is to ignore the typically Spinozistic grounding of his theory of equality and the fact that several, only slightly later, writers, like Tyssot de Patot, Lahontan, Gueudeville, Doria, Radicati, and Bernard, do in fact, and just as vehemently, assert universal equality in reference to non-European societies. Basic equality, for van den Enden, renders slavery totally reprehensible and illegitimate together with all forms of institutionalized subjection of non-white peoples. But this did not mean that no form of settlement overseas was legitimate. The Dutch were a trading nation and their republic the centre of a great global shipping and commercial network. In his *Vrye Politieke Stellingen* (1665), van den Enden summons his compatriots to end slavery and unjust subjection by embracing a new kind of 'free' colonialism partly as a means of countering the aggressive mercantilist schemes of the English and French monarchs who were seeking to topple Holland's commercial primacy and divert, he says, Dutch wealth, skills, and resources to their own lands thereby expanding their own trade and industry and rendering their realms more prosperous and powerful and their would-be absolutist monarchies stronger.[91]

Van den Enden urges the Dutch to abandon their once formidable, heavily armed joint-stock West India Company, now enfeebled by the collapse, in 1654, of its colony in northern Brazil, and create a network of free colonies of equal citizens in the New World only, this time, without subjecting or encroaching on the local inhabitants and

[85] Parker, *Agony of Asar*, 41, 164.

[86] May, *Enlightenment in America*, 70–1, 73, 134, 144; Schlenther, 'Religious Faith', 131–2.

[87] Marsden, *Jonathan Edwards*, 256–8.

[88] Ibid. 38–9; van den Enden, *Vrye Politieke Stellingen*, 160.

[89] Van den Enden, *Vrye Politieke Stellingen*, 169–70; Rosenberg, *Nicolas Gueudeville*, 89.

[90] Mertens, 'Natural Man, Colonialism', (forthcoming).

[91] Van den Enden, *Vrye Politieke Stellingen*, 131–3, 142–3, 225–6; Bedjaï, 'Franciscus van den Enden', 299, 303; Israel, *Dutch Primacy*, 197–291.

without any social hierarchy, church government, or slavery. By founding such centres of production and commerce they would support their homeland and also establish a fairer, more equal trade with the Amerindians. Such new colonies should be called, he thought, *vrye volx verbreidingen* [free people's settlements]. One plausible site, he thought, with the second Anglo-Dutch War (1664–7) beginning, might again be northern Brazil, where the West India Company had failed but the permanent abandonment of which, to the Portuguese, many Dutchmen, especially the Zeelanders, were reluctant to accept.[92] In particular, Amazonia, where the Zeelanders had established some small colonies in the early seventeenth century, seemed a possibility. Preferable, though, for such morally justifiable colonization, he suggested, was New Netherland (New York, New Jersey, and Delaware), territory colonized by the Dutch since 1611 and where he himself, together with some Collegiant utopians, was attempting to organize an autonomous, egalitarian, and self-reliant colony, at Zwanenburg, on the Delaware estuary. By the time he finished his book, in May 1665, however, New Netherland had been overrun by the English whose king claimed the colony's territory, refusing to accept the legitimacy of the Dutch presence anywhere on the North American seaboard.[93]

Colonies of settlers based on what van den Enden calls 'de natuirlijke even gelijke vryheit' [natural equal freedom], devoid of all social, political, and ecclesiastical subordination of part of the population to others, would, he held, create fresh and unrestricted markets for manufactures produced at home, as well as new commerce and shipping. Such settlements, he thought, would also have an openness, dynamism, and natural robustness, including a capacity for self-defence, enabling them successfully to resist the imperial designs of stronger powers such as England and France. Equality and free labour would be the essential basis of such colonies which would in turn serve to strengthen the fabric of human freedom and dignity.

3. EMPIRE AND NATIONAL IDENTITY

In the later seventeenth century and beginning of the eighteenth century, empire became integral to the formation of national identity and attitudes in Europe in a number of new ways and important new respects. The escalating global conflict between Britain and France from 1689 onwards was a great power contest in Europe, but for the first time in the history of European conflicts soon came to be viewed predominantly as a vast rivalry for empire outside Europe, especially in North America, India, West Africa, and the Caribbean. At the same time, the growing realization that it was successful 'colonizing' and imperial expansion, more than

[92] Israel, *Diasporas*, 347, 351–2.

[93] Van den Enden, *Vrye Politieke Stellingen*, preface; Smith, *Religion and Trade*, 234; Klever, 'Inleiding', 28–32, 37–8.

anything else, which accounted for the tremendous increase in British power, riches, and national glory in the century down to 1750[94] served greatly to enhance the value of empire in the eyes of British statesmen and public alike, not only subtly altering feelings of national identity but leading some to suppositions about the innate superiority of the British over others, that is over the non-white races in the first place but also over the French, Dutch, Spaniards, and other Europeans.

Not a few enthusiasts for empire deemed the looming prospect of global domination justification enough in itself. The news of Charles II's securing the transfer of Tangiers and Bombay from Portugal to England, under the 1661 Anglo-Portuguese pact, prompted a euphoric response from merchants and courtiers in London. One English commentator, in 1661, took it for granted that this was an admirable and invaluable step in 'perfecting the work of making our nation masters, when not of all, yet of the greatest part of the commerce of the world'.[95] Empire was proving a sure way of consolidating not just Britain's prosperity but also its evident superiority over the Portuguese, Spaniards, Italians, French, Jews, and Dutch, as well as the 'barbarous' Moors. Referring to plans for further expansion in North Africa, royal documents of Charles II's reign saw it as sufficient justification to add 'to our dominions' in order to 'gaine to our subjects the trade of Barbary and enlarge our dominions in that sea, and advance thereby the honour of our crowne and the general commerce and weale of our subjects'.[96]

But there were also many other ways in which empire was increasingly affecting different parts of Europe. Spain, Sweden, Russia, and Austria all had large empires within Europe and around its fringes and in the case of the Russia and Austria these rapidly expanded from the late seventeenth century onwards. On the other hand, Italy, parts of whose territory were under the rule of Spain and, for a time Austria, was experiencing a process of general economic decline which many ascribed in part to the impact of the colonial empires. This was a view strongly held by Doria, for instance, an acerbic critic of large empires, both in and outside Europe. Doria, it has been claimed, evinced a profound antagonism towards modern commercial society.[97] But actually this lifelong ardent republican and admirer of the Dutch Republic neither opposed commerce as such, nor the fluidity of social orders which commerce brings, but rather specifically the great global empires, arguing that these were based on conquest and force, and, while enslaving native peoples outside Europe, also reduced much of the populace inside Europe to a position of unjustified subordination. Here he was thinking especially of the long Spanish control of appreciable parts of Italy (Naples, Sicily, Sardinia, and the Milanese). At the same time, these great empires created an unhealthy imbalance of power, and dangerous tensions, within Europe by generating resources from outside wherewith to maintain

[94] Greene, 'Empire and Identity', 218–20.

[95] BL, MS Harl. 1595 'Sundry Particulars Relating to the Towne and Roade of Tanger', fos. 20^{v}, 22^{v}; Israel, *Diasporas*, 423–4.

[96] BL, MS Harl. 1595, fos. 11^{r-v}.

[97] Ferrone, 'Seneca', 43; Carpanetto and Ricuperati, *Italy*, 99–100.

far larger military and naval forces there than could otherwise have been maintained.[98] These were clearly criticisms aimed at Spain and Britain in particular.

Doria viewed great colonial empires as a system of global oppression which had decimated and enslaved the Indians of Spanish and Portuguese America and ravaged the West Indies, and also stripped Italy of its prosperity and even, he added, obstructed the progress of learning and philosophy. While his native city of Genoa, he remarked, is better located for the Levant trade than London or Amsterdam, it had nevertheless been wholly thwarted in recent times from participating in commerce with the Ottoman Empire, owing to lack of adequate naval forces with which to compete with the English and Dutch. He expressed intense indignation that 'quelle due Potenze Maritime vietano a tutte le altre nazioni il commercio di mare' [those two Maritime Powers forbid seaborne commerce to all the other nations].[99]

Far from resenting commerce, Doria considered seaborne trade the principal factor accounting for the greatness of fifteenth-and sixteenth-century Italy and what made it Europe's cultural centre. What he condemned and despised was, rather, the commerce of enforced systems, exploitation, blockades, and empire which he believed had ruined much of the world economically, including Italy. Giannone too, in *Civil History of the Kingdom of Naples* (1723), was a forceful critic of the vitiating effect of Spanish rule on Naples,[100] but Doria was unusual in this period in linking the ravages of Spanish imperialism in Europe into a wider critique of the Spanish mercantilist system as a whole, repeatedly contrasting Spanish and other imperial commerce with what he calls 'il commercio reale e naturale' [real and natural commerce].[101] Although inclined to view luxury as a cause of moral decline, tyranny, and the onset of scepticism, he did not hesitate to label the great commercial empires the prime cause of the growth of luxury in the world.

Philosophy, liberation, prosperity, political virtue, and the resurgence of Italy thus all combined in a remarkable fashion in Doria's anti-colonial radicalism. While his political thought chiefly concerned Italy, it was simultaneously a universal call for liberation and the establishment of republics. Resuming his lifelong diatribe against the pernicious 'tyranny' of Philip II of Spain, a bigoted tyrant, he says, who kept peoples ignorant and weak so that he could more easily dominate them, and nowhere more so than in Naples, he attributes his ability to marshal great fleets and armies to what he considered the hugely deleterious effects of the new global imperial navigation and commerce.[102] Spain's power stemmed from her control of the resources and wealth of her American viceroyalties of Mexico and Peru and only when that commerce 'becomes free and open to all nations, will the inhabitants of the western Indies buy their goods from all the nations of Europe' (including Italy) and not just the Spaniards and, then finally, not only will Italy have its fair share but

[98] Doria, *Manoscritti napoletani*, iv. 288–98.

[99] Ibid. i. 174; Israel, *Dutch Primacy*, 308, 414; Anderson, *English Consul*, 52–4.

[100] Giannone, *Opere*, 199–200, 252–3, 274–6; Tortarolo, *L'Illuminismo*, 122–3.

[101] Doria, *Manoscritti napoletani*, iv. 288–9, 299, 329.

[102] Ibid. iv. 292–3, 303, 326; Stone, *Vico's Cultural History*, 172–3.

'non potranno gli Spagnoli esercitare agl'Indiani la loro tirannia' [the Spaniards won't be able to exercise their tyranny over the Indians].[103]

An anti-colonialism based on equality, freedom of the individual, 'general will', and a republican rejection of monarchy, such as the Radical Enlightenment, could not confine its attention solely to problems posed by overseas colonial empires outside Europe. For insofar as its basic concepts provided the intellectual tools needed to unify rejection of racial hierarchies, slavery, religious justifications for empire, and systems of enforced economic subjection outside Europe, into a comprehensive system of anti-colonial theory, the same arguments had an obvious relevance to supranational, imperial claims to sovereignty in Ireland, Scotland, the recent Austrian conquests in Hungary and the Balkans, Venice's recent acquisition of the Peloponnese, and Russia's acquisition of the former Swedish Baltic provinces and claims to the Black Sea, as well as to the Spanish viceroyalties in Italy. Essentially the same foundational principles applied equally to imperial contexts inside and outside of Europe.

If absolutist ideology left small realms and peoples vulnerable to the grandiose designs of great monarchs like Louis XIV and Tsar Peter the Great, it was far from clear the 'Revolution principles' of 1688, as interpreted by Tories and most Whigs, did much to help either. Some argued that the Revolution of 1688–9 had actually betrayed its promises in Scotland by expanding Parliament's power, and absorbing Scotland's assembly into England's under the Act of Union (1707), further strengthening the position of London-based English interests within the functioning of the British state. Some Scots felt that an oppressive new imperial structure had been foisted on them against their will and at the expense of Scotland's separate institutions and political identity. Among these was Andrew Fletcher of Saltoun and Sir James Montgomerie of Skelmorlie, both republicans and originally ardent foes of Stuart absolutism.[104] Montgomerie approved of the fact that 'the last great Revolution in Britain', as he calls it, 'turned our hereditary monarchy into an elective', but so resented the prince of Orange's elevation to the throne and the 'weighty oppressions and manifest infractions of our choicest and most valuable rights which we at present feel' that he returned to arms, siding with the Jacobites against the Williamite regime.

Scotland nevertheless shared in many of England's gains accruing from the Revolution, and the growth in British power, commerce, and the overseas empire, so that it can hardly be said to have been reduced to colonial subjection either. The position was otherwise, though, with Ireland, which only finally submitted to the Williamite army, after a hard and bitter war, in 1691 and where the Catholic majority was placed in a clearly inferior position to the Protestants. The stark deterioration of the Catholic majority's position was then exacerbated further by what Montgomerie called the 'irregular and unheard of abuses and miscarriages of the [Protestant

[103] Doria, *Manoscritti napoletani*, iv. 326.

[104] Montgomerie, *Great Britain's Just Complaint*, 60; Worden, 'English Republicanism', 462.

Anglo-Dutch] Irish army, the desolations brought upon that miserable kingdom by them' being not a little reminiscent of the Cromwellian era.[105] Ireland, then, was reduced to the status virtually of a dependency, arguably little different from a colony in practice.

It was a situation resented not only by the Catholics but also by many Irish Protestants, William Molyneux, as we have seen, publishing his remarkable *The Case of Ireland* (Dublin, 1698) in protest. Although this was a text which, as he assured Locke, he trusted he had couched with enough 'caution and submission that it cannot justly give any offense', in fact it caused great offence in both Ireland and England and was publicly burnt on the orders of Parliament by the common hangman.[106] Molyneux's appeal to William III to rescue Ireland from its post-1688 plight, urging the king to fulfil the undertaking of his *Declaration* of The Hague, of October 1688, and 'rescue these nations from arbitrary power' by curbing the suddenly expanded sway of the London Parliament in Ireland, and making it respect the Irish (Protestant) Parliament, in Dublin, was based partly on Ireland's ancient constitution, precedent, and tradition but partly also on the wider Lockean and potentially radical claim that liberty is 'the inherent right of all mankind'.[107]

In addition to the actions of the occupying army, Irish resentment was fuelled by a recent ban on the free export of Irish woollens, aimed at boosting the English product at Irish expense, and the reassignment of land confiscated from exiled Jacobite rebels in a manner high-handedly imposed from London. But with Britain now a crowned republic and parliamentary empire, the stadtholder-king, who was by no means unsympathetic to (especially Protestant) Irish grievances, found himself impotent to afford Ireland any redress. Ignoring Irish complaints, Parliament, in London, simply directed William to remind Dublin that their country was now wholly dependent in such matters, and much else, on Parliament in London.[108]

Molyneux's was an argument later interesting to Americans, as well as Scots and Irishmen and, not surprisingly, came to feature in the libraries and thoughts of both Jefferson and Madison.[109] Yet in eighteenth-century Ireland, its argument did not, and perhaps could not yet, develop into a broadly conceived anti-colonialism any more than this was then, before the 1760s, feasible in the American colonies. This was not because of lack of resentment. On the contrary, the curbs placed by the British Parliament on Irish commerce, the general discrimination, in the administration, in favour of the English, as also in the Anglo-Irish church and assigning Irish peerages, as well as the humiliating way the Irish Parliament was treated, were all intensely resented, to a degree by Protestants as well as Catholics. The reason no anti-colonial ideology could develop was rather because those who opposed the English Parliament's policies in Ireland either viewed matters in religious terms or

[105] Montgomerie, *Great Britain's Just Complaint*, 35; Hayton, 'Williamite Revolution in Ireland', 211–13.

[106] McLoughlin, *Contesting Ireland*, 41, 44, 50.

[107] Molyneux, *The Case of Ireland*, 3; Davies, 'L'Irlande', 19; Hoppit, *A Land of Liberty?*, 260.

[108] Hoppit, *A Land of Liberty?*, 261; McLoughlin, *Contesting Ireland*, 43–4; Armitage, *Ideological Origins*, 157.

[109] Davies, 'L'Irlande', 19.

else, as in Molyneux's case, were mostly not so aggrieved as to condemn empire comprehensively or aspire to break away politically. Hence, on the one hand, the aggrieved Catholic majority thought primarily in traditional theological terms, while, on the other, what the Anglo-Irish elite wanted in practice was not political emancipation but rather the same or similar political and economic benefits to those enjoyed since 1707 by Scotland, that is elevation from the status of subordinate colonists to partnership in empire with Britain.[110]

110 Bartlett, 'This Famous Island', 260–1; Kidd, 'Constitutions', 53–4.

24

Rethinking Islam: Philosophy and the 'Other'

1. ISLAM AND TOLERATION

It was predictable perhaps, given the 'universalism' of the radical stream, and its eradication of theological criteria from its ethical system, that there would be a striking divergence between the two wings of the Enlightenment in their respective attitudes towards Islam. If both streams jettisoned much of the prejudice and wildly biased attitude of the past, and sought to be more objective and fairer, the moderate mainstream (other than the providential Deists, such as Voltaire) was still far from the partially positive attitude adopted by the radicals toward Muslim traditions of thought, moral teaching, revelation, and prophecy. If the radical stream, by contrast, still found much to be contemptuous of, particularly in Islamic popular piety and the attitudes of Muslim preachers, it showed a marked tendency to view these perceived negative features as imperfections or a falling away from the pure core of Muhammad's teaching.

Giannone, one of those who urged contemporaries to cultivate the study of Islamic religion and culture in their own interest,[1] called Islam a close 'sister' of Christianity and yet a religion of which, astonishingly, Christians knew next to nothing.[2] Respectable adjustments to the West's image of the Muslim religion were made by a number of scholars during this period prominent amongst whom was the Utrecht orientalist Adriaan Reland (1676–1718). His *De religione mohammedica libri duo* (1705), appearing in English in 1712, in German in 1717, and in French in 1721, though placed on the Roman Index in 1722, evidently had a wide impact, not least on Giannone who congratulated the Dutch *érudit* on initiating such badly needed research.[3] Reland's general approach was to urge a more balanced and tolerant view of Muhammad and his religion than had been usual hitherto, noting that the Jews had always been much fairer and more accurate than the Christians in their appraisals of Islam.[4] Wolff was among those who praised Reland as the scholar who, through his admirable erudition, did most to make the 'face of Islam more tolerable

[1] Giannone, *Opere*, 982. [2] Ibid. 976–7.

[3] Ibid. 983; *Bibliothèque choisie*, 8 (1706), 396–407; Hamilton, 'Western Attitudes', 75–7; Gunny, 'Images of Islam', 198–201. [4] Reland, *Religion des Mahométans*, ii. 91.

to us',[5] while Brucker, using Reland's work, introduced major corrections in the history of philosophy, emphasizing the centrality of belief in the immortality of the soul in Islam as well as the consequent irrelevance (and dubious intent) of Bayle's stressing, on the contrary, the soul's mortality in the philosophy of Averroes.[6]

Both dimensions of the Enlightenment seemed disposed in some degree to heed Giannone's summons by studying and learning more about the Muslim past. But the outcome in the two cases was very different. It is true that something of the old fierce hostility to the figure of Muhammad as an 'impostor' lingered on in the aggressively anti-religious and materialistic *Traité des trois imposteurs*—except that now Muhmmad is construed as following Moses and Jesus in deliberately deceiving the people,[7] much as Meslier, an implacable foe of all revealed religion, denigrates Muhammad as a purveyor 'de tromperie et d'imposture'.[8] It is true also that the Radical Enlightenment evinced some sharp criticism of post-medieval Islam, for lapsing from its early intellectual openness and love of philosophy and science, as well as its former commitment to toleration.[9] By and large, though, traditional antipathy yielded in radical texts to an image of Islam as a pure monotheism of high moral calibre which was also a revolutionary force for positive change and one which from the outset proved to be both more rational and less bound to the miraculous than Christianity or Judaism.[10]

This dissident complex of ideas about Islam began to emerge in the late seventeenth century in various writers the most important of whom was Bayle, who drew much of his information on the subject from first-hand travellers' accounts such as Pietro della Valle's *Viaggi* (1650–3).[11] The shift culminated in Boulainvilliers's openly subversive *Vie de Mahomed*, a formidable book proclaiming Islam's superior rationality and moral force composed probably some time before 1720 but not published until 1730, a text which, though thinly documented, was widely read and proved influential both in French and in translation, reappearing in English (1731) and German (1747). Muhammad's religious thought, according to Boulainvilliers, was wholly 'conforme aux lumières de la raison', retaining nothing 'grossier ni barbare', the goal of Islam's founder having been to lead men to a knowledge of truth and the practice of good works, that is activities thoroughly conducive to justice and the 'bien général de la société'.[12] The German ecclesiastical historian Johann Lorenz

[5] *Bibliothèque choisie*, 8 (1706), 404–5; Wolff, *Oratio*, 119–21; Brucker, *Historia critica philosophiae* (1742), iii. 112; Badir, *Voltaire et l'Islam*, 57–8.

[6] Brucker, *Historia critica philosophiae* (1742), iii. 131, 167.

[7] *Traité des trois imposteurs*, 148–55; Bolingbroke, *Philosophical Works*, ii. 235, 258; Mori, *Bayle philosophe*, 301; Brogi, *Cerchio*, 119–36; Harrison, *'Religion' and the Religions*, 111, 163; Thomson, 'L'Utilisation de L' Islam', 248, 251–3.

[8] Meslier, *Testament*, i. 37.

[9] D'Argens, *Jewish Spy*, iv. 66–7, 77, 79; Thomson, *Barbary and Enlightenment*, 27, 37–8.

[10] D'Argens, *Jewish Spy*, ii. 233–6, 238–45; Bolingbroke, *Philosophical Works*, ii. 235–6; Brogi, *Cerchio*, 119–36.

[11] After some years in papal service, Pietro della Valle (1586–1652) set out, in 1614, for Constantinople, where he stayed thirteen months before continuing on to Cairo, Jerusalem, Baghdad, and Persia (where he remained for four years), returning to Italy in 1626, Charnley, *Pierre Bayle*, 148.

[12] Boulainvilliers, *Vie de Mahomed*, 248–9; Hamilton, 'Western Attitudes', 79–80.

Mosheim (1695–1755), a pillar of Lutheran moderate mainstream, much regretted that Boulainvilliers, whom he rated as one of the most penetrating intellects of the age, should have been an overt disciple of Spinoza and hence someone who used his great gifts only to undermine generally received belief and opinion.[13]

Besides the writings of Bayle and Boulainvilliers, notable contributions to this new set of ideas about Islam were furnished by Toland,[14] Radicati, Jean-Frédéric Bernard, Fréret, and the marquis d'Argens who was among the most active at propagating the new radical construct, having, as a 21-year-old, around 1724, visited Algiers, Tunis, and Tripoli and spent half a year in Constantinople as a secretary to the French embassy.[15] Where Radicati extols the 'purity of [the Muslims'] divine worship', d'Argens, like Boulainvilliers, did not hesitate to project Muhammad as a proto-Deist.[16] Certain parts of their message, especially as regards toleration and Islam's high moral status, were strongly echoed also by mainstream writers like Veyssière de La Croze[17] and especially Voltaire who, on the question of Islam, partly converged with the radical tradition.[18] Voltaire substantially differed, however, from the likes of Bayle, Boulainvilliers, Toland, and d'Argens, in viewing Islam as powerful confirmation of Natural Theology, particularly divine providence, immortality of the soul, and the divinely ordained character of morality.

It was especially radical writers, then, who promoted the idea that the core of the faith of Muhammad, once stripped of some later irrational encrustation, and popular fanaticism, constitutes a morally more uplifting creed than those of Moses and Jesus and one clearer and more emphatic in its monotheism than Christianity, as well as more tolerant and less addicted to 'miracles' and superstition. If Muhammad became the leader of a people as ignorant and credulous as any, unlike Moses and Jesus, he made no claim to miraculous powers. It is striking, remarks Bayle, that Muhammad himself said 'qu'il ne faisoit point de miracles' and yet his followers 'lui en attribuent beaucoup'.[19] The intellectual coherence, consistency, and conformity to justice of Muhammad's teaching when compared with other faiths were stressed by all the radical writers and most of all Boulainvilliers,[20] Voltaire later giving further currency to the latter's conception of Muhammad as a great leader, legislator, and rational reformer rather than religious visionary and wonder-worker.[21] Cultivating philosophy and science as well as nurturing toleration, Islam seemed to the radicals and, in a different fashion, Voltaire a world in which human reason and 'enlightenment' had, in former times at least, made admirable advances precious to all mankind.

[13] Mosheim, 'Notes', ii. 1139–40.

[14] Champion, *Pillars of Priestcraft*, 127–32; Harrison, *'Religion' and the Religions*, 166.

[15] D'Argens, *Mémoires*, ed. Thomas, 201; d'Argens, *Jewish Spy*, i. 103–4, ii. 238–9; Bush, *Marquis d'Argens*, 57, 120–1, 126, 141; Harrison, *'Religion' and the Religions*, 111; Trousson, 'Cosmopolitisme', 23.

[16] Radicati, *Succinct History*, 42–3; Venturi, *Alberto Radicati*, 153.

[17] Mulsow, *Die drei Ringe*, 73–6.

[18] Voltaire, *Essai sur les mœurs*, i. 274, ii. 915; Richter, 'Europe and *The Other*', 30–1.

[19] Bayle, *Dictionnaire* (1740), iii, art. 'Mahomet', p. 257; Badir, *Voltaire et l'Islam*, 52–3.

[20] Boulainvilliers, *Vie de Mahomed*, 247, 249.

[21] Badir, *Voltaire et l'Islam*, 160–5, 215–17.

Muslims, from the time of Muhammad in the seventh century onwards, held Bayle, in his article 'Mahomed' in the *Dictionnaire* (1697), a claim later echoed by Voltaire in his *Traité sur la tolérance* (1762), were invariably more tolerant than the Christians.[22] Had Christians ruled the Ottoman Near East instead of the Turks, avers Bayle, there would remain today no 'trace of the Greek Church' and Islam would have been obliterated whereas, by contrast, 'ces infidèles' fully tolerated Christianity. Delighting in such paradoxes, Bayle suggests further that Muslims following the principles of their faith ought to use violence to liquidate other religions and yet they tolerate them instead. Christians, on the other hand, though commanded to eschew all violence and stick to purely peaceful preaching and proselytizing, from the outset strove to overthrow and exterminate with fire and sword everyone who was not of their religion.[23] Claiming men rarely live in accord with what they say they believe was of course a recurrent theme of Bayle's philosophy, from the *Pensées diverses* (1683) onwards, as also of Mandeville's thought, in his *Fable of the Bees*; both use the topos to reinforce their argument that since men rarely live in accordance with their professed beliefs atheists often live better lives than Christians.[24]

Stressing the superior tolerance and rationality of Islam's core teaching fitted well also with Bayle's unrelenting feud with his 'rationaux' opponents. For his revisionism regarding Islam reinforced his wider claim that Christianity is not demonstrated to be the true faith by reason. Le Clerc might argue that the obstinate Jews 'ne savent guère mieux raisonner que les Mahométans', both Muslims and Jews resisting only because they 'n'apprennent nullement à raisonner juste',[25] but Bayle retorted that although faith assures us Christianity is the true religion, by rational assessment and all worldly tests, Islam's claims are superior. For not only is the Islamic world more tolerant and less cruel but it has far less blood on its hands. 'Dans toutes leurs persécutions contre les Chrétiens', counters Bayle, the Muslims slaughtered far fewer people in the name of their religion than the Christians massacred during the St Bartholomew's Day Massacre of 1572 in Paris alone.[26]

Bayle was not, of course, the first to contradict the churches' ancient insistence on the uniquely providential character and miraculous, unparalleled impact of Christian revelation in the world. Spinoza, whose father and uncle had close trading links with both Morocco and Egypt,[27] had earlier stressed, besides the moral equivalence of Islam to Christianity, that Islam had swept the world faster than Christianity, and exerted a more unified dominion, as well as won over a still vaster

[22] Bayle, *Dictionnaire* (1740), iii, art. 'Mahomet', p. 265 and art. 'Mahomet II', p. 275; Voltaire, *Traité sur la tolérance*, 50; Charnley, *Pierre Bayle*, 52–3, 59, 86.

[23] Bayle, *Dictionnaire* (1740), iii, art. 'Mahomet', p. 265; Labrousse, *Pierre Bayle*, ii. 521; Bost, *Pierre Bayle*, 55–6.

[24] Bayle, *Dictionnaire* (1740), iii, art. 'Mahomet', p. 265; Mandeville, *Fable of the Bees*, ii. 214–16; Charnley, *Pierre Bayle*, 109.

[25] Le Clerc, *De l'incrédulité*, 80–1.

[26] Bayle, *Dictionnaire*, iv, Index 'Sarazins', p. 791.

[27] Nadler, *Spinoza*, 32–3; Israel, *Diasporas*, 279, 298, 310–11.

area,[28] perspectives which disgusted Henry More when he first saw Spinoza's published correspondence in 1678.[29] But Bayle (echoed in 1711 by Jean-Frédéric Bernard) took up and further elaborated Spinoza's argument, deliberately standing on its head the traditional Christian contention that Islam spread by using mere worldly force whilst Christianity triumphed, facing great persecution, miraculously, through divine intervention.[30]

If speed, completeness, and durability of worldly success are deemed tokens of providential backing for a revealed faith, then by this measure, held Bayle, like Spinoza and the Jewish writer Orobio de Castro, when disputing with van Limborch in the early 1680s, Islam clearly stands pre-eminent. The star of Islam decisively prevailed 'sur l'étoile du Christianisme' so that if one judges the worth of religions 'par la gloire des bons succès temporels, la Mahométane passeroit pour la meilleure'. Muslims are so sure of this, he observes, that they find no better proof of the superiority of their cause than 'les prospéritez éclatantes dont Dieu l'a favorisée'.[31] However, now that the Turks, he adds characteristically, had suffered a string of devastating defeats since their failed second siege of Vienna, in 1683, at Austrian, Venetian, and Russian hands, they are as unwilling to interpret these failures as signs of divine disfavour, as previously they had been to proclaim their successes the outcome of the divine will; this, says Bayle, is a splendid example of the inconstancy of human reasoning regarding success and failure.[32]

Byzantine and Visigothic Christian rule in the Near East, North Africa, and Spain was overthrown by the Muslims with stunning speed, held Spinoza, Bayle, Boulainvilliers, Radicati,[33] d'Argens, and other radicals, not due to Satan's assistance, inhuman violence, or sheer terror, as medieval Christians believed, but due to the many imperfections of Christian society. Admittedly, they were not alone in offering this reading. Socinians made a similar point, as, for instance, Arthur Bury does in his *Naked Gospel* (1690), where he remarks that Muslims can claim that if the 'victories of the Gospel' over the Jewish religion demonstrate the 'greater authority of the Gospel, so the victories of the Alcoran over that Gospel, must be an evidence that . . . the religion of Mahomet be better than that of Christ'; but his aim here was to prove the religious corruption of the Orthodox and Catholic churches, not imply the ultimate superiority of Muhammad's faith or suggest that that 'lewd impostor' can be compared with Christ as Man's universal guide.[34] Radical writers attributed Islam's stunning conquest of so many former Christian lands rather to the thirst for dominance and rapaciousness of the Christian clergy from whose ambitious grasp, according to them, the Arab conquerors freed a grateful population.[35]

28 Bayle, *Dictionnaire* (1740), iii, art. 'Mahomet', p. 256; Spinoza, *Letters*, 241, 303–12, 341–3.

29 Israel, *Radical Enlightenment*, 224–8.

30 Bayle, *Commentaire philosophique*, 155–6.

31 Bayle, *Dictionnaire* (1740), iii, art. 'Mahomet II', p. 273; Bernard, *Réflexions morales*, 222–3.

32 Bayle, *Dictionnaire*, iii. p 274.

33 Champion, *Pillars of Priestcraft*, 132.

34 [Bury], *Naked Gospel*, B1^{v}–2.

35 Radicati, *Recueil*, 93; Bernard, *Dialogues critiques*, 298; Simon, *Henry de Boulainviller*, 345; Venturino, *Ragioni*, 181–6.

From Spinoza and Bayle onwards, radical thought emphatically denied, against Le Clerc and Locke, that there exists any evidence of Christianity's moral superiority, a point Bernard especially stressed. Faith may assure us that Christianity is the truth delivered to Man by God, held Bayle, but no one can prove anything of the sort on the basis of moral superiority. If one cannot say Christians are more disorderly in their morals than Muslims, 'je n'oserois affirmer qu'ils le soient moins'.[36] Jean-Frédéric Bernard went further: his fictitious 'philosophe persan' travelling in the West, a man of sound reason and admirable generosity of spirit, disgusted by the immorality he finds everywhere in Christian lands, is made even more indignant at the astounding hypocrisy with which Christians deem every 'Turc, More ou Arabe' they meet untrustworthy, 'un homme sans foi, et en un mot . . . un parfait scélérat'. The Muslims now have a perfect right, he concludes, to retaliate daily by labelling everyone they meet, of whatever faith, who is especially dishonest, hypocritical, or unjust 'un Chrétien'.[37]

Christians, suggests Bernard, in his seditious *Dialogues critiques* (1730), should try to visualize the Crusades in reverse. Supposing, he asks, a host of 100,000 Saracens and others whom they call 'infidels' had invaded Germany and France to advance the sacred truth of their religion at the point of the sword and, authorized by their theologians, 'eussent pillé et ravagé vos terres', how would the Christians feel about that? Bernard, like Bayle, vehemently denounced the Crusades as totally contrary to the 'Droit de la Nature et du Droit des gens', the first forbidding the taking of life other than to save one's own, the second the despoiling of other men's property.[38] Christians seemingly forget, furthermore, that in the first centuries after Christ, it was they who were 'des infidelles, des impies et des hérétiques' in the eyes of the Roman authorities and that, when relentlessly persecuted, it was they who implored this very toleration 'que vous refusez maintenant aux autres'.[39]

2. BAYLE AND IBN RUSHD (AVERROES)

Islam fascinated the radical wing more than the moderate mainstream Enlightenment also because for centuries, during the Middle Ages, the Arab lands had been pre-eminent in philosophy. To the radical mentality this meant that the Muslim world had once played a crucial role in the history of humanity and of *l'esprit humain*. It also meant that there must have been a great struggle within Islam itself between the forces of reason which had then finally been defeated and the superior force of popular credulity, obscurantism, priestcraft, and fanaticism. Bayle raises this key complex of themes, among other places, in his *Dictionnaire* article

[36] Bayle, *Dictionnaire* (1740), iii, art. 'Mahomet', p. 261; Charnley, *Pierre Bayle*, 52.
[37] Bernard, *Réflexions morales*, 170.
[38] [Bernard], *Dialogues critiques*, 240–1.
[39] Ibid. 245–6.

'Takiddin', dealing with the medieval Damascene theologian Ibn Taymiyyah (d. 1328) (Taqi al-Din Ahmad Ibn Taymiyyah), a great 'Hanbali', or follower in the tradition of Imam Ahmad ibn Hanbal (d. 855), a traditionalist and opponent of philosophy who scorned all suggestion that the Koran was created and not an eternal attribute of God.[40]

The celebrated Abbasid Caliph al-Ma'mun, universally (if wrongly) reputed in later Arab and European historiography to be the ruler who initiated the great project of rendering the Greek philosophers into Arabic, was praised by the Arab philosophers but denounced by 'Taqi al-Din', notes Bayle, as someone who would undoubtedly be punished by God, 'pour avoir troublé la dévotion des Musulmans' by establishing 'des études philosophiques'.[41] Bayle lauds al Ma'mun for introducing philosophy into Islam and, more generally, promoting learning and science,[42] noting that the philosophically minded have always been persecuted and that, over the centuries, the common people continually murmur that the philosophers do not believe 'qu'il y ait des Dieux'.[43] The reason 'Taqi al-Din' desired divine retribution to be visited on al-Ma'mun, suggests Bayle, was his resentment at what he considered 'les mauvais effets de ces études', that is the doubts and questioning philosophy introduces in the minds of a few.

Bayle thought the Arab philosophers had actually opened many eyes to 'les sottises de la secte Mahométane' and that religious observance among them had, in consequence, 'souffert un prodigieux affoiblissement'.[44] There were reports, he notes, that the Arab philosophers, while refining moral ideas, deferred to their theologians only outwardly, being privately convinced that various articles of faith stipulated by the theologians were 'contraires à la raison'.[45] Their greatest obstacle, however, was the piety, or what Bayle calls the 'sotte crédulité', of the common man, reinforced by the likes of Ibn Taymiyya, something that reduces humans to blind submission before rulers and theologians who then avidly exploit them.[46] The Arab philosophers, he says, 'reconnurent par leur philosophie que l'Alcoran ne valoit rien' but, despite the immense value of such knowledge to everyone, had been obliged to keep it to themselves.[47]

D'Argens similarly heroicized the Arab philosophers and likewise scorned the credulity and bigotry of the common people. Since 'the vulgar' of all religions, including Islam, states the English version of his *Lettres juives*, 'favour those most that tell them the most chimeras and the most fables', Muslims heartily loathe their philosophers 'because they are enemies to miracles and superstition'.[48] 'The works

[40] Fakhry, *Philosophy, Dogma*, essays xviii, p. 94 and xix, p. 197; Leaman, *Brief Introduction*, 50, 64; Haleem, 'Early *Kalam*', 82, 85.

[41] Bayle, *Dictionnaire* (1740), iv, art. 'Takiddin', p. 315.

[42] Gundling, *Vollständige Historie*, ii. 1639; Gutas, *Greek Thought*, 77, 88, 93–4.

[43] Bayle, *Dictionnaire* (1740), iv, art. 'Takiddin', p. 315.

[44] Ibid.

[45] Ibid.; Bayle, *An Historical and Critical Dictionary*, 340.

[46] Bayle, *An Historical and Critical Dictionary*, 340–2; Labrousse, *Pierre Bayle*, ii. 483; Mori, *Bayle philosophe*, 257.

[47] Bayle, *Dictionnaire*, iv, art. 'Takiddin', p. 315; Bayle, *An Historical and Critical Dictionary*, 342.

[48] D'Argens, *Jewish Spy*, ii. 158.

of Macrisi'—presumably he meant al-Maqrisi (d. 1442), the Egyptian historian—'a famous author', he says, 'are not so much esteem'd as those of several mollas and imams, which are full of ridiculous fables'. He judged the Egyptians still 'more superstitious than the Turks', remarking that even 'the Spaniards are scarce a match for them'.[49] By contrast, medieval Muslim philosophy he saw as a distinct advance for mankind being altogether more rational and conducive to progress, in his opinion, than the turgid scholasticism of the Christian Middle Ages. It is true, he grants, that they were addicted to Aristotle, their thinkers being 'as great peripateticks anciently, as the friars'; at about the time 'Averroes brought the Arabians acquainted with this Greek philosopher', the French began to 'imbibe *his* opinions'.[50] This eager French reception of Averroes was indeed a sign of Muslim intellectual superiority at the time. If too timid and obscure, medieval Arab philosophers nevertheless made more sense and were less apt to paralyse students' minds, held d'Argens, than Duns Scotus and his ilk in Christian lands: in Avicenna or Averroes, one finds nothing, he says, 'qui approche du ridicule des *a parte rei*, ou *a parte mentis*'.[51]

For several reasons, Ibn Rushd (1126–1198), or Averroes as he was known to the Enlightenment, the Andalusian philosopher, physician, and—at the summit of his career—judge [*qadi*] of Córdoba, 'l'un des plus subtils philosophes qui aient paru entre les Arabes', according to Bayle,[52] became a particular focus of attention, as did Bayle's article in his *Dictionnaire* about him.[53] Relying chiefly on this piece, d'Argens later recounted how Averroes at terrible cost to himself experienced the tribulations entailed by a life devoted to the pursuit of reason, dangers heightened by his 'attempting to outstrip his brother-professors; and it was not, till after he had suffered much greater calamities than those which obliged Descartes to leave his native country, that he at last found an opportunity of pursuing undisturbed his philosophical studies'.[54] Averroes in this way was held up as the man who found the courage single-handedly to combat the bigotry, credulity and crassness of his time.

Last and perhaps greatest of the 'rationalist' philosophers of the medieval Arabic intellectual tradition, presiding over what has been dubbed the 'Averroist Enlightenment',[55] Ibn Rushd tried to advance the cause of reason by restricting philosophical knowledge to a small, sophisticated, and largely concealed (even at the Moroccan court in Marrakesh where he spent some time) intellectual coterie. Such extreme caution he believed unavoidable if one is to prevent the destructive fury generated by the collision of philosophy with popular theological notions from unsettling society and destroying everyone who dares to think independently. Only where the people's literal and unquestioning understanding of the anthropomorphic terms and images applied to God in the Koran remains publicly

[49] D'Argens, *Jewish Spy*, ii. 155–6; Bush, *Marquis d'Argens*, 71.
[50] D'Argens, *Jewish Spy*, iv. 67.
[51] D'Argens, *Mémoires*, ed. Thomas, 202.
[52] Bayle, *Dictionnaire*, i. 414.
[53] Anderson, *Treatise*, 132.
[54] Bush, *Marquis d'Argens*, 68–9, 71.
[55] Dethier, 'Siger van Brabant', 224.

unchallenged can a furtive, private independence of thought, and freedom to read and discuss, survive among the necessarily reticent, philosophical few.[56]

Given the precarious position of the philosophers in medieval Islam such rigorous segregation may indeed have been the only way to preserve philosophy from liquidation by popular piety and the anti-philosophical campaign of the religious scholars.[57] Seeking a peaceful *modus vivendi* between faith and philosophy of a kind that would legitimize *falsafa* within mainstream Muslim society—and making no plea for general liberty of expression or thought—Ibn Rushd nevertheless warned against the perils of religious teachers and sectarians deliberately exacerbating doctrinal faction and strife so as to be able to enforce their own notions of orthodoxy.[58] If revealed religion remains indispensable for the mass of humanity, the Koran being essential for teaching piety, respect, and obedience,[59] 'the first intention' of the Holy Law, urged Ibn Rushd, was precisely to guide those incapable of grasping basic philosophical truths concerning God and the world.[60] Even so, those who proclaim the supremacy of theology and teach doctrines such as 'Creation from Nothing' are founts of untruth, propagating notions contrary to any authentic understanding of Nature.

Not unlike Spinoza and Bayle in this respect, Ibn Rushd stressed the risks—both intellectual and practical—of mixing theology and philosophy: 'for if you do so you will be neither a rationalist nor a traditionalist'.[61] Such mixing is undesirable even for men 'who possess by nature a sound understanding, though such men are very scarce', and to broach profound philosophical questions 'with the masses is like bringing poisons to the bodies of many animals, for which they are real poisons'. For just as poisons 'are relative, and what is poison for one creature is nourishment for another' so it transpires, held Ibn Rushd, with ideas: 'that is, there are ideas which are poison for one kind of men but nourishment for another.'[62] The 'ignorant' and 'vulgar' always hate and despise those who are wise.[63] For this reason, Ibn Rushd, in his treatise the *Kitab Fasl al-Maqal* [the Decisive Treatise], while superficially adopting Aristotle's classification of men into three intellectual categories—a small intellectual elite capable of achieving knowledge of God through philosophy [*falsafa*]; the common people [*al-jumhur*] whose duty is to obey the divine law as expounded in the Koran; and finally, the theologians [*mutakallimun*, or *ahl al-Kalam*] who expound divine revelation for the people—in practice merges the last with the second, producing a sharply polarized duality between *hikma*—wisdom and philosophy—on the one side, and popular culture and theology, something extremely unstable, dangerous, and opaque, on the other.[64]

[56] Gauthier, *Théorie d'Ibn Rochd*, 5–6, 58, 164–6; Hyman, 'Maimonides', 176; Haddad-Chamakh, 'Foi et philosophie', 160–1; Leaman, *Brief Introduction*, 173–5.

[57] Gauthier, *Théorie d'Ibn Rochd*, 111, 166.

[58] Haddad-Chamakh, 'Foi et philosophie', 156, 162–3, 168–9.

[59] Ibid. 339; Gauthier, *Théorie d'Ibn Rochd*, 97; Leaman, *Brief Introduction*, 159–60.

[60] Ibn Rushd, *Tahafut al-tahafut*, 145.

[61] Ibid. 145–7; Anderson, *Treatise*, 134–5.

[62] Ibn Rushd, *Tahafut al-tahafut*, 146.

[63] Ibid. 87.

[64] Butterworth, 'The Source', 116–18; Haddad-Chamakh, 'Foi et philosophie', 168.

Ibn Rushd thus conceives the religious scholars who guide the people, not unlike Spinoza and Bayle, as being equally linked, by profession and ambition, to the chaotic mental world of the multitude and hence also those who pose the chief danger of civil strife if not effectively restrained.[65] There is, however, he insists, such a thing as a higher and truer theology, since whatever is true respectively in theology and philosophy cannot really contradict the other. Should they appear to, the best expedient is to resort to poetic allegory.[66] Although no champion of western Enlightenment could subscribe to Ibn Rushd's rigid dichotomy, segregating philosophy from the 'vulgar', and theology, to avoid social conflict, there were clear affinities nevertheless between his largely submerged and banned intellectual underworld and that of the radical stream which did not escape the notice of Bayle, Boulainvilliers, and d'Argens.

Although Ibn Rushd asserts the ultimate oneness and accord of Aristotelian rationalism and religion, of metaphysics (*ilahiyyat*), and thus could not have sanctioned the total severance of philosophy from theology urged by Spinoza and Bayle,[67] he did envisage philosophy and theology as being in a state of practical segregation for all intents and purposes since most men cannot grasp their ultimate convergence. His influence, moreover, remained confined to a tiny coterie among Muslims and Jews, mainly in southern Spain and the western Maghrib, though even there, seemingly, his philosophical, as opposed to medical and scientific works, soon disappeared from circulation amid the accelerating cultural and psychological as well as political disintegration of al-Andalus. The emotional backlash against 'philosophy' in the western Muslim world was further intensified shortly after Ibn Rushd's death by general dread and gloom stemming from Islam's most decisive defeat in Spain, the great catastrophe of Muslim arms at Las Navas de Tolosa in the Sierra Morena, in 1212.[68]

Nevertheless, via bilingual Toledo, northern Spain, Provence, and Naples, Averroes' doctrines powerfully penetrated thirteenth-century Latin Christendom (and western Jewry), as part of the wider Aristotelian revolution of the thirteenth century, seeding what soon became known, within Christendom, as the highly suspect philosophical heresy called 'Averroism'. Christian and Ibero-Jewish Averroism may have become to an extent detached from the real system of Ibn Rushd, and eventually even more radically heretical; nevertheless, this strain was still perceived as being rooted in Ibn Rushd's philosophy and hence in an authentically Arabic intellectual tradition.[69] A submerged Averroism survived, if after a certain point no longer within Islamic culture, in France, Italy, and not least among the Jews and New Christians in early modern Spain;[70] for in the universities (which the Islamic

[65] Haddad-Chamakh, 'Foi et philosophie', 161–2; van Dooren, 'Ibn Rushd's Attitude', 625–6, 633.

[66] van Dooren, 'Ibn Rushd's Attitude', 632; Endress, 'Le Projet d'Averroès', 8–14; Urvoy, 'Ibn Rushd', 338–9.

[67] Conrad, 'Through the Thin Veil', 240–1, 246–7; Butterworth, 'The Source', 105–6.

[68] Urvoy, 'Ibn Rushd', 343; Burnett, 'The "Sons of Averroes" ', 260, 266, 275–6.

[69] Burnett, 'The "Sons of Averroes" ', 272–3; Gauthier, *Théorie d'Ibn Rochd*, 2–5.

[70] Gauthier, *Théorie d'Ibn Rochd*, 233.

world lacked) this subterranean growth proved ineradicable while reaction against Averroism within late medieval Spanish and Provençal Judaism, though real, was less than within Islam and Christianity.[71]

Spanish clandestine academic Averroism became in fact the prime source of the underground Deism rife among the crypto-Jews in the Iberian world from at least as far back as the fifteenth century, a current of thought which persisted uninterrupted through the sixteenth and seventeenth centuries. Isaac Orobio de Castro encountered several such 'Deistas' among the university-trained New Christians in early seventeenth-century Castile.[72] Among the most active proselytizers of this sort was a certain Dr Juan Pinheiro who studied with both Orobio and Prado at Alcalà de Henares and later moved to Seville where he died around 1662.[73] It was reportedly Pinheiro who converted to philosophical Deism none other than Juan de Prado, Spinoza's closest companion and ally during the last year or so of his membership of the Sephardic Jewish community of Amsterdam (1655–6).

In Italy, too, this underground intellectual heresy remained deeply rooted. A key feature of the late seventeenth-century atheistic clandestine manuscript *Theophrastus redivivus* is its thesis that the truth about the universe, and in particular philosophical atheism and the impossibility of miracles, has always been known to the wisest minds since the age of the Greek philosophy schools, but that this knowledge has been generally suppressed, surviving only as a clandestine tradition hidden from the eyes of the theologians and common people. Averroes is identified as a prime mover of this concept as well as the connected idea that most men do not need to know anything about truth but must be exhorted to a code of orderly conduct for which purpose revealed religion, to which philosophers must outwardly conform, is indispensable.[74]

Among Averroism's most heretical strands was Ibn Rushd's rejection of the immortality of the individual soul.[75] On his deathbed, 'Averroes' was supposed during the Early Enlightenment to have declared 'moriatur anima mea morte philosophorum' [may my soul die the death of the philosophers].[76] He held that the intellect in an individual represents not the union of the body with an individual soul but rather the projection into that individual of the single, universal Intellect: 'the soul', he asserts in his *Tahafut al-tahafut*, 'is closely similar to light; light is divided by the division of illuminated bodies, and is unified when the bodies are annihilated, and this same relation holds between soul and bodies.'[77] All humans,

[71] Nadler, *Spinoza's Heresy*, 64–6.

[72] Révah, *Spinoza et le Dr Juan de Prado*, 90, 103, 109, 114; Kaplan, *From Christianity*, 142.

[73] Kaplan, *From Christianity*, 126; Nadler, *Spinoza*, 142–6; Muchnik, *Vie marrane*, 345–8, 365.

[74] Gregory, *Theophrastus redivivus*, 50, 58–9.

[75] Ibn Rushd, *Commentary on Aristotle's Metaphysics, Book Lam*, 103–4; Leibniz, *Theodicy*, 77, 363; Dethier, 'Siger van Brabant', 215–16; Genequand, *Ibn Rushd's Metaphysics*, 49; Nadler, *Spinoza's Heresy*, 65, 88–9.

[76] Bayle, *Dictionnaire*, i. 387 note H; *Algemeen Historisch, Geographisch*, i. A, p. 549; Brucker, *Historia critica philosophiae* (1742), iii. 109; Marchand, *Dictionnaire historique*, i. 314 note E; Renan, *Averroès et l'Averroisme*, 236.

[77] Ibn Rushd, *Tahafut al-tahafut*, 26.

consequently, are seen in this tradition, as Leibniz observes, as participating in the same universal soul and can think rationally precisely through sharing in this universal intelligence.[78] When they die their 'soul' reverts to the universal Active Intellect without any form of individual survival. Some Christian Averroists, notes Leibniz, combined acceptance of this proposition with the last resort strategy of 'double truth' rendering the soul mortal philosophically but immortal, theologically.[79]

Denial of divine providence as a cause of particular events and explaining miracles as natural phenomena, quintessential features of the Averroist legacy, plainly struck at the heart of all theological systems. Inherent also in the tradition was the legend of Ibn Rushd's alleged blasphemous view of the three revealed religions which persisted in humanist and libertine circles through the sixteenth, seventeenth, and eighteenth centuries.[80] A variant of the notorious *Traité des trois imposteurs*, copied from a manuscript belonging to the library of Prince Eugene de Savoy in 1716, and surviving in copies in London (BL, MS Add. 12064), Cracow, and Munich, bearing the title *Dissertation sur le Livre des trois imposteurs*, a text which, like the parent *Traité*, probably dates from the late 1670s or early 1680s,[81] has a preface claiming the *Traité* had been rumoured to exist for more than four hundred years and, while practically every religiously subversive thinker had, at one time or another, been suspected of having a hand in it, Averroes, famous Arab commentator on Aristotle's works, 'est le premier sur le compte duquel on l'ait mis'. Noting that Averroes wrote in the 'eleventh' (actually the twelfth) century when 'on a commencé à parler des *Trois Imposteurs*', this text repeats the legend that he inwardly denied all three revealed religions, choosing to die 'en philosophe', that is without subscribing to the opinions of the common people: was this not enough 'pour le publier ennemi des trois Religions qu'il avoit méprisées'?[82]

Plying his familiar paradox of the 'virtuous atheist', Bayle characteristically couples this reported apostasy from all revealed religion with Averroes' equally attested high moral character. Despite performing his functions as *qadi* (religious judge) in Seville and Córdoba impeccably, observes Bayle, his outstanding qualities did not prevent his enemies denouncing him as an abominable heretic and ruining his reputation. Disgraced at the behest of the theologians and people, discharged, humiliated, and exiled to the small town of Lucena, the religious scholars and people mightily concurred, recounts Bayle, that the only fitting punishment for such a man was public execution and eternal ignominy. However, the sultan in Marrakesh, he adds with delicate irony, chose banishment instead, deeming it unwise to execute for heresy so admirable a judge and philosopher, lest infidels, being completely ignorant of theology, should refuse to believe he was liquidated for heinous doctrinal

[78] Leibniz, *Philosophical Writings*, 38, 161. [79] Leibniz, *Theodicy*, 80.

[80] Gregory, 'Libertinisme érudit', 330–1; Niewöhner, *Veritas sive varietas*, 305–7.

[81] Charles-Daubert, '*Traité des trois imposteurs*', 449.

[82] BL, MS 12064, 'Dissertation sur Le Livre des trois imposteurs', fo. 1^{r-v}; Charles-Daubert, '*Traité des trois imposteurs*', 547.

unsoundness and come to suspect his death was authorized for some entirely base and inconsequential reason.[83]

Averroes' famous refutation of Al-Ghazali (AD 1058–1111), the flail of the philosophers, in his *Destructio destructionum contra Algazalem* [i.e. the *Tahafut al-tahafut*], avers Bayle, thoroughly destroyed the ridiculous accusations of Al-Ghazali. But how much use, he asks, should upright advocates of the 'good cause', right-thinking persons, make of such a dubious champion: someone who denies Creation from nothing and that God knows particular things or extends 'sa providence sur les individus de ce monde'?[84] In the *Dictionnaire* article 'Averroes', Bayle emphasizes both the incompatibility of Ibn Rushd's philosophy with revealed religion, and his contempt for Christianity.[85] Ibn Rushd's doctrine of the mind, he notes, however much anchored in Aristotle, is both 'impie et absurde', because it implies the individual soul vanishes with the body and because obviously opposed opinions 'ne sauroient loger ensemble dans un seul entendement'. This objection to those claiming this general intellect is God is also the route, he says, citing note N of the article on Spinoza, by which one refutes 'invinciblement le Spinozisme'.[86] Bayle's implication that the seeds of what would one day develop into Spinozism are, in part, discernible in Ibn Rushd's philosophy, however far-fetched it seems today, was also a view to which Leibniz inclined.[87] Since 'it is known that Spinoza recognizes only one substance in the world, whereof souls are but transient modifications', Leibniz followed Bayle in closely linking Spinoza (as well as Moses Germanus and Wachter) to Averroist tradition.[88]

Such a perspective was as fascinating to some as it worried others; for it followed from Bayle's and Leibniz's formulation that Spinozism was inherent in what had been passed down, and penetrated most forcefully into the European consciousness, from medieval Arabic thought.[89] This led moderate Enlightenment writers, like Reland, seeking to bring Islam (and Judaism) into closer alignment with Christianity on the key questions of immortality of the individual soul and reward and punishment in the hereafter, to heighten their stress on Averroes being an out-and-out heretic, blasphemer, and rebel against Islam. Where Islam was shown by Reland, contrary to what Christians had formerly believed, clearly to assert divine providence in particular processes and events and the immortality of the individual soul, Ibn Rushd denies immortality of the individual soul and, hence, reward and punishment in the hereafter and hence was an apostate from Islam.[90] The older Christian view that the Muslims envisage God to be corporeal rather than spiritual

[83] Bayle, *An Historical and Critical Dictionary*, i. 432; Bost, 'Regards critiques', 208.

[84] Bost, 'Regards critiques', 208.

[85] Bayle, *Dictionnaire*, i. 387 note G.

[86] Ibid. i. 386 note E.

[87] Leibniz, *Theodicy*, 79–81; Gundling, *Vollständige Historie*, ii. 1640–1; Kolakowski, 'Pierre Bayle', 75; Mori, *Bayle philosophe*, 165.

[88] Leibniz, *Theodicy*, 79; Woolhouse, *Descartes, Spinoza, Leibniz*, 155, 162.

[89] Brucker, *Historia critica philosophiae* (1742), iii. 112; Anderson, *Treatise*, 141.

[90] Reland, *Religion des Mahometans* i. 319–29, ii. 420, 25–8, 91,162; Leaman, *Brief Introduction*, 170; Nadler, *Spinoza's Heresy*, 88–91.

should now be scrupulously avoided and would in any case mean, warns Reland, 'qu'ils sont à peu près Spinosistes'.[91]

3. IBN TUFAYL AND THE HIDDEN WISDOM OF THE EAST

Bayle postulated a strong affinity between the Averroist and Spinozist conception of the soul. Further parallels between Spinozism and Averroism, to his mind, were that revelation and theology are completely distinct from, and irreconcilable with, philosophical truth, and that both strains deem revealed religion indispensable as a social and educational tool.[92] Further, there is their rejection of divine providence intervening in the workings of nature and *a priori* denial of the miraculous. Spinozism, held Bayle, can therefore be considered a later variant of Averroism with an alternative terminology substituted for its Aristotelianism. Bayle, indeed, recognized in Averroes, and other medieval Arabic rationalist freethinkers and philosophers, not just precursors of his own radical ideas but, like the 'Spinozist' circle in late seventeenth-century Holland and the anonymous Italian author of *Theophrastus redivivus*, a crucial link in an unbroken, if mostly hidden and subterranean, 'enlightened' philosophical chain connecting the materialist philosophy schools of ancient Greece with their own age.[93]

This tendency to envisage radical thought as a chain of tradition reaching back to the beginnings of philosophy, in Greece, became an integral feature of the Radical Enlightenment after Bayle; but there may also have been an incipient inclination in this direction from the outset, at Amsterdam. This is suggested, at any rate, by the eagerness with which Spinoza's Amsterdam circle greeted publication of the Latin translation of *The Life of Hai Ibn Yaqzan* by Ibn Rushd's friend, patron, and predecessor Abu Bakr Mohammed ben Abd-al-Malik Ibn Tufayl (Abentofal) (*c.*1100–1185) of Wadi-Ash [Guadix]. This work, published in Latin by the Oxford orientalist Edward Pocock in 1671, is a sophisticated philosophical novel about a child stranded on an uninhabited tropical island which he had reached floating in a chest and where he is mothered by a gazelle and, through good fortune, survives, grows up, and begins to reflect. As he matures, Ibn Yaqzan develops more and better survival techniques and begins to think out for himself the causes and workings of nature. Step by step, learning to apply his reason, he discovers the rational coherence of all that is and his part in it.

Central to Ibn Tufayl's vision, like that of Ibn Rushd, is the clash between the rational individual and society. After getting away from the island physically he tries,

[91] Reland, *Religion des Mahometans*, ii. 85, 90–1, 114–15, 162; Hazard, *European Mind*, 32–3; Concina, *Della religione rivelata*, i. 302–5.

[92] Gauthier, *Théorie d'Ibn Rochd*, 6, 97; Allison, *Benedict de Spinoza*, 223, 241.

[93] Gregory, 'Libertinisme érudit', 328–9, 331.

unsuccessfully, to rejoin the rest of humanity socially while continuing to lead a rational life but, defeated by the insuperable power of what is commonly thought, eventually abandons hope and returns to his desert island to die in isolation.[94] With its markedly rationalistic and Deistic tendency, emphasizing the isolated, vulnerable character of philosophical reason, it appealed strongly to Johannes Bouwmeester (1630–80), a close friend of Meyer and Spinoza, who, at a meeting of the Amsterdam literary society Nil Volentibus Arduum in December 1671, and at the request of his fellow members, undertook the task of preparing a Dutch version for publication.[95] One of the most learned of the Amsterdam 'Spinozists', Graevius informed Leibniz in 1674,[96] Bouwmeester esteemed Ibn Tufayl for showing 'how someone can, without any contact with other people, and without education, arrive at knowledge of himself, and of God'.[97]

An accomplished Latinist and connoisseur of theatre, science, the aesthetic, and the erotic, said to have returned from Italy with many antiquities and other 'fine things', Bouwmeester remained, over many years, powerfully committed to a radical perspective.[98] An anonymous pamphlet of 1677 lambasting the Nil Volentibus Arduum literary circle especially decries Bouwmeester as the reprobate who taught Koerbagh his atheistic ideas and obstinately upheld (Meyer's doctrine) that 'philosophy and natural reason is the interpreter of God's Holy Word'.[99] A person who agreed with all Meyer's and Spinoza's blasphemous views as expounded in the *Philosophia* and the *Tractatus theologico-politicus*, Bouwmeester, furthermore, reports this tract, possessed 'all the secret writings of Dr van den Enden who died in France high in the air', an allusion to the latter's execution in Paris, by hanging, in 1674.[100]

Ibn Tufayl took ten months to translate and, on 11 October 1672, with Bouwmeester himself chairing, copies were presented to Meyer (who is recorded as being present) and other members of the society.[101] The text was then published by Jan Rieuwertsz (who also published all Spinoza's works) under the title *De Natuurlijke Wijsgeer, of het Leven van Hai Ebn Jokdan* [The Natural Philosopher, or The Life of Hai Ibn Yaqzan]. This publication for popular consumption highlights Ibn Tufayl's advocacy of freedom to philosophize (one of Spinoza's chief concerns), and the fact that in medieval Islam there had existed a clandestine tradition of subversive philosophy which, as Bouwmeester's preface stresses, shows 'how far the human intellect can advance outside divine Revelation' on the exclusive basis of rational inference furthered by 'investigation of natural causes and effects'.[102]

94 Ibn Tufayl, *Hayy Ibn Yaqzan*, 164–5; Crone, *Medieval Islamic Political Thought*, 188–9.

95 Gundeling, *Vollständige Historie*, ii. 1649; Hubbeling, 'Inleiding', 47; Steenbakkers, *Spinoza's* Ethica, 17; Klever, *Een nieuwe Spinoza*, 105–6; Russell, 'Impact', 224–8.

96 Klever, *Sphinx*, 132.

97 Ibid. 138; Thijssen-Schoute, *Nederlands Cartesianisme*, 414.

98 *De koekoecx-zangh van de Nachtuylen*, 5.

99 Ibid. 5, 8, 10.

100 Ibid. 5, 8; van Suchtelen, '*Nil volentibus arduum*', 393.

101 van Suchtelen, '*Nil volentibus arduum*', 397.

102 Ibn Tufayl, *Hayy Ibn Yaqzan*, preface; Wielema, *Filosofen*, 87; Klever, *Een nieuwe Spinoza*, 106; Guerrero, 'Filósofos hispano-musulmanes', 130–1; Conrad, *World of Ibn Tufayl*, 275–6; Klever, *Sphinx*, 138; van Bunge et al. (eds.), *Dictionary*, i. 145.

The philosophy which inspired him, says Ibn Tufayl in his introduction, was actually a clandestine 'eastern' legacy he had imbibed in Andalusia by reading 'the great master Ibn Sina [Avicenna (AD 980–1037)]' who had shown how, through practice and meditation, the individual can elevate himself to the highest level of philosophical illumination and grasp the Supreme Truth.[103] The secrets of this esoteric 'eastern philosophy' (*al-hikmat al-mashriqiyyah*), introduced into Spain by Ibn Bajia of Zaragoza (d. 1139), known to medieval Christendom as Avempace, had been loudly denounced by Al-Ghazali addressing himself to a wide public but, insisted Ibn Tufayl, without solid or convincing grounds.[104] Extolling *al-hikmat al-mashriqiyyah*—a mysterious term still in dispute among scholars[105]—Ibn Tufayl implied there existed a precious and hidden eastern philosophical legacy, later transferred to himself and Ibn Rushd in Andalusia via Ibn Bajia. By rendering the novel into the vernacular, Bouwmeester may thus have deliberately hinted at a remarkable submerged chain of tradition linking the radical thought of the Early Enlightenment with a partly imagined and partly real eastern Arabic legacy of thought which, after Ibn Sina, took root in Spain and then Italy. Bouwmeester's rendering of Ibn Tufayl was later reissued, in 1701, in two different printings, at Amsterdam and Rotterdam, with revisions and notes added by Reland, plus the words 'translated by S.D.B.', which several modern scholars have conjectured might be a further hint, invoking the legendary initials 'B.D.S'—implying Spinoza himself may have urged the usefulness of translating the work, though others construe it as just a reference to [Seigneur?] Doctor Bouwmeester.[106]

Many contemporaries were interested in Ibn Tufayl, whose novel was widely read in Latin and translated into various vernacular languages besides English and Dutch. Le Clerc published a twenty-two-page French summary of the work in the third volume of his *Bibliothèque universelle* in 1686,[107] further posing the question of Ibn Tufayl's clandestine 'eastern philosophy', and that of the origin of Arabic freethinking and the legend of the Three Impostors. It was Bayle's thesis, though, that Ibn Rushd represented the culmination of a vigorous Aristotelian tendency which, since the beginnings of Islam, had generated a deep conflict between philosophy and Muslim popular religion that was to prove the most subversive. Outwardly philosophers conformed to the dictates of religion but not inwardly. Leading Arab thinkers had attached themselves so closely to Aristotle, he held, that so as not to contradict his principles Averroes, 'Alfarabius [i.e. al-Farabi (AD 870–950)], Abumassor [the astronomer Abu Ma'shar?] et assez d'autres philosophes arabes se sont éloignez des sentimens de leur Prophète'.[108] Inwardly, at least, they gave priority to philosophical reason. But was all this just a figment of Bayle's imagination or did such a

[103] Ibn Tufayl, *Hayy ben Yaqzan*, 4–5; Klever, *Sphinx*, 140.

[104] Ibn Tufayl, *Hayy ben Yaqzan*, 1–2, 9, 12; Conrad, 'Through the Thin Veil', 253–8.

[105] Nasr, 'Ibn Sina's "Oriental Philosophy" ', 247–9.

[106] Ibid.; Meinsma, *Spinoza et son cercle*, 212, 501; Thijssen-Schoute, *Nederlands Cartesianisme*, 415; Guerrero, 'Filósofos hispano-musulmanes', 129–31; Conrad, *World of Ibn Tufayl*, 276; Russell, 'Impact', 255 n. 16.

[107] Russell, 'Impact', 250.

[108] Bayle, *Dictionnaire*, i. 350.

clandestine radical philosophical campaign to undermine belief in revealed religion really exist and really reach back via an unbroken chain to late antiquity?

4. THE CLANDESTINE 'ENLIGHTENMENT' OF THE *ZINDIKITES*

According to Bayle and other radical writers, the evidence of recent Ottoman history showed that underground traditions based on philosophical reason had indeed persisted down to modern times and proved that an unbroken living legacy of monist thought infused the entire history of the Islamic world. The atheistic undercurrent revived in the al-Andalus of Ibn Rushd had later, according to Bayle, Mandeville, and Fréret,[109] resurfaced again in Ottoman Constantinople. Here, says Bayle, 'une secte nombreuse' took shape which consisted mainly of '*cadis*, et des personnes savants dans les livres Arabes', that is among the most literate and rational part of the population. These, he says, following Sir Paul Rycaut's well-known account of the Ottoman empire, a widely influential French version of which appeared in 1670,[110] evinced 'une amitié extraordinaire les uns pour les autres'. Typically stressing both the atheism and moral uprightness of the sect, Bayle describes the scandal which erupted, only a few years before, surrounding 'Mehmet Effendi', a prominent man executed, Rycaut reports, during his time in Constantinople, in the 1660s, for atheism and blasphemy.[111]

Effendi was executed for having 'advanc'd some notions against the existence of God', as Mandeville puts it, echoing Bayle, in his *Fable of the Bees*, and for belonging to a sect whose members were enjoined to treat each other with exemplary love and charity.[112] Preferring death to retracting his views, identically report both Bayle and Mandeville, Effendi went to his death despite having no hope of reward in an afterlife because 'the love of truth constrain'd him to suffer martyrdom in its defense'.[113] Returning to the theme, in his *Continuation* of 1705, Bayle again styles Mehmet Effendi's sect one which 'nie absolument la divinité'.[114] And here again Bayle was following his sources: for Rycaut does indeed claim not just that there were Turkish atheists who formed a clandestine movement, calling themselves 'Muserins', that is 'we possess the true secret', nurturing a secret doctrine that there is no God, but also that, for them, God is equivalent to nature, or the internal principle in everything which directs the course of all things.

There are, Rycaut had claimed, a 'large number of persons who are of this opinion in Constantinople, most of them being "cadis" and learned in the writings of the

[109] Fréret, *Œuvres philosophiques*, 95–6.

[110] Kors, *Atheism in France*, i. 151.

[111] Bayle, *Pensées diverses*, ii. 112–13; Charnley, *Pierre Bayle*, 129, 132.

[112] Bayle, *Pensées diverses*, ii. 137–8; Crousaz, *Examen*, 666; Reimmann, *Historia Universalis*, 539–40; Cantelli, *Teologia*, 104, 106; Kors, *Atheism in France*, i. 158–9; Corsano, *Bayle, Leibniz*, 30; Foucault, 'Pierre Bayle', 231.

[113] Bayle, *Pensées diverses*, ii. 137–8; Mandeville, *Fable of the Bees*, i. 215; Bouchardy, *Pierre Bayle*, 197.

[114] Mori, *Bayle philosophe*, 191; Bayle, *Continuation*, i. 68.

Arabs'.[115] Their chief martyr, Mahomet Effendi, he says, was executed 'during my stay in Constantinople, for having insolently uttered various blasphemies against the existence of God'. Reviewing a 1709 reissue of Rycaut's work, in the *Nouvelles de la République des Lettres*, Jacques Bernard, despite his own commitment to the principle of *consensus gentium* proving the existence of God, acknowledged that 'atheism has made great progress among the [Turks]', restating the views of the 'Muserim', as reported by Rycaut, and the absolute naturalism of Mehmet Effendi, adding that their philosophical concept of a nature capable of design from within itself leads to insuperable contradictions.[116] In the wake of Rycaut's report, it was thus by no means only Bayle who suspected there was a buried but pervasive strain of systematic naturalism within Islam.

All this served to tighten the widely perceived linkage between the legend of the Three Impostors and Islamic history and culture. In late seventeenth- and early eighteenth-century Europe, continued to be Averroes, widely considered the original inspirer of this notorious legend, and, if it existed, of the text of the 'Three Impostors',[117] the mythical medieval text purportedly denouncing as frauds all three revealed religions. According to Early Enlightenment versions of the legend, this age-old clandestine text denouncing Moses, Jesus, and Muhammad as the three prime 'impostors' who systematically misled and deceived mankind had been redacted under the auspices of the Emperor Friedrich II (Holy Roman Emperor: 1220–50) during his bitter dispute with the papacy.[118] Ibn Rushd's precise role in generating this powerfully seditious theme, and the historical perspectives it gave rise to, was of course a matter of surpassing interest to Bayle and the *philosophes* who followed in his wake.

Bayle's *Dictionnaire*, like the first European *encyclopedia*—the *Algemeen Historisch Geographisch en Genealogisch Woordenboek* (The Hague, 1724)—and subsequent eighteenth-century compendia, including Prosper Marchand's *Dictionnaire* (1758) and the great French *Encyclopédie*, all narrate the tale of Ibn Rushd devising the notion of the 'Three Impostors' simultaneously to negate and equate the three great revealed religions. Ibn Rushd, in all these compendia, is cited as denouncing the revealed faiths in highly offensive terms: 'quod Lex Moysi, est lex puerorum; Lex Christi, lex impossibilitum; lex Mahumeti, lex porcorum' [that the Law of Moses is a law for children; the Law of Christ an impossible law, and the Law of Muhammad a law of pigs].[119] The Hague encyclopedia of 1724 claims 'Averroes'

115 Bayle, *Continuation*, i. 68; Reimmann, *Historia Universalis*, 539–40.

116 Kors, *Atheisim in France*, i. 152.

117 Bayle, *Dictionnaire*, i. 384; Gauthier, *Théorie d'Ibn Rochd*, 52–3; Dethier, 'Siger van Brabant', 209, 215; Berriot, 'La "Littérature clandestine" ', 43.

118 Bayle, *Dictionnaire*, i. 387; Bayle, *An Historical and Critical Dictionary*, i. 430; *Algemeen Historisch, Geographisch*, i, A pp. 549–50; Brucker, *Historia critica philosophiae* (1742), iii. 108–9.

119 Marchand, *Dictionnaire historique*, i. 314–15; Berti, 'Introduzione', p. xvii; Charles-Daubert, '*Traite des trois imposteurs*', 11; Diderot, *Œuvres complètes*, xiv. 739; see also Schwarzbach and Fairbairn, 'History and Structure', 86, 89–90.

deemed Christianity doubly absurd since its followers chew the God they worship with their teeth.

Even though there was (and is) no definite evidence tying the legend to either al-Andalus or Ibn Rushd, there thus persisted through the Enlightenment a centuries-old linkage of 'Averroes' with the rise of the 'Three Impostors' legend. Actually, 'Averroes' here is probably just shorthand in the collective western memory for Islamic philosophy in some wider sense; for not only does the legend, as several modern scholars note, certainly pre-date both Friedrich II and Ibn Rushd (who lived a generation earlier), but systematic denial, on philosophical grounds, of revealed religion as the highest source of the truth, and equating the three great revealed faiths as equally invalid, certainly arose in the Islamic world centuries before Ibn Rushd's time. Indeed, it reaches back at least to the ninth-and tenth-century 'eastern' freethinking circles, culminating in the thought of Ibn al-Rawandi and Abu Bakr al-Razi, and very likely still further back.[120] Not only did awareness of Ibn al-Rawandi's and Al-Razi's critique of Islam, and the forceful arguments they used, create an intellectual milieu in which the idea of the Three Impostors could flourish but their influence is thought to have spread in a subterranean manner across the Arabic-speaking world as far as Spain;[121] and even though Bayle, Boulainvilliers, d'Argens, and their contemporaries knew practically nothing about Ibn al-Rawandi and Al-Razi, they did possess a few hints suggesting that such a radical clandestine tradition had existed in early Islam.

Abu al-Husayn ibn al-Rawandi (*c.*815–*c.*900), author of the *Kitab al-Zumurrudh* [Book of the Emerald], was a Persian who had studied under the Manichaean Abu 'Isa al-Warraq, and repudiated his Muslim faith, becoming a self-proclaimed *mulhid*, or arch-heretic,[122] who systematically questioned the foundations of revealed religion, and especially Islam. He did so on purely rational grounds, though detractors claimed his books to have been written among and in the pay of the Jews.[123] Reason, held Ibn al-Rawandi, is man's exclusive guide to truth, a quest in which revelation is of no help. Deriding the Koran as absurdly obscure and self-contradictory,[124] he renewed arguments, some scholars claim, originally introduced by the late pagan Greek philosophers Celsus, Porphyry, and Proclus to combat Christianity. He held, for example, that even where a revealed faith establishes a beneficial, rationally cogent code of good and evil, prohibition and obligation, there is no requirement to venerate the prophet proclaiming such a system but only the code itself and especially its rational basis; if the code decreed by religious

120 Badawi, 'Muhammad ibn Zakariya al-Razi', 437, 445–6, 448; Haq, 'Indian and Persian Background', 57–8; Stroumsa, *Freethinkers*, 74, 81–3, 99–100, 217.

121 Fierro, 'Ibn Hazm', 86; Balty-Guesdon, 'Al-Andalus', 336; Stroumsa, *Freethinkers*, 205, 208, 210.

122 Stroumsa, *Freethinkers*, 40; Stroumsa, 'Religion', 50–1; Niewöhner, *Veritas sive varietas*, 238–42.

123 Niewöhner, *Veritas sive varietas*, 242–3; Lewis, *Islam in History*, 230; Stroumsa, *Freethinkers*, 75, 207.

124 Stroumsa, *Freethinkers*, 81–2; Stroumsa, 'Religion', 48; Fakhry, *Philosophy, Dogma*, essay xxiv, p. 179; Fierro, 'Ibn Hazm', 84; Crone, *Medieval Islamic Political Thought*, 173.

revelation does not correspond to what reason ordains then there is even less reason to venerate such a prophet.

Ibn al-Rawandi roundly denounced the miracles of 'Ibrahim, Musa, 'Isa and Muhammed' as *makhariq* (fraudulent tricks) and lies, and the founders of the three revealed religions to be all impostors.[125] Abu Bakr al-Razi (*c.* AD 854–925), from Rayy (near modern Tehran), in the next generation, likewise an Arabic-writing Persian, attacked revealed religion in a still more acerbic fashion. Al-Razi, who knew various Greek sources in Arabic translation, and was said to have damaged his eyesight through excessive study and to have gone blind, was later remembered in the West as the learned Arab 'Rhazes' but solely as a great physician.[126] Diderot praises him in the *Encyclopédie* exclusively as an exponent of Greek natural philosophy, knowing nothing, seemingly, of his freethinking.[127] Of his philosophical work, only the titles and a few fragments survive. But enough is known from these, and subsequent reports, to show that Al-Razi, a critic of Galen influenced by Platonism, was not an atheist but believed in a benevolent and eternal God.[128] He categorically denied miracles, *Creatio ex nihilo*, and especially the miraculous status of the Koran, scorning claims that its inimitability proves its miraculous status, insisting it is possible to compose a better book in better style.[129] He rejected prophecy, and while allowing the great power of these 'revelations' denied them any divine sanction, ascribing their capacity to dominate men to the force of authority, tradition, and imitation as well as their indispensable function in upholding law and the social hierarchy.[130]

Philosophy is the only path to truth, in his opinion, religion's role being exclusively social and political.[131] There is no way to adjudicate the competing claims of the rival revelations theologically; meanwhile, they all aspire to dominate and are all politically and intellectually destabilizing and inflammatory, posing a constant threat to society. Because the claims of revelations and prophecy can only be judged philosophically, Al-Razi, quite differently from Ibn Rushd later, apparently thought it necessary for philosophical reason to be propagated among the common people as well as the intellectual elite. Philosophy he considered 'accessible to all men', and the religious scholars (who would inevitably oppose such a process) he deemed an inevitable enemy which had to be fought and overcome.[132]

Two of his titles, *Makhariq al-anbiya'* [Tricks of the Prophets] and *Hiyal al-mutanabbiyin* [Tricks of the Would-be Prophets], possibly referring to the same

[125] Niewöhner, 'Are the Founders?', 239; Kraemer, 'Heresy', 174–5; Stroumsa, *Freethinkers*, 83–4.

[126] Gundling, *Vollständige Historie*, ii. 1650–2; Bar-Asher, 'Abu Bakr al-Razi', 99–100.

[127] Diderot, *Œuvres complètes*, xiv. 732–3.

[128] Bar-Asher, 'Abu Bakr al-Razi', 109–10; Stroumsa, 'Religion', 52, 57.

[129] Badawi, 'Muhammed ibn Zakariya al-Razi', 446; Bar-Asher, 'Abu Bakr al-Razi', 103; Goodman, 'Muhammed ibn Zakariyya al-Razi', 203–4.

[130] 'Muhammed ibn Zakariya al-Razi', 446; Fakhry, *Philosophy, Dogma*, essay ii, pp. 11–12; Bar-Asher, 'Abu Bakr al-Razi', 108; Stroumsa, *Freethinkers*, 97–107.

[131] Crone, *Medieval Islamic Political Thought*, 172.

[132] Badawi, 'Muhammed ibn Zakariya al-Razi', 440; Hodgson, *Venture of Islam*, i. 431–2; Crone, *Medieval Islamic Political Thought*, 172, 267, 328, 397; Stroumsa, *Freethinkers*, 98–9, 104–5, 109.

text, reflect his particular emphasis on unmasking the mechanics of prophecy.[133] Moses, Jesus, and Muhammad, held Al-Razi, at key points all contradict each other and themselves. Jesus, for instance, announced that he came to fulfil the Torah but then proceeded to abrogate its law, replacing its precepts with others.[134] While Al-Razi and Ibn al-Rawandi both apparently drew on Zoroastrian and Manichaean, as well as Greek, ideas for their critique of revealed religion, this did not prevent al-Razi claiming these latter traditions too are rife with contradiction. Mani (AD 216–77) and Zoroaster, he notes, contradict Moses, Jesus, and Muhammad 'concerning the Eternal One' but also contradict each other on the subject of good and evil, ontological dualism being more systematic in Manichaeism than Zoroastrianism.[135]

Ibn al-Rawandi and Al-Razi lived in a troubled time. Waves of religious and political turmoil gravely troubled the early Abbasid caliphate, and Bayle followed by various subsequent European writers conceived the idea that it was precisely in this widespread unrest that we can discern, or at least can surmise, a formative early phase of radical thought in the Near East which he interprets as a clandestine atheistic and pantheistic tradition stemming from both Greek and Persian sources. When describing Spinozism, for example, Bayle says men had long believed that the entire universe consists of only one substance 'et que Dieu et le monde ne sont qu'un seul être',[136] offering as evidence the report of Pietro della Valle, the early seventeenth-century aristocratic scholar-traveller, concerning the Iranian sect della Valle calls *ahl-i tahqiq* and Bayle renders *Ehl Eltahik* 'ou hommes de vérité, gens de certitude' (i.e. *ahl al-haqq*). This was a sect which believed, according to Bayle and Giannone (both stripping the theology from della Valle's account), there is no other God but nature, consisting of Four Elements from which all things are composed, and no other life after this one, so that when we die we return to the Four Elements, Heaven and Hell existing only in this world, according to the well-being or misery in which men find themselves.[137]

In interpreting the sect, remnants of which della Valle encountered in Lar, as proto-Spinozists, Bayle and, following him, Giannone were, no doubt, adding a layer of philosophical sophistication scarcely plausible in the context of bands of rough tribesmen, easily aroused to violent action. Bayle depicts them as a quasi-Spinozist undercurrent, supposedly deriving from a mixture of Sadduceeism, Manichaeism, and older Greek monistic philosophy, forming an intellectual chain spanning the ages: with Spinoza's system, he declares, 'le fond est toujours le même'; the *ahl al-haqq*, like the modern Spinozists, claim the universe consists of only one

[133] Stroumsa, *Freethinkers*, 93–4; Badawi, 'Muhammed ibn Zakariya al-Razi', 445; Niewöhner, *Veritas sive varietas*, 246; Goodman, 'Muhammad ibn Zakariyya al-Razi', 202–3.

[134] Stroumsa, *Freethinkers*, 101.

[135] Ibid. 41–2, 100; Badawi, 'Muhammed ibn Zakariya al-Razi', 446; Haq, 'Indian and Persian Background', 58.

[136] Bayle, *Dictionnaire*, iii. 2767; Giannone, *Opere*, 954.

[137] Giannone, *Opere*, 954; Bayle, *Écrits*, 114; Charnley, *Pierre Bayle*, 76–7; Gurney, 'Pietro della Valle', 112–13.

substance 'et que tout ce qu'on appelle générations et corruptions, mort et vie, n'est qu'une certaine combinaison, ou dissolution de modes'.[138] Yet in a way, Bayle and Giannone were perhaps not so wide of the mark as may at first appear; for these were extremist Shi'ites inspired by ancient (in fact Gnostic) undercurrents, a sect calling themselves 'men of truth' or *ahl al-haqq*, to set themselves in open opposition to what most men believe, cultivating a hidden truth which would, eventually, be revealed in all its glory, and were thus at any rate an underground movement, reviving older impulses and opposing the sway of the revealed religions.[139]

That late antique anti-Christian Greek philosophical arguments really persisted in Islamic society, as Bayle supposed, by means of clandestine traditions nurtured by these extremist Shi'ite factions, such that reason, toleration, and equality continued to be revered, was of course far-fetched in the extreme. Yet it was an effective device because late pagan Greek philosophical attitudes encountered in anti-Christian writers such as Celsus, Proclus, and Simplikios probably did survive among the Persian intellectual elite as the reports concerning Ibn al-Rawandi and Al-Razi suggest, just as other late antique philosophical attitudes deeply influenced less subversive Muslim thinkers like Al-Farabi.[140] Ibn al-Rawandi and Al-Razi may indeed really have been links in a living chain of underground 'pagan reaction' against revealed religion reaching back ultimately to the age of Julian the Apostate (emperor AD 360–3) which might have interacted and become entwined with the Gnostic impulses reappearing in extremist Shi'ism.[141]

However uncertain these remote derivations, and the exact currents of thought, Bayle was on fairly solid ground in linking what were historically certain facts surrounding the anti-Umayyad and then anti-Abbasid political insurgency with hidden streams of thought and belief generating a quasi-revolutionary fervour aimed in part at the three revealed faiths. If he deliberately mixed fact and conjecture he also concocted thereby a new radical construct which did not lack a degree of historical plausibility. Thus, in his article 'Abumuslimus', in his *Dictionnaire*, he focuses on a historically certain figure, a legendary commander of non-Arab, possibly Iranian (and possibly slave) origins, Abu Muslim Khorasani (AD *c.*728–755) (or Abu Salama), the figure largely instrumental in bringing the Abbasids to power in Baghdad. Leading the Iranian insurrection of 749, with its raising of black banners, Abu Muslim first gained control of Khorosan—later the probable birthplace of Ibn al-Rawandi[142]—and then, with strong rural support from eastern Iran, definitively overthrew the Umayyad dynasty, installing the Abbasids as caliphs in their place.

Abu Muslim was then liquidated in or around AD 754 by the Caliph al-Mansur who feared his following in regions of the empire where there was continuing dangerous unrest.[143] 'Abumuslimus', asserts Bayle, with typical panache (and seditious

[138] Bayle, *Dictionnaire*, i. 38–9; Bayle, *Écrits*, 29, 114–15.
[139] Halm, *Shiism*, 166–7, 169–70; Crone, *Medieval Islamic Political Thought*, 83.
[140] Crone, *Medieval Islamic Political Thought*, 175.
[141] Bar-Asher, 'Abu Bakr al-Razi', 109; Stroumsa, *Freethinkers*, 142.
[142] Stroumsa, *Freethinkers*, 37.
[143] Ibid. 87 n., 95; Abid, 'Political Theory', 734.

intent), belonged to a heretical sect believing in the eternality of the world which denied divine providence and that there is a knowing God. He and his followers, he says, also rejected the immortality of the human soul and judgement in the hereafter.[144] His was a sect, he says, which proclaimed the oneness and unity of all substance, 'une secte, dont celle du malheureux Spinoza n'est pas dans le fond fort différente'.[145] The insurrectionary creed of Abu Muslim's movement, scholars agree, was actually built out of an explosive mix of Shi'ite, Zoroastrian, and Manichaean ingredients,[146] so that while there is no concrete evidence of any Greek strand, Bayle was probably not stretching the truth far in postulating a resurgence of religious impulses of late antiquity, Persian, and Greek, clandestinely opposed to all three revealed religions.

While it might be objected that Bayle was resorting to pure fantasy in thinking Abu Muslim's movement adhered to the fundamental unity of all substance, and was proto-Spinozist, the fact that it was against this background that the freethinking tradition, culminating in Ibn al-Rawandi and Al-Razi, arose means that his construct was perhaps, taking all forms of dissent in the Abbasid era into account, not so remote from the actual historical circumstances after all. For the philosophical freethinking of Al-Warraq, Al-Rawandi, and Al-Razi was an intellectual revolt against belief in the miraculous, revelation, prophecy, and the supremacy of theology over human life, and did arise against a backdrop of endemic spiritual revolt, heretical sects, and armed political insurrection simultaneously aimed against the Abbasid caliphate and orthodox religion.

One of Bayle's main sources of information, Herbelot's influential *Bibliothèque orientale* (Paris, 1697), identifies Al-Rawandi as 'Ahmed ben Iahia ben Ishak Ravendi', styling him a 'Saducéen', 'impie', and author of several books 'contraires aux principes de la religion mahométane', including the *Ketab alzumroud* [Book of Emeralds].[147] What Bayle found here and in della Valle gave him some reason to think a theologico-philosophical tradition linking antiquity with later Islamic philosophy had indeed evolved in Umayyad and Abbasid Iran, leading him to postulate a connection—possibly historically factual—between, on the one hand, an anti-Abbasid insurgency which opposed the revealed religions and owed something to Manichaeism and other pre-Islamic religious Persian traditions, and, on the other, a clandestine philosophical tradition, equally opposed to revealed religion and which also actually existed.[148]

A quarter of a century after Abu Muslim's demise, the Caliph al-Mahdi (ruled AD 775–85) reacted to further unrest—especially in Khorosan—and further resurgence of several Iranian anti-Islamic movements, especially Manichaeism, by instigating with the help of the religious scholars the first systematic persecution of

144 Reimmann, *Historia Universalis*, 531; Bayle, *Écrits*, 114–15.

145 Bayle, *Écrits*, 114; Kolakowski, 'Pierre Bayle', 74, 80; Mori, *Bayle philosophe*, 165.

146 Crone, *Medieval Islamic Political Thought*, 94–6.

147 Herbelot, *Bibliothèque orientale*, 711.

148 Hodgson, *Venture of Islam*, i. 273–5; Gutas, *Greek Thought*, 48–9.

zanadiqa (heretics), a large number of whom were executed.[149] Among those put to death was Ibn al-Muqaffa (d. 776), a master of Arabic prose who, though outwardly a Muslim, preceded Ibn al-Rawandi's teacher Ibn Warraq in welding together Zoroastrian, Manichaean, and possibly also Greek arguments against Islam, a writer who mocked the anthropomorphic thinking evident in the Jewish and Christian Bibles and the Koran.[150] Bayle utilized this episode by employing an invented plural form for the Arabic *zindiq* (plural=*zanadiqa*), a term originally applied in Abbasid times to Manichaean dualists but later broadened to cover all heretical beliefs particularly where suspected of endangering the social order,[151] to add a further layer to his astounding philosophico-historical concoction of anti-Abbasid insurgency, adducing another pseudo-Muslim 'sect', the 'Zindikites', who rejected revelation and miracles and, he says, following several earlier scholars, 'approchent des Sadducéens' from whom Early Enlightenment scholars thought they derived their name.[152]

Discussing this passage in Bayle in the 1720s, Reimmann, the German Lutheran historian of atheism, thought Bayle mistaken in construing Abu Muslim's sect and the 'Zindikites' as two different groups, citing Herbelot's entry on the subject as evidence that Abu Muslim was actually one of the 'Zindikites',[153] but agreed with his assessment that this Islamic sect proves the survival, under the Abbasids, of ancient Greek monist philosophical tendencies. Della Valle's account he too saw as evidence that Abu Muslim's teaching and that of the Zindikites were indeed akin to Spinozism.[154] According to the Zindikites, there was no providence, 'ni de résurrection des morts', as Bayle puts it, their creed being reducible to the principle that everything which exists 'dans le monde, que tout ce qui a été créé, est Dieu'.[155] Al-Rawandi, remarks Herbelot in his *Dictionnaire*, had been known as 'al-Zendik', the impious one or 'Sadducee', so that both Bayle himself and his learned readers readily made the connection, as indeed Reimmann does too, between Al-Rawandi the freethinker and Bayle's (and later Diderot's) Spinozistic 'Zindikites'.[156]

In this way what Brucker later called the 'secta Zindekaeorum cum duce Abu Muslimo, quam inter Spinozistas ante Spinozam referat P. Bayle' [sect of the Zindikites with the leader Abu Muslim whom Bayle includes among the Spinozists before Spinoza][157] provided the Radical Enlightenment with an interpretation of Islamic history which integrated it into the wider frame of history of the *l'esprit humain*. It could be flexibly worked backwards and forwards, and was to resurface in a variety of radical contexts. Thus, for example, it is clearly Bayle's

149 Lewis, *Islam in History*, 229; Kraemer, 'Heresy', 176–7; Gutas, *Greek Thought*, 65–6.

150 Gutas, *Greek Thought*, 165; Kraus, 'Zu Ibn al-Muqaffa', 17–20; Kraemer, 'Heresy', 168, 172, 174; Haq, 'Indian and Persian Background', 57; Urvoy, 'La Démystification', 92–3.

151 Lewis, *Islam in History*, 228; Stroumsa, 'Religion', 49–50; Stroumsa, *Freethinkers*, 124–6.

152 Bayle, *Écrits*, 29; Reimmann, *Historia universalis*, 531–2.

153 Herbelot, *Bibliothèque orientale*, 928–9.

154 Reimmann, *Historia universalis*, 531–2; Herbelot, *Bibliothèque orientale*, 928–9.

155 Bayle, *Écrits*, 29; Brucker, *Historia critica philosophiae* (1742), iii. 138–9; Ramond, 'Ne pas rire', 109.

156 Reimmann, *Historia universalis*, 532; Herbelot, *Bibliothèque orientale*, 711.

157 Brucker, *Historia criticia philosophiae* (1742), iii. 139.

device which lies behind Diderot's claim in his article 'Sarrasins' in the *Encyclopédie* where he declares that, among the Muslims, the impulse to mix theology with philosophy generated over the centuries 'une espèce de théosophisme, le plus détestable de tous les systèmes'; and that it was in reaction to this that those in whose eyes theology and philosophy should be kept apart, and are mutually debased by any such 'association ridicule' (including Ibn Rushd), inclined to atheism: 'tels furent les *Sendekéens*' [i.e. Zindikites] and the '*Dararianéens*'.[158] It was a construct, thanks chiefly to Bayle, especially apt to foment the idea that the 'esprit de Spinoza' spans the millennia, religions, and parts of the globe, infusing the world of Islam no less than Europe and China.

[158] Diderot, *Œuvres complètes*, xiv. 743.

25

Spinoza, Confucius, and Classical Chinese Philosophy

1. CHINA AND *SPINOZISMUS ANTE SPINOZAM*

A central challenge for the western Enlightenment as a whole in the eighteenth century was the question of how to classify 'the other'. Efforts were made by the Europeans to reach general assessments of Islamic, Indian, and Chinese thought. But as so often in cases of attempts at cross-cultural evaluation the result was curiously self-centred and limited. Western philosophers strove valiantly to grasp the fundamentals of classical Chinese philosophy but ended up, in the main, merely mirroring their own prior obsessions.

The Radical Enlightenment's enthusiasm for what it took to be classical Chinese thought originated during the third quarter of the seventeenth century, among a small but remarkable group of libertine Deist neo-Epicureans. The first *esprit fort*, or 'suspected atheist', Reimmann calls him,[1] to hit on the idea of using Chinese culture as a subversive strategy within western intellectual debate, apparently, was Isaac Vossius (1618–89), who deployed the evidence of Chinese antiquity and the ancient character of their philosophy during the late 1650s as part of his campaign to sap confidence in biblical chronology and notions of *prisca theologia* as well as the centrality of revelation. Also reliant on the exceptional antiquity of Chinese civilization was Vossius' (and Blount's) argument that the Flood engulfed only a restricted area of the world, essentially the land of the Jews themselves.[2] Vossius' many detractors fiercely deplored his taking it upon himself, despite knowing no Chinese, or having ever been to China, to laud Chinese thought, morality, and culture to the skies, exalting Chinese accomplishment out of all proportion to its real worth into one of humanity's supreme achievements.[3]

Chinese society, held Vossius, in his *Variarum observationum liber* (London, 1685), his foremost contribution to radical thought, was not just the oldest but

[1] Reimmann, *Historia universalis*, 480–1.

[2] Bayle, *Réponse*, iv. 65; Yuen-Ting Lai, 'Leibniz and Chinese Thought', 138–9; King, *Mr Blount's Oracles*, 21, 24.

[3] King, *Mr Blount's Oracles*, 179; Heumann, *Acta philosophorum*, 11 (1720), 717–20, 774, 778.

also the most praiseworthy section of civilized humanity if one measures men's achievements, as one should, in terms of peace, stability, and cultivation of the arts and sciences.[4] He extolled in particular Chinese science, technology, and medicine, stressing it was they, not the Europeans, who had invented printing and done so, moreover, 1,500 years before the West.[5] The reason for their unmatched success, he urged, was that they had approached closer to achieving a 'Platonic republic' than others, entrusting the most vital questions to 'philosophers and lovers of philosophy' so that 'were the rulers to err, the philosophers enjoy such great freedom to admonish those things as formerly was scarcely even found among the Israelite prophets'.[6]

Other early exponents of philosophical Sinophilia, that new 'principe des esprits forts', included the sieur de Saint-Évremond (1613–1703) and Sir William Temple (1628–99), the English diplomat; and it is not without significance that Vossius, Saint-Évremond, and Temple all knew each other and, in the later 1660s, all resided in the same town—The Hague—where they were virtual neighbours, and all acquainted with Spinoza. For theirs were minds very much in opposition to the received thinking of their time. Possibly no one ever thought 'aussi profondement, aussi solidement et, en même temps, aussi naturellement' as Saint-Évremond, remarked the marquis d'Argens, several decades later.[7] He was to remain a role model to many as a nobleman of 'advanced' views and would not hesitate to take Bayle's part when, on the publication of the first edition of the *Dictionnaire*, in 1697, the Parisian orientalist the Abbé Eusebe Renaudot denounced both its general impiety and what he considered its scholarly travesties concerning China.[8] Temple, for his part, was labelled an 'atheist' by his foes but praised by Dutch libertine friends as a wise republican, 'aimant la Hollande comme son propre pays, parce qu'elle étoit libre';[9] he fully endorsed Saint-Évremond's preference for Epicurean moral philosophy and the pursuit of calm enjoyment of life and philosophical peace of mind.

A true cosmopolitan, much influenced by Italian and French sceptics, libertines, and republicans, like Montaigne, Bocaccio, Machiavelli, and 'Padre Paolo' (i.e. Sarpi),[10] Temple too greatly admired what he had learned of China and especially Confucius, 'the most learned, wise and virtuous of all the Chineses'.[11] It was his opinion that there is no better model for men to emulate in organizing their lives than the wisdom of Confucius, Temple, like Vossius and Saint-Évremond, being struck especially by the close parallelism between philosophical insight based on reason and the practical ordering of human life and politics on earth. Confucius' 'chief principle', observed Temple, was that everyone ought 'to study and endeavour the improving and perfecting of his own natural reason to the greatest height he is

[4] Vossius, *Variarum observationum liber*, 56–7, 77; Reimmann, *Historia philosophiae Sinensis*, 47; *Gründliche Auszüge*, 9 (1741), 406; De Smet and Elias, 'Isaac Vossius', 156, 162–4.

[5] Vossius, *Variarum oberservationum liber*, 59, 75–6, 81.

[6] Ibid. 58–9; Hazard, *European Mind*, 36.

[7] D'Argens, *Réflexions historiques*, 43.

[8] Zoli, 'Pierre Bayle e la Cina', 467.

[9] Quoted in Monk, 'Introduction', p. viii.

[10] Temple, *Five Miscellaneous Essays*, 65.

[11] Ibid. 113.

capable, so as he may never (or as seldom as can be) err and deviate from the law of nature in the course and conduct of his life', being convinced that 'in this perfection of natural reason consists the perfection of body and mind and the utmost or supreme happiness of mankind'.[12] Such neo-Epicurean eulogy of Confucius and of Chinese thought later prompted Reimmann to exclaim, echoing Buddeus' maxim about Spinozism before Spinoza: 'fuisse in China Epicureanismum ante Epicurum et post Epicurum' [there was Epicureanism in China both before and after Epicurus].[13]

The Sinophilia of Vossius, Temple, and Saint-Évremond rapidly became an integral feature of radical thought and their sentiments in this area continued to be echoed for decades. Boulainvilliers closely identified the figure of Confucius with that of Spinoza.[14] Boulainvilliers's protégé Fréret in the second quarter of the eighteenth century fully endorsed Vossius' view that Confucius is so full of fine insights one would wish, 'pour le bonheur du genre humain', that all men would practise them.[15] Boulainvilliers, Tyssot de Patot, Dorthous de Mairan, Radicati, Bruzen de La Martinière,[16] Doria, and d'Argens all expressed similar opinions. 'The followers of Confucius', affirmed Radicati, 'have precepts which contain most excellent morals, with very sublime ideas of that Supreme Power which gives life and motion to created beings.'[17] What especially appealed to Bruzen was that Confucius' China was a meritocracy rather than a land governed by autocracy or nobility.[18]

Confucius' philosophy was viewed, then, by the *esprits forts*, as a moral and political system which had positively shaped China for millennia and was potentially a model for all mankind. Such a perspective remained highly problematic, though, from a Christian and moderate Enlightenment viewpoint, owing to its obvious and many worrying implications for morality, social theory, revealed religion, and education. While the origins of the western debate about Chinese philosophy reached back to Vossius, Saint-Évremond, and Temple, the main discussion began only when an extensive body of original source material became available with the publication in Latin, in 1687, of several translated classical Confucian texts under the title *Confucius Sinarum philosophus*.[19] With this project, a group of Jesuits, headed by Father Philippe Couplet, seeking to defend the long-standing Jesuit practice of mingling Confucian and Christian terms, concepts, and rituals in their missions in China, undertook to prove that Confucianism is not after all 'atheistic'. Their aim was to convince European opinion of the pervasive theism, as well as venerable antiquity and reasonableness, of Confucianism.[20] The *Confucius Sinarum philosophus* held Confucius' teaching centred around the idea of a providential God, and

[12] Temple, *Five Miscellaneous Essays*, 113–14; Mungello, 'European Philosophical Responses', 90; Israel, *Radical Enlightenment*, 606.

[13] Reimmann, *Historia philosophiae sinensis*, 9.

[14] Benítez, *Face cachée*, 405.

[15] Fréret, *Œuvres philosophiques*, 112.

[16] [Bruzen de La Martinière], *Entretiens*, i. 591–2, 596.

[17] Radicati, *A Succinct History*, 36.

[18] [Bruzen de La Martinière], *Entretiens*, i. 586–7.

[19] Pinot, *La Chine*, 151–2, 158, 418.

[20] Kors, *Atheism in France*, i. 163; Elisseeff-Poisle, *Nicolas Fréret*, 52.

that the terms *Tien* and *Xam-ti* in his thought designate not the universe, as opponents maintained, but the Divinity. The material looked impressive, though Le Clerc, reviewing the volume in his *Bibliothèque universelle*, worried that the Jesuits might have embellished Confucius' thought in some degree with some insights of their own and hence overly 'spiritualisé' the philosophy of the Chinese.[21]

To the Jesuits, modern Chinese philosophical 'atheism' was something real enough but in no way authentically Confucian. Couplet warned that to style as 'atheists' classical Confucians who most commentators agreed had been outstandingly wise and virtuous would have serious consequences; for that would clearly imply that 'virtuous atheists' exist, that virtue and piety are distinct, and that denial of God can arise from something other than utter moral depravity.[22] Thus while he agreed with Jesuit critics, such as Father Nicola Longobardi (1565–1655), that neo-Confucianism was 'atheistic', Couplet staunchly defended Confucius and his successors and his own endeavours to make their texts better known. For centuries before Moses, as well as Christ, he contended, the Chinese had possessed genuine knowledge of the true God, and of morality, gleaned from nature but especially tradition, a case powerfully reiterated, in 1696, with the publication of another work by a Jesuit missionary to China, Louis Le Comte's widely consulted *Nouveaux Mémoires sur l'état présent de la Chine*.[23] Unlike ancient Greece and Rome, where a mere handful of philosophers had grasped the truths of monotheism, and morality, while most men had remained mired in idolatrous superstition, in China, held Le Comte, *prisca theologia* had prevailed from the outset, shaping the religious traditions and culture of the people and enabling them robustly to resist atheism as well as crass credulity and idolatry.

From 1687, Europe's philosophers disposed of plausible renderings of Chinese thought and lost no time in exploring the fraught implications implicit in the existence of a great and ancient tradition of thought about which, hitherto, they had known next to nothing. But how were they to categorize that rich and complex philosophical 'otherness' in terms of their own theological and philosophical traditions? Not surprisingly, there was no consensus. Among the first to articulate a clear response was the Jansenist Cartesian Antoine Arnauld (1612–94) who, being no friend of the Jesuits, greatly preferred the counter-arguments of critics like Longobardi to those of Couplet. The ancient Confucians, he concluded, after examining the translations, had never known any 'spiritual substance' distinguished from mere matter and, consequently, had no correct notion 'ni de Dieu, ni des anges, ni de nôtre âme'.[24]

But it was above all Bayle, once again, who fixed the contours of the great controversy which now ensued, the full extent of the philosophical problem emerging

21 Le Clerc, *Bibliothèque universelle*, 7: 455; Pinot, *La Chine*, 152.

22 Kors, *Atheism in France*, i. 164.

23 Ibid. i. 169–70; Harrison, *'Religion' and the Religions*, 138.

24 Arnauld, *Morale pratique*, in *Œuvres*, xxxiv. 304; *Histoire des ouvrages des savants* (Oct. 1692), 94–9, reviewing Arnauld; Leibniz, *Opera omnia*, iv. i. 82.

only with his arguments about the moral feasibility of an atheistic society.[25] It was towards the end of his life, in the *Continuation des Pensées diverses* (1705) and the *Réponse aux questions d'un provincial* (1704), that the sage of Rotterdam chiefly developed his deliberately convoluted and perplexing double contention that while the classical Chinese thinkers held that the beauty, symmetry, and order which one sees in the universe are, as his critic Crousaz indignantly put it, 'l'ouvrage d'une nature qui n'a point de connoissance', that is were 'atheists', they also believed human happiness and social stability depend on morality, and were outstanding in their accomplishments in this sphere.[26] Bayle, while classifying classical Chinese philosophy as a form of Spinozistic monism, at the same time, as Crousaz saw it, had the effrontery to agree with the Jesuits that Confucianism upholds 'le bien public' on the basis of the highest and most praiseworthy moral and political values.[27] What seemed especially deplorable about Bayle's view, to Crousaz, was that he construed Confucianism not as a virtual or primitive undeveloped atheism, or *athéisme négatif*, like that of the Caribs, or Canadian Indians, but a philosophically sophisticated 'athéisme positif' with Confucius and Mencius confidently comparing metaphysics infused with the idea of God unfavourably with 'le système opposé—that is equating nature with God![28]

In his late works where he is at his most challenging and provocative, Bayle, then, deliberately equates 'les Spinozistes et les Lettrez de la Chine', both, he says, being as aware as the most 'pious' men of other nations of the rules of secular morality and of all the 'diverses sortes de bien' in human society.[29] The disturbing impact of his views about China was heightened further by his arguing that China was not the only focus of Spinozistic sentiment in the East, 'l'athéisme de Spinoza', as he had already proposed in his *Dictionnaire*, being 'le dogme de plusieurs sectes répandues dans l'Asie'.[30] In his long article 'Spinoza', he had pointed out that missionaries' and travellers' reports from the Indies confirm that Confucianism is only one particular style of expounding a dogma 'qui a un grand cours dans les Indes'.[31] He cites one travel writer, Bernier, as proof that such quasi-Spinozism pervades the thought, among others, of the Cabbalists, Sufis, and 'la plupart des gens de lettres en Perse'.[32] If the Chinese, according to Lévesque de Burigny, echoing Bayle, in 1724, 'ont aussi leurs Spinosistes, dont le principe est que tout est un', 'Spinosistes' maintaining that the univese 'n'est composé que d'une seule substance' and who are very numerous, the Japanese too, he asserts, again following Bayle, 'ne sont pas éloignés du systême, que Spinosa a tâché de faire valoir'.[33]

[25] Zoli, 'Pierre Bayle e la Cina', 468, 471; Zoli, *Europa libertina*, 206–9.

[26] Crousaz, *Examen*, 410–11, 675; Spink, *French Free-Thought*, 263–4; Yuen-Ting Lai, 'Linking of Spinoza', 153; Pocock, *Barbarism*, i. 167.

[27] Crousaz, *Examen*, 438, 689; Cantelli, *Teologia*, 263; Paganini, 'Avant la *Promenade*', 20, 45.

[28] Bayle, *Continuation*, ii. 728–9; Bayle, *Réponse*, iv. 139–41; Hazard, *European Mind*, 40.

[29] Bayle, *Réponse*, iv. 434; Bayle *Continuation*, i. 68–9, 73, 134–5.

[30] Bayle, *Continuation*, i. 68; Yuen-Ting Lai, 'Leibniz and Chinese Thought', 154.

[31] Yuen-Ting Lai, 'Leibniz and Chinese Thought', 35.

[32] Ibid.; Charnley, *Pierre Bayle*, 100.

[33] Lévesque de Burigny, *Histoire de la philosophie payenne*, i. 17–21.

The strange feature of the debate about China was that the very same claim that the classical Confucianists were 'atheistic' and virtual *Spinosistes* was now being continually advanced by key sections of both opposing parties to the dispute. Highly unusually, an almost identical argument figured centrally in diametrically opposed philosophical strategies; and not just briefly. For this curious juxtaposition remained deeply characteristic of the controversy surrounding Chinese philosophy for half a century. Where the anti-Jesuit moderate mainstream strove in this way to discredit and diminish the standing and prestige of China and the Chinese (as well, often, as the Jesuits) what the radicals implied, by linking China with Spinozism, was that the latter was not just an ancient way of thinking but also, however much decried in contemporary Europe, a wholly 'natural' way and potentially—or even perhaps actually—the mode of thought of most of mankind. Thus, Boureau-Deslandes in his *Histoire critique de la philosophie* of 1737 repeats Bayle's idea that 'la plupart des nations orientales sont encore dans le même sentiment [as Spinoza]', drawing an especially close parallel between Confucianism and Strato.[34] D'Argens, writing around the same time, has his Chinese visitor to Paris report back to China that innumerable Europeans now embrace a philosophy closely resembling that of the Chinese *literati* and that its European originator was a Dutch thinker, 'Spinoza', though he was perhaps just its 'restaurateur' as it also resembled that of various ancient philosophers.[35]

The same topos could also be deployed in a more complex way to argue that conventional, theological attacks on Spinozism as atheistic and immoral were a philosophically inadequate way of meeting the challenge of such a world-embracing system of impiety. Christian scholars, held the Abbé Pluquet, in the mid 1750s, needed to go beyond merely denouncing Spinoza as 'atheistic' and opposed to the church's teaching. For demonstrating that Spinoza overthrows all received ideas 'sur la nature de Dieu, et sappe tous les fondemens de la morale', as Christians see it, could have no beneficial results in China or India, since the professional philosophers of China and India 'regardent comme des vérités ordinaires ces conséquences si revoltantes' which faithful Christians so abhor in Spinozism. Had Bayle offered his refutation of Spinoza, in his *Dictionnaire* article, at Peking, remarked Pluquet, he would have been dismissed as 'un philosophe médiocre', hopelessly mired in popular thinking and prejudice.[36] In short, debating classical Chinese thought in terms of Spinoza and Spinozism rapidly evolved into a philosophical maze of astounding complexity and resonance.[37]

In the *Continuation*, Bayle distinguishes four different schools of classical Chinese philosophy; but claims they all conceived reality, with relatively minor variations, as a single unified coherent structure governed by a single set of rules, in

34 Boureau-Deslandes, *Histoire critique*, ii. 296–8, iv. 30; Vernière, *Spinoza*, 352.

35 Vernière, *Spinoza*, 353; d'Argens, *Lettres chinoises*, i. 106; Ehrard, *L'Idée*, 409; Israel, *Radical Enlightenment*, 588.

36 Pluquet, *Examen*, ii, p. iv.

37 Yuen-Ting Lai, 'Linking of Spinoza', 151; Mungello, 'Malebranche and Chinese Philosophy', 561–3; Mungello, 'European Philosophical Responses', 98.

other words as one or another form of monistic one-substance doctrine. This followed on from his earlier claim, in the *Dictionnaire*, that while Spinoza was a powerful and original synthesizer 'le fond de sa doctrine lui fut commun' with various other philosophers ancient and modern, western and oriental.[38] Bayle portrays classical Chinese philosophy, especially that of Confucius, as an 'atheistic', Spinozistic system very formidable in its grasp of moral precepts, in which one acknowledges nothing in nature except nature itself, the driving force being the principle of movement and rest, this being the prime factor which produces 'l'ordre dans les différentes parties de l'univers et qui cause tous les changemens qu'on y remarque'.[39] Hence ancient China was an atheistic society which proves 'atheism' can inspire a wholly admirable moral order and one superior, in practice, to that of the Christians.[40] His claiming classical Chinese moral philosophy was both atheistic and worthy of high praise, and had, he argues, citing the non-Jesuit missionary Simon de La Loubère's *Du royaume de Siam* (2 vols., Amsterdam, 1691),[41] spread generally among the Chinese, was clearly designed further to bolster the thesis first formulated in his *Pensées diverses* (Rotterdam, 1683) that the cause 'du dérèglement des mœurs' in society is not incredulity and that religion is not a brake 'capable de retenir nos passions'.[42]

Where Bayle had at least made a show of agreeing, in the *Dictionnaire*, out of deference to readers' sensibilities, that Chinese 'atheistic' ideas are a system so extravagant and so 'remplie de contradictions absurdes' that, despite having swayed vast numbers of people of diverse cultural backgrounds, it is hard to comprehend how anyone can embrace them, later, in the *Continuation*, even this pretence is dropped. In his last writings, Bayle concentrates on highlighting the rational coherence of this overarching Confucian-Spinozist construct emphatically aligning both with Stratonism, the philosophy he judges internally the most consistent of the Greek systems of 'atheism'.[43] The problem the Christian missionaries encounter in China in refuting Confucianism is, therefore, he concludes, basically the same as that which European philosophers face in trying to refute Stratonism.[44] Bayle then admits he does not know how to rebut either Stratonism or Confucianism but presumes Cartesianism with its rigorous dualism, and denial that movement can be inherent in matter, offers the best prospects for doing so.

Confucianism, then, for Bayle, like Malebranche, possessed a purely rational structure grounded in nature rather than any transcendental realm, one identifying nature as the totality of what is and exclusive source of its own laws and principles.[45] This radical construct was then taken up a few years later, as we have seen, by Anthony Collins, who similarly equates the 'Literati of China' with Strato and

[38] Bayle, *Écrits*, 29.
[39] Bayle, *Continuation*, ii. 537–40, 728–30; Crousaz, *Examen*, 41, 438, 675; Davis, 'China', 534.
[40] Crousaz, *Examen*, 689–91; Zoli, *Europa libertina*, 226, 232.
[41] Bayle, *Écrits*, 90; Charnley, *Pierre Bayle*, 100.
[42] Bayle, *Pensées diverses*, ii. 72, ii. 86.
[43] Bayle, *Continuation*, i. 134–5, ii. 540, 729.
[44] Ibid. ii. 553–4.
[45] Pinot, *La Chine*, 314–27, 332; Yuen-Ting Lai, 'Linking of Spinoza', 167.

Xenophanes as well as Spinozism.[46] While it was doubtless easier in the West to praise the moral integrity of 'atheists'—whether 'Spinozist' or Chinese—than insist on the logical coherence of their metaphysics, it seems clear, contrary to what has sometimes been maintained,[47] that Bayle and Collins were effectively asserting both the moral superiority *and* the greater coherence of Chinese and Japanese thought to that of the Europeans.

Meanwhile, the theological controversy in France and at Rome, between the Jesuit and anti-Jesuit factions in the Chinese Rites controversy, approached its climax. The Catholic world resounded with treatises on the subject, the Jesuits advancing the old *prisca theologia* concept but also deploying it in a novel way to fit the Chinese context. In the religious thought of ancient China, they held, one finds clear traces of an authentic ancient theology, the antiquity and genuineness of which were more convincing and certain than in the case of the *Corpus Hermeticum* or *Orphica*. The Chinese, held Le Comte and his allies, since over 2,000 years before Christ, had preserved intact an authentic knowledge of the true God and it was this that had enabled their society to uphold a wholly admirable moral code as pure as that taught by Christianity ever since.[48] However, these propositions proved deeply divisive within the church, arousing strenuous opposition from several dissident Jesuit scholars as well as Jansenist, Dominican, and Franciscan critics.

Where the official Jesuit position classified the ancient Chinese as monotheists and possessors of *prisca theologia* whose true faith had to an extent been corrupted by the neo-Confucians and especially the most eminent neo-Confucian, Chü Hsi (AD 1130–1200), opponents of their approach, like the Jesuit Longobardi and the Franciscan Antoine de Sainte-Marie, claimed the Confucian concept of *T'ien* as encountered in both ancient Confucian classics and in the neo-Confucians (all of whom Longobardi considered 'atheists') definitely excludes the existence of a providential God. It was also objected that the neo-Confucian *hun*—the spirit of man's vital force expressed in his intelligence and animation—could not, contrary to what most Jesuit missionaries claimed, correspond to the Christian soul.[49] Above all, Longobardi held that the First Principle of the universe, according to Confucianism, termed by them *Ly*, was inseparable from matter and wholly lacking in wisdom, goodness, and intelligence which meant that their system was irretrievably monist, materialist, non-providential, and quasi-Spinozist.[50]

To extricate themselves from the looming pitfall of 'atheism' *with* moral uprightness into which Bayle designed to steer them, theologians and mainstream enlightened philosophers had either to come up with a convincing demonstration that the classical Chinese were 'atheists' *and* lacked moral uprightness or else, alternatively,

[46] [Collins], *An Answer*, 89; Zoli, *Europa libertina*, 227; Israel, *Radical Enlightenment*, 617; Taranto, *Du déisme à l'athéisme*, 332.

[47] Yuen-Ting Lai, 'Linking of Spinoza', 177.

[48] Kors, *Atheism in France*, i. 169–70.

[49] Lundbaek, 'Image', 26; Wing-Tsit Chan, 'Study of Chu Hsi', 559–60.

[50] Wing-Tsit Chan, 'Study of Chu Hsi', 559–60; Roy, *Leibniz et la Chine*, 66–7.

that they were 'virtuous' but not 'atheists'.[51] After years of bitter wrangling and strenuous manoeuvring in Rome, the first position was endorsed by the cardinals and the *prisca theologia* thesis of the Jesuit *Confucionistes*, as Arnauld dubbed them, formally set aside. Accordingly, the proposition that *Ly* is a memory, notion, or premonition of the providential God of the Christians in classical Chinese civilization descended from *prisca theologia* was categorically condemned as error by the Sorbonne in 1700.[52]

It soon transpired, though, that banning the *Confucianiste* position was more fraught with philosophical pitfalls and risk for the church than had been supposed. For by rejecting Couplet's and Le Comte's arguments, and conceding that Chinese thought is essentially 'atheistic', the cardinals not only questioned the whole basis of decades of Jesuit missionizing in China but also the hitherto almost impregnable argument from *consensus gentium* for the existence of God. For rebuffing the Jesuit view meant that a great part of the world's population was, after all, 'atheistic'; worse still, it implied that a social code and ancient system of ethics which many judged surpassingly admirable had been devoutly preserved over many centuries by 'atheists'. Some effort was made to circumvent this seeming confirmation of Bayle's thesis that a well-ordered society of atheists is possible by holding that while the emperor, mandarins, and scholars were Confucianists, and hence atheists, the Chinese common people were not: the multitude adhered to praiseworthy moral standards because they remained loyal to religion, even if a false one.[53] But this was neither wholly convincing nor satisfying.

Yet, had the cardinals ruled, instead, that Chinese natural religion *does* provide a true conception of a providential God and his commandments whilst upholding a moral order equal or superior in uprightness and purity to that of Christendom, it would then have been even less clear why revelation and Christianity are needed for the well-being of society and Man's redemption. Meanwhile, with papacy, Sorbonne, and theologians all deeply entangled in these intricacies, the Jesuits refused to abandon their alternative view; indeed, a network of French Jesuits in China and Europe began devising a new and still bolder version of the *prisca theologia* thesis. This group, dubbed by Fréret the Jesuit *figuristes*, included Father Joachim Bouvet, who worked, from 1685 until his death, in 1730, mainly in China, from where he carried on a correspondence with Leibniz which was to have a not inconsiderable impact on the intensifying philosophical debate.[54] Another *figuriste* was Jean-François Foucquet, who laboured as a missionary in China from 1699 until 1722 when he was obliged to return to France for holding 'heterodox' views about the common sources of Chinese and Christian doctrine; later, he was also expelled from his order. Despite this, he continued to labour tirelessly,

[51] Roy, *Leibniz et la Chine*, 34–5; Kors, *Atheism in France*, 171–5.
[52] Charnley, *Pierre Bayle*, 22; Harrison, *'Religion' and the Religions*, 138; Zoli, *Europa libertina*, 208, 211.
[53] Bergier, *Apologie*, ii. 299.
[54] Rowbotham, 'Jesuit Figurists', 474; Poulouin, *Temps des origines*, 282.

impressing Ramsay among others,[55] mainly in Rome, where he settled in 1723 and composed his *Tabula chronologica historiae Sinicae* (1729), to change the papal view of China.

The *figuristes*—though Fréret considered their theories completely absurd[56]—had some success in impressing philosophical opinion. Leibniz and Ramsay in particular were sympathetic to arguments which they felt held out the promise of resolving a thoroughly intractable set of problems. Bouvet granted that ancient Chinese piety had subsequently become buried beneath obfuscating layers 'de l'idolâtrie et de l'athéisme' but insisted that the underlying bedrock of natural religion reaching back to the age and family of Noah survived and that he and his colleagues had found 'non sans une assistance du ciel toute spéciale, la clé du temple de l'ancienne sagesse'.[57] As to the proximity of the Chinese ancient canon to the essentials of Christian belief he refused to admit the least element of doubt: 'il n'y a aucun mystère dans la religion chrétienne', he assured the Abbé Bignon, no dogma 'dans notre théologie', no maxim in our holy morality 'qui ne soit exprimée dans ces livres avec une clarté surprenante'.[58]

The argument from *prisca theologia* relied on the notion of an austere, quasi-Christian pristine moral order, God's original revelation to man, delivered not by reason but a supreme lawgiver and teacher appointed by God to instruct humanity. This lawgiver, the progenitor and promulgator of all morality, science, and human knowledge, held the *figuristes*, was the Hermes Trismegistus of the Egyptians and Greeks, his Chinese name being Fu Hsi, the primal god-man, and founder of Chinese culture, identified by Foucquet with Enoch. Hence, there was no atheism in classical Chinese thought and not just an acknowledged providential God but likewise the doctrines of Heaven, Hell, the Fall, the Saviour, redemption, fallen angels, and the Immaculate Conception. Allusions to Christ, they insisted, featured integrally in the authentic Chinese classics.[59] This fitted with their conception of the universal presence of the Christian 'mysteries' and the submerged, coded embodiment of Christian truth to be found everywhere in symbols, words, and arcane traditions. The idea of a single source and primal tradition, superficially concealed behind but in fact uniting western and Chinese theological and religious traditions, was to prove a powerfully seductive one over several decades.

Leibniz responded positively to such reasoning but remained isolated among the major philosophers in supporting the Jesuit *figuristes*. The rest, both Catholic and Protestant, refused to be swayed. Malebranche, who had for years suffered from fierce Jesuit attacks on his own system, critically scrutinized the Jesuit conception of Chinese *prisca theologia* in his *Entretien d'un philosophe chrétien et d'un philosophe chinois sur l'existence et la nature de Dieu* of 1708. Confucianism, in his eyes, was a

[55] Baldi, *Verisimile, non vero*, 194.

[56] Pinot, *La Chine*, 149, 262–3, 266–7; Elisseeff-Poisle, *Nicolas Fréret*, 55–6; Larrère, 'Fréret et la Chine', 116.

[57] Poulouin, *Temps des origines*, 282–3.

[58] Rowbotham, 'Jesuit Figurists', 475.

[59] Ibid. 479; Spence, *Question of Hu*, 75–6, 108–9.

purely monistic philosophy which nowhere undertakes a thoroughgoing differentiation of body and mind. Classical Chinese thought, he contended, exactly like Bayle but with firmly opposite purposes, conflates body and mind into one, reducing the totality of what is to a single substance.[60] The neo-Confucianist principle of *Ly*, though an emanation notionally distinct from matter (*Ch'i*), is not conceived, stressed Malebranche, as existing independently of matter and while indubitably expressing the supreme rationality of the universe, lacks intelligence, benevolence, and freedom of will. Hence, the *Ly* of Malebranche's 'Chinese philosopher' acts only through the necessity of its nature without knowing or wishing anything that it creates or influences.[61] What in the West is called 'spirit' or 'soul' consists, therefore, for the Chinese not of pure spirit but 'de la matière organisée et subtilisée'.[62]

Malebranche abjures all such notions, of course, holding that the Chinese are grossly in error in supposing our perceptions 'ne soient que des modifications de la matière',[63] since Nature is demonstrably devoid of motion and sensibility, and hence wholly inert. The Spinozist-Confucian hypothesis of force and movement innate in bodies is thus utterly false, he insists, as well as morally pernicious. By depicting Confucianism as a system in which the active, creative force in the universe, *Ly* 'n'est pas libre ni intelligent', and is inseparable from the inert matter it infuses, Malebrache too firmly bracketed the debate about Chinese philosophy with that about Spinozism, albeit without explicitly saying so in the dialogue itself. Rather in unstated opposition to both, he urged that in our universe the rationality and energy animating Nature must derive wholly from outside, via a decree of God.[64] Malebranche had already attacked Spinoza, once before, in his *Entretiens sur la métaphysique* of 1688, and there too had chosen to do so only indirectly, by allusion and inexplicitly.[65]

No one was misled, however, by his not mentioning the obvious. When Malebranche says 'Chinois', retorted his Jesuit critics 'il pense Spinoza'.[66] Quite right. By proceeding in this fashion, Malebranche not only struck at his Jesuit foes, especially Father Josèphe René Tournemine (1661–1739), unsubtly tarring them with Spinoza—in effect paying Tournemine back in his own coin—but could reaffirm his own strict dualism in direct opposition to one-substance monism thereby convincingly demonstrating the wide gulf between his own philosophy and the Spinozism with which the Jesuits claimed he showed telling affinities.[67] His analysis of Confucian philosophy was thus partly incidental to what, to him, was a still more important undertaking, as he himself afterwards fully admitted when he answered

60 Yuen-Ting Lai, 'Linking of Spinoza', 156; Cantelli, *Teologia*, 263; Davis, 'China', 534; Mungello, 'European Philosophical Responses', 97–8.

61 Malebranche, *Entretien*, 3, 14; Robinet, *Malebranche*, 483.

62 Malebranche, *Entretien*, 12; Yuen-Ting Lai, 'Linking of Spinoza', 157; Mungello, 'Malebranche and Chinese Philosophy', 556, 559.

63 Malebranche, *Entretien*, 13; Moreau, 'Malebranche et le Spinozisme', 6–7.

64 Malebranche, *Entretien*, 40; Robinet, *Malebranche*, 487; Yuen-Ting Lai, 'Linking of Spinoza', 173–4.

65 Malebranche, *Dialogues*, 149–51; Moreau, 'Malebranche et le Spinozisme', 2–3.

66 Malebranche, *Entretien*, appendix pp. 42–3.

67 Yuen-Ting Lai, 'Linking of Spinoza', 167.

Jesuit complaints that his *Entretien d'un philosophe* was transparently an attack on them, by saying that he had written the tract not to injure them, or Christianity in China, but to combat Spinozism which he (like the Jesuits) thought was now making 'de grands ravages' in France.[68]

Malebranche used the debate about Chinese thought to promote the reputation of his rationalistic dualism as the most viable type of Christian metaphyics, and effective answer to Spinoza, in the eyes of the French clergy and court. It was a shrewd tactic which, however, incurred the disadvantage of provoking Tournemine and another Jesuit, Jean Hardouin (1646–1729), into redoubling their attacks on him.[69] The Jesuits granted that 'le systême de l'impie Spinosa fait icy [i.e. in France] de grands ravages', and that this lent added urgency also to the debate about China, but insisted that Malebranche by publishing a dialogue in which one finds 'beaucoup de rapport entre les impietez de Spinosa et celle de nôtre philosophe chinois' had merely slandered the Jesuits, lowered esteem for China, and concocted a ridiculous travesty of Confucianism, while doing nothing effective to combat Spinozism.

Yet virtually the same critique of classical Chinese thought as was advanced by Malebranche against the Jesuits could be employed, with only slight modification, in reverse, by exponents of radical ideas. One such was Fréret whose treatise on Chinese letters and scripts, though unpublished until 1731, was written for an address to the Parisian Académie des Inscriptions, in December 1718.[70] Fréret showed a sustained interest in China and had actually acquired some Chinese, having studied the language with Arcade Huang (d. 1716), a bilingual young Chinaman and protégé of Bignon attached to the Bibliothèque du Roi as a translator. Corresponding with missionaries active in China, Fréret, between 1714 and 1733 composed several discourses on Chinese culture, chronology, and literature.[71] Scorning the idea that the Chinese thinkers believed in 'natural religion', he contended rather, practically echoing Malebranche, that Chinese philosophy acknowledges neither Creation nor Providence and consequently 'ne reconnoit point de Dieu, c'est à dire, d'Être distingué de l'Univers, qui ait produit ou créé le monde', or who governs and conserves it in accordance with laws which he has established.[72]

In his notes on Couplet's *Confucius sinarum philosophus*, Fréret freely ridiculed the Jesuits' credulity and self-delusion regarding miracles and Natural Theology, holding that Confucius never speaks 'du souverain estre ni de l'immortalité de l'âme ni de l'autre vie'. This great Chinese sage, he insisted, exhorts men to virtue for its own sake and for the advantages 'qu'elle entraîne nécessairement avec elle par une suite naturelle', claiming everything the Jesuits asserted about Chinese conceptions of the Divinity and the universe was false.[73] Extolling

68 Pinot, *La Chine*, 331; Mungello, 'Malebranche and Chinese Philosophy', 561.
69 Mungello, 'Malebranche and Chinese Philosophy', 564.
70 Elisseeff-Poisle, *Nicolas Fréret*, 72; Pocock, *Barbarism*, i. 161.
71 Larrère, 'Fréret et la Chine', 109; Spence, *Question of Hu*, 16, 139.
72 Quoted in Spence, *Question of Hu*, 166; Pinot, *La Chine*, 345–6.
73 Quoted in Elisseeff-Poisle, *Nicolas Fréret*, 54, 91.

Confucius' aversion to metaphysics and theology, he explains the spirituality of which Confucius speaks as something which is intimately united to all things 'et qui n'en peut estre separé', as something hence resembling the world-soul 'ou à la vertu active des spinozistes'.[74] Confucius, concludes Fréret, had no conception of divine providence, his notion of the creative principle in nature being entirely that of 'l'action de la matière, suivant le système des hylozoïstes'.[75] Hence, in reality Confucianism stood totally at odds with what most western philosophers took to be the first principles and maxims of eternal truth 'en morale et métaphysique'.[76] Fréret entirely agreed with Malebranche, therefore, while simultaneously opposing his strategy, that the issue of Spinozism crucially underlay the whole of the European debate about Chinese thought.[77]

2. LEIBNIZ, WOLFF, AND CHINESE *PRISCA THEOLOGIA*

Leibniz, though intensely interested in the Jesuit mission in China at least since his visit to Rome, in 1689,[78] and long since persuaded 'there was nothing idolatrous or atheistic in the teachings of Confucius',[79] late in his life directly intervened in the hugely vexing deadlock about Chinese philosophy. Through corresponding with Father Bouvet during the period 1697 to 1704, he was won over to the idea of a conceivable common ancient source for Chinese and Judaeo-Christian religion, though this was not ultimately essential to his universalist position that insofar as both are based on reason and the search for eternal truths Christianity and classical Chinese thought are in close parallel and equally fix the main elements of Natural Theology. Then, in 1713, a young savant, Nicolas de Remond, contacted him, after reading his *Theodicée*, encouraging him to refute Malebranche's *Entretien* and the treatises of Longobardi and other adversaries of Jesuit Confucianist *prisca theologia*. Having annotated Malebranche's text in November 1715, Leibniz in the last months of his life composed his *Discours sur la théologie naturelle des Chinois* (1716) presented in the form of a letter to de Remond.[80] Here, the great German thinker roundly contradicts Malebranche, maintaining that genuine Confucianists do distinguish an *intelligentsia supra mundana* from the material cosmos, warmly approving the main tradition of classical Chinese philosophy, and broadly accepting the claims of Le Comte, Couplet, and Bouvet dismissed by Arnauld, Bayle, and Malebranche.

[74] Quoted in Elisseeff-Poisle, *Nicolas Fréret*, 54; Vernière, *Spinoza*, 352–3; Larrère, 'Fréret et la Chine', 113–14.

[75] Larrère, 'Fréret et la Chine', 114; Elisseeff-Poisle, *Nicolas Fréret*, 55.

[76] Quoted in Larrère, 'Fréret et la Chine', 163.

[77] Ibid. 114–15; Israel, *Radical Enlightenment*, 374.

[78] Cook and Rosemont, 'Leibniz', 257; Hsia, 'Euro-Sinica', 22–3.

[79] Leibniz, *Opera omnia*, iv. 82–4; Leibniz, *New Essays*, 501.

[80] Mungello, 'Malebranche and Chinese Philosophy', 575–7; Schmidt-Glintzer, '"Atheistische" Traditionen', 273–5.

Leibniz at this late stage in his career showed an altogether more eager and active interest in learning the truth about Chinese culture and philosophy than the other western philosophers.[81] To his mind it mattered fundamentally that the classical Chinese were, after all, not 'atheists' but believed in a God who is *intelligentia supramundana*, as well as in spiritual substance, divine providence, and the immortality of the soul.[82] Moreover, he was increasingly impressed by the unmatched antiquity of classical Chinese thought, seeing Confucius merely as the reformer of a much older tradition reaching back to Bouvet's shadowy Fu Hsi, convinced that one finds in Fu Hsi 'une méthode générale et très-parfaite des sciences, un système numéraire semblable à celui de Pythagoras'; this led him to ponder at least the notion that primal Chinese and western wisdom might perhaps descend from a common source in Hermes Trismegistus or some such equivalent,[83] though he did not go so far, as is sometimes suggested, as expressly to underwrite Bouvet's thesis that almost the entire system of true religion 'se trouve renfermé dans les livres classiques des Chinois'.[84]

In his passages about Strato, aimed against Spinoza and Bayle, in the *Theodicée*, Leibniz holds the notion of spontaneous creation of nature to be self-contradictory, such a thing being conceivable only if there is a God who pre-establishes both matter and the laws of motion.[85] For the same reason, Leibniz dismissed Longobardi's account of classical Chinese thought as self-contradictory, a rebuttal by no means lacking in irony given that Arnauld—whom Leibniz had unsuccessfully tried to win over to his cherished undertaking to reunify the Christian churches and whose opposite view of Confucius was well known to him—had declared, in 1691, that nothing could be more useful or beautiful 'pour bien connoître la religion des Chinois, que le traité du P. Longobardi'.[86] The doctrine of *Ly*, argued Leibniz, actually proves that Confucius and the ancient sages of China, unlike the atheistic neo-Confucianists of later times, did conceive 'substances spirituelles' to be separate from 'et tout à fait hors de la matière'.[87]

Leibniz repudiated the Baylean-Malebranchian view of ancient Chinese thought by pointing to apparent confusions in Longobardi and other critiques of the Jesuits, contending that these actually reveal the opposite of what they assert. Where the Spinozists envisage matter as having inherent within it 'le principe actif', Confucius had conceived of matter as 'une chose purement passive'.[88] Leibniz tried to show that Confucius and the other ancient Chinese sages by conceiving the spirit that governs the Heavens as the true God 'et le prenant pour le *Ly* même', that is the governing rule

[81] D'Argens, *Lettres chinoises*, i, preface pp. 2–3; Mungello, 'European Philosophical Responses', 88, 97.

[82] Leibniz, *Discours*, 170, 174, 204–5; Cook and Rosemont, 'Leibniz', 259; Davis, 'China', 535–6; Lach, 'Leibniz and China', 109–11.

[83] Wolff, *Oratio*, 40–5; Cook and Rosemont, 'Leibniz', 261–3; Albrecht, 'Einleitung', pp. xx, xxii.

[84] *Bibliothèque germanique*, 35 (1736), ii. 175.

[85] Leibniz, *Theodicy*, 245–7, 336; Roy, *Leibniz et la Chine*, 76.

[86] Arnauld, *Morale pratique*, in *Œuvres*, xxxiv. 305.

[87] Leibniz, *Discours*, 170–2, 188, 204–5; Yuen-Ting Lai, 'Leibniz and Chinese Thought', 155.

[88] Leibniz, *Discours*, 175–6, 180.

or 'sovereign reason', had indeed penetrated to the truth of things and were thus in no way 'Spinosistes';[89] rather, their conception of the universe stood much closer to the Christian rational universalism of his own divinely pre-established harmony, for the ancient Chinese, just as Le Comte and Bouvet urged, professed a form of 'théologie naturelle, vénérable pour son antiquité', developed around three thousand years ago which fully differentiated the existence of spiritual beings, and grasped the true nature of matter. Only the Chinese 'nouveaux philosophes', or neo-Confucianists, could rightly be said to identify nature with reason. But precisely by focusing too much on their views, especially those of Chü Hsi, Longobardi, held Leibniz, had severely distorted our picture of the Confucian tradition.[90]

Though the only front-rank philosopher openly to side with the Jesuits in the Chinese Rites controversy,[91] Leibniz was important enough single-handedly to exert a powerful influence on the subsequent debate. If he failed to resolve or calm the wider dispute about Confucianism, and still less the intensifying controversy among western thinkers as to whether 'natural religion' or Spinozism is the more universally prevalent tendency in Man's conception of reality,[92] he certainly evened up the balance between European *Confucianistes* and anti-*Confucianistes*, with his insistence that the true Confucius and ancient *lettrés* of China conceived of *Ly* as 'la souverain substance' which we worship under the name of God. He also pitted his 'universalist' concept of Natural Theology in harmony with Christianity more firmly than ever against the materialist conception of universal truth. His argument that the Chinese *had* outstripped the Europeans in 'practical philosophy', and hence were superior in moral wisdom to the Christians,[93] whilst also seeing Confucius as not the inventor but just the renovator of a classical Chinese philosophy which reached much further back, linked the entire quarrel to the question of 'natural religion' with a clarity and force previously lacking.

Leibniz's strongly positive view of ancient Chinese philosophy helped win over Barbeyrac;[94] but was only partly reaffirmed by his disciple, Christian Wolff, in the sensational public lecture on the subject of Chinese moral ideas which he delivered at Halle in July 1721. This was the year after the Thomasian Eclectic Heumann had published a long piece reaffirming the view that the classical Chinese thinkers had simply acquired their knowledge of moral truth from other peoples, dismissing Isaac Vossius' eulogy of Chinese philosophy as overblown.[95] Wolff's counter-blast to Heumann was thus both an eloquent eulogy of classical Chinese philosophy and a provocation to Pietist critics inclined to detect a suspicious naturalism in his

[89] Leibniz, *Discours*, 170–1, 188; Roy, *Leibniz et la Chine*, 93; Yuen-Ting Lai, 'Leibniz and Chinese Thought', 159–63; Stewart, *Courtier*, 275–6.

[90] Leibniz, *Discours*, 169–70, 197; Bilfinger, *Specimen*, 48; Lach, 'Leibniz and China', 110, 112; Lach, 'Sinophilism', 123.

[91] Wolff, *Oratio*, 40–5; Zoli, *Europa libertina*, 232; Lach, 'Leibniz and China', 108–9.

[92] Leibniz, *Discours*, 174; Wing-Tsit Chan, 'Study of Chu Hsi', 571.

[93] Ibid. 101; d'Argens, *Lettres chinoises*, i, preface pp. 2–3; Lach, 'Leibniz and China', 101; Perkins, 'Virtue, Reason', 452–4.

[94] Barbeyrac, 'Préface', pp. iii, xviii, xxxvii.

[95] Heumann, *Acta philosophorum*, 11 (1720), 753, 759, 774.

system. The result was the furious public quarrel which then erupted, leading to his being officially denounced as a crypto-Spinozist and his peremptory expulsion from Prussia by decree of King Friedrich Wilhelm I (reigned 1713–40) of 8 November 1723 and the immense philosophical controversy which followed.[96]

Quite recklessly, as it turned out, Wolff asserted in his lecture, which was published, after a long delay, in 1726 (following the appearance of an unauthorized printing), that the particular truth of Christianity, and its role in Man's salvation, intervenes in the context of a philosophical enquiry only at that point where the truths revealed by natural reason leave off. Thus any truly enlightened Christian philosophy must, as a matter of course, specify where that boundary lies. He held that in the context of metaphysical and moral truths there are, for the Christian philosopher, three sources of knowledge, namely, divine revelation, truths revealed by 'natural religion', and those revealed by natural reason.[97] While following Leibniz in holding the classical Chinese were not 'atheists', Wolff did not emulate Leibniz in stressing the spirituality and religious dimension of their thought or their accomplishments in 'natural religion'.[98] In fact, as far as Wolff could see, the Chinese had only a very vague, shadowy notion of God and had not in fact striven to base their morality on 'natural religion'. Rather, they based their moral philosophy, in his opinion, purely on natural reason, in the use of which they had gone further, and more successfully in the sphere of practical philosophy and ethics than any other nation.[99] This made China and the Chinese uniquely relevant, he thought, as a philosophical thought experiment for the Christian enlightened philosopher, enabling us to determine how far unaided human reason can attain valid moral concepts without revelation or 'natural religion'.

While discarding Leibniz's involvement with 'natural religion' and thereby avoiding the thorny complications of the latter's position, Wolff's strategy actually heightened the clash between natural reason and revelation implicit in Leibniz's conception. For if the Chinese established an even finer moral order than the Christians without the guidance of a clergy, relying on natural reason alone, then what exactly is the contribution and function, in the world, of Christian revelation? Since classical Chinese moral philosophy and education, according to Leibniz and Wolff alike, surpassed those of other peoples, this showed that moral and political excellence, and an admirable regulation of society, can be delivered by 'practical philosophy', applying the principles taught by reason unaided by anything else. Wolff, in fact, appears to have believed this and even declared in his lecture, momentarily forgetting that most people linked Confucianism with Spinozism, that Confucianism accorded in basic respects with his own moral philosophy.[100]

96 Wolff, *Oratio*, pp. xlvi–xlvii, l; Israel, *Radical Enlightenment*, 544–58.

97 Wolff, *Oratio*, 23, 25–7; Albrecht, 'Einleitung', pp. xliv, lxii.

98 Lach, 'Leibniz and China', 115; Lach, 'Sinophilism', 119.

99 Albrecht, 'Einleitung', p. xliv; Wolff, *Oratio*, 25–6; Perkins, 'Virtue, Reason', 457–8.

100 Wolff, *Oratio*, 64–5; Schneewind, *Invention of Autonomy*, 442; Hochstrasser, *Natural Law Theories*, 158.

The classical Chinese, held Wolff, undertook nothing which contradicted or went against human nature: for the exclusive criterion of truth in pure moral philosophy, unaided by 'natural religion', must be what best suits human nature and conduces to the happiness of the individual and society.[101] The 'highest good' of the Chinese, he held, was identical to his own, for they also held 'hominem beatiorem fieri haud quoquam posse, quam ut ad majores perfectiones indies progrediatur' [Man can in no way be happier than when he daily progresses to higher perfections].[102]

In the published version of 1726, Wolff stood his ground in the face of a vehement onslaught of criticism but prudently diluted the bold comparison drawn in the public lecture between Confucius and the three great lawgivers of revealed religion—Moses, Christ, and Muhammad—to the extent at least of removing Christ from the equation, remarking that he had not meant to reduce the true Messiah to the level of the others, or detract from his divinity, infallibility, and special role as Man's Saviour.[103] He again stressed that he was only discussing Man's philosophical 'highest good', citing Confucius to show that Man can attain to that highest good in the moral sphere through natural reason alone. He entirely accepted, he added, in deference to the theologians, that Man cannot aspire to full salvation by unaided natural means.

Wolff had been so bold on the issue of Chinese philosophy that it is scarcely surprising that his numerous followers supported him only half-heartedly on this issue. Bilfinger, as always, rushed to his aid, intervening with his *Specimen doctrinae vetorum Sinarum moralis et politicae* (1724), but was markedly more cautious, and conventional, than either Wolff or Leibniz, contending that for all its praiseworthy qualities, spiritual and moral, Chinese thought utterly lacks the 'perfection of Christianity'.[104] But the theologians remained unappeased, Lange, Wolff's foremost Pietist opponent, in particular insisting that the Chinese were out-and-out 'atheists',[105] and that Wolff both conceded this and yet dared to affirm, before Halle's entire professorial complement and hundreds of students, that the ancient Chinese, after and owing to Confucius, were the wisest, morally most upright, and politically most adept of men.[106] In his view, it was impossible to interpret his outrageous intervention as anything other than an attempt to spread a concealed Spinozism among the entire German Lutheran academic body.

Meanwhile, Wolff's Thomasian, Eclectic opponents, while leaving the main work of stirring up condemnation of Wolff to the theologians, quietly added their voice in the background. In 1724–5, Buddeus and Bilfinger clashed in an exchange of tracts in part over the question of Chinese thought, Buddeus having long before, in his *De Spinozismo ante Spinozam* (1701), endorsed Bayle's view that Confusianism

[101] Wolff, *Oratio*, 23, 25; Albrecht, 'Einleitung', pp. xl–xlii.

[102] Wolff, *Oratio*, 56; Schneewind, *Invention of Autonomy*, 441.

[103] Wolff, *Oratio*, 119–21; Cassirer, *Philosophy*, 166; Albrecht, 'Einleitung', p. lxiii.

[104] Bilfinger, *Specimen*, 36, 48–9; Reimmann, *Historia philosophiae sinensis*, 53; Lach, 'Leibniz and China', 115.

[105] Albrecht, 'Einleitung', p. lxxi; Walch *Einleitung*, i. 11.

[106] Lange, *Kurtzer Abriss*, 10; *Fortgesetzte Sammlung* (1737), ii. 577; Lach, 'Sinophilism', 118–20.

is essentially Spinozistic.[107] Reprimanded for this by Bilfinger and Wolff, Buddeus now reiterated his opinion that since the Chinese philosophers did not admit the principle of incorporeality, they must consequently have considered the universe to be purely physical in composition. Hence, it was impossible to classify the Confucians as anything other than virtual Spinozists.[108]

Christian Thomasius, for his part, publicly criticized Wolff's *Oratio* in 1726, rebuking him for shamelessly comparing 'sapientiam Confuciam' with his own moral philosophy.[109] Walch followed his master Buddeus, as Heumann followed Thomasius, noting that unlike Leibniz and Wolff, most German scholars, including himself, attached no particular value or importance to Chinese philosophy or social thought.[110] Another disciple of Buddeus, Johann David Leonhard, writing under the pseudonym 'Aelius Sabinus', roundly condemned Wolff's claims about Chinese philosophy in a pamphlet published at Leipzig in 1727, delighting in Thomasius' scathing reference to the Wolffians as 'Konfuzianer' [Confucians], which, in the heated context of the moment, was equivalent to calling them 'Spinozists'.[111]

3. VOLTAIRE, MONTESQUIEU, AND CHINA

That the issue of classical Chinese philosophy was peculiarly hazardous terrain for the scholar was a theme aired on more than one occasion in the 1730s and 1740s. Endorsing Bayle's view of the matter, in a letter of 1721, La Croze, rejecting his deceased friend Leibniz's pro-Jesuit perspective, insisted that Confucianism teaches 'omnia sunt unum', and *must* be equated with Spinozism, Confucius being essentially a 'pantheist'.[112] The public disputation held at Greifswald, in May 1739, concerning the perils inherent in studying Chinese thought, reminded students that both Buddeus and Bayle—albeit not Brucker who preferred to compare Confucianism with ancient Stoicism—judged Confucianism to be Spinozistic.[113] 'Since the Chinese do not acknowledge the highest God', concluded this disputation, it is unsurprising that they understand nothing of the duties one owes to the Deity.[114]

During the Early Enlightenment, culminating in the 1730s, the western philosophers' battle over Chinese philosophy became increasingly a tussle between radical writers following Bayle in equating ancient Chinese thought with Spinozism while also seeing it as expressing an exemplary ethics and social philosophy, on the one hand, and moderate mainstream providential Deists, on the other, following

[107] Buddeus, *De Spinozismo ante Spinozam*, 351–2; *Gründliche Auszüge*, 9 (1741), 412–13.
[108] Buddeus, *Compendium historiae philosophicae*, 530.
[109] Ibid. 121; Albrecht, 'Einleitung', p. lxxii; Diderot and d'Alembert, *Encyclopédie*, iii. 342.
[110] Walch, *Einleitung*, i. 11. [111] Albrecht, 'Einleitung', p. lxxiii.
[112] Leibniz, *Opera omnia*, iv. 212–13; d'Argens, *Lettres chinoises*, i, preface pp. 4–5.
[113] *Gründliche Auszüge*, 9 (1741), 407, 411–13. [114] Ibid. 414.

Leibniz in seeking to appropriate the prestige of Confucius and Confucianism in moral philosophy for the principle of a universal 'natural religion' decreed by a providential God. Voltaire was particularly emphatic in pursuing the anti-Spinozist and anti-Bayliste strategy of combining admiration for Chinese society and morality with stressing its basis in Natural Theology, in effect modifying and secularizing the stance of Leibniz. For him, the idea of moral uprightness among the Chinese sages, and their seeing 'le bien public comme le premier devoir', is concrete proof that 'natural religion' and morality while standing intellectually exclusively on reason yet cannot be said to function, in the actual world, independently of faith—for in his eyes a moral system intended for society can never be divorced from key elements of religion or popular faith.[115] Greatly impressed, like Fréret, by the antiquity and long stability of the Chinese empire, unlike him, Voltaire conceived that the Chinese from an early date had always consistently been 'théistes'.

Hence, Voltaire, in opposition to Arnauld, Bayle, Malebranche, Buddeus, and Fréret, adamantly refused to agree that classical Chinese philosophy was atheistic or can be aligned in any way with Spinozism, holding rather, like Leibniz and Saint-Hyacinthe, that, on the contrary, Confucian moral philosophy is anchored in the idea of a Creator-God and divine providence. Rejecting Bayle's thesis that a society of atheists is both conceivable and possible, Voltaire contended, like Leibniz, that the classical Chinese thinkers, always eschewing 'atheism', were (like himself) adherents of 'natural religion' without divine revelation.[116] If the Chinese were inferior to the modern Europeans in mathematics, physics, and medicine, as Dorthous de Mairan claimed in 1734, the Greeks and Romans, Voltaire pointed out, had been likewise but, in any case, it was the Chinese who had 'perfectionné la morale, qui est la première des sciences'.[117]

Claiming the ancient Chinese cult was characterized by 'l'adoration simple d'un seul Dieu' and that its very antiquity, together with a moral philosophy based on reason, places China at the fountain-head of humanity, rendering the Bible superfluous, Voltaire dubbed the ancient Chinese 'Noachides', in humorous allusion to Jesuit claims that China had been populated with Noah's descendants.[118] For Voltaire's approach, like that of Leibniz, was in essence a semi-secularized version of that of the Jesuits. How can anyone, he contends, call 'atheistic' a society most of the laws of which are 'fondées sur la connaissance d'un Être suprême, rémunérateur et vengeur?'[119] There is a blatant contradiction, he urged, again like Leibniz, in the arguments of the Jesuits' opponents, since they simultaneously insist, against Bayle, that an orderly society of 'atheists' is impossible and yet that what is in effect 'le plus sage empire de l'univers est fondé sur l'athéisme'.[120]

115 Voltaire, *Essai sur les mœurs*, i. 216; Cassirer, *Philosophy*, 166; Pocock, *Barbarism*, i. 155.

116 Lussu, *Bayle, Holbach*, 237–8; Schneewind, *Invention of Autonomy*, 459–62; Pocock, *Barbarism*, i. 168.

117 Voltaire, *Essai sur les mœurs*, i. 68; Pinot, *La Chine*, 417; Rihs, *Voltaire*, 122–3.

118 Voltaire, *Traité sur la tolérance*, 51; Pinot, *La Chine*, 279; Gay, *Enlightenment*, ii. 391–2.

119 Voltaire, *Essai sur les mœurs*, i. 70, 220–1.

120 Ibid. 71, 224; Hsia, 'Euro-Sinica', 22–4.

During the 1730s and 1740s, the problem of classical Chinese thought in relation to natural reason and natural religion, as bequeathed by Bayle, Leibniz, and Wolff, remained central to the European Enlightenment. Vico's friend Doria figured among those who joined in this convoluted contest though, being in a church-dominated Italy, he did so only in the privacy of his own study, composing, some time after 1728, a sixty-page manuscript treatise about Confucius, entitled *Lettera critica, metafisica, e istorica fatta a fine di esaminare qual sia stata la filosofia di Confugio filosofo cinese*, which remained unpublished for centuries. Like Wolff and Voltaire (with whom he was loath to agree about anything), Doria believed China and its history offered a crucial and inspiring exception to the usual dismal story of human brutality, aggression, self-deception, and failure and that for political stability, cultural cohesion, and the excellence of its moral system, the Chinese had indeed set an unparalleled example to the world.

If one wishes to know why China was exceptional, it was, he maintained, giving his perspective an anti-Jesuit twist and avoiding resort to 'natural theology', because there, unlike the rest of the world, a coherent philosophy based solely on reason, namely that of Confucius—and the *philosophia practica* he taught—had been made the general work-plan of society as a whole.[121] Unlike Vico, who stressed rather the moral influence of collective ancient institutions,[122] Doria did not doubt Confucius' philosophy was chiefly responsible for the high moral standards in China, the tradition of upright government and curbing antisocial impulses towards violence, persecution, and tyranny.[123] The main problem posed by classical Chinese thought for philosophers, argued Doria, remained as it had been for half a century, that of whether Confucius' philosophy is Spinozistic, or as he preferred to put it, whether Confucius was a follower of Plato or Spinoza. Until this question was resolved, it seemed to him nothing of importance could be said about Chinese thought. Had Confucius really declared the universe, or the world, to be God, it would mean, held Doria, that he bases his admirable moral philosophy on a metaphysics 'uniforme a Spinosa, e direttamente contrario a Platone' [at one with Spinoza and directly contrary to Plato].[124]

Assuredly, there were grounds to hesitate. Confucius enjoins the people to worship the heavens. 'But when I then consider that Confucius declared the soul immortal, and reward and punishment after death, I see Confucius resembles Plato more than Spinoza and only decreed worship of the heavens to instil a concept of God as something immense, beautiful and superior to men.'[125] But in finally classifying Confucius as ultimately Platonic, rather than Spinozistic, what counts most, averred Doria, is his attributing intelligence and providence to God.[126] If Confucius 'gave China the most perfect criteria of human morality and politics', this could

121 Doria, *Manoscritti napoletani*, iv. 17–18, 90, 112, 115.

122 Vico, *Nuova scienza terza* (1744), 32–3, 137.

123 Doria, *Manoscritti napoletani*, v. 108.

124 Ibid. iv. 33; Zambelli, *Formazione filosofica*, 306–8.

125 Doria, *Manoscritti napoletani*, iv. 89.

126 Ibid. iv. 36–7.

never have happened had he really nurtured the same idea of God as the *Spinosisti*: for from an idea of God as something material one cannot derive the ideal of brotherly love, or the foundational concepts of justice, constancy, sobriety, prudence, 'all virtues taught by Confucius and of which the *Deisti* deny the real existence and the real essence'.[127]

Montesquieu, whose account of Chinese political institutions noticeably helped lessen the prestige of China in the West, privately inclined more to a *Bayliste* than Leibnizian view of classical Chinese philosophy. His opinions on this topic, he reports, were influenced by conversations 'que j'ai eues avec M. Hoange', that is, once again, Arcade Huang with whom, in 1714, he became acquainted in Paris, presumably through their mutual acquaintance Fréret. Huang, a uniquely precious cultural asset in the West, having been assigned by Bignon to compile a handbook designed to promote knowledge of Chinese culture, society, and history,[128] from him Montesquieu learnt that Confucianism had long been the dominant philosophical sect in China, though the 'Tao' and the 'Foë' [Buddhists], in the latter case with monks of both sexes who remain celibate, were also integral to the picture.[129] In his early notes, or *Spicilège*, of around 1718, Montesquieu remarks that he had also discovered that Confucius did not, despite Jesuit claims, uphold the immortality of the soul.[130] Rather the soul, in Confucianism, is merely a thin material substance or vapour, permeating the body which entirely dissipates at death.

Returning to these themes several times, Montesquieu observed in some jottings, dating from the 1730s or early 1740s, that both Confucius and the Chinese *literati* more generally, doubtless in part because they lived some 500 years before Christ, had no notion at all 'de l'immatérialité, et sont à proprement parler athées ou spinozistes'. Their regarding *T'ien* as the world-soul or the world itself, something which acts necessarily and is 'fatalement déterminée et determine de même', nevertheless had good consequences for morality and social tranquillity even if it helped buttress an empire he deemed despotic and one which left little room for individual liberty.[131] Unlike Voltaire, Saint-Hyacinthe, and Doria, Montesquieu adopted a distinctly anti-Jesuit perspective on China but, at the same time, could never wholly escape from an element of contradiction in his conclusions on this vexed topic. Indeed, the undeniable excellence of Chinese moral philosophy he came to view as a paradox, a local peculiarity which his cultural relativism and stress on he cultural particularity of religions, helped him render specific to China. Confucianism, like Stoicism, he reiterates in *L'Esprit des lois*, despite denying immortality of the soul, nevertheless derives from such 'bad' principles consequences 'admirables pour la société'.[132]

Attempting to reconcile what he saw as both positive and negative features in the Chinese imperial political and cultural system, in his private notebooks, *Mes*

[127] Doria, *Manoscritti napoletani*, iv. 90.
[128] Ibid. iv. 47; Spence, *Question of Hu*, 16, 54.
[129] Montesquieu, *Œuvres complètes*, 368.
[130] Ibid. 395.
[131] Ibid. 369; Carrithers, 'Democratic and Aristocratic', 137.
[132] Montesquieu, *Œuvres complètes*, 702; Courtney, 'Montesquieu and Natural Law', 58.

pensées, he claimed the Chinese, for all the defects of their political constitution, lived under a moral code 'la plus parfaite et la plus pratique' that any people had developed in that part of the world.[133] One must simply accept, concluded Montesquieu, that the classical Chinese had forged a slavish political culture based on 'obedience' and the sway of the rod, and were at the same time virtual 'Spinozists' and yet, despite all this, had developed a surpassingly fine *philosophia practica* in the moral sphere. Indeed, it seemed clear to him that the Jesuits had falsely raised hopes for their Christian missionary enterprise with an inaccurate account of Chinese philosophy which misled Chinese and Europeans alike, deceiving the first into supposing the Christians 'étaient du culte chinois', and the latter into imagining that 'les Chinois avaient le culte Chrétien' which, particularly in terms of his own particularist cultural geography, made no sense at all.[134]

The Early Enlightenment's fundamental disagreement as to whether Confucianism was Spinozistic or not slowly lapsed but was never resolved. What did change was that by the middle of the century the Chinese 'card' had to a large extent been captured by Voltaire and the providential Deists and began to be dropped by the radical fringe as well as increasingly rejected by the churches and by disciples of Montesquieu repelled by the despotic character of the Chinese empire. Prior to 1750, for several decades, all strands of the Enlightenment (except perhaps the Thomasians) had agreed that classical Chinese society was a model society adhering to an ethical system and awareness of the law of nations equalled by no other. Whether one approached the question from a *Malebranchiste*-Baylean standpoint, or a Leibnizian-Jesuit, Wolffian, or Voltairean one, it seemed there was no need of the Gospels, or any revelation, to achieve an orderly, secure society based on wisdom, justice, virtue, and 'le bien public'. By around 1750, however, the position was perceptibly changing, with the radical tendency divesting itself of much of its former enthusiasm for China and the churches devising a counter-strategy to sap the arguments of both Voltaire and the non-providential Deists, by disparaging Chinese society itself and undermining the prestige of its *philosophia practica*.

The Abbé Nicolas-Sylvestre Bergier, for example, in his *Apologie de la religion chrétienne* (1769), accused the *philosophes* of having so few scruples about misleading the French public with lies that they missed no opportunity to belittle faith and religion by misinforming readers on the subject of Chinese morality and society. The *philosophes* habitually celebrate 'les mœurs et le gouvernement des Chinois comme un prodige'; yet reliable recent travellers' reports completely contradict them, presenting an entirely different picture.[135] Far from being exemplary products of Confusian virtue, the Chinese, countered Bergier, were lazy, obsequious, avaricious, and deceitful, diligent at nothing but the arts of trickery and deceit. The mandarins might all be diligent disciples of Confucius; but rather than employing their laws to curb crime and wrongdoing, he alleges, they mostly did so

133 Montesquieu, *Œuvres complètes*, 1075; Pinot, *La Chine*, 409–10.

134 Montesquieu, *Œuvres complètes*, 368; Kingston, 'Montesquieu on Religion', 379.

135 Bergier, *Apologie*, ii. 16–17.

to enrich themselves at the expense of everyone else. These wise magistrates 'ont tant fait de progrès dans la morale', he remarked sarcastically, that they conspire together with robbers to despoil strangers.

As more detailed reports about Chinese society and its shortcomings became available, and the image of Chinese society began to fray at the edges, radical thinkers such as Diderot, Boulanger, and Mably reacted to the change of mood by insisting on more realism and refusing to allow the question of Chinese thought the prominence it had enjoyed formerly, and finally by disengaging from the debate entirely, abandoning this topic to Voltaire and Montesquieu. Diderot, who personally prepared the substantial article 'Chinois', making extensive use of extracts from Le Comte and Brucker, published in the third volume of the *Encyclopédie* in November 1753, portrays Chinese society as basically idolatrous and corrupt, its arts and sciences as backward and stagnant, and its politics as slavish and based on abject obedience; yet while deeming Confucius' metaphysics absurd, he still at the same time warmly praised Confucian moral philosophy and social responsibility.[136]

This new radical perspective was thus a response partly to the widely influential views of Voltaire and Montesquieu, and partly to the aspersions of Christian writers and recent travellers' unfavourable accounts of China. It also reflected Diderot's and other radical *philosophes*' innate scepticism about the existence of any 'sages nations'.[137] Rather than extol a particular people, they preferred to promote the view that men are virtually the same everywhere, being determined by the same impulses and desires. Very likely, this post-1750 change of perspective was connected also to the strengthening anti-absolutist, republican tendency on the radical wing of the *parti philosophique* allied to a willingness to accept that Voltaire and Montesquieu were right to see Confucius and his followers as advocates of a monarchical despotism in which supreme authority is vested exclusively in the emperor.[138]

At the same time, Voltaire's claim in his *Essai sur les mœurs* that Chinese imperial rule was so benign that the emperor may justly be seen as 'premier philosophe' of China, a figure guided by wise councillors, was scornfully rejected by Diderot.[139] Chinese society thus came to be viewed by the radical stream as steeped in paternalism, subservience, and obsequiousness, a system of political tyranny reaching down from the court through every level of society to that of the humble peasant family; and to this was increasingly added their realization (again partly following Montesquieu) that, despite the deep impact of Confucius, Chinese popular culture was as steeped in superstition as any, Diderot accounting the 'three religions' of modern China—Taoisme, Buddhism, and neo-Confusianism—merely three different combinations of popular superstition, idolatry, polytheism, and atheism.[140]

[136] Koseki, 'Diderot', 126, 131; Roberts, 'L'Image', 94; Hsia, 'Euro-Sinica', 26–7; Cohen, 'Diderot and the Image', 223–4.

[137] Hsia, 'Euro-Sinica', 27.

[138] Proust, *Diderot*, 122, 368, 410; Benítez, *Face cachée*, 420; Cohen, 'Diderot and the Image', 225.

[139] Cohen, 'Diderot and the Image', 230.

[140] Diderot, 'Chine', 339–41; Roberts, 'L'Image', 94–5.

26

Is Religion Needed for a Well-Ordered Society?

1. SEPARATING MORALITY FROM THEOLOGY

Spinoza and his circle, followed by Bayle, Collins, Mandeville, and then the French materialists, formulated arguments, proclaiming divine revelation and miracles impossible and all religious authority based on interpreting divine revelation unreal, misleading, and, where insufficiently subjected to secular control, politically dangerous, which were hard to refute. At the same time, Spinoza and Bayle, and many lesser radical writers, taught that morality, while natural and essential to all human societies, is not innate in men's minds and cannot be cogently anchored in theology or religious authority, even though the vast majority think otherwise. Morality, for the radical fringe, is something grasped exclusively through the power of reason, though religion may perhaps be indispensable for propagating some of its most basic rules.

Of course, most contemporaries totally rejected such conclusions in favour of revealed religion. But this was insufficient to prevent radical ideas posing an overwhelming challenge to traditional conceptions of morality during the Early Enlightenment. For religious authority was undeniably everywhere deeply splintered and reduced owing to the unresolved Reformation splits within Christendom, and the post-1650 general intellectual crisis. In the new circumstances, even those most implacably opposed to radical ideas had to ask whether there really is, in fact, some clearly demonstrable, rational test proving revelation, faith, and ecclesiastical authority indispensable or at least incontestably beneficial to society's well-being. Few questioned religion's indispensability, or that Christianity was the faith on which society's proclaimed values, institutions, laws, and procedures should be based. But the fact defiance of religious authority and philosophical libertinism were spreading, along with growing awareness of the great variety of the world's religions and reports of the existence of 'atheistic' societies functioning without any organized religion, helped make Bayle's question 'whether organized religion is necessary for a well-regulated society?' the pivotal moral query of the era.[1]

[1] Harris, 'Answering', 229–30, 252.

Figure 3 Copper engraved portrait of Spinoza (1677) bound into some of the Latin and Dutch copies of the first edition of B.d.S. *Opera posthuma* (By courtesy of the Vereniging het Spinozahuis, Amsterdam)

This was not, admittedly, a wholly new debate. In essence, Giordano Bruno had already posed and answered this question along radical lines. Stressing the infinity, harmony, and unity of the cosmos it seemed to him that no revelation or confession can have any general validity. Justice and morality must rest on universal and purely worldly foundations. Drawn to the Protestant Reformers in part, especially their rejection of images, monasticism, and the cult of the saints, he later reacted strongly against both Calvinist intolerance and Luther's principle of salvation by 'faith alone' as ultimately destructive of morality; for good works can then no longer contribute to salvation, and grace becomes an undeserved gift bestowed in exchange merely for faith.[2] Their own doctrines convinced the philosopher of Nola that neither Catholicism, nor Calvinism, nor Lutheranism are morally persuasive and hence none of them is the truth. But Bruno could only search for the universal basis of morality in strict privacy, as a speculative philosopher in deep isolation; Spinoza and Bayle, by contrast, brought the issues of morality, charity, and justice, shorn of theology, directly into the public arena.

Van den Enden, Meyer, Koerbagh, Cuffeler, van Balen, Walten, and Beverland, in Holland, followed by Boulainvilliers, Toland, Collins, Mandeville, Radicati, Jean-Frédéric Bernard, Bruzen de La Martinière, Knutzen, Wagner, Stosch, Lau, Hatzfeld, Edelmann, Du Marsais, Fréret, Meslier, d'Argens, Diderot, Morelly, and doubtless dozens of others, strove to break the churches' hold over social and political values in their own societies while recognizing this makes little sense without simultaneously substituting a cogent secular ethics independent of religious tradition, anchored in Man's tangible social and political needs alone.

The only conceivable alternative to such a radical secession from the past, free of appeal to religious authority, was the essentially unphilosophical 'Christian Deism' of Chubb, Thomas Woolston (1670–1733), and Thomas Morgan (d. 1743). Morgan, a former dissenting minister, dismissed from his living at Frome, in Somerset, for Socinian leanings, in his major work, *The Moral Philosopher* (1737), rejects all 'sacerdotal superstition', irrational dogmas like the Trinity, prophecies, and miracles, but simultaneously insists the Chinese, Persians, Jews, and ancient Greeks all utterly failed to provide a sound moral basis for humanity using reason alone since only a rationalized Christianity, centred on the moral teachings of the Bible, reveals the 'most plain and necessary truths, such as are founded in the eternal immutable reason and fitness of things'.[3] Unless one adopted Morgan's, Woolston's or Chubb's passionately mystical, figurist and biblicist rejection of 'philosophy' and their emotional, quasi-theological rhetoric, the task of re-evaluating all values and reconstructing morality on an entirely universal and egalitarian basis could only devolve on those philosophers who wholly separated morality from religion and theology.

[2] Gatti, 'Giordano Bruno', 151–6; Mendoza, 'Metempsychosis', 280–4, 297.

[3] Morgan, *Moral Philosopher*, 144–5, 168; Young, *Religion and Enlightenment*, 38–9, 188–9; Trapnell, 'Peut-on dégager', 322.

One might label the kind of moral philosophy which rejects all religious underpinning, mysticism, and appeal to supernatural agency 'utilitarian' since it invokes only worldly functions and values. But this would not be altogether exact, given the term's close association with Jeremy Bentham (1748–1832) who, though in part an heir to the Radical Enlightenment, modified its legacy in some respects in a *dirigiste*, pro-colonial direction. The term 'utilitarian' hence hints at a governmental, top-down perspective ultimately incompatible with the Spinozists' libertarian premisses. Accordingly, it seems best to label the Spinozist-*Bayliste* approach to moral philosophy monist or simply radical.

In any case, their starting point was Hobbes's dictum, in the *Leviathan*: 'do not to another, which thou wouldest not have done to thy selfe.' The core of the Spinozistic moral code is already evident, if somewhat simplistically formulated, in Koerbagh's chapter 'on good and on bad' in *Een Ligt Schijnende in Duystere Plaatsen* (1668).[4] A human morality free of theological tutelage, held Koerbagh, must rest on the principle that everyone acts in their own interest, or according to what seems best to them, so that something is 'immoral', or 'wrong', only where it damages oneself or another: 'that is, all a person's doings are good before God wherever he is not being harmful to himself, or to his neighbour.'[5] Here was a premiss tied to a basic equality between oneself and all other men, resting on Hobbes's claim that it is a law of nature that 'every man acknowledge other for his equall by nature',[6] but widening it to apply more consistently than in Hobbes, becoming the overriding principle in politics and toleration as well as morality.

Koerbagh, though, is hardly very clear. What does it mean to say one is 'harming' or not harming oneself, or another? In what was probably his first work, the *Short Treatise*, of the late 1650s, Spinoza takes further the idea that 'goet en kwaad niet anders is als betrekkinge' [good and bad are nothing other than a relationship], holding that nothing is good or bad in itself but only in relation to something else: hence moral good and evil do not exist in nature and all judgements about the goodness or badness of anything exist only in the mind, as judgements about the usefulness of things to ourselves, comparisons between two things, or else judgements about whether something is a good or less good example of a type.[7] At this stage, however, he says little about the different categories of value relativity (utilitarian, comparative, and model-relative) capable of rescuing human value-judgements, and hence morality, from a complete relativism in which there is no way to rank one man's 'good' against another's 'evil', or a third man's 'less good' or 'better', subjectivity which prevents anyone's conduct or life-style being accounted better or worse than someone else's, or having improved, stood still, or got worse.

At first, it was easier to see what Spinoza was dismantling than what he was putting in its place. Indeed, for decades he was often portrayed exclusively as the

4 Koerbagh, *Een Ligt Schijnende*, 226.

5 Ibid. 227–9; Jongeneelen, 'Philosophie politique', 254–5.

6 Hobbes, *Leviathan*, ch. 15.

7 Spinoza, *Korte Verhandeling*, 289; Jarrett, 'Spinoza', 159–61, 166.

iconoclast of moral absolutes. Laurent François's *Preuves de la religion de Jésus-Christ contre les Spinosistes et les Déistes* (4 vols., Paris, 1751), for instance, rightly identifies Spinoza's moral thought as the underpinning of contemporary French materialism, but construes it as just a levelling of men to the status of animals and plants. By eliminating absolute good and evil Spinoza allegedly provided a purely libertine creed which legitimizes fornication, homosexuality, adultery, murder, and robbery. His morality of 'chacun pour sa propre conservation', held François, must inevitably reduce society to moral chaos and a general war of all against all.[8]

In his *Ethics*, though, Spinoza did strive to forge a viable moral framework reconciling his naturalistic relativism, maintaining that good and evil mean nothing in themselves, with an absolute standard of what is morally right or wrong. By developing a concept of type-relativity around the idea of greater and lesser perfection in human life, Spinoza made it possible to say that something is morally inherently good or bad, or that our passions harm or help us, in relation to a model of human perfectibility naturalistically defined and do so exclusively on the basis of reason, the only criterion of truth he allows.[9] While many different moralities and systems of values exist, he argues, they are by no means equally valid: for all but one stem in different proportions from tradition, revelations, and prophecy as well as reason. If it is disturbing to see that men produce innumerable different systems of morality, they all overlap to an extent and only one, the purely rational, can be absolutely 'true'.

Furthermore, Spinoza argued, men will always concur in acknowledging the moral force of this sole valid system of good and bad, insofar as they are rational, and this he seeks to prove in part iv of his chief work. A remarkable feature of this doctrine that the 'good' is the 'means by which we may approach nearer and nearer to the model of human nature that we set before ourselves' is that there is practically no difference between what is 'good' or bad' in relation to type (that is the rational man), and good and bad relative to what is useful to others, so that, as likewise in Du Marsais later, whoever is more, or less, rational is in society *ipso facto* more, or less, socially responsible, moral, and useful to others.[10]

A crucial question for Spinoza, like Bayle, Boulainvilliers, Du Marsais, Vauvenargues, Diderot, and Lévesque de Pouilly after him, is how to reconcile his morality with his determinism. This he does by tying together virtue, power, desire, and pleasure (joy) in a rather original fashion. Knowledge of good and evil and pursuit of the good are every person's business, he urges, because everyone wants to be happy which means everyone desires what he or she considers good, whether money, sensual pleasure, idleness, luxury, or a life of reason, and everyone shuns what he or she deems 'bad'.[11] This appetite, or desire, is the very 'essence' of man, and everyone is determined by it and in the same way. But the more one seeks one's

8 [François], *Preuves*, i. 370–81.

9 Spinoza, *Collected Works*, i. 545–7, Jarrett, 'Spinoza', 161–2, 165, 168.

10 Jarrett 'Spinoza', 168–9, 175; Spinoza, *Collected Works*, i. 545; [Du Marsais], *Le Philosophe*, 176–7, 188, 200.

11 Spinoza, *Collected Works*, i. 556; Bouchardy, *Pierre Bayle*, 183, 202, 205; Klever, *Ethicom*, 495–6.

own advantage, realistically understood, that is preserves one's being, the more one is 'endowed by virtue', according to Spinoza's terminology. But 'acting absolutely from virtue', holds proposition 24 of part iv of the *Ethics*, 'is nothing else in us but acting, living, and preserving our being (these things signify the same thing) by the guidance of reason, from the foundation of seeking one's own advantage'.[12] Hence insofar as we are rational we will always attempt to secure the best balance of good to evil that we can, for ourselves, and this, it is claimed, will *ipso facto* be the best outcome for everyone, tending to, and promoting, a wider contentment.

Herein lay both the moral content and the claimed objectivity of Spinoza's moral naturalism and the grounds for the claim that religion fails to encourage awareness of how greatly it furthers individual self-interest to adhere to what Du Marsais calls 'les loix de la société'.[13] It was the emancipation of desire and gratification which prompted many to deny there was any moral content here at all. In Spinozism, held François, in 1751, it is in practice only fear of punishment which deters men from violating the civil laws. Ethically speaking, Spinoza leaves the individual free to obey the laws of his country, or not obey them, as he pleases, his only real concern being to evade the rigour of the law as it might be enforced against him. Spinoza invokes intellectual love of God but what his morality really amounts to, held François, is some 'cruels paradoxes' legitimizing antisocial behaviour, even the most horrendous crimes.[14] Love of God here is no more than 'la cupidité ou l'amour des biens sensibles'. Are not sensuality, licentiousness, and adultery matters of complete indifference to the *esprits forts*? *Spinosistes* say individual happiness can not be 'détaché de celui de la société';[15] but this cannot alter the fact most men put their own selfish concerns before those of society.

The characteristic combination of determinism and 'liberty' advanced by Hobbes, Spinoza, Boulainvilliers, Collins, Du Marsais, and the rest was opposed by the main corpus of Enlightenment thought and by most churchmen. Yet, on the opposite side of the arena, there was a hint of support for the radical Deists' determinism from a surprising quarter: the hard-line Calvinist wing of the Counter-Enlightenment. The Lockean Enlightenment's stance, as well as Catholic, Lutheran, and Arminian insistence on free will, while simultaneously asserting God's omniscience and the impossibility of his foreknowledge of the contingent, seemed a blatant contradiction in terms not just to Bayle and the Spinozists but also to such Calvinist stalwarts as Jonathan Edwards who argued—in practice not unlike Bayle—that it is the 'Arminian scheme, and not the scheme of the Calvinists, that is utterly inconsistent with moral government, and with all the laws, precepts, prohibitions, promises and threatenings'.[16]

Insofar as Arminians and others consider it right to 'induce men to what is materially virtuous' by means of instruction, persuasion, precept, and example, held

12 Klever, *Ethicom*, 504–5; Spinoza, *Collected Works*, i. 558; Jarrett, 'Spinoza', 169–71.

13 [Du Marsais], *Le Philosophe*, 192–3.

14 [François], *Preuves*, i. 382–3.

15 Ibid i. 388.

16 Edwards, *Freedom of the Will*, 182, 212–13; Mori, *Bayle philosophe*, 227; Kueklick, *History*, 20–4.

Edwards, they blatantly contradict their own false notions of liberty and moral agency. Arminians not unnaturally retorted by accusing hard-line Calvinists like Edwards of 'agreeing with the ancient Stoics in their doctrine of fate, and with Mr Hobbes in his opinion of necessity',[17] to which Edwards replied that he had never read Hobbes and, in any case, not everything in Hobbes and other philosophical necessitarians is wrong. Edwards may not have read Spinoza either; but the Yale theologian certainly had examined, and was here citing, Clarke's account of Spinoza's system to reinforce his own claim that the Arminian position is self-contradictory.[18] Less cogent was his addendum that the moral necessity inherent in the 'perfect nature of the Divine Mind' must not be confused with the inferior and servile 'subjection to necessity' of the materialists.[19]

Spinoza's reformation of morality gained further ground thanks to Bayle's unrelenting efforts to drive in the wedge inserted by his predecessor between ethics and religion. Total separation of morality and theology was indeed the very cornerstone of Radical Enlightenment, the point at which the systems of Spinoza and Bayle almost totally converge. To detachment of morality from theology, Bayle added, to the consternation of the whole Huguenot diaspora, the proposition that revealed religion based on miracles, church dogma, and an afterlife, whether Christian or not, is neither requisite nor helpful, in upholding a moral order geared to the well-being of society. Here, Bayle and, later, Diderot ventured beyond Spinoza: for where Christianity, for the latter, teaches 'obedience' to socially useful moral principles, Bayle removes the force even of this, claiming a society sincere in upholding the Christian ethic would be ill adjusted to the realities of life and unable to survive for long. The more one studies the history of one's own time, and previous centuries, he argues, the more one sees that every society threatened by neighbours would soon collapse 'si elle se conformoit à l'esprit évangélique'.[20]

With this, Bayle professed not to be attacking religion but merely proving philosophy has nothing to do with faith and cannot support it.[21] Some took this pseudo-fideist stance at face value; but whether one accepted it or not, Bayle's last books, the *Continuation des Pensées diverses* and the *Réponse aux questions d'un provincial*, claim an 'atheistic' society can be morally viable, and more so than a Christian one, being better able to defend itself and far more likely to uphold toleration; his last works also held there are no grounds for considering religion, revealed or otherwise, requisite for upholding the core moral values essential for society.[22] Unquestioning submission of faith is justifiable, philosophically, says Bayle, only by means of Pyrrhonism, leading many later interpreters wrongly to assume that his

17 Edwards, *Freedom of the Will*, 257–9, 270, 284, 322.

18 Ibid. 259–60, 263–4; Marsden, *Jonathan Edwards*, 73.

19 Edwards, *Freedom of the Will*, 282, 284, 305–6, 311.

20 Bayle, *Continuation*, ii. 600; Pascual López, *Bernard Mandeville*, 97–8.

21 Bayle, *Réponse*, iii. 642–3.

22 Bayle, *Continuation*, ii. 591–2, 598–600, 757–9; Gros, 'Tolérance et le problème', 436–7; Brogi, *Teologia senza verità*, 177, 182.

'fideism' must therefore be 'Pyrrhonist' and his supposed Pyrrhonism applicable also to moral concepts.[23] Yet, nothing could be less Pyrrhonist than Bayle's system of moral, social, and political thought. Indeed, he vehemently rejects Pyrrhonism in these spheres, especially because (incomprehensibly for those who maintain Bayle's Calvinist piety) Pyrrhonism permits no proper conception of goodness and justice. Sound moral ideas, holds Bayle, can only be derived by natural reason and, hence, stand diametrically against both faith and every kind of scepticism including fideism.

Nor is there any inconsistency here. There is a basic contradiction only if one takes Bayle's 'fideism' seriously, which by the end of his life few of those who knew him any longer did.[24] Far from expounding Pyrrhonism, Bayle is really highlighting the morass of moral difficulties Pyrrhonism creates with the ostensible aim of showing that only fideism can justify faith which, he adds with a rhetorical flourish, everyone agrees is the true basis of our moral and social system. But his real intention, contemporary readers saw, is to convince us of the exact opposite, namely that faith can never be the basis of our moral system. What is 'divine' in Scripture can be known to be such only through testing its precepts and claims by means of our natural reason, and this alone proves or disproves their moral worth; hence religious faith can play no part in identifying what is ethically valuable in Scripture nor construct our edifice of moral *fundamenta*, a stance intended to be a *reductio ad absurdum* of fideist claims.

Whatever the truth of Bayle's ultimate religious convictions, the effect of his arguments, Leibniz notes in his *Theodicy*, is to reinforce Spinoza's contention that there is nothing miraculous in the operation of general laws, or any ground for believing in miracles as exceptions to those laws. The result is that natural, textual, and philosophical questions of whatever sort can only be genuinely investigated omitting all appeals to faith, God, theology, or ecclesiastical authority.[25] From this it follows that issues of morality, toleration, and politics, which he, no less than Spinoza, holds should be regulated according to 'reason', must always be settled independently of theology and faith. Even if there remain many believers in society, Christian values can then have no part in explaining or justifying ethics, laws, institutions, and the social ideals of the state. Already, in the *Commentaire philosophique* (1686), Bayle attempts to explain how we should frame a universal secular morality from basic principles: if we rely on natural reason alone, we have, he says, 'une règle sure et infaillible' by which we can judge every moral issue not excepting even the question whether 'une telle ou une telle chose est contenue dans l'Écriture', for without reason our ability to assess anything at all pertaining to life in this world, or any ethical dilemma whatsoever, wholly ceases.

Scepticism, according to Bayle, is the proper tool for judging metaphysical and spiritual questions; but repudiating reason on sceptical grounds when discussing

[23] McKenna, 'Pierre Bayle et la superstition', 59–60; Mori, 'Scepticisme', 277–8.

[24] Bayle, *Réponse*, iv. 139; [Jurieu], *Philosophe de Rotterdam*, 106–7.

[25] Leibniz, *Theodicy*, 334, 338.

worldly matters would, he says, create the most appalling moral chaos 'et le pyrrhonisme le plus exécrable qui se puisse imaginer'. Indeed, it is an essential rule of social and political debate that every particular dogma, whether one advocates it because it is clearly scriptural, or on some other grounds, must be deemed false if refuted 'par les notions claires et distinctes de la lumière naturelle, principalement à l'égard de la morale'.[26] Hence, when considering moral and social issues pure reason, by which he meant philosophical reason based on geometrical criteria, always has priority, for Bayle, over both faith and scepticism. His denial that theology—and 'fideism' as the chief prop to religion—can ground a universal morality, or society's rules, is all the more final in that he considers this morality ascertained solely via reason the only possible basis of the 'common good', and of all justice in politics and law. However different the style, his system thus delivers a firmly crypto-Spinozist message wholly opposite to that of Locke and Voltaire.

For Bayle, then, reason is far clearer and more authoritative than faith or theology when judging questions of social justice, legislation, politics, and institutions.[27] His contention that faith is irrelevant to morality and his disturbing topos of the 'virtuous atheist' were then further elaborated by Collins, Mandeville, Gueudeville, Radicati, Jean-Frédéric Bernard, d'Argens, and others in the next generation of radical writers for whom every religion is deemed inherently indifferent, and ultimately opposed, to the common interest and 'le bien civil'.[28] Morally and socially, therefore, radical thought as grounded by Spinoza and Bayle was indeed revolutionary and trebly so. First, it repudiates all theology and hence topples ecclesiastical authorities as arbiters or judges of the morality on which society and society's laws should be based. Secondly, it insists the good of society is the highest good in ethics and that society and the new morality must hence be exclusively built on the principles of equality and reciprocity so that, by implication at least, it destroys all legitimization of kingship, social hierarchy, and slavery. Finally, its basic equality included an equal right to property which seemed in some very vague sense to promote 'égalité de biens', or at any rate not too much inequality of means, an impulse at least towards modifying existing institutionalized and legalized gross inequality of wealth.

During the Early Enlightenment Spinoza's ethical system was restated in an astoundingly large number of different and often exotic contexts, including that of Lahontan's and Gueudeville's Canadian Hurons, accounted by Bruzen de La Martinière 'de tous les sauvages, les plus spirituels et les plus sages'.[29] The Huron 'Adario', in Gueudeville's 1705 version of Lahontan's *Voyages*, claims the morality of his people rests solely on the principles of 'bon-sens' and 'équité' and the injunction to harm neither oneself nor others, 'faire tout le bien raisonnablement possible à sa propre personne, et à ses semblables, voilà nôtre jurisprudence, ce sont toutes nos

[26] Ibid. 97; Gros, 'Tolérance et le problème', 417, 429; Mori, *Bayle philosophe*, 46.
[27] Bayle, *Continuation*, ii. 640–1; McKenna, 'Pierre Bayle: moralisme', 343.
[28] Bernard, *Réflexions morales*, 22–3, 170–1, 292; Taranto, *Du déisme à l'athéisme*, 417–24.
[29] Bruzen de La Martinière, *Abrégé portatif*, i. 273.

loix'.[30] Doing good to one self and to others is viewed here as an axiom as in Spinoza's doctrine that the 'greatest good of those who seek virtue is common to all, and can be enjoyed by all equally'.[31] This axiom governs their moral system, says Adario, because 'la raison est nôtre unique et souverain juge' and reason dictates that men should 'rendre heureux les uns les autres, et se concourir au bonheur commun par une égalité de biens'.[32] A like moral order prevails in the social utopias devised a few years later by Tyssot de Patot. Similarly, d'Argens in 1746 published at Berlin his ironic parable of a utopian society of *singes philosophiques* [philosophical apes] where the same moral order based on perfect equality prevails and the first principle is that we should not do to others what we do not wish to have done to ourselves.[33]

Morelly, who ardently believed human happiness rests on virtue, and unhappiness stems from lies, flattery, theft, and exploitation, developed a radical republicanism and primitive communism infused with an intense *moralisme*, urging rulers to understand that they exercise sovereignty not to defend the 'absurd' theses of Calvin, Luther, or Muhammad but exclusively to protect 'la République', the freedom and dignity of their subjects, and suppress 'le crime et tout phanatisme persécuteur'.[34] It was integral to this radical tradition that the true fundamental laws of society or what Morelly called the 'loix sacrées de l'humanité' cannot be upheld without simultaneously battling what he termed the 'vérités surnaturelles de la théologie'. Hence the new morality, translated into politics, categorically required either full separation of church and state or else Spinoza's and Meyer's subjection of the public church to supervision by office-holders of the state. In d'Argens's republic of the apes, egalitarian laws are based on the eternal values of the moral system; one still finds temples dedicated to virtue but they are devoid of priests since whoever lives 'virtuously' suffices on that ground to be deemed a *prêtre de la vérité*.[35]

The only real basis of morality is reason and nature, so that morality, or so Morelly, like other radicals, supposed, can be worked out with almost mathematical precision.[36] Anchored in the basic equality of all men, and of peoples as of individuals, such a morality requires an uncompromisingly republican politics and a duty to recognize, given the variety of the world's political systems that we actually see, that some peoples are far freer, and therefore happier, than others. Lahontan (Gueudeville) has his Adario depict Huron society as a republic of perfect liberty and equality built on an ethics governed exclusively by 'la droite raison', something, he says, European nations with their kings, ecclesiastics, and theology have, at vast cost to themselves, banished from their midst. To repair the harm, urges Adario,

30 Lahontan, rev. Gueudeville, *Voyages du baron*, ii. 269.

31 Spinoza, *Collected Works*, i. 564.

32 Lahontan, rev. Gueudeville, *Voyages du baron*, ii. 271.

33 [D'Argens], *Songes philosophiques*, 14; Ehrard, *L'Idée*, 682.

34 [Morelly], *Basiliade*, i. 166–9, 189; [Morelly], *Le Prince*, ii. 55.

35 [D'Argens], *Songes philosophiques*, 12–13; Ehrard, *L'Idée*, 484, 683.

36 [Morelly], *Basiliade*, i. 206–7, ii. 53; Coe, *Morelly*, 76.

European thinkers should learn from the Indians. 'C'est ici', he assures his French interlocutor, 'où vos prétendus sages devroient venir entendre la voix de la Nature qu'ils écoutent et qu'ils consultent si peu.'[37]

Jean-Frédéric Bernard, through the mouthpiece of his fictitious *philosophe persan* travelling in the West, in 1711, restates Bayle's strictures about Europe's twisted conventional morality in still sharper terms. Ridiculing the arrogance and hypocrisy of Christians in claiming a higher morality and then behaving like everyone else, he complains of the rank injustice of their supposing that by some special divine dispensation they will be 'saved', through faith in Christ, whilst others, morally no worse, or better, than themselves, must be eternally damned. Deeply unimpressed by western moral standards and reasoning alike, Bernard's 'Persian philosopher' accounts the frequent and terrible wars fought in Europe proof enough, were this much needed, of Christendom's moral bankruptcy. Where the proclaimed core of Christian morality is gentleness and patience, he protests, the actual ethics of the Christian is generally 'un zèle faux et cruel, mêlé de vengeance, de haine et d'orgueil'.[38] So blatant is the contradiction, and dire that religion's schisms, that he imagines the day might come when 'la désunion des incirconcis' will compel all their sects finally to submit to the superior unity and cohesion of Islam.[39]

No less subversive than Bayle's separation of philosophy and theology, and of morality from religion, and his demolition of *consensus gentium*, was his contention that paganism, idolatry, and superstition are more harmful to society than atheism, because they are morally more detrimental.[40] For the *rationaux*, like Locke and Leibniz, it was axiomatic that salvation through Christ is the sole path to individual redemption and simultaneously the best and most reliable basis for the social and moral order. Later, Montesquieu resumed the discussion, vigorously criticizing what he called this 'paradoxe de Bayle', rejecting the claim that it is less socially harmful to believe in no religion than a false one.[41] He held the reverse to be true, dismissing Bayle's contention that a truly Christian society would be ill equipped to survive in the real world as patently absurd. Where Bayle denies Christianity is what best sustains societies, claiming morality is independent of religion and a matter of conforming to reason, Montesquieu reverses this, reasserting the indispensability of organized religion for the upholding of morality.

One of Bayle's most provocative remarks was his observation that Spinoza's moral thought is 'un exemple éclatant' of the truth that even a system based on the most 'formal atheism' that has ever been taught may readily produce an impressive moral philosophy and a set of valuable maxims as to the duties of the honest man.[42] Against

37 Lahontan, rev. Gueudeville, *Voyages du baron*, ii. 258.

38 Bernard, *Reflexions morales*, 189.

39 Ibid. 222–3.

40 Brogi, *Teologia senza verità*, 175–6, 179.

41 Montesquieu, *L'Esprit des lois*, 698–9; Kingston, 'Montesquieu on Religion', 389–90; Ehrard, *L'Esprit des mots*, 273, 283–4.

42 Bayle, *Continuation*, ii. 728, 759; Brogi, *Teologia senza verità*, 163–5; Israel, 'Pierre Bayle's Political Thought', 379.

this, Jacques Bernard argued that the thesis of Machiavelli, Spinoza, and other 'atheists' that religion is the invention of 'politiques' to compel men to their duties amounts to an admission that religion, irrespective of which religion, is in general more effective for sustaining societies than 'atheism'.[43] Spinoza asks who can fail to see that 'both the Testaments are just a training for obedience, that each has its purpose in this alone, that men should sincerely hearken to God?'[44] But by arguing thus, held Bernard, he effectively grants that atheism destroys conscience, respect for duty, and all sense of obligation, things every society requires for its existence.

Society cannot subsist, contends Bernard, without 'la pratique de ces devoirs' and hence, 'atheism', in the sense of denial of a Creator, providence, and revelation, violates society's most precious concerns vastly more than idolatry or paganism, indeed entails 'la destruction totale des sociétez'.[45] But Bayle totally disagreed. Stressing the frightful consequences of bigotry, cruelty, and credulity, and noting that pagan Greek cults inculcate dread of wholly immoral gods mostly moved by base and violent passions, he argued that anyone reared in such a milieu will be incapable of grasping that pride, greed, ambition, lasciviousness, love of luxury, violence, and desire for vengeance are immoral. On the contrary, what the idolatrous cults of the Graeco-Roman world demanded of men, was exclusively subservience, adoration, and flattery. In Bayle's eyes, Greek pagan religion meant 'la renversement de la morale' which is why, he alleges, Socrates felt it requisite to stake his life against such idolatry.[46]

Bernard's thesis of the universal utility of religion, even false religion, for organizing and stabilizing societies Bayle dismisses as incoherent, firmly rejecting its basic premiss. He denies that the common people lack respect for the laws or mock their magistrates when these are not backed by religious doctrine, even a false religion.[47] It is untrue, he avers, that classical religion inspired virtue and frowned on wrongdoing, rendering pagans more orderly in their morality than those who worship 'ni les idoles ni le vrai Dieu'.[48] If the political leadership of the Hellenic city-states and republican Rome successfully countered the viciousness fostered by their publicly established cults this was entirely due, contends Bayle, to the influence on public life of reason and the philosophers. Atheistic thinkers like Epicurus, he remarked, believed in no gods but nevertheless had an admirable ability to formulate moral concepts by examining what was and what was not 'conforme aux règles de la raison'.[49] To appreciate the impressive political and moral achievements of the Greeks, he argues, one must consider the wisdom of their statesmen and especially their philosophers; for it was these who chiefly combated the effects of idolatry which nurtured, in his opinion, only moral disorder, vice, and superstition.[50]

43 Bayle, *Réponse*, iv. 249.
44 Spinoza, *TTP* 221.
45 Bayle, *Réponse*, iv. 267; Bernard, *De l'excellence de la religion*, 352–3.
46 Bayle, *Continuation*, ii. 560, 610–20, 630–1, 643, 658.
47 Ibid. ii. 519; Bost, *Pierre Bayle*, 105–9.
48 Bayle, *Continuation*, ii. 519, 566.
49 Ibid. ii. 722–3.
50 Ibid. ii. 574, 610–31, 640–3; Bayle, *Réponse*, iv. 267, 272–3, 348, 366–7.

The idea that ancient philosophers, before Christ, were capable of forging a viable system of moral theory 'whereof', as Locke put it, 'the world could be convinced', an ethics able to underpin law and institutions as, in their view, Christianity does, was precisely what the *rationaux*, together with Locke, denied. To them, it was self-evidently true that reason alone is inadequate. Locke, while rejecting innateness of ideas, judged the true principles of morality discoverable through experience and reason; but he too claimed this is insufficient to uphold the moral order society requires. Even were it possible 'that out of the sayings of the wise heathens before our Savior's time, there might be a collection made of all those rules of morality which are found in the Christian religion', he held, 'yet this would not at all hinder, but that the world, nevertheless, stood as much in need of our Savior and the morality delivered by him'.[51] Even if we suppose there had been a gatherer of precepts like Stobaeus 'in those times who had gathered the moral sayings from all the sages of the world', yet these would have had no 'authority'. Knowledge of truth is not the same as its effective propagation; for this, high authority is essential and if one does ascribe overriding authority to the ethical teachings of a particular ancient sage, say Epicurus, one would then have to regard all the rest of his doctrine as binding too, were such a thing conceivable. 'But such a body of ethics, proved to be the law of nature from the principles of reason and teaching all the duties of life', concludes Locke, 'I think nobody will say the world had before our Savior's time.'[52]

Locke's, Le Clerc's, and Benard's dictum 'the greatest part cannot know, and therefore they must believe' was indeed persuasive.[53] Philosophy and reason may be wholly ineffective guides for most, countered Bayle, but they sufficed to instruct the magistrates in the Greek city-states, and in Rome, and therefore for producing philosophically and morally based legislation which did effectively curb the untutored and restrain the religiously fomented immorality of the majority. All societies, Christian or not, require institutions embedded in laws anchored in accepted morality so that in pagan society too, thanks to philosophy—whether Socratic, Platonic, Stoic, or Epicurean—and the wisdom of a few statesmen, a social context was wisely and effectively stabilized, at least in the better periods, when a magistrate could not be publicly respected without passing for being a man of honour and probity.[54]

Morally and educationally, argues Bayle, religion and philosophy in ancient Greece and Rome stood in direct opposition. Their admirable administrative, legal, and civic achievements stemmed from philosophical reason locked in combat with 'la théologie fabuleuse'; the good they accomplished was not because but in spite of the latter. The Greek philosophers may have failed to point the way to heaven; but, equally, he retorted, their priests 'ne montrent point le chemin de la vertu',[55] a claim shrewdly tailored to recent research into and discussion of ancient religion. Locke

[51] Locke, *Reasonableness of Christianity*, 172, 175.
[52] Ibid. 172–3; James, *Passion and Action*, 241; Schneewind, 'Locke's Moral Philosophy', 218.
[53] Schneewind, 'Locke's Moral Philosophy', 218; Locke, *Reasonableness of Christianity*, 178–9.
[54] Bayle, *Continuation*, i, *avertissement* pp. 8^{V}–9, 238–9, ii. 635–6.
[55] Ibid. i. 238–9; Brogi, *Teologia senza verità*, 181–3.

too granted a degree of opposition in the pagan Graeco-Roman world between religion and ethics, noting that 'lustrations and processions' are much easier to organize than pursuit of moral truth and that the 'priests that delivered the oracles of heaven, and pretended to speak from the gods, spoke little of virtue and a good life'.[56] Yet to his mind this proves not the superiority of philosophy, urged by Bayle, but rather the indispensability of Christ's mission and the Gospels.

Yet Locke's theology was also, to a degree, a hindrance to later Enlightenment empiricists and sceptics locked in combat with radical thought. Hume jocularly speaks of Locke being 'the first Christian, who ventured openly to assert, that faith was nothing but a species of reason, that religion was only a branch of philosophy, and that a chain of arguments, similar to that which established any truth in morals, politics, or physics, was always employed in discovering all the principles of theology, natural and revealed'.[57] Yet while throwing over his reasoning, Hume nonetheless supports Locke, Le Clerc, and the *rationaux* on the key question of the necessity of revelation for teaching morality, praising Locke's stance as altogether opposed to the 'ill use which Bayle and other libertines made of the philosophical scepticism of the Fathers', in order to align reason, including scepticism itself, with materialism and 'atheism'.[58] It was not, of course, Bayle's 'atheism', or bogus scepticism, which Hume disliked and rejected so much as the overarching role in the social and moral sphere his predecessor accords philosophy. Brilliantly seeing through Bayle's paradoxes, Hume remained as antagonistic as Locke to the hegemony Bayle, like Spinoza and later Diderot, ascribes to reason.

A key point of contention remained the moral content of past religions. Let Bernard contemplate the terrible persecutions unleashed by the Roman provincial governors on the early Christians down to Diocletian's time, averred Bayle, and then see whether he still thinks Graeco-Roman cults better suited than atheism to maintain 'la tranquillité de l'état, et le bien des societez'.[59] The onslaught directed by the Roman governors, he says, was merciless, ferocious, and unspeakably harsh and unjust. But what drove the emperors to resort to such cruelty if not the power of faith and furious indignation of the people? Had the pagans who so afflicted the Christians consulted only the light of natural reason, as, he adds, Spinoza advises, who could doubt they would then *not* have thought of putting to death, torturing, or blighting the lives, of innumerable innocent people?[60] Religion furnished them with what 'la raison leur eût refusé', transforming rulers and magistrates into vile persecutors and 'perturbateurs du repos public'.

From pagan cults, Bayle moves on to all organized religion: no greater plague or misery besets any society than when the community is torn by competing religions or split into warring sects, as the frightful strife of the French Wars of Religion showed all too dreadfully. For whichever denomination temporarily gains the ear of

[56] Locke, *Reasonableness of Christianity*, 169–70, 176.
[57] Hume, *Dialogues*, 111; Fogelin, 'Hume's Scepticism', 90–1.
[58] Hume, *Dialogues*, 111.
[59] Bayle, *Réponse*, iv. 273.
[60] Ibid. iv. 276.

the king directly threatens the lives of the rest. Every citizen is then divided in his loyalties and filled with anxiety for his safety: what troubles and disorder result in the mind of anyone with such split loyalties, he adds, 'qui ne tombera jamais dans l'esprit d'un Spinoziste!'[61] What, he muses aloud, at one point in his argument would be preferable should an epidemic decimate England, for example: would it not be a better solution, for everyone, to repopulate the land with *Spinosistes* than with Catholics?[62]

Who doubts, he continued, with evident emotion, that every Huguenot uprooted and ejected from France by the despicable bigotry and tyranny of Louis XIV, even those least affected by the appalling *dragonades*, must admit, however reluctantly, that it would have been preferable for all the French Protestants, even the staunchest Calvinist pastors, as much as everyone else, had their country been ruled by 'un roi Spinoziste' all of whose subjects 'auroient été Spinosistes' rather than a king filled with Catholic zeal and veneration for the papacy, most of whose subjects 'étoient animé du même esprit'. With a *Spinosiste* firmly on the throne instead of Louis XIV, contended Bayle, everyone would have been better off and no one would have questioned the loyalty or patriotism of the Huguenots whilst they remained loyal to the state and obedient to its institutions and civil laws.[63]

Bernard's and Le Clerc's argument falls, asserts Bayle, because those who avow religious zeal have urgent reasons for destroying the civil peace, and destabilizing society, which atheists lack. In a society where most think theologically, toleration cannot develop from forbearance, scepticism, or indifference but only by means of some non-religious political mechanism which actively disciplines and curbs intolerance.[64] Exasperated by his opponent's evasive sliding between paganism and revealed religion, Bernard reminded Bayle that their dispute was not about pagans but rather whether Christianity 'est propre ou non à maintenir les sociétez', a question responsibly and rationally answered only in the affirmative. Indignant at Bayle's claiming a society of genuine Christians could not ward off their neighbours' envy, greed, and aggression, Bernard recommends that to disabuse himself of this 'étrange paradoxe' he might like to peruse the English Latitudinarians, Tillotson and Sharp, and learn from them that nothing is so well adjusted to the happiness of every man individually, 'et pour celui des sociétez en général', as the Christian faith.[65]

If we know, through faith, that Christianity is the true religion, answered Bayle, nothing proves Christianity offers better or more useful standards in the moral and political spheres than other creeds. For religious doctrine rests on faith alone whereas morality, something which all societies require, is solely a question of reason.[66] The *Spinosistes*, he asserts, like the Confucians of China (whom he considered atheists), see no less clearly than the most pious of Christians the aims and

61 Ibid. iv. 289–90. 62 Gros, 'Tolérance et le problème', 434. 63 Bayle, *Réponse*, iv. 285.

64 Gros, 'Tolérance et le problème', 437.

65 [Bernard], *Nouvelles de la republique des Lettres* (Jan.–June 1705), 322.

66 Bayle, *Continuation*, ii. 574, 591–2, 640–1, 726–7, 757–9.

varieties of moral and social good.[67] If Bernard would like to read Spinoza's writings, he retorted, with obvious intent to provoke, he will find there a moral system admirably expounded and adapted to the needs of civil society.[68] After all, he observes, citing Matthew 10: 34, 35, Jesus Christ does not say his gospel 'ne troubleroit pas les sociétez', rather he proclaimed the opposite—that he would throw society into turmoil;[69] and, indeed, Christianity had proven by and large more prone to strife and division than Islam or other religions and nothing is worse for whatever society than religious strife.

Removing revelation, divine commandment, and ecclesiastical authority as chief foundations for human justice, morality, and political institutions leaves Bayle, like Spinoza before and Mandeville after him, faced with providing a purely philosophical grounding for morality, rule of law, and political legitimacy. Regarding morality and justice, he proceeds according to the premisses expounded in the *Commentaire philosophique*, and later the *Continuation* and *Réponse*, lodging the true foundations of right conduct, or what he terms 'la loi naturelle et éternelle qui montre à tous les hommes les idées de l'honnêteté', purely in the dictates of reason.[70] The same logic which shows that the whole 'est plus grand que sa partie' infallibly demonstrates also, holds Bayle, the moral basis of equity, gratitude to our benefactors, and refraining from doing to others whatever 'nous ne voudrions pas que nous fût fait'.[71]

These moral laws we construct instinctively, that is naturally, and it is crucial to Bayle's thesis that it is through such natural concepts of 'goodness' and just dealing that we construct our idea of 'God', God being basic to men's thoughts and a being who adheres not voluntarily but, in our minds, he argues, necessarily, to goodness and justice. Bayle's 'God' is a powerful symbol in Man's inner mental world. But like Spinoza's, he seemingly has nothing to do with divine providence or actual regulation of the cosmos, it being only an idea in our minds that he rules our consciences and moral notions about conduct.[72] Admittedly, Bayle says this 'Être souverainement parfait, qui gouverne toutes choses' rewards some actions of men, and punishes others; but he does not say this happens supernaturally, or in the hereafter.[73]

Of course, there was never much doubt the *rationaux* and Lockean Latitudinarians would win their battle with Spinoza and Bayle before the public, in the periodicals and in the sermons of the day, nor that the moderate mainstream's intellectual hegemony would long endure. What was less clear, though, was whether they had surmounted Spinoza and Bayle on intellectual grounds, so that behind the scenes the struggle dragged on, requiring more and more elaborate intellectual

[67] Bayle, *Réponse*, iv. 434; Pinot, *La Chine*, 324–5.
[68] Bayle, *Réponse*, iv, 434–5; see also Bayle, *Continuation*, ii. 430, 470.
[69] Bayle, *Réponse*, iv. 456–7.
[70] Bayle, *Commentaire philosophique*, 92; Mori, *Bayle philosophe*, 42–3.
[71] Schlüter, *Französische Toleranzdebatte*, 196–7; McKenna, 'Rationalisme moral', 264, 269.
[72] McKenna 'Rationalisme moral', 267, 272; Mori, *Bayle philosophe*, 253, 338.
[73] Bayle, *Commentaire philosophique*, 98.

weaponry on the part of the moderate mainstream. Leibniz added new metaphysical depth and Barbeyrac the refinements of Pufendorfian Natural Law to the arsenal amassed by Le Clerc and Locke. While accepting the need to construct, via reason, a lay morality independent of churchmen and religious doctrine,[74] Barbeyrac, in contrast to Bayle, yet rejected the full secularization of ethics seeking rather, like Locke, to devolve ethical responsibility onto the individual, by demonstrating morality's dependence on the teachings of the Gospels, Christian doctrine for him being both rational and universally applicable precisely as Bayle denied.[75]

Agreeing with Locke that denial of a providential God dissolves all obligation, indeed the very idea of Natural Law, forfeiting all right to be tolerated in an 'enlightened' society,[76] Barbeyrac insisted on the necessary entwining of Christian values and theology with politics, morality, and law. In this respect, despite its Natural Law component, his thought was a typical product of the Arminian-Lockean Enlightenment, repudiation of Bayle's radical segregation of politics and religion being indeed integral to the Huguenot outlook of the time. Nowhere did their anti-Baylean campaign seem more urgent to the *rationaux* than in the context of the public debate about luxury, vice, and the corruption of morals, and especially the upsurge of libertinism and freethinking, a universal preoccupation in early eighteenth-century western Europe not least in France where, during the 1720s and 1730s, society rapidly became more tolerant, and susceptible to philosophical arguments.

Jaquelot's admonition that rational religion was the answer to the *esprits forts* and that the 'grande corruption des mœurs' affecting society was due to the fact that 'l'on n'enseigne pas d'une manière assez solide les véritez de la religion Chrétienne' was a sentiment widely shared.[77] But precisely this claim of Jaquelot's, that more Christian education and admonition, especially when rationally expounded, would counter freethinking and libertinism and ensure a high level of social and moral order, Bayle declared untenable and false.[78] Nothing is harder, urged Jacquelot, than to reform men's immorality and disorderly conduct. How then can society succeed in this task unless men are thoroughly persuaded of the truths of religion, of the sanctity of its laws and excellence of its promises?[79] It is certain then, he concluded, that the true origin of libertinism and irreligion derives from the inadequate education, and insufficient instruction in Christianity, given to young people.[80] Even among Christians, retorted Bayle, experience 'réfute cela invinciblement' despite their having notions of God's power and anger 'plus distinctes, et plus étendues' than those of idolaters and pagans.[81]

The real problem, argued Bayle, was not inadequate religious teaching but rather inadequacies of government, policing, and law enforcement. Restating his principle

74 Lomonaco, 'Jean Barbeyrac', 253–4; Lomonaco, 'Natural Right', 139–40, 150.
75 Lomonaco, 'Religious Truth', 422–3.
76 Gros, 'Tolérance et le problème', 434–5; Lomonaco, 'Natural Right', 137.
77 Jaquelot, *Conformité*, preface pp. 13–14, 16; Bayle, *Réponse*, v. 216.
78 Bayle, *Réponse*, iv. 434–6, v. 216, 237–8.
79 Jaquelot, *Conformité*, preface pp. 13–14.
80 Ibid., preface p. 16.
81 Bayle, *Continuation*, ii. 690; Mori, *Bayle philosophe*, 175–6; Braun, 'Diderot', 47.

that men do not behave according to their professed beliefs, Bayle cited the nobility, a group frequently the target of his social criticism. Nobles, he held, were usually well enough versed in religion but yet, in their daily lives, mostly adhere to their code of aristocratic honour and reputation, values exciting their ambition and desires in ways 'truths of religion' could not.[82] Aristocrats, therefore, generally engage in every known kind of dissolute, factious, and self-aggrandizing activity, from gambling, duelling, and seduction to political conspiracy, not through ignorance of religion but moved by their passions and against conscience. Aristocrats, then, continually disrupt and behave badly despite being 'très-persuadé qu'ils offensent Dieu'.[83]

To disprove the *rationaux*'s claim that Christian principles best ensure an orderly society, Bayle cites Lahontan's observation, from his Canadian experience, that the number of murders in a particular region rises and fall at different times of the year according to changes in circumstances. From this Bayle infers that religion does not restrain men's passions—and lack of it is not what unbridles appetites: passion for revenge 'et le peu de crainte de la justice humaine', he argues, is what explains seasonal, geographical, and circumstantial variations in the incidence of crime.[84] Overall, he says, experience shows that disorder and licentiousness abound with equal facility among peoples of all types and cults, Christianity no less than paganism, proving, he says, that religion does not repress 'la méchanceté de l'homme et qu'il faut attribuer à d'autres principes' the barriers which maintain the social order.[85] Only well-enforced laws can restrain the passions. He dismissed as a fallacy the notion that fear of worldly punishment has less effect on men than dread 'des loix divines': on the contrary, for every true Christian who prefers to obey God rather than men, urged Bayle, there are a thousand who, in practice, obey men rather than God.[86]

If religious belief teaches obedience, Bayle, like Diderot later, held that neither theology nor ecclesiastical authority can establish or uphold the core principles of ethics, or advance the cause of social stability and a viable politics.[87] Bayle's political thought, consequently, far from being purely 'passive', turns out, in some respects, above all the undermining of ecclesiastical authority and institutionalization of toleration and a secular morality, to be a surprisingly active tool for reforming society. For Bayle does not hesitate to redefine true 'religion', like Spinoza and many later radicals (but in a way vigorously resisted by Montesquieu),[88] to mean basing legislation on sound ethical principles. Human laws should be rooted in 'true religion', meaning, above all, equity, equality, individual liberty, and a comprehensive toleration. It was in this connection that Epicurus came to represent in Bayle's eyes—until Strato assumed this role in his last works—not just the thinker who most consistently explains the *conditio humana* in purely natural terms but equally the ancient

82 Bayle, *Réponse*, v. 226. 83 Ibid. v. 229–30. 84 Ibid. v. 236–8.
85 Ibid. v. 241; Gros, 'Tolérance et le problème', 432–3. 86 Bayle, *Continuation*, ii. 690.
87 Jenkinson, 'Introduction', p. xxxiv; Gros, 'Tolérance et le problème', 433–5.
88 [Bruzen de La Martinière], *Entretiens*, ii. 553–5; Montesquieu, *Œuvres complètes*, 698.

world's man of 'religion' *par excellence*. Bayle relished this paradox all the more in that it utterly flouted every conventional notion on the subject, Jaquelot, typically, deeming Epicurus the worst of 'atheists' and the ancient equivalent of Spinoza.[89]

2. 'MODERATE' ENLIGHTENMENT DEIST MORALITY

Leibniz agreed that 'good morality and true religion' is something natural reason itself teaches us but not that this is independent of divine providence and revelation.[90] For Leibniz, Malebranche, and Locke, like Montesquieu, Voltaire, and Hume, part of the challenge of moral philosophy in their age was precisely to counter the strategy towards a strict autonomy of ethics, and its exclusive grounding in natural need, arising from the systems of Spinoza, Bayle, Collins, Mandeville and the French materialists. This they proposed to do by constructing moral systems based, ultimately, on God's will and divine ordinances. Of those major thinkers who rejected the radicals' divorcing morality totally from religion, it was indeed Leibniz who delved deepest, and was most philosophically consistent and effective, in advancing a counter-strategy.[91]

But if, as Mendelssohn claimed in 1753, Leibniz and Wolff were deeper and more coherent in moral and general philosophy than French counterparts like Voltaire,[92] equally eager to reconcile philosophy with divine providence, it was nevertheless Voltaire who pre-eminently linked the French Enlightenment to a moral vision based on divine agency, physico-theology and supernatural reward and punishment and who, especially in France, proved most effective in countering the Spinozist-Baylean challenge. He was by no means alone, though, among the *parti philosophique* in this endeavour: Saint-Hyacinthe, Réaumur, Maupertuis, and Turgot, as well as such discreet unbelievers as Montesquieu, Hume, and Benjamin Franklin, also judged that Spinozism and materialism ineluctably reduce to moral cynicism and nihilism. Turgot, an ardent enthusiast for Locke, headed the most emphatically Christian wing of this anti-materialist tendency in the French High Enlightenment, claiming men are naturally selfish and perverse and that only religion, especially Christianity, can nurture both love of one's community and 'enlightened' devotion to humanity generally, making it possible for legislation and state-building to progress.[93] Turgot's philosophical writing, undeniably, was always aimed as much against Diderot, radical Deists, and atheists as against tradition, authority, and bigotry.

Here, then, was a vast unresolved disagreement about the social, as well as religious, basis of morality, law, and institutions, something many came to see

[89] Israel, *Radical Enlightenment*, 460.

[90] Leibniz, *New Essays*, 463.

[91] Schneewind, *Invention of Autonomy*, 237.

[92] Mendelssohn, *Philosophical Writings*, 106, 112.

[93] Turgot, *Discours sur les avantages*, 208–11; Turgot, *Plan de deux discours*, 284; Gay, *Enlightenment*, i. 373 n., ii. 110–11.

a pressing need to respond to using new strategies. For the older systems of Le Clerc, Locke, Bernard, Jaquelot, Basnage, Crousaz, Barbeyrac, Leibniz, and Thomasius, urging the harmony and interdependence of reason and faith, all entailed intractable intellectual difficulties especially in trying to replace Cartesian dualism with a more cogent treatment of substance differentiation. This problem could perhaps be better surmounted, or skirted around, using less theologically orientated approaches. Hence, emerged during the 1730s and 1740s more empirically based, less metaphysically charged, ways of combating Spinoza and Bayle on providence, free will, morality, society, and faith, strategies which came to dominate the moderate mainstream and were developed with particular flair by three of the Enlightenment's greatest thinkers—Montesquieu, Voltaire, and Hume.

Voltaire began by asserting the crucial ethical significance of belief in Creation of the cosmos by a knowing divinity and the idea that morality is divinely ordained. To this he added Locke's (very hesitant) defence of 'free will', claiming this too is essential to upholding the moral and social order, being indispensable to belief in reward and punishment in the hereafter.[94] Unlike the theologians, but like Shaftesbury and Hume, Voltaire agrees that the 'good of society' is the only authentic measure of moral good and evil.[95] He grants also that 'good' and 'evil' are in some degree relative rather than absolute notions while also insisting that a providential Supreme Being has instilled into man 'certain sentiments that he cannot get rid of' which determine the 'eternal ties and first laws' of human society.[96] Voltaire's moral thought, in other words, was anchored in a de-Christianized theology. While acknowledging the Greeks had accomplished much in ethics, he held, contradicting Bayle, that this was because their efforts here rested squarely on the principle of 'un Dieu suprême' and other key articles of natural theology.[97]

In his *Essai sur les mœurs* of the early 1740s, he pushes his critique of Bayle still further. While concurring that the Chinese had gone furthest in extrapolating from experience and constructing a praiseworthy moral system, creating the most enduring and stable of societies, he denied these accomplishments could be interpreted to mean, as Bayle contends, that an 'atheistic' society can be more moral and well ordered than a Christian one, classical Chinese ethics being based, according to him, on belief in an 'Être suprême, rémunérateur et vengeur'. Arguing, like Locke, that true moral law is the morality God ordained for us, Voltaire held, against Bayle, that all the Greek philosophy schools, aside from the Epicureans and Stratonists, acknowledged 'l'architecte du monde'.[98] Combining naturalism and voluntarism, he urges that the moral values God decrees, men discover through their natural impulses and needs; just as divinely given instinct guides humanity in forging institutions of family and social life along broadly similar lines throughout the world, so

94 Marshall, *John Locke*, 152–4; Schneewind, 'Locke's Moral Philosophy', 201, 204; Harris, *Of Liberty and Necessity*, 20–1.

95 Voltaire, *Traité de métaphysique*, 459, 475, 477.

96 Ibid.; Wade, *Intellectual Development*, 598, 631, 649–50.

97 Voltaire, *Essai sur les mœurs*, i. 70–1, 94; Ehrard, *L'Idée*, 409–10; Mason, 'Voltaire devant Bayle', 448–9.

98 Voltaire, *Essai sur les mœurs*, i. 94; Schneewind, 'Locke's Moral Philosophy', 204–5.

morality's content was discovered, step by step, over the course of history in ways which render basic moral truths essentially the same everywhere.[99] God did not proclaim the morality he intended for men through any revelation, or by sending a Saviour, or any miraculous means; yet morality is no less divinely ordained and supervised for that. Newton conclusively showed that divine providence usually proceeds not through miracles and revelations but through nature itself. God fixed a universal moral code, held Voltaire, his commandments being rationally coherent, orderly, and binding on all.

This universal coherence of moral norms, he argues, is reflected in what he saw as the unifying threads tying together all the world's major religions, a unifying essence at least rudimentarily diffused through all the world's many creeds, and it is this which he calls 'natural religion': 'j'entends par religion naturelle les principes de morale connues au genre humain.'[100] This tying together, moreover, he saw as a long process of diffusion occurring in particular through borrowing: one sees clearly, he averred, that the world's religions have borrowed 'tous leurs dogmes et tous leurs rites les unes des autres'.[101] Religious division and diversity is real, therefore, but behind it lies a veiled, primarily moral unity, ordained by a benign Creator.

To counter, on the one hand, Bayle's destruction of *consensus gentium* arguments, and on the other Lahontan's, Gueudeville's, and Jean-Frédéric Bernard's elevation of the 'noble savage', Voltaire revived the reasoning advanced earlier by Basnage, and in 1712 by Élie Benoist (against Toland as well as Bayle), that the proven 'atheism' of primitive peoples like the Caribs, a few African peoples, and Brazilian Indians and those of the Guyanas cannot detract from a higher *consensus gentium*, nor can their rudimentary notions of equity serve as the basis for a fully-fledged morality, primitive peoples, among whom reason is severely limited, being incapable of systematic thought: for knowledge of both God and morality, held Voltaire, requires 'une raison cultivée, et leur raison ne l'était pas'.[102] Humanity's progress had occurred chiefly in Europe, China, and also India, the three most developed societies, in his view, not the remote, less civilized regions.[103] As for Bayle's proofs, citing Greece and China, that strife and disruption abound everywhere, and under all religions, and that Christianity has not evinced any moral superiority to other creeds,[104] Voltaire's new universalist Deist stance was indeed much less vulnerable on this score than the systems of Le Clerc, Basnage, Leibniz, and Locke.

Providence in Voltaire's system, no less than in Newton's, governs our cosmos and all human history, decreeing human morality and duties through processes

[99] Voltaire, *Traité de métaphysique*, 475–7; Schneewind, *Invention of Autonomy*, 459–60.
[100] Voltaire, *Métaphysique de Newton*, 219, 221; Cassirer, *Philosophy*, 244–5.
[101] Voltaire, *Essai sur les mœurs*, i. 274; Tortarolo, *L'Illuminismo*, 35–6.
[102] Voltaire, *Essai sur les mœurs*, ii. 343; Benoist, *Mélange*, 80–1; Ehrard, *L'Idée*, 412.
[103] Voltaire, *Essai sur les mœurs*, i. 239; Rihs, *Voltaire*, 123.
[104] Bayle, *Continuation* ii. 566, 590–2, 610–20; Basnage, *Traité*, i. 10–11, ii. 9; Bayle, *Réponse*, v. 226–42.

predetermined and internal to Nature itself.[105] It was a system relying for its intellectual cogency—however disturbing in this context a catastrophe such as the Lisbon earthquake of 1755—on the Newtonian doctrine of a benign Deity who created and regulates the world on a basis of reason in accordance with mathematical principles.[106] Bayle's contrary claim that no one can rationally reconcile the universal dominion of a benign, knowing Creator with the immensity of evil and suffering the world endures, Voltaire roundly dismisses in his *Élémens de la philosophie de Neuton* (1738), as 'le grand refuge de l'athée', insisting that it is precisely Newtonianism supplemented by Clarke, affirming the 'connoissance d'un Être suprême qui a tout créé, tout arrangé librement', which definitively refutes such reasoning.[107]

Until the 1740s, the 'argument from design' did indeed hold Spinoza's and Bayle's strictures regarding divine providence in check. If Hume and Montesquieu, no less than Voltaire, judged some form of religion enthroning a divine Creator and universal legislator, and promising reward and punishment in the hereafter, indispensable, Voltaire diverged notably from Hume, as well as Bayle and the *Spinosistes*, in arguing that the Supreme Being's freedom must be mirrored in a small, fragmentary way also in the liberty of Man's will. For lacking this, how can anyone be held responsible for acting immorally? Were there only one substance, and all that is exists one continuum, functioning mechanically and necessarily, then humanity too would be 'déterminée nécessairement' just as Collins and Mandeville—following Spinoza—maintain; but this Voltaire deemed a fallacy highly inimical to morality and the social order.[108] Locke, Newton, and Clarke, held Voltaire, all show that 'l'être infiniment libre' has comunicated to man his creature a limited portion of this freedom.[109] This idea, basic, he thought, to human morality, was fundamental to his own system and demonstrable in a way immortality of the soul was not, though that too was something men generally should be urged to believe.[110]

Bayle's, Collins's, and Mandeville's arguments against free will were not easy to dismiss, however; nor was their contention that religion does not, after all, curb men's wickedness and wrongdoing 'et qu'il faut attribuer', as Bayle put it, 'à d'autres principes' the barrier which maintains societies, namely worldly curbs imposed by government.[111] After Du Marsais and Meslier, French radical thinkers of the 1730s and 1740s, like Vauvenargues, in his *Traité sur le libre arbitre* (*c.*1737), again argued that morality and 'good works' are not prejudiced 'en établissant la nécessité de nos actions' nor is determinism contradicted by proclaiming 'l'humanité' the chief of

[105] Bayle, *Réponse*, v. 226–42; Rihs, *Voltaire*, 111, 120–32, 144–5; Schneewind, *Invention of Autonomy*, 458–60.

[106] Fichera, *Il Deismo critico*, 100; Benelli, *Voltaire metafisico*, 78–9.

[107] Voltaire, *Métaphysique de Newton*, 196; Porset, 'Voltaire et Meslier', 196–8.

[108] Voltaire, *Lettres philosophiques*, 92; Wade, *Intellectual Development*, 698–9; Ehrard, *L'Idée*, 453–5; Walters and Barber, 'Introduction', 113; Berman, 'Determinism', 252.

[109] Voltaire, *Métaphysique de Newton*, 213–14, 216; Benelli, *Voltaire metafisico*, 72–3, 78–9, 96.

[110] Voltaire, *Traité de métaphysique*, 458; Diderot, *Œuvres philosophiques*, 23 n.

[111] Bayle, *Réponse*, v. 241; Pascaul López, *Bernard Mandeville*, 79–80.

virtues.[112] Punishment under this schema, as Collins had urged, is pragmatic and utilitarian, certainly, but is also 'just'.[113] From 1747, Diderot too emphatically rejected freedom of the will while, like Spinoza, Bayle, Collins, Mandeville, Boulainvilliers, Meslier, Du Marsais, and Vauvenargues, simultaneously championing the validity of an autonomous secular morality and the justice of punishment under the law.[114]

Montesquieu's strategy, meanwhile, reveals many parallels with that of Voltaire. After years of careful 'philosophical' historical research along the lines pioneered by Bayle, Boulainvilliers, and Fréret, pondering the issues he inherited from them, Montesquieu's great discovery about humanity, as elaborated in *L'Esprit des lois*, holds that human history is not, after all, a single continuum, as Bayle, Fontenelle, and Voltaire conceived, but rather a vast plurality of different contexts in which customs, laws, and institutions, as well as morality and religion, comprise intricate bundles of interrelated but particular sets of relations and conditions. While sharing Spinoza's and Bayle's dislike of tyranny, oppression, war, and ecclesiastical sway, and prepared to accept, like them, that there are preferable norms to which all societies ought to tend, especially those favouring social stability, toleration, and individual liberty, yet Montesquieu rejected the idea of a universal morality, in fact, as it has been aptly put, did not 'believe in universal solutions, indeed in no simple or final solutions at all'.[115]

The essence of wisdom, political and philosophical, to his mind lies in moderation and especially moderation adjusted to the nature of things as we find them.[116] On this ground, he develops the idea that there is not one but several divergent moralities, the typology of which requires meticulous study since different ethical principles are, depending on circumstances, more or less suited to particular types of government and society. Agreeing with Voltaire that religious belief together with popular credence in Heaven and Hell and supernatural reward and punishment are essential for both morality and rule of law, Montesquieu attacks Bayle on this question, in his *Spicilège*, a collection of jottings, of 1715.[117]

Where for Spinoza or Bayle there is no intrinsic difference between a Christian, pagan, or atheistic society as regards political and moral viability,[118] Montesquieu held that there is and must be a close concordance between religion and morality in Christian and non-Christian states alike, since religion, even where false, offers the best prospect we have 'de la probité des hommes'.[119] He expressly deploys this

[112] Vauvenargues, *Traité sur le libre arbitre*, 195, 197–8; McKenna, 'Vauvenargues', 217, 223–4.

[113] Taranto, *Du déisme à l'athéisme*, 422–3.

[114] Duflo, *Diderot philosophe*, 59–61, 406; Dupré, *Enlightenment*, 119.

[115] Berlin, 'Montesquieu', 284; Courtney, 'Montesquieu and Natural Law', 57–9.

[116] Ehrard, *L'Idée*, 378–9; Goyard-Fabre, *Montesquieu*, 273–4.

[117] Montesquieu, *Œuvres complètes*, 396.

[118] Bayle, *Continuation*, ii. 690–1; Hochstrasser, 'Claims', 32; Braun, 'Diderot', 48–9, 55; Gros, 'Tolérance et le problème', 432, 434, 439.

[119] Montesquieu, *Œuvres complètes*, 700; Kra, *Religion in Montesquieu's* Lettres persanes, 83; Bartlett, *Idea of Enlightenment*, 27, 37–8.

argument against *le Spinosisme*. Yet his manner of doing so, as the Abbé Jean-Baptiste Gaultier noted in 1752, contains within itself the 'vicious' seed of surrender to Spinoza's doctrine that religions are human constructions and that, rather than being divinely ordained, 'la justice dépend des conventions humaines'.[120]

We should hope God exists, mused Montesquieu, and if he does not, then accept that it is still advisable to defend and uphold religion.[121] This was a strategy which left him precariously vulnerable, however, to criticism from both left and right. Reminding readers that Spinoza's philosophy means society and the state should permit people to have as much of what they individually want as is compatible with everyone else doing the same, that is 'a political and moral philosophy based on the principle of equality of pleasure and satisfaction of desire', an essentially libertine creed, Montesquieu's Jansenist critics pointed out that despite his rejecting equality, his reservations concerning liberty of thought, and dislike of sexual freedom for women (particularly in republics), Montesquieu's conception of civil liberty is by no means wholly dissimilar to Spinoza's.[122] Montesquieu, complained Gaultier, seeks to avoid the consequences of Spinoza's notion of justice, conceding that if justice is not absolute and eternal, and if it depends solely on human ingenuity, 'ce seroit une vérité terrible' which must, as far as possible, be concealed from the common people. But by hinting, as he does, that Spinoza's 'principe peut être une vérité',[123] does not Montesquieu, at a deeper metaphysical level, unmask the ugly truth—that he is not really fighting Spinoza at all but rather simply retreating before him?

Montesquieu was indubitably more robust, though, in assailing Bayle's thesis that a society of atheists can function not just successfully, and durably, but also more amicably than one of believers in divine providence, and in reward and punishment in the hereafter, dismissing this as the Baylean paradox 'par excellence'. Against this 'sottise de Bayle', Montesquieu insists on the efficacy of religion, Christian and non-Christian, for strengthening respect for the laws and morality,[124] arguing that men are naturally so conditioned to fear and hope that any creed featuring neither Heaven nor Hell 'ne saurait guère leur plaire'; to be respected an organized religion must proclaim miracles and mysteries.[125] Even an unquestionably inferior religion, which Montesquieu considers Confucianism to be—since it fails to teach immortality of the soul—can nevertheless, he argues, provide indispensable social and moral benefits.[126]

120 [Gaultier], Lettres persanes *convaincues*, 34–6, 101; Masseau, *Ennemis des philosophes*, 55–6.

121 Kra, *Religion in Montesquieu's* Lettres persanes, 213.

122 [Gaultier], Lettres persanes *convaincues*, 35; Livesey, *Making Democracy*, 35; Carrithers, 'Democratic and Aristocratic', 133–4.

123 [Gaultier], Lettres persanes *convaincues*, 35–6, 101; Payne, *The Philosophes*, 68–9; Kra, *Religion in Montesquieu's* Lettres persanes, 83, 213; Bartlett, *Idea of Enlightenment*, 28.

124 Montesquieu, *Œuvres complètes*, 698–9, 810, 814, 1036; Schlüter, *Französische Toleranzdebatte*, 192; Bartlett, *Idea of Enlightenment*, 19–20.

125 Montesquieu, *Œuvres complètes*, 705; Ehrard, *L'Idée*, 466–7.

126 Montesquieu, *L'Esprit des lois*, 702; Bartlett, *Idea of Enlightenment*, 28–9.

Where Spinoza and Bayle propose to curb misconduct, and promote moral goals in society, using laws, legal deterrents, and penalties alone, without theological underpinning, affirming the viability of their moral code based exclusively on worldly values, Montesquieu claims the moral order must be based on transcendental values and religion. It was far more than just aristocratic *hauteur* that moved Montesquieu to declare, in his *Lettres persanes*, that the common people 'est un animal qui voit et qui entend, mais qui ne pense jamais'.[127] Rather this idea is integral to his critique of Spinoza and Bayle: since the people do not think, their moral responses and conduct are not a product of conviction or reason but follow from their veneration for and trust in the supernatural and in their creed. Here especially, but also in his support for the *thèse nobiliaire*, and rejection of equality, Montesquieu had some justification for protesting, in his apology for *L'Esprit des lois*, published at Geneva in February 1750, that his critics understood him so little that 'l'on a pris pour des opinions de Spinosa' the very novelties which he, Montesquieu, was advancing 'contre le Spinosisme'.[128]

Hume's approach to ethics and the social order stood, on the whole, rather closer to Montesquieu's than Voltaire's. For he too effectively eliminates divine providence along with free will and other elements of 'natural religion'.[129] Developing his moral theory, as a young thinker, at the same time as Voltaire, in the 1730s, Hume's philosophy was complete in essentials by the early 1740s[130]—the great Scotsman devising a highly distinctive method of reinstating tradition, the ecclesiastical order, monarchy, and aristocracy, commencing by attacking the idea that morality can be demonstrated by reason. In this, he closely followed the Ulster philosopher Francis Hutcheson (1694–1746), a Newtonian and a no less strong believer in divine providence than Voltaire who, however, powerfully disagreed with Clarke and other Newtonians about the relationship of reason to morality.[131]

Hutcheson incorporated within his Newtonianism Shaftesbury's theory of moral sense and natural benevolence, adapting it to a more specifically Christian context than had its originator. He staunchly opposed what he called, echoing Shaftesbury, the 'Epicurean Opinion', namely that 'all desires of the human mind, nay of all thinking natures, are reducible to self-love, or desire of private happiness'.[132] This to his mind pernicious tendency he saw culminating in Mandeville, whose Spinozistic moral theory had been Hutcheson's chief target in his *An Inquiry into the Original of our Ideas of Beauty and Virtue* (1725), the modern revival of the 'Epicurean Opinion' being something which Hutcheson, like Shaftesbury, expressly attributes to Hobbes and Spinoza.[133] These opposed positions Hutcheson, again like Shaftesbury, conceives as the two great traditions of

[127] Romani, 'All Montesquieu's Sons', 192.

[128] Montesquieu, *Œuvres complètes*, 809.

[129] Norton, 'Hume, Human Nature', 156, 158; Gaskin, 'Hume on Religion', 334–5; Stewart, *Opinion and Reform*, 150–1.

[130] Stewart, *Opinion and Reform*, 315.

[131] Hutcheson, *Essay*, 155–7; Turco, 'Moral Sense', 140–1; Haakonssen, 'Natural Jurisprudence', 206, 209.

[132] Hutcheson, *Essay*, 134–5.

[133] Ibid. 134; Klein, *Shaftesbury*, 61; Pascual López, *Bernard Mandeville*, 76–9, 83–5.

western moral theory. Advancing 'the opposite opinion' to that of the 'Epicureans', Hutcheson proposed we evince not only self-love but 'benevolent affections also toward others'.[134] Our approval of moral actions, he urged, does not, and should not, properly arise from their effects, social or personal. By also firmly denying that reason can reveal the content of morality, he incurred the contemptuous disapproval of Le Clerc but was followed by Hume who likewise stressed sensibility rather than reason as the basis of ethics.[135]

As regards miracles, Revelation, and supernatural agency, Hume, unlike Hutcheson, diverged only marginally—albeit the margin (his rejection of miracles being almost but not quite *a priori*) is not insignificant[136]—from the Spinozists. Yet his inferences from his scepticism about miracles and free will, with respect to religion, morality, and politics, were fundamentally different from those of the radicals, except perhaps for Collins. The *rationaux*, Locke, and Leibniz claimed we live in a God-ordained universe in which reason demonstrates the truth of moral rules conveyed to mankind through revelation, indeed that the perfection of Christian morality may be regarded as one of the proofs that Christianity is the true faith. Spinoza and Bayle deny this. But their moral philosophies were 'relativistic' only in the sense that they accepted what they took to be universal human needs and characteristics, rather than any external or revealed standard, as the measure of good and bad, virtue and vice, among men.

Echoing Shaftesbury and Hutcheson in stressing moral sense, Hume's moral theory combined sensibility in a remarkable fashion with elements taken from Mandeville.[137] While refusing to agree that reason can demonstrate the content of ethics, or that there is a universal morality, Hume did not disagree with Hobbes, Spinoza, Bayle, Collins, and Mandeville in holding that justice in all societies, and the public interest, have a universal and common origin, originating in the clash of individual appetites, and that it is in everyone's interest to bridle what would otherwise be wild and uncontrollable anarchy. For him too, 'the attainment of happiness' is the goal of every man, and even the savage, as he puts it, 'forgets not, for a moment, this grand object of his being'; indeed Hume combines liberty and necessity in a compatibilism directly parallel to that of Spinoza, Bayle, and—on this topic—the highly cogent Collins.[138]

For Hume, then, like Spinoza, Bayle, and Collins, morality is entirely independent of religion and there is no 'stronger foundation for our political duties than interest, and human conventions'.[139] Granting that 'self-interest is the original

[134] Hutcheson, *Essay*, 136–7; Norton, 'Hume, Human Nature', 154–5.

[135] Turco, 'Moral Sense', 141, 144; Darwall, 'Hume', 62, 64, 75; Stewart, *Opinion and Reform*, 80–97, 110–19.

[136] Gaskin, *Hume's Philosophy of Religion*, 6, 134; Fogelin, *Defence of Hume*, 18–19, 25.

[137] Turco, 'Moral Sense', 144–5; Himmelfarb, 'Two Enlightenments', 301–2; Haakonssen, 'Natural Jurisprudence', 211.

[138] Hume, *Essays*, 148; Fogelin, *Defense of Hume*, 59–61; Landucci, 'Mente e corpo', 130, 136; Bouchardy, *Pierre Bayle*, 257–60; Taranto, *Du déisme à l'athéisme*, 346–54.

[139] Hume, *Treatise*, 543; Gaskin, 'Hume on Religion', 333–4; Rothschild, *Economic Sentiments*, 230–1.

motive to the establishment of justice', he concurs also (while criticizing Mandeville for exaggerating the role of political artifice and overlooking the role of moral sensibility in individuals) that Man's developing a sense of sympathy for the common interest, and the principles of justice, is both a natural and a necessary thing. Such 'justice', moreover, had often been 'forwarded by the artifice of politicians, who, in order to govern men more easily, and preserve peace in human society, have endeavour'd to produce an esteem for justice, and an abhorrence of injustice'.[140]

Political allegiance and moral obligation are indeed human contrivances and have the same origin in nature, the same function in society, and the same status, being based on the common interest of all. Indeed, Hume's discarding of Hobbes's social contract', and reliance on continuing self-interest to explain political submission, parallels similar moves in Spinoza and Bayle.[141] Nor does Hume wholly rule out the revolutionary implications of such a stance, though, like the Thermidorean French enthusiast for Hume, Portalis, he is by no means willing to grant as a general principle that the sovereign power in society emanates from the people, he accepts that government is for the common good, and has no other basis, and that armed rebellion against insufferable tyrants like Nero or Philip II is therefore natural, inevitable, and justified.[142]

Hume, furthermore, rules 'superstition' an 'enemy to civil liberty', since, as he put it in 1741, it 'renders men tame and abject and fits them for slavery'.[143] Nor does he diverge far from Spinoza and Bayle in admonishing that armed rebellion against tyrants is proper only in extreme cases, since the 'convulsions, which always attend such revolutions' can cause great damage, tending 'directly to the subversion of all government, and the causing an universal anarchy and confusion among mankind'.[144] 'The common rule', affirmed Hume, 'requires submission; and tis only in cases of grievous tyranny and oppression, that the exception can take place.'[145] Rather it is in refusing to accept there is no moral legitimacy or validity in religions and social hierarchies simply because we doubt they are divinely ordained, and especially in refusing to judge religions, moral systems, or types of government, in terms of their rationality or alleged capacity to serve the common interest, that Hume diverges fundamentally from the Radical Enlightenment. For Hume claims his principle of the sentimental, non-rational origins of morality and justice 'gives authority to all the most establish'd governments of the world without exception: I mean, long possession in any one form of government, or succession of princes'.[146]

Of course, where one traces back far enough one finds all the monarchies and other regimes of the world were 'primarily founded on usurpation and rebellion',

140 Hume, *Treatise*, 500; Norton, 'Hume, Human Nature', 165–6.

141 Hume, *Treatise*, 550–1.

142 Ibid. 552; Hume, *Essays*, 94, 489–90; Gay, *Enlightenment*, ii. 454–5; Bongie, *David Hume*, 107, 198–201; Haakonssen, 'Structure', 203.

143 Hume, *Essays*, 73–8; Hume, 'Of Superstition', 250; Gaskin, 'Hume on Religion', 335; Himmelfarb, 'Two Enlightenments', 321; Stewart, 'Religion', 48.

144 Hume, *Treatise*, 553.

145 Ibid. 554; Hume, *Essays*, 511; Stewart, *Opinion and Reform*, 174, 242.

146 Hume, *Treatise*, 556; Wootton, 'David Hume "the Historian" ', 297.

with title 'worse than doubtful and uncertain'.[147] But legitimate succession, held Hume, is just as irrelevant to true legitimacy as divine sanction: it is the passage of time and force of custom, he argues, which 'gives solidity to their right' and confers authority. In this way, he devised a conservative relativism which closely parallels that of Montesquieu. Only, where, for the latter, what Hume terms 'physical causes'—geography, air, and climate—are decisive influences which help shape cultural continuities together with institutions, an 'esprit' which is a constant and active factor in future political development, for Hume it is rather the historical context and passage of time, and 'moral causes', that is circumstances that 'work on the mind as motives or reasons, and which render a peculiar set of manners habitual to us', that matter.[148] Indeed, Hume was apt to 'doubt altogether' that men 'owe anything of their temper or genius to the air, food or climate'.[149]

Hence, while Spinozist premisses about self-interest were correct, for Hume there exists no universal model, like democratic republicanism, or Bayle's secular absolutism, preferable in politics, or any universal rules of constitutionality or the 'common good': ' 'tis interest which gives the general instinct; but 'tis custom which gives the particular direction.'[150] Hume may have slightly preferred republics to monarchies, and did not share Montesquieu's view that republics are only suitable for small territories, but he firmly denied that political sovereignty emanates from the people.[151] Moreover religion, provided the state checks religious zeal and 'superstition', constitutes an essential part of the moral and political fabric of society and is requisite for a balanced and healthy politics, even if its claims to supernatural authorization are dubious and, in Hume's view,[152] it corrupts the highest forms of morality. Despite seeing no philosophical basis for faith, or theological basis for morality, Hume did not regard religion *per se* as mere superstition. Rather, he refused to exclude divine Creation and miracles *a priori*, granting that the 'whole frame of nature', as the Newtonians and Voltaire maintain, does seem to support, at least as a reasonable notion, the idea of an 'intelligent author'.[153]

This sceptical position enabled Hume to combine a conservative cast of mind with ardent support for the Glorious Revolution, 'that famous revolution, which has had such a happy influence on our constitution'.[154] No matter how dubious the dethroning of James II, and enthronement of the prince of Orange, in 1689, from a legitimist viewpoint, 'time and custom give authority to all forms of government, and all successions of princes, and that power which at first was founded only on

[147] Hume, *Treatise*, 556.

[148] Hume, *Essays*, 198; Westerman, *Disintegration*, 236, 232.

[149] Hume, *Essays*, 200; Gay, *Enlightenment*, ii. 330; Wootton, 'David Hume "the Historian" ', 294–5.

[150] Hume, *Treatise*, 556; Turco, 'Moral Sense', 145.

[151] Hume, *Essays*, 94, 515–16, 527; Stewart, *Opinion and Reform*, 284.

[152] Gaskin, *Hume's Philosophy of Religion*, 194–8.

[153] Hume, *Dialogues*, 191–4; Gaskin, 'Hume on Religion', 319–20, 338; Fogelin, *Defense of Hume*, 18–19.

[154] Hume, *Treatise*, 563; Haakonssen, 'Structure', 209; Wootton, 'David Hume "the Historian" ', 302, 306–7; Stewart, *Opinion and Reform*, 242–5.

injustice and violence, becomes in time legal and obligatory'.[155] Nor was the length of time needed to confer such validity upon a government, church, or moral system at all long. 'The kings of France have not been possess'd of absolute power for above two reigns', he remarked, and yet few in France question the French monarchy's legitimacy, indeed 'nothing will appear more extravagant to Frenchmen than to talk of their liberties', noted Hume who, while less inclined to French absolutism than British mixed government, nevertheless insisted on the civilizing and legitimate character of the eighteenth-century French crown, as also of other continental absolute monarchies.[156] Central to Hume's moral, no less than his political, system was the idea that 'right to authority is nothing but the constant possession of authority, maintain'd by the laws of society and the interests of mankind', a principle setting his philosophy squarely against the *Spinosiste* radicalism of the democratic republicans.[157]

Hume spurned Voltaire's Deism and, unlike Voltaire, embraced neither 'free will', nor immortality of the soul, nor indeed Barbeyrac's (and Pufendorf's) voluntarism, remaining, at least philosophically, ambivalent also about Newtonian 'argument from design'.[158] But he stood still further from the Radical Enlightenment and in three crucial respects. First, there was what is sometimes called his 'modesty' towards (meaning antipathy to) the sweeping application of philosophical reason to everything, one of his chief aims, we have seen, being to limit philosophy's competence by inculcating what he calls 'a notion of the imperfections and narrow limits of human understanding'.[159] Secondly, Hume denies rejection of miracles and supernatural agency means we must replace theology with an integrated conception of an orderly, coherently structured cosmos, a single set of rules governing the whole of reality from which nothing is exempt. The political, social, and moral conclusions Spinoza and Bayle draw from their toppling of theology seemed to him wholly unwarranted. Finally, Hume's conservatism encompassed morality itself, his moral theory, anchored in custom, tradition, and sensibility, helping to buttress his political and religious conservatism.

Now it was precisely this organizing tool of 'those who affirm that virtue is nothing but a conformity to reason, that there are eternal fitnesses and unfitnesses of things, which are the same to every rational being that considers them; that the immutable measures of right and wrong impose an obligation, not only on human creatures, but also on the Deity himself' that Hume, not unlike Montesquieu, firmly resists. This indeed was the target of his first major work, *A Treatise of Human Nature*, composed whilst residing in France, during the years 1734–7, just when Montesquieu began *L'Esprit des lois*.[160] Claiming reason has no influence on the

155 Hume, *Treatise*, 566; Hume, *Essays*, 506–8; Straka, 'Sixteen Eighty-Eight', 143, 146–7.

156 Hume, *Treatise*, 557; Hume, 'Of Superstition', 251; Gay, *Enlightenment*, ii. 335–6; Haakonssen, 'Structure', 204–5; Wootton, 'David Hume "the Historian" ', 296.

157 Hume, *Treatise*, 557.

158 Hume, *Dialogues*, 140–52, 184–5; Fogelin, 'Hume's Scepticism', 93; Stewart, *Opinion and Reform*, 150.

159 Wolheim, 'Introduction', 28–9; Fogelin, 'Hume's Scepticism', 90–1.

160 Hume, *Treatise*, 456; Hutcheson, *Essay*, 137–44.

human passions, or on conduct, whereas moral injunctions inculcated into men during their upbringing and education do influence attitudes, Hume holds the influence of moral ideas on our conduct derives primarily from non-rational causes.

That reason has a strictly mathematical quality, that 'truth or falsehood consists in an agreement or disagreement either as to the *real* relations of ideas, or to *real* existence and matter of fact', Hume did not deny. But, unlike his great predecessors from Descartes onwards, he did not think the remit of this precise, carefully crafted tool extends very far: 'whatever, therefore, is not susceptible of this agreement or disagreement, is incapable of being true or false, and can never be an object of our reason.'[161] Deeming it self-evident that our passions, wishes and actions 'are not susceptible of any such agreement or disagreement', he concludes ' 'tis impossible, that the distinction betwixt moral good and evil, can be made by reason; since that distinction has an influence upon our actions, of which reason alone is incapable'.[162]

Building on Locke and the real scepticism of Montaigne, rejecting Bayle's pseudo-scepticism, Hume endeavours to show there are actually many areas where philosophy can shed little or no light, and is incapable of yielding anything but utter uncertainty. Bayle's Stratonism, far from being the sole cogent outcome of a thorough philosophical examination of the facts, in Hume's opinion, was really just a leap of faith, a presumption unjustified by the limited capacities of our reason. 'While Newton seemed to draw off the veil from some of the mysteries of nature', he observed in his *History of England*, 'he showed at the same time the imperfections of the mechanical philosophy; and thereby restored her ultimate secrets to that obscurity in which they ever did and ever will remain.'[163] The 'obscure forces' Huygens, Leibniz, and Fontenelle deemed the most dubious feature of Newton's system, Hume considered a positive virtue.

3. RADICAL THOUGHT AND THE CONSTRUCTION OF A SECULAR MORALITY

If the thrust of his moral philosophy was conservative, what remained of 'religion', for Hume, especially in his last years when he increasingly became 'a staunch supporter of the established church',[164] was acceptance of religious practice and duties, in any given country, as they are, provided society and the individual are sufficiently protected by an established toleration and individual liberty from the 'errors' of religion.[165] This stance he combines with a remarkable hostility to any attempt to

[161] Hutcheson, *Essay*, 356; Hume, *Treatise*, 458.

[162] Hume, *Treatise*, 458; Dupré, *Enlightenment*, 131.

[163] Wolheim, 'Introduction', 29.

[164] Stewart, *Opinion and Reform*, 280; Himmelfarb, 'Two Enlightenments', 321.

[165] Stewart, 'Religion', 45–7.

breach society's conventional bounds and commonplaces by introducing new systems, creeds, or ideologies. Our moral judgements, rather than being drawn from reason, and built into a coherent system, must instead be drawn from the social context in which we live.[166] Although philosophy, by its very nature, can provide no positive content for what Voltaire called 'natural theology', Hume was nevertheless a 'non-atheist' in a particular eighteenth-century sense, since he recognizes no conclusive basis for finally ruling out supernatural agency and does not wholly reject the 'argument from design'.[167]

No sharper contrast can be found in the mid eighteenth century than that between Hume's moral thought and Diderot's. As early as his *Pensées philosophiques* (1746),[168] Diderot spurned Original Sin and the whole structure of Christian ethics, for which reason that work, together with his moral philosophy more generally, came to be identified later as one of the chief intellectual seeds of the French Revolution,[169] in particular by a former disciple of Voltaire, Jean-François La Harpe, who after the fall of Robespierre, in 1794, publicly abjured *la philosophie*, embracing *anti-philosophisme* instead as the new general panacea. Although, in 1746, still professing Deism, Diderot already then firmly detached morality from religion, custom, and 'superstition', seeking to emancipate the individual and his or her libido from association with sin, freeing men for the enjoyment of pleasures aesthetic, culinary, and sexual. It is now a long time, he exclaims, in one of his *pensées* of 1746, that the theologians have been asked how they reconcile the doctrine of eternal damnation and torment with the 'infinite mercy of God' and still they come up with no answer![170]

At the latest by mid 1747 Diderot was a materialist. But like Spinoza and Bayle, he took very seriously the task of demonstrating the distinction between moral right and wrong, just and unjust, and constructing a new morality.[171] In part, his moral philosophy was 'utilitarian'. But it was not quite 'utilitarian' in the sense in which this term came to be used in late eighteenth-century England. For in proclaiming 'that action is best, which procures the greatest happiness of the greatest number', a form of words first introduced by Hutcheson,[172] the Benthamite utilitarians later placed the main responsibility for defining 'the greatest good', and applying the criterion, in a somewhat imperious spirit appropriate to a colonial milieu, on the philosopher, legislator, administrator, and wise statesman. For the Radical Enlightenment, by contrast, the 'common good' as formulated from the late seventeenth century by the Spinozists is embedded in a republican theory of coexistence of equal volitions and hence inherent in collective decision-making, freedom of the individual, re-education of the public, and democratic politics, where the 'common

166 Stewart, *Opinion and Reform*, 138, 145–6, 149–51.

167 Stewart, 'Religion', 94; Hume, *Dialogues*, 204.

168 Diderot, *Pensées philosophiques*, 65–6.

169 Tarin, *Diderot*, 114–15.

170 Diderot, *Pensées philosophiques*, 66.

171 Duflo, *Diderot philosophe*, 382, 385, 394; Tortarolo, 'Epicurus and Diderot', 387–90.

172 Darwall, 'Hume', 58.

good' works as much (or more) unconsciously as consciously. Part of the strength of *Spinosiste* moral philosophy, and Diderot's in particular, is that human rationality is conceived as an extension of sensibility and the unconscious, rather than standing against or in conflict with it, proceeding along the same lines, only further and more efficiently.[173]

Philosophically, what shapes Diderot's treatment of the moral sphere, a topic to which he continually returned during his career, and examined from many angles, was his constant concern to construct the new morality on the basis of the individual quest for happiness and society's needs. As with Spinoza, Bayle, Boulainvilliers, Meslier, and Du Marsais, its core was the principle that 'l'humanité', as Vauvenargues put it, 'est la première des vertus'.[174] The morality of reason, held Diderot, requires us to abide by the 'general will', or *bien général* of his species, as he calls it in his 1745 notes on Shaftesbury, and therefore to ensure that our conduct and actions are consonant with 'the general and common interest'.[175] How to reconcile self-interest with the 'common good' in purely worldly terms without debasing virtue by offering future rewards, or eternal punishment, was, for Diderot, the chief question of moral philosophy and one which pivots on finding a viable balance of individual and general interest in contrast to Rousseau's sentimental, communitarian conception of 'general will', dubious, as Habermas notes, due to relying on the fiction of a homogeneous collective moral sense.[176]

Ridiculing moral psychologists appalled that men and women act out of selfish concerns and self-interest, Diderot claims all human conduct is motivated by self-love and that the question for the moral philosopher is not to concede or refuse to acknowledge this but rather clearly distinguish between self-interested conduct which does, and which does not, conduce to what all men and women yearn for, namely their happiness.[177] The atheist has an interest in the rewards of his moral lifestyle, as in the well-being of society, and society an interest in nurturing morality in him, as an individual, while, on the other hand, the interest of he who aspires, through his actions, to earn eternal bliss, as Bayle showed, is both cruder and more self-directed than that of the 'virtuous atheist', from which Diderot draws his conclusion that the morality of the 'virtuous atheist' is a higher ethic than that of the believer in eternal salvation for the faithful and even that of the truly virtuous believer.[178] Religious belief, he argues, inevitably has negative rather than beneficial moral consequences. In his view, the acme of discernment and a worthy ethics—Diderot repeatedly likens the quest for literary and artistic excellence to that for the sublime 'dans les mœurs'—is to know the true worth of things, that is to love oneself, seek one's advantage, and know 'son bonheur comme il faut'.[179]

[173] Quintili, *Pensée critique*, 476–8.

[174] Vauvenargues, *Traité sur le libre-arbitre*, 215; Gay, *Enlightenment*, i. 188.

[175] Diderot, *Essai sur le mérite*, 21; Schneewind, *Invention of Autonomy*, 467; Cherni, *Diderot*, 415, 417, 426.

[176] Dahlberg, 'Habermasian Public Sphere', 128–9; O'Hagan, *Rousseau*, 117–21, 129.

[177] Duflo, *Diderot philosophe*, 388.

[178] Ibid. 382–6, 390–3.

[179] Diderot, *Essai sur le mérite*, 44; Diderot, *Pensées philosophiques*, 9–11.

Seeking one's true happiness, however, is conceivable only on the basis of insight and reason and consists, in essence, in attuning one's conduct to pursue those goals where one's own desires and the 'bien général' coincide.[180] We are all born with, or develop in childhood, negative temperamental inclinations whether of timidity, greed, enviousness, idleness, lust for dominance, or conceit which can easily strengthen as we grow older. Curbing such harmful or useless impulses can only be accomplished, he argues, by mobilizing other ambitions and desires against these; but such counteraction can itself only be achieved through reason and cultivating our moral sensibility, a *Spinosiste* logic Morelly likewise adopts.[181] Free will is ruled out; men are determined beings; but virtue can still be cultivated by the individual in himself or herself through the lessons of experience and by striving for understanding and, by society, through education and admonition.[182] Feeling virtuous is pleasant, holds Diderot, and remorse painful;[183] but this is only part of the cost of failing to be 'virtuous' in Diderot's sense.

Happiness, then, in Diderot, is a psychological-physiological state, as befits the theory of a materialist thinker, combining aesthetic and erotic elements with feelings of tranquillity and well-being. As such, it is far removed from being a mere negative condition, a freedom from pain and anxiety as implicit in Condillac's ethics which Diderot criticizes in his *Lettre sur les aveugles* (1749).[184] Unhappiness, for him, does not consist in a mere absence, or loss, of happiness as shade is an absence of light, as in Condillac, any more than happiness is just a painless or trouble-free security. Rather, happiness, in Diderot's moral philosophy, is something striven for, a reward accruing to those who have earned it through their moral efforts, rationality, and 'virtue'. Its specifically moral quality arises precisely from the merging of self-love and interest with consideration, benevolence, and being of service to others, and the striving for this fusion on the basis of experience and understanding. Moral education, in this context, is something the individual cultivates in him-or herself and which society can institutionalize, though there is little chance of this happening satisfactorily where theological criteria interfere.

Diderot's solution, in direct conflict with traditional morality, involves promoting within society's proclaimed scale of values, if also carefully refining, a whole batch of qualities not previously thought of as moral attributes at all, like ambition, eagerness to excel, desire for fame, intellectual impartiality, lust for sexual pleasure, and insisting on the equality of others, as well as venerating, as Du Marsais had urged, around 1720, in his *Le Philosophe*, the rule of law in all respects; supporting the republic, particularly in defending domestic and international security and advancing freedom of the individual and freedom of expression, becomes here

180 Diderot, *Essai sur le mérite*, 44, 46; Duflo, *Diderot philosophe*, 399–402, 416–17.

181 [Morelly], *Basiliade*, ii. 138; Coe, 'Le Philosophe Morelly', 164, 183, 186.

182 Duflo, *Diderot philosophe*, 386–8; Dupré, *Enlightenment*, 119.

183 Diderot, *Pensées philosophiques*, 59–60.

184 Diderot, *Lettre sur les aveugles*, 140; Condillac, *Traité des systêmes*, 37–8; Duflo, *Diderot philosophe*, 418–19.

a personal virtue. This new ethic implied a full-scale collective and individual moral revolution, though, rather amazingly, some historians still manage to construe Diderot as a 'moral conservative'.[185] As also in d'Argens, Diderot's moral system is closely tied to the world of law and politics: man only lives well upholding 'les lois humaines' and 'en vivant en honnête homme'.[186]

As the job of a watch is to tell the time, so the happiness of individuals, held Diderot, in 1745, in his notes on Shaftesbury, 'est la fin principale de la société'.[187] At the same time, his approach entailed de-emphasizing or eliminating numerous former alleged 'virtues', especially those, like self-denial, meekness, chastity, piety, and abstinence from culinary and sexual pleasure, traditionally esteemed more highly than those now being urged. Diderot's 'general will', like that of Spinoza, Bayle, Boulainvilliers, Meslier, Du Marsais, d'Argens, and Vauvenargues, then, rests on the desire of all men to be happy. In his article 'Droit naturel' for the *Encyclopédie*, he characterizes the 'general will' as the core of the true moral system, labelling the man who thinks only of his own private concerns an enemy of humanity. 'Volonté générale', he contends, is what reason defines (when the passions do not interfere) as that which every individual may fairly demand from his fellow-man 'and his fellow-man has a right to demand of him'.[188] This moral principle is envisaged as simultaneously a guide to individual conduct, the proper basis of the legal system and rule of law in a given society, and also the principle that ought to guide relations between different societies or states.

True moral values then are those that benefit men both collectively and individually in this world and in this life. Transcendental values are rejected. All this highlights the fact that morality, according to this kind of ethical philosophy, must of necessity seek to escape from tutelage to theological notions and most of all those that envisage an overseeing deity who punishes evil-doing and rewards virtue, dismissing this as a form of bondage for both individual and society more broadly—something inherently inimical to true morality, indeed destructive. For those who piously follow the directives of theologians will always promote their leaders' desiderata, and urge religious dogma, over the worldly interests of all and especially against those who oppose their system of belief. At the same time this new ethics born exclusively of reason must seek new and purely secular methods to prod men in the right direction, and hence closely interact with both politics and law to create new norms and forms of correct behaviour.[189]

185 MacIntyre, *After Virtue*, 47; Gray, *Enlightenment's Wake*, 147.

186 D'Argens, *Thérèse philosophe*, 146–7.

187 Note of Diderot in Diderot, *Essai sur le mérite*, 87.

188 Cherni, *Diderot*, 423, 426–7; Quintili, *Pensée critique*, 473, 477; Diderot, *Political Writings*, 20–1.

189 Diderot, *Political Writings*, 20–1; Gay, *Enlightenment*, ii. 25–6; Domenech, *L'Éthique*, 22, 106–9, 145, 152.

Part VI

Radical *Philosophes*

27

The French Enlightenment prior to Voltaire's *Lettres philosophiques* (1734)

1. THE POST-1715 REACTION TO ABSOLUTISM

An especially dramatic change in the structure of thinking in a given society, history suggests, is apt to follow a sudden change in the composition of power, after a long period of concerted, sustained ideological pressure in a particular direction. Hence, a crucially formative if rather neglected aspect of the French Enlightenment is the remarkably complex and far-reaching intellectual upheaval intervening between the death of 'Louis the great', as he was then called, in 1715, and Voltaire's emergence as the pre-eminent figure in the French intellectual arena in the later 1730s. In just a few years, from 1715, the closely supervised, rigid, cultural system enforced in France by an increasingly intolerant and autocratic king since the 1670s largely disintegrated.

All at once, the ideologically tightly compressed system of Louis's absolutism with its cult of divine right monarchy, aristocratic militarism, comprehensive ecclesiastical control of faith, education, and moral values, and heavy-handed repression of Jansenists, Huguenots, Jews, and freethinkers, besides tight regulation of teaching in colleges and universities, lost its credibility, fell apart as a working apparatus, and generated a powerful reaction throughout French society commencing incipiently even before the king's demise as his last terrible war dragged to its prolix diplomatic conclusion at the great European peace congress of Utrecht (1712–13).

With the end of the War of the Spanish Succession (1702–13), reopening of sea-lanes, and resumption of trade with the rest of Europe and the world beyond, came an easing of Louis's stringent tax, recruitment, and censorship regime, the beginning of a slow recovery of commerce, shipping, and industry and a rapid process of cultural, intellectual, and artistic relaxation. While the censorship regulations, control of printing, and ban on propagating Jansenist and Protestant theology were only marginally modified in theory, lack of zeal for upholding the censorship priorities of the previous reign, and the new regime's half-hearted retention of the anti-Jansenist, anti-Protestant, and anti-Jewish legislation of the 1680s and 1690s, soon produced a far more tolerant and flexible cultural atmosphere.[1]

[1] Kreiser, *Miracles, Convulsions*, 26–7; Woodbridge, *Revolt*, 9, 12.

Many welcomed this easing of institutionalized intolerance and censorship, changes described, among other places, in Montesquieu's *Lettres persanes* (1721).[2] Driven by pent-up resentment at the long cultural repression, lifting of trade restrictions, and resumption of contact with neighbouring countries, this general relaxation of pressures at the same time brought to the surface numerous unresolved tensions and contradictions inherent in the tightly regulated cultural milieu of the previous half-century, especially the deep rifts between Jansenists and anti-Jansenists in the church, Aristotelian scholastics and their opponents in the colleges, and absolutists and constitutionalists among the politically conscious nobility and legal elite.

Backed by diverse factions among the French privileged elites all hopeful that, via the new noble-dominated regency council, they would recover influence lost under *le roi soleil*, as well as opponents of Louis's ecclesiastical policies, the regency of Philippe d'Orléans (1715–23) led to many prestigious offices of government being assigned to the old high aristocracy (whose role Louis had cut back) and an almost open debate among sections of the nobility about the true nature and historical roots of the monarchy.[3] The regency also enabled the regional high courts, or *parlements*, and high magistracy, known as the *noblesse de robe*, to recoup much of the influence they had lost under Louis, through the regent's restoring to the *parlements* their ancient constitutional right, quashed in the 1660s and 1670s, to 'remonstrate', or question, proposed royal legislation.[4] In this way emerged a less efficient, less centralized, and weaker but also politically less tense, more consensus-orientated monarchy and administration than had existed in the past. But if the sense of living through a significant transition was general whether in political, economic, religious, or military life, only in the intellectual and ideological sphere did the changes precipitate a truly profound and far-reaching crisis sapping the very foundations of monarchy, aristocracy, and religion.[5]

Basic to this 'revolution' of the mind was a prompt withering of the old scholasticism of the colleges, followed, in the 1720s, by disintegration also of the Cartesian world-view. Hardly had Louis's prohibition on teaching Cartesianism lapsed, and diffusion of Malebranche's works in France begun in earnest, than Cartesian dualism and Malebranche's *volontés générales* as ways of defending the sacred, miracles, freedom of the will, and immortality of the soul foundered on powerful objections and many a searching critique from both theological and philosophical opponents. Cartesianism and *Malebranchisme* seemingly no longer provided plausible answers to the most pressing questions facing society. Descartes's, Arnauld's, and Malebranche's insistence that no two substances can interact causally, and denial of the possibility of any interaction between body and spirit, all looked irredeemably problematic. Difficulties long apparent with the rifts between Arnauld, Régis,

[2] Montesquieu, *Lettres persanes*, 93; Ehrard, *L'Esprit des mots*, 110.

[3] Ellis, *Boulainvilliers*, 112–13, 119, 144–5, 156–7.

[4] Ibid.; Bell, *Cult of the Nation*, 52–5; Rogister, *Louis XV*, 12.

[5] Hazard, *European Mind*, 502–4; Israel, *Radical Enlightenment*, 6.

Malebranche, and Rohault appeared fatal after the critiques of Le Clerc, Bayle, and other expatriate Huguenot *érudits*, as well as foreign thinkers such as Locke, Newton, Clarke, and Leibniz. All this contributed to the post-1720 loss of prestige and receding of interest which, by the 1720s had largely undermined the viability of French Cartesianism.[6]

Despite shortages of paper and skilled printers, and continued refusal of the authorities to permit publication of Bayle, Le Clerc, and other key authors, a surge in publishing activity during these years at Paris and other major cities resulted in the appearance, both legally and illegally, of a torrent of previously banned or unavailable books A few were intellectually significant works like Fénelon's *Démonstration de l'existence de Dieu* (Paris, 1713), a text penned many years before but brought out now together with Tournemine's refutation of Spinoza, and (among the illegal category) Fontenelle's *L'Origine des fables* (Rouen, 1714), a text previously left unknown in manuscript since its composition in the 1680s.[7] But most of this soon vast outpouring of challenging reading matter consisted not of 'philosophical', scientific, or political publications but new kinds of pious literature, especially Jansenist works,[8] often entering illegally from the Netherlands.[9] This post-1713 opening up and diffusion during the regency period and the 1720s and 1730s rode on a spectacular surge of 'livres de Hollande' entering through Rouen and other sea ports, shipped from Rotterdam in particular. Holland in this way served to familiarize the French reading public for the first time with numerous authors banned and only very patchily known about under Louis XIV—notably Bayle, Pascal, Fénelon, Malebranche, Le Clerc, Basnage, and Richard Simon, creating a new framework in which philosophical debate outside the universities as well as the production and circulation of clandestine manuscripts could flourish.

Numerous individuals, after years of imposed discretion and near silence, now felt freer to express their opinions and began, as was widely noted around 1720, to do so more openly. Huguenots and Jansenists became more vocal as did intellectual dissidents who now dropped much of their previous furtiveness except, as with publication of irreligious and erotic books, where such activity remained definitely illegal. In June 1715, Boulainvilliers's *protégé* Fréret was released from the Bastille where he had spent his time reportedly learning Bayle's whole *Dictionnaire* by heart, having been imprisoned in the last December of Louis's reign for 'plusieurs libelles'.[10] From 1716, Voltaire began openly styling himself a 'Deist'; his brief incarceration in the Bastille by the new regime, in May 1717 (released April 1718), was unconnected with his Deism, resulting from his having penned some irreverent verses about the regent and Madame du Barry.[11] Despite being imprisoned,

6 Watson, *Breakdown*, 101–15.

7 BL, MS 4284, fo. 13. Ganeau to Des Maizeaux, Paris, 23 Mar. 1714?; Mothu, 'Un morceau', 37.

8 Maire, *De la cause de Dieu*, 136, 138–9.

9 Israel, 'Publishing', 233–43; Shank, 'Before Voltaire', 421–2, 433; Pevitt, *Man*, 320.

10 Wade, *Clandestine Organization*, 186; Grell and Volpilhac-Auger, *Nicolas Fréret*, 26–7; Schröder, *Ursprünge*, 38.

11 Schröder, *Ursprünge*, 26–7, 31; Pevitt, *Man*, 320.

Voltaire, like Montesquieu, actually greatly admired the regent's deftly reformist, pro-aristocratic politics, confining his revenge to later blackening the image of the Bastille.[12]

A degree of intellectual and religious freedom after a long era of stifling absolutism inevitably brings its own problems. Many who benefited from the weakening of royal and episcopal control, especially Jansenists and hard-line Calvinists, still disapproved of both liberty of conscience and toleration on principle. To advocates of religious uniformity, ecclesiastical authority, and divine right monarchy, the obvious changes during the regency and in the 1720s, and signs of an incipient secularization, seemed altogether pernicious, especially being accompanied as they were by a tide of *livres de Hollande*, previously difficult to obtain books, pamphlets, and periodicals, welcomed by many nobles, professionals, and more liberal clergy. The Orléans regency, noted Gundling, at Halle, presided over an unprecedented transformation in the French book trade, publishing, reading habits, and indeed the French state of mind itself.[13]

In aristocratic circles, intellectual libertinism, political debate, and an easygoing approach in the sexual sphere were trends encouraged, moreover, by the regent personally. Philippe d'Orléans (1674–1723), a man of pronounced freethinking views and liberal tastes who knew and esteemed both Boulainvilliers and Fontenelle, privately enjoyed discussion of 'philosophical' topics and, like others of his class, thoroughly despised the religious polemics of the age as well as taking a discreet interest in the surge of irreligious clandestine manuscripts at least one of which, by Fontenelle, is known to have been read aloud to him in his private rooms by the author.[14] With this enlarged freedom—but also disillusionment and growing cynicism about government—anti-absolutist, anti-ecclesiastical, and radical ideas rapidly spread behind the scenes and did so with a measure of official collusion. Fontenelle and Boulainvilliers were now men of influence. Montesquieu—who experienced the intellectual repression under the ageing Louis XIV as a student, in Paris, between 1709 and 1713—admitted after the regent's death, in January 1724, to actually regretting the demise of a ruler for the first time in his life. In his and Voltaire's eyes, the tactful, sophisticated, easygoing duke, despite being damaged by political failures and especially the disastrous scandal of the failed royal bank set up, in 1720, under John Law, remained the very image of a benign, near heroic agent of consensus and compromise, a kind of 'anti-Louis XIV'.[15]

Meanwhile, Jansenism, and, in the south, Protestantism, besides moderate Deism and radical thought, all now spread and increased their penetration, transforming France into what quickly became the headquarters of Europe's organized doctrinal opposition to established structures of power, authority, and doctrine. Deep divisions over church affairs, Jansenist agitation, and the volatility of Parisian

12 Lüsebrink and Reichardt, *The Bastille*, 27.
13 Gundling, *Vollständige Historie*, i. 159–60.
14 Mothu, 'Un morceau', 37–8; Pevitt, *Man*, 9.
15 Pevitt, *Man*, 320; Ehrard, *L'Esprit des mots*, 113–14.

popular religion in the 1720s, noted the Danish Lutheran Ludvig Holberg,[16] were particularly crucial agents of cultural change.

Of these, it was certainly Jansenism which, on the surface at least, had the greatest impact. For prior to 1715, the traditional religiosity of most Frenchmen was essentially an illiterate, non-doctrinal religious culture dependent on proclaimed authority and visual aids to piety such as relics, images, and ritual, all stoutly defended by the Jesuits in particular. By contrast, the Jansenist movement, systematically repressed by Louis XIV, after 1713 quickly gained the initiative in French lay religious culture despite the opposition of most of the episcopate, the Jesuits, and the crown, welling up strongly among the literate urban population and much of the lower clergy, especially in major cities such as Paris, Rouen, and Lyons, but also in many other places, aggravated by the papal bull *Unigenitus* (1713) which Louis had solicited and which roundly condemned Jansenism. The regent's efforts to check this rebellion, and curb Jansenist insubordination within the church, via a negotiated settlement of a long list of procedural, doctrinal, and church constitutional issues which had lain unresolved for decades, utterly backfired from the government's point of view: instead of resolving the tension, Philippe's efforts at compromise only inflamed opinion, hugely boosting urban popular Jansenist resentment, agitation, and rebellion, and visibly widening the deep fissures in French literate culture and society.[17]

This fundamental Counter-Reformation (or incipient Counter-Enlightenment) of a major part of the French (and Flemish) church and society welling up from within, primarily from among the urban population, is sometimes characterized as an 'interiorization' of French piety. But 'interiorization' hardly seems the appropriate term. For while Jansenist reformism sought to reduce use of visual images and the outward appurtenances of faith, de-emphasizing the cult of saints and the Virgin, eschewing pompous burials, semi-pagan carnivals, and processions, and urging more austerity of cult and lifestyle, Jansenist renewal, prioritizing repentance, submission, and a more orderly systematizing of belief, above all aspired to intensify lay spirituality and religious commitment through preaching, collective experience, and directed reading.[18]

The faithful were summoned to discard visual props and 'superstition' other than simple crucifixes and holy water fonts, and manifest devotion rather through purifying and projecting what they believed, both inwards and outwards, transforming piety from the visual and aesthetic participation of the illiterate, addicted to venerating saints and watching spectacles, into an essentially literate, text-based faith anchored in doctrinal and confessional rigour. The shift was from simple credulity to systematically organized belief, from ritual, and a profusion of objects and relics, to a specifically theological rather than 'superstitious' culture absorbed through

[16] Holberg, *Memoirs*, 69–70.

[17] Kreiser, *Miracles, Convulsions*, 27–8; Ellis, *Boulainvilliers*, 112–13.

[18] Vovelle, *Piété baroque*, 495–6, 534; Fairchilds, 'Marketing', 40, 42–3, 52.

preaching and reading. It was reminiscent of the Huguenot upsurge of the late sixteenth century, in some respects, especially in its stress on literacy, on reforming religion, and its power to grip the cities in spiritual agitation, but differed in its deep loyalty to Catholic doctrine.

Here was a religious outlook even more adamantly opposed to philosophical principles than traditional faith owing to its austere morality and insistent propagation of formulated doctrine in place of the old passive deference and lay illiteracy. Jansenism was particularly emphatic in seeking to guide Man's moral quest away from the this-wordly, and the social, to the individual, transcendental, and penitential. Montesquieu, though not unappreciative of Jansenist fortitude in the face of Louis XIV's persecution, nevertheless, like all the *philosophes*, moderate and radical, disliked both Jansenist dogma and morality, once remarking acidly that Jansenism leaves men with none of the worldly pleasures other than that of scratching ourselves.[19]

Jansenism was even more detested by Voltaire. One of his two earliest *contes philosophiques* [philosophical stories], *Cosi-Sancta*, penned around 1718 whilst a guest of the duchesse du Maine, at Sceaux, a lady fond of having stories read out at her all-night parties, is an elaborate joke ridiculing Jansenist austerity and belief in predestination. The heroine, *Cosi-Sancta*, a young woman strictly brought up on Jansenist principles, from St Augustine's birthplace, and the most beautiful of her province, whose sanctimonious husband collects the sayings of St Augustine, saves the lives of her husband, brother, and son by amply satisfying the lust of several unscrupulous but powerful men; for doing so much good she is canonized for her self-sacrifice after her death.[20] Of course, such aristocratic frivolities could not be published at the time and survived only in manuscript. But Voltaire's fierce antipathy to Jansenism remained, as with Diderot and Boulanger later, an abiding feature of his outlook. In an anonymous pamphlet, published in June 1750, he remarks that he who is a Jansenist 'est réellement un fou, un mauvais citoyen et un rebelle' who forsakes reason or he would see that a sect given to convulsions is a band of madmen, and is also a bad citizen 'parce qu'il trouble l'ordre de l'état'.[21]

The Jansenists built an impressively large following in the main cities after 1713, in no small part with the help of the illicit press. Indeed, quantitatively, printed Jansenist literature utterly dominated the clandestine category of publications in France between 1713 and the 1740s. Hence, the Jansenist revival owed much of its impact precisely to the new opportunities for communicating with the public which the post-1715 relaxation of the censorship and of royal ecclesiastical policies afforded. No less than 2,600 Jansenist and anti-Jansenist works long and short were published in France between 1713 and 1765. Especially before 1745, a veritable tidal wave of *littérature du jansénisme* and *de l'antijansénisme* poured from the presses, and while crown, episcopate, and Jesuits strove to generate an impressive counter-stream,

[19] Montesquieu, *Œuvres complètes*, 1001 (Pensée no. 1337); Van Kley, *Religious Origins*, 75–6; Kingston, 'Montesquieu on Religion', 385.

[20] Voltaire, *Romans*, 697–702; Pearson, *Fables*, 41–4, 47.

[21] [Voltaire], *La Voix du sage*, 427; Van Kley, *Religious Origins*, 98–9.

nevertheless, over two-thirds of this vast outpouring of theological protest, anger, and criticism was pro-Jansenist in orientation. Many hundreds of texts publicized new miracles, disputed ecclesiastical procedure, and protested over the papal bull *Unigenitus* (1713) which Louis XIV had requested of the papacy and which included provisions condemning active popular participation in the liturgy and lay reading of the Bible. Other polemics dealt with issues of sin, predestination, forms of spirituality, Jesuit policies, disputed points of Augustinian theology, and church–state relations.[22] The government's and episcopate's attempted crackdown was not so much on belief or religious practice as on public protest and incitement to protest, as well as 'convulsionary' excesses and publicizing Jansenist views. Of 332 Jansenists arrested in France during the period from 1715 to 1740, no less than 72 per cent, rather significantly, were interned for printing, editing, and bookselling offences. The imprisonment of Jansenist dissidents in the Bastille, both men and women, continued at exceptionally high levels through the 1740s.[23]

Jansenism differed from both traditional Catholicism and Protestantism especially in its insistence that the direct power of God, providence, repentance, and inner renewal should be closely linked not just to individual emotional religious experience, preaching, and reading, but also outward and collective events, thereby encouraging the spate of 'miracles', signs, public experiences, and 'convulsions' which occurred under Jansenist auspices during the second quarter of the eighteenth century, a spiritual impulse creating waves of collective religious agitation and excitement. In the late 1720s, 'miracles', accompanied by ecstatic manifestations in both men and especially women, convinced many in Paris that the Almighty did indeed favour the formerly persecuted, and still officially disapproved of, faction within French society and the church and that the official church was now discredited.[24]

Montesquieu notes that women were the driving force, the 'motrices de toute cette révolte' against papal and royal policy, and had dragged the men in their wake. Given both his discreet mockery of Jansenism and the subtle anti-feminism running through his *oeuvre*, it would seem his emphasis on this, in the *Lettres persanes*, is a way of gently ridiculing both women and Jansenism.[25] Like any *philosophe*, he had his reservations about both Jansenists and Jesuits; but he is by no means merely neutral on this subject. For though he disapproved of the strong government and ecclesiastical pressure brought to bear to stifle the movement, he also viewed the Jansenist popular upsurge as an irrational, dangerous, and destabilizing phenomenon, the neutralization of which by well-thought-out, non-violent, and non-oppressive means was an urgent priority.[26]

22 Phillips, *Church and Culture*, 108–10; Maire, *De la cause de Dieu*, 136–8.

23 Maire, *De la cause de Dieu*, 136–8; Cottret, *Jansénismes*, 295.

24 Cottret, *Jansénismes*, 295; Van Kley, *Religious Origins*, 97.

25 Montesquieu, *Lettres persanes*, 75, 115; Kingston, 'Montesquieu on Religion', 384–5; O'Reilly, 'Montesquieu: Anti-feminist', 144–8; Cottret, *Jansénismes*, 52–6.

26 Cottret, *Jansénismes*, 53–4, 79–81; [Diderot], *Suite*, 52–4; Mosher, 'Monarchy's Paradox', 195–6, 202.

The ardour of the *convulsionnaires* attached in particular to the Parisian cemetery of Saint-Médard around the tomb of a Jansenist hermit, François de Pâris (1690–1727), the site of a veritable thaumaturgical frenzy, especially miraculous curing of the disabled and long-term sick, alleged miracles later scathingly dismissed by Diderot among others, disagreement about the status of which, in 1751–2, played a considerable part in the wider dispute about miracles infusing the public quarrels surrounding the first two volumes of Diderot and d'Alembert's *Encyclopédie*.[27] 'The curing of the sick, giving hearing to the deaf and sight to the blind', records Hume, who lived in France for several years in the mid-1730s and undoubtedly also witnessed Jansenist fervour at first hand, 'were everywhere talked of as the most usual effects of that holy sepulcher.'[28] A miraculous cure which occurred there in 1731, the healing of a paralytic female neighbour, was attested to, among others, by Boulanger's parents, the future *encyclopédiste* being 9 at the time and his father, a paper merchant, a devout Jansenist.[29]

The irreproachably austere hermit de Pâris, notes d'Argens, proclaimed a morality of renunciation which thoroughly impressed the multitude though one which must be judged by any true philosopher 'pernicieuse à la société'.[30] Blunter still, Voltaire thought the *convulsionnaires* included some of the most fanatical, intolerant, and irrational minds in Europe.[31] What was most 'extraordinary' about the whole phenomenon, for Hume, was that 'many of the miracles were immediately proved upon the spot, before judges of unquestioned integrity, attested by witnesses of credit and distinction, in a learned age, and on the most eminent theater that now is in the world'.[32] The Jesuits, adds Hume, sought to discredit these 'miracles' but were never 'able distinctly to refute or detect them'. But this did nothing to soften the sarcasm of his dismissal of claims that the certainty of Jansenist miracles was as incontestable as those 'of our Saviour' and that the 'evidence for the latter is equal to that of the former'. It may be 'ridiculous', he comments, to compare the first with purely 'human testimony', but were one to allow the comparison, for the sake of discussion, treating Gospel as human testimony, then one 'might, with some appearance of reason, pretend that the Jansenist miracles much surpass the other in evidence and authority'.[33]

Occasionally embarrassed by their adherents' excesses of zeal, Jansenist clergy rarely disowned such outbursts. Historians, still today, sometimes associate Jansenism, particularly in Italian and Austrian contexts, with 'enlightened' attitudes, affirming links between Jansenism and moderate Enlightenment. But while, as in the Austria of Maria Theresa, there was often a pragmatic alliance between

27 Yvon et al., *Apologie*, seconde partie, 245–51, 264–74; Van Kley, *Religious Origins*, 97–100.

28 Hume, *Enquiry Concerning Human Understanding*, 132; Delumeau and Cottret, *Le Catholicisme*, 222, 277; Buckley, *At the Origins*, 208; Cottret, *Jansénismes*, 15, 59, 231, 244–5, 255.

29 Inguenaud, 'Famille', 361–2, 364.

30 D'Argens, *Lettres chinoises*, i. 73; Maire, *De la cause de Dieu*, 241–56.

31 Voltaire, *Traité sur la tolérance*, 56.

32 Hume, *Enquiry Concerning Human Understanding*, 132.

33 Ibid. 133 n.; Cottret, *Jansénismes*, 59.

Jansenism and moderate Enlightenment, both being committed to ecclesiastical reform, and purifying the cult, the two phenonema remained essentially quite distinct—and ultimately in conflict: the Jansenists were, in fact, the most implacable adversaries of Montesquieu, Voltaire, Buffon, Diderot, and Helvétius, and, professing a strict Augustinianism, denounced freedom of the individual, and unbelief, more stridently than any other wing of the church.[34] Far from participating in the Enlightenment, Jansenism strove to build, in opposition to secularism and *philosophie*, a spiritual counter-culture widening the gulf between reason and faith.

Research confirms that most *convulsionnaires* were women,[35] and the rest often artisans and workmen; but they also included some prominent persons, among them, ironically, Voltaire's own brother Armand Arouet, a government fiscal official (whom he despised), their father too having been a zealous Jansenist.[36] The bull *Unigenitus*' admonition against lay reading of the Bible, observes Montesquieu, in the *Lettres persanes*, was thought to be chiefly directed against the new fashion of women reading Scripture and, hence, frequently antagonized female devotees.[37] The *convulsionnaires*' fervour—urban, popular, semi-educated, and heavily orientated towards doctrine and belief—was further heightened by a passionate rhetoric proclaiming that pious rectitude, miraculous happenings seen and experienced, and most of all the simple faith of the humble, count for infinitely more in God's eyes—and on the arduous path to Heaven—than the arrogant and frivolous concerns of the irreligious lay educated and idly sophisticated.

In Paris, the agitation reached an extraordinary crescendo in the early 1730s, obliging the royal government, under the anti-Jansenist Cardinal Fleury, to close the Saint-Médard cemetery in January 1732, the year when Rousseau reached 20 and Diderot 19, and forbid all further manifestations of the 'convulsionary movement', though this only served to divert *convulsionnaire* fervour into other channels. Clandestine convulsionary gatherings proliferated more than before among the labouring poor, and elements of the Parisian middle classes, assembling regularly with between twenty and forty participants in private homes, especially of shopkeepers and artisans.[38] Likewise, elsewhere in France, informal prayer gatherings, convulsionary hysteria, and *figurisme* generated a Jansenist spiritual revival which culminated in the early and mid 1730s, the very years when Montesquieu's thought matured, Hume experienced France, the initially devout Diderot, living in the years 1730–5 in student lodgings in the Rue Saint-Victor, in the *quartier* of the *convulsionnaires*, studied theology and philosophy at the University of Paris, and the immature young Rousseau, residing as Madame de Warens's companion at Chambéry, became 'a half Jansenist', or so he claimed later, through reading

[34] Cottret, 'Jansenism', 284; Roger, *Buffon*, 186–7; Dupré, *Enlightenment*, 318.

[35] Maire, *De la cause de Dieu*, 295–6; Kreiser, *Miracles, Convulsions*, 252–5; Fairchilds, 'Marketing', 42.

[36] D'Argens, *Lettres chinoises*, i. 73, 76–7; Maire, *De la cause de Dieu*, 241–50.

[37] Montesquieu, *Lettres persanes*, 75.

[38] Vovelle, *Piété baroque*, 309, 365–6; Kreiser, *Miracles, Convulsions*, 67–8, 351; Van Kley, *Religious Origins*, 98; Maire, *De la cause de Dieu*, 289–94, 299, 327.

Jansenist literature, though 'their harsh theology scared me sometimes', and learned from them the true 'terror of Hell'.[39]

La Mettrie, intended by his family for a Jansenist career, switched to medicine at Paris where he studied in the years 1727–33;[40] he too, before proceeding to Leiden to study under Boerhaave in the mid 1730s, undoubtedly witnessed, like Diderot and Boulanger, Jansenist penitential fervour at first hand. Diderot describes one such eruption, in the streets of Paris, in his *Pensées philosophiques* (1746): the neighbourhood filled with shouts of 'Miracle! Miracle!' and he too began to run with the crowds through the streets to find a small lame 'impostor' who normally got about on crutches, being helped to walk without them by three or four others, inspiring vast exaltation.[41] This only confirmed, for him, that those who see ghosts are those who already believe in them and those who witness 'miracles' are they who already know there are miracles.

Diderot's observing in the streets of Paris what, in 1752, he called the 'spectacle abominable' of the *convulsionnaires* contributed both to his sweeping rejection of the possibility of miracles, a rejection as absolute as Spinoza's, and conviction that the common people, 'toujours avide du merveilleux', always find the miracles they are resolved to witness; it clearly reinforced his abiding dislike of displays of collective religious emotion and aversion to the proclaimed eternal damnation of much of humanity.[42] Serious consequences of many kinds flow, he, like Boulanger, became convinced, from the fears and anxieties inculcated by such a religion. All this, together with his ingrained anticlericalism, and long encounter with Jansenist doctrine whilst a full-time theology student in the years 1732–5, fed further a lasting antipathy to Pascal whom, in 1745, he called 'fearful and credulous' and someone who, though an elegant writer and good reasoner, potentially capable of helping to enlighten mankind, had unfortunately been led by providence into the hands of those [i.e. the Jansenists] who sacrifice their talents to their hatred.[43]

The Jansenist faithful were avid readers of a new style of religious commentary on, and prophesying about, social, historical, and political issues, making extensive use of biblical images and 'figures', symbols, and enigmas, a cultural-intellectual trend pronounced in early eighteenth-century French sermons and popular religious literature and known as *figurisme*. Much of the appeal and power of the Jansenist message was due to the success of the Jansenist clergy in firing up the people with a discourse which brought both Bible and doctrine closer to them. Figurative explanation was also an effective way of putting an elevated interpretation on the writhing of the *convulsionistes* deemed by Diderot both 'odious and ridiculous'.[44] Energizing popular opinion, Jansenist preachers encouraged the

[39] Rousseau, *Confessions*, 194, 202–3; Trousson, *Rousseau*, 114–15; Cottret, *Jansénismes*, 56, 76, 78–9.

[40] Vartanian, *La Mettrie's* L'Homme machine, 2, 10; Markovits, 'La Mettrie' (2003), 183.

[41] Diderot, *Pensées philosophiques*, 42–3; [Diderot], *Suite*, 53; Cottret, *Jansénismes*, 348 n. 93.

[42] [Diderot], *Suite*, 52–4; Yvon et al., *Apologie*, seconde partie, 228–9.

[43] Diderot, *Pensées philosophiques*, 15; Van Kley, *Religious Origins*, 245; Duflo, *Diderot philosophe*, 15; Inguenaud, 'Famille', 396.

[44] Yvon et al., *Apologie*, seconde partie, 247–8.

populace to judge, and react emotionally to, current events, and actively protest against the government and bishops; indeed, *figurisme* blended with *convulsionisme* produced a potent discourse the barely literate could readily grasp, and one which could quickly be mobilized against any opponent, indeed, according to Diderot, in 1752, was fully capable of obliterating every last remnant of *bon-sens* lingering in Jansenist heads.[45]

However, *figurisme*'s esoteric prophecies and cryptic symbolism also played into the hands of the *philosophes* and the *esprits forts*: for it further widened and deepened the rift in the church, weakening the episcopate, as well as further intensifying the popular character, intolerance, and vehement anti-intellectualism of Parisian Jansenism.[46] Among prominent early eighteenth-century Jansenist *figuristes* was the same highly skilled editor and orator Jean-Baptiste Gaultier (1684–1755) who later emerged as a leading critic of Montesquieu during the great public controversy over *L'Esprit des lois* in the years 1748–52. In Gaultier's eyes, those who use naturalistic arguments to belittle the divine order, and convert the duties of divinely given morality to general laws of society, are wicked betrayers of true doctrine who must be made to feel the people's anger. To be taken to heart by ordinary folk, held Gaultier, the laws of family, religion, politics, and society must be seen to emanate directly from the transcendent will of God to whom alone homage and adoration are due.[47] In his diatribe against Deism of 1746, entitled *Le Poème de Pope intitulé* Essai sur l'homme, *convaincu d'impiété*, Gaultier closely linked Bayle to the rise of French Deism, rightly stressing that Bayle, far from being a fideist, is someone who insidiously subjects 'Christian mysteries' to the light of reason.[48]

Hence, what was by far the strongest *cultural* current in Early Enlightenment France was a force quintessentially opposed to all forms of Enlightenment in intellectual matters.[49] Much of French urban culture was being powerfully reconfigured by a popular insurrection working from the bottom up, fomented by dissident parish clergy. It was the force of popular feeling which enabled clerical leaders of the revolt against state and church increasingly to throw the royal authorities and episcopate, Jesuits, and theology faculties, onto the defensive. But this powerful, textually disseminated extension of Catholic theology in French society and culture was, by the same token, potentially also an instrument for forging opinion in the streets into a potent engine of war for crushing intellectual dissent, impious books, irreligion, and 'philosophy'.

From 1728, the Jansenist leadership also wielded a regular, semi-clandestine, but soon well-established news review, a hard-hitting weekly journal which the government proved unable to locate and suppress, entitled the *Nouvelles ecclésiastiques*, a

[45] Ibid. 248. [46] Kreiser, *Miracles, Convulsions*, 248–9, 395; Chartier, *Cultural Origins*, 103–4.

[47] Maire, *De la cause de Dieu*, 112, 126, 403, 498, 650–1; Masseau, *Ennemis des philosophes*, 55–6; Sgard, 'Diderot', 13. [48] Gaultier, *Poème de Pope*, 124; Masseau, *Ennemis des philosophes*, 219.

[49] Vovelle, *Piété baroque*, 475, 477–8, 489; Hufton, *Europe*, 55–6, 63; Van Kley, 'Christianity', 1086, 1093.

journal destined to play a key role in mid eighteenth-century French cultural and intellectual controversies. Initially, it engaged only in theological polemics; but, from 1746, it began fulminating, as one historian aptly put it, 'against the whole secular temper of the age as well as the blasphemies of the *philosophes*'.[50] That year, in effect, marked a turning point in the Counter-Enlightenment: for it was the Jansenists who first established in France that potent independent press and large urban opposition readership, as well as oppositional habit of mind and reading, which, from the late 1740s, forced the *philosophes* into open combat against popular attitudes and 'religion', pushing them into organizing as the *parti philosophique* and seeking to infiltrate society, and counter-propagandize broadly, in their turn.[51]

For, however formidable, early eighteenth-century French Jansenism clearly suffered from a fatal limitation: a new phenomenon, being a public force peculiarly dependent on urban popular support, it was precisely its appeal to the man in the street which proved its undoing. For its irrationality, intolerance, and insistent demands increasingly alienated the more highly educated. Furthermore, after the closing of Saint-Médard, heightened pious fervour inspired a new style of group experience characterized by waves of collective religious emotion, frequent outbursts of a 'hysterical nature', and individual ecstatic experiences involving furious spasms and convulsions, screaming, and thrashing about on the floor, trends which alienated many others besides the *philosophes* and struck the latter as the very acme of irrationality.

Hence the Jansenist upsurge was in some respects counter-productive from its own standpoint, less through open defiance of ecclesiastical authority and evasion of censorship than via, on the one hand, its attack on toleration, secular values, and irreligion, and on the other, *convulsionnaire* excesses, a ferment creating more and more of those Diderot dubbed *Anti-Convulsionistes*.[52] In both respects, it seemed peculiarly apt to generate a broad-based urban counter-movement propagating an intense scepticism about miracles and prophecies, and support for what one worried senior ecclesiastic, Houtteville, in 1722 called 'le monstrueux système de la tolérance'. The Jansenists, held Diderot in 1752, by everywhere provoking such bitter disputes, and so much insubordination within the church, did incomparably more in the forty years prior to the appearance of the first volume of the *Encyclopédie* to diminish the laity's respect for the church, and raise philosophy's prestige, than did the *philosophes*.[53]

At the same time, Jansenism carved out a wider and wider sphere for public polemics and debate, as a consequence of which it also unwittingly extended freedom of thought, more and more polarizing society, by mobilizing the urban common man against the intellectual elite. Jansenism set out to reinforce faith, trust in miracles, and the pull of tradition, but simultaneously exacerbated strife in the

50 Hampson, *Enlightenment*, 135.
51 Kreiser, *Miracles, Convulsions*, 48–50; Masseau, *Ennemis des philosophes*, 139.
52 Ehrard, *L'Idée*, 86–7.
53 [Diderot], *Suite*, 52–4.

church, helped discredit the Jesuits and their schools, and alienated many of the highly educated. Finally, the movement depended for its active support on levels of popular fervour which it proved impossible to sustain indefinitely. As a popular movement, Jansenism, by the early 1740s, was already visibly ebbing.[54]

Houtteville, writing in the early 1720s, saw that behind France's ecclesiastical civil war was being waged a still deeper spiritual struggle linked to Jansenism, no doubt, but which ultimately far transcended it in its capacity to transform French society, namely the upsurge of philosophical doubt, freethinking, and impiety, driving on all sides a proliferation of *incrédules*. Amid the distractions of the Jansenist controversy and clamour of popular piety, traditional religious feeling and genuine Catholic piety were rapidly eroding if not among the people then certainly among those who demand positive evidence and rational arguments to justify so much, and such conspicuous, fervour, intolerance, and preoccupation with dogma. Already by the 1720s, nothing could be plainer than that freethinking and irreligion were systematically capturing the many who refused to be bullied by the Jansenist revolt and had cause to fear the power of popular belief.[55]

Admittedly, it was still rare, granted Houtteville, in 1722, for freethinkers openly to deny miracles, or defy established structures of belief, in public. But this was now definitely due, in his opinion, less to the constraints of royal laws weakened by the regency's policies, or ecclesiastical authority, than precisely—as Jean Meslier also judged—the refusal of the unlearned majority or what Meslier called 'l'empire de la multitude' to tolerate impiety: for in Paris it was now especially the people, backed by the *Parlement*, rather than the crown or church who would permit no talk against faith, sacraments, worship, piety, and miracles.

The more, therefore, the force of popular piety made itself felt, the stronger the reaction. In the big cities, an undisguised, provocative defiance of received opinion slowly reared its head in response. In 1729, the Paris police recorded that a certain 'Gautier' was regularly instigating open-air 'conferences', including in the Luxembourg gardens, denouncing revealed religion as a human contrivance and the popes as cunning fabricators of doctrines by which the French are misled, scorning Moses as a 'tyrant' who enslaved his people with a cult designed to deceive them while the powerful of the world profit from faith to keep their subjects in subjection.[56] It is wholly illogical to believe Jesus is God or engendered by God, and to believe in the Incarnation, he urged, while to believe that a woman can, through divine providence, conceive a child without sexual intercourse is surely 'la chose la plus absurde qu'on ait pu imaginer'. If anyone objected that belief derives from faith, he would reply that faith is God's gift, that it is up to him to give it or not; if he does not, no one need believe 'ce qu'on nous dit être incompréhensible'.

[54] Maire, *De la cause de Dieu*, 301.

[55] Houtteville, *Religion chrétienne prouvée*, i. pp. vi–viii.

[56] 'Notes et documents', *La Lettre clandestine*, 2 (1993), 214–15.

Where the first beginnings of radical thought in France, before 1713, had been furtive and inconspicuous, the clandestine techniques of the pre-1713 era now invaded the public sphere if not in a new way then certainly to a wholly new extent. Fostering ideas opposed to church dogma, popular belief, and divine right monarchy, as well as *Malebranchiste* thought structures, had earlier been veiled from the view of nearly everyone; now the phenomenon permeated elite culture in the main cities. The change in cultural climate after 1715 brought radical thought, if not yet quite into the open, then certainly out of the closet, radical thinking becoming a pervasive force even though, for the moment, it still relied on the clandestine methods perfected before 1713.

2. THE MATERIALIST CHALLENGE

Of the private Fontenelle the public knew nothing about, it has been aptly said that he was master of two subversive techniques—that of insinuating seditious ideas between published lines and undermining established views with anonymous 'philosophical' manuscripts.[57] The same was true of his allies, disciples, and their followers. Clandestine manuscripts, conversation, and insinuation in published writings, then, were their weapons and, in the long run, proved extremely formidable ones. Foremost among the *philosophes* clandestinely attacking, on the one hand, Louis XIV's legacy of enforced cultural uniformity and, on the other, the cultural and intellectual 'empire of the multitude', were Fontenelle, Boulainvilliers, Fréret, Lévesque de Burigny, Benoît de Maillet (1656–1738), the physicist Jean Jacques Dorthous de Mairan (1678–1771), the grammarian César Chesneau Du Marsais (1676–*c.*1756), the Deist *militaire philosophe* Robert Challe (1659–1721), Saint-Hyacinthe, the refractory priest Jean Meslier (1664–1729), and the atheistic critic Nicolas Boindin (1676–1751), as well as the reclusive, sickly aristocrat the marquis de Vauvenargues (1715–47), the veteran soldier thinker Jean-Baptiste de Mirabaud (1675–1760), and, by the early 1730s, the eloquent libertine the marquis d'Argens.

During the 1720s and 1730s, such men still conducted themselves with calculated caution, working in tiny discreet networks, or abroad, or largely in isolation, as with Vauvenargues, an ardent admirer of Boulainvilliers from whom, presumably, he derived his Spinozism but who, as far as is known, knew none of the others. All employed sophisticated techniques of masking, camouflage, and insinuation, but now did so in a usually less isolated, more concerted, fashion than before 1715. While propagating their views only indirectly, deviously, or, like Vauvenargues reclusively practising philosophy in almost total privacy, they explored both the human condition and our cosmos anew, laying the basis for an established materialist, pantheist, and *Spinosiste* coterie which by 1720, as

[57] Mothu, 'Un morceau', 36; Niderst, 'Fontenelle', 161, 173.

Houtteville attests, already unmistakably represented an intellectually formidable and unsettling underground intellectual opposition and one which discerning eyes could see might eventually exert a far more revolutionary impact than the Jansenist agitation to which in part it was a response, the dialectical other.

Philosophical writings fomenting irreligious, materialist, and radical Deist sentiments thus began to be diffused widely in French society, becoming to an extent a typical accoutrement of the cultural life of the social elites. Houtteville's (and others') remarks show that it was no longer uncommon to encounter French nobles, officials, and diplomats who scarcely troubled to conceal freethinking, libertine views from others and even considered such opinions proper for men of their station. D'Argens, in 1739, has one of his fictional French noblemen profess total scorn for popular ideas as well as the host of theologians and academically accredited 'philosophers' who, as he puts it, waste their energies combating the teachings of 'Spinosa et Vanini'. The new generation of French *esprits forts*, says d'Argens's fictional hero, felt only contempt for all these so-called 'philosophes qui leur [i.e. to Spinoza and Vanini] étoient contraires', that is ideologues employing Aristotle, Descartes, Malebranche, Houtteville, and other academically respectable authorities against Boulainvilliers, Fontenelle, Du Marsais, d'Argens, and their allies.[58]

Circulating seditious ideas by clandestine manuscript may seem a more tenuous way of propagating dissident ideas than the risky and—within France—still comparatively rare device of illegal printing. But in the main cities where such manuscripts circulated, the readership was sufficiently small, and reports about inaccessible but scandalous manuscripts sufficiently enticing, to foster a potent mystique surrounding the distribution of such literature. The *anti-philosophe* historian of philosophy Guillaume Maleville (1699–1771), for instance, remarks that before Boulainvilliers's *Essai de métaphysique* (1706), a reworking of Spinoza's *Ethics*, was illegally published in 1731, it caused him more anxiety circulating in manuscript than it did afterwards as a clandestine publication. For previously, as a young priest, having heard about it only from *esprits forts* lauding it as a work 'plein de subtilité et de force', he had felt a deep dread dispelled as soon as he read it, after publication, and found its arguments less terrible than he had feared.[59] Maleville was not the only Jansenist *anti-philosophe* greatly preoccupied with such literature; other pillars of Counter-Enlightenment, like the Jansenist priest Jean-Baptiste Gaultier, similarly pored over texts like Du Marsais's *Examen* with deep but fascinated loathing, anxious to uncover the true aims and intentions lurking behind the more restrained texts the *Spinosistes* did publish.[60]

The clandestine manuscripts mostly originated in a pre-1713 milieu of intellectual concealment but now circulated in a world emerging from the oppressive absolutism of Louis XIV, though those who copied, circulated, or otherwise participated

[58] [d'Argens], *Le Législateur moderne*, 5.

[59] Benítez, *Face cachée*, 34–5, 310; Mothu, 'Les Vanités manuscrites', 66.

[60] Gaultier, *Poëme de Pope*, 1–2.

in this refined form of disaffection could on occasion still be made examples of in a way which certainly deterred blatant indiscretion but also underlined, as the radical *philosophes* and their supporters saw it, the biased, prejudiced, and irrational character of the government's continued support for clerical and popular intolerance and hostility to freethinking. Among those severely punished was a priest, Étienne Guillaume, curé of Fresnes sur Berny since 1707, arrested and brought to the Bastille in April 1728, accused of writing against the Christian faith, spreading 'atheism', and presiding over impious discussions at the residence of the comte de Plélo, at Vaugirard, focal point of one of the more notorious aristocratic philosophical coteries of the 1720s.[61]

Louis, comte de Plélo (1699–1734), was a spendthrift and short-lived young Breton nobleman with a large library, destined to die fighting the Russians during the War of the Polish Succession, in a failed landing at the mouth of the Vistula designed to relieve the siege of Danzig. As a youth, he had lived in both Holland and England (where he acquired a detailed knowledge of Tindal among other freethinkers) and became a noted connoisseur of the latest European freethinking trends and literature, being well read in English and Italian as well as French. A vocal critic of absolute monarchy, he was a member, for a time, of the aristocratic discussion club the Entresol, which met weekly for much of the 1720s.[62] In 1728, at the age of 29, he was appointed French ambassador in Copenhagen. Guillaume, his intellectual accomplice, had composed a huge, two-folio subversive text (now lost), which seems, from reports and a few surviving fragments, to have compared Moses and Jesus unfavourably with Socrates, Plato, and Confucius, and claimed these philosophers to have taught a higher morality, and showed more moral integrity, than the founders of the revealed religions. Hints suggest that this lost text was unrelated to *L'Esprit de Spinosa* as some scholars formerly thought but rather another version of the Three Impostors concept.[63] After nine months' imprisonment, Guillaume was sent for further strict detention to the Abbey of Yvernaux where he remained confined until 1734.

Meanwhile, the flood of incoming French-language publications from Holland rendered the writings of Bayle, Malebranche, Arnauld, Pascal, Le Clerc, Abbadie, Jaquelot, Richard Simon, Basnage, Jacques Bernard, Jean-Frédéric Bernard, La Croze, Tyssot de Patot, Élie and Jacques Saurin, and other Huguenot *rationaux*, as well as masses of Jansenist and Protestant theology, that is all the many major and minor French writers Louis XIV and the bishops had tried to shut out and whose influence in French society had hitherto been restricted, integral to the post-1713 reconfiguring of French intellectual culture. There was a vast wealth of imported philosophical as well as theological material to digest, be stimulated by, and on

61 Vernière, *Spinoza*, 392–4, 397; Schröder, *Ursprünge*, 473; Benítez, *Face cachée*, 155–7.

62 Vernière, *Spinoza*, 397–8; Childs, *Political Academy*, 94.

63 Benítez, *Face cachée*, 166; Charles-Daubert, '*Traité des trois imposteurs*', 307–8 n.; Schröder, *Ursprünge*, 474.

which to comment. This needs to be stressed because much of the existing Anglo-American historiography, and some of the relevant continental literature, has persistently but quite wrongly claimed that the French Enlightenment was 'nourished by seventeenth-century English thought',[64] and that the essential and primary stimulus, before 1750, was coming from Britain, a view which now requires drastic revision.

English influence certainly played a key role, on the conservative side, later. Briefly, in the 1730s and 1740s, penetration of English ideas was, indeed, crucial to the making of the French moderate mainstream Enlightenment. Prior to about 1725, though, contrary to what has so often been claimed, 'English' ideas in fact played remarkably little part in the formation and propagation of French Enlightenment thought and, what is perhaps most important, an especially marginal role, indeed also long after the 1730s, in generating the more radical, thoroughgoing, and democratic dimensions of the French High Enlightenment.

Post-1715 France, in most respects, constituted an intellectual milieu markedly different from that prevailing in Britain, Italy, the Netherlands, or Germany. If outside intellectual influence played a large part in fostering French Enlightenment ideas, then without question overwhelmingly the chief input at work before the mid 1730s was Huguenot and French dissident literature banned under Louis XIV, seconded by the wider radical tendency emanating from the Netherlands. The evidence for this is unanswerable. The preface and main text of Challe's *Difficultés sur la religion proposées au Père Malebranche*, for instance, a huge work written in the years 1710–12 which has, with good reason, been dubbed the 'most important text of Deism of the French Enlightenment',[65] being the chief precursor of Voltaire and Saint-Hyacinthe, and a key marker of the French clandestine intellectual stage around 1713, reveals no foreign, other than Dutch (and Dutch Huguenot), influences whatsoever; and, as we shall see, this reflects the general pattern.

Challe sought to demolish Cartesianism, and especially Malebranche, and replace these with an anti-scripturalist providential Deism based not on belief but on 'certain' knowledge. He deemed mathematical demonstration, not facts, the ground of all certitude, claiming the rules for discovering the truth about religion are identical to those for finding the truth about anything else. Of course, Challe is much preoccupied with Spinoza.[66] But, unlike Fontenelle, Du Marsais, and Meslier he wholly rejects the Dutch philosopher's 'atheism' and elimination of all theism, free will and teleology;[67] he also discusses Jaquelot (who is likewise centrally preoccupied with Spinoza),[68] and cites Bayle and Le Clerc, as well as Jurieu whom he heartily detests.[69] However, no English authors, books, or influences are referred to at all and, if he differs markedly from Voltaire and other providential Deists in this,

64 Porter, *Enlightenment*, 6–9; Kennedy, *A Cultural History*, 55; Spallanzani, *Immagini*, 38.

65 Schröder, *Ursprünge*, 170, 484.

66 Challe, *Difficultés*, 227, 235.

67 Ibid. 57–8; Mori, 'Introduction', 13; Schröder, *Ursprünge*, 124, 148–9, 232.

68 Challe, *Difficultés*, 56, 677.

69 Ibid. 338.

he was, as we shall see, typical not atypical of the French Enlightenment as a whole before the mid 1730s.

Challe's providential Deist perspective is emphatically anti-Spinozist while yet centrally concerned with refuting Spinoza; it was also anti-Socinian insofar as Socinians reject the immortality of the soul, and proto-Voltairean in its stress on the reality of a divinely decreed morality emanating directly from God. While fiercely attacking all clergies, revelations, and organized religion, and denying the validity of 'faith', everything meaningful in human life being disclosed to us, in Challe's opinion, exclusively through reason rather than 'facts', this author also robustly defends the reality of an intelligent Creator, a God whom he proclaims 'parfaitement juste'.[70] The Almighty, he argues, never reveals his wishes to us via miracles and revelations but only through our powers of reason; yet he also administers reward and punishment to human souls after death.[71]

As with Challe, so with Meslier, the writer who was arguably the most coherently and systematically radical thinker of the French early eighteenth century, a key figure whose vast text, mostly written in the early 1720s, similarly cites no English sources at all and whose otherwise inexplicable neglect in conventional accounts of the Enlightenment may indeed be partly explicable in terms of his remarkable system obviously having nothing to do with English authors and ideas. This renegade priest built his elaborate atheistic materialism wholly on elements taken from Descartes, Malebranche, and Bayle as well as Tournemine's critique of Spinoza, most of his polemical barbs being directed against Malebranche and Fénelon.[72] And as with Challe and Meslier, so with Fontenelle, Boulainvilliers, Fréret, Mirabaud, Du Marsais, Lévesque de Burigny, and Vauvevenargues: far from generating, or being pivotal, the real influence of Locke, Newton, Clarke, Toland, and Collins on the formation of French radical ideas was exceedingly slight, only Locke having a noticeable influence and even then one restricted, in Boulainvilliers and Du Marsais, for instance, to some adjustments to Cartesio-Spinozistic epistemology. Grasping that this influence was very limited, moreover, is essential to a proper understanding of the basic intellectual mechanisms generating the French High Enlightenment.[73]

The term 'matérialistes' began to be used in France from around 1700. But it was certainly the post-1713 political, cultural, and ecclesiastical changes associated with Louis XIV's demise and the regency of Philippe, duc d'Orléans, which enabled coteries of *esprits forts* like the (in part, overlapping) circles of Boulainvilliers and Fontenelle and the Deistic group at the Parisian Académie des Inscriptions, as well as that surrounding the freethinking comte de Plélo—a close friend of the brother

[70] Ibid. 641; McKenna, 'Vauvenargues', 202.

[71] Challe, *Difficultés*, 58, 119, 121, 600–4; Mori, 'Introduction', 8.

[72] Wade, *Clandestine Organization*, 67–8, 73; Porset, 'Voltaire et Meslier', 198; Schröder, *Ursprünge*, 493–4.

[73] Ricuperati, 'Il problema', 384; Brogi, *Cerchio*, 144 n., 248, 195–202; Taranto, *Du déisme à l'athéisme*, 14, 433–4.

of the regent's mistress—to gather in select residences, forge links with highly placed persons, and meet regularly. This was a social milieu in which a radically new kind of intellectual framework and personal network could become entrenched,[74] making it possible to organize and concert intellectual strategies, and find posts for young freethinkers as tutors, editors, and secretaries.[75] Voltaire, looking back in 1767, described the French 'atheists' and *matérialistes* of the period of his youth as consisting of 'les Maillet, les Boulainvilliers, les Boulanger, les Meslier, le savant Fréret, le dialectician Du Marsais, l'intempérant La Mettrie, et bien d'autres'.[76]

Hence, it is no accident that the future *encyclopédiste* Du Marsais, originally from Marseilles but since 1701 permanently in Paris, only became known in society from 1716, or that his most formidable radical text, the *Examen de la religion*, though written around 1705, should have languished largely unnoticed until it began circulating in Parisian 'cabinets' and was increasingly copied and discussed from around 1720.[77] It circulated anonymously like all the clandestine manuscripts except where, as with Boulainvilliers after 1722, the author was safely dead. Voltaire, though, always hostile to atheistic materialism and *le spinosisme*, long suspected Du Marsais—someone he respected as a grammarian, scholar, and man of sense but despised as a philosopher—to be its author; the *Examen* itself he brusquely dismissed as poorly argued and badly written.[78] He could not deny, though, that it was, from the 1720s, among the most influential philosophical *clandestina* in France or that Diderot deemed Du Marsais not just the foremost of grammarians but at the same time, as he put it in 1751, 'un de nos meilleurs métaphysiciens'.[79]

'Le dialectician Du Marsais', as Voltaire disparagingly calls him, for whom there is nothing after death, was among the first systematically to employ the term *l'esprit philosophique* in its radical, specifically anti-Lockean, sense of meaning the sole correct instrument for interpreting reality.[80] A materialist and an atheist, he developed his mechanistic materialism from elements of Descartes, Fontenelle, Boulainvilliers, Challe, stripped-down Malebranche, and again Spinoza. Unlike Fontenelle, Bayle, Boulainvilliers, Challe, and Meslier, Du Marsais it is true does incorporate something of Locke; but it would be quite wrong to suggest that Locke was a centrally formative or guiding influence in his thought. Du Marsais's empiricism, like Spinoza's, wholly dissolves the residual dualism in Locke and is, *au fond*, in no way authentically Lockean. Sense impression in Du Marsais, like the subsequent French materialists and Diderot, is not just the exclusive source of 'facts', words, emotions, and ideas but also defines 'la certitude' in every respect and 'les bornes des connoissances humaines'. Revelation and divine authority, in his opinion, influence human affairs

[74] Ellis, *Boulainvilliers*, 93–4, 102–10; Bell, *Cult of the Nation*, 57.

[75] Vernière, *Spinoza*, 388–2, 395–6; Benítez, *Face cachée*, 157–9; Mori, 'Postface', 338–41.

[76] Voltaire, *Lettres à son altesse*, 350–1.

[77] Mori, 'Du Marsais philosophe', 181; Mori, 'Introduction', 50; Schwarzbach, 'Les Clandestins', 169.

[78] [Du Marsais], *Examen*, appendices 363–4; Voltaire, *Œuvres complètes*, xxv. 125.

[79] Diderot, *Lettre sur les sourds*, 414.

[80] Voltaire, *Lettres à son altesse*, 350; Ildefonse, 'Du Marsais', 40, 42, 55.

only negatively, being powerful fictions needful of demolition by the philosopher along with the force of popular credulity.[81]

Against the Lockeans, Du Marsais argues that 'toutes nos connoissances viennent des sens' and that Locke's 'faculties' of the mind are a fiction.[82] This uncompromising empiricism he uses to underpin a wholly materialist conflation of body and mind, rejecting the principal features of Locke's epistemology—quasi-substantial dualism of mind and body, using empiricism to protect belief in miracles and the fundamentals of Christian theology as delivered through revelation. Du Marsais also entirely rejects Locke's use of empiricism to restrict philosophy's scope, in the process fiercely criticizing but yet also incorporating strands of Malebranche. As in his metaphysics, Bible criticism, and epistemology, Du Marsais develops a moral philosophy in essence indisputably far closer to that of Spinoza and Bayle than that of Locke.[83]

In developing a *matéraliste* conception of Man, Du Marsais is more explicit than most of the others in claiming Man is merely part of nature, indeed pre-empts La Mettrie by three decades in accounting the *philosophe* 'a human machine like any other man but a machine which, by its mechanical construction, reflects on its movements'.[84] The core of his psychology and moral theory is the Spinozist principle that all men want to be happy in their particular way and that all their decisions are mechanistically determined by this impulse: 'dans toutes les actions que les hommes font ils ne cherchent que leur propre satisfaction actuelle, c'est le bien ou plutôt l'attrait présent suivant la disposition méchanique où ils se trouvent qui les fait agir' [in all the actions of men they search only their own present satisfaction, this is the good, or rather the present attraction following the mechanical disposition in which they find themselves, that makes them act].[85]

In his *Le Philosophe*, a text dating from the years 1716–20,[86] Du Marsais restates his view that we know things only via sense impressions *and* learning to gather the abstract from the particular—rather than the mind having, as Locke argues, innate functions and faculties enabling us to refine simple ideas derived from the senses into more complex ideas. This monist empiricism, anchored in an overarching materialist metaphysics and blanket denial of religious authority, miracles, and theological dogmas, renders sense impression not just the first but the only path to knowing anything at all.[87] Against Locke and Le Clerc, Du Marsais refuses to accept there can be a rational conjunction of reason and faith and attacks revealed religion precisely for lacking, in his opinion, all empirical grounding and, hence, being at odds with reason: 'la religion chrétienne', he even contends, 'est le tombeau de la raison.'[88]

81 Ildefonse, 'Du Marsais', 38; [Du Marsais], *Le Philosophe*, 176–8, 192.

82 [Du Marsais], *Le Philosophe*, 177.

83 Mori, 'Introduction', 14, 16.

84 [Du Marsais], *Le Philosophe*, 174–7; Gumbrecht and Reichardt, '*Philosophe*', 18–20; Romeo, 'Matérialisme et déterminisme', 104.

85 [Du Marsais], *Le Philosophe*, 196.

86 Mori, 'Introduction', 40–1.

87 [Du Marsais], *Le Philosophe*, 180; Geissler, '*Matérialisme*', 63–4; Ildefonse, 'Du Marsais', 36–7.

88 [Du Marsais], *Le Philosophe*, 176–7; [Du Marsais], *Examen*, 299.

When assailing metaphysics and *métaphysiciens*, as he does repeatedly, Du Marsais undoubtedly includes Locke, along with Descartes and Malebranche, in this category. If he agrees with Challe in no other respect, he wholeheartedly concurs that the *philosophe* should be defined as someone for whom reason is the exclusive and only criterion of what is true. To this rule, Du Marsais, like Challe and Meslier, allows absolutely no exemption. Hence, where *métaphysiciens*, Du Marsais's shorthand for false teachers, purveying mystifying obfuscation, urge men to delegate facts to 'historians', and leave languages to grammarians, and concentrate on construing the truth of things according to their *a priori* principles, he urges readers to reject such limited conceptions of history and literature, and truncated a view of philosophy, and grasp that true philosophers, unlike 'metaphysicians', see that human reason only proceeds reliably when dealing with 'facts' and data discovered through our senses, whether directly or indirectly, through researching history, languages, and literature or using devices such as the telescope and microscope.

Above all, Du Marsais, one of the creators of the new enlightened conception of *philosophe*, held that a veritable empiricism, scorning all 'metaphysics', must assign a key role to grammar. For it is grammar, not merely the grammar of individual languages but rather the underlying structure, common to all languages, termed by Du Marsais 'grammaire générale', which reveals the true relationship—at first unreflectively and unconsciously and later, in the minds of those capable of rational thought—between things and ideas.[89] 'Philosophy', for Du Marsais, is by definition something all-inclusive, excluding nothing real and concerned only with facts.

A striking consequence of the cultural-intellectual crisis gripping post-1713 France was the striking weakness, compared to Britain, the Netherlands, Germany, and Italy, of a distinctively Christian moderate mainstream championing premisses designed to reconcile faith with reason, and tradition with science. The royal ban on Cartesianism, the shoring up of Aristotelianism until the last moment, and the split between traditional religiosity and Jansenist reform, not only shattered the intellectual unity of the church but seemingly largely deprived it of an intellectually cogent and educationally influential middle ground. With the collapse of Cartesianism and *Malebranchisme* in the 1720s, the liberal Catholic intelligentsia, and universities, endeavouring to move beyond the scholasticism, dogmatism, and rigid anti-Cartesianism of Louis XIV's reign, and forge a new consensus with which to defend faith, dogma, and ecclesiastical authority in France, had no real option other than to fall back on the Huguenot *rationaux* and, eventually, through them, embrace the intellectual edifice of Locke and Newton.

However problematic and, for many, distasteful was the prospect of leaning on pro-toleration, reforming, Protestant *rationaux* in a Catholic land steeped in hostility to Protestantism, the French moderate mainstream after around 1730 had very little alternative but to borrow extensively—while simultaneously stripping out the

[89] Ildefonse, 'Du Marsais', 40–1.

Arminian theology—from precisely that milieu. Even the Jesuits, abandoning their former Aristotelianism, and modifying their anti-Cartesianism albeit keeping up their campaign, orchestrated by Father René-Josephe de Tournemine in the *Journal de Trévoux*,[90] against *Malebranchisme* as back-door Spinozism, found themselves in a growing quandary and some perplexity, and eventually obliged to look across the Channel for new philosophical principles with which to anchor their cultural strategies.

Intellectually, the middle tendency in the French intellectual arena thus remained for decades, from 1713, conspicuously lightly armed compared with the Latitudinarian, 'Arminian', and Thomasian blocs in Britain, Holland, and Germany. The best-known French enlightened mainstream apologies for faith were Jean Denyse's *La Vérité de la religion chrétienne démontrée par ordre géometrique* (Paris, 1717) and Houtteville's *La religion chrétienne prouvée par les faits* (1721); however, both works proved highly problematic intellectually. Denyse's, like Houtteville's work, aspiring to employ only 'demonstrations' accessible to 'tout le monde' against Spinoza and Spinozism,[91] was largely inspired by Abbadie's *Traité de la vérité de la religion chrétienne* (2 vols., Rotterdam, 1684) to which, Denyse, a Sorbonne philosophy professor, freely admits he owes 'ce qu'il a de meilleur' in his own treatise. He tries to counter Spinoza by reclaiming the 'geometric method', the prestige of which was then especially high in France, to substantiate the 'reality' of miracles, and especially Christ's Resurrection, as 'historical facts' akin to what we see with our own eyes, show that matter is wholly inert, and prove divine reward and punishment in the hereafter, something essential, he thought, to upholding the moral order.[92]

Both Denyse and Houtteville viewed the intellectual crisis in France 'today' as being due to the influence of new, dangerous, and pernicious 'philosophy', creating a situation very different from that prevailing under Louis XIV, a behind-the-scenes confrontation with 'des athées au milieu du Christianisme'. However, the only philosophical opponents actually discussed by Houtteville as undermining authority, tradition, and established structures of thought are Spinoza and Bayle, the former especially being identified as the prime spokesman of the atheistic and materialistic wing of the philosophical dissenters, a thinker so central to the *esprits forts*' campaign against faith, tradition, and authority that it would be a waste of time disputing other systems. Both Denyse and Houtteville concentrate on proving the reality of miracles, especially Christ's miracles and Resurrection, Houtteville's aim, he says, being to show the atheists and Deists that however sceptical one may be about the 'mysteries' proclaimed by the church, if the facts related in the Gospels prove 'incontestables', this alone sweeps away all the objections of the *esprits forts*.[93]

90 Allard, 'Angriffe', 2–3.

91 Denyse, *La Vérité*, preface p. liii and pp. 129, 308–9, 342.

92 Ibid., preface; *L'Europe savante*, 2 (1718), 257, 261; Kors, *Atheism in France*, i. 37–8, 92, 108; Ehrard, *L'Idée*, 111–12.

93 Houtteville, *Religion chrétienne prouvée*, i, preface p. xix, 13; Landucci, 'Introduction', 14, 18; Schröder, *Ursprünge*, 138–41.

For Denyse and Houtteville, the task of defending Christianity involves less reaffirming 'mysteries' which they admit stand 'above' human reason than persuading us that we should trust in the church's promises and dogmas, given the indisputable historical 'facts' recounted in the Gospels. What establishes the veracity of Christ's miracles, they hold, following Abbadie, Le Clerc, and Locke, is the thick, uninterrupted chain of testimony and tradition reaching back to the eyewitnesses of the First Century, the authenticity of which is 'unquestionable'. Hence, it is the incontestably attested events proclaimed in the Gospels which prove the sacred truth of Christ's mission and his being divinely sent. Such impregnable 'facts' as Christ's and the disciples' miracles, and the reports that the disciples, for his sake, suffered 'les plus affreux supplices',[94] in turn, avers Houtteville, securely underpin papal primacy over the church and the church's authority over mankind, morality, politics, education, and truth itself.

Houtteville's volumes sold briskly and attained the status of pre-eminent French Catholic apology of the early eighteenth century. Yet his work also drew some harsh criticism and by no means only from the radical fringe, negative appraisals emanating from both Jansenist and Jesuit circles, both parties eyeing with suspicion Houtteville's *Malebranchisme* and style of combining philosophy and natural philosophy with theology. 'Miracles', noted his critics, occur, according to Houtteville, only within God's general design, as part of what he terms 'l'ordre général de la nature', hence, are exceedingly rare and, despite being firmly attested, far surpass human understanding. Houtteville, furthermore, envisages miracles as consonant events embedded in a rationally ordered and coherent universe otherwise comprehensively explicable in philosophical and scientific terms.[95] Such overt *Malebranchisme* seemed a singularly risky strategy in a work seeking to defend Christianity by combating Spinoza to the exclusion of practically everyone else, given that Tournemine and the Jesuits had for decades denounced Malebranche's thought as a form of back-door Spinozism.

Houtteville was hence widely judged a precarious, even 'dangerous', writer since in practice his works were apt to foster the very thing, Spinozism, which he seeks to overthrow.[96] The bleakness of the outlook, from the French Catholic point of view, in the 1720s, with neither Denyse nor Houtteville offering true reassurance, left a wide gap which the adherents of Newton and Locke eventually filled. The Jesuits firmly rejected Houtteville but not philosophy and science and continued with their search for a surer path, leading them increasingly, during the 1730s, in France as in Italy, to embrace 'English' ideas. Locke and Newton were now an attractive and powerful option if still not an altogether reassuring one for traditional shades of opinion. For out-and-out traditionalists abjuring any such compromises, there was

[94] Denyse, *La Vérité*, 333; *L'Europe savante*, 2 (1718), 263, 268, 272; McKenna, 'Vauvenargues', 202.

[95] Masseau, *Ennemis des philosophes*, 219–20; Shank, 'Before Voltaire', 489–91.

[96] [Desfontaines], *Lettres . . . à Monsieur l'Abbé Houtteville*, 69–70; Houtteville, *Religion chrétienne prouvée*, i, preface pp. xi, xiii; *Notice des écrits*, 187; Kors, *Atheism in France*, i. 348–9, 377; Ehrard, *L'Idée*, 84–5.

only one other way to go. With Malebranche discredited, and radical ideas gaining ground, the sole remaining plausible option if 'pernicious philosophy' was to be blocked was to embrace *anti-philosophie*, Jansenist *figurisme*, and the uncompromising rejectionism of the Counter-Enlightenment *dévots*.

3. CLANDESTINITY

The 1720s appear to have been the most fertile decade for both the copying and proliferation of clandestine philosophical manuscripts in France, as well as a crucial transition period of retreat from the cultural absolutism of Louis XIV's reign, a juncture revealing both the precariousness of the middle ground and the pending force of the challenges from both right and left. Cartesianism was wrecked but as yet Locke and Newton had barely begun to penetrate in France. Bayle and Spinoza had obviously made much more massive inroads at this juncture, and since the *dévot* right, represented by out-and-out fideists like Huet and Baltus, was firmly committed to *anti-philosophisme* and the unqualified supremacy of theology, uniquely in Europe, the French radical fringe was presented with a remarkable strategic opening—the opportunity to seize the intellectual initiative among the elites of French society in countering ecclesiastical and popular thinking. For the moment, only they possessed the resources to assail authority, tradition, and conventional structures of thought using the methods of the new critique, new science, and new philosophy. Post-1713 cultural circumstances, including the impact of the Jansenist resurgence in the main cities, thus helped radical thought emerge as potentially the chief philosophical opponent of those in society who fulminated against new ideas, loudly denying reason is Man's primary path to truth, the massed ranks of those dubbed by Boureau-Deslandes the *anti-rationaux*.[97]

Boulainvilliers, Fréret, Du Marsais, and the brothers Lévesque de Pouilly and Lévesque de Burigny were reclusive *érudits* who mixed mainly with other like-minded men of learning. This helped them slowly advance their cause in part by conducting abstruse scholarly discussions of historical topics, thereby uncovering false revelations and mysteries, pious forgeries, imposture, and explaining irrational myths, a not ineffective, if indirect, line of attack, safe from censure but only marginally relevant to disseminating radical ideas more widely in society. Keeping a low profile, however, by no means barred 'ces penseurs libres', noted a police report of 1737, from forming clandestine networks and 'corrupting' more and more younger men.[98] If social constraints and the police could, for the moment, inhibit the spread of freethinking small-group discussion into the semi-public milieu of the Parisian cafés, the police could not easily interfere with the circulation of clandestine texts, or impious readings and conversation, in select households.

[97] Tortarolo, *L'Illuminismo*, 30. [98] Wade, *Clandestine Organization*, 306.

Resentment at being a generally decried and still sporadically hounded coterie confronted by an overwhelming apparatus of royal, ecclesiastical, academic, and popular power, as well as the vigorous Jansenist revival, no doubt explains the militancy and often virulent tone of the attack on authority, tradition, and faith, as well as the frequently sombre pessimism pervading the writings of the French radical fringe in these decades. While some of these men were unknown to the wider public and effectively had no other status than that of being hardened *esprits forts* moving inconspicuously in Parisian society, others, like Fontenelle, Dorthous de Mairan, and, more ambiguously, Montesquieu, were prominent men whose successful careers obliged them to preserve an image of respectability in society more widely. This fomented a culture of camouflage and studied ambiguity especially between public and private discourses, producing some distinctly odd situations. The price the more prominent paid for the precautions required to safeguard their public reputations was the embarrassment of appearing to have two incompatible sets of principles, resulting, especially in Montesquieu's case, in some fierce disparagement 'from the left'.

If Montesquieu injected a implicit clandestine Spinozist undercurrent in his *Lettres persanes* (1721) perceptible only to readers complicit in such things,[99] and, as Benoît de Maillet reported in November 1736, publicly concealed his private disbelief in Creation and biblical chronology, 'pour être admis dans une académie honorable', to those who knew him it was clear he no more believed the Bible accurately fixes the age of the earth than that we can count the grains of sand on the shore.[100] But the contradiction between his personal views and public stance later elicited some pointed remarks in radical circles. When Boureau-Deslandes, a more notorious atheist, proud of his libertine convictions, lay on his deathbed in 1757, he acidly enquired of a bystander whether it was true that Montesquieu (who died two years before) had accepted the last rites: 'est-il possible qu'un tel homme ait voulu déshonorer sa mémoire?'[101]

How rightly to die was a topic on which Boureau-Deslandes counted as an expert, having begun his philosophical career with his *Réflexions sur les grands hommes qui sont morts en plaisantant* (1712), recounting the cheerful manner in which the truly wise meet their end. Reviewing this book (which also appeared in English) with obvious repugnance, the Jesuit *Mémoires de Trévoux* explained that while it preferred to ignore such 'impious' writings, the well-worn tactic of passing over such irreligious books in silence carried severe risks, encouraging libertines to exult 'sur le silence qu'on garde en de semblables occasions'.[102] The *esprits forts*, held *dévot* ideology, however confident whilst healthy, soon change their tune when seriously ill, experiencing acute pain, or approaching death. Maleville rejoiced on reading the 1756 supplement to Moréry's *Dictionnaire* where it was

[99] Negroni, 'Le Rôle', 49–50. [100] Benítez, *Face cachée*, 233, 246 n.

[101] Quoted in Geissler, *Boureau-Deslandes*, 23; Salaün, *L'Ordre*, 109.

[102] *Mémoires de Trévoux*, 12 (1713), art. xxxii, p. 410; Geissler, *Boureau-Deslandes*, 64.

reported that Boulainvilliers had expired 'très repentant et dans des sentiments forts chrétiens'.[103] Better grounded were the stories that Montesquieu had received the last rites at the hands of a Jesuit (Castel) who also obtained his permission to publish the terms of his confession 'for the edification of posterity and to combat *les esprits forts*'.[104]

Significantly, nearly all clandestine manuscripts which figured prominently in the making of the French Enlightenment were conceived between 1670 and the early 1730s, that is before the irruption of Newtonianism and Locke's influence in France. By 1734, the formative phase of the French Radical Enlightenment was already over, most relevant intellectual positions having by then entered into circulation and debate. The *clandestina* composed in France included Challe's *Difficultés*, Boulainvilliers's *Essai*, Boulainvilliers's *Abrégé*, Du Marsais's *Examen* (*c.*1705), Du Marsais's *Le Philosophe* (*c.*1720), *La Religion chrétienne analysée*, Fréret's *Lettre de Thrasybule et Leucippe*,[105] Meslier's *Testament*, Maillet's *Telliamed* (1717–30), Maillet's *Sentimens* finalized in the 1720s, Mirabaud's *Opinions des anciens sur la nature de l'âme*, the *De l'examen de la religion*—not to be confused with Du Marsais's earlier text—and the *Examen critique des apologistes de la religion chrétienne*, both the latter probably by Jean Lévesque de Burigny (1692–1785).[106] While most of these date from before 1720, their availability before that date was very limited, and references to them exceedingly rare; it was only during the period of the regency, after 1715, the signs are that these works began circulating in earnest, penetrating the select 'cabinets' of Paris and attracting more attention.

The *Testament* of Jean Meslier (1664–1729) was typical of the genre with respect to date and the general thrust of its argument, if not the place and circumstances of its composition, or its hugely ambitious scale, systematic character, and scope. A graduate of the Catholic seminary in Rheims, Meslier became village priest at Etrépigny, in the Champagne region of north-eastern France, where he lived quietly until his death. Although there were no reports suggesting anything other than his being regarded in the locality as an exemplary priest prior to 1716, after that he seems to have emerged as something of a rebel in the eyes of the local ecclesiastical establishment, and came to be regarded as a person 'présomptueux' and 'opiniâtre' who paraded an exterior 'fort dévot et janséniste', even though he was inclined to neglect some of his routine duties; already then it was noticed that he was unusually ill disposed toward the local *noblesse*.[107]

In private, Meslier slowly refined his deeply sombre *Weltanschauung*, aiming to undermine the whole doctrinal ground-plan of existing society, to him a single, formidably coherent but corrupt edifice 'du gouvernement des hommes'. Like Challe and Du Marsais, he accepts no guide other than unaided human reason, the sole

[103] Mothu, 'Les Vanités manuscrites', 66. [104] Cottret, *Jansénismes*, 52.

[105] Wade, *Clandestine Organization*, 187; Cotoni, 'L'Exégèse', 97; Schröder, *Ursprünge*, 510.

[106] Schwarzbach, 'Critique biblique', 79; Landucci, 'Introduction', 9–11; Israel, *Radical Enlightenment*, 690. [107] Wade, *Clandestine Organization*, 66; Benítez, *Face cachée*, 202–3.

source of 'facts' and knowledge in his eyes.[108] Beyond Marana's *L'Espion turc* and some Bayle, he lacked familiarity with radical writings.[109] Yet his Cartesian training helped him construct an impressively unified system, combining a fierce critique of theology, popular culture, ecclesiastical authority, and academic learning with a relentless attack on monarchy and aristocracy.[110] Revolted by the extreme inequality found everywhere between 'les différens états et conditions des hommes', some born to domineer over other men, monopolizing all the pleasure and contentment in life, while the rest, unhappy and vile slaves, subsist as mere drudges 'et pour gémir toute leur vie dans la peine et dans la misère', he depicts French society in the grimmest, most unremitting terms.[111]

Both the ideas and social system prevailing in France Meslier judges wholly *contraire* to 'right reason', justice, and 'natural equity'.[112] To his mind, the mighty fortress of error which rules the world includes providential Deism which he conceives as rooted in a credulous notion of Creation not much better than that of the theologians, one of the bastions of imposture, replete with philosophical contradictions, designed to mislead and exploit men. More than most other radical thinkers of the time, Meslier lays a particular stress on the close collaboration of the religious, landed, and political exploiters, equally lambasting both governing hierarchies, spiritual and worldly, for oppressing the bulk of human kind primarily for the benefit of kings, *les grands*, the rest of the *noblesse*, and the priesthood. Devoting his whole inner life to elaborating his comprehensive revolutionary world-view embracing every dimension of reality, he proceeded step by step in his work of ruthless intellectual demolition while outwardly remaining a man of the church, keeping his innermost thoughts from even his closest colleagues. He worked silently, in a remote village beset by the crushing poverty of the peasantry, misery that saddened but, as also with Vauvenargues, repelled and angered him.[113]

Erudite in an old-fashioned way, familiar with Scripture, the Fathers, ancient history and some Roman authors, besides Montaigne and Pascal, Meslier was aware of remarkably few books published after 1700. He apparently knew nothing of Locke, Clarke, Toland, Collins, or Newton or indeed Hobbes. He knows about Spinoza, though, of whom he approves as a thinker who 'ne reconnoissoit aucune divinité', but only at second hand, thanks to Tournemine's widely read refutation of that thinker.[114] As it happens, Meslier's personal copy of the 1718 edition of Fénelon's *Démonstration de l'existence de Dieu*, with the Tournemine appendix attacking Spinoza, survives today filled with his own manuscript annotations, identifying nature with matter, scorning Tournemine's objections, and firmly aligning with

108 Meslier, *Testament*, ii. 99.

109 Ibid. i. 207, 314, ii. 173, 250–1; Desné, 'Meslier', 87; Mori, 'L'ateismo', 125.

110 Artigas-Menant, *Secret des clandestins*, 28, 185–6; Ehrard, *L'Idée*, 520–3, 739–40.

111 Meslier, *Testament*, ii. 169; Desné, 'Meslier', 88, 96–7.

112 Meslier, *Testament*, ii. 170–3, 178–80, 247; Ehrard, *L'Idée*, 521.

113 *Notice des écrits*, 190–1; Buckley, *At the Origins*, 268–9; Bove, 'Vauvenargues politique', 422.

114 Meslier, *Testament*, ii. 291; Ricuperati, 'Il problema', 372, 396–7.

Spinoza.[115] Until his death hardly anyone knew anything of his text, or the far-reaching character of his critique.

Working in secrecy, filled with pessimism for himself and those around him, Meslier yet also harboured a deep-seated, hidden ambition that some day, somehow, his intellectual legacy might after all help break the vast, all-encompassing web of 'erreurs' which men had spun over the ages in order to imprison themselves, collectively and individually, denying themselves what is rightfully theirs. Popular belief, court culture, monastic ethos, concepts taught in universities, and dogmas of the church he saw as forming a vast interlocking complex, pervasive throughout France and the entire world, and yet a system as erroneous, false, crass, and superstitious as it was powerful. Though far from supposing himself the only inhabitant of France to realize this, he believed those who had previously discerned the truth over the millennia, and did so now, were forced to keep it to themselves, as he himself did whilst he lived, appreciating the virtually irresistible force of intolerance, tradition, and authority, the overwhelming capacity of 'superstition' and the multitude to crush those who dissent from what the people believe. Privately, he allowed himself to dream that there might in the end be a way to undermine it: this is Man's only hope, though admittedly a faint one; it is the hope which lies in 'philosophy'.[116]

Shortly before his death, Meslier deposited with notaries three copies of his sensational book, written out in his own hand, in a package only to be opened after his demise. On being revealed, at his death, the package's contents caused uproar in the village, and consternation among the priests of the locality with whom he had been friends for forty years and among whom he had always presented himself as a faithful priest. The ensuing local scandal led to the intervention of the bishop and Meslier's corpse being refused a Christian burial. His text was impounded by the authorities. But, later, reportedly, one of the copies was somehow borrowed, by the comte de Caylus, and soon afterwards, notes Voltaire, a hundred copies were circulating in Paris selling at ten *louis* apiece, so that this work, so shocking to contemporaries, began to be known and talked about.[117] La Mettrie was among those that read it in the 1740s. Later, in 1762, Meslier's text was also clandestinely published by none other than Voltaire himself who, however, so drastically abridged and expurgated the original, under the title *Extrait des sentiments de Jean Meslier*, as entirely to twist and emasculate Meslier's legacy: for Voltaire opted to project him as a providential Deist, altogether erasing his atheism and materialism.[118]

At one point in his writing, without revealing he had been instrumental in the outcome, Voltaire remarks that Meslier's huge text, written, he thought, in a dreadful style, had appeared happily purged 'du poison de l'athéisme'.[119] He even inserted

[115] Meslier, *Testament*, ii. 67–8; Artigas-Menant, *Secret des clandestins*, 30; Benítez, 'Jean Meslier', 463, 467 n.

[116] Benítez, *Face cachée*, 202–5.

[117] Voltaire, *Lettres à son altesse*, 366; Wade, *Clandestine Organization*, 9, 73; Porset, 'Voltaire et Meslier', 194; Artigas-Menant, *Secret des clandestins*, 182–4, 186.

[118] [Voltaire], 'Extrait des sentiments', in Voltaire, *Œuvres complètes*, xliii. 326; Ehrard, *L'Idée*, 462–3; Ricuperati, 'Il problema', 370, 395; Buckley, *At the Origins*, 269; Pearson, *Voltaire*, 306–7.

[119] Voltaire, *Lettres à son altesse*, 365–7.

a completely bogus final prayer at the end of his doctored version where his fictitious 'Meslier' beseeches a God (in whom the real Meslier did not believe) to recall the Christians to 'la religion naturelle, dont le Christianisme est l'ennemi déclaré', to this holy religion [of Voltaire] which God has put into the hearts of all men (and which Meslier, in reality, detested). Voltaire loathed not only Meslier's atheism, materialism, and French style but also his social objectives. Why address something like Meslier's *Testament* to a people comprised largely of an illiterate peasantry? Why remove from their shoulders 'un joug salutaire', a necessary fear which alone can curb crime and rapine? Belief in reward and punishment after death, insisted Voltaire, 'est un frein dont le people a besoin'; a much better solution than Meslier's atheism, held Voltaire, would be a purified religion.[120]

Meslier's social and political criticism, and doctrine of the equality of all men, rests on a systematic materialism using strands of Plato, Aristotle, Epicurus, and Averroes but especially, as we have seen, Descartes, Bayle, Malebranche, and Tournemine's refutation of Spinoza.[121] For him our whole cosmos integrally coheres, unified by that same 'raison universelle' which yet has no author which *Malebranchisme* can be construed to hint at, on which Bayle's 'Stratonism' rests, and Bruzen de La Martinière rightly identified as the basis of Bayle's sedition.[122] All claims to revelations, prophecies, and visions verified by signs and miracles, like all pretensions to magical powers or the existence of magic and spirits, are dismissed by Meslier, no matter how widely believed or what their source, as always fraudulent and false. Like other authors of clandestine manuscripts, Meslier strongly affirms the unknowing working of motion on matter and materiality of the soul, denying that thought is something substantially apart from, and external to, matter.[123] Everything arises from matter, matter being his first principle, the surrogate for the Supreme Being in rival systems; our wishes and desires, he argues, like our feelings of pleasure, pain, love, hatred, joy, and sadness are always (whatever Descartes and Malebranche say) 'des modifications de la matière'.[124] Providential Creation, hence, is an impossibility and there is no divine direction of matter: for only matter itself, and the motion within it, can move and change what is material.[125]

All the works of nature, held Meslier, make and fashion themselves 'par le mouvement qui leur est propre et naturel'; consequently, all living things are produced by nature itself by causes 'nécessaires et fortuites' as well as 'aveugles et privées de raison'.[126] Hence, his work, like Spinoza's, implies a theory of evolution even though he lacks the scientific knowledge to provide one. Matter, for him, is the primary principle, source of all creative power in which the rational structure of the cosmos

[120] Ibid. 367; Porset, 'Voltaire et Meslier', 203.

[121] Artigas-Menant, *Secret des clandestins*, 30; Vartanian, 'Quelques réflexions', 154–5; Ehrard, *L'Idée*, 99–100, 520–2.

[122] Mori, 'L'ateismo', 148, 150–1, 159–60; [Bruzen de La Martinière], *Entretiens*, ii. 594–5, 598–9.

[123] Ehrard, *L'Idée*, 101; Meslier, *Testament*, ii. 377–82, iii. 8, 100; Wade, *Clandestine Organization*, 69–70.

[124] Meslier, *Testament*, iii. 292, 295; Schröder, *Ursprünge*, 338–9; Mori, 'L'ateismo', 128–9.

[125] Meslier, *Testament*, ii. 381, 386–7, 392–3; Benítez, 'Jean Meslier', 464–5.

[126] Meslier, *Testament*, ii. 387–400; Kors, 'Skepticism', 61; Mori, 'L'ateismo', 144–6.

inheres, the equivalent of Spinoza's *natura naturans*, that of which all other things are but 'modifications'. He grants there are difficulties with such a doctrine, notably regarding the origin of the movement in matter, and framing the laws of motion. But these he deems minor compared with the absurd 'contradictions' and 'impossibilities' inherent in Creationism Christian or Deist. What is truly insoluble is the collision between popular culture and philosophy. The truth of things being comparatively simple in his estimation, its principles could be grasped by the common people were their minds not wholly clouded with 'error'. Thus, nature's productions, contrary to Descartes, Fénelon, and Malebranche, do not demonstrate 'et ne prouvent nullement l'existence d'une souveraine intelligence'.[127] But the people believe otherwise and who is going to disabuse them of their fallacies?

Written around the same time, the early 1720s, Fréret's *Lettre de Thrasybule à Leucippe* stands, alongside Meslier's *Testament*, as the other of the two pre-eminent texts of French atheistic materialism, prior to Diderot's *Lettre sur les aveugles* (1749).[128] Here, too, reality is a rationally coherent structure and denial of God, Creation, and the soul's immortality emphatic, all knowledge comes through the senses, and all the world's religions are dismissed as imposture, using a sceptical-critical conception of 'reason' here more directly reminiscent of Bayle. God is a phantasm of the collective imagination. It is Man's misfortune that none of the religions dominating history since the remotest times, many of which terrorize the individual with their threats and fanaticism, is truly based on 'cette raison' precise and universal 'qui éclaire également tous les hommes', albeit some faiths are less irrational than others, and Zoroastrianism—a favourite topic of Bayle and of 'l'illustre et profound' Fréret, as Voltaire calls him—less irrational than the rest.[129]

Where Meslier kept his musings strictly to himself, and Fréret was a recluse, whose clandestine *Lettre* seemingly circulated only after his death (1749), Mirabaud, a former army officer who knew Boulainvilliers, Du Marsais, Lévesque, and Fréret, and was especially influenced by Fontenelle, passed his subversive manuscripts among small coteries of friends and sympathizers, among the closest being Du Marsais and Maillet's collaborator the Abbé Le Mascrier. An enthusiastic scholar of the ancient world, his contribution to the clandestine philosophical manuscript literature, the *Opinions* (probably composed before 1722), showed the subversive uses to which the new historical-critical method could be put by reconstructing, in reaction to Cartesian, *Malebranchiste*, and Lockean rejection of the past, the alleged thought and belief structures of the ancient Greek world. This text circulated in manuscript for two decades after 1722 before being published first in a short version, in Holland, by Jean-Frédéric Bernard, in his *Dissertations mêlées*

127 Meslier, *Testament*, iii. 201–2; Benítez, *Face cachée*, 206; Schröder, *Ursprünge*, 338–40.

128 Schröder, *Ursprünge*, 384–8; Tortarolo, *L'Illuminismo*, 29, 93; Paganini, *Philosophies clandestines*, 130–3; Mori, 'L'ateismo', 184.

129 Mori, 'L'ateismo', 184–5; Voltaire, *Lettres à son altesse*, 356, 361; Wade, *Clandestine Organization*, 191–2.

(1740),[130] and then the full version, in a clandestine collection published by Du Marsais and Le Mascrier, in 1751.[131]

The main tradition of ancient thought, since philosophy's beginnings, holds Mirabaud, was materialist and monist, based on the idea of the corporeality of the active principle. This original current, he argues, nurtured no notion of Creation *ex nihilo* or immortality of the soul but was later diverted to a different course by a mystifying metaphysics of spirituality introduced less by Plato (who, he alleges, adduced his notions of soul and world-soul merely as a thought experiment but did not really believe in them) than by the Neoplatonists.[132] Greek philosophy, he contends, following Bayle and Le Clerc, was then further debased by the Church Fathers who severed Platonism from its roots in the idea of an eternal spirit or world-soul pervading, rather than distinct from, the universe and adapted his ideas to Christianity.[133] Claiming immortality of the soul wholly alien to archaic and classical Greek and Roman culture, Mirabaud notes the absence of such a concept in classical religion, differentiating sharply between Plato and Neoplatonism, and claiming all Greek and Latin words designating soul or spirit to have originally denoted just 'breath' or 'breathing', there being originally no terms for immaterial spirits.

Descartes's and Malebranche's mechanistic dualism Mirabaud deems an absurd diversion from the true path, a duality deriving ultimately from Platonist and Christian tradition. Descartes's and Malebranche's systems he considers self-contradictory monstrosities justly derided by Pyrrhonian sceptics and disciples of Montaigne. If one yearns correctly to grasp the nature of the cosmos and the human soul one must revert to the authentic starting point, commencing with the pristine pre-Platonic world of Greek thought.[134] On the appearance of the 1751 edition, the Jesuits published an indignant appraisal of his critique of Platonism, roundly deploring his dissident approach to philosophy, ancient and modern, and especially the erudite subversion worked by his citations from Greek and Hebrew. Celsus and Julian had indeed endeavoured to overturn the Judaeo-Christian account of the Creation, but the Christian Fathers, Origen and St Cyril especially, they retorted, had thoroughly demolished their arguments.[135]

De l'examen de la religion, a work which dates, on internal evidence, from around 1730, likewise questions supernatural revelation and the claims of religious leaders and prophets to have been inspired by Heaven. Supernatural revelation, it urges, is impossible, miracles inconceivable, and the claims of all the revealed religions false, scorning Houtteville's contention that the 'facts' of the Gospels are unquestionable

130 Wade, *Clandestine Organization*, 209–10; note of Alain Mothu, *La Lettre clandestine*, 3 (1994), 357.

131 See the note of Gianluca Mori, *La Lettre clandestine*, 2 (1993), 132–3.

132 Wade, *Clandestine Organization*, 209, 212–15; Rétat, 'Mirabaud et l'antiquité', 92.

133 Rétat, 'Mirabaud et l'antiquité', 94–5; Wade, *Clandestine Organization*, 205, 213–14; Geissler, 'Boureau-Deslandes lecteur', 230–1; Artigas-Menant, *Secret des clandestins*, 26–7, 32.

134 [Lelarge de Lignac], *Élémens*, 116; Rétat, 'Mirabaud et l'antiquité', 97–8.

135 See the extracts in *La Lettre clandestine*, 3 (1994), 362–3; Geissler, '*Matérialisme*', 66.

and justify faith in the 'mysteries'.[136] When one examines the relevant passages with the necessary expertise—which most men lack—argues the author, probably Lévesque, it becomes clear such alleged 'facts' and certain 'miracles', far from being beyond question, are all thoroughly unreliable; meanwhile, interpreting such texts presents so many exegetical difficulties that no meaningful tradition of authority can be built on them.[137]

Another trenchant radical text rejecting revelation, Creation, miracles, prophecy, demonology, and martyrology was *La Religion chrétienne analysée*, also called the *Analyse de la religion chrétienne*, dating from around 1723.[138] Proclaiming 'reason' the sole criterion for sifting truth from delusion, and reminding readers that most of the world's population is not Christian, it pronounces the Bible's account of Creation an utterly bizarre concoction which shocks 'toutes les lumières de la raison'.[139] Against the major recent Christian apologists, Abbadie, Le Clerc, and Houtteville, it marshals radical authors, such as van Dale and Fontenelle, though the argument, exegetical technique, and general inspiration mostly derive directly from the Spinoza of the *Tractatus*, a work repeatedly cited in its French version under the title *Des cérémonies superstitieuses des Juifs*. The reader is even urged, at one point, to go himself to consult that book and find more material 'de quoi se satisfaire'.[140] Like Spinoza, the writer stresses Scripture's discrepancies, the 'contradictions sans nombre' between the Vulgate and the Septuagint, our ignorance of most of the biblical books' authors, and the countless difficulties posed by Hebrew expressions for which we can no longer reconstruct the original social or cultural context.

The assault on Houtteville who, we are assured, 'n'est pas plus solide' than Abbadie, resumes in a later clandestine text, of the early 1730s, again probably by Lévesque, the *Examen critique des apologistes de la religion chrétienne*.[141] Much of this erudite manuscript, later often attributed to Fréret, is devoted to examining one of the chief proofs of Christian claims offered by early apologists of the church, namely the dispelling through the power of Christ and the disciples, by prayer and exorcism, of the long-enduring evil 'empire' on earth operated by demons.[142] The Greek Christian Father Origen (AD 185–254) is derided for believing the very name of Christ something of such extraordinarily potency that even wicked men, merely by pronouncing it, could share in the wondrous power of driving out devils.[143] Celebrating van Dale's campaign to eradicate belief in demonic power, the author invokes the Dutch savant as his guiding light on this topic, though conceivably he knows him only indirectly, through Fontenelle.

136 Ehrard, *L'Idée*, 87; Landucci, 'Introduction', 12–13.

137 Landucci, 'Introduction', 13; [Lévesque de Burigny], *De l'examen*, 36–8.

138 Wade, *Clandestine Organization*, 164–77; Benítez, *Face cachée*, 47–8, 144–5.

139 MoBM Ms 338 'Analyse de la Religion chrétienne', 21.

140 Ibid. 37–40; Mori, 'Du Marsais philosophe', 181; Schröder, *Ursprünge*, 518–19.

141 [Lévesque de Burigny], *Examen critique*, 18, 23, 100–2.

142 Ibid. 170; see also the Paris variant entitled 'Histoire critique ou Examen de la religion chrétienne', PBN MS 1198/I 'Histoire critique', 76–83.

143 [Lévesque de Burigny], *Examen critique*, 72; Niderst, 'Fontenelle', 171.

A key radical strategy, illustrated by this text, was the adoption of van Dale's and Fontenelle's thesis that the ancient oracles ceased not through Christ's coming, or via miracles wrought by the disciples, but solely owing to the decrees of the Christian emperors who followed Constantine, especially Theodosius I (AD 346–95). Lévesque holds that paganism would linger still, and most of Europe still be pagan, had Constantine's successors not used their authority to abolish it 'et pour y substituer le Christianisme'.[144] Ironically complimenting Jurieu who also denied it is a sign of God's favour if overriding political power is wielded, as with Louis XIV, on behalf of a particular cult, Lévesque asserts that human power, however apt for changing a priesthood, is still worldly power, not divine intervention. In his *Histoire des oracles*, Fontenelle had been less radical than van Dale, not quite asserting, even if he implied, that the ancient oracles had never been operated by demons, or involved any magical power; nor did he categorically state, like van Dale, that it was not the gospel's power but the Christian emperors who suppressed the oracles. But even van Dale stopped short of saying, as Lévesque affirms here, that generally Christianity owes its 'principal accroissement à la violence des empereurs chrétiens'.[145]

For all its harsh, anti-Christian militancy, this text, like *De l'examen*, is plainly the work of a highly erudite man. It was also one of the last of the major radical clandestine texts, possibly dating no earlier than 1735, by which time the *anglomanie* had certainly taken firm hold. Yet here, too, strikingly, as with the other major early clandestine philosophical manuscripts, the functional role of English intellectual influence, far from being central, is minimal. While we find references to van Dale, Isaac Vossius, Richard Simon, Orobio de Castro, Fontenelle, and Boulainvilliers, with whose *Abrégé* the author is apparently familiar,[146] the philosophical inspiration to which this author, like Fréret, is most indebted is clearly the philosopher of Rotterdam, Bayle.[147] This tallies closely with other evidence for Lévesque including his survey of Greek thought of 1724, where he pronounces Bayle a *philosophe* 'qu'on ne peut assez admirer'.[148]

Among those who produced and collected clandestine philosophical manuscripts in the 1720s and 1730s, Bayle is never depicted as an essentially Calvinist or 'fideist' sceptic, as he is in Voltaire and the late twentieth-century historiography. Rather he is depicted as an atheistic rationalist closely aligned with Spinoza. A graphic illustration of this is a brief text, of around 1744, entitled 'Most celebrated writings, printed and manuscript, which favour incredulity or are dangerous when read by feeble minds'; for here not only do Bayle's *Pensées diverses* and 'presque tous ses ouvrages' appear in the 'dangerous' category, but Bayle himself is accounted someone who wrote against Spinoza, in his *Dictionnaire*, while yet being 'lui-même un vrai Spinosiste'.[149]

144 [Lévesque de Burigny], *Examen critique*, 106, 110.
145 PBM MS 1198/I 'Histoire critique', 112; Niderst, 'Fontenelle', 168–71.
146 Niderst, 'Fontenelle', 171; PBM MS 1198/I 'Histoire critique', 202.
147 PBM MS 1198/I 'Histoire critique', 91, 139, 161, 198, 202, 234.
148 [Lévesque de Burigny], *Histoire de la philosophie payenne*, i. 85.
149 *Notice des écrits*, 184, 187.

Irrespective of the continuing debate today, one must bear in mind when assessing the early, pre-Voltairean French Enlightenment that this, not the image of Bayle the 'fideist', was the usual and predominant way of understanding Bayle.

A constant focus of attack in the clandestine texts is Malebranche: again and again his principal doctrines are targeted. Lévesque, in his *De l'examen*, claims Malebranche cannot have reflected very deeply before making his, piously intended but nevertheless astounding, admission in his *Entretiens sur la métaphysique et sur la religion* (1688) that however convinced one is that Scripture is divine revelation there is nothing that conclusively proves it to be such or distinguishes it from other texts, other than the force of tradition and the church.[150] With this, Malebranche thinks he topples Protestantism and Socinianism, overturning their most cherished argument, namely that Christian truth derives *sola Scriptura*, but seems to have forgotten that such an admission, far from strengthening ecclesiastical authority, ultimately destroys 'la principale preuve de la religion chrétienne', interposing an insuperable objection to churchmen's claims. No matter how impressive the chain of tradition which for Malebranche, Houtteville, and Jurieu, in contrast to Le Clerc and the *rationaux*, constitute the ultimate guarantee, all this, contends Lévesque, assessed philosophically amounts to nothing at all cogent or convincing.

While he leaves open the possibility of a Supreme Being governing the universe in some fashion, and therefore is not precisely an 'atheist',[151] positive Deistic content of the sort characteristic of Challe and Voltaire is very sparse in Lévesque's *clandestina*. His typical trait is aversion to all 'metaphysics' and church authority and adamant insistence on the universality of reason. Like the rest of the French Early Enlightenment, his concern is above all with 'certainty' and, following Bayle (and ultimately Spinoza), he boldly radicalizes the criteria offered by Descartes and Malebranche, insisting on applying the test 'clear and certain' to everything without any exemption. Thus, his argument that none of the world's revealed religions is true rests on the argument that every faith the proofs of which are not 'à la portée de tous les hommes raisonnables' cannot be the true religion.[152] Since no revealed religion offers proofs which men who judge solely in accord with reason can embrace, obviously none of the revealed faiths is true. He accepts Denyse's and Houtteville's stricture that what are required for faith are 'indisputable facts', but wholly rejects their contention that it is Christianity alone which rests on reliable 'facts'. The only faith he is willing to endorse, he states repeatedly, is that of 'reason'.

150 Malebranche, *Dialogues*, 269–70; [Lévesque de Burigny], *De l'examen*, 37.

151 Schröder, *Ursprünge*, 516–17.

152 [Lévesque de Burigny], *De l'examen*, 34; Landucci, 'Introduction', 13–15.

28

Men, Animals, Plants, and Fossils: French Hylozoic *Matérialisme* before Diderot

The world of the clandestine manuscripts was one of furtiveness, conspiracy, anonymity, deception, manipulation, and collage, but it would be wrong to infer from this that the thought of the incipient *parti philosophique* before Diderot's entry on the scene was therefore not a sustained or coherent body of thought. For, on the contrary, what is most remarkable about Early Enlightenment French clandestine philosophical literature, or at least its major works, was precisely its intellectual seriousness and cogency. A corpus with a hidden core, and somewhat chaotic and eclectic façade, it is nevertheless a mistake to dismiss its authors and content (as they have often been dismissed) as a marginal dimension of the Enlightenment. If these *clandestina* were concocted from many sources recent and ancient and, when finally printed, were frequently heavily edited or doctored, this does not mean that they lacked a coherent common purpose or a clear philosophical orientation.

There were, of course, some important differences of view. The manuscripts diverge widely, for instance, over whether, and how far, organized religion benefits men. Where Meslier's *Testament* and Du Marsais's *Le Philosophe*, both written in the early 1720s, deny that revealed religions serve positive social and moral ends, the *Analyse de la religion*, like Spinoza and Boulainvilliers, maintains that revealed religion usefully serves to instil 'obedience'; and that at the end of the day Christian morality, despite questionable aspects, is 'bonne, en général'.[1] But unresolved questions such as this, or the lingering problems of the materiality of the soul, elementary human drives, and the 'first principles of morality', all pointing to residual philosophical disagreements, remained relatively few.

If most *matérialiste* writers, unlike Challe and the Deists, agreed the soul, and its drives, are something natural, and material, and therefore morally neutral, and potentially good, the question remained what *was* the soul? Whilst the clandestine manuscripts exerted their greatest impact during the 1720s and 1730s, two rival materialist solutions competed. On the one hand, an older conception of the soul as something consisting of invisible, superfine particles of matter, animating animals

[1] MoBM MS 338 'Analyse de la religion', 8–9; [Du Marsais], *Le Philosophe*, 191–3; Israel, *Radical Enlightenment*, 79–80; Artigas-Menant, *Secret des clandestins*, 29.

as well as men, and emanating, like fire or light, from heavier substances, associated with Epicureanism, Lucretius, and Gassendi, retained some support;[2] against this pushed a more specifically 'Spinozist' tendency, conflating body and mind into one, deploying hylozoism and one-substance doctrine to eliminate the notion of soul as something distinct from bodies.[3] An anonymous manuscript probably of the 1730s, entitled *L'Âme matérielle* or *L'Âme mortelle*, collating extracts from Bayle, Malebranche, and others,[4] used an eclectic method to bracket animal and human intelligence together, as one, but also classifies mind as something quite separate from body. Expressly rejecting Spinoza's rival thesis, it opts for an Epicurean approach, claiming the mortal soul must be a super-fine substance composed of corpuscles distinct from the body and varying from individual to individual, as well as species to species, a hypothesis supposedly accounting for why temperaments vary, some men feeling anger or sexual desire more strongly than others.[5] Generally, though, one-substance doctrine came to seem the most plausible solution and body and soul were increasingly merged into a single entity,[6] or as the *Dissertation sur la formation du monde* (1738) calls it 'la substance matérielle', 'la substance infinie', or 'la substance universelle', the only thing which is eternal.[7]

Although all the early eighteenth-century materialist systems (except La Mettrie's) converge in offering moral theories based on worldly concerns, and what is useful to society, some, like those of Boureau-Deslandes, place a heavier, Epicurean emphasis on the pleasure principle, and individual satisfaction in isolation, while others, perhaps most, are more strictly Spinozist in bracketing a wider range of elementary drives under the rubric *conatus* and coupling individual satisfaction with collective, social aims.[8] Additionally, one finds widely varying degrees of optimism and pessimism as to what can be hoped for. Many are, in fact, deeply pessimistic. Du Marsais, while asserting the social utility of philosophy and vowing to combat the superstitious masses, shares Bayle's scepticism about the chances of ever sufficiently re-educating the common people, by means of philosophy, the tool by which men uncover truth, to safeguard toleration, individual freedom, and political stability.

Nevertheless, the major examples circulating in Paris in the 1720s and 1730s shared most of their ultimate aims and are best viewed as a single intellectual, cultural, and political project despite their obvious divergences in style and inspiration.[9] The unifying metaphysical thrust is always the elimination of supernatural agency from Man's history and that of the cosmos and eradication of all magical powers and priestly status, combined with theories of imposture and priestcraft, together with

[2] PBM MS 1189/3 'L'Âme mortelle', 38, 63–4, 72; [Du Marsais] (ed.), *Nouvelles Libertés*, 90–7; Vernière, *Spinoza*, 372–3.

[3] Vartanian, 'Quelques réflexions', 149.

[4] Benítez, *Face cachée*, 217 n.; Mori, 'Du Marsais philosophe', 184; Schröder, *Ursprünge*, 497.

[5] PBM MS 1189/ 3 'L'Âme mortelle', 72; Vartanian, 'Quelques réflexions', 151, 153.

[6] Deneys-Tunney, 'Roman de la matière', 100–1.

[7] *Dissertation sur la formation*, 99, 101, 109, 113–14.

[8] Boureau-Deslandes, *Pygmalion*, 52–3, 63–6: Coulet, 'Présentation', 23; Bonacina, *Filosofia ellenistica*, 109–10.

[9] Wade, *Clandestine Organization*, 266; Stancati, 'Introduction', 4; Israel, *Radical Enlightenment*, 689.

locating sensibility, mind, and ideas in matter, and finding the origin of life and of species in movement in matter. Finally, they share in the elimination of all hierarchy: nobody, whatever their birth or blood, genuinely wields authority or is worthy of respect unless 'délivré des préjugés vulgaires' [freed from popular prejudices], as Boureau-Deslandes puts it, and this is the only kind of status that matters.[10] Here then is the unifying '*Spinosiste*' narrative infusing, in the main, all the major examples of this literary genre, those of Fontenelle, Boulainvilliers, Du Marsais, Fréret, Meslier, Boureau-Deslandes, Mirabaud, Maillet, and Lévesque de Burigny, despite the wide diversity of styles and sources invoked.

The heavily preponderant tendency in the lead texts, then, is emphatically towards an atheistic materialism and determinism, sometimes with pantheistic tendencies, deriving from an intellectual context closely linked to Descartes, Malebranche, Spinoza, and Bayle, all features, it is worth noting, already conspicuous in Fontenelle's *Traité de liberté* dating from the mid 1680s.[11] What we are presented with, then, is an impressively coherent corpus of materialist doctrine extending over more than half a century down to the mid 1730s when Voltaire arrived on the scene and stormed the French intellectual arena with his vigorously empiricist and anti-materialist *Lettres philosophiques* (1734) and *Élémens de la philosophie de Neuton* (1738). Voltaire is always uncompromisingly Anglophile; but also hostile to the tradition of Du Marsais, Meslier, and Fontanelle. By contrast, the clandestine materialist literature is strikingly devoid of English inspiration, even Locke, Toland, and Collins figuring only very marginally.

French one-substance monism then was strongly entrenched by the 1730s having been reached by many writers and a variety of routes. Boulainvilliers for his part is essentially a *Spinosiste*. Eliminating the soul by interpreting it as the sensibility of the body is also Meslier's preferred solution but one he arrives at by means of a thoroughgoing critique of 'Messieurs les Cartésiens' as he calls his chief opponents, and especially Malebranche. He proceeds not only without discussing Spinoza but also without altogether ruling out the Epicurean, or radicalized *Gassendiste*, approach, though he considers the latter route distinctly less plausible.[12] His strongest argument against the Cartesians is that they themselves have rendered the soul superfluous by demonstrating that human life, like animal life, is generated and sustained by the mechanisms of our bodies and that animals and birds, according to them, are born, live, reproduce, and die, as well as have instincts, and feel materially, even if they do not conceptualize their feelings, and supposedly do all this without having souls.[13]

Fréret's atheistic and anti-Deist *Lettre* of around 1722, rather less systematic and more tentative than Meslier, though Voltaire found it formidably armed with 'des raisonnements très forts',[14] sets out yet another impressive system, again denying

[10] Boureau-Deslandes, *Pygmalion*, 52.

[11] Niderst, 'Fontenelle', 161–6; Israel, *Radical Enlightenment*, 689; Romeo, 'Matérialisme et déterminisme', 103–5.

[12] Meslier, *Testament*, ii. 154–6.

[13] Ibid. ii. 306–7, 377–9, iii. 207–92.

[14] Artigas-Menant, *Secret des clandestins*, 315.

the immateriality and immortality of the soul as well as Creation, a First Cause, and providence. Fréret, having been close to Boulainvilliers, draws on a wide range of radical sources, but especially admired the critical-historical method of Bayle with whom he shared a certain anti-mathematicism which was later to surface still more strongly in Diderot; he is likewise familiar with Du Marsais, Mirabaud, and Lévesque de Burigny. For him, the chief purpose of philosophy is to change human life. There would be no point in men priding themselves on possessing reason, he urges, if we fail to use reason to procure that tranquillity of spirit and inner repose providing the pure, untroubled felicity which is the promise of 'true philosophy'—that is 'à nous rendre heureux'. To this end, he offers an undogmatic, one-substance monism, albeit continually reminding readers that difficulties, unresolved contradictions, and problems remain and that, by sticking scrupulously to the facts, we must combine firm confidence in what we do know with honest acknowledgement of the great deal we do not yet know or will never know.[15] Philosophy cannot enlarge our list of pleasures or make us something different from what we are; but what it can very effectively do, holds Fréret, is teach us to regulate our desires and impulses, restrain the unnecessary fears of which our untutored imagination is full and help men live in accordance with nature, emancipated from the worst oppressor there is—'l'empire de l'opinion'.[16]

Du Marsais is another firm opponent of every account of Man which introduces two separate substances. Since Man and all the rest of the animal world is composed of one single substance which is both body and sense, holds *Le Philosophe*, Man is simply a body, 'une machine humaine'.[17] The power of thinking Du Marsais characterizes as a sense, like sight or hearing, something depending 'également d'une constitution organique', a notion enabling him unreservedly to roll 'l'idée de la pensée avec l'idée de l'étendue' into one.[18] But besides Epicurean strands and this predominant monism, we find also, in some texts, a curious tendency to combine the divergent Epicurean and Spinozist conceptions by reworking Spinoza's doctrine of the mind, with Bayle's help, in a particular way, to yield a pseudo-*Spinosiste* materialist vitalist doctrine, as exemplified, for instance, in de Maillet's *Sentimens des philosophes sur la nature de l'âme*, dating from the 1720s and clandestinely published, in 1743, in Du Marsais's collection *Nouvelles Libertés de penser*.[19]

Benoît de Maillet (1656–1738), having reviewed the opinions of other philosophers, expounds in his third chapter as the 'Sentimen de Spinoza' what was in fact plainly his own personal view—a vitalist, semi-Averroist *Spinosisme*, inspired in part by Bayle's discussion of Averroism, envisaging human souls as emanations from an 'âme universelle du monde', pervading all matter including the air, and animating all living things. This universal soul, which Maillet expressly equates with Spinoza's

15 Artigas-Menant, *Secret des clandestins*, 383–4; Wade, *Clandestine Organization*, 186–9, 193–4; Benítez, 'Composition de la *Lettre*', 189–91; Kors, 'Scepticism', 62–3; Schröder, *Ursprünge*, 188–9, 210–11.

16 Schröder, *Ursprünge*, 19; Ehrard, *L'Idée*, 383.

17 Artigas-Menant, *Secret des clandestins*, 17; [Du Marsais], *Le Philosophe*, 174–6.

18 [Du Marsais], *Le Philosophe*, 180.

19 Mori, 'Benoît de Maillet', 13.

natura naturans,[20] is claimed to be definitely material but composed of 'une matière déliée', matter highly dynamic, like fire, which unites itself to things apt to be animated by it as flames seize hold of combustible things. A disciple of Fontenelle, closely linked to Mirabaud, Benoît de Maillet, was a well-known connoisseur of the French philosophical *clandestina* and, during the 1730s, an eager disseminator of Mirabaud's writings as well as Du Marsais's *Examen*.[21] He may not have been a Spinozist in any precise sense of the term; nevertheless, he certainly counted among the large number of Early Enlightenment French *Spinosistes* as the category was used then, that is as a thinker who envisages the universe, as the Jesuit *Mémoires de Trévoux* explained in 1749, when reviewing a newly revised published version of his text, published at Paris the year before, with 'Amsterdam' falsely stated on the title page, as something that creates and 'perpetuates itself' without the intervention of any external 'cause intelligente et supérieure' and wholly devoid of immaterial beings and substances.[22]

But such a theory of the world left much unexplained. More than the other clandestine radicals, apart from Fontenelle, Maillet took a keen, lifelong interest in natural philosophy. Over many years, he pondered the origin of life and of species as well as questions such as that first raised, in the late 1660s, by the Danish naturalist Steno, and later examined by Leibniz, concerning the marine fossils encountered in profusion on high ground, remnants arguably deposited over a much longer time span than the duration of the biblical Flood would allow for,[23] and the issue, again first raised by Steno and Leibniz, of the existence of geological strata of seemingly vastly different ages. Most early eighteenth-century contemporaries, while accepting that fossils really had once been living creatures, still adhered to the traditional explanation for their frequency on high ground, namely that these had been deposited by the biblical Flood.[24] But Maillet, like the great René-Antoine Ferchault de Réaumur (1683–1757), and other leading *naturalistes* of the time, granting the force of Steno's and Leibniz's objections to this—that the Flood had been too brief and too violent an event to account for vestiges deposited in very different geological *strata* which must have formed slowly over long periods and at different times—sought a different 'natural history' that would explain more satisfactorily why marine fossils and shells are found in large masses even on the highest mountains.[25]

Neither Steno nor Leibniz, nor many that came after them, had supposed a theory more satisfactorily explaining this phenomenon need be non-providential in character. In his *Theodicy*, Leibniz argues (against Bayle) that 'God has no less the quality of the best monarch than that of the greatest architect', claiming there had

[20] Ibid. 20–1; Maillet, 'Sentimens des philosophes', 26–7.
[21] See the note of Gianluca Mori, *La Lettre clandestine*, 3 (1994), 301–3.
[22] *Mémoires de Trévoux*, 49 (Apr. 1749), 636; Benítez, *Face cachée*, 208.
[23] Leibniz, *Protogaea*, 21–3; Barrande, 'Introduction', pp. xxii–xxiii; Roger, *Buffon*, 96.
[24] Roger, *Buffon*, 96–7; Ehrard, *L'Idée*, 200.
[25] Leibniz, *Protogaea*, 26–7, 30–1; Barrande, 'Introduction', p. xi.

been 'different deluges and inundations whereof traces and remains are found which show that the sea was in places that today are far remote from it,'[26] and that this complex sequence of things, even though it appears disorderly to us, in fact hides a hidden design and order, and a benign one, known only to the Almighty. But the clandestine radicals could accept no such conception of providence and design.

The unresolved difficulties and frequent invoking of ancient authors in favour of one, or another, theory of the world, matter, motion, and mind, meanwhile also stimulated, particularly in Fréret, Mirabaud, Lévesque de Burigny, and Boureau-Deslandes, renewed interest in Bayle's researches into the history of ancient philosophy. Ancient theories of the world and of matter were carefully scrutinized anew. A notable contribution here was that of Boureau-Deslandes, author of the three-volume *Histoire critique de la philosophie* (Amsterdam, 1737), the first full-scale French history of philosophy. Born and having spent his first ten years at Pondicherry, in French India, Boureau-Deslandes later developed into an accomplished amateur polymath while pursuing his career as a naval official, much of the time, between 1716 and 1735, at Brest.[27] Originally a follower of Malebranche, he early developed strong libertine and radical tendencies, under Fontenelle's influence, becoming a vehement foe of all pedantry and purely academic erudition. The bulk of theologians and philosophers who throng history were, in his view, immersed in 'de vaines chimères, idées superstitieuses' which they then ridiculously consider 'pour des oracles'.[28] The only useful books, he held, are those which teach men 'à bien vivre' and expound 'des sciences' the veritable goal of which is to procure 'des avantages réels', that is worldly improvements.[29]

Like de Maillet, Boureau-Deslandes was a materialist *Épicuro-Spinosiste*. His history of thought, like his other works, was long banned in France and has been only rarely consulted since. Less learned than Brucker's *Historia*, it is nevertheless not without interest, adapting Fontenelle's ideas about myth, fable, and the progress of *l'esprit humain* from its primitive beginnings to the rise of philosophy, forging interesting links between the French philosophical debate of the 1720s and 1730s and the study of ancient thought, and emphasizing the practical uses of philosophy. Its monist tendency, and concern with exploring the concept of 'matter' so as to integrate body and soul, forcefully reappear in the same author's banned clandestine philosophical fable *Pygmalion, ou La Statue animée* (1741) which mixes Spinozist, erotic, and sensationalist themes, equating God and the universe, describing the totality of reality as 'le Tout, qu'on appelle Dieu, la Nature, l'univers', as well as proclaiming gravity inherent in matter and 'thought' to be generated, through the action of movement in matter, from what was once inanimate matter.[30]

26 Leibniz, *Theodicy*, 278; Wilson, *Leibniz's Metaphysics*, 295–6.

27 Geissler, *Boureau-Deslandes*, 15, 18.

28 [Boureau-Deslandes], *Pygmalion*, preface p. 50; Guéroult, *Histoire*, 301–7; Braun, *Histoire*, 149; Kelley, *Descent of Ideas*, 80, 143.

29 [Boureau-Deslandes], *L'Apothéose du beau-sexe*, preface p. xxvi.

30 [Boureau-Deslandes], *Pygmalion*, 49, 60–1, 66–8; Deneys-Tunney, 'Roman', 102–3; Geissler, *Boureau-Deslandes*, 85, 87.

Clandestinely published 'à Londres', probably at Paris, it recounts, as if narrating a mythological allegory, how a statue wrought by an ancient Greek sculptor comes to life and experiences sensations, musing as to whether movement in matter is the ultimate origin of thought, and, if it is, whether this means movement is simply inherent in all matter, unchangingly, or whether there is a progressive genesis of sensation—and, if the latter, whether this should be conceived as innate or, echoing (and perhaps ridiculing) Locke and Voltaire, as a quality which some Divinity accorded to matter.[31] For the time being, all this found no clear resolution. Another work maintaining that the natural history of matter required closer scrutiny, that all life derives from movement in matter, and all matter has movement inherent in it, thereby effectively abolishing the distinction between animate and inanimate matter, is the fifty-eight-page anonymous *Dissertation sur la formation du monde*, probably by Maillet, which bears the date 1738. This text which shows many similarities with the thought of Du Marsais and Fréret, as well as Meslier, and others of the period, and is again wholly pre-Newtonian in its physics and cosmology, includes a remarkable discussion of stones as part of its wider attempt to explain how an infinity of distinct forms can emerge from a single 'substance universelle'.[32] It claims stones experience a 'purely passive life' and that it is contrary to experience to 'refuser un genre de vie aux pierres'. For their formation must entail movement, and movement 'est le caractère essentiel de la vie'.

The miracle of 'passive life' given to some bodies by 'la substance universelle', it was argued, is just as great as the gift of 'active life' which other bodies enjoy. No doubt Boureau-Deslandes was no more a strict 'Spinosiste' than Maillet, or for that matter Du Marsais, Meslier, Fréret, Lévesque de Burigny, or indeed Mirabaud whose clandestine texts he seems to have read at some point before 1737, and been influenced by. In Boureau-Deslandes, as with most French *matérialistes* of this period, there are enough ambiguities and points of confusion for overly clear-cut classification to be inadvisable.[33] Indeed, in him, a systematic materialism has not fully supplanted providential Deism, while Locke's 'thinking matter' divinely conferred remains at least a theoretically conceivable possibility to be considered. Even so, the central thrust, once again, is clear: Boureau-Deslandes deploys several of Spinoza's formulations, blending these with the insights of the Bayle of the *Dictionnaire* and strands of Locke, trying to impose order on the unresolved difficulties bequeathed by the collapsed legacy of Descartes and Malebranche.

Boureau-Deslandes's writing, indeed, like Maillet's, aptly illustrates both the crucial role of Spinozism as a tool for organizing and systematizing ideas during the formation of eighteenth-century French materialism and Bayle's no less vital function in clearing the path to *matérialisme*.[34] Following Mirabaud, and here going

[31] [Boureau-Deslandes], *Pygmalion*, pp. xi–xii, 57; Deneys-Tunney, 'Roman', 94, 96.

[32] *Dissertation sur la formation*, 113–14; Stancati, 'La *Dissertation*', 112; Benítez, *Face cachée*, 335.

[33] Vernière, *Spinoza*, 397–8; Geissler, 'Boureau-Deslandes lecteur', 230–1.

[34] Geissler, *Boureau-Deslandes*, 85, 89; Geissler, '*Matérialisme*', 64–5; Deneys-Tunney, 'Roman', 102–3.

beyond Bayle, he maintains that the idea there exists only 'une seule substance dans l'univers' and that spirituality and materiality 'étoient ses deux principaux attributs' represented the original and most authentic tendency of ancient Greek philosophy which, like Bayle, he considers a decisive step forward in Man's history.[35] This was clearly a reworking, but also an extension, of Bayle's and Buddeus' *Spinozismus ante Spinozam* thesis. Like Fontenelle, Boulainvilliers, Fréret, Mirabaud, and later Diderot, Boureau-Deslandes firmly equates 'history of philosophy' with the general progress of humanity and 'l'histoire de l'esprit humain'.[36]

Inextricably linked to the question of one substance, and the animation of matter, but still more crucial, was that of the creation of species or what, since around 1707, in the circle around Boulainvilliers, Fontenelle, and Fréret was dubbed that of the 'origine des êtres et espèces'.[37] Before French materialism could develop into a philosophically coherent system, it needed to work its way—as was not the case with the providential Deism of the Newtonians, or of Challe, Saint-Hyacinthe, Maupertuis, Réaumur, and Voltaire—towards an account not just of animate matter but also of the creation of species which, as the vague musings of Mirabaud, Meslier, Maillet, and Boureau-Deslandes on this subject amply demonstrate, was still largely lacking. Moreover, their path seemed to many to be wholly blocked by the triumphant natural philosophy of Boyle, Newton, and the Newtonians. Saint-Hyacinthe, who rightly envisaged providential Deism, such as his own, as being in total and unremitting opposition to the systems of the 'Spinosistes, Naturalistes, Stoiciens et Matérialistes' in that he (like his mortal enemy Voltaire) upheld a knowing active, providential Creator 'libre et non nécessité', likewise invokes the then weighty authority of 'le célèbre Boerhaave', who had undoubtedly 'mieux examiné la Nature que Straton, Zénon, Épicure et Spinoza', in favour of 'design', pronouncing it the 'folle présomption' of all the 'matérialistes et les Spinosistes' to postulate that the formation of living being is 'l'effet d'un concours aveugle'.[38]

Much was at stake in this contest. For in Saint-Hyacinthe, as in all the proponents of 'design', including the English Newtonians, there was a marked tendency to accept that the existing hierarchy of beings, and relationships between creatures, as well as males and females, constitutes a divinely intended ladder of being. Since, for them, the world does not exist at random, and was never 'left in a state of confusion or as a chaos', as Wollaston expressed it, it clearly followed that 'the several species of beings having their offices and provinces assigned to them; plants and animals subsistence set out for them; and as they go off, successors appointed to relieve them and carry on the scheme',[39] the existing relationship between men, animals, and plants is a matter of constant divine supervision and modification, of 'particular providence' as well as of 'a general providence'. Hence, hierarchy, natural and social, is divinely fixed.

35 Boureau-Deslandes, *Histoire critique*, i. 367.

36 Guéroult, *Histoire*, 303–4, 307.

37 Schröder, *Ursprünge*, 506–7.

38 [Saint-Hyacinthe], *Recherches philosophiques*, 387.

39 Wollaston, *Religion of Nature*, 98.

Against this broadly entrenched moderate mainstream stance of divine intention and 'design', radical thought as yet could find few natural philosophical data and, seemingly, few solid arguments. Mirabaud, from 1742 the Abbé Houtteville's successor as permanent secretary of the Académie Française, formerly friendly with Boulainvilliers and now a central figure of the budding *parti philosophique*, stoutly maintained in his *Le Monde, son origine et son antiquité*, composed probably before 1722 and later published clandestinely in 1751,[40] that the ancient Greek philosophers made no recourse to any 'Être intelligent' in order to explain 'la production des animaux'. The 'Stratonist' idea that all of nature is in continual flux and movement and that some of 'les anciens', as the radical Huguenot radical Jean-Frédéric Bernard also put it, repeating Mirabaud's words, did not appeal to 'un Être intelligent' to generate animals, and that it is perfectly conceivable that movement, pressure, heat, and humidity in varying degrees sufficed for this operation, already played, as it later continued to play, a central part in the argumentation of eighteenth-century French materialism.[41] But as articulated by Mirabaud the idea still seemed implausibly simplistic. For he got no further than surmising, like his favourite philosophical ancients, that men, animals, and plants just sprang or grew up out of the earth in some way, no doubt 'comme des champignons'—as a Jesuit critic commented sarcastically.[42]

Maillet strove to penetrate further. Gradually, he edged towards a remarkable new hypothesis concerning the history of the earth and the rise of species. Although Leibniz's *Protogaea* (1692) was not published until 1749, a year after Buffon's *Histoire naturelle*, its chief arguments had been published in the 1693 issue of the Leipzig *Acta eruditorum*. There Leibniz argues that solid substances betray a double origin, first in the cooling of fiery matter, in the first stage of the earth's history, and then from the action of the seas, dissolving and depositing solids into new formations.[43] Since the earth had passed through a long series of fundamentally different stages, it seemed to follow that fossils are the vestiges of creatures 'qu'on ne trouve plus aujourd'hui' just as the New World had also revealed previously unknown animals and other creatures.[44] But while Leibniz grants the indubitable evidence for the extinction and mutation of species and briefly ponders the plausibility of 'transformism', at the same time he quickly recoiled from such speculations partly because, he says, they entail 'inextricables difficultés' but also on the ground that such ideas are in conflict with Scripture.[45]

There the matter stood until Réaumur delivered a famous paper to the Académie Royale des Sciences in Paris in 1720, holding that the evidence the seas had once covered the inhabited parts of Europe was incontrovertible, especially given that the

[40] Mori, 'Du Marsais philosophe', 190–1; Mothu, 'L'Édition de 1751', 45–6.

[41] [Bernard], *Le Monde, son origine*, i. 204.

[42] Ibid. 53; [Mirabaud], *Le Monde, son origine*, i. 202–4.

[43] Leibniz, *Protogaea*, 23–5, 65; Spink, 'Un abbé philosophe', 153.

[44] Leibniz, *Protogaea*, 90–1; Ehrard, *L'Idée*, 202.

[45] Leibniz, *Protogaea*, 26–7; Leibniz, *New Essays*, 316–18; Barrande, 'Introduction', p. xxiv; Cohen, *Fate*, 57–8.

horizontal placement of fossil concentrations unearthed in Touraine conclusively proves these to have been deposited in water over time, slowly, rather than broken and jumbled by the pressure of overlaying geological strata.[46] Granting that among the fossils 'one finds many species unknown on these coasts', he remained, notwithstanding, even less willing than Leibniz to contemplate the possibility that these were the remnants of creatures and plants which became extinct long ago, or which mutated later into other species. Maillet, by contrast, in his conjectures about fossils and species *was* prepared to abandon all traditional inhibitions. His account, if more remote from a genuine evolutionist theory than is sometimes suggested, nevertheless helped focus attention on botanical and zoological mutations in a way which paved the way for the subsequent rise of meaningful proto-evolutionist thinking during the mid eighteenth century.[47]

Maillet's preoccupation with the interaction of sea and land, and the different proportions of sea and land on the earth's surface at different times, as the decisive factor in encouraging matter to yield the variety of species resurfaces in the (very likely his) *Dissertation sur la formation du monde*.[48] Although there is only one substance, 'la substance universelle', the earth, he observes, nevertheless contains 'millions' of species so that this immense variety must derive from the changing interaction of contrary or 'mixed' aspects of matter generating dry and moist, warm and cold, liquid and solid, sea and land.[49] The world then has a complex natural history that must be explained as a succession of stages. Some species 'more or less approaching the configuration of certain creatures that we know', we learn of, he notes, only from fossils found deep in mineshafts.

From an early stage, then, French radical thought leaned towards a hylozoic materialism which was later to culminate in Diderot and d'Holbach. According to this view, men, animals, birds, fish, and plants all arise from matter and there is no 'substantial' difference between them. From such a metaphysics it follows also that minds, being the sensibility of bodies, are encountered in many other living beings besides men, beings which hence have ideas, even if less developed ones than we do, a theme prominent in Maillet's *Dissertation*.[50] This in turn suggests that the difference between the minds of primitive animals and fish, on the one hand, and men, on the other, may be less considerable than we suppose. For primitive man's capacity for thought must have differed very greatly from ours: conceivably, conjectures Maillet, the first men were no more capable of what we call thinking than are oysters.[51]

The moderate mainstream, meanwhile, continued to champion physico-theology as the aptest counter-strategy which meant also upholding Creationism and fixity

46 Réaumur, 'Remarques', 412–13; Ehrard, *L'Idée*, 202, 205; Hampson, *Enlightenment*, 90.

47 Roger, *Life Sciences*, 420–5; Mori, 'Benoît de Maillet', 20; Benítez, *Face cachée*, 267, 270–3.

48 *Dissertation sur la formation*, 116–17; Benítez, *Face cachée*, 348–9.

49 *Dissertation sur la formation*, 117–18; Wade, *Clandestine Organization*, 234–5; Stancati, 'La *Dissertation*', 111.

50 *Dissertation sur la formation*, 127–30, 137.

51 Ibid. 119–20; Stancati, 'Introduction', 57.

of species. A distinctively French physico-theology, rooted in Fénelon and Réaumur, rapidly gained ground in France during the 1720s, reinforced from 1725 by the publication in Paris of Bernard Nieuwentijt's best-selling *L'Existence de Dieu démontrée par les merveilles de la nature*, a work of expressly anti-Spinozist reasoning heavily influenced by English thought, albeit less by Newtonianism than by Latitudinarian theology. This French physico-theological trend culminated in the appearance of *Le Spectacle de la nature*, by the Abbé Noël-Antoine de Pluche (1688–1761), one of the greatest literary sensations of the age, a work which eventually comprised nine best-selling volumes, appearing between 1732 and 1750. The first included extensive evidence marshalled in support of divine providence at work in nature supplied by Réaumur.[52]

Réaumur's own research culminated in his vast, if unsystematic, study of insects, the *Mémoires pour servir à l'histoire naturelle des insectes*, published between 1734 and 1742, which established its author as the pre-eminent French naturalist of the age. He was to prove an indefatigable defender of the 'argument from design' and dogged opponent of the *matérialistes*. An ardent Lockean empiricist, he vigorously shared Newton's antipathy to broad hypotheses, his *magnum opus* being, indeed, a classic example of the potentially narrowing effect of an overly dogmatic empiricism.[53] Impressive in bulk, and sophisticated in description, it immensely impressed readers with its vast scope and detail illustrating the range and variety of the entire insect world. However, relying excessively on exciting wonder, it proved in the end of limited use against the *matérialistes* since, as both Buffon and Diderot later disparagingly pointed out, it was deficient in classification and analysis, merely collecting facts and dogmatically asserting divine providence without providing real arguments.[54]

A staunch Catholic, Réaumur was unwavering in upholding Creation from nothing, and the immateriality and immortality of the soul, rejecting all suggestion of transformism and quasi-evolutionism, as proposed by the *Spinosistes* and Maillet, much as he later opposed the views of Diderot.[55] Though insisting on what is sometimes called 'fixist Creationism', like Pluche, unlike him Réaumur insisted on adhering strictly to natural evidence, discarding the biblical Flood as an authoritative explanation. Yet, as Montesquieu noted, he refused to accept that fossils of creatures no longer known are remnants of extinct or less developed species, proposing, instead, that these are remains of still extant animals albeit living in distant, warmer parts of the world, or deep under water, so that we are unlikely ever to see them without some vast upheaval in the world.[56] More generally, he urged readers to marvel at how wisely divine providence has ordered everything, helping provide for the needs of men, not least by depositing banks of crushed shells in areas of poor soil, like the Touraine, so that the peasants should be provided with

52 Ehrard, *L'Idée*, 128–31; Roger, *Buffon*, 73–4.
53 Roger, *Buffon*, 73, 75, 83; Dawson, *Nature's Enigma*, 26–8.
54 Diderot, *De l'interprétation de la nature*, 232; Roger, *Buffon*, 72–4, 189; Duflo, *Diderot philosophe*, 158.
55 Ehrard, *L'Idée*, 205, 207; Roger, *Buffon*, 72.
56 Réaumur, 'Remarques', 415–16; Montesquieu, *Œuvres complètes*, 958.

readily accessible material at hand for fertilizing the land and supporting their families.

This huge and unbridgeable rift between respectable mainstream and clandestine Radical Enlightenment extended also to a dramatic divergence of time-frames. The moderate mainstream, tied to Creationism, postulated short time-frames for the age of the world—Newton proposing 4004 BC as the date of Creation, his acolyte William Whiston preferring 2349 BC—whereas radical thinkers, from Boulainvilliers onwards, ignoring the biblical account, more freely experimented with the thesis that the earth is far older.[57] Characteristic in this respect was the work of Maillet, and later Buffon and Boulanger, study of fossils here again becoming a critical arena in the wider intellectual contest, there being no area of research over the previous fifty years, remarked Réaumur in 1720, more fought over and crucial to *naturalistes*.[58]

Benoît de Maillet, a former French consul in Egypt and man of means, though no great intellect, liked to collaborate in philosophical group endeavour, almost like a member of a modern research seminar. Bound to Fontenelle, whom he thanked in an extant letter of around 1726 for his encouragement of his work, in discussion, and for helping him develop his biological theories, he persevered over the years in propagating the same vitalist *Spinosisme* of the 'âme du monde' as one finds in his *Sentimens*, a hypothesis articulated in essentials as early as 1716, but which Maillet continued to espouse also later. Over the years, Maillet, who possessed copies of numerous naturalistic clandestine manuscripts which he often lent to others, entrusted manuscript copies of his slowly emerging natural history to various members of the Fontenelle and Boulainvilliers coteries, requesting comment and corrections. Through the 1730s, he persisted with the work of clandestine intellectual subversion, collaborating in particular with the Abbé Le Mascrier, an ally of both Mirabaud and Du Marsais.[59]

Devised in part in conscious opposition to Réaumur's physico-theology, and his theory of fossils in particular, Maillet tried to combine a 'long' history of the earth and its geology with the thesis that the entire surface of the earth was once covered by sea and all living creatures, including men, had first arisen in the oceans.[60] Elaborating an idea which, according to Leibniz in his *Protogaea*, already existed in embryonic form in the 1690s in some freethinking minds, dissenting from the scriptural account,[61] Maillet held that, as the seas receded plant life had been forced to adapt from water to soil, while creatures originally designed for life in the sea, living first amphibiously, slowly adapted their limbs, breathing, and skin for more sustained life on land. Late seventeenth-century Spinozists and Epicureans had devised a new perspective on the emergence of species but one that accounted only for the transformation of types under radically changed conditions, a thesis,

[57] Ehrard, *L'Idée*, 200. [58] Réaumur, 'Remarques', 400.

[59] Mothu, 'L'Édition de 1751', 45; Mori, 'Postface', 341; note of M. Benítez in *La Lettre clandestine*, 1 (1992), 25.

[60] La Mettrie, *Machine Man*, 98; Roger, *Buffon*, 223–4; Roger, *Life Sciences*, 420–1; Artigas-Menant, *Secret des clandestins*, 208.

[61] Leibniz, *Protogaea*, 26–7; Barrande, 'Introduction', p. xxiv.

rejected by Leibniz and reworked by Maillet, which fell well short of a full-fledged theory of evolution.[62] For here men, mammals, birds, reptiles, and plants were still conceived as intrinsically distinct categories which, far from evolving from lower forms, somehow arose separately, each in its own category, first in the sea and, then, gradually metamorphosed from marine through amphibious to land-based forms.

Over time, Maillet's text reportedly came into the hands of 'tous les gens de lettres'.[63] He, or someone in his circle, also liaised with radical circles in Holland. For a detailed account of his theory appears in the fourth volume of d'Argens's *Lettres juives* published at The Hague, in 1736, his remarkable new argument being jocularly ascribed by d'Argens to an 'auteur Arabe'.[64] The discussion about animal life and species then took a distinctly new turn, from 1742, with the publication, at Paris, of the sixth volume of Réaumur's monumental account of the insect world which additionally announced to the republic of letters a series of sensational experiments carried out using microscopes, magnifying glasses, and the ancestor of test-tubes in 1740–2 by the Swiss Huguenot Abraham Trembley (1710–84), by another Swiss, Charles Bonnet, and by himself, on polyps, worms, and water-worms, experiments which overturned some of the most widely accepted 'laws' and assumptions of contemporary biology. This was then followed up by Trembley's own treatise on freshwater polyps attached to aquatic plants, published at Leiden in 1744. These accounts reported the phenomenon of reproduction by these primitive creatures without any coupling of two individuals, or sexual differentiation, and still more sensationally, the rapid and apparently automatic regeneration of arms and legs which had been removed.

Trembley's research, carried out at Sorgvliet, the country house of the counts of Bentinck, near The Hague, where he then lived, meticulously documented, with the help of expert plates, left no doubt about the newly discovered phenomena, won him instant immortality, as La Mettrie remarked,[65] and posed a particular difficulty, for philosophers by demonstrating production of complete animals with mouths, stomachs, arms, and legs, from polyps not just cut in half, or into three, but even into multiple parts. The ability of these polyp slices swiftly to become whole and adapt new organs and limbs stunned contemporary opinion,[66] as did Trembley's experiments separating the 'grains' of the polyp which seemed to show that complex living organisms were basically aggregates of smaller 'molécules organiques' as Buffon was to call them.[67]

Since December 1740, Trembley stood in close contact with Réaumur, to whom he appealed not just to help interpret and publicize his findings, but in responding to the thorny 'questions métaphysiques' which they posed.[68] Réaumur admitted to experiencing the utmost difficulty accepting that sliced-off portions of the bodies

[62] Ehrard, *L'Idée*, 206–7; Roger, *Life Sciences*, 423–4.

[63] Benítez, *Face cachée*, 243.

[64] Ibid. 251–2; McKenna, 'Marquis d'Argens', 103.

[65] La Mettrie, *Machine Man*, 12, 85.

[66] Ibid.; Réaumur, *Mémoires pour servir*, vi, preface pp. xlix–l, lii, lvi, lxiv; Trembley, *Mémoires*, preface pp. 6–7, 25, 229–30, 235, 270.

[67] Ehrard, *L'Idée*, 219n.

[68] Trembley, *Mémoires*, preface p. vi, and p. 4; pp. li–liii.

of certain animals had the capacity to become a complete animal and that slices of its body, no matter which, could produce a head, mouth, stomach, and arms and legs and become complete. For this implied that nature can itself directly generate complex organized living beings, an idea destined to exert a profound effect on the generation of La Mettrie and Diderot, who were among the first to draw materialist implications from the research.[69] In the wake of Locke, observed Réaumur, few philosophers any longer doubted—unlike the Cartesians previously—that animals too have 'souls', or minds: but what kind of souls would they be which, like bodies, can be cut into pieces and then autonomously reproduce themselves in a short time?

This question had a considerable bearing on the problem of animal 'souls' as Réaumur calls them, and hence also of the human mind. Mind and matter for the moderate mainstream were wholly distinct. Since animals have ideas, Locke had affirmed, 'and are not bare machines (as some would have them)', it follows 'we cannot deny them to have some reason' and, therefore, minds.[70] Animals, therefore, receive ideas through sense experience in much the same way as humans do. But, at the same time, Locke effectively segregates the animal kingdom from humanity, as well as mind from matter, by pronouncing the structure of their minds quite different from ours in that 'the power of abstracting is not at all in them; and that the having of general ideas, is that which puts a perfect distinction betwixt Man and brutes; and is an excellency which the faculties of brutes by no means attain to'.[71] Hence, faculties of the human mind, as distinct from sense experience, something on which Locke lays much emphasis, is a 'proper difference wherein [men and animals] are wholly separated'. But if the part of the mind which yields simple ideas passes through slices of an animal into whole new animals, is not mind and thus ideas, if not 'reason' itself, shown in some way to inhere in matter?

Réaumur and Trembley readily confessed their astonishment at the new findings, and their difficulty in interpreting them. But of one thing they were certain: it was of paramount importance to adapt the newly found empirical data to their physico-theology and to Locke. For these *naturalistes* it was impossible to accept that nature has the creative power to form organized beings itself. Only God can do that. Since the data, on the face of it, could readily be construed by the *matérialistes* as proof of nature's power to create itself, one effect of the new experiments was to intensify Réaumur's and Trembley's insistence on Locke's strict empiricism and fervent conviction that 'l'auteur de l'univers' produces many marvellous things in large part incomprehensible to us and which will ever remain hidden.

The infinite complexity of animal life is something which we should wonder at and patiently study, Réaumur claims at the outset of his great project, but we must remain 'extrêmement retenus', extremely reserved, he admonishes, in attempting to explain the aims and purposes of 'l'Estre suprême' in organizing nature as he has.

69 Réaumur, *Mémoires pour servir*, vi, preface pp. lv, lvii, lxvi, lxvii; Hobohm, 'Le Progrès', 92; Roger, *Buffon*, 124; Spangler, 'Science', 90–1.

70 Locke, *Essay*, 160; Réaumur, *Mémoires pour servir*, vi, preface, p. lxvii; Dawson, *Nature's Enigma*, 34–5.

71 Dawson, *Nature's Enigma*, 127–8, 135; Locke, *Essay*, 159.

Rather we should patiently venerate him by describing his marvellous works without trying to delve too far into his ends, although we should not doubt that divine providence functions 'pour une fin, et pour la plus noble de toutes les fins'.[72] For Trembley too, the perplexing new finds most of all demonstrated how vital it is to lay aside all 'règles générales' and accept the inadequacy of human ideas for grasping 'l'ouvrage d'un Être infini à tous regards'. We must accept that there is simply a great deal we cannot explain.[73]

But the *matérialistes* put a very different construction on Trembley's, Réaumur's, and Bonnet's findings, seeing them, as La Mettrie does in his *L'Homme machine* (1748), as exciting confirmation of the reality of spontaneous generation.[74] Among the most daring articles of the first volume of the *Encyclopédie*, of 1751, partly written by Diderot personally, was the long article 'Animal', widely accounted one of the most subversive and transparently materialist pieces to be found in the early volumes, and one which has been aptly described as a kind of preface to the materialist writings of Diderot's philosophical maturity.[75] Here the physico-theological and fervently Lockean-Newtonian conception of the life sciences promulgated by Pluche and Réaumur, and heavily dominant in France in the 1730s and early 1740s, is totally rejected, partly using Buffon's research, but also, in large part, by reviewing the 1740–2 experiments and reports of Trembley, Bonnet, and Réaumur himself with a closely critical eye.[76]

Diderot relentlessly highlights Trembley's severe early doubts as to whether the polyps he was studying were really animals, or rather plants, and his suggestion at one point that we should perhaps best think of them as 'animaux-plantes'.[77] From this, Diderot launches into a long peroration depicting Trembley's research as proof that the generally accepted division of nature, differentiating nature's productions into fundamental categories of 'animals', 'plants', and 'minerals', is ultimately a false and meaningless one, since the new research proved that nature proceeds 'par des degrés nuancés', insensible shades of difference, from the animal to the vegetable and that ultimately the animate and living, rather than being a metaphysically separate category, is more appropriately conceived as an aspect, that is to say physical property of matter [une propriété physique de la matière] in general.[78]

Meanwhile, in the late 1740s, the greatest naturalist of the French Enlightenment, George-Louis Leclerc de Buffon (1708–88), following on from Maillet, and adopting the latter's idea (as Voltaire notes) that life evolved first in the sea at a time when the entire world was covered by the oceans,[79] sought, like Nicolas-Antoine Boulanger, to resume the discussion of fossils and their distribution, building on, but also

[72] Réaumur, *Mémoires pour servir*, i. 15, 23, 25; Dawson, *Nature's Enigma*, 28–9.

[73] Dawson, *Nature's Enigma*, 133–4; Trembley, *Mémoires*, 308–11.

[74] La Mettrie, *Machine Man*, 12, 24, 82, 85.

[75] Proust, *Diderot*, 137, 162, 258.

[76] Diderot and Daubenton, 'Animal', 468–74; Dawson, *Nature's Enigma*, 186–7.

[77] Diderot and Daubenton, 'Animal', 469–70, 472; Trembley, *Mémoires*, 307–8; Réaumur, *Mémoires pour servir*, p. vi, preface p. liii; Hazard, *European Mind*, 154.

[78] Diderot and Daubenton, 'Animal', 474; Proust, *Diderot*, 288, 393; Duflo, *Diderot philosophe*, 163–4; Cherni, *Diderot*, 236.

[79] Voltaire, *Œuvres complètes*, 164.

diverging from, the ideas of Réaumur. The aristocratic Buffon, having studied at the universities of his native Dijon and then Angers, and travelled in Italy, joined the erudite world of the Parisian academies, in 1732 and, from the mid 1730s, devoted himself increasingly to the study of the life sciences. In 1739, he was appointed *intendant* of the Jardin du Roi (Royal Gardens) in Paris. But it was not until the later 1740s that he became a major participant in the philosophical debate. For Buffon, as he put it in his *Histoire naturelle* in 1749, 'la certitude physique' and 'l'évidence mathématique' were the only criteria of what is true or false; everything else is just conjecture or probability. Although widely supposed, before the appearance of Voltaire's *Élémens*, to be 'tout anglois' in outlook, and one of those whom Voltaire was most anxious to win over during his attempt, in the years 1738–9, to dominate the Parisian intellectual scene,[80] later Buffon emerged as a *matérialiste* and firm anti-Voltairean, someone openly disdainful of Newton's unwillingness to ascribe a physical cause to gravity or separate theology from natural philosophy.[81]

From around 1740, Buffon was increasingly also at loggerheads with Réaumur. Considered proud and presumptuous even by his friends, Buffon avoided espousing most of the more obviously atheistic propositions of the *esprits forts*; but by the late 1740s he was nevertheless commonly classified among the virtual *incrédules* who, as it was put by one of his foes, the Oratorian Father Lelarge de Lignac, profess only 'extérieurement le christianisme' and suppose themselves entitled on that account to contradict revelation 'impunément'.[82] Buffon discerned in all natural things an 'ordre général' which sustained the processes of nature and unified their multiplicity into a single coherent structure which, however, was not a divine order.[83] A private materialist, he rejected all physico-theology and did much finally to separate natural history from theological preoccupations.

Buffon and Boulanger carried further Maillet's efforts to demonstrate that a history, or evolution, of natural forces, without the intervention of any supernatural agency, had, over an immense span of time, both slowly shaped the layers of the earth's geology and organized the development of species.[84] For Buffon, the earth, once a fiery liquid ball only slowly cooling, had passed through successive stages of evolution as had the (especially marine) species which arose and then later become extinct. Foremost among their critics was Voltaire who obdurately refused to accept either that seas had covered the whole earth or that land-based species could have begun in the oceans, and most of all that species have become extinct.[85] From his research Buffon concluded that fossils not only show that dry land, even very high terrain, was once covered by sea but since heavier layers of sedimentation containing

[80] Mignot de Montigny to Voltaire, Paris, 4 Feb. 1738; Voltaire to Helvétius, Paris, 3 Oct. 1739, Voltaire, *Correspondence*, v. 20–2, vii. 12–13.

[81] Roger, *Buffon*, 56–7, 109, 427; [Lelarge de Lignac], *Lettres à un Amériquain*, 1st Letter, 18, 47.

[82] Ibid. 1st Letter, 3–5; Cristani, 'Tradizione biblica', 95–6.

[83] Roger, 'Diderot et Buffon', 222, 235–6; Pappas, 'Buffon materialiste?', 235–6, 247.

[84] Ehrard, *L'Idée*, 209; Cristani, 'Tradizione biblica', 103; Cohen, *Fate*, 97, 98–9, 114.

[85] Voltaire, *Œuvres complètes*, xxv. 164; Roger, *Buffon*, 196; Martin-Haag, *Voltaire*, 48–51.

fossils overlay lighter layers, that these creatures were fossilized, just as the geological layers in which they are found developed, across immense spans of time,[86] evolving, he concluded, long before the world was habitable or inhabited by plants, animals, or men. Where Genesis recounts that the earth was covered by plants and trees before the sea was inhabited by fish, Buffon, like de Maillet, reversed the order proclaimed in Scripture, inhabiting the world with fish and other aquatic creatures before the emergence of plants.[87] Although the process proceeded extremely slowly, the conditions which made it possible followed from a tremendous initial upheaval dubbed by Buffon a *révolution générale*. Still more at odds with theological perspectives was his notion that the earth existed for thousands of centuries after this *révolution générale*, covered in oceans, during which time the only living things it produced were fish and shellfish destined to record their presence by depositing millions of fossils in rocks.[88]

Buffon, in part building on Trembley and Bonnet, developed a biology based on the principle that complex organisms are merely aggregates of simple organisms and these, at their simplest 'molécules organiques', are the basic building blocks of both living creatures and plants.[89] Here then was the basis of a systematic materialism but not necessarily of a monist system: for Buffon, unlike Diderot in his article 'Animal', firmly adheres to the distinction between what he calls *matière vivante* and inanimate, brute matter or *matière morte*.[90] The marine creatures and shellfish whose fossils are found everywhere on land were composed of the same living 'molecules', held Buffon, as subsequently were horses, dogs, and plants.[91] Each species evolved very slowly, he surmised, under different material circumstances; but he adduced no consistent theory to account for the extinction and transformation of species, nor to explain how life enters into his molecules in the first place. Once emerged, his species simply remained fixed, lingering unchanged for centuries. His was not, therefore, a fully evolutionary vision of our world though it was one in which species evolve from matter in stages (like the cosmos more generally), a conception which, on being published, in 1749, sufficed to scandalize many and most of all the Jansenists.[92]

The first three volumes of his *Histoire naturelle* of 1749 were worded prudently enough, though, to pass the censors, asserting among other requisite points that, in humans, the soul is distinct from the body. Even so, it was reported, the *matérialistes* excitedly recognized in his work an 'anti-Polignac' and 'le rétablissement de l'épicureanisme'.[93] If it remains unclear, in Buffon, exactly how animals, plants, and men came into existence, the undoubted implication was that they evolved without

[86] Roger, *Buffon*, 102–3; Pappas, 'Buffon matérialiste?', 236.
[87] Cherni, *Buffon*, 80–2; [Lelarge de Lignac], *Lettres à un Amériquain*, 3rd Letter, 13–14.
[88] [Lelarge de Lignac], *Lettres à un Amériquain*, 3rd Letter, 15–16, 18; Cristani, 'Tradizione biblica', 104.
[89] Cherni, *Buffon*, 79–81; Ehrard, *L'Idée*, 219–20.
[90] Ehrard, *L'Idée*, 221–3; Duflo, *Diderot philosophe*, 164.
[91] [Lelarge de Lignac], *Lettres à un Amériquain*, 3rd Letter, 9–11.
[92] Ibid., 3rd Letter, 5–6, 8–9; Pappas, 'Buffon matérialiste?,' 236.
[93] [Lelarge de Lignac], *Lettres à un Amériquain*, 1st Letter, 3, 5.

supernatural intervention from small 'éléments vivants', over long periods. Along with Buffon's accounts of generation nutrition, and growth, his approach conveyed a new, more sophisticated sense of how organic matter organizes into larger and more complex forms. What most attracted the *incrédules*, noted Lelarge de Lignac, was that they could now eliminate divine intervention from creation of species without postulating some highly implausible leap, or think of large animals emerging 'd'une motte de terre, ou du bouton d'un arbre fruitier' [from clods of earth, or from buds of fruit-trees].[94] They liked also the unifying tendency, Buffon openly scorning the complex classification system for plants formulated by his Lutheran Swedish rival Carolus Linnaeus (1707–78) in his *Systema naturae* (1735), claiming his pedantic adversary's proliferation of categories had rendered the language of science 'plus difficile que la science même'. Anti-materialists, of course, were uniformly hostile, Linnaeus, an avowed enemy of the *esprits forts*, complaining that Buffon in his books amply criticizes everyone else (including Linnaeus) but forgot to criticize himself.[95]

In this way, the life sciences in France came to be captured, from the mid 1740s, by the radical camp, albeit it was not until 1749 that this became obvious to the theologians and public, resulting in a call to arms against Buffon and his '*paradoxes*'; and, even then, the Jesuits, unlike the Jansenists, the Sorbonne, and Réaumur, preferred not to consider him a proper target since he was highly placed and inclined, as aristocrats were apt to do, to be publicly deferential to the church.[96] The tripartite division of French public intellectual and cultural life into a middle bloc, flanked on the one side by a powerful Jansenist Counter-Enlightenment and, on the other, by the radical thought, the configuration which was to characterize the rest of the French eighteenth century was now becoming clearly apparent; and what was most striking about it, despite the efforts of Voltaire and Réaumur, was the obvious weakness of the middle ground.

94 [Lelarge de Lignac], *Lettres à un Amériquain*, 1st Letter, 6, 9.

95 Koerner, *Linnaeus*, 28; Ehrard, *L'Idée*, 188–90.

96 Pappas, 'Buffon matérialiste?', 247–9.

29

Realigning the *Parti philosophique*: Voltaire, *Voltairianisme*, *Antivoltairianisme* (1732–1745)

1. VOLTAIRE'S ENLIGHTENMENT

The decisive period of Voltaire's formation as a philosopher was the years 1732–8 when he worked painstakingly to fashion a coherent system for himself and succeeded in reconfiguring, and briefly dominating, the French intellectual stage as a whole. By the mid 1730s, he could look forward to presiding over a wide-ranging programme of reform and renewal in French philosophy, science, and scholarship as well as the world of literature, based on Lockean-Newtonian principles. For these then seemed set to win over not only the French aristocratic courtly elite and royal authority, but also major elements within the church.

From the time of his contacts with Lord Bolingbroke (who had been in exile in France since 1715) in the years 1722–6, and participation in the latter's circle, Voltaire had been steadily learning about English culture, science, and thought.[1] His stay in England in 1726–8 and the opportunities, whilst there, to meet with English intellectual luminaries, notably his several conferences with Samuel Clarke,[2] exerted a lasting influence on his views about God, toleration, philosophy, and science. This set in motion a process of philosophical maturing and development which continued right through the 1730s. By 1732, Voltaire was an enthusiastic Newtonian as well as Lockean but not yet someone who had worked out, even in his own mind, the precise philosophical consequences of Newton, or the relationship between Locke and Newton, or indeed was yet especially confident in his grasp of Newtonian science and mathematics.

In the 1720s, the opposition to Newtonian ideas in France seemed distinctly formidable. The assessment of Newton's achievement delivered by Fontenelle, the academy's secretary, in his public *éloge de M. Newton*, celebrating the great scientist's memory, delivered in the academy's public assembly hall in Paris in November

[1] Barber, 'Newton de Voltaire', 118–21; Walters and Barber, 'Introduction', 30–2.

[2] Walters and Barber, 'Introduction', 32–3, 57; Voltaire, *Métaphysique de Newton*, 195; Fichera, *Il Deismo critico*, 89–92; Benelli, *Voltaire metafisico*, 70, 72–3; Barber, 'Newton de Voltaire', 120.

1727, warmly praised his mathematical achievement but firmly cast doubt, like Huygens, Leibniz, and Hartsoeker earlier, on his physico-theological interpretation of what he had demonstrated mathematically, broadly questioning his philosophy as such. Fontenelle especially highlighted what he took to be the shortcomings of Newton's theory of gravity, principle of 'attraction', and notions of absolute space, time, and motion, declaring Newton's physics 'occultist' and philosophically incoherent.[3] In thus publicly endorsing the anti-Newtonian critique of Huygens, Leibniz, Hartsoeker, and Bernoulli, Fontenelle deliberately introduced into contemporary French intellectual and scientific parlance a new polarizing terminology of 'impulsionnaires' versus 'attractionnaires' instead of 'Newtonians' versus 'Cartesians'. Rebuffing Newton's (and Le Clerc's) claims that Cartesianism is purely 'hypothetical' whereas Newtonian science, like English thought more generally, is quite differently structured and solidly 'empirical', Fontenelle insisted the correct antinomy was a post-Cartesian French science of clear reason and *évidence* as opposed to Newtonian occultism and obscurantism. This antithesis was, of course, rhetorical and misleading; but it was one which powerfully infused (as well as confused) much philosophical discussion in France over the next two decades.

By the late 1720s, then, Newtonianism had become a major complicating factor at the heart of French (and Italian) intellectual culture. The core issue, as Montesquieu's friend the Jesuit scientist Louis-Bertrand Castel (1688–1757) stressed in his review of the Leibniz–Clarke correspondence in 1728, was whether Clarke's thesis that no philosophy was ever less prone to encourage materialism than Newton's was really valid. Some were inclined to trust in Clarke's assurances; but Jesuit doctrinal experts, like Tournemine and Castel, remained distinctly dubious about this. Castel suspected (like Leibniz) that implicit in Newtonianism was a worrying tendency to spiritualize everything, and 'with Spinoza' conflate body and spirit, rendering not just absolute space but physical reality itself part of God.[4] Hence, the French public controversy about Newton coalesced for the moment around the, to us, irrelevant and confusingly formulated question of whether Newtonian 'attraction' ultimately advances or curbs materialism and Spinozism.

Eager to deepen his understanding of the subject, Voltaire entered into a correspondence, in the autumn of 1732, with Pierre-Louis Moreau de Maupertuis (1698–1759), son of an aristocratic family of Saint-Malo, and leading younger member, since 1723, of the Paris Académie Royale des Sciences, converted to Newtonianism in 1728, during his visit to London, and who had recently publicly assumed the role of chief advocate of Newtonianism in France. Shortly before, Maupertuis had delivered a celebrated *Discours* before the Parisian academy 'Sur les loix d'attraction', stressing that the 'Créateur et l'Ordonnateur' of everything could not have chosen a more efficient law of 'attraction' than Newton's laws of gravity for retaining the planets in their orbits and ensuring the stability and orderly

[3] Ehrard, *L'Idée*, 125–6; Shank, 'Before Voltaire', 393–7, 406.
[4] Shank, 'Before Voltaire', 486; Jammer, *Einstein and Religion*, 157.

functioning of our cosmos. He compared the systems of Descartes and Newton in a manner highly detrimental to the former, stressing particularly the universality of Newton's principle of 'attraction' and its divine inspiration, and the empirical basis of his argumentation. Maupertuis was now the leader of a lively Newtonian faction in France, head of a widening campaign, supported by a clique of young acolytes, championing Newton against Fontenelle, Dorthous de Mairan, and other opponents of Newton's cosmology and physics.[5]

An accomplished mathematician and naturalist, somewhat in the physico-theological mould of Réaumur, Maupertuis had been a regular at the Café Procope since the early 1720s and such a fixture of the Parisian café scene that, later, in July 1740, when Voltaire first heard that Frederick the Great wanted him in Berlin to head his newly revived royal academy there, Voltaire predicted he would stay in Paris while 's-Gravesande, whom the king also 'wanted', would exchange Holland for Prussia, both parts of his prediction proving wrong.[6] Whilst he remained in Paris, though, until 1745, Maupertuis remained one of the 'plus célèbres partisans du Newtonianisme',[7] as d'Alembert labelled him, and as such a prime adversary of the scientific neo-Cartesianism of the then French scientific establishment, his chief quality in the role being his formidable presence. Condorcet later characterized Maupertuis as an 'homme de beaucoup d'esprit, savant médiocre, et philosophe plus médiocre encore'.[8] Voltaire at this stage was content to play the disciple: Newton, he declared in a letter to Maupertuis, is our Christopher Columbus, having carried us to a new world, 'et je voudrois bien y voyager à votre suite'.[9]

During his stay in London, in 1728, where he was made a Fellow of the London Royal Society, Maupertuis, like Voltaire afterwards, had established particularly cordial relations with Clarke, then in the thick of the *vis viva* controversy with 's-Gravesande, over questions of force, dynamics, and inert or active matter.[10] Although Maupertuis was mostly less inclined than Voltaire, during the ensuing public intellectual battles, to stress the theological implications of Newton's system, or broadcast Clarke's views, he too always insisted that Newton's thought buttresses belief in God and divine providence; he also publicly aligned with the liberal Catholic camp in opposition to the *esprits forts* whose chief argument 'contre nous', as he expressed it in 1749, in his *Essai de philosophie morale*, is based 'sur l'impossibilité de nos dogmes'.[11] Certainly, he was more willing than 's-Gravesande to stress the defence

5 Maupertuis, 'Sur les loix d'attraction', 343–4, 347–8, 362; De Gandt, 'Qu'est-ce qu'être', 128–9, 133.

6 Voltaire to Maupertuis, Brussels, 7 July 1740, Voltaire, *Correspondence*, viii. 239.

7 D'Alembert, 'Attraction', in Diderot and d'Alembert, *Encyclopédie*, i. 855.

8 Condorcet, *Vie de Voltaire*, 116.

9 Voltaire to Maupertuis, Fontainebleau, 3 Nov. 1732, Voltaire, *Correspondence*, ii. 246; Ehrard, *L'Idée*, 132–3; Shank, 'Before Voltaire', 565–7, 583.

10 Shank, 'Before Voltaire', 518; M.A.F.C., *Lettres sur les Hollandois*, 28; Barber, 'Newton de Voltaire', 122–3; Vamboulis, 'La Discussion', 162, 167.

11 Maupertuis, 'Sur les loix d'attraction', 347; Maupertuis, 'Essai de philosophie morale', 246–7; Gumbrecht and Reichardt, '*Philosophe*', 30; Terrall, *Man who Flattened*, 67–70, 76, 80–1.

of revelation, providence, miracles, and ecclesiastical authority that Newtonianism and adherence to Locke affords.[12]

Convinced that 'English ' principles in philosophy and culture generally were the path of the future, the key to nurturing in France everything admirable, tolerant, balanced, cogent, and up to date in contemporary western thought, Voltaire also believed that such a 'revolution of the mind' must be introduced gently and gradually lest the latent religious bigotry, hostility to toleration and Protestantism, scholasticism of the universities, and anxieties of the court be aroused against his great project for reforming France. It was to advance the cause of this firmly Lockean-Newtonian Enlightenment, then, that Voltaire urged in his *Lettres philosophiques* (1734) that no one need fear his proposed intellectual innovations and that, anyhow, no development in 'philosophy', as such, *can* harm society, religion, or the political order since, as he put it, few read and fewer still both read and think.[13] Tact was never Voltaire's forte, however, and despite his concerting both text and tactics with Maupertuis, the book met with a stringently unfavourable reception. Indeed, shortly after its appearance, a *lettre de cachet* was issued for his arrest, for publishing without a royal licence. The printer was actually arrested, the remaining stock confiscated, and on 10 June 1734 the work was publicly prohibited by the *Parlement* of Paris, and lacerated and burnt in the courtyard of the Palais de Justice.

This crushing rebuff was mainly due, however, to the book's thoroughly disrespectful tone regarding the current state of French learning, in fact almost everything French, as well its approvingly labelling Newton a 'Socinien', and gratuitously suggesting that the Unitarians (i.e. Socinians) argue 'plus géométriquement que nous'.[14] Neither had it helped that his book claims it was not 'Locke, Bayle, Spinoza, Hobbes, Shaftesbury, Collins or Toland' who were responsible for the unsettling intellectual ferment of the times, or the discord and strife in Europe, but, rather, the theologians.[15] Alarmed, and forewarned about the possibility of arrest, Voltaire took the precaution of evacuating the capital in good time. On departing, he urged Maupertuis to be chief of their faction [chef de secte], promising that both he and his elegant young aristocratic companion, Émilie, Madame Du Châtelet—also an intimate of Maupertuis (who had converted her from Cartesianism to Newtonianism)—would prove ardent adherents. Maupertuis, though, chose not to exert himself unduly either for Voltaire or any such philosophical 'sect', enabling the more dynamic Voltaire, before long, to assume effective leadership of the faction championing Newtonianism in France, as well as gain sole possession (from April 1735) of Émilie's affections. This he did working from his retreat at her château at Cirey-en-Champagne, a place located on the eastern edge of the kingdom where he spent

12 Maupertuis, 'Sur les loix d'attraction', 348; Maupertuis, 'Essai de philosophie morale', 182, 250; Shank, 'Before Voltaire', 555–6.

13 Voltaire, *Lettres philosophiques*, 68–9; Voltaire, *Mémoires*, 40–1; Wellman, *La Mettrie*, 253.

14 Voltaire, *Lettres philosophiques*, 31; Shank, 'Before Voltaire', 34; Gumbrecht and Reichardt, '*Philosophe*', 17; Rahe, 'Book', 52, 55–6.

15 Voltaire, *Lettres philosophiques*, 94–5.

much time over the next years and which offered, should he need to flee in a hurry, a convenient choice of borders within easy reach.

The years immediately following publication of Voltaire's *Lettres philosophiques*, Condorcet recalled over half a century later, were among us 'l'époque d'une révolution'. By this, he meant that the controversy it stirred lent tremendous new impetus to the taste for English ideas, science, society, and literature, precipitating a veritable tide of French *anglicisme*.[16] For while Voltaire's Anglicizing bombshell had caused some irritation in official quarters; more broadly it also aroused much real intellectual enthusiasm and did so without provoking any real opposition from the forces of authority or the church; rather the contrary, it initiated a period of more general willingness to accept the offered double dose of Newtonian and Lockean inspiration from across the Channel. For the outcry against the *Lettres philosophiques* was almost entirely due to the book's presumptuous tone rather than its intellectual content.

The brief furore over the book taught Voltaire and other budding French *philosophes* of the 1730s the advantages of caution and trebly so: caution regarding the crown, caution regarding the church, and caution regarding popular opinion. Having sent his *Considérations* on the Romans to Amsterdam for publication in 1733, the circumspect Montesquieu, having already gone through the proofs with his Jesuit friend Father Louis Bertrand Castel in the spring of 1734, deleting everything construable as offensive to church or state, went through the text again, following the Voltaire affair, in the summer, censoring himself still more strenuously.[17] His anxieties seemed real enough at the time, though actually neither he nor, at this stage, Voltaire had any desire to appear to be criticizing either the monarchy or the church. In the end, Voltaire's career as a kind of intellectual 'outlaw' proved extremely brief and wholly unconnected with the core philosophical issues raised by his provocative book. If some resented the outspokenness of his assault on Descartes, and on Malebranche's 'illusions sublimes', and the Jansenists were indignant at his dismissing Pascal as 'un fanatique', little in the controversy surrounding the book indicated any real antagonism to the ideas of Bacon, Boyle, Locke, Newton, and Clarke which the work so vigorously extols.[18]

On the contrary, the Jesuits showed no sign of making an issue of the *Lettres philosophiques*, and at this juncture made editorial changes to their periodical the *Mémoires de Trévoux* which signalled further conciliatory intentions regarding the new developments in philosophy and science advocated by Maupertuis, Voltaire, Réaumur, and the Newtonians. Even the Jansenists, though immediately recognizing an implacable foe in Voltaire, at this juncture had nothing to say about his ardour for Locke and Newton.[19] All that was needed, seemingly, for Voltaire's

[16] Condorcet, *Vie de Voltaire*, pp. Dviii–ix, D11; Tillet, *Constitution anglaise*, 76, 78; Rahe, 'Book', 51.

[17] Rahe, 'Book', 51.

[18] Gaultier, *Poëme de Pope*, 56–7, 63; Shank, 'Before Voltaire', 589; Cottret, *Jansénismes*, 28; O'Keefe, *Contemporary Reactions*, 34–5.

[19] Condorcet, *Vie de Voltaire*, pp. E–E1; O'Keefe, *Contemporary Reactions*, 35; Cottret, *Jansénismes*, 28–30.

Enlightenment based on English ideas to achieve a major breakthrough was more tact and a more willingness to curb his disdain for theologians and pedants. Here was a definite opening for a long-term and wide-ranging *rapprochement* between Voltaire, Réaumur, Maupertuis, Condillac, Montesquieu, and 'English' ideas, on the one hand, and the forces of the French religious and political establishment on the other.[20]

From the mid 1730s, the middle ground hence increasingly edged towards embracing the Enlightenment of Newton, Locke, and Voltaire, and the latter could set seriously to work to exploit the liberalizing tendency in current Jesuit intellectual policy so as to position himself in the French intellectual arena, and society, more advantageously. This he did, in particular, via a prolonged epistolary exchange with his former teacher at the Collège Louis-le-Grand in Paris, the veteran Jesuit controversialist and anti-Spinozist Father René-Josèphe Tournemine (1661–1739). Despite his advanced years, Tournemine was still an influential figure and one of the editors of the Jesuit journal, on which he worked together with other noted moderates such as Father Pierre Julien Rouillé and Montesquieu's well-connected *confidant* Castel. Voltaire's objective was to win Tournemine and the *Journal de Trévoux* round to acceptance of Bacon, Boyle, Locke, Newton, and Clarke as the intellectual core of a new 'enlightened' Catholic philosophical world-view.[21]

As it happened, Voltaire's interaction with Tournemine coincided with his first serious attempt at systematic philosophy, the exploratory *Traité de métaphysique*, a text which remained unpublished in his lifetime,[22] but in which he worked out and refined the basic doctrines of his own system, the philosophical ground-plan, as it were, of the Voltairean Enlightenment. His aim in entering into extended dialogue with Tournemine was less to convince him of the jarring contrast in intellectual environment between England and France with the former flourishing amid toleration, Latitudinarianism, and freedom of the press, and dominated by Lockean-Newtonian ideas, while the latter languished under censorship, relative intolerance, and reverence for outdated authorities and old quarrels (though he did not neglect to deliver that message), than endeavour, without antagonizing the old man, to win him round to a positive attitude to Locke and Newton and in this way forestall the hitherto distinct risk that his Lockean-Newtonian construct would be opposed or condemned out of hand by the church as heretical or impious.

In pursuing this strategy, Voltaire was, for a time, remarkably successful. The ideas pondered with Tournemine were precisely those he himself was refining to strengthen his own system. In the *Lettres philosophiques*, Voltaire declares the Newtonian doctrine of 'attraction' a great and defining force ordering the universe, an inherent property of matter, doing so in a more emphatic way than had Maupertuis and distancing himself from 's-Gravesande who claimed, rather, that

20 Pappas, *Berthier's* Journal, 19–21.

21 Voltaire, *Traité de métaphysique*, 364; Wade, *Intellectual Development*, 367, 401–2, 405–8; Ehrard, *L'Idée*, 137; Reichardt, 'Einleitung', 115.

22 Voltaire, *Traité de métaphysique*, 359.

we cannot know bodies as they really exist or the forces that move them.[23] The two most crucial of Voltaire's propositions, and those Tournemine was most reluctant to embrace, were his claim that Newton's gravity could satisfactorily unite modern science with a conservative Catholic philosophy and theology and the idea that if it is possible for God, as Voltaire put it in his letter to Tournemine of June 1735, to lend to matter the property of gravitation, or 'attraction', as Newton showed, it is surely equally possible for him to impart to matter the capacity of thought, as Locke suggests.[24] The hardest part of his task, Voltaire perceived, was to overcome Tournemine's deep suspicion that Newtonian gravity could imply the innateness of motion in matter, and Locke's superadding of thought to matter that matter is capable of thought.

Voltaire's Newtonianism, unlike 's-Gravesande's, was designed to allay ecclesiastical worries regarding matter, motion, and thought, firmly upholding the inertness of matter as well as divine providence, while simultaneously exploiting the French Jesuits' traditional hostility to Cartesianism and aversion to Malebranche. It was a brilliant strategy. Very likely Voltaire calculated that if he could persuade the intellectual elite of the French church fully or in part of the advantages of Locke and Newton from their standpoint, he would subsequently be in an impregnable position from which to launch a campaign for more toleration and reduced censorship, and finally manage to curb ecclesiastical influence in France, using a philosophical ground-plan the clergy, once they had sanctioned it, would be largely impotent to attack.

To allay Tournemine's fears, Voltaire urged the special characteristics of Newton's principle of attraction, repeating that neither Newton, nor anyone 'digne du nom de philosophe', holds motion to be innate in matter. Newton, he insisted, conceives motion 'seulement comme une propriété donnée de Dieu'.[25] Furthermore, if God can communicate attraction and movement, imparting these to matter, on what basis can one then oppose Locke's doctrine that God can also 'communiquer le don de la pensée à la matière'?[26] Locke's aim, stressed Voltaire, was by no means to suggest that matter in itself is capable of thought as the 'atheists' delude themselves into supposing: 'ce sentiment est rejeté par M. Locke comme absurde.'[27]

Locke, 'le seul métaphysicien raisonnable', Voltaire called him, seeks only to show that God can, through his providence, miraculously impart the property of thought to matter. Not a few Frenchmen, Voltaire assured the elderly Jesuit, were at last beginning to glimpse this vital truth 'dont toute l'Angleterre, le pays des philosophes, commence à être instruite'. At the heart of his own system, Voltaire repeatedly assured Tournemine, as of those of Locke and Newton, stands the idea of

[23] Shank, 'Before Voltaire', 614–15.

[24] Voltaire, *Métaphysique de Newton*, 226; Wade, *Intellectual Development*, 401–2; Casini, 'Voltaire, la lumière', 41; Firode, 'Locke et les philosophes', 61–2.

[25] Voltaire to Tournemine, [Aug.] 1735, Voltaire, *Correspondence*, iii. 185.

[26] Ibid.; Voltaire, *Lettres à son altesse*, 318; Voltaire, *Mémoires*, 40; Benelli, *Voltaire metafisico*, 96.

[27] Voltaire, *Correspondence*, iii. 278, Voltaire to Tournemine, [Dec.] 1735.

a providential God and his governance of the universe. He rejoiced that Tournemine had grasped 'avec quelle supériorité de raison Locke a prouvé avec Clarke l'existence de cet Être Suprême'. Newton and Locke, much the two greatest geniuses of the modern age, are such, urged Voltaire, precisely because it was they who demonstrate God's 'existence avec le plus de force' so that all thoughtful men should glory in being their disciples.[28]

Working steadily on his book expounding the philosophy of Newton, Voltaire strove to turn the tables on Fontenelle and Dorthous, insisting that it was Descartes's 'tourbillons' (vortexes), and their principle of 'propulsion', not Newton's 'attraction', the fundamental law of the universe, which should be labelled 'occult', since the existence of these vortexes had never been demonstrated while Newton's 'attraction' is something demonstrably real, observable, and measurable albeit the cause of gravity remains hidden: 'la cause de cette cause est dans le sein de Dieu.'[29] This time, still proclaiming his ideological alliance with Maupertuis,[30] Voltaire prepared his ground well. However ironic it may seem in retrospect, especially when we consider what the future was to hold, publication of the *Élémens de la philosophie de Neuton* in 1738 met with no significant opposition from among the ecclesiastical or court establishment—indeed met with widespread approval, except from the Jansenists who remained doggedly silent.

The Jesuit *Journal de Trévoux* could see nothing that was not praiseworthy in the project of 'M. de Voltaire, de se rendre philosophe et de rendre, s'il est possible, tout l'univers newtonien'.[31] The lively resistance Voltaire did encounter was almost entirely from entrenched groups of philosophically inclined *érudits*, dismissed by him as 'Cartesians', among the academies and the intellectual avant-garde. Acknowledging that Newton always speaks of the Creator and his attributes 'avec décence', the Jesuits, by contrast, were now willing to endorse the general propagation of Newtonianism, together with Lockean epistemology, in the colleges, universities, and academies of France and, with it, the spread of Voltaire's national influence.[32] As far as major sections of the French establishment of church and state were concerned, Voltaire's Enlightenment based on 'English ideas' had in fact, by 1738, won the battle. At Paris, by the end of the 1730s and beginning of the 1740s, it was almost automatic for both Catholics interested in natural philosophy and students like Diderot (who was aged 25 when Voltaire's book appeared), aspiring to the status of *philosophe*, to be enthusiasts for Newton, Locke, and Voltaire.[33]

Having warmly welcomed the first edition of Voltaire's work on Newton, the Jesuits were even more positive in their reception of the second edition of June 1744. All the considerable advantages of Voltaire's 'Newtonian' Enlightenment,

[28] Voltaire, *Correspondence*, iii. 286; Ehrard, *L'Idée*, 137–8; Walters, 'Voltaire', 892; Gawlick, 'Epikur bei den Deisten', 334.

[29] Voltaire, *Lettres philosophiques*, 111.

[30] Terrall, *Man who Flattened*, 173.

[31] Quoted in Walters and Barber, 'Introduction', 85; O'Keefe, *Contemporary Reactions*, 52.

[32] O'Keefe, *Contemporary Reactions*, 52–3; Pappas, *Berthier's* Journal, 88–90.

[33] De Gandt, 'Qu'est-ce qu'être', 143–4; Duflo, *Diderot philosophe*, 107.

from a Jesuit standpoint, were pointedly noted on that occasion: Newton, held Voltaire's new Jesuit allies, reinforces the liberty of God and the freedom of will in man given by God; whereas the pernicious Cartesian system, as Voltaire stressed, is 'la source de celui de Spinoza'. Voltaire's Newtonianism, the world was assured, powerfully buttresses belief in divine providence, underpins the immateriality and eternality of the soul, shows how God imparts the gift of thought to matter, thereby underpinning Locke while safeguarding the externality of motion to matter, and demonstrating the impossibility of species and types in nature arising from mere movement allegedly internal to matter.[34]

The Jesuits regularly praised Voltaire's philosophical efforts, plays, and poetry during these years, continuing to support him also after Guillaume-François Berthier (1704–82), the pre-eminent Jesuit intellectual strategist of the mid eighteenth century, became editor-in-chief of the *Mémoires de Trévoux* in 1745.[35] Once the machinery of Jesuit publicity had set this fateful course, the initially welcoming clerical response to Voltaire and his allies was indeed to take many years to reverse. This is why when the first great struggles between the *parti philosophique* and the church erupted in France, at the end of the 1740s, Voltaire, disconcertingly for himself, found that he had been left on the sidelines; indeed, even in the most conservative 'enlightened' contexts, including papal Rome and the early Greek Enlightenment, Voltaire continued to be thought of, until the late 1750s, as essentially a proponent of the kind of enlightenment sanctioned by liberal churchmen—whether Catholic, Protestant, or Greek Orthodox: the guarantee of his loyalty and support for miracles, providence, and ecclesiastical authority, and of his opposition to the materialism and atheism of the *esprits forts*, lay precisely in his tireless invoking of Bacon, Locke, and Newton.

As in Paris, so in the Rome of Benedict XIV (pope 1740–58). No doubt Voltaire himself savoured the irony of Benedict's amicable letter to him and best wishes more than anyone and more and more saw the advantages of his good standing with the church. In these circumstances it is easy to see why during the 1740s and early 1750s Voltaire consistently denied his authorship of the clandestine manuscript the *Sermon des cinquante*, penned around 1740, a text which seems to have remained unpublished until 1763, despite the fact that the earliest printed copies carry the date '1749'.[36] The *Sermon* is a militant providential Deist tract, summoning men to adore the one Supreme Being and acknowledge him as Creator, benefactor, and legislator of the universe. It contained several elements which Voltaire wished, indeed at this juncture positively needed, to keep firmly hidden from sight. Strongly pro-Socinian, the text betrays a deep, underlying, and hitherto unsuspected aversion to traditional Christianity, a religion which he here denounces as an 'affreux pervertissement de la religion naturelle'; the *Sermon*, had it been known to be his, would have lifted the veil from his private but ardent fantasies about undermining

[34] Pappas, *Berthier's* Journal, 88–9; *Mémoires de Trévoux*, 44 (June 1744) 1008–28.

[35] Pappas, *Berthier's* Journal, 21, 53, 90.

[36] Lee, 'Le "Sermon" ', 143–6.

Christianity and the churches in favour of a 'natural religion' which he believed would unite rather than divide men.[37]

Meanwhile, by joining in alliance with Locke, Newton, and Voltaire, as well as Maupertuis, Montesquieu, and the new natural philosophy of Réaumur and Pluche, the French Jesuits, like other liberal wings of the main churches, elsewhere reaped numerous and solid benefits. As long as the main thrust of learned opinion in France, Italy, Spain, and the Netherlands, as in Britain, held that Newton and Locke represented what was most up to date, progressive, and convincing in the realms of science and philosophy, 'enlightened' churchmen could echo Le Clerc in proclaiming materialism, Spinozism, and all philosophical atheism outmoded remnants of ancient 'superstition' and pagan fanaticism, irrelevant vestiges of now finally discredited ways of thinking which were wholly unscientific. The claim that they were now more up to date and scientific than the *esprits forts* derived its entire plausibility precisely from their embracing Locke and Newton.

In its scathing review of Du Marsais's *Nouvelles Libertés de penser* in August 1743, for instance, the *Mémoires de Trévoux* labelled the authors of this collection of irreligious and materialist tracts spiritual offspring of Bayle, benighted 'atheists' who grasped scarcely anything 'de bonne physique ni aucune science de raisonnement'.[38] Where the *esprits forts* had long professed to scorn churchmen as 'd'ignorans et de petits esprits superstitieux', by espousing Voltaire's Enlightenment, the Jesuits, thanks to Locke and Newton, had now turned the tables on their bitterest enemies and aligned with the Huguenot *rationaux* in declaring Spinoza's and Bayle's disciples the true *ignorants* and impostors, whose impiety and maliciousness was equalled only by their ignorance and crassness, an ignorance which, aided by the avarice of corrupt booksellers, was inundating society with a new kind of false oracle worship and credulity.[39] Locke and Newton triumphant, celebrated, and venerated meant the moderate clergy could henceforth present themselves as altogether more reasonable, progressive, scientific, learned, and truly 'philosophical' than their materialist and atheistic opponents.

Partly for this reason, the incipient rift in what a few years later would be known as the *parti philosophique* into divergent Voltairean and radical camps, already perceptible by the mid 1730s, before the publication of Voltaire's *Élémens de la philosophie de Neuton* (1738), became distinctly clearer in its wake. Voltaire found the months immediately following the publication of his *Élémens* deeply frustrating, referring in letters to Dortous de Mairan and Maupertuis, in the autumn of 1738, for example, to the 'grande fermentation' in France resulting from the division among those interested in philosophical and scientific issues into two irreconcilable rival camps, 'deux partis' which he continued to label 'Cartesians' and 'Newtonians'; and indeed the clash of philosophies was real enough, despite Voltaire's refrain that such 'guerres civiles ne sont point faites pour des philosophes'.[40] In 1739, d'Argens

[37] HHL MS Fr. 79 [Voltaire], 'Le Sermon', 27^{r-v}; [Voltaire], *Sermon des cinquante*, 4.

[38] *Mémoires de Trévoux*, 43 (1743), 2278.

[39] Ibid. 43 (1743), 2284–5.

[40] Voltaire to Dorthous de Mairan, Cirey, 11 Sept. 1738, and to Maupertuis, Cirey, *c.*1 Oct. 1738, Voltaire, *Correspondence*, v. 286, 290–1, 307.

has his 'Chinese' visitor to Paris recounting a fight with fists in a Parisian café between ardent *Neutonistes* and latter-day 'Cartesians' who obdurately oppose 'attraction' and what they regard as Newton's 'occult' forces.[41]

Voltaire, who had hoped for a war of reason against Jansenists and *dévots*, in alliance with the Jesuits and the court, was undoubtedly irked and pained by the intensity of the angry schism among the natural philosophers and *philosophes*: 'les philosophes', he complained privately in August 1738, 'ne doivent pas ressembler aux Jésuites et aux Jansénistes.'[42] But while he continued to refer to his philosophical-scientific adversaries of these years disparagingly as 'Cartesians', the modern reader should not be misled by this. For the conflict of the late 1730s and 1740s was by no means between a group of old-fashioned dogmatists and 'rationalists' resisting up-to-date, 'enlightened' men espousing a more modern scientific empiricism, and still less anything remotely like the tremendous struggle, shortly to erupt, in the early 1750s, between the *parti philosophique* as a whole and the forces of reaction and Counter-Enlightenment.

Rather this was a battle between two rival philosophical factions in which Voltaire's basic strategy in the period 1738–9, before he left with Mme Du Châtelet for a long stay in Brussels, avowedly disgusted with Paris,[43] was to try to win the key *naturalistes* and philosophers, in particular Dorthous de Mairan, Buffon, d'Argens, the young Helvétius (who was very close to Buffon), Vauvenargues, and others, over to his point of view.[44] Moreover, this was an intellectual controversy in which the modern observer cannot easily pronounce as to which faction was the more up-to-date and 'scientific' from a modern viewpoint. For the party of Fontenelle, Dorthous de Mairan, Buffon, and others were not opposing Newton's mathematics, and still less the principle of experiment and demonstration, but rather the principle of 'attraction' as an unexplained general phenomenon and in particular Newton's, Clarke's, and Voltaire's physico-theology.

Admittedly, the schism was tinged with a hint of 'French' versus 'English' patriotism; certainly there was an element of settling old scores with Voltaire whose biting tongue and pen were not such as to endear him to everyone; but these were secondary factors. The central issue was 'impulsion' versus' attraction', and a consistent pure mechanism versus Newtonian physico-theology, with the materialist *esprits forts* supporting the elderly Fontenelle, and the church either standing completely aside (as with the Jansenists) or else, as with the Jesuits and Sorbonne, broadly supporting Voltaire. What then is the great difficulty, exclaimed Voltaire in exasperation in August 1738, with the idea that God has imparted gravitation to matter just as he has bestowed inertia, mobility, and impenetrability? God could not have created matter without extension, he adds, but could perhaps have done so without weight. 'Pour moi', Voltaire summed up, 'je ne reconnois, dans cette propriété

[41] D'Argens, *Lettres chinoises*, i. 134–5.

[42] Voltaire to Pitot, Cirey, 4 Aug. 1738, Voltaire, *Correspondence*, v. 234.

[43] Voltaire to Helvétius, Brussels, 24 Jan. 1740, ibid. vii. 83–4.

[44] Voltaire to Helvétius, Paris, 3 Oct. 1739, ibid. vii. 12–13.

[i.e. gravitation]' of bodies any other cause than the hand 'toute puissante de l'être Suprême'.[45] Physico-theology was, and remained, the real hub of the conflict.

2. THE DEFEAT OF VOLTAIRE AND THE FRENCH 'NEWTONIANS'

Le neutonianisme, as it was called in France at the time, was now, assuredly, very much *à la mode* in Paris in the late 1730s and early 1740s, an exciting novelty, supported by many.[46] But the many allies and heirs of Fontenelle, Boulainvilliers, Du Marsais, and Boureau-Deslandes simply refused to follow Voltaire in embracing providential Deism, 'attraction', and adulation of Bacon, Boyle, Newton, Locke, and Clarke, protesting incessantly about the Newtonians' introducing of 'causes occultes'. The split was basically philosophical and physico-theological rather than scientific but also a matter of personalities and potentially political. Encouraged though he was by his initial success, Voltaire by the end of the 1730s began to see the growing possibility that he might, after all, fail to carry through the Newtonian-Lockean 'revolution' for which he had hoped. Dorthous and Fontenelle refused to be swayed. Vauvenargues called him 'maître' but eschewed Locke and Newton. Buffon proved not just unwilling to follow Voltaire's lead but began actively to attack his and Réaumur's Creationism, views on fossils and species, and physico-theology along with the Newtonian account of gravity and force.[47]

Voltaire's position was further complicated by Mme Du Chatelet's following her own independent course. No sooner had he dedicated his *Élémens* to her, than she, now in her own right a significant voice in contemporary philosophical debate but hitherto championing Newtonianism, performed a well-publicized volte-face, renouncing Newtonianism, and proclaiming her conversion to the philosophy of Leibniz and Wolff. This introduced some brisk intellectual rivalry, albeit of a friendly sort, into his very household.[48] As a Leibnizian, one respect in which she immediately defected to the anti-Newtonian camp was in repudiating Newton's conception of gravity as a purely immaterial force lacking a mechanical cause. Indeed, she refused all talk of a direct emanation of divine providence in the physical workings of nature, like Wolff, pronouncing all nature's effects to be 'opérés par des causes mécaniques'.[49] Along with the Newtonian conception of motion and 'attraction', Mme Du Châtelet also discarded absolute time and space, espousing the Leibnizian principles of relative space and time and 'sufficient reason'.

The situation was convoluted further by the lingering unresolved *Querelle des forces vives*, though here there was scope for Voltaire to build bridges with the

45 Voltaire to Le Pour [*c.*3 Aug. 1738], ibid. v. 230–1.

46 D'Argens, *Lettres chinoises*, i. 135–6.

47 Roger, *Buffon*, 32–3, 190, 196; Hazard, *European Mind*, 326–7.

48 Hazard, *European Mind*, 279; Beeson, 'Il n'y a pas d'amour', 913; Walters, 'Voltaire', 889–90.

49 Walters, 'Voltaire', 895; Ehrard, *L'Idée*, 134, 150, 158–9.

'Cartesians'. For Dorthous de Mairan had replied to Bernoulli's *Discours* on the *vis viva* of 1726 in the Memoirs of the French Royal Academy of Sciences for 1728, rejecting Bernouilli's and Leibniz's view that the force of 'any body in motion is proportional not to its velocity', as Clarke expressed it in 1729, 'but to the square of its velocity'. On this point, the Cartesians and Newtonians were, in fact, united against Huygens, Leibniz, 's-Gravesande, and Bernoulli. But these latter natural philosophers 'in order to raise a dust of opposition against Sir Isaac Newton's philosophy', as Clarke put it, were advancing a principle which called Newton's whole dynamics into question, or as Clarke again expressed it 'which subverts all science, and which may easily be made to appear (even to an ordinary capacity) to be contrary to the necessary and essential nature of things'; moreover, these men, influential in Germany, Holland, and Switzerland, were gaining ground also in France.[50]

Newtonians and Cartesians had to join forces against the champions of *vis viva* because if force is the square of velocity, all that part of the force beyond what is proportional to velocity would, as Clarke observed, 'arise either out of nothing' or, as Leibniz maintained, out of the monads constituting matter, which to many seemed little different from locating live energy in matter itself. Voltaire found all this more than a little perplexing. After reading Dorthous's *Dissertation*, in August 1736, having already begun on his *Élémens de la philosophie de Neuton*, he adhered first to the united Cartesian-Newtonian line. But during his visit to Holland in the spring of 1737, where at Leiden he observed 's-Gravesande performing his demonstrations with ball bearings, he was temporarily converted to the principle of *forces vives*. Finally, however, following Mme Du Châtelet's defection to Leibnizio-Wolffianism in 1740, he reverted to his defence of his Newtonian creed, new considerations outweighing even his respect for 's-Gravesande. Leibniz's doctrine of monads Voltaire henceforth roundly disparaged as a veritable *absurdité* wholly obscure and incompatible with the observed operations of matter as well as 'attraction'.[51]

The fog of polemic surrounding *forces vives* was only finally dispelled in 1743, when the young d'Alembert published his judiciously couched tract on dynamics in which he showed that Newton and Leibniz were, in fact, both right, the dispute being essentially just a confusion of words over two different things—linear momentum versus quadratic impact. It was, he explained, an argument about quantities of motion defined as linear momentum and seen as a function of velocity which is, in fact, proportional to velocity, just as Newton contended, on the one hand, and energy proportional to mass times squared velocity, as Leibniz correctly asserts, where momentum is defined as kinetic energy, this energy then being a conserved quantity in elastic collisions.[52]

Yet d'Alembert's intervention, by treating the metaphysical aspects of Newton's and Leibniz's concepts of force as both unproven,[53] also subtly contributed to Newtonianism's receding and loss of prestige in France in the mid 1740s, by

50 Walters, 'Querelle', 199.

51 Ibid. 209–10; Voltaire, *Micromégas*, 146.

52 Gori, *Fondazione*, 118; Ehrard, *L'Idée*, 173–5; Paty, 'D'Alembert', 49–51.

53 D'Alembert, *Traité de dynamique*, pp. xix–xxiii; d'Alembert, *Élémens*, 196, 203–4, 206.

vindicating Newton in a rather qualified fashion which restricted and somewhat narrowed Newtonianism's viable scope when viewed as a system of natural philosophy. For d'Alembert gravity is not a 'cause' ontologically different from other causes of movement but (as with 's Gravesande) simply a physical cause which we know solely by its effects and of whose nature we are essentially ignorant.[54] Applying a Cartesian rather than Newtonian conception of 'certitude' in science, d'Alembert lumps all causation together as an unknown and simply refuses to discuss causes at all since these were 'obscures et métaphysiques', declaring meaningless the (Newtonian) doctrine of the 'proportionalité des causes à leurs effets' and confining himself to considering only measurable 'effects'.[55]

Admittedly, this did not prevent d'Alembert calling himself a 'Newtonian'.[56] But by this he meant something rather different from what Voltaire, Maupertuis, Clarke, MacLaurin, or indeed Newton himself meant by Newtonianism. In part, d'Alembert's use of the label was just a deft sleight of hand enabling him to incorporate the mathematically valid physics and astronomy while deliberately sheering off the 'argument from design' and the other dogmas of Newtonian metaphysics, divine providence as a regulating force, gravity as a causeless cause, inertness of matter, and absolute space, time, and motion. Hence, d'Alembert concludes that the laws of dynamics, as he redefines them in his *Traité de dynamique* (1743), reveal no element of contingency or adjustment that can be said to be interposed by an intelligent providence; they simply embody the necessary attributes inherent in freely existing matter itself.[57] The ways of the Supreme Being, he remarks, are too much hidden from us for us to be able to ascertain directly what does, or what does not, confirm to the ways of his wisdom, so that we only glimpse the 'effects of this wisdom by observing the laws of nature where mathematical reasoning will have shown the simplicity of these laws and experience shown their applications and extent'.[58]

Newtonianism as a creed had suffered a setback. But if Voltaire failed to dominate the French intellectual scene to the extent he had hoped and expected, he undoubtedly reached the peak of his acceptance as a semi-establishment figure in the decade from the late 1730s to the late 1740s. His relations with both the French royal and church authorities, as well as with the papacy and (from 1740) with the court at Berlin, were then at their best. In 1745 he was appointed royal *historiographe* and his contacts with Rome improved further;[59] in 1746 he was elected to the Académie Française. The high-water mark of this strategic *rapprochement* between the Lockean-Newtonian Enlightenment and the reformist wing of the clergy was

[54] D'Alembert, *Traité de dynamique*, preface pp. xi, xvii, xxiii; Le Ru, *D'Alembert philosophe*, 85–7.

[55] Le Ru, *D'Alembert philosophe*, 48–9, 53; d'Alembert, *Traité de dynamique*, pp, xvii–xix, xxi–xxii; d'Alembert, 'Éloge historique', 58; d'Alembert, *Élémens*, 196–8; Ehrard, *L'Idée*, 160.

[56] Paty, 'D'Alembert', 24–5, 36, 48–9.

[57] Ibid.; d'Alembert, *Traité de dynamique*, pp. xxviii–xxix.

[58] D'Alembert, *Traité de dynamique*, p, xxix; d'Alembert, *Élémens*, 211–18.

[59] Artigas-Menant, *Secret des clandestins*, 288–91.

reached in 1746, when Father de La Tour, principal of the Jesuit college Louis-le-Grand in Paris, where Voltaire had once been a pupil, published an open letter publicly praising his efforts and announcing that Voltaire and the Jesuit order were now in alliance engaged in a common undertaking to spread 'enlightenment' in all quarters and foster everywhere in the civilized world the supremacy 'de la religion et de la vertu', together with patriotism, loyalty to sovereigns, 'le goût de travaux utiles', and the 'repos commun de la société'.[60] This was too much for the Jansenists who reacted in disgust, thoroughly disdaining what they saw as a highly questionable fraternization. The *Nouvelles ecclésiastiques*, since 1728 chief organ of the Jansenist movement, under the editorship of the refractory priest Jacques Fontaine de La Roche, caustically labelled the Jesuits' support for Voltaire and the moderate *philosophes* a revival of the ancient alliance of 'Pharisees' and 'Sadducees'.

Opposition to the principles of Newton and Locke, then, as expounded by Voltaire emanated not from any part of the ecclesiastical, academic, or royal establishment but from the two opposite fringes, on the one side of the underground radical intellectual coterie, publicly masquerading in the academies as 'Cartesians' and, on the other, the equally clandestine but noisier Jansenist press, a staunch Counter-Enlightenment drawing strength from popular faith and opinion, firmly rejecting all modern philosophy in favour of an uncompromising purging of the church and its values. For the populace and Jansenists, however, Voltaire felt only contempt; he preferred to concentrate his fire on what he saw as the real challenge—that of the materialists and atheists.

Underlying the dialogue with Tournemine, and the central problem which Voltaire still needed to resolve, and which he consistently addressed in his *Traité de métaphysique*, was that of how to answer the anti-Newtonian, anti-Lockean critique of those 'atheistic' philosophers adhering to monistic systems who, advocating the innateness of motion in matter, denied divine providence, free will, and what Voltaire calls 'un être qui préside à l'univers'. The question of motion and matter was particularly awkward. Like Tournemine, Voltaire saw that the entire Newtonian vision of a divinely decreed cosmic order, based on the 'argument from design', collapses the moment one concedes the innateness of motion in matter: for that opens the door to notions of a universe 'existant par lui-même d'une nécessité absolue', removing the whole foundation of physico-theology and Lockean epistemology.[61] He recognized that he faced formidable philosophical difficulties but, at the same time, could not see how the materialists could circumvent his batch of arguments for 'design'. The laws of mathematics, he granted, were 'immuables'; but there is nothing necessary, he declared, about the fact that the world is located in space where it is. No mathematical law can function of itself, without being regulated, any more than any force can apply without motion; something which cannot be of itself must then be an emanation of the Deity. From this entrenchment he refused to retreat.

[60] *Nouvelles ecclésiastiques* (1746), 61 (17 Apr.), 69 (1 May); Pappas, *Berthier's* Journal, 91.

[61] Voltaire, *Traité de métaphysique*, 428–9; Roger, *Life Sciences*, 515–16; Geissler, '*Matérialisme*', 66–7.

Voltaire's 'maîtres dans l'art de raisonner, les Lockes, les Clarkes' were such precisely because these were the thinkers who, he thought, most clearly show that movement cannot exist 'par lui-même, donc il faut recourir à un premier moteur'.[62] Clarke, in his rebuttal of Spinoza, *A Demonstration of the Being and Attributes of God* (1705), argues, as was resumed later by Le Clerc in French in his review of this treatise, that both reason and natural philosophy prove matter cannot be self-moving and, hence, that necessity, mechanism, and determinism cannot govern the functioning of the universe. Le Clerc, rightly, it seemed to Voltaire, recognized in this argument the most effective weapon against Spinoza, whom Clarke identified as the supreme chief of the *esprits forts* and Le Clerc, in 1713, had dubbed 'le plus fameux athée de notre tems'.[63]

Voltaire's objective was to rework the argumentation of Clarke and Le Clerc into a system which would prove effective against the *Spinosistes modernes* of mid eighteenth-century France. This is why, in his *Notebooks*, covering the decisive years of his intellectual formation (1735–50), Spinoza is mentioned rather more often than Descartes, Pascal, Hobbes, Malebranche, or indeed any other major thinker of whom Voltaire disapproves.[64] While constantly invoking his philosophical heroes Newton, Locke, and Clarke, Voltaire never loses sight of the fact that his prime philosophical antagonist was neither Descartes nor Malebranche whom he disdains, nor the scorned Pascal, nor Leibniz whom he had to take rather more seriously after Mme Du Châtelet espoused his cause, nor Hobbes in whom, during these years, Voltaire—like the Early French Enlightenment more generally—took hardly any interest,[65] but specifically Spinoza, the deluded dreamer shut up in his study who duped himself, as Voltaire put it, with his 'esprit géométrique'.[66]

Voltaire the *philosophe* consistently viewed Spinoza as his prime philosophical opponent essentially because Spinoza's was the system most wholly opposed to physico-theology, and the 'argument from design', indeed all teleology, and, hence, the system most contrary to Newtonianism, the principal intellectual prop of natural religion, Deism, and the maintenance of the moral and social order as he saw things. Among many proofs of this are the marginal notes in Voltaire's own hand in his copy of Condillac's *Traité de systèmes* (1749): in this work, Condillac analyses six philosophers in some detail—Descartes, Malebranche, Leibniz, Spinoza, Locke, and Newton—and in his personal copy Voltaire made thirty-five notes in his own hand in the margins; of these no less than thirty-four concern Spinoza, and clearly express his deep and abiding hostility to that thinker.[67] Similarly, in reverse, he followed Clarke in viewing Newtonian 'argument from design' as the chief barrier to Spinozism and what Condillac calls 'les sectateurs de Spinosa'.[68] At the heart of his critique is his complaint that Spinoza 'n'examine point si les yeux sont faits pour

62 Voltaire, *Traité de métaphysique*, 432, 435; Benelli, *Voltaire metafisico*, 78–9; Ehrard, *L'Idée*, 134.

63 *Bibliothèque choisie*, 26 (1713), 293, 302, 308.

64 Wade, *Intellectual Development*, 695.

65 Glaziou, *Hobbes en France*, 106–7.

66 Voltaire, *Philosophe ignorant*, 38.

67 *Corpus des notes marginales*, ii. 703–10.

68 Voltaire, *Homélies prononcés à Londres*, 335–6.

voir', or the ears for hearing or feet for walking.[69] The threat of Spinozism, moreover, he sees on all sides and not just in the work of atheists like Du Marsais, Meslier, and La Mettrie. To reduce the system of Malebranche to something coherent, he concurs with Tournemine, one must 'recourir au spinosisme', that is recognize that the underlying logic of Malebranche's system ensures the primacy of an overall rational structure and identification of the whole universe with God; and that this God 'agit dans tous les êtres', feels in all creatures, thinks in all men, 'végète dans les arbres, est pensée et caillou'.[70] So many *philosophes* had been seduced by Spinoza's ideas that there were even some, asserts Voltaire, alluding presumably to Boulainvilliers, who began by writing against him, and yet afterwards 'se rangèrent à son opinion'.[71]

Here, as elsewhere amid Voltaire's musings about his prime philosophical antagonist, one detects a hint of admiration for an otherwise scorned rival. In general, Spinoza stood for many things Voltaire disdained—a life of pure thought, *esprit de système*, materialism, 'atheism', rejection of all teleology, a non-divine morality based on equality. He refused to be impressed by the serenity Spinoza sought, his spending his life closeted in study, remote from the wear and tear of the world, repeatedly attacking his 'système spécieux en quelques points et bien erroné dans le fond'.[72] Still, he could not help admiring the depth and range of Spinoza's unparalleled impact. If ever having illustrious *adversaires* rendered a writer glorious, he remarks, then plainly no man was ever so honoured as Spinoza; for his high-profile enemies included not only intellects of the caliber of Bayle, Fénelon, and Condillac, and a whole herd of lesser controversialists, Lamy and Pluquet among them, but also two senior cardinals of the French church (Polignac and Bernis) who wrote verses assailing him and his 'château enchanté' as he here terms Spinoza's system.[73]

In his *Traité de métaphysique*, Voltaire designates this chief enemy to Locke, Newton, and 'English ideas' sometimes *le spinosisme* and alternatively the *matérialistes*, clearly considering these near interchangeable terms. *Spinosisme*, in short, was the philosophical spearhead of contemporary French materialism, the chief weapon of the adversaries against whom he was pitting his ingenuity and efforts. Spinoza's 'principes', declares Voltaire, are that one substance cannot make another, entailing the non-interaction of substances; this, the principle that everything belongs to and inheres in 'l'être unique', he believed, was also the chief maxim of the ancient Stoics.[74] Because materialist 'atheists' claim the world exists necessarily 'of itself', they must also assert, holds Voltaire, that this material world has within itself 'essentiellement la pensée et le sentiment' since it cannot otherwise acquire these things which would then arise from 'nothing'. Hence, for Voltaire, a consistent doctrine eliminating the role of a First Mover is only even provisionally feasible if

[69] Voltaire, *Philosophe ignorant*, 37; Voltaire, *Lettres à son altesse*, 390–2; Voltaire, 'Notes de M. de Morza', 252–3.

[70] Voltaire, *Traité de métaphysique*, 444; Wade, *Intellectual Development*, 710.

[71] Voltaire, *Philosophe ignorant*, 35.

[72] Ibid. 40; Pearson, *Fables*, 141.

[73] Voltaire, 'Notes de M. de Morza', 253.

[74] Ibid. 252; Voltaire, *Notebooks*, i. 410, ii. 595, 599.

presented in the form of a monistic system, like Spinoza's, seeking to conflate body and mind, attributing thought and sentiment to matter.

But if Voltaire sees Spinoza as the great adversary, and the latter's system as the seed-bed of the atheism and materialism threatening to capture the French Enlightenment from out of his hands, there was, as likewise with Bayle, one solitary redeeming aspect of the Dutch thinker's *oeuvre* which Voltaire deemed useful and of which he approved, namely, his conception of *critique* and his Bible criticism. Indeed, Voltaire even argues at one point that the *Tractatus theologico-politicus*, a work he characterizes as 'très profond' and the best Spinoza wrote, represents a quite different set of views from the *Ethics*, being so far removed from 'atheism' that there Spinoza speaks of Jesus (as indeed he does) as the envoy of God. Voltaire saw no point in denying the value of Spinoza's erudition here, fully acknowledging the effectiveness of his critique of Scripture,[75] and rightly observing that not only Le Clerc but also many others had been profoundly influenced by it, including, he implausibly suggests, Newton.

If the materialists and 'atheists' had their Spinoza, the antidote to their materialism was assuredly Locke whom Voltaire styled 'l'Hercule de la métaphysique', the thinker who had imposed firm limits on 'l'esprit humain'.[76] After publishing the *Élémens*, Voltaire intensified his researches into Locke and Newtonianism, widening his philosophical grasp by also addressing Leibniz, and sought to clarify his ideas on all those points where he found himself still beset by difficulties. If he found Locke's doctrine that God has the power to 'communiquer la pensée à la matière', as he puts it in his philosophical tale *Micromégas* (1752), unassailable,[77] he remained greatly troubled, while continuing to view determinism with deep repugnance, by the increasing difficulty he encountered in defending 'liberty of the will';[78] here was a prickly conundrum he contemplated without either much assurance or any of the zeal of a Tournemine or Castel.

For Voltaire, the autonomy of the Deity must be reflected in a small and fragmentary way in the freedom of the human will: Locke's quasi-dualistic epistemology (however hesitantly) accommodates such a doctrine and, according to Newton and Clarke, the infinitely free Being has communicated to Man, 'sa créature, une portion limitée de cette liberté'.[79] If there *were* only one substance and all that exists in the universe exists within the same continuum, and necessarily, then Man too would be 'déterminé nécessairement', as had already been pointed out, he notes, by Clarke's opponent Anthony Collins (who had likewise cited Spinoza as the modern philosopher who most solidly grounds this kind of determinism).[80] But whatever

[75] Voltaire, *Lettres à son altesse*, 389–90; Vernière, *Spinoza*, 505, 509.

[76] Voltaire, *Micromégas*, 146–7; Hutchison, *Locke in France*, 203; Firode, 'Locke et les philosophes', 57.

[77] Voltaire, *Micromégas*, 147.

[78] Wade, *Intellectual Development*, 598; Vartanian, *La Mettrie's* L'Homme machine, 62, 66–7, 204; Salaün, 'Voltaire', 712.

[79] Roger, *Life Sciences*, 213–14, 216; Wade, *Intellectual Development*, 598, 631; Ferrone, *Intellectual Roots*, 266; Pearson, *Fables*, 230–1.

[80] Walters and Barber, 'Introduction', 113; Berman, 'Determinism', 252; Israel, *Radical Enlightenment*, 616–18.

the difficulties of grounding the doctrine clearly and convincingly, in practice freedom of the will seemed indispensable to Voltaire if his system was to stand, and the moral order itself be preserved, for he was as persuaded as Tournemine that materialistic determinism destroys the foundations of morality.[81]

God may not, held Voltaire, have proclaimed the rules of morality he wishes men to follow with any revelation, or by miracles; but through the universal needs and aspirations of men these moral rules are nonetheless discovered, empirically and haltingly, and indeed in more or less the same way, by all peoples, and are therefore assuredly God-given and universally valid and binding.[82] Providence, held Voltaire, governs history and shapes human morality, albeit not by intervening miraculously, contrary to the normal course of nature, as the Christians and Jews wrongly believe, but exclusively through processes inherent in Creation and nature itself.[83] In his *La Métaphysique de Neuton* (1740), afterwards amalgamated into later editions of his *Élémens*, Voltaire again invoked Newton, Clarke, and Locke in proclaiming a Divinity who is more than just eternal, infinite, and perfect—being also one who actively creates, intervenes in, and regulates the universe and governs men's souls. Voltaire here fully endorses Clarke's doctrine that an 'ens utcumque perfectum sine dominio non est dominus Deus' [a being however perfect without dominion is not the Lord God].[84]

Where the whole philosophy of Newton, and that of Locke, necessarily leads to the knowledge of 'un Être suprême qui a tout créé, tout arrangé librement', Cartesian arguments, whatever Descartes claimed, are infinitely less reliable as a path to this vital conclusion. In fact, contends Voltaire: 'je dis que le système cartésien a produit celui de Spinosa'.[85] He himself had known many, he remarks, who through Cartesianism were seduced into Spinozism and, hence, no longer acknowledge any other God than 'l'immensité des choses'; but, as against this, he had never met a single Newtonian who was not a 'théiste dans le sens le plus rigoureux'.[86] Here again, conceived as the primary adversary of the type of philosophy Voltaire prescribes for the world, 'le spinosisme' is highlighted and condemned as the principal 'other', the ultimate antithesis to 'English ideas', chief foe and rival of Voltaire's Enlightenment, something opposed to himself, his thought, and his *anglicisme*, at a far deeper and more comprehensive level than the spurned systems of Descartes, Pascal, Hobbes, Arnauld, Malebranche, Leibniz, and Wolff.

Voltaire ties his concept of a divine Creator who is wise, good, and purposeful and who made and regulates the world to the Newtonian conception of absolute space and time, dismissing as nonsensical Leibniz's notion of the relativity of space and time no less than the atheists' denial of providential Creation.[87] A decisive argument against Leibniz, he contends, is that if space and time were relative, this

[81] Wade, *Intellectual Development*, 698–9.
[82] Voltaire, *Métaphysique de Newton*, 219, 221.
[83] Cassirer, *Philosophy*, 244–5; Rihs, *Voltaire*, 111, 120–32, 144–5; Schneewind, *Invention of Autonomy*, 458–60.
[84] Voltaire, *Métaphysique de Newton*, 195.
[85] Ibid. 196; Ehrard, *L'Idée*, 135.
[86] Walters and Barber, 'Introduction', 100.
[87] Voltaire, *Métaphysique de Newton*, 201–2, 207; Pearson, *Fables of Reason*, 228–9.

would then make God 'corporel' and have the effect of undermining both 'la religion naturelle' and the moral order.[88] This would be ironic, he remarks, for no one had proved a stronger champion of 'natural religion' than Newton if not 'Leibnitz lui-même, son rival en science et en vertu'.[89] Leibniz remained, in Voltaire's eyes, a bumbling but well-intentioned philosopher whose metaphysics propounds a cosmology governed by a benevolent Creator, in roughly the same way as Newton and Voltaire, but who, in the end, did more harm than good by confusing many, and misguidedly opposing Newton and Locke.

The English had proved, contrary to Descartes and Spinoza, that a void is possible, which means, contended Voltaire, that they had also shown the physical universe to be finite and that there are specific and identifiable locations in absolute space where there is nothing. From the reality of void, he argued, it follows also that neither being nor non-being is, of itself, necessary, and since matter does not exist 'nécessairement, elle a donc reçu l'existence d'une cause libre'.[90] If the planets move in one direction, and not in another, are situated in one part of space and not elsewhere, and there is no mechanical cause of gravitation, the only cogent explanation, he concludes, the force of 'attraction' that holds everything in its course, is that the hand of their 'Créateur a donc dirigé leur cours en ce sens avec une liberté absolue'.[91] God, being infinitely free as well as infinitely powerful, declares Voltaire, echoing Newton, has created many things which have no reason for their existence other than 'sa seule volonté'.[92]

Voltaire's *La Métaphysique de Neuton*, first published in 1740, reappeared in an Italian version at Florence in 1742, and was greeted with considerable enthusiasm in Italy, not least among sections of the clergy which now included many *Neutoniani*.[93] Admittedly, Voltaire's system was not yet watertight, particularly as regards 'free will'. He acknowledged that the *Spinosistes* would inevitably answer that 'il n'y a point plusieurs substances'; and should this be correct then the universe must be everything that exists and must exist necessarily, creating itself ceaselessly. These antagonists, observes Voltaire, suppose the universe constitutes a single Being whose nature is unchangeable 'dans sa substance, et éternellement varié dans ses modifications'. The key to overcoming this idea, he urged, is to convince the 'atheists' that matter cannot be the origin and source of movement.[94] Through his efforts and those of his allies, the *Spinosistes* would in the end learn from 'les Newtoniens' that if there were in matter the slightest movement not posited there by an autonomous substance entirely external to matter, then not only would motion be innate and essential to the nature of matter but there would be no such thing as absolute rest. He admitted that he was somewhat unsure how to proceed should his conjectured Spinozist adversary reply that there is indeed no such thing

[88] Voltaire, *Métaphysique de Newton*, 218. [89] Ibid. 219.
[90] Ibid. 196; Ehrard, *L'Idée*, 134. [91] Voltaire, *Métaphysique de Newton*, 196.
[92] Ibid. 209; Roger, *Life Sciences*, 517–18.
[93] Moniglia, *Dissertazione contro i materialisti*, i. 47, 102; Ferrone, *Intellectual Roots*, 87, 250, 263–4.
[94] Voltaire, *Métaphysique de Newton*, 198; Geissler, *Matérialisme*, 66–7.

as rest, that rest is 'une fiction, une idée incompatible avec la nature de l'univers'. In such a case, the philosopher upholding a free and intelligent Deity, concludes Voltaire, would do best, yet again, to fall back on Newton's 'argument from design'.[95]

Here, as with 'fixity of species', and the *vives forces* dispute, Voltaire remained loyal to his 'Newtonian' creed, even where the evidence of experiments, arguments, and the facts seemed to tell against him.[96] Though he paid homage to experiment and research, he was apt to become dogmatic whenever the basic principles of Newton and Locke were challenged. Locke and Newton, what he called the 'superiority' of English philosophy, was always his anchor. Integrating elements of Newton, Locke, and Clarke, centring around the idea of a benevolent deity who governs the cosmos, a Supreme Being whom, he believed, the essential traditions of Greek, Chinese, Persian, and Indian philosophy also all upheld, he framed a philosophy which was at the same time a universal 'natural religion' comprising what he deemed the valid essence of all historical religions once these are stripped of their specific theology which he considered superfluous.[97] Thus, Christianity has, he thought, a pure core, just like Islam, Buddhism, Confucianism, and others, but only when purged of thick layers of useless obfuscation; that existing religion which he judged least obscured by theological mystification was in fact Confucianism. How utterly ridiculous and misguided it was on the part of contemporary philosophers and theologians, he complained, to condemn as 'atheistic' that very doctrine which represents the closest historical approximation to natural religion! How ridiculous to censure Bayle for claiming a society of 'atheists' can function in an orderly fashion and then maintain that China, 'le plus sage empire de l'univers est fondé sur l'athéisme'![98]

'Natural religion', held Voltaire, underlies and is more universal than any historically evolved religion. Indeed Voltaire claims in the *Essai sur les mœurs*, begun in 1739, and one of his most important texts of the early 1740s, that both the universality of God's justice and the universality of our 'natural' conceptions of him, and his requirements of men, underpin all actual religions among the more civilized peoples and not least that of the Chinese, ethically perhaps the most admirable. Hence, just as the main elements of moral truth are everywhere identical, so the world's higher religions have, historically, borrowed 'all their dogmas' and rites from each other.[99] Primitive men, for Voltaire, were morally, as well as intellectually and artistically, less refined, developed, and clear-sighted and, in this sense, definitely inferior to 'civilized' men. If, besides them, a few misguided and isolated ancient and modern thinkers likewise fail to acknowledge this 'supreme God', no developed, civilized peoples have ever failed to do so.

Since the Supreme Being freely created the various aspects and living species of nature, according to Voltaire, and since the creative power which shapes species, no

95 Voltaire, *Métaphysique de Newton*, 198–9; Roger, *Life Sciences*, 518, 521.

96 Pappas, 'Buffon matérialiste?', 248.

97 Voltaire, *Essai sur les mœurs*, i. 33, 70, 94, 216, 239.

98 Ibid. i. 224; Koseki, 'Diderot', 125–6; Tortarolo, *L'Illuminismo*, 33–4.

99 Voltaire, *Essai sur les mœurs*, i. 274; [François], *Preuves*, iv. 511–12.

less than regulates the motions of the cosmos, is wholly external to nature, nature possessing no creative power of its own, it must necessarily follow, he held, that no natural evolution is possible and that, consequently, the particularities and characteristics of plant and animal species remain fixed and invariable: nothing vegetable and nothing animal has changed, he declared in 1746, all species 'sont demeurées invariablement les mêmes'.[100] Not the least palatable feature of Voltaire's system to the Jesuits, and ecclesiastical authority generally, during the period of their alliance with Voltaire, the late 1730s and 1740s, was, indeed, his emphatic rejection of fossils as evidence of species mutation and his treating fossilists, like Buffon, who argued otherwise as accomplices of atheistic naturalism.[101] For Voltaire the philosopher, the creative process was now complete and transformism and evolutionism conceptual impossibilities, chimeras of the Spinozist imagination, like the doctrine of equality and that of the overarching and ultimate unity of mankind.[102]

3. BREAKDOWN OF THE LOCKEAN-NEWTONIAN SYNTHESIS

D'Alembert, in his article 'Cartesianism' in the second volume of the *Encyclopédie*, written around 1749, observed that it was only 'around eighteen years ago', hence from the early 1730s, that 'des Newtoniens' had emerged as a active force in French culture but that French Newtonianism had 'so prodigiously' advanced in French intellectual life that by the late 1740s 'toutes nos académies maintenant sont newtoniennes' while the professors of the Sorbonne openly taught their students Newtonianism as the now established way of thinking about philosophy and the *sciences*.[103] Historians of the Enlightenment, it seems, have hitherto insufficiently stressed the extent of the breakthrough of what d'Alembert called 'la philosophie angloise' in France, especially Locke and Newton, between the early 1730s and the mid 1740s, and the completeness of the Lockean-Newtonian hegemony over the respectable moderate mainstream Enlightenment in France by the early 1740s. The French establishment by 1745 was a Lockean-Newtonian culture.

This was not just a question of ideas, or ideas and science. Rather it has to be understood as a major cultural phenomenon affecting every aspect of French society and politics. A discerning observer of the intellectual scene in the mid 1740s would undoubtedly have predicted a lasting, as well as overwhelming, ascendancy for Locke, Newton, and the British model. For Cartesianism had now been largely discredited as a system, the Leibnizio-Wolffianism in France had been marginalized, while intellectual reaction as it had flourished in the last years of Louis XIV

[100] Voltaire, *Métaphysique de Neuton* 238; Voltaire *Œuvres complètes*, ed. Moland, 226; Alatri, *Voltaire, Diderot*, 422; Roger, *Life Sciences*, 516, 521, 524; Pappas, 'Buffon matérialiste?', 235.

[101] Pappas, *Berthier's* Journal, 88, 90–3, 96.

[102] Roger, *Life Sciences*, 516.

[103] D'Alembert, 'Cartésianisme', in Diderot and d'Alembert, *Encyclopédie*, ii. 725; Paty, 'D'Alembert', 43.

had been almost swept from the board. In a hierarchically ordered, tradition-bound society there was great need, psychologically, educationally, and culturally, for a viable method of reconfiguring the main elements of the prevailing social, religious, and institutional system in a coherent synthesis, making it possible to systematize intellectually and integrate the basic realities of science, learning, and philosophy, and of morality and religion, with the social and political order.

This impressive reintegrating of the disparate elements of culture via the thought structures of English empiricism and Newtonian natural philosophy, moreover, seemed to be part of a wider syndrome, long dominant in Britain and the Netherlands, which now appeared to have gained the upper hand also in Rome. Pope Benedict XIV was certainly not alone in the papal curia in admiring Voltaire, or rather the public Voltaire of the 1740s, or wanting his call for all Europe to imbibe the thought-world of Locke and Newton to succeed, though the Counter-Reformation mentality of the past still had its champions in the Vatican and Holy Office, and Benedict's drive to align Rome behind the moderate mainstream Enlightenment unleashed a veiled inner civil war within the bowels of the Vatican which was not finally resolved (against Benedict's legacy) until some time after the pope's death, towards the end of the 1750s.[104]

Meanwhile, if there were elements of the French intellectual avant-garde who resisted Voltaire's Enlightenment, dissenting forces, threatening to frustrate the new grand cultural synthesis based on 'English ideas' for which he strove, radical ideas on their own lacked the muscle and the support ever to challenge the hegemony of the Lockean-Newtonian symbiosis in the universities, colleges, and in official circles in France, and Italy, on their own. In fact, there was only one cultural, social, and psychological force in France powerful enough to unseat *Voltairianisme* from its current primacy in French cultural life and that was the Jansenist resurgence of the late 1740s. Hence it is with considerable justification that some historians in recent years have identified in the post-1715 growth of Jansenist support in the French cities the chief factor in the violent fragmentation and polarization of French intellectual and religious culture in the mid eighteenth century, leading to the eventual total shattering of the *ancien régime* cultural synthesis, helping pave the way for the French Revolution itself.

The vigorous Jansenist backlash was, indeed, the hammer which eventually broke the French moderate mainstream Enlightenment. For if the recent philosophical schisms between mainstream and radical wings originated, as we have seen, in the failure of Voltaire and the French Newtonians fully to consolidate the victory they seemed set to win in the late 1730s, thereby leaving the door just sufficiently ajar to enable the Radical Enlightenment to emerge strongly once the moderate mainstream weakened, there was little the radicals themselves could do to engineer such a collapse. What enabled them, after all, to capture the main apparatus of the French Enlightenment, within a few years, was the sudden break-up, from 1748, of

[104] Godman, *Geheime Inquisition*, 248–68.

the existing status quo, causing a full-scale polarization of cultural camps around the extremes; and this unheralded upheaval, as we shall see, chiefly resulted from the unsettling impact of Jansenist revolt and protest on the establishment. No sooner did the Jansenists declare open war on philosophical reason, as they did in 1748, leading to the great drama of the intellectual battles of 1748–52, than the middle camp largely disintegrated, leaving the radicals to take possession of much of the ground from which the *anglicistes* were to be unceremoniously driven.

Intellectually, the two rival French Enlightenment camps were, in the 1740s, as before, sharply and irreconcilably at odds at every level. Where Voltaire, Maupertuis, Réaumur, and by the late 1740s also Turgot fought to consolidate the links between science and theology forged by Newton and Locke, providing formulae readily compatible also with a fully de-Christianized Deistic metaphysics, most of the younger *philosophes* resisted their approach, effectively detaching *l'esprit philosophique* from all forms of theology, physico-theology, and teleology.[105] Where Locke, Newton, and Voltaire powerfully projected the 'argument from design', the intellectual heirs of Boulainvilliers, Fontenelle, and Fréret, grouped in the circles around Buffon, Helvétius, Diderot, and d'Alembert, rejected all such appeals to supernatural governance and providence and began experimenting with rudimentary 'transformist' and quasi-evolutionary ideas in place of the Creationist finalism of Réaumur, Pluche, and Voltaire.[106] Where Locke and Newton, amplified by Voltaire, upheld a quasi-dualism which saw both motion in general, and gravitation in particular, as wholly external to matter, the radical *philosophes* attacked these positions, declaring Newtonian notions of gravity and force neither cogent in themselves nor a proof of divine providence at work, advocating instead the Spinozistic idea that movement is inherent in matter and all movement mechanically caused.[107]

Free will was a particular and early casualty among the main planks of the Lockean-Newtonian symbiosis in France. Rejected by Vauvenargues, an eager admirer of Boulainvilliers, in his *Traité sur le libre-arbitre* of the late 1730s,[108] by 1738 other members of the budding *parti philosophique* also began urging that Locke's defence of free will is incoherent: 'vous avez raison assurément', replied Voltaire to Helvétius, rather perplexedly, in June 1738, 'de trouver de grandes difficultez dans le chapitre de Loke de la puissance, ou de la liberté.'[109] Yet where Voltaire, albeit also grappling with worrying doubts, refused to abandon 'free will', recognizing it as essential to the thought-world of Boyle, Locke, Newton, and Clarke and hence, in his view, something basic to true 'enlightenment', Helvétius, like Vauvenargues, began to oppose Locke's 'free will' and immortality of the soul, along with his idea of mind as an active category quasi-substantially separate from body.

105 Voltaire, *Métaphysique de Newton*, 195–6, 209, 213; Benelli, *Voltaire metafisico*, 100–1.
106 Postigliola, *Città della ragione*, 136.
107 Ibid. 135; Casini, 'Voltaire, la lumière', 40–1; Salaün, 'Voltaire', 705.
108 Vauvenargues, *Traité sur le libre-arbitre*, 98–9, 106; McKenna, 'Vauvenargues', 207, 214.
109 Voltaire to Helvétius, 11 Sept. 1738, Helvétius, *Correspondance générale*, i. 10.

From the late 1740s, Diderot, Buffon, Hélvetius, d'Holbach, and others, as has often been pointed out, incorporated into their systems a 'sensationalist' psychology and epistemology, introduced by the Abbé Étienne Bonnot de Condillac (1715–80). Like Voltaire, Condillac was greatly indebted to Locke and this has often been cited as additional evidence that the French High Enlightenment *was* essentially Lockean and Newtonian. Rousseau claims to have been the discoverer of Condillac and it was he who introduced him to Diderot at a time, in 1744, when he was still unknown but had just finished his 'Lockean' epistemological study, *L'Essai sur l'origine des connaissances humaines*, which was to make him famous. Though blocked at first by the censors, with Diderot's help he was able to get the book published[110] during 1746. Diderot, Rousseau, and Condillac, friends at the time, took to meeting for regular discussions or what Rousseau calls their 'weekly dinners', sometimes with Mably present also.[111]

Spurning Descartes, Malebranche, Spinoza, and Leibniz 'for having established metaphysical structures on general principles by a priori reasoning', Condillac did indeed fervently admire Locke and Newton, and their disciples, above all for relying only 'on observation and experiment, on accumulating and testing the data of experience, and on only using abstract terms as instruments of classification'.[112] Explaining Condillac's distinction between *l'esprit systématique*, the new empiricist approach which Ernst Cassirer and Peter Gay, like Condillac, considered an essential feature of 'enlightened' thought, and *l'esprit de système*, the approach of the seventeenth-century system-builders, Gay stressed that Condillac's heroes 'are Locke and Newton', two giants, the first of whom 'exposed the absurdity of building vast constructions on abstract principles' and the second of whom achieved his great feats by 'modestly contenting himself with observing the world without trying to create one out of his head'.[113]

Condillac did indeed dismiss the great system-builders of the seventeenth century in this fashion and indubitably 'admired Locke as the greatest of modern philosophers'.[114] Yet his 'sensationalism', worked out in the mid 1740s, is Lockean only in part, and while Condillac (who had studied theology for eight years and was an attested believer) was an authentically Lockean philosopher, especially in his approach to the mind–body problem with his quasi-substantial separation of body and soul, and stress on restricting philosophy's scope, it is wrong to infer that his sensationalism, as such, and hence his influence on the *philosophes* was Lockean in character. For, actually, this was not the case: while Locke eliminates 'innate ideas', attributing to sense experience the origin of all ideas, he also holds that the human intellect has innate faculties, or 'operations of the mind', without which ideas cannot be processed and knowledge is impossible. Among these, the powers of

110 Rousseau, *Confessions*, 291; Quarfood, *Condillac*, 21.

111 Rousseau, *Confessions*, 291; Roger, 'Diderot et Buffon', 233; Haechler, *L'Encylopédie*, 11.

112 Gay, *Enlightenment*, i. 139; see also Cassirer, *Philosophy*, 6–7.

113 Gay, *Enlightenment*, i. 139.

114 Aarsleff, 'Locke's Influence', 275.

'perception', 'reflection', willing, and 'retention' (or memory) are especially vital. They are also innate, being non-physical, procedures or capabilities of the mind.

Crucial was the mind's 'power' of abstraction. For it is this, held Locke, which grounds a basic category distinction between men and animals. Locke, unlike Descartes, as we have seen, thought that at least some animals 'in certain instances reason, as that they have sense; but it is only in particular ideas, just as they receiv'd them from their senses'. Even the most highly developed animals, he says, are 'tied up within those narrow bounds, and have not (as I think) the faculty to enlarge them by any kind of abstraction'.[115] Equally, despite hesitating as to how to formulate his guiding distinction between 'material' and 'immaterial' beings, Locke always maintains that 'there are but two sorts of beings in the world, that man knows or conceives'—those that 'are purely material, without sense, perception, or thought' and those 'sensible, thinking, perceiving beings', including men but some of which, like angels, are not tied to bodies.[116] This two-tiered ontology was basic not just to his own philosophical system but to the entire Lockean mainstream, because this enabled its proponents to retain his *de facto* spirit–body duality and endorse a comprehensive physico-theology—though, of course, Locke and Voltaire at the same time retained the possibility that 'God can, if he pleases, superadd to matter a faculty of thinking' without thought being inherent in, and intrinsic to, matter.

Whether or not postulating 'operations of the mind' which are non-physical states 'unequivocally' commits Locke 'to the truth of substance dualism' remains a matter of dispute among scholars.[117] But whether it does or not, Locke's system undeniably involves the assumption, or implication, of an ontology equivalent to 'substance dualism' in its consequences philosophical, moral, and theological, a quasi-dualism securing the separate existence of mind and soul as well, as Locke repeatedly reminds us, as of angels and other spirits—and, hence, a systematic rejection of materialism. Indeed, the whole junction between philosophy and theology, so central to Locke's, as to Newton's, system, crucially depends on this fundamental dualism, a duality which entails a conception of gesture, signs, and consequently of words, as something passively functional and quite distinct from the more formative conception of language developed by Du Marsais, Condillac, Rousseau, and Diderot. Condillac, though, found Locke's notion of language unconvincing.

Prompted by some lively debate with friends, including Diderot, and also by Leibniz's criticism of Locke's account of 'reflection' as contradicting his claim that all ideas arise from sense, Condillac fundamentally modified Locke's empiricism by eliminating his innate faculties, substituting instead a progression from pure sense and sensibility to signs and words, and from signs and words to a gradually more structured and analytical use of language, from which, in turn, evolve logical sequences and abstract ideas.[118] Sense perception, argues Condillac, leads first to

115 Locke, *An Essay*, 160; Jolley, *Locke*, 93; Chappell, 'Locke's Theory', 38–43.

116 Locke, *An Essay*, 622–3.

117 Jolley, *Locke*, 81, 83–4; Charrak, *Empiricisme*, 17–19.

118 Condillac, *Essay*, 91, 102–3, 214, 220; Cassirer, *Philosophy*, 25, 100; Jimack, 'French Enlightenment', i. 238; Roger, *Buffon*, 157; Charrak, *Empiricisme*, 16, 26–8, 32, 34, 37.

establishing signs, and hence ideas, through our directing our minds towards some object or another, driven by basic physical needs, and motivated by desire for pleasure and to avoid pain. Focusing the mind, in response to our drives on something, rather than something else, Condillac calls 'attention', one of his key terms. It is 'attention', he contends, which leads to connecting different perceptions and which, once we possess signs for them, and can recall them, leads in turn to our associating, comparing, and contrasting ideas, in particular by enabling us to reflect on a perception in the absence of the object that first gave rise to it.[119]

Hence, where for Locke memory is merely recall of a perception, for Condillac memory actively translates perception into a set of signs relevant to Man's wants and appetites. In this way Condillac grounds an empiricist epistemology which, unlike Locke's, designates no ontological duality and presents no clear intellectual barrier to a pure materialism. This shift (with its unconscious convergence with Spinoza in radically grounding all ideas in sensibility alone) was far-reaching in its consequences, revolutionizing the concept of mind and, among other things, making language and gesture prior to ideas.[120] One of the disturbing results for moderates was the consequent elimination of Locke's distinction between men and animals, leaving those embracing Condillac's argumentation to face the dilemma that either, by divine superaddition, matter thinks in animals as in men leaving no qualitative difference between men and brutes or else brutes too possess immortal souls.

In Locke, language transmits, and is moulded by, the non-material operations of the mind and is their passive medium whereas, with Condillac, and after him, the French sensationalists as a group heightened the stress on communication and language as the active agent enabling us to order and analyse our perceptions. Language hence becomes the key factor in the genesis of ideas, albeit initially language of primitive men, they thought, was very sparse and inexact, mostly just gesture and inchoate grunts and cries. Only gradually, through collective experience of its use, could language become more precise and complex.[121] This approach then, in turn, entailed a wholly different and more elevated conception of the history of languages and literature as tracing the main lines of the history of *l'esprit humain* itself. In this way, Condillac decisively, even fatally, weakened Locke's system but without himself actually abandoning either Locke's insistence on the immortality and immateriality of the soul, and its quasi-substantial separation from the body on which he always insisted, or Locke's summons to limit philosophy's brief, on both of which much of his readership congratulated him.[122]

Condillac defended his position by comparing the operations of the mind to Newton's principles of dynamics.[123] The philosopher's task, he held, is to analyse

[119] Condillac, *Essay*, 24–6, 78; Jimack, 'French Enlightenment', 238; Charrak, *Empiricisme*, 52–3.

[120] Charrak, *Empiricisme*, 52–3; Vinciguerra, *Spinoza*, 106–9, 118–20; Duchesnau, 'Condillac', 92–4.

[121] Duchesnau, 'Condillac', 82–5; Dagen, *L'Histoire*, 97–9; Aarsleff, 'Locke's Influence', 275–7; Cherni, *Diderot*, 88–9; Pariente, 'L'effacement', 79–83; Pécharman, 'Signification', 90–4.

[122] Niderst, 'Modernisme', 310; Stenger, 'La Théorie', 107; Charrak, *Empiricisme*, 17–18; McManners, *Church and Society*, i. 664–5; Falkenstein, 'Condillac's Paradox', 412, 414.

[123] Yvon et al., *Apologie*, seconde partie, 11; Cassirer, *Philosophy*, 66; Ricken, 'Condillac', 267.

and classify the movements he observes, the recorded effects, here the sensations, but not to delve into the ultimate causes of those operations, since these can be observed by no one. Other champions of Locke, such as Voltaire, Maupertuis, Réaumur, and numerous liberal ecclesiastics, on the other hand, while granting that simple ideas are sense impressions, made a particular point, after 1746, of adhering to Locke's priority of operations of the mind, defending the subsidiary, merely intermediary, role of language, as well as Locke's doctrine of the 'incommunicability' of material ideas in the making of comparisons, judgements, inferences, and so forth. For them, these positions remained indispensable protective trenches against 'les Spinosistes et les Déistes'.[124] For without such segregation, whatever Condillac thought, Locke's, Clarke's, and Voltaire's doctrine of 'the immateriality of the soul' as well as its immortality, and refusal to identify thought with the sensibility of matter, was bound to break down.[125] It was precisely Locke's vaguely formulated but fundamental dualism (however much it irritated Bayle) which rendered his philosophy the prime barrier to materialism and Spinozism—and radical ideas more generally. In opposing the 'Spinosiste' materialism of the mid eighteenth-century *esprits forts*, particular stress was laid by Voltaireans and genuine Lockeans on the argument that a purely material soul, should such a thing exist, could not of itself perform the functions of recollection, reasoning, comparison, and inference because these are essentially movements of the mind, whereas matter, as one ecclesiastic put it, 'n'a d'elle-même aucun mouvement'.[126]

Condillac, then, not only radicalized but also fatally undermined Locke's system by eliminating precisely its dualistic components. In Condillac, like the more radical of the *philosophes* whom he influenced but of whom he was not directly an ally, reflection, memory, judgement, and the other mental faculties are wholly discarded as innate functions of the mind so that physical sensation becomes the exclusive source not just of simple ideas but of all human consciousness, understanding, and thought.[127] As part of his work of demolition, Condillac held Locke to be mistaken not only in making 'operations of the mind' independent of, and prior to, sense experience but also in considering such operations of the mind prior to language. Reversing the order, Condillac and the radical *philosophes* (in the late 1740s including Rousseau) regarded the body's sensibility as coming first, after which develop primitive thoughts and language; these then, eventually, produce or at least nudge towards rational operations of the mind.[128]

Even if still only implicitly—for outside epistemology, his own general ontology remained dualistic[129]—Condillac's philosophy reduces all thought, and knowledge,

124 Locke, *An Essay*, 88–9, 92; [François], *Preuves*, i. 42–5, 47; Roger, *Buffon*, 157.

125 Roger, *Buffon*, 540–1; Dagen, *L'Histoire*, 99; Charrak, *Empiricisme*, 23–5.

126 [François], *Preuves*, i. 52–3, 96–102, 136–7.

127 Condillac, *Essay*, 14–15, 24, 28, 32; Wellman, *La Mettrie*, 152; Dedeyan, *Diderot*, 274–88; Grossman, *Philosophy of Helvétius*, 57, 63, 68; Smith, *Helvétius*, 13–14.

128 Condillac, *Essay*, 91, 104, 115–17; Charrak, *Empiricisme*, 72–5; Jimack, 'French Enlightenment', i. 238–40; Garrard, *Rousseau's Counter-Enlightenment*, 96–7.

129 Duchesnau, 'Condillac', 91–2; Vartanian, 'Quelques réflexions', 163; Charrak, *Empiricisme*, 53, 93.

to a function of body and physical sensibility, suggesting a mind–body monism diverging decisively from Locke and carrying quite different metaphysical and moral implications. Hence, this kind of sense- and experience-based epistemology, presenting sensibility as the source of all perception, expression, and ideas, inevitably savoured of Spinozism in its monistic implications. Assuredly, Condillac, a rather timid man, had not the slightest wish to appear to be championing materialism, or to be labelled a materialist, monist, or determinist. Locke, for him, remained the surpassing philosophical genius and unrivalled destroyer of bogus and pernicious systems. In true Lockean spirit, he strove to uphold both free will and the immateriality of the soul intact, trying to prevent his sensationalism evolving into a more general materialism—albeit not very cogently and at the cost of detaching both free will and his doctrine of the soul entirely from operations of the mind.[130] This powerful anxiety to block any widening of the implications of his destroying Locke's special operations of the mind stiffened not just his fierce opposition to systems, and *esprit de système* in general, but also in his *Traité de systèmes* (1749) led to the notion that a principle valid in one area of philosophy or science, such as his sensationalism in epistemology, can not automatically be ruled valid in other areas of thought.

Condillac denied that the totality of what is is governed by a single set of rules, denouncing those who believed this as materialists and atheists, including among them, rightly, Bayle whom he charged with extrapolating the 'goodness' attaching to our idea of God to construct a false 'system' making this abstraction of divine goodness and equity the basis of morality, toleration, and politics.[131] On such grounds Condillac also declined to be associated with the *Encyclopédie*, rejecting the broad conception of philosophy of the others, labouring rather to reconcile Locke with Leibniz and salvage 'soul', siding with Réaumur against Buffon, and emphatically distancing himself from Diderot after the latter clearly showed himself to be a materialist and atheist in the late 1740s.[132] Hence, the man who fatally undermined Locke's physico-theological system of empiricism tried nevertheless to limit philosophy's sway and uphold, strangely enough, with both Locke's and Leibniz's help, a viable junction of philosophy and theology.

By eliminating mind–body dualism and adopting 'sensationalism', the radical *philosophes*, invoking Condillac, not only destroyed Locke's doctrine of mental faculties, and the immateriality of the soul, but reinforced the idea of mind, and the emergence of reason, as something evolving by stages, the collective experience being reflected in the development of language, poetry, music, and other aesthetic representations of reality, a dimension broadly lacking in Lockean empiricism.[133] Here, the thought of Condillac, Helvétius, Boulanger, Diderot, and d'Holbach can

130 Proust, *Diderot*, 321; Firode, 'Locke et les philosophes', 61, 63; Duchesnau, 'Condillac', 90.

131 Condillac, *Traité des systèmes*, 15; Ehrard, *L'Idée*, 684–5.

132 Trousson, *Rousseau*, 133, 197; Van Kley, 'Christianity', 1095; Haechler, *L'Encyclopédie*, 17; Quarfood, *Condillac*, 23–4, 27–9.

133 Aarsleff, 'Introduction', pp. xv–xvi; Ehrard, *L'Esprit des mots*, 209.

be seen to stand closer to Fontenelle, Boulainvilliers, and Vico than Locke or Newton. Since irrational imagination and poetic wisdom precede rational concepts in the development of both the individual, and mankind generally, according to these *philosophes*, their systems carried very different implications for education, philosophy of morality, and aesthetics from Locke's. Rousseau may have gone his own way in many other respects but as regards the centrality of 'natural man', the importance of the early evolution of signs, language, and aesthetics, he is arguably more typical than untypical of the *philosophes* as a group.

Hence, for the younger and more radical *philosophes* of the mid eighteenth century, including La Mettrie who deliberately subverts Locke for materialist purposes, Locke's philosophy was altogether less pivotal, influential, inspiring, and in detail familiar than Enlightenment historians commonly claim.[134] As for d'Alembert, a *philosophe* who paid effusive homage to Locke and Newton without being in the least an authentic Lockean, it was precisely by claiming, in his Preface to the *Encyclopédie*, that the *encyclopédistes* derived their main inspiration and principles fervently and unreservedly from Bacon, Boyle, Locke, and Newton, a claim which was essentially tactical, highly misleading, and not at all reflected in the *Encyclopédie*'s actual content, that he reassured enough churchmen, academics, and royal officials for the project to be able to proceed. By trumpeting unshakeable allegiance to Locke and Newton from the rooftops, the editors performed a massive philosophical sleight of hand, initially disarmed the opposition, and momentously cleared the way for a devastating pre-emptive strike which was to have a profound effect on the future course of the West's Enlightenment.

[134] Ehrard, *L'Idée*, 684, 719; Duflo, *Diderot philosophe*, 124–35.

30

From Voltaire to Diderot

By the early 1740s, Voltaire's philosophy had matured, acquired a certain solidity, and was poised to dominate the French Enlightenment. Until 1752, moreover, he was generally perceived as an ally of the Jesuits, the reforming papacy of Benedict XIV, and the liberal wings of all the churches, Anglican Latitudinarian, Greek Orthodox, and Reformed no less than Catholic. Yet there was also an element of contradiction in all this. Privately, his closer philosophical allies (and enemies) knew perfectly well that his true position was ultimately more antagonistic to Christian tradition and ecclesiastical authority than this public stance and reputation at the time presupposed, a discrepancy sooner or later bound to create major complications.

Besides veiling the extent of his hostility to Christianity, Voltaire endeavoured to soften also other lines of potential antagonism. He evinced little desire to challenge the existing political and social status quo and in high society generally spoke as if he had no wish to 'enlighten' the lower orders. 'Le vulgaire', he assured the Countess Bentinck in June 1752, 'ne mérite pas qu'on pense à l'éclairer.'[1] Yet his deep-seated antipathy to ecclesiastical authority and traditional theology, however much veiled for the moment, a certain proselytizing zeal, and twinges of bad conscience about leaving the common people to languish in a morass of imposture and lies, occasionally nudged some part of him in a different direction. In the unpublished *Sermon des cinquante*, at any rate, he is distinctly troubled by the view of some 'qu'il faut des mystères au peuple; qu'il faut le tromper', exclaiming rhetorically: but how can enlightened men of conscience inflict such an 'outrage' on the human race?[2] Here was a tension which, from a Lockean-Newtonian perspective, was not easily resolved; and this was by no means his only dilemma: by the late 1730s there were also other worrying cracks appearing in the edifice of his Lockean-Newtonian Enlightenment.

One unresolved theoretical difficulty, we have seen, was Locke's extreme caution, and dithering, in successive editions of the *Essay* over what he called 'liberty in respect of willing'. In 1737 Voltaire's incisive young friend the officer-philosopher Vauvenargues, examining Locke's arguments about this in his *Traité sur le libre*

[1] Lee, 'Le "Sermon" ', 144; Himmelfarb, *Roads to Modernity*, 170–1.

[2] HHL MS Fr, 79 [Voltaire], 'Le Sermon', 26^{v}; [Voltaire], *Sermon des cinquante*, 21.

arbitre, roundly rejected his position, opting instead for a strict necessitarianism in the style of Boulainvilliers and Spinoza.[3] Where, for Voltaire, Locke remained the towering hero who was, in metaphysics, 'ce que Neuton est dans la connaissance de la nature',[4] Vauvenargues, though willing to grant Locke was an important philosopher, also complains in this (then unpublished) text of the Englishman's prolixity, obscurity, indecisiveness, 'contradictions', adding the acerbic remark that his philosophy appeals mainly to 'des esprits pesants', pedestrian minds.[5] Unsettled by such objections, Voltaire too, as we have seen, privately became uneasy about free will but also persisted in championing Locke, assuring Helvétius, in June 1738, that human liberty consists, exactly as Locke affirms, in not doing what one feels tempted or attracted to do where one's conscience makes one aware of the morally negative character of the action so that judgement counteracts desire.[6]

Morality, contended Voltaire, absolutely requires the belief that moral choice is divinely given and the will free; and, further, that this 'choice' is inherently part of God's design. Admittedly, Helvétius', Vauvenargues's, and Du Marsais's contrary arguments, and his own growing doubts, induced Voltaire to admit privately that he could not see how to counter the proposition that we are not more free in repressing our desire than in letting ourselves be carried away by impulses and inclinations: for in both cases we irresistibly follow 'notre dernière idée' and this last idea is necessary; consequently, 'je fais nécessairement ce qu'elle me dicte'.[7] Yet 'free will' remained an indispensable article of Voltairean 'natural religion' and his public stance: proclaiming a Supreme Being who created the universe, held Voltaire, must mean God endows men with freedom of moral choice.

Nor, at this stage, could those who disagreed reveal their divergence from the great Voltaire in more than the odd private remonstrance, gentle nudge, or discreet disavowal. For, in the eyes of the public and the authorities, the opinions of his radical critics were altogether less respectable than Voltaire's publicly stated views, indeed were totally unacceptable. If Locke's conception of mind and the will failed to convince, if Newton's 'forces occultes' and views on chronology met with tenacious resistance,[8] and Fontenelle, Buffon, Fréret, Dorthous de Mairan, and Montesquieu all privately derided Voltaire's Newtonian physico-theology and views on Creation, providence, and the divine origin of morality, it hardly suited them to make a public spectacle of this.[9] Voltaire was now widely acclaimed the foremost champion of toleration, liberty of thought, and 'philosophy', a larger-than-life figure making splendid progress everywhere, not least at the courts of Paris and Berlin, and in the Vatican, a circumstance which ensured that publicly,

[3] Brykman, 'Locke', 173–6, 180, 183–5; Charrak, 'Statut', 188–9; Bove, 'Vauvenargues, une philosophie', 227, 234.

[4] Voltaire to Nicolas Claude Thieriot, 30 Nov. 1735, in Voltaire, *Correspondence*, iii. 262.

[5] Brykman, 'Locke', 176–7.

[6] Voltaire to Helvétius, [June? 1738], in Voltaire, *Correspondence*, v. 149.

[7] Voltaire, *Notebooks*, ii. 438; Wade, *Intellectual Development*, 630–1.

[8] Du Châtelet, *Réponse*, 36; De Pater, 'Inleiding', 19, 48–51.

[9] Roger, *Buffon*, 196; Ehrard, 'Voltaire', 950; Ehrard, *L'Esprit des mots*, 209.

at least, he both deserved, and would get, not opposition and criticism but the backing of (nearly) all the *philosophes*.

Behind the scenes, though, there were many more personal tensions than were disclosed in public. Voltaire and Montesquieu were simultaneously 'allies and enemies', eyeing each other, as has been aptly observed, with a distrust verging on outright animosity. Montesquieu, whom, in public, Voltaire had to praise as 'le plus modéré et le plus fin des *philosophes*', was likewise discretion itself in public, but in private freely permitted himself the luxury of deriding the Newtonians' 'occult' properties and dismissing Voltaire as a mediocre historian and still more mediocre philosopher.[10] D'Argens, far more radical than Montesquieu, and an ally philosophically of the materialists, firmly inclining to the determinism and eroticism later explicit in his *Thérèse philosophe* (1748),[11] not only disagreed with Voltaire about Bayle but also much else, while confining his public criticism of the *Élémens* to suggesting Voltaire should have eulogized Newton less and 'traité tous les anciens avec moins de mépris'.[12]

Meanwhile, with Voltaire away much of the time at Cirey-en-Champagne where he spent long periods from 1734 down to Madame Du Châtelet's death in childbirth in 1749, or else in Brussels or Berlin, lively philosophical circles gathered regularly in Paris, mostly in his absence. Only during the pivotally important years 1745–8 prior to her death, and again after her death from October 1749 until June 1750, did Voltaire, now on excellent terms with the royal government, again spend significant periods in Paris, enabling him to participate to an extent at the most decisive stage in the formation of the French *parti philosophique*—albeit apparently without once meeting Diderot. When away, he sustained lively correspondences with Maupertuis until the latter's departure for Berlin, in 1745, Helvétius, and Vauvenargues with whom he conducted an intense literary and philosophical dialogue, for some years hoping to get that young *philosophe* to follow him as his 'maître', but, in general, his position among the *philosophes* gradually weakened.

Among the *philosophes*' favourite meeting places were the Café Procope, Café Palais-Royal, Café Rotonde, Café Gradot, Café Laurent—much patronized by Fontenelle—and Café de la Régence where Diderot first met Rousseau in August 1742, places where one consumed coffee, chocolate, ices, and lemonade and could express irreverent views relatively freely, albeit by no means wholly without precautions.[13] (Boindin, when holding forth, reportedly often referred to God as 'Monsieur de L'Être' to confuse police spies.) Much of the debate, naturally, revolved around the great questions posed by Newton and Voltaire, but also Bayle whom Diderot read a great deal of during these years. These encounters often pitted radical-minded atheists and non-providential deists, like Boindin, Lévesque de Burigny, Fréret, Du Marsais, and, until his premature death in May 1747, Vauvenargues,

10 Ehrard, *L'Esprit des mots*, 195–7, 207–9; Voltaire, *Lettres à son altesse*, 363; Lacouture, *Montesquieu*, 287.

11 [D'Argens], *Thérèse philosophe*, 85, 141.

12 Ehrard, 'Voltaire', 949–1; Walters and Barber, 'Introduction', 92–3.

13 Dagen, *L'Histoire*, 161–2; Artigas-Menant, *Secret des clandestins*, 18.

whose intellectual culture had been chiefly moulded by Fontenelle, Bayle, and Boulainvilliers, against the advocates of Newton, Locke and 'English' ideas, among them Maupertuis until he left, in August 1745. Initially, the latter camp included the young Diderot, son of a pious provincial Catholic family, who in life style, tastes, and attitude seemingly already counted as early as 1741 as one of the Parisian *philosophes*; at that early stage, he recorded later, he dreamt of following in Voltaire's footsteps and publishing a general commentary on Newton.[14]

Not only Diderot but also Helvétius, d'Alembert, and Buffon had originally followed Voltaire in parading as ardent disciples of Locke and Newton. From around 1745, one of the liveliest of their coteries, both philosophically and socially, was in fact that formed by the young Diderot who had a special gift for creating collaborative networks and discussion groups, together with Rousseau, after the latter's return to Paris from Venice in October 1744, Condillac, and Mably.[15] A fine talker, fond of the cafés where he spent much of his time, Diderot was on close terms, moreover, with several of the foremost Parisian publishers, including those most skilled at putting out clandestine works, like Laurent Durand who published his *Pensées philosophiques* and *Les Bijoux indiscrets*. and, still more important, Antoine-Claude Briasson (1700–75), the future entrepreneurial driving force behind the *Encyclopédie*, an entrepreneur with important ties abroad, especially, from 1737, with the Imperial Academy at St Petersburg.[16]

The point at which most of the younger *philosophes* broke with *Voltairianisme* was precisely in the mid 1740s.The Parisian cafés and discussion groups formed one forum in which this drama was played out. But there was also another and related arena which certainly influenced the development of the younger *philosophes* where the 1740s represent a clear watershed in terms of quantity and reach: for this decade marked the peak in the surge of clandestine manuscripts circulating in the French capital and among high society.[17] The *manuscrits clandestins*, though far from being a novelty, were now circulating in the capital in unprecedented numbers and certainly exerted a growing effect on the discussion groups. In 1747, well after assuming effective charge of the directorship of the *Encyclopédie*, Diderot is known to have personally copied out by hand a version of *La Religion chrétienne analysée*, one of the hardest hitting pieces and, as we have seen, one of the most Spinozistic, a fiercely anti-Christian text written around 1723 in reply to Houtteville's defence of Christianity of 1722.[18] It was of no small relevance to Diderot's development at this point, and his formative role in the building of the *parti philosophique*, as we shall see, that both Houtteville's text and the clandestine manuscript rejoinder were centrally concerned with Spinoza.

14 Damiron, *Mémoires sur Diderot*, 41; Proust, *Diderot*, 238–9; Quintili, *Pensée critique*, 86, 100.

15 Trousson, *Rousseau*, 146–7, 197–9; Haechler, *L'Encyclopédie*, 11–16.

16 Kopanev, 'Libraire-éditeur', 188–90.

17 Paganini, 'Scepsi clandestina', 93–5; Varloot, 'Introduction', 15.

18 Varloot, 'Introduction', 15; ABM MS 63 (580), 118; Benítez, *Face cachée*, 144–5; Israel, *Radical Enlightenment*, 689–90.

Soon to become the most influential opinion-former among the younger generation of *philosophes*, Diderot began his philosophical career in the late 1730s by studying mathematics and Newton, but from around 1740 sought to widen his humanistic culture by studying English and Italian (he already possessed good Greek and Latin). Before long, he was equipped to respond to the Paris *libraires*' eagerness for hard-working editors with English competent to prepare renderings of English authors for French consumption.[19] From late 1741, he launched into a hectic bout of translation and editing, and by May 1742 had already completed his first major undertaking, translating, under the title *Histoire de la Grèce*, the newly expanded 1739 edition of Temple Stanyan's *Grecian History* (1707).

Temple Stanyan (1677–1752) provided Diderot with some useful perspective on ancient Greece and contributed to the early genesis of his political thought, since the question of how the Greeks had lost their liberty is central to Stanyan's account and ancient Greece was subsequently always central in Diderot's moral, social, and political philosophy.[20] Stanyan also raised interesting questions of chronology. With his efforts to promote Newton's system for amending the accepted dates of the earliest history, Stanyan prompted Diderot to investigate problems of ancient and biblical chronology, thereby very likely contributing to his then only incipient anti-Newtonianism.[21] Subsequently, he translated a multi-volume medical dictionary, laborious work which, however, orientated him in the current state of the medical sciences. Intellectually the most rewarding of these projects, however, was certainly his rendering of Shaftesbury's *An Inquiry Concerning Virtue and Merit*, his French version appearing in Amsterdam, under the title *Principes de la philosophie morale*, in 1745.

Diderot thus first became known in Parisian intellectual circles as a leader of the then prevailing *anglomanie* and prime French champion of Shaftesbury. Given the latter's anti-Christian Deist orientation, the Jesuit *Journal de Trévoux* gave Diderot's reworking of the English thinker a surprisingly enthusiastic reception, proclaiming the young *philosophe* a sound disciple of Locke, advocate of an absolute moral order, and supporter of 'English' principles generally.[22] The *Journal des savants*, while criticizing Shaftesbury—as well as the unnamed translator, Diderot—for failing to show the 'necessity of Revelation', and the superiority of Christianity to all other religions, nevertheless also reviewed the book rather favourably, congratulating Diderot especially for showing how much atheism 'est opposé à la vertu' and that true virtue definitely requires belief in a 'Dieu juste, bon et rémunérateur'.[23]

Such plaudits from the intellectual and academic mainstream reinforced the standing and self-confidence of the young *philosophe*, associating him closely with 'English' ideas and the Voltairean Deist camp. At the same time, the encounter with Shaftesbury exerted a profound and in some respects lasting impact on the evolution

19 Trousson, 'Diderot helléniste', 182; Robb, 'Making of Denis Diderot', 137; Dziembowski, 'Défense du modèle', 90.

20 Dedeyan, *Diderot*, 23–4.

21 Ibid. 20–6.

22 Pappas, *Berthier's* Journal, 163; Saada, *Inventer Diderot*, 70.

23 *Journal des savants*, (Apr. 1746), 211, 218–19; Harris, 'Answering', 242.

of his thought. For Diderot, moral philosophy *à la Shaftesbury*, wholly detached from religion and assumptions of Original Sin but linked to rejection of all 'superstition'—though he renounced what he saw as Shaftesbury's excessive asceticism—always remained central to his concerns, and directly linked to what he conceived of as the ordered, coherent structure of the cosmos, or 'l'ordre universel des choses'.[24] This overarching cohesion applied also to issues of morality, aesthetics, and art, and here too the stimulus and influence of Shaftesbury proved of enduring significance.

Shaftesbury's stressing the need for a system which—in opposition to Locke, Newton, and Condillac—distinguishes even Diderot's earliest forays into the realm of philosophy remained a pervasive preoccupation, as indeed it was of the Radical Enlightenment generally, and something which is indeed rather ironic given his lifelong proneness to be unsystematic in presenting his ideas. But, above all, Shaftesbury inspired Diderot's initial Deism, though it is important to remember that Diderot, with his rather free translation, not only absorbed but also, in some degree, tailored a new 'Shaftesbury' adapted to the contemporary French milieu.[25] If it was only briefly that Diderot agreed that ''tis very apparent how conducing a perfect theism must be to virtue and how great deficiency there is in atheism',[26] he never ceased to endorse Shaftesbury's view that there is an insufficiency of well-grounded moral philosophy in contemporary culture and that modern philosophers had paid inadequate attention to this important sector. Shaftesbury's idea that there is a 'natural sense of right and wrong' in Man and that this moral sensibility is prior to—the mature Diderot would say independent of—ideas about God seemed to him something of fundamental importance. Harder to judge is whether Shaftesbury also contributed to Diderot's incipient republicanism.

Initially, Diderot backed Voltaire's campaign against deterministic materialism and atheism, maintaining, like both Voltaire and Shaftesbury, that atheism undermines all morality.[27] It is sometimes suggested that, while morality figured among Diderot's 'most enduring concerns', he never developed a systematic moral theory;[28] but this, as we have seen, seems to underestimate the extent to which he developed a coherent view of moral problems and gravitated towards a particular type of moral theory which he emphatically linked to the political sphere, later endorsing naturalistic egalitarian principles in such articles for the *Encyclopédie* as those on 'Natural Right' and 'Citizen'; but the original impulse to formulate a secularized moral theory wholly detached from, and intrinsically opposed to, theological criteria clearly began, in the early 1740s, with his encounter with Shaftesbury before evolving further in his *Pensées philosophiques* (1746).[29]

24 Diderot, *Essai sur le mérite*, 41–2; Tortarolo, 'Epicurus and Diderot', 386–7.

25 Pommier, *Diderot*, 20–5; Robb, 'Making of Denis Diderot', 142; Venturi, *Pagine*, 45.

26 Löpelmann, *Der junge Diderot*, 97–8; Dedeyan, *Diderot*, 37–45.

27 Diderot, *Essai sur le mérite*, 30–1, 80; Ehrard, *L'Idée*, 369–70, 449–50.

28 Dedeyan, *Diderot*, 289, 295; Schneewind, *Invention of Autonomy*, 466–7.

29 See the notes of Diderot in Diderot, *Essai sur le mérite*, 19–25, 27–31, 33–4, 37–44, 46, 49–53, 55–8, 143–4; also Diderot, *Pensées philosophiques*, 59–70.

In the first of Diderot's preserved letters documenting serious philosophical concerns, a letter about faith and religion written in 1745 to his brother—who, the following year, became an ordained priest—just before, or just after, publication of the Shaftesbury translation (which, indeed, was dedicated to his brother), his determination to detach theology and religion completely from morality (as well as philosophy) is striking and emphatic. Nor can it be an accident that he here expresses his utter horror of the effects of religious fanaticism in terms strongly reminiscent of Bayle, who was undoubtedly a prime influence on the radicalization of his thought at this time. Recalling the effects of the French Wars of Religion in which half the French nation bathed its hands 'par piété', in the blood of the other, wholly suppressing, supposedly to sustain God's cause, 'les premiers sentiments de l'humanité', as if one must cease to be human 'pour se montre religieux', he bitterly deplored the inhuman consequences of religious fanaticism.[30] Shaftesbury's separation of morality from religion and theory of the prior nature of moral sentiment never lost its appeal for Diderot though he later became profoundly aware of the philosophical difficulties of such a position. In Diderot's mind, though, the tension between belief and true morality, sharpened by discussion between the rival Parisian philosophical coteries, was already working to destabilize his commitment to Shaftesbury's brand of theism, as well as, more broadly, Voltairean principles based on Locke and Newton and Condillac's sweeping rejection of *esprit de système*.

Doubtless it was because his own philosophical odyssey was shaped in this way, by regular and lively discussion groups, that, from the outset, dialogue became, for Diderot, both overtly and sometimes less obviously, a paramount feature of his own writing. During 1746, the year Condillac's book appeared, debate, questioning, ambiguity, and disagreement, especially about divine providence, Deism, and the 'argument from design', permeated Diderot's thoughts and his own first work, the *Pensées philosophiques*, published anonymously in April 1746 with 'à La Haye' falsely declared on the title page. In July, the book was forbidden by the Paris *Parlement* and condemned to be torn up and burnt by the public executioner together with La Mettrie's *Histoire naturelle de l'âme*, both as 'scandaleux, contraires à la religion et aux bonnes mœurs'. Its ambivalence has prompted some scholars to interpret this text as expounding less the providential Deism it purports to advocate than a veiled 'crypto-materialism and implied atheism'.[31] More likely, though, the latter was just one of two warring currents fighting for predominance in Diderot's mind.

In any case, the *Pensées philosophiques* clearly reflects the intensity of the current Parisian intellectual battle between Newtonian-Voltairean Deism and 'atheistic' monism over how far modern research in natural history does or does not substantiate the 'argument from design' and disprove one-substance doctrine.[32] In his summing up, the *président* of the *Parlement* condemned Diderot's work for reducing all

[30] Diderot, *Correspondence*, i. 51–2.

[31] Diderot, *Pensées philosophiques*, 15–26; Vernière, *Spinoza*, 567; Vartanian, 'La Mettrie and Diderot', 158–9; Ehrard, *L'Idée*, 449–50, 452; Stenger, 'L'Atomisme', 76.

[32] Pommier, *Diderot*, 36–7; Dedeyan, *Diderot*, 301–3; Bourdin, *Diderot*, 18, 20, 26.

religions to equivalence, refusing to acknowledge any as supreme, and advising men to base their moral conduct purely on their own social wants and concerns, 'leurs seules passions'.[33] Turgot, intellectually always one of Diderot's most determined opponents from within the Enlightenment camp, remarked that the anonymous work seemed more dangerous than other irreligious texts in circulation in Paris at the time because of its intellectual conciseness and the brilliance of its written style.[34]

Philosophically, perhaps the work's most striking feature is its uncompromising redefinition of scepticism and insistence on turning scepticism into a tool, or first step, of reason itself. Instead of taking scepticism to be chiefly a means of questioning reason, as was usual in Montaigne and many others, Diderot, here emulating Bayle and several of the clandestine manuscripts, turns scepticism into an instrument primarily for questioning what men believe. A true philosopher to his mind is someone who weighs all arguments carefully, doubting everything which he and others have been taught or urged to believe, embracing as true only what reason and empirical observation confirm to be true.[35] What is unequivocal here is the rejection of all fideist, Pascalian, and Lockean solutions to the problems of faith, Creation, and miracles, and emulation of Bayle and Spinoza in rejecting all attempted distinctions between truth 'au-dessus de la raison' and truth 'contre la raison', that is to judge what is true exclusively on the ground of rational demonstration. 'Si je renonce à ma raison', remarks Diderot, in his later additions to the text, 'je n'ai plus de guide.'[36] While still ostensibly repudiating atheism, he also strongly reaffirms Bayle's cardinal principle that 'superstition' is a greater evil than atheism.[37]

The chief line of enquiry in the *Pensées philosophiques* is whether the 'argument from design' on which the Newtonian system, and hence Voltaire's strategy, hinges remains cogent. In the prevailing Lockean-Newtonian climate of the time this was, of course, no easy doctrine to call into question. Is it not the very height of absurdity, exclaimed one French Newtonian in 1751, to deny that eyes are for seeing, ears for hearing, and teeth intended for chewing? yet, observes this writer, 'c'est ce que nie Spinosa' in his *Ethics*.[38] Diderot, at this point, still partly aligned with Voltaire, Réaumur, and Maupertuis, grants that scientific enquiry and debate seem to confirm the validity of the doctrine. Indeed, affirms Diderot, it is assuredly only in the works of Newton, Musschenbroek, Hartsoeker, and Nieuwentyt that one finds 'des preuves satisfaisantes de l'existence d'un être souverainement intelligent'; he adds, clearly alluding to Spinoza, that it is solely thanks to these great men that 'le monde n'est plus un dieu'.[39] However, the work also represents a marked degree of slippage

33 *Nouvelles ecclésiastiques* (1746), 136 (21 Aug.); Paganini, 'Scepsi clandestina', 89.

34 Turgot, *Réflexions sur les Pensées*, 87; Trousson, *Denis Diderot*, 90–1.

35 Diderot, *Pensées philosophiques* 24, 27–8; Benítez, *Face cachée*, 316–17; Paganini, 'Scepsi clandestina', 83, 86; McKenna, 'Vauvenargues', 203–4; Quintili, *Pensée critique*, 104–6, 109, 141.

36 Diderot, *Pensées philosophiques*, 58; McKenna, 'Vauvenargues', 201–3, 207, 210.

37 Diderot, *Pensées philosophiques*, 14; Bonacina, *Filosofia ellenistica*, 80–1.

38 [François], *Preuves*, i. 281

39 Diderot, *Pensées philosophiques*, 17–18; Venturi, *Jeunesse de Diderot*, 86; Vartanian, 'From Deist to Atheist', 53; Sejten, *Diderot*, 50–1, 82–4.

from basic Lockean and Newtonian premisses, including in *Pensée* number XXI Diderot's first affirmation that motion is innate in matter, at which point Voltaire pointedly annotated his own personal copy (today in St Petersburg) with the objection that Diderot's motion innate in matter is just a 'supposition'.[40]

As against Condillac (besides Locke and Newton), the *Pensées philosophiques* is also a powerful reaffirmation of reason as Man's sole and exclusive guide and the need for reason to be both consistent and coherent. However, Diderot's text betrays throughout an unmistakable instability of both perspective and argument, a continual wavering, the author perceiving serious objections to physico-theology, and hence Newtonianism and Voltaireanism more broadly, while also perceiving, like Helvétius and Vauvenargues, that Lockean free will may be no more than a common prejudice which philosophers should dismantle. Such reservations potentially aligned him, in the Paris of that period, with Du Marsais, Lévesque de Burigny, Buffon, Boureau-Deslandes, Boindin, La Mettrie, Boulanger, and the materialist tradition.[41] He was moved also by a powerful sense, as emerges from his *De la suffisance de la religion naturelle* (1746), a short text and the last of his so-called 'English' period, with Shaftesbury, Tindal, and Wollaston still among the prime influences on his thought, of the need for men to emancipate themselves from a long-endured and oppressive burden of misery and self-imposed suffering caused by bigotry, factionalism, fanaticism, and credulity, the main blame for which he attributes to revealed religion while still trusting that the victory of 'la religion naturelle', a pure Deism with a God-ordained morality delivered without revelation, such as that urged by Voltaire, would set this process of universal emancipation in motion.[42]

In 1746, the young *philosophe*, about to find himself at the head of the great project of the *Encyclopédie*, was not yet unequivocally committed to materialism or atheism; but he was already vehement in his rejection of revelation, organized religion, and all theological claims, and on grounds which already clearly point to what has rightly been called 'le spinozime radical de Diderot'.[43] While at this date still agreeing with Voltaire that the moral superiority of natural religion and its treating all men as equals is rationally evident, and requires the true philosopher to dismiss all the actual religions of the world as mere 'sects' of natural religion, classifying Christians, Jews, Muslims, and pagans alike as 'naturalistes hérétiques et schismatiques', he was already readier than Voltaire to attack core Christian doctrines.[44] Shortly after the public burning of his *Pensées philosophiques*, the police received a complaint from the curé of Saint-Médard characterizing Diderot as an extremely dangerous person 'qui parle des saints mystères de notre religion avec mépris'.[45]

[40] Voltaire's MS annotation, RNLP MS Russian ИНВ N2577, p. 42.

[41] Brykman, 'Locke', 176–7; Bove, 'Vauvenargues, une philosophie', 234 n.; McKenna, 'Vauvenargues', 203, 210.

[42] Diderot, 'De la suffisance', 55, 62–4; Duflo, *Diderot philosophe*, 72; Cherni, *Diderot*, 31–2.

[43] Quintili, *Pensée critique*, 189–90.

[44] Diderot, 'De la suffisance', 62.

[45] Diderot, *Correspondence*, i. 54; Trousson, *Rousseau*, 205; De Booy, *Histoire*, 19.

Meanwhile, growing doubts about Deism and the 'argument from design' to which he had only latterly become prone were further explored in his next work, *La Promenade du sceptique* (1747), a turning point in the evolution of his thought which has a curious history. The text's existence was reported to the Paris police at a time, in 1746–7, when the young author was already under regular surveillance.[46] Unable to publish it, and prudently refraining from putting it into clandestine circulation, given the furore provoked by the *Pensées philosophiques*, Diderot kept his single personal copy at home where it was discovered, during a police search, in 1752, and confiscated.[47] Later, after being buried away in the personal library of the lieutenant-general of police at the time for many years, the manuscript disappeared without trace and was supposed lost. It resurfaced, though, decades later, after the Revolution when it was offered for auction by a Paris bookseller in 1800, only to become the object of a dispute between the latter and Diderot's daughter regarding rightful ownership, resulting in the work's sole copy gaining the remarkable distinction, for any philosophical text, of being confiscated by the Paris police for the second time.[48]

Though not finally published until well into the nineteenth century, the *Promenade* reveals much concerning Diderot's intellectual development in the pivotal years 1746–7. He locates the imaginary scene in which he sets his small gathering of 'philosophes', rather intriguingly, in the aftermath of the French victory at Fontenoy in 1745, which indeed was precisely when Diderot's participation in such philosophical symposia most crucially influenced the evolution of his own thinking.[49] The tone is now very different from in the *Pensées philosophiques*. The first part consists of a blistering assault on revealed religion much in the style of the pre-1740 clandestine manuscripts, questioning outright the integrity of the Bible, and expressing wonder that the Supreme Being should have delivered two such contrasting testaments to mankind couched in literary styles so divergent, and with such different content, as to make the Almighty look rather careless about his choice of secretaries, or else he suggests darkly 'qu'on a souvent abusé de sa confiance.'[50]

Those who venerate the second Testament condemn devotees of the first as 'aveugles', while those faithful to the first label the former intruders 'et des usurpateurs'. How perfectly absurd! Meanwhile, those who believe the second Testament to be the truth are so lacking in critical sense as not to realize that all first-century AD accounts written by non-Christians, including Philo and Josephus, totally fail to mention anything that might corroborate Christian claims, indeed say virtually nothing of any substance at all about Christ or his alleged miracles. Indeed, Josephus, who loathed Herod and includes everything denigrating he could possibly find to say about him, breathes not a word about the (presumably cynically fabricated) story of the Massacre of the Innocents of Bethlehem. Christians must be blind

46 De Booy, *Histoire*, 16–17; Diderot, *Œuvres*, i. 67–9.

47 De Booy, *Histoire*, 26–7; Pommier, *Diderot*, 39.

48 De Booy, *Histoire*, 39, 42–3.

49 Diderot, *Promenade*, 177; Trousson, *Rousseau*, 199–200; Cherni, *Diderot*, 26–7.

50 Diderot, *Promenade*, 191.

indeed, contends Diderot, not to see the implications of this humiliating silence 'des historiens contemporains de leur chef'.[51]

But all this was just a preface. What is chiefly significant about the *Promenade* is not the attack on revelation and miracles but the subsequent convoluted philosophical debate presented in the second part. For this reflects Diderot's deeply introspective, and still private, but also conclusive, break with the world of Voltaire, Newtonianism, physico-theology, and the entire enterprise of a French Enlightenment based on Locke and Newton. Vividly recounted here in the form of a long and convoluted dialogue, the defection of the main body of *philosophes* away from the 'British' model to materialism, one-substance determinism, atheism, and a systematic anti-Newtonianism, as well as a rebellious, ironic attitude towards Voltaire, the English philosophers' apostle and chief French and European apologist, was hence certainly complete before the first great intellectual controversy of mid-eighteenth-century France, the 'Querelle de *L'Esprit des lois*', erupted in 1748. By 1746–7, Diderot had inwardly broken with Voltaire's 'enlightenment'; and very soon this was to be announced to the world.

Meanwhile, other key figures such as d'Alembert, Buffon, Helvétius, and Boulanger were likewise shifting away from Voltaire's orbit. D'Alembert, admittedly, was much less obviously opposed to the values of Locke and Newton than Diderot. What has recently been termed d'Alembert's 'Spinosisme' may, at first glance, seem to amount merely to discarding all metaphysical and theological considerations, freeing him to ponder the whole of natural and human reality in purely physico-mathematical and material terms.[52] His public but heavily truncated 'Locke', and private Spinoza, might even be deemed interchangeable since both constructs, the first silently and indirectly, and the second explicitly, eliminate all immaterial and Newtonian 'occult forces' leaving the philosopher autonomous of all existing authority and tradition, in principle and practice. But while such a procedure is consistent with Spinozism, viewed from a Lockean perspective it was really a form of imposture. For Locke, for all his empiricism and iconoclasm regarding 'essences' and Cartesianism, remained always resolutely committed philosophically to a system of divine providence, God's 'Creation of the World', 'the soul's immateriality', Man's separateness from other creatures, and his doctrine that God's existence is 'of that consequence, that all religion and genuine morality depend thereon'.[53]

The authentically Newtonian inspiration of Voltaire's thought, then, and his deep veneration of Locke, reflected the main line of the French Enlightenment only briefly, as it developed in the 1730s down to the mid 1740s. Voltaire, furthermore, however brilliant and confrontational his writing, and however vast the impact of his caustic personality on his century, was a social and intellectual reformer in only a very few, restricted areas. If his name later came to be associated with a fundamental

51 Ibid. 211; Pommier, *Diderot*, 43–4.

52 Dagen, *L'Histoire*, 382–3; Ehrard, *L'Idée*, 159–61; Le Ru, *D'Alembert philosophe*, 132–7, 169–70.

53 Locke, *Essay*, 622; Harris, *Of Liberty and Necessity*, 21, 28–30, 34.

shift in religiosity, it was never the case that his battle cry 'écrasez l'infame!', even much later, after he openly broken with the church, was a summons to crush the traditional, conventional piety of the people: his target was always chiefly intolerance and ecclesiastical authority as it affected the cultural life of the elites. Still less was he a political reformer. To kings, princes, noblemen, and, before 1752, even the right sort of ecclesiastics, he had no real challenge to offer. His intellectual adversaries within the Enlightenment camp were very different in this respect.

If it seems paradoxical that so towering a figure and one so central to the cultural and intellectual life of his time should have been simultaneously a champion and opponent of the establishment, his philosophy and general strategy remained remarkably consistent throughout his long career from the time of his stay in England onwards. In Britain itself, and its American colonies, Voltaire was initially viewed, especially during the period that he dominated the French philosophical scene, rather positively, owing to his ardent declarations in favour of English institutions, freedoms, and philosophers. But if this too changed, from the 1760s, and he later came to be looked on in the English-speaking world disapprovingly, as a seditious force fomenting irreligious attitudes, the Voltaire of the 1760s and 1770s could still with every justification remind Locke's no longer sympathetic countrymen: 'j'ai été vôtre apôtre et vôtre martyr.'[54]

The intellectual and cultural ascendancy of the 'British Enlightenment' in France, then, was a short-lived affair, never consolidated, and by the time of the Battle of Fontenoy (1745) among the leading younger *philosophes* was for, all practical purposes, already over. If both Voltaire, in his private thoughts, and clerical opponents like François and the Abbé François-André Pluquet (1716–90), labelled the new men, no less than the generation of Boulainvilliers, Du Marsais, and Fréret, *Spinosistes*, Diderot in private, and at one point, rather obviously, even in the *Encyclopédie*, designated his own party 'Spinosistes modernes', or 'nouveaux Spinosistes'.[55] And this, far from being 'loose usage', or a mere propaganda label, had a clear logic to it since this faction were exclusively concerned with the here and now, claimed the whole of reality is governed by a single set of rules, rigidly excluded all supernatural agency, roundly rejected free will and the immortality of the soul along with Heaven and Hell, admitted no demons or other spirits divorced from bodies, scorned all talk of alchemy and magic as well as Newton's mystical chronology, placed a new emphasis on equality and freedom of the individual, and were broadly atheistic and hylozoic in tendency. Not only did they differ profoundly from, and oppose, Locke and Newton regarding supernatural agency, the soul, and Man's redemption, as well as in moral theory and such political topics as toleration and the common good, they did so no less in their views on physics

54 Voltaire to Horace Walpole, 15 July 1768, Voltaire, *Correspondence*, xxxiii. 449; Willey, *Eighteenth-Century Background*, 235; Hutchison, *Locke in France*, 203; May, *The Enlightenment in America*, 39–40.

55 Diderot and d'Alembert, *Encyclopédie*, xv, 'art. 'Spinosiste', p. 474; Vernière, *Spinoza*, 596; Vartanian, 'Diderot and Maupertuis', 55–8; Israel, *Radical Enlightenment*, 711–13.

and biology, especially with their doctrine of the self-contained, self-regulating character, as well as internal material coherence of all (physical) reality and the human condition. After 1746, Diderot and his allies were not at all Lockeans or Newtonians; on the contrary, they were outright if tacit opponents of their legacies.

From its inception, the western transatlantic Enlightenment had been essentially a duality of moderate and Radical Enlightenment—a duality of both conflict and dialectical interaction. The Enlightenment had never been a single movement, and could not be in the intellectual context of the time. But only from the late 1740s, owing to the wider impact of the escalating intellectual and cultural tensions in France, did it become apparent that what was taking place was a sustained and general struggle between two rival interpretations of Man and the universe and two competing programmes of social and moral action, one intellectually moderate and socially conservative, the other, in essence, revolutionary; while against both, directly influencing the outcome, surged the anger, hatred, and frustration of a still more widely supported Counter-Enlightenment. Here was a tripartite intellectual struggle which in general terms was to continue to grip the western world for the next two centuries.

31

The 'Unvirtuous Atheist'

1. THE 'AFFAIRE LA METTRIE' (1745–1752)

A most remarkable and prolonged controversy affecting the course of the Radical Enlightenment erupted in the mid 1740s around the figure of physician-philosopher, Julien Offray de La Mettrie (1709–51), a native of Saint-Malo. This philosophical but also rather public affair not only greatly scandalized respectable opinion but called into question the fundamental values and meaning of radical thought, and the relationship of the radical fringe to existing society, in a way which had far-reaching implications for the future as well as highlighting the peculiarities of established methods of intellectual censorship and intensifying the long-standing controversy over toleration and freedom of the press. Most importantly, it caused a permanent and complete rupture between La Mettrie and the main body of radical *philosophes*.

The episode began with the furore in Paris provoked by the clandestine publication in 1745—with 'The Hague' declared on the title page—of La Mettrie's *L'Histoire naturelle de l'âme*. Despite lip-service to physico-theology, curiously combined with a brisk dismissal of Newton's philosophy,[1] immortality of the soul, and condemning Spinoza for denying God and making Man a 'vèritable automate', a machine 'assujettie à la plus constante necessité', no one failed to discern the book's essentially irreligious core.[2] Its sweeping claim that nothing is either 'good' or 'bad' in nature, 'just' or 'unjust' absolutely,[3] as Xenophanes, Melissus, and Parmenides had stated long ago, and the materialist implications of its physiological account of the mind with its claim that our capacity to think stems from a particular organization of the brain and machinery of our bodies—predictably provoked both ecclesiastical condemnation and a public outcry.[4] La Mettrie, who knew Meslier, de Maillet's *Telliamed*, d'Argens's works, and, like Diderot, Du Marsais's *Examen*, while professing to admire Locke, totally subverts his epistemology by eradicating his non-material mental 'faculties' and turning mental states and procedures into purely anatomical and physiological processes while, like Du Marsais but unlike Condillac, simultaneously discarding his theological grounding.[5]

[1] Masseau, *Ennemis des philosophes*, 205, 225; Panizza, 'L'Étrange matérialisme', 100.

[2] La Mettrie, *Histoire naturelle*, 248.

[3] Ibid. 250–1.

[4] Frederick the Great, *Éloge*, 108; Vartanian, *La Mettrie's* L' Homme machine, 5.

[5] Panizza, 'L'Étrange materialisme', 101; Wellman, *La Mettrie*, 149–55; Thomson, 'L'*Examen*', 367–8.

The professors of the Sorbonne, seeing that he 'reduces everything to materialism and, while not acknowledging any spiritual being, even denies the existence of God', unreservedly condemned the anonymous author as an 'atheist'.[6] Plainly, protested one critic, 'c'est un disciple de Spinosa' who acknowledges no substance distinct from matter, someone who sees matter as the unique source of 'l'ordre et de l'arrangement de l'univers', and sole ground of movement, acknowledging no First Mover distinct from the universe itself:[7] this is 'en quoi consiste essentiellement le spinosisme'.[8] With all literary Paris discussing the scandal, in June 1745, the remaining stock of copies was seized by the police and transferred to the Bastille.[9]

Spurning Cartesian and *Malebranchiste* notions of matter as something defined in terms of extension alone, La Mettrie insists matter possesses also two other inherent properties: the power of self-motion ('la puissance de se mouvoir') and inherent sensibility.[10] No one failed to notice that far from being anchored in Locke (or Newton), this was a philosophy which completely demolishes the Lockean-Newtonian construct and was broadly equivalent, at least in its metaphysics, to 'le Spinosisme'. Admittedly, La Mettrie at this early stage denied either he himself or his Dutch medical hero Herman Boerhaave were *Spinosistes*, denouncing Spinoza as a 'monstre d'incrédulité'.[11] But this struck contemporaries as blatant imposture, calculated to divert attention from the book's scarcely veiled 'atheism'. Arguing that motion, 'la force motrice et pensante', is inherent in matter and that matter-motion-thought is the only creative force in nature, emphatically conflating body and mind, La Mettrie rules out all teleology and all prospect of the permeating presence of a world-soul along Platonic or Stoic lines.[12] Blind nature, not providence, is responsible for the appearance of 'design' in the universe, held La Mettrie, as of the great variety of species. Here again, he stood close to Spinoza, Meslier, de Maillet, and (subsequently) Diderot, albeit La Mettrie's probing in the direction of a theory of evolution remained much less sophisticated than that which Diderot expressed a few years later, in his *Pensées sur l'interpretation de la nature* (1753).[13]

On 7 July 1746 the Paris *Parlement* (in the same decree as also banned Diderot's *Pensées philosophiques*), condemned La Mettrie's book as one which, under pretence of investigating nature and the working of the human mind, reduces mind to matter, thereby sapping 'les fondements de toute religion et de toute vertu'.[14] It was sentenced to be symbolically torn up and burnt in the *Parlement*'s courtyard, its further sale being forbidden under stern penalties. La Mettrie, a man of distinctly bizarre inclinations, at this point wrote recounting details of the public outcry to Mme Du Châtelet (with whom, like Maupertuis, he too had conducted an amorous

[6] *Lettre de M., maître en chirurgie*, 113.

[7] Ibid. 114, 117; Vartanian, *La Mettrie's* L'Homme machine, 42

[8] *Lettre de M., maître en chirurgie*, 120.

[9] *Archives de la Bastille*, xi. 261, de Rochebrune à Marville, 28 June 1745.

[10] *Lettre de M., maître en chirurgie*, 121–2; Morilhat, *La Mettrie*, 54–5.

[11] La Mettrie, *Histoire naturelle*, 247–8.

[12] *Lettre de M., maître en chirurgie*, 117–18; Ehrard, *L'Idée*, 237–8; Morilhat, *La Mettrie*, 51–2, 59; Panizza, 'L'Étrange matérialisme', 107.

[13] Wellman, *La Mettrie*, 199, 204–5.

[14] 'Documents', in *Corpus*, 5/6 (1987), 131.

affair), teasing her by professing to be shocked by the atheistic contents of his own anonymously published book.

However, connoisseurs of such things did not take long to identify La Mettrie as the author of *l'Histoire naturelle*, reports to this effect being notably more confident and emphatic than those claiming Diderot as author of the *Pensées philosophiques*. Indeed, an anonymous diatribe against the *Pensées*, appearing at Rouen in 1747, attributed that text too to La Mettrie, despite the fact that it contains some veiled criticism of him.[15] It was left to La Mettrie himself to attempt to put the record straight a few months later, in his *L'Homme machine* (1747) where he remarks that the *Pensées* had actually been written by Diderot (whom he had probably known since the late 1720s when they were both students at the Collège d'Harcourt, in Paris) and had doubtless encountered further after returning to Paris, from Saint-Malo, in 1742, and whom he, in turn, now criticized.[16] However, as *L'Homme machine* too appeared anonymously, and abroad, the presumption that La Mettrie in fact wrote both works remained quite widespread over the next few years both in Holland and Germany.

While Epicurean elements gradually became more prominent in the structure of his thought, La Mettrie's materialism was in crucial respects more Spinozist than Epicurean especially as regards the mind. This he interprets as physically indistinguishable from the body, and something wholly determined, in the same way that bodies are, our capacity to think arising from the organization of our brains, nerves, and other organs rather than owing to the existence of a material 'soul' composed of some subtly elusive substance. La Mettrie evinced that same strong commitment to 'system' which Cassirer mistakenly thought was not a characteristic of the Enlightenment and which actually characterizes Meslier, Du Marsais, and the entire Radical Enlightenment (as well as Voltaire and Montesquieu), firmly adhering to one substance doctrine.[17] By 1747, he had dropped his earlier pretence to the contrary, openly confessing to being a follower of Spinoza, on the final page of his *L'Homme machine* where he asserts that 'il n'y a dans tout l'univers qu'une substance diversement modifiée', a statement which could only be read in Europe at the time as an open declaration of Spinozism.[18] It was wholly consistent, then, with the new work's content, as well as the States General's general ban on Spinozistic writings, that, in February 1748, the executive committee of the States of Holland suppressed *L'Homme machine*, published a few weeks before at Leiden, on the ground that it contains the 'harmful and impious views of Spinosa'.[19]

Despite the strong empiricist bent of La Mettrie's writing, his habit of anchoring his arguments in physiological and medical observations,[20] and familiarity with

[15] Saada, *Inventer Diderot*, 63, 66–9, 76.

[16] La Mettrie, *Machine Man*, 24; Vernière, *Spinoza*, 537.

[17] *Lettre de M., maître en chirurgie*, 120–1; Cassirer, *Philosophy*, 55; Thomson, 'La Mettrie ou la machine', 21–2; Morilhat, *La Mettrie*, 49–50.

[18] La Mettrie, *Machine Man*, 39; *Nouvelle Bibliothèque germanique*, 5 (1748/9), 335; Dupré, *Enlightenment*, 27; Duflo, *Diderot philosophe*, 220.

[19] Jongenelen, *Van Smaad tot erger*, 1.

[20] Cassirer, *Philosophy*, 66; Wellman, *La Mettrie*, 149–50.

Locke, the contemporary debate about his work never focused to any significant extent on Locke, Hobbes (whom he practically never mentions), or Newton, whose physico-theology he rejected outright,[21] but always rather on Descartes, Malebranche, and Spinoza—and with good reason, for the most challenging question posed by La Mettrie's empirical materialism, as the Oratorian Lelarge de Lignac observed, in 1753, was whether there is some valid empirical means of proving there is in man a spiritual 'substance' wholly separate from, but temporarily coexisting with, physical 'substance'.[22] To rescue Descartes and Malebranche's substance dualism, Lelarge develops a theory of the *sens intime*, a pervasive sense of the self of which everyone has experience and which he argues must be both a certain and a non-material reality.

However, what is genuinely Spinozistic in La Mettrie is confined to his approach to the mind–body problem, rejection of providence and all teleology, and conception of matter, that is to his philosophy of nature, life, physiology, and the human body, and his eliminating 'free will', seeing all human action as invariably determined.[23] The rest, on the other hand, was by no means Spinozistic. Given his growing emphasis on the pleasure principle, and his stripping Descartes's dualism down to what he considered its cogent grounding, he did not lack justification for also calling his thought a 'système épicuro-cartésien'.[24] No contradiction was involved, in any case, when in the final summation of his philosophy, the *Discours préliminaire* to his *Œuvres philosophiques* ('Londres' [Berlin], 1751), he designates himself a *Spinosiste* while also claiming to be a thinker who revives 'le système d'Épicure'.[25] While the term 'Spinosisme' was frequently affixed to La Mettrie in the late 1740s and early 1750s,[26] in his case there are good grounds to consider the label somewhat problematic. For while his conception of matter diverges markedly from that of Epicureanism with its atoms and atomic swerve, his theory of motivation and the passions, and holding the pleasure principle to be the prime determinant, does follow a distinctively Epicurean line.[27] Especially crucial, by substituting a modified Epicureanism for Spinoza's ethics, he avoids, unlike other radical writers, any requirement to draw Spinozistic social, moral, and political consequences from hylozoic materialism, consequences they, in contrast to him, judged essential for the moral order and the well-being of society.

Soon after the initial scandal broke, in Paris, La Mettrie was expelled from the crack regiment of guards where he had served as regimental physician since 1742; but, owing to his medical expertise and the war, not yet altogether disgraced, being assigned, instead, away from the capital, as an inspector of military hospitals in French-occupied Flanders. After the formal prohibition of his book, however, and

21 Ibid. 282.

22 [Lelarge de Lignac], *Élémens*, 237–54; Vartanian, *La Mettrie's* L'Homme machine, 106–8.

23 Morilhat, *La Mettrie*, 93.

24 Ibid. 90.

25 La Mettrie, *Discours préliminaire*, 48.

26 Vartanian, *La Mettrie's* L'Homme machine, 110.

27 Comte-Sponville, 'La Mettrie: Un Spinoza moderne?', 112; Thomson, 'La Mettrie et l'épicurisme', 361, 370–2.

publication of his pamphlet *Politique du médecin de Machiavel* (1746), a vitriolic attack on the French medical profession, his position in France became finally untenable. In August or September 1746, he fled first to Middelburg and then Leiden where he had formerly studied, in 1733–4, under Boerhaave. He commented later that he went by choice to the place 'qui me forma', though it is unclear whether he meant by this that Holland was his true spiritual home, or merely that this was where he had imbibed his medical knowledge, attended Boerhaave's lectures, and procured many of his books.[28] In any case, the Dutch professor's solidly empirical and mechanistic medical teaching had inspired his own practice as an army physician and, together with Spinoza, formed the intellectual grounding of the physiological materialism he so sensationally deployed against both his philosophical opponents and the French medical establishment.[29]

At Leiden, La Mettrie reportedly spread his Epicurean 'evangelium' of pleasure among a small band of acolytes especially, apparently, some visiting English 'mylords', philosophy, for him, being a kind of extension of the medical art of healing individual cases.[30] Having translated most of Boerhaave's works into French whilst practising as a physician in Saint-Malo in the late 1730s and early 1740s, La Mettrie knew his writings better than probably anyone in France or indeed in Holland. More than his zealous empiricism, he stressed Boerhaave's ability to build arguments on observation: in La Mettrie's eyes he was above all 'le grand théoricien', system being just as important as experiment in his estimation.[31] A 'modern' who deemed physiology, clinical observation, and recording data, the basis of sound medical knowledge, Boerhaave strove to relate empirical knowledge to a particular conception of the human body, illness, and physiology which was comprehensively mechanistic in spirit. Above all, La Mettrie admired his fondness—which is precisely what led the Franeker professor Regius to accuse him of Spinozism—for dealing with the mind–body relationship in mechanistic terms. Boerhaave, asserted La Mettrie (rather questionably) explains 'par le seul mécanisme toutes les facultés de l'âme raisonnable', even when discussing the highest metaphysical questions 'ce grand théoricien soumet tout aux loix de mouvement', a designation making Boerhaave sound distinctly more Spinozistic than he probably was in reality.[32]

La Mettrie's interpretation of Boerhaave's medical thought in any case buttressed his own system which was characterized by the complete elimination of the immaterial will or soul from Man's being and a conception of thought as something that arises from sensibility purely through the nerves.[33] In *L'Homme machine* (1747), La Mettrie also emphatically rejects Voltairean Deism, and, equally, that expressed in Diderot's *Pensées philosophiques* (1746), arguing that one does not need to suppose intentional 'design', any more than the blind 'chance' of Epicurus, to explain the marvellous intricacy of the works of nature all of which can be satisfactorily

[28] Vartanian, *La Mettrie's* L'Homme machine, 6. [29] Wellman, *La Mettrie*, 61.

[30] Pontoppidan, *Kraft der Wahrheit*, 401–3; Gay, *Enlightenment*, i. 15.

[31] Wellman, *La Mettrie*, 7, 37, 60–1; Vartanian, *La Mettrie's* L'Homme machine, 77.

[32] Ibid. 79. [33] Wellman, *La Mettrie*, 122–3; Tortarolo, *L'Illuminismo*, 42, 77.

accounted for in terms of the blind and inherent laws of nature itself.[34] Man for La Mettrie, as for Diderot, is distinguished from animals only by superior intelligence and ability to talk, neither of which is considered an absolute difference but merely one of degree.[35]

In the Netherlands, La Mettrie resumed his double campaign against ignorance, medical and philosophical, preparing two texts, *La Faculté vengée*, aimed at the Parisian medical establishment, and what became his most notorious philosophical text—*L'Homme machine*. Finished seemingly in the summer of 1747, publication of the latter, late in 1747, by Élie Luzac (1723–96), a Dutch Huguenot of mostly conservative opinions who, however, was uncompromisingly radical regarding freedom of the press,[36] unleashed a furore which was dramatically to affect the lives of both men. No sooner did the book appear than it 'met', as the preface to the English translation put it, 'with the severest and bitterest treatment from almost every quarter'.[37] As Frederick the Great noted, from Berlin, Calvinists, Catholics, and Lutherans momentarily forgot they were divided by 'consubstantion, le libre arbitre, la messe des morts et l'infaillibilité du Pape' and instead combined their best efforts to suppress *L'Homme machine*.[38] While the spectacle appealed to the Prussian monarch's somewhat perverse sense of humour, raising La Mettrie's stock in Berlin, in Holland the outcry led to La Mettrie's book being publicly burnt at The Hague as proof that the new Orangist regime of William IV wished to crack down hard on libertines, freethinkers, and atheists.

On 18 December 1747, Luzac was summoned before the *consistoire* of the Église Wallonne of Leiden and required to surrender all remaining copies, reveal the anonymous author's identity, and show appropriate contrition for having published so offensive a work. He solemnly undertook never to do the like again,[39] complying with the first and third demands, but declined to name the author to protect La Mettrie who was still in Leiden, sticking to the story told in his publisher's preface that the manuscript had arrived anonymously on his desk, sent through the post from Berlin with a request only to send six of the printed copies 'à l'adresse de M. le marquis d'Argens', though d'Argens, he was certain, was not the author.[40] Some weeks later, the culprit's name was discovered anyhow, obliging La Mettrie promptly to remove himself to Germany where his notoriety had long preceded him and where, at this time, the reviews in the German journals show, he was considerably better known than Diderot.[41] Luzac too was obliged to flee when the States of Holland ordered the arrest of author and publisher, taking refuge in Göttingen where he worked for two years for a doctorate and studied Wolff.[42]

[34] Thomson, 'La Mettrie et l'épicurisme', 364–5.

[35] Ehrard, *L'Idée*, 197–8; Duflo, *Diderot philosophe*, 164, 216 n. 425; Morilhat, *La Mettrie*, 68–9.

[36] Velema, 'Introduction', 14, 19–20; Israel, *Dutch Republic*, 1074–5, 1085.

[37] [La Mettrie], *Man a Machine*, preface.

[38] Ibid. 7; Frederick the Great, *Éloge*, 110.

[39] Marx, 'Grand Imprimeur', 782; Velema, 'Introduction', 15–16.

[40] [La Mettrie], *Œuvres philosophiques*, i, *L'Homme machine* 'avertissement de l'imprimeur', 3^{V}.

[41] Saada, *Inventer Diderot*, 62–3, 66–9, 71.

[42] Marx, 'Grand Imprimeur', 783.

La Mettrie's arrival in Berlin, the new haven of banned writers and *esprits forts*, on 7 February 1748, electrified the literary world of northern Europe. The spectacle of Europe's most notorious atheist, a hounded refugee philosopher-physician, being publicly received at one of Europe's principal monarchical courts was both unprecedented and bizarre. Establishing himself in Prussia with the help of d'Argens to whom he was close for a while and many of whose books graced his Potsdam library,[43] and Maupertuis, a fellow native of Saint-Malo to whom La Mettrie had had the effrontery to dedicate his *Histoire naturelle de l'âme*, obliging him to intervene with the Paris publishers to delete the claims that he agreed with La Mettrie's views, the latter was now a courtier, man of fame, and, seemingly, in a impregnable position. Maupertuis, who now presided over the newly revived Prussian royal academy, found himself obliged to treat the new arrival with studied respect, since the king had latterly followed his career with interest, drawn less out of admiration for his ideas than because the burning of La Mettrie's books in France and Holland had rendered his new protégé Europe's foremost victim, as he put it characteristically, 'des théologiens et des sots'.[44]

The remarkable European controversy which was to continue for several years surrounding La Mettrie, and his *L'Homme machine*, carried on in three capitals, and especially among the Huguenot diaspora in Holland and Berlin, in which, besides various more orthodox figures, Luzac, Rousset de Missy, Marchand, d'Argens, and Formey all participated, ranged from the proper limits of freedom of the press and expression to the existence or otherwise of God.[45] In structure this controversy was a quadrangular battle in which the familiar struggle between religion and incredulity was paralleled by a more specialized contest, purely within the Enlightenment camp, between what Luzac called *immatérialisme* and *matérialisme*,[46] meaning the Deistic and atheistic philosophical world-views, a clash convoluted by a further split within the ranks of the *matérialistes* between the Diderot camp and La Mettrie, who in his *Discours préliminaire* was to refer disparagingly to his radical critics, in Paris, as 'nos beaux esprits'.[47]

Christians and Deists could agree that *L'Homme machine* was 'atheistic' and apt to subvert 'all order, encourage every vice, and, in a word, destroy the essence of virtue'.[48] But where the orthodox and many moderates insisted the text should be banned outright and no discussion of its arguments permitted, champions of full toleration and a freer press, led by Luzac, held that a number of vital issues were involved which required close consideration and that without open discussion of such an atheistic work its theses could neither be properly examined nor genuinely refuted.[49] Defeating La Mettrie's materialism should be clear and open, argued

43 Pia Jauch, 'Wenn Therese philosophiert', 141.

44 Weil, 'La Diffusion', 209; Wellman, *La Mettrie*, 170, 266, 283.

45 Marx, 'Grand Imprimeur', 782; [Luzac], *L'Homme plus que machine*, preface.

46 [Luzac], *L'Homme plus que machine*, 41.

47 La Mettrie, *Discours préliminaire*, 49.

48 [La Mettrie], *Man a Machine*, preface; Pia Jauch, 'Wenn Therese philosophiert', 143.

49 [Luzac], *L'Homme plus que machine*, 30, 35–6.

Luzac, something witnessed by the public, in which his defeat was incontestably secured by superior arguments rather than censorship and repression. On the same grounds, Luzac assiduously persisted, until his flight to Germany, in distributing La Mettrie's text despite its being banned in France, the Netherlands, and much of Germany alike, the Paris police, for example, receiving information in November 1748 that a clandestine shipment of *L'Homme machine* was *en route* from Holland.[50]

Publisher and distributor Luzac was likewise himself an eager controversialist. Having studied La Mettrie's writings and Diderot's *Pensées philosophiques* closely,[51] he propounded a thesis with which Deists and Christians alike, he claimed, could conclusively trounce La Mettrie and all the *matérialistes*, proving the human soul 'une substance immatérielle'. If ideas are just the effects of a 'movement communicated to the nerves', as La Mettrie maintained, then human thought cannot, he proposed, be an active self-motivating and self-producing process but must be 'au contraire toujours passive'. Experience, and our thoughts and minds, however, plainly prove thought is an active force so that La Mettrie is clearly shown to be wrong.[52] Meanwhile, a remarkable anonymous tolerationist tract clandestinely published, in 1749, 'au pays libre, pour le bien public', amusingly 'avec privilège de tous les véritables philosophes', either in Leiden or Amsterdam, entitled *Essai sur la liberté de produire des sentimens*, usually thought to be by Luzac, vigorously criticized by implication the censorship policy of the new Dutch Orangist regime (which Luzac otherwise strongly supported). Liberty to express opinions, argues this tract, exists by virtue of Man's very nature, and the wish of the Creator, and is surely also intimately linked to maintaining the 'public good'.

Most commentators were in agreement that whatever is prejudicial to society should be prevented. But before society is justified, in Natural Law, in forbidding expression of a given opinion it must first be demonstrated that such an opinion really is damaging.[53] Without first exposing the issues involved to an open and free discussion there can be no such proof, added to which, remarks the author, were it true, as Bayle holds, that 'la superstition' harms society more than atheism, we should perhaps begin by suppressing opinions promoting superstition before attempting to ban atheism.[54] Against this, more conventionally minded observers urged that a middle way had to be found between excessive restriction of the press and an unrestricted freedom tending to licentiousness. Since 'atheism' was a crime against the state, as well as God, and since Pufendorf, Barbeyrac, and all reputable Natural Lawyers agreed it should be banned, 'athées dogmatisans' like the writer of *L'Homme machine* were rightly condemned by the authorities.[55]

One commentator who argued that books encouraging vice and undermining generally accepted rules of morality should be comprehensively banned engaged Luzac in a particularly long and arduous dispute. After several exchanges, Luzac's

[50] *Archives de la Bastille*, xi. 297, Bonin to Berryer, 14 Nov. 1748.

[51] [Luzac], *L'Homme plus que machine*, 30, 35–6, 40.

[52] Ibid. 44.

[53] [Luzac], *Essai sur la liberté*, 15–16, 30.

[54] Ibid. 76.

[55] *Nouvelle Bibliothèque germanique*, 5 (1748/9), 329–30, 340–3.

adversary, writing in the *Nouvelle Bibliothèque germanique*, remarked that men's powers of persuasion are not unlimited and even if Luzac's arguments against Spinoza and La Mettrie are valid this would not carry his point regarding liberty of the press. How often, he exclaims, has 'le Spinosisme', of which La Mettrie publicly owns himself a partisan, been proven harmful and thoroughly refuted?[56] Yet all these refutations do nothing to curb the further spread of Spinozism. Against this, Luzac retorted that it is not easy adequately to define 'Spinozism' for purposes of censorship; an eminent German theologian, for instance, claimed 'le Leibnitzianisme étoit un Spinosisme caché'; were the authorities therefore obliged to suppress the writings of the great Leibniz?[57]

The controversy was complicated by continuing uncertainty as to the identity of *L'Homme machine*'s author. The English translation published in London and Dublin, in 1749, states on the title page (despite repeated denials that the Provençal nobleman was its author) that the work was 'translated from the French of the Marquiss d'Argens', the (radical) translator's preface remarking that the Dutch authorities had refrained from pursuing the book resolutely because it was 'whisper'd into the ears of the leading men, that it had for its author no less a person than the marquess d'Argens, the known favourite of the [Prussian] court, the darling of the ladies, the terror of bigots, and the delight of men of sense'. Rumours that d'Argens was in fact the author and that the Dutch regents were unable to act vigorously, because d'Argens was Frederick's intimate friend, further enhanced the book's notoriety, reportedly causing a 'sudden revolution in the fate of the work' and rousing the 'attention of all parties, so that *Man a Machine* is now as well known in foreign parts as any book in Europe'.[58] This was true; La Mettrie, book and journal research shows, was, with the possible exception of d'Argens, easily the best known of the materialists to the general public in the years 1745–50 and remained one of the best-selling materialist authors in France, Germany, and the Netherlands alike for several decades thereafter.[59]

The fast-unfolding controversy was closely followed by Prosper Marchand, at The Hague, who carefully annotated his own copies of La Mettrie's texts (of which he possessed four, among them the *Histoire naturelle de l'âme)*. He also compiled a detailed *Catalogue des ouvrages de Monsieur La Mettrie* which appeared in his *Éloge du Sieur La Mettrie* published at The Hague, after that *philosophe*'s premature death, in 1751.[60] Rousset de Missy likewise closely followed the proceedings, as La Mettrie, securely ensconced in Potsdam, turned out more works in rapid succession further elaborating his materialist system. Among the most notable of these, *L'Anti-Sénèque* (1748) proved too much even for the freethinking Frederick the Great, being immediately banned and withdrawn from circulation by personal order of

[56] *Nouvelle Bibliothèque germanique*, 6 (1750), 431–4 and 11 (1752), 353.
[57] Ibid. 6 (1750), 433–4.
[58] [La Mettrie], *Man a Machine*, preface.
[59] Darnton, *Forbidden Best-Sellers*, 68, 71, 73; Chartier, *Cultural Origins*, 76, 79.
[60] Berkvens-Stevelinck, *Prosper Marchand*, 158.

the king.[61] Frederick readily supported La Mettrie the outcast, enjoyed his witty conversation, and admired his one-man contest with the clergy; likewise, he had no difficulty with his principle that nature is self-creating and does so blindly, Man being purely a product of nature so that, paradoxically, nature 'a fait sans penser, une machine qui pense'.[62] Neither did he worry overly that there was no real moral basis to La Mettrie's system; but he could hardly be expected to countenance the Frenchman's openly preaching immoralism and his insolent contention that monarchy is something altogether arbitrary and hence devoid of any moral principle.[63]

2. ATHEISTIC AMORALISM

At the close of an earlier work, *La Volupté* (1745), La Mettrie expresses confidence that however many bigots denounced him, the partisans of 'true virtue' and sworn enemies of superstition, 'plein de sentiments pour l'humanité', would rally to his support.[64] At the time, he had some grounds for confidence in this expectation, being close in particular to d'Argens whom *La Volupté* seems to have strongly influenced and whose *Thérèse philosophe* (1748), a work which appeared, anonymously, shortly after La Mettrie's arrival in Potsdam, it helped shape,[65] while at the same time further fomenting the confusion about authors, Lessing, for instance, considering this erotic novel quite 'dégoûtant' and thus presumably by La Mettrie rather than the more respectable and respected d'Argens.[66] But, after 1748, it by no means proved to be the case that La Mettrie could rely on the support of the other *philosophes*. If, in the Parisian cafés, there was backing for materialist positions of all kinds as well as for La Mettrie's war on the churches, the Parisian police, and the 'charlatans' of the medical profession, this was more than outweighed by the perception that he had overstepped all bounds, not in assailing conventional ideas but through his moral and social cynicism.

La Mettrie, self-proclaimed prophet of pleasurable indulgence, culinary as well as sexual, died suddenly in Berlin at the age of 43 on 11 November 1751, from food poisoning, after consuming a spoiled game and truffle pâté pie. Few expressed much sorrow. His official obituary, as a member of the Berlin academy, composed, to the deep embarrassment of most of the academy, by the Prussian monarch himself, was declaimed at a public session of that body by a royal secretary, subsequently published under the title *Éloge de M. Julien Offray de la Mettrie . . . prononcé par S.M. le roi de Prusse dans son Académie, à Berlin* (Berlin, 1752), a text then reissued

[61] Thomson, 'La Mettrie ou la machine', 15–16; Falvey, 'Politique textuelle', 33.
[62] Voltaire, *Mémoires*, 80–1; Morilhat, *La Mettrie*, 53.
[63] Wellman, *La Mettrie*, 266–9; Falvey, 'Politique textuelle', 33–4; Markovits, 'La Mettrie', 84.
[64] La Mettrie, *La Volupté*, 136.
[65] Pia Jauch, 'Wenn Therese philosophiert', 146–7, 149–50.
[66] Seifert, 'C'est un pays', 250.

by the publisher Pierre Gosse, at The Hague, the same year.[67] The king also assigned a pension to the lady-companion whom La Mettrie (having apparently abandoned his wife and children in Paris) had brought with him to Prussia. Voltaire, whose 'Berlin period' (1750–3) converged geographically with the last phase of La Mettrie's career, assured Frederick in September 1752, in the obsequious tone he adopted when writing to that monarch, that the royal eulogy was assuredly 'plus philosophique' than anything La Mettrie himself had ever written.[68]

All who disregard calumny and bigotry, including the Prussian royal academy, declared the Prussian monarch, would continue to honour La Mettrie as 'un honnête homme et un savant médecin'. Few were prepared to agree. He was actually a dreadful physician, complained Voltaire, and a madman,[69] while Rousset de Missy who irreverently remarked of the Reformed preachers who denounced La Mettrie at The Hague that these were 'des J.F. comme tous les Prêtres partout ailleurs', nevertheless assured Marchand, on reading the *éloge* in July 1752, that it was bizarre indeed that a monarch should extol such 'un extravagant'.[70] In his opinion, La Mettrie had outrageously overstepped all bounds. La Beaumelle similarly thought La Mettrie an author whose fearless audacity should be admired but who was certainly the craziest of the 'atheistic' writers; more significantly still, Dorthous de Mairan, himself a 'bon athée' and private *Spinosiste*, according to La Beaumelle, had remarked that even in a 'society of atheists' La Mettrie would be condemned and punished.[71]

Although, Rousset, writing to Marchand in February 1752, designates Diderot 'ce second La Mettrie', actually significant differences and tensions had by this time emerged between La Mettrie and the radical wing of the *parti philosophique* whether in France, Holland, or Prussia.[72] While d'Argens, Dorthous, Rousset, Diderot, Buffon, Boulanger, Helvétius, d'Alembert, and d'Holbach doubtless largely agreed with the atheistic materialism of *L'Homme machine*, and several of these men did initially defend La Mettrie, a consensus rapidly emerged which was vehemently critical of, and increasingly negative towards, the moral and political system of the prematurely deceased *matérialiste*. For if La Mettrie was broadly *Spinosiste* in his materialism and naturalism, in arguing that philosophy, 'aux recherches de laquelle tout est soumis, est soumise elle-même à la Nature', and claiming that body and soul are one and that no supernatural agency or event is possible, the rest of his system, especially his *immoralisme*, threw up an insuperable barrier between him and the maturing Radical Enlightenment.[73]

Ultimately at issue was La Mettrie's abandonment of the *Spinosistes*' moral naturalism. While genuine philosophy, for La Mettrie, must be based on the study of

67 Voltaire, *Mémoires*, 83; Berkvens-Stevelinck and Vercruysse (eds.), *Métier*, 139; Salaün, *L'Ordre*, 82.

68 Voltaire to Frederick, Potsdam, 5 Sept. 1752, *Correspondence*, xiii. 179.

69 Frederick the Great, *Éloge*, 111; Markovits, 'La Mettrie' (2003), 180.

70 Berkvens-Stevelinck, *Métier de journaliste*, 152.

71 La Beaumelle, *Mes pensées*, 384–6, 429; Lauriol, *La Beaumelle*, 245.

72 Lauriol, *La Beaumelle*, 137.

73 La Mettrie, *Discours préliminaire*, 4; Fossati, 'Maximum Influence', 50; Bourdin, *Matérialistes*, 59–60.

nature, morality has nothing to do with nature but is really just an indispensable fiction, a 'fruit arbitraire de la politique', devised for purely social reasons and arbitrarily as well as forcibly imposed by society. Since men are determined in what they do by nature and governed by natural impulse, we are no more criminal in following our basic drives, contends La Mettrie, than is the Nile in inundating precious farmland.[74] Happiness, according to La Mettrie's moral schema, is an essentially individual affair unconnected alike with the common good, on the one hand and the moral and intellectual progress of the individual on the other. The world is full of contented imbeciles, he declared, and unhappy *gens d'esprit*.[75] Philosophy and morality, being opposites, he argues, are in permanent, irresolvable conflict with each other: 'diamétricalement opposées jusqu'à se tourner le dos'; what can one conclude from this other than that 'la philosophie est absolument inconciliable avec la morale, la religion et la politique'?[76]

This was totally unacceptable to Diderot, Dorthous de Mairan, d'Argens, and the *Spinosistes modernes*. The point at which La Mettrie parts company with the Radical Enlightenment was hence precisely where he diverges from Spinozism itself: precisely, in the sharp differentiation he introduces between nature, reason, and philosophy, on the one hand, which reveal what is true and 'natural' and what he deems the utilitarian myths of virtue, equity, and justice, on the other, all arbitrary political constructions devised to uphold one or another kind of social order. La Mettrie, unlike Spinoza, Bayle, Du Marsais, and Diderot, forges a naturalism which offers no ethic of equality based on the equivalence of volitions and consciences, or moral system rooted in the idea of equity, or any concept of 'virtue' linked to a 'common good' in which men rationally and naturally share. Although he agrees with Spinoza's thesis in the *Tractatus* that government is justified by its social functions, not authority conferred by supernatural agency, and that it is necessary that rulers uphold law and order, he diverges dramatically from Spinozist thinking in claiming the principles of government and justice are nevertheless wholly arbitrary.[77] Displaying no particular reverence for monarchy, he showed no commitment to republican ideals either.

Since 'virtue', indeed any altruistic motive for sharing in an enterprise, or sense of social and political responsibility, is for La Mettrie purely fictional, the veritable 'morale de la nature' in his view is merely the pursuit of physical pleasures combined with the investigation of nature.[78] One's aim in life is to seek satisfaction of one's desires and thereby attain pleasure: 'le plaisir', wrote La Mettrie, in his *La Volupté* (1745), 'est l'essence de l'homme, et de l'ordre de l'univers'.[79] Every person, he held, carries within himself or herself the germ of their own well-being in their

74 Ehrard, *L'Idée*, 390; Morilhat, *La Mettrie*, 96–9; Dupré, *Enlightenment*, 112, 120; Salaün, *L'Ordre*, 252.
75 La Mettrie, *Anti-Sénèque*, 241, 243.
76 La Mettrie, *Discours préliminaire*, 1, 9; Falvey, 'Politique textuelle', 31.
77 Wellman, *La Mettrie*, 266–8; Markovits, 'La Mettrie', 84, 99.
78 Falvey, 'Politique textuelle', 32.
79 Ibid.; La Mettrie, *La Volupté*, 119; Morilhat, *La Mettrie*, 97.

erotic feelings, though true hedonism for La Mettrie is something different from sensual pleasure as commonly understood. Real satisfaction, for him, is a cumulative state and refined synthesis of the most satisfying pleasures, transporting the individual into a lasting state of tender indolence which reconciles to the world.[80] Despising the Stoics who, all soul, make an abstraction of their bodies, he and his adherents—dubbed by him the Anti-Stoïciens—being all body make an abstraction, he avows, of their souls.[81]

Like sexual gratification, to which it is directly linked, human happiness, being morally neutral, and detached from all ethical schemes conventional or otherwise, is equally available, according to La Mettrie, to everyone, benevolent and malicious alike.[82] For no one is better or worse than anyone else in nature. Hence, there is no essential difference, he contends, between 'virtues' and 'vices' as generally understood.[83] Remorse for misdeeds, cruel acts, or satisfying appetites at someone else's expense, like bad conscience generally, all needlessly hamper enjoyment and uselessly trouble men's equanimity.[84] A sentiment inculcated by religion and education to impose constraints on the individual, guilty conscience merely spoils Man's enjoyment, hampering gratification in doing what humans are anyhow determined by their physical constitution to do and cannot avoid doing.

La Mettrie in this way introduced a sharp disparity, what has aptly been called a 'fundamental dissonance between individual constitutions—and satisfying our desires—and the interests of society'.[85] While La Mettrie did not deny that society requires moral guidelines and must protect itself, ensure maintenance of law and order, and impose its own discipline on people's behaviour, agreeing with Spinoza that rabid dogs must be killed and poisonous snakes eliminated,[86] he thought the laws society enforces to accomplish this are inherently arbitrary and ungrounded in either reason or nature.[87] For Diderot and the new *Spinosistes*, by contrast, human happiness requires us to live consciously, in thought and action, in conformity with the universal laws of nature and reason, not in the Stoic sense of attempting to tame the passions with reason, a goal Diderot, like Spinoza, believed conflicts with nature, but rather, through moderating our passions in accord with the natural circumstances, shaping and improving the human condition, our common good, and meeting society's needs.[88]

From a Postmodernist perspective, and that of such contemporary thinkers as Alasdair MacIntyre or Charles Taylor critical of the Enlightenment's efforts to construct a universal secular morality, the disowning of La Mettrie by the *philosophes* places the latter in a poor light. For it implies they unjustly hounded and vilified

80 La Mettrie, *La Volupté*, 109; Philippaki, 'La Mettrie on Descartes' (forthcoming).
81 La Mettrie, *Anti-Sénèque*, 238.
82 Schneewind, *Invention of Autonomy*, 463–4; Morilhat, *La Mettrie*, 99.
83 [Luzac], *Essai sur la liberté*, 32; Fossati, 'Maximum Influence', 49.
84 La Mettrie, *Anti-Sénèque*, 257; Morilhat, *La Mettrie*, 98; Thomson, 'La Mettrie et l'épicurisme', 374.
85 Wellman, *La Mettrie*, 244; Salaün, *L'Ordre*, 251–2.
86 Morilhat, *La Mettrie*, 99. 87 La Mettrie, *Discours préliminaire*, 4.
88 Duflo, *Diderot philosophe*, 412, 490, 504.

someone who had seen through the illusions, pretensions, and contradictions they themselves could not resolve. Interpreted thus, La Mettrie emerges as the perceptive and candid thinker who grasped the ugly reality Diderot and the rest were blind to, a victim of dogmatists, hypocrites, and moral cowards who had aroused their fears of having persecution brought down on their own heads, by pointing out the weaknesses in their system and the obstacles to constructing a secular morality on the basis of materialism.[89] For Diderot, holds MacIntyre, while otherwise sharing La Mettrie's physiological materialism, undermined his own attempt 'to find a basis for morality in human physiological nature' by arbitrarily distinguishing between 'desires that are natural to man' and artificially aroused and corrupt impulses nurtured by civilized society.[90] The marquis de Sade, adds Charles Taylor, was merely following La Mettrie, when later in the century he 'showed how the utter rejection of all social limits could be embraced as the most consistent and thoroughgoing liberation from traditional religion and metaphysics. Morals, law and virtue are to be thrown off.'[91]

La Mettrie has hence proved useful to Postmodernists seeking to press their campaign to discredit and sap the moral foundations of what they disparage as the 'Enlightenment project'. One author claims La Mettrie '"barbarized" the Enlightenment and set it on a course toward materialism and mechanism which proved to be irreversible', arguing that despite being a mediocre thinker, La Mettrie 'proved to be a devastating force in the demise of the old regime'.[92] But while it is perfectly true to say that Europe's 'political and social revolution did not commence in 1789' and that the 'revolution which unalterably pitted science against metaphysics began in the 1740s', as well as that one finds in La Mettrie a nihilistic moral philosophy based purely on egoism and the pursuit of pleasure,[93] it is wholly incorrect to suppose that La Mettrie did in fact typify eighteenth-century French materialism, much less drag any of the materialist main body in his wake.

La Mettrie may have propounded what Charles Taylor terms 'a morality of purely egoistic gratification' and his philosophy was certainly grounded in the radical materialism developing in France during the first half of the eighteenth century.[94] But there were many other radical materialists prior to 1750, with Boulainvilliers, Meslier, Du Marsais, Boulanger, Vauvenargues, d'Argens, Fréret, Helvetius, Boindin, de Maillet, and Diderot prominent among them and he was neither a characteristic representative of the moral thinking of this group nor a major influence on the post-1750 French *parti philosophique* as a whole. If Diderot and other exponents of Radical Enlightenment vociferously protested against La Mettrie's moral theory this was not because they feared that, through La Mettrie, the compromising truth was being told, or inconsistencies in their own thought uncovered, or persecution being brought down on themselves, but because they genuinely abhorred and were angered by his views.

89 Wellman, *La Mettrie*, 213, 215, 240, 244, 272, 284; Taylor, *Sources of the Self*, 334.

90 MacIntyre, *After Virtue*, 48.

91 Ibid. 335.

92 Fossati, 'Maximum Influence', 49, 52.

93 Ibid. 57.

94 Taylor, *Sources of the Self*, 334–5.

The Postmodernist attack on the Enlightenment, defenders of the Enlightenment, and the Enlightenment legacy today have frequently repeated the charge that Enlightenment thinking about moral issues was confused and incoherent, leading to a failure to establish a viable secular morality independent of theology and traditional metaphysics which allegedly encouraged and contributed to the disintegration and pulverizing of the modern secular moral identity and the collapse of efforts meaningfully to combine moral values with social benevolence. The 'breakdown' of this project of enlightenment, holds Alasdair MacIntyre, a leading theorist of this view, 'provided the historical background against which the predicaments of our own culture can become intelligible'.[95] A number of prominent philosophers and social theorists have offered elaborate accounts of this alleged process of failure and 'breakdown', MacIntyre, Charles Taylor, and John Gray among them, all of which, however, founder on what is arguably a seriously erroneous understanding of the historical context.[96]

Failure to distinguish adequately between moderate mainstream and Radical Enlightenment must always invalidate any general assessment of the Enlightenment. Hence to invoke the moral philosophies of Locke, Hume, Voltaire, Montesquieu, and Kant who all strove to circumvent the thoroughgoing naturalism of the materialists which they recognized must lead to a complete divorce between morality and Christian tradition makes no sense if the object of the exercise is to fault an 'Enlightenment' project which tried to base morality purely on natural premisses. MacIntyre himself, criticizing Kant, affirms that it is 'of the essence of reason that it lays down principles which are universal, categorical, and internally consistent' and that 'a rational morality will lay down principles which both can and ought to be held by all men, independent of circumstances and conditions, and which could consistently be obeyed by every rational agent on every occasion.'[97] It is this critique itself which is a complete contradiction. For the conservative moral and social theories of Locke, Voltaire, Montesquieu, Hume, and Kant were all expressly intended to avoid forging moral philosophy systematically on the basis of philosophical reason and nature, in the interest of salvaging major elements of tradition, custom, and theology.

All these moral philosophers are by definition and by design not just inconsistent but wholly at odds with the consistent naturalism sought by Spinoza, Bayle, Boulainvilliers, Diderot, and d'Holbach. It was the moral theories of the hard-core French High Enlightenment, Du Marsais, Diderot, d'Argens, Helvétius, d'Holbach, and Condorcet, which follow Spinoza and Bayle in adopting a fully secular and universalist ethic based exclusively on the 'common good', equity, and equality, that were designed to be philosophically coherent and consistent; and, for this very reason, the Postmodernist critique of the Enlightenment entirely lacks force in relation to them. The radicals disowned La Mettrie precisely because he ran counter

95 MacIntyre, *After Virtue*, 39.

96 Ibid. 36–78; Taylor, *Sources of the Self*, 248–390; Gray, *Enlightenment's Wake*, 1–3, 7, 144–70.

97 MacIntyre, *After Virtue*, 45.

to their systematic moral, political, and social naturalism, threatening to break its cohesion and introduce dissonances and disjunctions they altogether rejected.

The moral code society enforces, holds La Mettrie, has no basis in Man's natural disposition. Consequently, laws and social norms, he thought, lack genuine moral force and since law is the only criterion of 'right' and 'wrong', obeying the laws wherever popular and theological ideas hold sway, that is to say in practically every state, obliges he who possesses philosophical insight to live a make-believe life, abide by a charade of hypocrisy, myth, lies, and pretence, systematic deception being indispensable, in his view, to managing the human herd.[98] It was this sweeping nihilism and moral cynicism and La Mettrie's explicit contention in his *Discours préliminaire* that all government and legal systems are morally equivalent in being built on 'superstition', 'prejudice', and 'myth' which prompted even the Prussian king to prohibit his *Œuvres philosophiques* in 1751.

La Mettrie, then, in the end diverged drastically from radical thought. For he refused to accept either that the moral conscience of the true *philosophe* must, in Diderot's words, be in perfect accord with 'morale universelle',[99] or d'Argens's principle that laws are made to make individuals 'heureux', and not to oppress them, and that to promote human happiness, laws must ensure and promote the general interest. La Mettrie's *épicuro-spinosisme* hence brutally departs from the radical principle that whoever is 'virtuous', as d'Argens expresses it, is a priest of truth, 'et par conséquent de l'Être Suprême, qui lui-même est la vérité'.[100] While Diderot and the radicals, and d'Argens most of all, agreed that *la volupté* is something vastly different from debauchery and that eighteenth-century society had inherited severely deformed and mutilated ideas about human sexuality from its past, and while, for them, no less than La Mettrie, sexual issues require discussion in a natural, balanced way, and pleasure-seeking is central,[101] none of this can alter, or detract from, the binding validity of the principles of equity, reciprocity, and justice or the need for the rational individual to conform to the 'common good'.

While Diderot and the Radical Enlightenment pressed for the sexual emancipation of the individual, male and female, and scorned—as d'Argens does in his *Songes philosophiques*—traditional Christian conceptions of marriage and especially the irrational cult of female chastity, condemnation of homosexuality, and denial of the right of divorce, and considered the keeping of unwilling and incompatible couples together as a particularly repellent aspect of the tyranny of the family,[102] La Mettrie's anarchic brand of hedonism detached from any moral framework was something they whole-heartedly repudiated. To La Mettrie, the voluptuous person loves life more than others, having a healthy body and a free spirit, and is more tranquil and better able to adore nature's beauties 'parce qu'il les connoît mieux qu'un autre'.[103]

[98] Wellman, *La Mettrie*, 256.

[99] Ibid. 256; Dagen, *L'Histoire*, 495 n.; Fossati, 'Maximum Influence', 50.

[100] [D'Argens], *Songes philosophiques*, 11–12.

[101] La Mettrie, *La Volupté*, 96–8, 108–9.

[102] [D'Argens], *Songes philosophiques*, 11.

[103] La Mettrie, *La Volupté*, 119; La Mettrie, *Anti-Sénèque*, 237–9.

To reduce the pursuit of happiness to pleasure-seeking and conceive pleasure as a purely physical process—a continual soothing of the nerves, with the pleasures of love, especially sexual intercourse, ranked highest—seemed to his radical critics to violate the most basic principles on which their social, moral, and political reform programme rested.

This amoralism of his last works sets La Mettrie firmly at odds with the neo-*Spinosistes* and materialists and hence with the Radical Enlightenment. For his system implies that crime, egoism, spite, and perversion are ultimately no less 'moral', legitimate, and apt for producing happiness than the 'charity and justice' Spinoza, Bayle, and Diderot proclaim the eternal and unalterable grounding of secular morality. Here indeed was a war *à l'outrance* between what Charles Taylor called 'purely egoistic materialism' and a materialism 'predicated on universal benevolence', Shaftesbury's and Diderot's 'doing good in the world'.[104] The gulf was further widened by La Mettrie's inference that knowledge and understanding, and therefore emancipation of the individual, are in practice feasible only for a small elite. Most men must remain steeped in superstition and, hence, unemancipated. However clearly thinkers might demonstrate Man is but a machine, he says, 'le peuple n'en croira jamais rien'.[105] The masses, he asserts, can never be brought to change their outlook or superstitions by philosophy.[106]

Voltaire reserved his harshest words for La Mettrie even though it was with him alone that he agreed that the *philosophes* should not try to propagate 'philosophical' awareness of fundamental truths about Man, God, and the universe among the common people, as this would be both dangerous to attempt[107] and anyway in practice impossible to accomplish.[108] Where the Radical Enlightenment believed it possible not only intellectually, but also in practice, to build a more just, equal, democratic, and humane society by spreading among the general populace consciousness of the systematic falsity of commonly received ideas, the impostures of priesthood, and irrationality of monarchy, aristocracy, and ecclesiastical power, for Voltaire and the moderate mainstream, but also La Mettrie, it seemed advisable, and ultimately unavoidable, to leave the illusions and ignorance of the great majority largely intact while striving to transform the thinking of elites, and especially strengthen toleration.

Hence, La Mettrie, like Voltaire who despised La Mettrie's atheism and materialism, no less than his immoralism, styling him 'ce fou de La Mettrie',[109] but was in fact closer to La Mettrie's political stance than to the social and political theories of the other materialists,[110] grounded not equality but a new and fundamental kind of

104 Taylor, *Sources of the Self*, 335.

105 La Mettrie, *Discours préliminaire*, 22, 28; Falvey, 'Politique textuelle', 37–8.

106 Falvey, 'Politique textuelle', 39; Markovits, 'La Mettrie', 83–4; Morilhat, *La Mettrie*, 20–1.

107 Wellman, *La Mettrie*, 258–60.

108 Ibid.; Payne, *The* Philosophes, 94.

109 Voltaire to Charlotte Sophia, Countess Bentinck, Potsdam, [May 1752], Voltaire, *Correspondence*, xiii. 62; Voltaire, *Homélies prononcées à Londres*, 356; Ehrard, *L'Idée*, 242.

110 Wellman, *La Mettrie*, 219, 231; Salaün, *L'Ordre*, 170–1.

inequality. This then, in turn, posed a vexing problem for Diderot, challenging him and his allies to show how their materialism could support the kind of values, and the species of politics, they hinted—and privately if not yet publicly announced—it could. If Man's mind is biologically determined by his physical make-up what sense does it make to say that the best as well as wisest and most philosophical way is to seek individual happiness through a life based on virtue, especially since in La Mettrie's opinion men are naturally born malicious and bad rather than good?[111] To this question Diderot had to produce a cogent and practicable answer, embodying his principle that there is an organic condition of the body underlying all our states of mind and emotional turns. Our decisions and intellectual processes, he agreed with La Mettrie, are determined by our bodily states, thought deriving from perception and perception arising, by stages, from sensation and sensation ultimately being nothing but 'un toucher diversifié'.[112] But there nonetheless remains, for Diderot, a crucial difference between order and disorder in our states of mind where, for La Mettrie, the deranged individual is as much the product of a blind nature shaping humanity as the happy, tranquil individual.[113] More mechanistic than Diderot's conception, La Mettrie's materialism places less emphasis on the idea of Man and animals as dynamic organic wholes producing harmonies and disharmonies in terms of their own make-up and conduct.[114]

Here again, Diderot is *Spinosiste*; La Mettrie is not. Diderot in effect counters La Mettrie by distinguishing between health and sickness, the balanced life and the unbalanced. The mind of the wise man who loves virtue and the good of all is not something extraneously introduced into human life by an external agent or force, is not a repressive imposition, and is not a metaphysical ideal, but rather the considered, logical stance of the balanced healthy mind combining intelligence, intuition, and understanding with properly considered self-interest.[115] Passions, says Diderot, echoing Spinoza, are internal movements. If everyone's state of mind is a constant flux yielding a mêlée of good and bad passions, the good and the bad passions, for Diderot, cannot be straightforwardly equated with those that conduce to more or less tranquillity or feelings of pleasure. Vital for survival, effectiveness, tranquillity and health is to curb and control emotions that are damaging and disrupt the proper continuities and harmony of the individual's existence, bearing in mind that everyone depends for his or her security and well-being on their relations with those around him, and society more generally.

If La Mettrie's challenge rests on reasoning derived from the world of medical experience and theory, Diderot's answer relies on a medical analogy, the ideal of the man or woman living well and in health, attuned to the world, to his or her fellows, and him- or herself. If La Mettrie's nature is driven by a blind necessity producing disorder, mistakes, and cruelty, no less than harmony, Diderot's blind nature is

111 La Mettrie, *Anti-Sénèque*, 251, 254.
112 Cherni, *Diderot*, 74; Ehrard, *L'Idée*, 234–5.
113 Ehrard, *L'Idée*, 236.
114 Ibid. 241–2.
115 Ibid. 243–4; Domenech, *L'Éthique*, 172–4; Duflo, *Diderot philosophe*, 492–3.

more of a coherent whole, a single substance in a more meaningful sense than La Mettrie's, one in which the overarching coherence of the whole gives its oneness a pervasive significance which extends also to the realms of ethics and politics. Diderot no less than Spinoza or La Mettrie banishes all teleology from our world-view. Everything in nature is a product of a blind and unintelligent creative force; nevertheless, there remains a physico-moral quasi-teleology in which the freak, misfit, despot, and deranged violate and detract from the whole and are not what nature intended.

The organic coherence of the cosmos is what makes the 'general good' conceivable and politics a proper sphere of action for the *philosophe*. It was La Mettrie's theory of the biological inequality of men, and ineligibility of most for a rational life free from credulity and prejudice, that served to justify limiting the application of philosophy to the purely private and intellectual, underpinning his thesis that neither politics, nor social organization, nor morality can be guided by the *philosophes*, or even be their proper concern. Here, as in his rejection of a secular morality based on equality, and endorsement of Frederick's despotism and arbitrary power, La Mettrie's physiological materialism reveals itself to be rather a tool of social hierarchy and political absolutism, and (according to d'Argens) even of the theologians, than a ground for general enlightenment, democratic republicanism, and equality; and this was all the more so in that for him, the few capable of understanding, and of being emancipated, are not a social or political hierarchy but ultimately a biological elite—those whose physiology and brains happen to be best organized for grasping the workings of nature. To be fully themselves such 'enlightened' men must therefore withdraw from the rest of society. La Mettrie's biological amoralism, then, could only exacerbate the tension between his system of *matérialisme* and the politics, ethics, and social theory of the radical *philosophes* leading them scornfully to reject him.[116]

That the *parti philosophique* must uphold morality and political ideals, and do so fervently, had long since been proclaimed, among others by van Leenhof, Bayle, Toland, Boulainvilliers, Radicati, Meslier, Du Marsais, and Rousset de Missy. In his *La Liberté de penser défendue* Rousset declares the unrelenting attacks of the clergy on the *esprits forts* doubly irrational in that the 'partisans de la liberté de penser' clearly desire nothing more, as he put it, than to promote 'les sentiments de la piété et de la morale la plus pure et la plus droite'.[117] One only had to consider the identities of the most illustrious recent defenders of freedom of thought, he declared, tendentiously citing 'les Lockes, les Bailes, les Tillotson, les Burnets, les Whistone; [et] Collins même l'auteur du *Discours de la Liberté de Penser*' to appreciate that this was so: what virtues 'n'a-t-on pas vû briller' in each of these great men?' What possible reason, he enquired, had their furious and implacable enemies, Jurieu, Hickes, and Bentley, ever had to reproach them with respect to morals?

116 Wellman, *La Mettrie*, 240–3; Schneewind, *Invention of Autonomy*, 463–4.
117 [Rousset de Missy], *Liberté de penser défendue*, 7–8, 29–30.

La Mettrie's positions, it has been claimed, 'seemed much too radical to be acceptable in the 1740s' and to be more unconventional than those of Diderot and his allies.[118] But there are many reasons to contest this judgement. La Mettrie, though a Spinozist in his naturalism, materialism, and critique of ecclesiastical authority, belonged to the Radical Enlightenment only in part. If there was a profoundly subversive impulse behind his system which he thought would help cure the world of theological strife and restore nature to its purity, and primacy in human life, his provoking the ire of Diderot, d'Argens, Dorthous de Mairan, d'Holbach, and other radical thinkers arose not from any advocacy of radical positions but due to political, moral, and social views which should rather be accounted conservative and timid than 'radical'. His repeated assurances that philosophy cannot change the people or influence the political world, though in part obvious imposture, combined a resigned and negative, as well as dismissive, view of most men with a desire to confine 'enlightenment' to courts and princes, and in this way hopefully mitigate the effects of despotism and intolerance. The 'unenlightened' spirits to be assailed, clergy, moralists, traditionalists, and the Galenist medical profession, were enemies only because they obstruct, needlessly from his philosophical standpoint, the flow of nature, repressing men's natural desire for personal gratification.[119]

For Diderot and the radical *philosophes*, morality can be wholly secularized, shown to correspond to Man's natural disposition, and adopted as the basis of the political and legal order.[120] Thus both the radical wing and the moderate mainstream agreed that La Mettrie's philosophical amoralism, his principle that happiness, like voluptuousness, is available to everyone equally, 'des bons comme des méchants', leaving the virtuous no happier than the immoral, a doctrine forcefully restated shortly before his death in his *Anti-Sénèque*, not only justified but positively required the *philosophes* to disown both the man and his books.[121] In the 1760s, d'Argens, having long since renounced his former collaboration with La Mettrie, spoke for all the *philosophes* in accounting him a kind of Trojan Horse,[122] someone who was not in any meaningful way one of them, insisting that all true *philosophes* were both horrified and astonished that anyone 'aussi pernicieux à la société' should pretend to 'le nom de philosophe' and cast an eternal shame on 'la philosophie'.[123]

118 Wellman, *La Mettrie*, 281; Salaün, *L'Ordre*, 251.
119 Cassirer, *Philosophy*, 70–1, 355; Morilhat, *La Mettrie*, 32–5.
120 Morilhat, *La Mettrie*, 101–2; Cherni, *Diderot*, 471; Duflo, *Diderot philosophe*, 412.
121 Vartanian, *La Mettrie's* L'Homme machine, 115.
122 Häseler, 'Marquis d'Argens', 89; Seifert, 'C'est un pays', 250.
123 Vartanian, *La Mettrie's* L'Homme machine, 115; Wellman, *La Mettrie*, 275.

32

The *Parti philosophique* Embraces the Radical Enlightenment

1. RADICALIZATION OF THE DIDEROT CIRCLE

The years 1748–52, as has often been noted, marked the onset of a new stage in the history of the French Enlightenment: the emergence of the *parti philosophique* into the open as a publicly identifiable bloc, an organized opposition not to the crown but to censorship, ecclesiastical power, institutionalized intolerance, and the cultural primacy of theology and tradition within France and, by extension, soon all Europe. The resulting generalized conflict between 'philosophy' and accepted ideas, the process of philosophical polarization and party formation which ended with setting virtually the entire camp of theologians, *dévots, gazetiers ecclésiastiques, anti-philosophes*, and most of the educational establishment publicly at odds with the *parti philosophique*, a struggle in which, from 1748, large sectors of society became involved, turned the intellectual encounter into a general struggle which ultimately permeated the whole of society, indirectly including the poor and illiterate.

Of course, this newly emerged opposition bloc seizing the attention of the reading public, and even of many who were unable to read the ensuing torrent of reading material, was an alliance of two very different camps, albeit pushed together for the time being by circumstances. The evidence very clearly shows that the French Enlightenment remained throughout a tense and deeply divided duality. But if this point has by now become familiar to the reader and no longer seems particularly extraordinary, what is truly remarkable about the drama of 1748–52 is that it was the Radical Enlightenment which at this juncture emerged as the dominant partner, squeezing the Lockean-Newtonian Enlightenment into a subordinate, marginalized status.

While the eruption of major new intellectual controversies in the years from 1748, the year of the publication of Montesquieu's *L'Esprit des lois*, down to the early1750s, has long been recognized as a decisive turning point, indeed in the past was often mistaken for the start of the French Enlightenment itself, the crucial importance of the controversies of 1748–52 lies less in any injection of new ideas—for intellectually almost nothing changed—than in a general reconfiguring of the French cultural-ideological factions and parties. This dramatic transformation of the French cultural scene occurred at this moment, due to the convergence and interaction of four simultaneous major controversies which together exerted a remarkable impact on thinking and attitudes throughout Europe. Besides the scandal over La Mettrie's *L'Homme machine*, these were the furore surrounding Montesquieu's *L'Esprit des lois*, the opening battles surrounding the *Encyclopédie*, and the disputes about biology triggered by Buffon's *Histoire naturelle*. The task of reconstructing these key 'controversies' in their full intellectual, cultural, social, ecclesiastical, and political context results, moreover, in a considerable readjustment of our historical perspective. For it emerges that despite what has so often been claimed, Locke, Newton, and the British Enlightenment had practically nothing to do with what was at issue, playing no part in the disputes, or promotion of new ideas, or the challenge to established structures of authority; nothing could be more mistaken than to suppose, as many still do, that the French High Enlightenment which emerged from the struggles of 1748–52 was in essence Newtonian and Lockean. Indeed, Voltaire, chief standard-bearer of Locke and Newton, played only a minor part in the struggle itself as in the process of party formation. Secondly, and still more important, the debates driving the process of polarization, placing the question of 'philosophy' at the top of the agenda of French cultural life, arose not from innovations in thinking, or approaches newly introduced in the 1740s, but rather from the unresolved questions left by the collisions of late seventeenth-century systems. The most conspicuous feature of the culminating controversies of the French Enlightenment in the years 1748–52, in short, is the very high degree of intellectual continuity with the key debates of the Early Enlightenment.

By the mid 1740s, 'la philosophie angloise' had been culturally dominant in France and Italy for a decade: Locke and Newton had been very widely embraced by French scholarship and the church and (leaving aside Jansenist views) there was almost no antagonism to Voltaire's Enlightenment detectable either in the ecclesiastical periodicals, papal policy, or among the secular authorities.[1] Even so implacable an anti-*philosophe* as the Jansenist polemicist, *figuriste*, and pro-*parlementaire* publicist Jean-Baptiste Gaultier, when firing off some opening shots against Voltaire in 1745–6, took good care to say nothing about Locke or Newton or, beyond reminding readers that Voltaire's *Lettres philosophiques* had been banned by the crown, criticize the Lockean-Newtonian concepts expressed in his writings, knowing full well the total irrelevance of this to the looming conflict.

Rather Gaultier adopted a wholly different strategy, accusing Voltaire of denying Original Sin and endorsing a purely secular morality based on Spinoza's maxim that men should live exclusively by reason and 'ce qui nous est véritablement utile', as well as encouraging erotic ideas by adopting Spinoza's principle that all men's actions are naturally determined by appetite and desire. All this Gaultier did by the curious procedure of linking Voltaire's Deism to one of the *philosophe*'s favourite poems, Alexander Pope's *Essay on Man* (1733), a text published in French, and

[1] O'Keefe, *Contemporary Reactions*, 34–5, 42–3, 52–3.

reviewed fairly positively by the Jesuits, in 1736. Gaultier's tactic was to link Pope's Deism (however dubiously) with Spinoza's *Tractatus theologico-politicus* from which Gaultier, in his tract, quotes a number of lengthy passages verbatim.[2] Gaultier's 152-page opening assault on Voltaire, and by implication the Jesuits,[3] of 1746 is tactically shrewd and carefully thought out: his strategy being to try to pin *le Spinosisme* on Voltaire, by expounding 'les principes de Pope et de Voltaire puisés dans Spinosa'.[4] He 'proves' his central accusation by 'demonstrating' that Pope embraces one-substance doctrine and the principle that nothing is contingent, and hence worked 'à l'imitation de Spinoza'.[5] Gaultier's argument may be nonsense but he was right about one thing: at that stage, this was the way, not talk of Locke and Newton, by which Voltaire, the Jesuits, and the French moderate mainstream Enlightenment could be undermined.

Jansenists aside, French Catholic writers in the mid 1740s were consciously reaching out to Voltaire and his allies and coming to terms with the Enlightenment of Locke and Newton; and this was also clearly the policy, since 1740, of the pope in Rome. Father Castel, protégé of Tournemine and, since 1720, natural philosophy editor of the *Mémoires de Trévoux*, the leading Jesuit mathematician and spokesman on scientific matters, had his reservations about what in Rome at this time was dubbed 'Neutonianismo', including some aspects of Newtonian physico-theology. From a letter of Castel's about Newtonianism, published in 1739, we see that he, like Tournemine before him, was still worried Newtonianism might be open to abuse, tending to 'divinise la matière' and engender a type of 'Spinosisme spirituel' paralleling the 'Spinosisme matériel' spread under cover of the name 'du célèbre Descartes'.[6] Yet, on courteous terms with Académie de Sciences since the 1720s, he remained nevertheless deeply committed to the new science and his own version of physico-theology which, like that of the Abbé de La Pluche, showed broad affinities to Newton's;[7] he also remained on friendly terms with Montesquieu, being also the priest who administered the last rites to him in February 1755, and published his dying declaration of reconciliation with the church.[8]

Castel and Montesquieu were in firm agreement, moreover, that the public scandal surrounding Voltaire's *Lettres philosophiques* in 1734 had been regrettable and damaging and also something perfectly avoidable given the prevailing consensus in society and the (official) church about natural philosophy, English empiricism, and Locke.[9] In any case, even before the Jesuits had espoused Newtonianism in the late 1730s, the earlier disputes about Newton had tended to range the Jesuits with the reforming clique of Fontenelle rather than promote any split between the church and *philosophes* as such. On the basis of 'English' ideas there were no grounds for such a split. Castel warmly endorsed English-style physico-theology in general and

[2] Gaultier, *Poëme de Pope*, 55–6, 58–9, 67, 69, 92; Ehrard, *L'Idée*, 388, 642–4.

[3] Ehrard, *L'Idée*, 643, 645, 51–2.

[4] Ibid. 133; Vernière, *Spinoza*, 505.

[5] Gaultier, *Poëme de Pope*, 72, 100–1, 104.

[6] Ibid. 151, 157.

[7] Shank, 'Before Voltaire', 388.

[8] Ehrard, *L'Esprit des mots*, 213, 215, 223, 259 n.

[9] Ibid. 220–1; Ehrard, *L'Idée*, 117–21.

remained eager to demonstrate the church's openness to the new experimental science and philosophy; he was also anxious to prevent the elements of his lingering disagreement with Voltaire and Maupertuis regarding Newton's notions of gravity and void causing unwelcome tensions or difficulties.

Still more striking, throughout the early and mid 1740s neither the ecclesiastical journals, nor the French periodicals more generally, sought to attack the *philosophes* as a group or denounce them as foes of French religion, culture, and society. While the Jansenist press simply ignored the *philosophes* (being entirely absorbed in theological polemics), a key Jesuit 'avis au lecteur' of January 1746, while noting the *philosophes* as a now formidable grouping in French society and culture, led by Voltaire and Maupertuis, showed no hint of hostility.[10] Even the Jansenist controversialist Maleville, zealously seething over the arguments of the clandestine manuscripts and such subversive compilations as Du Marsais's *Nouvelles Libertés de penser*, as well as other perceived dire threats to Catholic orthodoxy—Spinoza, Bayle, d'Argens, Le Clerc, Barbeyrac, Hobbes, Clarke, and Shaftesbury and, after its publication, Diderot's *Pensées philosophiques* (1746)—took no interest in Locke, Newton, Montesquieu, Voltaire, and Maupertuis. Before 1748, none of the latter could be presented as challenging or dangerously innovative.[11]

No less remarkable, Condillac's *Essai sur l'origine des connaissances humaines* (1746), widely assumed to be a device for spreading Locke's influence, met with no objection or opposition at all either from Father Guillaume-François Berthier (1704–82), since 1745 editor-in-chief of the *Journal de Trévoux*, or the other French journals, on grounds of encouraging materialist philosophical tendencies (which, in fact, it did). On the contrary, so convinced was Berthier, among others, that Locke's philosophical influence was desirable and benign and Condillac a staunch Lockean that it seemed impossible that Condillac could do anything other than strengthen the church's position in French thought and culture, in particular by reinforcing the principle, so vital to the Jesuits, that thought cannot be a 'modification de la matière'.[12] This was so despite widespread realization that Condillac revised Locke in significant respects. In the same spirit of boundless confidence in everything Lockean, Berthier, friend and ally of Father Castel, warmly applauded Diderot's *Essai sur le mérite* in February 1746, hailing it as an excellent work, altogether reminiscent of Locke.[13] He also reviewed the second edition of Montesquieu's *Considérations*, in 1748, wholly favourably. Nothing could be clearer than that there was no objection from the official church, or academe or the state, to the spread of the Enlightenment in France on the basis of Locke, Newton, and *la philosophie anglaise*.

The eruption of full-scale intellectual warfare in 1748 was hence hard to foresee in 1746–7; but, once begun, the effects of the upheaval were crucially affected by the

10 Masseau, *Ennemis des philosophes*, 120–1.
11 Schwarzbach, 'Les Clandestins', 168–71, 179.
12 *Mémoires de Trévoux*, 47 (May 1747), 801–3; Schøsler, *Bibliothèque raisonnée*, 54–5.
13 Diderot, *Lettre au R. P. Berthier*, 4, 9; Pappas, *Berthier's* Journal, 163.

widening rift within the ranks of the *parti philosophique* itself, a revolt against Voltaire and 'English ideas' which simultaneously came to a head in the late 1740s, with the radicalization of Diderot in particular. While the roles of d'Alembert, Buffon, Helvétius, the recently arrived d'Holbach, and others were all significant, Diderot emerged as the pre-eminent figure among the philosophical vanguard, especially through his function, from 1746, as chief editor of the *Encyclopédie*.

Diderot proved to be an intellectual strategist of genius, an extraordinarily capable operator both on a personal level and in the domain of public opinion. What Rousseau called his 'numberless acquaintances', his captivating wit, fluency, and sociability, enabled him to function almost like an orchestral conductor, concerting discussion, literary collaboration, propaganda, evasion of the censorship, and lines of communication across a wide spectrum. A much liked and generous spirit, he was the linchpin who, by 1747, knew practically everyone that counted (apart from Voltaire and the aloof Montesquieu): among his many associates were Condillac, Buffon, d'Alembert, Fontenelle, Du Marsais, Boureau-Deslandes, Helvétius, Réaumur, Rousseau, La Beaumelle, Raynal, the baron d'Holbach, almost as soon as he arrived in Paris, and, on his arrival in 1749, his henceforth lifelong friend Friedrich Melchior Grimm (1723–1807).[14]

Within the *parti philosophique*, the decisive shift to radical ideas, in terms of both Diderot's own personal intellectual development, and the group as a whole, occurred in the years 1745–8, after the appearance of his *Pensées philosophiques*. This was when he penned his philosophical allegory, entitled the *Promenade du sceptique* [Sceptic's Walk] (1747), a text which provides a glimpse of the fraught and crucially formative philosophical debates gripping the *philosophes*' radical wing, among other places at the Café Procope, Café de la Régence, and the tavern Panier fleuri, the location of weekly lunches, in the later 1740s, where Diderot met with Rousseau, Condillac, and sometimes Mably.[15] Long recognized as representing a key step in Diderot's intellectual formation—especially in his abandonment of Deism and switch to the one-substance atheistic materialism which characterized his thought for the rest of his career—the *Promenade* is a veiled, rather mysterious text recounting a four-or five-cornered intellectual tussle in the form of a dialogue placed in a pseudo-mythical ancient setting.[16]

A striking feature of the *Promenade* is that the party of the *athées* in Diderot's nomenclature, headed by 'Atheos', represents an unsatisfactory, incomplete, and rather crudely mechanistic immoral 'atheism' which has been plausibly equated with the thought of La Mettrie; for Diderot seems already to have had some 'inside' knowledge of his materialist antagonist's final position, even though the latter's *L'Homme machine* did not appear until the following year.[17] It may also include

[14] Rousseau, *Confessions*, 309–10; Pommier, *Diderot*, 104; Geissler, *Boureau-Deslandes*, 19; Roger, *Buffon*, 154; Stenger, 'L'Atomisme', 90.

[15] Diderot, *Œuvres complètes*, i. 345; Haechler, *L'Encylopédie*, 11.

[16] Venturi, *Jeunesse de Diderot*, 116; Quintili, *Pensée critique*, 158–9; Duflo, *Diderot philosophe*, 73–9.

[17] Venturi, *Jeunesse de Diderot*, 116; Vartanian, 'La Mettrie and Diderot', 168–9.

elements of an older, more moralistic brand of philosophical atheism long bandied about the Café Procope and similar places by the likes of Nicolas Boindin, a declared unbeliever whose ideas were drawn from his holy 'trinity' of Descartes, Bayle, and Fontenelle.[18] Even lower down in the author's esteem comes the party of Pyrrhonist sceptics which Diderot, with his firmly *Bayliste* rejection (or rather redefinition) of scepticism, assigns no positive role to.[19] Deism rates more highly but is represented by two contrasting figures, one of which is Cléobule, a reticent aesthete who despairs of enlightening mankind [éclairer les hommes] and who has convincingly been identified with Shaftesbury.[20]

Cléobule grants that enlightening men would, indeed, be the greatest service one could render them, were the task feasible; but, he contends, it is quite impossible. Were men crass and ignorant merely through not having learnt much, the task might be conceivable, 'mais', holds Cléobule, 'leur aveuglement est systématique'.[21] In the decisive intellectual encounter, however, the Deists are headed not by 'Shaftesbury' but by a more vigorous advocate, Phyloxène, who, we learn, preaches Newtonian providential Deism but in a hectoring, conceited manner unfitting for a true philosopher. Plainly, he stands for Voltaire or else a conflation of Voltaire, Maupertuis, and Réaumur.[22] The highly charged encounter which unfolds leads to the triumph of one particular intellectual faction, but the triumphant school of thought proves to be neither the 'atheists', nor the sceptics, nor the Newtonian-Voltairean Deists, nor the 'Shaftesbury' Deists. Rather, the debate ends, to the amazement of those assembled, with the defeat of the Newtonian-Voltaireans by 'Oribaze' and 'Alcmeon' who Diderot expressly states are *Spinosistes*.[23]

Clearly, the central issue here is Spinozism, as Venturi observed;[24] nor is this fact at all surprising, though some scholars have considered it highly perplexing.[25] The 'Spinozist' denouement to Diderot's *Promenade*, far from being inexplicable, reflects the actual process of Diderot's evolution from Voltaire's positions to Spinozism occurring at the time and is indeed essential to a proper grasp of Diderot's intellectual trajectory at this vital juncture. The first part of the *Promenade* with its uncompromising claim that revealed religion and theology cannot be either true, or part of what is meaningful and universal in human life, claims only philosophies that wholly discard theology and separate faith from reason—like Shaftesbury's Deism, Voltaire's Deism, philosophical atheism, and Spinozism—qualify for consideration by the true philosopher. The systems of Malebranche, Leibniz, Le Clerc, and Locke are all rather disdainfully excluded *a priori*, just as they doubtless were in the café discussions in Paris during the mid 1740s, as confused and irrelevant

[18] Lauriol, *La Beaumelle*, 176.
[19] Paganini, 'Avant la *Promenade*', 46; Paganini, 'Scepsi clandestina', 92.
[20] Diderot, *Promenade*, 178–9. [21] Ibid. 181; Dedeyan, *Diderot*, 304–5.
[22] Venturi, *Jeunesse de Diderot*, 117; Diderot, *Promenade*, 228.
[23] Diderot, *Promenade*, 228; Vernière, *Spinoza*, 568–70; Vartanian, 'From Deist to Atheist', 54; Trousson, *Rousseau*, 199; Quintili, *Pensée critique*, 150–1.
[24] See, for instance, Venturi, *Jeunesse de Diderot*, 117–18.
[25] Brugmans, *Diderot*, 25; Duflo, *Diderot philosophe*, 77; Quintili, *Pensée critique*, 150, 159.

precisely because they unite philosophy with theology. Seeing 'la connaissance des phénomènes de la nature' as the sole and exclusive business of philosophy, he denounced the mixing of theology with philosophy as the worst syncretism, a perfidious threat to intellectual freedom, rationality, and society. Nor was this just a question of theory and ideas. Much like Bayle, a philosopher whom he greatly admired but was prevented by the royal censorship from openly eulogizing,[26] Diderot sought to divorce all moral and social issues from theology, ecclesiastical authority, and every form of faith-based justification and authorization.

In the *Promenade*, then, not just Locke's system but all philosophical systems which accommodate, and are linked to, miracles, revelations, and theological criteria are disqualified from the outset. Supernatural agency, including a revised Newtonianism, nevertheless remains firmly on the agenda in the shape of Deist divine providence. The *athée* (and to begin with the *Spinosistes*) is indeed, overwhelmed by the eloquent discourse of the Deists. Phyloxène and his followers proclaim the 'argument from design' proven by close investigation of nature's workings, using microscopes, the intricate construction of small living bodies in particular demonstrating, as La Pluche and Réaumur urged, 'design' for a purpose and hence divine intelligence behind Creation. Given the wondrous intricacy of the minute, as well as the grandeur and overarching coherence of the universe: 'sa structure n'annonce-t-elle pas un auteur?'[27]

Yet at the very moment the Deists appear victorious, Oribaze, the chief 'Spinosiste', arises among the assembled participants, asserting that there cannot have been a Maker of the cosmos prior to the existence of physical structures and beings: if there had ever not been physical beings 'il n'y en aurait jamais' since to impart existence 'il faut agir, et pour agir il faut être'.[28] Rather than being the work of a far-seeing, intelligent Creator, the substance and coherence of the universe, he argues, must ensue from an order immanent in nature itself. Contrary to what Réaumur supposed, his laborious research on insects reveals not the truth of physico-theology, and hence religion, but only that 'la matière est organisée'. It follows, holds Oribaze, that both 'l'être intelligent et l'être corporel sont éternels', that these two dimensions make up the universe, 'et que l'univers est Dieu'.[29]

Philoxène counters by assuring the audience the *Spinosistes* are merely introducing new forms of obscurity and mystification, 'deifying' the emergence of insects, drops of water, 'et toutes les molécules, de la matière'. Oribaze denies 'deifying' matter or anything else, averring that if his adversary listened, he would appreciate he was attempting, on the contrary, to eradicate 'la présomption, le mensonge et les dieux'.[30] Already in his *Pensées philosophiques* (1746), Diderot advocates a form of scepticism quite different from that of Montaigne and the Pyrrhonists, a scepticism

[26] Gordon and Torrey, *Censoring*, 48–51; Proust, *Diderot*, 238–40.

[27] Diderot, *Promenade*, 229; Bourdin, *Diderot*, 36.

[28] Diderot, *Promenade*, 234.

[29] Ibid.; Diderot, *Correspondence*, i. 77; Bourdin, *Diderot*, 54–5.

[30] Diderot, *Promenade*, 234; Vartanian, 'From Deist to Atheist', 55; Duflo, *Diderot philosophe*, 77; Stenger, 'L'Atomisme', 80.

deriving directly from Bayle which operates chiefly against beliefs and theological doctrines. What is a sceptic, he asks? It is a philosopher, he replies, who has doubted everything which he believes and who believes only what legitimate usage of his reason 'et de ses sens lui a démontré vrai'.[31] It was this *Bayliste* anti-Pyrrhonist scepticism, labelling as delusion and mad presumption practically everything most men believe, and eschewing everything one's own independent reason and senses cannot verify, which had brought Diderot, finally, to reject his own prior Deism, as well as Newton's, Fénelon's, Réaumur's, Maupertuis's, and Voltaire's 'argument from design'. For Diderot this was decisive.

Philoxène (Voltaire) is used to success and inclined, notes Diderot, to treat everyone else condescendingly, and, hence, taken aback by this vigorous sortie on the part of an adversary 'dont il avait fait peu de cas', suddenly becomes disconcerted. Attempting to rally himself, he is all at once paralysed by the sight of 'une maligne joie', spreading on the faces all around him, prompted by hidden feelings of jealousy to which, comments Diderot, even the most philosophical of men are never altogether immune. The philosophico-historical psychology of the situation seems clear: the Newtonian-Voltairean faction, not without a certain arrogance, having dominated Parisian intellectual life for over a decade, had become accustomed to their ascendancy; but now suddenly their hegemony collapsed and the whole assembly, all the factions, enjoyed witnessing the public humiliation of the overbearing Philoxène at the hands of an antagonist whom he had treated 'assez cavalièrement'.[32]

The old-style *athées* are partly blamed for the long primacy of the Newtonian-Voltairean Deists, their thinking and discourse allegedly having been insufficiently flexible, even simplistic. For if they too maintain that 'la matière est organisée', they fail to develop this idea cogently or demonstrate that life may arise from matter and that matter and perhaps even 'son arrangement, sont éternels'.[33] A key difference between the La Mettrie *athées* and *Spinosistes*, according to Diderot, who had presumably witnessed this himself in the cafés, was that the former infer there is no moral order to uphold, and rely on a rather cynical immoralism—which is precisely what Diderot later accused La Mettrie of doing—while the *Spinosistes*, more high-mindedly, strive to uphold not the theologically deformed or conventional but the true moral order.[34]

Through the late 1740s, during the years of the great public drama over philosophy, Diderot, encouraged, as his future collaborator Naigeon later remarked, by the success his *Pensées philosophiques* enjoyed among 'les bons esprits, les seuls juges qu'il reconnût', added some further thoughts, refining these into what became his clandestine *Addition aux Pensées philosophiques*.[35] These he closeted away 'prudemment', as Naigeon put it, the notes only appearing in print in a collection of material

[31] Diderot, *Pensées philosophiques*, xxx. 27–8; Paganini, 'Avant la *Promenade*', 33–4, 46.

[32] Diderot, *Promenade*, 235.

[33] Ibid. 234; Stenger, 'L'Atomisme', 81.

[34] Stenger, 'L'Atomisme', 81; Vartanian, 'La Mettrie and Diderot', 192–3.

[35] Diderot, *Œuvres philosophiques*, 53.

which Naigeon clandestinely published, under the title *Recueil philosophique* ('Londres' [Amsterdam], 1770), in Holland more than twenty years later, though in France this *Addition* remained largely unknown until after the Revolution. Here, Diderot vigorously reaffirms his (Spinozist-Baylean) principle that reason and faith cannot be made to support each other: if reason is a gift from Heaven, and so is faith, Heaven 'nous a fait deux présents incompatibles et contradictoires'.[36] The only option, once this is grasped, is to judge faith 'un principe chimérique, et qui n'existe point dans la nature'. Any organized, structured religion relevant to all men, at all times, and in all places, he says, must be 'éternelle, universelle et évidente': clearly, none such actually exists: all religions are consequently 'trois fois démontrées fausses'. From this, he asserts, follows the total invalidity of all theological criteria no less for the fixing of moral boundaries and determining what is best in society, politics, and education than in the search for philosophical truth. Such a stance need not mean denying the utility of religion for society altogether; but in Diderot's case, it does.

The anonymous publication of his next philosophical work, with 'à Londres' falsely declared on the title page, the notorious *Lettre sur les aveugles* (1749), in effect publicly announced the decisive shift in Diderot's thinking, that is his abandonment of physico-theology, Locke, Newton, and Deism, all of which he here unequivocally rejects, and adoption of a deterministic evolutionary 'naturalisme' henceforth unambiguous and systematic.[37] As we have seen,[38] this text centres on a deathbed scene in which an expiring, blind philosopher, 'Saunderson', rebuffs the efforts of a Newtonian clergyman, emphatically invoking the 'argument from design', to persuade him that the universe was intended as it is by an intelligent and providential Creator. Saunderson, however, ends by abjuring the 'God of Clarke, Leibniz and Newton', embracing instead a vision of the universe driven by blind fatality which generates, through the activity innate in matter, a natural evolution of species without Creation or supernatural direction. Condillac's epistemology is invoked to rule out traditional forms of metaphysics, and support denial of the existence of any being, or reality, beyond the bounds of the tangible physical universe. Clearly, Diderot's new-found rigorous monism was not just un-Lockean, and contrary to Condillac, but one which, on Locke's premisses—which were also Voltaire's—Diderot had no right to draw.[39] Disagreeing, Voltaire noted in his clear, inimitable, hand, in his own personal copy of Diderot's *Lettre* preserved today in the Russian National Library in St Petersburg, that Saunderson seemed to him 'to reason very badly'.[40]

As was known in Paris at the time, Diderot's *Lettre* alludes to and recreates a recent clash over an operation performed by a German oculist on the eyes of

[36] Diderot, *Œuvres philosophiques*, 58.

[37] Vartanian, 'From Deist to Atheist', 53–4, 61; Jimack, 'French Enlightenment', 244; Cherni, *Diderot*, 63–9.

[38] Israel, *Radical Enlightenment*, 710.

[39] Wartofsky, 'Diderot', 280–6; Dupré, *Enlightenment*, 28–9; Curran, 'Diderot's Revisionism', 92; Buckley, *At the Origins*, 214–22; Roger, *Buffon*, 157.

[40] RNLP Ms. ИНВ N2635, p. 111; *Corpus des notes marginales*, iii, no. 494.

a young girl, blind from birth, presided over by the celebrated Réaumur. Réaumur, keen to confirm Locke's quasi-dualism, expected the 'experiment' to prove, from the girl's reactions, the validity of Locke's response to the 'Molyneux problem', that is the question whether a blind person who can distinguish a globe and a cube by touch can, if suddenly given sight, distinguish between the two without touching them. Locke agreed with Molyneux that, 'at first sight', a newly sighted person would not distinguish globe and cube but need a period of 'experience' before being able to do so, since our mental power to 'abstract' from, and impose order on, sense impressions, though functioning independently of the senses, needs direct experience via the relevant sense which takes time.[41]

Condillac, however, in his treatise of 1746, held that while the eye must first learn to focus, the power to distinguish would be instant with the capacity to see since the senses are closely interrelated and there is no such thing as a non-sensory power to 'abstract'; the man born blind and given sight 'will thus distinguish the globe from the cube on sight, because he will recognize in them the same ideas which he has formed by touch'.[42] This potentially anti-Lockean move which Condillac later retracted, in 1754, claiming to have earlier paid insufficient attention to Locke's argument, Diderot adopts, in the *Lettre* and again in his subsequent *Lettre sur les sourds et muets* (1751), categorically denying that judgement is an action of the soul posterior to, or distinct from, the act of perception; however, differently from Condillac, judgement here also becomes a critical reflection of perception.[43] Diderot, consequently, had been eager to attend the operation; but Réaumur prevented this in a manner which caused a row. In the *Lettre*, Diderot complains that a precious opportunity for scientific experiment had been thus lost, since no witnesses of account were present, thereby further exacerbating the quarrel.

Diderot's *Lettre* sold briskly, much to Réaumur's disgust, and brought him the praise of his many acquaintances, including that of Buffon, now on the worst terms with Réaumur. The *Lettre* also had a immediate impact in Germany, being reviewed in many German-language periodicals prior to 1750.[44] Its author was further gratified to receive his first communication from the great Voltaire, who (having no knowledge of the unpublished *Promenade du sceptique*) had no inkling that the younger man had already, in a sense, set in motion an underground struggle between their rival conceptions of enlightenment. Writing soon after the *Lettre* went on sale, Voltaire congratulated Diderot on his success but also firmly disagreed that a blind philosopher, reasoning like Saunderson, would deny the existence of a divine Creator. Had he himself been blind, he wrote, he would still have inferred, from the infinite connections of all things, the existence of an 'ouvrier infiniment

41 Locke, *An Essay*, 146; Diderot, *Œuvres philosophiques*, 128–32; Cassirer, *Philosophy*, 108–9; Aarsleff, 'Locke's Influence', 266–7; Sejten, *Diderot*, 134–6.

42 Condillac, *Essay*, 104, 107; Falkenstein, 'Condillac's Paradox', 410–12; Charrak, *Empiricisme*, 131.

43 Charrak, *Empiricisme*, 131–2; Diderot, *Œuvres philosophiques*, 81–2; Diderot, *Lettre sur les sourds*, 369, 371, 374; d'Alembert, 'Aveugles', in Diderot and d'Alembert, *Encyclopédie*, i. 873; Roger, *Buffon*, 157–8; Stenger, 'La Théorie', 108–10; Duflo, *Diderot philosophe*, 83, 128, 139–40.

44 Saada, *Inventer Diderot*, 83–5.

habile'.[45] Inviting Diderot to visit him, Voltaire desired 'passionément' to know whether *enfin* the younger man counted himself among the *ouvrages* of the divine Creator or as a portion 'nécessairement organisée d'une matière éternelle et nécessaire', a witty way of enquiring whether Diderot adhered to Voltairean-Newtonian-Lockean ideas or was now a hylozoist *Spinosiste*.[46]

Diderot's reply is not without interest given the direction of his recent writing. Assuring Voltaire that his letter marked a supreme moment of his life, and that he would answer his question, he declined to pay the requested visit for the time being, under pretext of domestic problems. (He was not to meet Voltaire, in person, until nearly thirty years later, in 1778.) His answering letter, remarkably, reiterates, in places almost verbatim, Oribaze's critique of Philoxène in the *Promenade*: if ever there had been no physical beings in the universe, there could never have been any, for physical beings are, by their nature, ontologically and conceptually, if not chronologically, prior to 'êtres spirituels'.[47] Minds, he asserts, are accordingly modes 'ou du moins des effets' of matter which, he points out, directly conflicts with Voltaire's view.[48] Both physical and spiritual substance being eternal, he concludes, with a sweeping and, in the circumstances, almost insolent Spinozistic flourish, plainly both of these simultaneously compose our universe and hence 'l'univers est Dieu'.[49]

This confirms, as Venturi saw,[50] that it was the *Spinosistes* rather than the Deists, Newtonians, and Lockeans with whom Diderot identified at the most decisive moment in his personal development. Moreover, the position he adopted in 1746–7, a deterministic, one-substance materialist *naturalisme* allied to a form of social and moral utilitarianism wholly distinct from La Mettrie's moral theory, was the philosophical stance he adhered to whilst writing the *Lettre* and throughout his maturity. The explicit Spinozism of the *Promenade*, in other words, far from indicating any 'mediating role of Spinozism' intervening between the *Pensées philosophiques* and *Lettre*, as some have suggested, or an immature vagary, as others suppose, signals rather a decisive, permanent shift from the *anglicisme* of his youth to a radical *Spinosiste* stance.[51]

2. THE 'QUARREL' OF THE *ESPRIT DES LOIS* (1748–1752)

Consequently, it is hardly surprising that Voltaire wanted nothing to do with, and totally ignored the early progress of, the *Encyclopédie*, at any rate down to the public furore which greeted publication of the first volume in 1751; and, equally, Diderot

[45] Wade, *Structure*, ii. 78; Voltaire to Diderot, 9 June 1749, in Diderot, *Correspondence*, i. 74.

[46] Diderot, *Correspondence*, i. 74; Torrey, 'Voltaire's Reaction', 1108, 1117, 1120–2; Buckley, *At the Origins*, 224–5; Trousson, *Rousseau*, 205.

[47] Diderot to Voltaire, Paris, 11 June 1749, Diderot, *Correspondence*, i. 75–80.

[48] Ibid. i. 76.

[49] Ibid. i. 77; Wartofsky, 'Diderot', 283–4; Bourdin, *Diderot*, 54–5.

[50] Venturi, *Jeunesse de Diderot*, 117.

[51] Wade, *Structure*, ii. 101; Proust, *Diderot*, 217–20; Duflo, *Diderot philosophe*, 96–109.

and his team extended no invitation to Voltaire to participate and largely ignored him.[52] But Voltaire was equally left on the sidelines with regard to the other great battles which were brewing. The year 1748, the year of Diderot's *Lettre* and Montesquieu's *L'Esprit des lois*, has traditionally been identified as a major landmark in the history of the Enlightenment, a moment witnessing a remarkable surge of publications of subversive philosophical, critical, and erotic works, marking the effective start of the long post-1750 contest between the French radical philosophical fringe and their adversaries in the church, at court, and among the public. For the first time, public controversy enveloped the entire *parti philosophique*, reconfiguring it as a publicly defined grouping, with the directors of the *Encyclopédie* emerging as the leaders of a radical tendency proclaiming *la philosophie* the path not just to genuine human knowledge but to a general improvement of humanity and a wider happiness.

Opponents loudly decried what they saw as a rising tide of materialism, naturalism, and Spinozism, for the first time portraying *l'esprit philosophique* as a concerted, immanent, and now specifically French intellectual, moral, and political conspiracy affecting the whole kingdom, something designed to undermine tradition, authority, faith, and Christian values.[53] The years 1748–52, then, may justly be described as 'an extraordinary moment' in the history of European culture and society, one in which, in the space of just a few years, the 'intellectual topography of France was transformed'.[54] But this occurred not only, or even primarily, owing to intellectual developments but also, we have seen, to the unusually fraught general political context of France at the end of the 1740s. At the close of the War of the Austrian Succession, the kingdom was thoroughly on edge owing to a whole combination of adverse factors and acute difficulties intensified by the humiliating failure of French royal diplomacy to translate French victories on the ground into tangible gains in territory, colonies, or commerce. France suffered much greater damage in trade and shipping than Britain—the Marseilles records show that 688 French vessels were lost in the Mediterranean alone during the years 1744–9[55]—and, of the two countries, experienced much the more serious general economic recession as well as colonial losses; yet, militarily, the French had won important victories in the Netherlands and in India. The fact that Britain had not done well in the fighting but somehow managed to get the better of France at the peace table, mainly the result of the acute economic pressures and strains within France, translated into a serious loss of prestige in international relations.[56]

Worse was the heavy toll in men, money, colonies, and ships which the war had exacted and the pressure of war taxation which weighed heavily on the populace, and remained in force for some time after the fighting ended, indeed had to be stepped up. In particular, the court's Controller General, Jean-Baptiste de Machault

[52] Haechler, *L'Encyclopédie*, 179–80, 186–7.

[53] Dagen, *L'Histoire*, 365, 367, 369–72; Gumbrecht and Reichardt, '*Philosophe*', 37, 40.

[54] Darnton, *Forbidden Best-Sellers*, 89–90.

[55] Riley, *Seven Years War*, 118.

[56] Anderson, *War of the Austrian Succession*, 199.

d'Arnouville, in 1749 attempted to introduce a major new tax, the *vingtième*, to be levied also on the privileged orders besides the general population, in the hope of bringing the burgeoning royal debt under control. Machault's refusal to exempt the privileged, or even the clergy, from the new taxation provoked a mood of mounting criticism and obstreperousness among the magistrates of the Paris *Parlement* which soon led on to a full-scale constitutional crisis between *parlements* and the crown.

Worst of all, though, and exacerbating all the rest, was a further resurgence of Jansenist resentment. The new archbishop of Paris (since 1746), the stubborn and pugnacious Christophe Beaumont du Repaire, in 1749, with the half-hearted backing of the court and the support of roughly two-thirds of the bishops, initiated a carefully planned repression of Jansenist supporters and clergy in Paris, seeking to intimidate the refractory lower Jansenist priesthood by denying parishioners sacraments, including the last sacraments, where unable to produce *billets de confession* signed by priests who had submitted to the bull *Unigenitus*. The result was an eruption of disaffection which also served to sharpen the struggle between the crown and the *parlements*, which were generally pro-Jansenist in sympathy and opposed the episcopate's sacramental policy. These various collisions, and especially the crown's fiscal and Jansenist entanglements, impacted also at a popular level, causing rioting in Paris in the spring of 1750.

Beaumont paraded a zeal to do battle with the Jansenists which even many of his colleagues among the constitutionary bishops deemed ill advised; but he refused to hold back.[57] An important factor here was the monarch's personal piety. Louis XV, though profoundly worried by the crisis, tended to the view, encouraged by Beaumont, that on matters such as sacraments and *billets de confession* he had no authority, in the sight of God, to interfere, other than to reject the complaints of the *parlements* against the bishops, but was obliged to defer to ecclesiastical authority.[58] As a consequence, both church and state fell into increasing disarray, a situation which made Montesquieu's *L'Esprit des lois* (1748), and the flurry of illegal lesser philosophical publications of the moment, appear more directly relevant to the fraught conjuncture in which they appeared than they actually were. Whatever their authors' original motives, many of these texts published without royal licence during these years looked like and often were part of an attempt to highlight the shortcomings of both crown and church, and pronounce on who was responsible and what should be done.

In June 1750, Voltaire anonymously published his pamphlet *La Voix du sage et du peuple*, a text renewing his attack on Jansenism but yet subsequently placed on the Index by the Vatican, for ridiculing ecclesiastical objections to the threatened loss of the church's fiscal immunities.[59] Given the dimensions of the crisis economic, constitutional, ecclesiastical, and intellectual, it was unsurprising that an English

[57] Rogister, *Louis XV*, 77–8, 80, 119–20; McManners, *Church and Society*, ii. 489–94.

[58] Van Kley, *Religious Origins*, 142–5; Van Kley, *Damiens Affair*, 121–2.

[59] [Voltaire], *La Voix du sage*, 423–4, 427; Godman, *Geheime Inquisition*, 262.

parliamentarian, disgruntled that Britain and the United Provinces had failed to press the war against France longer and with more resolution, in 1748 published a hostile tract, purporting to be by a Dutch regent, highlighting the unprecedentedly vulnerable state of France at this time. French trade and shipping, urged this writer, had been decimated to the advantage of both Protestant powers while the strain of the conflict had generated so much internal stress as to point to a fundamental crisis of confidence. 'Such a tumour was gathering in the bowels of France', asserts this pamphleteer, 'as might, if artfully nurs'd up, endanger her very existence, I mean in her present state of absolute and abject subjection to the will of an individual. It is well known that the murmurs of the French were general and loud. They are of late become as Free-Thinkers in religious matters, as you in England or we in Holland; and if well managed, and touch'd properly by your and our statesmen, might be soon brought to wish to be eased as well of the Papal as regal yoke. I could say much more of this topic. I could say what I know to be a truth as clear as Day, that such ill blood was gathering in France as made the French courtiers shudder and tremble for the consequences.'[60]

Compared to the rift within the church, fiscal resentment, problems of demobilized and injured men, loss of commerce, and diplomatic humiliation, the upsurge of illicit Deistic and radical books and pamphlets appearing in the years 1748–51 might seem a comparatively minor irritant in the eyes of the court. But philosophy was now a real political and social issue in that it underlined the elements of dysfunction threatening to induce a breakdown of the monarchy, tended to question, if not discredit, precedent, tradition, and custom as validating factors, and cast a critical eye on the ferocious but irresolvable wrangling within the church. The common factor uniting all these illegal publications was the rejection of accepted structures of authority and values and the urging of readers critically to examine existing institutions and ideas. Besides Montesquieu's *L'Esprit*, works like La Beaumelle's *L'Asiatique tolérant* ('Amsterdam' [Geneva?], 1748), Diderot's *Les Bijoux indiscrets* (1748), François-Vincent Toussaint's *Les Mœurs* (1748)—a work widely attributed at the time to 'Diderot'—La Mettrie's *L'Homme machine* issuing at Leiden in late 1747, Benoît de Maillet's *Telliamed* (Amsterdam, 1748), d'Argens's *Thérèse philosophe* (Amsterdam?, 1748),[61] the Abbé Morelly's *Physique de la beauté*,[62] and Diderot's *Lettre sur les aveugles* (1749) all appeared and circulated at this time in the capital and, in some cases, other major provincial cities and added to the mounting criticism of court, church, and social structure.

All but *L'Esprit des lois* could be safely ignored by church and state and treated as if practically no one ever read or noticed them. The contrast between France and Germany in this respect is remarkable. Diderot's *Pensées philosophiques*, widely reviewed and denounced in Germany, was discussed by none of the French journals; La Mettrie, still more widely decried in Holland and Germany, was condemned

[60] *The Genuine Speech of an Eminent Dutch Patriot*, 22–3.

[61] Conlon, *Siècle*, vi. 31.

[62] Goulemot, '1748: année littéraire', 26.

only behind the scenes in France where, in 1748, neither the *Journal des savants* nor the Jesuit or Jansenist journals even mentioned him.[63] La Beaumelle's *L'Asiatique tolérant*, written in Geneva and radical in its vigorous advocacy of a *Bayliste* conception of toleration,[64] was publicly burnt by the *Parlement* at Grenoble as a work destructive of the foundations of religion and government in 1751, but beyond Grenoble seemingly made little impression.[65] Diderot's erotic novel *Les Bijoux indiscrets* got its author placed on the police blacklist of insidious authors but could be laughed aside; the next year the same author's *Lettre sur les aveugles* appeared clandestinely in Paris, and caused a temporary stir, but never penetrated widely enough to be worth denouncing in the press.

But it was all very different with *L'Esprit de lois*, published in the autumn of 1748. Not only did this work apply a strikingly novel conceptual framework to the whole range of social institutions, from religion and marriage to types of political system and morality, but it discussed issues of absolutism versus constitutional monarchy in a manner bound to have an effect, at a moment of rising tension between crown and *parlements*. Equally important in the context, Montesquieu's book was a phenomenal publishing success, especially among the sophisticated reading public of the professional and aristocratic classes, though the *Mémoires de Trévoux* reports that its impact was such that it also became well known, at least by name, to people quite incapable of reading or understanding it.[66] Montesquieu, then, from 1748, became impossible to ignore, especially because the wide-ranging character of the work generated anxiety (and not only in France) that a sophisticated new form of political opposition had come into being and that freethinking and naturalism were fast eroding the very fabric of society. In Rome, despite Montesquieu being looked upon there favourably by the pope, an internal battle began within the Vatican over whether or not to ban *L'Esprit des lois*.[67]

Anonymously published at Geneva, to shield Montesquieu, *L'Esprit* was reissued, again anonymously (which added to the considerable annoyance it caused in government circles), by two different publishing houses in Paris, late in 1748 and in 1749, and republished four more times during the latter year alone and again in 1750. It was also clandestinely brought out at Lyons, in March 1749, with 'Leyde' [Leiden] falsely given as place of publication. It proved an immediate sensation. Likewise abroad, *L'Esprit des lois* was very widely and enthusiastically read from the outset.[68] Turgot already, within weeks of the appearance of *L'Esprit*, decribed Montesquieu as 'un des plus beaux génies de notre siècle'.[69] The moment *L'Esprit des lois* appeared, recalled La Beaumelle in 1750, it was as eagerly sought

63 Ibid. 27; Saada, *Inventer Diderot*, 71–2, 78, 80.

64 [La Beaumelle], *L'Asiatique tolérant*, pp. xxvii, 31, 35.

65 Susong, 'Montesquieu, La Beaumelle', 133; Volpilhac-Auger, 'Lire en 1748', 54.

66 *Mémoires de Trévoux*, 49 (Apr. 1749), 718.

67 Macé, 'Lumières françaises', 17, 21; Godman, *Geheime Inquisition*, 239–45.

68 D'Alembert to Gabriel Cramer, 21 Sept. 1749, in *DHS* 28 (1996), 246–7; Haechler, *L'Encyclopédie*, 46.

69 Turgot, *Recherches sur les causes*, 140.

after everywhere as it had, for years, been impatiently awaited by his friends; in fact, he asserted, everyone who was not 'Jésuite ou Janséniste, dévôt ou bel-esprit' (an admission that the real *esprits forts* were unimpressed), judged it the triumph of 'l'humanité, le chef d'œuvre du génie, la Bible des politiques'.[70]

Additionally in 1749, there were two French-language editions at Amsterdam and another at London. During 1750 a further French-language version appeared at Edinburgh as well as an English version published at London in 1750 and 1752, at Edinburgh in 1750, and Dublin in 1751. An (anonymous) Italian version appeared at Naples in 1750, bringing closer the Vatican's condemnation of Montesquieu, and a German at Frankfurt, in 1752.[71] La Beaumelle's claim that a dozen editions of *L'Esprit des lois* sold out in six months was by no means an exaggeration: for around fifteen editions had appeared by the end of 1749 in four different countries.[72] From Ireland to Italy, *L'Esprit des lois* resoundingly won the unprecedented status of being a philosophical best-seller, something which undoubtedly struck some royal officials, as well as many churchmen, as distinctly disturbing in itself: for this hardly seems to bear out Voltaire's maxim that few men both read and think. How could any work of *philosophie* become a best-seller?

Admittedly, not everyone thought so highly of it. Although d'Alembert failed to read it until September 1749, he was not overly impressed when he did, concluding that Montesquieu's factual basis was insufficient to sustain such a sweeping 'système général' cogently. Voltaire covered his two personal copies (the earlier, of the 1749 Lyons edition) with mostly disparaging annotations,[73] though he also noted that what especially won favour among French readers was Montesquieu's praise of English mixed monarchy, a sure sign that some at least were interpreting the book as political criticism.[74] Helvétius, writing to Montesquieu in December 1748, a mere few weeks after *L'Esprit* had gone on sale at Geneva, warmly complimented the author on his success but also remarked that Montesquieu seemed to him too preoccupied with how things were and insufficiently concerned with how to improve them;[75] he also warned that while the court had provisionally decided not to forbid its sale and republication, his book had deeply angered numerous highly placed persons, including several government ministers.[76]

In any case, nothing else made an even remotely comparable impact, albeit d'Argens's *Thérèse philosophe*, with its erotic-philosophical caption that 'voluptuousness and philosophy produce the happiness of the sensible man', also caused high-level irritation. Asserting the materiality of the soul and laying down a Spinozist determinism, *Thérèse philosophe* offended especially through its uninhibited celebration of sexual pleasure with its particular emphasis on the innocence of female masturbation and highly unflattering portrayal of Christianity as a perverted form

70 [La Beaumelle], *Suite de la défense*, 68; Hampson, *Enlightenment*, 128; Lauriol, *La Beaumelle*, 190.

71 Godman, *Geheime Inquisition*, 242; Courtney, '*L'Esprit des lois*', 65, 78–81; Macé, 'Lumières françaises', 18.

72 Macé, 'Lumières françaises', 78–80; [La Beaumelle], *Suite de la défense*, 69.

73 *Corpus des notes marginales*, v. 727–59.

74 Voltaire, *Œuvres complètes*, xxv. 178.

75 Lacouture, *Montesquieu*, 263–4, 285.

76 Desgraves, 'Montesquieu en 1748', 115.

of seduction and the clergy as skilled seducers. But what irritated most of all was the subversive manner of its distribution, copies being 'planted' in august places around the capital, even concealed in confessionals in the royal chapel and in the Orangerie at Versailles.[77]

The 'querelle de *L'Esprit des lois*', in short, erupted against a polemical backcloth seething with popular grievance and theological ire, as well as radical publications, rapidly becoming a great furore with wide international ramifications and a massive internal impact intensified by rising domestic political tensions. To begin with, in 1748 and 1749, those soon to join forces as adversaries of the *philosophes* did not, as yet try to coordinate a generalized, concerted campaign against *la philosophie*, Deism, or the *Encyclopédie*; nor did they yet clearly envisage the *parti philosophique* as a publicly defined group or permanent ideological foe. Rather this was to be the outcome of the reconfiguration of forces which now began. When such extremely grave charges as 'Spinozism' and naturalism first began to be levelled against Montesquieu, in the autumn of 1749, initially there was no attempt to connect his ideas with other contemporary figures in the French and German intellectual arenas or yet talk of a wider philosophical conspiracy to subvert religion, society, and the state. All this emerged, though, during the course of the furore and partly due to its cultural and political impact.

What the opening phases of the controversy clearly revealed was that the impulses in French society towards toleration, freethinking, desacralization and libertinism, welded together philosophically by earlier debates, were suddenly resurfacing in a potentially highly explosive mix of philosophy, social criticism, moral debate, and politics. A tremendous struggle was brewing. Predictably, though, neither the court, nor the bishops, universities, Jesuits, Inquisition, nor papacy took the initiative in declaring war on the irreligious *parti philosophique*; this, of course, was the work of the Jansenists. Indeed, at first, the Jesuits persevered with their declared policy of conciliation and bridge-building while the bishops preferred to stick to their conflict with the Jansenists.

Following the *rapprochement* between Voltaire and the Jesuits in the mid 1730s, and their welcoming his *Élémens* in 1738, the *Mémoires de Trévoux*, conscious no doubt of the heavy price the order had formerly paid in lost prestige for long opposing Cartesianism prior to 1720, aspired to remain as conciliatory and flexible as they could regarding the new leading lights of philosophy, natural philosophy, and erudition, as indeed did the now predominantly Newtonian and Lockian Sorbonne.[78] An ardent enthusiast for Locke's conception of rational religion,[79] and physico-theology, Father Berthier continued, throughout the period from 1734 down to the end of the 1740s, to see no danger in keeping up friendly relations with the *parti philosophique* defined as the *parti* of Voltaire, Montesquieu, Maupertuis, Turgot, and Réaumur. However, this papal, episcopal, and Jesuit moderation entailed

[77] Darnton, *Forbidden Best-Sellers*, 90–114; Goulemot, '1748: année littéraire', 25.

[78] O'Keefe, *Contemporary Reactions*, 34–5; Roger, *Buffon*, 185; Pappas, *Berthier's* Journal, 53, 67, 88–92, 96.

[79] Pappas, *Berthier's* Journal, 201–2, 220–2.

appreciable difficulties with the out-and-out *dévots* both within the Vatican and more generally. It was this which gave the clandestine Jansenist periodical *Nouvelles ecclésiastiques*, headed, since 1732, by the Abbé Fontaine de La Roche, its opportunity publicly to brand the Jesuits, anti-Jansenist bishops, and Sorbonne alike as lamentably half-hearted, mediocre, and intellectually incompetent defenders of the faith.[80]

The charge that the official church and scholarly establishment, as well as the court and aristocracy, were making too many concessions to, and excessive compromises with, highly pernicious philosophical systems, being more concerned with defending their influence and privileges than true Catholic doctrine, discipline, and moral values, was to prove a devastating weapon both socially and intellectually. The clear implication, as already in Gaultier's *Poëme de Pope* (1746), was that the Jesuits were the allies of Voltaire and were hence serving as accessories to the spread of irreligion and Deism in France. Consequently, as La Roche rather brutally expressed his point in January 1746, the Jesuits were now at best 'moitié Chrétiens, moitié payens'.[81] Until 1748, the Jansenists had been too engrossed in their feud with the episcopate and the Jesuits to divert energy to distracting wrangling about erudition and philosophy, and despite their 1746 denunciation of Voltaire as a *Spinosiste* had not yet openly declared general war on the *parti philosophique* as such, and the tensions over philosophy within society had not been great enough to make such a strategy worth their while. But this changed when, in 1749, the Jansenist press suddenly instigated a general offensive against pernicious 'philosophy', relentlessly targeting not Voltaire, Locke, Newtonianism, or 'English ideas', nor, indeed, initially Diderot, Buffon, or La Mettrie (who were still thought best ignored), but rather Montesquieu portrayed as the mouthpiece of the *Spinosistes*.

The real issue confronting religion, society, morality, and state in France, contended the Jansenist press (accurately enough), was the challenge of Spinoza and Bayle. Earlier, during the first months of the 'querelle de *L'Esprit des lois*', the *Mémoires de Trévoux*, though uneasy about Montesquieu's attitude to religion, as well as his treatment of the varieties of marriage, different moralities, apparent praise of Julian the Apostate, and vigorous support for toleration, displayed a cool determination to avoid clashing with Montesquieu and his acolytes and made no effort to declare him an enemy of the faith. On the contrary, the initial Jesuit reaction combined some mild criticism of detail with praise for his learning and written style.[82] Father Castel was nevertheless sufficiently worried by the signs of a possible major eruption, and by Montesquieu's failure to confide in him fully or early enough, to step up his close collaboration with the latter among other steps to try to head off a major collision.[83]

[80] Roger, *Buffon*, 185–6.

[81] Ibid. 42–3, 77; *Nouvelles ecclésiastiques* (1746), 2 (Jan.); [La Beaumelle], *Suite de la défense*, 67; Susong, 'Montesquieu, La Beaumelle', 115–16.

[82] *Mémoires de Trévoux*, 49 (Apr. 1749), 719, 735, 740–1; Pappas, *Berthier's* Journal, 65, 67; Cottret, *Jansénismes*, 60; Masseau, *Ennemis des philosophes*, 121–2.

[83] Ehrard, *L'Esprit des mots*, 22–3; Desgraves, 'Montesquieu en 1748', 115–16.

Montesquieu's secularism and advocacy of toleration were certain to complicate life for those many Catholic priests sympathetic to the aims of the moderate *philosophes*. Particularly unfortunate, from their standpoint, was Montesquieu's thesis that minorities adhering to tolerated opinions are usually 'plus utiles à leur patrie' than those who conform to the dominant faith,[84] an obvious plea for greater appreciation as well as a wider toleration of Jansenists, Protestants, and Jews bound to be read as criticism of crown, church, and society. Though expressed relatively discreetly in *L'Esprit des lois* itself, this idea was immediately recycled in more bracing terms in La Beaumelle's *L'Asiatique tolérant*. The argument that religious minorities, being cut off from court favour and honours, devote themselves more industriously to commerce and the crafts, instead, and that the Huguenots and Jews are, therefore, more useful to society than most others, possessed a logic as odious to defenders of the religious and social status quo as it was welcome to members of the long oppressed religious minorities.

Then, in October 1749, the Jansenists, seized, as La Beaumelle put it, by a paraxysm of 'saint enthousiasme', initiated a public onslaught on *L'Esprit* as a subversive work of philosophical naturalism, permeated by *Spinosisme* and wholly incompatible with a Christian society.[85] The Jansenist critique, reprinted the following April, in the Amsterdam edition of the *Journal des savants*, simultaneously accused the Jesuits of responding to *L'Esprit des lois*, in their review the previous April, in an irresponsibly non-committal fashion highly damaging to a Catholic nation. Jansenist complaints that the Jesuits were combating irreligion and naturalism but 'très-foiblement'[86] thus became incorporated into a wider Jansenist strategy, implying that it was they, not the Jesuits or the Sorbonne (or, indeed, the papacy), who were the true champions of society's holy fight against the raging tide of *Spinosisme*, sexual libertinism, pornography, republicanism, and naturalism. Following the example of Philippe-Louis Joly's *Remarques critiques sur le Dictionnaire de Pierre Bayle* (Paris, 1748), the chorus of angry condemnation which had so suddenly started up particularly stressed the links between the spread of intellectual and moral libertinism, thereby intensifying the now head-on collision between *la philosophie* and Jansenist pressure for moral reform. As in Gaultier's *Poëme de Pope* of 1746, the blame for the crisis of irreligion in France was pinned squarely on Spinoza and Spinozism, and the subversive literary-sexual libertinism of Bayle, a threat reportedly nurtured in France by Bayle's innumerable 'partisans' and a blind predilection in his favour among a 'multitude de personnes' who think themselves free of prejudgement and prejudice.[87]

Stepping up the campaign, in October 1749, the Abbé de La Roche denounced Montesquieu as a follower of 'natural religion' and purveyor of *Spinosisme* infused with the pernicious influence of Bayle, launching a campaign in which the *Journal*

[84] [La Beaumelle], *L'Asiatique tolérant*, 63.

[85] [La Beaumelle], *Suite de la défense*, 69; Havinga, *Nouvelles ecclésiastiques*, 66; Pappas, *Berthier's* Journal, 68, 70; Masseau, *Ennemis des philosophes*, 115–16; Goulemot, '1748: année littéraire', 19.

[86] O'Keefe, *Contemporary Reactions*, 77.

[87] [Joly], *Remarques critiques*, pp. vii–x.

des savants and, then, Jesuit *Mémoires de Trévoux* found themselves, through pressure of public opinion, compelled to join. Bayle was especially decried for his deviousness and 'mauvaise foi' [bad faith].[88] Throughout the great controversies of 1748–52, Spinoza and Bayle were indeed continually linked as the two publicly declared primary philosophical targets of *anti-philosophie*.[89] Meanwhile, throughout 1748–9, official concern was reflected in a wave of detentions of subversive pamphleteers, authors, *libraires*, printers, and even Sorbonne professors due less to the effect of any particular books than the circulation of scurrilous and politically motivated verses and libels and the nervous state of the court and capital at the time.[90] The repression was prompted as much as anything by a backlash in Parisian society at the flurry of irreligious, 'philosophical', and erotic books suddenly proliferating all around and a desire to deflect criticism from the court. Among those arrested was Diderot, taken into custody on 24 July 1749.

The basis of the charge of 'Spinozisme' was that Montesquieu, challenging traditional notions of what laws and systems of morality are, depicts 'les mœurs' as the natural context of habit, usage, and attitude in a society, and something which determines the evolution of its laws, customs, and social relations.[91] What Montesquieu defines as the 'esprit général' of a people not only appears as the prime agent of social change but is shaped by blind and necessary forces, often climatic; these climactic and other unknowing natural factors govern a universe in which God, or at least the God of the Bible and of revelation, appears to play no role and miracles and the miraculous are seemingly irrelevant to human existence.[92] A satirical poem preserved at Grenoble and entitled 'L'Esprit de *L'Esprit des lois*' summed the matter up by proclaiming Montesquieu's message as being that 'le climat seul est l'arbitre des Dieux et du Gouvernement'.[93] It was especially this aspect of Montesquieu's thought, stressed by the *gazetiers ecclésiastiques*, which led subsequently to the banning of *L'Esprit* in Turin and Vienna in 1750, and, after a long internecine battle in the Vatican, its being placed on the Index in November 1751.[94]

Montesquieu's published defence of *L'Esprit des lois*, written against his critics, and in particular the Jansenists, after consulting his allies, was anonymously published at Geneva in February 1750. Rebutting the accusations of naturalism, determinism, and *Spinosisme* and alleged partiality for Bayle, rather than responding to what his more sympathetic readers identified as basic difficulties of argument, or errors of scholarship, he still had at this point, before the papal ban, good prospects of winning sections of the church round and did in fact succeed with a good many

88 Ibid. pp. v–vi; d'Alembert, 'Éloge de Montesquieu', 27; Holberg, *Remarques*, B6; Havinga, *Nouvelles ecclésiastiques*, 67–9; Glaziou, *Hobbes en France*, 71–2; Goyard-Fabre, *Montesquieu*, 127; Goulemot, '1748: année litterarire', 28.

89 Cottret, *Jansénismes*, 60–2; Masseau, *Ennemis des philosophes*, 116; Lacouture, *Montesquieu*, 295–6.

90 Rousseau, *Confessions*, 292–5; Saada, *Inventer Diderot*, 84.

91 Saada, *Inventer Diderot*, 84; Krause, 'History', 238.

92 Benrekassa, 'Mœurs', 172–3; Ehrard, *L'Idée*, 691–2, 718; Bonacina, *Filosofia ellenistica*, 99.

93 Larrère and Volpilhac-Auger (eds.), *1748, l'année*, 164.

94 Borghero, 'L'Italia in Bayle', 18; Israel, *Radical Enlightenment*, 12, 108; Haechler, *L'Encyclopédie*, 47.

clergy, including figures high in the papal curia.[95] It was absurd, he contends, to charge him with *Spinosisme*, when he expressly denies blind fatality had produced 'tous les effets que nous voyons dans le monde' and clearly avoids attributing the formation of 'des êtres intelligents' to a blind fatality lacking intelligence. Had he not repudiated mechanistic determinism in favour of 'free will', or soul?[96] His view of God's relationship to the universe, he claimed, is that of a Creator and *conservateur* who ordains and upholds laws which he understands because he has created them out of his wisdom. Montesquieu claims further to be fighting Spinozism by demonstrating that the laws of justice and equity are prior to all positive laws made by men and that the truth that impresses the idea of a divine Creator on our minds and carries us to him is the first 'des lois naturelles par son importance'.[97] In speaking, as his enterprise obliged him to do, a good deal about Christianity he had sought not to impugn faith but rather enhance the consideration and respect in which religion is held. How *could* he justly be denounced as a *Spinosiste*, he complained, when he continually combats Bayle's paradox 'qu'il vaut mieux être athée qu'idolâtre', a principle, he agrees, from which atheists draw the most pernicious consequences.[98]

On its appearance, Father Castel wrote enthusiastically to Montesquieu, reporting that he was urging all his Jesuit colleagues to read his *Défense* and was assuring them of Montesquieu's esteem and love 'for all of us'.[99] Though a model of prudent restraint, and one that convinced many liberal clergy that the baron did indeed view *le Spinosisme* with detestation and horror, Montesquieu's *Défense*, nevertheless, predictably only further stoked up the flames of controversy widening the scope of the *querelle*.[100] While the Jesuit review, published the same month, rebuked him on some points but still kept criticism to a minimum,[101] the *Nouvelles ecclésiastiques* assailed Montesquieu with renewed virulence in April and May. Unmoved by his disavowal of Spinozism, the *Nouvelles ecclésiastiques* retorted that Montesquieu's remarks on 'the laws' which God follows in governing the world show that to his mind these are 'invariables' just like the fatal necessity of the philosophical atheists. If Montesquieu were to be believed, admonished La Roche, miracles would no longer be miracles but 'des suites nécessaires des loix générales', which is what Spinoza undertakes to prove in the sixth chapter of his *Tractatus theologico-politicus* while with consummate insolence claiming that he too is rebutting 'atheists'.[102]

95 Bonacina, *Filosofia ellenistica*, 99; Courtney, 'Montesquieu and Natural Law', 50; Negroni, 'Le Rôle', 50; Godman, *Geheime Inquisition*, 240.

96 Montesquieu, *Œuvres complètes*, 808–9; Krause, 'History', 238–40, 261.

97 Montesquieu, *Œuvres complètes*, 809; *Nouvelles ecclésiastiques* (1750), 66 (24 Apr.); Glaziou, *Hobbes en France*, 76; [La Beaumelle], *Suite de la défense*, 121.

98 [La Beaumelle], *Suite de la défense*, 120–1; Montesquieu, *Œuvres complètes*, 809; Niderst, 'Modernisme', 310.

99 Pappas, *Berthier's* Journal, 70.

100 [La Beaumelle], *Suite de la défense*, 69–73; Lauriol, *La Beaumelle*, 186; Niderst, 'Modernisme', 310–11; Ehrard, *L'Esprit des mots*, 223.

101 *Mémoires de Trévoux*, (Feb. 1750), 532–41; Diderot, *Lettre au R. P. Berthier*, 4.

102 *Nouvelles ecclésiastiques* (1750), 66–7 (24 Apr.) and 68 (1 May).

Spinoza's argument that nothing happens in nature which contravenes, or fails to accord with, or is not an infallible consequence of, *loix universelles* exactly converges, held La Roche, with Montesquieu's key principle. Jesuits might be amenable to such ruinous notions; but as for the Jansenists, 'nous soutenons hautement que les miracles ne sont point les effets des loix ordinaires'.[103]

Many pens were taken up on Montesquieu's behalf, of course, but not always, in this fraught atmosphere, in ways which were to his liking. According to La Beaumelle—rather unfairly bracketing the Jansenists and Jesuits together—the Catholic press had violated the first rule of the erudite periodicals' code and, instead of adjudicating arguments with scholarly impartiality, had, with their harsh, sweeping accusations, become a form of censorship.[104] Also appearing in May 1750 was an anonymous pamphlet the acidic style of which, widely departing, it was noted, from Montesquieu's 'modération philosophique', smacked unmistakably of Voltaire. Although originally, in March 1749, one of *L'Esprit*'s detractors, publicly (if anonymously) Voltaire was keen to join the counter-attack against Jansenism and show solidarity with Montesquieu if only for his own purposes, that is he championed Montesquieu by emphasizing his debt to Locke and advocating Deistic natural religion, clearly implying that this was also Montesquieu's creed. With brilliant sarcasm, Voltaire thanked the *Nouvelles ecclésiastiques* for alerting everybody to such fearsome perils as the spread of an 'esprit de tolérantisme qui est la ruine du monde' and a philosophy which will doubtless destabilize whole kingdoms and instigate civil wars; he concludes by congratulating the editor of the *Nouvelles ecclésiastiques* on being not just the most implacable enemy to be found of the *Esprit des lois* but surely of 'toute sorte d'esprit'.[105]

Voltaire mockingly suggested that *L'Esprit des lois* should be immediately burnt along with all the writings of Bayle, Pope, and Locke. Thanks to the *Nouvelles*, he added, 'as soon as I shall see a wise man who, everywhere in his philosophy recognizes the Supreme Being, and venerates Providence in what is infinitely large, as well what is infinitely small, in the Creation of worlds no less than that of insects, I shall conclude it is impossible this man is a Christian'.[106] Although Voltaire does mention that Montesquieu stood accused, along with the English poet Pope—and, by allusion, Voltaire—of being 'disciples de Spinosa' and adhering to Bayle's principles,[107] his real concern, as the exasperated tone of the pamphlet suggests, was that while France was now experiencing the greatest furore over philosophy, science, and religion hitherto seen, only Montesquieu, Spinoza, and Bayle were centre stage, with he himself, Locke, and Newton being largely ignored. Apart from lambasting the Jansenists, the main point of Voltaire's pamphlet seemed to be to divert attention

[103] Ibid. 67; Froeschlé-Chopard, 'Les *Nouvelles ecclésiastiques*', 83–4.

[104] [La Beaumelle], *Suite de la défense*, 73.

[105] [Voltaire], *Remerciement sincère*, 2; [Boulenger de Rivery], *Apologie de* L'Esprit des loix, 13; Lauriol, *La Beaumelle*, 186; Ehrard, *L'Esprit des mots*, 198; Ehrard, 'Voltaire', 941–2; Conlon, *Siècle*, vi. 309.

[106] [Voltaire], *Remerciement sincère*, 2; Lacouture, *Montesquieu*, 287–8.

[107] [Voltaire], *Remerciement sincère*, 1.

back to Locke, providential Deism, and himself, which, however, nobody else seemingly thought relevant.

Relations between Voltaire and Montesquieu had been strained for some time; and it was highly inconvenient to the latter that just when he published his public disavowal of *Spinosisme* and 'natural religion', Voltaire should assail the Jansenists using highly provocative language seemingly confirming their charge that he was a Deist and naturalist.[108] Voltaire employed imagery which graphically suggested, even if only in burlesque, and to ridicule the Jansenists, that philosophy was indeed now revolutionizing France, and all the world. It made sensational reading but did nothing to rescue Montesquieu from what, for him, was a most disconcerting predicament. It was at this point that La Beaumelle, having arrived in Paris from Geneva, began to compose his continuation of Montesquieu's *Défense*, doing so in consultation with his hero. This tract was completed in September 1750 and, since no licence for publication could be obtained in France, dispatched for publication to Amsterdam.[109] This too appeared anonymously and on its appearance, the editors of the *Nouvelles ecclésiastiques* and other journals supposed, not unnaturally, but mistakenly, that this was a further intervention by Montesquieu himself, a supposition which dragged the latter still deeper into difficulties over Spinozism, materialism, and determinism. For it was here that La Beaumelle tried to detach Spinoza's toleration theory from the rest of his philosophy, arguing that Spinozist full toleration had now become compatible with a Christian standpoint.

Since the 1720s, a growing *de facto* religious toleration, defended by the *philosophes*, was a fact of life in France; something the *dévots* had little choice but to put up with. But some participants in the controversy felt Montesquieu went far beyond advocating a limited religious toleration and, while stopping short of the comprehensive toleration of Bayle or Spinoza, was nevertheless recommending a general 'liberté du raisonnement',[110] a feature deemed generally characteristic of libertine systems. Against this, La Beaumelle countered that in the new French context, under Louis XV, this particular strand of *Spinosisme* should no longer be considered shocking, atheistic, or undesirable and could now be safely detached from the rest of Spinoza's philosophy. Spinoza, contends La Beaumelle, in his defence of Montesquieu of 1751, expounds atheism only in his *Ethics*, there being no trace of his 'système impie' in the *Tractatus thelogico-politicus*, aspects of which, like the impressive argument for toleration and freedom of thought, could now respectably be recommended for French society, as Montesquieu does, without embracing Spinoza's impious system more generally: 'si c'est-là être Spinosiste', asserts La Beaumelle, more strikingly than accurately, 'tout bon citoyen, tout bon Chrétien doit être Spinosiste'.[111] This was playing with fire and directly into the hands of the Jansenists and *dévot* foes of Benedict XIV and certainly angered Montesquieu.

[108] [Voltaire], *Remerciement sincère*, 1–2; Ehrard, *L'Esprit des mots*, 198–9.

[109] Lauriol, *La Beaumelle*, 189; Havinga, *Nouvelles ecclésiastiques*, 73.

[110] Haringa, *Nouvelles ecclésiastiques*, 135; Cottret, *Jansénismes*, 185.

[111] [La Beaumelle], *Suite de la défense*, 119–20, 136; Lauriol, *La Beaumelle*, 193.

What mattered from a theological standpoint, urged La Beaumelle, was that Montesquieu refuses to reduce Man to the status of a 'machine' or 'automate, un individu esclave des loix du monde matériel', despite the claims of his Jansenist critics.[112] As for the charge that he eulogizes Bayle, designating him 'un grand homme', La Beaumelle, like Montesquieu himself, retorts that everyone knew Bayle had 'un grand esprit dont il avait abusé', assuring readers that Montesquieu combats Bayle's errors and *sophismes* no less assiduously and competently than Spinoza's.[113] Predictably, the Jansenists then cited this sequel to his defence of *L'Esprit des lois*, to show that 'Montesquieu' claims Spinoza reasons like a 'Christian philosopher' and does so in the very text [the *Tractatus theologico-politicus*] where he lays down the foundations of his deadly 'atheism'. Spinoza defines the laws of nature in the same way as Montesquieu, they reiterated, and expounds 'la tolérance la plus affreuse en matière de religion' that exists, and with this Montesquieu now publicly proclaims that he is in entire agreement.[114] Gaultier afterwards followed this up with a tract affirming that there was nothing new about Montesquieu's *Spinosisme* and that the *Lettres persanes* (1721) had already been permeated with this fatal poison.[115]

The 'Querelle de *L'Esprit des lois*' culminated, in August 1750, when the Sorbonne announced that a panel of commissioners had been named to examine Montesquieu's text along with Buffon's *Histoire naturelle*—the first three volumes of which had been published in 1749 and which was also an immediate and outstanding success in the bookshops, indeed in France was destined to become the best-selling publication of the century.[116] Buffon's volumes, though greeted initially by the Jesuit journal with almost unmitigated praise, and by the *Journal des savants* with only hints of protest, were soon likewise squarely accused, by the Jansenists and Sorbonne, of promoting materialism and naturalism as well as rejecting biblical chronology and impugning physico-theology.[117] Diderot, with whom Buffon had been friendly for some years, and in whose research and ideas he was intensely interested, had studied the proofs and compiled notes on Buffon's volumes whilst in prison at Vincennes (with his feud with Réaumur at its height), although his notes were then confiscated by the police and destroyed.[118]

Despite a substantial list of charges, the inquest into Buffon remained both tactically and doctrinally subordinate to the larger controversy surrounding Montesquieu. Actually, there was scant desire to make an example of Buffon for he was of even higher social status than Montesquieu and only slightly less adroit at veiling his materialist views, besides which he had previously received even more

112 [La Beaumelle], *Suite de la défense*, 140.

113 Montesquieu, *Œuvres complètes*, 811; Holberg, *Remarques*, B6; [La Beaumelle], *Suite de la défense*, 128–30.

114 *Nouvelles Ecclésiastiques* (1752), 91–2 (4 June).

115 [Gaultier], Lettres persanes *convaincues*, 34–6, 101; Israel, *Radical Enlightenment*, 12, 729.

116 Hazard, *European Mind*, 156; Roger, *Buffon*, 184.

117 *Mémoires de Trévoux*, 49 (Sep. 1749), 1853–72; *Journal des savants* (Oct. 1749), 648–57; *Nouvelles ecclésiastiques* (1750), 120 (1 May), (1751), 21–3 (6 Feb.); d'Alembert, 'Éloge de Montesquieu', 27; Ehrard, *L'Esprit des mots*, 284; Montesquieu, *Œuvres complètes*, 823; O'Keefe, *Contemporary Reactions*, 79–80.

118 Roger, *Buffon*, 199.

praise than Montesquieu from the Jesuits.[119] But precisely this also ensured that he would remain at least a subsidiary target of the anti-philosophical campaign waged in the pages of the Jansenist press. Here he was charged with flagrantly contradicting the Book of Genesis, ruining morality, and dishonouring God, by reducing Man to much the same status as the animal world, treating all men as in some sense equivalent, and denying the Creation as a unitary process, his fish and shellfish, for example, existing for thousands of centuries before the appearance of plants and animals.[120]

By late 1750, the Sorbonne had identified fourteen objectionable propositions in Buffon. Both author and university wished to resolve matters with as little further commotion as possible and, once Buffon had made the required public gesture of submission in April 1751, signing various documents declaring his unqualified acceptance of what Scripture says about Creation, the immortal soul, and Man, his perfunctory retraction and apology, however hypocritical, were immediately accepted, reportedly by 115 votes out of 120, by the full convention of the Sorbonne's theology faculty. According to Voltaire, the Sorbonne was also prompted to smooth things over quickly through fear of appearing ridiculous to the public, given the enthusiasm for both Montesquieu and Buffon among sophisticated readers.[121] Printed later, with the preface to the fourth volume of the *Histoire naturelle*, in 1753, Buffon's retraction was also accepted with good grace by the Jesuits. Less easily mollified, however, were the Jansenists and the thoroughly incensed Réaumur, who refused to desist from his behind-the-scenes campaign to undermine Buffon.[122] His main success in this regard was to inspire a long and detailed anti-Buffon diatribe, mainly by his ally the Oratorian Father Lelarge de Lignac. This text, which appeared anonymously, with 'Hambourg' falsely printed on the title page, in 1751,[123] though thoroughly despised by Diderot, and widely criticized, was warmly applauded by the Jansenist public and the *Nouvelles ecclésiastiques*.

Montesquieu, meanwhile, inspired by Buffon's aristocratic adroitness, was equally keen to assure the Sorbonne of his spirit of Christian contrition, likewise offering whatever clarifications the theologians judged necessary. However, the examination of his book dragged on for months, attention still focusing on the allegedly Spinozistic determinism of his views on climate. When, finally, matters drew to a conclusion, Montesquieu had to accept a substantial list of deletions and revisions, obligatory in all subsequent authorized printings, especially regarding influence of climate on religion and morality, and the role of virtue in monarchies, as well as alter remarks about Aristotelianism, the Aztec Emperor Montezuma, Julian the Apostate, polygamy, and suicide. Finally, he had to modify his comment

119 Roger, *Buffon*, 185–6; Pappas, 'Buffon matérialiste?', 237, 239; Masseau, *Ennemis des philosophes*, 115.

120 *Nouvelles ecclésiastiques* (1751), 1–3 (6 Feb.); Lelarge de Lignac, *Lettres à un Amériquain*, 3rd Letter, 6, 11, 15–16, 18–19; Roger, *Life Sciences*, 435–6; 471, 478; Roger, *Buffon*, 185–7.

121 Roger, *Buffon*, 188; Voltaire, *Lettres à son altesse*, 363; Voltaire, *Œuvres complètes*, xxv. 178.

122 Pappas, 'Buffon matérialiste?', 240–2; Froeschlé-Chopard, 'Les *Nouvelles ecclésiastiques*', 84–5.

123 Roger, *Buffon*, 190–3; Cherni, *Diderot*, 221–2.

about the English king Henry VIII reforming the church in England, changing 'suppressing the monks, an idle species', to suppressing the monks whom he considered 'une nation paresseuse'. With his public submission, Montesquieu's apologies too were formally accepted,[124] albeit not in the Vatican where, after a long internal battle, and despite Benedict's sympathy and the French ambassador's intercession on Montesquieu's behalf, *L'Esprit* was finally manœuvred onto the Index by the Counter-Enlightenment cardinals, led by Lorenzo Ganganelli (the future Pope Clement XIV), in November 1751.[125]

124 Montesquieu, *Œuvres complètes*, 828–9; [La Beaumelle], *Suite de défense*, 115, 118.
125 Israel, *Radical Enlightenment*, 12; Godman, *Geheime Inquisition*, 239–47.

33

The 'War of the *Encyclopédie*': The First Stage (1746–1752)

Diderot's situation at the end of the 1740s was indeed embattled. The atmosphere in the country, and Paris especially, was unusually tense. The interruption in the work on the *Encyclopédie*, by the summer of 1749 already a vast and diversifying body of up-to-date material on all the arts, sciences, and crafts, gravely threatened the whole project. Serious in itself, his suspected authorship of the anonymously published *Lettre sur les aveugles* with its clear materialistic and atheistic tendencies, while precipitating his incarceration at Vincennes under a royal *lettre de cachet* on 9 July 1749, was by no means the sole reason for his arrest. Rather it capped a considerable list of complaints, and charges of illicit publication, which the Paris police, having had him under surveillance for some time, had gradually accumulated.

The 36-year-old *philosophe* was now a prominent figure in Parisian intellectual life, an *érudit* and café personality of exceptional range, intellectual acuteness, and versatility, as well as one of the more experienced editors and compilers in the capital. It was therefore with some justification that the consortium of publishers investing in the project of the *Encyclopédie* reacted with unusual consternation to his arrest. Jointly petitioning the comte d'Argenson, pleading for his release, they styled Diderot an 'homme de lettres' of acknowledged merit and probity who alone was capable of controlling such a vast enterprise, 'et qui possède seul la clef de toute l'opération;'[1] for it was true that it was he who had all along, and latterly more and more, shouldered most of the editing burden, rather than his (then close) friend d'Alembert who prior to 1751 was still nationally and internationally the better known of the two.[2]

Interrogated at Vincennes by the lieutenant-general of police, Berryer, on 31 July, Diderot initially stuck to his refusal to admit any offence, denying all knowledge of the anonymously published *Pensées philosophiques*, *Bijoux indiscrets*, and *Lettres sur les aveugles*, claiming he had been unjustly arrested and that various prominent persons, Mme Du Châtelet, d'Alembert, Buffon, the aged Fontenelle, and Voltaire among them, would vouch for his good character. It was not until mid August 1749

[1] Diderot, *Correspondance*, i. 81; Venturi, *Jeunesse de Diderot*, 170–1, 178; Diderot, *Œuvres complètes*, i. 278.

[2] Gordon and Torrey, *Censoring*, 12–13.

that he became more cooperative, admitting being the author of the three works in question, terming them 'des intempérances d'esprit qui me sont échappées', and engaging his honour that they were the only ones and would be his last. Throughout his period in prison, a frantic Rousseau, then his closest ally, experienced bouts of extreme agitation at the prospect of seeing his friend and mentor languishing for years in prison. Classified, as his police file puts it, as a thoroughly subversive writer 'plein d'esprit, mais extrêmement dangereux', Diderot, his wife, and Rousseau had every reason to fear a much longer spell of imprisonment than he actually received and, in other circumstances, this might well have been his fate. He was released, after three months in custody, on 3 November 1749, under stringent oath of better behaviour, as a gesture to various powerful patrons, including the prison governor (who became another of his innumerable 'friends') and especially the publishers whose investments in the *Encyclopédie* were considerable.[3]

Initiated, in 1745, by a consortium of publishers who thought originally merely in terms of a French equivalent of Chambers's *Cyclopaedia* of 1728, Diderot had originally been taken on, in December 1745, like d'Alembert (who was needed to oversee the articles on science and mathematics), as a mere editorial assistant. Almost from the first, though, these two rapidly expanded their roles and infused the project with more grandiose ambitions. By the time the incompetent original chief editor, the Abbé Gua de Malves, withdrew in October 1747, it was already clear the two young *philosophes*, had *de facto* gained editorial control of what was fast becoming a very different sort of compendium from that originally envisaged, one destined to become the most innovative and influential publishing project of the Enlightenment.[4]

Warned by the authorities at the time of his release that the most serious consequences would ensue were he again to offend by publishing writings irreligious or 'contraire aux bonnes mœurs', Diderot was left in no doubt that he must scrupulously avoid whatever could lead to further encounters with the police and his rearrest. Nothing could have been clearer than that dire consequences would follow, not just for his wife and child, and friends, but for the great enterprise and its publishers, should he offend further and return to prison.[5] But though he became wilier and more careful, temperamentally he simply could not desist. His ardent nature made it impossible for him to abandon his efforts to undermine structures of belief, thinking, and authority which he saw as oppressing and constricting humanity. Thus, the entire enterprise of the *Encyclopédie* continued to be seriously endangered by his persisting with his clandestine propagation of atheistic and materialist views, at a time when freethinking books were being publicly burned and copies of illicit writings actively searched for.

It was this ardent but calculating radical mind directing the *Encyclopédie*, combined with immense diligence, hard work, and the vast sweep of his interests, as well as an

[3] Diop, 'L'Anonymat', 84 n. [4] Ibid. 11–13; Proust, *Diderot*, 92; Blom, Encyclopédie, 46–8.

[5] Blom, Encyclopédie, 93, 150, 205; Diderot, *Correspondance*, i. 96; Duflo, *Diderot philosophe*, 56.

acute eye for what was best in Montesquieu and Voltaire—if not Réaumur and Maupertuis whom he scorned—that ensured in the end that the *Encyclopédie* indeed became more 'emblematic of the Enlightenment', as Bernard Williams put it, than anything else.[6] As it grew in complexity and size, the great publishing project also became still more dependent on Diderot's unmatched skills as editor, researcher, *érudit*, translator, in effect orchestrator of the whole operation. This also meant that for all the veiled language and necessary concessions to prevailing ideas, from this point on the *Encyclopédie* became more and more subtly oppositional, in intent, being designed, as one scholar has aptly put it, to carry through a general 'reformation of the Republic of Letters',[7] creating a new framework of knowledge and understanding emancipated from the academies and the closed closets of men of learning that would be both a public asset and possession available, in principle, to anyone. It was intended to be a summation of all existing knowledge but also to order what we know in such a way as to make human knowledge accessible, meaningful, and clear, that is it was now firmly intended to be quintessentially *philosophique*. Furthermore, as it grew, Diderot at least always planned it to be also an antidote to English cultural and intellectual hegemony, thinking of it in part, as he assured the judicial authorities from his cell at Vincennes in August 1749, as something undertaken 'à la gloire de la France et à la honte de l'Angleterre'.[8] Its anti-Baconianism and anti-Newtonianism were indeed to be among its prime features.

The pending struggle which opponents were to dub *la guerre de l'Encyclopédie* was arguably the most decisive of all Enlightenment controversies. Recruiting more and more contributors—their ranks eventually swelled to around 160—the editors assembled a remarkable team, though only a probably quite small minority, including Du Marsais who was responsible for the articles on grammar and d'Holbach who had settled in Paris, after completing his studies at Leiden in 1749, and quickly became a close ally of Diderot's, held atheistic and radical opinions broadly in line with those of the chief editors. However, there was also a sizeable middle group, at this stage including Rousseau, Claude Yvon, and the Abbé de Prades, who in ways subtle and not so subtle were being dragged along by Diderot. The years 1746–9 being the most intense phase of the friendship between Diderot and Rousseau, it was only natural the latter should be reckoned one of the team and directly involved, being entrusted, early on, with the articles on music.[9] The various contributors, noted Rousseau, were given three months to write their articles on the fields assigned to them, though he alone completed his assignment on time; Diderot and d'Alembert themselves, especially the former, wrote much of the first volume.[10]

As the most forceful personality in the team, Diderot fixed the general strategy and tone. No doubt something of the gradually mounting tension between

[6] Williams, *Truth and Truthfulness*, 186.
[7] Goodman, *Republic of Letters*, 27–8.
[8] Diderot to d'Aguesseau, Vincennes, 10 Aug, 1749, Diderot, *Correspondance*, i. 83.
[9] Trousson, *Rousseau*, 201, 203–4.
[10] Rousseau, *Confessions*, 292; Blom, Encyclopédie, 44–5.

Rousseau's intense Deism and Diderot's atheistic materialism, as well as between d'Alembert's and Diderot's differing conceptions of encyclopedism, was already discernible well before 1750, when Rousseau first made his name by winning the Academy of Dijon annual prize competition for his essay arguing that the progress of the sciences and arts had contributed to the corruption, rather than the advance, of morality. But in the late 1740s and during the first phase of the war of the *Enyclopédie*, down to 1752, Rousseau, shy, less articulate, and less developed intellectually than his slightly younger comrade, bottled up his steadily growing worries and doubts and let himself be swept along, in Diderot's wake, *en route*, that is, to materialism, philosophical atheism, and Spinozism. Undoubtedly, this long-bottled-up reluctance helped prepare the ground for the subsequent violent quarrel between the two men, and the sharpness of the later ideological break between Rousseau and the *encyclopédistes*, a group to which, until the early 1750s, he certainly belonged. This was also the reason Rousseau was later accused of blatant hypocrisy, and abjuring his own earlier views, in denouncing the *encyclopédistes*' philosophy as 'atheistic' and their books as even more insidious and dangerous than the 'rêveries' 'des Hobbes et des Spinoza'.[11]

For the moment, in any case, Rousseau collaborated energetically. Not just for Diderot and d'Alembert but for their entire intellectual fraternity, the *Encyclopédie* was a golden opportunity, nothing less than being entrusted with the ideal vehicle, eventually totalling twenty-eight lavishly illustrated folio volumes, for reshaping French high culture and attitudes, as well as the perfect instrument with which to insinuate their radical *Weltanschauung* surreptitiously, using devious procedures, into the main arteries of French society, embedding their revolutionary philosophic manifesto in a vast compilation ostensibly designed to provide plain information and basic orientation but in fact subtly challenging and transforming attitudes in every respect. It was an opportunity substantially, and perhaps decisively, to educate the public in philosophy, religion, and science, raising the prestige and widening the influence of the *philosophes* and of *philosophie* in the new sense forged by the pre-Voltaire generation.

If much of the paranoid logic of Jansenist *anti-philosophie* with its talk of *Spinosiste* conspiracies was wildly exaggerated and distorted, Diderot's prime contribution, the *Encyclopédie*, undeniably, despite mounds of camouflage, did fit their accusations; it was, in essence, a 'Spinosiste' conspiracy or what an anti-philosophic journal in Paris in 1802 called an assemblage of 'scepticism, materialism, and atheism'.[12] It was what *L'Esprit des lois* was at this very time accused of being but was not. During the 'Querelle de *L'Esprit des lois*', Spinoza again became the main focus of the debate about naturalism in France. Partly, this was because the charge of 'Spinozism' was the most potent that could be levelled against Montesquieu but it was also

11 Trousson, *Rousseau*, 200–1; Salaün, *L'Ordre*, 121–2; O'Hagan, *Rousseau*, 12, 20, 233, 235, 252.

12 Gumbrecht and Reichardt, '*Philosophe*', 11, 18, 20, 23, 29; Van Kley, *Religious Origins*, 3; Quintili, *Pensée critique*, 164, 185–90, 257–62, 264–76; McMahon, *Enemies of the Enlightenment*, 126–7.

because his multiple assailants preferred not to draw attention to the little-read materialist works of Diderot and La Mettrie and because they assumed that by toppling the 'maître' of the *esprits forts*, as Laurent François dubbed Spinoza in 1751, his French underlings, Diderot above all, would more or less automatically founder in his wake. It was in this fraught situation, with French materialism being presented as essentially a branch of the doughty tree of Spinozism, that Diderot and d'Alembert, observing the ominous 'Querelle de *L'Esprit des lois*' with an anxious eye, and seeing Montesquieu's struggle very much also as their own fight, a fight against 'les tyrans, les prêtres, les ministres et les publicains', forged ahead with their great project of the *Encyclopédie*.[13]

With so much labour and publishers' investment involved, and so much at stake, the project was always bound to be immensely challenging, requiring vast stamina, powers of organization, and resolve, besides endless tact, strategy, and finesse. It also required at least some unimpeachable intellectual solidity and would clearly have benefited from offering more internationally reputed names of high scholarly prestige. But Diderot's radical views and devious intellectual strategy rendered the enterprise far more precarious also in this respect than it would have been in the hands of a genuine Lockean or Newtonian, adherent of the *voltairianisme* of the 1740s, or even the much more cautious and more 'Baconian' d'Alembert.

In November 1750, Diderot politely asked Voltaire to embellish the project with 'quelques morceaux' of his hand. But at this stage, the latter seemingly preferred not to become involved. For his part, d'Alembert, despite his lack of enthusiasm for *L'Esprit des lois*, asked Montesquieu to contribute the articles 'Démocratie' and 'Despotisme', and others on politics, which would likewise have lent greater stature and respectability to the enterprise. However, again doubtless at least in part owing to reservations about Diderot, he too declined, claiming to have nothing new to say—though he did later contribute a relatively minor article on 'taste'.[14] Doubtless Voltaire's and Montesquieu's pointed non-participation in a way suited Diderot who, while admiring Montesquieu's written style, and having learnt much from his secular, sociological approach to religion and politics, and fully supporting him in the 'Querelle de *L'Esprit des lois*', was by no means attracted to his aristocratic style of political thought and tended more and more to diverge personally from the anti-republican, monarchical proclivities pervading both Montesquieu's and Voltaire's intellectual systems.[15]

After his release from prison, Diderot resumed his labours on the *Encyclopédie* with redoubled energy, working flat out over many months. Many of the articles already existed, in masses of drafts, at the time of his arrest but these were now extensively revised and put in order. In October 1750 he published the *Encyclopédie*'s *Prospectus*, a text intended to drum up public support for the rapidly advancing

[13] Ehrard, *L'Esprit des mots*, 279.

[14] Damiron, *Mémoires sur d'Alembert*, 16–17; Trousson, *Denis Diderot*, 167; Ehrard, *L'Esprit des mots*, 225, 278.

[15] Ehrard, *L'Esprit des mots*, 280–4; Proust, *Diderot*, 348–9; Salmon, 'Liberty', 99, 105–6.

project, announcing an eventual compilation of ten volumes and explaining the scheme of the project. Diderot's *Prospectus* created a thoroughly favourable impression in some circles, being glowingly reviewed among others by the Abbé Raynal, in the *Mercure de France*;[16] but this was counterbalanced, as was hardly surprising given the now highly suspect reputation of its author, by an ominously negative reaction in others. Jansenist hostility could, of course, be taken for granted; but the Jesuits and the Sorbonne, having had their fingers burnt by the 'Querelle de *L'Esprit des lois*', were also now distinctly less than encouraging. On the contrary, even before the first volume of the *Encyclopédie* appeared in 1751, there was an unmistakable tension in the air, it being widely rumoured, according to d'Alembert, that the Jesuits had already made up their minds to oppose the *Encyclopédie* and those responsible for it.[17]

As yet, however, there were no clear lines of combat or any definite linkage between the Montesquieu furore and the affair of the *Encyclopédie*. Still less was there any general rift between the *parti philosophique* and the church, universities, and *parlements*; but, equally, the intellectual arena was rapidly developing into a public contest and potentially one on a huge, national scale in which precisely such an unprecedented formalized scenario was now a real possibility. The editor of the Jesuit *Mémoires de Trévoux*, Father Berthier, abandoning the friendly attitude he had earlier displayed towards Voltaire and Condillac, and deeply shocked by (but having completely ignored) the *Lettre sur les aveugles*, reviewed the *Prospectus* in January 1751, reacting to Diderot's statement of his plans with a menacing mix of sarcasm, criticism, and unease.[18] Granting the literary *monde* deemed the brochure impeccably written, Berthier noted in a decidedly ironic tone Diderot's claim that no one had ever before conceived or executed so vast and innovative a publishing project. (Given Johann Heinrich Zedler's prior and larger, if admittedly less philosophical, *Universallexicon* (Leipzig, 1731–54) in sixty-four volumes, Diderot's boast as to priority and scale was not in fact justified). Complimenting Diderot on his modesty as well as his success in assembling a team distinguished alike for ability, courtesy, morals, and religion, Berthier pointedly queried his overall concept, strongly implying the inferiority of Diderot's and d'Alembert's design to Bacon's vision of the relationship of the sciences and crafts to society.

Diderot's conception of encyclopedism was indeed somewhat distinct from (and opposed to) Bacon's, though there was an element of disagreement between Diderot and d'Alembert in this respect. D'Alembert did not in fact share Fontenelle's, Boulainvilliers's, and Diderot's master-conception of a general order of knowledge reflecting the progress of *l'esprit humain*, or the latter's insistence that abstraction and system is just as vital as organized experiments and observation, tending more towards the English empiricist inductive notion of factuality as a set of primary,

[16] *Journal des savants* (1751), 624; Proust, *Diderot*, 46; Pommier, *Diderot*, 106; Haechler, *L'Encyclopédie*, 56–7.
[17] D'Alembert to Gabriel Cramer, Paris, 15 Feb. 1751, *DHS* 28 (1996), 251.
[18] Proust, *Diderot*, 62–3; Masseau, *Ennemis des philosophes*, 122; Cottret, *Jansénismes*, 72–3; Saada, *Inventer Diderot*, 94–6.

untested data more or less randomly chosen or come upon and subjected to experiment and observation. Diderot entirely agreed that all knowledge comes through the senses but put an equal stress on adequate interpretation of phenomena, perceptions, and impressions in terms of reason, *critique*, and historical context.[19] For him, this was the essence of *l'esprit philosophique*. D'Alembert's preference for gathering observed data and postponing efforts to seek reasons he attributed to excessive attachment to a mathematical model of knowledge unsuited, in his view, to explicating what we know of Man, society, morality, and politics, as well as of many aspects of nature, and hence apt to divide the mathematical sciences from the rest of 'philosophy'.

To Berthier's attack, Diderot responded by publishing an equally cutting *Lettre de M. Diderot au R.P. Berthier, Jésuite* (1751) after which each published a further caustic open letter. The clash between the *Encyclopédie*'s editors and the Jesuits's Baconism soon developed into a full-scale battle with the appearance, in February 1751, of Diderot's anonymous *Lettre sur les sourds et les muets* and especially, in June, of the first volume of the *Encyclopédie*, in 2,000 copies. For the latter proved an instant but also challenging and provocative success.[20] Additional copies had to be printed to supply the subscribers who, by 1752, numbered over 4,000. Assailed by Berthier in a long review the following April, the *Encyclopédie's* opening volume also proved highly divisive. This was despite d'Alembert's deftly accommodating preface, or *Discours préliminaire*, on which he had expended many weeks of labour, grandly proclaiming the 'progrès de l'esprit' since the 'Renaissance' of letters in the sixteenth century as the most significant development in the history of the world and avoiding all mention of the current controversies, aside from alluding to the (unnamed) Montesquieu's *L'Esprit* as a work which, despite some objections in France, was otherwise 'estimé de toute l'Europe'.[21] In his *Discours préliminaire*, d'Alembert bent head over heels to be conciliatory, heavily emphasizing the editors' supposed veneration of Bacon, Boyle, Locke, and Newton and the matchless superiority of *la philosophie anglaise*.[22] Many were enthusiastic, Montesquieu being among those who dashed off letters of support to d'Alembert.

But d'Alembert's promise of a rigorously Lockean-Newtonian enterprise was in no way lived up to in the main body of the *Encyclopédie*. Bacon, Locke, Newton, and Clarke do not in fact figure prominently in the major articles on philosophy, religion, politics, and society or even, more surprisingly, in much of the discussion of natural philosophy where the influence of d'Alembert himself often predominated albeit balanced by the conspicuous influence here of the anti-Newtonian Buffon. Buffon, a cosmologist as well as biologist, was a long-standing materialist and opponent of physico-theology who, in the recently published first three volumes of his *Histoire naturelle*, not only set out his innovative ideas on the formation of the

[19] Saada, *Inventer Diderot*, 94–6; Le Ru, *D'Alembert philosophe*, 201–9, 213.

[20] Proust, *Diderot*, 52.

[21] Ibid. 67, 69; d'Alembert, *Discours préliminaire*, p. xxxii.

[22] Diderot, *Lettre au R.P. Berthier*, 11–12, 20, 32–3, 47–8; Firode, 'Locke et les philosophes', 58, 61.

world, fossils, men, and species without invoking the 'argument from design' and shocking many, but even went so far as to praise expressly Diderot's banned *Lettre sur les aveugles* for its 'métaphysique très fine et très vraie'.[23] He and Diderot were close allies.

No doubt it was never Diderot's intention that *la philosophie anglaise* should be the guiding inspiration behind the *Encyclopédie.* But even d'Alembert, however willing publicly to exalt Locke and Newton, was by no means above suspicion; in fact, he too soon became deeply embroiled in the fight with the Jesuits. If his preface to the first volume was widely applauded, and the Paris *Journal des savants* took pride in a French achievement which, indeed, dwarfed Chambers, that journal also sarcastically thanked d'Alembert for ensuring that divine providence and the spirituality of the soul were remembered, complaining of his conspicuous brevity here: one might easily suspect in this preface 'un laconisme affecté sur ce qui regarde la religion'.[24] Still more indicative of d'Alembert's unsoundness in Newtonian, Lockean, and Jesuit eyes was his article on the blind ('aveugles') where he invokes Diderot's *Lettre sur les aveugles*, strictly forbidden by the *Parlement* of Paris, as a book by an anonymous author 'très-philosophique et très bien écrit', quoting whole passages from it and agreeing with its arguments.[25]

Much of the first volume rapidly aroused anxiety and indignation in mainstream as well as Jansenist quarters. Superficially, it might seem the editorial aim was a balance of respectable philosophical influences, including Leibniz and Wolff, the article on 'athéisme' for example being mainly drawn from the papers of the Berlin Huguenot Formey, an ardent Wolffian. But there were abundant grounds to suspect, in many places, a concerted campaign of insinuation and subversion. It was impossible not to recognize the signs of radical infiltration in the article on the soul, 'Âme', for instance, where the treatment of the soul's immortality struck Berthier in the *Mémoires de Trévoux* as suspicious throughout, no less in the part by the Abbé Claude Yvon than in the latter section, by Diderot, stressing the close interaction of body and soul in inducing moods while rejecting the idea that the soul has a 'seat' in the body.[26]

Yvon's section rather oddly drew much of its argumentation from Jaquelot's now obsolete *Dissertations* (1697), a laborious Protestant Cartesian text chiefly concerned with trying to counter Spinoza's demolition of that very doctrine; still odder was the suspiciously large amount of space assigned here to 'le trop fameux Spinosa' himself and his premiss that there is only one substance in the universe as well as his denial of the soul's immortality. Any reader was bound to wonder why he was reading whole passages about Spinoza in an article supposedly about immortality of the soul. Yvon, moreover, had incautiously followed Bayle in tying Aristotelian Averroism

[23] Roger, 'Diderot et Buffon', 222, 236.

[24] *Journal des savants* (1751), 626; White, *Anti-Philosophers*, 104.

[25] Diderot and d'Alembert, *Encyclopédie*, i. 870–3; Duflo, *Diderot philosophe*, 137.

[26] Vernière, *Spinoza*, 585–6; Proust, *Diderot*, 124, 287; Crampe-Crasnabet, 'Les Articles', 92–3, 95, 98–9.

to Spinozism, attributing to Spinoza the idea of a 'universal soul permeating all matter',[27] ending with the curious remark that Spinoza's 'absurde système' had also been embraced by Hobbes.[28] In their apologetic preface to the third volume of the *Encyclopédie*, published in 1753, Diderot cites this particular article rather slyly as one which, admittedly, spends so much time adducing arduous proofs of the soul's immortality as to make this holy dogma appear positively dubious 'si elle pouvoit jamais l'être'.[29]

Particular annoyance stemmed from the fact that several articles while not directly propagating materialist views could be construed to be doing so indirectly, often by reviewing ancient and modern reasoning against the 'argument from design' in an ostensibly neutral fashion but without sufficiently balancing such reasoning with counter-arguments in its favour. This is the procedure, for example, in the piece—probably by d'Alembert—on 'atomisme' where claims that the totality of what is 's'est fait par hasard', denying that the body's parts were designed by a knowing, intelligent Creator, are emphatically expounded with responsibility being fobbed off onto Leucippus, Democritus, and Lucretius.[30] The long and highly contentious article 'Aristotélisme', a piece largely drawn from Bayle, Boureau-Deslandes, and Brucker which was fiercely attacked by Berthier,[31] d'Alembert privately admitted had purposely been designed to antagonize and ridicule the Jesuits.[32] Among other provocative strategies, the anonymous authors, probably Yvon, Diderot, and d'Alembert together, focus unduly on Strato. Certainly they assert that it was ridiculous for Strato to contend that a nature that feels and knows nothing should nevertheless invariably conform to eternal laws but the way it does so, rhetorically asking whether anyone can conceive that nature's eternal laws were not established by 'une cause intelligente', prompted suspicion that the real aim here was precisely to implant such a conception in the reader's mind. Claiming it was Strato's system which Spinoza renewed in modern times, the authors point out that the only significant difference between the systems of Strato and Spinoza is the one-substance doctrine which, they say, Spinoza borrowed from Xenophanes, Melissus, and Parmenides.[33]

After this, this same key article continues with an obviously subversive account of Pomponazzi, depicted here as a loyal Aristotelian in some respects but one who nevertheless ridiculed everything to be found in the Gospels and Fathers. Pomponazzi was a major figure in the history of philosophy, according to the *Encyclopédie*, but one primarily concerned to undermine basic Catholic dogma,

27 *Mémoires de Trévoux*, 52 (Feb. 1752), 296–322, (Mar. 1752), 468; Spallanzani, *Immagini*, 145.

28 Yvon, art. 'Âme', in Diderot and d'Alembert, *Encyclopédie*, i. 335.

29 Diderot and d'Alembert, 'Avertissement des éditeurs', ibid., 1. p. vii.

30 D'Alembert, 'Atomisme', ibid. i. 823; Proust, *Diderot*, 128.

31 Proust, *Diderot*, 256–7; Jehl, 'Brucker', 247–9.

32 D'Alembert to Gabriel Cramer, 10 Sept. 1751 *DHS* 28 (1996), 256; Diderot and d'Alembert, 'Avertissement des éditeurs', p. ix; Geissler, 'Boureau-Deslandes, historien', 147.

33 Proust, *Diderot*, 18, 123, 157, 247 n.; Yvon, 'Aristotélisme', in Diderot and d'Alembert, *Encyclopédie*, i. 661.

holding that either Man does not possess free will or else God is ignorant of future events and does not intervene in the course of human affairs, since the doctrine of divine providence is logically wholly incompatible with human liberty.[34] Though basically just a hack for Diderot, Yvon carried responsibility for this and other offending articles and soon faced such an outcry that he found himself obliged to go into exile, fleeing to Holland where, among others, he consorted with Rousset de Missy, though years later he apologized, firmly abjured Diderot's views, and declared publicly for theism.[35]

Nowhere in the initial volume of the *Encyclopédie*, though, was it clearer that what was being laid before the French public was a veiled but systematic attack on physico-theology, and hence the entire Christian Enlightenment, than in the article 'Animal'. This article, composed by Diderot himself, together with Buffon's assistant Louis-Jean-Marie Daubenton, using extracts from Buffon, focused, as we have seen, mainly on the experiments and debates conducted in 1740–2 by Réaumur and his disciples Trembley and Bonnet.[36] But one quickly sees that the design here is the utter overthrow of Réaumur's long-standing hegemony over the life sciences in western Europe as well as underhandedly to propagate materialism. Réaumur, in the *Encyclopédie*'s account of the animal realm, is firmly unseated chiefly by being ignored, and replaced by a Buffon who had only recently become famous, almost overnight, albeit a Buffon subtly doctored by Diderot to erase the residual dualism of his 'molécules vivantes' and inanimate matter.[37] Not only does Diderot here largely remove the distinction between the animal and vegetable realms 'par des nuances insensibles de l'animal au végétal' but, despite ambivalently acknowledging that there may be a clear difference between plant and mineral life, effectively erodes that too with his prediction that further research would probably identify 'des êtres intermédiaires' (intermediary beings), organized bodies without the power to reproduce like animals and plants but capable of movement and with some semblance of life.[38] The whole thrust of the article was to render redundant the traditionally and conventionally firm divisions between animal, vegetable, and inanimate matter.

While new discoveries and ideas, not least those of Montesquieu, Condillac, Buffon, Trembley, Boulanger, Brucker, Wolff, Diderot himself, and, in dynamics, d'Alembert, played a considerable part in shaping the content and general conception of the *Encyclopédie*, overall its key philosophical, religious, and scientific articles consisted less of new material or perspectives than a continuation and further elaboration of older controversies solidly anchored in Spinoza, Bayle, Boulainvilliers, Locke, Newton, Le Clerc, Jaquelot, Fontenelle, and Leibniz. In inspiration and basic orientation not only did the *Encyclopédie* conspicuously fail to further the Enlightenment of Bacon, Boyle, Locke, Newton, and Clarke, neither did it reflect the

[34] Yvon, 'Aristotélisme' i. 665–7. [35] Jacob, *Radical Enlightenment*, 281–2.

[36] Quintili, *Pensée critique*, 295–8; Martin-Haag, *Aspect de la pensée*, 35.

[37] Martin-Haag, *Aspect de la pensée*, 35; Roger, *Buffon*, 199; Proust, *Diderot*, 258, 260, 288; Cherni, *Diderot*, 50, 187, 225, 254–5, 264–5; Malherbe, 'Introduction', 55–6.

[38] Diderot and Daubenton, 'Animal', 469; Wartofsky, 'Diderot', 323–7; Roger, *Buffon*, 339.

views and perspectives of the leading figures of the French moderate mainstream—Voltaire, Montesquieu, Maupertuis, and Turgot. Hence not only were the Jesuits angered and the Jansenists up in arms but such powerful contemporary figures as Voltaire, Montesquieu, Maupertuis, and Réaumur, all towering figures in French and European intellectual life, not only felt affronted but from their standpoint had every reason to be extremely indignant. D'Argens, admittedly, viewing the proceedings from Berlin, rebuked those *philosophes* who continually criticized the early volumes of the *Encyclopédie*, suggesting they were reacting negatively merely out of pique at being ignored and deploring their pettiness exclaiming, as he expressed it in a letter to Maupertuis of March 1752, 'o folie humaine!'[39] But he viewed the matter from a much more radical perspective.

The moderate *philosophes* were furious. More immediately ominous from Diderot's and d'Alembert's point of view, however, was the affair which erupted surrounding one of their key contributors, the Abbé Jean-Martin de Prades (1724–82), a youthful scholar and friend of Yvon not given to expressing unacceptable ideas who, though never close to Diderot, had been engaged by the editors as part of a team of young theologians, including Yvon and the Abbé Pestré, who afterwards disappeared from the body of contributors to the later volumes. These were recruited to provide the early articles on religion, metaphysics, and theology, basically as a ruse to shield Diderot and d'Alembert from direct responsibility.[40] The irony of this new affair was that de Prades, unlike Diderot, d'Alembert, Buffon, or, at the time, Yvon, was actually a believing Christian and sincere admirer of Locke who had previously encountered no difficulty with the theologians.

De Prades successfully defended his rambling, unusually wide-ranging doctoral thesis during a twelve-hour session before the theology faculty of the Sorbonne on 18 November 1751. Affirming the certainty and 'l'authenticité du Pentateuque', and reality of Christ's miracles (here following Locke and Houtteville), he rejects outright the Bible criticism of Hobbes, Spinoza, and Richard Simon and even criticizes at some length Leibniz's account of fossils together with those of de Maillet, in his *Telliamed*, and Buffon,[41] arguing the physical evidence proves that the distribution of fossils is due to the biblical Flood. He expressly attacks Spinoza's theory of miracles, heaping lavish praise on Newton and Locke.[42] Yet his thesis, unfortunately for him, also included some odd wording regarding Christ's driving out of demons and miraculous cures, comparing these with other supposedly miraculous ancient healings, a scornful reference to the 'indécentes et scandaleuses' excesses of the Jansenist *convulsionnaires*—though few in the Sorbonne were likely to object to that[43]—the statement contradicting Le Clerc that 'Baylius recte animadvertit Stratoni et Spinosae patrocinari Cudwortum cum suis formis plasticis' [Bayle rightly remarked that

[39] Häseler, 'Marquis d'Argens', 84.
[40] Proust, *Diderot*, 22, 153, 156; Spallanzani, *Immagini*, 36–7, 66.
[41] De Prades, *Thèse*, 27–33; Spink, 'Abbé philosophe', 146–7.
[42] Spink, 'Abbé philosophe' 155; de Prades, *Thèse*, 62–3; Firode, 'Locke et les philosophes', 58.
[43] De Prades, *Thèse*, 67.

Cudworth is helping Strato and Spinoza with his plastic forms], and a stress on the distinction between 'religion surnaturelle' and revealed religion, declaring all revealed religions (except the true one) to have corrupted the truth by proclaiming false miracles, oracles, martyrs, and visions, that could be construed as an oblique defence of Deist Natural Theology.[44]

Theologically, there was not much that was unambiguously fit to take issue with. But in the ideologically charged atmosphere of the moment this sufficed to precipitate a major new furore. Although the Sorbonne's faculty jury accepted his thesis without seeing any problem, de Prades soon learned, to his consternation, that the Jesuits demurred and wished to lodge a formal protest. Their intervention led to his thesis being brought before the full assembly of 146 doctors of the theology faculty in December 1751, primarily owing to its strange reading of the Book of Genesis, suspect wording regarding Christ's miracles, and supposed cunning camouflage of 'monstrous errors, irreligion, and impiety' which included citing the pernicious Bayle with approval.[45] To this the Jansenist *Nouvelles ecclésiastiques* added that de Prades was 'intimately connected' with the *encyclopédistes* and that his thesis formed part of a vile conspiracy of the *esprits forts* using philosophy 'contre la religion', a prime goal of which was to subvert the Paris faculty of theology.[46]

It was also widely reported that de Prades had not written his thesis himself but been extensively assisted, notably by Diderot or various combinations of Diderot, d'Alembert, Montesquieu, Buffon, and Yvon.[47] Formal condemnation of the work by the Sorbonne followed—albeit with some dissenting voices—in January 1752, with a list of ten censured propositions, 'fundamenta religionis Christianae subvertentes' [undermining the fundamentals of the Christian religion], including the idea, associated with Spinoza, that the Mosaic Law was originally a political device, the doctrine, based on Locke and Condillac, but now being misused for materialist ends, that 'toutes les connoissances de l'homme naissent des sensations', his insinuatingly questioning the status of Christ's driving out demons from sick persons, and the authority of the Fathers and, eighth, while purporting to acknowledge the truth of miracles, surreptitiously seeking to undermine belief in them by means of philosophical quibbles.[48] De Prades's original examiners were officially reprimanded and his doctorate revoked.

With both the Jesuits and Jansenists now fully aroused, and the Sorbonne impelled by a chorus of outrage to protest at the treatment of religion in the *Encyclopédie* and condemn de Prades and all dangerous 'philosophy', the archbishop

[44] Ibid. 10–11; Diderot, *Œuvres complètes*, i. 435; Spink, 'Abbé philosophe', 152.

[45] *Nouvelles ecclésiastiques* (1752), 33 (27 Feb.); Cottret, *Jansénismes*, 72–6; Ehrard, *L'Idée*, 416; Masseau, *Ennemis des philosophes*, 117–18.

[46] *Nouvelles ecclésiastiques* (1752), 34–6, 44 (27 Feb., 12 Mar.); Yvon et al., *Apologie*, preface pp. A2^{v}, 10; [Diderot], *Suite*, 6–7; Wellman, *La Mettrie*, 276; Chartier, *Cultural Origins*, 42; Sgard, 'Diderot', 12–13.

[47] Yvon et al., *Apologie*, 6–7; Saada, *Inventer Diderot*, 119–20.

[48] Yvon et al., *Apologie*, seconde partie, 150, 156, 173, 187–93; *Nouvelles ecclésiastiques* (1752), 45 (12 Mar.); Pappas, *Berthier's* Journal, 72; Spallanzani, *Immagini*, 36; Ricken, 'Condillac', 266; Masseau, *Ennemis des philosophes*, 118.

of Paris, Christophe de Beaumont, felt that he could not afford to be left behind. Six days after the second volume of the *Encyclopédie* came off the presses, and without bothering this time with the prior enquiries and courtesies extended to Buffon and Montesquieu, Beaumont issued his own public condemnation of de Prades's thesis, denouncing it on 29 January 1752 for casting doubt on the miracles of Christ and advancing propositions both scandalous and offensive, apt to corrupt morals and assist the impiety of the 'philosophes matérialistes'. This last was widely construed as an allusion to Diderot confirming he was now effectively head of a movement in the country. The primate of the French church also deplored the new philosophical movement itself, that is anti-Lockean, anti-Newtonian materialism, 'cette philosophie superbe et téméraire' daily gaining ground in France but which existed also, he noted, in ancient times and which St Paul denounced for raising against Christianity 'une opposition générale à tous ses mystères'.[49]

The archbishop mounted his onslaught on the *Encyclopédie* and the *philosophes matérialistes*, including de Prades, averred the Jansenist journal, in view of 'la grandeur du mal'; according to the *encyclopédistes*, he did so under pressure of public reaction and the Jesuits, though this did not prevent his being rebuked by Jansenist *dévots* for not condemning de Prades and freethinking robustly enough.[50] The marquis d'Argenson, Louis XV's minister of foreign affairs and no friend of the Jesuits, commented in his journal on the curious rivalry in progress between Jesuits and Jansenists, and now also the archbishop, as to who abominated *le matérialisme* most.[51] Beaumont's intervention had a crucially important impact, however, placards denouncing materialism being posted up in the streets and read out in the churches, something which was a decided error on the part of the church, according to some observers, since many Parisians previously wholly unaware there was anything scandalous about the *philosophes*, nor in the least inclined to read them, were sufficiently impressed by the commotion to think perhaps they should pay more attention to this strange business of philosophy. Almost overnight de Prades, materialist philosophy, and the *Encyclopédie*, an expensive work affordable only to a small elite, became a *cause célèbre* known to the entire population of Paris.

The Paris *Parlement*, for its part, ordered de Prades's thesis to be burned and a warrant issued for his arrest, prompting him to flee to Holland. It rapidly emerged, meanwhile, that the second volume of the *Encyclopédie* again included numerous suspect passages, some rumoured to have been illegally interpolated afterwards into articles cleared by the censors. The entry on the Canadian Indians, for example, cites Lahontan, who was roundly classified by theological authors like Loescher as a 'Spinozist',[52] as the chief authority on the topic, as someone who had lived among them for ten years, though it admits his Indians are so scornful of

[49] Masseau, *Ennemis des philosophes*, 119; Diderot, *Correspondance*, i. 137–8; Concina, *Della religione rivelata*, i. 20–1; Haechler, *L'Encyclopédie*, 135, 144; Pappas, *Berthier's* Journal, 185.

[50] *Nouvelles ecclésiastiques* (1751), 191 (27 Nov.); Yvon et al., *Apologie*, 32, 38; [Diderot], *Suite*, 5; Spink, 'Abbé philosophe', 165–6.

[51] Diderot, *Œuvres complètes*, i. 432.

[52] Loescher, *Praenotiones*, 146.

Christianity that one wonders whether he may perhaps have doctored their comments.[53] Another offending article was 'Certitude' by de Prades, a piece containing many of the same points just censured in his thesis and judged, in particular, to erode belief in miracles by questioning the value of supposed eyewitness testimony in his attack on Houtteville.[54] This piece contained, in addition, a suspiciously feeble attack on the *Pensées philosophiques*, here billed as a pre-eminent assault on miracles and the certitude of 'faits surnaturels', a particularly bizarre touch given that this embattled text, lately praised by Buffon but banned in France by order of the *Parlement*, was the work of the editor-in-chief, Diderot himself![55]

The uproar now moved towards its climax. Numerous contemporaries had now gathered the vague (but not incorrect) impression that the *Encyclopédie* insidiously assails the fundamentals of religion and were persuaded, consequently, that it should be suppressed. The crescendo of complaints led a week later to the interim decision of the royal *Conseil d'état*, of 7 February 1752, to ban the first two volumes of the *Encyclopédie*, forbidding their further sale or distribution in the kingdom under pain of heavy fines and the halting of the project overall. Diderot's papers were seized by the royal police and there was talk of his being sent back to prison, this time with d'Alembert along with him.[56] The *Encyclopédie* significantly, was suppressed by order of the crown not just as inimical to religion, and apt to promote incredulity and corruption of morals, but in part also for the strikingly naturalistic and republican-sounding account of political power in the article 'Autorité politique', an anonymous entry by Diderot, and his first important contribution to political thought, shrewdly highlighted and attacked by Berthier and the Jesuit press in order to damage him further.[57] This article, long to be recalled by *anti-philosophes* as the first open betrayal of monarchy by the *philosophes*, explicitly states that the *bonheur des peuples* is the chief function of government, that absolute power cannot be 'légitime', and that there exists an underlying contract between crown and people carrying reciprocal responsibilities; it also daringly extols Henri IV, religious toleration, and the Edict of Nantes.[58] Not surprisingly, all this was judged detrimental to the crown's prestige, at court, and apt to foster the spirit 'de l'indépendance et de la révolte'.[59] Things looked dire indeed for Diderot and d'Alembert and many had reason to hope that it was now all over with *la philosophie*.

A mood of deep depression descended over the *encyclopédistes*, the publishers, and the project. D'Alembert withdrew into his shell and was henceforth more

[53] Diderot and d'Alembert, *Encyclopédie*, ii, 'Canadiens', 581–3; Proust, *Diderot*, 122, 128.

[54] Vernière, *Spinoza*, 579; de Prades, art. 'Certitude', in Diderot and d'Alembert, *Encyclopédie*, ii. 851–2.

[55] De Prades, 'Certitude', 851–2; Yvon et al., *Apologie*, seconde partie, 80–6; Haechler, *L'Encyclopédie*, 132–3.

[56] Diderot, *Œuvres complètes*, i. 28; Diderot, *Correspondance*, i. 139.

[57] Proust, *Diderot*, 345–5, 352–3.

[58] Diderot, 'L'Autorité politique', in Diderot and d'Alembert, *Encyclopédie*, i. 898–901; McMahon, *Enemies of the Enlightenment*, 29–30.

[59] Pappas, *Berthier's* Journal, 185; *Mémoires de Trévoux*, 52 (Mar. 1752), 456–9; O'Keefe, *Contemporary Reactions*, 90; Darnton, *Business*, 10; Chartier, *Cultural Origins*, 42; Diop, 'L'Anonymat', 85; Tarin, *Diderot*, 66–7, 69; Salaün, *L'Ordre*, 140.

than ever prone to leave everything philosophically, theologically, or politically contentious to Diderot, a withdrawal which led to a marked cooling of relations between the two at this time.[60] Likewise Rousseau largely lost his appetite for his friends' embattled enterprise. Several allies urged Diderot to emulate Yvon and de Prades and thwart his opponents by escaping to Holland or Prussia. But he decided to risk staying on, for the sake of the *Encyclopédie*, the *parti philosophique*, and what he had come to stand for, in the streets, encouraged by a last few staunch supporters, notably the literary critic and musical enthusiast Grimm, who was well connected in Germany, and his new ally d'Holbach. D'Alembert, by contrast, *was* converted to the idea of transferring the whole operation to Berlin where Frederick would doubtless have permitted its continuance. He was dissuaded, though, by Voltaire, who firmly opposed the suggestion. Warning that many arts and techniques were unknown in Prussia, that essential facilities were lacking, that Berlin contained prodigious quantities of bayonets but hardly any books, Voltaire insisted that only in Paris could such 'un ouvrage qui sera la gloire de la France et l'opprobre de ceux qui vous ont persécutés' successfully be completed. Furthermore, in the end, he believed, several key royal ministers could be counted on for support.[61]

Above all, Diderot refused to consider such an evacuation.[62] At the French court, meanwhile, there was much wavering over whether or not to confirm and enforce the ban on the *Encyclopédie*—and a flurry of intrigue around the king. Since the official clergy were still obstructing the *vingtième* tax and proving intractable over *billets de confession* there was a lingering element of political tension between crown and church which helped the *encyclopédistes* in some degree.[63] Royal ministers saw that the affair could end by making the court look foolish, especially as Diderot, early in 1751, had been made an honorary member of the Berlin Academy by the Prussian king, prodded by d'Argens and Voltaire, as a way of strengthening Diderot's hand.[64] Among those hesitantly resisting the urging of Beaumont, of the dauphin's tutor, the bishop of Mirepoix, the other bishops, and Jesuits, were Madame de Pompadour (1721–64), who held mildly anticlerical views and respected Diderot, and especially Malesherbes, a highly placed friend of Condillac and Mably charged with reforming the royal censorship who was himself a target of Jansenist ire.[65] The Jesuits, aware that it was not over yet, proceeded circumspectly, holding back from going all out against Messieurs Diderot and d'Alembert (much less Voltaire or Montesquieu) for this would have meant antagonizing powerful courtiers as well as have obliged them wholly to ditch their strategy of the last two decades and throw in their lot with *anti-philosophie* which they were not yet ready to do, though soon they would be forced to.

[60] Vandeul, *Mémoires*, p. xlv.
[61] Voltaire to d'Alembert, Potsdam, 5 Sept. 1752, Voltaire, *Correspondence*, xii. 176.
[62] Proust, *Diderot*, 153; Cherni, *Diderot*, 19; Haechler, *L'Encyclopédie*, 159.
[63] Rogister, *Louis XV*, 102–3.
[64] Diderot, *Correspondance*, i. 113–14.
[65] Hobohm, 'Le Progrès', 79–82; Haechler, *L'Encyclopédie*, 161.

Whatever the mood in the country, the Jesuits, in any case, *could* not really join hands with their most implacable theological antagonists the Jansenists, and deliberately eschewed their strident tone. They were, in fact, in a deep quandary and tried to hedge their bets. The reviews of the *Encyclopédie* in the *Mémoires de Trêvoux* for 1752, while sternly rebuking the *encyclopédistes* for plagiarism and irreverence, still sought to balance their complaints that in many places 'la religion n'a point été respectée' with approval of the purely scientific articles and the scholarly labours of most contributors, including Rousseau, whose talents the Jesuits hoped to see enrich subsequent volumes even while reproaching him for his arguments 'contre les sciences et les arts'.[66] Many suspected from such remarks that the Jesuit strategy was less to scotch the *Encyclopédie* altogether than emasculate it by forcing a situation in which it could continue only in a drastically altered form, under new management and their own supervision.

Meanwhile the affair had become an international spectacle. From Holland, de Prades moved on, in August, to Berlin, d'Argens and Voltaire having persuaded Frederick to take him under his protection. Widely reported, this news hardly improved the mood at the French court. Even so, his flight, and the *Parlement*'s warrant for his arrest, looked like a triumph of sorts for the *anti-encyclopédistes*, especially since both the *Parlement* and the archbishop of Paris had now formally condemned the *Encyclopédie* and there was mounting talk of Diderot's files of draft articles being transferred by ministers to the Jesuits who, it was rumoured, would be entrusted with a surviving revamped version. Circumstances, seemingly, had pushed Jesuits, episcopate, and Sorbonne alike, together with the *Parlement* and the court, into pulling in their oars regarding 'enlightened' ideas if only temporarily. A broad moderate mainstream based on Locke and Newton had come into being in France in the 1730s but this middle ground had suddenly become virtually untenable and the whole edifice built on it visibly threatened with collapse. This was a resounding success for the *dévot* party up to a point, but one that was double-edged and in several respects awkward for them and which, as some officials and Jesuits quickly realized, could easily trap the court, dauphin, and party of authority and religion generally in outright opposition to the combined *parti philosophique*, a body profoundly split internally, no doubt, but not publicly divided.

This greatly complicated matters for the *anti-encyclopédistes*. But the real strength of Diderot's hand was that precisely because the *Encyclopédie* had generated an unprecedented coalition of *anti-philosophes*, headed by Jansenists and *dévots*, Voltaire, Maupertuis, Turgot and their adherents were in practice left with no alternative but to withdraw from their former alliance with the Jesuits and side with him.[67] Publicly, moderate and radical wings, Voltaire, Montesquieu, Diderot, and Buffon included, showing a healthy sense of self-preservation and all feeling threatened at this critical juncture, maintained a united front. Were their opponents

[66] *Mémoires de Trévoux*, 52 (1752), 160–90, 296–322, 424–68; Voltaire, *Lettres à son altesse*, 371.
[67] Condorcet, *Vie de Voltaire*, 165–7; Spallanzani, *Immagini*, 3, 8–41, 55–6 n. 28.

to press any harder, it would seem crown and church had gone to war with Bacon, Locke, Newton, and Voltaire, historiographer royal of France, as much as the *philosophes matérialistes*.

If Voltaire and Montesquieu had ever been in two minds about helping to save the *Encyclopedie*, it must soon have occurred to them that they simply could not align with the Jesuits in a situation in which the *encyclopédistes* were claiming, with a considerable show of plausibility, that they were being unjustly hounded by a self-interested coalition of the credulous and the cynical. The atmosphere in Paris was now so threatening, even to the likes of Montesquieu and Buffon, that it obliged all the *philosophes*, moderate and radical, despite their private backbiting, to stand together, thereby helping vindicate Diderot's and d'Alembert's hypocritical protestations that since de Prades and the *Encyclopédie* were chiefly based on Locke and Newton, philosophers of whom Jesuits, episcopate, and Sorbonne were equally in favour, they were being maliciously and cynically persecuted on grounds that were intellectually nonsensical. While Jesuits, Sorbonne, and the journal the *Bibliothèque raisonnée*, in these changed circumstances, tried to justify themselves by saying that, in some instances, Locke could be misused in an undesirable materialist direction, this indeed looked like nothing but a cynical manoeuvre to cement the coalition against the *Encyclopédie*. All serious commentators, as the Oratorian Lelarge de Lignac stressed, in 1753, agreed that Locke does not argue that matter can think, and firmly denies any inherent capacity in matter to move or feel, and that, in contrast to the materialists, as indeed Voltaire emphasized more than anyone, Locke argues only that, by natural reason, we cannot know whether God can give matter the power to perceive, feel, and think or not.[68] Locke and Newton, the inspiration of the moderate mainstream, had at the same time now become the stumbling-block of the anti-*encyclopédistes*.

Contemplating the scene from Berlin and Potsdam, Voltaire understood perfectly how much was at stake. His comments about the first volume of the *Encyclopédie* show he was lukewarm at best about the project and was as much as ever opposed to Diderot's anti-Lockean and anti-Newtonian philosophy.[69] But he also had a shrewd eye for the international impact of the affair and saw at once that de Prades's arrival in Prussia offered a splendid opportunity to present himself, on the stage of Europe, as the champion of the unreasonably oppressed. He promptly arranged for both de Prades and Yvon to stay at his lodgings at Potsdam, and dine daily at his personal table.[70] This eloquent piece of theatre spoke volumes. For it made starkly evident at this crucial juncture that while there were indeed two intellectually irreconcilable and completely opposed enlightenments pitted against each other in Europe—the conservative (or 'English') and the radical—at odds now as much as ever, yet, in the wider context of French and European society, culture, and

[68] [Lelarge de Lignac], *Élémens*, 382–3; Jolley, *Locke*, 86–7.

[69] D'Alembert to Voltaire, Paris, 24 Aug. 1752, Voltaire, *Correspondence*, xiii. 160–1.

[70] Voltaire to de Prades, Potsdam, 18 July 1752, Voltaire, *Correspondence*, xiii. 109, 111; Haechler, *L'Encyclopédie*, 144.

politics, an open split needed to be and could be avoided. Voltairianisme, in short, was so boxed in by the play of forces in France that Voltaire had to come out against the Sorbonne, archbishop, and Jesuits as well as the *parlements* and Jansenists, and to an extent even the French court, embarking on a course pregnant with consequences for the future from which he could never subsequently turn back.

Nor, compelled though he was so to act, did Voltaire, in the end, go against the grain of his own feelings. For if he detested *le Spinosisme*, materialism, and atheism, he did not dislike Diderot personally—or indeed d'Argens, though his relations with the latter at this juncture were tense[71]—and never doubted that the 'monsters called Jansenists and Molinists' remained a far greater and more fatal threat to mankind, a more total, vengeful, and abiding enemy of the 'partisans of reason and humanity' than the *Spinosistes*. For Voltaire and Montesquieu, the *anti-encyclopédistes* were the very acme of unreason, intolerance, and unjust persecution. Hence, Voltaire and the providential Deist centre bloc were pushed by the logic of events and circumstances into a marriage of convenience with the radical stream, from which circumstances prevented them from ever subsequently extricating themselves on a public level.

Voltaire, then, had to choose but there was only one way he could go—publicly, to stand with Diderot and d'Alembert, which meant, as he must have known, not just that the *guerre de l'Encyclopédie* would involve the complete destruction of his ties with the Jesuits, the Catholic episcopate, and the papacy but that virtually the entire bandwagon of the French Enlightenment would now be captured by Diderot's *matérialistes*.[72] Meanwhile, he played his part with aplomb, helping make the *anti-encyclopédiste* double-talk about Locke look unreasonable. In August 1752 it was announced by the editors of the *Encyclopédie*, in Paris, that at Potsdam the great Voltaire and the marquis d'Argens had generously taken de Prades and Yvon under their wing, rescuing them from their persecutors and from ruin, and that d'Alembert was now sending an open letter to the Prussian king and another to Voltaire, thanking both for what they had done to assist the two young refugee scholars 'injustement persécutés par la cabale des dévots', missives to be sent in the name of all the French *philosophes* collectively 'et au nom de l'humanité même'.[73]

In attacking de Prades as they had, it was beginning to dawn on both Voltaire and Diderot, the *dévots* had made a remarkable error of judgement: for he was not another 'La Mettrie', as Voltaire put it, but a genuine Lockean and Newtonian sincerely attacking 'atheism' and materialism; it seemed he was being persecuted in France, as Voltaire put it, 'assez mal à propos par des fanatiques et des imbéciles'.[74] If for the first time Jesuits and Jansenists had in a way joined forces, their precarious common front against the *Encyclopédie* remained evidently unsteady and self-contradictory,

71 Voltaire to d'Argens, Potsdam, [July?] 1752, Voltaire, *Correspondence*, xiii. 112–13.

72 Torrey, 'Voltaire's Reaction', 1107, 1111; Haechler, *L'Encyclopédie*, 159.

73 Voltaire, *Correspondence*, xiii. 138–9.

74 Voltaire to Charlotte Sophia, Countess Bentinck, Potsdam, *c.*20 Aug. 1752, Voltaire to Marie Louise Denis, Potsdam, 19 Aug. 1752, Voltaire, *Correspondence*, xiii. 155, 157–8.

appearing thoroughly muddled intellectually. In their *Apologie* for de Prades's thesis, completed in the early summer of 1752, a text composed by de Prades and Yvon under Diderot's direction and heavily edited and illegally published by him, the authors made splendid capital out of this disarray, playing particularly on the frequent Jansenist reminders that the Jesuits had encouraged the dissemination of Locke in Catholic Europe.[75]

De Prades's thesis, Diderot and Yvon stressed, was essentially Lockean. Locke categorically upholds the spirituality and immateriality of the soul and defends the existence of purely spiritual beings, championing miracles and divine judgement of men with particular insistence. Indeed, Locke, arguably, had done no more than return to the principle that all ideas come from the senses which, before Descartes, had generally been accepted in the schools by the entire scholastic establishment, in France, and especially the Jesuits. Since all philosophers agree that at least some ideas derive from the senses, how can Locke's thesis that ideas derive from the senses in itself compromise the immateriality, and hence also the immortality, of the soul or freedom of the will? Diderot and his sub-editors granted that Condillac had gone beyond Locke towards sensationalism but pointed out that he too had nevertheless insisted that 'la matière ne peut pas penser' and that the Jesuits' *Mémoires de Trévoux*, notwithstanding their great piety, had warmly praised his treatise.[76] The essence of Locke's system, Diderot reminded his opponents, is to separate spirit from matter. With his thoroughgoing empiricism, Locke not only fully acknowledges the existence of spirits without bodies but also that there is no impediment to angels and demons having ideas merely because as pure spirits they are detached from bodies.[77] In fact, contended Diderot and his team, nothing could be older, more innocuous, more conservative, more palatable to men of moderation, or less challenging from a Catholic theological standpoint than the main principles of Locke's epistemology and philosophy of the mind. In short, nothing could be less apt to favour 'le matérialisme' than Locke's empiricism.[78]

Even though the *anti-encyclopédistes* continually insisted that the real issue was materialism and the attack on miracles, in the circumstances Diderot's tactically adroit reply—Locke, Locke, Locke—completely undermined their position. There *can* be no Catholic objection to Locke, he retorted, except perhaps to complain that under certain circumstances Locke's system could be perverted into materialism by the ill intentioned. But if that is the case, contended Diderot and Yvon, why do not de Prades's adversaries still more stridently decry the Sorbonne's former, and now apparently reviving, defence of Descartes's innate ideas? Now that they seem to be questioning their own prior endorsement of Locke, de Prades's critics seemed to be ridiculously resorting to the wholly discredited 'innate ideas' of Descartes and

[75] De Prades to Voltaire, 19 May 1752, ibid. xiii. 57; Diderot, *Correspondance*, i. 140; Yvon et al., *Apologie*, seconde partie, 3–7.

[76] *Apologie*, seconde partie, 11.

[77] Ibid., seconde partie, 17–18; Quarfood, *Condillac*, 30–1.

[78] *Apologie*, seconde partie, 17–18; Damiron, *Mémoires sur Diderot*, 58; Cassirer, *Philosophy*, 99.

Malebranche.[79] Surely they must be denounced? For there is no one who does not know that it was by taking Descartes's principles too far that 'Spinosa a bâti son système'. Yet 'I do not believe', adds the *Apologie*, with consummate irony, that any antagonist of de Prades regards himself or wishes to be regarded 'comme un Spinosiste'.[80]

A tactically brilliant polemical masterpiece, Diderot's section of the *Apologie* proved a highly potent defence of the *Encyclopédie*. He could now maintain that a horde of dangerous, furious, and thoroughly irrational enemies were charging that the *Encyclopédie* overthrows religion with no better justification than that it destroys their hopelessly muddled 'prétentions' and venerates Locke, preposterous grounds indeed.[81] It was beginning to become clear how much the *anti-encyclopédistes* had risked by committing themselves to an all-out onslaught on the *Encyclopédie*. Matters were beginning to look potentially disastrous from a conservative standpoint, especially as there were also now growing signs of support for the *encyclopédistes* among critics of the unrelenting Beaumont at court. At this crucial juncture, the *anti-philosophes*' major weakness was that their indictment of the *Encyclopédie* suddenly began to look much less solidly based and persuasive than it actually was, especially since the German and Dutch journals, during 1752, came out with mostly positive appraisals. Undoubtedly, there were numerous impieties in the *Encyclopédie* but so skilfully scattered and buried among much else, of an innocent or plainly useful character, noted the irreproachably orthodox Swiss Protestant medical professor Albrecht von Haller, reviewing the second volume in the *Göttingische Zeitungen von gelehrten Sachen* in July 1752, that most moderate, well-meaning Christian readers found it hard to convince themselves that the whole project deserved to be suppressed.[82] A still more supportive review appeared around the same time in the *Bibliothèque impartiale* of Leiden published by Luzac, who once again was chiefly concerned to promote freedom of thought and expression.[83]

All this not only further convoluted an already highly complex situation but enabled Diderot to edge closer and closer to capturing the whole philosophical movement and steering it in head-on opposition to existing structures of authority, tradition, and thought. Confirming the ban on the *Encyclopédie* would mean joining in a generalized attack on the *parti philosophique* in alliance with all factions of the church which would certainly damage the court's prestige, as some saw it, by making it look as if the crown was clerically dominated, and so antiquated in intellectual matters as to be lagging some considerable distance behind the pope. Such a break, furthermore, would force the Jesuits finally to abandon their policy of studied moderation of the last two decades and their alliance with Voltaire, forcing Voltaire to go to war with them and into a behind-the-scenes, marginalized, but permanent solidarity not just with d'Alembert, whom he esteemed more highly than Diderot, but Diderot himself.[84]

[79] Yvon et al., *Apologie*, seconde partie, 8.
[80] Ibid. 11; Spallanzani, *Immagini*, 138–9, 142–3.
[81] Yvon et al., *Apologie*, seconde partie, 63–4.
[82] Saada, *Inventer Diderot*, 110–12.
[83] Proust, *Diderot*, 65.
[84] Torrey, 'Voltaire's Reaction', 1108–9; Ehrard, *L'Esprit des mots*, 198.

From both the *dévot* and liberal ecclesiastical points of view, the position was all the riskier in that the *Apologie* for de Prades cleverly concentrated its fire on the *anti-philosophisme* of the Jansenists, while pretending to sympathize with the Jesuits, and also because the bishops' nagging efforts to get the ban on the *Encyclopédie* confirmed only rendered the court still more divided and hesitant as to how to proceed. Indeed, ministers were already backtracking from their decision to suppress the *Encyclopédie*. In May, Madame de Pompadour, d'Argenson, and other courtiers let Diderot and d'Alembert know, unofficially, that they should not give up yet: at court the mood was shifting and indeed they could quietly resume their editorial work provided they steered clear of everything theologically controversial.[85] Over the next weeks the news from court continued to improve. Finally, the draft articles and Diderot's papers were released and it was made official that preparations for the third volume could resume—under Diderot's and d'Alembert's editorship.[86] Against all the odds, for the moment, it seemed, Diderot had won. It was indeed an astounding outcome. Without a truly singular combination of circumstances, Condorcet later remarked, above all Diderot's courage, but also the unity of the *parti philosophique* and support of many others, and the deep divisions within the church and at court, its enemies would certainly have succeeded in destroying what he called 'le plus beau monument dont jamais l'esprit humain ait conçu l'idée'.[87]

Jansenists, Jesuits, archbishop, and *Parlement* alike were stunned. The *Encyclopédie* had somehow survived 'une violente tempête' as d'Alembert described the ups and downs of the previous months to Voltaire. It was time to capitalize on victory. Swinging from dejection to euphoria, Diderot came out, in October 1752, again anonymously and illegally with his *Suite de l'apologie de M. l'abbé de Prades*, in which the ostensible author, de Prades (in fact, Diderot), supposedly writing in a country (Holland) where he could express himself freely 'sans danger pour ma liberté, pour mon repos, et pour ma vie',[88] indignantly rejects the charge of materialism, denying 'his thesis' was the collective product of a 'société d'incrédules'. Archbishop, Jesuits, and the Sorbonne are witheringly assailed while the Jansenists are reckoned to have convicted themselves before all the world, without any help from him, of 'beaucoup d'ignorance et de témérité' such that all just and impartial men could see the injustice and unreasonableness of their conduct. Singling out for special rebuke the recent pastoral letter of the Jansenist Bishop Caylus of Auxerre sternly condemning de Prades together with the *encyclopédistes*, Diderot took the opportunity to air his views on the alleged philosophical conspiracy which, through de Prades, had supposedly spread its tentacles into the Paris theology faculty, providing abundant evidence of his finely tuned literary and propagandistic skills.

[85] Blom, *Encyclopédie*, 118; Haechler, *L'Encyclopédie*, 162.

[86] Diderot and d'Alembert, 'Avertissement des éditeurs', 1; Leca-Tsiomis, *Écrire l'*Encyclopédie, 232–3.

[87] Condorcet, *Vie de Voltaire*, 167–8; Haechler, *L'Encyclopédie*, 164.

[88] [Diderot], *Suite*, 53–4.

Assuming the guise of a loyal Catholic, anxious to defend religion and fight the *incrédules*, Diderot, by turns amusing and scathing, redoubled his pseudo-Lockean attack on the coalition ranged against him. Delighting in the humiliation of the Sorbonne which had originally passed de Prades's thesis, he proclaimed a basic dualism, in Man, of body and soul, announcing that he was taking his stand with Locke, and only Locke, which surely neither they, nor anyone else in alliance with them, could possibly object to given that around two-thirds of the university's professors were clearly Lockeans too.[89] Against the Jansenist *dévots*, he turned the arguments Jaquelot and the *rationaux* had used against Bayle, emphasizing especially the ruinous and paradoxical effects, for religion, of denigrating the claims of reason.[90] From listening to them, he admonished, one would suppose that men can only enter into the bosom of Christianity like a herd of animals being driven into the stables. For our understanding to submit fully to faith it must first be satisfied on grounds of reason.[91] He would not abandon reason; he would not retract his praise of Bayle the sceptic for his demolition of Cudworth's 'formes plastiques';[92] admittedly, he had spurned Descartes, Malebranche, and Clarke, but only out of preference for the discoveries of 'la physique expérimentale' over against 'leurs méditations abstraites' as Locke would approve.[93]

This, of course, was perfectly true. Indeed, everybody except for the Jansenists—either sincerely or hypocritically, as in Diderot's case, was continually invoking Locke. For the *anti-encyclopédistes*, Jesuits and Jansenists alike, this was a wholly disastrous outcome; for the failure of their tactics had the final result of immeasurably strengthening Diderot's position while his unrelenting 'Locke! Locke!', completely disarmed them, throwing the coalition between the ecclesiastical factions into disarray while cementing the tactical alliance between mainstream and radical *philosophes*. Diderot concludes his fifty-page tirade with a remarkable rebuke of the bishop of Auxerre and the Jansenists. They were taking the lead in the onslaught against *la philosophie*. But is it not they who are the true enemies of Jesus Christ with their constant fomenting of disobedience, rebellion, and discord and inflexible opposition to the decrees of the church? It is you, he says, you who have taught the people to question things which previously they accepted in all humility, and to begin to 'reason' when they should simply believe, to discuss when they should merely 'adore'.

It is the 'spectacle abominable' of your convulsions, he says, which has undermined the testimony of miracles and your proceedings which have enabled the freethinkers to say that all talk of miracles proves nothing, requiring only some adroit impostors 'et des témoins imbéciles'.[94] It was due to their fomenting endless disputes and trouble all over France, finally, the Jansenists should now admit, that irreligion had spread so rapidly in the kingdom. How, then, was it possible to doubt that it was

[89] Ibid. 12, 42; Ricken, 'Condillac', 267; Cottret, *Jansénismes*, 75. [90] Ibid. 9.
[91] Ibid. 10; Brugmans, *Diderot*, 47; Haechler, *L'Encyclopédie*, 148–50. [92] [Diderot], *Suite*, 46.
[93] Ibid. 46–7. [94] Ibid. 79; Trousson, *Denis Diderot*, 187–8.

they who, for more than forty years, 'ont fait plus d'indifférents, plus d'incrédules que toutes les productions de la philosophie?'[95] If the pope, bishops, priests, monks, and the ordinary faithful, indeed the whole church with its mysteries, sacraments, sanctuaries, ceremonies, indeed the whole of religion, had fallen into disrepute: 'c'est votre ouvrage'.[96]

The third volume of the *Encyclopédie* appeared in 1753, by which time the first two volumes, thanks to Briasson, were on sale as far away as St Petersburg.[97] In their announcement introducing the new volume, the editors, in effect Diderot, offered an almost insultingly minimal apology to their Jesuit, Jansenist, episcopal, and academic opponents and even felt strongly enough placed to venture a carefully crafted rebuke to the entire church. Acknowledging how disheartened they had been just a few months before, they declared themselves greatly encouraged by the evidence of support 'from all sides', so much so that the editors had latterly been able to take up their pens once again with renewed confidence. They warned in measured, deliberate tones that 'religion' was now being used as a cynical pretext by bigoted and self-interested enemies of the *Encyclopédie* who, ridiculously citing just a small number 'd'expressions équivoques' which could easily slip in, unnoticed, by the editors, had purposely fomented 'un grand scandale' in the hope of blighting a project which was urgently needed in the view of all responsible-minded persons to enlighten the people. This was a serious abuse and showed there was a need, suggested the editors, for a serious and well-reasoned work to appear against 'les personnes mal-intentionnées et peu instruites' who without any legitimate justification thus betrayed the true interests of religion and truth to attack *les philosophes*: 'c'est un ouvrage qui manque à notre siècle'.[98]

Despite its comical aspects, the first stage of the 'guerre de l'*Encyclopédie*', down to the autumn of 1752, thus has a crucial significance in both intellectual and wider social-cultural history. Historians have often noted that it was at this point that the lines of ideological confrontation in France were reconfigured in a new way and that the *parti philosophique* first acquired its public profile as a 'sect' or party within French society and cultural life. The importance of this is considerable in itself. But, equally important, there is a second point which has not really been made before. The circumstances of the struggle locked together two opposed philosophical traditions which had long acknowledged, and continued to acknowledge, their own mutual antagonism and incompatibility but saw themselves as obliged to work together against a vastly more popular and more powerful force, namely that of *anti-philosophie* and Jansenism. This was a unique situation in Europe, differentiating the French Enlightenment from Enlightenment in Britain, Germany, the Netherlands, and elsewhere, and one which had a crucial consequence: it enabled the radical wing to come out from the closet and become, in the French-speaking world, the dominant partner.

[95] [Diderot], *Suite*, 52–3. [96] Ibid. 53. [97] Kopanev, 'Libraire-éditeur', 199.
[98] Diderot and d'Alembert, 'Avertissement des éditeurs', pp. i–ii, vi, xii.

34

Postscript

The pleas for the great diversity and heterogeneity of the Enlightenment fuelling the current lively debate over 'which Enlightenment?'[1] lose much of their intellectual force, and their usefulness as a teaching guide to the Enlightenment, arguably, when one highlights the core intellectual issues of that age and the controversies about them. The 'which Enlightenment?' debate is fundamentally misleading because all our current classifications of the Enlightenment in terms of plurality and difference, whether national, denominational, or subcultural, are inherently unable to encompass much of the intellectual ground covered by the chief Enlightenment controversies. Ultimately, the view that there was not one Enlightenment but rather a 'family of enlightenments' leads to distraction from the core issues, and even a meaningless relativism contributing to the loss of basic values needed by modern society, and hence also to the advance of Counter-Enlightenment and Postmodernism.

But the 'family of enlightenments' idea is by no means the only danger. While preference for intellectual isolationism, for adopting an essentially 'national' approach to the topic focusing on the 'British Enlightenment', the 'American Enlightenment', or 'French Enlightenment', may encapsulate some of the most essential ground and some of the most vital issues, it inevitably does so in a partial, insular, distorting, and philosophically inadequate fashion. In the past there was a strong tendency to assert the primacy of the 'French Enlightenment' which nowadays has thankfully been broadly discarded. Since France, from the 1730s onwards, was simultaneously the main base of the Radical Enlightenment *and* the chief branch of the Voltairean variant of the Lockean-Newtonian 'British Enlightenment', strictly speaking, there is no such thing as a 'French Enlightenment' at all. But what especially needs to be guarded against is the notion that an alternative particular national or social context is of surpassing importance for understanding the main lines and trends of the Enlightenment, and especially that one particular 'national' tradition retains an overriding value or relevance in our contemporary world.

Claiming that what is best and most valuable to us in 'the Enlightenment' should be attributed, indeed restored, 'to its progenitor, the British', as one historian

1 Schmidt, *What is Enlightenment?*, 1–44; Umbach, *Federalism and Enlightenment*, 25–8; Jürgens, 'Welke Verlichting?', 28–9, 38, 52–3; Schaich, 'A War of Words?', 29–31.

recently expressed her agenda,[2] is all too apt to encourage intellectual insularity and narrowness, and a tendency to belittle, ignore, and discount the contributions of other key national contexts. Furthermore, the growing emphasis on this particular 'national' and linguistic legacy is, for a variety of reasons, an increasingly powerful cultural construct of our time. For in the Far East, southern Asia, and eastern Europe today, pivotal areas of the world which have largely lost their former interest in learning French, German, and Italian, and for most intents and purposes now communicate with the West only in English, this approach has proven to be the obvious and most convenient means to introduce, explain, and impart an ostensible coherence and appearance of direction to the Enlightenment. Hence, the mounting pressure to acknowledge, or rather assume, that books and ideas expressed in what is today the world language must surely have been, from Locke and Newton onwards, the main path to the western Enlightenment by no means emanates only from anglophone countries. Rather, the mounting chorus calling for recognition of the supposedly specially hegemonic role for the 'British Enlightenment', often giving a particularly strong emphasis to the Scottish dimension, has become a powerful global phenomenon as evident in Taiwan and other fringes of China, or in contemporary Greece or Poland, for instance, as it is in Australia or India.

There is good reason to worry about this tendency in contemporary Enlightenment studies. For its effect is not just to unbalance and distort our picture of the intellectual course of the West's Enlightenment but actually to obscure indispensable parts of the historical reality: of the five most crucial 'national' contexts in the making of the eighteenth-century Enlightenment—the Dutch, French, British, German, and Italian—the British Enlightenment was actually never at any stage the principal arena in the making of the egalitarian, democratic 'Radical Enlightenment', the main source of 'modernity' understood as a philosophical 'package'. Rather the main line here transferred from the late seventeenth- and early eighteenth-century Dutch Republic to France, which consequently was the Enlightenment's true epicentre for most of the eighteenth century.

Finally, there is also a third substantial danger in the fashion for stressing the plurality and diversity of the Enlightenment. For focusing on subcultural enlightenments of sociability, Freemasonry, clubs, societies, the journals, and so forth[3] readily diverts us still further away from the goal, namely to survey the chief Enlightenment controversies in a balanced fashion. Indeed, such a desideratum is almost completely obscured if one adopts, as many do, a denominational standpoint such as 'Catholic', Anglican, Lutheran, 'Jewish',[4] 'Methodist', 'Unitarian', Orthodox, or Arminian[5] Enlightenment. Meanwhile, some scholars encourage a particular preoccupation with Freemasonry as a way not just to focus more attention on subcultures *per se* but as part of a wider plea to get scholars and students to accord primacy to the 'social' over the 'intellectual', thereby creating a wholly false

[2] Himmelfarb, *Roads to Modernity*, 5.
[3] Dupré, *Enlightenment*, 5–12.
[4] Schulte, *Jüdische Aufklärung*, 17–47; Feiner, *Jewish Enlightenment*, 1–20.
[5] Pocock, *Barbarism*, i. 51–8.

antithesis between the 'Enlightenment of the *philosophe*' and a so-called 'popular Enlightenment'.[6] Such a distinction may have some relevance with regard to purely learned disputes about ancient philosophy or Newtonian dynamics. But it is largely irrelevant to the major ideological controversies of the Enlightenment over toleration, press freedom, aristocracy, biology, the Glorious Revolution, Jacobitism, Orangism, the Bekker furore about magic and witchcraft, the Wertheim Bible, marriage, sexuality, and, indeed, as many contemporary sources show, about Newtonianism in general or Deist freethinking, great controversies which infused the whole of society. For popular participation, anxiety, and pressure was a constant factor in all these debates.

Indeed, from a strictly 'enlightened' viewpoint Freemasonry turns out, after further research, to be a rather peripheral phenomenon and not the significant key some have represented it as being. Although it did sometimes employ a rhetoric of equality, eighteenth-century French and German Freemasonry in reality hardly ever tried to erase distinctions between aristocracy and commoners, or between high bourgeoisie and the common man; rather such modes of sociability mostly sought to preserve and emphasize hierarchy in the context of their own rules and activities more than they endeavoured to break down existing lines of social hierarchy.[7] By and large, Masonic lodges were social mechanisms for muting rather than stimulating discussion of the difficult issues posed by the Enlightenment. If our aim is to get to the heart of the Enlightenment as a decisively important world-historical phenomenon, arguably the less said about Freemasonry the better.

The Enlightenment chiefly emphasized and prized by historians in the twentieth century was that most favoured by liberal churchmen and governments in the eighteenth century, namely the Enlightenment of Locke, Newton, Hume, Voltaire, Montesquieu, Turgot, and Kant. Its primary characteristics were the impulse to limit both the scope of 'reason' in philosophy and the use of reformist philosophy as a tool, mixing the new criteria of rationality and criticism with theology (especially central in Locke) whether Christian or 'natural' (providential Deist) as well as with respect for tradition, monarchy, social hierarchy, and existing political and moral institutions. This is the Enlightenment which fills the older textbooks and whose philosophical and scientific principles have until recently been urged to be authoritative, compelling, and sensible. But this was not the impulse which dominated the High Enlightenment in France from the late 1740s onwards. Neither was the moderate Enlightenment the impulse which shaped the French Revolution or had the greatest impact on the eighteenth century generally. Neither, finally, was it the moderate mainstream Enlightenment which has had the greatest continuing impact on modernity since the eighteenth century. Viewed from the democratic, egalitarian, and anti-colonial perspective of the post-1945 western world, the more important Enlightenment was surely that of the radical stream which also drew on many

[6] Jacob, *Radical Enlightenment*, 117–52; Jacob, *Living the Enlightenment*, 46, 215–24.

[7] Gayot, 'War die französische Freimauerei', 235–7, 246–8; Schrader, 'Aufklärungssoziabilität', 260–2, 272–3; Schaich, 'A War of Words?', 32–5; Robertson, *The Case*, 19,112.

sources, and figured many writers and thinkers, Descartes and Hobbes prominent among them, but was intellectually unified and crafted into a powerful philosophical apparatus primarily by Spinoza, Bayle, and Diderot.

Radical Enlightenment conceived as a package of basic concepts and values may be summarized in eight cardinal points: (1) adoption of philosophical (mathematical-historical) reason as the only and exclusive criterion of what is true; (2) rejection of all supernatural agency, magic, disembodied spirits, and divine providence; (3) equality of all mankind (racial and sexual); (4) secular 'universalism' in ethics anchored in equality and chiefly stressing equity, justice, and charity; (5) comprehensive toleration and freedom of thought based on independent critical thinking; (6) personal liberty of lifestyle and sexual conduct between consenting adults, safeguarding the dignity and freedom of the unmarried and homosexuals; (7) freedom of expression, political criticism, and the press, in the public sphere; (8) democratic republicanism as the most legitimate form of politics. This then is the essence of 'philosophical modernity' and this crucial core cannot usefully be linked to any one 'national', linguistic, religious, or subcultural context. On the contrary, it seems rather important in terms of both moral and cultural integrity, and historical accuracy, emphatically to reject the notion that one particular nation, religion, or cultural tradition played a hegemonic role in forging 'modernity' conceived as an interlocking system of values.

Abandoning the 'national' approach, and granting that the main issue is indeed to see how democratic, egalitarian, libertarian, and comprehensively tolerant values emerged, a number of recent scholars have adopted a rather different tactic for diverting attention from the radical monism of Spinoza, Bayle, Diderot, and the 'nouveaux Spinosistes', urging the tremendous diversity of intellectual and cultural contexts from which a given writer, thinker, or controversialist could move towards or embrace parts of the democratic, anti-colonial, egalitarian package.[8] It is perfectly true, of course, that clashes or convergences of distinct religious, cultural, and intellectual traditions often produced points of view enabling a writer or spokesmen, like Poulain de La Barre, Saint-Hyacinthe, or indeed Locke with respect to his *Second Treatise of Government*, to be radical in some respects but not in others: 'a certain degree of moderation in one area', it has aptly been said, 'often made radicalism in another possible and vice versa, radicalism in one area often went hand-in-hand with moderation in another'.[9]

However, adopting this in some ways novel and flexible approach can also lead to an unfortunate glossing over the intellectual incoherence characteristic of such positions. For if it was very common to be 'radical' in some respects but 'moderate' in others, it was assuredly not possible to be so coherently, with the result that parts

[8] Jacob, *Radical Enlightenment*, pp. xiv, 23, 27–59, 80, 151–3; Stuurman, *François Poulain de La Barre*, 15, 274–7; Mulsow, *Moderne*, 20–3, 339–40.

[9] Mulsow, *Moderne* 439–43; Martin Mulsow, 'The Radical Enlightenment: Problems and Perspectives', unpublished paper submitted at the Los Angeles Radical Enlightenment conference in Oct. 2003, p. 2.

of such a writer's legacy inevitably came to be detached from other parts. Hence, Poulain's insistence on the equality of the sexes is hard to square (not least in his own mind) with his acknowledgement of biblical authority, while respectable, mainstream Enlightenment in the eighteenth century almost invariably tended to detach the *Second Treatise* from its conception of Locke's thought, veneration of Locke in both Britain and continental Europe being mainly focused on his epistemology, limited toleration, theories of property, and method of reintegrating theology with philosophy, rather than on his politics of popular sovereignty and justified resistance to tyrannical kings. On the very rare occasions when this latter, radical strand of Locke's thought was deployed, as for instance by Rousset de Missy in Holland during the Revolution of 1747–8, it was always firmly detached from the rest of his thought. A further risk inherent in this type of pluralism is that it readily lends itself to asserting the primacy of social over intellectual factors, once again serving to shift attention from intellectual currents to a patchwork of local underground networks, locations, and regional contexts, encouraging students to focus on what are often rather peripheral topics, underground associations, and forms of sociability rather than on intellectual arguments and patterns of thought and controversy.

In this present work, over seventy writers French, Dutch, German, Italian, and British active within the period between 1660 and 1750 have been identified as significantly contributing to formulating and publicizing the ideas which drove the Radical Enlightenment, in conjunction with social forces and grievances where these helped produce the ideas and shape the controversies. National contexts doubtless played some part here, in particular by giving rise to more or less conducive situations and hence to the unequal distribution of these writers by nationality: among the five main 'national' contingents, the French group turns out to have been by far the largest, the Dutch the second largest, and the British group seemingly the smallest.

Equally clearly, the philosophical sources of inspiration of these seventy or so writers were extremely disparate: among the older thinkers from whom they drew their inspiration were Pomponazzi, Machiavelli, Bruno, Galileo, Gassendi, Descartes, Hobbes, Locke, Toland, Spinoza, Bayle, Malebranche, Leibniz, Fontenelle, and Boulainvilliers. The diverse intellectual currents which fed into the Radical Enlightenment ranged from late medieval Averroism to Renaissance naturalism, from early eighteenth-century English Deism and pantheism to Polish and Collegiant Socinianism, from liberal Sephardic Judaism to forms of Cartesianism and the rhetoric of the English Levellers. But this vast diversity notwithstanding, the only kind of philosophy which could (and can) coherently integrate and hold together such a far-reaching value condominium in the social, moral, and political spheres, as well as in 'philosophy', was the monist, hylozoic systems of the Radical Enlightenment generally labelled 'Spinozist' in the 'long' eighteenth century, even though in some cases, such as those of Du Marsais, Meslier, and, perhaps, Toland and Collins, there may possibly have been little or no direct derivation.

Only these kinds of system with their powerful unifying tendency and intellectual cohesion were included by Diderot in the corpus of philosophy which, in his remarks on Helvétius of 1773, he called 'clear, distinct and frank'.[10] Intellectually and ideologically, nothing else could so effectively bind all the elements of the Radical Enlightenment into a cohesive whole and this, as was widely acknowledged at the time, was the reason why so many of the key controversies in France, the Netherlands, Germany, and Italy revolved principally around propositions and constructions originally formulated by Spinoza or Bayle.

Important sources also were the Greek Presocratics, ancient Stoicism, Epicureanism, scepticism, variant forms of Aristotelianism, and eclecticism. Some also immensely admired what they knew of classical Chinese culture and philosophy. But while it is easy to draw attention to the diversity of any historical phenomenon, it is often far more important for the historian to try to explain the general direction and pattern of convergence, viewing 'Enlightenment' not just as a European or 'Atlantic' phenomenon but something operating across the entire globe. Thus, Postcolonialism has proved very useful for getting more scholars and students to recognize 'how colonialism created injustice in the colonized regions', as one scholar puts it,[11] and to see that there was much of originality, beauty, and integrity in pre-colonial cultures. But, equally, Postcolonialism has proved generally useless for helping us to discern how pre-colonial integrity relates to, and can feed into, the core values, including anti-colonialism, of philosophical 'modernity' as expressed by the Radical Enlightenment. The European anti-colonial and democratic Enlightenment absorbed a great many influences and, in that sense, was a thoroughly varied and plural phenomenon; but from the 1660s it also exhibited a high degree of continuity, coherence, and unity whether in the form of published books, clandestine manuscripts, or reconstructions of its ideas in academic disputations, and this can only be explained in terms of the centrality in its formation of monist philosophies and specifically the thinking patterns of Spinoza, Bayle, and Diderot.

Postcolonialists together with Postmodernist philosophers such as Alasdair MacIntyre and Charles Taylor were mistaken in supposing there is no coherent or viable moral core to the Enlightenment and in claiming to have 'exposed the moral fictions that mask modern morality's lack of a foundation and cover up the fact that what it presents as values are nothing but 'the preferences of arbitrary will and desire'.[12] However, these commentators were to some extent correct—even if they never managed to express the point clearly or accurately—in their suspicion that a consistent and coherent Enlightenment moral philosophy was never very strongly promoted, or adequately expounded, in the thought of many of those philosophers and scientists traditionally acknowledged as the principal heroes of the Enlightenment, most notably Locke, Newton, Hume, Voltaire, Montesquieu, and Kant.

[10] Bourdin, *Diderot*, 9. [11] Lee, 'Post-modernist/Post-colonialist Nationalism', 95.
[12] Gutting, *Pragmatic Liberalism*, 74.

Postmodernist and Postcolonialist thinkers called in question the validity of the Enlightenment's conception of reason and sought to discredit its efforts to further the general welfare of society and the general good.[13] But in doing so Postmodernists and Postcolonialists so thoroughly muddled the two main dimensions of the Enlightenment as wholly to invalidate their own analysis and perpetrate a highly questionable conflation of disparate strands, providing massive if spurious leverage for a wide range of social conservatives, nationalists, fundamentalists, anti-democrats, and adherents of Counter-Enlightenment. Postmodernist and Postcolonialist 'difference' and plurality judged as a critique of, and as an answer to, Enlightenment is simply too inaccurate, and incoherent, both historically and philosophically, to be taken seriously in appraising 'modernity' whether defined philosophically or historically. But a wrong appraisal if sufficiently modish can still lend powerful support, as indeed both Postmodernism and Postcolonialism do, to claims that a range of national, religious, non-western, and subcultural approaches to the complexities of ordering modern life are morally and politically of equivalent or superior validity to the visions of 'modernity' forged by the Enlightenment merely because they are anti-Enlightenment and often non-western.

The Postmodernist and Postcolonialist claim that 'all values are equally valid' is thus a major threat to democratic, egalitarian values and individual liberty and, as such, reveals itself to be just as devoid of moral and political as of intellectual cogency. Both theoretically and in practice, they provide a gigantic fig-leaf of wholly spurious moral justification to what amounts to systematic infringement of individual liberty, democratic integrity, and the basic equality of all men, tacitly endorsing the subordination and disadvantaging of long despised minorities, as well as of women and homosexuals.

For anyone who believes human societies are best ruled by reason as defined by the Radical Enlightenment, ordering modern societies on the basis of individual liberty, democracy, equality, equity, sexual freedom, and freedom of expression and publication clearly constitutes a package of rationally validated values which not only were, but remain today, inherently superior morally, politically, and intellectually not only to Postmodernist claims but to *all* actual or possible alternatives, no matter how *different*, national, and Postcolonial and no matter how illiberal, non-western, and traditional. The social values of the Radical Enlightenment, in short, have an absolute quality in terms of reason which places them above any possible alternative, always provided we bear in mind, as Isaac Vossius, William Temple, and Saint-Évremond pointed out in the late seventeenth century, and a new wave of Chinese reformers stressed in the 1890s, there is no reason why one should search only in western philosophical traditions to find the intellectual roots of, or a cultural basis for, personal liberty, comprehensive toleration, equality sexual and racial, and a secular morality of equity—any less, indeed, than for grounding anti-slavery or anti-colonialism.

[13] Ibid. 70–7; MacIntyre, *After Virtue*, 265–6; Gray, *Enlightenment's Wake*, 153.

For if a universalist secular ethic is indeed superior on rational grounds to other moralities, this means there must be multiple intellectual and cultural sources of such ideas whether European, Asian, American, or African. As Kang Youwei observed in the context of his attempted reform of Confucianism in the 1890s, no matter how deeply rooted obedience, family control over the individual, and social hierarchy are within a given cultural-ideological heritage, moral universalism based on equality, democracy, and personal liberty is ultimately both superior to, and compatible with, cultural difference where ancient cultural traditions are suitably adjusted, reformed, adapted, and 'modernized' in the light of these universal values.[14] It is precisely this continuing, universal relevance of its values on all continents, and among all branches of humanity, together with the unprecedented intellectual cohesion it gave to these moral and social ideals, which accounts for what Bernard Williams called the 'intellectual irreversibility of the Enlightenment', its uniquely central importance in the history of humanity.[15] Parenthetically, it might be worth adding that nothing could be more fundamentally mistaken, as well as politically injudicious, than for the European Union to endorse the deeply mistaken notion that 'European values' if not nationally particular are at least religiously specific and should be recognized as essentially 'Christian' values. That the religion of the papacy, Inquisition, and Puritanism should be labelled the quintessence of 'Europeanness' would rightly be considered a wholly unacceptable affront by a great number of thoroughly 'European' Europeans.

Hence, the formidable strength of the current opposition to the values of the Radical Enlightenment whether Postmodern, Postcolonialist, nationalist, religious, or traditionalist is by no means a proof of their invalidity or their failure. Quite the reverse. Far from it being true that the 'problems of modern moral theory emerge clearly as the product of the failure of the Enlightenment project',[16] as MacIntyre holds, the crisis of modern morality can much more compellingly be shown to result from the continuing and fierce worldwide resistance to the equity and equality, as well as democracy, of the radical stream's 'common good', an opposition which began in the late seventeenth century and which continues today at the expense of vast sections of humanity. The irony is that while Postmodernist and Postcolonialist philosophers insist on the moral 'failure of the Enlightenment project', it is actually their assortment of 'post-Enlightenment' philosophies (frequently mere invitations to Counter-Enlightenment), their slogan that there can be no adjudication of the 'culture wars' of our time since 'all values are equally valid', which, as one scholar aptly put it, actually have least of 'ethical importance' to offer the world's 'excluded and exploited'.[17]

This is unquestionably true. But if Postmodernists and Postcolonialists make no claim to be seeking what is universal, what is conceivably 'worst of all', as some alert observers have warned, is that 'the fashionable despair about the prospects for

[14] Spence, *Gate of Heavenly Peace*, 31–42, 50–2, 63–74.
[15] Williams, *Truth and Truthfulness*, 254.
[16] MacIntyre, *After Virtue*, 62; Gray, *Enlightenment's Wake*, 148.
[17] Bronner, *Reclaiming*, 13.

humankind fostered by Postmodernism could easily prove to be a self-fulfilling prophecy'.[18] Yes, indeed. The democratic, egalitarian, and libertarian quest of the Radical Enlightenment might very well fail in the end—or rather be defeated and overwhelmed. But, if so, this will be at least partly due to the late twentieth- and early twenty-first-century failure not just of philosophy on all continents but more broadly of the humanities, and the world's universities, both in general terms and, more specifically, their failure to teach humanity about the historical origins and true character of the 'modern' ideas of democracy, equality, individual freedom, full toleration, liberty of expression, anti-colonialism, and our universalist secular morality based on equity.

[18] Meynell, *Postmodernism*, 185.

Bibliography

Primary

AALSTIUS, JOHANNES, *Inleiding to de Zeden-leer* (Dordrecht, 1705) BL.

Aan de Waarde Meede-Burgers van Amsterdam (Knuttel 17986) (Amsterdam, 1748) KBH.

Aan de Weledle Grootachbaare Heeren Burgemeesteren en de Vroedschappen der Stadt Amsterdam (Knuttel 17971) (Amsterdam, 1748) HKB.

Acta eruditorum (Acta Lipsiensia) periodical: (Leipzig, 1682–1750).

Acta Stoschiana (1694; Leipzig, 1749), in Stosch, *Concordia*, 239–312.

ALEMBERT, J. LE ROND d', *Traité de dynamique* (1743; 2nd edn. Paris, 1758).

—— 'Éloge historique de M. Jean Bernoulli' (1748), in *Mélanges* (1770), ii. 11–66.

—— *Discours préliminaire*, in vol. i (1751) of the *Encyclopédie*, pp. i–xlv.

—— *Essai sur les élémens de philosophie ou sur les principes des connoissances humaines* (1759), in *Mélanges* (1770), iv. 1–298.

—— *Mélanges de littérature, d'histoire et de philosophie* (2 vols., Berlin, 1753) BL.

—— *Mélanges de littérature, d'histoire et de philosophie* (5 vols., Amsterdam, 1770).

—— *Recherches sur différens points importans du système du monde* (3 vols., Paris, 1754–6) BL.

—— *Essai sur les élémens de philosophie, ou sur les principes des connoissances humaines*, in d'Alembert, *Mélanges* (1770), iv. 1–298.

—— 'Éloge de Montesquieu', in Montesquieu, *Œuvres complètes*, ed. Oster, 21–32.

Het Algemeen Historisch, Geographisch en Genealogisch Woordenboek, ed. A. G. Luïscius (8 vols., The Hague, 1724–30) BL.

ALLAMAND, J. N. S., *Histoire de la vie et des ouvrages de Mr 's Gravesande*, in 's-Gravesande, *Œuvres philosophiques et mathématiques*, i, pp. ix–lix.

Antwoord aen den Opstelder van de Aanmerkingen op de vergaderingen in de Schutters Doelen (Knuttel 18001) (Amsterdam, 1748) HKB.

Archives de la Bastille: documents inédits, ed. F. Ravaisson (19 vols., Paris, 1866–1904).

—— *Mémoires de Monsieur le marquis d'Argens* (2nd edn. 'Londres', 1737) UCLA.

—— *Lettres morales et critiques sur les différens états et les diverses occupations des hommes* (1737; new edn. Amsterdam, 1746) PBM.

ARGENS, JEAN-BAPTISTE DE BOYER, MARQUIS d', *Lettres cabalistiques, ou Correspondance philosophique, historique et critique* (1739–40; 2nd edn., 7 vols., The Hague, 1759) UCLA.

—— *La Philosophie du bons-sens ou Réflexions philosophiques sur l'incertitude des connoissances humaines* (1737 2 vols., new edn., The Hague, 1747) UCLA.

—— *Lettres chinoises, ou Correspondance philosophique, historique et critique* (5 vols., The Hague, 1739–40) UCLA.

—— *Lettres juives ou Correspondance philosophique, historique et critique entre un Juif voiageur en différens états de l'Europe et ses correspondans en divers endroits* (1735–7; new edn., 6 vols, The Hague, 1742) PrF.

—— *Le Législateur moderne, ou Les Mémoires du chevalier de Meillcourt* (Amsterdam, 1739) WLC.

—— *Réflexions historiques et critiques sur le goût et sur les principaux auteurs anciens et modernes* (Berlin, 1743) GUB.

—— *Mémoires secrets de la République des Lettres ou le théâtre de la vérité* (7 vols., Amsterdam, 1744) ABM.

—— *Songes philosophiques par l'auteur des* Lettres juives (Berlin, 1746) PBM.

—— *Thérèse philosophe*, ed. G. Pigeard de Gurbert (n.p., 1992).

—— *The Impartial Philosopher; or, The Philosophy of Common Sense* (2 vols., London, 1749) WLC.

—— *The Jewish Spy: Being a Philosophical, Historical and Critical Correspondence, by Letters which Lately Pass'd between Certain Jews in Turkey, Italy, France etc.* (4 vols., Dublin, 1753) WLC.

—— *Mémoires du Marquis d'Argens*, ed. Louis Thomas (Paris, 1941).

Arnauld, Antoine, *Morale pratique des Jésuites* (1691), in Arnauld, *Œuvres*, xxxiv (Paris, 1780).

—— *Œuvres* (43 vols., Paris, 1775–83) PFL.

Arnim, Johann von (ed.), *Stoicorum veterum fragmenta* (4 vols., Leipzig, 1905–24).

Arnold, Johann Konrad (praes.), *Universalista in theologia naturali planeta* (Giessen, 1719), repr. in Pott (ed.), *Philosophische, clandestina*, ser. 1, vol. i.

Arrian, *Epictetus' Discourses*, trans. W. A. Oldfather (1925; repr. 2 vols., Cambridge, Mass., 2000).

Atwood, William, *The History, and Reasons, of the Dependency of Ireland upon the Imperial Crown of the Kingdom of England* (London, 1698) BL.

Aubert de Versé, Noël, *L'Impie convaincu ou Dissertation contre Spinosa* (Amsterdam, 1685) UCLA.

—— *Traité de la liberté de conscience ou de l'authorité des souverains sur la religion des peuples* ('Cologne' [Amsterdam], 1687; repr. Paris, 1998).

Auserlesene theologische Bibliothec oder Gründliche Nachrichten von denen neuesten und besten theologische Büchern (periodical: Leipzig, from 1724) GUB.

Avalon, Cousin d', *D'Alembertiana, ou Recueil d'anecdotes, bons mots, plaisanteries, maximes, réflections et pensées de d'Alembert* (Paris, 1813) BL.

Averroes (Abu'l Walid Ibn-Rushd), *Grand commentaire de la métaphysique d'Aristote*, trans. and ed. A. Martin (Paris, 1984).

Balling, Pieter, *Het Licht op den Kandelaer* (Amsterdam, 1662) AUB.

Baltus, Jean-François, *Jugement des SS pères sur la morale de la philosophie payenne* (Strasbourg, 1719) PBM.

—— 'Sentiment du R.P. Baltus Jesuite, sur le traité *De la foiblese de l'esprit humain*', *Bibliothèque françoise*, 10 (1727), art. iv, pp. 49–118.

Barbeyrac, Jean, 'Préface' to Pufendorf, *Le Droit de la nature et des gens* (Amsterdam, 1706), pp. i–xcii.

—— *Éloge historique de feu Mr. Jean Le Clerc* (Amsterdam, 1736) UBA.

Basnage, Jacques, *Traité de la conscience* (2 vols., Amsterdam, 1696) KB.

—— *Histoire des Juifs depuis Jésus-Christ jusqu'à présent* (16 vols., The Hague, 1716) BL.

Basnage de Beauval, Henri, *Tolérance des religions* (1684; New York, 1970).

Bayle, Pierre, *Pensées diverses sur la comète*, ed. A. Prat (Paris, 1994).

—— *Commentaire philosophique sur les paroles de Jésus-Christ, 'Contrains-les d'entrer'*, ed. Jean-Michel Gros (1686; n.p. [Paris?], 1992).

Bayle, Pierre, *Ce que c'est que la France toute Catholique sous le règne de Louis le Grand*, ed. E. Labrousse (Paris, 1973).
——*Nouvelles de la République des Lettres* (4 vols., Amsterdam, 1684–7) BL.
——*La Cabale chimérique* ('Cologne' [Amsterdam], 1691) BL.
——*Supplément du Commentaire philosophique* (1688), ed. M. Pécharman, in Zarka et al. (eds.), *Fondements philosophiques*, ii. 19–259.
——*Projet et fragmens d'un dictionnire critique* (Rotterdam, 1692) BL.
——*Dictionnaire historique et critique* (1697; 3 vols., Rotterdam, 1702) BL.
——*Dictionnaire historique et critique* (1697; rev. 4 vols., Amsterdam, 1740).
——*An Historical and Critical Dictionary* (4 vols., London, 1710).
——*Continuation des Pensées diverses sur la comète* (2 vols., Rotterdam, 1705) BL.
——*Continuation des Pensées diverses sur la comète* (4 vols., Rotterdam, 1721) BL.
——*Réponse aux questions d'un provincial* (5 vols., Rotterdam, 1704–7) BL.
——*Entretiens de Maxime et de Thémiste* (Rotterdam, 1707), in *Œuvres diverses*, iv. 3–106.
——*Lettres de Mr Bayle*, ed. Pierre Des Maizeaux (3 vols., Amsterdam, 1729) BL.
——*Écrits sur Spinoza*, ed. Françoise Charles-Daubert and Pierre-François Moreau (Paris, 1983).
——*Political Writings*, ed. S. L. Jenkinson (Cambridge, 2000).
——*Correspondance*, ed. E. Labrousse, E. James, A. McKenna, M. C. Pitassi and R. Whelan (3 vols. so far; Oxford, 1999–).
——*Œuvres diverses* (1731; 4 vols., repr. Hildesheim, 2001).
——'Mémoire communiqué par Mr. Bayle pour servir de réponse à ce qui le peut intéresser dans . . . 5 tome de la *Bibliothèque choisie*', in Bayle, *Œuvres diverses*, iv. 179–84.
Beermann, S., *Impietas atheistica scoptico-sceptica detecta et confutata* (Leipzig, 1720) GUB.
Bekker, Balthasar, *Kort Begryp der Algemene Kerkelyke Historien Zedert het Jaar 1666 daar Hornius eindigt tot den Jare 1684* (Amsterdam, 1686) BL.
——*De Betoverde Weereld* (1691–4; new edn., 4 vols., Deventer, 1739) BL.
——*Kort Beright . . . Aangaande alle de schriften, welke over sijn Boek* De Betoverde Weereld *enen tijd lang heen en weder verwisseld zijn* (Franeker, 1692) BL.
Benoist, Élie, *Mélange de remarques critiques, historiques, philosophiques, théologiques sur les deux dissertations de M. Toland* (Delft, 1712) BL.
Benthem, Heinrich Ludolff, *Holländischer Kirch- und Schulen-Staat* (2 vols., Frankfurt, 1698) BL.
Bentley, Richard, *Eight Boyle Lectures on Atheism* (London, 1692; repr. Garland, 1976).
——*Remarks upon a Late Discourse of Free-Thinking* (London, 1713) BL.
——*La Friponnerie laïque des prétendus esprits-forts d'Angleterre* (new edn. Amsterdam, 1738) AUB.
——*The Folly of Atheism: and (What is now Called) Deism, even with Respect to the Present Life* (London, 1692).
——*The Works*, ed. A. Dyce (3 vols., London, 1836–8; repr. 1971).
Bergier, Nicolas-Sylvestre, *Apologie de la religion chrétienne* (1769; 2nd edn., 2 vols., Paris, 1776).
Berkeley, George, *Alciphron, or The Minute Philosopher*, ed. David Berman (London, 1993).
Bernard, Jacques, *De l'excellence de la religion* (Amsterdam, 1714) GUB.
——*Nouvelles de la République des Lettres* (Amsterdam, 1699–1710 and 1716–18).
——*Supplément aux anciennes éditions du* Grand Dictionnaire historique *de Mr. Louis Moreri* (2 vols., Amsterdam, 1716) BL.

Bernard, Jean-Frédéric, *Réflexions morales, satiriques et comiques, sur les mœurs de notre siècle* ('Cologne. Chez Pierre Marteau' [Amsterdam?], 1711) PFL.

—— *Dialogues critiques et philosophiques* (Amsterdam, 1730) PFL.

—— *Superstitions anciennes et modernes* (2 vols., Amsterdam, 1733) PFL.

—— *Le Monde, son origine, et son antiquité* (2 vols., 'Londres' [Amsterdam?]) PFL.

—— (ed.), *Bibliothèque françoise* (13 vols., Amsterdam, 1723–9) GUB.

—— *Dissertations mêlées sur divers sujets importans et curieux* (2 vols., Amsterdam, 1740) BL.

—— *Lettre à Monsieur G. J. 's-Gravesande professeur en philosophie à Leide, sur son Introduction à la philosophie* (Amsterdam, 1736) AUB.

—— and Picart, Bernard, *Cérémonies et coûtumes religieuses des peuples idolâtres* [i.e. vol. i of the *Cérémonies et coutûmes religieuses de tous les peuples du monde*] (1723 Amsterdam, 1735) AUB.

—— *The Ceremonies and Religious Customs of the Various Nations of the Known World* (7 vols., London, 1733–4) BL.

—— *Céremonies et coûtumes religieuses de tous les peuples du monde*, v: *Qui contient les cérémonies des Mahométans* (Amsterdam, 1737) AUB.

Beverland, Hadrianus, *De peccato originali* (Leiden, 1679) BL.

—— *Histoire de l'état de l'homme dans le péché originel* (1678; n.p. [Amsterdam?, 1714]) AUB.

Bibliothèque ancienne et moderne, ed. Jean le Clerc (periodical: Amsterdam, 1714–26) BL.

Bibliothèque choisie, ed. Jean Le Clerc (periodical: Amsterdam, 1703–13) BL.

Bibliothèque françoise, ou Histoire littéraire de la France (periodical: Amsterdam, 1723–46).

Bibliothèque germanique (periodical: Amsterdam, 1720–41) GUB.

Bibliothèque universelle et historique, ed. Jean Le Clerc (periodical: Amsterdam, 1686–93) BL.

Bierling, Friedrich Wilhelm, *Dissertatio theologica de origine mali* (Rinteln, 1719; repr. in Bierling, *Dissertationes selectae*, ed. M. Mulsow (Lecce, 1999) (unpaginated).

Bilfinger, Georg Berhard, *Specimen doctrinae veterum Sinarum moralis et politicae* (Frankfurt am Main, 1724) PFL.

Blount, Charles, *Anima mundi, or, An Historical Narration of the Opinions of the Ancients Concerning Man's Soul after this Life* (London, 1679) PFL.

—— *Great is Diana of the Ephesians or, The Original of Idolatry* (London, 1695) PFL.

Bluhme, Christophorus, *Exercitatio philosophica de eo quod pulchrum est in theologia naturali* (Copenhagen, 1732) GUB.

De Boekzaal van Europe, ed. Pieter Rabus (periodical: Rotterdam, 1692–1702) BL.

Bolingbroke, Henry St John, Viscount, *The Philosophical Works*, ed. R.Wellek (5 vols., New York, 1977).

—— *Political Writings*, ed. David Armitage (Cambridge, 1997).

Boulainvilliers, Henri de, *Œuvres philosophiques*, ed. Renée Simon (2 vols., The Hague, 1973–5).

—— *La Vie de Mahomed* ('Londres' [Amsterdam?], 1730) BL.

—— *Essais sur la noblesse de France contenans une dissertation sur son origine et établissement*, ed. J. F. de Tabary ('Amsterdam'[Rouen], 1732) YML.

—— *État de la France* (8 vols., 'à Londres', 1752) YSL.

—— *The Life of Mahomet* (London, 1743) BL.

—— M.L.C.D.C.D.B. [Monsieur le Comte etc.... Boulainvilliers], *Abrégé d'histoire universelle* (MS version, 2 vols.) IAS.

[Boulanger, Nicolas-Antoine], B.I.D.P.E.C., *Recherches sur l'origine du despotisme oriental* ('Londres' [Amsterdam?], 1762) PFL.

[Boulenger de Rivery, Claude François-Félix], *Apologie de* L'Esprit des loix, *ou Réponse aux Observations de M. de L.P.* (Amsterdam, 1751) BL.

Boureau-Deslandes, André-François, *A Philological Essay, or Reflections on the Death of Free-Thinkers* (London, 1713) BL.

—— *Histoire critique de la philosophie* (3 vols., Amsterdam, 1737) BL.

—— *De Konst om zonder verdriet in de Weereld te leeven* (Amsterdam, 1740) AUB.

—— *De la certitude des connoissances ou Examen philosophique des diverses prérogatives de la raison et de la foi* ('Londres' [Amsterdam?], 1741) BL.

—— *Pygmalion ou la statue animée* (1742), in H. Coulet (ed.), *Pygmalions des Lumières* (Paris, 1998), 47–70.

—— *L'Apothéose du beau-sexe* ('à Londres' [Amsterdam?], 1712) YML.

—— *Réflexions sur les grands hommes qui sont morts en plaisantant* (new edn. Amsterdam, 1758) AUB.

Boyle, Robert, *A Free Enquiry into the Vulgarly Received Notion of Nature*, ed. E. B. Davis and Michael Hunter (Cambridge, 1996).

Brink, Henricus, *Ongenoegsame satisfactie, gedaan door den auteur van het boek*, De Betoverde Weereld *genaamt* (Utrecht, 1692).

Brucker, Jakobus, *Historia philosophica doctrinae de ideis* (Augsburg, 1723) AUB.

—— *Otium vindelicum, sive maletematum historico-philosophicorum triga* (Augsburg, 1729) GUB.

—— *De Stratonis Lampsaceni atheismo dissertatio epistolaris*, in *Amoenitates literariae quibus variae observationes scripta item quaedam anecdota et rariora opuscula exhibentur*, vols. xiii–xiv (Frankfurt, 1730), 311–23 BL.

—— *Kurtze Fragen aus der philosophischen Historie von den Anfang der Welt bis auf die Geburt Christi* (2 vols., Ulm, 1731) BL.

—— *Historia critica philosophiae* (1st edn., 5 vols., Leipzig, 1742; repr. Hildesheim, 1975).

—— *Historia critica philosophiae* (2nd edn., 6 vols., Leipzig, 1767) BL.

[Bruzen de la Martinière, Antoine], *Entretiens des ombres aux Champs Élisées sur divers sujets d'histoire, de politique et de morale* (2nd edn., 2 vols., Amsterdam, 1723) UBA.

—— *Abrégé portatif du Dictionnaire géographique de La Martinière* (2 vols., The Hague, 1762).

Buddeus, Franz, *De Spinozismo ante Spinozam* (1701), repr. in Buddeus, *Analecta*, 309–59 BL.

—— *Elementa philosophiae instrumentalis* (2nd edn., 2 vols., Halle, 1706) BL.

—— *Theses theologicae de atheismo et superstitione* (1717; new edn. Utrecht, 1737) UCLA.

—— *Analecta historiae philosophicae* (2nd edn. Halle, 1724) BL.

—— *Miscellanea sacra* (3 vols., Jena, 1727) KBJ.

—— *Introductio ad philosophiam stoicam ex mente M. Antonini* (Leipzig, 1729) BL.

—— *Compendium historiae philosophicae* (Halle, 1731) KBJ.

—— *Traité de l'athéisme et de la superstition* (Amsterdam, 1740) UCLA.

Burke, Edmund, *Pre-Revolutionary Writings* (Cambridge, 1993).

—— *Reflections on the Revolution in France* (1790; New York, 1987).

Burmannus, Franciscus (the younger), *Burmannorum pietas, gratissimae beati parentis memoriae communi nomine exhibita* (Utrecht, 1700) BL.

—— *'t Hoogste Goed der Spinozisten vergeleken met den* Hemel op Aarden (Enkhuizen, 1704) AUB.

Burmannus, Frans, *Exercitationum academicarum pars prior* [et posterior] (Rotterdam, 1688) AUB.
Burnet, Gilbert, *History of his Own Time* (6 vols., Oxford, 1833).
[Bury, Arthur], *The Naked Gospel* (London, 1690) BL.
Capasso, Giambattista, *Historiae philosophiae synopsis* (Naples, 1728) NBN.
Capitein, Jacobus Johannes, *Political-Theological Dissertation Examining the Question: Is Slavery Compatible with Christian Freedom or not?* (1742), trans. G. Parker in Parker, *Agony of Asar*, 81–132.
Carroll, William, *Spinoza Reviv'd* (London, 1709) BL.
——*Spinoza Reviv'd, Part the Second, or, A Letter to Monsieur Le Clerc* (London, 1711) LDrW.
Challe, Robert, *Difficultés sur la religion proposées au Père Malebranche* (ed.) F. Deloffre and F. Moureau (Geneva, 2000).
Chaufepié, Jaques Georges, *Nouveau Dictionnaire historique et critique pour servir de supplément ou de continuation au Dictionnaire de... Pierre Bayle* (4 vols., Amsterdam, 1750) BL.
Chubb, Thomas, *A Discourse Concerning Reason with Regard to Religion* (London, 1731).
Clarke, Samuel, *The Works* (4 vols., London, 1738).
——*A Demonstration of the Being and Attributes of God*, (ed.) E. Vailati (Cambridge, 1998).
——*A Third Defense of an Argument Made Use of in a Letter [by S. Clarke] to Mr Dodwel, to Prove the Immateriality and Natural Immortality of the Soul* (London, 1708).
Clement of Alexandria, *Protreptikos pros Hellenas (The Exhortation to the Greeks)*, trans. G. W. Butterworth (Loeb, 1919; Cambridge, Mass., repr. 1999).
Colerus, Johannes, *La Vie de B. de Spinoza* (The Hague, 1706) UCLA.
Collins, Anthony, *A Discourse of Free-Thinking* (London, 1713; repr. New York, 1984).
——*An Essay Concerning the Use of Reason in Propositions* (London, 1707) BL.
——*An Answer to Mr Clark's Third Defence of his Letter to Mr. Dodwell* (London, 1708) BL.
——*Priestcraft in Perfection* (1709; 3rd edn. 1710) YBL.
——*Discours sur la liberté de penser. Écrit à l'occasion d'une nouvelle secte d'esprits forts ou de gens qui pensent librement* ('à Londres' [The Hague], 1714) GUB.
——*A Philosophical Inquiry Concerning Human Liberty* (2nd edn. London, 1717) BL.
——*A Discourse of the Grounds and Reasons of the Christian Religion* (London, 1724) BL.
Concina, Daniele, *Della religione rivelata contro gli ateisti* (2 vols., Venice, 1754) VBM.
Condillac, Étienne Bonnot de, *Essay on the Origin of Human Knowledge* (1746), ed. H. Aarsleff (Cambridge, 2001).
——*Traité des sistêmes* (1749; Paris, 1991).
Condorcet, Jean-Antoine-Nicolas de Caritat, marquis de, *Vie de Voltaire*, vol. i ('Londres' [Paris?], 1791).
——*Réflexions sur la Révolution de 1688, et celle du 10 août 1792* (n.p., n.d. [Paris, 1792]).
——*Esquisse d'un tableau historique des progrès de l'esprit humain* (Paris, 1795) PBN.
Conti, Antonio, *Prose e poesie* (2 vols., Venice, 1739) NYPL.
——*Illustrazione del Parmenide di Platone con una dissertazione preliminare* (Venice, 1743) VBM.
——*Scritti filosofici*, ed. N. Badaloni (Naples, 1972).
Corpus des notes marginales de Voltaire, ed. T. Voronova (5 vols. thus far, Berlin, 1979–94).

Crousaz, Jean-Pierre de, *Examen du Pyrrhonisme ancien et moderne* (The Hague, 1733) UCLA.

Cudworth, Ralph, *The True Intellectual System of the Universe* (1678; 2 vols., New York, 1978).

—— *Systema intellectuale huius universi*, ed. and annotated by J. L. Mosheim (2 vols., Jena, 1733) AUB.

—— *A Treatise Concerning Eternal and Immutable Morality*, ed. Sarah Hutton (Cambridge, 1996).

Cuffeler, Abraham, *Specimen artis ratiocinandi* (3 vols., 'Hamburg' [Amsterdam], 1684) BL.

Cymbalum mundi sive Symbolum sapientiae, ed. G. Canziani et al. (Milan, 2000).

Dale, Anthonie van, *De oraculis veterum ethnicorum* (1683; 2nd edn. Amsterdam, 1700) BL.

—— *Verhandeling van de Oude Orakelen der Heydenen* (1687; new edn. Amsterdam, 1718) HHL.

—— 'Aanmerkinge op de Getuigenisse wegens den Zaligmaker Jezus Christus Die men in Josefus vind', preface to Rabus, *Griekse, Latijnse*, p. xviii.

—— *Dissertatio super Aristea De LXX interpretibus* (Amsterdam, 1705) WLC.

Denyse, Jean, *La Vérité de la religion chrétienne démontrée par ordre géometrique* (Paris, 1719) BL.

Derham, William, *Dimostrazione della essenza, ed attributi d'Iddio del'opere della sua Creazione* (Florence, 1719) VBM.

Desaguliers, J. T., 'A Letter to the Translator (John Chaberlayne) (2 Feb. 1718)', prefix to Nieuwentyt, *Religious Philosopher*.

Deschamps, Léger-Marie, *Œuvres philosophiques* (2 vols., Paris, 1993).

[Desfontaines, Abbé], *Lettres . . . à Monsieur l'Abbé Houtteville au sujet du livre de La Religion chrétienne prouvée par les faits* (Paris, 1722) MBN.

Des Maizeaux, Pierre, *La Vie de Monsieur de Saint-Évremond*, in vol. ii of *Œuvres de Monsieur de Saint-Évremond*, ed. P. Des Marzeaux (5 vols., Amsterdam, 1726) BL.

—— *La Vie de Monsieur Bayle*, in Pierre Bayle, *Dictionnaire historique et critique* (5th edn. Amsterdam, 1740), i, pp. xvii–cxii.

Deurhoff, Willem, *Voorleeringen van de H. Godgeleerdheid* (Amsterdam, 1687) AUB.

Diderot, Denis, *Œuvres complètes*, ed. R. Lewinter (15 vols., Paris, 1969–73).

—— *Œuvres philosophiques*, ed. P. Vernière (Paris, 1990).

—— *Correspondance*, ed. G. Roth and J. Varloot (15 vols., Paris, 1955–70).

—— [based on Shaftesbury], *Essai sur le mérite et la vertu* (repr. Paris, 1998).

—— *Pensées philosophiques*, in Diderot, *Œuvres philosophiques*, 9–55.

—— *Additions aux Pensées philosophiques*, in Diderot, *Œuvres philosophiques* (1763; Paris,1990), 53–72.

—— 'De la suffisance de la religion naturelle' (1745), in *Œuvres*, ed. Versini, i. 55–64.

—— *La Promenade du sceptique* (1746), in Diderot, *Œuvres complètes*, i. 307–401.

—— *Lettre de M. Diderot au R.P. Berthier, Jésuite* (n.p. [Paris], 1751) YSL.

—— *Lettre sur les sourds et muets à l'usage de ceux qui entendent et qui parlent*, in *Œuvres complètes de Diderot*, ed. J. Assezat, i (Paris, 1875), 343–428.

—— *Suite de l'Apologie de Mr. L'Abbé de Prades ou Réponse à l'instruction pastorale de Mr l'Évêque d'Auxerre* (1752; new edn. Amsterdam, 1753) PBN.

—— *De l'interprétation de la nature* (1753), in *Œuvres complètes*, 165–245.
—— *Political Writings*, trans. and ed. J. Hope Mason and Robert Wokler (Cambridge, 1992).
—— *Supplément au voyage de Bougainville*, ed. A. Adam (Paris, 1972).
—— *Œuvres*, ed. Laurent Versini (4 vols., Paris, 1994).
—— 'Chine', in Diderot and d'Alembert, *Encyclopédie*, iii (1753), 339–41.
—— *Lettre sur les aveugles à l'usage de ceux qui voient*, in Diderot, *Œuvres philosophiques*, ed. Vernière, 81–146.
—— and Alembert, Jean le Rond d', *Encyclopédie ou Dictionnaire raisonné des sciences, des arts et des métiers* (17 vols., Paris, 1751–72).
—— 'Avertissement des éditeurs', in Diderot and d'Alembert, *Encyclopédie*, iii (1753), pp. i–xvi.
—— and Daubenton, Louis-Jean-Marie, 'Animal', in Diderot and d'Alembert, *Encyclopédie*, i. 468–74.
Diels, Hermann (ed.), *Poetarum philosophorum fragmenta* (Berlin, 1901).
Diogenes Laertius, *Lives of Eminent Philosophers*, trans. R. D. Hicks (1925; repr. 2 vols., Cambridge, Mass., 1995).
Dissertation sur la formation du monde (1738), ed. C. Stancati (Paris, 2001).
Doria, P. M., *Discorsi critici filosofici intorno all filosifia degl'antichi, e dei moderni* (Venice, 1724) VBM.
—— *La vita civile* (1709; new edn. Naples, 1729) FBN.
—— *Ragionamenti . . . ne' quali si dimostra la donna in quasi che tutte le virtù più grandi, non essere all'uomo inferiore* ('Francfort' [Naples], 1726) VBM.
—— *Filosofia di Pado Mattia Doria con la quale si schiarisce quella di Platone* (2 vols., 'Amsterdam' [Geneva?], 1728) VBM.
—— *Difesa della metafisica degli antichi filosofi contro il signor Giovanni Locke ed alcuni altri moderni autori* (2 vols., 'Venice', 1732) VBM.
—— *Ragionamenti e poesie varie*, (Venice, 1737) VBM.
—— *Manoscritti napoletani*, ed. G. Belgioioso, A. Spedicati, P. da Fabrizio, and M. de Marangio (5 vols., Galatina, 1981–2).
—— *Lettere e ragionamenti vari dedicati alli celebri e sapientissimi signori dell'Accademia Etrusca* (3 vols., Perugina, 1741) PBP.
Dorn, Johann Christoph, *Bibliotheca theologia critica* (2 vols., Frankfurt, 1721) GUB.
Du Châtelet, émilie, marquise, *Réponse de Madame la marquise du Chastelet, à la Lettre que M. de Mairan . . . lui a écrite le 18. Février 1741* ('Bruxelles', 1741).
Du Marsais, César Chesneau, *Examen de la religion*, ed. Gianluca Mori (Oxford, 1998).
—— *Le Philosophe*, in Du Marsais (ed.), *Nouvelles Libertés*, 173–204.
—— (ed.), *Nouvelles Libertés de penser* ('Amsterdam', 1743) BL.
Durand, David, *La Vie et les sentiments de Lucilio Vanini* (Rotterdam, 1717).
Edelmann, Johann Christian, *Abgenöthigtes jedoch andern nicht wieder aufgenöthigtes Glaubens-Bekentniss* (n.p. [Neuwied?], 1746) BL.
—— *Moses mit aufgedeckten Angesichte* (3 vols., 'Freyburg' [Berleburg], 1740) BL.
Edwards, Jonathan, *The Religious Affections* (1746; Edinburgh, 2001).
—— *The Freedom of the Will* (1753; Morgan, Pa., 1996).
De Eerste en Voornaamste Oorzaken van de Laatste Onlusten en het Verval van Koophandel binnen de stad Amsterdam ('Antwerpen' [Amsterdam?], 1747) KBH.

EMPEDOCLES, *The Extant Fragments*, ed. M. R. Wright (New Haven, 1981).

ENDEN, FRANCISCUS VAN DEN, *Vrye Politieke Stellingen en Consideratien van Staat* (1665; Amsterdam, 1992).

—— *Kort Verhael van Nieuw Nederlants Gelegenheit, Deughden, Natuerlijke Voorrechten, en Byzondere Bequaemheidt ter Bevolkingh* (n.p. [Amsterdam], 1662) BL.

Entretiens sur divers sujets d'histoire et de religion entre Mylord Bolingbroke, et Isaac d'Orobio, rabin des Juifs portugais à Amsterdam ('Londres' [Paris?], 1770) BL.

EPICTETUS, *The Discourses*, ed. W. A. Oldfather (2 vols., Cambridge, Mass; 1925; repr. 2000).

[EPISCOPIUS, SIMON], *Vrye Godes-dienst* (Knuttel 3753) (n.p., n.d. [1627]).

L'Europe savante (periodical: The Hague, 1718–20) BL.

FABRICIUS, JOHANNES ALBERTUS, *Delectus argumentorum et syllabus scriptorum qui veritatem religionis christianum adversus atheos... assuerunt* (Hamburg, 1725) AUB.

FALCK, NATHANAEL, *De daemonologia novatorum autorum falsa* (2nd edn. Wittenberg, 1694) BL.

[FAYDIT, PIERRE VALENTIN], *Remarques sur Virgile et sur Homère et sur le style poëtique de l'Écriture-Sainte; où l'on refute les inductions pernicieuses que Spinoza, Grotius et Mr Le Clerc en ont tirées* (Paris, 1705) UCLA.

FÉNELON, FRANÇOIS DE SALIGNAC DE LA MOTHE, *Démonstration de l'existence de Dieu* (2nd edn. Paris, 1713) BL.

FEUERLEIN, JAKOB WILHELM (praes.) and ROSCHMANN, TOBIAS (resp.), *Dissertatio historico-philosophica de Xenophane* (Altdorf, 1729) GUB.

FINETTI, GIOVANNI FRANCESCO, *Apologia del genere umano accusato d'essere stato una volta bestia* (Venice, 1768) VBM.

FLETCHER, ANDREW, *The Political Works* (London, 1737) BL.

FONTENELLE, BERNARD LE BOVIER DE, *Histoire des oracles* (1686; new edn. Paris, 1698) BL.

—— *Traité de la liberté*, in [Du Marsais] (ed.), *Nouvelles Libertés*, 112–51 BL.

—— 'De la diversité des religions' (1695), ed. Alain Mothu, in A. Mothu and A. Sandrier (eds.), *Minora clandestina*, i: *Le Philosophe antichrétien* (Paris, 2003), 77–96.

—— *De l'origine des fables* (1724), ed. J. R. Carré (Paris, 1932).

Fortgesetzte Sammlung von alten und neuen theologischen Sachen, Büchern, Urkunden, Controversien (Leipzig periodical) GUB.

Four Treatises Concerning the Doctrine, Discipline and Worship of the Mahometans (London, 1712) PFL.

[FRANÇOIS, LAURENT], *Preuves de la religion de Jésus-Christ, contre les Spinosistes et Déistes* (4 vols., Paris, 1751) IAS.

FRANKLIN, BENJAMIN, *Autobiography*, ed. L. W. Laboree et al. (New Haven, 1964).

[FREDERICK THE GREAT], *Éloge du Sieur La Mettrie, médecin de la Faculté de Paris et membre de l'Académie Roiale des Sciences de Berlin* (The Hague, 1752) AUB.

FRÉRET, NICOLAS, *Œuvres complètes* (20 vols., Paris, 'an IV' [1796]) PFL.

—— *Œuvres philosophiques* ('Londres' [Paris ?], 1776).

—— *Lettre de Thrasybule à Leucippe*, ed. S. Landucci (Florence, 1986).

FREUDENTHAL, J. (ed.), *Die Lebensgeschichte Spinozas in Quellenschriften, Urkunden und nichtamtlichen Nachrichten* (Leipzig, 1899).

The Genuine Speech of an Eminent Dutch Patriot Lately Made in the Assembly of the States General on the... General Peace (Knuttel 17830) (London, 1748) KBH.

[GAULTIER, ABBÉ JEAN-BAPTISTE], *Le Poëme de Pope intitulé* Essay sur l'homme *convaincu d'impiété* (The Hague, 1746) PBN.

—— *Les* Lettres persanes *convaincues d'impiété* (n.p., 1751) BL.

Genovesi, Antonio, *Discorso sopra il vero fine delle lettere e delle scienze* (1753), in F. Venturi (ed.), *Illuminati italiani*, vol. v (Milan, 1965), 84–131.

—— *Elementa metaphysicae* (4th edn., 5 vols., Naples, 1760) BL.

—— *Elementorum artis logicocriticae libri V* (1745; 4th edn. Naples, 1759) VBM.

—— *Lettere filosofiche ad un amico provinciale* (2 vols., Naples, 1759) VBM.

Giannone, Pietro, *Opere*, ed. S. Bertelli and Giuseppe Ricuperati (Milan, 1971).

Goeree, Willem, *De kerklyke en weereldlyke historien* (new edn. Leiden, 1729) UCLA.

—— *Mosaize historie der hebreeuwse kerke* (4 vols., Amsterdam, 1700) AUB.

Gordon, George, *Remarks on the Newtonian Philosophy, as Propos'd by Sir Isaac Newton, in his* Principia Philosophiæ Naturalis*... Wherein the fallacies of the... demonstrations... are laid open and the philosophy itself proved to be false* (London, 1719) BL.

Graevius, J. G. (ed.), *Callimachi hymni, epigrammata, et fragmenta* (2 vols., Utrecht, 1697) BL.

Grau, Abraham de, *Historia philosophica* (2 vols., Franeker, 1674) BL.

Gravina, Gianvincenzo, *Orationes* (1699), ed. F. Lomonaco (Naples, 1997).

Gründliche Auszüge aus denen neuesten theologisch-philosophisch und philologischen Disputationibus welche auf denen hohen Schulen in Deutschland gehalten worden (11 vols., Leipzig, 1735–45) GUB.

[Gueudeville, Nicolas], *Critique du premier tome des* Avantures de Télémaque ('Cologne' [Amsterdam?], 1700).

Gundling, Nikolaus Hieronymus, 'Hobbesius ab atheismo liberatus', in *Observationum selectarum ad rem litterarium*, i (Frankfurt, 1707) YSL.

—— *Gundlingiana* (5 vols., Halle, 1715–28) YSL.

—— *Historiae philosophiae moralis pars prima* (Halle, 1726) BL.

—— *Vollständige Historie der Gelahrsamkeit* (5 vols., Frankfurt, 1734–6) YSL.

—— *Sammlung kleiner teutscher Schriften und Anmerckungen* (Halle, 1737) YSL.

Haigold, Johann Joseph, *Beylagen zum neuveränderten Russland* (2 vols., Riga-Mitau, 1769–70) BL.

Halma, François, *Aanmerkingen op't Vervolg van Philopater* (Utrecht, 1698) BL.

[Hamer, Petrus], 'Iiratiel Leetsosoneus', *Den Swadder, die E.W. op Cartesianen en Coccejanen Geworpen heeft, in sijn twee Deelen van Aardige Duivelarye* (Amsterdam, 1692) WLC.

Hanssen, Peter, *Anmerckungen über Johann Christian Edelmanns Irrthümer* (Lübeck, 1745) WUL.

Harenberg, Johann Christoph, *Die gerettete Religion, oder Gründliche Wiederlegung des Glaubensbekentnisses* [von . . .] *Johann Christian Edelmann* (Brunswick, 1747) WUL.

Hartsoeker, Nicolas, *Recueil de plusieurs pièces de physique où l'on fait principalement voir l'invalidité du système de Mr Newton* (Utrecht, 1722) BL.

Hase, T., and Lampe, F. A. (eds.), *Bibliotheca historico-philologico-theologica* (Bremen, 1718–20) BL.

Hassel, David, 'Voorreden' to Wittichius, *Ondersoek*, pp. i–ix KBH.

Hattem, Pontiaan van, *Den Val van 's Werelts Af-God, Ofte het Geloove der Heyligen* (4 vols., The Hague, 1718–27) KBH.

Hatzfeld, Johann Conrad Franz von, *The Case of the Learned* (London, 1724) BL.

Hatzfeld, Johann Conrad Franz von, pseud. 'Veridicus Nassviensis', *La Découverte de la vérité et le monde détrompé à l'égard de la philosophie* (The Hague, 1745) HARA.

Helvétius, Claude-Adrien, *De l'homme: de ses facultés intellectuelles et de son éducation* (1773; repr. 2 vols., Paris, 1989).

—— *Correspondance générale*, ed. A. Dainard et al. (3 vols., Toronto, 1981–91).

Herbelot de Molainville, *La Bibliothèque orientale, ou Dictionnaire universel contenant généralement tout ce qui regarde la connoissance des peuples de l'Orient* (Paris, 1697) AUB.

Herslev, Georg Peter (pres.), *De vera notione miraculi* (Greifswald, 1752) UUL.

Heumann, Christoph August, *Acta philosophorum, das ist: Gründl. Nachrichten aus der Historia philosophica* (18 vols., Halle, 1715–27).

Histoire des ouvrages des savants, ed. Henri Basnage de Beauval (periodical: Rotterdam, 1687–1709) BL.

Historie der Gelehrsamkeit unserer Zeiten, darinne Nachrichten von neuen Büchern... ertheilet werden (12 parts but continuous pagination) (Leipzig, 1721–5) GUB.

Hobbes, Thomas, *Leviathan*, ed. A. D. Lindsay (1914; repr. London, 1962).

Holberg, Ludvig, *Memoirs*, ed. S. E. Fraser (Leiden, 1970).

—— *Remarques sur quelques positions, qui se trouvent dans* L'Esprit des loix (Copenhagen, 1753) BL.

Hooghe, Romeyn de, *Spiegel van Staat des Vereenigde Nederlands* (2 vols., Amsterdam, 1706) BL.

—— *Nieuw Oproer op Parnassus* (The Hague?), n.d. [1690?] AUB.

—— *Postwagen-Praetjen tussen een Hagenaer, Amsterdammer Beneficiant, Schipper en Frans Koopman* (n.p. [The Hague?], 1690) AUB.

—— *De Nyd en Twist-sucht nae 't Leeven Afgebeedt* (Utrecht, 1690) BL.

Hoogstraten, D. van, and Schuer, J. L., *Groot Algemeen Historisch, Geographisch, Genealogisch en Oordeelkundig Woordenboek* (7 vols., Amsterdam, 1733) BL.

Hornius, Georgius, *Historiae philosophiae libri septem* (Leiden, 1655) AUB.

[Houbraken, Arnold], *Philalethes Brieven* (2 vols., Amsterdam, 1713) AUB.

Houtteville, Alexandre Claude François, *La Religion chrétienne prouvée par les faits* (1722; 2 vols., Paris, 1740) UCLA.

Hume, David, *Treatise of Human Nature* (1739; Buffalo, NY, 1992).

—— 'Of Superstition and Enthusiasm' (1741), in *Hume on Religion*, ed. R. Wolheim (1963; London, 1971).

—— *Essays Moral, Political and Literary*, ed. E. F. Miller (1741; Indianapolis, 1985).

—— *Dialogues Concerning Natural Religion*, in *Hume on Religion*, ed. R. Wolheim (1966; London, 1971), 99–204.

—— *An Enquiry Concerning Human Understanding* (1748), ed. E. Steinberg (2nd edn. Indianapolis, 1993).

—— *An Enquiry Concerning the Principles of Morals* (1751; Indianapolis, 1957).

—— *The Natural History of Religion* (1757), in *Principal Writings on Religion*, ed. J. C. A. Gaskin (Oxford, 1993), 134–93.

Hutcheson, Francis, *An Essay on the Nature and Conduct of the Passions and Affections, with Illustrations on the Moral Sense*, ed. A. Garrett (Indianapolis, 2002).

Ibn Rushd, Abu al-Walid Muhammad ibn Ahmad, *Tahafut al-tahafut* (The Incoherence of Incoherence), E-text edition trans. Simon van den Bergh (n.p., n.d.).

—— *Commentary on Aristotle's Metaphysics, Book Lam*, trans. Ch. Genequand (Leiden, 1984).

Jäger, Johann Wolfgang, *Spinocismus sive Benedicti Spinosae famosi atheistae vita et doctrinalia* (Tübingen, 1710) JUB.

[Jaquelot, Isaac], *Dissertations sur l'existence de Dieu, où l'on démontre cette vérité... par la réfutation du système d'Épicure et de Spinoza* (The Hague, 1697) BL.

——*Conformité de la foi avec la raison; ou Défense de la religion contre les principales difficultés répandues dans le* Dictionnaire*... de Mr Bayle* (Amsterdam, 1705) BL.

——*Examen de la théologie de Mr. Bayle* (Amsterdam, 1706) BL.

Jelles, Jarig, *Belydenisse des algemeenen en christelyken geloofs* (1684; Macerata, 2004).

Jenichen, Gottlob Friedrich, *Historia Spinozismi Leenhofiani* (Leipzig, 1707) BL.

Jens, Petrus, *Examen philosophicum sextae definitionis Part. 1 Eth. Benedicti de Spinosa* (Dordrecht, 1697).

Jöcher, Christian Gottlieb, *Allgemeines gelehrten Lexicon* (4 vols., Leipzig, 1750).

Johnson, Samuel, *An Argument Proving that the Abrogation of King James by the People of England from the Royal Throne... was According to the Constitution* (London, 1692) BL.

[Joly, Philippe Louis], *Remarques critiques sur le Dictionnaire de Bayle* (1748; 2nd edn., 2 vols., Paris, 1752) AUB.

Jordan, Charles Étienne, *Histoire de la vie et des ouvrages de Mr La Croze, avec des remarques de cet auteur sur divers sujets* (Amsterdam, 1741) BL.

Journal littéraire (periodical: The Hague, 1713–22, 1729–39).

[Jurieu, Pierre], *Le Philosophe de Rotterdam accusé, atteint et convaincu* (Amsterdam, 1706) BL.

De Koeckoecx-Zangh van de Nachtuylen van het Collegie Nil Volentibus Arduum (Knuttel 11543) (Zwolle, 1677) AUB.

Justin Martyr, St, *Apologies I et II avec Tryphon: la philosophie passe au Christ*, trans. L. Pautigny and G. Archambault (Condé-sur-l'Escaut, 1982).

Kant, Immanuel, *Gedanken von der wahren Schätzung der lebendigen Kräfte* (1747), in *Kant's gesammelte Schriften*, vol. i (Berlin, 1902), 5–181.

[Katephoros, Antonios], *Vita di Pietro il Grande Imperador della Russia* (Venice, 1736) BL.

King, Josiah, *Mr Blount's Oracles of Reason Examined and Answered* (Exeter, 1698) LDrW.

Knutzen, Matthias, 'Ein Gespräch zwischen einem lateinischen Gastgeber und drei ungleichen Religionsgästen, gehalten zu Altona', in Pfoh, *Matthias Knutzen*, 45–55.

——'Schriften', in vol. ii of J. Ch. Edelmann, *Moses* ('Freyburg' [Berleburg], 1740).

Koelman, Jacobus, *Ericus Walten, Quanswijs Apologist* (Knuttel 13321) (Amsterdam, 1689) AUB.

——*Het Vergift van de Cartesiaansche Philosophie Grondig Ontdekt* (Amsterdam, 1692) AUB.

——*Wederlegging van B. Bekkers Betoverd Wereldt* (Amstedam, 1692) BL.

[Koerbagh, Adriaen], *Een Bloemhof van Allerley Lieflijkheyd sonder Verdriet* (Amsterdam, 1668) HKB.

——*Een Ligt Schijnende in Duystere Plaatsen*, ed. H. Vandenbossche (Brussels, 1974).

Kortholt, Christian, *De tribus impostoribus magnis* (Kiel, 1680) BL.

K[uyper], F[rans], *Bewys dat noch de Schepping van de Natuur, noch de Mirakelen, die de H. Schrift Vertaalt, op Eenigerhande Wijz, Teegen de Natuurlijke Reeden Strijdig zijn* (Amsterdam, 1685) AUB.

La Beaumelle, Laurent Angliviel de, *Mes pensées ou Le qu'en dira-t-on*, ed. C. Lauriol (Geneva, 1997).

——, L.B.L.D.A., *L'Asiatique tolérant* ('Paris' [Amsterdam], 1748) AUB.

La Beaumelle, Laurent Angliviel de, *Suite de la defénse de* L'Esprit des loix (1751; repr. Geneva, 1753) IAS.

[La Court, Johan] *Consideratien van Staat, Ofte Politike Weeg-Schaal* (1660; Amsterdam, 1662) LUB.

—— and La Court, Pieter de, *Politike Discoursen* (2 vols., Amsterdam, 1662) LUB.

[La Court, Pieter de], *Interest van Holland, ofte gronden van Hollands-Welvaren* (Amsterdam, 1662) BL.

—— *Aanwijsing der Heilsame Politike Gronden en Maximen van de Republike van Holland en West-Vriesland* (Leiden, 1669) BL.

—— *The True Interest and Political Maxims of the Republic of Holland and West-Friesland Written by John de Witt and Other Great Men in Holland* (London, 1702) BL.

La Croze, Mathurin Veyssière de, *Entretiens sur divers subjets d'histoire, de littērature, de religion et de critique* ('Cologne' [Amsterdam], 1711) BL.

—— *Abrégé chronologique de l'histoire universelle*, ed. J. H. S. Formey (1754; new edn. Leiden, 1799) AUB.

—— *Merkwaardig en Zonderling Mond-gesprek, Tusschen een Gereformeerd Christen en een Portugeesche Jood mitsgaders de Bekering dezer Laatste*, trans from French (Amsterdam, 1757) AUB.

—— *Dissertations historiques sur divers sujets* (Rotterdam, 1707) PFL.

—— *Historical and Critical Reflections upon Mahometanism and Socinianism* in *Four Treatises*, 151–254, PFL.

Lahontan (or La Hontan), Louis Armand Lom d'Arce, baron de, *Nouveaux Voyages dans l'Amérique septentrionale* (3 vols., The Hague, '1703' [1702]) BL.

—— *Voyages du baron de La Hontan dans l'Amérique septentrionale* (2 vols., Amsterdam, 1705) AUB.

—— *Suite du Voyage de l'Amérique, ou Dialogues de Monsieur le baron de Lahontan et d'un sauvage de l'Amérique* (Amsterdam, 1728) BL.

La Mettrie, Julien Offray de, *La Volupté*, in *Œuvres philosophiques* (1987), ii. 87–137.

—— *Histoire naturelle de l'âme* (The Hague, 1745) BL.

—— *L'Homme machine* (Leiden, 1748) BL.

—— *Man a Machine: Translated from the French of the Marquiss d'Argens* (Dublin, 1749) BL.

—— *Œuvres philosophiques* (2 vols., Paris, 1987).

—— *Réponse à l'auteur de la Machine terrassée* (1749), *Corpus*, 5/6 (1987), 149–66.

—— *Réflexions philosophiques sur l'origine des animaux* (1750), *Corpus*, 5/6 (1987), 167–79.

—— *Discours préliminaire*, in *Œuvres philosophiques* (1751; 2 vols., Amsterdam, 1753) BL.

—— *Anti-Sénèque, ou Discours sur le bonheur*, in *Œuvres philosophiques* (1987), ii. 237–95.

—— *Machine Man and Other Writings*, ed. Ann Thomson (Cambridge, 1996).

Landucci, Sergio (ed.), 'Appendice: la polémique entre Jurieu et Saurin', in [Jean Lévesque de Burigny,] *De l'examen de la religion*, 77–129.

Lange, Joachim, *Kurtzer Abriss derjenigen Lehr-Sätze welche in der Wolffischen Philosophie der natürlichen und geoffenbahrten Religion nachtheilig sind* (n.p. [Halle?], n.d. [1736]) BL.

—— *Der philosophische Religions-Spötter* (Leipzig, 1736) WHA.

—— 'Jucundus de Laboribus', *Freye Gedancken von Realis de Vienna Prüfung des Versuchs vom Wesen des Geistes* (1710), in S. Wollgast (ed). *Gabriel Wagner (1660–717): Ausgewählte Schriften* (Stuttgart, 1997), 461–532.

La Placette, Jean, *Traité de la conscience* (Amsterdam, 1699).

L[a] P[orte], Abbé Josephe de, *Observations sur* L'Esprit des loix, *ou L'Art de lire ce livre, de l'entendre, d'en juger* (Amsterdam, 1751) BL.

Larkin, S., *Correspondance entre Prosper Marchand et le marquis d'Argens* (Oxford, 1984).

Larousse, Pierre (ed.), *Grand Dictionnaire universel du XIXe siècle, français, historique, géographique, mythologique, bibliographique, littéraire, artistique, scientifique, etc.* (Paris, 1866–[90]).

Lau, Theodor Ludwig, *Meditationes philosophicae de Deo, mundo, homine* (1717), in M. Pott (ed.), *Philosophische clandestina der deutschen Aufklärung*, ser. 1, vol. i (Stuttgart, 1992), 55–104.

—— *Meditationes, theses, dubia philosophico-theologica* (1719), in M. Pott (ed.), *Philosophische Clandestina der deutschen Aufklärung*, sec. 1, vol. i (Stuttgart, 1992), 105–52.

Le Clerc, Jean, *Règles de critique*, *Bibliothèque universelle*, 10 (1688), 309–78.

—— *Sentimens de quelques théologiens de Hollande* (Amsterdam, 1685) BL.

—— *De l'incrédulité où l'on examine les motifs et les raisons générales qui portent les incrédules à rejeter la religion chrétienne* (1696; 2nd edn. Amsterdam, 1714) PFL.

—— *Ars critica* (2 vols., Amsterdam, 1697) BL.

—— *Parrhasiana; or Thoughts upon Several Subjects* (London, 1700) BL.

—— *The Lives of the Primitive Fathers* (London, 1701) WLC.

—— *A Funeral Oration upon the Death of Mr Philip Limborch, Professor of Divinity among the Remonstrants at Amsterdam* (London, 1713) BL.

—— *Epistolario*, ed. M. Sina and M. Grazia (4 vols., Florence, 1987–97).

Leenhof, Frederik van, *De Prediker van de Wijzen en Magtigen Konink Salomon* (Zwolle, 1700) AUB.

—— *Het Leven van den Wijzen en Magtigen Konink Salomon* (Zwolle, 1700) AUB.

—— *Den Hemel op Aarden; of een Korte en Klare Beschryvinge van de Waare en Stantvastige Blydschap, zoo naar reden als de H. Schrift voor alle slag van menschen* (2nd edn. Amsterdam, 1704) AUB.

Leibniz, G. W., *Opera omnia, nunc primum collecta*, ed. Ludovicus Dutens (6 vols., Geneva, 1768) BL.

—— *Protogaea* (1692), ed. Jean-Marie Barrande (Toulouse, 1993).

—— *Political Writings*, trans. and ed. P. Riley (1972; 2nd edn. Cambridge, 1988).

—— *Philosophical Essays*, ed. and trans. R. Ariew and D. Garber (Indianapolis, 1989).

—— *Philosophical Writings*, ed. G. H. R. Parkinson (London, 1973).

—— *New Essays on Human Understanding*, ed. P. Remnant and J. Bennett (Cambridge, 1996).

—— *Theodicy*, trans E. M. Huggard, ed. A. Farrer (LaSalle, Ill., 1985).

—— *Discours* (1716) ['Lettre de Mr G. G. de Leibniz sur la philosophie chinoise'], in Leibniz, *Opera omnia*, iv/1. 169–210.

The Leibniz–Clarke Correspondence, ed. H. G. Alexander (1956; Manchester, new edn. 1998).

Leidekker, Melchior, *Historische en Theolgische Redeneringe over het Onlangs Uitgegeve Boek van den Seer Vermaarden Balthsar Bekker* (Utrecht, 1692) WLC.

—— *Verder Vervolg van de Kerkelyke Historie, van de Hr Hornius Beginnende met het Jaar 1666* (Amsterdam, 1696) UCLA.

—— *Dissertatio historico-theologica De vulgate nuper cl. Bekkeri volumine* (Utrecht, 1692) GUB.

Leland, John, *A View of the Principal Deistical Writers* (3 vols., London, 1755–7; repr. New York, 1978).

Lelarge de Lignac, Abbé Josephe-Adrien, *Lettres à un Amériquain sur l'*Histoire naturelle générale et particulière *de M. de Buffon* ('Hambourg' [Paris], 1751) PBN.

——, *Élémens de métaphysique tirés de l'experience: ou Lettres à un matérialiste* (Paris, 1753) PBN.

Lenglet Dufresnoy, Nicolas, *Méthode pour étudier l'histoire* (4 vols., Paris, 1729) WLC.
—— *Histoire de la philosophie hermétique* (3 vols., Paris, 1744) WLC.
—— *Traité historique et dogmatique sur les apparitions, les visions et les révélations particulières* (2 vols., Avignon, 1751) WLC.
—— *Réfutation des erreurs de Benoît de Spinosa* ('Bruxelles' [Amsterdam], 1731) BL.
Leti, Gregorio, *La Monarchie universelle de Louys XIV* (2 vols., Amsterdam, 1688–90) BL.
—— *Teatro Belgico* (2 vols., Amsterdam, 1690) BL.
—— *Raguagli historici e politici* (2 vols., Amsterdam, 1700) BL.
Lettre de M, maître en chirurgie, à M*, médecin sur le livre intitulé* 'Histoire naturelle de l'âme', *Corpus*:, 5/6 (1987), 113–30.
Lettre de M.N... à un de ses amis. Où il dit son sentiment sur les Parrhasiana [of Le Clerc] (n.p. n.d.) LUB.
Lettre du Chevalier... à Mylord... sur le danger que court la liberté angloise (n.p. [Amsterdam], 1718) LUB.
Lettres sur la vie et sur la mort de Monsieur Louis de Wolzogue (Amsterdam, 1692) BL.
Leuckfeld, Georg, *Die verführliche Atheisten Hauffe und das ungottische Wesen unter den Christen* (Frankfurt, 1699) GUB.
Lévesque de Burigny, Jean, *Théologie payenne* (2 vols., Paris, 1754) UCLA.
—— *Histoire de la philosophie payenne* (2 vols., The Hague, 1724) BL.
—— *De l'examen de la religion*, ed. S. Landucci (Oxford, 1996).
—— (attrib. to 'M. Fréret'), *Examen critique des apologistes de la religion chrétienne* (n.p. [Paris?], 1767) BL.
Lévesque de Pouilly, Louis-Jean, *Théorie des sentimens agréables* (Paris, 1774) WLC.
Leydekker, Jacobus, *Dr Bekkers Philosophise Duyvel* (Dordrecht, 1692) BL.
Lilienthal, Michael, *Theologische Bibliothec* (Königsberg, 1741) BL.
Locke, John, *Epistola de tolerantia*, ed. R. Klibansky (Oxford, 1968).
—— *Political Writings*, ed. David Wootton (London, 1993).
—— *Two Treatises of Government*, ed. Peter Laslett (1960; repr. Cambridge, 1991).
—— *The Second Treatise of Government* (*c.*1681), in Locke, *Political Writings*, 261–387.
—— *A Third Letter for Toleration* (London, 1692) DrWL.
—— *An Essay Concerning Human Understanding*, ed. P. H. Nidditch (Oxford, 1975).
—— *The Reasonableness of Christianity* (1695), ed. G. W. Ewing (repr. Washington, 1989).
—— *Some Thoughts Concerning Education*, ed. J. W. and J. S. Yolton (Oxford, 1989; repr. 2003).
—— *The Correspondence of John Locke*, ed. E. S. De Beer (8 vols., Oxford, 1976–89).
Loescher, Valentin Ernst, *Praenotiones theologicae contra naturalistarum et fanaticorum omne genus atheos, deistas, indifferentistas, antiscriptuarios*, etc. (Wittenberg, 1708) BL.
Lucas, Jean-Maximilien, *La Vie de Monsieur Benoit de Spinosa*, in S. Berti (ed), *Trattato dei tre impostori* (Turin, 1994), 1–58.
Luzac, Élie, *Bibliothèque impartiale*, vol. i (Leiden, 1750) GUB.
—— *L'Homme plus que machine* ('à Londres' [Leiden?], 1748) AUB.
—— *Essai sur la liberté de produire des sentimens* ('au pays libre pour le bien public' [Amsterdam?], 1749) AUB.
Mably, Gabriel Bonnot de, *Collection complète des œuvres de l'Abbé de Mably* (15 vols., Paris, 'l'an III de la République' [1794/5]) PFL.
—— *Parallèle des Romains et des Français par rapport au gouvernement* (2 vols., Paris, 1740) YBL.

—— *Le Droit public de l'Europe fondé jusqu'en l'année 1740* (2 vols., Paris, 1746) YML.
—— *Observations sur les Grecs* (1749; 2nd edn. Geneva, 1766) YSL.
—— *Observations sur les Romains* (2 vols., Geneva, 1751) YSL.
—— *Observations sur le gouvernement et les lois des États-Unis d'Amérique* (1783), in *Collection complète*, viii. 337–85.
—— *Du gouvernement et des lois de Pologne* (1770), in *Collection complète*, viii. 1–336.
MacLaurin, Colin, *An Account of Sir Isaac Newton's Philosophical Discoveries* (1748; 2nd edn. London, 1750) BL.
McKenna, Antony (ed.), *Pierre Bayle: témoin et conscience de son temps* (Paris, 2001).
M.A.F.C., *Lettres sur les Hollandois* ('Londres' [Amsterdam?], 1735) LUB.
Maffei, Scipio, *Arte magica dileguata* (2nd edn. Verona, 1750) PBP.
—— *Arte magica annichilata libri tre* (Verona, 1754) NBN.
Maichelius, Daniel, *De philosophia theologiae domina et serva* (Tübingen, 1737) WHA.
[Maillet, Benoît de?], 'Sentimens des philosophes sur la nature de l'âme', *La Lettre clandestine*, 4 (1995), 21–9.
Malebranche, Nicolas, *Entretien d'un philosophe chrétien et d'un philosophe chinois* (1708), ed. A. Robinet, *Œuvres complètes*, xv (Paris, 1958).
—— *Dialogues on Metaphysics and Religion*, ed. N. Jolley and D. Scott (Cambridge, 1997).
—— *Correspondance avec J. J. Dortous de Mairan*, ed. J. Moreau (Paris, 1947).
Mandeville, Bernard, *The Fable of the Bees*, ed. F. B. Kaye (2 vols., Indianapolis, 1988).
—— *The Virgin Unmask'd* (London, 1709) BL.
—— *Free Thoughts on Religion, the Church and National Happiness* (London, 1720) BL.
Marchand, Prosper, *Dictionnaire historique* (2 vols., The Hague, 1758) BL.
Marcus Aurelius, *Meditations*, ed. C. R. Haines (1916; Cambridge, Mass., repr. 1994).
Maréchal, Sylvain, *Dictionnaire des athées anciens et modernes* (Brussels, 1833).
Masius, Hector Gottfried, *Dissertationes academicae* (2 vols., Hamburg, 1719) BPK.
Mastricht, Petrus van, *Novitatum Cartesianarum gangraena* (Amsterdam, 1677) WHA.
Maupertuis, Pierre-Louis M. de, *Œuvres de Mr de Maupertuis* (new edn., 4 vols., Lyons, 1756) AUB.
—— 'Sur les loix de l'attraction', *Histoire de l'Académie Royale des Sciences*, 1732 (Paris, 1735), 343–62.
—— 'Essai de philosophie morale', in *Œuvres*, i. 171–252.
Mavrocordatos, Nicolaos, *Les Loisirs de Philothée*, ed. C. Dimaras (Athens, 1989).
—— *Les Loisirs de Philothée/Philothéou Parerga*, ed. and trans. Jacques Bouchard (Montréal, 1989).
[M. de R.] *Apologie de* L'Esprit des loix *ou Réponses aux Observations de M. de L.P.* (Amsterdam, 1751) BL.
Memorie van Rechten by Mr Adraen Bakker... in de Criminiele Saak Tegens Romein de Hooge, etser (Amsterdam, 1690) BL.
Mendelssohn, Moses, *Philosophical Writings*, ed. D. O. Dahlstrohm (Cambridge, 1997).
Meslier, Jean, *Le Testament*, ed. R. Charles (3 vols., Amsterdam, 1864).
Meyer, Johann, *Die Närrische Welt in ihrer Narrheit, oder Endeckte Quellen der Atheisterey und Freydenckerey* (Breslau, 1752) GUB.
[Meyer, Lodewijk] *De jure ecclesiasticorum* (Amsterdam, 1665) BL.
—— *Philosophia S. Scripturae interpres* (Eleutheropoli [Amsterdam], 1666) BL.
—— *Philosophie d'Uytleghster der H. Schrifture* (Vrystadt [Amsterdam], 1667) KBH.

Mirabaud, Jean Baptiste, *Le Monde, son origine et son antiquité* (2 vols., 'Londres', 1751) BL.

Molinaeus, Johannes, *De* Betoverde Werelt *van D. Balthazar Bekker Onderzogt en Wederlegdt* (Rotterdam, 1692) GUB.

Molyneux, William, *The Case of Ireland* (Dublin, 1698) BL.

Moniglia, Tommaso Vincenzo, *Dissertazione contro i fatalisti* (2 vols., Lucca, 1744) PBP.

—— *Dissertazione contro i materialisti e altri increduli* (2 vols., Padua, 1750) PBP.

Montesquieu, Charles de Secondat, baron de, *Œuvres complètes*, ed. D. Oster (Paris, 1964).

—— *Lettres persanes* ('Cologne' [Amsterdam], 1721), in Montesquieu, *Œuvres complètes*, 61–151.

—— *De L'esprit des lois*, in Montesquieu, *Œuvres complètes*, 528–808.

—— *Défense de L'Esprit des lois*, in *Œuvres complètes*, 808–22.

Montgomerie, Sir James, *Great Britain's Just Complaint* (n.p., 1692) BL.

[Morelly], *Essai sur le cœur humain, ou Principes naturels de l'éducation* (Paris, 1745) PBN.

—— *Le Prince: les délices des cœurs* (2 vols., Amsterdam, 1751) PBN.

—— [*Basiliade*], *Naufrages des isles flottantes, ou Basiliade* (2 vols., 'Messine' [Paris?], 1753) PBN.

—— *Code de la nature, ou Le Véritable Esprit de ses loix* ([Amsterdam?] 1755) PFL.

Morgan, Thomas, *The Moral Philosopher* (1737; Repr. New York 1977)

Mosheim, J. L., 'Notes' to R. Cudworth, *Systema intellectuale huius universi* (2 vols., Jena, 1733) AUB.

—— *Vindiciae antiquae Christianorum disciplinae* (Kiel, 1720) BL.

—— *Versuch einer unparteiischen und gründlichen Ketzergeschichte* (1746; 2 vols., Hildesheim, 1998).

Mothu, A., and Sandrier, A. (eds.), *Minora clandestina*, vol. i (Paris, 2003).

Moyle, Walter, *The Whole Works of Walter Moyle, Esq.* (London, 1727) BL.

Münter, Balthasar, *Theologiae naturalis polemicae specimen exhibens historiam et refutationem systematis illius quod a Benedicto de Spinoza nomen habet* (n.p., 1758) GUB.

Musaeus, Johann, *Ableinung des ausgesprengten abscheulichen Verleumdung ob wäre... in Jena eine neue Secte, der so genannten Gewissener entstanden* (Jena, 1674) WHA.

—— *Tractatus theologico-politicus... ad veritatis lancem examinatus* (Jena, 1674) CRL.

Nadere Aanmerkingen op de Drie Artykelenm, als meede Aanspraken van en aan de Burgers van Amsterdam, die op den Colveniers Doelen zyn Vergadert (Knuttel 17984) (Amsterdam, 1748) KBH.

Nannestad, Christian, *De libertate philosophandi* (Copenhagen, 1719) GUB.

*Neuer Zeitungen van gelehrten Sachen (*Leipzig periodical) GUB.

Newton, Isaac, *Philosophiae naturalis principia mathematica* (Amsterdam, 1714).

—— *Mathematical Principles of Natural Philosophy* (2 vols., London, 1729).

Nieto, David, *Matteh Dan* (London, 1714).

Nieuhoff, Bernard, *Over Spinozisme* (Harderwijk, 1799).

Nieuwentyt, Bernard, *Gronden van Zekerheid* (Amsterdam, 1720) BL.

—— *The Religious Philosopher, or The Right Use of Contemplating the Works of the Creator* (1718; 3rd edn., 3 vols., London, 1724).

—— *L'Existence de Dieu démontrée par les merveilles de la nature* (Amsterdam, 1727) BL.

Notice des écrits les plus célèbres, tant imprimés que manuscrits, qui favorisent l'incrédulité, ou dont la lecture est dangereuse aux esprits foibles (*c.*1744), *La Lecture clandestine*, 2 (1993), 178–92.

Notice historique sur le marquis d'Argens à la cour de Prusse et ses ouvrages, in *Mémoires du marquis d'Argens* (new edn. Paris, 1807), 1–114 PrF.

Nouvelle Bibliothèque germanique (periodical: Amsterdam, 1746–59, from 1750 ed. J. H. S. Formey).

[OEDER, GEORG LUDWIG], *Anmerckungen über die Vorrede des wertheimischen Bibelwerks*. (Frankfurt, 1736) WHA.

OLIVET, ABBÉ D', *Histoire de l'Académie française depuis 1652 jusqu'à 1700* (Amsterdam, 1730) GUB.

OROBIO DE CASTRO, ISAAC [BALTHASAR], *Certamen philosophicum* (2nd edn. Amsterdam, 1703) BL.

OSTERMANN, A. I., *Einrichtung der Studien Ihro Kayserl: Majest. Petri des Andern Kaysers und Souverains von Gantz Russland* (n.p., 1730) BL.

PAINE, THOMAS, *The Rights of Man* (1790), ed. E. Foner (New York, 1985).

PAPIN, ISAAC, *The Toleration of Protestants, and the Authority of the Church* (London, 1733) BL.

PHILIPPS, J. TH., *Dissertatio historico-philosophica de atheismo* (London, 1716) UCLA.

PICO DELLA MIRANDOLA, GIOVANNI, *Oration on the Dignity of Man*, in E. Cassirer and P. O. Kristeller (eds.), *The Renaissance Philosophy of Man* (Chicago, 1948), 233–54.

—— *The Heptaplus* (1489), in Giovanni Pico della Mirandola, *On the Dignity of Man*, ed. P. J. W. Miller. (1965; Indianapolis, repr. 1998), 67–174.

PINTO, ISAAC DE, *Précis des arguments contre les matérialistes* (The Hague, 1740) BL.

PLATO, *Timaeus*, ed. H. D. P. Lee (Harmondsworth, 1965).

PLOUQUET, GODFROY, *Dissertatio de materialismo* (Tübingen, 1751) GUB.

PLUQUET, ABBÉ FRANÇOIS, *Examen du fatalisme* (3 vols., Paris, 1757) UCLA.

POLIGNAC, MELCHIOR, CARDINAL DE, *L'Anti-Lucrèce* (2 vols., Paris, 1750) UCLA.

POMPONAZZI, PIETRO, *De immortalitate anima* [On the Immortality of the Soul], in E. Cassirer and P. O. Kristeller (eds.), *The Renaissance Philosophy of Man* (Chicago, 1948), 280–381.

PONTOPPIDAN, ERIC, *Abhandlung von der Neuigkeit der Welt* (2 vols., Copenhagen, 1758) GUB.

—— *Kraft der Wahrheit den atheistischen und naturalistischen Unglauben zu besiegen* (Copenhagen, 1763) GUB.

—— *Sanheds Kraft til at Overwinde den Atheistike og Naturalistike Vantroe* (Copenhagen, 1768) CRL.

POPPO, VOLCKERTSZ CONRAD, *Spinozismus Detectus* (Weimar, 1721) HUB.

PORTALIS, J. E. M., *De l'usage et de l'abus de l'esprit philosophique durant le XVIIIe siècle* (1798; 3rd edn., 2 vols., Paris, 1834) PFL.

POULAIN DE LA BARRE, FRANÇOIS, *The Equality of the Sexes*, ed. D. M. Clarke (Manchester, 1990).

PRADES, JEAN-MARTIN DE, *Thèse soutenue en Sorbonne le 18 novembre 1751* (Amsterdam, 1753) PBN.

PRATJE, J. H., *Historische Nachrichten von Joh. Chr. Edelmanns, eines beruchtigten Religionspötters* (Hamburg, 1755) BL.

Préface historique et critique sur les ouvrages de M. Antoine Arnauld (1777), in *Œuvres de Arnauld*, x. 39–377.

PRITIUS, JOHANN GEORG, *De atheismo et in se foedo, et humano generi noscio* (Leipzig, 1695).

PROAST, JONAS, *The Argument of the Letter Concerning Toleration Briefly Consider'd and Answer'd* (Oxford, 1690).

Proast, Jonas, *A Third Letter Concerning Toleration* (Oxford, 1691) DrWL.
Prokopovich, Feofan, *Vorschläge wie ein Printz in der christlichen Religion soll unterrichtet werden* (n.p., n.d. [1750?]) BL.
—— *Peters des Grossen Geistliches Reglement* (St Petersburg, 1721) BL.
Raap, Daniel, *Korte Schets of Dag-Verhaal van het tegenwoordig Gedrag der Burgeren van Amsterdam* (Knuttel 17961B) (Amsterdam, 1748) HKB.
Rabus, Pieter, *Griekse, Latijnse en Neerduitse Vermakelykheden der Taalkunde* (2nd edn. Rotterdam, 1692) BL.
Radicati di Passerano, Alberto, *A Philosophical Dissertation upon Death* (London, 1732) BL.
—— *Twelve Discourses Concerning Religion and Government, Inscribed to all Lovers of Truth and Liberty* (2nd edn. London, 1734) BL.
—— *Recueil de pièces curieuses sur les matières les plus intéressantes* (Rotterdam, 1736) BL.
—— *A Succinct History of Priesthood, Ancient and Modern* (London, 1737) YBL.
—— *Sermon préché dans la grande assemblée des Quakers de Londres par le fameux frère E. Elwall dit l'Inspiré* ('Londres' [Rotterdam?], 1737).
—— *Christianity set in a True Light in XII Discourses, Political and Historical by a Pagan Philosopher Newly Converted* (London, 1730).
—— *La Religion Muhammédane comparée à la paienne de l'Indostan, par Ali-Ebn-Omar* ('Londres' [Rotterdam?], 1737).
—— *A Parallel between Muhamed and Sosem, the Great Deliverer of the Jews by Zelim Musulman* (London, 1732) YBL.
Ramsay, Andrew Michael, *Les Principes philosophiques de la religion naturelle et révélée*, ed. G. Lamoine (Paris, 2002).
—— *Anecdotes de la vie de M. Andre Michel de Ramsay*, in Baldi, *Verisimile, non vero*, 423–76.
Raynal, Guillaume Thomas François, *Histoire du stadhoudérat depuis son origine jusqu'à présent* (4th edn. The Hague, 1748) KB.
Réaumur, René-Antoine Feschault de, 'Remarques sur les coquilles fossilles de quelques cantons de la Touraine', *Histoire de l'Académie Royale des Sciences*, 1720 (Paris, 1722), 400–16.
—— *Mémoires pour servir à l'histoire des insectes* (7 vols., Paris, 1734–42) IAS.
Reimmann, J. F., *Versuch einer Einleitung in die Historiam literariam* (6 vols., Halle, 1713) GUB.
—— *Historia universalis atheismi et atheorum* (Hildesheim, 1725) UCLA.
—— *Historia philosophia Sinensis* (new edn. Brunswick, 1741) GUB.
Reland, Adriaan, *La Religion des Mahometans*, trans. D. Durand (1705; 2 vols., The Hague, 1721) BL.
—— *Of the Mahometan Religion*, in *Four Treatises*, 1–150 PFL.
—— *Dissertationum miscellanearum* (3 vols., Utrecht, 1706) GrUB.
Rencontre de Bayle et de Spinosa dans l'autre monde ('Cologne' [Amsterdam], 1711) WLC.
Ries, Franz Ulrich (praes.), and Hermann, Wilh. Lud. (resp.), *Dissertatio philosophica de atheis, eorumque stultitia* (Marburg, 1725) GUB.
[Risteau, François], *Réponse aux questions sur* L'Esprit des loix (Amsterdam, 1751) BL.
Roggeveen, Jacob, 'Voor-reden' to van Hattem, *Den Val*, vol. i (The Hague, 1718) KBH.
Rousseau, Jean-Jacques, *The Social Contract and Discourses*, ed. G. D. H. Cole, J. H. Brumfitt, J. C. Hall, and P. D. Jimack (repr. London, 1993).

——*A Discourse on the Origin of Inequality*, in Rousseau, *Social Contract*, 31–126.

——*The Confessions*, ed. Chr. Kelly et al. (Hanover, NH, 1995).

[Rousset de Missy, Jean], j.l.r., *Réponse à la dissertation de M. de La Monnoye sur le 'Traité des trois imposteurs'* (Rotterdam, 1716).

——*La Liberté de penser défendue contre les attaques du clergé* (n.p. [The Hague], 1717) GUB.

——*Le Chevalier de St George réhabilité dans sa qualité de Jaques III* (Knuttel 16135) ('Whitehall' [The Hague?], 1713) KBH.

——[R.D.M.], *Les Intérêts et la tranquilité de l'Europe défendus*... (Knuttel 17829) (n.p., 1748) KBH.

——L.C.R.D.M. A.D.P., 'Avertissement sur cette cinquième edition', in *Du gouvernement civil, par Mr. Locke* (Amsterdam, 1755) AUB.

Ruyter, Johan, *Funus philosophico theologicum* (Groningen, 1708) UCLA.

Ryssenius, Leonardus, *Dagon: den Politiken Afgod Verbroken... tegen een Godlasterlijk Schrift van eenen Ericus Walten* (Knuttel 13500) (The Hague, 1690) GrUB.

Sabatier de Castres, M., *Apologie de Spinosa et du Spinosisme* (Altona, 1805) AUB.

Saint-Évremond, Charles, sieur de, *Écrits philosophiques*, ed. Jean-Pierre Jackson (Paris, 1996).

Saint-Hyacinthe, Thémiseul de, *Matanasiana, ou Mémoires littéraires, historiques et critiques* (1715; new edn., 2 vols., The Hague, 1740) BL.

——*Recherches philosophiques* (Rotterdam, 1743) BL.

[Sallengre, Henri de], *Mémoires de littérature* (3 vols., The Hague, 1715) BL.

Saurin, Élie, *Traité de l'amour de Dieu* (Amsterdam, 1700) BL.

Saurin, Jacques, *L'État du Christianisme en France* (The Hague, 1725) BL.

Schlosser, Friedrich Philipp (praes.), *De Stratone Lampsaceno cognomento physico et atheismo hylozoico vulgo ipsi tributo* (Wittenberg, 1728) BL.

Schmauss, Johann Jacob, *Neues Systema des Rechts der Natur* (Göttingen, 1754) GUB.

[Schmidt, Johann Lorenz], 'Vorrede' to *Die göttlichen Schriften vor den Zeiten des Messie Jesus. Der erste Theil* (Wertheim, 1735), 1–48 WHA.

[Schmidt, Johann Lorenz], *Die veste gegründete Wahrheit der Vernunft und Religion* (Wertheim, 1735) GUB.

——*Vertheidigung der freyen Uebersetzung von den göttlichen Schriften* (Wertheim, 1736) GUB.

——*Beantwortung verschiedener Einwürfe... durch der Verfasser derselben* (Wertheim, 1736) WHA.

——*Sammlung derienigen Schriften welche bey Gelegenheit des Wertheimischen Bibelwerks für oder gegen dasselbe zum Vorschein gekommen sind* (Frankfurt, 1738) WHA.

——'Vorbericht' to [Tindal], *Beweis dass das Christenthum so alt als die Welt sey* (Frankfurt, 1741) WHA.

——'Vorrede' to B.D.S., *Sittenlehre widerleget von dem berühmten weltweisen unserer Zeit Heren. Christian Wolf* (Frankfurt, 1744) HHL.

Schröder, Carolus Gustav, *Dissertatio gradualis ideam libertismi philosophici, sistens* ('Londini Gothorum', 1738) GUB.

Seckendorff, Veit Ludwig von, *Christen-Staat* (2 vols., Leipzig, 1693) BL.

Sentiments d'un voyageur sur plusieurs libelles de ce temps (n.p., n.d. [Amsterdam? 1677?]).

's-Gravesande, Willem Jacob van, *Œuvres philosophiques et mathématiques*, ed. J. N. S. Allamand (2 vols., Amsterdam, 1774) AUB.

's-Gravesande, Willem Jacob van, 'Rede over de ware, nooit misprezen filosofie', in 's Gravesande, *Welzijn, wijsbegeerte en wetenschap*, ed. C. De Pater (Gouda, 1988), 60–71.

——*Mathematical Elements of Natural Philosophy Confirm'd by Experiments* (3rd edn., 2 vols., London, 1726).

——*Essai d'une nouvelle théorie du choc des corps*, in 's-Gravesande, *Œuvres philosophiques et mathématiques*, i. 215–51.

Shaftesbury, Anthony Ashley Cooper, third earl of, *Characteristics* (Cambridge, 1999).

Simon, Richard, *A Critical History of the Old Testament* (London, 1682) BL.

Simplicius, *Corollaries on Place and Time*, trans. J. O. Urmson, annotated by L. Siorvanes (Ithaca, NY, 1992).

Sinnhold, Johann Nikolaus, *Ausführliche Historie der verruffenen sogenannten Wertheimischen Bibel* (Erfurt, 1739) WUB.

——*Historische Nachricht von der bekanten und verruffenen sogenannten Wertheimische Bibel* (Erfurt, 1737) WHA.

Sluiter, Johannes, *Overeenstemming tusschen den heer Fredericus van Leenhof en Spinoza en* Philopater *Vertoont* (Amsterdam, 1704) GUB.

Sluiter, Wilhem, *Idea theologiae Stoicae* (Leiden, 1726) AUB.

[Souverain, M.], *Le Platonisme desvoilé* ('à Cologne' [London?], 1700) GUB.

Spandaw, Willem, *De Bedekte Spinosist Ontdekt* (Goes, 1700) KBH.

Spinelli, Francesco Maria, *Riflessioni... su le principale materie della prima filosofia* (Naples, 1733) NBN.

Spinoza, Benedict de, *Opera*, ed. Carl Gebhardt (4 vols., Heidelberg, 1925).

——*Ethics*, ed. and trans. G. H. R. Parkinson (Oxford, 2000).

——*Korte Verhandeling van God, de Mensch en dezelvs welstand*, in Spinoza, *Korte geschriften*, 223–392.

——*The Political Works*, ed. A. G. Wernham (Oxford, 1958).

——*The Letters*, trans. S. Shirley (Indianapolis, 1995).

——*Korte Geschriften*, ed. F. Akkerman et al. (Amsterdam, 1982).

——*Briefwisseling*, ed. F. Akkerman et al. (Amsterdam, 1992).

——*Tractatus theologico-politicus* (Gebhardt edn. 1925), trans. S. Shirley (Leiden, 1989).

——*Een Rechtsinnige Theologant, of Godgeleerde Staatkunde* ('Bremen' [Amsterdam], 1694).

——*Tractatus politicus*, in *The Political Works*.

——*Collected Works*, ed. E. Curley (1 vol. so far, Princeton, 1985).

Staalkopf, Jakob, *De atheismo Benedicti de Spinoza... adversus Io. Georgium Wachtervm* (1707), repr. as appendix to Wachter, *De primordiis christianae*, ed. Schröder.

Stanley, Thomas, *The History of Philosophy* (3 vols., 2nd edn. London, 1687) (facs. repr. 1978).

Stosch, Friedrich Wilhelm, *Concordia rationis et fidei* (1692), ed. W. Schröder (Stuttgart, 1992).

Temple, Sir William, *Observations* (1672; Cambridge, 1932).

——*Five Miscellaneous Essays*, ed. S. H. Monk (Ann Arbor, 1963).

Thomasius, Christian, *Elender Zustand eines in die Atheisterey verfallenen Gelehrten* (1720), in Pott (ed.), *Philosophische clandestina*, ser. 1, i. 191–316.

Thomasius, Jakob, *Exercitatio de Stoica mundi exustione* (Leipzig, 1676) KBH.

——*Dissertationes ad Stoicae philosophiae et caeterem philosophiam historiam facientes argumenti varii* (Leipzig, 1682) GUB.

THORSCHMID, URBAN GOTTLOB, *Critische Lebensgeschichte Anton Collins des ersten Freydenckers in Engelland* (Dresden, 1755) BL.
TIETZMANN, HEINRICH (praes.), *Atheismi inculpati monstrum* (Wittenberg, 1696)
TIL, SALOMON VAN, *Het Voor-Hof der Heydenen voor alle Ongeloovigen Geopent* (Dordrecht, 1694) BL.
—— *'t Vervolg op het voorhof der heydenen* (Dordrecht, 1696).
TINDAL, MATTHEW, *Christianity as Old as the Creation* (London, 1731) BL.
—— *A New Catechism with Hickes's Thirty Nine Articles* (1709; 3rd edn. London, 1710) YBL.
TOLAND, JOHN, *Christianity not Mysterious* (1696; repr. New York, 1978).
—— *Anglia libera* (London, 1701) BL.
—— *Letters to Serena* (1704; New York, 1976).
—— *The Jacobitism, Perjury and Popery of High Church-Priests* (London, 1710) BL.
—— *An Appeal to Honest People against Wicked Priests* (London, 1710) YBL.
—— *Reasons for Naturalizing the Jews in Great Britain and Ireland*, (1714), ed. H. Mainusch, Studia Delitzschiana 9 (Stuttgart, 1965).
—— *A Specimen of the Critical History of the Celtic Religion and Learning* (1718–19), in J. Toland, *A Collection of Several Pieces* (1726; repr. 2 vols., New York, 1977), i. 3–228.
—— 'A Large Introduction' to *Letters from the Right Honourable The Late Earl of Shaftesbury to Robert Molesworth, Esq.* (London, 1721) YBL.
—— *The Danger of Mercenary Parliaments* (London, 1698) BL.
—— *The Art of Governing Partys* (London, 1701) BL.
TOURNEMINE, RENÉ-JOSEPHE, 'Preface' to Fénelon's *Démonstration* (Paris, 1713) BL.
Traité des trois imposteurs [*Trattato dei tre impostori*], ed. S. Berti (Turin, 1994).
TREBY, SIR GEORGE, *The Speech of Sir George Treby Kt., Recorder of the Honourable City of London to His Highness the Prince of Orange, December the 20th 1688* (London, 1688) BL.
TREMBLEY, ABRAHAM, *Mémoires pour servir à l'histoire d'un genre de polypes d'eau douce* (Leiden, 1744) IAS.
TUFAYL, ABU BAKR MOHAMMED BEN ABD-AL-MALIK IBN, *Hayy ibn Yaqzan*, trans. and ed. L. E. Goodman (4th edn. Los Angeles, 1996).
—— *Het Leven van Hai Ebn Yokdhan . . . vert. d. S.D.B.* (Amsterdam, 1701) UCLA.
TUINMAN, CAROLUS, *De Liegende en Bedriegende Vrygeest Ontmaskeert in een Antwoord Aan den Vermomden Constantius Prudens* (Middelburg, 1715) AUB.
—— *Het Helsche Gruwelheim der Heilloose Vrygeesten* (Middelburg, 1717) AUB.
—— *Korte Afschetzing der Ysselykheden, welke van de Spinozistische Vrygeesten Uitdrukkelyk worden Geleert* (Rotterdam, 1719) AUB.
TURGOT, ANNE-ROBERT-JACQUES, BARON DE L'AULNE, 'Réflexions sur les *Pensées philosophiques* de Diderot' (1746), in *Œuvres*, i. 87–97.
—— *Recherches sur les causes des progrès et de la décadence des sciences et des arts ou Réflexions sur l'histoire des progrès de l'esprit humain*, in Turgot, *Œuvres*, i. 116–42.
—— *Discours sur les avantages que l'établissement du christianisme a procurés au genre humain* (1750), in Turgot, *Œuvres*, i. 194–214.
—— *Tableau philosophique des progrès successifs de l'esprit humain* (1750), in Turgot, *Œuvres*, i. 214–35.
—— *Plan de deux discours sur l'histoire universelle* (*c.*1751), in Turgot, *Œuvres*, i. 275–323.
—— *Œuvres*, ed. G. Schelle (5 vols., Paris, 1913).
TURRETTINI, JEAN-ALPHONSE, 'Réfutation du système de Spinosa' (*c.*1728), *NAKG* (1988), 68 191–212.

Tyssot de Patot, Simon, *Voyages et avantures de Jaques Massé*, ed. A. Rosenberg (Oxford, 1993).

—— *La Vie, les aventures et le voyage de Groenland du Réverend Père Cordelier Pierre de Mésange* (2. vols., Amsterdam, 1720; repr. Geneva, 1979).

—— *Lettres choisies et Discours sur la chronologie*, ed. A. Rosenberg (Paris, 2002).

Undereyck, Theodor, *Der närrische Atheist entdeckt und seiner Thorheit überzeuget* (Bremen, 1689) BPK.

Valla, Lorenzo, *Scritti filosofici e religiosi*, ed. G. Radetti (Florence, 1953).

Valsecchi, Antonio, *Ritratti o vite letterarie e paralleli di G. J. Rousseau, del sig. di Voltaire, di Obbes, e di Spinosa, e vita di Pietro Bayle* (Venice, 1816) BL.

Vandeul, Mme de, *Mémoires pour servir à l'histoire de la vie et des ouvrages de Diderot*, in *Œuvres complètes de Diderot*, ed. J. Assezat, i (Paris, 1875), pp. xxix–lxviii.

Vauvenargues, Luc de Clapiers, marquis de, *Œuvres*, ed. P. Varillon (3 vols., Paris, 1929).

—— *Traité sur le libre arbitre* (1737), in Vauvenargues, *Œuvres posthumes et œuvres inédites*, ed. D. L. Gilbert (2 vols., Paris, 1857), i. 191–219.

Velthuysen, Lambert van, *Tractatus de cultu naturali*, in Velthuysen, *Opera omnia* (2 vols., Rotterdam, 1680) CUL.

Vervolg van 't leven van Philopater (1697) [attrib. Johannes Duijkerius], ed. G. Maréchal (Amsterdam, 1991).

[Verwer, Adriaen], *'t Mom Aensicht der Atheisterey Afgerukt* (Amsterdam, 1683) AUB.

Vico, Giambattista, *De nostri temporis studiorum ratione* [On the Study Methods of our Time] (1709), trans. and ed. Elio Gianturco (Ithaca, NY, 1990).

—— *De antiquissima Italorum sapientia* [On the Most Ancient Wisdom of the Italians] (1710), trans. and ed. L. M. Palmer (Ithaca, NY, 1988).

—— '*Disputation* with the *Giornale de' Letterati d'Italia*', in Vico, *De antiquissima*, 113–87.

—— *The First New Science* (1725), ed. L. Pompa (Cambridge, 2002).

—— *The New Science* (3rd edn. 1744), trans. and ed. Th. G. Bergin and M. H. Fisch (1948; 5th printing Ithaca, NY, 1994).

—— *Autobiography*, trans. and ed. M. J. Fisch and Th. G. Bergin (Ithaca, NY, 4th printing 1993)

La Vie et l'esprit de Mr. Benoit de Spinosa (The Hague, 1719; repr. ed. S. Berti, Turin, 1994).

Voltaire, François-Marie Arouet de, *Œuvres complètes de Voltaire*, ed. M. Auguis et al. (97 vols., Paris, 1828–34).

—— *Correspondence and Related Documents*, ed. Th. Besterman (51 vols., Toronto 1968–77).

—— *Lettres philosophiques* (1733), ed. R. Naves (Paris, 1988).

—— *Notebooks*, ed. Th. Besterman (2 vols., Geneva, 1968).

—— *Traité de métaphysique* (1734/5), ed. W. H. Barber, in *The Complete Works of Voltaire* (The Voltaire Foundation), xiv (Oxford, 1992), 357–503.

—— *Eléments de la philosophie de Newton* (1738), ed. R. L. Walters and W. H. Barber in *The Complete Works of Voltaire* (The Voltaire Foundation), xv (Oxford, 1992).

—— *La Métaphysique de Newton* (1740), in *Élements*, 195–252.

—— *Essai sur les mœurs et l'esprit des nations et sur les principaux faits de l'histoire depuis Charlemagne jusqu'à Louis XIII*, ed. R. Pomeau (2 vols., Paris, 1963).

—— 'Micromégas', in Voltaire, *Romans*, 131–47.

—— *Romans et contes*, ed. R. Pomeau (Paris, 1966).

—— *Œuvres complètes*, ed. Louis Moland (52 vols., Paris, 1877–85).

—— *Histoire de l'empire de Russie sous Pierre-le-Grand* (2 vols., Paris, 1761–3) PBN.
—— *Extrait des sentiments de Jean Meslier*, in Voltaire, *Œuvres complètes*, xliii. 254–327.
—— *Traité sur la tolérance*, ed. R. Pomeau (Paris, 1989).
—— *Dictionnaire philosophique*, ed. Chr. Mervaud (2 vols., Oxford, 1994).
—— *Homélies prononcées à Londres en 1765 dans une assemblée particulière* in Voltaire, *Œuvres complètes*, xliii. 331–417.
—— *Le Philosophe ignorant* (1766), in Voltaire, *Œuvres complètes*, xliv. 1–87.
—— *Lettres à son altesse M. le prince de Brunsvick* (1767), in Voltaire, *Œuvres complètes*, xliv.
—— 'Notes de M. de Morza sur les systèmes' (1772), in Voltaire, *Œuvres complètes*, xvi. 248–76.
—— *Mémoires pour servir à la vie de M. de Voltaire écrits par lui-même*, vol. ii of Condorcet, *Vie de Voltaire* (London, 1791) PBN.
—— 'Manifesto of the King of France in Favour of Prince Charles Edward', in Th. Besterman, *Voltaire* (Paris, 1969), 565–7.
—— 'Remerciement sincère à un homme charitable' (n.p., 1750).
—— 'La Voix du sage et du peuple' (1750), in *Collection complète des œuvres de Monsieur de Voltaire*, xvii (new edn. Amsterdam, 1764), 423–8.
—— *Sermon des cinquante* (n.p. [Paris?], 1749) BL.
Vossius, Gerardus Johannes, *De theologia gentili* (new edn. Amsterdam, 1668) AUB.
—— *De philosophorum sectis*, in Vossius, *Opera* (Amsterdam, 1697), iii. 281–315.
Vossius, Isaac, *De Sibyllinis aliisque quae Christi natalem praecessent oraculis* (Oxford, 1679) BL.
—— *Variarum observationum liber* (London, 1685) BL.
Wachter, Johann Georg, *Der Spinozismus in Jüdenthumb*, ed. W. Schröder (Stuttgart, 1994).
Wachter, Johann Georg, *Origines juris naturalis* (Berlin, 1704), repr. in W. Schröder (ed.), *Freidenker der europäischen Aufklärung* (Stuttgart, 1995), part 1, ii. 201–60.
—— 'Leben Herrn Johann George Wachters, aus sein eigener Handschrift' in W. Schröder (ed.), *Freidenker der europäischen Aufklärung* (Stuttgart, 1995), part 1, ii. 279–90.
—— *De primordiis Christianae religionis* (Stuttgart, 1995).
Wagner, Gabriel [Realis de Vienna], *Discursus et dubia in Christ. Thomasii Introductionem ad philosophiam aulicam* ('Regensburg' [Frankfurt an der Oder?], 1691) WUL.
—— *Prüfung des Versuchs vom Wesen des Geistes* (1707), in S.Wollgast (ed.), *Gabriel Wagner (1660–1717): Ausgewählte Schriften* (Stuttgart, 1997), 371–452.
—— F.M.v.G., *Antwort auff Jucundi de Laboribus Unverschämtheit* (1710), in S. Wollgast. (ed.), *Gabriel Wagner (1660–1717): Ausgewählte Schriften* (Stuttgart, 1997), 533–630.
Wagner, Georg Thomas, *Johan Christian Edelmanns verblendete Anblicke des Moses mit aufgedeckten Angesicht* (3 vols, Frankfurt, 1747) BL.
Walch, Johann Georg, *Einleitung in die Philosophie* (1727; repr. of the 1738 edn., 2 vols., Bristol, 2001).
—— *Philosophisches Lexicon* (3 vols., Leipzig, 1733; repr. Bristol, 2001).
Walten, Ericus, *De Regtsinnige Policey* (The Hague, 1689) BL.
—— *Onwederleggelyk Bewys van het Regt, de Magt en Pligt der Overheden in Kerkelyke Saken* (The Hague, 1689) PC.
—— *Portret van Jacobus Koelman* (The Hague, 1689) AUB.
—— *Brief aan een Regent der Stad Amsterdam* (Knuttel 13840) (The Hague, 1692) AUB.
—— *Brief aan sijn Excellentie, de Heer Graaf van Portland* (Knuttel 13895) (The Hague, 1692) WLC.

WALTEN, ERICUS, *Remonstrantie van Mr Ericus Walten, Doctor in de Theologie, Regten en Philosophie* (n.p., n.d. [1692]) AUB.

—— *'t Samenspraeck Gehouden tusschen Twee Reysigers, zynde de een een Haagenaer en de Andere een Amsterdammer* (n.p., 1690) AUB.

—— *Weerklank op de Uitvlugtige Antwoord van een Onbekenden Auteur, tegen den Brief van den Heer Raad-Pensionaris Fagel* (n.p. [The Hague?], 1688) BL.

—— E.W., *Wederlegginge van het Schend-schrift Genaamt* Parlementum pacificum*: of Een Verdeedinge van het Gemene belang der Waarheid* ('Keulen' [Amsterdam?], 1688) NYPC.

—— *Spiegel der Waerheyd, ofte 't Samesprekinge tusschen een Arminiaan ende Vroom Patriot.* (Knuttel 13480) (n.p., 1690) PC.

—— *Aardige Duyvelary Voorvallende in dese Dagen* (Knuttel 13712) (n.p., n.d. [Amsterdam? 1691]) WLC.

—— *Vervolg van de Aardige Duyvelary Voorvallende in dese Dagen* (Knuttel 13713) (Rotterdam, 1691) BL.

—— *Beschryvinge van een Vremd Nagt-Gezigte, Vertoont aan een Toehoorder der Predikatie, die Door de Remonstrantsche Leeraer Ds Johannes Molinaeus voor't Vermogen des Duivels, en tegen den Aucteur van't Boek de Betooverde Weereld, onlangs te Rotterdam Gedaan is* (n.p., n.d. [The Hague?, 1691?]) UCLA.

—— *Den Triumpheerende Duyvel Spookende omtrent den Berg van Parnassus* (Middelburg, 1692) WHA.

—— *Triumph-Digt op de Medailje of Penning . . . van . . . Balthasar Bekker* (Rotterdam, 1692) AUB.

WATER, J. VAN DE, *Groot Placaat-Boeck Vervattende alle Placcaten . . . der Staten 's Lands van Utrecht* (3 vols., Utrecht, 1729) LIHR.

WEBER, IMMANUEL, *Beurtheilung der Atheisterey wie auch derer mehresten deshalben berüchtigsten Schrifften* (Frankfurt am Main, 1697) HUL.

WEHRLI, FRITZ, *Die Schule des Aristoteles*, v: *Straton von Lampsakos* (Basel, 1950).

WILDMAN, SIR JOHN, *A Letter to a Friend, Advising in this Extraordinary Juncture, how to Free the Nation from Slavery*, in *A Sixth Collection of Papers Relating to the Present Juncture of Affairs in England* (London, 1689), no. iii, pp. 13–16.

WILSON, JOHN, *The Scriptures Genuine Interpreter Asserted* (London, 1678) BL.

WISZOWATY, ANDREAS, *Religio rationalis* (Amsterdam, 1685) AUB.

—— *Spooren der Deugden en Breidels der Zonden* (2nd edn. Amsterdam,1703) AUB.

WITSIUS (Witz), H., *Het Aenstootelijcke Nieuw, in Waerheyt en Liefde Ontdeckt* (Amsterdam, 1673) AUB.

WITTICHIUS, CHRISTOPHER, *Consensus veritatis in Scriptura divina et infallibili revelatione cum veritate philosophica a Renato Des Cartes detecta* (2nd edn. Leiden, 1682) AUB.

—— *Anti-Spinoza, sive Examen Ethices Benedicti de Spinoza* (Amsterdam, 1690) BL.

—— *Ondersoek van de Zede-konst van Benedictus de Spinoza* (Amsterdam, 1695) UCLA.

WOLFF, CHRISTIAN, *Oratio de Sinarum philosophia* (1721), ed. M. Albert (Hamburg, 1985).

WOLLASTON, WILLIAM, *The Religion of Nature Delineated* (London, 1724).

WOLZOGEN, LOUIS, *De Scriptuarum interprete* (Utrecht, 1668) BL.

[WOTTON, WILLIAM], *A Letter to Eusebia* (London, 1704) BL.

WYERMARS, HENDRIK, *Den Ingebeelde Chaos* (Amsterdam, 1710) AUB.

XENOPHANES OF COLOPHON, *Fragments*, trans. and commentary by J. H. Lesher (Toronto, 1992).

YVON, CLAUDE, article 'Âme', in Diderot et d'Alembert, *Encyclopédie*, i.

—— article 'Aristotélisme', in Diderot et d'Alembert, *Encyclopédie*, i.

—— Prades, Jean-Martin de and Diderot Denis, *Apologie de Monsieur l'Abbé de Prades.* (Amsterdam, 1753) PBN.

YVON, PIERRE, *L'Impiété convaincue* (Amsterdam, 1681) AUB.

ZEDLER, JOHANN HEINRICH, *Grosses volständiges universal Lexicon* (64 vols., Leipzig, 1732–1754).

ZIMMERMANN, JOHANN JACOBUS, *Vindiciae dissertationis de atheismo Platonis contra ea, quae... monuit D. Nicol. Hieron. Gundlingius* (Frankfurt, 1729) BL.

Secondary

AARSLEFF, HANS, 'Introduction' to Condillac, *Essay*, ed. Aarsleff, pp. xi–xxxviii.

—— 'Locke's Influence', in Chappell (ed.), *Cambridge Companion to Locke*, 252–89.

ABID, SYED ABID ALI, 'Political Theory of the Shi'ites', in Sharif (ed.), *History*, i. 732–46.

ABUN-NASR, JAMIL M., *A History of the Maghrib in the Islamic Period* (1987; Cambridge, repr. 1983).

AGRIMI, MARIO, 'Paragrafi sul "Platonismo" di Vico', *Studi filosofici* (Naples), 5/6 (1982–3), 83–130.

AKKERMAN, FOKKE, *Studies in the Posthumous Works of Spinoza* (Meppel, 1980).

ALATRI, PAOLO, *Voltaire, Diderot e il 'partito filosofico'* (Messina, 1965).

ALBERTI, A., *Alberto Radicati di Passerano* (Turin, 1931).

ALBRECHT, MICHAEL, 'Einleitung to Wolff', *Oratio*, pp. ix–ciii.

ALBRECHT, MICHAEL, *Eklektik: Eine Begriffsgeschichte* (Stuttgart, 1993).

ALGRA, KEIMPE, 'Stoic Theology', in Inwood (ed.), *The Cambridge Companion to the Stoics*, 153–78.

—— 'The Beginnings of Cosmology', in A. A. Long (ed.), *The Cambridge Companion to Early Greek Philosophy* (Cambridge, 1999), 45–65.

—— BARNES, JONATHAN, MANSFELD J., and SCHOFIELD, M. (eds.), *The Cambridge History of Hellenistic Philosophy* (Cambridge, 1999).

ALLARD, E., 'Die Angriffe gegen Descartes und Malebranche im *Journal de Trévoux*, 1701–1715', *Abhandlungen zur Philosophe und ihrer Geschichte*, 43 (Halle, 1914), 1–58.

ALLEN, M. J. B., and REES, V. *Marsilio Ficino: His Theology, His Philosophy, his Legacy* (Leiden, 2002).

ALLISON, H. E. *Benedict de Spinoza: An Introduction* (New Haven, 1987).

ALPHEN, G. VAN, *De stemming van de Engelschen tegen de Hollanders in Engeland tijdens de regering van den de koning-stadhouder Willem III, 1688–1702* (Assen, 1938).

ALTMANN, ALEXANDER, *Moses Mendelssohn: A Biographical Study* (London, 1973).

ANDERSON, ABRAHAM, 'Sallengre, La Monnoye, and the *Traité des trois imposteurs*', in Berti et al. (eds.), *Heterodoxy*, 255–71.

—— *The* Treatise of the Three Impostors *and the Problem of Enlightenment* (Lanham, NY, 1997).

ANDERSON, M. S., *The War of the Austrian Succession 1740–1748* (London, 1995).

ANDERSON, S., *An Engish Consul in Turkey: Paul Rycaut at Smyrna, 1667–1678* (Oxford, 1989).

Armitage, David, 'Introduction' to Bolingbroke, *Political Writings* (Cambridge, 1997), pp. vii–xxiv.
—— *The Ideological Origins of the British Empire* (Cambridge, 2000).
—— ' "That Excellent Forme of Government": New Light on Locke and Carolina', *Times Literary Supplement*, 5299 (22 Oct. 2004), 14–15.
—— 'Empire and Liberty: A Republican Dilemma', in van Gelderen and Skinner (eds.), *Republicanism*, ii. 29–46.
Artigas-Menant, G., *Du secret des clandestins à la propagande voltairienne* (Paris, 2001).
Ascoli, Georges, 'Bayle et l'*Avis aux réfugiés* d'après des documents inédits', *Revue d' histoire littéraire de la France*, 20 (1913).
Ashcraft, R., *Revolutionary Politics and Locke's* Two Treatises of Government (Princeton, 1986).
—— 'Locke's Political Philosophy', in Chappell (ed.), *The Cambridge Companion to Locke*, 226–51.
Assmann, Jan, *Moses the Egyptian* (Cambridge, Mass., 1997).
—— ' "Hen kai pan": Ralph Cudworth und die Rehabilitierung der hermetischen Tradition', in M. Neugebauer-Wölk (ed.), *Auflärung und Esoterik* (Hamburg, 1999), 38–52.
Athanassiadi, P., and Fredę Michael, (eds.), *Pagan Monotheism in Late Antiquity* (Oxford, 1999).
Aubery, Pierre, 'Montesquieu et les Juifs', *SVEC* 87 (Banbury, 6 1972), 87–99.
Badaloni, Nicola, *Introduzione a G. B. Vico* (Milan, 1961).
—— 'Vico nell'ambito della filosofia europea', in *Omagio a Vico* (Naples, 1968), 235–65.
—— 'Vico prima della Scienza nuova', in the *Atti del convegno internazionale sul tema: Campanella e Vico* (Rome, 1969), 339–55.
—— *Antonio Conti* (Milan, 1968).
Badawi, Abdulrahman, 'Muhammad ibn Zakariya al-Razi', in Sharif (ed.), *History*, 434–49.
Badir, Magdy Gabriel, *Voltaire et l'Islam* (Banbury, 1974).
Baker, K.M., 'Revolution', in Colin Lucas (ed.), *The Political Culture of the French Revolution* (Oxford, 1988), 41–62.
—— and Reill, P. H. (eds.), *What's Left of Enlightenment?* (Stanford, Calif., 2001).
Baldi, M., *Verisimile, non vero: filosofia e politica in Andrew Michael Ramsay* (Milan, 2002).
Balduzzi, Maria Annunziata, 'Problemi interpretativi nell'opera di Pierre Bayle', in G. Salinas (ed.), *Saggi sull'Illuminismo* (Cagliari, 1973), 451–501.
Balibar, Étienne, *Spinoza and Politics* (London, 1998).
—— 'Jus, pactum, lex: sur la constitution du sujet dans le *Traité théologico-politique*', *Studia Spinozana*, 1 (1985), 105–42.
Balty-Guesdon, M. G., 'Al-Andalus et l'héritage grec d'après les *Tabaqat al-umam*, de Sha'id al-Andalusi', in Hasnawi et al. (eds.), *Perspectives*, 331–42.
Bar-Asher, M. M., 'Abu Bakr al-Razi (865–925)', in F. Niewöhner (ed.), *Klassiker der Religionsphilosophie von Platon bis Kierkegaard*, (Munich, 1995), 99–111.
Barber, W. H., 'Le Newton de Voltaire', in De Gandt (ed.), *Cirey*, 115–25.
Barbour, J. B., *The Discovery of Dynamics*, vol. i of Barbour, *Absolute or Relative Motion?* (Cambridge, 1989).
Barebone, S., and Rice, L. C., 'La Naissance d' une nouvelle politique', in Moreau (ed.), *Architectures*, 47–61.

Baridon, M., 'Les Concepts de nature humaine et de perfectibilité dans l'historiographie des Lumières de Fontenelle à Condorcet', in *L'Histoire au dix-huitième siècle: Centre Aixois d'Études et de Recherches sur le XVIIIème siècle* (Aix-en-Provence, 1980), 353–74.

Barnes, Annie, *Jean Le Clerc (1656–1736) et la République des Lettres* (Paris, 1938).

Barnes, Jonathan, *The Presocratic Philosophers* (rev. edn. 1982; repr. London, 2002).

Barnouw, J., 'The Psychological Sense and Moral and Political Significance of "Endeavour" in Hobbes', in Bostrenghi (ed.), *Hobbes e Spinoza*, 399–416.

Barnouw, P. J., *Philippus van Limborch* (The Hague, 1963).

Barrande, Jean-Marie, 'Introduction' to Leibniz, *Protogaea* (Toulouse, 1993), pp. i–xxxi.

Bartlett, R. C., *The Idea of Enlightenment: A Post-mortem Study* (Toronto, 2001).

Barlett, Thomas, ' "This Famous Island Set in a Virginian Sea": Ireland in the British Empire 1690–1801', in P. J. Marshall (ed.), *The Oxford History of the British Empire*, ii. 253–75.

Bartuschat, Wolfgang, 'The Ontological Basis of Spinoza's Theory of Politics', in C. de Deugd (ed.), *Spinoza's Political and Theological Thought* (Amsterdam, 1984), 30–6.

Batalden, S. K., 'Notes from a Leningrad Manuscript: Eugenios Voulgaris' Autograph List of his Own Works', 'ο' *Ερανιστής*, 18 (1976), 1–22.

Becker, C. L., *The Heavenly City of the Eighteenth-Century Philosophers* (New Haven, 1932).

Beddard, Robert, *A Kingdom without a King* (Oxford, 1988).

Bedjaï, Marc, 'Franciscus van den Enden: maître spirituel de Spinoza', *Revue de l'histoire des religions*, 207 (1990), 289–311.

—— 'Libertins et politiques', *Revue de la Bibliothèque nationale*, 44 (1992), 29–33.

—— 'Les Circonstances de la publication du *Philedonius* (1657) Franciscus van den Enden', in F. van den Enden, *Philedonius, édition critique*, ed. M. Bedjaï (Paris, 1985), 9–55.

Beeson, D., ' "Il n'y a pas d'amour heureux": Voltaire, Émilie and the Debate on *Force vive*', in Kölving and Mervaud (eds.), *Voltaire et ses combats*, ii. 901–13.

Beiser, F. C., *The Sovereignty of Reason* (Princeton, 1996).

Belgioioso, G., 'Introduzione' to Doria, *Manoscritti napoletani*, 5–47.

Belgrado, A. M., 'Voltaire, Bayle e la polemica sull'idolatria pagana', *Saggi e Ricerche di letteratura francese*, 18 (1979), 381–422.

Bell, D., *The Cult of the Nation in France: Inventing Nationalism, 1680–1800* (Cambridge, Mass., 2001).

Bellinghen, J., van, 'David van Dinant', in Dethier and Vandenbossche (eds.), *Woordenboek*, i. 81–100.

Benelli, Giuseppe, *Voltaire metafisico* (Genoa, 2000).

Benítez, Miguel, *La Face cachée des Lumières* (Paris, 1996).

—— 'Jean Meslier et l'argument ontologique', in Fink and Stenger (eds.), *Être matérialiste*, 67–80.

—— 'La Composition de la *Lettre de Thrasybule à Leucippe*', in Grell and Volpilhac-Auger (eds.), *Nicolas Fréret*, 177–92.

Bennett, C. V., *White Kennett, 1660–1728: Bishop of Peterborough* (London, 1957).

—— 'King William III and the Episcopate', in C. V. Bennett and J. D. Walsh (eds.), *Essays in Modern English Church History* (London, 1966), 104–32.

Bennett, J., 'Locke's Philosophy of Mind', in Chappell (ed.), *Cambridge Companion to Locke*, 89–114.

Bénot, Yves, *Diderot, de l'athéisme à l'anticolonialisme* (Paris, 1981).

—— 'Y a- t- il une morale materialiste?', in Fink and Stenger (eds.), *Être matérialiste*, 81–91.

Benrekassa, G., 'Mœurs', in *HPSGF* xv/xviii. 159–205.

Bergh, C. J. van den, *The Life and Work of Gerard Noodt (1647–1725)* (Oxford, 1988).

Berkvens-Stevelinck, Chr., *Prosper Marchand: la vie et l'œuvre (1678–1756)* (Leiden, 1987).

—— 'La Tentation de l'arminianisme', in Magdalaine et al. (eds.), *De l'humanisme aux Lumières*, 219–29.

—— 'L'*Epilogueur* épilogué, ou L'Antivoltairianisme acide de Rousset de Missy et Prosper Marchand', in Kölving and Mervaud (eds.), *Voltaire et ses combats*, ii. 977–84.

—— Vercruysse, J. (eds.), *Le Métier de journaliste au dix-huitième siècle* (Oxford, 1993).

—— Israel, J. I., and Posthumus Meyjes, G. H. M. (eds.), *The Emergence of Tolerance in the Dutch Republic* (Leiden, 1997).

Berlin, Isaiah, 'Montesquieu', *Proceedings of the British Academy*, 41 (1956), 267–96.

—— *Three Critics of the Enlightenment: Vico, Hamann, Herder* (Princeton, 2000).

Berman, David, 'Determinism and Freewill: Anthony Collins', *Studies: An Irish Quarterly Review* (summer/autumn 1977), 251–4.

—— *A History of Atheism* (Beckenham, 1988).

—— 'Disclaimers as Offence Mechanisms in Charles Blount and John Toland', in Hunter and Wootton (eds.), *Atheism*, 255–72.

Bernasconi, R., 'Kant as an Unfamiliar Source of Racism', in Ward and Lott (eds.), *Philosophers on Race*, 145–66.

Berriot, François, 'La "Littérature clandestine": le cas des hétérodoxes du Moyen Âge et de la Renaissance', in McKenna and Mothu (eds.), *La Philosophie clandestine*, 39–47.

Berry, C. J., 'Lusty Women and Loose Imagination: Hume's Philosophical Anthropology of Chastity', *HPTh* 24 (2003), 415–33.

Bertelli, Sergio, *Erudizione e storia in Lodovico Antonio Muratori* (Naples, 1960).

Berti, Silvia, 'The First Edition of the *Traité des trois imposteurs* and its Debt to Spinoza's *Ethics*', in Hunter and Wootton (eds.), *Atheism*, 182–220.

—— 'Introduzione' to S. Berti (ed.), *Trattato dei tre impostori* (Turin, 1994), pp. xv–lxxxiv.

—— 'L'*Esprit de Spinosa*: ses origines et sa première édition dans leur contexte spinozien', in Berti et al. (eds.), *Heterodoxy*, 3–51.

—— 'Radicali ai margini: materialsmo, libero pensiero e diritto al suicidio in Radicati di Passerano', *RSI* 116 (2004), 794–811.

—— Charles-Daubert, F., and Popkin, R. H. (eds.), *Heterodoxy, Spinozism and Free Thought in Early Eighteenth-Century Europe: Studies on the* Traité des trois imposteurs (Dordrecht, 1996).

Betts, C.J., *Early Deism in France* (The Hague, 1984).

Bevir, M., 'The Role of Contexts in Understanding and Explanation', Bödeker (ed.), *Begriffsgeschichte*, 159–208.

Bianchi, Lorenzo, *Tradizione libertine e critica storica: da Naudé a Bayle* (Milan, 1988).

—— 'Religione e tolleranza in Montesquieu', *RCSF* 49 (1994), 49–71.

—— 'Pierre Bayle et le libertinage érudit', in Bots (ed.), *Critique, savoir et érudition*, 251–67.

—— 'Histoire et nature: la religion dans *L'Esprit des lois*', in Porret and Volpilhac-Auger (eds.), *Temps de Montesquieu*, 289–304.

—— 'Impostura religiosa e critica storica', in G. Canziani (ed.), *Filosofia e religione nella letteratura clandestine (secoli XVII–XVIII)* (Milan, 1994), 235–64.

—— (ed.), *Pierre Bayle e l'Italia* (Naples, 1996).

Bientjes, J., *Holland und die Holländer im Urteil deutscher Reisender 1400–1800* (Groningen, 1967).

Bietenholz, P. G., *Historia and Fabula: Myths and Legends in Historical Thought from Antiquity to the Modern Age* (Leiden, 1994).
—— *Daniel Zwicker (1612–1678): Peace, Tolerance and God the One and Only* (Florence, 1997).
Bijl, M. van der, *Idee en interest* (Groningen, 1981).
Birnstiel, E., 'Frédéric II et le *Dictionnaire* de Bayle', in Bost and Robert (eds.), *Pierre Bayle*, 143–57.
Black, Jeremy, *Convergence or Divergence: Britain and the Continent* (Basingstoke, 1994).
Blackwell, C. 'The Logic of History of Philosophy: Morhof's *De variis methodis* and the *Polyhistor philosophicus*', in Waquet (ed.), *Mapping the World of Learning*,
Blair, Ann, 'The Practices of Erudition According to Morhof', in Waquet (ed.), *Mapping the World of Learning*, 59–74.
Blanning, T. C. W., *The Culture of Power and the Power of Culture: Old Regime Europe, 1660–1789* (Oxford, 2002).
Bloch, O., 'L'Héritage libertin dans le matérialisme des Lumières', *DHS* 24 (1992), 73–82.
—— (ed.), *Le Materialisme du XVIIIe siècle et la littérature clandestine* (Paris, 1982).
—— (ed.), *Spinoza au XVIIIe siècle* (Paris, 1990).
Blom, H. W., 'Politics, Virtue and Political Science: An Interpretation of Spinoza's Political Philosophy', *Studia Spinozana*, 1 (1985), 209–30.
—— ' "Our Prince is King!" The Impact of the Glorious Revolution on Political Debate in the Dutch Republic', *Parliaments, Estates and Representation*, 10 (1990), 45–58.
—— 'Politieke filosofie in het Nederland van de zeventiende eeuw', *GWN* 4 (1993), 167–78.
—— *Morality and Causality in Politics* (Utrecht, 1995).
Blom, H. W. 'Citizens and the Ideology of Citizenship in the Dutch Republic', *Yearbook of European Studies*, 8 (1995), 131–52.
—— 'Burger en belang: Pieter de La Court over de politieke betekenis van burgers', in Joost Kloek and Karin Tilmans (eds.), *Burger: een geschiedenis van het begrip burger in de Nederlanden van de Middeleeuwen tot de 21 ste eeuw* (Amsterdam, 2002), 99–112.
—— 'The Republican Mirror: The Dutch Idea of Europe', in A. Pagden (ed.), *The Idea of Europe* (Cambridge, 2002), 91–115.
Blom, Philip, Encyclopédie: *The Triumph of Reason in an Unreasonable Age* (London, 2004).
Bödeker, H. E., 'Reflexionen über Begriffsgeschichte als methode', in Bödeker (ed.), *Begriffsgeschichte*, 73–121.
—— 'Debating the *Respublica mixta*: German and Dutch Political Discourses around 1700', in van Gelderen and Skinner (eds.), *Republicanism*, ii. 219–46.
—— (ed.), *Begriffsgeschichte, Diskursgeschichte, Metapherngeschichte* (Göttingen, 2002).
Bonacina, Giovanni, *Filosofia ellenistica e cultura moderna* (Florence, 1996).
Bondì, Roberto, ' "Spiritus" e "anima" in Bernardino Telesio', *GCFI* 72 (1993), 405–17.
Bongie, L. L., *David Hume: Prophet of the Counter-Revolution* (1965; 2nd edn. Indianapolis, 2000).
Bonney, Richard, *The European Dynastic States, 1494–1660* (Oxford, 1991).
Bordoli, Roberto, *Ragione e scrittura tra Descartes e Spinoza* (Milan, 1997).
—— 'Account of a Curious Traveller', *Studia Spinozana*, 10 (1994), 175–82.
Borghero, Carlo, 'L'Italia in Bayle, Bayle in Italia', in Bianchi (ed.), *Pierre Bayle*, 3–33.
—— 'I ritmi del moderno', *Archivio storico italiano*, 162 (2004), 313–45.
Borrelli, Gian Franco, 'Hobbes e la teoria moderna della democrazia', *Trimestre*, 24 (1991), 243–63.
Boss, Gilbert, 'L'Histoire chez Spinoza et Leibniz', *Studia Spinozana*, 6 (1990), 179–200.

Bost, Hubert, *Pierre Bayle et la religion* (Paris, 1994).

—— 'L'Écriture ironique et critique d'un contre-révocationnaire', in Magdalaine et al. (eds.), *De l'humanisme aux Lumières*, 665–78.

—— 'Regards critiques ou complices sur les hérétiques', in Bost and de Robert (eds.), *Pierre Bayle*, 199–213.

—— Robert, Ph. de (eds.), *Pierre Bayle, citoyen du monde* (Paris, 1999).

Bostrenghi, D. (ed.), *Hobbes e Spinoza: scienza e politica* (Naples, 1992).

Bots, Hans, 'Le Plaidoyer des journalistes de Hollande pour la tolérance (1684–1750)', in Magdalaine et al. (eds.), *De l'humanisme aux Lumières*, 547–59.

—— (ed.), *Henri Basnage de Beauval en de* Histoire des ouvrages des savans *(1687–1709)* (2 vols., Amsterdam, 1976).

—— (ed.), *Critique, savoir et érudition à la veille des Lumières: le Dictionnaire historique et critique de Pierre Bayle (1647–1706)* (Amsterdam, 1998).

—— and Evers, M., 'Jean Leclerc et la réunion des églises protestantes dans la *Bibliothèque ancienne et moderne* (1714–1727)', *NAKG* 66 (1986), 54–67.

Bouchard, J., 'Les Relations épistolaires de Nicolas Mavrocordatos avec Jean Le Clerc et William Wake', 'O' *Ερανιστήζ*, 11 (1980), 67–92.

—— 'Nicolas Mavrocordatos et l'aube des Lumières', *Revue des études sud-est européennes*, 20 (1982), 237–46.

Bouchardy, Jean-Jacques, *Pierre Bayle: la nature et la 'nature des choses'* (Paris, 2001).

Boudou, B., 'La Poétique d'Henri Estienne', *BHR* 52 (1990), 571–92.

Bourdin, Jean-Claude, *Diderot: le matérialisme* (Paris, 1998).

—— *Les Matérialistes au XVIIIe siècle* (Paris, 1996).

Bourel, D., 'Le Marquis d'Argens à Berlin', in Vissière (ed.), *Marquis d'Argens*, 29–39.

Bouveresse, Renée, *Spinoza et Leibniz: l'idée d'animisme universel* (Paris, 1992).

—— (ed.), *Spinoza, science et religion* (Paris, 1988).

Bove, Laurent, 'Vauvenargues politique: l'héritage machiavélien et spinoziste', in Dagen (ed.), *Entre Epicure*, 403–26.

—— *La Stratégie du conatus: affirmation et résistance chez Spinoza* (Paris, 1996).

—— 'C'est la résistance qui fait le citoyen', in Moreau (ed.), *Architectures*, 73–85.

—— 'Vauvenargues, une philosophie pour la "seconde nature" ', in Bove (ed.) *Vauvenargues*, 227–49.

—— 'Introduction' to Spinoza, *Traité politique* (Paris, 2002), 9–101.

—— (ed.), *Vauvevenargues: philosophie de la force active* (Paris, 2000).

Bowersock, G. W., *Julian the Apostate* (1978; Cambridge, Mass, 5th printing 1997).

Box, M. A., *The Suasive Art of David Hume* (Princeton, 1990).

Bracken, H. M., *Freedom of Speech: Words are not Deeds* (Westport, Conn., 1994).

Braida, Lodovica, 'Censure et circulation du livre en Italie au XVIIIe siècle', *Journal of Modern European History*, 3 (2005), 81–99.

Brann, N. L., *The Debate over the Origin of Genius during the Italian Renaissance* (Leiden, 2002).

Braun, Lucien, *Histoire de l'histoire de la philosophie* (Paris, 1973).

Braun, Th. E. D., 'Diderot, the Ghost of Bayle', *Diderot Studies*, 27 (1998), 45–55.

Bremmer, J. N., *The Rise and Fall of the Afterlife* (London, 2002).

Briggs, E. R., 'Bayle ou Laroque?', in Magdalaine et al. (eds.), *De l'humanisme aux Lumières*, 509–24.

Briggs, R., *Communities of Belief* (1989; new edn. Oxford, 1995).

BROADIE, ALEXANDER (ed.), *The Cambridge Companion to the Scottish Enlightenment* (Cambridge, 2003).
—— 'The Human Mind and its Powers', in Broadie (ed.), *Cambridge Companion to the Scottish Enlightenment*, 60–78.
BROGI, STEFANO, *Il cerchio dell'universo: libertinismo, spinozismo e filosofia della natura in Boulainvilliers* (Florence, 1993).
—— *Teologia senza verità: Bayle contro i 'rationaux'* (Milan, 1998).
BRONNER, S. E., *Reclaiming the Enlightenment* (New York, 2004).
BROWN, STUART, 'Monodology and the Reception of Bruno in the Young Leibniz', in Gatti (ed.), *Giordano Bruno*, 381–401.
—— 'Introduction' to Stuart Brown (ed.), *British Philosophy and the Age of Enlightenment* (London, 1996).
BRUGMANS, H., *Diderot (1713–1784)* (Amsterdam, 1937).
BRUNNER, O., CONZE, W., and KOSELLEK, R. (eds.), *Geschichtliche Grundbegriffe: Historisches Lexicon zur politisch-sozialen Sprache in Deutschland* (9 vols., Stuttgart, 1972–90).
BRUNSCHWIG, J., 'Skepticism', in Brunschwig and Lloyd (eds.), *Greek Thought*, 937–56.
—— 'Introduction: The Beginnings of Hellenistic Epistemology', in Algra et al. (eds.), *Hellenistic Philosophy*, 229–59.
—— and LLOYD, G. (eds.), *Greek Thought: A Guide to Classical Knowledge* (Cambridge, Mass., 2000).
BRYKMAN, G., 'Bayle's Case for Spinoza', *Aristotelian Society*, NS 83 (1988), 259–70.
—— 'Locke dans le *Traité sur le libre arbitre* de Vauvenargues', in Bove (ed.), *Vauvenargues*, 173–86.
BUCK, AUGUST, 'Diderot und die Antike', in Toellner (ed.), *Aufklärung und Humanismus*, 131–44.
BUCKLEY, M. J., *At the Origins of Modern Atheism* (New Haven, 1987).
BUIJNSTERS, P. J, 'Les Lumières hollandaises', *SVEC* 87 (1972), 197–215.
—— 'Hendrik Smeeks', in Dethier and Vandenbossche (eds.), *Woordenboek*, i. 231–6.
BUNGE, WIEP VAN, *Johannes Bredenburg (1643–1691)* (Rotterdam, 1990).
—— 'Spinoza's Atheisme', in E. Kuypers (ed.), *Sporen van Spinoza* (Leuven, 1993).
—— 'Pierre Bayle et *l'animal machine*', in Bots (ed.), *Critique, savoir et érudition*, 7, 375–88.
—— 'Rationaliteit en Verlichting', *De Achttiende Eeuw*, 32 (2000), 145–64.
—— 'Balthasar Bekker over Daniel', *It Beaken: Tydskrift fan de Fryske Akademy*, 58 (1996), 138–48.
—— 'Ericus Walten (1663–1697)', in van Bunge and Klever (eds.), *Disguised and Overt Spinozism*, 41–54.
—— *From Stevin to Spinoza* (Leiden, 2001).
—— 'Spinoza en de waarheid van de Godsdienst', in P. Hoftijizer and Theo Verbeek (eds.), *Leven na Descartes* (Hilversum, 2005), 55–67.
—— (ed.), *The Early Enlightenment in the Dutch Republic, 1650–1750* (Leiden, 2003).
—— and KLEVER, WIM (eds.), *Disguised and Overt Spinozism around 1700* (Leiden, 1996).
—— KROP, HENRI, et al. (eds.), *The Dictionary of Seventeenth and Eighteenth-Century. Dutch Philosophers* (2 vols., Bristol, 2003).
BURGER, PIERRE-FRANÇOIS, 'La Prohibition du *Dictionnaire historique et critique* de Pierre Bayle par l'Abbé Renaudot (1648–1720)', in Bots (ed.), *Critique, savoir et érudition*.

Burnett, Charles, 'The "Sons of Averroes with the Emperor Frederick" and the Transmission of the Philosophical Works of Ibn Rushd', in Endress and Aertsen (eds.), *Averroes*, 259–99.

Burns, J. H., 'The Idea of Absolutism', in J. Miller (ed.), *Absolutism in Seventeenth-Century Europe* (London, 1990), 21–42.

Bush, N. R., *The Marquis d'Argens and his Philosophical Correspondence* (Ann Arbor, 1953).

Butterworth, Ch. E., 'The Source that, Nourishes, Averroes's Decisive Determination', *Arabic Sciences and Philosophy*, 5 (1995), 93–119.

Cabanel, P., 'La Faute à Voltaire et le nécessaire révisionnisme historique: la question de l'oubli de Bayle au XIXe siécle', in Bost and de Robert (eds.), *Pierre Bayle*, 105–25.

Candea, V., 'Les Intellectuels du sud-est européen au XVIIe siècle', *Revue des études sud-est européennes*, 8 (1970), 181–230, 623–67.

Cantelli, G., *Teologia e ateismo: saggio su pensiero filosofico e religioso di Pierre Bayle* (Florence, 1969).

—— 'Mito e storia in Leclerc, Tournemine e Fontenelle', *RCSF* 27 (1972), 269–86, 385–400.

—— 'La virtù degli atei nei *Pensieri diversi sulla cometa* di Pierre Bayle', in Méchoulan et al. (eds.), *Formazione*, ii. 679–706.

—— 'Nicola Fréret, tradizione religiosa e allegoria nell' interpretazione storica dei miti pagani', *RCSF* 29 (1974), 264–83.

Canziani, Guido, 'Critica della religione e fonti moderne nel *Cymbalum mundio Symbolum sapientiae*', in Canziani (ed.), *Filosofia e religione*, 35–81.

—— 'Les Philosophes de la Renaissance italienne dans le *Dictionnaire*', in Bots (ed.), *Critique, savoir et érudition*, 143–64.

—— (ed.), *Filosofia e religione nella letteratura clandestine: secoli XVII e XVIII* (Milan, 1994).

Caporali, Riccardo, 'Ragione e natura nella filosofia di Vico', *BCSV* 12/13 (1982/3), 151–95.

Caprariis, Vittorio de, 'Religione e politica in Saint-Évremond', *RSI* 66 (1954), 204–39.

Carayol, E., *Thémiseul de Saint-Hyacinthe* (Oxford, 1984).

Carpanetto, Dino, and Ricuperati, Giuseppe, *Italy in the Age of Reason, 1685–1789* (London, 1987).

Carrithers, D. W., 'Democratic and Aristocratic Republics', in Carrithers et al. (eds.), *Montesquieu's Science*, 109–58.

—— Mosher, M. A., and Rahe, P. A. (eds.), *Montesquieu's Science of Politics* (Lanham, Md. 2001).

Casini, Paolo, 'Diderot et les philosophes de l'antiquité', in Anne-Marie Chouillet (ed.), *Colloque international Diderot (1713–1784)* (Paris, 1985), 33–43.

—— 'Voltaire, la lumière et la théorie de la connaissance', in Kölving and Mervaud (eds.), *Voltaire et ses combats*, i. 39–45.

Cassirer, Ernst, *The Philosophy of the Enlightenment* (1932; Princeton, 1979).

—— *Kant's Life and Thought* (New Haven, *c.*1981).

Cerny, G., *Theology, Politics and Letters at the Crossroads of European Civilization: Jacques Basnage and the Baylean Huguenot Refugees in the Dutch Republic* (Dordrecht, 1987).

—— 'Jacques Basnage and Pierre Bayle', in Magdalaine et al. (eds.), *De l'humanisme aux Lumières*, 495–507.

Champion, Justin, *The Pillars of Priestcraft Shaken* (Cambridge, 1992).

—— 'John Toland: The Politics of Pantheism', *Revue de synthèse*, 116 (1995), 269–70.

—— 'Père Richard Simon and English Biblical Criticism, 1680–1692', in D. Katz and J. Force (eds.), *Everything Connects* (Leiden, 1999), 37–62.

—— 'Making Authority: Belief, Conviction and Reason in the Public Sphere in Late Seventeenth Century England', *Libertinage et philosophie*, 3 (Saint-Étienne, 1995), 143–90.

—— *Republican Learning: John Toland and the Crisis of Christian Culture, 1696–1722* (Manchester, 2003).

Chappell, V. (ed.), *The Cambridge Companion to Locke* (Cambridge, 1994).

—— 'Locke's Theory of Ideas', in Chappell (ed.), *Cambridge Companion to Locke*, 26–55.

Charles-Daubert, Françoise, *Le 'Traité des trois imposteurs' et 'L'Esprit de Spinosa': philosophie clandestine entre 1678 et 1768* (Oxford, 1999).

—— 'La Fortune de Cremonini chez les libertins érudits du XVIIe siècle', in Riondato and Poppi (eds.), *Cesare Cremonini*, i. 169–91.

Charnley, J., 'Near and Far East in the Works of Pierre Bayle', *Seventeenth Century*, 5 (1990), 173–83.

—— *Pierre Bayle: Reader of Travel Literature* (Bern, 1998).

Charrak, André, *Empiricisme et métaphysique: 'L'Essai sur l'origine des connaisances humaines' de Condillac* (Paris, 2003).

—— 'Le Statut de la volonté chez Vauvenargues', in Bove (ed.), *Vauvenargues*, 187–200.

Chartier, Roger, *The Cultural Origins of the French Revolution* (Durham, NC, 1991).

Cherni, A., *Buffon, la nature et son histoire* (Paris, 1998).

—— *Diderot: l'ordre et le devenir* (Geneva, 2002).

Childs, N., *A Political Academy in Paris, 1724–1731: The Entresol and its Members* (Oxford, 2000).

Ching J., and Oxtoby, G., *Discovering China: European Interpretations in the Enlightenment* (Rochester, NY, 1992).

Christophersen, H. O., *A Bibliographical Introduction to the Study of John Locke* (Oslo, 1930).

Chukwudi Eze, E., *Race and the Enlightenment* (Oxford, 1997).

Cicanci, O., *Companile Greceşti din Transilvania şi comertul European în anii 1636–1746* (Bucharest, 1981).

Ciornanescu, A., *Bibliographie de la littérature française du dix-huitième siècle* (3 vols., Paris, 1969).

Clark, D. H., and Clark, S. P. H., *Newton's Tyranny* (New York, 2000).

Clark, R. W., *Einstein: The Life and Times* (1974; New York, repr. 1994).

Clarke, D. M., 'Introduction' to François Poulain de La Barre, *The Equality of the Sexes* (Manchester, 1990).

—— 'Locke and Toland on Toleration', in O'Dea and Whelan (eds.), *Nations*, 261–71.

Claydon, T., *William III and the Godly Revolution* (Cambridge, 1996).

Cleve, F. M., *The Giants of Pre-Socratic Greek Philosophy*, vol. i (The Hague, 1965).

Cobban, Alfred, *Aspects of the French Revolution* (1968; London, 1971).

Coe, R. N. C., '"Le Philosophe Morelly": An Examination of the Political Philosophy' (unpublished University of Leeds Ph.D. thesis, 2 parts, 1954).

—— *Morelly: Ein Rationalist auf dem Wege zum Sozialismus* (Berlin, 1961).

Cohen, Claudine, *The Fate of the Mammoth: Fossils, Myth and History* (Chicago, 1994).

Cohen, H., 'Diderot and the Image of China in Eighteenth-Century France', *SVEC* 242 (Oxford, 1986), 219–32.

Cohen, I. Bernard, 'The Eighteenth-Century Origins of the Concept of Scientific Revolution', *JHI* 37 (1976), 257–88.

Coleman, F. M. *Hobbes and America: Exploring the Constitutional Foundations* (Toronto, *c.*1977).

Colilli, P., 'Giordano Bruno's Mnemonics and Giambattista Vico's Recollective Philology', in Gatti (ed.), *Giordano Bruno*, 345–64.

Collingwood, R. G., *The Idea of History* (1946; Oxford, 1961).

Colombero, Carlo, 'Andrea Cesalpino e la polemica anti-aristotelica ed anti-spinoziana', *RCSF* 35 (1980), 343–56.

Comte-Sponville, A., 'La Mettrie: un "Spinoza moderne"?', in Bloch (ed.), *Spinoza*, 133–50.

Conlon, Pierre, *Le Siècle de Lumières: bibliographie chronologique*, i: *1716–1722*; ii: *1723–1729*; iii: *1730–1736* (Geneva, 1983–4).

Conrad, L. I. (ed.), *The World of Ibn Tufayl: Interdisciplinary Perspectives on Hayy ibn Yaqzan* (Leiden, 1996), 1–37.

—— 'Through the Thin Veil: On the Question of Communication and the Socialization of Knowledge in Hayy b. Yaqzan', in Conrad (ed.), *The World of Ibn Tufayl*, 238–66.

Cook, D. J., and Rosemont, H., 'The Pre-established Harmony between Leibniz and Chinese Thought', *JHI* 42 (1981), 253–67.

Cook, Harold J., 'Bernard Mandeville and the Therapy of the "Clever Politician" ', *JHI* 61 (1999), 101–24.

—— 'Body and Passions: Materialism and the Early Modern State', *Osiris* (The History of Science Society, 2002), 25–48.

Cook, R. I., 'The Great Leviathan of Lechery', in Primer (ed.), *Mandeville Studies*, 22–33.

Copenhaver, B. P., 'Astrology and Magic', in Schmitt and Skinner (eds.), *CHRPh* 264–300.

Corsano, Antonio, *Bayle, Leibniz e la storia* (Naples, 1971).

Costa, Gustavo, 'Bayle, l "anima mundi" e Vico', in Bianchi (ed.), *Pierre Bayle*, 107–22.

—— 'La santa sede di fronte a Locke', *NRL* (2003), 37–122.

Cotoni, M. H., 'L'Exégèse du Nouveau Testament dans la philosophie française du dix-huitième siècle', *SVEC* 220 (Oxford, 1984).

Cottret, M., *Jansénismes et Lumières: pour un autre XVIIIe siècle* (Paris, 1998).

—— 'Jansenism', in Kors (ed.), *Encyclopedia*, iv. 278–84.

Coudert, Allison, *Leibniz and the Kabbalah* (Dordrecht, 1995).

—— Popkin, R. H., and Weiner, G. M. (eds.), *Leibniz, Mysticism and Religion* (Dordrecht, 1998).

Coulet, Henri, 'Présentation' to *Pygmalions des Lumières* (Paris, 1998).

Courtney, C. P., 'Montesquieu and Natural Law', in Carrithers et al. (eds.), *Montesquieu's Science*, 41–67.

—— 'Montesquieu and English Liberty', in Carrithers et al. (eds.), *Montesquieu's Science*, 273–90.

—— '*L'Esprit des lois* dans la perspective de l'histoire du livre (1748–1800)', in Porret and Volpilhac-Auger (eds.), *Temps de Montesquieu*, 65–96.

Courtois, Jean-Patrice, 'Temps, corruption et l'histoire dans *L'Esprit des lois*', in Porret and Volpilhac-Auger (eds.), *Temps de Montesquieu*, 305–17.

Cover, J. A., and Kulstad, M. (eds.), *Central Themes in Early Modern Philosophy* (Indianapolis, 1990).

Cracraft, J., *The Church Reform of Peter the Great* (London, 1971).

—— *The Revolution of Peter the Great* (Cambridge, Mass., 2003).

—— *The Petrine Revolution in Russian Culture* (Cambridge, Mass., 2004).
Cragg, G. R., *The Church and the Age of Reason, 1648–1789* (Harmondsworth, 1960).
Crampe-Crasnabet, M., 'Les Articles ame dans l'*Encyclopédie*', *RDIE* 25 (1998), 91–9.
Cristani, G., 'Tradizione biblica, miti e rivoluzioni geologiche negli *Anecdotes de la nature* di Nicolas-Antoine Boulanger', *GCFI* 14 (1994), 92–123.
Cristofolini, Paolo (ed.), *L'Hérésie Spinoziste* (Amsterdam, 1995).
Croce, Benedetto, *La filosofia di Giambattista Vico* (1911; new edn. Bari, 1965).
Crone, Patricia, *Medieval Islamic Political Thought* (Edinburgh, 2004).
Curd, P., *The Legacy of Parmenides: Eleatic Monism and Later Presocratic Thought* (1997; new edn. 2004).
Curley, Edwin, 'Spinoza as an Expositor of Descartes', in S. Hessing (ed.), *Speculum Spinozanum 1677–1977* (London, 1977), 133–42.
—— *Behind the Geometric Method: A Reading of Spinoza's* Ethics (Princeton, 1988).
—— 'Notes on a Neglected Masterpiece', in Cover and Kulstad (eds.), *Central Themes*, 109–59.
—— 'I durst not write so boldly', in Bostrenghi (ed.), *Hobbes e Spinoza*, 497–593.
—— 'Kissinger, Spinoza and Genghis Khan', in Garrett (ed.), *Cambridge Companion to Spinoza*, 315–42.
Curran, Andrew, 'Diderot's Revisionism: Enlightenment and Blindness in the *Lettre sur les aveugles*', *Diderot Studies*, 28 (2000), 75–94.
Curtis, D. E., 'Pierre Bayle and the Range of Cartesian Reason', *Yale French Studies*, 49 (1973), 71–81.
Dagen, J., *L'Histoire de l'esprit humain dans la pensée française de Fontenelle à Condorcet* (Paris, 1977).
—— (ed.), *Entre Épicure et Vauvenargues* (Paris, 1999).
Dagron, Tristan, 'Toland et l'hétérodoxie', *Historia philosophica*, 2 (2004), 79–96.
—— 'Toland (1670–1722)', introduction to John Toland, *Clidophorus* (Paris, 2002).
—— 'Toland et l'hétérodoxie: de la conformité occasionelle au panthéisme', *Historia philosophica*, 2 (2004), 79–96.
Dahlberg, L., 'The Habermasian Public Sphere: Taking Difference Seriously?', *Theory and Society*, 24 (2005), 111–36.
Daiber, Hans, 'Rebellion gegen Gott: Formen atheistischen Denkens im frühen Islam', in Niewöhner and Pluta (eds.), *Atheismus*, 23–44.
Dakin, D., *Turgot and the* Ancien Regime *in France* (New York, 1980).
Damasio, A. *Looking for Spinoza: Joy, Sorrow and the Feeling Brain* (New York, 2003).
Damiron, Jean-Philibert, *Mémoires sur Diderot* (1852; repr. Geneva, 1968).
—— *Mémoires sur d'Alembert* (1852; Geneva, 1968).
Darnton, Robert, *The Business of Enlightenment* (Cambridge, Mass., 1979).
—— *The Forbidden Best-Sellers of Pre-Revolutionary France* (London, 1996).
—— 'Two Paths through the Social History of Ideas', in Mason (ed.), *Darnton Debate*, 251–94.
Darwall, S., 'Hume and the Invention of Utilitarianism', in Stewart and Wright (eds.), *Hume*, 58–82.
Davidson, N., 'Unbelief and Atheism in Italy, 1500–1700', in Hunter and Wootton (eds.), *Atheism*, 55–85.
Davies, S., 'L'Irlande et les Lumières', *DHS* 30 (1998), 17–35.
Davis, D. B., 'New Sidelights on Early Antislavery Radicalism', *William and Mary Quarterly*, 3rd ser. 28 (1971), 585–94.
—— *The Problem of Slavery in the Age of Revolution, 1770–1823* (New York, 1999).

DAVIS, W. W., 'China, the Confucian Ideal, and the European Enlightenment', *JHI* 44 (1983), 521–48.

DAWSON, V. P., *Nature's Enigma: The Problem of the Polyp in the Letters of Bonnet, Trembley and Réaumur* (Philadelphia, 1987).

DE BOOY, J. TH., *Histoire d'un manuscript de Diderot 'La Promenade du sceptique'* (Frankfurt, 1964).

DEDEYAN, CHARLES, *Diderot et la pensée anglaise* (Florence, 1987).

DE DIJN, H., 'Was van den Enden het meesterbrein achter Spinoza?', *ANTW* 86 (1994), 71–9.

—— *Spinoza: The Way to Wisdom* (West Lafayette, Ind., 1996).

—— 'Spinoza and Revealed Religion', *Studia Spinozana*, 11 (1995), 39–52.

DE GANDT, F., 'Qu'est-ce qu'être newtonien en 1740?', in De Gandt (ed.), *Cirey*, 126–47.

—— (ed.), *Cirey dans la vie intellectuelle: la réception de Newton en France* (Oxford, 2001).

DE JONG, K. H. E., *Spinoza en de Stoa, MVSH* (Leiden, 1939).

DEKKER, RUDOLF, 'Private Vices, Public Virtues Revisited: The Dutch Background of Bernard Mandeville', *History of European Ideas*, 14 (1992), 481–98.

DELEUZE, GILLES, *Spinoza, Practical Philosophy*, trans. R. Hurley (San Francisco, 1988).

—— *Expressionism in Philosophy: Spinoza*, trans. M. Joughin (New York, 1992).

DELOFFRE, F., 'Du vrai sauvage au bon sauvage: La Hontan, Robert Challe et "La Grand Gueule" ', *University of Ottawa Quarterly*, 56 (1986), 67–79.

DELON, M., 'Tyssot de Patot et le recours à la fiction', *Revue d'histoire littéraire de la France*, 80 (1980), 707–19.

DELUMEAU, JEAN, and COTTRET, M., *Le Catholicisme entre Luther et Voltaire* (Paris, 1971).

DEN UYL, D. J., 'Passion, State and Progress: Spinoza and Mandeville on the Nature of Human Association', *JHPh* 25 (1987), 369–95.

—— 'Sociality and Social Contract: A Spinozistic Perspective', *Studia Spinozana*, 1 (1985), 19–51.

—— and Warner, S. D., 'Liberalism, Hobbes and Spinoza', *Studia Spinozana*, 3 (1987), 261–318.

DENEYS-TUNNEY, ANNE, 'Le Roman de la matière dans *Pigmalion ou La Statue animée* (1741) d'A.-F. Boureau-Deslandes', in Fink and Stenger (eds.), *Être matérialiste*, 93–108.

DE PATER, C., 'Inleiding' to Willem Jacob's Gravesande, *Welzijn, wijsbegeerte en wetenschap* (Gouda, 1988), 13–58.

DESGRAVES, LOUIS, 'Montesquieu en 1748', in Larrère and Volpilhac-Auger (eds.), *1748, l'année*, 11–16.

DESNÉ, ROLAND, 'Meslier, lecteur de La Bruyère', in *Études sur le Curé Meslier: actes du colloque international d'Aix-en-Provence* (Paris, 1966), 87–105.

DETHIER, HUBERT, 'Siger van Brabant', in Dethier and Vandenbossche (eds.), *Woordenboek*, i. 199–229.

—— and VANDENBOSSCHE, HUBERT (eds.), *Woordenboek van Belgische en Nederlandse vrijdenkers* (2 vols., Brussels, 1979).

DEUGD, C. de, (ed.), *Spinoza's Political and Theological Thought* (Amsterdam, 1984).

DE VET, J. J. V. M., 'Learned Periodicals from the Dutch Republic and the Early Debate on Spinoza in England', in C. W. Schoneveld (ed.), *Miscellanea Anglo-Belgica* (Leiden, 1987), 27–39.

—— 'La "Bibliothèque universelle et historique": témoignage d'une revue à propos de la lutte autour de Spinoza', *LIAS* 16 (1989), 81–110.

—— 'Spinoza en Spinozisme en enkele "Journaux de Hollande" ', *MvSH* 83 (2002), 3–32.

—— 'Jean Rousset de Missy (1686–1762) against "Le Courier" of Avignon', *LIAS* 26 (1999), 133–41.

—— 'Spinoza's "systema" afgewezen in de *Examinator*', *MSJCW* 26 (2003).

De Voogd, N. J. J., *De Doelistenbeweging te Amsterdam in 1748* (Utrecht, 1914).

De Vries, Jan, and van der Woude, A., *The First Modern Economy* (Cambridge, 1997).

Dibon, P. A. G. (ed.), *Pierre Bayle: Le Philosophe de Rotterdam* (Amsterdam, 1959).

Dickinson, H. T., 'The Politics of Bernard Mandeville' in Primer (ed.), *Mandeville Studies*, 80–97.

Di Luca, G., *La teologia razionale di Spinoza* (L'Aquila, 1993).

Dimaras, C. Th., *La Grèce au temps des Lumières* (Geneva, 1969).

Diop, D., 'L'Anonymat dans les articles politiques de l'*Encyclopédie*', *La Lettre clandestine*, 8 (1999), 102.

Domenech, Jacques, 'L'Egypte dans les *Lettres juives* et les *Lettres cabalistiques*' in Vissière (ed.), *Marquis d'Argens*, 95–110.

—— *L'Éthique des Lumières* (Paris, 1989).

Donini, Pierluigi, 'The History of the Concept of Eclecticism', in J. M. Dillon and A. A. Long (eds.), *The Question of Eclecticism* (Berkeley and Los Angeles, 1988), 15–33.

Donini, Pierluigi, 'Stoic Ethics', in Algra et al. (eds.), *Cambridge History of Hellenistic Philosophy*, 705–38.

Dooren, W. van, 'Ibn Rushd's Attitude towards Authority', in Hasnawi et al. (eds.), *Perspectives*, 623–33.

Drake, H. A., *Constantine and the Bishops: The Politics of Intolerance* (Baltimore, 2000).

Dreitzel, Horst, 'Zur Entwicklung und Eigenart der "Eklektischen Philosophie" ', *Zeitschrift für historische Forschung*, 18 (1991), 281–337.

Driessen, Jozien, *Tsaar Peter de Grote en zijn Amsterdamse vrienden* (Utrecht, 1996).

Duchesnau, F., 'Condillac critique de Locke', *International Studies in Philosophy* (Turin), 6 (1974), 77–98.

Duflo, Colas, *Diderot philosophe* (Paris, 2003).

Dunn, John, *The Political Thought of John Locke* (1969; Cambridge, repr. 1995).

—— *Locke* (Oxford, 1984).

—— 'The Claim to Freedom of Conscience', in O. P. Grell, J. I. Israel, and N. Tyacke (eds.), *From Persecution to Toleration*, (Oxford, 1991) 171–93.

—— 'What History can Show? Jeremy Waldron's Reading of Locke's Christian Politics', *Review of Politics* (Notre Dame, Ind.), 67 (2005), 433–50.

Dupré, Louis, *The Enlightenment and the Intellectual Foundations of Modern Culture* (New Haven, 2004).

Dziembowski, E., 'La Defense du modèle anglais pendant la Guerre de Sept Ans', in Kölving and Mervaud (eds.), *Voltaire et ses combats*, i. 89–97.

Earle, Peter, *The World of Defoe* (Newton Abbot, 1977).

Edwards, Paul (ed.), *The Encyclopedia of Philosophy* (8 vols., New York, 1967).

Eeghen, I. H. van, *De Amsterdamse boekhandel* (5 vols., Amsterdam, 1963–78).

—— 'Bernard Picart en de joodse godsdienstplichten', *Maandblaad Amstelodamum*, 65 (1978).

Ehrard, Jean, *L'Idée de nature en France dans la première moitié du XVIIIe siècle* (Geneva, 1981).

—— 'Voltaire vu par Montesquieu', in Kölving and Mervaud (eds.), *Voltaire et ses combats*, ii. 939–51.

—— *L'Esprit des mots: Montesquieu en lui-même et parmi les siens* (Geneva, 1998).

EIJNATTEN, JORIS VAN, *Mutua Christianorum tolerantia: Irenicism and Toleration in the Netherlands: The Stinstra Affair, 1740–1745* (Florence, 1998).

——'Gerard Noodt's Standing in the Eighteenth-Century Dutch Debates on Religious Freedom', *NAKG* 79 (1999), 74–98.

——'The Huguenot Clerisy in the United Provinces', in Pott et al. (eds.), *The Berlin Refuge*, 207–35.

——*Liberty and Concord in the United Provinces: Religious Toleration and the Public in the Eighteenth-Century Netherlands* (Leiden, 2003).

——'The Church Fathers Assessed: Nature, Bible and Morality in Jean Barbeyrac', *De Achttiende Eeuw*, 35 (2003), 15–25.

ELIAS, WILLEM, 'Het Spinozistisch Eroticisme van Adriaen Beverland', *TvSV* 2 (1974), 283–320.

ELISSEEFF-POISLE, DANIELLE, *Nicolas Fréret (1688–1749): réflexions d'un humaniste du XVIIIe siècle sur la Chine.* memoires de l'Institut des Hautes Études Chinoises (Paris, 1978).

ELLENZWEIG, S., 'The Faith of Unbelief', *Journal of British Studies*, 44 (2005), 27–45.

ELLIOTT, J. H., 'Revolution and Continuity in Early Modern Europe' (1969), in J. H. Elliott, *Spain and its World, 1500–1700* (New Haven, 1989), 92–113.

ELLIS, H. A., *Boulainvilliers and the French Monarchy* (Ithaca, NY, 1988).

ENDRESS, GERHARD, 'Le Projet d'Averroès', in Endress and Aertsen (eds.), *Averroes*, 3–31.

——and Aertsen, J. A. (eds.), *Averroes and the Aristotelian Tradition* (Leiden, 1999).

ENGELS, EVE-MARIE, 'Wissenschaftliche Revolution: Die variantenreiche Geschichte eines Begriffs', *Archiv für Begriffsgeschichte*, 34 (1991), 237–61.

EVERS, MEINDERT, 'Die "Orakel" von Antonius van Dale (1638–1708): Eine Streitschrift', *LIAS* 8 (1981), 225–67.

——'Jean Le Clerc versus G. W. Leibniz', *LIAS* 19 (1992), 93–117.

FAIRCHILDS, C., 'Marketing the Counter-Reformation', in Ch. Adams et al. (eds.), *Visions and Revisions of Eighteenth-Century France* (University Park, Pa., 1997), 31–57.

FAKHRY, MAJID, *Philosophy, Dogma and the Impact of Greek Thought in Islam* (Aldershot, 1994).

FALKENSTEIN, L., 'Condillac's Paradox', *JHPh* 43 (2005), 403–35.

FALVEY, JOHN, 'La Politique textuelle du Discours préliminaire: l'anarchisme de La Mettrie', *Corpus*, 5/6 (1987), 27–61.

FARR, J., ' "So vile and miserable an estate": The Problem of Slavery in Locke's Political Thought', *Political Theory*, 14 (1987), 263–89.

FAULKNER, R. K., 'Political Philosophy', in Kors (ed.), *Encyclopedia*, iii. 314–23.

FAUVERGUE, C., 'Diderot traducteur de Leibniz', *RDIE* 36 (2004), 109–23.

FEDERICI VESCOVINI, G., 'Il problema dell' ateismo di Biagio Pelacani da Parma, Doctor Diabolicus', in Niewöhner and Pluta (eds.), *Atheismus*, 193–214.

FEINER, SHMUEL, *The Jewish Enlightenment* (Philadelphia, 2003).

FEINGOLD, M., 'Huygens and the Royal Society', *De Zeventiende Eeuw*, 12 (1996), 22–36.

FERRONE, VINCENZO, 'Seneca e Cristo: la "Respublica Christiana" di Paolo Mattia Doria', *RSI* 96 (1984), 5–68.

——*The Intellectual Roots of the Italian Enlightenment* (1982; Atlantic Highlands, NJ, 1995).

——*I profeti dell'Illuminismo* (1989; 2nd edn. Bari, 2000).

——and ROCHE, DANIEL (eds.), *Le Monde des Lumières* (1997; French trans. Paris, 1999).

FICHERA, GIUSEPPE, *Il Deismo critico di Voltaire* (Catania, 1993).

FIERRO, M., 'Ibn Hazm et le *Zindiq* juif', *Revue de l'Occident et de la Méditerranée*, 63/4 (1992), 81–9.

FINK, B., and STENGER, G. (eds.), *Être matérialiste à l'âge des Lumières* (Paris, 1999).

FINKELBERG, A., 'Studies in Xenophanes', *Harvard Studies in Classical Philology*, 93 (1990), 103–67.

FINOCCHIARO, M. A., 'Philosophy versus Religion and Science versus Religion: The Trials of Bruno and Galileo', in Gatti (ed.), *Giordano Bruno*, 145–66.

FIRODE, A., 'Locke et les philosophes français', in De Gandt (ed.), *Cirey*, 7–72.

FIRPO, LUIGI, *Il processo di Giordano Bruno* (Rome, 1998).

FISCH, MAX HAROLD, 'Introduction' to Vico, *Autobiography*, 1–107.

FITZPATRICK, M., 'Toleration and the Enlightenment Movement', in Grell and Porter (eds.), *Toleration*, 23–68.

FIX, ANDREW, *Prophecy and Reason: The Dutch Collegiants in the Early Enlightenment* (Princeton, 1991).

—— *Fallen Angels: Balthasar Bekker, Spirit Belief, and Confessionalism in the Seventeenth-Century Dutch Republic* (Dordrecht, 1999).

—— 'Bekker and Bayle on Comets', *GWN* 11 (2000), 81–96.

FOCKEMA ANDREAE, S. J., 'Montesquieu in Nederland', *De Gids*, 12 (Dec. 1949), 176–83.

FOGELIN, R. J., 'Hume's Scepticism', in Norton (ed.), *Cambridge Companion to Hume*, 90–116.

—— *A Defense of Hume on Miracles* (Princeton, 2003).

FONTIUS, M., 'Critique', in R. Reichardt and E. Schmitt (eds.), *HPSGF* v. 7–26.

FORCE, J. E., 'Newton's God of Dominion', in Force and Popkin (eds.), *Essays*, 75–102.

—— 'The Newtonians and Deism', in Force and Popkin (eds.), *Essays*, 43–73.

—— 'The Breakdown of the Newtonian Synthesis of Science and Religion', in Force and Popkin (eds.), *Essays*, 143–63.

—— and KATZ, D. (eds.), *Everything Connects: In Conference with Richard H. Popkin* (Leiden, 1999).

—— and POPKIN, R. H. (eds.), *Essays on the Context, Nature and Influence of Isaac Newton's Theology* (Dordrecht, 1990).

FORD, PHILIP, 'Classical Myth and its Interpretation in Sixteenth-Century France', in G. Sandy (ed.), *The Classical Heritage in France* (Leiden, 2002), 331–49.

FORSCHNER, M., *Die stoische Ethik* (Stuttgart, 1981).

FOSSATI, W. J., 'Maximum Influence from Minimum Abilities: La Mettrie and Radical Materialism', in B. Sweetman (ed.), *The Failure of Modernism* (Mishawaka, Ind. 1999), 45–57.

FOUCAULT, DIDIER, 'Pierre Bayle et Vanini', in Bost and Robert (eds.), *Pierre Bayle*, 227–41.

FOUCAULT, MICHEL, *The Order of Things: An Archaeology of the Human Sciences* (New York, 1994).

FRANK, GUSTAV, 'Die Wertheimer Bibelübersetzung vor dem Reichshofrat in Wien', *Zeitschrift für Kirchegeschichte*, 12 (1891), 279–302.

FREDE, D., 'Stoic Determinism', in Inwood (ed.), *The Cambridge Companion to the Stoics*, 179–205.

FREDE, MICHAEL, 'Monotheism and Pagan Philosophy in Late Antiquity', in Athanassiadi and Frede (eds.), *Pagan Monotheism*, 41–67.

FREDERIKSEN, PAULA, *Jesus of Nazareth, King of the Jews* (London, 2000).

FRIEDEBURG, ROBERT VON, 'Natural Jurisprudence, Argument from History and Constitutional Struggle in the Early Enlightenment', in Hochstrasser and Schröder (eds.), *Early Modern Natural Law Theories*, 141–67.

FRIJHOFF, WILLEM, 'Religious Toleration in the United Provinces: From "Case" to "Model" ', in Hsia and van Nierop (eds.), *Calvinism and Religious Toleration*, 27–52.

—— and SPIES, MARIJKE, *1650: Bevochten eendracht* (The Hague, 1999).

FROESCHLÉ-CHOPARD, MARIE-HÉLÈNE, 'Les *Nouvelles ecclésiastiques* et les Lumières (année 1750)', *DHS* 34 (2002), 77–89.

FUBINI, RICCARDO, *Humanism and Secularization* (Durham, NC, 2003).

FUCHS, J. L., 'Borrowed Criticism and Bayle Criticism', *NRL* (1985), 97–110.

FUNKE, HANS-GÜNTER, *Studien zur Reiseutopie der Frühaufklärung* (2 vols., Heidelberg, 1982).

FUNKENSTEIN, AMOS, *Theology and the Scientific Imagination from the Middle Ages to the Seventeenth Century* (Princeton, 1986).

FURET, F., and OZOUF, M., 'Deux légitimations historiques de la société française au XVIIIe siècle: Mably et Boulainvilliers', in *L'Histoire au dix-huitième siècle* (Aix-en-Provence, 1980), 233–49.

FURLEY, DAVID, 'Cosmology', in Algra et al. (eds.), *Cambridge History of Hellenistic Philosophy*, 412–51.

GABBEY, ALAN, 'Spinoza's Natural Science and Methodology', in Garrett (ed.), *Cambridge Companion to Spinoza*, 142–91.

GAIFFE, FELIX, *L'Envers du Grand Siècle* (Paris, 1924).

GALLIANI, R., 'Mably et Voltaire', *DHS* 3 (1971), 181–94.

GARBER, DAN, *Descartes' Metaphysical Physics* (Chicago, 1992).

—— 'Soul and Mind: Life and Thought in the Seventeenth Century', in Garber and Ayers (eds.), *CHSPh* i. 759–95.

—— 'Leibniz: Physics and Philosophy', in Jolley (ed.), *Cambridge Companion to Leibniz*, 270–352.

—— and AYERS, M. (eds.), *CHSPh* (2 vols., Cambridge, 1998).

GARDAIR, JEAN-MICHEL, *Le 'Giornale de' letterati' de Rome (1668–1681)* (Florence, 1984).

GARRARD, G., *Rousseau's Counter-Enlightenment* (Albany, NY, 2003).

GARRETT, AARON, *Meaning in Spinoza's Method* (Cambridge 2003).

GARRETT, DON, 'Spinoza's Ethical Theory', in D. Garrett (ed.), *Cambridge Companion to Spinoza* (Cambridge, 1995), 267–314.

GASKIN, J. C. A., *Hume's Philosophy of Religion* (1978; Basingstoke, 1988).

—— 'Hume on Religion', in Norton (ed.), *Cambridge Companion to Hume*, 313–44.

GASTER, MOSES, *History of the Ancient Synagogue of the Spanish and Portuguese Jews* (London, 1901).

GATTI, H. (ed.), *Giordano Bruno: Philosopher of the Renaissance* (Aldershot, 2002).

GATZEMEIER, M., *Die Naturphilosophie des Straton von Lampsakos* (Meisenheim, 1970).

GAUCHET, M., *The Disenchantment of the World: A Political History of Religion* (new edn. Princeton, 1999).

GAUKROGER, STEPHEN, *Descartes' System of Natural Philosophy* (Cambridge, 2002).

GAUTHIER, L., *Théorie d'Ibn Rochd (Averroès) sur les rapports de la religion et de la philosophie* (Paris, 1909).

GAVROGLU, KOSTAS, and PATINIOTIS, M., 'Patterns of Appropriation in the Greek Intellectual Life of the 18th Century', in A. Ashtekar et al. (eds.), *Revisiting the Foundations of Relativistic Physics* (Dordrecht, 2003), 569–91.

Gawlick, Günter, 'Thomasius und die Denkfreiheit', in W. Schneider (ed.), *Christian Thomasius, 1655–1728: Interpretationen zu Werk und Wirkung* (Hamburg, 1989), 256–73.

——'Epikur bei den Deisten', in G. Paganini and E. Tortarolo (eds.), *Der Garten und die Moderne* (Stuttgart, 2004), 323–39.

Gay, Peter, *The Enlightenment: An Interpretation*, i: *The Rise of Modern Paganism* (1966; New York, 1977).

——*The Enlightenment: An Interpretation*, ii: *The Science of Freedom* (1969; New York, 1977).

Gayot, G., 'War die französische Freimauererei des 18. Jahrhunderts eine Schule der Gleichheit?', in H. E. Bödecker and E. François (eds.), *Aufklärung und Politik* (Leipzig, 1996), 235–48.

Gebhardt, M., 'Spinoza on Self-Preservation and Self-Destruction', *JHPh* 37 (1999), 613–28.

Geissler, Rolf, *Boureau-Deslandes: Ein Materialist der Frühaufklärung* (Berlin, 1967).

——'Boureau-Deslandes lecteur des manuscripts clandestins', Bloch (ed.), *Matérialisme*, 227–34.

——'*Matérialisme, matérialiste*', in *HPSGF* v. 61–88.

Geissler, Rolf, 'Boureau-Deslandes, historien de la philosophie', in *L'Histoire au dix-huitième siècle: Centre Aixois d'Études et de Recherches sur le XVIIIeme siècle* (Aix-en-Provence, 1980), 135–52.

Gelder, H. A. Enno van, *Getemperde vrijheid* (Groningen, 1972).

Gelderblom, Arie-Jan, 'The Publisher of Hobbes' Dutch Leviathan', in S. Roach (ed.), *Across the Narrow Seas* (London, 1991), 162–6.

Gelderen, Martin van, and Skinner, Quentin (eds.), *Republicanism: A Shared European Heritage* (2 vols., Cambridge, 2002).

Genequand, Charles, *Ibn Rushd's Metaphysics* (Leiden, 1984).

Ghachem, M. W., 'Montesquieu in the Caribbean', *Historical Reflections/Réflexions historiques*, 25 (1999), 183–210.

Giancotti-Boscherini, E., 'Liberté, démocratie et révolution chez Spinoza', *TSV* 6 (1978), 82–95.

Gierl, Martin, *Pietismus und Aufklärung* (Göttingen, 1997).

Gilley, Sheridan, 'Christianity and Enlightenment: An Historical Survey', *History of European Ideas*, 1 (1981), 103–21.

Giuntini, Chiara, 'Toland e Bruno: ermetismo "riviluzionario"?', *RDF* 2 (1975), 199–235.

Glausser, W., 'Three Approaches to Locke and the Slave Trade', *JHI* 51 (1990), 199–216.

Glaziou, Yves, *Hobbes en France au XVIIIe siècle* (Paris, 1993).

Glebe-Møller, Jens, *Vi fornaegter Gud og foragter øverigheden* (Copenhagen, 2004).

Göbel, Helmut, 'Lessing und Cardano: Ein Beitrag zu Lessings Renaissance-Rezeption', in Toellner (ed.), *Aufklärung und Humanizmus*, 167–86.

Godman, Peter, *From Poliziano to Machiavelli* (Princeton, 1998).

——*Die geheime Inquisition: Aus den verbotenen Archiven des Vatikans* (Munich, 2001).

Goetschel, Willi, *Spinoza's Modernity* (Madison, 2004).

Goldenbaum, U., 'Die philosophische Methodendiskussion des 17. Jahrhunderts in ihrer Bedeutung für den Modernisierungsschub in der Historiographie', in W. Küttler et al.

(eds.), *Geschichtsdiskurs*, ii: *Anfänge modernen historischen Denkens* (Frankfurt, 1994), 148–61.

——'Die erste deutsche Übersetzung der Spinozischen "Ethik" ', in H. Delf et al. (eds.), *Spinoza in der europäischen Geistesgeschichte* (Berlin, 1994), 107–25.

——'Leibniz as a Lutheran', in Coudert et al. (eds.), *Leibniz*, 169–92.

——'Der Skandal der Wertheimer Bibel' in U. Goldenbaum et al. (eds.), *Appell an das Publikum. Die öffentliche Debatte in der deutschen Aufklärung, 1687–1796*, vol. 1 (Berlin, 2004), 175–508.

Goldgar, Anne, *Impolite Learning: Conduct and Community in the Republic of Letters, 1680–1750* (New Haven, 1995).

Goldie, Mark, 'The Roots of True Whiggism, 1688–94', *HPTh* 1 (1980), 195–236.

——'The Political Thought of the Anglican Revolution', in R. Beddard (ed.), *The Revolutions of 1688* (Oxford, 1991), 102–136.

——'The Reception of Hobbes', in J. H. Burns (ed.), *The Cambridge History of Political Thought, 1450–1700* (Cambridge, 1991), 589–615.

——'The Revolution of 1689 and the Structure of Political Argument', *Bulletin of Research in the Humanities*, 83 (1980), 473–564.

Goodman, D., *The Republic of Letters* (New York, 1994).

Goodman, L.E., 'Muhammed ibn Zakariyya al-Razi', in Nasr and Leaman (eds.), *History*, 198–215.

Gordon, Daniel, 'The Great Enlightenment Massacre', in Mason (ed.), *Darnton Debate*, 129–56.

——*Postmodernism and the Enlightenment: New Perspectives in Eighteenth-Century French Intellectual History* (New York, 2001).

Gordon, D. H., and Torrey, N. L., *The Censoring of Diderot's* Encyclopédie *and the Re-established Text* (New York, 1947).

Gori, Giambattista, *La fondazione dell'esperienza in 's-Gravesande* (Milan, 1972).

Gottschalk, H., 'Strato of Lampsacus: Some Texts', *Proceedings of the Leeds Philosophical and Literary Society* (1965).

Goulemot, Jean-Marie, 'Le Mot *révolution* et la formation du concept de *révolution politique*', *Annales historiques de la Révolution française*, 39 (1967), 417–44.

——'Démons, merveilles et philosophie à l'âge classique', *Annales*, 25 (1980), 1223–50.

——'1748: année littéraire ou année de l'imprimé?', in Porret and Volpilhac-Auger (eds.), *Temps de Montesquieu*, 17–31.

Goyard-Fabre, Simone, *Montesquieu: la nature, les lois, la liberté* (Paris, 1993).

Graeser, Andreas, *Zenon von Kition: Positionen und Probleme* (Berlin, 1975).

Graesse, J. G. Th., *Trésor des livers rares et précieux ou Nouveau Dictionnaire bibliographique* (8 vols., Dresden, 1858–69).

Grafton, Anthony, 'The Availability of Ancient Works', in Schmitt and Skinner (eds.), *CHRPh*, 767–91.

——*Defenders of the Text* (Cambridge, Mass., 1991).

——*The Footnote: A Curious History* (Cambridge, Mass., 1997).

——*Joseph Scaliger: A Study in the History of Classical Scholarship*, ii (Oxford, 1993).

——*Cardano's Cosmos: The Worlds and Works of a Renaissance Astrologer* (Cambridge, Mass., 1999).

——*Bring out your Dead: The Past as Revelation* (Cambridge, Mass., 2001).

GRAVER, M., *Cicero on the Emotions* (Chicago, 2002).

GRAY, JOHN, *Enlightenment's Wake* (London, 1995).

GREENE, J. P., 'Empire and Identity from the Glorious Revolution to the American Revolution', in. P. J. Marshall (ed.), *The Oxford History of the British Empire* (Oxford, 1998), ii. 208–30.

GREGG, E., 'The Financial Vicissitudes of James III in Rome', in E. Corp (ed.), *The Stuart Court in Rome* (Aldershot, 2003), 65–83.

GREGORY, TULLIO, *Theophrastus redivivus: erudizione e ateismo ne Seicento* (Naples, 1979).

—— 'Pensiero medievale e modernità', *GCFI* 6th ser. 16 (1996), 149–73.

—— ' "Libertinisme érudit" in Seventeenth-Century France and Italy', *BJHP* 6 (1998), 323–49.

—— 'Apologeti e libertini', *GCFI* 6th ser. 20 (2000), 1–35.

GRELL, CHANTAL, 'Nicolas Fréret, la critique et l'histoire ancienne', in Grell and Volpilhac-Auger (eds.), *Nicolas Fréret*, 51–71.

—— and VOLPITHAC-AUGER, C. (eds.), *Nicolas Fréret, légende et vérité* (Oxford, 1994).

GRELL, O. P., and PORTER, ROY, 'Toleration in Enlightenment Europe', in Grell and Porter (eds.), *Toleration*, 1–22.

—— —— (eds.), *Toleration in Enlightenment Europe* (Cambridge, 2000).

GRIMSLEY, R., *Jean d'Alembert (1717–83)* (Oxford, 1963).

GROS, JEAN-MICHEL, 'Sens et limites de la tolérance chez Bayle', in O. Abel and P. F. Moreau (eds.), *Pierre Bayle: la foi dans le doute* (Geneva, 1995).

—— 'Introduction' to Bayle, *Commentaire philosophique* (Paris, 1992), 7–41.

—— 'Pierre Bayle et la République des Lettres', in *Libertinage et philosophie au XVIIe siècle*, 6 (Saint-Étienne, 2002), 131–8.

—— 'Bayle: de la tolérance à la liberté de conscience', in Zarka et al. (eds.), *Fondements philosphiques*, i. 295–311.

—— 'La Tolérance et problème théologico-politique', in McKenna and Paganini (eds.), *Pierre Bayle dans la République des Lettres*, 411–39.

GROSSMAN, M., *The Philosophy of Helvétius* (New York, 1926).

GROSSMANN, W., *Johann Christian Edelmann: From Orthodoxy to Enlightenment* (The Hague, 1976).

GRÜNDER, KARLFRIED, and SCHMIDT-BIGGEMANN, W. (eds.), *Spinoza in der Frühzeit seiner religiösen Wirkung* (Heidelberg, 1984).

GRUNERT, F., 'The Reception of Hugo Grotius' *De jure belli ac pacis* in the Early German Enlightenment', in Hochstrasser and Schröder (eds.), *Early Modern Natural Law Theories*, 89–105.

GUERLAC, H., *Newton on the Continent* (Ithaca, NY, 1981).

—— and JACOB, MARGARET, 'Bentley, Newton, and Providence: The Boyle Lectures Once More', *JHI* 30 (1969), 307–18.

GUÉROULT, MARTIAL, *Histoire de l'histoire de la philosophie* (Paris, 1984).

GUERRERO, RAFAEL RAMÓN, 'Filósofos hispano-musulmanes y Spinoza: Avempace y Abentofail', in A. Domínguez (ed.), *Spinoza y España* (Murcia, 1994), 125–32.

GUMBRECHT, H., and REICHARDT, R., '*Philosophe, philosophie*', in *HPSGF* iii. 7–82.

GUNNY, AHMAD, 'Images of Islam in Some French Writings of the First Half of the Eighteeenth Century', *BJEC* 14 (1991), 191–201.

GURNEY, J. D., 'Pietro della Valle: The Limits of Perception', *Bulletin of the School of Oriental and African Studies*, 49 (1986), 103–16.

Gutas, D., *Greek Thought, Arabic Culture* (London, 1999).

Gutting, Gary, *Pragmatic Liberalism and the Critique of Modernity* (Cambridge, 1999).

Gwynn, R. D., 'Disorder and Innovation: The Reshaping of the French Churches of London after the Glorious Revolution', O. P. Grell, J. I. Israel, and N. Tyacke (eds.), *From Persecution to Toleration* (Oxford, 1991), 251–73.

Haakonssen, Knud, 'The Structure of Hume's Political Theory', in Norton (ed.), *Cambridge Companion to Hume*, 182–221.

—— 'Natural Jurisprudence and the Theory of Justice', in Broadie (ed.), *Scottish Enlightenment*, 205–21.

Haddad-Chamakh, F., 'Foi et philosophie chez Spinoza et les Péripatéticiens Arabes: Spinoza et Averroès', in R. Bouveresse (ed.), *Spinoza: science et religion* (Paris, 1988), 155–70.

Haechler, Jean, *L'Encyclopédie: les combats et les hommes* (Paris, 1998).

Häfner, Ralph, 'Johann Lorenz Mosheim und die Origines-Rezeption in der ersten Hälfte des 18. Jahrhunderts', in Mulsow (ed.), *Johann Lorenz Mosheim*, 230–60.

—— 'Jacob Thomasius und das Problem der Häresien', in F. Vollhardt (ed.), *Christian Thomasius (1655–1728): Neue Forschungen im Kontext der Frühaufklarung* (Tübingen, 1997), 141–64.

—— 'Das Erkenntnisproblem in der Philologie um 1700', in R. Häfner (ed.), *Philologie und Erkenntnis* (Tübingen, 2001), 95–128.

Haitsma Mulier, E. O. G., *The Myth of Venice and Dutch Republican Thought in the Seventeenth Century* (Assen, 1980).

Haleem, Abdel, 'Early *Kalam*', in Nasr and Leaman (eds.), *History*, 71–88.

Halm, Heinz, *Shiism* (Edinburgh, 1991).

Halper, E. C., 'Spinoza on the Political Value of Freedom of Religion', *History of Philosophy Quarterly*, 21 (2004), 167–82.

Hamilton, Alastair, *The Apocryphal Apocalypse: The Reception of the Second Book of Esdras (4 Ezra) from the Renaissance to the Enlightenment* (Oxford, 1999).

—— 'Western Attitudes to Islam in the Enlightenment', *Middle Eastern Lectures*, 3 (1999).

—— and Richard F., *André Du Ryer and Oriental Studies in Seventeenth-Century France* (London, 2004).

Hammacher, Klaus, 'Ambition and Social Engagement in Hobbes' and Spinoza's political thought', in C. de Deugd (ed.), *Spinoza's Political and Theological Thought* (Amsterdam, 1984), 56–62.

Hampshire, Stuart, *Spinoza and Spinozism* (Oxford, 2005).

Hampson, Norman, *The Enlightenment* (Harmondsworth, 1968).

Hampton, John, *Nicolas-Antoine Boulanger et la science de son temps* (Geneva, 1955).

Hankinson, R. J., 'Science', in Jonathan Barnes (ed.), *The Cambridge Companion to Aristotle* (Cambridge, 1995), 140–67.

Haq, S. N., 'The Indian and Persian Background', in Nasr and Leaman (eds.), *History*, 52–70.

Hardt, M., and Negri, A., *Empire* (Cambridge, Mass., 2000).

—— *Multitude* (New York, 2004).

Harris, E. E., *Spinoza's Philosophy: An Outline* (Atlantic Highlands, NJ, 1992).

Harris, J. A., *Of Liberty and Necessity: The Free Will Debate in Eighteenth-Century British Philosophy* (Oxford, 2005).

—— 'Answering Bayle's Question: Religious Belief in the Moral Philosophy of the Scottish Enlightenment', in Daniel Garber and Steven Nadler (eds.), *OSEMPh* i (Oxford, 2003), 229–53.

Harris, I., *The Mind of John Locke* (Cambridge, 1994).
Harrison, Peter, *'Religion' and the Religions in the English Enlightenment* (Cambridge, 1990).
—— *The Bible, Protestantism and the Rise of Natural Science* (Cambridge, 1998).
Häseler, J., *Ein Wanderer zwischen den Welten: Charles Étienne Jordan (1700–1745)* (Sigmaringen, 1993).
—— 'Refugiés français à Berlin lecteurs de manuscrits clandestins', in Canziani (ed.), *Filosofia e religione*, 373–85.
—— ' "Liberté de pensée": éléments d'histoire et rayonnement d'un concept', in McKenna and Mothu (eds.), *La Philosophie clandestine*, 495–507.
—— 'Der Marquis d'Argens und die Berliner Akademie', in Seifert and Seban (eds.), *Marquis d'Argens*, 77–91.
Hasnawi, Ahmad, et al. (eds.), *Perspectives arabes et médiévales sur la tradition scientifique et philosophique grecque* (Leuven, 1997).
Havinga, J. Ch. A., *Les* Nouvelles ecclésiastiques *dans leur lutte contre l'esprit philosophique* (Amersfoort, 1925).
Hayton, D., 'The Williamite Revolution in Ireland, 1688–91', in Israel (ed.), *Anglo-Dutch Moment*, 185–213.
Hazard, Paul, 'Les Rationaux (1670–1700)', *Revue de littérature comparée*, 12 (1932), 677–711.
—— *La Crise de la conscience européenne, 1680–1715* (new edn. Paris, 1961).
—— *The European Mind, 1680–1715* (London, 1964).
Hazewinkel, H. C., 'Pierre Bayle à Rotterdam', in Dibon (ed.), *Pierre Bayle*, 20–47.
Heck, Paul van, 'In het Spoor van Machiavelli: de *Politieke Discoursen*, 1662, van Johan en Pieter de La Court', *LIAS*, 27 (2000), 277–318.
Hellinga, Lotte, et al. (eds.), *The Bookshop of the World: The Role of the Low Countries in the Book Trade, 1473–1941* ('t Goy-Houten, 2001).
Henderson, G. P., *The Revival of Greek Thought, 1620–1830* (Albany, NY, 1970).
Henry, John, 'The Scientific Revolution in England', in Roy Porter and M.Teich (eds.), *The Scientific Revolution in National Context* (Cambridge, 1993), 178–209.
Hershbell, J. P., 'The Oral-Poetic Religion of Xenophanes', in Kevin Robb (ed.), *Language and Thought in Early Greek Philosophy* (La Salle, Ill., 1983), 125–33.
Hertzberg, Arthur, *The French Enlightenment and the Jews* (New York, 1968).
Heyd, M., 'A Distinguished Atheist or a Sincere Christian? The Enigma of Pierre Bayle', *BHR* 39 (1977), 157–65.
—— *'Be Sober and Reasonable': The Critique of Enthusiasm in the Seventeenth and Early Eighteenth Centuries* (Leiden, 1995).
Hill, Christopher, *Some Intellectual Consequences of the English Revolution* (1980; new edn. London, 1997).
Himmelfarb, G., 'Two Enlightenments: A Contrast in Social Ethics', *Proceedings of the British Academy*, 117 (2001), 297–324.
—— *Roads to Modernity* (New York, 2004).
Hirschmann, Albert, *The Passions and the Interests* (1977; Princeton, 1996).
Hobohm, Hans-Christoph, 'Le Progrès de l'*Encyclopédie*: la censure face au discours encyclopédique', in Mass and Knabe (eds.), *L'Encyclopédie*, 69–96.
Hochstrasser, T. J., 'The Claims of Conscience: Natural Law Theory, Obligation, and Resistance in the Huguenot Diaspora', in Laursen (ed.), *New Essays*, 15–51.
—— *Natural Law Theories in the Early Enlightenment* (Cambridge, 2000).
—— and Schröder, P. (eds.), *Early Modern Natural Law Theories* (Dordrecht, 2003).

Hodgson, M. G. S., *The Venture of Islam* (1974–5; new edn., 3 vols., Chicago, 1977).
Hoekstra, Kinch, 'Hobbes on Law, Nature and Reason', *JHPh* 41 (2003), 111–20.
—— 'Tyrannus rex vs. Leviathan', *Pacific Philosophical Quarterly*, 82 (2001), 420–46.
—— 'Disarming the Prophets: Thomas Hobbes and Predictive Power', *RSF* 1 (2004), 97–153.
Hofmeier, Thomas, 'Cudworth versus Casaubon', in Carlos Gilly and C. van Heertum (eds.), *Magic, Alchemy and Science 15th to 18th Centuries: The Influence of Hermes Trismegistus*, vol. i (Florence, 2002), 569–72, 579–86.
Holmes, George, *The Florentine Enlightenment, 1400–1450* (Oxford, 1969).
Holt, P. M., Lambton. A. K. S., and Lewis, Bernard (eds.), *The Cambridge History of Islam* (2 vols., Cambridge, 1970).
Hope, Nicholas, *German and Scandinavian Protestantism 1700 to 1918* (Oxford, 1995).
Hope Mason, John, 'Materialism and History: Diderot and the *Histoire des deux Indes*', *European Review of History*, 3 (1996), 151–60.
—— and Wokler, Robert, 'Introduction' to Diderot, *Political Writings*, pp. ix–xxxv.
Hoppit, Julian, *A Land of Liberty? England, 1689–1727* (Oxford, 2000).
Horkheimer, Max, and Adorno, Theodor W., *Dialectic of Enlightenment* (New York, 2000).
Horowitz, I. L., *Claude Helvétius: Philosopher of Democracy and Enlightenment* (New York, 1954).
Hosking, G., *Russia and the Russians* (London, 2001).
Hösle, Vittorio, 'Philosophy and the Interpretation of the Bible', *Internationale Zertschrift Für Philosophie* (1999), 181–210.
—— *Philosophiegeschichte und objektiver Idealismus* (Munich, 1996).
—— *Objective Idealism, Ethics and Politics* (Notre Dame, Ind., 1998).
—— *Morals and Politics* (Notre Dame, Ind., 2004).
Hourcade, Ph., 'Jet de plume ou projet: *sur l'histoire*, de Fontenelle', *Corpus*, 44 (2003), 17–33.
Hsia, Adrian, 'Euro-Sinica: The Past and Future', *TJEAS* 1 (2004), 17–58.
Hsia, R. Po-Chia, and Nierop, H. F. K. van (eds.), *Calvinism and Religious Toleration in the Dutch Golden Age* (Cambridge, 2002).
Hubbeling, H. G., *Spinoza* (Baarn, 1966).
—— 'Inleiding' to Spinoza, *Briefwisseling*, 29–48.
—— 'Zur frühen Spinozarezeption in den Niederlanden', in Gründer and Schmidt-Biggemann (eds.), *Spinoza in der Frühzeit*, 149–200.
Huenemann, Charles, 'The Middle Spinoza', in O. Koistinen and J. Biro (eds.), *Spinoza: Metaphysical Themes* (Oxford, 2002), 210–20.
Hufton, O., *Europe: Privilege and Protest, 1730–1789* (1980; 2nd edn. Oxford, 2000).
Hughes, Lindsey, *Peter the Great: A Biography* (New Haven 2002).
—— *Russia in the Age of Peter the Great* (1998; New Haven, new edn. 2000).
—— *Sophia, Regent of Russia 1657–1704* (New Haven, 1990).
Hüning, Dieter, 'Die Grenzen der Toleranz und die Rechtsstellung der Atheisten', in L. Danneberg et al. (eds.), *Säkularisierung in den Wissenschaften seit der Frühen Neuzeit*, ii (Berlin, 2002), 219–73.
Hundert, E. J., *The Enlightenment's Fable* (Cambridge, 1994).
—— 'Bernard Mandeville and the Enlightenment's Maxims of Modernity', *JHI* 56 (1995), 577–93.
Hunter, Ian, *Rival Enlightenments* (Cambridge, 2001).

—— 'The Passions of the Prince: Moral Philosophy and *Staatskirchenrecht* in Thomasius' Conception of Sovereignty', *Cultural and Social History*, 2 (2005), 113–29.

Hunter, M., and Wootton, D. (eds.), *Atheism from the Reformation to the Enlightenment* (Oxford, 1992).

Hussey, Edward, *The Presocratics* (1972; new edn. London, 1995).

Hutchison, R., *Locke in France 1688–1734* (Oxford, 1991).

Hutton, Sarah, 'Reason and Revelation in the Cambridge Platonists, and their Reception of Spinoza', in Gründer and Schmidt-Biggemann (eds.), *Spinoza in der Frühzeit*, 181–200.

—— 'Introduction' to Cudworth, *A Treatise*, pp. ix–xxxiv.

—— 'Classicism and Baroque: A Note on Mosheim's Footnotes to Cudworth's *The True Intellectual System of the Universe*', in Mulsow et al. (eds.), *Johann Lorenz Mosheim*, 211–27.

Huussen, A. H., 'Onderwijs in de Groningse rechtenfaculteit gedurende de eerste helft van de 18e eeuw', in A. H. Huussen (ed.), *Onderwijs en onderzoek* (Hilversum, 2003), 161–84.

Hyman, A., 'Maimonides on Creation and Emanation', in J. Wippel (ed.), *Studies in Philosophy and the History of Philosophy* (Washington, 1987), 45–61.

Ildefonse, F., 'Du Marsais, le grammairien philosophe', *Corpus*, 14/15 (1990), 35–60.

Ingegno, A., 'The New Philosophy of Nature', in Schmitt and Skinner (eds.), *CHRPh* 236–63.

Inguenaud, Marie-Thérèse, 'La Famille de Nicolas-Antoine Boulanger et les milieux Jansénistes', *DHS* 30 (1998), 361–72.

Inwood, B., *Ethics and Human Action in Early Stoicism* (Oxford, 1985).

—— 'Stoic Ethics', in Algra et al. (eds.), *Cambridge History of Hellenistic Philosophy*, 675–705.

—— *The Cambridge Companion to the Stoics* (Cambridge, 2003).

Iofrida, M., 'Linguaggio e verità in Lodewijk Meyer (1629–1681)', in Cristofolini (ed.), *L'Hérésie Spinoziste*, 25–35.

Irwin, T. H., 'Stoic Naturalism and its Critics', in Inwood (ed.), *The Cambridge Companion to the Stoics*, 345–64.

Israel, Jonathan I., *Dutch Primacy in World Trade, 1585–1740* (Oxford, 1989).

—— *Empires and Entrepots: The Dutch, the Spanish Monarchy and the Jews, 1585–1713* (London, 1990).

—— 'Meyer, Koerbagh and the Radical Enlightenment Critique of Socinianism', *GWN* 14 (2003), 197–208.

—— 'William III and Toleration', in Ole Grell, J. I. Israel, and Nicholas Tyacke (eds.), *From Persecution to Toleration* (Oxford, 1991), 129–70.

—— 'Propaganda in the Making of the Glorious Revolution', in S. Roach (ed.), *Across the Narrow Seas* (London, 1991), 167–77.

—— 'Toleration in Seventeenth-Century Dutch and English Thought', in S. Groenveld and M. Wintle (eds.), *Britain and the Netherlands*, xi (Zutphen, 1994).

—— *The Dutch Republic: Its Rise, Greatness and Fall, 1477–1806* (Oxford, 1995).

—— 'Locke, Spinoza, and the Philosophical Debate Concerning Toleration in the Early Enlightenment (*c.*1670–*c.*1750)', Koninklijke Nederlandse Akademie van Wetenschappen. *Mededelingen van de Afdeling Letterkunde*, NS 62/6 (1999), 5–19.

—— 'Spinoza, Locke and the Enlightenment Battle for Toleration', in Grell and Porter (eds.), *Toleration*, 102–13.

—— *Radical Enlightenment: Philosophy and the Making of Modernity* (Oxford, 2001).

—— 'The Publishing of Forbidden Philosophical Works in the Dutch Republic (1666–1710) and their European Distribution', in Hellinga et al. (eds.), *Bookshop*, 233–43.

Israel, Jonathan I., *Diasporas within a Diaspora: Jews, Crypto-Jews and the World Maritime Empires (1540–1740)* (Leiden, 2002).

—— 'Religious Toleration and Radical Philosophy in the Later Dutch Golden Age (1668–1710)', in Hsia and van Nierop (eds.), *Calvinism and Religious Toleration*, 148–58.

—— 'The Early Dutch Enlightenment as a Factor in the Wider European Enlightenment', in van Bunge (ed.), *Early Enlightenment*, 215–30.

—— 'The Intellectual Origins of Modern Democratic Republicanism (1660–1720)', *European Journal of Political Theory*, 3 (2004), 7–36.

—— 'Pierre Bayle's Political Thought', in A. McKenna and G. Paganini (eds.), *Pierre Bayle dans la République des Lettres: philosophie, religion, critique* (Paris, 2004), 349–79.

—— 'The Banning of Spinoza's Works in the Dutch Republic', in van Bunge and Klever (eds.), *Disguised and Overt Spinozism*, 3–14.

—— 'The Intellectual Debate about Toleration in the Dutch Republic', in Berkvens-Stevelinck et al. (eds.), *The Emergence of Tolerance*, 3–36.

—— 'John Locke and the Intellectual Legacy of the Early Enlightenment', *Eighteenth-Century Thought*, 3 (2005), (forthcoming).

—— 'Monarchy, Orangism and Republicanism in the Later Dutch Golden Age', Second Golden Age Lecture of the Amsterdams Centrum voor de Studie van de Gouden Eeuw (Amsterdam, 2004).

—— 'Spinoza, King Solomon, and Frederik van Leenhof's Spinozistic Republicanism', *Studia Spinozana*, 11 (1995), 303–17.

—— *European Jewry in the Age of Mercantilism 1550–1750* (1985; new edn. Oxford, 1998).

—— (ed.), *The Anglo-Dutch Moment: Essays on the Glorious Revolution and its World Impact* (Cambridge, 1991).

Israël, Nicolas, *Spinoza: le temps de la vigilance* (Paris, 2001).

Jack, M. R., 'Religion and Ethics in Mandeville', in Primer (ed.), *Mandeville Studies*, 34–42.

Jackson, C., 'Revolution Principles, *Ius naturae* and *Ius gentium* in Early-Enlightenment Scotland', in Hochstrasser and Schröder (eds.), *Early Modern Natural Law Theories*, 107–40.

Jacob, Margaret C., 'John Toland and the Newtonian Ideology', *Journal of the Warburg and Courtauld Institutes*, 32 (1969), 307–31.

—— *The Radical Enlightenment* (London, 1981).

—— *Living the Enlightenment* (New York, 1991).

—— 'Radicalism in the Dutch Enlightenment', in Jacob and Mijnhardt (eds.), *Dutch Republic*, 224–40.

—— 'Bernard Picart and the Turn towards Modernity', *De Achttiende Eeuw*, 37 (2005), 3–16.

—— and Mijnhardt, Wijnand (eds.), *The Dutch Republic in the Eighteenth Century* (Ithaca, NY, 1992).

Jacobitti, E. E., *Revolutionary Humanism and Historicism in Modern Italy* (New Haven, 1981).

Jaffro, Laurent, 'Les *Exercices* de Shaftesbury: un stoïcisme crépusculaire', in Lagrée (ed.), *Le Stoïcisme*, 204–17.

James, E. D., 'Faith, Sincerity and Morality: Mandeville and Bayle', in Primer (ed.), *Mandeville Studies*, 43–65.

—— 'Schism and the Spirit of Toleration in Bernard Mandeville's *Free Thoughts on Religion*', in Magdalaine et al. (eds.), *De L'humanisme aux Lumières*, 693–700.

James, Susan, 'Spinoza the Stoic', in Sorell (ed.), *Rise of Modern Philosophy*, 289–316.

—— 'Reason, the Passions, and the Good Life', in Garber and Ayers (eds.), *CHSP* ii. 1358–96.

—— *Passion and Action: The Emotions in Seventeenth-Century Philosophy* (new edn. Oxford, 1999).

JAMMER, MAX, *Einstein and Religion* (Princeton, 1999).

JARRETT, CH., 'Spinoza on the Relativity of Good and Evil', in Koistinen and Biro (eds.), *Spinoza*, 159–81.

JAUMANN, HERBERT, *Critica: Untersuchungen zur Geschichte der Literaturkritik zwischen Quintilian und Thomasius* (Leiden, 1995).

—— 'Frühe Aufklärung als historische Kritik: Pierre Bayle und Christian Thomasius', in S. Neumeister (ed.), *Frühaufklärung* (Munich, 1994), 149–70.

JAUMANN, HERBERT, 'Jakob Friedrich Zimmermanns Bayle-Kritik und das Konzept der "Historia literaria" ', in Mulsow and Zedelmeier (eds.), *Skepsis, Providenz, Polyhistorie*, 200–13.

—— 'Der *Refuge* und der Journalismus um 1700: Gabriel d'Artis (*c.*1650–*c.*1730)', in Pott et al. (eds.), *The Berlin Refuge*, 155–82.

JEHASSE, JEAN, *La Renaissance de la critique* (Paris, 2002).

JEHL, RAINER, 'Jacob Brucker und die *Encyclopédie*', in Schmidt-Biggemann and Stammen (eds.), *Jacob Brucker*, 238–56.

JENKINSON, S., 'Two Concepts of Tolerance: Or Why Bayle is not Locke', *Journal of Political Philosophy*, 4 (1996), 302–21.

—— 'Nourishing Men's Anger and Inflaming the Fires of Hatred: Bayle on Religious Violence and the "Novus Ordo Saeclorum" ', *Terrorism and Political Violence*, 10 (1998), 64–79.

—— 'Introduction' to Bayle, *Political Writings*, pp. xviii–xli.

JIMACK, P., 'The French Enlightenment 1: Science, Materialism and Determinism', in S. Brown (ed.), *British Philosophy and the Age of Enlightenment* (London, 1996), 228–50.

JOARY, JEAN-PAUL, *Diderot et la matière vivante* (Paris, 1992).

JOHNSON, R. R., 'The Revolution of 1688–9 in the American Colonies', in Israel (ed.), *Anglo-Dutch Moment*, 215–40.

JOLLEY, NICHOLAS, *Locke: His Philosophical Thought* (Oxford, 1999).

JONGENELEN, G., 'La Philosophie politique d'Adrien Koerbagh', *Cahiers Spinoza*, 6 (1991), 247–67.

—— 'Disguised Spinozism in Adriaen Verwer's *Momaensicht*', in van Bunge and Klever (eds.), *Disguised and Overt Spinozism*, 15–21.

—— 'Adriaan Koerbagh: een voorlooper van de Verlichting?', *GWN* 5 (1994), 27–34.

—— *Van smaad tot erger, Amsterdamse boekverboden 1747–1794* (Amsterdam, 1998).

JONGSTE, J. A. F. DE, *Onrust aan het Spaarne: Haarlem in de jaren 1747–51* (The Hague, 1984).

—— 'The Restoration of the Orangist Regime in 1747', in Jacob and Mijnhardt (eds.), *Dutch Republic*, 32–59.

JUFFERMANS, PAUL, *Drie perspectieven op religie in het denken van Spinoza* (n.p., 2003).

JÜRGENS, HANCO, 'Welke Verlichting? Tijdaanduidingen en plaatsbepalingen van een begrip', *De Achttiende Eeuw*, 35 (2003), 28–53.

KAPLAN, YOSEF, ' "Karaites" in Early Eighteenth-Century Amsterdam', in D. S. Katz and J. I. Israel (eds.), *Sceptics, Millenarians and Jews* (Leiden, 1990).

—— 'The Intellectual Ferment in the Spanish-Portuguese Community of Seventeenth-Century Amsterdam', in Haim Beinart (ed.), *The Sephardic Legacy*, vol. ii (Jerusalem, 1992), 288–314.

—— *From Christianity to Judaism: The Story of Isaac Orobio de Castro* (Oxford, 1989).

KELLEY, DONALD, *Fortunes of History: Historical Inquiry from Herder to Huizinga* (New Haven, 2003).
—— *The Descent of Ideas* (Aldershot, 2002).
—— (ed.), *History and the Disciplines* (Rochester, NY, 1997).
KENNEDY, E., *A Cultural History of the French Revolution* (New Haven, 1989).
KENYON, JOHN, *Revolution Principles: The Politics of Party, 1689–1720* (Cambridge, 1977).
KERKHOVEN, J. M., and BLOM, H. W., 'De La Court en Spinoza: van correspondenties en correspondenten', in H. W. Blom and I. W. Wildenberg (eds.), *Pieter de La Court in zijn tijd* (Maarssen, 1986), 137–60.
KERVÉGAN, JEAN-FRANÇOIS, 'Société civile et droit privé: entre Hobbes et Hegel', in Moreau (ed.), *Architectures*, 145–64.
KESSLER, E., 'The Intellective Soul', in Schmitt and Skinner (eds.), *CHRPh* 485–34.
KIDD, COLIN, 'Constitutions and Character in the Eighteenth-Century British World', in P. M. Kitromilides (ed.), *From Republican Polity to National Community* (Oxford, 2003), 40–61.
—— *Subverting Scotland's Past: Scottish Whig Historians and the Creation of an Anglo-British Identity 1689–1830* (Cambridge, 1993).
KILCULLEN, JOHN, *Sincerity and Truth: Essays on Arnauld, Bayle and Toleration* (Oxford, 1988).
KINGSTON, R. E., 'Montesquieu on Religion and on the Question of Toleration', in Carrithers et al. (eds.), *Montesquieu's Science*, 375–408.
KIRK, G. S., RAVEN, J. E., and SCHOFIELD, M. (eds.), *The Presocratic Philosophers* (1957; 2nd edn. Cambridge, 1983).
KITROMILIDES, PASCHALIS M., 'Tradition, Enlightenment, and Revolution: Ideological Change in Eighteenth and Nineteenth Century Greece' (unpublished Harvard Ph.D. thesis, Sept. 1978).
—— *The Enlightenment as Social Criticism: Iosipos Moisiodax and Greek Culture in the Eighteenth Century* (Princeton, 1992).
—— 'John Locke and the Greek Intellectual Tradition: An Episode in Locke's Reception in South-East Europe', in G. A. J. Rogers (ed.), *Locke's Philosophy: Content and Context* (Oxford, 1994), 217–35.
—— 'Athos and the Enlightenment', in A. Bryer and M. Cunningham (eds.), *Mount Athos and Byzantine Monasticism* (Aldershot, 1996), 257–72.
KLEIN, L. E., *Shaftesbury and the Culture of Politeness* (Cambridge, 1994).
KLEVER, WIM, 'De Spinozistische prediking van Pieter Balling', *Doopsgezinde Bijdragen*, NS 14 (1988), 55–65.
—— 'Proto-Spinoza: Franciscus van den Enden', *Studia Spinozana*, 6 (1990), 281–301.
—— 'A New Source of Spinozism: Franciscus van den Enden', *JHPh* 29 (1991), 613–31.
—— 'Spinoza's Vindication of Meyer's Hermeneutics', *Studia Spinozana*, 7 (1991), 215–19.
—— 'Een zwarte bladzijde? Spinoza over de vrouw', *ANTW* 84 (1992), 38–51.
—— 'Inleiding' to van den Enden, *Vrye Politieke Stellingen*, 13–119.
—— *Ethicom: Spinoza's Ethica vertolkt in tekst en commentaar* (Delft, 1996).
—— *Mannen rond Spinoza (1650–1700)* (Hilversum, 1997).
—— *Definitie van het Christendom: Spinoza* Tractatus theologico-politicus *opnieuw vertaald en toegelicht* (Delft, 1999).

—— *The Sphinx: Spinoza Reconsidered in Three Essays* ('Vrijstad', 2000).
—— *Democratische vernieuwing in Nederland en de Europese Unie op historische en filosofische grondslag* ('Vrijstad', 2003).
—— 'Bernard Mandeville and his Spinozistic Appraisal of Vices', E-publication: *Foglio spinoziano*, 20.
—— 'Burchardus de Volder (1643–1709): A Crypto-Spinozist on a Leiden Cathedra', *LIAS* 15 (1988), 191–241.
—— 'Krijgsmacht en defensie in Spinoza's politieke theorie', *Transaktie*, 19 (1990), 150–66.
—— *Spinoza classicus: antieke bronnen van en moderne denker* (Budel, 2005).
—— ' "Conflicting" Considerations of State', *Foglio Spinoziano*, 17 (2001), 1–14.
—— *Een nieuwe Spinoza in veertig facetten* (Amsterdam, 1995).
—— 'Power: Conditional and Unconditional', in C. De Deugd (ed.), *Spinoza's Political and Theological Thought* (Amsterdam, 1984), 95–106.
Kloeck, Joost and Mijnhardt, Wijnand, *1800: Blueprints for a National Community* (Assen, 2004).
Knetsch, F. R. J., *Pierre Jurieu, Theoloog en politicus der Refuge* (Kampen, 1967).
Knuttel, W. P. C., 'Ericus Walten', *Bijdragen voor Vaderlandsche Geschiedenis en Oudheidkunde*, 4th ser. 1 (1900), 345–455.
—— *Balthasar Bekker de bestrijder van het bijgeloof* (1906; repr. Groningen, 1979).
—— *Verboden boeken in de Republiek der Verenigde Nederlanden* (The Hague, 1914).
Kobuch, A., *Zensur und Aufklärung in Kursachsen* (Weimar, 1988).
Koerner, L., *Linnaeus: Nature and Nation* (Cambridge, Mass., 1999).
Koistinen, O., and Biro, J. (eds.), *Spinoza: Metaphysical Themes* (Oxford, 2002).
Kolakowski, Leszek, *Chrétiens sans église* (Paris, 1969).
—— 'Pierre Bayle, critique de la métaphysique Spinoziste de la substance', in P. A. G. Dibon (ed.), *Pierre Bayle: Le Philosophe de Rotterdam* (Amsterdam, 1959), 66–80.
Kölving, U., and Mervaud, Ch., (eds.), *Voltaire et ses combats* (2 vols., Oxford,1997).
Kopanev, N. A., 'Le Libraire-éditeur parisien Antoine Claude Briasson et la culture russe au milieu du XVIIIe siècle', in J. P. Poussou et al. (eds.), *L'Influence française en Russie au XVIIIe siècle* (Paris, 2005), 185–200.
Kopitzsch, F., 'Altona-ein Zentrum der Aufklärung am Rande des dänischen Gesamtstaats', in K. Bohnen and S. A. Jorgensen (eds.), *Der dänische Gesamtstaat* (Tübingen, 1992), 91–118.
Korkman, P., 'Voluntarism and Moral Obligation: Barbeyrac's Defence of Pufendorf Revisited', in Hochstrasser and Schröder (eds.), *Early Modern Natural Law Theories*, 195–225.
Kors, Alan, *Atheism in France, 1650–1729*, vol. i (no more so far; Princeton, 1990).
—— 'Skepticism and the Problem of Atheism in Early-Modern France', in G. Paganini et al. (eds.), *Scepticisme, clandestinité et libre pensée* (Paris, 2002), 47–65.
—— (ed.), *Encyclopedia of the Enlightenment* (4 vols., Oxford, 2003).
Koseki, T., 'Diderot et le Confucianisme', *RDl'E* 16 (1994), 125–31.
Koselleck, Reinhart, 'Hinweise auf die temporalen Strukturen begriffsgeschichtlichen Wandels', in Bödeker (ed.), *Begriffsgeschichte*, 29–47.
—— 'Revolution, Rebellion, Aufruhr: Bürgerkrieg von der Frühen Neuzeit bis zur französischen Revolution', in *Geschichtliche Grundbegriffe*, 5 (1984), 689–788.

Kossmann, Ernst, *Politieke theorie in het zeventiende-eeuwse Nederland* (Amsterdam, 1960).
—— *Politieke theorie en geschiedenis* (Amsterdam, 1987).
—— 'Freedom in Seventeenth-Century Dutch Thought and Practice', in Israel (ed.), *Anglo-Dutch Moment*, 281–98.
—— *Political Thought in the Republic: Three Studies* (Amsterdam, 2000).
Kra, P., *Religion in Montesquieu's* Lettres persanes (Geneva, 1970).
Kraemer, J. L., 'Heresy versus the State in Medieval Islam', in *Studies in Judaica, Karaitica and Islamica Presented to Leon Nemoy on his Eightieth Birthday* (Bar-Ilan, 1982), 167–80.
Krakauer, Moses, *Zur Geschichte des Spinozismus in Deutschland während der ersten Hälfte des achtzehnte Jahrhunderts* (Breslau, 1881).
Kraus, P., 'Zu Ibn al-Muqaffa', *Rivista degli studi orientali*, 14 (Rome, 1934), 1–20.
Krause, Sharon, 'History and the Human Soul in Montesquieu', *HPTh* 24 (2033), 235–61.
Kraye, J., 'Ficino in the Firing Line', in M. J. B. Allen and V. Rees (eds.), *Marsilio Ficino* (Leiden, 2002), 377–97.
Kreiser, B. R., *Miracles, Convulsions, and Ecclesiastical Politics in Early Eighteenth-Century Paris* (Princeton, 1978).
Kristeller, Paul Oskar, *Eight Philosophers of the Italian Renaissance* (Stanford, Calif., 1964).
—— *Greek Philosophers of the Hellenistic Age* (New York, 1993).
—— 'The Myth of Renaissance Atheism', *JHPh* 6 (1968), 233–43.
Krop, H. A., 'Northern Humanism and Philosophy', in F. Akkerman, A. J. Vanderjagt, and A. H. van der Laan (eds.), *Northern Humanism in European Context, 1469–1625* (Leiden, 1999), 149–66.
—— 'Inleiding and Notes to Spinoza', *Ethica*, ed. H. Krop (Amsterdam, 2002).
Krüger, Reinhard, '*Geroglifici* und *scrittura*—Priesterbetrug und Freiheit', in H. C. Jacobs and G. Schlüter (eds.), *Beiträge zur Begriffsgeschichte der italienischen Aufklärung im europäischen Kontext* (Frankfurt, 2000), 351–71.
Kucklick, Bruce, *A History of Philosophy in America, 1720–2000* (Oxford, 2001).
Kuehn, Manfred, *Kant: A Biography* (Cambridge, 2001).
Kühler, W. J., *Het Socinianisme in Nederland* (1912; repr. Leeuwarden, 1980).
Kuhn, Thomas S., *The Structure of Scientific Revolutions* (1962; 3rd edn. Chicago, 1996).
Labrousse, Elisabeth, *Pierre Bayle* (1964; 2 vols., Paris, 1996).
—— 'Introduction' to Basnage de Beauval, *Tolérance*, i–cliii.
—— 'Le Refuge hollandais: Bayle et Jurieu', *XVIIe siècle*, 77 (1967), 75–93.
—— 'The Political Ideas of the Huguenot Diaspora (Bayle and Jurieu)', in R. M. Golden (ed.), *Church and Society under the Bourbon Kings of France* (Lawrence, Kan. 1982).
LaCapra, D., *Rethinking Intellectual History* (Ithaca, NY, 1983).
Lach, D. F., 'Leibniz and China', in Ching and Oxtoby (eds.), *Discovering China*, 97–116.
—— 'The Sinophilism of Christian Wolff (1679–1754)', in Ching and Oxtoby (eds.), *Discovering China*, 117–30.
Lacouture, Jean, *Montesquieu: les vendanges de la liberté* (Paris, 2003).
Laeven, A. H., *De 'Acta eruditorum' onder redactie van Otto Mencke* (Amsterdam, 1986).
Lagrée, Jacqueline, 'Le Thème des deux livres de la mature et de l'écriture', in *Travaux et documents du Groupe de Recherches Spinozistes*, iv (Paris, 1992), 11–40.
—— (ed.), *Le Stoicisme aux XVIe et XVIIe siècles* (Caen, 1994).
—— 'Y a-t-il une théodicée chez Spinoza?', in Z. van Martels et al. (eds.), *Limae labor et mora: Opstellen voor Fokke Akkerman* (Leende, 2000), 195–205.

——'Du magistère spirituel à la *medicina mentis*', in Bostrenghi (ed.), *Hobbes e Spinoza*, 595–621.
——*Spinoza et le débat Religieux* (Rennes, 2004).
LAMBERTON, R., *Homer the Theologian: Neoplatonist Allegorical Reading and the Growth of the Epic Tradition* (1986; Berkeley and Los Angeles, 1989).
LANDUCCI, SERGIO, 'Introduction' to [Jean Lévesque de Burigny], *De l'examen de la religion* (Oxford, 1996).
——'Mente e corpo nel dibattito fra Collins e Clarke', in Santucci (ed.), *L'età dei Lumi*, 125–42.
LANG, B., 'The Politics of Interpetation: Spinoza's Modernist Turn', *Review of Metaphysics*, 43 (1989), 327–56.
LAQUEUR, THOMAS, *Solitary Sex: A Cultural History of Masturbation* (New York, 2004).
LARRÈRE, C., 'Fréret et la Chine', in Grell and Volpilhac-Auger (eds.), *Nicolas Fréret*, 109–29.
——'*L'Esprit des lois*, tradition et modernité', in Larrère and Volpilhac-Auger (eds.), *1748, l'année*, 141–60.
——'Diderot et l'atomisme', in J. Salem (ed.), *L'Atomisme aux XVIIe et XVIIIe siècles* (Paris, 1999), 151–65.
——'D'Alembert and Diderot: les mathématiques contre la nature?', *Corpus*, 38 (2001), 75–94.
——and VOLPILHAC-AUGER, C. (eds.), *1748, l'année de L'Esprit des lois* (Paris, 1999).
LASLETT, PETER, 'Introduction' to John Locke, *Two Treatises of Government* (1960; new edn. Cambridge, 1988), 3–126.
LAURIOL, CLAUDE, *La Beaumelle: un Protestant cévenol entre Montesquieu et Voltaire* (Geneva, 1978).
LAURSEN, J. CH., *The Politics of Skepticism in the Ancients, Montaigne, Hume and Kant* (Leiden, 1992).
——'The Politics of a Publishing Event', in Berti et al. (eds.), *Heterodoxy*, 273–96.
——'Impostors and Liars: Clandestine Manuscripts and the Limits of Freedom of the Press in the Huguenot Netherlands', in Laursen (ed.), *New Essays*, 73–100.
——'Baylean Liberalism: Tolerance requires Nontolerance', in J. Ch. Laursen and C. J. Nederman (eds.), *Beyond the Persecuting Society: Religious Toleration before the Enlightenment* (Philadelphia, 1998).
——'Temporizing after Bayle: Isaac de Beausobre and the Manichaeans', in Pott et al. (eds.), *The Berlin Refuge*, 89–110.
——'Censorship in the Nordic Countries, *c*.1750–1890', *Journal of Modern European History*, 3 (2005), 100–16.
——(ed.), *New Essays on the Political Thought of the Refuge* (Leiden, 1995).
LA VOLPA, A. J., 'Conceiving a Public: Ideas and Society in Eighteenth-Century Europe', *Journal of Modern History*, 64 (1992), 79–116.
LEAMAN, OLIVER, *A Brief Introduction to Islamic Philosophy* (Cambridge, 1999).
LECA-TSIOMIS, M., *Écrire l'*Encyclopédie. *Diderot: de l'usage des dictionnaires à la grammaire philosophique* (Oxford, 1999).
LEE, J. PATRICK, 'Le "Sermon des cinquante" de Voltaire, manuscrit clandestin', in McKenna and Mothu (eds.), *Philosophie clandestine*, 143–51.
LEE, THOMAS H. C., 'Post-modernist/Post-colonialist Nationalism and the Historiography of China', *TJEAS* (2004), 89–118.

Leeb, I. L., *The Ideological Origins of the Batavian Revolution* (The Hague, 1973).

Leemans, Inger, *Het woord is aan de onderkant: Radicale ideeën in Nederlandse pornografische romans, 1670–1700* (Utrecht, 2002).

Leeuwenburgh, B., 'Meten is weten: Pierre Bayles populariteit in de Republiek', *GWN* 13 (2002), 81–93.

Lennon, Th. M., 'Bayle, Locke and the Metaphysics of Toleration', in M. A. Stewart (ed.), *Studies in Seventeenth-Century European Philosophy* (Oxford, 1997), 177–95.

—— *Reading Bayle* (Toronto, 1999).

—— 'Did Bayle read Saint-Évremond?', *JHI* 63 (2002), 225–37.

—— 'Bayle and Socinianism', in A. McKenna and G. Paganini (eds.), *Pierre Bayle dans la République, des lettres* (Paris, 2004), 171–91.

Leroux, Serge, 'Un Dieu rémunérateur et vengeur comme fondement-garantie de la morale', in Kölving and Mervaud (eds.), *Voltaire et ses combats*, i. 739–50.

Leroy, Pierre, 'Le Royaume de France dans le *Dictionnaire* de Pierre Bayle', in Bots (ed), *Critique, savoir et érudition*, 165–79.

Le Ru, Véronique., *D'Alembert philosophe* (Paris, 1994).

—— 'L'Aigle à deux têtes de l'*Encyclopédie*: accords et divergences de Diderot et de d'Alembert de 1751 à 1759', *RDIE* 26 (1999), 17–26.

Lesher, J. H., *Xenophanes of Colophon: Fragments* (Toronto, 1992).

—— *The Greek Philosophers: Selected Greek Texts from the Presocratics, Plato, and Aristotle* (London, 1988).

Lestringant, F., 'L'Utopie amoureuse: espace et sexualité dans la "Basiliade" d'Étienne Gabriel Morelly', in F. Moureau and Alain-Marc Rieu (eds.), *Éros philosophe* (Paris, 1984), 83–107.

Levene, J. M., 'Giambattista Vico and the Quarrel between the Ancients and the Moderns', *JHI* 52 (1991), 55–79.

Levillain, Charles-Édouard, 'William III's Military and Political Career in Neo-Roman Context, 1672–1702', *Historical Journal*, 48 (2005), 321–50.

Lewis, Bernard, *Islam in History: Ideas, Men and Events in the Middle East* (La Salle, Ill., 1973).

Lewitter, L. R., 'Peter the Great's Attitude towards Religion', in R. P. Barlett et al. (eds.), *Russia and the World of the Eighteenth Century* (Columbus, Oh., 1988), 62–77.

Lieshout, L. van, 'Op de drempel van de Verlichting', in Bots (ed.), *Henri Basnage*, ii. 81–160.

Lilla, Mark, *G. B. Vico: The Making of an Anti-Modern* (Cambridge, Mass., 1993).

Livesey, J., *Making Democracy in the French Revolution* (Cambridge, Mass., 2001).

Locqueneux, Robert, 'L'Abbé Pluche, ou l'accord de la foi et de la raison à l'aube des Lumières', *Sciences et techniques en perspective*, 2nd ser. 2 (1998), 235–88.

Lohr, C., 'Metaphysics', in Ch. B. Schmitt (ed.), *The Cambridge History of Renaissance Philosophy* (Cambridge, 1988), 537–638.

Lomonaco, Fabrizio, 'Readers of Locke: Cartesianism and Historical Criticism from Perizonius to Le Clerc', *GWN* 8 (1997), 103–11.

—— '"Natural Right", Liberty of Conscience and "Summa Potestas" in Jean Barbeyrac', in Pott et al. (eds.), *Berlin Refuge*, 137–51.

—— *Lex regia: diritto, filologia e fides historica nella cultura politico-filosofica dell'Olanda di fine seicento* (Naples, 1990).

——'Tra erudizione e critica storica: note sull'epistolario Le Clerc (1679–1689)', *BCSV* 20 (1990), 157–68.

——'Jean Barbeyrac et le "Pyrrhonisme historique" ', in J. Häseler and A. McKenna (eds.), *La Vie intellectuelle aux refuges protestants* (Paris, 1999), 253–67.

——'Jean Barbeyrac als Ausleger Pufendorfs', in M. Beetz and G. Cacciatore (eds.), *Die Hermeneutik im Zeitalter der Aufklärung* (Cologne, 2000), 197–207.

——'Religious Truth and Freedom of Conscience in Noodt and Barbeyrac', in G. Paganini (ed.), *The Return of Scepticism from Hobbes and Descartes to Bayle* (Dordrecht, 2003), 415–27.

——*Tolleranza: momenti e percorsi della modernità fino a Voltaire* (Naples, 2005).

Long, A. A., 'Freedom and Determinism in the Stoic Theory of Human Action', in Long (ed.), *Problems in Stoicism*, 173–99.

——*Hellenistic Philosophy: Stoics, Epicureans, Sceptics* (1974; 2nd edn. repr. 1996).

——*Stoic Studies* (Berkeley and Los Angeles, 1996).

——'Stoicism in the Philosophical Tradition', in Inwood (ed.), *The Cambridge Companion to the Stoics*, 365–92.

——'Stoicism in the Philosophical Tradition: Spinoza, Lipsius, Butler', in Miller and Inwood (eds.), *Hellenistic and Early Modern Philosophy*, 7–29.

——*Epictetus: A Stoic and Socratic Guide to Life* (Oxford, 2002).

——(ed.), *Problems in Stoicism* (1971; new edn. London, 1996).

——and Sedley, D. N., *The Hellenistic Philosophers* (2 vols., Cambridge, 1987).

Longo, Mario, 'Geistige Anregungen und Quellen der Bruckerschen Historiographie', in Schmidt-Biggemann (ed.), *Jacob Brucker*, 159–86.

Löpelmann, Martin, *Der junge Diderot* (Berlin, 1934).

Lott, T. L., 'Patriarchy and Slavery in Hobbes's Political Philosophy', in Ward and Lott (eds.), *Philosophers on Race*, 63–80.

Luciani, Paola, 'Les Répercussions de la propagande philosophique des tragédies de Voltaire en Italie: Mahomet', in Kölving and Mervaud (eds.), *Voltaire et ses combats*, ii. 1501–12.

Luft, S. R., 'A Genetic Interpretation of Divine Providence in Vico's *New Science*' *JHPh* 20 (1982), 151–69.

Lundbaek, K., 'The Image of Neo-Confucianism in *Confucius Sinarum philosophus*', *JHI* 44 (1983), 19–30.

Lurbe, Pierre, 'Le Spinozisme de John Toland', in Bloch (ed.), *Spinoza*, 33–47.

——'John Toland, Cosmopolitanism, and the Concept of Nation', in O'Dea and Whelan, *Nations*, 251–9.

Lüsebrink, Hans-Jürgen, 'Zur Verhüllung und sukzessiven Aufdeckung der Autorschaft Diderots an der *Histoire des deux Indes*', in T. Heydenreich (ed.), *Denis Diderot (1713–1784): Zeit, Werk, Wirkung* (Erlangen, 1985), 107–26.

——and Reichardt, R., *The Bastille: A History of a Symbol of Despotism and Freedom* (Durham, NC, 1997).

Lussu, Maria Luisa, *Bayle, Holbach e il dibattito sull'ateo virtuoso* (Genua, 1997).

Lynch, A. J., 'Montesquieu and the Ecclesiastical Critics of *L'Esprit des lois*', *JHI* 38 (1977), 487–500.

McDowall, David, *A Modern History of the Kurds* (1996; 2nd rev. edn. London, 2000).

Macé, Laurence, 'Les Lumières françaises au tribunal de l'Index et du Saint-Office', *DHS* 34 (2002), 13–25.

McGuirre, J. E., 'Predicates of Pure Existence: Newton on God's Space and Time', in P. Bricker and R. I. Hughes (eds.), *Philosophical Perspectives on Newtonian Science* (Cambridge, Mass., 1990), 91–108.

Macherey, P., 'À propos de la différence entre Hobbes et Spinoza', in Bostrenghi (ed.), *Hobbes e Spinoza*, 689–98.

Macintyre, Alasdair, *After Virtue* (1981; 2nd edn. Notre Dame, Ind., 1984).

—— *Whose Justice? Which Rationality?* (Notre Dame, Ind., 1988).

Mack, P., *Renaissance Argument* (Leiden, 1993).

McKenna, Antony, 'Sur l'hérésie dans la littérature clandestine', *DHS* 22 (1990), 301–13.

—— 'Le Marquis d' Argens et les manuscrits clandestins', in Vissière (ed.), *Marquis d' Argens*, 113–40.

—— 'L'*Éclaircissement sur les Pyrrhoniens*, 1702', in *Le Dictionnaire de Pierre Bayle (Actes de Colloque de Nimègue, 24–7 Oct. 1996)* (Amsterdam, 1997), 297–320.

—— 'Recherches sur la philosophie clandestine à l'Âge Classique', in McKenna and Mothu (eds.), *La Philosophie clandestine*, 3–14.

—— Pierre Bayle et la superstition', in B. Dompnier (ed.), *La Superstition à l'âge des Lumières* (Paris, 1998), 49–65.

—— 'Le Marquis d'Argens et les manuscrits clandestins', *La Lettre clandestine*, 12 (2003), 97–120.

—— 'Rationalisme moral et fidéisme', in Hubert Bost and Philippe de Robert (eds.), *Pierre Bayle, citoyen du monde* (Paris, 1999), 257–74.

—— 'Vauvenargues, lecteur de Pascal et de l'anti-Pascal', in Bove (ed.), *Vauvenargues*, 201–26.

—— 'La Norme et la transgression: Pierre Bayle et le socinianisme', in *Normes et transgression au XVIIe siècle*, Sillages critiques (Paris, 2002), 117–36.

—— 'Molière et l'imposture dévote', *Libertinage et philosophie*, 6 (2002), 97–129.

—— 'Pierre Bayle: moralisme et anthropologie', in Mckenna and Paganini (eds.), *Pierre Bayle*, 321–47.

—— and Mothu, Alain (eds.), *La Philosophie clandestine à l'Âge Classique* (Paris, 1997).

McLoughlin, T. O., *Contesting Ireland: Irish Voices against England in the Eighteenth Century* (Portland, Ore., 1999).

McMahon, D. M., *Enemies of the Enlightenment* (Oxford, 2001).

McManners, John, *Church and Society in Eighteenth-Century France* (2 vols., Oxford, 1998).

McNally, D., 'Locke, Levellers and Liberty', in Milton (ed.), *Locke's Moral*, 87–110.

McShea, R. J., *The Political Philosophy of Spinoza* (New York, 1968).

Magdalaine, M., Pitassi, M. C., Whelan, R., and McKenna, A. (eds.), *De l'humanisme aux Lumières: Bayle et le protestantisme: mélanges en l'honneur d'Élisabeth Labrousse* (Paris, 1996).

Maiolani, D., 'Mably e il repubblicanesimo dei lumi', *Il pensiero politico*, 34 (2001), 73–94.

Maire, C., *De la cause de Dieu à la cause de la nation: le Jansénisme au XVIIIe siècle* (Paris, 1998).

Malcolm, Noel, *Aspects of Hobbes* (Oxford, 2002).

Malherbe, Michel, 'The Impact on Europe', in Broadie (ed.), *Cambridge Companion to the Scottish Enlightenment*, 298–315.

—— 'Introduction' to Condillac, *Traité des animaux* (1755) (Paris, 2004), 7–106.

Malssen, P. J. W. van, *Louis XIV d'après les pamphlets répandus en Hollande* (Paris, n.d.).

Malusa, Luciano, 'Renaissance Antecedents to the Historiography of Philosophy', in Santinello (ed.), *Models*, 3–65.

—— 'The First General Histories of Philosophy in England and the Low Countries', in Santinello (ed.), *Models*, 161–370.

Mamiani, M., 'La rivoluzione incompiuta', in A. Santucci (ed.), *L'età dei Lumi* (Bologna, 1998).

Mandonnet, Pierre, *Siger de Brabant et l'Averroïsme latin au XIIIe siècle* (2nd edn. Louvain, 1911).

Mannarino, L., *Le mille favole degli antichi: ebraismo e cultura europea nel pensiero religioso di Pietro Giannone* (Florence, 1999).

Manuel, F. A., *The Prophets of Paris* (Cambridge, Mass., 1962).

—— *The Broken Staff: Judaism through Christian Eyes* (Cambridge, Mass., 1992).

Manusov-Verhage, C. G., 'Jan Rieuwertsz, marchand libraire et éditeur de Spinoza', in F. Akkerman and P. Steenbakkers (eds.), *Spinoza to the Letter* (Leiden, 2005), 237–50.

Marcolungo, F., 'L'uomo e Dio nei primi scritti di Giambattista Vico', in A. Lamacchia (ed.), *Vestigia: studi e strumenti di storiografia filosofica* (Bari, 1992), 83–102.

Maréchal, G., 'Inleiding' to *Het Leven van Philopater: een spinozistische sleutelroman uit 1691/1697* (Amsterdam, 1991), 11–38.

Marilli, Massimo, 'Cartesianesimo e tolleranza: il *Commentaire philosophique* di Pierre Bayle', *RSF* 3 (1963), 555–79.

—— 'Il Cartesianesimo di Pierre Bayle', *Annali della Facoltà di Lettere e Filosofia. Università di Siena*, 5 (1984), 181–230.

Markley, R., *Fallen Languages: Crises of Representation in Newtonian England, 1660–1740* (Ithaca, NY, 1993).

Markovits, F., 'La Mettrie, l'anonyme et le sceptique', *Corpus*, 5/6 (1987), 83–105.

—— 'La Mettrie: une éthique de l'inconstance', *DHS* 35 (2003), 171–85.

Marsden, G. M., *Jonathan Edwards: A Life* (New Haven, 2003).

Marshall, John, *John Locke: Resistance, Religion and Responsibility* (Cambridge, 1994).

—— *Locke and 'Early Enlightenment Culture': Religious Intolerance and Arguments for Religious Toleration in Early Modern and 'Early Enlightenment' Europe* (Cambridge, forthcoming).

Martels, Z. von, Steenbakkers, Piet and Vanderjagt, A. (eds.), *Limae labor et mora: opstellen voor Fokke Akkerman ter gelegenheid van zijn zeventigste verjaardag* (Leende, 2000).

Martin-Haag, E., *Un aspect de la pensée politique de Diderot* (Paris, 1999).

—— *Voltaire. Du Cartésianisme aux Lumières* (Paris, 2002).

Martino, Pierre, 'Mahomet en France', in *Actes du XIVe congrès international des orientalistes, Alger 1905* (Paris, 1907), 3rd part 'Langues musulmans', 206–40.

Marx, J., 'Un grand imprimeur au XVIIIe siècle: Élie Luzac fils (1723–96)', *Revue belge de philologie et d'histoire*, 46 (1968), 779–86.

Marx, Karl, *Economic and Philosophic Manuscripts* (Moscow 1959).

Mason, Haydn T., 'Voltaire devant Bayle', in A. McKenna and G. Paganini (eds.), *Pierre Bayle dans la République des lettres* (Paris, 2004), 443–56.

—— *The Darnton Debate: Books and Revolution in the Eighteenth Century* (Oxford, 1998).

Mason, Richard, *The God of Spinoza: A Philosophical Study* (Cambridge, 1997).

Mass, E., and Knabe, P. E. (eds.), *L'Encyclopédie et Diderot* (Cologne, 1985).

Masseau, D., *Les Ennemis des philosophes: l'antiphilosophie au temps des Lumières* (Paris, 2000).

MASSIGNON, LOUIS, *Opera minora*, ed. Y. Moubarac (3 vols., Paris, 1969).

MASTELLONE, SALVO, 'Italian Enlightenment and the Swedish Constitution during the Age of Liberty (1719–1772)', in N. Stjernquist (ed.), *The Swedish Riksdag in an International Perspective* (Stockholm, 1989), 112–17.

MATAR, NABIL, 'John Locke and the Jews', *Journal of Ecclesiastical History*, 44 (1993), 45–62.

MATHERON, ALEXANDRE, *Individu et communauté chez Spinoza* (1969; new edn. Paris, 1988).

—— *Le Christ et le salut des ignorants chez Spinoza* (Paris, 1971).

—— 'Femmes et serviteurs dans la démocratie Spinoziste', in S. Hessing (ed.), *Speculum Spinozanum 1677–1977* (London, 1977), 368–86.

—— 'Spinoza et la propriété', *TvSV* 5 (1978), 96–110.

—— 'La Fonction théorique de la démocratie chez Spinoza', *Studia Spinozana*, 1 (1985), 259–73.

—— 'Le Moment stoïcien de *l'Éthique* de Spinoza', in. J. Lagrée (ed.), *Le Stoicisme*, 147–61.

—— 'Le Problème de l'évolution de Spinoza du *Traité théologico politique* au *Traité politique*', in Curley and Moreau (eds.), *Spinoza: Issues and Directions. The Proceedings of the Chicago Spinoza Conference (1986)* (Leiden, 1990), 258–70.

MAUTHNER, FRITZ, *Der Atheismus und seine Geschichte im Abendlande* (3 vols., Stuttgart, 1920–2).

MAY, H. F., *The Enlightenment in America* (1976; new edn. New York, 1978).

MAZAURIC, S., 'Fontenelle et la construction polémique de l'histoire des sciences', *Corpus*, 44 (2003), 73–97.

MAZZOTTA, G., *The New Map of the World: The Poetic Philosophy of Giambattista Vico* (Princeton, 1999).

—— 'Newton for Ladies', *BJHS* 27 (2004), 119–46.

MÉCHOULAN, HENRY, POPKIN, R. H., RICUPERATI, G., and SIMONUTTI, L. (eds.), *La formazione storica della alterità: studi di storia della tolleranza nell'età moderna offerti a Antonio Rotondò* (3 vols., Florence, 2001).

MEIJERING, E., *Irenaeus, Grondlegger van het christelijk denken* (Amsterdam, 2001).

MEINSMA, K. O., *Spinoza et son cercle: étude critique historique sur les hétérodoxes hollandais* (new edn. Paris, 1983).

MENDOZA, R. G., 'Metempsychosis and Monism in Bruno's *Nova filosofia*', in H. Gatti (ed.), *Giordano Bruno: Philosopher of the Renaissance* (Aldershot, 2002), 273–97.

MERTENS, F., 'Franciscus van den Enden: tijd voor een herziening van diens role in het ontstaan van het Spinozisme?', *Tijdschrift voor filosofie*, 56 (1994), 717–37.

MEYNELL, H. A., *Postmodernism and the New Enlightenment* (Washington, 1999).

MICHAEL, M., 'Locke, Religious Toleration and the Limits of Social Contract Theory', *History of Philosophy Quarterly*, 20 (2003), 21–40.

MIGNINI, FILIPPO, 'Données et problèmes de la chronologie Spinozienne entre 1656 et 1665', *RSPhTh* 76 (1987), 9–21.

—— *L'*Etica *di Spinoza: introduzione alla lettura* (Rome, 1995).

—— 'La dottrina spinoziana della religione razionale', *Studia Spinozana*, 11 (1995), 53–80.

—— 'Taal en communicatie bij Spinoza', in Martels et al. (eds.), *Limae labor et mora*, 172–83.

MIHAILA, I., 'L'*hylozoïsme* de Diderot', in Fink and Stenger (eds.), *Être matérialiste*, 185–97.

MIJNHARDT, WIJNAND, 'The Dutch Enlightenment', in Jacob and Mijnhardt (eds.), *Dutch Republic*, 197–223.

—— *Over de moderniteit van de Nederlandse Republiek* (Utrecht, 2001).

—— 'The Construction of Silence: Religious and Political Radicalism in Dutch History', in van Bunge (ed.), *Early Enlightenment*, 231–62.

Miller, J., 'Stoics, Grotius, and Spinoza on Moral Deliberation', in Miller and Inwood (eds.), *Hellenistic and Early Modern Philosophy*, 116–40.

—— and Inwood, B., *Hellenistic and Early Modern Philosophy* (Cambridge, 2003).

Miller, John, 'Britain', in J. Miller (ed.), *Absolutism in Seventeenth-Century Europe* (Basingstoke,1990), 195–224.

Milton, J. R.(ed.), *Locke's Moral, Political and Legal Philosophy* (Aldershot, 1999).

Miner, R. C., *Vico: Genealogist of Modernity* (Notre Dame, Ind. 2002).

Minuti, R., 'Orientalismo e idea di tolleranza nella "*Lettres chinoises*" di Boyer d'Argens', in Méchoulan et al. (eds.), *Formazione*, iii. 887–920.

Mogyoródi, Emese, 'Xenophanes as a Philosopher: Theology and Theodicy', in André Laks and Claire Louguet (eds.), *Qu'est-ce que la philosophie présocratique* (Lille, 2002), 253–86.

Monk, S. H., 'Introduction' to Sir William Temple, *Five Miscellaneous Essays*, ed. S. H. Monk (Ann Arbor, 1963).

Monro, D. H., *The Ambivalence of Bernard Mandeville* (Oxford, 1975).

Montag, Warren, *Bodies, Masses, Power: Spinoza and his Contemporaries* (London, 1999).

Moreau, Joseph, 'Malebranche et le Spinozisme', in Malebranche, *Correspondance*, 1–98.

Moreau, Pierre François, 'Spinoza et le *Jus circa sacra*', *Studia Rosenthaliana*, 1 (1985), 35–44.

—— 'Louis Meyer et l'*Interpres*', *RSPhTh* 76 (1992), 73–84.

—— 'Les Principes de la lecture de l'Écriture Sainte dans le TTP', *GRSTD* 4 (1992), 119–31.

—— 'La Méthode d'interprétation de l'Écriture Sainte', in Bouveresse (ed.), *Spinoza*, 109–13.

—— 'Spinoza's Reception and Influence', in Garrett (ed.), *Cambridge Companion to Spinoza*, 408–33.

—— 'Sacerdos levita pontifex: les prêtres dans le lexique du *Traité theologico-politique*', *Kairos*, 11 (1998) 33–40.

—— 'Les Sept raisons des *Pensées diverses sur la comète*', in D. Abel and P. F. Moreau (eds.), *Pierre Bayle: la foi dans le doute* (Geneva 1995).

—— (ed.), *Architectures de la raison* (Paris, 1996).

—— and Thomson A., (eds.), *Matérialisme et passions* (Lyons, 2004).

Morgan, E. S., *Benjamin Franklin* (New Haven, 2002).

Mori, Gianluca, 'Sullo Spinoza di Bayle', *GCFI* 67 (1988), 348–68.

—— 'Interpréter la philosophie de Bayle', in Bost and de Robert (eds.), *Pierre Bayle*, 303–24.

—— 'Benoît de Maillet et son traité "Sur la nature de l'âme" ', *La Lettre clandestine*, 4 (1995), 13–21.

—— 'L'ateismo "Malebranchiano" di Meslier', in Canziani (ed.), *Filosofia e religione*, 123–60.

—— 'Pierre Bayle, the Rights of Conscience, the "Remedy" of Toleration', *Ratio juris*, 10 (1997), 45–60.

—— 'Baruch de Spinoza: athée vertueux, athée de système', in Bots (eds.), *Critique, savoir et érudition*, 341–58.

—— 'Introduction' and 'Postface' to C. Ch. du Marsais, *Examen de la religion* (Oxford, 1998), 3–139, 337–59.

—— *Bayle philosophe* (Paris, 1999).

—— 'Scepticisme ancien et moderne chez Bayle', *Libertinage et philosophie*, 7 (2003), 271–90.

MORI, GIANLUCA, 'Einleitung' to [Du Marsais], *Die wahre Religion oder die Religionsprüfung* (Stuttgart, 2003), pp.vii–liii.

——'Athéisme et philosophie chez Bayle', in Mckenna and Paganini (eds.), *Pierre Bayle*, 381–410.

—— 'Du Marsais Philosophe clandestin', in McKenna and Mothu (eds.), *La Philosophe clandestine*, 169–92.

MORILHAT, CLAUDE, *La Mettrie: un matérialisme radical* (Paris, 1997).

MORIN, ROBERT, *Les* Pensées philosophiques *de Diderot devant leurs principaux contradicteurs au XVIIIe siècle* (Paris, 1975).

MORMAN, P. J., *Noël Aubert de Versé: A Study in the Concept of Toleration* (Lewiston, NY, 1987).

MORRISON, J. C., 'How to Interpret the Idea of Divine Providence in Vico's *New Science*', *Philosophy and Rhetoric*, 12 (1979), 256–61.

——'Vico and Spinoza', *JHI* 41 (1980), 49–68.

——'Spinoza and History', in R. Kennington (ed.), *The Philosophy of Baruch Spinoza*, Studies in Philosophy and the History of Philosophy 7, ed. J. P. Dougherty (Washington, 1980), 173–95.

MORTIER, ROLAND, *Lumières du XVIIIe siècle* (Athens, 2003).

——'Diversités culturelles: *Aufklärung* allemande—Lumières françaises', in F. Grunert and in F. Vollhardt (eds.), *Aufklärung als praktische Philosophie* (Tübingen, 1998), 21–30.

MOSHER, M. A., 'Monarchy's Paradox: Honour in the Face of Sovereign Power', in Carrithers et al. (eds.), *Montesquieu's Science*, 159–229.

MOST, G. W., 'Rhetorik und Hermeneutik: Zur Konstitution der Neuzeitlichkeit', *Antike und Abendland*, 30 (1984), 62–79.

MOTHU, ALAIN, 'L'Édition de 1751 des *Opinions des anciens*', *La Lettre clandestine*, 3 (1994), 45–53.

——'Les Vanités manuscrites des esprits forts', *La Lettre clandestine*, 6 (1997), 65–9.

——'Un curé "Janséniste" lecteur et concepteur de manuscrits clandestins: Guillaume Maleville', *La Lettre clandestine*, 6 (1997), 25–50.

——'Un morceau des plus hardis et des plus philosophiques qui aient été faits dans ce pays-ci', *Corpus*, 44 (2003), 35–56.

MOUREAU, F., 'Du clandestin et de son bon usage au XVIIIe siècle', *La Lettre clandestine*, 6 (1997), 271–83.

MOWBRAY, MALCOLM DE, 'What is philosophy? *Historia philosophica* in the Dutch Republic, 1640–1669' (forthcoming).

MUCHEMBLED, ROBERT, *A History of the Devil* (Cambridge, 2003).

MUCHNIK, N., *Une vie marrane: les pérégrinations de Juan de Prado dans l'Europe du XVIIe siècle* (Paris, 2005).

MÜHLPFORDT, G., 'Die Petersburger Aufklärung', *Canadian American Slavic Studies*, 13 (1979), 488–509.

MÜLLER, M. G., 'Toleration in Eastern Europe', in Grell and Porter (eds.), *Toleration*, 212–29.

MULSOW, MARTIN, *Monadenlehre, Hermetik und Deismus: Georg Schades geheime Aufklärungsgesellschaft, 1747–1760* (Hamburg, 1998).

——'The "New Socinians"', in M. Mulsow and J. Rohls (eds.), *Socinianism and Arminianism: Antitrinitarians, Calvinists and Cultural Exchange in Seventeenth-Century Europe* (Leiden, 2005), 49–78.

——*Die drei Ringe: Toleranz und clandestine Gelehrsamkeit bei Mathurin Veyssière La Croze (1661–1739)* (Tübingen, 2001).

——*Moderne aus dem Untergrund: Radikale Frühaufklärung in Deutschland, 1680–1720* (Hamburg, 2002).

——'Gundling *versus* Buddeus: Competing Models of the History of Philosophy', in Kelley (ed.), *History*, 103–25.

——'Reaktionärer Hermetismus vor 1600?', in Mulsow (ed.), *Ende des Hermetismus*, 161–85.

——'Views of the Berlin *Refuge*: Scholarly Projects, Literary Interests, Marginal Fields', in Pott et al. (eds.), *The Berlin Refuge*, 25–46.

MULSOW, MARTIN, 'Eine "Rettung" des Servet und der Ophiten? Der junge Mosheim und die häretische Tradition', in Mulsow et al. (eds.), *Johann Lorenz Mosheim*, 45–92.

——(ed.), *Das Ende des Hermetismus: Historische Kritik und neue Naturphilosophie in der Spätrenaissance* (Tübingen, 2002).

——and ZEDELMAIER, H., (eds.), *Skepsis, Providenz, Polyhistorie: Jakob Friedrich Reimmann (1668–1743)* (Tübingen, 1998).

——et al. (eds.), *Johann Lorenz Mosheim (1693–1755): Theologie im Spannungsfeld von Philosophie, Philologie und Geschichte* (Wiesbaden, 1997).

MUNGELLO, D. E., 'Malebranche and Chinese Philosophy', *JHI* 41 (1980), 551–78.

——'European Philosophical Responses to Non-European Culture', in Garber and Ayers (eds.), *CHSPH* i. 87–100.

MUTHU, SANKAR, *Enlightenment against Empire* (Princeton, 2003).

NADLER, STEVEN, *Spinoza: A Life* (Cambridge, 1999).

——*Spinoza's Heresy: Immortality and the Jewish Mind* (Oxford, 2001).

——'Spinoza's Theory of Divine Providence', *MvSH* 87 (2005), 3–30.

NAMER, ÉMILE, *La Vie et l'œuvre de J. C. Vanini, prince des libertins* (Paris, 1980).

NASR, SEYYED HOSSEIN, 'Ibn Sina's "Oriental Philosophy" ', in Nasr and Leaman (eds.), *History*, 247–51.

——and LEAMAN OLIVER (eds.), *History of Islamic Philosophy* (London, 1996).

NAUERT, CH. G., *Humanism and the Culture of Renaissance Europe* (Cambridge, 1995).

NEGRI, ANTONIO, *The Savage Anomaly* (Minneapolis, 1991).

NEGRONI, B. DE, 'Le Rôle de la citation de Bayle à Voltaire', *La Lettre clandestine*, 8 (1999), 35–54.

NELLEN, H., 'Controverses binnen de *Refuge*: Bayle, Jurieu en Basnage', in Bots (ed.), *Henri Basnage*, i. 177–215.

NEIMAN, SUSAN, *Evil in Modern Thought: An Alternative History of Philosophy* (Princeton, 2002).

NIDERST, A., 'Fontenelle et la littérature clandestine', in Canziani (ed.), *Filosofia e religione* 161–73.

——'Scepticisme ou fidéisme de Bayle?', *Seventeenth-Century French Studies*, 21 (1999), 205–14.

——'Modernisme et catholicisme de L'abbé Trublet', *DHS* 34 (2002), 303–13.

NIEWÖHNER, FRIEDRICH, 'Are the Founders of Religions Impostors?', in S. Pines and Y. Yovel (eds.), *Maimonides and Philosophy* (Dordrecht, 1986), 233–45.

——*Veritas sive varietas: Lessings Toleranzparabel und das Buch von den drei Betrügern* (Heidelberg, 1988).

——and PLUTA, P. (eds.), *Atheismus im Mittelalter und in der Renaissance* (Wiesbaden, 1999).

NIJENHUIS, I. J. A., *Een joodse* philosophe, *Isaac de Pinto (1717–1787)* (Amsterdam, 1992).

NOORDENBOS, O., 'De eeuw der Verlichting', *De Gids*, 134 (1971), 446–53.

Norton, D. F., 'Hume, Human Nature, and the Foundations of Morality', in Norton (ed.), *Cambridge Companion to Hume*, 148–81.

—— (ed.), *The Cambridge Companion to Hume* (Cambridge, 1993).

Nuzzo, E., 'Vico e Bayle: ancora una mesa a punto', in Bianchi (ed.), *Pierre Bayle*, 123–202.

O'Cathasaigh, S., 'Bayle and Locke on Toleration', in Magdalaine et al. (eds.), *De l'humanisme aux Lumières*, 679–92.

O'Dea, M., and Whelan, K. (eds.), *Nations and Nationalisms* (Oxford, 1995).

O'Hagan, T., *Rousseau* (London, 1999).

O'Higgins, J., *Anthony Collins: The Man and his Works* (The Hague, 1970).

O'Keefe, C. B., *Contemporary Reactions to the Enlightenment (1728–1762)* (Paris, 1974).

Okenfuss, M. J., *The Rise and Fall of Latin Humanism in Early-Modern Russia* (Leiden, 1995).

Oliel-Grausz, E., 'Relations, coopération et conflits intercommunautaires dans la diaspora séfarade: l'affaire Nieto', in H. Méchoulan and G. Nahon (eds.), *Mémorial I. S. Révah* (Paris, 2001), 371–402.

Olscamp, P. J., *The Moral Philosophy of George Berkeley* (The Hague, 1970).

Orcibal, J., 'Les Jansénistes face à Spinoza', *Revue de littérature comparée*, 23 (1949), 441–68.

O'Reilly, R. F., 'Montesquieu: Anti-feminist', *SVEC* 102 (1973), 143–56.

Osborne, Catherine, *Rethinking Early Greek Philosophy* (Ithaca, NY, 1987).

Osier, Jean Pierre, 'L'Hermeneutique de Hobbes et Spinoza', *Studia Spinozana*, 3 (1987), 319–47.

Osler, M. J., 'Ancients, Moderns, and the History of Philosophy: Gassendi's Epicurean Project', in Sorell (ed.), *Rise of Modern Philosophy*, 129–43.

Otegem, Matthijs van, 'Twee Enkhuizer predikanten over het cartesianisme: filosofie en politiek in het rampjaar', *GWN* 11 (2000), 51–60.

Otto, R., *Studien zur Spinozarezeption in Deutschland im 18. Jahrhundert* (Frankfurt, 1994).

Paganini, Gianni, 'Tra Epicuro e Stratone: Bayle e l'imagine di Epicuro dal Sei al Settecento', *RCSF* 33 (1978), 72–115.

—— *Analisi della fede e critica della ragione nella filosofia di Pierre Bayle* (Florence, 1980).

—— 'Hume et Bayle: conjonction locale et immatérialité de l'âme', in Magdalaine et al. (eds.), *De l'humanisme aux Lumières*, 701–13.

—— 'Scepsi clandestina: i Doutes des Pyrrhoniens', in Canziani (ed.), *Filosofia e religione*, 83–122.

—— 'Avant la *Promenade du sceptique*: Pyrrhonisme et clandestinité de Bayle à Diderot', in Paganini, et al. (eds.), *Scepticisme*, 17–46.

—— 'Haupttendenzen der clandestinen Philosophie', in J. P. Schobinger (ed.), *Die Philosophie des 17. Jahrhunderts*, Grundriss der Geschichte der Philosophie (Basel, 1998), i. 121–95.

—— *Les Philosophies clandestines à l'âge classique* (Paris, 2005).

—— Benítez, Miguel, and Dybikowski, J., (eds.), *Scepticisme, clandestinité et libre pensée* (Paris, 2002).

Pagden, Anthony, 'The Effacement of Difference: Colonialism and the Origins of Nationalism in Diderot and Herder', in G. Prakash (ed.), *After Colonialism: Imperial Histories and Postcolonial Displacements* (Princeton, 1995), 129–52.

Palmer, L. M., 'Introduction' to Vico, *De antiquissima*, 1–34.

Palmer, R. R., *The Age of Democratic Revolution* (2 vols., Princeton, 1959).

Palsits, V. H., *A Bibliography of the Writings of Baron Lahontan* (Chicago, 1905).

Panizza, Giulio, 'L'Étrange Matérialisme de La Mettrie', *Corpus*, 14–15 (1990), 97–109.

Pappas, J. N., *Berthier's* Journal de Trévoux *and the Philosophes* (Geneva, 1957).
—— 'Buffon matérialiste?', in Fink and Stenger (eds.), *Être matérialiste*, 233–49.
Paradis, Michel, 'Les Fondements de la tolérance universelle chez Bayle', in E. Groffier and M. Paradis (eds.), *The Notion of Tolerance and Human Rights* (Montreal, 1991), 25–35.
Pariente, Jean-Claude, 'L'effacement du logique chez Condillac', in A. Bertrand (ed.), *Condillac l'origine du langage* (Paris, 2002).
Parikh, I., 'The Need of the Third World for Humanism', in P. Kurtz and T. J. Madigan (eds.), *Challenges to the Enlightenment: In Defence of Reason and Science* (New York, 1994).
Park, D., 'John Locke: Toleration and Civic Virtues', in E. Groffier and M. Paradis (eds.), *The Notion of Tolerance and Human Rights* (Mantreal, 1991), 13–24.
Parker, Grant, *The Agony of Asar* (Princeton, 2001).
Parrochia, D., 'Physique et politique chez Spinoza', *Kairos: revue de philosophie* (Toulouse), 11 (1998), 59–95.
Pascual López, Esther, *Bernard Mandeville: legitimación de la fantasía y orden espontáneo* (Madrid, 2000).
Patrides, C. A., *The Cambridge Platonists* (Cambridge, 1969).
Paty, M., 'D'Alembert, la science newtonienne et l'héritage cartésien', *Corpus*, 38 (2001), 19–64.
Pätzold, D., *Spinoza, Aufklärung, Idealismus: Die Substanz der Moderne* (1995; 2nd edn. Assen, 2002).
Payne, H. G., *The* Philosophes *and the People* (New Haven, 1976).
Peabody, S., '*There are no Slaves in France*' (New York, 1996).
Pearson, R., *The Fables of Reason: A Study of Voltaire's* Contes philosophiques (Oxford, 1993).
—— *Voltaire Almighty: A Life in Pursuit of Freedom* (London, 2005).
Pecharman, M., 'Signification et langage dans l'*Essai* de Condillac', *Revue de Métaphysique et de Morale*, 1 (1999), 81–103.
Pérez-Ramos, Antonio, 'Giambattista Vico', in S. Brown (ed.), *Routledge History of Philosophy*, v: *British Philosophy and the Age of Enlightenment* (London, 1996), 332–53.
Perkins, Francis, 'Virtue, Reason and Cultural Exchange: Leibniz's Praise of Chinese Morality', *JHI* 63 (2002), 447–64.
Perkins, J. A., 'Voltaire and La Mettrie', *SVEC* 10 (1959), 49–100.
Petry, M. J., 'Hobbes and the Early Dutch Spinozists', in de Deugd (ed.), *Spinoza's Political and Theological Thought*, 150–70.
—— 'Nieuwentijt's Criticism of Spinoza', in *MvSH* 40 (1979), 1–16.
Petuchowski, Jacob T., *The Theology of Haham David Nieto* (New York, 1954).
Pevitt, Christine, *The Man Who Would Be King: The Life of Philippe d'Orléans, Regent of France* (London, 1998).
Pfoh, Werner, *Matthias Knutzen: Ein deutscher Atheist und revolutionärer Demokrat des 17. Jahrhunderts* (Berlin, 1965).
Phillips, H., *Church and Culture in Seventeenth-Century France* (Cambridge, 1997).
Piaia, Gregorio, 'Brucker versus Rorty? On the "Models" of the Historiography of Philosophy', *BJHP* 9 (2001), 69–81.
—— 'Jacob Bruckers Wirkungsgeschichte in Frankreich und Italian', in Schmidt-Biggemann and Stammen (eds.), *Jacob Brucker*, 218–37.
Pia Jauch, Ursula, ' "Wenn Therese philosophiert": Einige Fussnoten zum Verhältnis von d'Argens und La Mettrie', in Seifert and Seban (eds.), *Marquis d'Argens*, 139–51.

Pigeard de Gurbert, G., 'La Philosophie du bon sens de Boyer d'Argens', in McKenna and Mothu (eds.), *La Philosophie clandestine*, 367–74.

Pii, Eluggero, 'Republicanism and Commercial Society in Eighteenth-Century Italy', in van Gelderen and Skinner (eds.), *Republicanism*, ii. 249–74.

Pine, M. L., 'Pietro Pomponazzi's Attack on Religion and the Problem of the *De fato*', in Niewöhner and Pluta (eds.), *Atheismus*, 145–72.

Pinot, Virgile, *La Chine et la formation de l'esprit philosophique en France (1640–1740)* (1932; repr. Geneva, 1971).

Pitassi, M. C., 'L'Écho des discussions métaphysiques dans la correspondance entre Isaac Papin et Jean Le Clerc', *Revue de théologie et de philosophie*, 114 (1982), 259–75.

—— *Entre croire et savoir: le problème de la méthode critique chez Jean Le Clerc* (Leiden, 1987).

—— 'De la courtoisie à la dénonciation: la reception du *Dictionnaire historique et critique* de Pierre Bayle à Genève', in Bots (ed.), *Critique, savoir et érudition*, 65–79.

—— 'Réfutation du système de Spinosa par Mr. Turrettini', *NAKG* 68 (1988), 191–212.

—— 'Entre *libido* et savoir: l'image de la femme chez Bayle', in McKenna and Paganini (eds.), *Pierre Bayle*, 307–19.

Pocock, J. G. A., *The Machiavellian Moment* (Princeton, 1975).

—— 'The Dutch Republican Tradition', in Jacob and Mijnhardt (eds.), *Dutch Republic*, 197–223.

—— *Virtue, Commerce and History* (Cambridge, 1985).

—— 'The Significance of 1688', in R. Beddard (ed.), *The Revolutions of 1688* (Oxford, 1991), 271–92.

—— *Barbarism and Religion* (3 vols. so far, Cambridge, 1999–2003).

Pomeau, René, *Politique de Voltaire* (Paris, 1963).

Pomian, K., 'Piotr Bayle wobec Socynianizmu', *Archiwum Historii Filozofii I Myśli Społecznej*, 6 (1960), 102–82.

Pommier, Jean, *Diderot avant Vincennes* (Paris, 1939).

Pompa, Leon, *Vico: A Study of the 'New Science'* (1975; 2nd edn. Cambridge, 1990).

Popkin, J. D., 'Robert Darnton's Alternative (to the) Enlightenment', in Mason (ed.), *Darnton Debate*, 105–28.

Popkin, R. H., 'The Philosophical Basis of Eighteenth-Century Racism', in H. E. Pagliaro (ed.), *Racism in the Eighteenth Century* (Cleveland, 1973), 245–62.

—— *The History of Scepticism from Erasmus to Spinoza* (Berkeley and Los Angeles, 1979).

—— 'Jewish Anti-Christian Arguments as a Source of Irreligion from Seventeenth to the Early Nineteeth Century', in Hunter and Wootton (eds.), *Atheism*, 159–81.

—— 'The Deist Challenge', in O. P. Grell, J. I. Israel, and N. Tyacke (eds.), *From Persecution to Toleration* (Oxford, 1991), 195–215.

—— 'Spinoza and Bible Scholarship', in J. E. Force and R. H. Popkin (eds.), *The Books of Nature and Scripture* (Dordrecht, 1994), 1–20.

—— 'The First Published Reaction to Spinoza's *Tractatus*', in Cristofolini (ed.), *L'Hérésie Spinoziste*, 6–12.

—— *Spinoza* (Oxford, 2004).

—— 'Les Caraïtes et l'émancipation des Juifs', *DHS* 13 (1981), 134–47.

—— *The Third Force in Seventeenth-Century Thought* (Leiden, 1992).

—— and Vanderjagt, A. (eds.), *Scepticism and Irreligion in the Seventeenth and Eighteenth Centuries* (Leiden, 1993).

Poppi, Antonino, 'Fate, Fortune, Providence and Human Freedom', in Schmitt and Skinner (eds.), *CHRPh* 641–67.

Porret, Michel, and Volpilhac-Auger, C. (eds.), *Le Temps de Montesquieu: actes du colloque international de Genève (28–31 Oct. 1998)* (Geneva, 2002).

Porset, Charles, 'Voltaire et Meslier: état de la question', in Bloch (ed.), *Matérialisme*, 193–204.

—— 'Position de la philosophie de Voltaire', in Kölving and Mervaud (eds.), *Voltaire et ses combats*, i. 727–38.

Porter, Roy, 'The Scientific Revolution: A Spoke in the Wheel?', in R. Porter and M. Teich (eds.), *Revolution in History* (Cambridge, 1986), 290–316.

—— *Enlightenment: Britain and the Creation of the Modern World* (London, 2000).

—— *Flesh in the Age of Reason* (London, 2003).

Postigliola, Alberto, *La città della ragione: per una storia filosofica del settecento francese* (Rome, 1992).

Pott, M., 'Einleitung' to *Philosophische Clandestina der deutschen Aufklärung*, ser. 1, vol. i (Stuttgart, 1992).

Pott, S., Mulsow, M., and Danneberg, L. (eds.), *The Berlin Refuge, 1680–1780* (Leiden, 2003).

Poulouin, Claudine, *Le Temps des origines: L'Éden, le Déluge et 'les temps reculés'. De Pascal à l'*Encyclopédie (Paris, 1998).

—— 'Fontenelle et la vérité des fables', *Corpus*, 13 (1989), 35–50.

Prak, Maarten, *Gezeten burgers: de elite in een Hollandse stad, Leiden 1700–1780* (n.p., 1985).

—— *Gouden Eeuw: het raadsel van den Republiek* (Nijmegen, 2002).

Preus, J. Samuel, 'Spinoza, Vico, and the Imagination of Religion', *JHI* l (1989), 71–93.

—— *Spinoza and the Irrelevance of Biblical Authority* (Cambridge, 2001).

Primer, Irwin, 'Mandeville and Shaftesbury', in Primer (ed.), *Mandeville Studies*, 126–41.

—— (ed.), *Mandeville Studies* (The Hague, 1975).

Prokhovnik, R., *Spinoza and Republicanism* (Basingstoke, 2004).

Proust, Jacques, *Diderot et l'Encyclopédie* (1962; Paris, 1995).

Puisais, Eric, 'Deschamps entre Spinoza et Hegel', in E. Puisais (ed.), *Léger-Marie Deschamps, un philosophe entre Lumières et oubli* (Paris, 2001).

Quarfood, Christine, *Condillac, la statue et l'enfant* (Paris, 2002).

Quintili, Paolo, *La Pensée critique de Diderot* (Paris, 2001).

Rachum, I., *'Revolution': The Entrance of a New World into Western Political Discourse* (Lanham, Md., 1999).

Rademaker, C. S. M., *Life and Work of Gerardus Joannes Vossius (1577–1649)* (Assen, 1981).

Raeff, Marc, *Origins of the Russian Intelligentsia* (New York, 1966).

Rahe, Paul A., 'The Book that never was: Montesquieu's *Considerations on the Romans* in Historical Context', *HPTh* 26 (2005), 43–89.

Ramond, Charles, ' "Ne pas rire, mais comprendre": la réception historique et le sens général du spinozisme', *Kairos: revue de philosophie*, 11 (1998), 97–125.

Raphael, D. D., *Hobbes: Morals and Politics* (1977; new edn. 2004).

Raptschinsky, B., *Peter de Groote in Holland in 1697–1698* (Amsterdam, 1925).

Réau, Louis, *L'Europe française au siècle des Lumières* (1938; repr. Paris, 1971).

Redwood, John, *Reason, Ridicule and Religion* (London, 1976).

Rees, O. van, *Verhandeling over de* Aanwijsing der Politieke Gronden... *van Pieter de La Court* (Utrecht, 1851).

REESOR, M., *The Nature of Man in Early Stoic Philosophy* (London, 1989).

REICHARDT, ROLF, 'Einleitung' to Reichardt, Lüsebrink, and Schmitt (eds.), *HPSGF* i. 39–148.

—— and LÜSEBRINK, JANS-JÜRGEN, '*Révolution* à la fin du 18e siècle: pour une relecture d'un concept-clé du siècle des Lumières', *Mots*, 16 (1988), 35–68.

—— and SCHMITT, E. (eds.), *Handbuch politisch-sozialer Grundbegriffe in Frankreich, 1680–1820* (20 vols. thus far, Munich, 1985–96).

REILL, P. H., *The German Enlightenment and the Rise of Historicism* (Berkeley and Los Angeles, 1975).

RENAN, ERNEST, *Averroès et l'Averroisme* (Paris, 1852).

REPICI, LUCIANA, *La Natura e l'anima: saggi su Stratone di Lampsaco* (Turin, 1988).

RÉTAT, PIERRE, *Le Dictionnaire de Bayle et la lutte philosophique au XVIIIe siècle* (Paris, 1971).

—— 'Érudition et philosophie: Mirabaud et l'antiquité', in Bloch (ed.), *Matérialisme*, 91–9.

RÉVAH, I. S., *Spinoza et le Dr Juan de Prado* (Paris, 1959).

—— 'Aux origines de la rupture spinozienne', *Revue des études juives*, 123 (1964), 359–431.

—— *Des Marranes à Spinoza* (Paris, 1995).

REVENTLOW, HENNING GRAF, 'Johann Lorenz Mosheims Auseinandersetzung mit John Toland', in Mulsow et al. (eds.), *Johann Lorenz Mosheim*, 93–110.

REX, WALTER, *Pierre Bayle and Religious Controversy* (The Hague, 1965).

RIASANOVSKY, N. V., *The Image of Peter the Great in Russian History and Thought* (New York, 1985).

RICCI, SALVERIO, 'Bruno "Spinozista", Bruno "martire luterano": la polemica tra La Croze et Heumann', *GCFI* 45 (1986), 42–61.

RICHARDSON, D., 'The British Empire and the Atlantic Slave Trade, 1660–1870', in P. J. Marshall (ed.), *The Oxford History of the British Empire*, ii: *The Eighteenth Century* (Oxford, 1998), 440–64

RICHTER, L., *Leibniz und sein Russlandbild* (Berlin,1946).

RICHTER, MELVIN, 'Europe and *The Other* in Eighteenth-Century Thought', *Politisches Denken* (1997), 25–47.

—— 'Competing Concepts and Practices of Comparison in the Political and Social Thought of Eighteenth-Century Europe', *Archiv für Begriffsgeschichte*, 44 (2002), 199–219.

—— 'Towards a Lexicon of European Political and Legal Concepts: A Comparison of the *Begriffsgeschichte* and the "Cambridge School" ', *Critical Review of International Social and Political Philosophy*, 6 (2003), 91–120.

RICKEN, ULRICH, 'Condillac et le soupçon de matérialisme', in Fink and Stenger (eds.), *Être matérialiste*, 265–74.

RICUPERATI, GIUSEPPE, 'A proposito di Paolo Mattia Doria', *RSI* 91 (1979), 261–85.

—— 'Il problema della corporeità dell'anima dai libertini ai deisti', in S. Bertelli (ed.), *Il libertinismo in Europa* (Naples, 1980), 369–415.

—— ' "Universal History": innovazioni e limiti di un progetto della "Crisis della coscienza europea" ', in F. Fagiani and E. G. Valera (eds.), *Categorie del reale e storiografia* (Milan, 1986), 408–34.

—— 'Paul Hazard e la storiografia dell'illuminismo', *RSI* 86 (1974), 372–404.

—— 'In margine al *Radical Enlightenment* di Jonathan I. Israel', *RSI* 115 (2003), 285–329.

—— *Nella costellazione del* 'Triregno' (San Marco in Limis, 2004).

RIHS, CHARLES, *Voltaire: recherches sur les origines du matérialisme historique* (Paris, 1962).

—— *Les Philosophes utopistes* (Paris, 1970).

Riley, J. C., *The Seven Years War and the Old Regime in France* (Princeton, 1986).
Riley, P., 'General and Particular Will in the Political Thought of Pierre Bayle', *JHPh* 24 (1986), 173–95.
Riondato, E., and Poppi, A. (eds.), *Cesare Cremonini: aspetti del pensiero e scritti* (2 vols., Padua, 2000).
Robb, Bonnie Arden, 'The Making of Denis Diderot: Translation as Apprenticeship', *Diderot Studies*, 24(1991), 137–54.
Robbins, C., *The Eighteenth-Century Commonwealthman* (Cambridge, Mass., 1961).
Roberts, J. A. G., 'L'Image de la Chine dans l'*Encyclopédie*', *RDIE* 22 (1997), 87–105.
Robertson, John, *The Case for the Enlightenment* (Cambridge, 2005).
Robinet, André, *Malebranche et Leibniz: relations personelles* (Paris, 1955).
Rodier, G., *La Physique de Straton de Lampsaque* (Paris, 1891).
Roe, Sh. A., 'Voltaire versus Needham', *JHI* 46 (1985), 65–87.
Roger, Jacques, 'Diderot et Buffon en 1749', *Diderot Studies*, 4 (1963), 221–36.
—— *The Life Sciences in Eighteenth-Century French Thought* (1963; Stanford, Calif. 1997).
—— *Buffon: A Life in Natural History* (1989; Ithaca, NY, 1997).
Rogers, G. A. J., 'Science and British Philosophy: Boyle and Newton', in Brown(ed.), *British Philosophy and the Age of Enlightenment*, 43–68.
Rogister, John, *Louis XV and the Parlement of Paris, 1737–1755* (Cambridge, 1995).
Roldanus, C. W., 'Adriaen Paets, een Republikein uit de nadagen', *Tijdschrift voor Geschiedenis*, l (1935), 134–66.
Romani, Roberto, 'All Montesquieu's Sons: The Place of *Esprit général, Caractère national*, and *Mœurs* in French Political Philosophy, 1748–1789', *SVEC* 362 (1998), 189–235.
Romeo, C., 'Matérialisme, et déterminisme dans le *Traité de la liberté* de Fontenelle', in Bloch (ed.), *Le Matérialisme*, 101–7.
Rooden, P. T., 'Spinoza's Bijbeluitleg', *Studia Rosenthaliana*, 18 (1984), 120–33.
—— and Wesselius, J. W., 'The Early Enlightenment and Judaism', *Studia Rosenthaliana*, 21(1987), 140–5.
Roothaan, Angela, 'Pontiaan van Hattem: een vroege kentheoretische criticus van Spinoza', *Tijdschrift voor Filosofie*, 50 (1988), 525–35.
—— *Vroomheid, vrede, vrijheid: een interpretatie van Spinoza's* Tractatus theologico-politicus (Assen, 1996).
Rorty, Richard, *Consequences of Pragmatism* (Minneapolis, 1982).
—— 'The Continuity between the Enlightenment and "Postmodernism" ', in Baker and Reill (eds.), *What's Left of Enlightenment?*, 19–36.
Rosen, Stanley, *The Ancients and the Moderns: Rethinking Modernity* (New Haven, 1989).
Rosenberg, Aubrey, *Tyssot de Patot and his Work (1655–1738)* (The Hague, 1972).
—— *Nicolas Gueudeville and his Work (1652–172?)* (The Hague, 1982).
—— 'Introduction' to Simon Tyssot de Patot, *Lettres choisies*, 9–33.
Rosenthal, M. A., 'Persuasive Passions: Rhetoric and the Interpetation of Spinoza's *Theological-Political Treatise*', *AGPh* 85 (2003), 249–68.
—— 'Spinoza's Republican Argument for Toleration', *Journal of Political Philosophy*, 11 (2003), 320–37.
Rothschild, E., *Economic Sentiments: Adam Smith, Condorcet, and the Enlightenment* (Cambridge, Mass., 2001).
Rowbotham, A. H., 'The Jesuit Figurists and Eighteenth-Century Religious Thought', *JHI* 17 (1956), 471–85.

Roy, Olivier, *Leibniz et la Chine* (Paris, 1972).

Ruderman, D. B., *Jewish Enlightenment in an English Key* (Princeton, 2000).

Ruler, J. A. van, *The Crisis of Causality* (Leiden, 1995).

Russell, G. A., 'The Impact of the *Philosophus autodidactus*', in G. A. Russell (ed.), *The 'Arabick' Interest of the Natural Philosophers in Seventeenth-Century England* (Leiden, 1994), 224–65.

Rutherford, D., 'Leibniz and Mysticism', in Coudert et al. (eds.), *Leibniz*, 22–46.

Rutherford, R. B., *The Meditations of Marcus Aurelius* (Oxford, 1989).

Ruyer, R., *L'Utopie et les utopies* (Paris, 1950).

Saada, A., *Inventer Diderot: les constructions d'un auteur dans l'Allemagne des Lumières* (Paris, 2003).

Salaün, F., 'Voltaire face aux courants matérialistes de son temps', in Kölving and Mervaud (eds.), *Voltaire et ses combats*, i. 705–18.

—— *L'Ordre des mœurs: essai sur la place du matérialisme dans la société française du XVIIIe siècle (1734–1784)* (Paris, 1996).

Salmon, J. H. M., 'Liberty by Degrees: Raynal and Diderot on the British Constitution', *HPTh* 20 (1999), 87–106.

Sandbach, F. H., *The Stoics* (1975; 2nd edn. repr. London, 1994).

Sanna, Manuela, 'Un'amicizia alla luce del Cartesianesimo', in Pina Totaro (ed.), *Donne filosofia e cultura nel seicento* (Rome, 1999), 173–8.

Santinello, Giovanni (ed.), *Models of the History of Philosophy* (1991; Dordrecht, 1993).

Santucci, Antonio (ed.), *L'età dei Lumi: saggi sulla cultura settecentesca* (Bologna, 1998).

Sassen, F., *Het wijsgerig onderwijs aan de Illustre School te 's-Hertogenbosch* (Amsterdam, 1963).

Saul, J. R., *Voltaire's Bastards: The Dictatorship of Reason in the West* (New York, 1993).

Schaich, Michael, 'A War of Words? Old and New Perspectives on the Enlightenment', *Bulletin of the German Historical Institute, London*, 24 (2002), 29–56.

Schettino, E., 'The Necessity of the Minima in the Nolan Philosophy', in H. Gatti (ed.), *Giordano Bruno: Philosopher of the Renaissance* (Aldershot, 2002), 299–325.

Schilderagtige en Naeuwkeurige Brief van een Amsterdam Heer, Geschreven aan zyn Vriend te Rotterdam (Knuttel 17911) (Amsterdam, 1748) KBH.

Schilling, B. N., *Conservative England and the Case against Voltaire* (New York, 1950).

Schleich, Thomas, *Aufklärung und Revolution* (Stuttgart, 1981).

Schlenther, B. S., 'Religious Faith and Commercial Empire', in P. J. Marshall (ed.), *The Oxford History of the British Empire*, ii (Oxford, 1998), 128–50.

Schlüter, G., *Die französische Toleranzdebatte im Zeitalter der Aufklärung* (Tübingen, 1992).

Schmidt, James, *What is Enlightenment? Eighteenth-Century Answers and Twentieth-Century Questions* (Berkeley and Los Angeles, 1996).

Schmidt-Biggemann, W., 'Platonismus, Kirchen- und Ketzergeschichte: Mosheims dogmatisch-historische Kategorien', in Mulsow et al. (eds.), *Johann Lorenz Mosheim*, 193–210.

—— *Theodizee und Tatsachen. Das philosophische Profil der deutschen Aufklärung* (Frankfurt, 1988).

—— 'Jacob Bruckers philosophiegeschichtliches Konzept', in Schmidt-Biggemann and Stammen (eds.), *Jacob Brucker*, 113–34.

—— *Philosophia perennis* (Dordrecht, 2004).

—— and STAMMEN, THEO (eds.), *Jacob Brucker (1696–1770): Philosoph und Historiker der europäischen Aufklärung* (Berlin, 1998).

SCHMIDT-GLINTZER, H., ' "Atheistische" Traditionen in China', in Niewöhner and Pluta (eds.), *Atheismus*, 271–90.

SCHMITT, CH. B., and SKINNER, QU. (eds.), *The Cambridge History of Renaissance Philosophy* (Cambridge, 1988).

SCHNEEWIND, J. B., *The Invention of Autonomy: A History of Modern Moral Philosophy* (Cambridge, 1998).

—— 'Locke's Moral Philosophy', in Chappell (ed.), *Cambridge Companion to Locke*, 199–225.

SCHNEIDER, R. A., *Public Life in Toulouse, 1463–1789* (Ithaca, NY, 1989).

SCHNEIDER, ULRICH JOHANNES, 'Eclecticism and the History of Philosophy', in Kelley (ed.), *History and the Disciplines*, 83–101.

SCHOBER, ANGELIKA, 'Diderot als Philosoph', in T. Heydenreich (ed.), *Denis Diderot (1713–1784): Zeit, Werk, Wirkung. Zehn Beiträge* (Erlangen, 1984), 35–42.

SCHOLDER, KLAUS, *The Birth of Modern Critical Theology* (1966; London, 1990).

SCHÖNFELD, M., *The Philosophy of the Young Kant* (Oxford, 2000).

SCHÖRDER, P., 'Liberté et pouvoir chez Hobbes et Spinoza', in Porret and Volpilhac-Auger (eds.), *Temps de Montesquieu*, 147–69.

SCHØSLER, JØRN, 'Jaquelot et Le Clerc juges de la critique de Locke par Bayle', in *Actes du 9e congrès des Romanistes scandinaves: Helsinki 13–17 août 1984* (Helsinki, 1986), 333–9.

—— *La Bibliothèque raisonnée, 1728–1753* (Odense, 1985).

SCHOULS, P. A., *Descartes and the Enlightenment* (Edinburgh, 1989).

—— 'Descartes as Revolutionary', *Philosophia reformata*, 52 (1987), 4–23.

SCHRADER, F. E., 'Aufklärungssoziabilität in Bordeaux', in H. E. Bödecker and E. François (eds.), *Aufklärung und Politik* (Leipzig, 1996), 249–74.

SCHREINER, KLAUS, 'Toleranz', in *Geschichtliche Grundbegriffe*, 6 (1990), 524–605.

SCHRÖDER, PETER, 'Liberté et pouvoir chez Hobbes et Montesqueieu', in Porret and Volpilhac-Auger (eds.), *Le Temps de Montesquieu*, 147–69.

SCHRÖDER, WINFRIED, *Spinoza in der deutschen Frühaufklärung* (Würzburg, 1987).

—— 'Das "Symbolum sapientiae"/"Cymbalum mundi" und der *Tractatus theologico-politicus*', *Studia Spinozana*, 7 (1991), 227–39.

—— 'Il contesto storico', in *Cymbalum mundi sive Symbolum sapientiae*, 9–67.

—— *Ursprünge des Atheismus: Untersuchungen zur Metaphysik- und Religionskritik des 17. und 18. Jahrhunderts* (Stuttgart, 1998).

—— ' "Spinozam tota armenta in Belgio sequi ducem": The Reception of the Early Dutch Spinozists in Germany', in van Bunge and Klever (eds.), *Disguised and Overt Spinozism*, 157–69.

—— 'Einleitung' to Wachter, *De primordiis*, 7–28.

SCHULTE, CHRISTOPH, *Die jüdische Aufklärung: Philosophie, Religion Geschichte* (Munich, 2002).

SCHUURMAN, PAUL, 'Locke and the Dutch: A Preliminary Survey', *GWN* 11 (2000), 119–40.

SCHWARZBACH, B. E., 'La Critique biblique dans les *Examens* de la Bible et dans certains autres traités clandestins', *La Lettre clandestine*, 4 (1995), 69–86.

—— 'Les Clandestins du Père Guillaume Maleville et ses autres lectures hétérodoxes', *La Lettre clandestine*, 10 (2001), 161–82.

—— and FAIRBAIRN, A. W., 'History and Structure of our *Traité des trois imposteurs*', in S. Berti, F. Charles-Daubert, and R. H. Popkin (eds.), *Heterodoxy, Spinozism and Free Thought in Early Eighteenth-Century Europe* (Dordrecht, 1996), 75–129.

Scott, Jonathan, *England's Troubles* (Cambridge, 2000).

—— *Algernon Sidney and the Restoration Crisis, 1677–83* (Cambridge, 1991).

Scribano, Emanuela, 'Animismo, origine della religione e interpretazione delle favole da Fontenelle a Voltaire', *Annali dell'Istituto di Filosofia* (Florence), 1 (1979), 237–59.

—— 'Johannes Bredenburg (1643–1691) confutore di Spinoza?', in Cristofolini (ed.), *L'Hérésie Spinoziste*, 66–76.

Scruton, Roger, *Spinoza* (Oxford, 1986).

Secretan, Catherine, 'La Réception de Hobbes aux Pays Bas', *Studia Spinozana*, 3 (1987), 27–46.

—— 'L'Urgence et la raison', *XVIIe siècle*, 49 (1997), 265–79.

Sedley, David, 'The School, from Zeno to Arius Didymus', in Inwood (ed.), *The Cambridge Companion to the Stoics*, 7–32.

Seeber, E. D., *Anti-Slavery Opinion in France during the Second Half of the Eighteenth Century* (Baltimore, 1937).

Seidler, M. J., 'The Politics of Self-Preservation', in Hochstrasser and Schröder (eds.), *Early Modern Natural Law Theories*, 227–55.

Seif, U., 'Der missverstandene Montesquieu', *Zeitschrift für neuere Rechtsgeschichte*, 22 (2000), 149–66.

Seifert, Hans-Ulrich, ' "C'est un pays singulier celui-ci": d'Argens et l'Allemagne', in Seifert and Seban (eds.), *Marquis d'Argens*, 231–53.

—— and Seban, Jean-Loup (eds.), *Der Marquis d'Argens* (Wiesbaden, 2004).

Sejten, A. E., *Diderot ou le défi esthétique* (Paris, 1999).

Sella, Domenico, *Italy in the Seventeenth Century* (London, 1997).

Senarclens, Vanessa de, *Montesquieu, historien de Rome* (Geneva, 2003).

Setton, K. M., *Venice, Austria and the Turks in the Seventeenth Century* (Philadelphia, 1991).

Sévérac, P., 'Convenir avec soi, convenir avec autrui: éthique stoïcienne et éthique spinoziste', *Studia Spinozana*, 12 (1996), 105–19.

Sgard, Jean, 'Diderot vu par les *Nouvelles ecclésiastiques*' *RDl'E* 25 (1998), pp. 9–19.

Shank, J. B., 'Before Voltaire: Newtonianism and the Origins of the Enlightenment in France, 1687–1734' (unpublished Stanford University doctoral thesis, 2000).

Shapin, Steven, *The Scientific Revolution* (Chicago, 1996).

Sharif, M. M. (ed.), *A History of Muslim Philosophy* (2 vols., Wiesbaden, 1963–6).

Sharpe, Kevin, ' "An Image Doting Rabble": The Failure of Republican Culture in Seventeenth-Century England', in K. Sharpe and S. N. Zwicker (eds.), *Refiguring Revolutions* (Berkeley and Los Angeles, 1998), 25–56.

Sheehan, Jonathan, *The Enlightenment Bible: Translation, Scholarship, Culture* (Princeton, 2005).

Sheridan, G., *Nicolas Lenglet Dufresnoy and the Literary Underworld of the* Ancien régime (Oxford, 1989).

Shklar, J. N., 'Jean d'Alembert and the Rehabilitation of History', *JHI* 42 (1981), 643–64.

Simon, R., *Henry de Boulainvillier: historien politique, philosophe, astrologue, 1658–1722* (Paris, n.d.).

Simonutti, L., *Arminianesimo e tolleranza nei Seicento olandese* (Florence, 1984).

—— 'Bayle and Le Clerc as Readers of Cudworth: Elements of the Debate on Plastic Nature in the Dutch Learned Journals', *GWN* 4 (1993), 147–66.

—— 'Between Political Loyalty and Religious Liberty: Political Theory and Toleration in Huguenot Thought in the Epoch of Bayle', *HPTh* 17 (1996), 523–54.

—— 'Religion, Philosophy, and Science: John Locke and Limborch's Circle in Amsterdam', in Force and Katz (eds.), *Everything Connects*, 293–324.

—— 'Absolute, Universal and Inviolable Liberty of Conscience', in Méchoulan *et al.* (eds.), *Formazione*, ii. 707–49.

—— 'Premières réactions anglaises au *Traité théologico-politique*', in Cristofolini, *L'Hérésie spinoziste*, 123–37.

SINA, MARIO, *L'avvento della ragione* (Milan, 1976).

—— *Vico e Le Clerc: tra filosofia e filologia* (Naples, 1978).

—— 'Le *Dictionaire historique et critique* de Pierre Bayle à travers la correspondance de Jean Le Clerc', in Bots (ed.), *Critique, savoir et érudition*, 217–33.

SKINNER, QUENTIN, 'Meaning and Understanding in the History of Ideas', *History and Theory*, 8 (1969), 3–53.

—— *Reason and Rhetoric in the Philosophy of Hobbes* (Cambridge, 1996).

—— *Liberty before Liberalism* (Cambridge, 1998).

SKRZYPEK, MARIAN, 'Le Libertinisme polonais et la littérature clandestine', in McKenna and Mothu (eds.), *La Philosophie clandestine*, 509–20.

SLEE, J. C. VAN, *De Rijnsburger Collegianten* (1895, repr. Utrecht, 1980).

SLUIS, JACOB VAN, *Herman Alexander Röell* (Leeuwarden, 1998).

SMET, RUDOLF DE, *Hadrianus Beverlandus (1650–1716)* (Brussels, 1988).

SMITH, D. W., *Helvétius: A Study in Persecution* (Oxford, 1965).

SMITH, G. L., *Religion and Trade in New Netherland* (Ithaca, NY, 1973).

SMITH, S. B., 'Spinoza's Democratic Turn: Chapter 16 of the *Theologico-Political Treatise*', *Review of Metaphysics*, 48 (1994), 359–88.

—— *Spinoza, Liberalism and the Question of Jewish Identity* (New Haven, 1997).

—— *Spinoza's Book of Life: Freedom and Redemption in the* Ethics (New Haven, 2003).

—— 'What Kind of Democrat was Spinoza?', *Political Theory* 33 (2005), 6–27.

SORELL, TOM (ed.), *The Rise of Modern Philosophy* (Oxford, 1993).

SORKIN, D., 'The Early Haskalah', in Shmuel Feiner and D. Sorkin (eds.), *New Perspectives on the Haskalah* (London, 2001), 9–27.

—— *The Berlin Haskalah and German Religious Thought* (London, 2000).

SPALDING, P. S., *Seize the Book, Jail the Author: Johann Lorenz Schmidt and Censorship in Eighteenth-Century Germany* (West Lafayette, Ind., 1998).

SPALLANZANI, M., *Immagini di Descartes nell'*Encyclopédie (Bologna, 1990).

SPANG, R. L., 'Paradigms and Paranoia: How Modern is the French Revolution?', *American Historical Review*, 108 (2003), 119–47.

SPANGLER, M., 'Science, philosophie et littérature: le polype de Diderot', *RDIE* 23 (1997), 89–107.

SPANNEUT, MICHEL, *Permanence du stoïcisme de Zenon à Malraux* (Gembloux, 1973).

SPARN, WALTER, 'Die Krise der protestantischen Orthodoxie, gespiegelt in ihrer Auseinandersetzung mit Spinoza', in Gründer and Schmidt-Biggemann (eds.), *Spinoza in der Frühzeit*, 27–63.

—— 'Omnis nostra fides pendet ab historia', in Mulsow and Zedelmaier (eds.), *Skepsis, Providenz, Polyhistorie*, 76–94.

SPECK, WILLIAM, 'Britain and Dutch Republic', in K. Davids and J. Lucassen (eds.), *A Miracle Mirrored* (Cambridge, 1995), 173–95.

—— *Reluctant Revolutionaries: Englishmen and the Revolution of 1688* (Oxford, 1988).

SPECTOR, CELINE, 'Des *Lettres persanes* à L'Esprit des lois', in Larrère and Volpilhac-Auger (eds.), *1748, l'année*, 177–39.

Spellman, W. M., *The Latitudinarians and the Church of England, 1660–1700* (Athens, Ga., 1993).

Spence, Jonathan, *The Question of Hu* (London, 1988).

—— *The Gate of Heavenly Peace: The Chinese and their Revolution, 1895–1980* (London, 1982).

Spink, J. S., *French Free-Thought from Gassendi to Voltaire* (London, 1960).

—— 'Un abbé philosophe: l'affaire de J. M. de Prades', *DHS* 3 (1971), 145–80.

Spitz, Jean-Fabien, 'Quelques difficultés de la théorie lockienne de la tolérance', in Zarka *et al.* (eds.) *Fondements, philosophiques*, i. 114–50.

Sprigge, T. L. S., 'Is Spinozism a Religion?', *Studia Spinozana*, 11 (1995), 137–63.

Spruit, Leen, 'Introduzione' to Jelles, *Belydenisse*, pp. xiii–lxiii.

Squadrito, K., 'Locke and the Dispossession of the American Indian', in Ward and Lott (eds.), *Philosophers on Race*, 101–24.

Stancati, Claudia, 'La *Dissertation sur la formation du monde* et les origines du matérialisme', in Bloch (ed.), *Matérialisme*,109–13.

—— 'Introduction' to *Disseration sur la formation du monde*, ed C. Stancati (Paris, 2001), 9–21.

Stedman Jones, G., *An End to Poverty?* (London, 2004).

Steenbakkers, Piet, *Spinoza's* Ethica *from Manuscript to Print* (Assen, 1994).

—— 'Johannes Braun (1628–1708), Cartesiaan in Groningen', *NAKG* 77 (1997), 198–210.

—— 'Spinoza over verdraagzaamheid', in Martels et al. (eds.), *Limae labor et mora*, 189–94.

Stein, Heinrich von, 'Der Streit über den angeblichen Platonismus der Kirchenvater, *Zeitschrift für die historische Theologie*, 31 (1861), pp. 319–418.

Steinmetz, P., 'Xenophanesstudien', *Rheinisches Museum für Philologie*, NS 109 (1966), 13–73.

Stenger, G., 'Le Matérialisme de Voltaire', in Fink and Stenger (eds.), *Être matérialiste*, 275–85.

—— 'L'Atomisme dans les *Pensées philosophiques*', *DHS* 35 (2003), 75–100.

—— 'La Théorie de la connaissance dans la *Lettre sur les aveugles*', *RDIE* 26 (1999), 99–111.

Stewart, J. B., *Opinion and Reform in Hume's Political Philosophy* (Princeton, 1992).

Stewart, M. A., 'Religion and Rational Theology', in Broadie (ed.), *Scottish Enlightenment*, 31–59.

—— 'Hume's Historical View of Miracles', in Stewart and Wright (eds.), *Hume*, 171–200.

—— Wright J. P., (eds.), *Hume and Hume's Connexions* (Edinburgh, 1994).

Stewart, Mathew, *The Courtier and the Heretic* (New Haven and London, 2005).

Stiehler, Gottfried, 'Gabriel Wagner (Realis de Vienna)', in G. Stiehler (ed.), *Beiträge zur Geschichte des vormarxistischen Materialismus* (Berlin, 1961), 63–123.

Stinger, Ch. L., *The Renaissance in Rome* (1985; repr. Bloomington, Ind., 1998).

Stone, H. S., *Vico's Cultural History, 1685–1750* (Leiden, 1997).

Stough, Ch., 'Stoic Determinism and Moral Responsibility', in J. M. Rist (ed.), *The Stoics* (Berkeley and Los Angles, 1978), 203–31.

Stoye, J., 'Europe and the Revolutions of 1688', in R. Beddard (ed.), *The Revolutions of 1688* (Oxford, 1991), 191–212.

Straka, G. M., 'Sixteen Eighty-Eight as the Year One: Eighteenth-Century Attitudes towards the Glorious Revolution', in L. T. Milic (ed.), *The Modernity of the Eighteenth Century* (Cleveland, 1971).

Strauss, Leo, *Spinoza's Critique of Religion* (1930; Chicago, 1997).

Stroumsa, G. G., 'Richard Simon: From Philology to Comparison', *Archiv für Religionsgeschichte* 3 (2001), 89–107.

Stroumsa, Sarah, *Freethinkers of Medieval Islam* (Leiden, 1999).

—— 'The Religion of the Freethinkers of Medieval Islam', in Niewöhner and Pluta (eds.), *Atheismus*, 45–59.

—— and Stroumsa G. G., 'Aspects of Anti-Manichaean Polemics in Late Antiquity and under Early Islam', *Harvard Theological Review*, 81 (1988), 37–58.

Stuurman, Siep, 'The Canon of the History of Political Thought: Its Critique and a Proposed Alternative', *History and Theory* 39 (2000), 147–66.

—— 'François Bernier and the Invention of Racial Classification', *History Workshop Journal*, 50 (2000), 1–21.

—— 'Pathways to the Enlightenment', *History Workshop Journal*, 54 (2002), 227–35.

—— *François Poulain de La Barre and the Invention of Modern Equality* (Cambridge, Mass., 2004).

—— 'The Voice of Thersites: Reflections on the Origins of the Idea of Equality', *JHI* (2004), 171–89.

—— 'How to Write a History of Equality', *Leidschrift*, 19 (2004), forthcoming.

Suchtelen, G. van, 'Franciscus van den Enden', in Dethier and Vandenbossche (eds.), *Woordenboek*, ii. 141–8.

—— '*Nil volentibus arduum*; les amis de Spinoza au travail', *Studia Spinozana*, 3 (1987), 391–404.

Susong, Gilles, 'Montesquieu, La Beaumelle, Genève', in Porret and Volpilhac-Auger (eds.), *Temps de Montesquieu*.

Sutcliffe, Adam, *Judaism and Enlightenment* (Cambridge, 2003).

—— 'Sephardi Amsterdam and the European Radical Enlightenment', in J. Targarona Borrás and A. Sáenz-Badillos (eds.), *Jewish Studies at the Turn of the Twentieth Century* (Leiden, 1999), 399–405.

—— 'Can a Jew Be a *Philosophe*? Isaac de Pinto, Voltaire and Jewish Participation in the European Enlightenment', *Jewish Social Studies*, 6 (2000), 31–51.

—— 'Judaism and Jewish Arguments in the Clandestine Radical Enlightenment', in Paganini et al. (eds.), *Scepticisme*, 97–113.

Swart, K. W., *The Miracle of the Dutch Republic as Seen in the Seventeenth Century* (Inaugural Lecture; University College London) (London, 1969).

Symcox, G., *Victor Amadeus II: Absolutism in the Savoyard State, 1675–1730* (Berkeley, 1983).

Szechi, Daniel, 'The Image of the Court: Idealism, Politics and the Evolution of the Stuart Court, 1689–1730', in E. Corp (ed.), *The Stuart Court in Rome* (Aldershot, 2003), 49–64.

Talmon, J. L., *The Origins of Totalitarian Democracy* (1952; London, 1970).

Taranto, Pascal, *Du déisme à l'athéisme: la libre-pensée d'Anthony Collins* (Paris, 2000).

Tarin, R., *Diderot et la Révolution française* (Paris, 2001).

Taylor, Charles, *Sources of the Self* (1989; Cambridge, Mass., 9th printing, 2000).

Terrall, M., *The Man who Flattened the Earth: Maupertuis and the Sciences* (Chicago, 2002).

Thijssen-Schoute, C. L., 'Lodewijk Meyer en diens verhouding tot Descartes en Spinoza', *MvSH* (Leiden, 1954).

—— *Nederlands Cartesianisme* (1954; repr. Utrecht, 1989).

Thomas, Keith, *Religion and the Decline of Magic* (1971; new edn. New York, 1997).

THOMSON, ANN, *Barbary and Enlightenment* (Leiden, 1987).

—— 'D'Argens et le monde islamique', in Vissière (ed.), *Marquis d'Argens*, 167–79.

—— 'L' *Examen de la religion*', in Canziani (ed.), *Filosofia e religione*, 355–72.

—— 'La Mettrie et la littérature clandestine', in Bloch (ed), *Matérialisme*, 235–44.

THOMSON, ANN, 'L'Utilisation de l'Islam dans la literature clandestine', in McKenna and Mothu (eds.), *La Philosophie clandestine*, 247–56.

—— 'Le Bonheur matérialiste selon La Mettrie', Fink and Stenger (eds.), *Être matérialiste*, 299–314.

—— 'Le *Discourse of Free-Thinking* d'Anthony Collins et sa traduction française', *La Lettre clandestine*, 9 (2000), 95–116.

—— 'Déterminisme et passions', in Moreau and Thomson (eds.), *Matérialisme*, 79–95.

—— 'La Mettrie ou la machine infernale', *Corpus*, 5/6 (1999), 15–26.

—— 'La Mettrie et l'épicurisme', in G. Paganini and E. Tortarolo (eds.), *Der Garten und die Moderne* (Stuttgart, 2004), 361–81.

TIETZ, M., 'Diderot und das Spanien der Aufklärung', in T. Heydenreich (ed.), *Denis Diderot (1713–1784): Zeit, Werk, Wirkung* (Erlangen, 1985), 127–50.

TILLET, E., *La Constitution anglaise, un modèle politique et institutionnel dans la France des Lumières* (Aix-en-Provence, 2001).

TINSLEY, B. S., *Pierre Bayle's Reformation* (Selinsgrove, Pa., 2001).

TODD, R. B., 'Monism and Immanence: The Foundations of Stoic Physics', in J. M. Rist (ed.), *The Stoics* (Berkeley and Los Angeles, 1978).

TOELLNER, R. (ed.), *Aufklärung und Humanismus*, Wolfenbütteler Studien zur Aufklärung 6 (Heidelberg, 1980).

TOMASONI, FRANCESCO, 'Il "sistema intellettuale" di Cudworth fra l'edizione originale e la traduzione Latina di Mosheim', *RCSF* 46 (1991), 629–60.

—— 'Critica al Cartesianesimo nella filosofia eclecttica di Christian Thomasius', in M. T. Marcialis and F. M. Crasta (eds.), *Descartes e l'eredità cartesiana nell'Europa sei-settecentesca* (Lecce, 2002), 147–69.

TORREY, N. L., 'Voltaire's Reaction to Diderot', *Proceedings of the Modern Language Association of America*, 50 (1935), 1107–47.

TORTAROLO, EDOARDO, *L'Illuminismo* (Rome, 1999).

—— *La ragione interpretata: la mediazione culturale tra Italia e Germania nell'età dell'Illuminismo* (Rome, 2003).

—— 'Hatzfeld: la vita di un radicale tedesco nella prima metà del XVIII secolo', *RSI* 116 (2004), 812–33.

—— 'Epicurus and Diderot', in G. Paganini and E. Tortarolo (eds.), *Der Garten und die Moderne* (Stuttgart, 2004), 383–98.

TOTARO, PINA, 'Niels Stensen (1638–1686) e la prima diffusione della filosofia di Spinoza nella Firenze di Cosimo III', in Cristofolini (ed.), *L'Hérésie Spinoziste*, 147–68.

—— 'La formazione storica dell'alterità in Spinoza', in *La formazione storica della alterità studi di storia della tolleranza nell'età moderna offerti a Antonio Rotondò*, ii (Florence, 2001), 577–94.

TRAPNELL, W. H., 'Peut-on dégager une pensée cohérente des écrits de Woolston?', *Revue de l'histoire des religions*, 213 (1996), 321–44.

TREVOR-ROPER, HUGH, *Religion, the Reformation and Social Change* (London, 1967).

TRINKHAUS, CHARLES, *In our Image and Likeness* (2 vols., London, 1970).

TROUSSON, RAYMOND, 'Voltaire et le Marquis d'Argens', *Studi francesi*, 29 (1966), 226–39.

—— 'Diderot helléniste', *Diderot Studies*, 12 (1969), 141–326.

——*Jean-Jacques Rousseau* (Paris, 2003).

——'Le Cosmopolitisme du marquis d'Argens', in Seifert and Seban (eds.), *Marquis d'Argens*, 15–34.

——*Denis Diderot ou le vrai Prométhée* (Paris, 2005).

TUCK, RICHARD, *Philosophy and Government, 1572–1651* (Cambridge, 1993).

——*Natural Rights Theories* (Cambridge, 1982).

TULLY, JAMES, 'Rediscovering America: The *Two Treatises* and Aboriginal Rights', in G. A. J. Rogers (ed.) *Locke's Philosophy* (Oxford, 1994), 165–96.

TURCHETTI, MARIO, 'La Liberté de conscience et l'autorité du magistrat au lendemain de la Révocation', in H. R. Guggisberg, F. Lestringant, and J. C. Margolin (eds.), *La Liberté de conscience (XVIe–XVIIe siècles)* (Geneva, 1991), 289–367.

——'Élie Saurin (1639–1703) et ses *Réflexions sur les droits de conscience*', in Berkevens-Stevelinck et al. (eds.), *Emergence of Tolerance*, 173–97.

TURCO, LUIGI, 'Moral Sense and the Foundations of Morals', in Broadie (ed.), *Scottish Enlightenment*, 136–56.

TYACKE, NICHOLAS, 'Introduction', in O. P. Grell, J. I. Israel, and N. Tyacke (eds.), *From Persecution to Toleration* (Oxford, 1991), 1–16.

——'The "Rise of Puritanism" and the Legalizing of Dissent, 1571–1719' in O. P. Grell, J. I. Israel, and N. Tyacke (eds.), *From Persecution to Toleration* (Oxford, 1991), 17–49.

——'Arminianism and the Theology of the Restoration Church', in S. Groenveld and M. Wintle (eds.), *Britain and the Netherlands*, xi (Zutphen, 1994), 68–83.

——'Religious Controversy', in Tyacke (ed.), *Seventeenth-Century Oxford*, 569–619.

——(ed.), *Seventeenth-Century Oxford: The History of the University of Oxford*, (Oxford, 1997).

UMBACH, M., *Federalism and Enlightenment in Germany, 1740–1806* (London, 2000).

URVOY, DOMINIQUE, 'Ibn Rushd', in Nasr and Leaman (eds.), *History*, 330–45.

——'La Démystification de la religion dans les textes attribués à Ibn al-Muqaffa', in Niewöhner and Pluta (eds.), *Atheismus*, 85–94.

UZGALIS, W., 'On Locke and Racism', in Ward and Lott (eds.), *Philosophers on Race*, 81–100.

——'An Inconsistency not to be Excused: On Locke and Racism', in J. K. Ward and T. L. Lott (eds.), *Philosophers on Race* (Oxford, 2002), 81–100.

VAMBOULIS, E., 'La Discussion de l'attraction chez Voltaire', in De Gandt (ed.), *Cirey*, 159–70.

VANDENBOSSCHE, HUBERT, 'Quelques idées politiques de Koerbagh', *TSV* 6 (1978), 223–40.

——'Adriaan en Jan Koerbagh', in Dethier and Vandenbossche (eds.), *Woordenboek*, i. 167–92.

——'Hendrik Wyermars', in Dethier and Vandenbossche (eds.), *Woordenboek*, i. 281–7.

VAN DER BIJL, M., 'Pieter de La Court en de politieke werkelijkheid', in H. W. Blom and I. W. Wildenberg (eds.), *Pieter de La Court in zijn tijd* (Amsterdam, 1986), 65–91.

VAN KLEY, D. K., 'Christianity as Casualty and Chrysalis of Modernity', *American Historical Review*, 108 (2003), 1081–104.

——*The Damiens Affair* (Princeton, 1984).

——*The Religious Origins of the French Revolution* (New Haven, 1996).

VANPAEMEL, G., 'The Culture of Mathematics in the Early Dutch Enlightenment', in van Bunge (ed), *Early Enlightenment*, 197–211.

VARLOOT, JEAN, 'Introduction' to Diderot, *Textes choisies* (3 vols., Paris, 1952).

VARTANIAN, ARAM, 'From Deist to Atheist: Diderot's Philosophical Orientation, 1746–1749', *Diderot Studies*, 1 (1949), 46–63.

——'La Mettrie and Diderot', *Diderot Studies*, 21 (1983), 155–97.

Vartanian, Aram, 'Quelques réflexions sur le concept d'âme dans la littérature clandestine', in Bloch (ed.), *Matérialisme*, 149–65.

—— *La Mettrie's* L'Homme machine: *A Study in the Origins of an Idea* (Princeton, 1960).

—— 'Diderot and Maupertuis', *Revue internationale de Philosophie*, 38 (1984), 46–56.

Vasoli, Cesare, 'Vico, Tommaso d'Aquino e il Tomismo', *BCSV* 4 (1974), 5–35.

—— 'Der Mythos der *Prisci theologi* als "Ideologie" der *Renovatio*', in Mulsow (ed.), *Ende des Hermetismus*, 17–60.

—— 'Reflessioni sul "problema" Vanini', in S. Bertelli (ed.), *Il libertinismo in Europa* (Naples, 1980), 125–67.

—— 'Vanini e il suo processo per ateismo', in Niewöhner and Pluta (eds.), *Atheismus*, 129–44.

Vaz Dias, A. M., and Tak, W. G. van der, 'Spinoza Merchant and Autodidact', *Studia Rosenthaliana*, 16 (1982), 113–95.

Velema, W. R. E., 'Verlichting in Nederland: het voorbeeld van de politieke theorie', *GWN* s (1994), 45–53.

—— 'Introduction to Élie Luzac's *An Essay on Freedom of Expression*', in J. Ch. Laursen and J. vander Zande (eds.), *Early French and German Defenses of Freedom of the Press* (Leiden, 2003), 11–33.

Venturi, Franco, *Jeunesse de Diderot (1713–1753)* (Paris, 1939).

—— *L'antichità svelata e l'idea del progreso in N. A. Boulanger (1722–1759)* (Bari, 1947).

—— *Pagine repubblicane* (Turin, 2004).

—— *Alberto Radicati di Passerano* (1954; new edn. Turin, 2005).

—— *Utopia and Reform in the Enlightenment* (Cambridge, 1971).

Venturino, Diego, *La ragioni della tradizione* (Turin, 1993).

Verbeek, Theo, *Descartes and the Dutch* (Carbondale, Ill., 1992).

—— *Spinoza's Theological-political Treatise: Exploring 'The Will of God'* (Aldershot, 2003).

—— 'Spinoza on Theocracy and Democracy', in Force and Katz, *Everything Connects*, 325–38.

—— 'Baruch de Spinoza', in Kors (ed.), *Encyclopedia*, iv. 117–20.

Vercruysse, J., *Voltaire et la Hollande* (Geneva, 1966).

Verene, D. Ph., *Vico's Science of the Imagination* (1981; Ithaca, NY, Repr., 1994).

Vermij, Rink, *Secularisering en natuurwetenschap in de zeventiende en achttiende eeuw: Bernard Nieuwetijt* (Amsterdam, 1991).

—— 'The Formation of the Newtonian philosophy', *BJHS* 36 (2003), 183–200.

—— *The Calvinist Copernicans* (Amsterdam, 2002)

—— (ed.), *Bernard Nieuwentijt: een zekere, zakelijke wijsbegeerte* (Baarn, 1988).

Vernière, Paul, *Spinoza et la pensée française avant la Révolution* (1954; 2nd edn. Paris, 1982).

—— 'Introduction' to Diderot, *Œuvres philosophiques*, pp. i–xl.

Vichert, G. S., 'Bernard Mandeville's *The Virgin Unmask'd*', in Primer (ed.), *Mandeville Studies*, 1–10.

Vinciguerra, Lorenzo, *Spinoza et le signe: la genèse de l'imagination* (Paris, 2005).

Vissière, Jean-Louis (ed.), *Le Marquis d'Argens: colloque international de 1988* (Aix-en-Provence, 1990).

Vliet, Rietje van, *Élie Luzac (1721–1796)* (n.p. 2005)

Voelke, André-Jean, *L'Idée de volonté dans le stoïcisme* (Paris, 1973).

Volpilhac-Auger, Catherine, 'Nicolas Fréret: histoire d'un image', in Grell and Volpilhac-Auger (eds.), *Nicolas Fréret*, 3–16.

——'Lire en 1748: l'année merveilleuse?', in Larrère and Volpilhac-Auger (eds.), *1748, l' année*, 47–60.

Voogt, N. J. de, *De Doelistenbeweging te Amsterdam in 1748* (Utrecht, 1914).

Vovelle, Michel, *Piété baroque et déchristianisation en Provence au XVIIIe siècle* (n.p., 1973).

Vrijer, M. J. A. de, *Petrus van Balen, medicinae et juris doctor* (Utrecht, 1928).

Vucinich, A., *Science in Russian Culture: A History to 1860* (2 vols., London, 1963).

Wade, I. O., *The Clandestine Organization and Diffusion of Philosophic Ideas in France from 1700 to 1750* (Princeton, 1938).

——*Studies on Voltaire* (Princeton, 1947).

Wade, I. O., *The Intellectual Development of Voltaire* (Princeton, 1969).

——*The Intellectual Origins of the French Enlightenment* (Princeton, 1971).

——*The Structure and Form of the French Enlightenment* (2 vols., Princeton, 1977).

Wagner, Nicolas, *Morelly, le méconnu des Lumières* (Paris, 1978).

Wal, G. A. van der, 'Politieke vrijheid en demokratie bij Spinoza', *MvSH* 41 (1980).

Waldron, Jeremy, *God, Locke, and Equality* (Cambridge, 2002).

Walker, D. P., *The Decline of Hell* (London, 1964).

——*Spiritual and Demonic Magic from Ficino to Campanella* (1958; repr. University Park, Pa., 2000).

Wall, Ernestine van der, *De mystieke chiliast Petrus Serrarius (1600–1669) en zijn wereld* (Leiden, 1987).

——'Cartesianism and Cocceianism: A Natural Alliance?', in Magdalaine et al. (eds.), *De l'humanisme aux Lumières*, 445–55.

——'Orthodoxy and Scepticism in the Early Dutch Enlightenment', in Popkin and Vanderjagt (eds.), *Scepticism and Irreligion*, 121–41.

——'The *Tractatus theologico-politicus* and Dutch Calvinism', *Studia Spinozana*, 11 (1995), 201–26.

——'The Religious Context of the Early Dutch Enlightenment', in van Bunge (ed.), *Early Enlightenment*, 39–57.

Walters, R. L., 'Voltaire and Mme. Du Châtelet's continuing Scientific Quarrel', in Kölving and Mervaud (eds.), *Voltaire et ses combats*, ii. 889–99.

——'La Querelle des forces vives et le rôle de Mme Du Châtelet', in De Gandt (ed.), *Cirey*, 198–211.

——Barber, W. H., 'Introduction' to Voltaire, *Eléments*.

Walther, Manfred, 'Die Transformation des Naturrechts in der Rechtsphilosophie Spinozas', *Studia Spinozana*, 1 (1985), 73–104.

——'Biblische Hermeneutik und/oder theologische Politik bei Hobbes und Spinoza', in Bostrenghi (ed.), *Hobbes e Spinoza*, 623–69.

——'Philosophy and Politics in Spinoza', *Studia Spinozana*, 9 (1993), 49–57.

——'Spinoza's Critique of Miracles: A Miracle of Criticism?', in G. Hunter (ed.), *Spinoza: The Enduring Questions* (Toronto, 1994), 100–12.

——'Biblische Hermeneutik und historische Erklärung: Lodewijk Meyer und Benedikt de Spinoza', *Studia Spinozana*, 11 (1995), 227–300.

——'*Machina civilis* oder Von deutscher Freiheit', in P. Cristofolini (ed.), *L'Hérésie spinoziste* (Amsterdam, 1991), 184–221.

Walzer, Michael, et al. (eds.), *The Jewish Political Tradition*, vol. i (New Haven, 2000).

WAQUET, FRANÇOISE (ed.), *Mapping the World of Learning: The* Polyhistor *of Daniel Georg Morhof* (Wiesbaden, 2000).

WARD, J. K., and LOTT, T. L. (eds.), *Philosophers on Race: Critical Essays* (Oxford, 2002).

WARE, TIMOTHY, *Eustratios Argenti: A Study of the Greek Church under Turkish Rule* (Oxford, 1964).

WARTOFSKY, M. W., 'Diderot and the Development of Materialist Monism', *Diderot Studies*, 2 (1952), 279–329.

WATSON, G., 'The Natural Law and Stoicism', in Long (ed.), *Problems*, 216–38.

WATSON, R. A., *The Breakdown of Cartesian Metaphysics* (Atlantic Highlands, NJ, 1987).

WEEKHOUT, I., *Boekencensuur in de Noordelijke Nederlanden: de vrijheid van drukpers in de zeventiende eeuw* (The Hague, 1998).

WEHRLI, F., *Die Schule des Aristoteles: Texte und Kommentar*, v: *Straton von Lampsakos* (Basel, 1950).

WEIL, FRANÇOISE, 'La Diffusion en France avant 1750 d'éditions de textes dits clandestins', in Bloch (ed.), *Matérialisme*, 207–11.

WELLMAN, K., *La Mettrie: Medicine, Philosophy, and Enlightenment* (Durham, NC, 1992).

WERTHEIM-GIJSE WEENINK, A. H., *Democratische bewegingen in Gelderland, 1672–1795* (Amsterdam, 1973).

WEST, M. L., 'Towards Monotheism', in Athanassiadi and Frede (eds.), *Pagan Monotheism*, 21–40.

WESTERMAN, P. C., *The Disintegration of Natural Law Theory* (Leiden, 1998).

WESTFALL, RICHARD, *The Life of Isaac Newton* (Cambridge, 1993).

WHALEY, JOACHIM, *Religious Toleration and Social Change in Hamburg 1529–1819* (Cambridge, 1985).

—— 'A Tolerant Society? Religious Toleration in the Holy Roman Empire, 1648–1806', in O. P. Grell and Roy Porter (eds.), *Toleration in Enlightenment Europe* (Cambridge, 2000), 175–95.

WHELAN, RUTH, *The Anatomy of Superstition: A Study of the Historical Theory and Practice of Pierre Bayle* (Oxford, 1989).

—— 'The Wisdom of Simonides: Bayle and La Mothe le Vayer', in Popkin and Vanderjagt (eds.), *Scepticism and Irreligion*, 230–53.

—— 'Reason and Belief: the Bayle–Jacquelot Debate', *RCSF* 48 (1993), 101–10.

WHITE, R. J., *The Anti-Philosophers: A Study of the Philosophes in Eighteenth-Century France* (London, 1970).

WHITMORE, P. J. S., 'Bayle's Criticism of Locke', in Dibon (ed.), *Pierre Bayle*, 81–96.

WIELEMA, M. A., *Filosofen aan de Maas* (Baarn, 1991).

—— 'Een onbekende aanhanger van Spinoza: Antony van Dalen (1644–na1690)', *GWN* 4 (1993), 23–40.

—— 'Spinoza in Zeeland: The Growth and Suppression of "Popular Spinozism" (*c.*1700–1720)', in van Bunge and Klever (eds), *Disguised and Overt Spinozism*, 103–15.

—— '"Dezen groten, verhevenen tekst onzer hora!": het verlichtingsbegrip van Bernard Nieuhoff', *GWN* 5v (1994), 169–92.

—— 'Ketters en Verlichters: de invloed van het Spinozisme en Wolfianisme op de Verlichting in Gereformeerd Nederland' (doctoral thesis of the Free University of Amsterdam, 1999).

—— 'Frederik van Leenhof, een radicale Spinozist?', *MSJCW* 25 (2002), 13–19.

—— 'Johann Conrad Franz von Hatzfeld (*c*.1685–na 1751)', in A. de Hass (ed.) *Achter slot en grendel* (Zutphen, 2002), 82–92.

—— 'Adriaan Koerbagh: Biblical Criticism and Enlightenment', in van Bunge (ed.), *Early Enlightenment*, 61–80.

—— *The March of the Libertines: Spinozists and the Dutch Reformed Church (1660–1750)* (Hilversum, 2004).

Wijngaards, G. N. M., *De 'Bibliothèque choisie' van Jean Le Clerc (1657–1736)* (Amsterdam, 1986).

Wildenberg, I. W., 'Appreciaties van de gebroeders de La Court ten tijde van de Republiek', *Tijdschrift voor Geschiedenis*, 98 (1985), 540–56.

—— *Johan en Pieter de La Court (1622–1660 & 1618–1685)* (Amsterdam, 1986).

Wille, Dagmar von, 'Apologie häretischen Denkens: Johann Jakob Zimmermanns Rehabilitierung der "Atheisten" Pomponazzi und Vanini', in Niewöhner and Pluta (eds.), *Atheismus*, 215–37.

Willey, Basil, *The Eighteenth-Century Background* (Harmondsworth, 1962).

Williams, Bernard, *Truth and Truthfulness* (Princeton, 2002).

Williams, David, *Condorcet and Modernity* (Cambridge, 2004).

Wilson, Catherine, *Leibniz's Metaphysics* (Manchester, 1989).

Wing-Tsit Chan, 'The Study of Chu Hsi in the West', *Journal of Asian Studies*, 35 (1976), 555–75.

Winkle, Stefan, *Die heimlichen Spinozisten in Altona und der Spinozastreit* (Hamburg, 1988).

Wladimiroff, Igor, 'Andries Winius and Nicolaas Witsen: Tsar Peter's Dutch Connection', in C. Horstmeier et al., *Around Peter the Great* (Groningen, 1997), 5–23.

Woitkewitsch, Thomas, 'Thomasius' "Monatgespräche": Eine Charakteristik', *Archiv für Geschichte des Buchwesens*, 10 (1969/70), 655–78.

Wokler, Robert, 'The Enlightenment Project as Betrayed by Modernity', *History of European Ideas*, 24 (1998), 301–13.

—— *Rousseau* (1995; Oxford, new edn. 1996).

Woldring, H. E. S., *Identiteit en tolerantie: Nederlandse filosofen aan het begin van de nieuwe tijd* (Baarn, 1995).

Wolff, L., *Inventing Eastern Europe* (Stanford, Calif., 1994).

—— *The Enlightenment and the Orthodox World* (Athens, 2001).

Wolff, Michael, 'Hipparchus and the Stoic Theory of Motion', in J. Barnes and M. Mignucci (eds.), *Matter and Metaphysics* (Naples, 1989), 346–419.

Wolfson, H. A., *The Philosophy of Spinoza* (1934; Cambridge, Mass., 1962).

Wolheim, R., 'Introduction' to R. Wolheim (ed.), *Hume on Religion* (1966; London, 1971), 7–30.

Wolin, Richard, *The Seduction of Unreason: The Intellectual Romance with Fascism from Nietzsche to Postmodernism* (Princeton, 2004).

Wollgast, S., 'Spinoza und die deutsche Frühaufklärung', *Studia Spinozana*, 9 (1993), 163–79.

—— 'Einleitung' to Gabriel Wagner, *Ausgewählte Schriften und Dokumente* (Stuttgart, 1997), 7–73.

Wood, G. S., *The Radicalism of the American Revolution* (1991; new edn. New York, 1993).

Wood, Paul, 'The Scientific Revolution in Scotland', in Porter and Teich (eds.), *The Scientific Revolution*, 263–87.

Woodbridge, J. D., *Revolt in Prerevolutionary France* (Baltimore, 1995).

Woolhouse, R. S., *Descartes, Spinoza, Leibniz: The Concept of Substance in Seventeenth-Century Metaphysics* (London, 1993).

Wootton, David, 'Leveller Democracy and the Puritan Revolution', in J. H. Burns (ed.), *The Cambridge History of Political Thought, 1450–1700* (Cambridge, 1991), 412–42.

—— 'Introduction' to *John Locke: Political Writings* (London, 1993), 94–110.

—— 'David Hume "the Historian"', in Norton (ed.), *Cambridge Companion to Hume*, 281–312.

—— 'Pierre Bayle, Libertine?', in M. A. Stewart (ed.), *Studies in Seventeenth-Century European Philosophy* (Oxford, 1997), 197–226.

—— 'Helvétius: From Radical Enlightenment to Revolution', *Political Theory*, 28 (2000), 307–36.

Worden, Blair, 'The Revolution of 1688–9 and the English Republican Tradition', in Israel (ed.), *Anglo-Dutch Moment*, 241–77.

—— 'English Republicanism', in J. H. Burns (ed.), *The Cambridge History of Political Thought, 1450–1700* (Cambridge, 1991), 443–75.

Wright, J. K., *A Classical Republican in Eighteenth-Century France: The Political Thought of Mably* (Stanford, Calif., 1997).

—— 'The Idea of a Republican Constitution in Old Regime France', in van Gelderen and Skinner (eds.), *Republicanism*, i. 289–306.

Wybrands, A. W., 'Marinus Booms, eene bladzijde uit de geschiedenis der Spinozisterij in Nederland', *Archief voor Nederlandsche Kerkgeschiedenis*, 1 (1885), 51–128.

Yardeni, Miriam, *Anti-Jewish Mentalities in Early Modern Europe* (Lanham, Md., 1990).

—— 'La France de Louis XIV après la Révocation dans le *Dictionnaire historique et critique*', in Bots (ed.), *Critique, savoir et érudition*, 181–90.

Yates, Francis, *Giordano Bruno and the Hermetic Tradition* (1964; new edn. Chicago, 1991).

Yolton, J. W., *Locke and the Way of Ideas* (1956; 2nd imp., Bristol, 1996).

Young, B. W., *Religion and Enlightenment in Eighteenth-Century England* (Oxford, 1998).

Young, J. C., *Colonial Desire, Hybridity in Theory, Culture and Race* (London, 1995).

Yovel, Y., *Spinoza and Other Heretics: The Marrano of Reason* (Princeton, 1989).

Yuen-Ting Lai, 'The Linking of Spinoza to Chinese Thought by Bayle and Malebranche', *JHPh* 23 (1985), 151–78.

—— 'Leibniz and Chinese Thought', in Coudert *et al.* (eds.), *Leibniz*, 136–68.

Yusuf, S. M., 'Arabic Literature: Poetic and Prose Forms', in Sharif (ed.), *History*, ii. 985–1015.

Zac, S., 'Spinoza et l'interprétion de l'Écriture', *Revue philosophique*, 95 (1970), 191–205.

Zagorin, Perez, *How the Idea of Religious Toleration Came to the West* (Princeton, 2003).

—— 'Prologemena to the Comparative History of Revolution in Early Modern Europe', *Comparative Studies and History*, 18 (1976), 151–74.

Zakai, Avihu, *Jonathan Edwards's Philosophy of History* (Princeton, 2003).

Zambelli, P., *La formazione filosofica di Antonio Genovesi* (Naples, 1972).

—— 'Il rogo postumo di Paolo Mattia Doria', in P. Zambelli (ed.), *Ricerche sulla cultura dell' Italia moderna* (Rome, 1973), 149–98.

Zarka, Yves Charles, Lessay, F., and Rogers, J. (eds.), *Les Fondements philosophiques de la tolérance* (3 vols., Paris, 2002).

Zedelmaier, H., 'Aporien frühaufgeklärter Gelehrsamkeit', in Mulsow and Zedelmaier (eds.), *Skepsis, Providenz, Polyhistorie*, 97–129.

Zeppi, Stelio, 'Intorno al pensiero di Senofane', *RCSF* 16 (1961), 385–98.

Zoli, Sergio, *Europa libertina tra controriforma e illuminismo* (Bologna, 1989).
—— 'Pierre Bayle e la Cina', *Studi francesi*, 33 (1990), 467–72.
Zuber, Roger, 'Spinozisme et tolérance chez le jeune Papin', *DHS* 4 (1972), 217–27.
—— 'Isaac Papin, lecteur de Spinoza', *BAASp* 11 (1983), 1–14.
Zuckert, M. P., 'Locke—Religion—Equality', *Review of Politics* (Notre Dame, Ind.), 67 (2005), 419–31.
Zurbuchen, Simone, 'Republicanism and Toleration', in van Gelderen and Skinner (eds.), *Republicanism*, ii. 47–71.

Index